8th Edition

North Carolina Real Estate
Principles & Practices

By E. Thomas Mangum

North Carolina Real Estate Principles and Practices, Eighth Edition

E. Thomas Mangum

Executive Editor: Sara Glassmeyer

Project Manager: Elizabeth King, Linda Francis

Composition: Cenveo Publisher Services

Cover Designer: Brian Brogaard

Cover Image: Simonkr/Getty Images

Chapter Opener Image Credits:
© KentWeakley/Thinkstock
© bbbrrn/Thinkstock
© Rawpixel/Thinkstock

© 2019, 2014, 2008 OnCourse Learning

ALL RIGHTS RESERVED. No part of this work covered by the copyright herein may be reproduced, transmitted, stored, or used in any form or by any means graphic, electronic, or mechanical, including but not limited to photocopying, recording, scanning, digitizing, taping, web distribution, information networks, or information storage and retrieval systems, except as permitted under Section 107 or 108 of the 1976 United States Copyright Act, without the prior written permission of the publisher.

For product information and technology assistance, contact us at
www.oncourselearning.com

Library of Congress Control Number: 2018965762
ISBN-13: 978-1-62980-232-9
ISBN-10: 1-62980-232-8

OnCourse Learning
20225 Water Tower Blvd., 4th Floor
Brookfield, WI 53045
USA
Visit our website at **www.oncoursepublishing.com**

Printed in the United States of America
3 4 5 6 7 24 23 22 21 20

BRIEF CONTENTS

	Preface	xxi
1	Basic Real Estate Concepts	1
2	Property Ownership and Interests	16
3	Property Taxation and Assessment	58
4	Transfer of Title to Real Property	66
5	Land Use Controls	95
6	Environmental Issues in Real Estate	120
7	Brokerage Relationships: Laws and Practices	133
8	Agency Contracts (Sales) and Related Practices	192
9	Basic Contract Law	251
10	Sales Contracts and Related Procedures	272
11	Real Estate Financing	333
12	Closing a Sales Transaction	401
13	Real Property Valuation	453
14	Property Insurance	496
15	Landlord and Tenant	508
16	Property Management	546
17	Fair Housing	568
18	Federal Income Taxation of Home Ownership/Sale	585
19	Basic Construction	599
20	Basic Real Estate Investment	621
	Appendix A: Exam Preparation Tips and Strategies and Practice National and State Examinations	628
	Appendix B: Real Estate Math	666
	Appendix C: North Carolina Real Estate License Law, North Carolina Real Estate Commission Rules, and License Law and Rule Comments	696
	Appendix D: Residential Square Footage Guidelines	857
	Appendix E: Safety Issues for Real Estate Brokers	885
	Appendix F: Real Estate Forms and Addenda	889
	Answer Key	936
	Glossary	957
	Index	986

CONTENTS

Preface	xxi

1 Basic Real Estate Concepts — 1
  Key Terms — 1
  Learning Objectives — 1
  In this Chapter — 1
  Basic Real Estate Concepts — 2
    Basic Terminology and Definitions — 2
    Economic Characteristics of Land — 3
    Physical Characteristics of Land — 4
  General Concepts of Land Use and Investment — 6
    The Highest and Best Use Concept — 6
    Public and Private Land Use Restrictions — 6
    Real Estate Investment Objectives — 7
  Scope of the Real Estate Business — 8
    Defining Broker and REALTOR® — 8
    The Real Estate Market — 10
    The Real Estate Practitioner — 11
  Summary of Important Points — 12
  Review Questions — 14

2 Property Ownership and Interests — 16
  Key Terms — 16
  Learning Objectives — 17
  In this Chapter — 17
  The Concept of Property — 17
    Real Property — 18
    Appurtenances — 19
    Personal Property — 21

Estates in Real Property ... 26
   Definition of Estate ... 26
   Types of Estate in Land ... 26
Ownership of Real Property ... 33
   Ownership in Severalty ... 33
   Concurrent (Joint) Ownership ... 33
   Combination (Hybrid) Forms of Ownership ... 36
Encumbrances to Real Property ... 42
   Liens ... 42
   Writ of Attachment ... 46
   Restrictive (Protective) Covenants ... 47
   Lis Pendens ... 47
   Easements ... 47
   Encroachments ... 51
Summary of Important Points ... 51
Review Questions ... 54

3 Property Taxation and Assessment ... 58
Key Terms ... 58
Learning Objectives ... 58
In this Chapter ... 58
Tax Rate and Calculations ... 59
   Property Subject to Taxation ... 60
   Listing Property for Taxation ... 60
   Appraisal and Assessment ... 60
   Timetable for Listing and Tax Collection ... 61
Summary of Important Points ... 63
Review Questions ... 64

4 Transfer of Title to Real Property ... 66
Key Terms ... 66
Learning Objectives ... 66
In this Chapter ... 67
Property Description ... 67
   Adequacy of Description ... 67
   Methods of Describing Real Property ... 67
   Government Rectangular Survey System ... 68
   Property Survey ... 71

Methods of Transferring Title	72
By Descent (Intestate Succession)	72
By Will	72
By Deed (Voluntary Alienation)	72
By Involuntary Alienation	73
Deeds	74
Nonessential Elements of a Deed	76
Title Assurance	82
Covenants of Title in Deeds	82
Title Examination Procedures	82
Attorney's Opinion of Title	83
Title Insurance	84
Marketable Title Act	87
The Torrens System	87
Summary of Important Points	89
Review Questions	91

5 Land Use Controls — 95

Key Terms	95
Learning Objectives	95
In this Chapter	95
Historical Development of Land Use Controls	96
Importance to Real Estate Practitioners and Buyers	96
Public Land Use Controls	97
Planning and Zoning	97
Urban and Regional Planning	103
Subdivision Regulations	103
Regulation of Special Land Types	107
Highway Access Controls	107
Interstate Land Sales Full Disclosure Act	108
Private Land Use Controls	110
Individual Deed Restrictions	110
Restrictive or Protective Covenants	111
Responsibility of Real Estate Agents	114
Agent Responsibilities Regarding Potential Land Use Problems	114
Summary of Important Points	114
Review Questions	116

6 Environmental Issues in Real Estate — 120
- Key Terms — 120
- Learning Objectives — 120
- In this Chapter — 120
- Lead Poisoning (Lead-Based Paint) — 121
  - *North Carolina Lead-Based Paint Hazard Management Program* — 124
- Asbestos — 125
- Radon — 126
- Formaldehyde — 127
- Toxic Mold — 128
- Leaking Underground Storage Tanks — 129
- Comprehensive Environmental Response, Compensation, and Liability Act — 129
- Summary of Important Points — 130
- Review Questions — 131

7 Brokerage Relationships: Laws and Practice — 133
- Key Terms — 133
- Learning Objectives — 133
- In this Chapter — 134
- General Agency Concepts and Definitions — 134
- Classification of Agency Relationships — 136
  - *Universal Agency* — 136
  - *General Agency* — 136
  - *Special Agency* — 136
- Creation of Agency Relationships — 137
  - *Relationships between Transaction Parties* — 137
  - *Relationships between Brokers and Firms* — 137
  - *Implied Agency* — 137
  - *Estoppel* — 138
  - *Scope of Agent's Authority* — 138
  - *Agency and Agent Compensation* — 139
- Agency and Subagency Relationships — 139
  - *Single Agency* — 140
  - *Exclusive Seller Agency* — 140
  - *Cooperating with Other Brokers* — 141
  - *Cooperating Firm Acting as Seller's Agent* — 141
  - *Exclusive Buyer Agency* — 142

Buyer as Principal	142
Both Seller and Buyer Agency with Dual Agency for In-House Sales	144
Agency Relationships in Real Estate Rentals	144
Agency's Effect on Communication Requirements for Contracts	145
Agency's Effect on Disclosure of Material Facts	146
Termination of Agency	146
Disclosure of Agency Relationships	147
First Substantial Contact	148
First Contact versus First Substantial Contact	154
Duties and Liabilities of Agents	154
Agent's Duties to Principal	154
Loyalty	155
Obedience	155
Confidentiality	156
Skill, Care, and Diligence	156
Disclosure of Information	158
Accounting	158
Agent's Duties to Principal under Real Estate License Law and Commission Rules	159
Agent's Duties to Third Parties	160
Material Facts	160
Quick Review of Material Facts	163
Misrepresentation	164
Omission	166
Other Laws Governing the Disclosure of Information in Real Estate Transactions	167
Stigmatized and Psychologically Affected Properties	167
Consumer Legislation	169
Seller's and Buyer's Responsibilities under Common Law	169
North Carolina Residential Property Disclosure Act	170
"As Is" Sale	171
Lead-Based Paint Disclosure	177
Synthetic Stucco Disclosure	177
Liabilities and Consequences of Agent's Breach of Duties	178
Dual Agency	179
Dual Agency Basics	179
Inherent Potential Conflicts of Interest	180

	Unintentional, Undisclosed Dual Agency	180
	How to Handle Intentional, Disclosed Dual Agency in North Carolina	181
	Designated Agency	182
	Individual Broker Dual Agent	184
Duties and Liabilities of Principals		184
	Principal's Duties to Agent	184
	Principal's Duties to Third Parties	185
	Liabilities and Consequences of Principal's Breach of Duties	185
Summary of Important Points		185
Review Questions		187

8 Agency Contracts (Sales) and Related Practices — 192

Key Terms	192
Learning Objectives	192
In this Chapter	192
Important Note Regarding Math Calculations for this Chapter	193
Broker's Entitlement to a Commission	193
In-House Sales	194
Co-Brokered Sales	195
Co-Brokerage with an Out-of-State Broker	195
Earning Commission as a Buyer's Broker	196
Legal Payment to Expired or Inactive Broker	196
General Requirements for Agency Contracts (Sales and Rental Transactions)	197
Listing Contracts and Practices	198
Definition and Purpose of Listing Contracts	198
Types of Listing Contracts	199
Full-Service Listing Agreements	199
Brokerage Fee	214
Flat Fee and Limited Service Agreements	214
Duration of the Listing	216
Property Data Sheet	217
Termination of Listing Contracts	217
Multiple Listing Service Arrangements	218
Antitrust Law	218
Laws Affecting Solicitation of Clients or Customers	219
Solicitation of Active Clients of Other Firms or Brokers	219
Federal and North Carolina Do Not Call Laws and Rules	219
"Junk Fax" Laws and Rules	220

"CAN-SPAM Act" 221
Listing Procedures 221
   Preliminary Listing Procedures 221
   Final Listing Procedures 222
Buyer Agency Contracts 226
   Agency Disclosure and Nonexclusive Buyer Agency Agreement 226
   Typical Provisions of a Buyer Agency Contract 231
Working with Buyers 238
   Working with Buyers as a Seller Subagent 239
Procedures for Buyers' Agents 240
Summary of Important Points 243
Review Questions 247

9 Basic Contract Law — 251

Key Terms 251
Learning Objectives 251
In this Chapter 252
Basic Contract Law 252
   Basic Contract Terms and Classifications 252
   Essential Elements of a Valid Contract 255
   Requirements for Reality of Consent 259
   Performance Dates and Times 262
   Statute of Frauds 262
   Uniform Electronic Transaction Act 263
   Agreement of the Parties 263
   Full Performance 264
   Impossibility of Performance 264
   Operation of Law 265
   Money Damages 267
   Specific Performance 268
   Rescission 268
Summary of Important Points 269
Review Questions 270

10 Sales Contracts and Related Procedures — 272

Key Terms 272
Learning Objectives 272
In this Chapter 273

Introduction ... 273
   "Drafting" the Sales Contracts ... 273
   Importance of Appropriate Sales Contract Form (Including Sources) ... 274
The Offer to Purchase and Contract ... 277
   The Offer to Purchase and Contract Standard Form 2-T ... 291
   Commonly Used Standard Addenda Forms ... 310
   Form for Sale/Purchase of Vacant Lot/Land (2A12-T) ... 313
Sales Contract Procedures ... 313
   Offer and Acceptance ... 313
   Submitting Offers to Sellers ... 317
   Handling Contract Modifications and Counteroffers ... 318
   Electronically Submitted Offer and Acceptance ... 320
   Handling Earnest Money and Due Diligence Fee ... 321
   Furnishing Copies of Offers and Contracts to Buyer and Seller ... 323
   Installment Land Contracts ... 323
   Advantages and Disadvantages ... 326
Option to Purchase Real Estate ... 327
   Agreements for Preemptive Rights ... 328
Summary of Important Points ... 329
Review Questions ... 330

11 Real Estate Financing ... 333

Key Terms ... 333
Learning Objectives ... 334
In this Chapter ... 335
Section 1: Basic Finance Concepts, Terminology, and Calculations ... 335
Principal, Interest, Taxes, and Insurance ... 335
   Amortization and Debt Service ... 336
   Equity ... 336
   Usury ... 339
   Loan Fees, Loan Values, and Loan-to-Value Ratio ... 340
Mortgage Basics ... 342
   The Mortgage Note (Promissory Note) ... 342
   Mortgage and Deed of Trust ... 345
   Rights of Mortgage Borrowers ... 352
   Rights of Lender ... 353

Short Sale	356
Sales of Mortgaged Properties	356
Cash Sales	357
Loan Assumption	357
Taking Title "Subject to" a Loan	358
Categories of Residential First Mortgage Loans	358
Conventional Loans	359
FHA-Insured Loans	360
FHA 203(b) Regular Loan Program	361
VA-Guaranteed Loan Program	363
Eligibility	363
Contract Requirements	364
VA Funding Fee	364
Qualifying for VA Loans	364
Restoration of Entitlement	365
History of Loan Guarantees	365
Negotiability of VA Interest Rate	365
Other Aspects of FHA and VA Loans	366
Escrow Account	366
Down Payment	366
Miscellaneous	366
RD and FSA Mortgage Loans	367
Fixed Rate—Level-Payment Plan	368
Adjustable (Variable) Interest Rate	368
Graduated Payment Plan	369
Term Loan	369
Growing Equity Mortgage	370
Buydown Loan	370
Types of Loans by Purpose or Special Feature	371
Purchase Money Mortgages (Seller-Financed Loans)	371
Construction Loan	371
Open-End Mortgage	372
Blanket Mortgage	372
Package Mortgage	372
Types of Loans by Mortgage Priorities	373
First (or Senior) Mortgage	373
Junior Mortgage	373

Mortgage Priorities	373
Effect of Recordation	373
Subordination of Mortgages	374
Releases	374
The Role of the Federal Reserve Bank	374
Section 2: Primary Sources of Real Estate Finance	376
Primary Sources of Mortgage Funds	376
Savings and Loan Associations	376
Savings Banks	377
Commercial Banks	377
Mortgage Bankers and Mortgage Brokers	377
Life Insurance Companies	378
Credit Unions	378
Real Estate Investment Trusts	378
Individual Investors	378
Government Agencies	378
Employers	379
Secondary Mortgage Market	379
Activities among Lending Institutions	380
Sale to Organizations	380
Residential Lending Practices and Procedures in Transactions Subject to Truth in Lending Act/Real Estate Settlement Procedures Act Integrated Disclosure	382
Loan Application Procedures	382
Loan Underwriting	384
Borrower Analysis	384
Property Analysis	385
Loan Analysis	386
Loan Commitment and Closing	386
Financing Legislation	386
Dodd-Frank Wall Street Reform and Consumer Protection Act	386
Consumer Financial Protection Bureau	387
Truth in Lending Act	387
Fair Credit Reporting Act	390
The Equal Credit Opportunity Act	391
North Carolina Lending Acts	391
Summary of Important Points	394
Review Questions	396

12 Closing a Sales Transaction — 401

- Key Terms — 401
- Learning Objectives — 401
- In this Chapter — 401
- Preclosing Procedures — 402
- Selecting and Providing Information to Closing Attorney — 402
  - *Buyer's Due Diligence Process* — 403
  - *Other Preclosing Matters* — 408
- Closing Procedures — 409
  - *Closing Methods and Procedures* — 410
  - *Procedures after the Settlement Meeting* — 411
  - *Real Estate Settlement Procedures Act* — 412
- Summary of RESPA Requirements — 412
  - *Penalties for RESPA Violations* — 421
  - *The Loan Estimate* — 421
  - *Permissible Variations* — 425
  - *The Closing Disclosures* — 425
- Closing Statement (with LE and CD Worksheet) — 426
  - *Settlement Statement Entries and Calculations* — 426
  - *Prorations and Prepaids* — 435
- Summary of Important Points — 446
- Review Questions — 449

13 Real Property Valuation — 453

- Key Terms — 453
- Learning Objectives — 453
- In this Chapter — 454
- Appraiser Regulation — 455
  - *Licensure and Certification* — 455
- Basic Appraisal Concepts — 455
  - *Definition of Appraisal* — 455
  - *Broker Price Opinion/Comparative Market Analysis* — 455
  - *Valuation versus Evaluation* — 457
  - *Additional Concepts of Value* — 458
  - *Forces and Factors Influencing Value* — 459
  - *Basic Economic Principles of Value* — 459
- The Valuation Process — 462

Approaches to Value ... 463
　　　　Sales Comparison (Market Data) Approach ... 463
　　　　Key Points about Sales Comparison Approach ... 464
　　　　Reconciliation ... 475
　　　　The Cost Approach ... 476
　　　　The Income Approach ... 481
　　　　Gross Rent Multiplier ... 485
　　　Reconciliation and Appraisal Report ... 486
　　　Broker Price Opinion/Comparative Market Analysis ... 487
　　　　Key Elements of the Appraisers Act Revision ... 488
　　　　Standards for CMA/BPO ... 489
　　　Summary of Important Points ... 489
　　　Review Questions ... 491

14　Property Insurance ... 496
　　　Key Terms ... 496
　　　Learning Objectives ... 496
　　　In this Chapter ... 496
　　　Property Insurance Basics ... 497
　　　　Basic Concepts and Terminology ... 497
　　　　Standardized Homeowner's Insurance ... 497
　　　　Common Homeowner's Insurance Policies ... 498
　　　Select Legal Issues ... 500
　　　　Insurable Interest ... 500
　　　　Unoccupied Building Exclusion ... 501
　　　　Residential Sales Transaction Concerns ... 504
　　　Summary of Important Points ... 506
　　　Review Questions ... 506

15　Landlord and Tenant ... 508
　　　Key Terms ... 508
　　　Learning Objectives ... 508
　　　In this Chapter ... 509
　　　Definitions ... 509
　　　Estates and Contracts ... 509
　　　The Residential Rental Agreements Act ... 510
　　　　Obligations of Landlord and Tenant ... 510
　　　　Landlord's Statutory Duties ... 510

Tenant's Statutory Duties	511
Tenant Remedies for Breach by Landlord	511
Application of the Law of Negligence	511
Retaliatory Eviction	512
North Carolina Tenant Security Deposit Act	512
Permitted Uses of Tenant Security Deposits	512
Maximum Amounts for Security Deposits	513
Typical Examples of Normal Wear and Tear	514
Common Examples of "Other Damage"	514
Limits on Late Payment Fees	515
Residential Eviction Remedies	515
Discrimination and Sexual Harassment	515
Rights of Tenants in Public Housing	515
Vacation Rental Act	516
Purpose	516
Nonfreehold Estates	519
Estate for Years	519
Estate from Period to Period	520
Estate at Will	520
Estate at Sufferance	520
Types of Leases	521
Common Lease Provisions	523
Essential Provisions	523
Other Provisions	524
Landlord's Implied Covenant of Quiet Enjoyment	537
Termination of Leases	537
Application of the Statute of Frauds	538
Recordation of Leases	538
Summary of Important Points	539
Review Questions	542

16 Property Management — **546**

Key Terms	546
Learning Objectives	546
In this Chapter	546
The Owner–Property Manager Relationship	546
Purposes of Property Management	546
Types of Property Requiring Management	547

	Property Management Fee	547
	Travel Agent Referral Fees in Vacation Rentals	548
	Agency Relationship in Rentals	548
	Property Management Contracts	549
	Duties of the Property Manager	559
	Principal Functions of Property Managers	560
	Preparing the Management Plan	560
	Marketing and Renting the Property	561
	Qualifying and Selecting Tenants	561
	Collecting Rents and Security Deposits	563
	Instituting Legal Actions	563
	Maintaining the Property	563
	Performing the Landlord's Duties	564
	Maintaining Records and Reporting to the Owner	564
	Americans with Disabilities Act and Fair Housing Laws	564
	Summary of Important Points	565
	Review Questions	566
17	**Fair Housing**	**568**
	Key Terms	568
	Learning Objectives	568
	In this Chapter	568
	Federal Fair Housing Act	569
	Definitions	569
	Exemptions	574
	Enforcement	575
	North Carolina Fair Housing Act	576
	Unlawful Discrimination	576
	Exemptions	576
	Enforcement and Penalties	576
	Federal Civil Rights Act of 1866	577
	Additional Regulation of Fair Housing in North Carolina	577
	Equal Housing Opportunity Today	578
	Americans with Disabilities Act	578
	Sexual Harassment	579
	Summary of Important Points	579
	Review Questions	581

18 Federal Income Taxation of Home Ownership/Sale — 585

Key Terms — 585
Learning Objectives — 585
In this Chapter — 585
   Tax Deductions For Homeowners — 586
   Real Property Taxes — 586
   Mortgage Interest — 586
Sale of a Personal Residence Basis — 587
   Effect of Purchase and Sale — 589
Rules for Taxation of Capital Gain — 592
   Reporting Features — 594
Special Rules that May Apply to Some Residential Transactions — 594
   Installment Sales — 594
   Like-Kind Exchange — 595
   Vacation Homes — 595
   Home Office — 596
Summary of Important Points — 596
Review Questions — 597

19 Basic Construction — 599

Key Terms — 599
Learning Objectives — 599
In this Chapter — 600
Architectural Types and Styles — 600
Location on Site — 601
Foundations — 602
   Footings — 602
   Foundation Walls — 602
Framing — 603
   Flooring — 603
   Walls — 605
   Ceiling Framing and Roof — 606
Exterior Walls — 607
Windows — 608
   Sliding Windows — 608
   Swinging Windows — 609
   Fixed Windows — 610

	Doors	610
	Roofing	610
	Insulation	611
	Moisture Control	611
	Heating/Air Conditioning Systems	612
	Solar Heat	613
	Electrical Systems	614
	Plumbing Systems	614
	Government Regulation	614
	North Carolina Uniform Residential Building Code	614
	FHA/VA Minimum Standards	615
	Contractor Licensing	615
	Summary of Important Points	616
	Review Questions	618
20	**Basic Real Estate Investment**	**621**
	Key Terms	621
	Learning Objectives	621
	In this Chapter	621
	Basic Real Estate Investment	622
	Investing versus Speculation	622
	Basic Concepts	623
	Summary of Important Points	625
	Review Questions	626

Appendix A: Exam Preparation Tips and Strategies and Practice National and State Examinations — 628
Appendix B: Real Estate Math — 666
Appendix C: North Carolina Real Estate License Law, North Carolina Real Estate Commission Rules, and License Law and Rule Comments — 696
Appendix D: Residential Square Footage Guidelines — 857
Appendix E: Safety Issues for Real Estate Brokers — 885
Appendix F: Real Estate Forms and Addenda — 889
Answer Key — 936
Glossary — 957
Index — 986

PREFACE

Revised and fully updated, *North Carolina Real Estate: Principles and Practices, Eighth Edition*, provides the knowledge that is fundamental to a successful career in real estate. This text blends information regarding national laws and concepts with information specific to North Carolina statutes, principles, and practices. The subject matter and study materials are based on the North Carolina Real Estate Prelicense Course Syllabus.

We have made every effort to present step-by-step explanations and to offer guidance regarding the most effective use of this material. Each chapter begins with key terms and learning objectives and concludes with a summary of important points, which reviews the chapter's key ideas in a succinct list that facilitates review. Most chapters also include review questions to allow students to self-test and a useful section of items to consider for the state exam, designed to focus students' preparation for the North Carolina State Licensing Exam. Finally, practice exams, separated into national and state portions to match the new state format, are included in the appendix. Many other resources can also be found in the appendix, including a math review, sample forms and addendum, the *Residential Square Footage Guidelines*, *Safety Issues for Real Estate Brokers*, and the most recent *North Carolina Real Estate License Law and Commission Rules*.

SPECIAL FEATURES

- Each chapter begins with Key Terms and Learning Objectives designed to help you focus on the chapter's key concepts.
- Summaries of Important Points and Review Questions are included at the end of each chapter to help you review the material.
- Practical advice including numerous highlights of important points of emphasis and test tips throughout make this textbook a great guide for preparing to sit for the exam and make a career in real estate.
- A complete Instructor's Manual is available, which includes learning objectives and suggested lecture discussion ideas.

NEW TO THIS EDITION

Chapter 1 – Key terms added including *deed*, *hereditaments*, and *tenements*

Chapter 2 – Expanded coverage of Bundle of Rights and personal property; new discussion of factory-built (manufactured) housing

Chapter 4 – Expanded coverage of Voluntary and Involuntary Alienation as well as the addition of Bargain and Sale Deed, Trustee's Deed, and Sherriff's Deed; added Math Concepts Related to Area.

Chapter 5 – Addition of Street Maintenance Disclosure Requirements specific to NC as well as discussion of Onsite Septic System requirements

Chapter 6 – Added Test Tip related to lead based paint, asbestos, and radon

Chapter 7 – Added Facilitator/transactional broker as well as expanded discussion of Buyer as Principal, Basic Duties of Agent to Principal, Confidentiality, Agent's Duties to Third parties, and Agent's Handling of Their Own Property

Chapter 8 – Added discussion of North Carolina—specific requirements regarding Legal Payment to Expired or Inactive Broker

Chapter 9 – Discussion of "time is of the essence" in contracts and rules for interpretation of contracts

Chapter 10 – Updated coverage of how brokers can use the array of industry created forms (with clarifying language stating that such use does not relieve a broker from responsibility to include required data)

Chapter 11 – Updated terminology to reflect changes within the lending industry as well as new concise coverage of math problems related to finance

Chapter 12 – Updated presentation to reflect changes in the closing forms used in NC

Chapter 13 – Expanded section under "other Pre-Closing Matters"

Chapter 14 – New Insurance chapter

Chapter 15 – Revised coverage of the Residential Rental Agreements Act and how it is applicable to all private owners and not just licensees; maximum Amounts for Deposit including for pets, service animals, and damages caused by animals; added coverage under Residential Eviction Remedies

Chapter 16 – Added Math Concepts for Property management

Chapter 17 – Added coverage under "Americans with Disabilities Act"

Chapter 19 – Deleted sections that are no longer part of the NC outline

Chapter 20 – Deleted sections that are no longer applicable to the NC outline

Appendix A – Revised exam question formats to reflect new methods of testing on state exams and revised number of questions in each section

Appendix C – Updated the North Carolina License Law and Commission Rules section

Appendix F – Included new forms for this edition

ABOUT THE AUTHORS

Tom Mangum. Tom Mangum has been a real estate broker since 1975 and a real estate instructor since 1978. Since 1989, he has served as the director of the HPW Real Estate School in Raleigh, North Carolina. He is an active member of the North Carolina Real Estate Educator's Association (NCREEA) and has served as secretary-treasurer as well as state president. He has twice been the recipient of the NCREEA "Educator of the Year" and "Program of the Year" award for his "Guaranteed to Pass" audio series, and the HPW school has been named as "Program of the Year." Tom has served on the North Carolina Real Estate Commission's Exam Review Committee. He is also the author of numerous continuing education courses and is a well-known instructor. He is a graduate of Chowan College and Appalachian State University. Tom currently resides in Raleigh with his wife Jo and their two "fur children" Abi and Mollie Mae.

ACKNOWLEDGMENTS

I would like to express my sincere appreciation to Deb Carpenter, and the North Carolina Real Estate Commission staff who reviewed this text and offered suggestions toward its improvement.

Certainly no project of this magnitude can be completed without the valuable input of many people. The team of Sara Glassmeyer, Executive Editor, and Linda Francis, Project Manager, makes the job of an author so much more efficient. They take the unfinished product and do their magic and make you feel as though you are much better at this than you really are, but never remind you of that fact. I would like to acknowledge Nancy Keck, the previous author, who left me some very good "bones" to work with, and I feel honored to have taken possession of her "book baby" and hopefully made her proud to have recommended me for this project.

Many other individuals contributed to this new text. I am deeply indebted to the following excellent instructors for their assistance: Kim Frye and Kevin Sensing. Certainly, I am always grateful for the endless support and enthusiasm of my assistant, Kim Spence, who keeps me focused and grounded on the task at hand. You simply cannot imagine how grateful I am for all that you do.

I also want to acknowledge my parents, Gene and Billie Mangum, who allowed me to go to college and graduate without one single dime of college debt. They also supported me in the early years and encouraged me tremendously when the opportunity to pursue real estate education presented itself.

Lastly, the lovely bride, My Funny Valentine, who constantly helped with technology issues, supported me and gave me much-appreciated advice on writing a book, and kept me focused on what was really important. Thank you, Jo Mangum, for all you do and who you are! *On se voit a paris?*

WELCOME TO A SUPERIOR ADVENTURE!

We appreciate the trust and confidence you have placed in us by choosing Superior School of Real Estate as your educational partner in obtaining your real estate license. Our students come to us because of the experience, the atmosphere, and the fun and excitement we bring into the classroom.

You have made a commitment to reach new heights in your life. Don't lose sight of the primary objective—you are here to obtain a real estate license. Collectively the instructors at Superior have over 100,000 hours of teaching in the classroom. Over the past few decades they have helped thousands of people like you succeed at the goals you have set.

Many of our instructors have achieved the designation of Distinguished Real Estate Instructor (DREI) from the national Real Estate Educators Association. There are fewer than 100 DREI's throughout the country and Superior School of Real Estate has more DREI instructors and candidates than any other school in the United States. They utilize top of the line PowerPoints, teaching techniques, and state-of-the-art technology to help you succeed. We have crafted our own customized material like no other real estate school you can find.

So welcome to the family, welcome aboard, and welcome to the Adventure. With your dedication and commitment and our knowledge and experience we can succeed together. More importantly we want you to have a grand adventure full of new experiences, new acquaintances, new knowledge, and new opportunities. We can't wait to help you Reach New Heights in your life and your career.

If I can help or be of assistance to you at any point along your journey, please feel free to reach out and contact me. We are honored to have you as a Superior student.

Len Elder, DREI, JD
Senior Instructor
Superior School of Real Estate
lelder@superiorschoolnc.com
877-944-4260

North Carolina Real Estate Principles and Practices

CHAPTER 1

BASIC REAL ESTATE CONCEPTS

KEY TERMS

appurtenance
bill of sale
chattel
deed
hereditaments
highest and best use
immobility
improvements

indestructibility
land use controls
land
nonhomogeneity
personal property
personalty
real estate
real property

REALTOR®
realty
scarcity
situs
specific performance
tenements

LEARNING OBJECTIVES

At the conclusion of this chapter, you should be able to:

1. Describe the characteristics of real estate, including classes of property, physical characteristics of land, and economic characteristics of land.
2. Describe the concepts of land use and investment, including highest and best use, land use controls, investment objectives, scope of the real estate business, and the real estate market.

IN THIS CHAPTER

This text is designed to help you master the fundamentals of real estate by introducing information in a step-by-step format that requires no real estate background. This chapter provides an overview of the entire real estate business. Each topic introduced in this chapter is discussed in more detail in the following chapters.

You should use this chapter to become familiar with the format of the book, including objectives, summary of important points, and questions. Each of these sections is designed to help you study the

material efficiently to master this information. Finally, this text offers advice on preparation for the North Carolina Real Estate Licensing Examination.

BASIC REAL ESTATE CONCEPTS

Real property has certain physical and economic characteristics that set it apart from other marketable commodities. These characteristics are so interrelated that they have a definite effect on one another and are sometimes difficult to separate in a practical sense. This chapter discusses these characteristics and their effects on real property value.

Basic Terminology and Definitions

Real estate, real property, realty, and **land**—These terms often are used interchangeably to describe the combination of land, improvements, and rights and privileges. Title (ownership) is conveyed by **deed**.

Personal property, personalty, or **chattel**—Anything that is *not* considered to be real property. Title is conveyed by **bill of sale**.

The first thing students will have to master in this course is the concept that all property is either real or personal. The concept of real property is made up of three components: land, improvements, and rights and privileges. (These components are addressed in more detail in the forthcoming chapters, but the following gives a brief introduction.)

Land—The surface of the earth with the boundaries extending downward to the middle of the earth extended back upward to the highest heavens. Land consists of three components: surface, subsurface, and airspace.

This concept shows us that much of what is considered "land" is, in fact, made up of air. In common usage, the term "land" often is used in much the same way as the terms real estate, real property, and realty.

Improvements—Anything used to better or "improve" the use of the land. These are artificially attached items and are considered to be real property and not personal.

Appurtenance—Any right or privilege that is considered to *run with the land*.

Not all rights and privileges are considered to run with the land and may be "personal" in nature. The concept of runs with the land is that the right or privilege is an integral part of the property, much like structures or other improvements, and are conveyed as a normal part of the deed transferring title to the real property. For example, municipal water and sewer lines are an example of a right or privilege the government has to place the pipes to provide utility service to the property and likely others. When the title is conveyed to a subsequent owner, that right remains intact. The same would apply if a property owner has the right to cross over adjoining property to access theirs. Most likely, this would be a permanent right that would convey upon transfer.

Tenements—Ownership interest in anything immobile and is considered part of the real property.

Hereditaments—Any rights capable of being inherited.

Economic Characteristics of Land

Scarcity

An important economic characteristic of real property (Figure 1.1) is its availability or **scarcity.** Land is a commodity that has a fixed supply base. No additional physical supply of land is being produced to keep pace with the ever-increasing population. The problems created by an ever-increasing demand for the limited supply of land, however, have been eased substantially by an increase in the economic supply of land. This increase has come about as a result of the greater utilization of the existing physical supply of land. Farmers are continuing to increase the use of land in the agricultural area. Greater crop yields per acre are being achieved as a result of scientific and technological advances. Today, the agricultural industry is producing more cattle per acre and more bushels of crops per acre than it did just a few years ago.

In urban areas, land is being utilized to a greater extent through high-density development. Advances in science and technology result in the creation of high-rise office buildings, apartment complexes, and multilevel shopping centers. Consequently, 1 acre of land serves many times the number of people who could use the land in the absence of these improvements.

Modification by improvement is another factor that has increased the *economic supply* of land. These modifications can include the construction of highways, bridges, water reservoirs, purification plants, and public utilities. The improvements and expansions of public air and land transportation systems also make a significant contribution in this regard. These accomplishments in the fields of

---

1. Scarcity
2. Permanence of investment
3. Location

FIGURE 1.1 Economic characteristics of real property.
Source: © 2019 OnCourse Learning

construction and transportation have converted land that had not been accessible and useful in a practical sense into land that can now be used. A substantial increase in the economic supply of land has resulted from these improvements *to* the land (rather than improvements *on* the land).

Permanence of Investment

Because of the physical characteristics of immobility and indestructibility of land, the investment of capital and labor to create improvements to the land and improvements on the land is a long-term investment. It takes many years to recoup the investment made to improve the value and quality of land. If a developer misjudges the demand for land-specific improvements or if economic conditions, including real estate market conditions, change dramatically, the developer may never recoup his full investment.

Location (Situs) *most important*

The *location of land*, or **situs**, is an extremely important economic (or more precisely, socioeconomic) characteristic of land, and it is the characteristic that has the greatest effect on property value. The physical characteristic of immobility dictates that the location of a parcel of land is permanent. Therefore, if the land is located in an area where demand is high, the land will have a substantially increasing value. Conversely, if the land is inaccessible from a practical standpoint or is located in an area with little or no demand, its economic value will be depressed.

Although the location of land cannot be changed, the value of the location (and consequently, the value of the land) can be increased by improvements to access and other modifications. Additionally, the value of the location can change as the result of the changes in preferences of people. In the 1950s there was a great flight from the urban centers to the suburbs. This resulted in property value reductions in urban areas. This trend has moderated in recent years. People are rediscovering the inner cities, rehabilitating older properties, and restoring lost urban property values.

Physical Characteristics of Land

Immobility

An essential physical characteristic of land (Figure 1.2) is its **immobility.** That *land cannot be relocated from one place to another* is an obvious feature of land as a commodity and is the primary distinguishing feature between land and personal property. The physical characteristic of immobility is the reason the economic characteristic of location significantly affects land value, thus making the market for land a strictly local market. This requires brokers and agents to have specific

1. Immobility
2. Permanence
3. Uniqueness

FIGURE 1.2 Physical characteristics of land.
Source: © 2019 OnCourse Learning

knowledge of their local real estate market to serve buyers and sellers in their respective market areas.

Permanence (Indestructibility)

Another unique feature of land is its physical characteristic of **indestructibility**. *Land is a permanent commodity, and it cannot be destroyed.* It may be altered substantially in its topography or other aspects of its appearance, but its geographic coordinates remain. Land values can change positively or negatively as a result of changing conditions in the surrounding area and are said to suffer from *economic obsolescence* when such changes adversely affect the value of land. For example, the construction of an interstate highway can radically affect land values. Do not confuse economic obsolescence with physical depreciation, which is a loss in value from deterioration of the improvements on the property itself (see Chapter 13).

The permanence or indestructibility of land makes it attractive as a long-term investment, but an investor should be alert to changing conditions that can affect the value of the investment.

Uniqueness (Nonhomogeneity)

An important feature of the land is that no two parcels are identical, in either a physical or a legal sense. For example, two tracts of land are quite different from two cars that come off an assembly line. Two cars may be nearly identical, and one could be substituted for the other; this is clearly not the case with real estate. Even two apparently identical adjoining parcels differ in aspects such as soil, drainage, view, and vegetation, to name a few.

This *uniqueness*, or **nonhomogeneity**, of each parcel of land gives rise to the concept of **specific performance.** *If a seller contracts to sell her real property, the law does not consider money a substitute for this duty.* Thus, if a seller tried to breach the contract and pay financial damages instead, *the buyer could refuse to accept the money and insist on taking title to the land as the only acceptable performance of the contract.* For example, one might sign a purchase agreement for a home in a particular neighborhood because it was next to friends, family, or schools. If the seller changed her mind and offered another, better home on the other side of town, the buyer could hold the seller to specific performance of the original contract for the unique advantages of that property.

> "Other textbook resources list four economic characteristics of land: scarcity, location, improvements, and permanence and three physical characteristics: immobility, indestructibility, and uniqueness."
> —Tim Terry, DREI

GENERAL CONCEPTS OF LAND USE AND INVESTMENT

The Highest and Best Use Concept

The concept of highest and best use is of extreme importance and considers all the physical and economic factors affecting the land. The **highest and best use** of land is *that use that will provide the property owner the best possible return on an investment over a specified time period, resulting in the highest possible present value of land. Present value* is defined as the value at the time of the appraisal; therefore, highest and best use can and does change with time. The use must be legal and must comply with zoning ordinances, government regulations, legally enforceable private deed restrictions, and restrictive covenants. The highest and best use of land is attained by the intelligent use of capital, labor, and other resources to improve the land and its productivity.

The task of coordinating and combining capital, labor, and resources to create an improvement is performed by an expert in real estate. The expert may be an individual developer or may be a general partner in a limited partnership with the other investors providing the capital as limited partners. The expert must determine the use of the land that will provide the necessary income from the land after labor and capital have been paid. For example, the expert will establish the optimum size of a building to be constructed on a particular site. The space should not be overimproved or underimproved. The building must not contain more space than can be rented in the market, nor should it fail to provide the space that the market demands. An overimprovement or an underimprovement does not provide the optimum income to the land, and as a result, the land is not put to its highest and best possible use.

A particular parcel of land has only one highest and best use at any particular time. The loss of residual income to the land resulting from failure to employ the land to its highest and best use causes the value of the property to diminish.

Public and Private Land Use Restrictions

Even though most land in the United States is privately owned, there is a vested public interest in land because the type of property use affects surrounding property owners and the general public. Because of this interest of the general public and of other property owners, the use of land requires regulation for the benefit of all. The need for **land use controls** has existed since the country's founding. This is especially true in areas of extremely dense population, where land uses radically affect a great number of people.

Public land use controls exist in the form of city planning and zoning, state and regional planning, building codes, suitability for occupancy requirements, and environmental control laws. Additionally, there is substantial public control of land use as a result of government ownership. Examples of government ownership include public buildings, public parks, watersheds, streets, and highways.

Regulation of land use in the private sector exists in the form of *protective* or *restrictive covenants* established by developers, restrictions in individual deeds (private deed restrictions) requiring the continuation of a specified land use or prohibiting a specified land use, and use restrictions imposed on a lessee in a lease contract.

Real Estate Investment Objectives

Real estate investors come in many varieties, ranging from the individual who buys one rundown property and fixes it up for resale or rental to the individuals or corporations who buy large commercial complexes such as shopping centers and factories.

The primary purpose of any investment is to produce income or profit, balancing the profit the investor desires against the risk he is willing to take. Real estate offers the opportunity to make a profit in three ways: appreciation, positive cash flow, and tax advantage.

Appreciation is the increase in market value during the time the investor holds the property. If an investor buys a property for $100,000 and it increases 3% in value annually, and he holds the property for 10 years, the property will have appreciated to a value of $134,391.46.

A *positive cash flow* exists when the gross effective income produced by the property exceeds the total of operating expenses. (See Chapter 13, "Real Property Valuation," for the discussion of gross effective income and expense.)

Tax advantages may result from appreciation or gains being taxed at a capital gain rate lower than the investor's marginal tax rate when the property is sold and from deductions of property taxes, insurance, and other expenses during the time the investor owns the property. Depreciation may provide an annual tax reduction, postponing the tax on the depreciated amount until the property is sold.

While appreciation, positive cash flow, and tax advantage are ways to make money on real estate investments, leverage allows more money to be made on less investment. For a simplified example, suppose an investor buys a $100,000 property with an initial investment of $10,000 for down payment and closing costs. The property appreciates $3,000 the first year, has a positive before-tax cash flow of $50 a month, and produces a tax savings of $400 for the year. This $4,000 is only 4% of $100,000, which is not a very good return on an investment. However, it is 40% of $10,000, which is an excellent return on an investment.

Real estate, like any investment, has risks. The real estate's market value can decline, the property can deteriorate, or the area surrounding the property can change, adversely affecting the property value. Rent or income may not meet expectations. Plants or military installations nearby can close. An "oil glut" can change to an "oil bust," leaving an overabundance of office space, homes, and so on. Environmental problems may adversely affect the property. If any of these things occurs, the effect may be compounded by the real estate's lack of liquidity. The investor most likely cannot sell the property instantly for its full value.

SCOPE OF THE REAL ESTATE BUSINESS

The real estate business is extensive in scope and is a complex industry. Usually, when people think of the real estate business, they think only of residential brokerage. This is just one of several specializations within the real estate business, however. In fact, within the field of brokerage, there are several specializations, including farm and land brokerage, residential property brokerage, and commercial and investment property brokerage. In addition to brokerage, other specializations in real estate include property management, appraising, financing, construction, property development, real estate education, and government service.

Real estate transactions can be traced to early written records from biblical times, but those transactions were between the seller and buyer directly, without the participation of a real estate broker. The business of real estate brokerage is a product of the twentieth century. In the early 1900s, states began enacting licensing law legislation, and today all states in the nation require real estate brokers or salespeople to be licensed. North Carolina adopted its Real Estate License Law statute in 1957.

The establishment of the National Association of Real Estate Boards in 1908 was a major factor in the development of real estate brokerage. During the 1970s, the name of this trade group was changed to the National Association of REALTORS® (NAR). The term **REALTOR®** *is a registered trademark of NAR, and it identifies licensees who are also members of the local, the state, and the national association.*

It is important to remember that all licensees are not REALTORS® and that only the active members of these associations may use the term REALTOR® or REALTOR ASSOCIATE®. One of the most important accomplishments of NAR and its predecessor organization was the creation of a Code of Ethics in 1913. This code has contributed significantly to the professional stature of real estate brokerage. Strong parallels exist between licensing laws and this original Code of Ethics.

Defining Broker and REALTOR®

The general public has a poor understanding of the distinction between a broker and a REALTOR®.

The North Carolina Real Estate Commission issues real estate broker licenses and regulates broker's practices. The term REALTOR® designates a licensee (broker) who is also a member of the local association of REALTORS® at the city or county level, a state association of REALTORS®, such as the North Carolina Association of REALTORS® (NCAR), and NAR. The REALTOR® association is in no way associated with or regulated by the Real Estate Commission, although the two groups work together for the advancement of professionalism in the real estate business.

Not all licensees are REALTORS®. North Carolina has approximately 94,500 licensees, of whom only roughly about one-third are REALTORS®. In addition to being answerable to the Real Estate Commission and to the civil and criminal courts for wrong-doing or failure of duty, the REALTOR® is also accountable under the Code of Ethics to the local association of REALTORS®.

Other significant contributions of NAR include efforts that have resulted in licensing laws being enacted in all states, legislative activity on the federal level to prevent unnecessary and harmful legislation from diminishing rights of private ownership in real property, and excellent programs of continuing education for members and nonmembers through NAR and its affiliated organizations.

Relocation is a growing part of the real estate business. A vast relocation network exists. Many corporations offer transferring employees generous relocation packages, including paying the closing costs for selling old homes and purchasing new homes. Some corporations have in-house relocation departments to assist employees with every aspect of their move. Others contract with third-party relocation companies to provide these services. Many corporations, relocation companies, real estate brokerage firms, appraisers, attorneys, and others who work with relocation belong to the Employees Relocation Council, which provides networking, research, education, and so on, to its members. In-depth coverage of relocation is beyond the scope of the text; however, new agents are advised to become familiar with the wants, needs, and expectations of relocating individuals, families, and employers, as well as relocation companies.

Real estate brokerage is the bringing together of buyers and sellers or landlords and tenants for the temporary or permanent transfer of an interest in real property owned by others through purchase, sale, lease, or rental by a real estate broker for compensation. In North Carolina, such brokerage activities require a North Carolina broker's license.

The fact that real estate represents a growing percentage of the wealth in the United States illustrates the extremely broad scope and importance of the real estate business. The complexity of this business requires that agents have continual interaction with people in a variety of other professions. Today's real estate practitioner needs a basic knowledge of the many functions performed by other members of the real estate and allied professions.

Real estate professionals must work with mortgage bankers or brokers to secure financing for their clients; appraisers to validate the value of the property; home inspectors and wood-destroying insect inspectors to determine the condition of the property; developers and contractors when selling new construction; attorneys, surveyors, and insurance agents when closing properties; and governmental officials, such as tax assessors, environmental health specialists, and city and county planners when necessary.

Successful real estate practitioners are also counselors and educators who must recognize the limits of their knowledge and guard against giving legal, accounting, or tax advice.

The Real Estate Market

A **free market** is *one in which the buyer and seller negotiate a purchase and sale without undue pressure, urgency, or outside influence other than the principle of supply and demand.* Although government regulations may indirectly affect the price of real estate or the costs of borrowing money to buy real estate, the government does not set real estate prices. The principle of supply and demand determines real estate prices; thus, the real estate market is an excellent example of the free market concept. Market value, which is discussed in Chapter 13, depends on the free market concept.

Special Characteristics

The physical characteristics of land create special characteristics of the real estate market that do not exist in other markets. As noted previously, the immobility of real estate causes the market to be local in character, requiring local specialists who are currently familiar with local market conditions, property values, and availability. The nonhomogeneity, or uniqueness, of each parcel of real estate also requires that the market be local. Each parcel of real estate is unique, primarily because of its location.

The physical characteristic of immobility also results in a market that is slow to react to changes in supply and demand. When supply substantially exceeds demand, existing properties cannot be withdrawn from a local market area and relocated to an area in which there is a higher demand. Conversely, when the demand exceeds supply, new supplies of housing and business properties cannot be constructed quickly. Therefore, after a recession, it takes many months for the supply to equal or exceed demand in the real estate market.

Factors Affecting Supply and Demand

Several factors affect supply and demand in the real estate market, on both the local and national levels. Examples of these factors include interest rates; availability of financing for purchase and construction; population migrations; variations in population trends and family formations; government regulations; local and national economic conditions; and the availability and cost of building sites, construction materials, and labor.

Historical Trends

Just as the economy as a whole is subject to peaks and valleys of activity that have recurred over the years with fairly reasonable regularity, the real estate industry, as a part of this economy, is similarly subjected to recurring periods of recession and prosperity.

The real estate industry is often the first industry to feel the adverse effects of depressed conditions in the national and local economies. It may take the real estate industry longer than the economy as a whole to climb out of a recession because of the inability of the real estate industry to react quickly to radical changes in supply and demand. But that is not always the case. In recent times, real estate has sometimes remained strong during a recession or led the recovery from an economic downturn.

Another characteristic of the real estate cycle is that the real estate industry usually attains a much higher level of activity in prosperous times than does the economy in general.

The Real Estate Practitioner

North Carolina defines only one real estate license category, broker, since it became an all-broker state on April 1, 2006, eliminating the "salesperson" license category. All individuals or entities who want to engage in real estate brokerage activities in North Carolina must first be licensed as brokers. Many current brokers have received their licenses under previous criteria of either education and experience (criterion one) and the passing of a state examination (criterion two). Some have been licensed based on reciprocal licensing arrangements in other states. Those who met the criteria for and were licensed as brokers before April 1, 2006, can remain brokers with no provisional status attached to their licenses. Those who were licensed as salespersons as of that date were licensed automatically as brokers at that time, although with provisional status. All new brokers licensed after April 1, 2006, were granted licenses on provisional status. To remove provisional status, all provisional brokers must complete three 30-hour post-licensing courses and pass the course exams.

A broker without provisional status is able to practice independently. A broker with attached provisional status is not. She must work under the supervision of a broker who is a broker-in-charge (BIC) until she has completed all post-licensing requirements to remove the provisional status and to practice independently. A provisional broker cannot become a BIC. A BIC must have a minimum of two years' full-time real estate experience, which may be met as a broker regardless of provisional status or lack thereof; however, provisional status must be removed before becoming a BIC. Although the broker-in-charge is ultimately responsible for all actions of the provisional brokers she supervises, the provisional broker cannot escape responsibility for her duties and actions.

Relationships between brokers and clients/customers, as well as relationships among brokers, are discussed extensively in Chapter 7. They are mentioned in this chapter only to clarify the terminology used in this text. The word *broker* or *agent* is used when the text is referring to a broker or a provisional broker when differentiation between the two is not required. The terms *broker* and *provisional broker* are used to differentiate the two categories of licensees, when necessary.

The successful real estate practitioner is not engaged in applying techniques of the "hard sell." Rather, he is a counselor or an adviser working diligently to solve the problems of buyers, sellers, and renters of real estate. Everyone who contacts a real estate office has a problem. The problem involves real property—the need to buy, sell, or lease. The real estate practitioner's ability to solve these problems for the benefit of others results in a successful career. Like any good counselor, the real estate practitioner provides information to, but does not make decisions for, the clients and customers. What information can and cannot be provided depends on several factors, but especially on the law of agency, which is discussed in Chapter 7.

A career in real estate can provide the practitioner with satisfaction from serving the needs of people and with accompanying financial rewards. Success in the real estate business is built on knowledge, service to others, and ethical conduct in all dealings.

The real estate practitioner must be knowledgeable in a variety of other subjects necessary to satisfactorily perform one's obligations in real estate transactions. These other subjects, which are discussed in depth in later chapters, include property ownership and interests, transfer of title to real property, fundamentals of residential construction, valuation of real estate, land use controls, fair housing laws, property management, insurance, and federal income tax implications of real estate ownership and sale. The real estate practitioner also must understand the meaning of the various real estate and legal terms used in real estate transactions. Finally, the practitioner must have a basic understanding of the various arithmetic problems that are common in the activities of real estate brokerage.

Summary of Important Points

1. Real property includes the surface of the land, all improvements that are attached to the property, everything beneath the surface, and the airspace above the land.
2. Personal property (also called personalty or chattel) is the opposite of real property—that is, everything that is not real property is considered personal property. Things that are readily movable—that is, not attached to the land—are personal property.
3. Real property has the physical characteristics of immobility, permanence, and uniqueness.

4. Real property has unique economic characteristics based on its physical location (situs).
5. The principle of highest and best use of land is an all-important concept in land use. Failure to make the highest and best use of land results in a lower value.
6. Controls of land use are necessary to protect the vested interests of the general public as well as the interests of surrounding landowners. Land use controls can be private, such as private deed restrictions and restrictive covenants, or public, such as zoning ordinances.
7. The real estate business involves many specialties besides residential brokerage and requires knowledge of many fields, including finance, housing codes, government regulations, contract law, and appraisal.
8. A real estate market is local and is an example of the free market concept wherein buyers and sellers have adequate time and information to reach a purchase and sale agreement without undue pressure, and with factual knowledge of all important aspects of the transaction. The physical and economic characteristics of land create a market that is local and slow to react to fluctuations in supply and demand.
9. The effects of depressed economic conditions are sometimes felt by the real estate industry before other segments of the economy. Traditionally, the real estate industry has been slower to pull out of depressed economic periods, but typically it reaches higher peaks of activity and prosperity during prosperous times than many other segments of the economy. In recent times, however, the real estate market has remained strong during a recession and sometimes has led the recovery from an economic downturn.
10. The real estate agent acts as an advisor or problem solver for the benefit of one's clients and customers. Because the purchase of a home involves the seller's most important financial asset and creates long-term financial obligations for the buyer, the agent must be thoroughly knowledgeable, competent, and responsible.
11. Real estate investment offers the opportunity to earn profits through appreciation of the property value, tax advantages, and positive cash flow. Leverage allows an investor to earn a greater return on a smaller initial investment. Some of the risks involved in real estate investments are market value declines, property deterioration, and adverse changes in the surrounding area.

Review Questions

Answers to the review questions are in the Answer Key at the back of the book.

1. All of the following are separable ownerships in land EXCEPT:
   A. surface of the land.
   B. area below the surface.
   C. nonhomogeneity.
   D. air rights.

2. The characteristic of land that causes the real estate market to be essentially a local market is the physical characteristic of:
   A. indestructibility.
   B. immobility.
   C. availability.
   D. natural features.

3. The nonhomogeneity of land:
   A. is the basis for the legal remedy of specific performance.
   B. results from the uniqueness of every parcel of real estate.
   C. is a physical characteristic of land.
   D. all of the above.

4. An increase in the economic supply of land has resulted from:
   A. increased utilization of the physical supply of land.
   B. modification by improvements to the land.
   C. high-density development.
   D. all of the above.

5. The quality of the location of land and, consequently, the value of the land can be changed by:
   A. the principle of nonhomogeneity.
   B. relocation of the land.
   C. changes in the national scope of the real estate business.
   D. improvements to the land that result in accessibility not previously available.

6. The employment of the concept of highest and best use:
   A. includes consideration of the physical and economic factors affecting land use.
   B. results in the greatest present value of the land.
   C. must be a use feasible in the near future.
   D. all of the above.

7. An example of public land use controls is:
   A. restrictive covenants.
   B. zoning laws.
   C. deed restrictions.
   D. protective covenants.

8. Real estate investment offers the opportunity to produce a profit in the following ways EXCEPT:
   A. appreciation.
   B. positive cash flow.
   C. specific performance.
   D. tax advantages.

9. The real estate market may be described in all the following ways EXCEPT:
   A. a free market.
   B. a local market.
   C. a movable market.
   D. a market that is slow to react to changes in supply and demand.

10. The function of a real estate agent in dealings with buyers and sellers in the real estate market may best be described as which of the following?
    A. financier
    B. counselor or advisor
    C. contractor
    D. salesperson

11. The real estate agent must have specialized knowledge of a variety of subjects that include all of the following EXCEPT:
    A. financing.
    B. contracts.
    C. legal advice.
    D. valuation of property.

12. Economic characteristics of real property include which of the following?
    A. location
    B. immobility
    C. indestructibility
    D. nonhomogeneity

13. Which of the following has the greatest effect on real property value?
    A. tax rates
    B. location
    C. availability
    D. indestructibility

14. Which of the following is an example of the private control of land use?
    A. zoning
    B. restrictive covenants
    C. building codes
    D. environmental controls

15. The term REALTOR® designates:
    A. any real estate licensee.
    B. a real estate licensee who is a member of the national, state, and local association of REALTORS®.
    C. only licensees who hold broker's licenses.
    D. all of the above.

16. Physical characteristics of land include all of the following EXCEPT:
    A. location.
    B. nonhomogeneity.
    C. permanence.
    D. immobility.

17. The National Association of REALTORS® is:
    A. a government organization.
    B. a trade group.
    C. an organization for buyers and sellers of commercial real estate.
    D. all of the above.

18. Factors affecting supply and demand in real estate include all of these items EXCEPT:
    A. government regulations.
    B. interest rates.
    C. local economic conditions.
    D. real estate investment trusts.

19. Scarcity and location are examples of:
    A. physical characteristics of the land.
    B. highest and best use.
    C. permanence of investment.
    D. economic characteristics of the land.

20. All of the following are public land use restrictions EXCEPT:
    A. building codes.
    B. protective covenants.
    C. zoning.
    D. regional planning.

CHAPTER 2
PROPERTY OWNERSHIP AND INTERESTS

KEY TERMS

- air rights
- alienation
- appurtenance
- appurtenant easement
- bundle of rights
- condemnation
- condominium
- cooperative
- co-ownership
- curtesy
- declaration of restrictions
- defeasible fee
- dower
- easement
- easement in gross
- emblements
- eminent domain
- encroachment
- encumbrance
- estate
- estovers
- fee simple absolute
- fixture
- foreshore
- freehold estate
- fruits of industry (*fructus industriales*)
- fruits of the soil (*fructus naturales*)
- hereditament
- intestate succession
- joint tenancy
- judgment lien
- land
- lateral support
- leasehold estates
- levy
- lien
- life estate
- life tenant
- *lis pendens*
- littoral rights
- marital life estates
- mineral lease
- nonfreehold estate
- North Carolina Condominium Act
- partition
- party wall
- prescription
- profit or profit à prendre
- *pur autre vie*
- remainderman
- reversionary interest
- riparian rights
- severalty
- subjacent support
- survivorship
- tenancy by the entirety
- tenancy in common
- tenements
- time sharing
- townhouse
- Uniform Commercial Code (UCC)

LEARNING OBJECTIVES

At the conclusion of this chapter, you should be able to:

1. Define and give examples of real property and personal property.
2. Define and give examples of fixtures, as well as describe tests for determining whether an item is a fixture.
3. Define and list the freehold estates.
4. Define severalty and concurrent property ownership, including condominiums, townhouses, cooperatives, planned unit developments (PUDs), and time-share property.
5. List and define types of lien.
6. List and define types of easement.
7. Define encroachments and appurtenances such as water, air, and subsurface rights.
8. Describe real property taxation and special assessment systems in North Carolina.

IN THIS CHAPTER

This chapter begins the discussion of the various forms of real property ownership. Real estate is defined by (and is subject to) a complex and unique body of laws. Although you will be exploring a variety of legal terms, you should not give legal advice. Providing legal advice or opinions is defined as the practice of law, which only attorneys are authorized to do. It is, however, the duty of real estate agents to recognize basic concepts of law as they affect clients and customers and to see that they are properly informed of their rights and obligations through appropriate legal counsel.

THE CONCEPT OF PROPERTY

Property is an individual's, a group's, or an entity's ownership rights, interest, and legal relationship to something, tangible or intangible, to the exclusion of other individuals, groups, and entities. Property, therefore, may be considered a legally created and protected bundle of rights, which an individual, a group, or an entity has in a tangible item or an intangible concept. A **bundle of rights** includes the right to possession of the property; the right of quiet enjoyment of the property; the right to exclude others; the right to dispose of the property by gift, by sale, or by will; and the right to control the use of the property and profits within the limits of the law. The components of the bundle can belong to one owner or can be separated with rights or groups of rights belonging to different owners. Examples of separate ownership of various rights in the bundle abound. For example, Hertz, a corporate entity, owns cars (tangible property) but rents the right to use those cars (intangible property) to individuals; an owner of an office building leases office space (right to possess and use) to a corporation; and a landowner sells the mineral rights to his property while retaining all other rights. Note that ownership and lease rights may coexist within the same property at the same time.

> "When you purchase a property, you get a bundle of rights. The items in the bundle can be remembered by the acronym DEEPC: Disposition, Enjoyment, Exclusivity, Possession, and Control."
> —Terry Wilson, DREI

Property is divided into real property and personal property. Real estate practitioners must have a thorough understanding of the differences between real and personal property. Different laws apply to each type of property. Most items of personal property do not require written documentation of transfer of ownership, but all transfers of ownership of an interest in real property must be in writing. Personal and real property are taxed differently. Owners' and creditors' rights differ depending on whether the property is real or personal.

Real Property

In Chapter 1, real property, also called real estate and realty, was defined as **land and everything permanently attached to the land.** A concept of the law of real property is that real property consists of lands, tenements, and hereditaments; therefore, everything included in the following definitions of these terms is a component of the property owner's bundle of rights.

Land is the surface of the earth; the area below the surface to the center of the earth; and the area above the surface, theoretically, to the highest heavens.

> 🔑 Plants are either annuals or perennials. Annuals must be planted each year and are considered personal property. Annuals are also called *fructus industriales*.
>
> Perennials do not require annual cultivation and are considered real property unless planted in a moveable container. Perennials are also called *fructus naturales*.

Land includes structures and other improvements (such as fences, swimming pools, flagpoles, and retaining walls) that have been placed there with the intention that they be a permanent part of the land.

Tenements and Hereditaments

Tenements *include all those things that are included in the definition of land and include both corporeal and incorporeal rights in land.* Corporeal rights are tangible things—things that can be touched and seen. *Incorporeal* rights are things that are intangible. Tenements include buildings (corporeal). Tenements also include rights in the property of another, such as an easement (incorporeal). In addition, tenements include *intangible rights in the land of another, such as the right to take minerals, soils, timber, fish, or game from that land.* This right is called **profit à prendre**, or simply **profit.**

Hereditament is a term that *includes everything in the term* land *and everything in the term* tenements *that is capable of being inherited.* The land and buildings are capable of being inherited and are therefore hereditaments. Some personal rights in land, such as the right to fish and some easements, may not be inheritable. If these rights are not inheritable, they are not hereditaments.

Things that grow in the soil may be included in the definition of real property. *Growing things that do not require planting or cultivation but that grow naturally and are perennial are* **fruits of the soil** (*fructus naturales*) and are designated in law as real property. Examples include forest trees, native shrubs, and wild berries. *Growing things that require planting and cultivation are* **fruits of industry** (*fructus industriales*) or **emblements** and are defined as *personal property*. These are usually annual crops, and examples include corn, wheat, melons, and soybeans. The term *emblements* also is used to denote the right of a tenant to reenter the property and harvest the emblements after the termination of the tenancy.

Appurtenances

An **appurtenance** is any right or privilege that is said to "run with the land." Therefore, it transfers with title to the land. Several of the items discussed next are examples of common appurtenances, such as subsurface, air, and riparian (water) rights. These three examples illustrate that an appurtenance cannot exist by itself; that is, the easement must attach to the primary item, the land that it affects. Other examples of appurtenances include appurtenant easements and the benefits of restrictive (protective) covenants (discussed later in this chapter).

Subsurface Rights

A subsurface right, or mineral right, is an interest in real property that allows the owner to take minerals from the earth. The owner may conduct mining operations or drilling operations personally or may sell or lease these rights to others on a royalty basis. A **mineral lease** *permits the use of land for mineral exploration and mining operations.* (The Statute of Frauds, discussed in Chapter 4, requires that such a lease be in writing to be enforceable.) The lease may be for a definite term or for a period as long as the land is productive. A mineral royalty is income received from leases of mineral land.

"Mineral, oil, gas and subsurface leases must be in writing in North Carolina."
—Melea Lemon, DREI

Air Rights

Ownership of land includes *ownership of and the rights to the area above the surface of the earth* (**air rights**). The right of ownership of the airspace enables the landowner to use that space to construct improvements, to lease, or to sell to others.

The right of ownership and control of the airspace is limited, however, by zoning ordinances and federal laws. Zoning ordinances often restrict the height of improvements constructed on the land, and federal laws permit the use of the airspace by air traffic flying at an altitude specified by the government. As a practical matter, a property owner is entitled to claim only the area above his land that he might reasonably be expected to use.

Water Rights

The *appurtenant rights of an owner of property bordering a flowing body of water* are **riparian rights.** Riparian rights attach to the land but cannot exist by themselves. Generally, property adjacent to a river or watercourse affords the landowner the right to access and use the water for purposes such as drawing water for personal use and entering the water via a boat pier. Actual ownership of the water depends on a number of factors. North Carolina recognizes the distinction between a *navigable* and a nonnavigable watercourse. In the former, adjacent owners are limited to the banks of the watercourse, whereas the state owns the body of water and the right to use it. If one owner owns all of the land surrounding a nonnavigable body of water, that owner owns all of the land under the water. If more than one owner owns property surrounding a nonnavigable body of water, ownership extends to the center of the water, unless the deed states otherwise.

Littoral rights are *the rights of landowners whose property borders an ocean or a lake.* If the water levels fluctuate, as with ocean tides, the landowner owns to the mean high watermark. The state owns the **foreshore,** which is *the land between the mean high watermark and low watermark.*

An owner's riparian property and property rights can be affected by changes in boundaries caused by the natural forces interacting with land and water. Although the geographic coordinates of land do not change, the part of the surface covered by the land and water can and do change over time.

The real estate practitioner should understand the following four natural processes that affect riparian boundaries.

1. Accretion is a gradual process in which the boundary of riparian land is extended by natural forces, usually water from a river, a lake, or an ocean depositing soil, sand, or rock onto areas previously covered by water. This acquired land becomes the property of the riparian property owner.
2. Reliction is also a gradual process and results from the permanent receding of the water that leaves the ground under it dry and exposed. This acquired land becomes the property of the riparian property owner.
3. Erosion, the reverse of accretion, is a natural process in which the flow or movement of water gradually produces a loss of riparian land—for example, beach erosion. The riparian property owner loses title to the land.
4. Avulsion, unlike accretion, reliction, and erosion, is not a gradual process. It is a rapid or sudden change in riparian land, either loss or gain, resulting from violent natural forces. There is no legal boundary change for land

> "When the river or stream is navigable, you own to the water's edge. When it is nonnavigable, you own to the center of the river or stream."
> —Tim Terry, DREI

affected by avulsion. The owner can reclaim the lost land. Theoretically, an owner retains title to and can reclaim land lost through avulsion; however, environmental laws may limit or void his right to do so.

5. Doctrine of prior appropriation is based on the theory that the first person to use the water has a continued right to do so and the later owners can make reasonable use of what is left.

Lateral and Subjacent Support

Land previously was defined as the surface of the earth; the area below the surface to the center of the earth; the air above the earth, theoretically, to the highest heavens; and everything permanently attached to the earth. For purposes of understanding lateral and subjacent support, consider only the solid surface of the earth. The ground is surrounded by more ground or by water. Riparian rights, the rights of landowners whose property borders water, are well defined in law. The solid surface of land can be gained or lost by forces of nature or by man's activity. What would happen if your neighbor decided to excavate the dirt from her land bordering your property for a project elsewhere? Unless your land is solid rock, the solid surface could shift, perhaps destroying or undermining the support of improvements on your land. Your neighbor cannot remove the dirt because you have a right of **lateral support,** which means the right of land to be supported in its natural state by adjacent land.

Now consider the part of the land that is below the surface of the earth. Suppose you sell the mineral rights. The owner of those subsurface rights can mine beneath your surface, but she must support your surface rights from below. She cannot cause the surface of your land to collapse. **Subjacent support** is the right to have one's land supported from below.

Personal Property

Personal property (also referred to as chattel or personalty) is anything that is not real property; therefore, it is not land or anything permanently attached to land. Unlike real property, it is readily, although not necessarily easily, movable. Some personal property can be severed, or removed, from the property (such as crops) and other property becomes a part of the real property by attaching or annexation (such as planting trees obtained from a nursery). Once attached, it becomes part of the real property unless excluded. Factory-built homes are another example of personal property unless steps have been taken to permanently affix it to the land including the requisite paperwork needed to convert it to being considered real property. Its "bundle of rights" is not identical to that of real property. Some property can be classified as real or personal property, depending on circumstances. Ownership of personal property is conveyed by a bill of sale.

Fixtures

> Intent is the major determinant in deciding if an item is a fixture.

A **fixture** is an item of personal property that is attached to the land or a permanent improvement on the land in such a manner that the law deems it to be part of the real property to which it is attached. Fixtures cause many problems because of misunderstandings by the parties involved. Real estate practitioners can avoid problems by thoroughly understanding the criteria for a fixture and paying careful attention to detail when listing and selling property.

Total circumstance test. This test, composed of four criteria or factors, may be used to determine an item's identification as a fixture *in the absence of a contractual agreement by the parties.*

1. *Intention:* Did the person making the attachment intend to make a permanent improvement? Would it be evident to a reasonable, rational person that the annexor's intention was that the improvement be permanent? For example, the owner of a property installs a ceiling fan in the family room. This criterion should be used in conjunction with the other criteria. If the owner expressly states her intention that the attachment is permanent, such as the sales contract stating the item is considered a fixture, and all parties involved are aware of the express intention, the express intention will rule without regard to the other three criteria.

2. *Relation of the attacher:* An owner is presumed to make a permanent improvement, whereas a renter may be presumed to make a temporary attachment. However, the real estate agent should not presume anything about the annexor's ownership but should ask questions if a tenant is involved. If the real property owner has permanently attached personal property to his real property during his ownership, the attached property is usually considered real property. (See the paragraph "Effect of the Uniform Commercial Code" for an exception.) Once the item becomes real property, its ownership passes to the new owner when the present owner sells or otherwise disposes of the property, absent a contract or an agreement to the contrary. Take the example regarding the ceiling fan. If a tenant instead of the owner of the property were to install the fan, would his intention be that the ceiling fan remain with the property or would he plan to take down the ceiling fan he had purchased and replace it with the original fixture?

3. *Method:* Does the method of attachment mean that removal of the item will damage the property? Answering this question is a bit tricky. What constitutes damage? Is a small nail or screw hole damage? What is "permanently attached"? It may not actually need to be attached. This criterion absolutely

must be used in conjunction with the other circumstances. A small picture hanger on a wall likely does not constitute substantial or permanent attachment, but a pair of thousand-pound statues sitting on custom-made concrete pillars may.

4. *Adaptation:* How is the item being used? Is the item adapted to the real property to which it is attached? An example would be blinds custom made to fit nonstandard windows. The more "site specific" an item is the less obviously attached it needs to be in order to be considered an attachment.

Courts have not been consistent in their application of the total circumstance test. If the courts cannot agree, buyers, sellers, and real estate agents are unlikely to always agree. Although real estate agents must understand these criteria, they should not give legal advice as to what is or is not a fixture in a given circumstance. That would be practicing law without a license. They can avoid, however, most problems in this area by using and understanding the North Carolina Bar Association/North Carolina Association of REALTORS® (NCBA/NCAR) Standard Form No. 2-T, Offer to Purchase and Contract, found in Chapter 10, page 276. Familiarizing the seller with this form at the time of listing and the buyer at the initial buyer interview, or at least by the time of the offer, is an excellent way to prevent misunderstandings.

Test Tip!

For an excellent list of fixtures that are important for testing purposes, refer to paragraph 2 of the Offer to Purchase and Contract (Chapter 10, Figure 10.2).

The practitioner must ensure that all parties understand all contracts. This can be accomplished by clearly identifying fixtures and personal property in both the listing and the sales contracts. Real property can become personal property by contract. For example, a chandelier is personal property until it is installed in the house and then becomes a fixture upon installation. If the contract provides for the chandelier to be replaced with a less expensive one, the original chandelier again becomes personal property upon removal according to the contract, and the new, less expensive chandelier, which is personal property when it is purchased, becomes real property when it is installed according to the contract. If the contract were silent about the chandelier, the buyers could reasonably expect the chandelier to be a fixture and to convey as real property. In some instances, something is considered a fixture simply because the contract states that it is a fixture even though the item does not appear to meet the standards for a fixture listed previously, such as a stove. Simply stated, if the contract says that an item is a fixture, then it is a fixture.

"At the end of a lease, trade fixtures remaining after the lease term are considered abandoned by the tenant and become the real property of the landlord through the process of 'accession.'"
—Tim Terry, DREI

Trade fixtures. A special category of fixtures is recognized for the items of personal property that are used in the course of a business operating in a leased property. For example, a merchant may rent a store and install shelves to display merchandise. These shelves are a temporary attachment necessary for the operation of the business. A more complex situation would arise in the operation of a restaurant in a rented space. Consider all the items required in this operation, including stoves, ovens, grills, chairs, tables, and so on. Such attachments are recognized as trade fixtures, and they retain their personal property classification such that the restaurant tenant can remove them at the termination of the lease. The tenant remains liable for any damages caused by the removal of the trade fixture at the expiration of the lease.

Again, the agent must ensure that all understandings of the parties are supported by terms of a rental contract. Recall, however, that only attorneys can draft contracts. Real estate practitioners would exceed their authority and be entering the prohibited practice of law if they attempted to write legal clauses in a contract.

Agricultural fixtures. Agricultural fixtures are those fixtures installed by a property owner for the purposes of agricultural use. Although historically treated differently, they are now treated the same as trade fixtures.

Effect of the Uniform Commercial Code. A special situation occurs when an owner has financed the purchase of an item installed in her property. The Uniform Commercial Code provides for the lender to retain a security interest in a chattel (personal property) until the lender is paid in full. An instrument called a security agreement, which is put on the public record by the filing of a notice called a financing statement, creates the security interest. This notice is filed in the office of the Register of Deeds. The filing of the financing statement provides constructive notice to the world that a security interest exists in the item. As a result, the attached item is not legally classified as a fixture, or a part of the real property, until the security agreement has been satisfied by full payment. It is treated as personal property of the homeowner until such time as it has been paid for in full. Before that time it can be repossessed by the creditor to satisfy repayment.

"The application of the UCC to fixtures keeps these items as personal property or personalty until the debt has been repaid."
—Tim Terry, DREI

Consequently, the lender can remove the item in the event the buyer/borrower defaults in payment, even though the item has been attached to real property. Subsequent purchasers, as well as a subsequent lender, are bound by the filing of the financing statement. Therefore, a purchaser of the home or a lender accepting the property as security for a mortgage must complete the payments or permit the removal of the item by the lender in the event the property owner does not satisfy the debt.

Improvements

Numerous improvements must be made to and on raw land to make it accessible and suitable for the various uses people have for it. An improvement is anything of value that is added to real property or anything that alters real property in such a way as to increase its utility or value; however, these improvements do not include repairs and replacements. The definition has two parts: (1) private improvements, usually done *on the land* by the property owner; and (2) public improvements such as streets, sewers, water, and sidewalks done *to the land* by government or quasi-government organizations. From a practical point of view, the agent should make certain that all parties understand the meaning each party intends to convey when using the terms *improvements, improvements to the land, improvements on the land, improved land,* or *improved lot.*

Improvements on the land done by property owners include structures such as buildings, paved driveways and walkways, tennis courts, fences, walls, and swimming pools. They do not include routine maintenance, repairs, or replacements.

Improvements to the land done by government or quasi-government entities may include the following:

1. Roads, highways, and bridges built to make the land accessible.
2. Utilities such as electric power, water, sewer, gas lines, and phone lines brought to the site.
3. Modifications or improvements such as clearing, grading, and draining to make it suitable for its intended use.

"Improved land" or "improved lot" could mean the land or lot has had improvements to it to prepare it for a building, or it could mean that improvements such as buildings have already been constructed on it. The important thing is for the agent to make certain that the meaning is clear when listing, advertising, and negotiating offers to purchase and in all other aspects of the transaction.

Test Tip!

For the National Exam section, the student should treat an improvement as an appurtance.

Factory-Built (Manufactured) Housing

Just like many components of a house today that are manufactured in a factory so is the case for entire homes. Although historically these type homes have been viewed as "less desirable" than a stick-built home, the reality is that manufacturing tolerances and conditions are superior to that of many site-built structures. The absence of weather-related delays, reduced theft, and the ability to literally work around the clock make this type of construction attractive in many ways.

The reference to a "manufactured" home is a modern term for what many people traditionally have called a mobile home or house trailer. Today's manufactured home is built according to rigid U.S. Department of Housing and Urban Development (HUD) standards and will have a HUD certification label affixed to the exterior of the structure. This type of housing can be considered either personal or real property depending on the steps taken by the owner. Initially the manufactured home is considered personal property and will be titled with the North Carolina Department of Motor Vehicles (DMV) much the same as an automobile is registered. One of the characteristics of the manufactured home is that it will be constructed on a permanent nonremovable steel chassis, although brokers need to be aware that some modular homes may utilize a steel chassis as well.

The owner can convert a manufactured home to real property status by removing the wheels, axle, and moving hitch and affixing the structure to a permanent foundation owned by the homeowner. Once this work has been completed, the owner can file an affidavit of conversion that cancels the title with the DMV, which will finalize the conversion from personal to real property. Once this is done, the owner will need to change the tax listing to show the unit is now real property and the bill of sale and lien will need to be changed to a deed and deed of trust as applicable. Unlike many other situations involving attaching personal property so that it may be considered real property, the manufactured home does not automatically convey to real property merely upon attachment. Until the appropriate paperwork has been completed and filed, the unit will remain personal property.

Many people confuse modular housing as merely a type of manufactured housing. Although both examples are clearly built in a factory, the modular home is built in accordance with state building codes and once constructed on the permanent foundation will be considered real property. These type of units also will have an identifying label, including a serial number, that typically is affixed next to the electrical panel, under the sink area, or on the back of the unit.

Most subdivision protective covenants that prohibit the construction of a manufactured home will not affect the ability of the property owner to construct a modular home on the lot.

ESTATES IN REAL PROPERTY

Definition of Estate

An **estate** in real property is an interest in the property sufficient to give the owner of the estate the right to possession of the property. It is essential to understand the difference between the right of possession and the right of use. The owner of an estate in land has the right of possession of the land in addition to the right to use it. An easement owner, in contrast, has the use of the land but not the right to possess it; therefore, the easement is a nonpossessory interest in land. The Latin translation for the word *estate* is "status." This indicates the relationship in which the estate owner stands with reference to rights in the property, and it establishes the degree, quantity, nature, and extent of interest a person has in real property.

Types of Estate in Land

Estates in land are divided into two groups: estates of freehold and estates of less than freehold (also called leasehold estates and nonfreehold estates). Two estates can exist simultaneously in land. The owner (lessor) of a property has a freehold estate. If she leases the property, the tenant (lessee) has a leasehold estate. Each of these two major divisions contains various groupings or subheadings.

Freehold Estates

Freehold is defined as *an interest in land of at least a lifetime and therefore generally is identified with the concept of title or ownership.* **Freehold estates** may be fee simple estates or life estates (see Figure 2.1). Fee simple estates are inheritable; most life estates are not.

Freehold estates are divided into two categories: estates of inheritance and estates not of inheritance.

> "'Freehold' means that you are 'free to hold' the property. You are the owner of it. A leasehold estate is anything less than ownership."
> —Jim Hriso

I. ESTATES OF INHERITANCE

Estates of inheritance last a lifetime and continue after the death of the titleholder as they are passed on to one's heirs.

A. Fee simple estates

1. *Fee simple absolute.* The estate of **fee simple absolute** *provides the greatest form of ownership available in real property.*

   This estate may be described as fee simple absolute, fee simple, or ownership in fee. Ownership in fee simple absolute provides certain legal rights usually described as a *bundle of rights*. The owner in fee simple absolute may convey a life estate to another, may pledge the property as security for a mortgage debt, may convey a leasehold estate to another, may grant

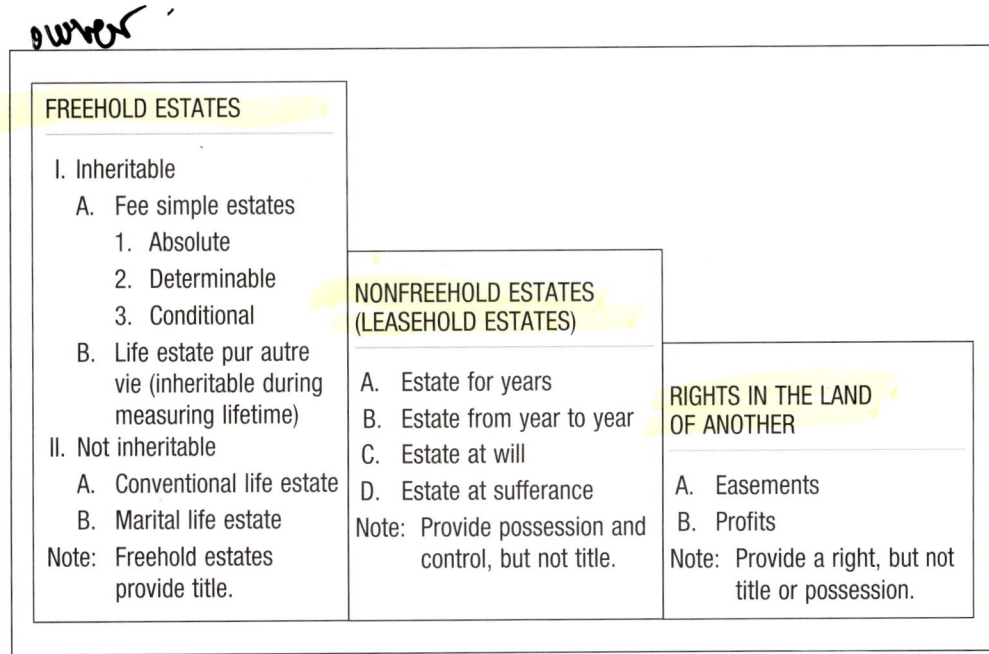

FIGURE 2.1 Estates and rights in real estate property (in descending order of importance).
Source: © 2019 OnCourse Learning

an easement in the land to another, or may give a license to conduct some activity on the property to another. Some of these rights may be removed from the bundle, leaving the other rights intact. For example, if the owner conveyed a lease or an easement to another, the owner's remaining rights would be a fee simple subject to the lease or easement. Fee simple ownership should not be confused with the quality of title. Ownership in fee means that the grantee owns it forever, not that it is free of title defects. Certainly an owner cannot expect to live forever, so the ownership consists of two periods of time, from receipt of title until the owner dies, and the period of time after the owner dies. The owner has the rights of ownership and use during his lifetime and then the ownership shall convey to his heirs (either by will or by the law of descent.).

> The word "fee" denotes ownership that is inheritable. Fee simple absolute, also known as fee simple or fee, means ownership forever or for at least a lifetime. Because the ownership is considered "for at least a lifetime" the use of the term "fee" does not mean that ownership is free and clear of any liens. It speaks more to the quantity of title (at least a lifetime) than to the quality (free of liens).

> "Fee simple defeasible, sometimes known as a fee with a condition subsequent or a fee simple determinable, can be defeated and taken away."
> —Terry Wilson, DREI

2. *Fee simple determinable.* This **defeasible fee** or **qualified fee** estate is also an inheritable freehold estate in the form of a fee simple estate; however, the grantor can terminate the title under certain conditions. An example of a fee simple determinable is a situation in which a grantor conveys title to a college and in the conveyance stipulates that the title is good "so long as" the property is used for scholastic purposes. Title received by the college can be for an infinite period of time. If the property is not used for the purpose specified in the conveyance, however, the title will automatically terminate and revert to the original grantor or the grantor's heirs.

3. *Fee simple subject to a condition subsequent.* The fee simple subject to a condition subsequent can continue for an infinite period, as is the case with the fee simple absolute. The fee simple subject to a condition subsequent also can be defeated and, therefore, is a defeasible title. The fee simple subject to a condition subsequent is created by the grantor (the one conveying title), who restricts the future use of the property in some way. For example, a grantor may convey property with the condition that it can never be used as a landfill. As long as the property is never used for this purpose, the title will continue indefinitely in the name of the initial grantee or any subsequent grantee. Any use of the property for a landfill will violate the covenant in the deed and the original grantor or her heirs may reenter the property and take

possession or go to court and sue to regain possession. By doing so, the titleholder's estate is terminated.

A grantor may want to convey a title this way for several reasons. In the case of the landfill, the owner may be protecting the property he owns that is close to the landfill. In the case of the college, the grantor may be highly committed to education but may not want to give up ownership of the property for any other reason. Notice that in the case of a fee simple determinable, the estate in the grantee automatically terminates in the event the designated use of the property is not continued or a prohibited use is undertaken. This is contrasted with the fee simple subject to a condition subsequent, in which the termination is not automatic. In the latter case, the grantor and/or the heirs must either reenter the property or go to court to obtain possession of the property and to terminate the estate in the grantee. It should be noted that qualified fee or use conditions based on race, color, sex, national origin, familial status, handicap, or religion are void because they are against public policy; therefore, if a qualified fee or use condition based on any of these factors appears as a condition of title, the title is really a fee simple absolute.

B. *Estates pur autre vie (for the life of another)*. *These estates are measured by the lifetime of a person other than the person receiving the title.* They may be willed or inherited by heirs of the life estate grantee if the grantee dies before the person who is the measuring life. These rights should not be confused with the more traditional, and noninheritable, conventional life estates. The **pur autre vie** is an inheritable right, should the life interest person die before the measuring life person deceases.

For example, Dad may grant title to his son for as long as Mom (his widow) is still alive. If the son dies before Mom, the title to the life estate *pur autre vie* would pass to the son's heirs, such as a grandson or a granddaughter. Therefore, the life estate is not only for the duration of the son's life, but will last until Mom's death, as hers is still the measuring life. At Mom's death, the life estate terminates.

II ESTATES NOT OF INHERITANCE

Estates not of inheritance are good only for the life of the tenant (freehold) and do not pass on to his heirs, but rather are disposed of by some other method.

In addition to being created by an intentional conveyance, life estates also can be created by operation of law. Life estates created by act of the parties are called conventional life estates, whereas life estates created by operation of law are called **marital life estates.**

A. *Conventional life estates (estate for tenant's own life).* A **life estate** is a noninheritable **freehold estate.** It is created only for the life of the named **life**

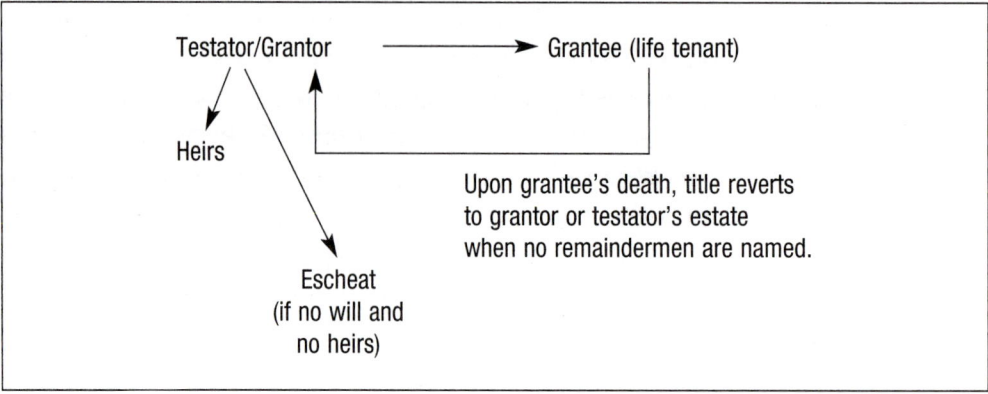

FIGURE 2.2 Life estate in reversion.
Source: © 2019 OnCourse Learning

> "Do not memorize that a remainderman means a 3rd party. It is better to remember that any time a life estate ends and the reversionary interest does not return to the grantor then a remainder interest exists."
>
> —Len Elder, DREI

tenant; that is, *one who holds a life estate.* The question arises as to what will happen to the estate at the death of the life tenant. *If nothing else is specified in the conveyance of the life estate, it will revert to the grantor or to his heirs at the death of the life tenant.* The grantor or his heirs thus would have a **reversionary interest** in this case (see Figure 2.2). Alternatively, the conveyance of the life estate could specify that the estate pass on to someone other than the grantor or his heirs. This person would be called a **remainderman** and has a *remainder, or future, interest in the property.* After the death of the life tenant, the remainderman would then have title in fee simple absolute (see Figure 2.3).

B. *Marital life estates.* A marital life estate is created in North Carolina by the **intestate succession** statutes governing the distribution of property of one who dies intestate, that is, dies without leaving a valid

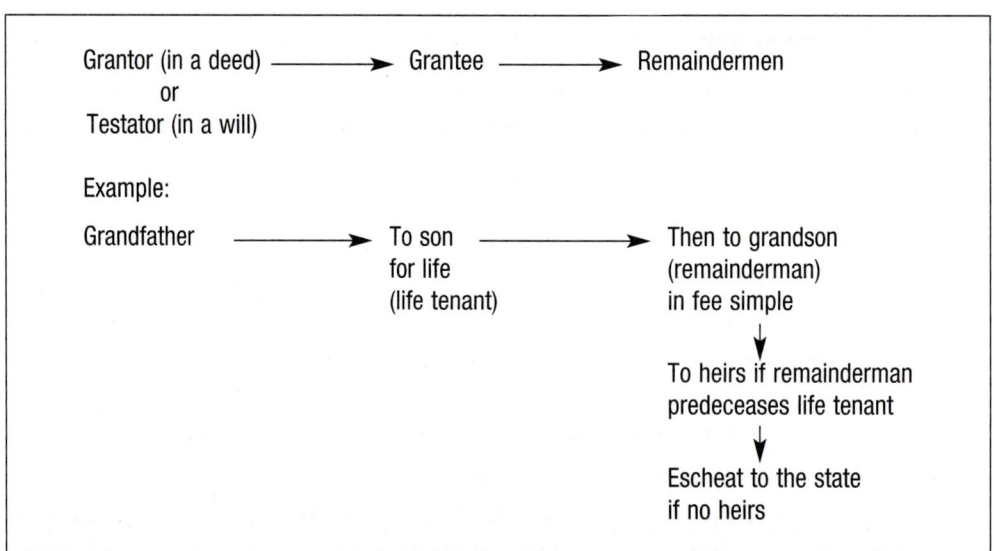

FIGURE 2.3 Life estate in remainder.
Source: © 2019 OnCourse Learning

will. This statute allows the surviving spouse to choose a life estate in one-third of the real property owned in severalty (sole ownership) by the deceased spouse at any time during the marriage under certain conditions. If the surviving spouse is entitled to any property of the deceased spouse through a will or intestate succession statutes and the surviving spouse has not joined in the transfer of such property by signing the deed, the surviving spouse must forfeit any interest in the deceased spouse's property resulting from a will or an inheritance to claim her marital estate. Few surviving spouses elect the marital life estate option because it is seldom advantageous for them to do so. Several important points pertain to marital life estates:

- A will cannot defeat the marital interest of a surviving spouse.
- Statutes do not apply to property owned as tenants by the entirety.
- A surviving spouse has a choice of either marital life estate or property of the deceased spouse willed to the surviving spouse.

From these requirements, you can see that it is extremely important for both husband and wife to join in the conveyance of any property owned by either of them while they are married. Otherwise, the grantee's title could be affected by a marital interest of the surviving spouse.

Some states still provide dower and curtesy rights to a surviving spouse. **Dower** is *the wife's right* and **curtesy** is *the husband's right to a life estate in the property owned by a deceased spouse* during the marriage. North Carolina's intestate succession statutes abolished dower and curtesy rights and provided a substitute, which sets forth the manner in which the property of an intestate (one who has died without leaving a valid will) is distributed to the heirs.

Rights and responsibilities of life tenants. A life tenant has the right of **alienation.** That is, the life tenant can *transfer her title to another person or pledge the title as security for a debt.* Of course, the individual cannot give a title for a duration longer than her life or the life of the person named in the creation of a life estate to establish its duration. The life tenant also has the right to the net income produced by the property, if any. The life tenant can legally mortgage the life estate. It is unlikely that a lending institution would accept a life estate as security for a mortgage, however, because the estate terminates on the death of the life tenant. If the life tenant were able to do this, however, she would be responsible for the principal and interest on that mortgage note. An outstanding mortgage on the property is the responsibility of the grantor or the remainderman, and the life tenant must pay the interest but not the principal.

A life tenant has certain responsibilities. He must not commit waste and must preserve the estate for the benefit of the remainderman or for the person who holds the reversionary interest. Otherwise, the life tenant is not answerable to the future holder of the estate. The life tenant has a legal right called the right to **estovers,** which allows him *to cut and use a reasonable amount of* *timber from the land to repair buildings or to use it for fuel, but does not allow the tenant to cut and sell the timber for profit.* A violation of the right of estovers is called an *act of waste*.

A life tenant has an obligation to pay the real property taxes on the property in which he has a life estate. The tenant also has the duty to pay any assessments levied against the property by a county or municipality for improvements to the property. Assessments are levied against land for improvements made to the land, such as paving streets and laying water and sewer lines.

The life tenant also has a duty to make repairs to the improvements on the land. He cannot permit the property to deteriorate because of lack of repairs and thus cause depreciation to existing improvements.

Many states recognize the primary home as a sort of life estate that can provide some degree of protection from creditors. The North Carolina Homestead Exemption Law protects an amount of interest, or equity, in the debtor's personal residence, whether it is real or personal property, from creditors in the event of lawsuits, including bankruptcy filings. The current amount of protection is $35,000, which was increased from $18,500 in December 2009. Additionally, this act increases the amount of protection to a maximum of $60,000 in cases in which the resident is over the age of 65 and the property was previously owned in tenancy by entireties, or in joint tenancy with rights of survivorship, in which one of the former co-owners is now deceased. The property owner is helped by this act in the event of judgment liens obtained against her. The owner still would be obligated to pay property taxes and any mortgage balances due.

Homestead exemptions in other states are relatively similar, although many are more extensive than those in North Carolina.

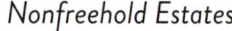

Nonfreehold Estates

The **nonfreehold estates,** also known as less-than-freehold or **leasehold estates,** *confer a rental interest in real property.* Four estates are recognized:

1. *Estate for years* is for any fixed period of time and automatically terminates at the end of that period.
2. *Estate from year to year* is a periodic estate that automatically renews at the end of its period if the parties do not provide otherwise.
3. An *estate at will* is for an indefinite time and may be terminated by either party instantaneously by giving notice to the other party.
4. An *estate at sufferance* is not truly an estate but rather a holdover situation created when the tenant's lease has expired and she fails to vacate the premises.

These nonfreehold estates are described in more detail in Chapter 15.

OWNERSHIP OF REAL PROPERTY

Ownership in Severalty

When *title to real property is held in the name of only one person* or entity, it is called ownership in **severalty**. Not to be confused with the word several, the concept of severalty is actually a derivative from the word "sever." The person holding title is the sole or only owner. This is the form of ownership that a corporation likely would have even though the corporation has many owners or stockholders (i.e., IBM Corporation). The fact that title is held in severalty does not eliminate the possibility of marital rights. This is the case when a single person acquires title to a property in severalty and later gets married. Even though the new spouse does not have his names on the title to the property, he still would obtain marital rights upon marriage.

Concurrent (Joint) Ownership

Simultaneous ownership of real property by two or more people is called concurrent ownership or **co-ownership**. There are various types of co-ownership, and the rights of the owners depend on the type of ownership they have. The types of co-ownership are tenancy in common, joint tenancy, and tenancy by the entirety.

The co-owners may hold title in the same manner as owners in severalty—for example, fee simple absolute, fee simple subject to a condition subsequent, and fee simple determinable.

Tenancy in Common

Tenancy in common is characterized by *two or more persons holding title to a property at the same time, with no right of survivorship*. Anyone can hold title as a tenant in common. The concept of unity of possession means that each owner holds an undivided interest in the entire property, rather than one specific part of it. Upon the death of a tenant in common, the deceased's share goes to his heirs.

A tenant in common may sell his share to anybody without destroying the tenancy relationship. Each tenant in common may also pledge her share of the property as security for a loan. This creates an encumbrance against that share only, not against the entire property. Tenants in common do not need to have the same amount of interest in the property. For example, one tenant may hold a 50% interest, with two other tenants holding 25% each. If the deed does not specify the interest each holds, their interest will be considered equal.

A tenant in common may bring legal action to have the property **partitioned** so *each tenant has a specific portion of the property exclusively*. If this can be done fairly with a piece of land, each tenant receives title to a tract according to his share of interest. If the land cannot be divided to the satisfaction of the co-owners, the court may order its sale, with appropriate shares of the proceeds distributed to the tenants. Tenancy in common is also the form of concurrent ownership that is recognized when either a joint tenancy, or tenancy by entireties, is destroyed but when there are still multiple owners, such as the case when a married couple obtains a divorce but remains in a co-ownership position.

Joint Tenancy

This form of co-ownership requires the four unities of time, title, interest, and possession. People with **joint tenancy** *must have the same interest in the property, must receive their title at the same time from the same source, and must have the same degree of undivided ownership and right to possession in the property.* For example, if there are three joint tenants, each must own an undivided one-third interest in the property, they must all receive their title from the same source at the same time, and they must continue to hold possession concurrently.

"Joint Tenancy exists where there are four fundamental unities; time, title, interest and possession. Remember TTIP."
—Derrin Dunzweiler

If a joint tenant sells her share of ownership, the sale violates the requirement of unity of time, title, interest, and possession as far as the new buyer is concerned. Upon the sale of an interest by a joint tenant, the person buying this share does not become a joint tenant with the other tenants, but rather joins them as a tenant in common.

Other states, but not North Carolina, provide the concept of automatic rights of **survivorship** in joint tenancies, wherein *the surviving partners automatically take over the share of a deceased partner.* Today, the automatic right of survivorship is not favored in law except in joint ownership by husband and wife as tenants by the entirety.

As indicated in the previous paragraph, North Carolina tends not to recognize the automatic rights of survivorship, but rather requires the parties to *specifically* indicate in the deed that it is to be joint tenancy with the rights of survivorship. A common illustration might be "to Sam Smith and Tracy Jones as joint tenants with rights of survivorship," which shows a specific intent. Examples such as "to Robert Bellamy and Sally Browne jointly" or to "Angie Smith and Stephanie Clark as joint tenants" fail to expressly provide for survivorship and therefore will not be recognized as joint tenancy but rather tenancy in common. Additionally, in contrast to the more "national" interpretation of joint tenancy, in 2009, North Carolina provided for the ability to have unequal ownership interests in joint tenancy as long as the right of survivorship was clearly addressed.

The concept of joint tenancy, with rights of survivorship, is increasing in popularity among unmarried couples, many of whom are not able to partake in tenancy by entireties, as a means to acquire title and have the ownership automatically go to the surviving member of the couple and therefore avoid the risks, costs, and consequences of an inheritance.

> **Test Tip!**
>
> Joint tenancy ownership requires the following four unities:
>
> - Time—Must acquire interests at the same time
> - Title—Must acquire title on the same document (deed)
> - Interest—Considered equal shares unless stated otherwise
> - Possession—Has the right to use and possess the entire property

Tenancy by the Entirety

Ownership through **tenancy by the entirety** *is limited to husband and wife.* To receive a title as tenants by the entirety, *there must be a legal marriage at the time that the husband and wife receive title to the property.* It is not necessary for the deed to read "to husband and wife as tenants by the entirety" to create a tenancy by the entirety. The deed only needs to convey the property "to John A. Jones and Mary A. Jones, who are husband and wife," and a tenancy by the entirety is automatically created. Tenancy by the entirety does contain the right of survivorship. The surviving spouse receives title to the property automatically by operation of law. Creation of tenancy by the entirety requires the five unities of time, title, interest, possession, and marriage.

A husband or wife owning land as tenants by the entirety may not legally convey property to a third party without the other spouse joining in the deed. There can be no partition of real property held by tenants by the entirety.

Tenancy by the entirety exists as long as the tenants hold title to the property and are legally married. Tenancy by the entirety is abolished by decree of divorce or in the event of death of one of the owners. A mere legal separation is not sufficient. When a final decree of absolute divorce is obtained, however, the ownership is automatically changed to tenancy in common by operation of law, eliminating the right of survivorship. In the event of death, the remaining spouse will now be considered to hold title in severalty.

Married people may, if they elect to do so, own property as tenants in common. It is not necessary for them to take title as tenants by the entirety.

In North Carolina, one spouse can purchase a property, but it usually takes the signature of the husband and the wife to convey and give a clear title to a grantee, regardless of how the property is held. If a mortgage or deed of trust is given to secure a note for a property being purchased by one spouse, the lender usually requires the other spouse to sign the deed of trust or mortgage but does not require the nonpurchasing spouse to sign the note unless that spouse's income is used to qualify for the loan.

Many times a property is owned by one spouse before the marriage. Upon marriage, title will remain in severalty but coupled with a marital right. In another

> "In North Carolina a married individual can take title in his or her name alone without the spouse having an interest in the property. The document which waives and relinquishes the spouse's interest is called a Free Trader Agreement."
> —Tim Terry, DREI

situation, a couple may have acquired title to a property together as co-owners, such as tenancy in common or joint tenancy, before their marriage. As in the illustration regarding severalty ownership just mentioned, the ownership does not convert to tenancy by entireties upon marriage. The deed would have to be conveyed by the couple, to the couple, after marriage to make it tenancy by entireties.

Combination (Hybrid) Forms of Ownership

Condominiums

Condominium ownership is a form of ownership in real estate that is now recognized in all states. North Carolina statutes define this type of ownership, set forth the requirements for the creation of a condominium, and set special restrictions on the offering of a condominium for sale.

A condominium purchaser receives a fee simple title to an apartment. Condominium unit owners can hold ownership of their units in the same ways owners of any freehold estate hold ownership—that is, in severalty, as tenants in common, as joint tenants, or as tenants by the entirety. Individuals, groups, and business entities can hold ownership in condominium units in the same ways they can hold ownership in other freehold estates, providing they meet the criteria for the specific type of ownership. For example, only a married couple can own real estate as tenants by the entirety. The owner can convey title by deed or leave it to an heir by will. **Condominium** ownership includes *ownership of the airspace of the individual unit as well as co-ownership in the common areas* of the condominium along with the other unit owners. This co-ownership is as a tenant in common in the common areas, including the corridors, grounds, parking areas, and recreational facilities. The right to partition is waived in this tenancy in common ownership of common areas (see Figure 2.4).

North Carolina statutes prescribe the manner in which a condominium is to be created. This includes a declaration, bylaws, and a copy of the construction plans. To be valid, the declaration, articles, and bylaws must be recorded on the public record in the Register of Deeds office in the county where the property is located.

The declaration includes a legal description of the property; a plat of the property with the location of the buildings, plans, and specifications for the buildings and the various units; a description of the common areas; and the degree of ownership in the common areas available to each unit owner. It also includes covenants, conditions, and restrictions affecting the property. It also may include a "right of first refusal" clause, giving the association the first opportunity to purchase a unit if the owner wishes to sell.

The articles of association establish an association to provide for the maintenance and management of the common areas and other services for the

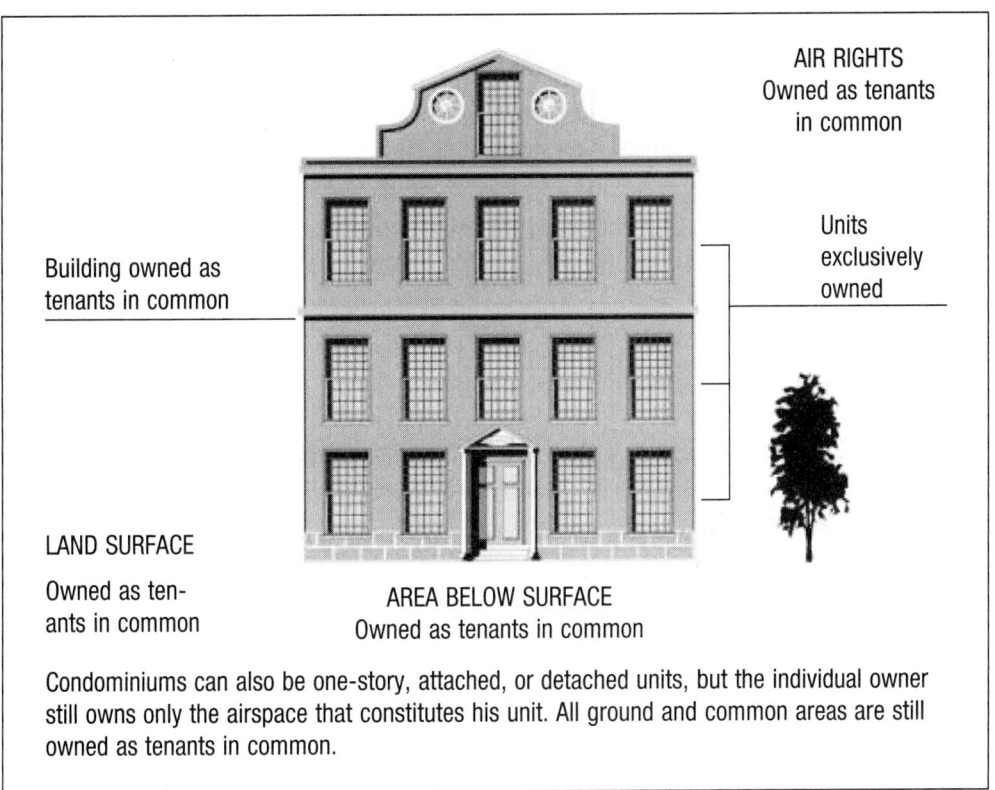

FIGURE 2.4 Condominium ownership.

owner-members. Owners, as members of the association, are assessed to pay for these necessary services. Such assessments are usually in the form of monthly dues, but periodic special assessments also can be levied. The bylaws set forth the various officers in the association and the way they are elected, and they set forth the requirements for amending the bylaws.

The creation of a condominium is not limited to residential purposes. Virtually anything can utilize the condominium form of ownership. Other purposes may include office space, parking space, and an industrial park. Indeed, it would seem as the potential uses of a condominium form of ownership are limited only by the developer's imagination. The purpose of the condominium must be set forth in the declaration as required by state statute.

Condominiums can also be one-story, attached, or detached units, but the individual owner still owns only the airspace that constitutes his unit. It is not uncommon that an owner may be granted exclusive use of some limited common areas such as balconies, assigned parking spaces and storage units. All ground and common areas are still owned as tenants in common.

A condominium unit can be mortgaged just as any other property. Federal Housing Administration (FHA) financing has been available for condominiums since 1961, and the Department of Veterans Affairs (VA) guarantees mortgage loans for the purchase of condominiums. A condominium project must have FHA or VA approval before FHA will make loans on any of the units. FHA further requires that condominium projects have a specified percentage of owner-occupancy before FHA will make a loan on any of the units. The occupancy rate is monitored. That percentage can vary by region.

The **North Carolina Condominium Act** (1986) sets specific requirements on offering for sale or resale a condominium created on or after October 1, 1986, although these rights can be waived, and typically are, when the condo is used for nonresidential purposes. Essentially, the act offers the following consumer protections (these protections apply only to condominiums, not to townhouses or PUDs).

1. *Public offering statement:* The developer must provide a public offering statement to the prospective buyer of a new condominium before the contract is signed. The North Carolina Condominium Act requires that the developer disclose certain information pertaining to the condominium project, including the purchaser's right to cancel. The public offering statement is not required for resale of units.

2. *Purchaser's right to cancel:* A purchaser has the right to cancel, absolutely and without penalty, the purchase of a new condominium unit from the developer for any reason during the first seven days after signing the contract. Title cannot pass during this seven-day period. Like the public offering statement, the purchaser's right to cancel does not apply to resale units.

3. *Escrow of deposit:* Any deposits made by the purchaser must remain in the developer's or his agent's escrow account the full seven days, unless the purchaser cancels the contract earlier. In that case, the money is to be refunded to the purchaser. All escrow accounts must be held in an insured bank or savings and loan in North Carolina.

4. *Resale certificates:* When reselling a condominium built on or after October 1, 1986, the unit's owner or owner's agent must provide a resale certificate to the purchasers that discloses monthly assessment for the common areas and other fees for which unit owners are responsible. A public offering statement or a right to cancel is *not* required for resale of a unit.

5. *Warranties:* There is an implied warranty that the unit is constructed in an acceptable manner, free from defects, and suitable for the purpose intended unless there is an agreement to the contrary or the warranty has been disclaimed in such a manner as to make it void.

The agent must provide his client with a public offering statement if the client is purchasing a new condominium or a resale certificate if reselling a unit subject to this statute. Failure to do so violates the agency relationship and, therefore, the Real Estate License Law. It also leaves the agent potentially liable to the purchaser in civil court.

> **Test Tip!**
> - New condominium sales require a public offering statement and contain rescission dates.
> - A resale condominium requires a property disclosure statement and a resale certificate and does not contain rescission dates.

Townhouse Ownership

> The **townhouse** form of ownership is somewhat different from the condominium form in that the townhouse *provides for the ownership of the unit as well as the specific portion of land upon which the individual unit is located.*

Because each unit rests on its own foundation and its own piece of land, it cannot have another unit above it. A townhouse is, therefore, a vertical structure that is attached horizontally to other units, which also rest on their own foundations. The townhouse may be two or three stories, but all the stories are part of one unit. This is in contrast to condominium units, which are attached vertically but whose horizontal stacks of units share a foundation and ground.

There is another significant difference in the ownership of the common grounds. Because the townhouse owner owns the land of his specific unit, the owners association owns the remainder of the common areas, such as the walks and swimming pool, in severalty. This is different from condominium ownership, in which the owners association owns nothing itself because the owners own the common elements together as tenants in common. Maintenance is provided by periodic fees and assessments that are charged to the individual unit owners.

Cooperatives

Ownership in a **cooperative** (co-op) results from *ownership of shares of stock in a corporation that owns a building containing cooperative apartments.* The right of stockholders to occupy an apartment is provided by a proprietary lease and therefore there is no deed. The only real property interest of the stockholders is a leasehold estate providing the right to possession of an apartment. The stockholders, as lessees, pay no rent but do pay an assessment to cover the cost of maintaining and operating the building, real property taxes, and debt service if there is a mortgage against the building. The owners' rights and obligations are specified in the lease and the stock certificate. Proprietary lease tenants do not "own" real property. The cooperative ownership requires that prospective purchasers are voted on to determine whether they will be allowed to purchase the share of stock and be allowed to occupy the unit. Because the purchaser is purchasing only shares of stock, as opposed to actual ownership of real property, this is not in violation of federal fair housing laws. Co-ops involving ownership of real property are not a popular form of ownership in North Carolina but are a common form of ownership in some larger metropolitan areas around the country.

Time Sharing

Time sharing is a fairly recent innovation. North Carolina has specific statutes defining and regulating time-shares. **Time sharing** is defined as *any right to occupy a property for five or more separated time periods over a span of five or more years.* Any interest meeting this definition is classified as real property, and the laws pertaining to real estate transactions apply. Article IV of the Real Estate License Law sets specific regulations on the sale of time-share property. The developer must obtain a registration certificate from the Real Estate Commission before offering the units for sale to the public, and all people selling an interest in a time-share must have a real estate license. Additionally, purchasers must be given a public offering statement meeting North Carolina Real Estate Commission guidelines before a contract is signed and must have a five-day right of rescission after executing such a contract. See Appendix C for rules and regulations for time-shares and real estate laws.

"North Carolina Statute 93A-39-58 found in Appendix C in the textbook contains significant detail on timeshares that is on the course syllabus. Read this statute in conjunction with the material in the Adventure Guide regarding timeshares."

—Tim Terry, DREI

Time sharing is a type of real estate innovation that allows participants to acquire the right to occupy a unit of real estate, most likely a resort, for a brief period of time. Because most people are unable to take more than a week to few weeks of vacation time each year this has become a popular method for people who prefer to pay only for the time they use. Unfortunately, this type of conveyance has created many problems, including high-pressure sales tactics that have left many people regretting the purchase almost immediately afterward. Numerous examples exist in which conveyances were never recorded and liens were not paid off. As a result, North Carolina has adopted numerous laws and rules pertaining to time-shares.

Test Tip!

Students should be aware that time-shares are tested in two different areas of the exam. They may be tested on for Chapter 2 as well as under License Law. Because of that importance, the following list gives the most important elements of these rules.

Key Time-Share Facts for North Carolina

- A time-share is considered to be five or more separate time periods spread over a period of at least five years.
- All time-shares are considered real property.

- All persons selling, or attempting to sell time-shares in North Carolina must have a valid active real estate license.
- There is no separate time-share license.
- There is no exemption for employee of developer status.
- The developer must obtain a certificate of registration from the North Carolina Real Estate Commission.
- The developer must record a time-share instrument (1) no less than 6 days nor more than 45 days from date of purchase, and (2) no more than 180 days from the date of sale if monies were paid to an independent escrow agent at the end of the 10-day period.
- The developer must give the purchaser the public offering statement by the date of purchase.
- The time-share contract is voidable without penalty for five days from contract of sale.
- Monies collected on the time-share purchase must be deposited immediately within 10 days upon receipt.
- Such payments are considered to belong to the purchaser and not to the developer during this period.
- If the developer, or his or her agent, fails to give the purchaser a copy of the public offering statement by the date of purchase: the purchaser may obtain from the developer an amount equal to 10% of the purchase price not to exceed $3,000; and (2) the North Carolina Real Estate Commission can fine the developer $500 for each violation. NOTE: Only the developer can be fined and not the salesperson.
- Time-share projects must have a time-share registrar and no sales may be made until such registrar has been designated.
- The developer also must designate a project broker.
- The project broker must supervise both brokers and provisional brokers licensees at the project location.
- Upon cancellation of the time-share contract, all refunds shall be made no later than 30 days from the date of purchase (not cancellation).

Trusts

A trust is an arrangement whereby a person's assets are being held by a third party (trustee) for the benefit of that person (trustor). This trustee is quite often a bank, attorney, or another person. This arrangement is considered to be a fiduciary relationship and often will involve real property. One of the distinct advantages of such a trust is that it allows property to pass outside of probate as well as provides privacy. In probate, the courts will want to verify the validity of the will, obtain an inventory and value of any property, pay relevant debts, and then distribute any remaining assets to the appropriate parties, such as the heirs. Another advantage of creating such a trust is that it allows much of this to be taken care of in advance, thereby relieving the executor, or administrator, of estate of tasks with which they may have little experience.

Living trusts often are referred to as "revocable trusts" and are created during the lifetime of the person setting up the trust. These documents place assets into a trust for a person's benefit during their lifetime and then transfer the assets to a designated beneficiary at death.

Testamentary trusts often involve the leaving of assets to children or others in cases in which the distribution may be set to occur at a particular time, such as a 30th birthday, or when a specific event, such as graduation from college or marriage, occurs. This type of trust often involves potentially large sums of money that may not be acquired by the person setting up the trust until their death, such as life insurance proceeds.

Land trusts are agreements in which the trustee agrees to hold ownership of real property for the benefit of the trustor. One of the benefits of this type arrangement is that it potentially provides privacy for the person who owns the property.

It is entirely possible that the recipient of a trust may be able to act only through the actions of the trustee. It is not unheard of for a future recipient (beneficiary) to represent to another person their desire to dispose of assets that are not yet within the control of that recipient. For example a person wants to sell a parcel of real property she "inherited" and is willing to sign the listing agreement. In this situation, the broker will need to determine whether the beneficiary actually has the right to sell independently or if the trustee must be willing to allow the conveyance.

ENCUMBRANCES TO REAL PROPERTY

An **encumbrance** is *anything that diminishes the bundle of rights of real property. As such, it is usually considered a burden on the property.* Charges, claims, restrictions, or infringements on a property reduce its overall value in some manner. In some instances, however, an encumbrance has a positive effect on the value of the property; one example might be a restrictive covenant, discussed later in this chapter. Therefore, an encumbrance can affect value either positively or negatively.

This section discusses liens, easements, and encroachments. Chapter 5 discusses other land use controls, such as zoning ordinances and deed restrictions.

Liens

A **lien** is *a claim or a charge against the property that can result from a contractual agreement or from the operation of law.* For example, a lien can result from an owner's contracting to have work done on property and not fulfilling part of the contract, from the owner's failure to pay taxes, or as a result of a lawsuit. A lien creates a cloud on the title. If this claim is not satisfied in the required time, the lien holder may execute the lien by process of foreclosure, which forces the property to be sold at public auction. Proceeds of the foreclosure sale are applied to outstanding liens in the order of priority of the liens, which is discussed later in this chapter.

Liens fall into two groups, which are shown in Figure 2.5:

1. *Specific liens* are claims against a specific property, such as mortgages, property taxes, and mechanic's liens.
2. *General liens* are claims against a person or that person's property, such as judgment liens, personal property tax liens, income tax liens, and estate and inheritance tax liens.

> "Liens are categorized as specific and general. Specific liens are 'specific' because they are tied to a particular individual property."
> —Len Elder, DREI

Specific Liens

Mortgage liens. A mortgage or deed of trust pledges a specific property, such as a home, as security for a debt. If the borrower does not pay the debt as promised (defaults), the lender can foreclose the mortgage by having the property sold at public auction and applying the proceeds of the sale to the debt.

Real property (ad valorem) tax and special assessment liens. The taxes levied by a local government constitute a specific lien against the real estate. State laws provide that real property tax liens have priority over all other liens. An assessment is a **levy,** or *tax, against a property for payment of a share of the cost of improvements made to areas adjoining the property.* Examples of these improvements are paving streets, installing sewer or water lines, and constructing sidewalks. Special assessments constitute a specific lien against the property until paid. Ad valorem and special tax liens are valid for 10 years.

---

1. Specific Liens: Claims against a particular property
    a. Mortgage
    b. Real property tax and special assessment
    c. Mechanic's
2. General Liens: Claims against all assets of a person
    a. Judgment
    b. Personal property tax
    c. Income tax
    d. Estate and inheritance tax

FIGURE 2.5 Classification of liens.
Source: © 2019 OnCourse Learning

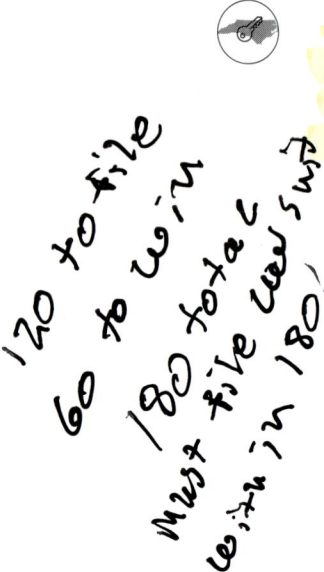

"Mechanic's liens are retroactive to the FIRST day the contractor, subcontractor, or supplier began work or provided labor or materials to the property."
—Steve Robinson

Mechanic's liens. In North Carolina, the term *mechanic's (materialman or laborer) lien* includes a lien filed by anyone (such as carpenters, lumber companies, appraisers, and surveyors) who provides labor or material to a property or property improvement. If these people are not paid according to the terms of their contract, they can file a lien against the property to which they provided work or materials any time up to 120 days after the last day that any labor or material was furnished to the property. The mechanic's lien is unique in that when it is filed, it becomes effective as of the first day any labor or material was furnished rather than on the day the lien is recorded. The mechanic's lien holder has up to 180 days after the last labor or materials were furnished to take court action to enforce her lien, provided she filed the lien within the 120-day filing period. The Statute of Limitations sets the time limit for the filing of lawsuits in various situations. If a lawsuit is not filed within the statutory time period, the injured party loses the right of legal remedy by operation of law. Therefore, the mechanic's lien must be filed within the statutory period. The special treatment the mechanic's lien receives as to effective date makes it necessary to verify that all work done on a property within 120 days before closing has been paid for. The mechanic's lien is the one type of lien that may not show up in a title search but, once subsequently recorded, would constitute a valid lien on the property. To avoid the risks of mechanic's liens being filed at a later date, most lenders will require the seller to produce a lien waiver in which the parties, who have produced labor or materials within the statutory period of time, have signed a document stating that they will waive their rights to file a lien against the property.

Legislation, effective April 1, 2013, applies to projects for which the anticipated cost exceeds $30,000 at the time of permitting. This law requires the owner to designate a "lien agent" to whom the lien claimants will be required to give notice. Anyone with a potential claim will be afforded a 15-day period from beginning work or risk loss of the mechanic lien priority. This new law does not apply to situations involving an existing single-family residence that is owner occupied.

Commercial Real Estate Broker Lien

North Carolina enacted the Commercial Real Estate Broker Lien Act effective October 1, 2011. This act enabled the commercial broker/firm to be able to file a lien to protect their claim to a sales or leasing commission. This became necessary because commercial brokers often have invested long periods of time and large sums of money in a transaction that can result in large amounts of monies due for the commission. As a result, commission disputes can arise that cannot be resolved before the closing date. Further compounding the problem is the fact that the broker generally had no right to place a lien on the property and had virtually no "leverage" to force the owner to pay after the title was transferred. The primary avenue available to the broker was to file a suit, which often resulted in long periods of costly litigation.

As a result, this legislation was passed allowing the broker/firm to file a lien for the earned commission in sales or lease transactions. This ability to file a lien is limited to only the listing broker/firm who had the written agreement to sell or lease the property as opposed to the cooperating broker/firm. The lien must be filed before the title is transferred in a sale and can be filed up to 30 days before the closing or by the date of possession in a lease. Once the lien has been filed, the broker/firm has up to 18 months to file a suit to enforce the lien.

General Liens

Judgment liens. A judgment is a court decree establishing that one person is indebted to another and specifying the amount of that indebtedness. A **judgment lien** constitutes *a general lien against all real and personal property the judgment debtor owns* in the county in which the judgment is recorded. The lien takes effect from the time the judgment is recorded. A judgment creditor may record a judgment in any county in the state, and it will constitute a general lien against all of the judgment debtor's property in that county. The creditor also may file notice of the lien in other counties where the debtor may own property and be protected for the debt in those counties as well. The judgment also creates a lien against any property the judgment debtor acquires subsequent to the judgment during the existence of the judgment.

A general lien does not apply to real property owned by husband and wife by the entirety or as joint tenants if the judgment is against only one of them. For the lien to attach to property in such cases, the judgment must be obtained against husband and wife on a debt they both incurred. A judgment lien remains in effect for 10 years in North Carolina unless the judgment is paid. Judgments may be renewed and kept in force for an additional period if the creditor brings another action on the original judgment before the original period has elapsed. Judgment liens have a priority relationship based on the time of recording. The creditor who records a lien before another creditor records a lien against the same judgment debtor has a higher priority claim. The judgment debtor's obligation to the creditor who has priority must be satisfied before creditors with a lower priority. Judgment liens are enforced by an order called an execution. This is an order signed by the clerk of court that instructs the sheriff to sell the property of the judgment debtor and apply the proceeds of the sale to the satisfaction of the judgment.

Personal property tax liens. Personal property taxes are assessed on certain personal property owned as of January 1 of the tax year. If these taxes are not paid, they become a general lien against all of the property the individual owns. Like the real property tax lien, this lien takes priority over other liens. The tax on licensed motor vehicles no longer constitutes a lien on real property.

Federal tax liens. The U.S. IRS can create a general lien against all of a taxpayer's property for overdue federal taxes. This lien is created by obtaining a judgment in a federal court against the taxpayer and by filing a certificate of lien against the landowner in the office of the clerk of the superior court in the county in which the taxpayer's land is located. A federal tax lien does not have a special priority. Its priority is established by time of recording, and its validity extends for 10 years. The federal government imposes a tax on the estate of deceased persons, which is called the federal estate tax. This tax creates a lien that attaches to all real and personal property in the estate and continues until the tax is paid.

State tax liens. The NC Commissioner of Revenue can create a general lien against all of a taxpayer's property for overdue state taxes. This lien becomes effective from the time of docketing in the superior court clerk's office in the county where the delinquent taxpayer's property is located and remains effective for 10 years.

All states impose a state inheritance tax upon the inheritance of real and personal property. This tax is paid by the heirs to the estate and remains a lien on the property until it is paid. The estate can sell property to satisfy the tax bill.

Priority of Liens

The priority of most liens in relation to other liens is based on the time (day and hour) they were recorded. North Carolina practices this *"pure race system."* This system provides that liens are established in priority by the time they are recorded—that is, the person who wins the race to the courthouse is at the head of the list. When the proceeds from the foreclosure sale are distributed, the lien holder with the highest priority gets paid first. With the exception of lien holders with special priority, the first to record is the first to be paid. However, certain liens have special priority by North Carolina statute, as is the case with mechanic's liens, where lien priority relates to the first day of work on the job rather than to the date of recordation. The highest priority of all liens is given to liens for real property taxes.

> "If there is a foreclosure the cost of the sale is always paid first, then real estate taxes, then special assessments, and then other liens based on the order of recordation, except mechanic's liens which have a priority based on when the work was begun."
> —Tim Terry, DREI

Homestead Exemption

North Carolina has a law that prevents the homeowner from total loss in the event of bankruptcy. Homeowners may exempt up to $35,000 ($70,000 for married couples filing jointly) of their home or any other real or personal property protected by the NC homestead exemption. If the homeowner is 65 or older and the spouse is deceased, the exemption protects up to $60,000 if the property was owned as tenancy by entirety or as joint tenancy with rights of survivorship.

Writ of Attachment

North Carolina allows a type of pre-judgment right to creditors called a writ of attachment. This right exists for creditors of debts, other than mortgages, and is obtained as the result of a judgment being passed down in a court of law against the debtor. By obtaining the writ of attachment, the creditor makes certain the debtor's property will be available to satisfy the debt once the judgment is finalized. Upon obtaining the judgment, the sheriff will be instructed to sell the property to satisfy the debt.

Restrictive (Protective) Covenants

Restrictive (protective) covenants are private restrictions that limit the way land may be used. They attach to the land, and they pass with title to successive purchasers. Often a developer defines such covenants to establish characteristics of a new residential subdivision. They may limit construction to single-family homes on a specific lot size, or they may require a given size or type of architecture. Agents, and consumers alike, should be cautious that restrictive covenants in a given subdivision can change within different areas of the development. The covenants can address anything that is legal. Careful consideration should go into establishing restrictive covenants because property becomes more difficult to sell as the number of restrictions increases. The *restrictions may be written in the individual deed or recorded as a master instrument,* a **declaration of restrictions.**

Lis Pendens

This *notice of pending litigation* indicates the existence of an unresolved lawsuit that affects title to all or part of the property of the defendant. Recording of the **lis pendens** *(lawsuit pending)* provides constructive, or effective, notice of the forthcoming legal action and its possible outcome. As a result, if the property is transferred to a new owner after the notice of lis pendens is placed on the public record in the county where the property is located, any court order or lien resulting from the lawsuit will affect the new owner's title to the property. Notices of lis pendens are routinely filed in boundary dispute cases.

Easements

An **easement** is a *nonpossessory right or interest in land owned by another*. It provides a right of use in land and not a right of possession.

General Classification of Easements

Easements can exist for a variety of legal uses, such as right-of-way for ingress and egress; a party wall; the right to take water from the land of another; the right to receive air, light, or heat from above the land of another; the right to obtain water from a well or spring on the land of another; and a right-of-way for the purpose of putting utility lines under and above the surface of the land.

Appurtenant Easement

An appurtenance is *something that has been added to something else and, as a result, becomes an inherent part of that to which it has been added*. In real property law, an appurtenance is the right that one property owner has in the property of another as a result of the first property owner's ownership in a particular

> "There must be at least two parcels for an easement appurtenant since they always benefit an adjacent parcel. Only one parcel is technically required for an easement in gross since it benefits a third party."
> —Steve Robinson

parcel of real estate. For example, if a purchaser receives a title to a tract of land and included in this title is an easement in the form of a right-of-way across the adjoining land of another, this easement is an appurtenance to that title. *Whenever the titleholder conveys that title to another, the conveyance includes the easement because the easement is appurtenant to the title.* Because an **appurtenant easement** moves with a title, it is said to *run with the land*. The land that is benefited by the easement is described as the *dominant tenement,* dominant land, or dominant estate, and the land encumbered by the easement (the land on which the easement exists) is described as the *servient tenement, servient land,* or *servient estate* (see Figure 2.6).

Easements in Gross

Unlike appurtenant easements, **easements in gross** *are not dependent upon ownership of an adjoining property.* Easements in gross have no dominant tenement, only a servient one. Typically, the owner of an easement in gross does not necessarily own property in the area of the property in which the easement exists. The owner of an easement in gross usually receives an easement by contract.

The most prevalent use of easements in gross is in the form of commercial easements. Commercial easements are common throughout the United States and typically are held by utility companies for the purpose of installing power lines, telephone lines, and gas lines above the surface of the earth, on the earth itself, or underground. Railroad rights-of-way are another prominent example of a commercial easement. These commercial easements are typically for long periods of time, perhaps indefinitely, and are binding on future owners of the servient estate. Commercial easements in gross are assignable and can be conveyed.

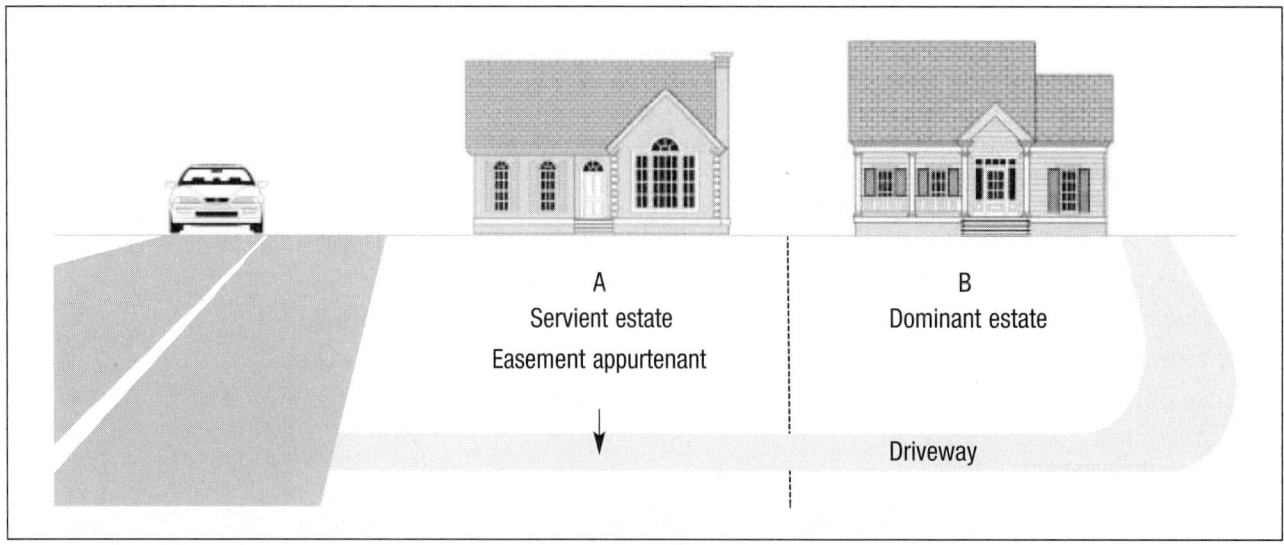

FIGURE 2.6 An example of an appurtenant easement.

Personal easements in gross are a form of personal, nonassignable, and uninheritable rights to use a property for a particular purpose or for the duration of the recipient's life unless stated otherwise. Many personal easements are not recorded and therefore are not enforceable against the grantor. If recorded, however, the easement would be binding upon any future owner of the servient property for as long as the easement exists. Personal easements are not to be confused with a license agreement. A license agreement is the right to occupy a property only for a relatively brief period of time and is not considered to be a conveyance of binding property rights. Examples of a license agreement would be tickets to a movie or sporting event where the holder's right is for only the duration of the named event.

Creation of Easements

Easements may be created by the use of an express written agreement, may be implied by the actions of a person, or may be created by the operation of law (see Figure 2.7). The Statute of Frauds requires that all transfers of interest in real property be in writing; therefore, an express easement cannot be created orally.

Express Easements

Express easements must be in writing according to the Statute of Frauds and should be recorded. An owner selling his land can expressly grant an easement to a buyer by using the appropriate language in the deed. In Figure 2.6, if A sold the land to B, A could grant the easement to B to cross A's land. If the situation were reversed, and B sold the land to A, B would reserve the easement. The party walls illustrated in Figure 2.8 are another example of express written easements. A **party wall** *is used by two adjoining neighbors to support the sidewall of each unit.* If the property line ran down the middle of the wall, each party would have a cross easement in the other or would have a tenancy in common. If the wall were

---

1. Express (must be in writing according to statute of frauds)
    a. Grant or reserve
    b. Party walls
    c. Dedication
2. Implied (actions of the parties)
    a. Necessity
    b. Reference to a recorded plat
3. Operation of law (court order)
    a. Prescription
    b. Condemnation

FIGURE 2.7 The way easements arise.
Source: © 2019 OnCourse Learning

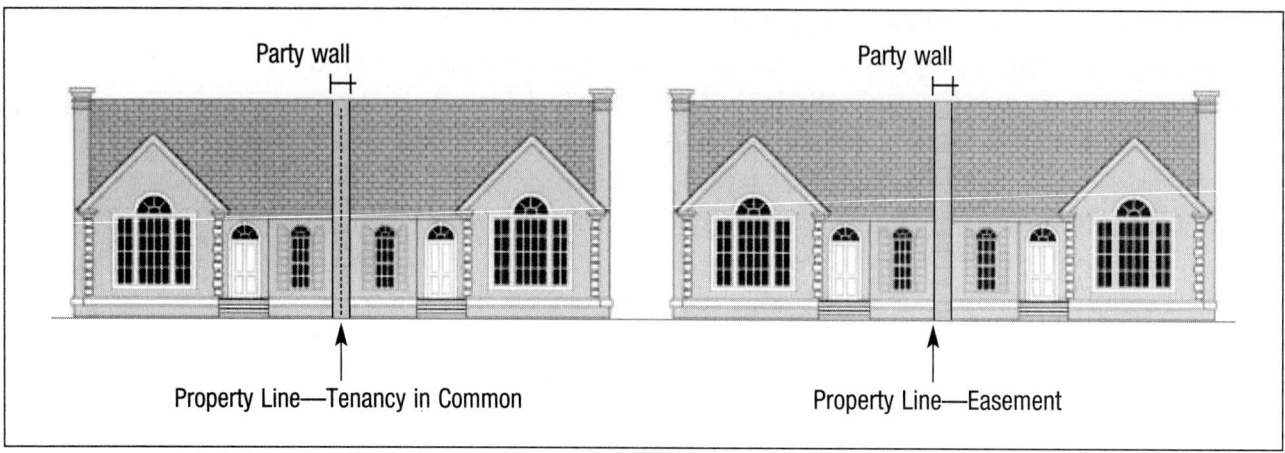

FIGURE 2.8 Party wall.

entirely within the property of one party, however, the other party would have an easement in the use of the wall. Easements may be created by express dedication, in which a portion of a property is set aside for use by the public. For example, a developer who is building a residential subdivision may dedicate a portion of the land for use by the public, such as roadways or recreational parks.

Implied Easements

In contrast to express easements, implied easements have no documentation. In certain cases, the actions of a party create an easement when these actions demonstrate an intent to create an easement. An *easement by necessity* is implied if a seller conveys title to a buyer who would be landlocked without access to a road. In Figure 2.6, if A sold the property to B and did not grant B the easement shown, B would have the right to claim such an easement by reason of the necessity to get to the public road. An *easement by dedication* may be implied as well as express. If the developer described in the preceding section had not expressly granted the roadways in the new subdivision but had described the property by referring to a map showing the existence of such streets, the easement would be implied.

Easements by Operation of Law

An easement may be obtained by **prescription,** that is, by *using another's land for a prescribed period of time.* The use must be open and well known to others (notorious) and must be continued and uninterrupted for the period of time required by laws of the state. Users must prove in court that they have satisfied all the requirements for the intended use. An easement also can be created by **condemnation** under the power of **eminent domain** of the government. This power enables the government to take private land for the benefit of the general public. In all cases, the property owner must be compensated for differences in value before and after the action by the government. Usually, condemnations for rights-of-way for various public uses are for the purpose of obtaining an easement rather than for acquiring title.

A statutory cartway proceeding is another easement that can arise by operation of law. The owner of a landlocked parcel of property can petition to have a cartway sectioned off over someone else's property. A three-person jury decides where the cartway is to be and what damages the owner of the landlocked property must pay the owners of the land where the cartway is located. Specific statutes govern this proceeding. A cartway of at least 18 feet in width may be obtained to connect the landlocked property to a public highway if the cartway is for the purpose of cultivation or for using the land for one of the purposes listed in the statute.

Termination of Easements

Easements may be terminated as follows: by the release of the easement by the dominant owner to the servient owner, by combining the dominant and servient lands into one tract of land, by abandonment of the easement by the dominant owner, by the cessation of the purpose for which an easement was created, and by the expiration of a specified period of time for which the easement was created.

Encroachments

An **encroachment** is a *trespass on the land of another as a result of an intrusion or invasion by some structure or other object,* such as a wall, fence, overhanging balcony, or driveway. The encroaching owner may obtain title to the area of the land upon which the encroachment exists by adverse possession (discussed in Chapter 4) or may obtain an easement by prescription in the case of the encroaching driveway if the owner of the land subject to the encroachment does not take appropriate legal action. Because encroachments are illegal, the owner who is being encroached upon can sue for damages (a judgment by the court requiring the encroacher to compensate the owner for the encroachment) or can petition the court for a decree ordering the encroachment to be removed.

Encroachments caused by building improvements straddling property boundaries are a major reason why lending institutions require surveys that specify the location of all improvements on the property. Typically, the existence of an encroachment is established by an accurate survey.

Summary of Important Points

1. Real property consists of land and everything attached to the land, including things that grow naturally without requiring planting and cultivation. Real property ownership is often described as a bundle of rights because it involves many attributes.

2. Annual crops that require planting and cultivation are personal property and are called emblements or *fructus industriales*.
3. Ownership in land includes the surface of the earth and the areas above and below the surface.
4. A fixture begins as personal property and becomes real property when attached to land improvements or the land. Since fixtures create many practical problems in real estate transactions, practitioners need to pay careful attention to this concept.
5. Private ownership of property is subject to four powers of government: eminent domain, police power, taxation, and escheat.
6. Estates involve the definition of the scope of one's interest in real property. Estates in land are divided into two groups: freehold and estates of less than freehold (leasehold). In freehold estates, one has an ownership interest in realty that lasts at least a lifetime. The nonfreehold, or rental, interests last less than a lifetime.
7. The freehold estates are the fee simple estates, which are inheritable, and life estates, which are not inheritable unless the life estate is for the life of another (*pur autre vie*).
8. The most comprehensive form of ownership in real property is fee simple absolute.
9. Life estates revert to the grantor or pass on to a remainderman.
10. The duration of a life estate is measured by the life of the life tenant.
11. Conventional life estates are created by someone's intentional act. Legal life estates, such as marital life estates, are created by operation of law.
12. A life tenant has the right of alienation, the right of encumbrance, the right of estovers, and the rights of possession and enjoyment of the property and of deriving certain income from it.
13. A life tenant is obligated to preserve and maintain the property for the benefit of the future interest.
14. Title held in the name of one person only is called ownership in severalty.
15. When title is held concurrently by two or more persons or organizations, it is called co-ownership (also, concurrent, or joint ownership). The forms of co-ownership are tenancy in common, joint tenancy, tenancy by the entirety, and certain aspects of condominiums and cooperatives.
16. Joint tenancy and tenancy by the entirety require the four unities of time, title, interest, and possession. Tenancy by the entirety is limited to husband and wife and requires a fifth unity, marriage (or unity of person), and includes the right of survivorship.
17. The owner of a condominium unit holds title to the unit either in severalty or as a co-owner with another, and she and any co-owners of the individual unit hold title to the common areas as a tenant in common with the owners of the other units.

18. The creation of a condominium requires the recording of a declaration, articles of association, bylaws, and construction plans.
19. The North Carolina Condominium Act applies to the sale or resale of condominiums created on or after October 1, 1986. This act provides consumer protection by requiring a developer to disclose certain information on new condominiums before a contract is signed, allowing the purchaser of a new condominium a seven-day right to cancel the purchase, requiring owners of resale units to disclose monthly assessments and other fees, and providing an implied warranty that the unit is constructed in an acceptable manner.
20. Ownership in a cooperative results from stock ownership in a corporation that owns a building containing cooperative apartments. Stockholders occupy apartments under a lease.
21. Business organizations may receive, hold, and convey title to real property.
22. Less-than-freehold estates also are called leasehold estates and are estates of limited duration, providing possession and control but not title (as in the case of freehold estates).
23. The leasehold estates are estate for years, estate from year to year, estate at will, and estate at sufferance.
24. Encumbrances are things that diminish the bundle of rights. They may take the form of a claim, lien, charge, or liability attached to and binding upon real property. Examples are encroachments, liens, restrictive (protective) covenants, easements, marital life estates, and deed restrictions. A lien is a claim or charge against property that may result in the loss of title through foreclosure. Restrictive covenants, lis pendens, easements, and encroachments also encumber, or diminish, the full interest in title.
25. An appurtenance is a right or privilege that results from ownership of a particular property and transfers with the title. An appurtenance depends on a principal item or the real estate. It belongs to that to which it is attached. It cannot stand alone.
26. A fee simple absolute title is freely transferable by the owner because he has the highest rights in the property, but the title may not always be free of encumbrances. Fee simple titles often have encumbrances, which pass with the title. To be effective, however, such encumbrances need to be recorded where they are easily discoverable (with certain exceptions, such as the potential for a mechanic's lien).
27. A freehold and a nonfreehold estate can exist at the same time in a rental property. The landlord retains the title (freehold) but has handed over the right of possession (nonfreehold) for a period of time.

28. Riparian rights are the rights of property owners adjoining a watercourse, such as a river. Such owners have the right to draw reasonable amounts of water from and enjoy access to the watercourse.

    Boundary lines of property bordering water include the following:

    a. Navigable waterway: Adjacent landowners own to banks.

    b. Nonnavigable waterway:

       1. One owner owning all the land surrounding water also owns the land under water.

       2. If more than one owner owns surrounding land, each owns land to center of water.

    c. Oceans or lakes where water levels fluctuate: Adjacent owners own to mean high watermark.

    d. State-owned land under navigable waterway and the foreshore (land between high and low watermarks) of oceans and lakes.

29. A manufactured home can be considered either personal or real property depending on whether the appropriate paperwork has been filed.

30. To be considered real property, the manufactured homeowner must remove the wheels, axles, and towing hitch and also file an affidavit attesting to such.

31. Manufactured housing is built according to HUD standards.

32. Modular construction is built according to "stick-built" state building codes.

33. Modular construction is considered to be real property as soon as erected on the foundation.

34. The most important elements of time-share rules are given in the Key Time-Share Facts for North Carolina list on page 40 (the list is not repeated in its entirety because of length and number of points).

Review Questions

Answers to the review questions are in the Answer Key at the back of the book.

1. Personal property attached to real property is prevented from becoming real property by which of the following?
   A. value
   B. an appurtenance
   C. security agreement and financing statement
   D. mineral rights

2. Which of the following is a right in the property of another that results from ownership in a particular parcel of real estate?
   A. easement in gross
   B. appurtenant easement
   C. license
   D. condemnation

3. Which of the following is (are) correct?
   A. An easement provides a nonpossessory interest in land.
   B. The land on which an easement exists is the dominant tenement.
   C. The land that benefits from an easement is the servient tenement.
   D. All of the above

4. Easements may be created in all of the following ways EXCEPT:
   A. condemnation.
   B. dedication.
   C. prescription.
   D. assessment.

5. An easement is terminated:
   A. when the purpose for which the easement was created ceases to exist.
   B. when the adjoining dominant and servient tenements are combined into one tract of land.
   C. by abandonment of the easement by the dominant owner.
   D. all of the above.

6. If a property owner gives a specific person permission to cross his property, this is a(n):
   A. easement in gross.
   B. easement appurtenant.
   C. lease.
   D. encroachment.

7. The creation of an easement by condemnation results from the exercise of which of the following?
   A. prescription
   B. eminent domain
   C. dedication
   D. implication

8. A fee simple determinable:
   A. is an example of a nonfreehold estate.
   B. typically stipulates the conveyance is "as long as" it is used for a particular purpose.
   C. is an example of pur autre vie (for the life of another).
   D. is an example of freehold rights until the original owner's rights are determined to be invalid.

9. If a widow inherits an estate by will granting her the right of use and possession of a parcel of land for the rest of her life, with the provision that the estate will go to her children in fee simple upon her death, she has received:
   A. an inheritable freehold estate.
   B. a life estate with remainder.
   C. a life estate pur autre vie.
   D. none of the above.

10. The highest and best form of estate in real property is which of the following?
    A. appurtenant easement
    B. defeasible fee
    C. life estate in reversion
    D. fee simple absolute

11. Estate for years, estates from year to year, estates at will, and estates by sufferance:
    A. are leasehold estates
    B. create a legal relationship between the parties of landlord and tenant
    C. are nonfreehold estates
    D. all of the above

12. Title held in the name of a corporation with many stockholders is considered to be held as:
    A. severalty.
    B. joint tenancy.
    C. tenancy in common.
    D. tenancy by entireties.

13. Which of the following types of ownership requires unity of interest, title, time, and possession?
    A. cooperative
    B. tenancy in common
    C. joint tenancy
    D. condominium

14. None of the following includes the right of survivorship in North Carolina EXCEPT:
    A. tenancy in common.
    B. tenancy by the entirety.
    C. life estate.
    D. joint tenancy.

15. The purchaser of a condominium unit receives title to the land on which the condominium is situated as a:
    A. tenant by the entirety.
    B. tenant in common.
    C. joint tenant.
    D. tenant at sufferance.

16. The purchaser of a condominium time-share:
    A. takes title for a specified time period (or periods) each calendar year.
    B. may not convey title to anyone else.
    C. has a 30-day right to rescind the purchase contract.
    D. all of the above.

17. In the cooperative form of ownership:
    A. the owner owns his unit in severalty.
    B. each owner owns an interest in the common areas.
    C. the owners own the building as tenants in common.
    D. none of the above.

18. A tenant in common:
    A. may sell her interest in the property.
    B. may pledge the entire property as security for a mortgaged loan.
    C. may not bring legal action to partition the property.
    D. has the right of survivorship in the property.

19. Ownership as tenants by the entirety includes which of the following?
    A. the right of one owner to convey title to his share of ownership without the participation of the other owner
    B. the right of survivorship
    C. ownership of an unequal interest in the property with another
    D. conversion to ownership as joint tenants if the owners are divorced

20. An encumbrance always:
    A. has a positive effect on property value.
    B. has a negative effect on property value.
    C. is a lien.
    D. none of the above.

21. All of the following are examples of specific liens EXCEPT:
    A. income tax liens.
    B. mortgage liens.
    C. mechanic's liens.
    D. real property tax liens.

22. Which of the following statements regarding judgment liens is correct?
    A. Judgment liens will not attach to property to which title is held by a husband and wife as tenants by the entirety unless both participated in the creation of the debt and are both named as defendants in the judgment.
    B. Judgment liens have a priority over the real property tax assessment.
    C. Judgment liens have a priority over all liens other than property tax liens.
    D. None of the above.

23. Liens, easements, encroachments, and restrictive covenants are examples of which of the following?
    A. emblements
    B. estovers
    C. estates
    D. encumbrances

24. Which of the following is an estate that automatically renews itself for consecutive periods?
    A. estate at will
    B. life estate
    C. estate from year to year
    D. estate for years

25. New construction time-share properties in North Carolina require:
    A. the developer to have a real estate license before sales are made.
    B. project registration with the Commission before marketing the units for sale.
    C. all time-share salespersons must have a time-share license in NC.
    D. the purchaser to be given a right of rescission for 3 days from purchase.

26. Time-share property in North Carolina:
    A. must be for a residential use.
    B. is considered personal property.
    C. is the right to occupy a property during five or more separated time periods over five or more years.
    D. allows a bona-fide employee of the developer to sell the units without a real estate license.

27. An example of an appurtenant easement would be:
    A. city water and sewer easement.
    B. easement for a neighbor friend to cross a nearby property to access the beach.
    C. an easement for the adjoining property to have a driveway over the subject property.
    D. a railroad right-of-way easement.

28. All of the following involve ownership of real property EXCEPT:
    A. cooperatives.
    B. condominiums.
    C. townhouses.
    D. time-shares.

29. All of the following are real property EXCEPT:
    A. standing timber.
    B. underground minerals.
    C. readily movable items.
    D. naturally growing vegetation.

30. The item(s) included as real estate is (are):
    A. trees.
    B. fences.
    C. a built-in microwave.
    D. all of the above.

31. A manufactured home that is towed to the land and placed upon a permanent foundation but still has the wheels, axles, and towing hitch attached will be considered:
    A. personal property.
    B. real property.
    C. an improvement.
    D. a fixture.

CHAPTER 3
PROPERTY TAXATION AND ASSESSMENT

KEY TERMS

ad valorem
appraisal
assessed value

assessment
market value

mill rate
mills

LEARNING OBJECTIVES

At the conclusion of this chapter, you should be able to:

1. Describe real property taxation and special assessment systems in North Carolina.
2. Describe the mill rate system used in the majority of other states.

IN THIS CHAPTER

The taxation on real property is the major source of revenue for the local units of government, including both the county and the city or township. Taxes are imposed on real property **ad valorem**, that is, according to value. North Carolina's statute, known as the Machinery Act, sets forth the details of property taxation. A key point of the act is that it requires the **assessed value,** or *the value placed upon property for purposes of taxation*, to be set at true market value, or **market value**, a 100% assessment, at least once every eight years. This reappraisal of property every eight years is called an *octennial reappraisal.* A horizontal adjustment upward or downward may be made at the four-year interval between the eight-year adjustments.

An official called a tax assessor is responsible for the valuation of property for tax purposes. Property values must be reasonably uniform to provide equal taxation of property owners. Many property owners take advantage of an appeal process when they believe their property has been overvalued. As a practical matter, a real estate agent can expect numerous phone calls from past clients asking

for information to support a value of their property that is less than the new assessment if they believe that assessment is higher than the actual market value. Often all they need is information on the selling prices of similar homes in their neighborhood. If they need an appraisal, the agent should refer them to a licensed appraiser.

Students will need to be prepared for questions regarding the mill rate method of tax computation and for other rules regarding assessment rates that commonly are used in other states. Such information is included in the sections Tax Rate and Calculations and Appraisal and Assessment.

TAX RATE AND CALCULATIONS

Each local government sets a tax rate annually to meet the needs of its budget. It does this by dividing the total assessed value of all the property subject to taxation by the amount of money needed for the budget. The rate is then applied to the assessed value of the individual properties subject to taxation. The rate must be sufficient to provide the revenue for the local government's budget and may be changed every year. North Carolina uses the formula of a tax rate per $100 of assessed valuation. Given the assessed value of the property and the current tax rate, you can easily calculate the annual property taxes. For example, if the assessed value is $185,500 and the tax rate is $1.50 per $100 of assessed value, the annual tax is calculated as ($185,500 ÷ $100) × $1.50 = 1,855 units of $100 × $1.50 = $2,782.50.

Nationally, a more common form of tax calculation involves the mill rate. A **mill rate** is a tax rate based upon one-tenth of one cent, or one mill. This equates to one-thousandth of a dollar (i.e., 0.1 × 0.01 = 0.001 one mill). The tax rate is typically stated in terms of "x" number of **mills** (i.e., 15 **mills**).

> "There are two zeros in 100 and three zeros in 1,000. Therefore, in doing tax rate math you can simply move the decimal point two places to the left for problems using a tax rate per $100 and move the decimal point three places to the left for problems using a tax rate per $1000."
> —Steve Robinson

Test Tip!

Students need to be prepared for property tax problems using the "mill rate" when taking the national portion of the state exam and using the "tax rate per $100" in the state portion.

There are basically two easy ways to calculate taxes involving the mill rate:

1. Multiply the number of mills × 0.1 of 1 cent (i.e., 0.1 × 0.01 × number of mills = mill rate as a decimal).
2. Divide the assessed value by $1,000 and then multiply by the mill rate.

Example: What would be the tax bill for a property with an assessed value of $185,500 that has a tax rate of 15 mills?

Answer: Solution is provided by illustrating both methods just addressed.

1. $1 \times 0.01 \times 15 = 0.015$ (15 mills as a decimal)
2. $\$185,500 \times 0.015 = \$2,782.50$ Tax Bill

OR

3. $\$185,500 \div \$1,000 = 185.5$ (# of $1,000)
4. $185.5 \times 15 = \$2,782.50$

Students need to understand how to compute NC *ad valorem* property taxes.

Property Subject to Taxation

Generally, at some point, all real and personal property is subject to taxation in North Carolina. Most people know of several exceptions to this generalization, however, such as property owned by churches and nonprofit charities. According to new tax laws, licensed personal property (such as automobiles) is now taxed upon relicensing. The legislature also has exempted household goods from personal property taxation and eliminated the intangibles tax on funds in the bank. Additionally, special cases exist for historic and certain types of agricultural property and for the property of elderly and disabled people.

Listing Property for Taxation

All property subject to taxation must be listed with the local tax office. Real property is listed in the county where the property is located; personal property is listed in the county where the owner has her permanent residence, if this is different. The Machinery Act requires property to be listed during January, even though the localities operate on a July 1 fiscal year. In certain circumstances in which the taxing authority considers it necessary, it has a local option to extend the listing period for another month.

Appraisal and Assessment

The distinction between appraisal and assessment often confuses people. **Appraisal** is the process of determining a market value; it is discussed in detail in Chapter 13. **Assessment** is the determination of a value of the property for taxation purposes. As noted previously, real property in North Carolina must be revalued, or reappraised, at least every eight years, at which time the assessed value is set at 100% of the market value. As a practical matter, however, one would not expect the two values to be identical at times other than this revaluation, as the property usually appreciates in value over the course of the eight years. As a result, the true market value, or simply market value, is historically higher than the assessed value, although the economic conditions of the past few years has certainly shown the assessed value can be much higher than the present market value of a given property.

In many other states, it is quite common to see the implementation of an assessed rate. The assessed rate is a percentage of the market value that is being taxed. For example, if a state is taxing property at 75% of the market value, then you would multiply 75% times whatever the market value is set to determine the value for tax computation purposes (i.e., $160,000 market value × 75% = $120,000 assessed value). Typically, if the assessed value is reduced, the amount required to be charged as the tax rate will be increased to collect the amount needed for taxes.

Timetable for Listing and Tax Collection

Real and personal property taxes attach to the property on January 1 when the property is due for listing. The property owner has until January 31 to list the property. Property taxes are due September 1 and are paid in arrears. Penalties are assessed at the beginning of January if taxes are not paid at that time. Many property owners think the taxes are due January 1 of the year after they are billed in September because they do not have to pay a penalty for late payment until then. All real estate agents should be aware that this is not the case; the taxes are due September 1.

Important Dates for North Carolina Property Taxation
January 1 = tax lien attaches to property
January 31 = taxable property listed
July 1 = annual tax rate must be set
September 1 = tax bill is due and payable
January 5 of next year = last day to pay tax bill without late penalty

Property Tax Lien

In North Carolina, unpaid property taxes legally constitute a valid lien against the property as of the first day of the tax year (January 1) even though the tax bills will not be sent out until after July 1 and are not due until September 1.

As noted in the discussion of liens, the real property tax lien takes the first priority. As such, it is an exception to North Carolina's pure race system because, in essence, the tax collector has already won the race to the courthouse, even before the others start.

"Know the following tax dates. Tax bills become a lien in advance on January 1st. Tax bills generally go out in July. The due date for taxes is September 1st. Taxes become delinquent January 1st of the following year."
—Len Elder, DREI

> Property taxes are lawfully considered a lien as of January 1 of the current tax year even though tax bills are not due and payable until September 1.

Special Priority of the Tax Lien

Even though a lien is recorded against a property in one year, a subsequent default in the payment of property taxes years later will take precedence over the earlier recorded lien. As a practical matter, most creditors understand this situation and see to the payment of taxes so their lien priority is not disturbed. For example, mortgage lenders prefer to collect monthly tax escrow payments from the borrower so the lender has the funds to pay the taxes on time to protect the mortgage lien.

Special Assessments

In addition to the ordinary property taxes that are collected by the local government for normal operating expenses, taxes may be levied for special county, city, or town projects (such as paving streets, building sidewalks, or installing sewer or water lines) that benefit certain properties. The statutes allow a number of ways to determine the amount of these assessments. A common way is to base the assessments on the number of feet a property has that borders on the improvement. This is referred to as a "front foot" and is a linear measurement along the distance of what is being "fronted" (e.g., road, waterway, railroad).

By County

> "Late fees for real estate taxes in NC are called 'Late Listing Fees.' They are payable and due from the seller and are not tax deductible."
> —Tim Terry, DREI

Counties have the authority to establish special assessments for new utilities to the area, such as a new water reservoir or sewage treatment facility, that benefit all properties within the jurisdiction. The statutes specify a detailed process of determining the cost of the project, publishing a notice of the intended assessment, and setting a schedule for the payment of the tax by the individual property owners.

By City and Town

Procedures also are established for cities and towns to levy and collect special assessments that are similar to those established for the counties.

Special Assessment Liens

As a real property tax lien, the special assessment attaches to the land and enjoys a high, although unique, priority. This lien is behind the real and personal property tax liens, but it takes priority over other liens.

Math Concepts for this Chapter

- Calculation of ad valorem property taxes given the tax rate and assessed value.
- Students should be able to perform calculations by using BOTH the North Carolina rate of "per $100" or the mill rate (National Exam section).

Tax Calculations Using North Carolina Tax Rate

1. Kevin's property has an assessed value of $178,500 and is being taxed at the rate of $1.15 per $100. What would be the amount due for annual taxes for this property?
2. Renee has a house located within the city limits that has an assessed value of $145,000. The tax rate per $100 is $0.85 for the city and $0.50 for the county. What are her annual taxes for this property?

Tax Calculations Using Mill Rate

3. Pam has a property that is assessed at $225,500 and is being taxed at the rate of 15 mills. What are the annual taxes due for this property?

Solutions

1. $178,500 ÷ $100 = 1,785 number of $100 increments
   $1.15 × 1,785 = $2,052.75 annual taxes due

2. $0.85 + $0.50 = $1.35 tax rate per $100 for city and county
   $145,000 ÷ $100 = 1,450 number of $100 increments
   $1.35 × 1,450 = $1,957.50 annual taxes due

3. $225,500 ÷ 1,000 = $225.50
   $225.50 × 15 = $3,382.50 annual taxes due

Summary of Important Points

1. The Machinery Act established the rules for property taxation in North Carolina.
2. The assessed rate for property in North Carolina is 100% of market value.
3. The assessed value is the value placed on property for purposes of taxation. Historically, the assessed value will be less than the active market value.
4. Tax rates for North Carolina are per $100 of assessed value.
5. Students will be required to calculate property taxes by using both the North Carolina system of "per $100" as well as the mill rate method.
6. Tax rates can be changed annually. Do not confuse this with the fact that tax values are to be adjusted at least every eight years.

7. Tax values may be modified every four years by using a horizontal adjustment. A horizontal adjustment is different than the eight-year reappraisal in that a horizontal adjustment simply applies a set percentage increase for all properties in the affected area. For example, if the county wishes to implement a 20% horizontal adjustment, all properties in that area will be increased in value by 20%. The eight-year reappraisal is more of a "door-to-door" analysis of property value.
8. Property that is owned as of January 1 of each year is to be listed for tax purposes no later than January 30.
9. Tax bills must be mailed out by September 1, at which time they are payable.
10. Taxes are to be paid by December 31. There will be interest penalties charged if taxes are not paid by January 5 of the following year.
11. An assessment is the pro rata share of the cost of some improvement, such as sidewalks, water and sewer lines, and street improvements.
12. Assessments typically are charged by the front foot.
13. A front foot is a linear measurement of the width of the property along the side that is being improved.
14. The mill rate system is used for most states in the United States.
15. One mill is the equivalent of 0.1 of 0.01.

Review Questions

Answers to review questions are in the Answer Key at the back of the book.

1. The tax levy against real property to provide the funds to pay all or part of the cost of an improvement to the property is which of the following?
   A. mechanic's lien
   B. special assessment
   C. general lien
   D. judgment lien

2. Real property taxation in North Carolina:
   A. requires listing the property by December 30.
   B. makes September 1 the due date of the tax.
   C. requires penalties for paying after September 1.
   D. none of the above.

3. How often may the North Carolina property tax rate be changed?
   A. every eight years
   B. every four years
   C. every two years
   D. each year

4. The Jones's home has an assessed value of $100,000 in a locality where the tax rate is $1.45 per $100. What is their monthly payment for tax escrow?
   A. $83
   B. $100
   C. $121
   D. $1,450

5. The tax rate is calculated on every $100 of the:
   A. sales price.
   B. appraised value.
   C. listing price.
   D. assessed value.

6. According to the Machinery Act in North Carolina, all real property must be reassessed for tax purposes at least:
   A. every year.
   B. every two years.
   C. every four years.
   D. every eight years.

7. Kim's house is located within the city limits and has a market value of $240,000. The local tax office is assessing her property at 75% and there are tax rates per $100 of $0.95 for the city and $0.35 for the county. What are her annual taxes for this property?
   A. $1,710.00
   B. $2,280.00
   C. $2,340.00
   D. $3,120.00

8. Carol's property has an annual tax bill of $1,495.00 and an assessed value $130,000. What is her tax rate per $100? (rounded)
   A. $11.50
   B. $1.15
   C. $0.87
   D. $0.01

9. A municipality has total assessed value of property located within its environs of $18,057,000. They have recently adopted an annual budget of $162,513. At what rate per $100 must they tax the local properties in order to meet this budget?
   A. $0.90
   B. $1.14
   C. $9.00
   D. $11.43

10. George's property recently sold for $235,000 and has an assessed value of $215,000. If the local tax rate is $1.40 per $100 how much would the annual taxes for this property be?
    A. $3,290
    B. $3,150
    C. $3,010
    D. $250.83

11. A parcel of land is being taxed at a rate of 25 mills. Assuming that it has a market value of $175,000 and is being assessed at 70%, what would the annual tax liability be?
    A. $4,900.00
    B. $4,375.00
    C. $3,062.50
    D. $1,225.00

12. A parcel of property (not a corner lot) that measures 95 feet wide by 175 feet deep is being assessed $8.50 per front foot for water and sewer lines that are being installed. How much will the assessment be for this particular property?
    A. $2,295.00
    B. $1,615.00
    C. $1,487.50
    D. $807.50

CHAPTER 4
TRANSFER OF TITLE TO REAL PROPERTY

KEY TERMS

- acknowledgment
- adverse possession
- beneficiary
- bequest
- bounds
- chain of title
- cloud on a title
- color of title
- condemnation
- Conner Act
- constructive notice
- covenant against encumbrances
- covenant of quiet enjoyment
- covenant of right to convey
- covenant of seisin
- covenant of warranty
- deed
- descent
- devise
- devisee
- eminent domain
- excise tax
- executor
- executrix
- foreclosure
- government rectangular survey system
- grantee
- grantor
- intestate
- judicial deed
- legal description
- lien foreclosure sale
- Marketable Title Act
- meridian
- plat
- point of beginning
- section
- special warranty deed
- Statute of Frauds
- suit to quiet title
- testate
- testator
- testatrix
- title examination
- title insurance
- township
- will
- words of conveyance

LEARNING OBJECTIVES

At the conclusion of this chapter, you should be able to:

1. List the methods of transferring title by the four categories of alienation—voluntary, involuntary, during life, and at death.
2. List and describe the essential elements of deeds in North Carolina.
3. Describe the three primary types of deed in North Carolina.

4. List the miscellaneous types of special purpose deed in North Carolina.
5. Describe excise tax, defining the rate and calculating the cost.
6. Describe the process of title examination.
7. Describe title insurance and the types of coverage.
8. Describe the importance and process of title recordation.
9. Explain the system of property description used in North Carolina.

IN THIS CHAPTER

The transfer of a title to real property is described in law as alienation. The property owner is alienated, or separated, from the title by transfer of the title to another. The alienation may be voluntary or involuntary and may occur during life or after death.

PROPERTY DESCRIPTION

Adequacy of Description

Any method that enables a surveyor or civil engineer to locate property with certainty is an acceptable legal method; however, the three most acceptable types of property description are metes and bounds, the government rectangular survey system, and description by reference. One should avoid using a simple street address, a tax description, or any ambiguous description. Although a description containing a latent ambiguity (one in which the property can be identified by extrinsic information) is legally sufficient, it is not professionally acceptable. A description containing a patent ambiguity (one in which the property cannot be identified with any certainty) is neither legally nor professionally acceptable.

Contracts should include an adequate legal description. If none exists, an attorney should be consulted. Real estate brokers are not allowed to write legal descriptions.

Methods of Describing Real Property

Metes and Bounds

The property description primarily used in North Carolina (and commonly used in the states that were part of the original 13 colonies) is the metes and bounds description and is based on distances and directions. In the metes and bounds description, the **metes** are the *distances from point to point in the description* and the **bounds** are the *directions from one point to another in the description*.

A metes and bounds description is made from a survey performed by a licensed registered land surveyor. One of the most important aspects of the metes and bounds description is the selection of the **point of beginning (POB)**. This point should be *one that is reasonably easy to locate and tied to a reference point that is well established.* After selecting the POB, the surveyor identifies the boundaries of the property by a series of "calls" that consist of distances (metes) and directions (bounds) between natural or artificial markers called landmarks or monuments. The term *monument* may lead one to assume that it represents some degree of magnitude in size. In reality, it is quite common that the monument is nothing more than an iron stake, pile of rocks, or any inanimate object. After all the calls have been made, the description must close; that is, the last call must end at the point of beginning. The directions in the metes and bounds description might read "N-45° E." There may be a further refinement of the direction. Degrees (°) are divided into minutes ('), with 1 degree containing 60 minutes, and each minute is divided into 60 seconds ("). A description then might read "N-45°, 30′,10″ E." These bearings are illustrated in Figure 4.1.

> The metes and bounds property description must have "closure" and must "close the loop" in that it must begin and end at precisely the same point.

Often a description also contains a statement as to the number of acres or quantity of land being conveyed. In the event this quantity is inconsistent with the description by metes and bounds, the quantity of land yields to the number of acres as actually established by the metes and bounds description.

Government Rectangular Survey System

The **government rectangular survey system** is the land description method used throughout the United States but not within North Carolina or any of the original 13 colonies.

In the government rectangular survey system, which is based on the longitude and latitude lines, the country is divided by north-south lines called principal **meridians** and by east-west lines called base lines. The areas between the base lines and north-south meridians are called ranges. Within the ranges are townships. Each **township** is *a square, 6 miles by 6 miles*, and is, therefore, 36 square miles in area. Each township is divided into 36 sections. Each **section** is *1 mile square, or 1 square mile*. A section is divided into quarter sections and may be subdivided into areas smaller than one-quarter sections. Each section contains 640 acres; therefore, a quarter section is 160 acres. Following is an example of a legal description using the government rectangular survey system: "All of the southwest quarter of the northwest quarter of section 25, range 1 east, township 1 north, Huntsville meridian and

Property Description 69

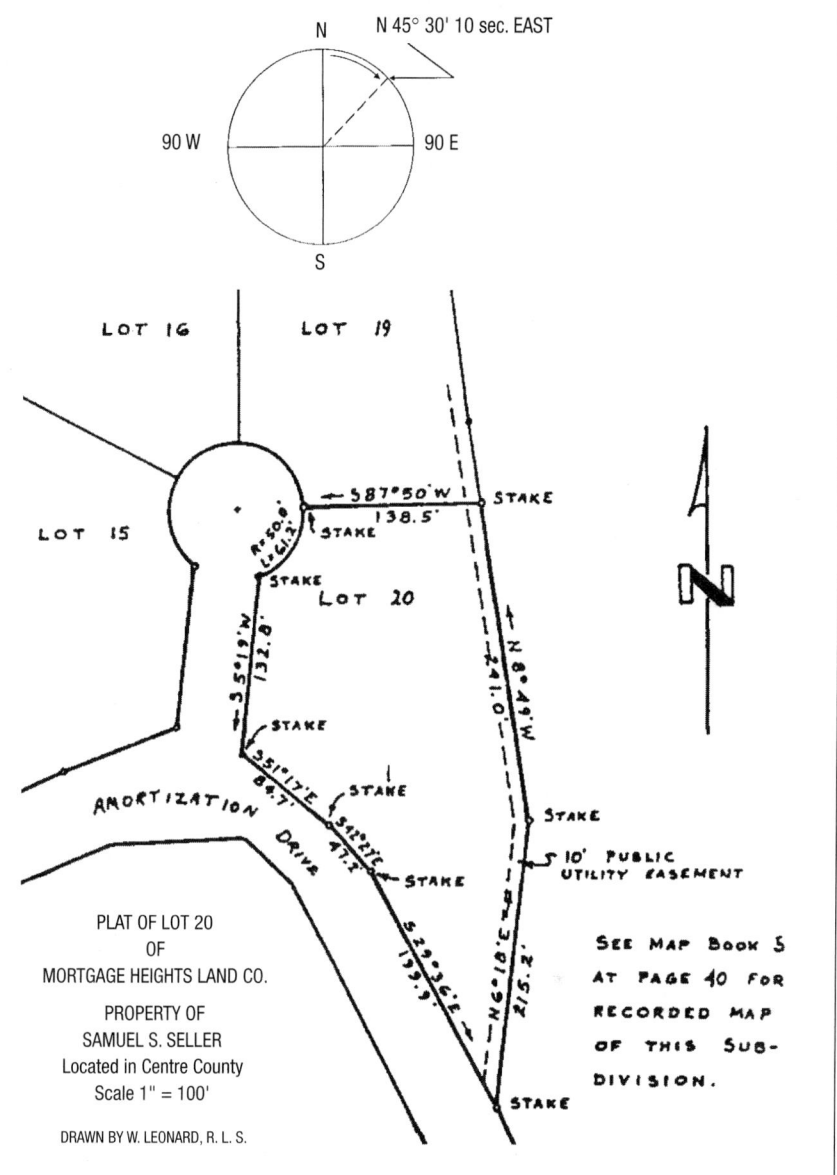

An example of a typical metes and bounds description and the plat resulting from that description follow.

*Being all of Lot No. 20 of the subdivision of a portion of the property of Mortgage Heights Land Company, Inc., Centre County, as shown by plat thereof prepared by Worley and Gray, Consulting Engineers, dated October 1, 1995, and recorded in Book 5, page 40, Records of Plats for Centre County, and more particularly bounded and described as follows:

**BEGINNING on a stake in the northeast margin of Amortization Drive, south corner of Lot No. 20 of the subdivision or a portion of the property of Mortgage Heights Land Company, Inc., and running thence North 6° 18' East 215.2 feet to a stake; thence North 8° 49' West 241.0 feet to a stake, common corner of Lot Nos. 20 and 19 of said subdivision; thence with the dividing line between said Lot Nos. 19 and 20, South 87° 50' West 138.5 feet to a stake in the east margin of a cul-de-sac; thence with the east margin of said cul-de-sac in a southwesterly direction along a curve with the radius of 50.0 feet, 61.2 feet to a stake in said margin; thence with the east margin of a drive leading to Amortization Drive, South 5° 19' West 132.8 feet to a stake in the point of intersection of said margin of said drive with Amortization Drive; thence with the northeast margin of said Amortization Drive, South 51° 17' East 84.7 feet to a stake in said margin; thence still with said margin of said drive, South 42° 27' East 47.2 feet to a stake in said margin; thence still said margin of said drive, South 29° 36' East 199.9 feet to the BEGINNING.

*Description by reference
**Description by metes and bounds

FIGURE 4.1 A sample metes and bounds description in conjunction with a description by reference.
Source: © 2019 OnCourse Learning

base line." Each township has a consistent numerical pattern to the layout for sections. The numerical pattern is to start each section from right to left, starting at the upper right-hand corner, and so forth in a "checkerboard" pattern until the section numbered 36 ends in the bottom right-hand corner (see Figure 4.2).

Description by Reference

A description by reference is a valid legal description. Sometimes an attorney incorporates into the deed a description by reference in addition to a metes and bounds description. Sometimes the description by reference is the only description in the deed.

6	5	4	3	2	1
7	8	9	10	11	12
18	17	16	15	14	13
19	20	21	22	23	24
30	29	28	27	26	25
31	32	33	34	35	36

Numerical layout of a typical township

FIGURE 4.2 Government rectangular survey system.
Source: © 2019 OnCourse Learning

Reference to recorded plat (lot and book). A description by reference is one in which a reference is made to a **plat**, or a *property map,* and a lot number that has been recorded. The description states the plat book number and page number in which the plat is recorded. The reader can refer to the plat and determine the exact location and dimensions of the property. An example of description by reference to a subdivision plat is shown in Figure 4.3.

Reference to publicly recorded documents. Some legal descriptions tell you what is actually being conveyed, whereas others will tell you where to look it up. Such is the case with the reference to publicly recorded documents method of land description. In this description, reference is made to another document that has been recorded in the public records. That previously recorded document will contain a more in-depth property description. For example, a contract might reference a tract as being "all of the land known as the Thomas Estate as referenced in a deed from John Wakefield to Henry Thomas dated April 11, 1959, recorded in deed book 468, page 92, Office of the Register of Deeds of Wake County, NC."

Informal reference. An informal reference such as a street address, a tax parcel number, or a word picture describing the property is a legally acceptable method if such a description identifies the property to the exclusion of all other properties. However, there is a huge potential for error. Street names can change. Streets can have similar names; for example, Plantation Place and Plantation Road.

> "An informal reference such as 'the house on Baker Street' is never adequate enough to transfer or convey real estate."
>
> —Tim Terry, DREI

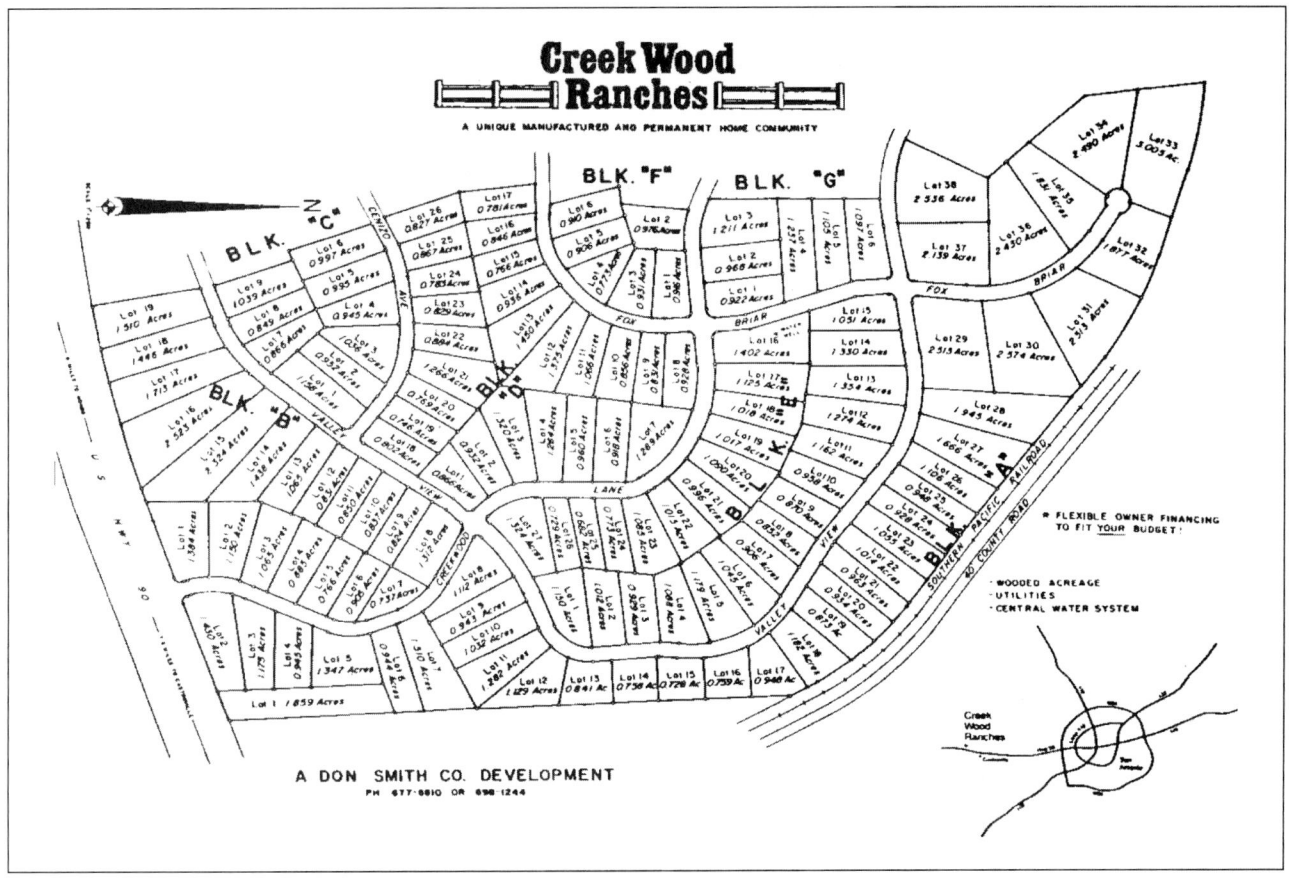

FIGURE 4.3 A sample subdivision plat map.
Source: © 2019 OnCourse Learning

An individual can own several adjoining lots that are not part of the property identified by the street address. Mr. Jones, the owner of several farms, can convey his farm described only as adjacent to widow Smith's property, unaware that another widow named Smith recently purchased property adjoining another of his farms. This description does not adequately describe the property, although it may have done so before the second widow Smith purchased her farm. The informal reference method should never serve as an adequate legal description in a deed or deed of trust. It is best utilized in a listing or short-term rental agreement. Often it is used as a secondary and more recognizable reference to a primary legal description such as "also known as 321 Shady Lane, Purlear, NC."

Property Survey

A property survey is used to determine the boundaries of a specific tract of land that is done by a licensed surveyor or civil engineer. After determining the boundaries of a tract, the surveyor or engineer prepares a map or plat of the parcel of land. In addition to the boundaries of a property, a survey includes such important information as the location of buildings, fences, and other structures and the location of easements and rights-of-way. The survey usually indicates the existence of an encroachment.

It is not uncommon for survey markers (monuments or landmarks) to become lost over time and for boundaries to become indistinct. Additionally, encroachments on another's property may have occurred. When a garage was built, it may have violated setback requirements or encroached upon a neighbor's property. A survey conducted before closing on a property will identify problems while the seller can still correct them. Real estate practitioners should not venture opinions as to this information; instead, they should refer their clients to a licensed surveyor or engineer. The purchaser traditionally pays for the survey when it is obtained for a loan closing.

METHODS OF TRANSFERRING TITLE

By Descent (Intestate Succession)

If *a person dies without leaving a valid will* (**intestate**), *property is distributed to the heirs* by **descent** according to laws called intestate succession statutes. The person appointed by a court to distribute the property of an intestate according to the provisions of the statute is called an *administrator* if a man or *administratrix* if a woman.

By Will

A **will** is *a legal instrument designed to dispose of a decedent's property according to her instructions*. If *a person dies and leaves a valid will*, he is said to have died **testate**. The deceased is the **testator** or **testatrix**. A *person appointed in a will to carry out the provisions of that will* is an **executor** or **executrix**. **Probate** is the *judicial determination of the validity of a will by the courts*. A *gift of real property by will* is a **devise**, and the *recipient of real property* is a **devisee**. A *gift of personal property by will* is a **bequest**, and the *recipient of personal property* is the **beneficiary**.

By Deed (Voluntary Alienation)

The concept of alienation is to remove oneself from ownership. This can be achieved either voluntarily or involuntarily. In a voluntary alienation the grantor is willingly transferring his interest in the property to the grantee. In the transfer of real property, this is accomplished by the transfer of a deed. A **deed** is a *written instrument that transfers an interest in real property when delivered to and voluntarily accepted by the grantee*. The contract of sale for real property is consummated by this delivery as required in the contract. The seller traditionally pays for the deed at the closing along with the required revenue stamps.

> "There are two main categories of alienation (transfer) of real estate: voluntary and involuntary. The most common type of voluntary alienation is a sale. The most common type on involuntary alienation is a foreclosure."
>
> —Jim Fletemier

By Involuntary Alienation

Title to real property also may be transferred during life by involuntary alienation (against the owner's wishes) as a result of a **lien foreclosure sale**, adverse possession, or under the power of eminent domain. In a transfer of involuntary alienation, the transfer will occur without the support of the grantor. In essence the owner is being removed from title without her cooperation. Title may be transferred by involuntary alienation after death as a result of escheat.

Lien Foreclosure Sale

Chapter 2 notes that real property can be sold at public auction to satisfy a specific or a general lien against the property. These lien **foreclosure** sales are *conducted without the consent of the property owner who incurred the debt that resulted in a lien*. Foreclosure sales are either ordered by a court or conducted under a *power of sale* clause of a deed of trust, and title is conveyed to a purchaser at the sale by a judicial deed or a trustee's deed. A **judicial deed** is *executed by the official authorized by the court to conduct the sale and transfer the title*. In these cases, titles typically are conveyed by a sheriff's deed or trustee's deed, generally without the participation of the property owner who lost the title as the result of the foreclosure.

Adverse Possession

Adverse possession is a *method of acquiring title to real property by conforming to statutory requirement*. A person other than the owner can claim title to real property if the other person takes use of the land under the following conditions:

1. The possession or occupation must be open and well known to others (notorious).
2. The possession must be without the permission of the true owner (hostile) and must be exclusive (not shared with the true owner).
3. The possession must be available to view by the public (open and notorious) and must not be hidden or secret so all can see that the use or claim is being made.
4. The possession must be continuous and uninterrupted for a period specified by statute. North Carolina provides by statute a shorter period of time if possession is under **color of title**. Color of title exists when someone has *a document (such as a will, a deed, or a divorce decree) that appears to give him or her title to the property but actually does not*. For example, the document may be defective or the person who created the document may not have owned the property or may not have had the authority to convey it. In North Carolina, the period is as short as 7 years when claiming individual land and

> "In order to take real estate away from another private owner through the concept of adverse possession you have to do an OCEAN of work. You must prove that the use was open, continuous, exclusive, adverse, and notorious."
> —Terry Wilson, DREI

21 years when claiming state land under color of title. The period is as long as 20 years when claiming individual land and 30 years when claiming state land without color of title.

The adverse possessor does not automatically acquire title to the property by merely meeting the requirements just listed. To obtain marketable title to the property, the claimant must satisfy the court that she has *fulfilled the requirements of the adverse possession statute in the particular state* by **suit to quiet title**. If the court is satisfied that the statutory requirements have been met, the court will award the title by court order to the claimant under adverse possession.

> A permissive use cannot be later acquired by adverse possession claims.

Escheat

Escheat occurs when no one is eligible to receive the property of the intestate. If no heirs can be found as specified by the statute, the property escheats (falls back) to the state. This means that in the absence of heirs, the state takes title to the property of the deceased. The deceased has no control over the transfer of title to the state, resulting in an involuntary alienation at death.

Eminent Domain

"When condemnation occurs regarding a rental property, the lease is terminated without further liability between the parties; however, the government may have to compensate both the owner and the tenant."
—Deb Cox

The federal government, states and their agencies, counties, cities, and towns have the power of eminent domain. This power provides the right to take private property for public use and benefit. The taking of the property under the power of eminent domain is called condemnation. The property owner must be compensated for the fair market value of the property lost through condemnation. The condemning authority must use due process of law, and the property owner must have the right to appeal the value of the property as established by the condemning authority through the court system. The property owner cannot prevent the condemnation; therefore, the loss of title is involuntary.

> **Eminent domain** is the *right* to take the property. **Condemnation** is the *process of actually taking* the property.

Deeds

Essential Elements of a Valid Deed

The following is a discussion of the requirements for the creation of a valid deed and the conveyance of title.

Named parties (grantor/grantee): The deed must contain the legal names of both the grantor as well as the grantee. The **grantor** conveys the title and the **grantee** receives the title.

Words of conveyance: The deed must contain *words demonstrating that it is the grantor's intention to transfer the title to the named* **grantee**, or the *one receiving title to the real property.* These **words of conveyance** are contained in the granting clause. Typical wording is "has given, granted, bargained, sold, and conveyed" in the case of warranty deeds. If the property is being sold subject to specific encumbrances of record, such as easements or a mortgage lien, the deed should recite these encumbrances. Please note two items in regard to encumbrances: The transfer of a **fee simple absolute title** does not mean there are no encumbrances, and the covenant against encumbrances in a deed (to be discussed) is only a **covenant against encumbrances** that have not been disclosed.

Property description: The deed must contain an adequate **legal description**, or a *description of land recognized by law.* The three most acceptable methods of providing such a description are discussed at the beginning of this chapter (see the section "Property Description").

Grantor: The **grantor** *(the one conveying the title)* must be legally competent; that is, the individual must have the capacity to contract. This requirement exists for all parties to a valid contract. The grantor must have reached the age of majority and must be mentally competent at the time of deed execution. Also, the grantor must be named with a certainty (for grantee requirements, see the paragraph "Execution"). It must be possible to positively identify the grantor. A corporation may be a grantor. Although title may be held and transferred in an assumed name, title may not be held or transferred in the name of a fictitious person or organization. The person or organization must exist. If a corporation is a grantor, it must be legally incorporated, the person signing for the corporation must be authorized to do so, and the corporate seal must be on the deed.

> "Only the Grantor must sign a deed. Only the trustor (borrower) must sign a Deed of Trust. Generally, only the person who is giving something up must sign the document for it to be binding."
> —Len Elder, DREI

Test Tip!

Throughout the text, students will encounter words ending in "or" or "ee" such as grantor and grantee. Always remember the "ee's" receive and the "or's" convey.

Acknowledgment: For a deed to be eligible for recording, it must be acknowledged. The grantor must appear before a public officer, such as a notary public, who is eligible to take an **acknowledgment** and state that *the signing of the deed was done by the grantor and was a voluntary act.* A deed is perfectly valid and enforceable between the grantor and grantee without an acknowledgment, but without the acknowledgment, the deed cannot be recorded by the grantee. Therefore, it will not provide the grantee protection of title against subsequent creditors or purchasers of the same property from the same grantor if the subsequent creditors or purchasers record their lien or deed before the original grantee records his deed. Therefore, the grantee should insist on receiving a deed that has been acknowledged and then promptly record it.

Historically, the acknowledgment process was carried out by having the person to sign "under seal," which involved the imprint of the person's seal next to the signature. The idea is the signature and the seal was from the same person. The idea of signing under seal in modern times is no more than the word seal being present next to the signature line. Today, students should simply treat the words witnessed, sealed, notarized, and acknowledged as interchangeable terms for practical purposes.

Delivery and acceptance: To affect a transfer of title by deed, there must be a delivery of a valid deed by the grantor to the grantee and the deed must be voluntarily accepted by the grantee. Delivery is made directly to the grantee or to an agent of the grantee. Typically, the agent for this purpose is the grantee's attorney, her real estate broker, or the lending institution providing the mortgage loan to finance the purchase of the property. If delivery is made to a real estate broker or to an agent, that person must be an agent of the grantee, not an agent of the grantor. In almost every case, acceptance by the grantee is presumed. This presumption is especially strong if the deed has been recorded and the conveyance is beneficial to the grantee.

Writing: The **Statute of Frauds** is *a law in effect in all states requiring that every deed must be written to be valid.* An oral conveyance is ineffective. The written form of the deed must meet the legal requirements of the state.

Nonessential Elements of a Deed

The following items, although usually found in a deed, are not required to create a valid deed.

Consideration: A deed does not need to recite the actual amount of consideration (money) involved. However, it must provide evidence that consideration (something of value, such as money) is present. A phrase such as "for a valuable consideration paid by the grantee, the receipt of which is hereby acknowledged," as is used in the current North Carolina Bar Association General Warranty Deed form, is sufficient to accomplish this purpose.

Seal: In North Carolina, deeds do not have to be sealed to be valid even if the deed form has the word "seal" after the signature. See the paragraph "Acknowledgment."

Recording: The purpose of **recording** the deed, or *registering the document on public record,* is to protect the grantee's title. This protection is provided by **constructive notice**, meaning that *all the world is bound by knowledge of the existence of the conveyance of title* and the fact that the title is now vested in the grantee. This protection is against everyone, including subsequent purchasers of the same property from the same grantor.

Witnessing: North Carolina is not one of the few states that requires the grantor's signature to be *witnessed* on the deed by one or more witnesses for the deed to be valid. See the paragraph "Acknowledgment."

Date: A deed does not need to be dated to be valid between the parties. If the grantee wants to record the deed to protect his interest against future claims on the property, he must have it acknowledged. The acknowledgment will provide a date. Because a gift deed must be recorded within two years, a date is needed to establish the time of the gift, and acknowledgment is needed to allow the deed to be recorded so it remains valid after the two-year period.

Types of Deed

Variations in types of deed result from the forms of warranty of title contained in the deed and from a special purpose for which the deed is drawn. Warranties, or covenants, in a deed are promises or guarantees made by the grantor to the grantee to protect the grantee against specific defects in the title. The following is a discussion of the various types of deed, by type of warranty and special purpose, that are common in North Carolina.

> "'Witnessing' a documents is the formal action of validating a signature. It can also be called 'seal,' 'notarize,' or an 'acknowledgment.' No document must be acknowledged in order to be valid; however, it may need to be acknowledged or notarized in order to be recorded."
> —Len Elder, DREI

> All deeds do two things: convey title and convey a warranty. General, special, and non-warranty deeds convey title equally as well. The difference is in the warranty. General warranty = maximum warranty, against the claims of all persons whomsoever. Special warranty = warranty limited to claims during the grantor's period of ownership. Non-warranty = no warranty conveyed or necessary.

General Warranty Deed

> The general warranty deed (often referred to as simply a warranty deed) contains the strongest and broadest form of guarantee of title of any type of deed; therefore, it provides the greatest protection to the grantee and the greatest liability to the grantor.

The North Carolina general warranty deed specifies the "grantor will warrant and defend the title against the lawful claims of all persons whomsoever." The general warranty deed usually contains the following covenants outlined in Figure 4.4.

Covenant of seisin (seizin). The typical wording of a covenant of seisin (pronounced like "season") is "grantor covenants that she is seised of said premises in fee." This covenant *provides an assurance to the grantees that the grantors hold the title that they specify in the deed that they are conveying to the grantees.* The grantors promise the grantees that they have fee simple title to the property.

Covenant of right to convey. This covenant usually follows the covenant of seisin in the general warranty deed and typically reads, "and has the right to convey the same in fee simple." By this covenant, the grantor *provides an assurance to the grantee that the grantor has legal capacity to convey the title* and also has the title to convey.

Covenant against encumbrances. This covenant typically states, "that said premises are free from encumbrances (with the exceptions below stated, if any)." The grantor is *assuring the grantee that there are no encumbrances against the title except those of record.* Typical encumbrances that are acceptable to grantees are the encumbrances of a mortgage lien when the grantee is assuming the grantor's existing mortgage, of recorded easements, and of restrictive covenants. As noted previously, this does *not* mean there are no encumbrances, only that there are none other than those of public record, such as easements, restrictive covenants, or zoning regulations.

> "A General Warranty Deed is the most powerful deed that can be used to convey property. It contains the most promises and offers the most protection for the buyer. The highest ranking office in the army is the General, who is very powerful."
> —Jim Hriso

Covenant of quiet enjoyment. This covenant typically reads, "the grantee, her heirs and assigns, shall quietly and peaceably have, hold, use, possess, and enjoy the premises." This covenant is an *assurance by the grantor to the grantee that the grantee shall have a quiet possession and enjoyment of the property being conveyed and that the grantee will not be disturbed in the use and enjoyment of the property because of a defect in the title being conveyed by the grantor.* In warranty deeds that do not contain this specific covenant, such as the North Carolina Warranty Deed shown in Figure 4.4, the covenant of warranty assures the grantee of quiet enjoyment of the property.

Covenant of warranty. The warranty of title in the general warranty deed provides that *the grantor "will warrant and defend the title to the grantee against the lawful claims of all persons whomsoever."* This is the best form of warranty for the protection of the grantee and contains no limitations as to possible claimants protected against, because the grantor specifies that he will defend the title against

NORTH CAROLINA GENERAL WARRANTY DEED

Excise Tax:

Parcel Identifier No. ______ Verified by ______ County on the __ day of ______, 20__

By: ______

Mail/Box to: ______

This instrument was prepared by: ______

Brief description for the Index: ______

THIS DEED made this ______ day of ______, 20__, by and between

GRANTOR	GRANTEE

Enter in appropriate block for each party: name, address, and, if appropriate, character of entity, e.g. corporation or partnership.

The designation Grantor and Grantee as used herein shall include said parties, their heirs, successors, and assigns, and shall include singular, plural, masculine, feminine or neuter as required by context.

WITNESSETH, that the Grantor, for a valuable consideration paid by the Grantee, the receipt of which is hereby acknowledged, has and by these presents does grant, bargain, sell and convey unto the Grantee in fee simple, all that certain lot or parcel of land situated in the City of ______, ______ Township, ______ County, North Carolina and more particularly described as follows:

The property hereinabove described was acquired by Grantor by instrument recorded in Book ___ page _.

A map showing the above described property is recorded in Plat Book ____ page ___.

NC Bar Association Form No. 3 © 1976, Revised © 1977, 2002
Printed by Agreement with the NC Bar Association - 1981

+ James Williams & Co., Inc.
www.JamesWilliams.com

Printed with permission by the North Carolina Bar Association.

TO HAVE AND TO HOLD the aforesaid lot or parcel of land and all privileges and appurtenances thereto belonging to the Grantee in fee simple.

And the Grantor covenants with the Grantee, that Grantor is seized of the premises in fee simple, has the right to convey the same in fee simple, that title is marketable and free and clear of all encumbrances, and that Grantor will warrant and defend the title against the lawful claims of all persons whomsoever, other than the following exceptions:

IN WITNESS WHEREOF, the Grantor has duly executed the foregoing as of the day and year first above written.

______ (Entity Name)

By: ______ Title: ______

By: ______ Title: ______

By: ______ Title: ______

USE BLACK INK ONLY

______(SEAL)

______(SEAL)

______(SEAL)

______(SEAL)

SEAL-STAMP

USE BLACK INK ONLY

State of North Carolina - County of ______
I, the undersigned Notary Public of the County and State aforesaid, certify that ______ personally appeared before me this day and acknowledged the due execution of the foregoing instrument for the purposes therein expressed. Witness my hand and Notarial stamp or seal this ______ day of ______, 20__.
My Commission Expires: ______ ______ Notary Public

SEAL-STAMP

USE BLACK INK ONLY

State of North Carolina - County of ______
I, the undersigned Notary Public of the County and State aforesaid, certify that ______ personally appeared before me this day and acknowledged that _he is the ______ of ______, a North Carolina or ______ corporation/limited liability company/general partnership/limited partnership (strike through the inapplicable), and that by authority duly given and as the act of each entity, _he signed the forgoing instrument in its name on its behalf as its act and deed. Witness my hand and Notarial stamp or seal this ______ day of ______, 20__.
My Commission Expires: ______ ______ Notary Public

SEAL-STAMP

USE BLACK INK ONLY

State of North Carolina - County of ______
I, the undersigned Notary Public of the County and State aforesaid, certify that ______ Witness my hand and Notarial stamp or seal this ______ day of ______, 20__.
My Commission Expires: ______ ______ Notary Public

The foregoing Certificate(s) of ____ is/are certified to be correct. This instrument and this certificate are duly registered at the date and time and in the Book and Page shown on the first page hereof.
______ Register of Deeds for ______ County
By: ______ Deputy/Assistant - Register of Deeds

NC Bar Association Form No. 3 © 1976, Revised © 1977, 2002
Printed by Agreement with the NC Bar Association - 1981

*James Williams & Co., Inc.
www.JamesWilliams.com

SAMPLE

FIGURE 4.4 North Carolina warranty deed.

"the lawful claims of all persons whomsoever." The covenant of warranty is the most important of all the covenants.

NOTE: The covenants of seisin and the right to convey are often considered one covenant, as are the covenants of warranty and quiet enjoyment.

Grantee's rights to recovery. If the covenant of seisin or the covenant of warranty is broken, a grantee may recover from the seller any financial loss up to the price paid for the property. If the covenant against encumbrances is broken, the grantee may recover from the grantor any expense incurred to pay off the encumbrance. The amount the grantee may recover in this case is limited to the price paid for the property.

Special Warranty Deed

In the **special warranty deed**, the *warranty is limited to claims against the title arising out of the period of ownership of the grantor.* Therefore, the warranty goes back in time only to the date when the grantor acquired the title, as contrasted with the general warranty deed, in which the warranty is against defects in the title going back for an unlimited period of time.

Quitclaim Deed

The **quitclaim deed** *contains no warranties whatsoever but is simply a deed of release.* It releases or conveys to the grantee any interest, including title, that the grantor may have. Even fee simple absolute title can be passed by a quitclaim deed if the grantor holds fee simple absolute title. However, the grantor does not state in the deed that she has any title or interest in the property. Execution of the quitclaim deed by the grantor prevents the grantor from asserting any claim against the title at any time in the future.

Quitclaim deeds may be used to clear a **cloud on a title**, a situation that occurs when someone has *a possible claim against a title.* As long as this possibility exists, the title is cloudy and therefore is not a good and marketable title. To remove this cloud and create a good and marketable title, the possible claimant must execute a quitclaim deed as grantor to the true titleholder as grantee. The granting clause in a quitclaim deed contains the words "remise, release, and quitclaim" instead of "grant, bargain, sell, and convey," as used in warranty deeds.

Bargain and Sale Deed

A bargain and sale deed typically is not used in North Carolina, but it is used in many other states where it is essentially serving the same purpose as a quitclaim, or non-warranty, deed.

Special Purpose Deeds

Trustee's deed. This deed is used by a person serving in the role of trustee. This can range from serving in the capacity for a trust to transfer the title to property for that trust or to the capacity of a trustee for a foreclosure proceeding.

Sheriff's deed. This deed is conveyed by the sheriff in the event of transfer of real property required to be handled by someone in this capacity. This type deed will be seldom, if ever, encountered in North Carolina.

Deed of gift. A gift of real property may be made by general warranty deed, by special warranty deed, or by quitclaim deed. If the warranty deed is used, however, the warranties cannot be enforced against the grantor by the grantee. This is because the grantor received no compensation for conveying the title to the grantee because the conveyance was a gift. Any type of deed will convey the property, provided the grantor has title to convey. The deed of gift must be recorded to protect the grantee's interest. In North Carolina, **a deed of gift must be recorded within two years to remain valid**. This is the only time that there is a time element in which a deed has to be recorded or the rights will cease to exist. Two other important points about a gift deed are these: It requires no excise tax, and it is fraudulent to convey property with a gift deed to defeat a creditor's rights.

Excise Tax

> North Carolina statutes require an **excise tax** to be paid by the seller. Excise stamps are commonly referred to as revenue or transfer stamps. The amount of tax is *based on the consideration received by the seller in the sale of the real property by deed.* The statute requires the amount of the excise tax *to be $1 per $500,* or a fraction thereof, *based on the full purchase price.*

Excise tax is assessed only in multiples of $1. There are no fractional prices, only a $1 increment for each portion of $500 of sales price. An easy way to calculate the excise tax is to round up the sales price to the next $500 and divide that number by 500. The answer is the amount of excise tax required. For example:

$74,000 cash sale, no rounding required; $74,000 ÷ $500 = $148 tax
$74,100 cash sale, round up to $74,500; $74,500 ÷ $500 = $149 tax
$74,700 cash sale, round up to $75,000; $75,000 ÷ $500 = $150 tax

The excise tax on deeds is often used as a rough indication of value paid for the property. The state has a statute requiring the amount of the tax to properly reflect the sales price. Because this information is a part of the public record, brokers draw information from these data for their comparable property sales files.

County Transfer Tax

A few counties in North Carolina impose a transfer tax on the sale of real property. These taxes require approval on a county-by-county basis from the North Carolina General Assembly. Fourteen such bills have been introduced and defeated by the General Assembly since 1991. The North Carolina Association of REALTORS® opposes the land transfer tax because it affects housing affordability. Passage of such bills would diminish the effects of federal and state programs designed to make homeownership more affordable.

TITLE ASSURANCE

Covenants of Title in Deeds

Covenants of title in deeds is a method of title assurance. In addition to other methods of protecting the purchaser with regard to the quality of title, *covenants of title in deeds* provides the grantee with the added assurance that the grantor can be sued if a covenant is breached. See the discussion of the various covenants starting on page 70.

Title Examination Procedures

Regardless of the warranties in a deed, the grantee should retain the services of an attorney to conduct an examination of the public record to verify if, in fact, the grantee is receiving a good and marketable title free from encumbrances, except those he has agreed to accept. The purpose of a **title examination** is *to determine the quality of a title.* Anyone can do a title search; however, only an attorney can give a legal opinion as to the quality of a title.

The title search consists of an examination of all public records that possibly affect a title to real estate. The examiner uses the grantor and grantee indexes maintained by the Register of Deeds office to trace the successive conveyance of title from the present to an appropriate time in the past, typically 40 to 60 years. The examiner must be able to show a consecutive and unbroken **chain of title** for the statutory time period (see the section "Marketable Title Act," page 70, for statutory time period). A chain of title refers to *successive conveyances of title to a piece of land.* If links are missing in the grantor and grantee indexes, the examiner must check other recorded documents, such as wills, to establish the required unbroken chain of title. A missing link could be the result of such things as failure to record a deed, a name change during ownership of the property whereby a person takes title under one name and grants that title to someone else under another name, or fraud. The sale should not close until proper documents are found to clear the title. If the missing link cannot be found, ownership may need to be established by a suit to quiet title. Additionally, the examiner searches all other public records, such as records of judgments, special proceedings, liens, restrictive covenants, easements, and any other recordings or documents that could affect the title.

A title search is done by name. For example, Jim Jones contracts to sell a property to John Smith. Jim is the grantor and John is the grantee when the property is conveyed. A title examination is done before this conveyance occurs. Jim, the grantor, was the grantee when he received the title to the property; therefore, the title examiner begins his search by finding Jim Jones in the grantee index. The grantee index also identifies the grantor, Jeff Best, and the book and page number for the deed. The examiner determines the time period in which Jim Jones owned the property and searches the public records for anything Jim may have done to affect the title during his ownership.

Because Jeff Best was the grantor to Jim Jones, Jeff was the grantee when he acquired title. The examiner finds Jeff Best in the grantee index, identifies the grantor in the transaction as Ann Todd, and determines Jeff's period of ownership. The examiner then searches the public records under Jeff's name for anything Jeff may have done to affect the title.

The title examiner follows the same procedure for Ann Todd and other previous owners until the appropriate time period has been searched.

Attorney's Opinion of Title

Upon completion of the title examination, the examining attorney provides an opinion of title, which sets forth the legal description of the property, a statement that the records have been carefully examined, the period of time covered by the examination, specific information about any liens or other encumbrances against the title, and the examiner's opinion of the quality of the title.

A **title examination** is concerned only with *recorded documents on the public record*. Circumstances affecting the property that are not a part of the public record are not covered. For example, the record may not reflect a missing heir, a mentally incapacitated grantor, or a forgery.

Therefore, even though a title examination indicates that a title is good and marketable, this may not actually be the case. The attorney may make a mistake, or the defect may be one not evident in the public record. An example of that includes forgery. The warranties in the deed and the attorney's opinion of title may be adequate protection provided the grantor and attorney are alive, available, and financially solvent. A lawsuit may become necessary should the grantor or attorney refuse to fulfill their responsibilities voluntarily.

Title Insurance

For maximum protection against a financial loss, the grantee should take advantage of the protection afforded by a **title insurance** policy. A title insurance policy is *an indemnity contract that protects the purchaser or mortgagee against loss resulting from a defect in title that is covered in the policy and is in existence when the policy becomes effective.* Conversely, it does not cover defects that are listed as exceptions in the policy or defects arising after the effective date of the policy. A one-time premium provides coverage for as long as the insured or his heirs have an interest in the property.

A rule of thumb for calculating title insurance is to estimate $2 per thousand. For example, insuring a $100,000 property requires a one-time premium of $200. The rate per thousand decreases for amounts over $100,000. Each $1,000 of value over $100,000 is typically charged at $1.50 per thousand. For example, the premium for a $200,000 property could be $350, calculated as $200 for the first $100,000, and $150 for the second $100,000. Rates for values over $500,000 can be even lower. Rates are significantly lower when the new buyer purchases a new policy from the company that issued the seller's policy. Considering the substantial financial loss that may occur as a result of a defective title, this cost is quite reasonable. A purchaser may save money on the policy by purchasing it from the company holding the seller's policy, thus *tacking on* to the previous policy.

Although title insurance companies perform their own title searches in many states, they rely on approved attorneys to do the searches in North Carolina. An attorney searches the title, submits a preliminary title opinion to the insurance company, and receives a preliminary title commitment.

After closing but before recording closing documents such as the deed and deed of trust, the attorney does a final search to ensure that nothing affecting title has been recorded since the initial search. He then records the documents and issues a final title opinion to the title insurance company, which issues the title policy to the insured owner or mortgagee.

Although a title insurance policy is usually the best form of insurance, it has limitations. Ordinarily, it limits coverage to the purchase price of the property, not covering future improvements or increased values resulting from appreciation. There are usually exceptions to the policy. Major commercial real estate purchases may exceed the title company's ability or willingness to insure. Title insurance companies are often easier to find and more financially solvent than many grantors or attorneys; however, these companies can become insolvent and dissolve if claims exceed their assets.

The major advantage of a title insurance policy is the title company's responsibility to defend the title against defects not evident in the public record and errors made in the title search.

Owner's Policy

The owner's policy is for the protection of the owner and is written for the amount that the owner paid for the property. The amount of coverage remains the same for the life of the policy. The policy remains in effect for the duration of the insured's ownership of the property and continues in effect after the owner's death to benefit heirs who receive an interest in the property. Although the owner's title policy is optional, real estate agents should advise buyers of the advantages of purchasing this policy.

Mortgagee's Policy

This policy protects only the mortgagee (lender). Under the terms of the policy, the mortgagee is insured against defects in the title pledged as security in the mortgage. The mortgagee's insurable interest is only to the extent of the outstanding loan balance at any given time. Therefore, the mortgagee's policy is one of diminishing liability; it provides coverage equivalent to the amount of the loan balance, which decreases as the loan principal decreases. Because most lenders require a mortgagee's policy and there is little or no increase in premium to the buyer to purchase both a mortgagee's policy and an owner's policy (typically, these policies together are referred to as a simultaneous policy), it is prudent and cost-effective for the buyer to purchase both.

Leasehold Policy

A leasehold policy is written to protect a lessee (leaseholder) or a mortgagee against defects in the lessor's title. This policy is issued to a mortgagee if the mortgagor has pledged a leasehold interest instead of a fee simple title as security for the mortgage debt.

Title Recordation

Although the recording of title is not required in North Carolina, it should be considered essential by all people. By recording the title, constructive notice is established that puts all the world on notice as to the claim in title. North Carolina has two statutes that make the recording of title extremely important.

The Conner Act

The North Carolina **Conner Act** provides that certain real estate documents *are not valid against third parties until recorded, therefore creating the need of protection.* This act places a great potential burden on the grantee. If the grantee does not record the document and a subsequent purchaser does, the latter would take priority. Because of this concern, the Conner Act makes North Carolina a pure race state. This means that, with only a few exceptions (such as for real property tax liens), the first party to record shall be recognized as the rightful owner or the higher priority lien. Therefore, it is important to know which documents must be recorded. The Conner Act requires that the following documents be recorded: purchase and option contracts, deeds, mortgage instruments (deeds of trust and mortgages), assignments of interest in real property, leases that cannot be completed in less than three years from the date of their making, easements, and restrictive covenants. A good rule of thumb is that if a document has to be in writing according to the Statute of Frauds, it has to be recorded to protect that interest.

> **Test Tip!**
>
> The Conner Act deals only with recordation, whereas the Statute of Frauds deals with the requirement to be in writing. A good rule of thumb is that if a contract for an interest in real estate has to be in writing under the Statute of Frauds, it will have to be recorded under the Conner Act.

"In order to remember what has to be recorded in North Carolina use the acronym DREAMOIL. Deeds, Restrictive Covenants, Easements, Assignments, Mortgages, Options, Installment Land Contracts, and Leases longer than 3 years all have to be recorded."
—Bill Gallagher, DREI

Recording contracts. In theory, any real estate contract that grants the purchaser the right to receive title at some future time should be recorded. This way, a purchaser is protected against the owner's reselling the property to another party. This is especially important in the case of contracts in which there will be an extended amount of time before title is to be conveyed, such as option and installment land contracts. However, most standard offers to purchase and contract for residential property call for closing to take place within a relatively short time. In actual practice, these contracts are rarely recorded because of the short duration (usually less than 60 days) and because problems arising from lack of recordation are rare. Should a purchaser raise the question of recording a standard residential offer to purchase and contract, the purchaser should be advised to consult an attorney. Since October 1, 2010, the seller is responsible for the recordation of installment land contracts (contracts for deed) and leases with an option to purchase within five days of closing.

Recording procedures. Document recordation is done at the Register of Deeds office in the county where the property is located. Copies of each instrument are placed in a book in the chronological order in which they are received. The documents then are recorded in the grantor and grantee indexes. After recordation, the original document is returned to the owners or the owner's designee.

In 2011, North Carolina adopted changes that provide for the recordation of a "memorandum of contract" in certain real estate transactions. This allows a memorandum to be registered that sets forth the name of the parties, property description, the expiration dates of the contract, and references sufficient to identify the agreement between the parties instead of requiring registration of the entire agreement.

Marketable Title Act

The North Carolina **Marketable Title Act** *aims to extinguish old defects in the title by providing that if a chain of title can be established for 30 years without conflicts, claims outside this chain are extinguished.* Paired with the Conner Act, this act emphasizes the importance of recording instruments and upholds the value of examining the record.

The Torrens System

North Carolina is one of about a dozen states that has a statute providing for title registration under the Torrens System. Essentially, land under this system is registered in a way similar to motor vehicle registration. A change in the status of the property, such as a transfer of ownership or placement of a lien on the property, requires that the old registration certificate be destroyed and replaced with a new one. The single registration certificate on the property at a particular time reflects the current status of the property. Anything not on the certificate does affect the title.

One advantage of the Torrens System is that it does not allow property to be taken by adverse possession. This feature may make it attractive to an owner of thousands of acres of mountain property who does not want to be bothered with policing her land to prevent adverse possession. This feature, however, has major disadvantages. The process of initially registering property under the system is lengthy and costly. Each issuance of a new registration certificate is time-consuming.

Action to Quiet Title. There are times in which the parties will have to resort to court action to establish an adverse possession claim or some other conflict. The problem with adverse possession claims is that they are not a part of the public record, so the claimant typically will not have a marketable title without having the courts to declare who the rightful owner is. This action will involve a lawsuit to settle the issue of who the legal owner is and the public record will reflect the court's ruling. Future title searches will be able to use this declaration to eliminate potential title disputes arising from this action.

Math Concepts Related to Area

The discussion of area-related math is introduced in this chapter because of its relevance to land. For more detailed explanations of how to complete this type of question, including examples of irregular-shaped properties, please review Appendix B at the end of this text. Solutions to these questions follow the examples.

Area and Related Calculations

- Conversion of acreage to square footage and vice versa
- Square footage of variously shaped buildings and land (see Appendix B)
- Square yards
- Cost/price per square foot/acre/front foot

> **Test Tip!**
>
> - There are 43,560 square feet per acre.
> - There are 9 square feet in 1 square yard.
> - In front footage examples, the first number is the width unless otherwise stated.

Conversion of Acreage to Square Footage and Vice Versa

1. A property contains 2.58 acres. How many square feet does it contain?
2. A property contains 52,250 square feet. How many acres does it contain?
3. A parcel of land containing 6.58 acres was recently sold for $114,650. What was the price per square foot?

Square Footage of Variously Shaped Buildings and Land

1. A triangular-shaped parcel of land was recently sold. It is a right-angle triangle with a base of 250 feet and a depth of 450. How many acres does this tract contain?

Square Yards

1. A building contains 1,449 square feet. The owner wishes to install carpeting throughout the area. Without consideration for any walls, other impediments, or waste, how many square yards of carpeting will he need?
2. An owner has been told that a large meeting room will require 54.7 square yards of flooring. Without considering any waste, how many square feet does this room contain?

Cost /Price per Square Foot/Acre/Front Foot

1. A developer is being asked to pay $35,000 per acre. If the tract contains 14.68 acres, what will the sales price be?
2. A tract of land is priced at $25,875 and is 225 feet wide and 350 feet deep. What is the price per front foot?
3. Sam is selling a parcel of land that measures 190 feet wide and 321 feet deep. Similar properties have sold for roughly $10,890 per acre. Based on the price of the similar properties, how much should Sam ask for his property?

Solutions to Area-Related Questions

Conversion of Acreage to Square Footage and Vice Versa

1. 43,560 × 2.58 = 112,384.8 square feet in property
2. 52,250 ÷ 43,560 = 1.2 acres
3. 43,560 × 6.58 = 286,624.8 square feet in property
   $114,650 ÷ 286,624.8 = $0.40 price per square foot

Square Footage of Variously Shaped Buildings and Land

1. 0.5 × 250 × 450 = 56,250 square feet in tract
   56,250 ÷ 43,560 = 1.29 acres

Square Yards

1. 1,449 ÷ 9 = 161 square yards in building
2. 54.7 × 9 = 492.3 square feet in room

Cost/Price per Square Foot/Acre/Front Foot

1. $35,000 × 14.68 = $513,800 price for the tract of land
2. $25,875 ÷ 225 = $115 price per front foot
3. 190 × 321 = 60,990 square feet in tract
   60,990 ÷ 43,560 = 1.4 acres
   $10,890 × 1.4 = $15,246 sales price for the tract

Summary of Important Points

1. A complete legal description of a property is essential for proper conveyance of title. A simple street address will not be considered adequate for the actual conveyance of title such as in a deed or deed of trust. A street address can be used for a listing or rental agreement if there is no confusion over the boundaries.
2. The primary method of property description in the original 13 colonies is metes and bounds.
3. In the government rectangular survey system, *land is divided into townships, which measure 6 miles by 6 miles. Each township is then divided into 1-mile-square increments referred to as sections. There are 36 sections in a township. Each section contains 640 acres.*
4. Transfer of title is known as alienation. Involuntary alienation occurs when a owner is removed from the title but not by his own free will. Involuntary

alienation occurs during life as a result of adverse possession, lien foreclosure sale, and condemnation under the power of eminent domain. Involuntary alienation at death is escheat. Voluntary alienation during life can occur only by delivery of a valid deed.

5. The requirements for deed validity are as follows: (1) the deed must be written, (2) the grantor must be competent, (3) the grantor and grantee must be named with a certainty, (4) there must be an adequate property description, (5) there must be words of conveyance, (6) the deed must be properly executed by the grantor, and (7) delivery and acceptance must occur to convey title. Real estate practitioners have no authority to prepare wills or deeds for others, but they should be familiar with the essential elements of the common forms of deeds used in the state.

6. To be eligible for recording on the public record, a deed must be acknowledged. Recording protects the grantee's title against creditors of the grantor and subsequent conveyances by the grantor. Recordation does NOT convey title but rather *protection* of what is already owned.

7. A general warranty deed is the strongest and broadest form of title guarantee. The general warranty deed typically contains five covenants: seisin, right to convey, against encumbrances, quiet enjoyment, and warranty. It provides the most protection for the grantee and the most liability for the grantor.

8. A quitclaim deed is a deed that contains no warranties. It conveys any interest, including fee simple absolute, the grantor may have, if any. Quitclaim deeds typically are used when there is no warranty expected, nor necessary, in the conveyance. The primary use of the quitclaim deed is to fulfill some special purpose such as a public official that conveys property in their official capacity or to remove clouds from the title if there are title issues.

9. Other types of deeds are special warranty, confirmation, release, surrender, gift, and judicial.

10. North Carolina state law requires the grantor to pay a tax of $1 per $500, or any portion thereof, based on the purchase price. Because the tax is accrued in multiples of $500 of purchase price, examination of the tax provides a rough indication of purchase price and is a valuable data source for the broker's office records.

11. The purpose of a title examination is to determine the quality of a title. Only an attorney can legally give an opinion as to quality of title. The Conner Act and the Marketable Title Act lend significance to the value of a record. The Conner Act provides possible penalties for failure to record and the Marketable Title Act establishes a limit of 30 years for most title defects.

12. A title insurance policy protects the insured against a financial loss caused by a title defect. The three types of policies are owner's, mortgagee's, and leasehold policies. A title insurance policy is the best form of title assurance.

Review Questions

Answers to the review questions are in the Answer Key at the back of the book.

1. All of the following are methods of title assurance EXCEPT:
   A. color of title.
   B. title insurance.
   C. covenants of title in the deed.
   D. title examination by an attorney.

2. Voluntary alienation during life occurs only in which of the following ways?
   A. will
   B. foreclosure sale
   C. deed delivery
   D. devise

3. Essential elements of a valid deed include all of the following EXCEPT:
   A. acknowledgment.
   B. writing.
   C. competent grantor.
   D. execution by grantor.

4. The purpose of a deed's being acknowledged is to:
   A. make the deed valid.
   B. make the deed eligible for delivery.
   C. make the deed eligible for recording.
   D. identify the grantee with certainty.

5. Which of the following is the type of notice provided by recording?
   A. actual
   B. reasonable
   C. protective
   D. constructive

6. Of the following types of deed, which provides the grantee with the greatest assurance of title?
   A. special warranty
   B. deed of confirmation
   C. grant deed
   D. general warranty

7. Which of the following covenants assures the grantee that the grantor has the legal capacity to transfer title?
   A. covenant of quiet enjoyment.
   B. covenant of right to convey.
   C. covenant of seisin.
   D. covenant of warranty.

8. Which of the following types of deeds is typically used where one is releasing any interest he/she may have in a parcel of real estate?
   A. quitclaim deed
   B. special warranty deeds
   C. grant deed
   D. general warranty deeds

9. A general warranty deed and a quitclaim deed are equally suitable for which of the following?
   A. judicial deed.
   B. deed of confirmation.
   C. official deed.
   D. deed of gift.

10. A grantor left a deed for the grantee to find after the grantor's death. The result was to:
    A. convey the title during the grantor's life.
    B. convey the title after the grantor's death.
    C. have the title automatically escheat to the state.
    D. none of the above.

11. The type of deed used to remove a mortgage lien when the debt is satisfied is a:
    A. deed of surrender.
    B. grant deed.
    C. deed of release.
    D. special warranty deed.

12. If the covenants in a general warranty deed are broken, the grantee's remedy is which of the following?
    A. Sue the grantor for damages in the amount of the loss up to the amount of the purchase price only.
    B. Require the grantor to execute a deed of confirmation only.
    C. Both sue the grantor for damages in the amount of the loss up to the amount of the purchase price and require the grantor to execute a deed of confirmation.
    D. None of the above.

13. The covenants in a general warranty deed will protect the grantee:
    A. against the lawful claims of "all persons whomsoever."
    B. only against the lawful claims arising from the grantor's period of ownership.
    C. only if the grantee acquires a valid title insurance policy.
    D. never; the general warranty deed provides no protection from the grantor to the grantee.

14. A claim of title by adverse possession may be defeated by the property owner by which of the following?
    A. permission
    B. confirmation
    C. will
    D. condemnation

15. The type of deed that guarantees the title only against defects that were created during the grantor's ownership is which of the following?
    A. general warranty
    B. special warranty
    C. surrender
    D. release

16. Which of the following statements regarding a title examination is correct?
    A. The purpose of the title examination is to reassure the purchaser the seller had good and marketable title.
    B. To determine if there are any items, recorded or not, that might negatively impact the seller's title.
    C. The purpose is to determine the quality of title.
    D. The title examination only includes items related to title and does not typically include liens or property tax matters.

17. The successive conveyances of a title are called:
    A. releases.
    B. remises.
    C. links in the chain of title.
    D. abstracts of title.

18. A title insurance policy can be written to protect all of the following EXCEPT:
    A. owner.
    B. seller.
    C. lessee.
    D. mortgagee.

19. A title insurance policy protects the insured against loss caused by:
    A. defects in the title existing at the time the insured acquired title.
    B. defects in the title created during the insured's ownership.
    C. defects in the title created after the insured's ownership.
    D. all of the above.

20. With reference to the metes and bounds property description, which of the following is correct?
    A. It is a description by distances and directions.
    B. It is the primary method of description used in the original 13 colonies.
    C. It must have a point of beginning.
    D. All of the above.

21. Which of the following legal descriptions would not be considered adequate for conveyance in a deed?
    A. reference to metes and bounds
    B. reference to a previously recorded deed
    C. informal reference
    D. reference to plat book and page

22. Of the following types of deed, which provides the grantor with the greatest liability?
    A. special warranty
    B. deed of confirmation
    C. grant deed
    D. general warranty deed

23. In a metes and bounds description, the description must close; that is, it must do which of the following?
    A. end at the northeast corner of property
    B. end at the point of beginning
    C. end at a known government marker
    D. none of the above

24. Lucy Landlord owns a house that she leases to Tim Tenant. Which of the following estates in real property exists during the time of Tim Tenant's lease?
    A. leasehold estate
    B. freehold estate
    C. neither a leasehold nor a freehold
    D. both a leasehold and a freehold

25. Which of the following is an adequate property description?
    A. 123 Smith Road, North Carolina
    B. the old Martin place
    C. Book 1968, page 924, Halifax County, North Carolina
    D. none of the above

26. A _____ property description has a point of beginning.
    A. government rectangular system
    B. legal
    C. points and calls
    D. metes and bounds

27. If a person dies intestate and has no heirs, his property will _____ to the state.
    A. devise
    B. escheat
    C. demise
    D. grant

28. A home is sold for $103,250. What is the amount of excise tax to be paid by the seller?
  A. $206
  B. $207
  C. $103
  D. $104

29. Two adjoining lots contain the same front footage. Lot A is 900 feet deep and Lot B is 780 feet deep. If Lot A contains 3.45 acres, how many acres are in Lot B? (Round width to whole number.)
  A. 2.99 acres
  B. 3.98 acres
  C. 5.56 acres
  D. 16.11 acres

30. A tract of land measuring 165 wide 350 deep recently sold for $138,600. What is its price per front foot? (Round to the nearest whole dollar.)
  A. $0.41
  B. $269
  C. $396
  D. $840

31. Carla recently purchased a tract containing 6.48 acres for $79,035. What would be the selling price of a 50 × 225 foot section of this land if she sells it for the same cost per square foot that she had originally paid for it? (Round answer to the whole dollar.)
  A. $3,150
  B. $6,300
  C. $11,250
  D. $40,178

32. A tract of land measuring 750′ × 825′ is divided into two tracts by a stream that runs diagonally through the property. How many acres are in each portion of the property?
  A. 14.20 acres
  B. 10.65 acres
  C. 7.10 acres
  D. 3.55 acres

33. A house was recently sold for $329,560. How much is due for the revenue stamps in this transaction?
  A. $660
  B. $330
  C. $659
  D. $329

34. A buyer recently purchased a lot containing .3817 acres. How many square feet does this lot contain?
  A. 24,275
  B. 21,875
  C. 17,825
  D. 16,627

CHAPTER 5

LAND USE CONTROLS

KEY TERMS

amendment
building codes
Certificate of Occupancy (CO)
conditions
covenant
deed restrictions
enabling acts
injunction
Interstate Land Sales Full Disclosure Act
master plan
negative covenants or easements
nonconforming use
overlay district
planned unit developments (PUDs)
police powers
private land use controls
property report
public land use controls
restrictive or protective covenants
run with the land
setback
special use
spot zoning
statement of record
subdivision regulations (ordinances)
variance
zoning ordinance

LEARNING OBJECTIVES

At the conclusion of this chapter, you should be able to:

1. Describe the general methods of creating land use controls and give examples of public land use controls and private restrictions.
2. Describe zoning concepts, including terminology, authority, purposes, and procedures.

IN THIS CHAPTER

Land use controls are very important to the real estate agent. Almost every property is subject to some form of control, whether it is the zoning ordinance of a city, subdivision ordinances, or restrictive (protective) covenants; the general restrictions of a subdivision plan; the unique deed restrictions of one parcel of land; or the impact of federal legislation. Any of these can have a major impact on the owner's rights.

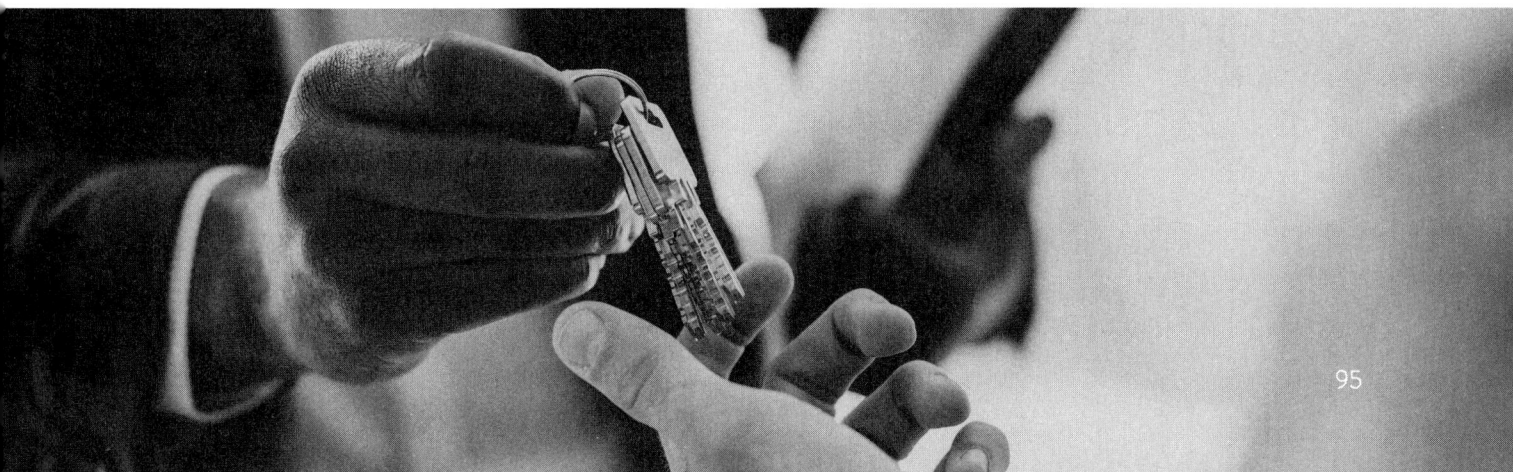

HISTORICAL DEVELOPMENT OF LAND USE CONTROLS

Private control of land use was the forerunner of public controls. In 1848, the U.S. Supreme Court first recognized and enforced restrictive covenants regulating land use in residential subdivisions, but it was not until 1926, when the Court upheld the validity of zoning ordinances, that **public land use controls** became legally reliable. These controls are commonly referred to as the right of **police powers**, which refers to *the government regulation of land use through zoning laws, building codes, subdivision ordinances, and environmental protection laws*. Before these two important legal events, a developer or government unit had no way to regulate land use, even though the need for such controls was apparent.

The increase in population density dictates the necessity for land use controls. The abuses of a few property owners in the use of their land can have a substantial adverse effect on the rights of other property owners and can cause the property value of those other owners to depreciate.

IMPORTANCE TO REAL ESTATE PRACTITIONERS AND BUYERS

Real estate practitioners must realize that all land is subject to restrictive controls, whether they are public laws or privately imposed restrictions. Rather than ask whether restrictions apply to a given property, a safer approach is to assume that many restrictions do apply and then seek to identify which controls affect the given property. We recommend giving a potential buyer a copy of subdivision covenants and any deed restrictions before he makes an offer. An agent should be aware of zoning issues in his area, but should avoid giving advice about the suitability of zoning for an intended use. The buyer may check with the zoning board or an attorney to ascertain how zoning will affect his intended use of a property. This is best done before making an offer or by making an offer contingent upon proper zoning for his intended use. Additionally, it is not appropriate to assume that an existing use by the present owner is in compliance with regulations. In documented cases, such unfortunate assumptions have worked adversely against the unwary buyer.

In some instances, a purchaser's intended use of property may be contrary to that allowed by the present regulations. Of course, the agent should not make representations as to the likelihood of obtaining approval for a different use. One should never make assumptions about the legality of a particular use, especially if that use is different from the present one. Rather, one should urge appropriate investigation before any purchase contract is signed. Although it is one thing to provide for a specific contingency approval in a purchase offer, it is quite another to make any such promises or representations.

The duty of real estate professionals is to be knowledgeable about the types of restriction that can affect property they are representing and to ensure that appropriate disclosures are made to the parties.

PUBLIC LAND USE CONTROLS

The **public land use controls** shown in Figure 5.1 are *limited in scope, and only a specific area can be subject to private use controls in the form of restrictive covenants.* The owners of property in subdivisions in which restrictive covenants exist have no control over surrounding land uses. Therefore, a subdivision may be affected adversely by an uncontrolled use of an adjoining property outside the subdivision. As a result, people became aware of the need for planning and land use controls for large areas.

> "Like we enable our children to make decisions, the state of NC enables local municipalities to make decisions regarding land use controls. Thus there are no statewide zoning laws."
> —Terry Wilson, DREI

Test Tip!

Protective covenants are the primary means of *private* land use control, whereas the others are types of *public* controls.

Zoning starts with city or county planning, which is implemented and enforced by zoning laws. Violations of zoning laws can be corrected by a court **injunction,** an *action of the court that requires the violation to be discontinued,* even to the extent of ordering an unlawful structure removed.

Planning and Zoning

The purpose of planning is to provide for the orderly growth of a community that will result in the greatest social and economic benefits to the people in the community. The North Carolina General Assembly has passed **enabling acts** that *provide the legal basis for the local cities and counties to develop long-range plans for growth.* Therefore, the state delegates authority to the local government to develop its own plan. An example of this delegation of authority was seen in Asheville some years ago, when the city wanted to develop comprehensive regulation of the cutting of trees in the front **setback** area of private property.

---

1. Zoning
2. Urban and regional planning
3. Subdivision regulations
4. Building codes
5. Highway access controls
6. Federal legislation
   A. Interstate land sales
   B. Environmental laws

FIGURE 5.1 Public land use controls.
Source: © 2019 OnCourse Learning

A setback refers to the *distance from a front or interior property line to the point where a structure can be located.* The city realized that this type of ordinance was not within its current authority and that it had to go to the state legislature for additional enabling legislation for the proposed regulation of trees. Zoning ordinances are one example of the rights of police power, which is the right of government to make and pass reasonable rules and regulations to promote and protect the public welfare. Ordinances must be reasonable, clear, precise, nondiscriminatory, and fairly applied; otherwise, they may not be valid.

The first step in developing a **master plan** is to determine what the city, municipality, or county contains by making a survey of the community's physical and economic assets. With this information as a basis, a master plan for orderly growth can be created. As a result of the plan, the various uses to which property may be put in specific areas are designated. The plan addresses such issues as land use, public resources and facilities, and transportation, as well as environmental concerns such as noise and air pollution. The zoning ordinances implement the plan by controlling population density and traffic congestion and promoting health and general welfare by providing water, sewer, adequate light, clean air, fire and environmental protection, schools, parks, and recreational facilities.

Zoning divides land within a county or municipality into areas, districts, or zones and specifies how the land within the zones may or may not be used. Zoning classifications usually include residential, commercial, industrial, and agricultural, which are then subclassified. For example, land zoned as "residential" may be divided into single family or multifamily, and land zoned as "industrial" may be divided into light industry or heavy industry. In actuality, each classification can be subdivided into numerous subclasses. Zoning classifications vary by locality. A zoning classification in Raleigh may not have the same regulations as a classification with the same name in Charlotte.

A **zoning ordinance** consists of two parts: the *zoning map, which divides the community into various designated districts, and the text of the ordinance, which sets forth the type of use permitted under each zoning classification and specific requirements for compliance.* The extent of authority for zoning ordinances is prescribed by the enabling acts passed by the state legislatures. These acts specify the types of use subject to regulation and limit the geographic area subject to the ordinances to the boundaries of the government unit enacting the zoning laws and to certain authorized extraterritorial areas outside a municipality's border.

For example, city zoning may extend for some specified distance into the county. In North Carolina, the extraterritorial jurisdiction rules allow a municipality to claim a distance up to 1 mile if its population is less than 10,000, up to 2 miles if their population is between 10,000 and 25,000, and up to 3 miles if the population exceeds 25,000. In instances in which two adjoining towns are both trying to claim the same limited amount of land that lies between them, the towns will be limited to splitting the distance between them equally.

Several types of zones are established by local ordinances: residential (which can be subdivided into single-family and various levels of multifamily dwellings), commercial, light manufacturing, heavy industrial, and multiple use or cluster zoning. The last category provides for **planned unit developments (PUDs),** which *create a neighborhood of cluster housing and supporting business establishments.*

Zoning ordinances provide for either exclusive-use zoning or cumulative-use zoning. In *exclusive-use zoning,* only the specific uses specified for a particular zone may be made of property in that zone. For example, if a zone is commercial, residential uses will not be permitted. In contrast, under *cumulative-use zoning,* more protected or higher category uses that are not designated are permitted in the zone. For instance, if an area is zoned for commercial use, a residential use could be made of the property. In cumulative-use zoning, uses are placed in an order of priority; therefore, a use of a higher priority may be made in an area where the zoned use has a lower priority. The priorities are in the following order: residential, commercial, and industrial. In addition to simply specifying the permitted use or uses in a zone, zoning laws define certain standards and requirements that must be met for each permitted type of use. These requirements include such things as minimum setbacks from front property lines to the building line as well as setbacks from the interior property lines, lot size on which a structure may be placed, height restrictions to prevent interference with the reception of sunlight and air to other properties, regulations against building on floodplains, and requirements for off-street parking.

A property owner is not reimbursed for loss of property value caused by a zoning change; however, the government must compensate a property owner whose land it takes under the power of eminent domain. These two very different powers of the government have different purposes, methods of implementation, and results. A municipality cannot "take" land without compensation by downzoning it to the point of making it unusable to avoid acquiring it by paying fair market value under eminent domain.

Zoning concepts and regulations undergo change as society's demographics, lifestyles, needs, and desires change.

Zoning Concepts and Terms

 Nonconforming use.

> A legal **nonconforming use** occurs when the *use of property in a zoned area is different from that specified by the zoning code for the area.*

When zoning is first imposed on an area or when property is rezoned, the zoning authority cannot require the property owners to immediately discontinue an existing use that does not conform to the new zoning ordinance (see Figure 5.2

"Planned Unit Developments (PUD's) and Mixed Use Developments (MUD's) are really the result of cluster or mixed use zoning."
—Derrin Dunzweiler

1. Nonconforming use
2. Illegal use
3. Zoning amendments
4. Variance
5. Special use (exception)
6. Overlay districts
7. Historic preservation zoning
8. Aesthetic zoning
9. Spot zoning

FIGURE 5.2 Zoning concepts.
Source: © 2019 OnCourse Learning

for all zoning concepts). The nonconforming use must be permitted because it may be unconstitutional to require the property owners to terminate the nonconforming use. Therefore, in these cases, the property owner is permitted to continue a nonconforming use, which is lawful. However, the nonconforming user is subject to certain requirements that exist to make everything conform eventually by gradually eliminating the nonconforming use. Examples of these requirements are as follows:

1. If the property owner abandons the nonconforming use, the owner cannot resume that type of use at a later date but may use the property only in a manner that conforms to the zoning ordinance.
2. The property owner cannot make structural changes to the property to expand the nonconforming use or to change the use to a different nonconforming use. The owner is permitted to make only normal necessary repairs to the structure.
3. The nonconforming use cannot be changed from one type of nonconforming use to another type of nonconforming use.
4. If a nonconforming structure is destroyed by fire or another disaster, it often cannot be replaced by another nonconforming structure. Some zoning ordinances, however, do allow for a nonconforming structure that has been destroyed to be replaced by one of the same type and size if done within a reasonable time period, such as one year.
5. Some ordinances provide for a long-term amortization period during which the nonconforming owner is permitted to continue the nonconforming use. At the end of this period, the owner must change the use to conform to the zoning ordinance, rebuilding the structure if necessary.

Test Tip!

Students should have a good working knowledge of the terminology related to zoning.

Despite these restrictions, however, nonconforming uses may be sold with full rights to continue the nonconforming use.

Illegal use. An illegal use is one that is contrary to the existing ordinance at the time the use is instituted. The difference between this concept and that of the nonconforming use is that the latter was preexisting (existed at the time the zoning regulation was instituted). Note that the illegal use and the nonconforming use give rise to apparently the same situation, namely a violation of the current code. Because the illegal use is a violation of the present law, however, it may be stopped or removed by an injunction, which is the exercise of the police power of the government. It is also important to not confuse an illegal use with an illegal building, or one that has been constructed without obtaining the necessary building permits before construction. The illegal use is perhaps being carried out in a legal building, whereas an illegal building cannot be utilized for a legal purpose.

Attempting to convert a single-family home into a business activity in an area that is zoned for residential use is an illegal use that can be prevented by enforcement of the code.

"Don't forget that a variance when approved does not change the zoning ordinance for the respective property. It merely allows for something to be done or performed on the property that the zoning ordinance would not permit. Changing of the zoning itself is considered to be rezoning, downzoning, or spot zoning."
—Steve Robinson

Zoning amendments. An actual *change in the zoning code* itself is known as an **amendment**. It is often difficult for individuals to persuade the city to amend its current regulations to allow a use of their property that is prevented by the code. A formal process is necessary to obtain a zoning change. The process usually includes such things as applications, fees, postings of intent to rezone, and public hearings before the zoning authority rules on the request. The real estate agent is cautioned not to promise or imply to a buyer that she can obtain such a change but to point out the difficulty of obtaining this result if it is essential to the purchaser's intended use.

Variance.

> A **variance** is a *permitted deviation from specific requirements of the existing zoning ordinance.*

For example, if an owner's lot is slightly smaller than the requirements of the zoning ordinance as to the minimum lot size upon which a structure may be built, the owner can be granted a variance by petitioning the appropriate authorities.

Variances are permitted if the deviation is not substantial and if strict compliance would impose an undue hardship on the property owner. The hardship must be applicable to one property only and must be a peculiar or special hardship for that property under the zoning law. The special hardship does not exist if all property owners in the zoned area have the same difficulty.

Special use permit (special exception). In contrast to the difficult and unpredictable process of obtaining a variance for a specific use for a property, the application of **special use** is essentially automatic in that the use is already provided for in the code. One of the pitfalls in just looking at the symbols on a zoning map to infer what uses may be made of the respective land is that underlying provisions of the text of the code in the given area may have provided for an unexpected application.

Although an area may be zoned generally for residential use, the planners could have provided for the location of a medical office building in the area for the benefit of the local owners. Thus, one wishing to establish such a use need conform only to the provisions established for the special use or exception. Note the difference between the process of obtaining a special use and obtaining a variance. For a variance, there is no requirement for the authority to grant the petition, whereas for a special use permit, there is no basis to deny the application provided required conditions are being met.

> "Early Planned Unit Developments (PUD's) began as overlay districts. The purpose was to cluster services for the residents."
> —Tim Terry, DREI

Overlay districts. An **overlay district** is a *zoning device that superimposes one zoning area over another.* Visualize a plastic transparency placed on top of a map that shows further restricted areas of the map. Suppose a river runs through the middle of a town, establishing the northern part of the town as residential and the southern half as commercial. As indicated by the general map, landowners south of the river could engage in the permitted commercial uses anywhere along the southern banks of the river. If an overlay transparency restricted the high-water floodplain of the river, however, only certain uses would be permitted. Instead of establishing a building close to the river, the owners may be able to use the land only for something such as a parking lot.

A special application of a floodplain ordinance created a landmark Supreme Court decision in 1987. In the particular instance, the California courts had ruled that the danger of the floodplain prevented all use of the land. The Supreme Court subsequently ruled that this action constituted the "taking" of land and required compensation to the owners as provided by the Constitution. Many people then tried, to no avail, to interpret this decision as requiring compensation to owners for any diminution of property by zoning. Thus, zoning or downgrading still is not considered taking of land requiring compensation to the owner.

Historic preservation zoning. Many cities have established specific zoning regulations to preserve the irreplaceable historic legacies of its architecture. In areas where such regulations have been established, one must obtain required approvals before materially modifying the exterior of a structure. This can cause significant problems for the owners or purchasers of property in the affected area if they want to remove existing structures to make way for modern improvements. Several areas have historic resource commissions that seek to provide comprehensive protection of existing buildings. Agents need to stay informed about current and proposed regulations that preserve the heritage of their area.

Aesthetic zoning. North Carolina also has specific interpretations providing that an area can be regulated for essentially aesthetic considerations. This can be viewed as an application of the historic preservation areas, designed to achieve a specific impact on a given property or area.

Spot zoning. Spot zoning occurs when a *certain property within a zoned area is rezoned to permit a use that is different from the zoning requirements for that zoned area.* If the rezoning of a particular property is simply for the benefit of the property owner and has the effect of increasing the land value, the spot zoning is illegal and invalid. It also is illegal to single out one person's property for spot zoning that will place a burden on that property and not on surrounding properties. North Carolina courts have ruled spot zoning to be legal in some cases in which a reasonable basis for it can be clearly demonstrated.

Cluster zoning. Unlike more traditional zoning that specifies the same density for every parcel within a subdivision, cluster zoning seeks to create an overall density for the whole area. This allows a developer to create some areas that reflect a higher density, such as apartments, and other areas, such as larger single-family home lots, that reflect a much lower density. Rather than have a singular standard with which every lot must comply, cluster zoning allows a variety of densities but still achieves the overall effect of traditional zoning.

Buffer zones. Buffer zones are transitional sorts of spaces that are used between two separate types of land uses, or even open spaces contained within a subdivision to allow privacy and some degree of visual or noise control from other neighbors.

Urban and Regional Planning

This form of long-range planning takes into account wide areas or multicounty regions and uses zoning as a local method to implement the overall plan. Topics addressed in the wide-region plan include predicted population trends; the development of water resources; and the placement of major utilities, power plants, airports, and sanitary landfills, as well as the location of present and contemplated railroads, streets and highways, historic preservation, and school sites.

Subdivision Regulations

There is no national planning or land development legislation; rather, the state empowers *local governments, cities, and counties to regulate the creation of subdivisions within their particular jurisdictions.* North Carolina General Statute (N.C.G.S.) 153A-335 defines subdivision as "all divisions of a tract or parcel of land into two or more lots, building sites or other divisions for the purpose of sale or building development (whether immediate or future) and includes all divisions of land involving the dedication of a new street or a change in an existing street."

Some exemptions apply when parts of previously subdivided and recorded lots are combined or recombined, when the government purchases land to develop or widen streets, and when land is subdivided into plots of more than 10 acres, or a 2-acre or smaller tract is subdivided into three or fewer lots without street right-of-way dedication.

The purpose of **subdivision regulations (ordinances)** is to protect purchasers of property within the subdivisions and to protect the taxpayers in the city or county from significantly increased tax burdens resulting from the demands for services generated by a new subdivision.

Subdivision regulations (ordinances) typically address the following requirements:

1. Streets must be of a specified width, be curbed, have storm drains, and not exceed certain maximum grade specifications.
2. Lots may not be smaller than a specified minimum size.
3. Dwellings in certain areas must be for single-family occupancy only. Specific areas may be set aside for multifamily dwellings.
4. Utilities, including water, sewer, electric, and telephone, must be available to each lot.
5. All houses must be placed on lots to meet specified minimum standards for setbacks from the front property line as well as from interior property lines.
6. Adequate area drainage must provide for satisfactory runoff of rainfall to avoid damage to properties.

Once a subdivision ordinance has been adopted, subdivision developers must obtain the approval of the appropriate officials; then the final subdivision plat is recorded on the public record and development can begin. North Carolina changed the law regulating the sale or lease of subdivision lots effective January 1, 2006. Owners, developers, or their agents may offer to sell or lease lots in a subdivision after obtaining preliminary approval of the subdivision plat provided all required statutory provisions are included in the contracts.

These required statutory provisions are as follows:

1. A copy of the preliminary map must be attached to the contract and language in the contract must require delivery of a copy of the final recorded plat to the buyer before closing and conveyance.
2. Owner, developer, or agent notifies the buyer or lessee of the following in a plain and conspicuous manner:

    - Final plat is not yet recorded.
    - No obligation by any government body to buyer or lessee exists as to final plat approval.

- Final recorded plat may differ from preliminary plat.
- Buyer or lessee has right to terminate contract without penalty if there is a material difference between the preliminary and final recorded plats.

3. The buyer or lessee has at least five days to close after receiving from the seller or lessor a copy of a final recorded plat provided the preliminary and final plats have no material difference.
4. The buyer has 15 days after receiving the final recorded plat to terminate the contract without penalty provided the preliminary and final plats have material differences.

These statutory provisions apply to anyone contracting to purchase or lease land whose purpose it is to construct any type of building on the land.

Real estate licensees must be careful in offering lots for sale or lease between the time of approval of the preliminary plat and approval and recording of the final plat. Violation of the statutes is a Class 1 misdemeanor and can subject the licensee to both criminal prosecution in the courts and disciplinary action by the Real Estate Commission.

In no circumstance can a conveyance or lease become effective until the final plat is recorded. A careful and prudent licensee will verify the approval of the preliminary plat and the approval and recording of the final plat before taking any action requiring these approvals.

Licensees are advised to use a contract form that meets the statutory requirements and that was drafted by an attorney because currently no standard form exists for this specific purpose. As always, the licensee must never draft a contract or improvise one from existing standard forms, as that would be an unauthorized practice of law.

Street Maintenance Disclosure Requirements

Once the developer acquires the land for the proposed subdivision, he will utilize the services of engineering companies to map the layout of the lots and the streets to service them. Once completed, the plat will be presented to the local planning department, which will approve or disapprove them. Once any concerns are worked out, the approved plat will receive the planning department's stamp of approval, which allows the plat to be recorded. Once recorded, the land shown as streets will be considered a *dedication* to the public. A dedication is simply to convey for public use or ownership and does NOT imply ultimate acceptance into the public road system. At this time, the developer will construct the streets to required specifications. Once completed, the streets will either be placed on the local government meeting schedule for inclusion as a "public" maintained street or the street will remain private. Even though many streets are "public" in accessibility, they will remain as a "privately" maintained street if not accepted into the public road system. For a complete listing of streets that are publicly maintained, the public is directed to the local highway department or website.

Before a developer or seller of a property in a (new) subdivision contracts to sell or convey a property, she must furnish a *subdivision street disclosure statement* to the purchaser and receive a signed acknowledgment by the purchaser that he has received it. This disclosure statement must indicate whether the street in front of the property is public or private. If public, the seller must certify that the Division of Highways has approved the design and right-of-way and that the street meets or will meet, upon completion, the Board of Transportation's criteria for acceptance into the system. If private, the developer or seller must disclose who will be responsible for the construction and maintenance of the street, explain the consequences involved in maintaining the street, and disclose that the street does not meet the minimum criteria for state maintenance (see N.C.G.S. 136-102.6).

Private roads can present practical problems. If the road maintenance agreement provides that responsibility for road maintenance be turned over to the property owners whose property fronts the road, the property owners must have some organizational structure for implementing the agreement.

Sometimes a problem arises in an older subdivision with private streets and no recorded private road maintenance agreement. In such cases, a street maintenance agreement may need to be signed by the property owners, notarized, and recorded before the lender will approve a buyer's loan for a property on the street.

The fact that a particular street was designated as "public" means that the North Carolina Department of Transportation (NCDOT) Division of Highways approved the plans for the street before the subdivision plat was recorded. This does NOT constitute, however, an acceptance into the state highway maintenance system, which is a separate process. Agents should be careful to explain that just because a street has been constructed to NCDOT requirements and is shown as being "public," it does not mean that the street will be publicly maintained. In the event the broker is not totally certain as to whether any street is "public" or "private," the broker should recommend that the buyer make inquiry into who is responsible for future street maintenance.

Building Codes

Building codes provide another form of *control of land use for the protection of the public.* These codes regulate such things as materials used in construction, electrical wiring, fire and safety standards, and sanitary equipment facilities. The codes require that a permit be obtained from the appropriate local government authority before the construction or renovation of any property is begun. While construction is in progress, local government inspectors perform frequent inspections to make certain that the code requirements are being met.

> After a satisfactory final inspection, a **Certificate of Occupancy (CO)** is issued. This *permits the occupation of the structure by tenants or the owner.*

Today, some cities require that a CO, *based on a satisfactory inspection of the property,* be issued before occupancy by a new owner or tenant of any structure even though it is not new construction or has not been renovated. Inspection is required to reveal deficiencies in the structure that require correction before the city will issue a CO for the protection of the new purchaser or tenant.

REGULATION OF SPECIAL LAND TYPES

Real estate that is designated as being in a **flood hazard area** is subject to certain federal laws and regulations, including whether improvements can be made in that area, the location of the improvements, and the elevation. The Federal Emergency Management Agency (FEMA) issues maps that designate flood hazard areas. These maps are updated constantly, and coupled with area construction, could result in an area being later included within the designated federal flood hazard area. Generally, real estate in flood hazard areas that is mortgaged through any federally related loan program (Federal Housing Administration, Department of Veterans Affairs, and most secondary mortgage market loans) must be covered by flood insurance under the National Flood Insurance Program. This flood insurance is purchased through local insurance companies, although the actual flood insurance is provided through the National Flood Insurance Program. Agents should disclose the existence of any part of a property that is in a designated flood hazard area as a material fact and encourage the purchaser to consult flood maps as maintained by the U.S. Army Corps of Engineers.

The coastal area of North Carolina is also prone to areas known as "wetlands." Although not limited to just the coastal area, wetlands are those areas that serve an important environmental purpose in that they allow settlement and filtering of natural contaminants to reduce the effect of such pollutants in more public bodies of water. Wetlands are not always "wet." The Army Corps of Engineers is responsible for identifying which areas qualify as wetlands. Before proceeding with construction, dredging, draining, or other use of lands subject to these regulations, the developer must obtain a permit from the Army Corps of Engineers.

Highway Access Controls

A major danger could exist to the public if unlimited access were permitted to high-speed roads with significant traffic. Therefore, the NCDOT has the statutory authority to restrict highway access when needed for safety. Just as the state can condemn property to build a highway, it can condemn property adjacent to a highway and restrict highway access. This requires compensation to the present owner but could well provide problems for a future owner. For example, a developer may want to purchase a tract of land for the construction of single-family homes. Next to an area where highway access has been restricted, the developer may not be able to connect individual driveways to the highway and would need to construct a single-access road.

Interstate Land Sales Full Disclosure Act

The **Interstate Land Sales Full Disclosure Act** is a *federal regulation of the interstate (across state lines) sale of unimproved lots* that became effective in 1969 and was made more restrictive by an amendment in 1980. The act is administered by the secretary of the U.S. Department of Housing and Urban Development (HUD) through the office of Interstate Land Sales Registration.

The purpose of the act is to prevent fraudulent marketing schemes when land is sold by misleading sales practices on a sight-unseen basis. The act requires that a developer file a **statement of record** with HUD before offering unimproved lots in interstate commerce by telephone or through the mail. The statement of record *requires disclosure of information about the property as specified by HUD.*

The developer is required to provide each purchaser or lessee of property with a printed **property report,** which *discloses specific information about the land before a purchase contract or lease is signed by the purchaser or lessee.* The property report contains specific information about the land for the protection of the purchaser or lessee. Required information includes such things as the type of title a buyer will receive, the number of homes currently occupied, availability of recreation facilities, distance to nearby communities, utility services and charges, and soil or other foundation problems in construction. If the purchaser or lessee is not supplied with a copy of the property report before signing a purchase contract or lease, the purchaser or lessee can void the contract. In addition, the act provides the purchaser with the right of rescission for a period of seven days from the date of purchase.

The act provides for several exemptions, the most important of which are as follows:

1. Subdivisions in which the lots are of 5 acres or more.
2. Subdivisions that consist of fewer than 100 lots are exempt from the registration requirements of the Act. Subdivisions of fewer than 25 lots are exempt from the act, including both the registration and antifraud provisions.
3. Lots that are offered for sale exclusively to building contractors.
4. Lots on which a building exists or where a contract obligates the lot seller to construct a building within two years.

If a developer offered only part of the total tract owned and thereby limited the subdivision to fewer than 100 lots to acquire an exemption, the developer could not then sell additional lots within the tract. HUD considers these additional lots part of a common plan for development and marketing, thereby eliminating the developer's opportunity for several exemptions as a result of a piecemeal development of a large tract in sections of fewer than 100 lots at a time.

The act provides severe penalties for violation by a developer or real estate agent participating in marketing the property. The offender can be sued for damages by a purchaser or lessee and is potentially subject to a criminal penalty by fine of up to $5,000 or imprisonment for up to five years or both. Therefore, before acting as an agent for a developer in marketing property, real estate agents must ascertain that a developer has complied with the law or is exempt.

Onsite Septic Systems

Property owners are required to have all wastewater created by use of the property to be discharged into an approved facility. For many properties located within municipal areas, this may be achieved by connecting to public sewer systems although not all properties will be connected to such system. It is not uncommon for older neighborhoods to have properties that have not yet connected to the public system. In cases in which the structure is not connected to a public system, it will be required to connect to a private system. In most of these cases, the private system will be an onsite system known as a septic tank.

Before a private septic system can be installed, a septic permit must be obtained from the local health department. The health department will conduct a soil suitability (or perc) test to analyze the soil conditions to determine its suitability for the installation of such system. The inspection will denote the property as "suitable," "provisionally suitable," or "unsuitable." The indication of "suitable" will allow for the installation of a conventional septic system that will be based on the number of bedrooms in the structure. Such a permit may limit the location and any other issues that might lead to overload of the system. An indication of "provisionally suitable" will not preclude the installation of a system but typically will involve a more complex installation than the basic conventional system. A prospective purchaser will want to always obtain the necessary septic permits before proceeding with the purchase of the property.

Brokers and prospective purchasers will want to obtain copies of previously issued permits to determine the capacity of an installed septic system. North Carolina regulations require retention of all septic permits as long as the system is still in use. These permits can be obtained through local health departments, although they may be difficult to locate in some cases. There has been no consistent standard by which these older permits have been registered. In the case in which a broker is unable to locate and produce a septic permit, the prospective owner should be notified of this situation and likely will want to have a septic inspection made to determine the adequacy of the installed system.

Brokers are reminded to be cautious when indicating the occupancy for any property served by a private septic system. Permits are not based on the number of bathrooms within the property but rather on the number of bedrooms. Capacity is based on 2 persons per bedroom. For example, a three-bedroom septic permit indicates the system is appropriate for 6 people. Any broker that is found guilty of misrepresenting the occupancy capacity limits of a property will be subject to disciplinary action by the Real Estate Commission as well as potential civil liability.

In the event that a property is not connected to an approved municipal or private system, the discharged waste simply may be "straight-piped" into the yard or a nearby body of water. Such straight-piping may be for the entire house or just for a particular use, such as a washing machine discharge. Such straight-piping is always illegal and is a material fact that must be disclosed by the broker.

Government Ownership

Federal and state governments own literally in excess of hundreds of millions of acres of land in the form of parks, roads, and other public buildings. These lands are strictly controlled by regulations concerning use access and easements.

PRIVATE LAND USE CONTROLS

Individual Deed Restrictions

Individual **deed restrictions,** or *limits on land use,* exist in the form of covenants or in the form of conditions. A **covenant,** or a *promise in writing,* exists in a deed to benefit property that is sold or to benefit a property that is retained, as in the case of a sale of adjoining property. For example, an owner selling an adjoining property provides in the deed that a structure may not be erected in a certain area of the property sold to protect the view from the property retained or to prevent the loss of reception of light and air to the property retained. Conversely, the purchaser of a property may require as part of the purchase that the owner restrict the part of the property he is retaining. For example, a buyer purchases a piece of property to use

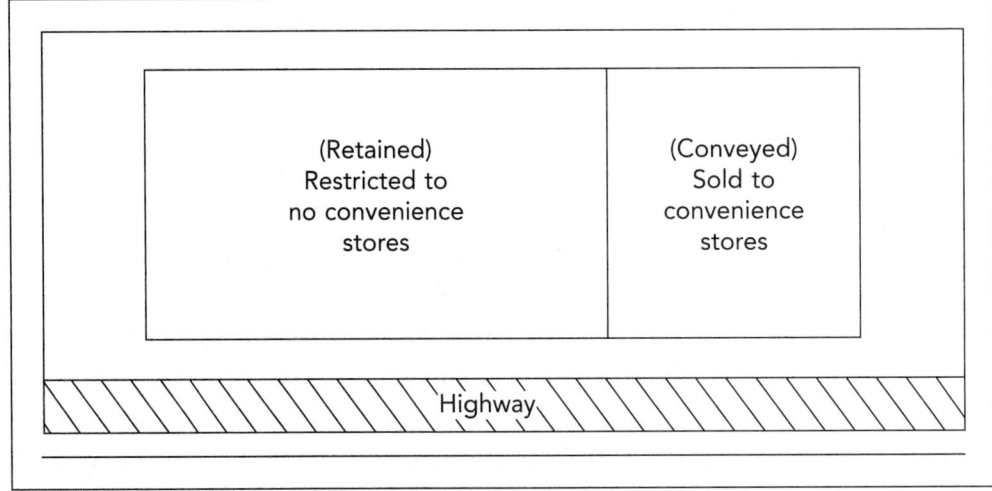

FIGURE 5.3 Restrictions applied to land retained.

as a convenience store and requires the owner to restrict the remaining property to prohibit convenience stores (see Figure 5.3). These restrictions are covenants that **run with the land,** meaning that they *move with the title in any subsequent conveyance.* Covenants are enforced by a suit for damages or by injunction. *Restrictions that provide for a reversion of title if they are violated* are called **conditions.** If a condition is violated, ownership reverts to the grantor, his heirs, or assigns.

Restrictive or Protective Covenants

> **Restrictive or protective covenants** are *restrictions in a deed placed on the use of land by the grantor. Such covenants are widely used by the developers of residential subdivisions.*

Historically, these covenants have been called "restrictive covenants," but current usage favors "protective covenants" to emphasize their positive aspects. The purpose of subdivision protective covenants is to protect all property owners against undesirable land uses by some property owners and to maximize land values by requiring the homogeneous or compatible use of land by purchasers of property in a subdivision. The covenants are *promises on the part of the purchasers of property in the subdivision to limit their use of their property to comply with the requirements of the restrictive or protective covenants* and therefore sometimes are referred to as **negative covenants** or **easements.** The deed conveying title to property in the subdivision contains a reference to a recorded plat of the subdivision and a reference to the separately recorded declaration of restrictive or protective covenants, or the restrictions may be recited in each deed of conveyance. Subdivision restrictive covenants must apply equally to all properties in the subdivision.

> When faced with a conflict between zoning regulations and protective covenants, the more restrictive of the two will control.

If the subdivision is in a zoned area, the restrictive or protective covenants have priority over the zoning ordinance, to the extent that the covenants are more restrictive than the zoning requirements. For example, if the zoning permits multifamily dwellings and the restrictive or protective covenants limit land use to single-family dwellings, the restrictive or protective covenants will be enforced. Covenants contrary to public law and public policy will not be enforced. For example, a restrictive or protective covenant requiring discrimination on the basis of race, color, religion, sex, national origin, disability, or familial status is invalid. Also, restrictive or protective covenants are not binding on the general public unless they are recorded on the public record in the county where the land is located (Conner Act; see Chapter 4).

Restrictive or protective covenants are land use limitations that provide a general plan for development of a subdivision. Before the start of development, the developer establishes a list of rules each lot purchaser is required to adhere to in the use of the property. These rules controlling the use of the land are then recorded in an instrument called the declaration of restrictions (or declaration of restrictive or protective covenants). The declaration is recorded simultaneously with the plat and includes a reference to the plat. A few examples of matters commonly addressed in restrictive/ protective covenants are as follows:

1. Only single-family dwellings may be constructed in the subdivision.
2. Dwellings must contain a specified minimum number of square feet of living area.
3. Only one single-family dwelling may be constructed on a lot.
4. No lot may be subdivided.
5. Dwellings must be of a harmonious architectural style. To ensure this, a site plan and plans and specifications for the structure must be submitted to and approved by a committee before the start of construction.
6. Structures must be set back a specified distance from the front property line and a specified distance from interior property lines.
7. Temporary structures may not be placed on any lot.
8. Covenants may be enforced by any one property owner or several property owners of land within the subdivision (or the homeowners association) by taking appropriate legal steps, which is typically a lawsuit seeking an injunction against the offending property owner.
9. Modern covenants typically specify a time period (e.g., 25 years) after which they will expire unless renewed by a specified percentage of property owners, or where there may be specified automatic renewal periods unless the property owners vote otherwise. The covenants usually prescribe how the property owners may amend the covenants.

Real estate practitioners are expected to be aware of the existence of restrictive or protective covenants in subdivisions, condominiums, townhouses, and multifamily developments where they are selling property. NCBA/NCAR Standard Form No. 2T, Offer to Purchase and Contract, contains a note advising the buyer to review restrictive covenants and other documents pertaining to the property before making an offer. The broker may assist the prospective buyer in locating a copy of the protective/restrictive covenants if the buyer requests one. Copies may be obtained from the Register of Deeds Office in the county where the property is located or from the developer if she is still on site. When providing the buyer a copy of the protective/restrictive covenants, ensure that the ones given are for the right phase of the subdivision, as covenants sometimes differ from phase to phase. It is also important to realize that building permits can be issued even though the construction might violate the restrictive, or protective, covenants. Remember that building permits are public, whereas restrictive or protective covenants are private.

Termination of Covenants

Covenants are terminated in the following ways:

1. Expiration of the time period for which the covenants were created.
2. Unanimous vote of the property owners to terminate the covenants, unless the covenants provide for termination by vote of a smaller number of landowners.
3. Changes in the character of the subdivision that make it unsatisfactory for the type of use specified by the covenants to continue. For example, as a result of the failure of property owners in a subdivision restricted to single-family residential use to enforce that restriction, the area gradually changes to commercial use. Consequently, the subdivision is no longer suitable for limitation to residential use.
4. The right to enforce particular restriction in the protective covenants may be lost by abandonment, which occurs when the property owners have violated their covenants and many of them have participated in the violations. As a result, a court may rule that there has been an abandonment of the original general plan by the property owners; therefore, the court will not enforce the covenants.
5. Failure to enforce restrictions on a timely basis. An owner or owners cannot sit idly by and watch someone complete a structure in a subdivision in violation of the protective covenants and then attempt to enforce the restriction by court action. The court will not apply the restriction against the violator. Therefore, the restriction is terminated by the property owners' failure to take action on a timely basis to enforce protective covenants.

Enforcement of Covenants

Private land use controls are enforced by public law but not by public officials or agencies. This is accomplished by the action of a court, known as an injunction. An injunction prevents a use contrary to the restrictions of record or orders the removal of any such uses that have been implemented. In a practical sense, the individuals who bear the primary responsibility for seeing that the restrictions are enforced are the developer or other owners of property in the affected area. Any property owner within the subdivision can enforce the covenants. If property owners do not enforce the subdivision covenants within the period of time required by the Statute of Limitations, they can lose their right to enforce. Very similar to this statute of limitations is the doctrine of laches in which case the homeowners association may lose its ability to enforce the regulations because even though the problem was known at the time of installation, there was no action taken for such a long period that it is no longer reasonable to make the property owner comply with the rule. Remember that it is possible for a property owner to acquire a building permit to construct in accordance with the local zoning laws but in direct violation of the protective covenants of a particular area. The fact that a building permit was issued in no way indicates compliance with the protective covenants.

Enforcement of the covenants is not limited to the original purchasers of property in the subdivision. Subsequent purchasers must abide by and can enforce the protective covenants until such time as the covenants are terminated, as previously discussed—that is, the restrictions run with the land.

RESPONSIBILITY OF REAL ESTATE AGENTS

Agent Responsibilities Regarding Potential Land Use Problems

There are likely not many issues more emotional than one person telling another what he can, and cannot do, with his property. As such, agents must be diligent to keep buyers fully informed as to any land use restrictions that may affect the buyers' decision to purchase any parcel of property. Agents should be cautious about any potential misrepresentation regarding permitted uses of the property as well as nondisclosures regarding flood hazard and protective covenants. If buyers express interest in making modifications to the property after the purchase, the agent should be diligent in making certain the buyers know the impact of zoning and protective covenants on the prospective improvements. Another "red flag" that is easily overlooked is the issue of flood hazards. If a property is in an area that is located near a stream, creek, river, or body of water, the agent should inquire as to the location of flood hazard areas in the general area as established by the flood zone maps provided by FEMA. The agent also should be aware of any major road or planned highway projects in the vicinity of the property and disclose such information to the buyer as appropriate. This knowledge is necessary to enable real estate agents to fulfill their obligations to their principals as well as to the buying public. Lack of knowledge in these areas may subject real estate agents to civil liability to injured parties and possible criminal liability under certain federal laws.

Summary of Important Points

1. The purpose of planning is to provide for the orderly growth of a community that will result in the greatest social and economic benefits to the people. Therefore, a real estate practitioner has a clear duty to identify and disclose which controls affect any given property.
2. Land use controls are grouped in two general categories. Public land use controls are best recognized in the form of zoning ordinances. Although

zoning is strictly a local regulation, other public controls such as building codes and environmental protection legislation add a state and federal level of land use regulation. Private land use controls arise from a grantor of title who wishes to restrict the way a property is used by successive grantees. Often this is done to maintain the essential residential character of a new development. Once restrictions are properly developed and recorded, they pass with the title—that is, they run with the land.

3. The plan for development is enforced by zoning ordinances. Planning and zoning are exercises of police power.
4. Typical zones include residential, commercial, PUDs, industrial, and agricultural. Zoning may be either exclusive use or cumulative use.
5. In addition to specifying permitted uses, zoning ordinances define standards and requirements that must be met for each type of use.
6. Urban and regional planning provide for long-term planning in a wide area that may affect several counties.
7. Subdivision ordinances regulate the development of residential subdivisions to protect property purchasers as well as to protect area taxpayers from increased tax burdens resulting from the demand for services generated by the subdivisions.
8. Building codes require that certain standards of construction be met. The codes are primarily concerned with electrical systems, fire and safety standards, and sanitary systems and equipment.
9. Highway access controls represent condemnation of areas of a property for connection to areas of major highways.
10. The Interstate Land Sales Full Disclosure Act is a federal law that regulates the sale of unimproved lots in interstate commerce to prevent fraudulent schemes that may occur when land is sold on a sight-unseen basis.
11. Environmental protection laws are a form of land use control to protect the public against abuses of the environment.
12. Private land use controls are in the form of deed restrictions and restrictive or protective covenants.
13. Restrictive or protective covenants for a subdivision must apply equally to all property owners in the subdivision.
14. Restrictive or protective covenants are recorded on the public record in an instrument called a declaration of restrictive or protective covenants. They are not enforceable unless recorded.
15. Restrictive or protective covenants are enforced by court injunction upon a petition by one or more property owners on a timely basis.
16. There are many examples of public land use controls such as zoning, building codes, highway access controls, and environmental regulations, but there is one primary example of private land use controls, that is, protective covenants.

17. Nonconforming use is use that was already in effect before the conflicting zoning ordinance was passed. It is allowed to continue but not to be expanded, and it can be freely marketed with the same reservation. If abandoned, it cannot be reinstituted. If destroyed, local zoning ordinances may or may not allow it to be reinstituted within a short period of time.

18. Illegal use is use contrary to the existing zoning ordinance at the time the use was instituted and may be prevented or removed by an exercise of the state's police power through an injunction. Prolonged illegal use does not mature into a legal use.

19. Some cities maintain their code in a loose-leaf notebook so new amendments can be easily substituted.

20. Zoning amendment. A municipality has the right to alter or modify the existing zoning classification to another use to reflect current changes in land use. These changes are typically made after a thorough review of the long range plans for that area and private as well as public input.

21. If owners can establish that a given zoning provision works an undue hardship on their property that prevents a fair return on their ownership, they can seek approval for a variance that is a permitted violation of the ordinance. There is no requirement for the city to approve the petition.

22. Under a special use permit, special use, or a special exception, is provided for in the zoning code itself. No appeal process is necessary if the requested use complies with the established provisions of the special exception. In contrast to a variance, the city does not have authority to deny this request.

23. Spot zoning that is the rezoning of one person's property solely for personal benefit is illegal. Spot zoning must have a clear, reasonable basis to be legal.

24. Public access streets will be be privately maintained until such time as accepted for public road maintenance by a governing body.

25. On-site septic system permits are based upon the number of bedrooms with an assumed occupancy of 2 persons per bedroom.

Review Questions

Answers to the review questions are in the Answer Key at the back of the book.

1. The instrument used for recording restrictive/ protective covenants is a:
   A. plat.
   B. master deed.
   C. covenant.
   D. declaration of restrictions.

2. Deed restrictions that run with the land are which of the following?
   A. ordinances
   B. variances
   C. declarations
   D. covenants

3. All of the following statements about restrictive/protective covenants are correct EXCEPT:
   A. They must be reasonable.
   B. They are enforceable even though not recorded.
   C. They are not enforceable if contrary to law.
   D. They provide for a general plan for development.

4. Which of the following statements about land use controls is NOT correct?
   A. Deed restrictions are a form of private land use control.
   B. Public land use controls are an exercise of police power.
   C. Subdivision covenants are a form of public land use controls.
   D. Localities receive their power to develop long-range plans for growth and the power to zone from the North Carolina General Assembly.

5. Restrictive/protective covenants are terminated in all of the following ways EXCEPT:
   A. expiration
   B. transfer of title
   C. failure to enforce on a timely basis
   D. abandonment

6. Restrictive/protective covenants are enforced by which of the following?
   A. zoning
   B. injunction
   C. police power
   D. condemnation

7. The type of zoning that permits a higher priority use in a lower priority zone is called:
   A. exclusive use
   B. nonconforming use
   C. amortizing use
   D. cumulative use

8. Which of the following is NOT a permitted deviation from the standards of a zoning ordinance?
   A. variance
   B. nonconforming use
   C. spot zoning
   D. special use

9. Which of the following is an illegal rezoning of a particular property solely for the benefit of the owner?
   A. variance
   B. nonconforming use
   C. spot zoning
   D. special use

10. Which of the following statements about subdivision ordinances is (are) correct?
    A. the purpose is to protect taxpayers from increased taxes caused by increased demand for services to subdivisions
    B. the purpose is to protect developers during the development period from excessive costs and thereby to encourage residential development
    C. the purpose is to provide uniformity of structures within the subdivision
    D. all of the above

11. Which of the following powers gives the government the right to zone?
    A. power of eminent domain
    B. police power
    C. power of escheat
    D. power of taxation

12. Building codes require which of the following?
    A. property report
    B. PUDs
    C. Certificate of Occupancy
    D. statement of record

13. Which of the following statements concerning the Interstate Land Sales Full Disclosure Act is correct?
    A. The Act regulates sales of large parcels of unimproved land (over 5 acres) across state lines.
    B. The Act is administered by the Environmental Protection Agency.
    C. The Act is administered by HUD.
    D. The Act only covers land with buildings on it.

14. Exemptions to the registration requirements of the Interstate Land Sales Full Disclosure Act include all of the following EXCEPT:
    A. subdivisions of fewer than 25 lots
    B. lots offered only to building contractors
    C. lots on which there is a building
    D. subdivisions in which the lots are 4 acres or more

15. John starts operating a five-unit apartment building in an area that has been zoned for a duplex only. John lists the property with Larry Listing Agent who eventually sells the property to Bob Buyer. Bob continues to operate the five-unit building for the next 20 years. Which of the following statements is correct?
    A. John had a legal nonconforming use.
    B. Larry was responsible for discovering and disclosing the situation to Bob.
    C. John had a legal nonconforming use and Bob has obtained a legal nonconforming use.
    D. John had a legal nonconforming use, Larry was responsible for discovering and disclosing the situation to Bob, and Bob has obtained a legal nonconforming use.

16. Twenty years ago John constructed a duplex on a lot that permitted multiple family housing to be constructed. Five years ago this was changed by zoning laws to permit only single family house construction. Which of the following best describes John's rights for this property?
    A. This is an example of an illegal use.
    B. This is an example of a legal nonconforming use.
    C. This is an example of a variance.
    D. This qualifies as a special use exception.

17. Which of the following statements concerning flood hazard areas is correct?
    A. Real estate designated as being in a flood hazard area cannot be financed through any federally related loan program.
    B. The Department of Housing and Urban Development issues maps that designate flood hazard areas.
    C. There are currently no federal laws or regulations concerning flood hazard areas.
    D. Flood insurance is available under the National Flood Insurance Program.

18. A property owner is reimbursed for loss when:
    A. a loss of property value is caused by a zoning change.
    B. a property is taken under the power of eminent domain.
    C. aesthetic zoning causes an undue hardship.
    D. all of the above.

19. A "public" street means that:
   A. the NCDOT has approved the street plans prior to the subdivision plat being recorded.
   B. it is publicly maintained but can be privately access such as a gated community.
   C. it is publicly maintained and is publicly accessed.
   D. it is not privately maintained.

20. Which of the following statements concerning zoning ordinances is/are true?
   A. Zoning ordinances must adhere to federal and state due process provisions.
   B. Zoning ordinances must be reasonable and nondiscriminatory.
   C. Zoning ordinances must provide for the health and safety of the general public.
   D. All of the above.

21. Clark has operated a small convenience store in a rural area for 20 years. Recent development has changed the rural area into a thriving residential area. The property the convenience store is located on is now zoned for residential only. Which of the following statements is true?
   A. This is an illegal use and must be stopped.
   B. Clark can expand the convenience store to sell gasoline.
   C. Clark can continue operating the store but may be prohibited from rebuilding in the event the building is destroyed.
   D. Clark must petition for a variance to continue doing business as a convenience store.

22. Private land controls are enforced by:
   A. deed restrictions.
   B. the Interstate Land Sales Full Disclosure Act.
   C. the Conner Act.
   D. court injunction.

23. A variance can be obtained in which of the following scenarios?
   A. placing a factory in an area zoned for residential only
   B. placing a daycare in an area zoned for residential only
   C. changing the setback lines for an entire subdivision
   D. none of the above

24. The government regulates all of the following EXCEPT:
   A. creation of subdivisions.
   B. building codes.
   C. subdivision regulations.
   D. protective covenants.

25. Which of the following requires a property owner to go before the planning commission?
   A. a variance
   B. a special use permit
   C. a nonconforming use
   D. all of the above

26. All of the following are public land use restrictions EXCEPT:
   A. building codes.
   B. protective covenants.
   C. zoning.
   D. regional planning.

CHAPTER 6
ENVIRONMENTAL ISSUES IN REAL ESTATE

KEY TERMS

asbestos
Comprehensive Environmental Response, Compensation, and Liability Act (CERCLA)
formaldehyde
friable
lead poisoning
nonfriable
radon
toxic mold

LEARNING OBJECTIVES

At the conclusion of this chapter, you should be able to:

1. Understand the health risks associated with lead poisoning, especially from lead-based paints.
2. Understand the health risks associated with asbestos.
3. Understand the health risks associated with radon exposure.
4. Understand the health risks associated with formaldehyde, including urea-formaldehyde.
5. Understand the health risks associated with toxic mold.
6. Understand the health risks associated with leaking underground storage tanks.
7. Understand how to reduce the health risks associated with each of the noted environmental issues.
8. Understand the basic elements of the Comprehensive Environmental Response, Compensation, and Liability Act (CERCLA).

IN THIS CHAPTER

Real estate agents must have a good basic knowledge of the various environmental issues that face the typical homeowner in today's market. Although the normal home-buying experience may focus on such elements as the attractiveness of the home, the value, and condition of the home, it is vitally important for the agent to be able to recognize some of the basic signs associated with common environmental concerns. As much as homeowners want to purchase the right home, it is easy to overlook

the very basic question of whether the house will provide a healthy environment in which to live. This chapter will provide a basic look at common issues that face today's real estate industry.

> **Test Tip!**
>
> Students should be familiar with the health risks of each of the environmental hazards as well as what can be done to reduce those risks.

LEAD POISONING (LEAD-BASED PAINT)

The health effects of lead contamination have been known for decades, but the issue has been prominent since the mid-1970s when many consumers were made aware of the issues. Automobiles converted to unleaded gasoline starting with the 1975 model year followed by a ban on lead-based paint in 1978. Although statistics will often indicate a large number of pre-1978 houses containing lead-based paint, houses constructed since 1960 have greatly reduced areas of lead-based paint, particularly on exterior doors and windows. Such a great reduction in lead-based paint was not related to health concerns but rather to a desire to use latex paint, which could be cleaned up with soap and water.

Lead poisoning *results in damage to the central nervous system and is not often diagnosed until many years after exposure.* Sources of lead contamination include paint, soldering material used in water pipes, and lead dust from soil. Lead contamination is an ongoing concern because lead does not rust or fade away over time. And just the smallest amount of friction—such as when raising or lowering a window, or when scraping or sanding old layers of paint—can send tiny particles of lead dust into the air, where it can be easily inhaled.

Lead dust can be picked up by the hands and feet of small infants as they crawl on the floor or play in the dirt next to an old house where the scrapings and deterioration of decades of lead-based paint has landed. Children under the age of six are particularly vulnerable, as their bodies' defense mechanisms are not yet sufficiently developed. The mere presence of lead-based paint is not a health concern, but rather, much like friable asbestos (discussed later), it quickly becomes a concern once it has been disturbed or otherwise dislodged.

The Residential Lead-Based Paint Hazard Reduction Act was passed by Congress in 1992 and both the U.S. Environmental Protection Agency (EPA) and U.S. Department of Housing and Urban Development (HUD) were granted rule-making authority to implement its directives, which they issued in 1996. Although these rules do not require that homeowners have their house tested for lead-based paint, they do require the disclosure of known lead-based paint hazards as well as the disclosure of any records and reports pertaining to lead-based

LEAD-BASED PAINT OR LEAD-BASED PAINT HAZARD ADDENDUM

Property: _____

Seller: _____

Buyer: _____

This Addendum is attached to and made a part of the Offer to Purchase and Contract ("Contract") between Seller and Buyer for the Property.

During the Due Diligence Period, Buyer shall have the right to obtain a risk assessment or inspection of the Property for the presence of lead-based paint and/or lead-based paint hazards* at Buyer's expense. Buyer may waive the right to obtain a risk assessment or inspection of the Property for the presence of lead-based paint and/or lead-based paint hazards at any time without cause.

*Intact lead-based paint that is in good condition is not necessarily a hazard. See EPA pamphlet "Protect Your Family From Lead in Your Home" for more information.

Disclosure of Information on Lead-Based Paint and Lead-Based Paint Hazards

> **Lead Warning Statement**
> *Every Buyer of any interest in residential real property on which a residential dwelling was built prior to 1978 is notified that such property may present exposure to lead from lead-based paint that may place young children at risk of developing lead poisoning. Lead poisoning in young children may produce permanent neurological damage, including learning disabilities, reduced intelligence quotient, behavioral problems, and impaired memory. Lead poisoning also poses a particular risk to pregnant women. The Seller of any interest in residential real property is required to provide the Buyer with any information on lead-based paint hazards from risk assessments or inspections in the Seller's possession and notify the Buyer of any known lead-based paint hazards. A risk assessment or inspection for possible lead-based hazards is recommended prior to purchase.*

Seller's Disclosure (initial)

_____ (a) Presence of lead-based paint and/or lead-based paint hazards (check one below):
  ❑ Known lead-based paint and/or lead-based paint hazards are present in the housing (explain).
  _____
  _____

  ❑ Seller has no knowledge of lead-based paint and/or lead-based paint hazards in the housing.

_____ (b) Records and reports available to the Seller (check one)
  ❑ Seller has provided the Buyer with all available records and reports pertaining to lead-based paint and/or lead-based paint hazards in the housing (list documents below).
  _____
  _____

  ❑ Seller has no reports or records pertaining to lead-based paint and/or lead-based paint hazards in the housing.

Buyer's Acknowledgement (initial)

_____ (c) Buyer has received copies of all information listed above.
_____ (d) Buyer has received the pamphlet *Protect Your Family from Lead in Your Home*.
_____ (e) Buyer has (check one below):
  ❑ Received the opportunity during the Due Diligence Period to conduct a risk assessment or inspection for the presence of lead-based paint and/or lead-based paint hazards; or
  ❑ Waived the opportunity to conduct a risk assessment or inspection for the presence of lead-based paint and/or lead-based paint hazards.

Page 1 of 2

This form jointly approved by:
North Carolina Bar Association
North Carolina Association of REALTORS®, Inc.

STANDARD FORM 2A9–T
Revised 7/2015
© 7/2018

Buyer Initials _____ _____   Seller Initials _____ _____

Agent's Acknowledgment (initial)

_____   (f)   Agent has informed the Seller of the Seller's obligations under 42 U.S.C. 4852d and is aware of his/her responsibility to ensure compliance.

Certification of Accuracy
The following parties have reviewed the information above and certify, to the best of their knowledge, that the information provided by the signatory is true and accurate.

IN THE EVENT OF A CONFLICT BETWEEN THIS ADDENDUM AND THE CONTRACT, THIS ADDENDUM SHALL CONTROL, EXCEPT THAT IN THE CASE OF SUCH A CONFLICT AS TO THE DESCRIPTION OF THE PROPERTY OR THE IDENTITY OF THE BUYER OR SELLER, THE CONTRACT SHALL CONTROL.

THE NORTH CAROLINA ASSOCIATION OF REALTORS®, INC. AND THE NORTH CAROLINA BAR ASSOCIATION MAKE NO REPRESENTATION AS TO THE LEGAL VALIDITY OR ADEQUACY OF ANY PROVISION OF THIS FORM IN ANY SPECIFIC TRANSACTION. IF YOU DO NOT UNDERSTAND THIS FORM OR FEEL THAT IT DOES NOT PROVIDE FOR YOUR LEGAL NEEDS, YOU SHOULD CONSULT A NORTH CAROLINA REAL ESTATE ATTORNEY BEFORE YOU SIGN IT.

Buyer:_____ Date:_____

Buyer:_____ Date:_____

Entity Buyer:_____
(Name of LLC/Corporation/Partnership/Trust/etc.)

By: _____ Date:_____

Name:_____ Title:_____

Agent:_____ Date:_____

Seller:_____ Date:_____

Seller:_____ Date:_____

Entity Seller: _____
(Name of LLC/Corporation/Partnership/Trust/etc.)

By: _____ Date_____

Name:_____ Title:_____

Agent:_____ Date:_____

paint or lead-based paint hazards. There are also requirements that all purchasers and renters of a pre-1978 dwelling be given a federal lead-based paint disclosure form. States are free to develop their own such form as long as it is significantly similar to the federal form, which North Carolina has chosen to do. This form also requires that all purchasers and tenants of pre-1978 residential dwellings be given a copy of the Environmental Protection Agency (EPA) pamphlet, "Protect Your Family from Lead in Your Home," before signing a purchase or lease agreement. Residential tenants need only be given this pamphlet, and form, upon initial leasing; the landlord is not required to give the tenant this form upon lease renewal. Another requirement of the act is that purchasers be given at least 10 days to undertake a lead-based paint assessment and testing, although this right can be either waived or extended. The current North Carolina Lead-Based Paint or Lead-Based Paint Hazard Addendum currently extends this right of assessment until the Due Diligence Date if that date is beyond the 10-day period. In an interesting twist, this addendum also includes the real estate agent as having responsibilities under this act, even though the real estate agent is not a party to the contract, in that the agent must acknowledge that the seller has been informed of his obligations under the act as well.

The EPA pamphlet "Protect Your Family from Lead in Your Home" identifies the following three groups as being particularly at risk of the effects of lead-based paint:

1. Children under the age of six
2. Women who are pregnant
3. Women of childbearing age

Test Tip!

- Houses built before 1978 are subject to this act.
- The Lead-Based Paint Addendum must be given to buyers before the first offer.
- The addendum does not state the house is free of lead-based paint.
- Buyers are allowed a 10-day assessment period.
- Health risks of lead-based paint include damage to the central nervous system.

North Carolina Lead-Based Paint Hazard Management Program

The North Carolina Lead-Based Paint Hazard Management Program (LHMP) was established in North Carolina in 1998 to address hazards associated with the improper removal of lead-based paint. Affecting properties constructed before 1978, the LHMP requires people who perform inspections, risk assessments, or abatement in a child-occupied facility, or other targeted housing, to be certified. The LHMP also requires a permit to be obtained by the contractor before any abatement work on such structures can proceed.

Since January 1, 2010, dust-sampling technicians, individuals, and firms undertaking renovation, repair, and painting (RRP) for compensation that will disturb lead-based paint in homes or other child-occupied facilities constructed before 1978 must be certified and follow specific work practices established by the LHMP-RRP. A child-occupied facility is defined as any residential building where children under the age of six will spend at least three hours per day for two days per week or more.

Contractors, property managers, and others working for compensation in target housing and facilities must be properly trained and must provide a copy of the EPA pamphlet, "Renovate Right," to owners and occupants before starting any RRP work. Such information also must be available to the parents and guardians of children who are under the age of six and attend such facilities.

Some exemptions are available under the LHMP-RRP:

- Post-1978 constructed buildings
- Properties found to be lead-free by a certified inspector or risk assessor
- Owners undertaking RRP work on their principal residences
- Areas where the interior space to be disturbed is less than 6 square feet, or less than 20 square feet when it is exterior work, except for window replacement or demolition work that is not exempt under LHMP-RRP

Violations of the Residential Lead-Based Paint Hazard Reduction Act and RRP regulations can result in severe penalties. Violators of the North Carolina Act can be fined $750 per day, although the EPA allows that violations can result in fines up to $35,500 per day. Additionally, courts are allowed to award triple damages for violations under the act.

ASBESTOS

Asbestos is *a fibrous mineral that has been used since the early ages because of its strengthening characteristics as well as its ability to retard heat and general fire resistance.* As a result, asbestos has been a popular choice for insulation, gaskets, siding, roofing, and flooring. Because of health-related concerns, the use of asbestos as an insulation was effectively banned in 1978.

The health risk of asbestos is due to its tiny, microscopic particles that are inhaled and become trapped in the soft tissue lining of the lungs, leading to various respiratory diseases including lung cancer. Unlike radon, lead poisoning, and many other known environmental hazards, there is no known safe level of asbestos. Unfortunately, the health effects caused by asbestos exposure do not surface until many years, often decades, later.

Not all asbestos is a health concern. Asbestos can be either friable or nonfriable. **Friable** is the more concerning form and *refers to asbestos that will become* *airborne particles if it is disturbed.* A typical example of friable asbestos would be from crumbling insulation found in older buildings. **Nonfriable** asbestos *will not become airborne if normal contact is made, such as in flooring, siding, and roofing products.* In the situation of repair, renovation, or removal, the normally nonhazardous installations of a nonfriable asbestos product could easily become friable.

Perhaps the easiest way to deal with asbestos is simply to avoid contact with it and leave it alone. A common method to reduce the health risk of asbestos is to encapsulate, or to seal it off, so as to eliminate or reduce the risk of airborne particles. If removal is desired, it should be undertaken only by state-licensed asbestos abatement contractors who will dispose of the asbestos in accordance with state environmental requirements.

Test Tip!

- Friable asbestos will become airborne if disturbed.
- Nonfriable asbestos will NOT become airborne if normal contact is made.
- A common method of dealing with asbestos is to leave it undisturbed.
- There is no "safe" level of asbestos exposure.
- Health risks include respiratory diseases and cancer.

RADON

Radon is *a colorless, odorless gas that occurs naturally from decaying uranium deposits.* As uranium deteriorates, it releases a radioactive gas (radon) that eventually rises through the cracks and crevices and porous materials of the earth until it reaches the surface and then rises to the highest heavens. Radon is the only naturally occurring radioactive material and is the second leading cause of lung cancer. The risk of lung cancer is greatly increased when a smoker is involved. Once radon enters a structure, it can become trapped and create a health concern for those occupants who inhale the gas over extended periods of time. Radon gas can easily enter a structure by rising through cracks in flooring as well as around pipes and other small openings. This gas can literally be sucked into the home by a "draft effect" caused by ventilation and exhaust fans, chimney flues, and vent pipes. As it enters the house, it becomes trapped and leads to elevated levels within the home. Although what is considered as a safe level of radon varies among different countries, the United States considers a level not exceeding 4.0 picocuries to be the maximum safe level. It is better NOT to think of the 4.0 picocuries as being "safe," but rather that the EPA recommends remediation to lower the level when that level meets or exceeds 4.0. Short-term exposure, even to relatively high levels of radon, is not the health concern that long-term exposure creates. It is impossible to determine whether a house has elevated levels of radon without proper testing. Note that radon levels are not consistently a single digit but rather typically fluctuate over the course of a day. A number rating, such as 4.0, is essentially the average over the testing period.

The North Carolina Real Estate Commission considers that a radon reading of 4.0 or higher is a material fact and must be disclosed by the broker. In the majority of cases, a high radon level can be remediated by a mitigation system. These mitigation systems can range from the simple, involving literally no more than a pipe to allow the gases to escape, to more involved methods that involve fans to remove the dangerous gases. It is most likely that older mitigation systems were installed to reduce radon levels once testing was conducted. Many builders are now installing radon mitigation systems as a safety net feature in all their houses before any testing is done to be proactive. Brokers should determine whether any mitigation system was installed as a proactive measure or in an effort to reduce high levels of radon.

Many radon-testing kits are available for home use, although professional testing is more accurate and is available at a moderate cost. These testing kits typically are placed on the lowest living level of a home in two to three separate locations and 24 inches from the floor, such as on a chair seat.

Recent testing conducted by the EPA indicates that the majority of North Carolina is subject to elevated levels of radon and counties that for years have been considered nonproblematic now have been found to have higher levels than originally thought.

Test Tip!

- Radon levels equal to or greater than 4.0 are considered a material fact.
- This colorless, odorless gas is radioactive.
- Remediation is the process of lowering radon levels.
- Radon is the second leading cause of lung cancer in the U.S.

FORMALDEHYDE

Formaldehyde is *a colorless gas that is emitted by many common construction materials and consumer products found within the home.* Like many other environmental hazards, formaldehyde serves many useful purposes and therefore it is found within a wide array of products, such as glues used in the manufacture of particle board and plywood, adhesives used in laminates, as a preservative in some paints and coating products, as a stiffening agent that allows permanent press qualities in clothing and draperies, and as an ingredient in foam that was used for home insulation until the early 1980s. In addition, many of the new furniture, drapery, and upholstery items within the home have the ability to emit higher levels of formaldehyde.

> "UFFI is a spray-on insulation which contains formaldehyde. Formaldehyde was used in homes built without traditional insulation and utilized in manufactured housing. It was banned in the 1980s."
> —Tim Terry, DREI

Formaldehyde has been shown to cause cancer in animals, but there is no definite evidence linking the chemical to cancer in humans. Higher-than-normal levels of formaldehyde in the home atmosphere can trigger asthma attacks in individuals who have this condition. Other health hazards attributed to formaldehyde include skin rashes; watery eyes, burning sensations in the eyes, throat, and nasal passages; and breathing difficulties.

Remediation to lower the effects of formaldehyde often can be quite simple. Initial procedures include steps to increase ventilation and improve circulation of outside air through the home. If new furniture, drapery, or other sources are contributing to higher-than-normal levels of formaldehyde, removal of these items (or limiting the number of new items introduced into the home) may be all that is needed. If the problem is emanating from the building materials, such as the plywood, paneling, and insulation, remediation may be more involved and disruptive. In many cases, the effects of formaldehyde will dissipate over time, but in more serious cases, the materials actually may have to be removed. Such a process will be costly and time-consuming to the homeowner.

TOXIC MOLD

Of all the various environmental hazards facing the homeowner, the issue of **toxic mold** perhaps may be the most frustrating. Molds can grow without the presence of light and often expand within the house without the owner having any idea there is a problem. Many molds are neither toxic nor a health risk, but given the media coverage of the topic over the past few years, it is understandable that wary homebuyers often consider any mold in the worst-case scenario. Further compounding the issue is that many people can live in a house that has mold and suffer no ill effects and yet another individual might have many health-related complications in the same situation. In reality, every house has mold to some extent. Molds can create serious health risks, especially respiratory problems along with severe allergic reactions. In less serious cases, the effects are much like those caused by the common cold.

In the past several years, there have been numerous high-profile cases of homes inundated with toxic mold. In some situations, the homeowner even burned the house to the ground to get rid of the problem, as it was cheaper and more certain than remediation. In many cases, juries have returned verdicts of literally millions of dollars against builders, sellers, and insurance companies for damages, including health-related claims, due to toxic mold. With such excessive awards, it is no wonder that many insurance companies have exempted mold claims from coverage, and many insurers refuse to extend coverage to homes that have had a history of water damage claims. How can any insurance company expect to withstand potential losses in the millions of dollars for a policy that might sell for only a few hundred dollars?

Molds can grow virtually anywhere in the presence of moisture, a food source, and mold spores. When you consider that many building materials contained in the average home qualify as a food source and that mold spores are present in the air everywhere, it is apparent that moisture is the only one of these factors over which the homeowner has any real control. Unfortunately, the homeowner often is not aware of any moisture or water issues until the mold has had ample opportunity to grow. Further compounding the problem is that once the moisture issue is eliminated, the mold dries and is then more easily distributed in the event the area is later disturbed.

Mold remediation can range from the fairly simple to the very involved. In cases in which a fairly small area is being affected, the homeowner can clean the mold with a bleach and water solution and let it dry thoroughly. In more serious cases, the affected area may have to be removed and professional assistance may be sought to remediate the contamination. Those involved in such removal process must be careful not to further spread the mold spores, and proper clothing and masks should be worn, as once the mold is disturbed, the spore count can dramatically increase in a relatively confined area.

> "The mere presence of mold is not a material fact in North Carolina unless it exists in large amounts and in unusual places."
> —Tim Terry, DREI

LEAKING UNDERGROUND STORAGE TANKS

North Carolina has adopted the North Carolina Leaking Petroleum Underground Storage Tank Cleanup Act to regulate the installation of underground storage tanks and control the risk of leakage and discharge. The focus is on storage tanks containing hazardous substances, including gas, oil, pesticides, and solvents used in commercial as well as some home installations. The property owners where such tanks are installed may face heavy fines and penalties for improper installation and leakage even though they did not either install the tanks or create the reason for the leakage.

Brokers and property owners need to consider the age of the house to determine whether it was likely that an oil furnace had been utilized at a previous point in time. Since the early 1970s, the older installations have been replaced with newer and more energy efficient electric and gas furnaces, but in many cases, the owners did not remove the oil tanks because they were not considered to be a problem for many years. Any property that was originally constructed before this time needs to be inspected to determine whether an underground tank is remaining, and for those that have been removed previously, to determine whether any contamination had occurred.

COMPREHENSIVE ENVIRONMENTAL RESPONSE, COMPENSATION, AND LIABILITY ACT

The purpose of the **Comprehensive Environmental Response, Compensation, and Liability Act (CERCLA)** was to detect and clean up sites where hazardous waste is a problem. Created in 1980 and updated in 1986, CERCLA is perhaps known to most consumers as the Superfund. Under CERCLA regulations, a landowner is responsible for hazardous waste problems occurring on her property even in cases in which the landowner did not directly cause the problem or have any knowledge of its existence. Regardless of who caused the problem, the landowner is responsible for the cleanup costs. The problem is that the cleanup costs can easily exceed the ability of most landowners to pay. The contaminating party could be a prior owner of the property, and if the landowner is unsuccessful in getting that party to pay, the landowner may be able to apply to the Superfund for financial assistance in cleaning the property of the hazardous waste. Because this requirement has the ability to financially ruin many landowners who had no responsibility in causing the contamination as well as no knowledge of its existence, CERCLA was updated in 1986 to include a provision called Innocent Landowner Immunity. Its purpose was to recognize that in many cases the landowner was indeed innocent of the cause of the problem, had acquired the property after the contamination had occurred, and had displayed reasonable efforts to determine if there were any contaminations of hazardous waste before purchasing the property, and therefore should not be held accountable for liability for the cleanup.

Summary of Important Points

1. The important year for lead-based paint is 1978. For residential properties constructed before 1978, real estate agents must provide both buyers, as well as tenants, a copy of the EPA pamphlet, *"Protect Your Family from Lead in the Home."*
2. This pamphlet must be provided before the buyer makes the first offer. Tenants need be provided with this form only before the initial lease period. It is not required for subsequent renewals.
3. According to the EPA, the groups at highest risk for the effects of lead-based paint contamination are (1) children under the age of six, (2) pregnant women, and (3) women of child-bearing age.
4. Beginning in 2010, individuals and firms undertaking RRP for compensation must be certified and perform all work in accordance with LHMP.
5. Asbestos is a fibrous mineral that has been used in many different types of building materials and products. Its use in insulation was banned in 1978.
6. The health risk of asbestos is from tiny, airborne particles becoming trapped in the lungs where they can cause lung-related diseases that may not show up for decades after exposure.
7. Asbestos can be either friable or nonfriable. Friable relates to the fact that the asbestos will become airborne particles when you come into physical contact with it. If normal contact will not result in airborne particles, it is considered nonfriable. Nonfriable asbestos is not considered a health risk.

8. There is no known safe level of exposure to asbestos.
9. Radon is a colorless, odorless gas that is emitted from decaying uranium deposits beneath the surface of the earth. It can become trapped within a home where long-term exposure can lead to the increased risk of lung cancer. It is considered the second leading cause of lung cancer in America.
10. The EPA considers that a radon level of less than 4.0 picocuries does not present a health concern.
11. Elevated levels of radon gas can be remediated simply by ventilating it out of the house or sealing up openings and cracks to reduce the ability of the gas to enter the home.
12. Formaldehyde is a colorless, odorless gas that is emitted from many products used within the home. Typically, the level of urea-formaldehyde will dissipate over time.
13. One of the leading causes of formaldehyde gas in the home is from some of the earlier forms of foam-based insulations. NOTE: The more recent forms of foam insulations are not urea-formaldehyde based.
14. Molds occur naturally on every continent and in every state in America. The best way to control molds in the home is to reduce the moisture content in the home.
15. Most molds are not toxic but some can be, especially to people who suffer from asthma and other respiratory diseases.
16. CERCLA is also known as the Superfund. CERCLA provides funding to clean up toxic waste sites where the current owner is unable to pay for cleanup.

Review Questions

Answers to the review questions are in the Answer Key at the back of the book.

1. The type of asbestos that can become airborne particles when you come into physical contact with it is referred to as:
   A. friable.
   B. nonfriable.
   C. encapsulated.
   D. organic.

2. The maximum "safe level" of asbestos exposure as determined by the EPA is:
   A. 1.0 picocuries.
   B. 2.0 picocuries.
   C. 4.0 picocuries.
   D. not known.

3. The predominant health risk of asbestos exposure is to the:
   A. central nervous system.
   B. lungs.
   C. memory.
   D. brain.

4. Radon is a colorless, odorless gas that is emitted by:
   A. improperly vented appliances.
   B. volatile organic compound paints.
   C. decaying uranium deposits.
   D. urea-formaldehyde.

5. The EPA _____ the maximum acceptable level of radon gas in the home.
   A. has established as 1.0
   B. has established as 2.0
   C. has established as 4.0
   D. has not established

6. According to the Federal Lead-Based Paint Hazard and Reduction Act, which of the following is NOT true?
   A. All pre-1978 housing must be tested for lead-based paint.
   B. All purchasers of pre-1978 housing must be given 10 days to test for lead-based paint.
   C. The buyers and sellers of pre-1978 housing may agree to waive the number of days to test for lead-based paint.
   D. Both purchasers and tenants of pre-1978 housing must be given a copy of the EPA pamphlet, "Protect Your Family From Lead In The Home."

7. The primary source of formaldehyde is from:
   A. lead-based paint.
   B. radon gas.
   C. asbestos.
   D. foam insulation.

8. In order to reduce the risk of mold contamination in the home, the homeowner should:
   A. control moisture and water intrusion.
   B. tightly seal cracks and openings.
   C. control the amount of sunlight the home receives.
   D. eliminate the opportunity for spores to enter the home.

9. Which of the following represents the best placement for the radon-testing mechanism in order to achieve the most accurate results?
   A. on the deck or patio
   B. on the lowest living floor
   C. on the second living floor
   D. in the attic

10. Which of the following is most likely to occur through prolonged mold exposure?
    A. central nervous system damage
    B. migraine headaches
    C. asthma and other respiratory issues
    D. liver and kidney diseases

CHAPTER 7
BROKERAGE RELATIONSHIPS: LAWS AND PRACTICE

KEY TERMS

- agent
- apparent authority
- breach of duty
- buyer agency agreement
- caveat emptor
- civil penalty
- client
- customer
- disclosure of information
- dual agency agreement
- employment authority
- estoppel
- express agency
- facilitator
- fiduciary
- first substantial contact
- general agency
- implied authority
- loyalty
- misdemeanor
- negligent misrepresentation
- negligent omission
- omission
- principal
- special or limited agency
- subagent
- third party
- transactional broker
- universal agency
- willful misrepresentation
- willful omission

LEARNING OBJECTIVES

At the conclusion of this chapter, you should be able to:

1. Define the basic concepts of agency.
2. Define three types of agency.
3. Define the employment authority of real estate agents.
4. Describe agency and subagency relationships in real estate contracts.
5. Define duties and liabilities of principals and real estate agents.
6. Describe examples of willful misrepresentation and negligent misrepresentation.

IN THIS CHAPTER

The body of laws and regulations that govern the relationship of agents to their principals and to one another is known as the law of agency. Inasmuch as most brokerage relationships are based on contractual agreements, contract law also governs real estate transactions. In addition, the North Carolina Real Estate License Law and the Rules and Regulations of the Real Estate Commission govern the conduct of real estate agents. Real estate agents are also responsible for complying with federal and state statutes that address consumer protection and unfair trade or business practices, as well as the common law of fraud and tort law.

GENERAL AGENCY CONCEPTS AND DEFINITIONS

Agency—Agency is the relationship that exists in which one person is empowered to act on behalf of another.

Principal/Client—The **principal** is the person for whom the agent acts. The principal is typically the party who hires the agents to act on his behalf and is responsible for compensation to the agent absent any other agreement. In a real estate transaction, the principal could be the buyer, such as in a buyer agency agreement, or the seller, such as is the case in a listing agreement.

Agent—The **agent** is the party who acts on behalf of the principal. The agent can be a person, such as the agent, who actually lists the property on behalf of the firm, or the agent could be the firm itself.

Subagent (Subagency)—Literally the agent of the agent. If the agent is considered to be the firm itself, the **subagent**(s) would be those agents who work for that firm. Likewise, if Firm "A" is the listing agent, any other firm who would like to sell the property, and is not acting in the capacity of a buyer agent, would be considered to be a subagent of the listing firm (i.e., the selling firm would also represent who the listing firm represents, the seller). The term, subagent, can also refer to the actual agent persons themselves. In this usage, the agent would have the capacity of subagent to the firm for whom she works. In its most literal sense, subagency is used to describe representation of the seller whether it is from the listing firm and its agents, or a co-brokering company and its agents, who are working with a buyer but not serving in the capacity of buyer agents. In that situation, the co-broker company and its agents actually would be representing the seller's interests and not the buyer.

Third Party—The **third party** is the party that you do not represent. In the case of a listing agreement, the listing agent and firm would represent the seller as their principal. The buyer would be their third party.

> "Agency is the largest category of test questions on the examination. Most of the agency questions are level-3-type questions, meaning you have to be able to apply and analyze these concepts, which are in fact pattern-type questions."
> —Len Elder, DREI

In buyer agency, the buyer agent represents the buyer as the principal, and the seller would be the third party. An agent working with a third party is obligated to be honest with that party and provide full disclosure of material facts. An agent must disclose personal information about a third party to their principal but cannot disclose personal information about the principal to the third party without first obtaining permission from the principal.

Fiduciary—A fiduciary relationship is based on trust. Agency is automatically considered a relationship based on trust as one party, the agent, is entrusted to represent the best interest of the principal client (another name for the principal or the person that the agent represents).

Customer—The person the agent does not represent, although the agent may have a relationship with this person. An example would be an agent who is showing houses to a buyer but represents the interests of the seller. The seller is the client and the buyer would be the customer.

Facilitator/transactional broker—Not allowed in North Carolina but is used in some other states. This is a type of "nonagency" relationship in which the licensee assists buyers and seller in a transaction but does not actually represent either party. It involves essentially treating each party as a customer rather than a client. The disclosure of material facts is still required.

Test Tip!

Students should be very familiar with each of the general agency concepts and definitions.

Agency relationships have existed throughout history and are not restricted to real estate. Literally any relationship in which one party represents the interests of another would be considered an agency. Because of this long history, the courts have established several tenets of agency law. These elements are considered to be standard in any agency relationship and do not have to be addressed specifically in the agency agreement. The agent is to represent the interests of the party for whom he acts without regard for his own self-interest. The principal will be held accountable for the reasonable actions of his agent. Additionally, the principal is responsible for the compensation of his agent. The North Carolina Real Estate Commission requires that all agency agreements be in writing from their inception with the exception of nonexclusive buyer agency agreements, which may be verbal under certain circumstances.

Agency relationships place the agents in a fiduciary role in that they are entrusted to look after the best interests of the party whom they represent. Such trust means the agents must place their principal's interests ahead of any others, even their own. Agents must disclose to their principal all material facts that they know, or reasonably should know, as well as any personal information about the third party. An agent does not necessarily represent the party who pays him. It is quite common that buyer agents will be hired by the buyer but yet be required to seek compensation from the seller through the listing agent.

CLASSIFICATION OF AGENCY RELATIONSHIPS

Three general classifications of agency are recognized: universal, general, and special. The first two are included for background material only and do not represent the typical real estate transaction.

Universal Agency

A **universal agency** provides for an agent to have all-encompassing powers to make decisions and act on behalf of the principal. Such a situation might arise under a power of attorney signed by parents entrusting all their property and assets to their adult children for the general welfare and benefit of the parents. In this case, the children could be authorized to sell the parents' home and automobile and to make investment decisions with the proceeds to provide the best income for the parents. Essentially, the children have been authorized to manage all the affairs of their parents. Universal agency rarely occurs in real estate relationships.

General Agency

General agency confers a broad scope of authority on the agent, but the authority is not as broad as the universal agency and is limited to some particular field. When a real estate licensee becomes associated with a brokerage firm, the licensee becomes a general agent of the broker/principal. As a sales associate, the licensee is permitted to solicit real estate business from the public on behalf of the broker, to place advertising in various publications, to place real estate signs on listed properties, and so on. The sales associate represents the broker in the field of real estate. However, the sales associate is not given the authority to hire or fire the broker's secretary, to make deposits or withdrawals from the trust account, or to otherwise make decisions regarding management of the broker's business. Sales associates are given a broad range of duties limited to real estate brokerage and are not assigned duties related to the management of a real estate office.

Special Agency

A **special** or **limited agency** is limited to one well-defined task one time. Once the task or the time period has been fulfilled, the agency relationship will no longer exist. In this situation, the agent is not authorized to make decisions on the part of the principal but only to stand in the principal's place to receive information and to bring this information to the principal for a decision. The agent is not empowered to evaluate offers but is required to transmit such information to the principal immediately for an evaluation and a decision. A real estate agency contract, such as a listing agreement, buyer agency agreement, or property management agreement for a single property, creates a special agency.

CREATION OF AGENCY RELATIONSHIPS

Relationships between Transaction Parties

Agency relationships can be created by contractual agreements between the firm and the person it represents. In the listing agreement, the firm is the agent and the principal is the seller. The firm is being hired to use its best efforts to secure a ready, willing, and able buyer for the seller's property. The buyer's agency agreement finds the firm in a position of representing the buyer in locating the desired property to purchase. In each of these agreements, the firm represents either the seller or the buyer's interests. In the **dual agency agreement**, the firm is actually representing both the buyer and the seller. Such agreements have a much higher risk because of the inherent conflicts of interest that dual agency creates. There are also agency agreements for leasing such as property management contracts, in which the firm is hired to lease and manage the property in an ongoing fashion for the owner, as well as the tenant representation agreement in which the firm will represent the tenant's interest in locating a suitable property to lease.

Relationships between Brokers and Firms

Agency agreements also are formed within the firm the agent works for. Most firms will want to enter into an in-house brokerage employment agreement to address the relationship between the firm and the agent. Such agreements will address what the firm expects of the agent, what the agent can expect of the firm, and what happens when the agent leaves. There is also an agency relationship formed when one firm is involved in the brokerage of another firm's listing. These agreements will address the division of commissions as well as create an understanding of whom the various parties represent. In many of these co-brokerage agreements, the firms will both be members of a local Multiple Listing Service (MLS) and these co-brokerage agreements will be addressed within the membership.

Implied Agency

When the actions of the principal and agent indicate that they have an agency agreement, this is called an implied agency or ostensible agency. For example, a broker who puts himself in the position in which she appears to be an agent of the buyer (i.e., showing homes, gathering information on properties, referring to herself as the buyer's real estate agent), she is, in fact, the implied agent of the prospective purchaser. The duties and responsibilities created by an implied agency are the same as those created by an **express agency**. Implied agency is highly unlikely in real estate brokerage practice today because both General Statute (G.S.) 93A-13 and the North Carolina Real Estate Commission Rule 58A, section A.0104, require all agency relationships to be in writing. Providing the Commission's brochure *Working with Real Estate Agents*, reviewing it with clients, and determining whether the agent will work for the buyer or seller in the transaction at first substantial contact, as required by A.0104, substantially reduces the possibility of an inadvertent dual agency. The agent, when dealing with a third party, must continue to avoid acting in such a way as to imply an agency relationship.

Estoppel

An agency relationship also can be created by **estoppel.** This occurs when an individual claims incorrectly that a person is his agent and a third party relies on the incorrect representation. In these cases, the person making the incorrect statement is stopped and prohibited from later claiming that the agency relationship does not exist. For example, Broker A states to Mr. and Mrs. R that Betty is an agent in Broker A's office, when he knows this is not true. If Mr. and Mrs. R rely on this incorrect statement, Broker A cannot later claim that Betty is not an agent, and Broker A is liable for Betty's actions.

Scope of Agent's Authority

Agency authority can be created in much the same fashion as the agency agreements themselves—expressed, implied, and apparent. Whereas the agency agreement is required to be expressed in writing by G.S. 93A-13 and North Carolina Real Estate Commission Rule 58A.0104, the full extent of an agent's authority may not be detailed in the written agreement. Certainly, the written agency agreement will contain much of the detail regarding the agent's authority, but it is unrealistic to think that every single detail will be reduced to writing. For example, a seller may instruct her agent to get a landscaper to mow the grass and trim the bushes. The agent therefore is authorized to obtain the services in question and compensate the contractor.

An agent also can be found to possess granted **implied authority.** Implied authority is based on custom and may very well be the result of an expressed agreement. For example, an agent may have just listed a real-estate-owned property (i.e., foreclosure) to sell for the bank. The bank's agreement with the broker states the broker is to maintain the property and do whatever is reasonably necessary to secure the premises. Even though the contract did not specifically state what those necessary steps might be, the agent is allowed to do whatever is reasonable to accomplish those tasks. The contract implied the agent had the right to hire the maintenance contractors and incur the expenses to secure the premises.

Apparent authority *occurs when an agent gives the impression that she has certain authority that a third party might reasonably rely upon, when in fact the agent does not actually hold such authority.* Suppose an agent is acting in a manner that she is not authorized to by her principal. The principal is aware the agent is acting in such fashion but does nothing to stop, or rein back in, the agent—even though the principal is aware that a third party is led to believe that the agent is acting within his authority. The third party believes the agent is acting within her authority because the principal has done nothing to lead her to think otherwise. It is entirely possible that the principal could be bound by the actions of her agent because the principal did not stop the agent from acting beyond his authority and did not inform the third party the agent was not authorized to act in the manner in which she performed. This concept is referred to as the *theory of estoppel*. In this case, the principal was estopped (stopped) from denying the existence of the agency agreement because she knew the agent was acting beyond her authority and she did nothing to stop the third party from incorrectly assuming the agent had such authority.

Agency and Agent Compensation

The source of compensation is not an accurate indicator of agency representation. Historically, it was believed that the agent worked for the person who paid his commission. This is probably based on the theory that the person who hires an agent is responsible for the compensation of the agent unless otherwise agreed and stipulated. With the evolution of buyer agency, agency representation is no longer determined solely by who compensates the agent. Today, an agent may be compensated by the buyer, the seller, or even a third party whose interest actually conflicts with that of the agent's principal. Regardless of who is compensating the agent, the agent still owes his fiduciary duty to his principal. For example, a buyer's agent may be paid from the seller's proceeds at closing, but nonetheless, the agent still represents the buyer, not the seller.

AGENCY AND SUBAGENCY RELATIONSHIPS

Agency practices can vary greatly and are not dictated by state law but rather by company policy. There are firms that handle only residential, commercial, or property management as well as those that handle all three. Companies that try to be all things to all people will be frustrated by the magnitude of the undertaking. Likewise, companies that try to focus in too narrow an area of expertise will find the going tough when the market contracts. In the same sense that companies will establish their own policy for which area they wish to practice real estate, they also will need to decide how they wish to practice their agency relationships.

Companies can practice single agency or dual agency as they prefer. The ultimate decision comes down to money and risks.

Single Agency

The primary advantage to the practice of single agency is that of risk. Regardless of whether the firm chooses to represent only sellers or only buyers, the least risk is involved with this form of relationship. There is no liability for the firm regarding the agents associated with another firm. One of the major disadvantages associated with agency representation is that a principal is generally responsible for the actions of its agents. Real estate firms are clearly aware of the costs of defending lawsuits, and even when they win, it can be quite expensive.

The major disadvantage of single agency is the limitation of being able to represent only one of the parties in a given transaction. Many parties that will want to list their properties are doing so because they wish to buy another. Many buyers will need to sell their existing property to be able to make a purchase.

Exclusive Seller Agency

Listing with an Independent Broker

The simplest and clearest relationship between principal and agent is that of a one-person brokerage firm. In the case of a one-person office, there is a very close one-to-one relationship between the principal and the broker. There is relatively little opportunity for confusion in the fulfillment of the broker's role to the principal as long as the broker represents only one principal.

Listing with a Multi-agent Firm

A brokerage firm consists of two or more licensed individuals working in the same office and sharing information. The agency agreement is between the principal and the brokerage firm. When an agent affiliated with a real estate firm enters into an agency contract with a buyer or seller, the *firm* owns the agency agreement and is the agent for that buyer or seller.

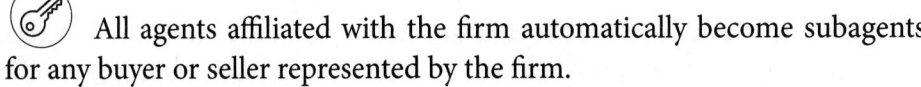 All agents affiliated with the firm automatically become subagents for any buyer or seller represented by the firm.

This presents an interesting situation in regard to communication of the acceptance, rejection, or withdrawal of an offer. Communication to any agent within the firm fulfills the communication requirement; therefore, agents should note the date and time of any such communication. This will prevent conflicts when an acceptance has been communicated to one agent and a withdrawal has been communicated to another agent in the same firm. The existence of a contract depends on which communication came first.

Subagency

The sales associates affiliated with the brokerage firm are agents of the broker and subagents of the brokerage firm's principals (clients). The fiduciary duty of sales associates thus extends both to their employing brokerage firm and to the firm's principals.

In this situation, the broker is in two separate agency relationships. The broker is the agent of the principal under the agency agreement; the broker is also the principal of the sales associates under an agency agreement in the brokerage firm. Therefore, the broker is responsible for the actions of the sales associates even though in almost all cases the sales associates are independent contractors. As general agents of the broker and subagents of the seller in reference to the listing agreements, the sales associates are required to comply with the terms of all the firm's agency agreements and with all rules of the brokerage firm.

Cooperating with Other Brokers

When a cooperating broker associated with another firm accepts the offer of subagency associated with a listing, she and her firm work through the listing broker; therefore, she and her firm are the principal's subagent, just as the sales associates in the listing agency's office are. The listing agent and the subagent work with—not for—the buyer; therefore, the buyer is a customer. The cooperating broker acting as a subagent has the same responsibility as the listing broker does—to work for the best interest of the seller.

Cooperating Firm Acting as Seller's Agent

Agency is a legal relationship that considers agents, subagents, and principals as the same legal entity. Figure 7.1 illustrates a cooperating broker relationship in which listing and selling brokers work exclusively for the seller. The buyer should acknowledge in writing that he has been informed that the agent is working for the seller. This can be accomplished when reviewing the Commission's brochure *Working with Real Estate Agents* (see Figure 7.4 later in this chapter). A buyer who will be a customer (not a client) should check the box and initial the section of the signature panel entitled "Disclosure of Seller Subagency." Everyone above the line of separation is, therefore, the same legal entity and is presumed to share all information. The agent has a duty to transmit all information about the transaction to the principal to ensure that the principal has all the information the agent knows. In this case, the buyer is alone on the other side of the line of separation. The agent must inform the buyer of the agent's duty to transmit all information to the seller or listing agent. This lets the buyer know he should not tell the agent any confidential information he does not want the seller to know.

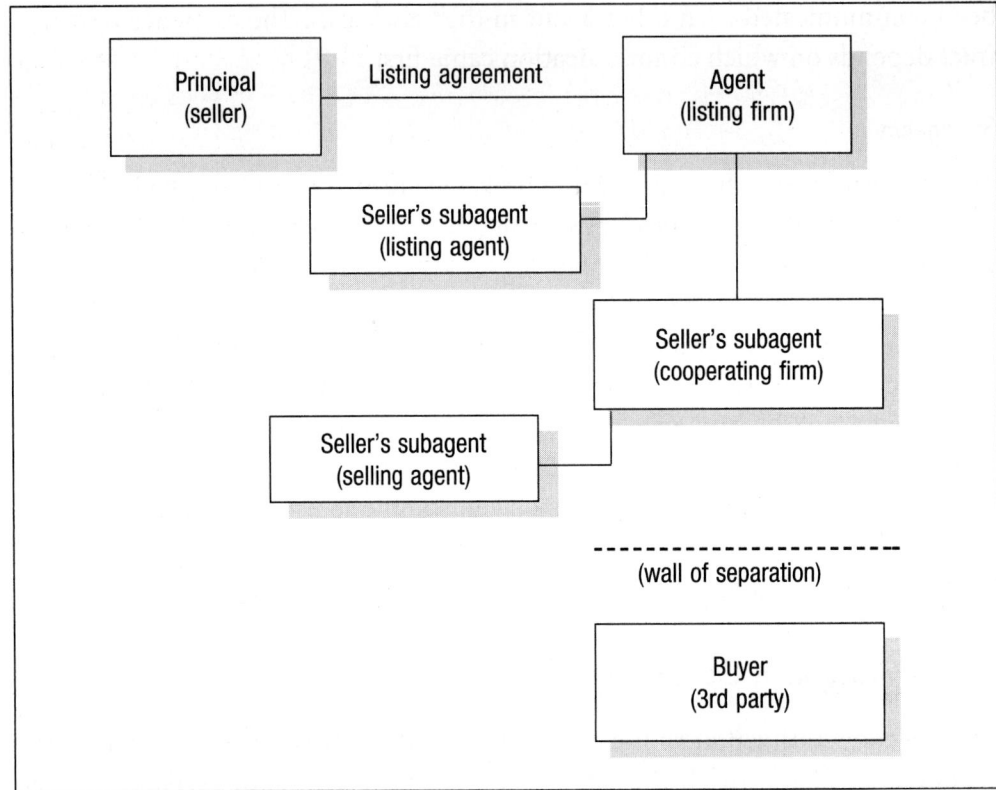

FIGURE 7.1 Agency relationships when seller is principal. Both listing and selling agents represent the seller.
Source: © 2019 OnCourse Learning

NOTE: Both agent and subagent owe to the buyer certain duties, which are discussed in the section "Agent's Duties to Third Parties."

Exclusive Buyer Agency

Many real estate buyers now hire brokers to represent them. Under an exclusive **buyer agency agreement** (see Chapter 8, Figure 8.6) the buyer is the broker's principal (client), and the agency relationship is between the buyer and the broker. As a principal of the brokerage firm, buyers also are due the fiduciary duties of agency from the firm's sales associates.

Buyer as Principal

Figure 7.1 illustrates the fact that the buyer is alone when all agents are working for the seller. She has no one to help her negotiate, to advise her on value, or to look out primarily for her interest. It is not difficult to understand why buyers are increasingly demanding their own advocates, their own agents, and a level playing field. Figure 7.2 shows the buyer with her agent on her side of the line of separation. Because of this demand by the buyer, it is now common that brokers will be asked to serve in the capacity of a buyer agent. The buyer's agent can now provide the same level of knowledge to the buyer that the seller has always had.

> "Technically licensees are always subagents since they are always acting as subagents of the brokerage or firm hired by the client. Buyer's subagency is different. It presumes that the buyer did not hire the agent and therefore the agent must work on behalf of the seller and will need permission from both the buyer and the seller to do so."
> —Steve Robinson

She knows that when she has a confidential discussion with her agent, the information will not cross the line of separation. As a result, any personal information the buyer shares with her buyer agent will not be shared with the seller.

In situations in which the broker has an ownership interest in a residential listing, the broker will not be permitted to represent the buyer in that transaction. It would be impractical to think that an owner could adequately represent the interests of the buyer. As a result dual, as well as designated agency, will not be allowed. The broker-owner is permitted to serve in the capacity of owner only in this transaction and could resume the role of buyer agent for other properties the buyer is contemplating. There is a different view of the broker-owner's role in transactions involving commercial properties. The broker can represent the buyer as buyer agent in commercial transactions in which the broker owns less than a 25% interest in the property being sold. This would still require the informed consent of any buyer before proceeding. One of the reasons for this variation is that commercial properties frequently have many owners and the theory is that a minor interest in the property should not preclude participation as a buyer agent.

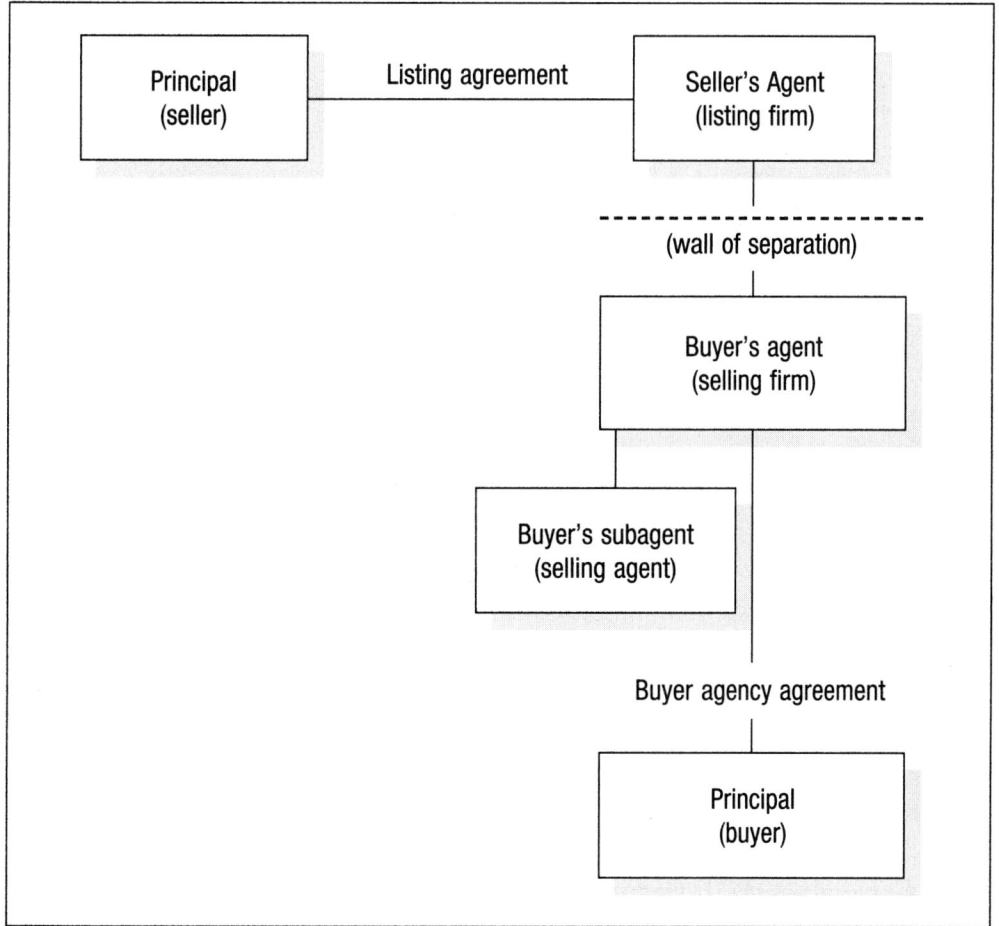

FIGURE 7.2 Agency relationships when both seller and buyer have their own agents.
Source: © 2019 OnCourse Learning

NOTE: The buyer's agent owes to the seller the duties that will be discussed in the section "Agent's Duties to Third Parties." Also see in Figures 7.1 and 7.2 that confidential information does not cross the wall of separation.

Both Seller and Buyer Agency with Dual Agency for In-House Sales

> "Dual agency limits a licensee's ability to advocate or negotiate on behalf of the client. The licensee is required to treat everyone in a manner which is fair, equal, and impartial."
> —Bill Gallagher, DREI

In some situations, the listing firm also will represent a buyer who expresses interest in that listing. In cases in which the same firm represents BOTH the buyer as well as the seller, it will be considered a dual agency transaction (see Figure 7.3). License Law 93A-6(4) prohibits a firm from *"acting for more than one party in a transaction without the prior knowledge and consent of all parties for whom he or she acts."* Real Estate Commission Rule A.0104(d) further states that *"a real estate broker representing one party in a transaction shall not undertake to represent another party in the transaction without the written authority of each party."* As evident from these two laws and rules, dual agency cannot be entered into without the fact being disclosed and the "informed consent" of each party must be obtained in writing. Therefore, any undisclosed dual agency shall constitute a violation of License Law as well as Real Estate Commission Rule.

North Carolina also allows a variation of basic dual agency utilized in which a firm shall designate one of its agents to represent strictly the seller's interest and another agent to represent strictly the buyer's interest. Such a situation is considered designated agency and is allowed under certain conditions.

There is a much more detailed explanation of the dual and designated agency concepts toward the end of this chapter.

Agency Relationships in Real Estate Rentals

Agency law also applies to real estate agents and firms who act as property managers. When a landlord contracts with a broker to manage properties on his behalf,

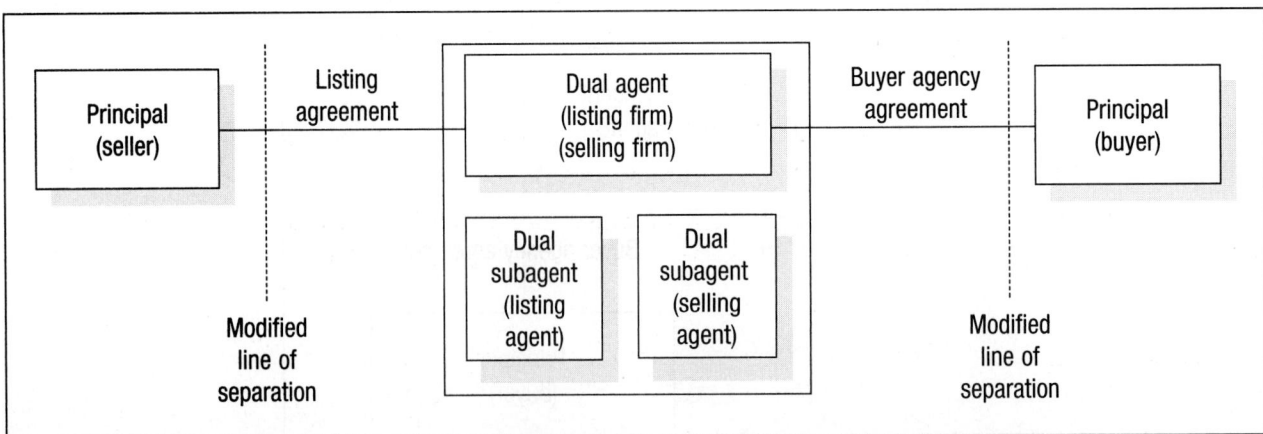

FIGURE 7.3 Agency relationship when both seller and buyer have the same agent (dual agent).
Source: © 2019 OnCourse Learning

the landlord is the agent's principal. It is important that the broker disclose to prospective tenants her representation of the landlord. Likewise, a prospective tenant may hire a broker to find a suitable rental property. In this case, the tenant is the broker's principal. In the unlikely event an agent finds herself in the potential position of representing a tenant and a landlord in the same transaction, all the rules and duties of dual agency apply. See Chapter 15 for further discussion of agency relationships with landlords and tenants.

Agency's Effect on Communication Requirements for Contracts

Agency status is often an important determinant of when the communication of the acceptance, rejection, or withdrawal of an offer has occurred. The following example illustrates how agency status affects the communication requirement in the acceptance of a contract.

A seller signs and accepts offer to purchase and contract in listing agent's presence, thus notifying listing agent of acceptance:

- If the listing agent is an exclusive seller's agent and the buyer has no agent or has an exclusive buyer's agent, communication has not occurred.
- If the listing agent is an exclusive seller's agent and the buyer is working with a subagent, communication has not occurred.
- If the listing agent or subagent notifies either the buyer or the buyer's agent, communication has occurred.
- If the listing agent is also the buyer's agent (consequently, a dual agent), communication has occurred as soon as the listing/dual agent knows of acceptance.

The following example illustrates how communication requirements are met in a counteroffer situation.

A seller receives an offer from a buyer and makes a counteroffer. (Seller thus rejects the offer and makes a new offer.) The rejection is considered communicated according to the same rules as listed previously. Acceptance or rejection by the buyer of the new offer from the seller is considered to be officially communicated as follows:

- If the buyer has no agent, communication occurs when he communicates his acceptance or rejection to the seller, his agent, or subagent.
- If the buyer has a buyer's agent, communication does not occur when he notifies his buyer's agent. It occurs only when he or his agent notifies the seller, his agent, or a seller's subagent.
- If the buyer's agent is the same agent as the seller's agent (dual agent), communication occurs as soon as the dual agent is notified.

NOTE: An agent should never make a judgment call as to whether there is a contract. An attorney should be consulted immediately in any situation that requires such a judgment.

Agency's Effect on Disclosure of Material Facts

In an agency relationship with a single principal (buyer or seller), material facts that an agent would present to her principal include *any* fact that might influence the principal's decisions in the transaction. This includes any confidential information that an agent is privy to regarding a third party in the transaction. For example, if a buyer's agent knows that a seller is in the midst of a divorce and believes that this personal financial situation may lead the seller to negotiate a lower sales price, the agent can and should make her buyer aware of this situation.

> An agent *must* disclose to all parties all material facts she knows, or reasonably should have known, regardless of who she represents. An agent *must* disclose personal information about a third party to the principal but *cannot*, without permission, disclose personal information about the principal to the third party.

In the practice of dual agency, contractual agreements, such as those in the dual agency addendum and a dual agency agreement, alter an agent's duties to disclose. These duties to both parties become, in effect, those duties owed to a third party in a transaction rather than those disclosure duties of an agent to a principal. In a dual agency situation in which the agency agreement forms of the North Carolina Association of REALTORS® (NCAR) are used to authorize the dual agency, material facts requiring disclosure are limited to facts about the property itself (e.g., defects), matters affecting the property or property value (e.g., pending zoning changes), and facts relating to a principal's ability to complete the transaction. Matters not directly related to the property, such as a seller's personal financial situation, are facts that should not be disclosed.

Termination of Agency

An agency relationship ends in accordance with the terms of the agency contract. All agency contracts must have an expiration date with no provision for automatic renewal. When the contract expires, the agency relationship terminates and so does any authority of the agent to act on behalf of the principal. An agency relationship also is terminated by completion of the terms of the agency—that is, completion of the sale of the listed real estate and the payment of commission. Agency agreements are personal service contracts that are not assignable; therefore, the death or insanity of a broker in a single-broker firm would terminate the contract. In some cases, operation of law may terminate the agency relationship. For instance, a power of attorney terminates automatically at the death of either principal or agent. Another example is the termination of a listing agreement held by a broker whose license is revoked or by a brokerage firm that closes or dissolves. If a listed property is totally destroyed, the listing contract terminates. If the property is partially destroyed, the listing contract would likely be voidable by either party. The injured party can terminate the listing contract if either agent or principal **breaches agency duties**.

Except in certain atypical circumstances, an agent's duties to a principal under the common law of agency terminate upon termination of the agency relationship. Thus, as a general rule, a broker does not owe any duty of confidentiality to a former client, especially when representing a new client in dealings with the former client.

Disclosure of Agency Relationships

The Real Estate License Law carefully regulates agency agreements and disclosures. North Carolina Real Estate License Law provision G.S. 93A-18 and Commission Rule 58A.0104 specifically require all real estate agency contracts to be in writing. All agency agreements, including listing agreements, exclusive buyer agency agreements, property management agreements, and any other real estate brokerage service agreements other than oral buyer agency agreements that do not bind the buyer to an agent or a time period must be in writing and provide for a definitive period of time, at the end of which the agreement automatically terminates with no prior notice required.

All such agreements must conspicuously incorporate the nondiscrimination language (Rule A.0104) as follows: "*The Agent (Firm) shall conduct all brokerage activities in regard to this agreement without respect to the race, color, religion, sex, national origin, handicap, or familial status of any party or prospective party to the agreement.*" All preprinted offers or sales contracts must provide for the identification of each real estate agent and firm involved and for the disclosure of whom each agent and firm represents.

The same rule (58A.0104e) requires an agent to review the Commission's brochure *Working with Real Estate Agents* (see Figure 7.4), with a potential client or customer, whether buyer or seller, at first substantial contact and to have the client or customer sign that he received the brochure and that it was reviewed with him. Merely providing the brochure and having the buyer sign it is not sufficient. The agent must review the entire brochure before obtaining the buyer's signature. Written disclosure by seller's agent to buyer at first substantial contact is also required. The agent and potential client or customer can then agree upon the desired agency relationship, if any. This form is for sales situations, residential and commercial only, and does not apply to rental scenarios.

If the agent will be working as an agent or a subagent of the seller and working directly with the buyer (customer), then when reviewing the brochure, the agent must disclose to the buyer that he works in the seller's interest and have the

"The disclosure of agency to consumers and clients happens at first substantial contact. Disclosure to other agents should occur at initial contact. The contract also requires a confirmation of agency status at the time of contract."
—Tim Terry, DREI

buyer acknowledge disclosure by initialing the section called "Disclosure of Seller Subagency" on the acknowledgment panel.

If a buyer wants buyer agency but does not want to sign an exclusive buyer agency agreement for a specific period of time, the agent can work as a buyer agent and/or a dual agent under an oral agreement under certain conditions. The buyer must sign the acknowledgment panel on the Commission's brochure *Working with Real Estate Agents*, and the buyer and/or dual agency agreement must be committed to writing before an offer on a property is made. The oral agreement cannot bind the buyer to work exclusively with the agent or be for a specific period of time. An agent working as a buyer's agent should disclose this relationship to the seller's agent at initial contact and follow the oral disclosure with the written disclosure to the seller or the seller's agent before or with the delivery of the offer to purchase (see Chapter 9).

An agent selling a buyer (client) a property offered directly by the seller must review the brochure with the seller at first substantial contact and have the seller sign the acknowledgment of receipt. He must notify the seller that he is acting as a buyer's agent, just as he would notify the seller's agent (if the seller had one) of that fact. NCAR Form 150 (not shown) may be used to notify a For Sale by Owner of agency status. NCAR Form 220, Confirmation of Agency, Relationship Appointment, and Compensation, may be used to notify a seller's agent of the status of the agent working with or for the buyer. If the seller wants to allow dual agency, both buyer and seller must agree to that arrangement and the appropriate documents must be signed.

A listing agent must review with a potential seller the Commission's brochure *Working with Real Estate Agents* and have him sign it at first substantial contact. If the seller lists his property, the listing agent will become a seller's agent with or without the potential of being a dual agent, depending on the agreement between the agent and the seller.

If after presentation of the Commission's brochure *Working with Real Estate Agents*, the customer does not wish to sign the acknowledgment, the agent is required to indicate this fact on the brochure acknowledgment panel. This does not alleviate the requirement that the agent retain the acknowledgment panel.

First Substantial Contact

> **First substantial contact** is that flexible point in time in which an agent must disclose to the buyer that she represents the seller and that the buyer should not disclose to the agent any personal information that she would not want the seller to know. This is also true in cases involving buyer agency where the agent must disclose to the seller that she represents the buyer and that the seller should not disclose to the agent any personal information that she would not want the buyer to know.

FIGURE 7.4 Working with real estate agents.
Source: © NC Real Estate Commission (Working with Real Estate Agents brochure)

The flexible part of this ends at the moment the agent shows the buyer the first house. This topic will be addressed in more detail later in this section, but it is important to note the concern is regarding personal information as opposed to materials facts. The basic rules of agency require the agent to disclose any and all material facts of which the agent is aware or reasonably should have been aware. This requirement goes both ways, and an agent owes the same disclosure of material facts to both her principal as well as the third party. It is the disclosure of personal information that creates the issue for first substantial contact. The agency requirement is that the agent must disclose personal information about the third party to the agent's principal but cannot disclose personal information about her principal to the third party without the consent of the principal. The assumption is that an agent represents the seller until, and unless, there is an agreement for the agent to represent the buyer. Because of this assumption, the buyer is treated as a third party when first meeting (as a **dual agent**). Or you may agree to let them represent only the seller (**seller's agent** or **subagent**). Some agents will offer you a choice of these services. Others may not.

Buyer's Agent

Duties to Buyer: If the real estate firm and its agents represent you, they must • promote your best interests • be loyal to you • follow your lawful instructions • provide you with all material facts that could influence your decisions • use reasonable skill, care and diligence, and • account for all monies they handle for you. Once you have agreed (either orally or in writing) for the firm and its agents to be your *buyer's agent*, they may not give any confidential information about you to sellers or their agents without your permission so long as they represent you. But **until you make this agreement with your buyer's agent, you should avoid telling the agent anything you would *not* want a seller to know.**

Unwritten Agreements: To make sure that you and the real estate firm have a clear understanding of what your relationship will be and what the firm will do for you, you may want to have a written agreement. However, some firms may be willing to represent and assist you for a time

Continued on the back

FOR BUYER/SELLER

_____
Agent Name   License Number

_____
Firm Name

_____
Date

WORKING WITH REAL ESTATE AGENTS

Agents must retain this acknowledgment for their files.

This is not a contract

By signing, I acknowledge that the agent named below furnished a copy of this brochure and reviewed it with me.

_____
Buyer or Seller Name (Print or Type)

_____
Buyer or Seller Signature

_____
Buyer or Seller Name (Print or Type)

_____
Buyer or Seller Signature

_____
Date

_____
Firm Name

_____
Agent Name   License Number

Disclosure of Seller Subagency
(Complete, if applicable)

❏ When showing you property and assisting you in the purchase of a property, the above agent and firm will represent the SELLER. For more information, see "Seller's Agent Working with a Buyer" in the brochure.

Buyer's Initials Acknowledging Disclosure: _____

FIGURE 7.4 (*Continued*)

with the agent, so any personal information the buyer might disclose is required to be disclosed to the agent's seller. Certainly, many buyers would not have disclosed such personal information had they known the agent must disclose it to the seller. For this reason, it is this point at which the agent must first disclose to the buyer that she represents the seller and the buyer should not disclose any personal information that she would not wish the seller to know. If the buyer decides to anoint the agent as her buyer agent, the buyer can freely disclose personal information to the agent with the assurance the agent is not allowed to share such information with the seller without first obtaining permission from the buyer. This is true regardless of whether the agreement is legally in writing or oral. Even in the event that dual agency should ensue, the agent cannot disclose this personal information gathered from the buyer without consent of the buyer in the typical North Carolina dual agency situation.

as a *buyer's agent* without a written agreement. But if you decide to make an offer to purchase a particular property, the agent must obtain a written agency agreement before writing the offer. If you do not sign it, the agent can no longer represent and assist you and is no longer required to keep information about you confidential.

Be sure to read and understand any agency agreement before you sign it. Once you sign it, the agent must give you a copy of it.

Services and Compensation: Whether you have a written or unwritten agreement, a *buyer's agent* will perform a number of services for you. These may include helping you • find a suitable property • arrange financing • learn more about the property and • otherwise promote your best interests. If you have a **written** agency agreement, the agent can also help you prepare and submit a written offer to the seller.

A *buyer's agent* can be compensated in different ways. For example, you can pay the agent out of your own pocket. Or the agent may seek compensation from the seller or listing agent first, but require you to pay if the listing agent refuses. Whatever the case, be sure your compensation arrangement with your *buyer's agent* is spelled out in a buyer agency agreement before you make an offer to purchase property and that you carefully read and understand the compensation provision.

Dual Agent

You may permit an agent or firm to represent you **and** the seller at the same time. This "dual agency relationship" is most likely to happen if you become interested in a property listed with your *buyer's agent* or the agent's firm. If this occurs and you have not already agreed to a dual agency relationship in your (written or oral) buyer agency agreement, your *buyer's agent* will ask you to amend the buyer agency agreement or sign a separate agreement or document permitting him or her to act as agent for both you and the seller. It may be difficult for a *dual agent* to advance the interests of both the buyer and seller. Nevertheless, a *dual agent* must treat buyers and sellers fairly and equally. Although the *dual agent* owes them the same duties, buyers and sellers can prohibit *dual agents* from divulging **certain** confidential information about them to the other party.

Some firms also offer a form of dual agency called "designated agency" where one agent in the firm represents the seller and another agent represents the buyer. This option (when available) may allow each "designated agent" to more fully represent each party.

If you choose the "dual agency" option, remember that since a *dual agent's* loyalty is divided between parties with competing interests, it is especially important that you have a clear understanding of • what your relationship is with the *dual agent* and • what the agent will be doing for you in the transaction. This can best be accomplished by putting the agreement in writing at the earliest possible time.

Seller's Agent Working With a Buyer

If the real estate agent or firm that you contact does not offer *buyer agency* or you do not want them to act as your *buyer agent*, you can still work with the firm and its agents. However, they will be acting as the *seller's agent* (or "subagent"). The agent can still help you find and purchase property and provide many of the same services as a *buyer's agent*. The agent must be fair with you and provide you with any "material facts" (such as a leaky roof) about properties.

But remember, the agent represents the seller—not you—and therefore must try to obtain for the seller the best possible price and terms for the seller's property. Furthermore, a *seller's agent* is required to give the seller any information about you (even personal, financial or confidential information) that would help the seller in the sale of his or her property. Agents must tell you *in writing* if they are *sellers' agents* before you say anything that can help the seller. But **until you are sure that an agent is not a *seller's agent*, you should avoid saying anything you do *not* want a seller to know.**

Sellers' agents are compensated by the sellers.

Disclosure of Seller Subagency (Complete, if applicable)

❏ *When showing you property and assisting you in the purchase of a property, the above agent and firm will represent the SELLER. For more information, see "Seller's Agent Working with a Buyer" in the brochure.*

Agent's Initials Acknowledging Disclosure:

(Note: This brochure is for informational purposes only and does not constitute a contract for service.)

The North Carolina Real Estate Commission
P.O. Box 17100 • Raleigh, North Carolina 27619-7100
919/875-3700 • Web Site: www.ncrec.gov
REC 3.45 3/1/12
00,000 copies of this public document were printed at a cost of $.000 per copy.

FIGURE 7.4 *(Continued)*

Real Estate Commission Rule A.0104(e) requires a broker who is the agent or subagent of a seller and who is working directly with a buyer to disclose to that buyer in writing at first substantial contact that she is working for the seller. This does not mean the agent must disclose his status immediately after she says hello. The North Carolina Real Estate Commission realizes that it is not always necessary or appropriate to make this disclosure at the very "first" contact. The standard is flexible, but agency status of a seller's agent or subagent working with a "customer" (not a "client") must be disclosed in writing before obtaining any confidential information. Once the discussion centers on properties or financing, the buyer is likely to volunteer confidential information; therefore, one should disclose before such a discussion begins.

Although the best approach is to disclose agency status as soon as possible, this is not always practical (e.g., at an open house or on the phone). Not every person who attends an open house is a legitimate buyer. Many people will frequent open houses to simply see what the house looks like inside or perhaps to check out the decorating. Only when a prospect visiting an open house shows a sincere interest in the property would the agent need to provide and review the Commission's brochure *Working with Real Estate Agents*, before the buyer volunteers any confidential information. Agents will have to use their judgment regarding who might be a serious buyer and who is out for entertainment. This is not always easy as many buyers will say things to make the agent think they are just curious and not serious simply to avoid having a salesperson contact them.

It is best to keep the conversation with a phone prospect brief and general by making an appointment to discuss the firm's agency policies and disclosure requirements. Rule A.0104(e) states: "If the first substantial contact occurs by telephone or by means of other electronic communication where it's not practical to provide written disclosure, the broker or salesperson shall immediately disclose by similar means whom he represents and shall immediately, but in no event later than three days from the date of first substantial contact, mail or otherwise transmit a copy of the written disclosure to the buyer." In today's technological environment, many firms will have a copy of the *Working with Real Estate Agents* brochure posted on their website so that the form can be delivered within the appropriate timeframe.

Certain exemptions apply to auction sale situations (Rule A.0104). The auction sale environment does not generally have a history of confusing buyers as to whom the auctioneer represents. The seller's agent is exempt from the agency disclosure requirement; the buyer's agent must disclose orally to the seller or seller's agent at initial contact but has until the time the written contract confirming the buyer's purchase is executed to put the disclosure in writing.

Examples of First Substantial Contact Situations Requiring the Commission's Brochure, Working with Real Estate Agents

Example 1. Macon, a real estate agent, is introduced to Karen at a party where Karen informs her that she is starting to look for a house to buy. Macon informs Karen that she is a real estate agent and would love to work with her. Later, before leaving, Macon approaches Karen and gives her a business card and suggests Karen give her a call if she is interested in having Macon work with her. Two days later Karen calls Macon and sets up an appointment to meet with Macon the next day. The next day Karen meets Macon at her office, where Macon proceeds to ask Karen specific questions about the type of house she is looking for and obtains information that would allow her to determine the price range that Karen can afford. It is at this point that first substantial contact is made, even though there had been several prior contacts between the two parties. None of the prior contacts had risen to the point of disclosure of any personal information that Karen would have not wanted to disclose to a seller.

Example 2. Gary receives a call from Bob Buyer who informs him that a friend highly recommended him as an agent. Bob proceeds to tell Gary what type of house he is looking for and Gary promises to look around and find some suitable properties to show him. The next day Gary meets Bob and shows him several houses. They meet again the next day after and Bob finds the house that would like to make an offer on. At the time that the offer is being prepared, Gary produces the *Working with Real Estate Agents* brochure and asks Bob to sign it along with a buyer agency agreement.

This example is all too common within the real estate world and is a violation of first substantial contact rules. First substantial contact was met within the very first contact between Gary and Bob when details about the type of house Bob was interested in and could afford were addressed. It was clearly violated again as first substantial contact always occurs before you show the first house. This situation illustrates the opportunities for Bob to have disclosed personal information to Gary that he would not have wanted a seller to know.

Example 3. Jaimie is hosting an open house for one of her listings when she is confronted with a large group of relatives who have been visiting with a family member who is a recent homebuyer down the street. Many of these family members are from out of state and have no intention of moving to the neighborhood. The family members are accompanied by several teenagers who are just accompanying the group. During the course of showing the house to this large group, one of the teens asks Jaimie to state what the house payments on this house would be. In this situation, Jaimie is not likely to be of the opinion that the teenager asking the question is a serious and potential buyer. She would not be required to present the *Working with Real Estate Agents* brochure or embark in a full disclosure of buyer and dual agency.

Test Tip!

Working with Real Estate Agents Important Points

- Must be given to the every prospective buyer or seller (residential or commercial) at first substantial contact.
- Brokers should review contents of the brochure.
- Complete the brochure and retain a copy of the acknowledgment panel in the brochure (including any evidence of a customer's refusal to sign the acknowledgment panel)
- Brokers must ascertain in what agency capacity they will work with the consumer before attempting to acquire any personal or confidential information.
- The acknowledgment panel must be retained as part of required trust records for minimum of three years.

First Contact versus First Substantial Contact

As indicated earlier, first substantial contact may or may not be triggered at the very first contact. In many ways the real issue is what constitutes "substantial." One possible way to consider this is when the agent "gets in the buyer's wallet" in the sense that he tries to determine, for example, how much the buyer makes, owes, can afford, or is motivated to spend. It is entirely possible that first *substantial* contact will not occur until after several instances of contact between the agent and the buyer. By comparison, first contact always occurs at the first contact. It is important that agents recognize the difference between the two. The agent must disclose to a seller, at first contact, that he represents the buyer. For example, when an agent calls to make an appointment to show the buyer another agent's listing, the agent must disclose at that first contact whose interests he represents. If the agent represents the buyer, the seller would know not to disclose any personal information he would not want the buyer to know. If the agent indicates that he represents the seller's interest, as a seller subagent, the seller could be more forthcoming in his disclosure of personal information. The seller's agent has to disclose to the buyer, by first substantial contact, that he represents the interests of the seller and that the buyer should not to tell the agent anything that he did not want a seller to know. One illustrates a flexible standard, whereas the other does not allow flexibility at all.

DUTIES AND LIABILITIES OF AGENTS

Agent's Duties to Principal

The broker is in a fiduciary (trust) relationship to the principal. The broker's principal may be a buyer, seller, landlord, or tenant. A firm's broker is also the principal of the agents who work for the firm. The firm's agents are agents of the broker and subagents of the principal whether the principal is buyer, seller, landlord, or tenant. Brokers and agents of firms co-brokering with a listing firm are subagents of the listing firm and the seller if they are not buyer's agents. The broker has certain obligations to the principal as required of every agent by law. The agent's duties and responsibilities are the same whether her principal is the buyer, seller, landlord, tenant, or broker; these duties are described next.

Basic List of Duties of Agents to a Principal

- Loyalty
- Obedience
- Confidentiality
- Skill, Care, and Diligence
- Disclosure of Information
- Accounting

Loyalty

The real estate broker must be loyal to the principal (her client) and must work diligently to serve the best interests of the principal under the terms of the employment contract creating the agency. The agent cannot work for personal interests or the interests of others to the adverse interests of the principal. The real estate broker cannot legally represent any other person in the activities of his agency without disclosing this fact to the principal and obtaining the principal's consent. Therefore, a real estate broker cannot represent buyer and seller in the same transaction and receive a commission from both without the knowledge and informed consent of both buyer and seller. It is a violation of the requirement of loyalty for a broker to purchase the listed property without knowledge by the principal that the broker is, in fact, the purchaser. It is also a violation of agency for a buyer's agent to sell a client a property in which the buyer's agent has an interest without disclosing that interest.

Loyalty requires that the agent put the client's interest above his own. For example, suppose a listing agent receives two offers on a property he has listed: one from another company and one from his customer. The agent gets the whole commission if his customer's offer is accepted. However, the offer from the other company is better. The agent's customer will not pay more than she has offered. Loyalty to the principal (and other laws, rules, and regulations) prohibits the agent from not disclosing the offer from the other company. If the agent did not actually have the offer in hand but knew the offer was coming, loyalty (and other laws, rules, and regulations) would still require him to disclose this to the seller.

Loyalty to a buyer/principal requires the agent to help the buyer find a property that best suits the buyer's need rather than show only the agent's listings or properties that pay the highest commission. If the buyer is paying his agent a flat commission, the commission will not be a significant factor. If the buyer is paying a commission based on a percentage of the sales price or the buyer's agent is being paid by the seller as offered through the listing agreement or MLS, the commission could become a significant factor. Agents should be careful not to let the amount of commission influence the advice and professional services they give to their buyer/clients.

Obedience

The duty of the agent is to obey all reasonable and legal instructions from her seller/principal. For example, the seller may specify that the property be shown only during certain times of the day or that it not be shown on days of religious observance. Or the seller might instruct the agent not to place the listing in the MLS or place signs on the property. If, however, the seller were to instruct the agent to do an illegal act, such as promoting the property in violation of the fair housing laws, the agent could not comply. Because the agent cannot disobey, she

> "Fiduciary duties require all of the following obligations. OLDCAR: Obedience, Loyalty, Disclosure, Confidentiality, Accounting, Reasonable Skill and Care."
> —Bill Gallagher, DREI

must withdraw from the agency relationship, if the seller insists. For example, a buyer/principal may specify that she does not want certain facts about her identity or planned use of the property disclosed. The agent must obey these directives. A buyer/principal may want to make an offer on a property for which she obviously does not qualify. She may instruct her agent not to inform the seller of this fact. The agent cannot obey this request; therefore, she must withdraw from the agency relationship if the buyer will not reconsider his instructions. Although it may seem incomprehensible that anyone would want to make an offer for which they do not qualify, it happens occasionally. Some buyers are eternal optimists, always hoping for a miracle. Although loyalty and obedience are shown as two separate topics, it is customary to use them together as a singular reference (i.e., loyalty and obedience).

Confidentiality

The issue of what can and must remain confidential and what has to be disclosed is essential for a broker. In the case of material facts, the broker must disclose to all parties to the transaction any and all material facts that he either knows or reasonably should have known. Therefore, there is no ability to remain confidential regarding material fact issues. Personal or confidential information is another matter. Brokers must disclose personal/confidential information regarding a third party to the broker's principal but cannot disclose any personal/confidential information regarding the principal to a third party without the knowledge and prior consent of the principal. For example, if a seller discloses to the listing broker a willingness to accept $2,500 less than the asking price, that would constitute personal information regarding the principal. If the seller instructs the listing broker to disclose this fact to the buyer, then no breach of confidentiality has occurred. If a buyer were to disclose to his buyer agent a willingness to pay a higher price than has been offered, sharing this information with the seller would constitute a breach of confidentiality if the buyer had not indicated an approval for such disclosure to the seller.

Skill, Care, and Diligence

In offering services as a real estate broker to the public, the broker is asserting that she possesses the necessary skill and training to perform the employment requirements. In performing duties as an agent, the broker must exercise the degree of skill, care, and diligence the public is entitled to expect of real estate brokers. If a broker's principal incurs a financial loss as a result of the broker's negligence and failure to meet these standards of skill, care, and diligence, the broker is liable for any loss incurred by the principal. Additionally, the principal would not be required to pay compensation to the broker as agreed in the employment contract.

A real estate agent is expected to perform with a degree of care and skill that is common to other reasonable, prudent professionals engaged in similar undertakings. For example, if an agent listed a property several months ago and property values increased or decreased since the time the agent did the market analysis for the seller, the agent has the responsibility to advise the seller of the change in the property's value. A seller relies on an agent's knowledge of the market in setting a list price and has a right to expect her agent to be knowledgeable about the value of his property. Real estate agents have the responsibility to ascertain all material facts concerning a property they are listing, and a buyer's agent also has a responsibility to verify information about a property for a prospective buyer. A *material fact* is any fact about a property that is important to a party in making decisions about a transaction. A material fact can be information about a property's features, defects, condition, or value. The agent should investigate the property for defects as well as all matters relating to the property. She should not offer, however, opinions or give advice outside or beyond her area of expertise. Rather, she should suggest that clients and customers seek competent professional advice when necessary. Matters relating to the property include any public or private restrictions, as well as public policies and proposed legislation affecting the property. For example, if a proposed highway will directly affect a property, this becomes a material fact affecting the property, which the agent should disclose. An agent is responsible not only for *known* facts relating to a property but also for facts that the agent *reasonably should have known*. This means that if an agent is unaware of the proposed highway, but this highway's location has been well publicized in local newspapers, the agent could be held to the *reasonably should have known* doctrine. That is, if a prudent agent using reasonable skill and care would have known about this proposed highway, the agent could be held responsible for having known and disclosed this information.

An agent's duty to perform with care and skill does not end with the signing of a contract. An agent has the duty to perform any tasks required to get the contract to closing. If a buyer is represented by a buyer's agent, the buyer's and seller's agents have the responsibility of working together to ensure that all preparations for closing are completed. If the buyer is not represented by a buyer's agent, the seller's agent may need to perform such tasks as assisting the buyer in obtaining financing. It is in the seller's best interest that the buyer be able to complete the transaction.

An agent's failure to exercise skill, care, and diligence is not only a breach of duties under agency law, it is also grounds for disciplinary action by the North Carolina Real Estate Commission. Brokers and agents should constantly strive to improve their knowledge and skill, considering their real estate license as a license to continue learning. The required eight hours of continuing education is just a beginning; all the knowledge in the world will not help if the agent does not take the time and effort to apply it. This may mean limiting the number of clients to ensure sufficient time to perform all the duties required to bring each transaction to a successful conclusion.

Disclosure of Information

A real estate broker is required to keep the principal fully informed of all important matters involved with the purpose of the broker's employment. Any information that is material to the transaction for which the broker is employed must be communicated promptly and totally to the principal. This requirement for **disclosure of information** is first discussed from the perspective of the seller/listing broker relationship. It includes the requirement that the broker present all offers to the seller. It is the seller's prerogative to decide whether to reject or accept an offer for the purchase of the property. In presenting the offer, the broker should provide the principal with knowledge of all circumstances surrounding the offer. An offer must be presented even though the seller may have several offers under consideration at the time an additional offer is made. The broker must continue to present offers during the term of the listing contract until the property sale is closed. Thus, even if an offer has been accepted, all subsequent offers must be presented until the sale is completed, unless the seller has instructed the broker otherwise.

A broker and any subagents of the seller working through him also have an obligation to the principal NOT to disclose certain information to third parties. A third party is the person in a transaction other than the principal and his agent. In this case, the third party is the buyer. When a buyer's agent is involved, however, the seller becomes the third party to the buyer's agent and any subagents. For example, if a listing broker knows that a seller will actually accept a price for the property lower than the listed price, the broker is obligated NOT to disclose this information to others. The listing broker and any subagents may offer the property only at the listed price. It is a violation of the broker's fiduciary obligation to the seller to offer the property at any price other than the listed price.

Even though one of the broker's obligations to the seller includes the requirement not to disclose certain confidential information to third parties that would be injurious to the seller, the broker cannot misrepresent the property in any way to the buyer. The law provides that liability may be imposed on a broker for the misrepresentation of the existence of a defect in the real estate, for concealing defects in the property, or for failing to disclose the existence of defects (omission). This liability may be imposed for both willful (intentional) and negligent (unintentional) misrepresentation or omission by the broker (see the section "Agent's Duties to Third Parties"). In summary, the agent must disclose to his principal BOTH any and all material facts of which the agent knows or reasonably should have known, including personal information about the third party.

Accounting

A real estate broker must account for and promptly remit as required all money or property entrusted to the broker for the benefit of others. The broker is required to keep adequate and accurate records of all receipts and expenditures of other people's money so a complete accounting can be provided. A real estate broker must maintain a special account for the deposit of other people's money. This account must be titled either "trust account" or "escrow account" and must be maintained in a federally insured depository institution lawfully doing business in North Carolina (see G.S. 93A-6(g)). It is a violation of the law of agency and the Real Estate Licensing Law for a broker to commingle funds or property she is holding in trust for others with personal money or property or with the operating account of her business. A broker is required to deliver immediately to the employing broker all monies received. This is essentially the only duty a broker other than the broker-in-charge (BIC) has regarding accounting for funds and record keeping. See Appendix C for the North Carolina Real Estate Commission's rules regarding accounting.

Agent's Duties to Principal under Real Estate License Law and Commission Rules

Many duties that an agent owes his principal are imposed by Licensing Law as well as the laws of agency. These duties will be addressed more specifically in Appendix C, Licensing Law and Rules and Regulations. Additionally, many of these duties also are owed to third parties, as described in the following section.

- Duty to avoid any willful or negligent misrepresentation of a material fact to the principal, and to disclose to the principal all material facts about which the agent has knowledge or should reasonably have acquired knowledge. (G.S. 93A-6(a)(1) and (3))
- Duty to avoid making any false promises to the principal. (G.S. 93A-6(a)(2) and (3))
- Duty to avoid any undisclosed conflict of interest. (G.S. 93A-6(a)(4); Rule A.0104(d)–(f), (i), and (j))
- Duty to properly account for funds held in trust for the principal. (G.S. 93A-6(a)(7), (12), and (14); Rules A.0116, A.0117, and A.0118)
- Duty to act competently in the performance of services required by the agency relationship. (G.S.93-A-6(a)(8); various rules)
- Duty to avoid improper conduct and to be honest in all dealings with the principal (as well as in dealings with other parties). (G.S. 93-A-6(a)(10))
- Duty to deliver a copy of any written agency and transactional documents to client within three days of broker's receipt of the executed document.(G.S. 93-A-6(a)(13); Rule A.0106)
- Duty to disclose any commissions, referral fees, kickbacks, and similar payments from third parties. (Rule A.0109)

Agent's Duties to Third Parties

The fact that a broker does not represent the interests of the third party does not alleviate her of all responsibilities to that person. The basic responsibilities to the third parties are the same whether they are buyers, sellers, or tenants.

Basic List of Broker's Duties to Third Parties

- Honesty
- Basic Fairness
- Disclosure of Known or Reasonably Known Material Facts

Honesty and Fairness

The broker's primary duty to the principal does not excuse him from his duty to make complete honest representations to the third party. A broker must remember, however, that being honest with a third party does not mean the broker should violate his/her duties to the client. For example the broker has been informed by his seller that he is willing to accept a lower offer of $175,000. In response to a question from the buyer inquiring about how low the seller might consider the broker replies "I don't know but if you would like to present an offer I will be more than happy to present it for you." In reality, it could be argued the broker does know how low his seller would accept and he was not being honest with the third party buyer. In reality if the broker had disclosed the willingness of the seller to accept less than the asking price, the broker would have been in violation of agency disclosure rules. The concept of honesty and fairness does not allow the broker to violate the basic elements of disclosure rules.

MATERIAL FACTS

It is essential that real estate brokers know the basic guidelines for which items constitute a material fact and which items likely do not. In actual practice there will always be items or situations where it is not readily apparent if a material fact exists or not. The best advice will typically be: when in doubt, it is best to disclose.

The following are considered to be material facts:

1. *Facts about the property itself (defects)*: These items typically involve something that needs to be repaired or replaced, such as a defective water heater, malfunctioning dishwasher, a leaking roof, or a house that needs painting. These factors are contained within the property itself and may or may not be readily apparent.

2. *Facts relating directly to the property (surrounding influences)*: These items are not located within the property itself but rather in proximity where they might influence the buyer's decision as to the desirability or attractiveness to purchase the property. Common examples would include plans to widen a

roadway in proximity to a house, air traffic, automobile, industrial, or military noise or odors that would have a perceived negative impact on the property, or even pending actions such as zoning, annexation, or other types of regulations that might be of interest to the buyer.

3. Facts that relate directly to the ability of the agents' principal to conclude the transaction, including foreclosure, short-sale approval necessity, and inability to obtain financing. It is often assumed that simply because someone has signed a contract to either purchase or sell a piece of property that they have the ability to act on it. In today's economic environment, it is quite common to encounter properties that are being foreclosed upon and where the seller may not be able to convey clear title. The same goes for short-sale transactions where the seller is incapable of conveying clear title to the property without first obtaining approval from a third-party lender. This inability to convey clear title, along with any other reason someone cannot perform the contract as presented, constitutes a material fact situation.

4. *Facts known to be of specific importance to a particular party (unique to that particular party)*: This category of material fact items is perhaps the most unique in that it involves things that are not necessarily material facts to another party. In this situation, it is incumbent on the party to make the importance known to their agent. Examples might include a statement by a buyer that he does not wish to purchase a house containing polybutylene plumbing pipe, or that he must be able to construct a fence around the back yard, or perhaps that he does not wish to locate near any registered sex offenders. In each of these instances, the agent would have the obligation to research to see whether this property complies with the buyer's requests or to at least lead the buyer in the appropriate direction so the buyer can ascertain the facts for himself.

> "A licensee owes fiduciary duties to clients. The obligations owed to customers and third parties are the duties of fairness, honesty, disclosure of material facts, and the prompt presentation of offers."
> —Tim Terry, DREI

In addition to the requirements of disclosure of the material facts just listed, agents must be aware of what constitutes personal, sometimes called confidential, information about the third party. When an agent learns these personal information items about the third party, it becomes a material fact that must now be disclosed to the agent's principal.

Again, the North Carolina Real Estate Commission has addressed these as being any one of the following three elements:

1. The third party's willingness to agree to terms other than those stated previously. Perhaps the most common example of this occurs when the seller is willing to accept a price less than what she is asking or when the buyer expresses a willingness to pay a price higher than what she initially offered.

2. Motivation. A person's motivation might injure a party's negotiating capability. A highly motivated buyer might be willing to pay more simply to finalize the deal. Conversely a motivated seller might accept much less than

> "A 'material fact' is anything that would affect a buyer's willingness to buy or a seller's willingness to sell."
> —Steve Robinson

the asking price to avoid some negative outcome. There are some caveats in dealing with motivation, however, as the motivating factors might actually constitute a material fact in a given situation. For example, a seller is placing his house on the market because a relative who works at the highway department privately told him that a proposed highway is going to be built directly behind his house. The seller fears this will negatively affect how much his house will be worth, so he wants to sell before word gets out about the proposed route of the highway. He instructs the agent not to say anything about this because his relative could get in a lot of trouble if word got out. This constitutes a material fact in this case and not personal information.

3. Any information that might influence the principal's decision in a transaction.

As has been stated previously, an agent has an obligation to disclose to his principal any and all material facts that the agent either knows or reasonably should have known in addition to disclosing any personal information about the third party. The agent has a more limited disclosure requirement in regards to the third party. An agent must only disclose any and all material facts that he knows or reasonably should have known to a third party and is not to disclose any personal information about his principal without first obtaining permission from the principal.

The agent's primary duty to the principal does not excuse the agent from his duty to make complete, honest representations to a third party, who is also referred to as the customer.

The agent must inform the third party of all material facts about the property that the agent knows or should reasonably have known by making a prudent and diligent investigation. This requirement of the agent to disclose any and all material facts that he knows or reasonably should have known does not extend to the disclosure of personal (confidential) information of the agent's principal. The North Carolina Real Estate Commission; agency law; and other laws, rules, and regulations require that any disclosure or representation be accurate; that is, any assertions, disclosures, or representation an agent chooses to make must be true. This duty cannot be avoided by a statement in an *agency* agreement, an advertisement, or MLS disclaiming liability. The affirmative duty to disclose material fact applies to any party whether they are clients (principals) or customers (third parties). It also applies to others involved in the transaction, such as attorneys, lenders, and home inspectors. An agent may not disregard information from a reputable source, such as a home inspector and engage another professional to give them a report without the material fact in it while hiding the original defect from the second inspector or the original report from the buyer.

The duty to disclose material fact may be breached by willful or negligent misrepresentation, as well as by willful or negligent omission. An agent's duty to disclose is closely related to duties of honesty, skill, care, and diligence. If an agent performs due diligence to discover problems and honestly communicates these problems to the proper parties, she should have no problems with her duty to disclose.

The agent cannot escape this duty simply by representing a property "as is." Rather, the agent needs to document that he disclosed to the customer what the "as is" conditions really are. Is the agent responsible for information published in the local newspaper relating to conditions that would adversely affect the property, such as a zoning change or annexation to the city? The answer is clearly yes, in that the agent must disclose all pertinent material facts to the third party.

Specifically, Chapter 93A-6 of the North Carolina G.S. prohibits the following acts in regard to the agent's duty to the third party:

1. **Willful misrepresentation**, which is intentionally informing the third party of something the agent knows to be false, or without regard for its truth, such as telling the third party that the property is subject only to county taxes when he knows the property is within the jurisdiction of the city, or when he does not know, and answers anyway as though he did know.
2. **Negligent misrepresentation**, which is unintentionally informing the third party of something that is false but that the agent does not know to be false because he did not exercise proper skill, care, or diligence. The agent is deemed to "reasonably should have known" and if reasonable skill, care, and due diligence had been utilized, this misrepresentation would not have occurred.
3. **Willful omission**, which is deliberately failing to inform the third party of a known defect in the property regardless of whether the agent was asked or not.
4. **Negligent omission**, which is unintentionally failing to inform the third party of something that the agent should have known but did not know because he did not exercise proper skill, care, or diligence. The fact the agent was not asked a question is irrelevant.

Quick Review of Material Facts

An understanding of the meaning of "material fact" is necessary to understand what should and should not be disclosed. Material facts that would affect a buyer's decision to buy or a seller's decision to accept an offer must be revealed to all parties to a transaction, whether they are a buyer, seller, or other agent. Material facts relate to the property itself, such as specified defects, and to external factors outside of the property that may affect the property such as new roads, airplane flight patterns, zoning changes, and commercial development. Agency status does not determine disclosure of these material facts.

Facts relating to a buyer's or seller's ability to complete the transaction also must be disclosed as material fact. The seller's inability to give clear title because of foreclosure proceedings or a buyer's inability to qualify for a loan are both examples of facts affecting a party's ability to complete a transaction. A third type of material fact is one that is known to be important to a party. This type of material fact must be disclosed to that party. For example, a truck driver wants to park his 18-wheeler on his property. The agent knows that restrictive (protective) covenants forbid this. It becomes a material fact. Other facts that have to be disclosed only to the agent's principal are the third party's motivation for entering the transaction and the third party's willingness to pay more or accept less for the property. These are not material facts.

An agent must disclose any interest he has in the property to the third party. Any funds the agent is furnishing to the buyer must be disclosed to the seller. Other offers and the potential for other offers must be disclosed to the seller. The duty to submit all offers to the principal remains until the transaction is closed. Conversely, there is an obligation not to disclose certain things to third parties. Nonmaterial facts include confidential information about an agent's principal that might compromise the principal's bargaining position, such as the principal's motivation for selling or buying or that the principal is willing to pay more or accept less for the property. When the buyer is the principal (client), the agent may not disclose his client's planned use of the property or motivation for purchasing it to the seller (third party) without authorization from the principal to do so.

Misrepresentation

The communication of false or incorrect information is a *misrepresentation*. **Willful misrepresentation** occurs when an agent knowingly communicates information she knows to be false or when an agent provides false information with no regard for the truth of such a statement. For example, an agent who tells a prospective buyer that she can place a mobile home on a vacant lot when she knows the restrictive covenants prohibit mobile homes is guilty of willful misrepresentation. The agent knows that statement of material fact is wrong and lies about it. Likewise, an agent who assures a prospective buyer that a mobile home can be placed on this same lot without knowing whether this is true and without checking to verify the truth of this statement is also considered to have made a willful misrepresentation. In the first example, the agent clearly made a willful misrepresentation by communicating information the agent knew to be false. In the second example, the agent still made a willful misrepresentation (even though the agent did not know the statement to be false) because the agent made the false statement intentionally and without regard for the truth of the statement. That is, the agent knew she did not know, made no effort to find out, and made the statement, anyway. She may try to justify this action by the thought process "If I do not know the answer, it is not a lie," but this would be absolutely wrong. "I don't know, but I'll find out" is a much better answer than lying. Willful misrepresentation is fraud.

While willful misrepresentation involves an intentional act, **negligent misrepresentation** involves an unintentional act. Negligent misrepresentation results from the failure to exercise reasonable care. If an agent does not know the information she is conveying is false, she is guilty of negligent misrepresentation. She thought it was true; therefore, she saw no need to check it out, and she acted in good faith. It doesn't matter. She is guilty, anyway, but not of fraud.

If an agent misinforms a party regarding a material fact about a property and the agent *reasonably should have known* the truth, the agent is guilty of negligent misrepresentation. Remember that an agent is held to a standard based on what a reasonably prudent agent could have been expected to know. Suppose an agent advertises a home and incorrectly states the home's heated square footage based on information on a tax sheet without actually measuring the home personally. If the standard of practice in the local market is for agents to measure a home when they list it, the agent is guilty of negligent misrepresentation.

Agents cannot avoid responsibility for negligent misrepresentation because information was obtained from a seller/principal, another agent, the MLS, or another source. An agent bears the responsibility of investigating facts whenever a reasonably prudent agent should have suspected that the information was incorrect.

A listing agent is held accountable for the accuracy of information placed in an MLS or on a listing information sheet. Because the seller's agent is responsible for compiling this information, the listing agent is held to a high standard regarding accuracy of information on a property. The selling agent, however, still will be held to the "reasonableness" standard and should not rely solely on information provided by the listing agent. For example, if a home is advertised as containing 1,500 square feet of heated living space and it actually contains only 1,483 square feet, the selling agent probably would not be considered negligent. If, however, the home actually contained only 1,300 square feet, the selling agent probably would be considered negligent in not verifying that the stated square footage was accurate, the premise being that a reasonably careful agent would have noticed that the house appeared smaller than the advertised size.

The basis for the imposition of liability in misrepresentation consists of a false representation of a material fact; that is, the fact that the person making the false representation knew or should have known it to be false, the fact that the misrepresentation was made with an intent to induce the party to act or refrain from acting in reliance on the misrepresentation, the fact that the party relied on the misrepresentation in acting or failing to act, and the fact that there was damage to the party who relied on the misrepresentation in acting or not acting. The agent cannot disclaim liability for misrepresentation by using a liability disclaimer in the MLS and in advertising.

Puffing differs from material fact in that it is a statement of opinion, often exaggerated, which should be recognized as an opinion. For example, an agent may describe a property as the most beautiful setting in Wayne County. It may or may not be, but that is only one person's opinion. It is not a representation of material fact. As a result, the use of *puffing* is not considered to be a misrepresentation.

Omission

Unlike misrepresentation, which is the communication of false or incorrect information, **omission** is the failure to disclose information. Omission may be willful or negligent.

Willful omission is the *deliberate failure to disclose material facts known to the agent.* The buyer's agent has a duty to disclose to the seller when the agent is aware of a financial problem that might affect the buyer's ability to close the transaction. This seems to be in conflict with the agent's duty to his principal, the buyer; however, an agent's duty to his principal does not relieve the agent of the duty to disclose material facts and to deal with third parties in a fair and honest manner. A seller's agent is obligated to disclose known material facts about the property to third parties, such as prospective buyers or tenants. Deliberate failure to disclose such known facts constitutes willful omission. **Negligent omission** *is the unintentional failure to disclose material facts that should have been but are not known to the agent.* When an agent knows a material fact and unintentionally rather than deliberately neglects to disclose it, the agent is guilty of negligent omission. The two facts could be the same. The classification of willful or negligent hinges on whether the agent knew the facts and whether he deliberately chose not to reveal the material facts he did know. An agent has a duty to discover and disclose material facts to third parties in a transaction, limited to facts about the property or to matters relating directly to the property and a party's ability to complete the transaction. This duty does not include the obligation to disclose facts not directly related to the property, such as a seller's motivation for selling (unless that motivation is the result of a defect or another fact affecting the property).

North Carolina has several exceptions to the duty to disclose. The fact that a person died or was seriously ill in a house listed for sale or in a residential rental unit is not deemed a material fact that an agent must disclose. However, an agent may not make a false statement about past occupancy. Therefore, the agent must answer truthfully about a past occupant if asked by a prospective purchaser. A special rule applies to deaths resulting from acquired immune deficiency syndrome (AIDS). People with AIDS are considered legally handicapped and, therefore, are a protected class under the federal fair housing laws. If a real estate agent is asked by a prospective purchaser whether the previous occupant had AIDS, she should treat the question as impermissible.

Negligent omission is perhaps the most likely way a real estate practitioner can inadvertently violate his duties to her principals and to third parties, consequently violating the law of agency and the Real Estate Licensing Law. When the agent knowingly misrepresents or omits something, he knows he is doing wrong. When he negligently misrepresents a fact, he does not know the correct answer, but believes the answer he gives to be correct. With negligent omission, the agent may not have a clue he is doing anything wrong. He either does not know the facts or knows the facts but negligently, rather than deliberately, does not reveal them. This act arises from not taking the necessary precautions to stay informed about properties, external factors affecting properties, and issues that would affect a client's or customer's decision to buy or sell. For example, the agent may not make a visual inspection of a property he lists, thereby missing defects that a reasonable, prudent agent would have known and disclosed. An agent may be oblivious to what is going on in his area, such as proposed new roads, zoning changes, or emerging environmental issues. When this knowledge is readily available to the public, the agent has a duty to know and disclose. Some agents may consider themselves too busy to keep up with the current environment or to visually inspect houses they list or sell, but ignorance is no excuse. The only way to avoid negligent omission is to constantly practice due diligence.

Many other duties arise from Real Estate License Law as well as Commission rules:

1. Duty to avoid making any false promises to a third party. (G.S. 93A-6(a)(2) and (3))
2. Duty to properly account for any funds belonging to others that come into the agent's possession. (G.S. 93A-6(a)(7), (12) and (14); Rule A.0107)
3. General duty to act competently in handling real estate transactions. (G.S. 93A-6(a)(8); various rules)
4. Duty to deliver a copy of any written agency and transactional documents to customer within three days of broker's receipt of the executed document. (G.S. 93A-6(a)(13); Rule A.0106)
5. Duty to disclose to third parties for whom services are recommended or procured any referral fees or kickbacks received for such recommendation or procurement. (Rule A.0109)

OTHER LAWS GOVERNING THE DISCLOSURE OF INFORMATION IN REAL ESTATE TRANSACTIONS

Stigmatized and Psychologically Affected Properties

The issue of stigmatized properties does not fit neatly within the confines of whether they constitute a material fact or personal information. They do not indicate a physical defect within the property nor do they relate to a surrounding property or limit the ability of a party to conclude the transaction. They can be very important, however, to the decision-making process as to whether to purchase a particular property. For this reason, these are not considered to be material facts, and an agent is not required to disclose such facts. In the event the agent is asked a direct question, he is not required to answer the question, but if he chooses to do so, the agent must provide a truthful answer. An agent may choose to disclose such facts, unless his principal (the seller) objects. It is not considered a violation to disclose.

There are several examples of stigmatized properties. One of the most common examples is that of a serious illness, or death, of a prior occupant, which is governed by G.S. 39-50 and 42.142. In cases involving old homes, especially in rural areas, it is quite common that a prior occupant has died in the home. In some cases potential buyers are more affected by the fact the death may have occurred as the result of a murder or suicide. It is not unusual that in some high-profile deaths, the house has proven to be quite difficult to sell as well as having its value greatly diminished.

The issue of serious illness, or death, is treated differently in the case of AIDS. AIDS is considered a handicapping condition by federal fair housing laws and is not to be disclosed even in the event the agent is asked a direct question. In the event an agent is asked by a prospective purchaser whether the prior occupant had an HIV infection or AIDS, the agent must respond that according to federal fair housing laws that is considered an impermissible question and that the agent is not allowed to answer it.

In North Carolina the issue of a registered sex offender is now essentially treated the same as the serious illness or death of a prior occupant in that it is not considered to be a material fact and need not be disclosed unless the agent is asked a direct question. One major distinction between examples of serious illness or death and a registered sex offender is that the sex offender is not as likely to be living in the house in question but rather to be living in the nearby vicinity of the property in question. The question quickly becomes one of *"how close is too close?"* That is a question that has no easy answer and varies greatly when you consider areas where the nearest neighbor lives a quarter of a mile away as opposed to a subdivision containing one-fifth-acre lots. In North Carolina, sex offenders must register with the local sheriff's office within 10 days of establishing residence. This information is forwarded to a state-maintained website that is updated daily so that interested people can determine whether registered sex offenders are located nearby. It is highly recommended that agents simply refer prospective buyers to the sex offender registry rather than point registered sex offenders out to prospective buyers. Insurance generally will not protect the agent in the case of misidentifying someone as a registered sex offender. For this reason, agents would be wise to direct interested parties to a search of the state sex offender registry website.

The reputation of the property as being haunted is another issue in which the broker needs to be aware. Although there is no shortage of old houses depicted in movies or in towns all across America that are purported to be haunted, this is not as obvious as a situation in which a person actually died or a registered sex offender lived in the home. In many cases, the buyer will simply shrug off the idea that some house was supposed to be haunted where another buyer will take it quite seriously to the extent they may not want to consider the purchase at all. As in all other cases of stigmatized or psychologically affected properties, the broker is not required to disclose this as a material fact unless asked a direct question, at which time the agent should answer as truthfully as possible. Besides . . . who you gonna call?

Consumer Legislation

The North Carolina Unfair and Deceptive Trade Practices Act prohibits the use of unfair or deceptive practices in commerce. Essentially, the conduct and practices prohibited under this act also are prohibited by the North Carolina Real Estate License Law and case law. Unfair and deceptive acts include the offering of a misleading opinion, failure to disclose a material fact, misleading advertising, misrepresentation, and false inducement. North Carolina allows the awarding of treble damages for violations of this act.

Seller's and Buyer's Responsibilities under Common Law

> Under the doctrine of **caveat emptor** (let the buyer beware), the seller has no disclosure of information obligation to the buyer beyond avoiding intentionally fraudulent acts, including misrepresentation.

A purchaser bears certain responsibilities for investigating a property before entering into a contract. It is for this reason that the seller has the opportunity to indicate "no representation" to many questions contained in the Residential Property and Owners' Association Disclosure Statement.

Although the doctrine of *caveat emptor* may be the acceptable legal standard between buyer and seller, it is not the standard under which the agent must perform. Regardless of the fact that the seller may choose to not disclose problems, even in situations in which the seller actually knows of problems with the house, the agent is still held to a standard that he must disclose things that he either knows or reasonably should know. Therefore, if an agent should have been able to reasonably observe some defective situation, and a buyer is harmed by the agent's negligent omission in not discovering and disclosing the defect, the agent may have violated the Real Estate License Law and may be held civilly liable even though the seller can hide behind caveat emptor.

Although real estate agents are held accountable to consumers for negligent as well as willful misrepresentations and omissions, this fact does not relieve the buyer of all responsibility for verifying easily verifiable information and examining the property. If a defect or misinformation regarding the property is so obvious that a buyer acting in a reasonable manner should have discovered the inaccuracy, the courts may find that the agent did not behave in an unlawful manner under the common law.

Even if an agent's misrepresentation or failure to disclose a material fact when selling a house is found to be insufficient to make the agent civilly liable, this *will not* relieve the agent of responsibility for his actions under the North Carolina Real Estate License Law. When representing a purchaser as a buyer's agent, the agent has the duty to assist the buyer in verifying information and adequately inspecting the property.

> **Test Tip!**
>
> A broker's disclosure responsibilities under License Law are NOT affected by the *doctrine of caveat emptor*.

North Carolina Residential Property Disclosure Act

The Residential Property Disclosure Act applies to most residential real estate transfers and requires sellers (including owners selling their own property and relocation companies) to furnish purchasers with a statutorily prescribed Residential Property and Owners' Association Disclosure Statement.

The seller must answer questions regarding the property with one of three answers: yes, none known, or no representation. Because of the doctrine of *caveat emptor*, if the seller chooses to make no representation as to the condition of the property, the seller is relieved of the obligation to disclose any condition even if the seller knew or should have known it.

Certain properties are exempt from the Residential Property Disclosure Act. These include properties that have never been occupied; transfers by lease with an option to purchase, where the purchaser will occupy the property before the purchase; transfers between co-owners, spouses, or heirs; and transfers by fiduciaries or pursuant to legal proceedings. In the case of the Mineral Oil and Gas Disclosure, there are fewer exempt transfers. This form will be required even in transactions involving properties never occupied; lease with option to purchase, where the purchaser will occupy the property; and cases where the parties agree to exempt this requirement.

The four-page form must be provided to a buyer no later than the time at which the Offer to Purchase and Contract is signed by the buyer. If the disclosure statement is *not* delivered before the time a buyer makes an offer, the buyer has the right to cancel any resulting contract within these limitations:

1. If the disclosure statement is delivered after an offer is made but *before acceptance,* the purchaser has three days after receipt of disclosure to cancel the contract.

2. If the disclosure statement is delivered *after acceptance* (or never delivered), the purchaser has three days after date of acceptance of contract to cancel.

The buyer's right to cancel under the law expires when settlement takes place or the buyer occupies the property. The implementation of the new Offer to Purchase and Contract of Sale has made the purchaser's right to cancel within three days to be meaningless in most transactions, as the buyer would have the right to terminate the contract for any reason up until 5:00 p.m. of the due diligence date.

The act also requires that the seller amend the statement if the seller discovers a material inaccuracy in the statement or if events change so as to render the statement inaccurate at any time up until the time of closing.

The Residential Property Disclosure Act provides that *any* agent involved in an affected residential transaction has a duty to inform her client of the client's rights and obligations under the act. This duty falls on seller's agents and buyer's agents. The act does *not* relieve an agent of responsibility to discover and disclose material facts under the Real Estate License Law.

In addition to advising a seller of his rights and obligations under this law, the Real Estate Commission expects a listing agent to—

1. Provide the seller with the disclosure form, including the Mineral and Oil and Gas Rights Mandatory Disclosure Statement;
2. Assist the seller in assessing the property and completing the form (but should not advise the seller which disclosure option to choose);
3. Deliver the completed disclosure form to prospective buyers or their agents; and
4. Retain a copy of the completed form signed by the buyer in transaction records.

"As Is" Sale

The listing of a property "as is" or an "as is" provision in the contract does *not* relieve the agent of the responsibility to reveal material facts, including defects, to a prospective purchaser. The problem with "as is" is that typically no one really knows what "as is" really is. The new sales contract forms used in North Carolina since January 1, 2011, also tend to make any attempt at an "as is" sale to be a moot point because the buyer has the ability to terminate the agreement before the due diligence date for any reason whatsoever.

Test Tip!

Brokers' disclosure responsibilities under Real Estate License Law are NOT affected by "as is" status.

STATE OF NORTH CAROLINA
RESIDENTIAL PROPERTY AND OWNERS' ASSOCIATION DISCLOSURE STATEMENT

Instructions to Property Owners

1. The Residential Property Disclosure Act (G.S. 47E) ("Disclosure Act") requires owners of residential real estate (single-family homes, individual condominiums, townhouses, and the like, and buildings with up to four dwelling units) to furnish purchasers a Residential Property and Owners' Association Disclosure Statement ("Disclosure Statement"). This form is the only one approved for this purpose. A disclosure statement must be furnished in connection with the sale, exchange, option, and sale under a lease with option to purchase where the tenant does not occupy or intend to occupy the dwelling. A disclosure statement is not required for some transactions, including the first sale of a dwelling which has never been inhabited and transactions of residential property made pursuant to a lease with option to purchase where the lessee occupies or intends to occupy the dwelling. For a complete list of exemptions, see G.S. 47E-2.

2. You must respond to each of the questions on the following pages of this form by filling in the requested information or by placing a check (√) in the appropriate box. In responding to the questions, you are only obligated to disclose information about which you have actual knowledge.

    a. If you check "Yes" for any question, you must explain your answer and either describe any problem or attach a report from an attorney, engineer, contractor, pest control operator or other expert or public agency describing it. If you attach a report, you will not be liable for any inaccurate or incomplete information contained in it so long as you were not grossly negligent in obtaining or transmitting the information.

    b. If you check "No," you are stating that you have no actual knowledge of any problem. If you check "No" and you know there is a problem, you may be liable for making an intentional misstatement.

    c. If you check "No Representation," you are choosing not to disclose the conditions or characteristics of the property, even if you have actual knowledge of them or should have known of them.

    d. If you check "Yes" or "No" and something happens to the property to make your Disclosure Statement incorrect or inaccurate (for example, the roof begins to leak), you must promptly give the purchaser a corrected Disclosure Statement or correct the problem.

3. If you are assisted in the sale of your property by a licensed real estate broker, you are still responsible for completing and delivering the Disclosure Statement to the purchasers; and the broker must disclose any material facts about your property which he or she knows or reasonably should know, regardless of your responses on the Disclosure Statement.

4. You must give the completed Disclosure Statement to the purchaser no later than the time the purchaser makes an offer to purchase your property. If you do not, the purchaser can, under certain conditions, cancel any resulting contract (See **"Note to Purchasers"** below). You should give the purchaser a copy of the Disclosure Statement containing your signature and keep a copy signed by the purchaser for your records.

Note to Purchasers: If the owner does not give you a Residential Property and Owners' Association Disclosure Statement by the time you make your offer to purchase the property, you may under certain conditions cancel any resulting contract without penalty to you as the purchaser. To cancel the contract, you must personally deliver or mail written notice of your decision to cancel to the owner or the owner's agent within three calendar days following your receipt of the Disclosure Statement, or three calendar days following the date of the contract, whichever occurs first. However, in no event does the Disclosure Act permit you to cancel a contract after settlement of the transaction or (in the case of a sale or exchange) after you have occupied the property, whichever occurs first.

---

5. In the space below, type or print in ink the address of the property (sufficient to identify it) and your name. Then sign and date.

    Property Address: _____
    Owner's Name(s): _____
    Owner(s) acknowledge(s) having examined this Disclosure Statement before signing and that all information is true and correct as of the date signed.
    Owner Signature: _____ Date _____, ____
    Owner Signature: _____ Date _____, ____

    Purchasers acknowledge receipt of a copy of this Disclosure Statement; that they have examined it before signing; that they understand that this is not a warranty by owners or owners' agents; that it is not a substitute for any inspections they may wish to obtain; and that the representations are made by the owners and not the owners' agents or subagents. Purchasers are strongly encouraged to obtain their own inspections from a licensed home inspector or other professional. As used herein, words in the plural include the singular, as appropriate.

    Purchaser Signature: _____ Date _____, ____
    Purchaser Signature: _____ Date _____, ____

REC 4.22
REV 7/14

Other Laws Governing the Disclosure of Information in Real Estate Transactions

Property Address/Description: _____

The following questions address the characteristics and condition of the property identified above about which the owner has *actual knowledge*. Where the question refers to "dwelling," it is intended to refer to the dwelling unit, or units if more than one, to be conveyed with the property. The term "dwelling unit" refers to any structure intended for human habitation.

		Yes	No	No Representation
1.	In what year was the dwelling constructed? _____. Explain if necessary: _____			☐
2.	Is there any problem, malfunction or defect with the dwelling's foundation, slab, fireplaces/chimneys, floors, windows (including storm windows and screens), doors, ceilings, interior and exterior walls, attached garage, patio, deck or other structural components including any modifications to them?	☐	☐	☐
3.	The dwelling's exterior walls are made of what type of material? ☐ Brick Veneer ☐ Wood ☐ Stone ☐ Vinyl ☐ Synthetic Stucco ☐ Composition/Hardboard ☐ Concrete ☐ Fiber Cement ☐ Aluminum ☐ Asbestos ☐ Other _____ (Check all that apply)			☐
4.	In what year was the dwelling's roof covering installed? _____ (Approximate if no records are available) Explain if necessary: _____			☐
5.	Is there any leakage or other problem with the dwelling's roof?	☐	☐	☐
6.	Is there any water seepage, leakage, dampness or standing water in the dwelling's basement, crawl space, or slab?	☐	☐	☐
7.	Is there any problem, malfunction or defect with the dwelling's electrical system (outlets, wiring, panel, switches, fixtures, generator, etc.)?	☐	☐	☐
8.	Is there any problem, malfunction or defect with the dwelling's plumbing system (pipes, fixtures, water heater, etc.)?	☐	☐	☐
9.	Is there any problem, malfunction or defect with the dwelling's heating and/or air conditioning?	☐	☐	☐
10.	What is the dwelling's heat source? ☐ Furnace ☐ Heat Pump ☐ Baseboard ☐ Other _____ _____ (Check all that apply) Age of system: _____			☐
11.	What is the dwelling's cooling source? ☐ Central Forced Air ☐ Wall/Window Unit(s) ☐ Other _____ _____ (Check all that apply) Age of system: _____			☐
12.	What are the dwelling's fuel sources? ☐ Electricity ☐ Natural Gas ☐ Propane ☐ Oil ☐ Other _____ _____ (Check all that apply) If the fuel source is stored in a tank, identify whether the tank is ☐ above ground or ☐ below ground, and whether the tank is ☐ leased by seller or ☐ owned by seller. (Check all that apply)			☐
13.	What is the dwelling's water supply source? ☐ City/County ☐ Community System ☐ Private Well ☐ Shared Well ☐ Other _____ (Check all that apply)			☐
14.	The dwelling's water pipes are made of what type of material? ☐ Copper ☐ Galvanized ☐ Plastic ☐ Polybutylene ☐ Other _____ (Check all that apply)			☐
15.	Is there any problem, malfunction or defect with the dwelling's water supply (including water quality, quantity, or water pressure)?	☐	☐	☐
16.	What is the dwelling's sewage disposal system? ☐ Septic Tank ☐ Septic Tank with Pump ☐ Community System ☐ Connected to City/County System ☐ City/County System available ☐ Straight pipe (wastewater does not go into a septic or other sewer system [note: use of this type of system violates state law]) ☐ Other _____ (Check all that apply)			☐
17.	If the dwelling is serviced by a septic system, do you know how many bedrooms are allowed by the septic system permit? If your answer is "yes," how many bedrooms are allowed? _____ ☐ No records available	☐	☐	☐
18.	Is there any problem, malfunction or defect with the dwelling's sewer and/or septic system?	☐	☐	☐
19.	Is there any problem, malfunction or defect with the dwelling's central vacuum, pool, hot tub, spa, attic fan, exhaust fan, ceiling fans, sump pump, irrigation system, TV cable wiring or satellite dish, garage door openers, gas logs, or other systems?	☐	☐	☐
20.	Is there any problem, malfunction or defect with any appliances that may be included in the conveyance (range/oven, attached microwave, hood/fan, dishwasher, disposal, etc.)?	☐	☐	☐

Owner Initials and Date_____ Owner Initials and Date_____
Purchaser Initials and Date_____ Purchaser Initials and Date_____

	Yes	No	No Representation

21. Is there any problem with present infestation of the dwelling, or damage from past infestation of wood destroying insects or organisms which has not been repaired?.. ☐ ☐ ☐

22. Is there any problem, malfunction or defect with the drainage, grading or soil stability of the property?.......... ☐ ☐ ☐

23. Are there any structural additions or other structural or mechanical changes to the dwelling(s) to be conveyed with the property?.. ☐ ☐ ☐

24. Is the property to be conveyed in violation of any local zoning ordinances, restrictive covenants, or other land-use restrictions, or building codes (including the failure to obtain proper permits for room additions or other changes/improvements)?... ☐ ☐ ☐

25. Are there any hazardous or toxic substances, materials, or products (such as asbestos, formaldehyde, radon gas, methane gas, lead-based paint) which exceed government safety standards, any debris (whether buried or covered) or underground storage tanks, or any environmentally hazardous conditions (such as contaminated soil or water, or other environmental contamination) which affect the property?... ☐ ☐ ☐

26. Is there any noise, odor, smoke, etc. from commercial, industrial, or military sources which affects the property? ☐ ☐ ☐

27. Is the property subject to any utility or other easements, shared driveways, party walls or encroachments from or on adjacent property?.. ☐ ☐ ☐

28. Is the property the subject of any lawsuits, foreclosures, bankruptcy, leases or rental agreements, judgments, tax liens, proposed assessments, mechanics' liens, materialmens' liens, or notices from any governmental agency that could affect title to the property?.. ☐ ☐ ☐

29. Is the property subject to a flood hazard or is the property located in a federally-designated flood hazard area? ☐ ☐ ☐

30. Does the property abut or adjoin any private road(s) or street(s)?... ☐ ☐ ☐

31. If there is a private road or street adjoining the property, is there in existence any owners' association or maintenance agreements dealing with the maintenance of the road or street?.. ☐ ☐ ☐

If you answered "yes" to any of the questions listed above (1-31) please explain (attach additional sheets if necessary):
_____
_____
_____

In lieu of providing a written explanation, you may attach a written report to this Disclosure Statement by a public agency, or by an attorney, engineer, land surveyor, geologist, pest control operator, contractor, home inspector, or other expert, dealing with matters within the scope of that public agency's functions or the expert's license or expertise.

The following questions pertain to the property identified above, including the lot to be conveyed and any dwelling unit(s), sheds, detached garages, or other buildings located thereon.

	Yes	No	No Representation

32. To your knowledge, is the property subject to regulation by one or more owners' association(s) or governing documents which impose various mandatory covenants, conditions, and restrictions upon the lot, including, but not limited to obligations to pay regular assessments or dues and special assessments? If your answer is "yes," please provide the information requested below as to each owners' association to which the property is subject [insert N/A into any blank that does not apply]: ☐ ☐ ☐

•(specify name)_____ whose regular assessments ("dues") are $_____ per _____. The name, address, and telephone number of the president of the owners' association or the association manager are_____
_____
_____.

•(specify name)_____ whose regular assessments ("dues") are $_____ per _____. The name, address, and telephone number of the president of the owners' association or the association manager are_____
_____
_____.

* If you answered "Yes" to question 32 above, you must complete the remainder of this Disclosure Statement. If you answered "No" or "No Representation" to question 32 above, you do not need to answer the remaining questions on this Disclosure Statement. Skip to the bottom of the last page and initial and date the page.

Owner Initials and Date_____   Owner Initials and Date_____
Purchaser Initials and Date_____   Purchaser Initials and Date_____

			No
	Yes	No	Representation

33. Are any fees charged by the association or by the association's management company in connection with the conveyance or transfer of the lot or property to a new owner? If your answer is "yes," please state the amount of the fees:_____ ☐ ☐ ☐

34. As of the date this Disclosure Statement is signed, are there any dues, fees, or special assessments which have been duly approved as required by the applicable declaration or bylaws, and that are payable to an association to which the lot is subject? If your answer is "yes," please state the nature and amount of the dues, fees, or special assessments to which the property is subject: _____ ☐ ☐ ☐

35. As of the date this Disclosure Statement is signed, are there any unsatisfied judgments against, or pending lawsuits *involving the property or lot to be conveyed*? If your answer is "yes," please state the nature of each pending lawsuit, and the amount of each unsatisfied judgment:_____ ☐ ☐ ☐

36. As of the date this Disclosure Statement is signed, are there any unsatisfied judgments against, or pending lawsuits *involving the planned community or the association to which the property and lot are subject*, with the exception of any action filed by the association for the collection of delinquent assessments on lots other than the property and lot to be conveyed? If your answer is "yes," please state the nature of each pending lawsuit, and the amount of each unsatisfied judgment:_____ ☐ ☐ ☐

37. Which of the following services and amenities are paid for by the owners' association(s) identified above out of the association's regular assessments ("dues")? (Check all that apply).

	Yes	No	No Representation
Management Fees	☐	☐	☐
Exterior Building Maintenance of Property to be Conveyed	☐	☐	☐
Exterior Yard/Landscaping Maintenance of Lot to be Conveyed	☐	☐	☐
Common Areas Maintenance	☐	☐	☐
Trash Removal	☐	☐	☐
Recreational Amenity Maintenance (specify amenities covered)_____	☐	☐	☐
Pest Treatment/Extermination	☐	☐	☐
Street Lights	☐	☐	☐
Water	☐	☐	☐
Sewer	☐	☐	☐
Storm water Management/Drainage/Ponds	☐	☐	☐
Internet Service	☐	☐	☐
Cable	☐	☐	☐
Private Road Maintenance	☐	☐	☐
Parking Area Maintenance	☐	☐	☐
Gate and/or Security	☐	☐	☐

Other: (specify) _____

Owner Initials and Date_____   Owner Initials and Date_____
Purchaser Initials and Date_____   Purchaser Initials and Date_____

STATE OF NORTH CAROLINA
MINERAL AND OIL AND GAS RIGHTS MANDATORY DISCLOSURE STATEMENT

Instructions to Property Owners

1. The Residential Property Disclosure Act (G.S. 47E) ("Disclosure Act") requires owners of certain residential real estate such as single-family homes, individual condominiums, townhouses, and the like, and buildings with up to four dwelling units, to furnish purchasers a Mineral and Oil and Gas Rights Disclosure Statement ("Disclosure Statement"). This form is the only one approved for this purpose.
2. A disclosure statement is not required for some transactions. For a complete list of exemptions, see G.S. 47E-2(a). **A DISCLOSURE STATEMENT IS REQUIRED FOR THE TRANSFERS IDENTIFIED IN G.S. 47E-2(b),** including transfers involving the first sale of a dwelling never inhabited, lease with option to purchase contracts where the lessee occupies or intends to occupy the dwelling, and transfers between parties when both parties agree not to provide the Residential Property and Owner's Association Disclosure Statement.
3. You must respond to each of the following by placing a check √ in the appropriate box.

MINERAL AND OIL AND GAS RIGHTS DISCLOSURE

Mineral rights and/or oil and gas rights can be severed from the title to real property by conveyance (deed) of the mineral rights and/or oil and gas rights from the owner or by reservation of the mineral rights and/or oil and gas rights by the owner. If mineral rights and/or oil and gas rights are or will be severed from the property, the owner of those rights may have the perpetual right to drill, mine, explore, and remove any of the subsurface mineral and/or oil or gas resources on or from the property either directly from the surface of the property or from a nearby location. With regard to the severance of mineral rights and/or oil and gas rights, Seller makes the following disclosures:

		Yes	No	No Representation
_____ Buyer Initials	1. Mineral rights were severed from the property by a previous owner.	☐	☐	☐
_____ Buyer Initials	2. Seller has severed the mineral rights from the property.	☐	☐	
_____ Buyer Initials	3. Seller intends to sever the mineral rights from the property prior to transfer of title to the Buyer.	☐	☐	
_____ Buyer Initials	4. Oil and gas rights were severed from the property by a previous owner.	☐	☐	☐
_____ Buyer Initials	5. Seller has severed the oil and gas rights from the property.	☐	☐	
_____ Buyer Initials	6. Seller intends to sever the oil and gas rights from the property prior to transfer of title to Buyer.	☐	☐	

Note to Purchasers

If the owner does not give you a Mineral and Oil and Gas Rights Disclosure Statement by the time you make your offer to purchase the property, or exercise an option to purchase the property pursuant to a lease with an option to purchase, you may under certain conditions cancel any resulting contract without penalty to you as the purchaser. To cancel the contract, you must personally deliver or mail written notice of your decision to cancel to the owner or the owner's agent within three calendar days following your receipt of this Disclosure Statement, or three calendar days following the date of the contract, whichever occurs first. However, in no event does the Disclosure Act permit you to cancel a contract after settlement of the transaction or (in the case of a sale or exchange) after you have occupied the property, whichever occurs first.

Property Address: _____

Owner's Name(s): _____

Owner(s) acknowledge having examined this Disclosure Statement before signing and that all information is true and correct as of the date signed.

Owner Signature: _____ Date _____, ____

Owner Signature: _____ Date _____, ____

Purchaser(s) acknowledge receipt of a copy of this Disclosure Statement; that they have examined it before signing; that they understand that this is not a warranty by owner or owner's agent; and that the representations are made by the owner and not the owner's agent(s) or subagent(s).

Purchaser Signature: _____ Date _____, ____

Purchaser Signature: _____ Date _____, ____

REC 4.25
1/1/15

Lead-Based Paint Disclosure

> 🔑 For properties built before 1978, the seller or lessor of a property and any agents representing sellers or lessors must provide to the buyers or lessees the U.S. Environmental Protection Agency pamphlet *Protect Your Family from Lead in Your Home*, must disclose the presence of any known lead-based paint, and must provide any available records or reports pertaining to lead-based paint or hazards.

The agent has a duty to her principal, whether her principal is a seller/lessor or buyer/lessee, to make her aware of rights and responsibilities under the Residential Lead-Based Paint Hazard Reduction Act of 1992 (see Chapter 6 for a full discussion of the act).

Synthetic Stucco Disclosure

Synthetic stucco is a term commonly used to describe the exterior finish product that is properly known as exterior insulating and finishing system (EIFS). This so-called synthetic stucco differs from real stucco in several ways. The most important is that unlike real stucco, synthetic stucco, or EIFS, is impervious to water. This means that no water is absorbed by the EIFS. Unfortunately, it also means that any water that enters through a seam or break in the finish becomes trapped in the wall. This trapped water can cause significant damage to wall framing because of excess moisture. For this reason, the North Carolina Real Estate Commission considers the existence of synthetic stucco to be a *material fact* that should be discovered and disclosed to prospective buyers.

If siding material looks like stucco, the agent has a duty to investigate and ascertain whether the material is real or synthetic stucco. If an agent knows or "reasonably should have known" that a structure was *formerly* sided with synthetic stucco, this is also considered a material fact, which the agent has a duty to disclose. An example of a situation in which it might be determined that an agent "reasonably should have known" that a structure was formerly sided with synthetic stucco is if all homes in a subdivision were sided with this product. The former existence of synthetic stucco must be disclosed even if the agent has reliable information that all moisture damage was corrected, although the agent can provide this repair information to the prospective buyer.

If a structure has or formerly had synthetic stucco, the agent has a duty to *disclose* its existence, *explain* the fact that there have been numerous instances of moisture damage to structures sided with this product, and recommend that the buyer have the property inspected by a qualified inspector for excess moisture and moisture damage.

Liabilities and Consequences of Agent's Breach of Duties

There are four major areas of accountability of an agent's failure to fulfill his agency duties:

1. *Accountability to the North Carolina Real Estate Commission for disciplinary action against a licensee.* The Commission is the only regulatory body that can take action against an agent's license. The actions include, in order of severity, reprimand, censure, suspension, and revocation.
2. *Civil Liability of Agent.* A **civil penalty** may result from a suit for monetary damages or injunctive relief. Thus, if an agent's action costs a client or prospect any financial loss, the injured party may sue to recover damages.
3. *Criminal Liability of Agent.* In more serious cases, such as fraud, the agent can be held liable for a criminal penalty by the court system. In addition, violation of the real estate law is a criminal violation (a misdemeanor) and is punishable by fine or imprisonment.
4. *Civil Liability of Principal (for Agent's Misconduct).* One of the basic premises of agency is that the principal can be held liable for the actions of his agent. If an agent's actions cause the third party to incur damages, the third party may be able to recover civil damages from the agent's principal in addition to the agent.

Agent's Handling of Their Own Property

As we complete the discussion regarding the agency responsibilities of the licensee, it is important to review some key elements. The first is that the licensee always will be considered to be under the jurisdiction of the North Carolina Real Estate Commission whether he is transacting for his own property or that of someone else. For example, a seller in North Carolina enjoys the rights of caveat emptor and is allowed to remain silent on material fact issues even when that person knows there is a problem with the property. Much like our court system, that rule does not require people to take the stand, but if they do, the requirement is they cannot perjure themselves. In other words, you don't have to say anything, but if you choose to do so, then you have to tell the truth. Licensees, on the other hand, are required to disclose any and all material facts they know or reasonably should know. An individual who holds an *active or inactive* real estate license is subject to License Law and Commission Rules whenever he or she is engaging in real estate transaction, even as a party to the transaction.

The issue of a licensee having to disclose material facts and not having the rights of *caveat emptor* is an important consideration when completing the Residential Property Owner and Disclosure Statement as the form contains numerous questions that allow for a *"no representation"* answer. There is no requirement that a licensee not be allowed to answer "no representation," but there IS a requirement that the licensee disclose material facts as required. Certainly, it is easiest for the licensee to simply answer "Yes" or "No" to all questions, but as long as the licensee is truthful in disclosing all material facts required, he does NOT have to do so on this particular form. One advantage is that the licensee likely will want to have evidence of such disclosures in writing and answering the questions on this form is convenient. For example, what if a licensee simply did not honestly know whether some particular condition existed and wanted to indicate "no representation" on the form. This would be allowed as an answer choice.

The question is also raised if the licensee *must* always disclose his ownership interest in the property. This is somewhat confusing to many people, but the reality is that the Commission does NOT require the licensee to always disclose his ownership interest. Clearly, the Commission strongly recommends such disclosure but currently has no rule in place requiring such. Note that REALTORS® must disclose the fact they are a REALTOR® as mandated by the REALTOR® Code of Ethics.

As indicated earlier in this chapter, a licensee who is selling his own residential property will NOT be allowed to serve in the capacity of a buyer agent. As such, this would prohibit the role of a dual or designated agency role as well. The licensee CAN act in the capacity of seller agent. He will NOT be permitted to act as buyer agent even if the purchaser allows such to occur.

DUAL AGENCY

Dual Agency Basics

> A dual agency exists when a real estate firm attempts to represent the buyer as well as the seller in the same transaction.

It is actually quite commonly practiced in North Carolina as many agents/firms do not wish to lose out on potential commissions to firms that practice only buyer or seller agency. These firms prefer to keep it all "in house" and represent anyone and everyone who may need to buy or sell a house.

One of the challenges for many agents is recognizing when dual agency exists and when it does not. Dual agency most typically exists when a firm, representing a buyer as the buyer agent, has a buyer who is interested in a property that is listed with that firm. It does NOT exist when a firm has the listing and one of its agents, who is working with a buyer but does not have any type of oral or written buyer agency agreement to represent that buyer, attempts to show and sell the listing to that buyer. It is not sufficient that the agent is *working* with the buyer. She must actually be *representing* the buyer, whether it is an exclusive or nonexclusive relationship. In this case, the firm would represent ONLY the seller's interest and would not represent the buyer's interests at all. In a co-brokered transaction, there would be no question of dual agency because the seller and buyer agents do not work for the same firm. It is not a requirement that both dual agents work from the same branch office, but rather they must both work for the same firm.

Inherent Potential Conflicts of Interest

The practice of dual agency is more complicated than an agency relationship in which the agent represents only one party, whether it's the buyer or the seller. The question is how to fulfill all of the duties the agent owes to both a principal as well as the third party when the same firm represents both parties. It is helpful to remember *the firm is the agent*. As mentioned previously in this chapter, an agent owes the *principal* a wide range of duties, including loyalty, obedience, skill, care, and diligence, accounting, and disclosure of material facts. By contrast, the agent owes the *third party* fairness, honesty, avoidance of misrepresentation, and disclosure of material facts. The issue that arises in dual agency is identifying who the principal is and who the third party is. In dual agency, does the firm have two principals or does it have two third parties?

As discussed previously in this chapter, basic agency law requires the agent to disclose any and all material facts the agent knows or reasonably should know to all parties regardless of who the agent represents or whether or not the agent is asked. This material fact disclosure requirement states the agent must disclose material facts to both the party the agent represents as well as to the party that he does not. The requirement for disclosure of personal information is challenging in that the agent must disclose personal, or confidential, information about the third party to the principal, but the agent cannot disclose personal, or confidential, information about the principal to the third party without first receiving the principal's consent. It is therefore considered that personal, or confidential, information about the third party creates a material fact that must be disclosed to the principal. That is not the case, however, regarding personal information about the principal because the agent cannot disclose that information without the consent of the principal. The issue then becomes what should the agent do when he possesses personal information about one principal that would benefit the other principal but is prohibited from disclosing personal information about the principal to the other party?

Unintentional, Undisclosed Dual Agency

G.S. 93A-6(a)(4) clearly states that real estate agents are prohibited from "acting for more than one party in a transaction without the knowledge of all parties for whom he or she acts." In addition, the Real Estate Commission Rule A.0104(d) carries this further when it states that a firm, or broker, cannot represent more than one party in a transaction without the written authority of each party. Very often this situation will arise from an agent having a written authorization to represent one party, but the agent acts in such a manner to benefit the other party without the principal's knowledge or consent. In this case, the agent has a written agreement to represent one party but "behaviorally" represents the other. This is clearly a violation of "loyalty" to the principal.

Consider the following example: An agent is showing a property, in which she is the listing agent, to a buyer for whom she does not have an oral or written agency agreement to represent. To facilitate a quick sale, the agent tells the buyer that the seller is desperate to sell and that the buyer probably could buy this house for much less than the listed price. This is clearly a case in which the agent and firm have a written contractual agreement to represent the seller but have behaviorally benefited the buyer without the knowledge and consent of the seller, thus constituting an undisclosed dual agency.

Another illustration of an unintentional, undisclosed dual agency situation would involve self-dealing. In this case, the agent has an agreement to represent one party but later acts in such a way as to benefit herself without the principal's knowledge or consent.

Consider another example: An agent has a listing on a parcel of land. After the property has been listed, the agent learns there are plans to construct a major highway nearby that would likely greatly increase the value of the land. Rather than inform the seller, the agent proceeds to purchase the property for her own investment without disclosing the potential highway construction to the seller. In this case, the agent has a written agreement to represent the seller but has acted in such manner as to represent herself to the detriment of her principal. This would also constitute an example of an unintentional, undisclosed dual agency.

How to Handle Intentional, Disclosed Dual Agency in North Carolina

The advent of buyer agency in the mid-1990s created the need for some type of dual agency agreement between the parties. Before this time, every broker was considered to represent the interests of the seller, and no one represented the buyer. With the gaining popularity of buyer agency, firms found themselves often with a buyer they represented expressing interest in a house where the firm represented the seller. As mentioned, the question rapidly became how to best handle the conflict of personal information disclosure to the principal when the firm represented both the buyer as well as the seller. A variety of laws and rules emerged to provide some degree of guidance on this matter, including the Restatement of the Law, 3d, Agency, North Carolina Licensing Law G.S. 93A-6(a)(4), and Real Estate Commission Rule (58A.0104). In general, these combined regulations stated that dual agency could be practiced legally if it was disclosed in advance and had the written and "informed consent" of each party. Furthermore, according to NCAR standard agency agreements, the firm shall not disclose the following to the other party:

- That either party will agree to a price, terms, or condition other than those offered.

- The motivation of either party unless such disclosure is required by law or rule.
- Any information either party has identified as confidential unless such disclosure is required by law or rule.

These named items have been mentioned previously in this chapter and constitute the basic list of items considered as personal or confidential information.

In essence, dual agency is permitted in cases in which the firm has disclosed to each party that dual agency exists, has obtained the prior informed written consent of each party for whom the firm acts, and has acted in a *fair and balanced manner*. The agreement to limit the disclosure of certain information to the principals, shown earlier, means that both parties have agreed to concede to the same restrictions and neither party should emerge with either an advantage, or disadvantage, from such limitations. As a result, it is important for agents to discuss with their parties, before dual agency consent, the fact the agent will not act in the role of an advocate for either party, but rather, as a facilitator for the flow of information between the two opposing parties.

It is an important element of dual agency to understand when the agreement has to be reduced to writing. Real Estate Commission Rule 58A.0104(d) requires *all dual agency agreements to be in writing*. Additionally the rule stipulates, "A real estate broker representing one party in a transaction shall not undertake to represent another party in the transaction without the written authority of each party." This clearly indicates the dual agency agreement must be in writing from the inception of the agreement; however, there is one notable exception. In cases in which the buyer agency agreement is legally allowed to be oral, the dual agency agreement is allowed to be oral as well until such time as the buyer agency agreement is required to be reduced to writing. Do not confuse oral with not being able to discuss the ability to engage in dual agency or its ramifications to the principal. The disclosure, and informed consent, still must be obtained before *first substantial contact* and engaging in dual agency acts, but it will not be required to be reduced to writing until such time as the nonexclusive buyer agency agreement has to be in writing, such as when the agent presents an offer on behalf of the buyer or wishes to limit or restrict the buyer's ability to work with another agent. The dual agency relationship, just like buyer agency, must be disclosed to the other party at the point of *first contact*.

Designated Agency

Certainly, one of the major areas of concern for principals is the reduction of the agent's obligations to provide the full range of agency disclosures. Because of this concern, the Commission adopted rules allowing a variation of dual agency, known as *designated agency*, in 1997. In essence, the parties reach an agreement in which the principals agree, "I'll let you keep your agent if you let me keep mine," where the agent will remain an advocate for his principal. In other words, the dual agent can act as though he is engaged in a single-agency transaction and the principal retains a more full representation. This is accomplished by the firm having to first adopt a company policy that will permit designated agency to be practiced as well as the details of how that will be accomplished. The firm will designate one agent to specifically represent the interests of the seller and the other to represent the interests of the buyer. Once the two agents are designated to represent a particular party, they will be able to more specifically advocate for their principal even though the firm is still technically in a dual agency role. This designation may be allowed only when the principals have provided their informed consent before such designation.

> Some important features of designated agency exist, and agents will need to have a good working knowledge of these facts and limitations.
>
> - Designated agency does not eliminate dual agency, but rather it is simply a type of dual agency.
> - Designated agency is applicable only to in-house transactions, although it is not restricted between different branch offices of the same firm. An agent based in one branch office of a multi-office firm is not prohibited from engaging in designated agency with another agent from one of the other branch offices of the firm.
> - An individual agent cannot engage in designated agency. It is limited to situations in which one individual agent will be designated to specifically represent the interests of the seller and the other agent to represent those of the buyer.
> - Permission to engage in designated agency is required to be obtained at the same time that dual agency consent is obtained. Ideally this will be addressed in the listing and buyer agency forms at the time they are signed. In cases in which the buyer agent is working under a legal oral agreement, the designated agency must be reduced to writing at such time as the dual agency agreement is required to be reduced to writing.
> - An agent is not allowed to practice designated agency in cases in which the agent has obtained personal or confidential information about the other party before becoming designated. In such cases, the agent would have been required to disclose such personal information to his principal once the designated agency relationship was implemented. It does not matter if the agent agrees to not disclose the personal information that was previously obtained. If there was personal information known about the other party before accepting such a designation, the relationship will not be allowed. The agent could continue to practice as a dual agent, but designated agency would not be an option.

"When a BIC and a provisional broker are involved in a transaction representing a seller and a buyer they will always be dual agents. Dual agency is permitted. Only designated dual agency is prohibited."
—Steve Robinson

- A BIC will not be allowed to engage in designated agency with a provisional broker (PB) under his supervision. The reasoning is that the BIC, in his supervisory capacity, has the right and obligation to know of the important facts in any transaction, thus potentially giving him an unfair advantage in a designated agency situation. There is no prohibition for a BIC to engage in designated agency with a PB from another of the firm's branch offices, as that BIC does not have supervisory responsibilities over the agents of another office. The BIC can engage in designated agency with a nonprovisional broker from his own office because he would not have the same supervisory responsibilities over the "full broker" as he would over the PB. Certainly, a PB could engage in designated agency with other "full brokers" or PBs without limitation unless by company policy or the fact of having possession of prior personal information about the other party.
- Designated agency must commence before submission of the first offer. Once the first offer has been submitted, the agent will not be allowed to convert to a designated agency role.

There are some practical issues involving designated agency that agents and firms will need to keep in mind. It will be rather difficult for designated agency to be practiced in a small office due to the fact everyone seems to know everybody else's business, making it very likely that personal information will be obtained about the other party before designation. Firms will need to be careful to protect clients' personal information. Once the designation has been made, any personal information learned by either agent is to be shared with the agent's principal. Every firm that wishes to engage in designated agency should adopt strict policies regarding the sharing of personal information in the office. A good policy guideline should focus on sharing information about the property and not the client.

Individual Broker Dual Agent

Commission rules allow individual agents to engage in dual agency and enjoy the same benefits as a designated agent. If an individual listing agent has a buyer client that expresses interest in the agent's listing, the agent is permitted to engage in dual agency with the same limitations on the sharing of her client's personal information as discussed in the previous section on designated agency. As always, these limitations must be discussed, and agreed upon, by the clients before such a relationship may proceed.

"An individual broker dual agent cannot become an advocate for either party and is required to treat the parties fairly, equally and impartial."
—Tim Terry, DREI

DUTIES AND LIABILITIES OF PRINCIPALS

Principal's Duties to Agent

The principal has definite duties to the agent. The principal must cooperate with the broker—that is, act in good faith. Therefore, a seller must cooperate with the listing broker in making the property available for inspection by prospective buyers at reasonable times. The principal is required to compensate the agent at the time when the agent accomplishes what she contracted to do. When the seller is the principal, the agent's duty is to find a buyer who is ready, willing, and able to purchase the property at terms acceptable to the seller. When the agent brings an offer from a buyer for the full terms of the listing contract, does the owner have to sell the property? No, but the agent has earned a commission. Compensation or the source of compensation alone does not determine the agency relationship. A seller/principal can pay the buyer's agent or provide for the buyer's agent to be paid out of the transaction's proceeds without creating any agency relationship with the buyer's agent.

Principal's Duties to Third Parties

Caveat emptor is a legal maxim that means "let the buyer beware." In the context of a real estate transaction, this doctrine places the burden on the buyer to inspect the property, and absolves the seller of responsibility for any defects that should have been discovered during a reasonable inspection. The law places no duty on the seller to disclose a defect. The only duties owed by a seller are a duty not to conceal defects (such as painting over a water stain to conceal evidence of a leak) and a duty to be truthful in the disclosures a seller *chooses* to make. The consumer protection concept of implied warranty—that the property is as it is represented—is the current prevailing force in legal actions.

Liabilities and Consequences of Principal's Breach of Duties

Because the principal is not likely to have a real estate license, he would not be accountable to the Real Estate Commission for disciplinary action as the agent would be, but the principal is fully responsible to the public—through the courts—for both civil and criminal wrongdoings. He is further responsible to the agent if he withholds information or gives false information that causes the agent relying on the information to be liable for misrepresentation to a third party. The principal must indemnify the agent for any legal action brought against the agent by an innocent third party by repaying the agent's losses.

The principal is also responsible to third parties for the actions of the agent. For example, if the principal properly discloses material facts to his agent, who then willfully misrepresents or neglects to disclose to the third party, the principal may be civilly liable for the wrongful actions of his agent. However, he may have some legal recourse against the agent for his losses. These civil wrongs are considered to be torts.

Summary of Important Points

1. An agent is a fiduciary and therefore has the following obligations to the principal: loyalty; obedience; skill, care, and diligence; accounting; and

disclosure of all material facts. The broker becomes an agent by the employment authority of the listing agreement, the property management agreement, the buyer agency agreement, or the tenant agency agreement. The principal and the agent have duties to each other under the contract.

2. All agents have the affirmative duty to represent the property honestly, fairly, and accurately to all prospective purchasers, making full disclosure of any facts that would adversely affect the property.

3. Subagency relationships are viewed in two contexts. The first is the in-house situation, in which a sales associate works for a broker. The sales associate is simultaneously an agent for the broker and a subagent of all the principals who have employed the broker as their agent. The second subagency situation occurs in the listing/selling context with the cooperating broker of another firm. All cooperating selling brokers and their sales associates are presumed to be subagents of the seller/principal unless a buyer has employed the cooperating broker through the use of a written buyer agency agreement and that fact is disclosed at first contact between the firms. In both subagency situations, the subagent has the same duties to the principal as the primary agent has.

4. A buyer agency relationship is created when a broker is hired under a buyer agency agreement to represent the buyer. The buyer's agent owes the duties of agency to the buyer.

5. Disclosed dual agency exists when a real estate firm attempts to represent the buyer and the seller in the same transaction with the full knowledge and consent of both. Undisclosed dual agency is a violation of North Carolina Real Estate Law. A designated agency is a type of dual agency in which the firm acts as a dual agent, but one agent in the firm represents only the seller's interest and another only the buyer's interest.

6. The National Association of REALTORS® requires all multiple listing services owned by boards and associations to allow participants to offer subagency, buyer's agency, or both at the discretion of the listing broker.

7. The North Carolina General Statutes specifically prohibit willful misrepresentation, negligent misrepresentation, willful omission, and negligent omission. The agent is accountable not only to the North Carolina Real Estate Commission, but also to the civil and criminal courts.

8. The brochure *Working with Real Estate Agents* is created and published by the North Carolina Real Estate Commission. All agents must review this document with sellers, potential sellers, buyers, and potential buyers at first substantial contact. Sellers, potential sellers, buyers, and potential buyers must sign the acknowledgment panel. The agent retains this panel for three years from the time it is signed or three years after the finalization of the transaction, whichever comes later.

Review Questions

Answers to the review questions are in the Answer Key at the back of the book.

1. A real estate listing agent advised a buyer (customer) that a property was zoned for the type of commercial use for which the buyer intended to use the property. Relying on the agent's advice, the buyer contracted to purchase the property. In making the statement regarding the zoning, the agent did not know what zoning applied to the property. The buyer subsequently learned that the zoning was such that he could not use the property as he intended. Which of the following is correct?
   A. The agent committed an act of misrepresentation and is liable to the buyer for any loss the buyer suffered as a consequence.
   B. Since the agent did not know the true facts regarding the zoning, no misrepresentation of the property to the buyer took place; therefore, the agent is not liable.
   C. Since the listing agent was not representing the interests of the buyer in this case, he is not liable for his statement.
   D. Commercial transactions are exempt from liability for brokers since these type facts can easily be determined by the buyer.

2. Misrepresentation occurs when:
   A. the party making a false representation knows it to be false.
   B. the party making a false representation does not know if the statement is true or false, but should have known.
   C. the party making the false representation makes no effort to determine if it is true.
   D. all of the above.

3. A broker is NOT held liable for misrepresentation or omission of material fact when:
   A. the broker fails to disclose a defect he reasonably should have known.
   B. the broker, who does not know the answer to the buyer's question, answers without regard for the facts of the situation.
   C. the misrepresentation or omission was made to a buyer the broker did not represent.
   D. the broker was not aware of the mis-statement and there was no way he reasonably could have been expected to know.

4. A contract in which a property owner employs a broker to market her property creates an agency relationship between which of the following?
   A. buyer and seller
   B. buyer and broker
   C. broker and seller
   D. broker, seller, and buyer

5. An agent's duties to the principal include all of the following EXCEPT:
   A. loyalty.
   B. accountability.
   C. obedience.
   D. legal advice.

6. Which of the following is NOT an agency relationship?
   A. the relationship between a sales associate and the broker with whom the associate is associated
   B. the relationship between a listing broker and a cooperating broker acting as a subagent of the seller
   C. the relationship between a seller's agent and a buyer's agent
   D. the relationship between a seller and the listing agent

7. A real estate broker presented an offer to the property owner during the listing term for the listed price payable in cash with no contingencies and a 10% deposit. This offer met all the terms of the listing agreement. In this situation, which of the following is correct?
   A. The property owner is required to accept the offer.
   B. The listing brokerage company is legally entitled to the commission agreed upon in the listing contract only if the property owner accepts the offer.
   C. The property owner is not required to accept the offer but is legally obligated to pay the listing company the commission agreed upon in the listing agreement.
   D. The buyer can sue the property owner for damages if the owner refuses to accept the buyer's offer.

8. A broker should present:
   A. all offers even if the property is currently under contract to be sold.
   B. only those offers that appear to be in the seller's best interest.
   C. only those offers the broker knows have been properly pre-qualified for the mortgage.
   D. only those offers that are for more money than the seller has indicated as his minimum for consideration.

9. The employment authority of the listing agreement:
   A. binds the broker to the best interests of the seller.
   B. gives the broker authority to screen offers for the seller.
   C. gives the broker the authority to either sell or rent the property.
   D. authorizes the broker to reject any offers that the broker feels are unacceptable.

10. A listing broker has the duty to disclose to the buyer (customer):
    A. the amount of the commission.
    B. the seller's financial status.
    C. the seller's reason for selling.
    D. structural defects.

11. Working for Beth Buyer under an exclusive buyer agency agreement, Babs Broker of ABC Realty sells Beth a house listed by XYZ Realty. Sabrina Seller pays Babs Broker's commission through Sabrina's listing agent at XYZ Realty, Lois Lister. Which one of the following statements is TRUE?
    A. Beth Buyer is Babs Broker's customer.
    B. Beth Buyer is Lois Lister's client.
    C. Sabrina Seller is Lois Lister's customer.
    D. Beth Buyer is Babs Broker's client.

12. The Residential Property Owners and Disclosure Statement (RPOADS) form must be provided to purchasers in which of the following transactions?
    A. transaction where the purchaser already occupies the property
    B. transaction where the parties agree to exempt each other from compliance
    C. new construction never occupied
    D. property purchased where the buyer will not be the new occupant

13. Which of the following statements is true regarding the Residential Property Disclosure Act?
    A. The Act relieves agents of the responsibility to discover and disclose material facts regarding a property.
    B. Once a seller has completed the disclosure statement, he is under no obligation to amend the statement if the condition of the property changes.
    C. A seller of residential property who does not complete the Residential Property Disclosure Statement may be fined $500.
    D. A disclosure statement should be provided to the buyer no later than the time at which an offer to purchase and contract is signed by the buyer.

14. Barbara, an agent at ABC Realty, presented an offer to Sandra of XYZ Realty. Barbara is a buyer's agent, and Sandra is the listing agent. Sandra presents a counteroffer from her seller to Barbara, who contacts her buyer. At 11:30 a.m., the buyer accepts the counteroffer in Barbara's presence. Meanwhile, at 11:45 a.m. on the same day, Sandra's seller receives a better offer, which she wants to accept, and tells Sandra to withdraw the counteroffer. Sandra immediately communicates this to Barbara before Barbara can tell her of her buyer's acceptance. Which of the following is (are) true?
    A. Sandra's seller cannot withdraw the counteroffer since Barbara has been notified of the acceptance of the counteroffer.
    B. Sandra's seller can withdraw the counteroffer since neither Sandra nor her seller has been notified of acceptance.
    C. Sandra's seller cannot withdraw the counteroffer because it was accepted before the seller received the new offer.
    D. Sandra must provide Barbara's buyer with an equal opportunity to match or exceed the new buyer's offer.

15. Sally Smith and Bob Broker are dual agents at XYZ Realty. Bob presented an offer to Sally on one of her listings. Sally presents a counteroffer from the seller to Bob, who contacts his buyer/client. At 11:30 a.m., the buyer accepts the counteroffer in Bob's presence. Meanwhile, at 11:45 a.m. on the same day, the seller receives a better offer, which he wants to accept, and tells Sally to withdraw the counteroffer. Sally immediately communicates this to Bob before Bob can tell her of the buyer's acceptance. Which of the following is true?
    A. Sally's seller cannot withdraw the counteroffer because acceptance in Bob's presence provides notification to the seller.
    B. Sally's seller can withdraw the counteroffer because the new offer is a better offer.
    C. Sally's seller can withdraw the counteroffer because Bob did not notify Sally of the acceptance before the seller asked Sally to withdraw the counteroffer.
    D. Sally must provide Bob's buyer with an equal opportunity to match or exceed the new buyer's offer.

16. Which of the following statements is true concerning designated dual agency?
    A. A broker-in-charge can be a designated dual agent if the other agent is a provisional broker under his direct supervision.
    B. A broker cannot be appointed as a designated dual agent if the broker has prior knowledge of confidential information about the other party to the transaction.
    C. Only the broker-in-charge can serve as a designated agent for both parties in a transaction.
    D. There is no provision that allows for an oral designated dual agency to exist.

17. Oral buyer agency:
    A. is no longer permitted in North Carolina since buyer agency agreements must be in writing from the inception.
    B. is permitted in North Carolina until the time an offer is presented on the buyer's behalf.
    C. must be converted to writing no later than the time of acceptance of offer by the seller.
    D. is allowed only if the buyer agrees not to work with another agent.

18. The *Working with Real Estate Agents* brochure:
    A. must be presented at first substantial contact.
    B. has the same legal weight as the listing or buyer's agency contract.
    C. should not be used if the customer desires oral buyer agency.
    D. should be presented at the same time as the Offer to Purchase.

19. Designated agency is permitted:
    A. only when the designated agents each work within the same office for the firm.
    B. as long as the designated agent does not learn any confidential information about the other agent's principal after becoming designated.
    C. when the listing agent is also the buyer agent and has the written consent of both parties.
    D. if the designated agent is not directly supervised by the other designated agent.

20. Which type of agency agreement does NOT have to be in writing from the time of its inception?
    A. Exclusive Right to Sell agreements
    B. Exclusive Right to Represent Buyer agreements
    C. Non-exclusive buyer agency agreements
    D. Property management agreements

21. Which of the following is NOT an appropriate action for the broker to undertake when acting as a seller subagent?
    A. disclosure of all known material facts even when disadvantageous to the seller
    B. preparing a CMA for a buyer
    C. showing the buyer some comparables of similar properties to the one listed
    D. disclosing to the seller how high the buyer is willing to pay

22. Which of the following must be disclosed to a buyer/customer by the listing agent?
    A. the reason the seller needs to sell quickly
    B. the death of the previous occupant from AIDS
    C. only the material facts the seller has authorized the agent to disclose
    D. all material facts including those detrimental to the seller

23. Which of the following does NOT constitute a material fact?
    A. a readily noticeable crack in the foundation
    B. the location of a landfill nearby the house that cannot be observed
    C. pending zoning changes
    D. willingness of the seller to accept a lower offer

24. The typical listing contract is a form of:
    A. universal agency.
    B. general agency.
    C. special agency.
    D. free agency.

25. An agent meets prospective buyers at an open house he is holding. The buyers walk through the property but have no interest in the house because it does not serve their needs. Which of the following best describes the broker's role in this transaction?

    A. The broker was required to provide them a copy of the *Working with Real Estate Agents* brochure as soon as they entered the open house.

    B. The broker was not required to provide the buyers with a copy of *Working with Real Estate Agents* brochure as he was considered a buyer agent already.

    C. The broker would only have to provide the *Working with Real Estate Agents* brochure at the time the buyers decided to actually make an offer.

    D. The broker was not required to provide a copy of the *Working with Real Estate Agents* brochure or discuss agency alternatives with them.

26. Allen Agent of ABC Realty is working with Betty Buyer under an oral buyer agency agreement. He shows her a house listed by Beatrice Broker of XYZ Realty. Betty wants to buy the home. Which contract does Allen prepare first?

    A. the Residential Property Owners and Disclosure Statement
    B. the Oral Agency Conversion
    C. the Exclusive Right to Represent Buyer
    D. the Offer to Purchase

CHAPTER 8
AGENCY CONTRACTS (SALES) AND RELATED PRACTICES

KEY TERMS

Do Not Call Registry
exclusive agency
exclusive buyer agency contract
exclusive right to sell
extender clause
flat fee listing

multiple listing service (MLS)
net listing
nonexclusive buyer agency agreement
open listing
override clause protection period

procuring cause of sale
protection agreements
ready, willing, and able buyer
retainer fee
success fee

LEARNING OBJECTIVES

At the conclusion of this chapter, you should be able to:

1. Define types and characteristics of the listing contract.
2. Describe function and agency characteristics of the multiple listing service.
3. Define the essential and common provisions of the listing contract.
4. Define the broker's entitlement to commission.
5. Describe the various commission arrangements.
6. Describe the termination of listing contracts.
7. Describe the property data sheet.
8. Describe the North Carolina Residential Property Disclosure Act and related forms.

IN THIS CHAPTER

The North Carolina Real Estate Commission requires all agency agreements to be in writing from their inception with some limited exemption for some buyer agency agreements. We will explore the more commonly used agency agreements in use today as well as address issues relating to compensation,

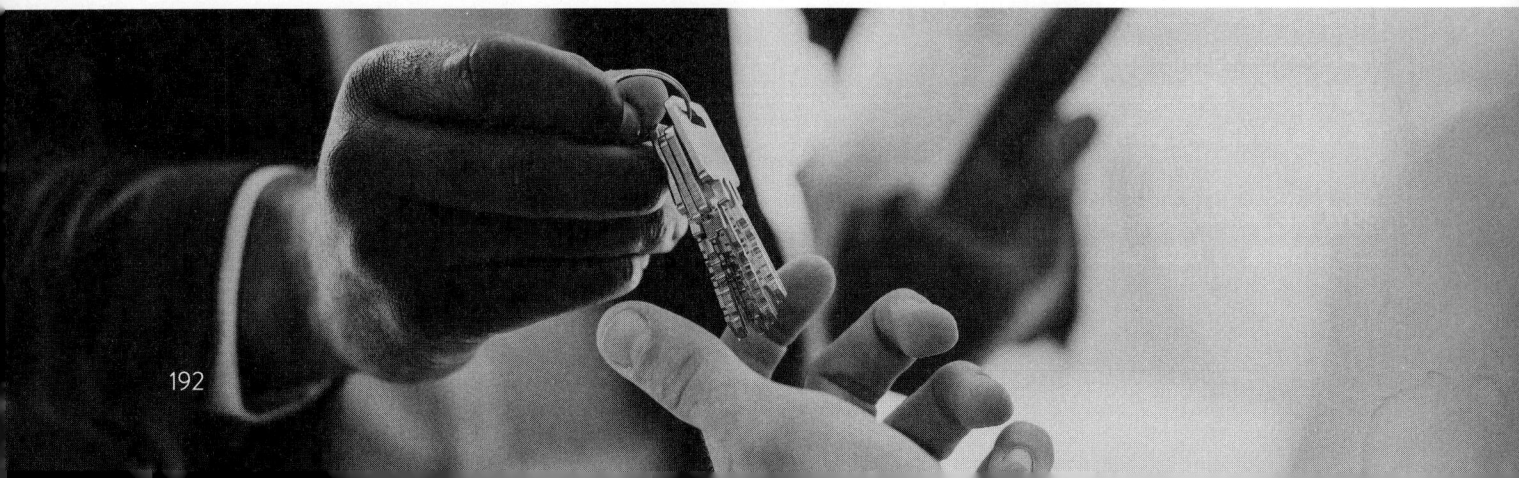

duties of both buyer and seller agents, measurement of square footage by using acceptable standards of practice, and other issues facing the real estate agents in the field.

IMPORTANT NOTE REGARDING MATH CALCULATIONS FOR THIS CHAPTER

This chapter includes numerous areas of math computations that are extremely important for students to learn. Students should anticipate being tested on all of the following areas:

- Conversion of acreage to square footage and vice versa
- Square footage of variously shaped buildings and parcels of land with straight-line sides (squares, rectangles, trapezoids, and right triangles)
- Square yards
- Cost/price per square foot/square yard/front foot
- Calculation of sales price needed to net "X" amount to seller
- Estimating net to seller with various sales prices
- Calculation of net profit/loss to seller on sale

BROKER'S ENTITLEMENT TO A COMMISSION

Three primary elements govern a broker's right to claim a commission:

- License in good standing
- Valid listing agreement
- Procurement of "ready, willing, and able buyer"

First, the broker must have a valid real estate license. Unlicensed people are not entitled to claim a commission in any negotiation of real estate and would be in violation of the real estate licensing statutes if they did so. Second, there must be a valid written contract of employment (listing) between the principal and the agent. Third, an agent must produce a ready, willing, and able buyer according to the listing terms or such other price, terms, and conditions that the parties later agree to. Whereas there is no particular form this employment authority must take, there must be a definite promise to pay a commission or fee to the broker. Depending on the form of the listing arrangement, the broker may need to demonstrate that he was the procuring cause of the sale. The **procuring cause of sale** requires an agent to prove that he was the primary foundation upon which negotiations have begun, the predominant factor in bringing about a conclusion to the transaction, and not in violation of agency law. This is especially true of the open listing, but it is not a requirement of the **exclusive right to sell** listing (see the section "Exclusive Right to Sell Listing") because in that situation, the agent is to be paid his commission regardless of who sells the property, even the seller.

The exclusive agency listing falls somewhere in between. It entitles the broker to a commission if he or another broker is the procuring cause of sale but not if the owner sells the property himself. The exclusive right to sell listing contract *entitles the broker to a commission if the property is sold during the listing term,* even though the broker may not have been the procuring cause of the sale.

Under the listing contract, the broker's entitlement to commission is determined by two tests. The first is the **ready, willing, and able** test. If the broker brings a buyer to the seller who is *ready to buy, is willing to buy, and is able (financially) to buy under the price, terms, and conditions of the listing contract, or such other price terms and conditions as are later agreed upon,* the broker is legally entitled to the commission. The broker has done the job he was hired to do in the listing contract, that is, find a buyer who will pay the listed price in cash under all terms of the listing agreement. When the broker does this, the commission has been earned under the ready, willing, and able test. It does not matter whether the owner actually agrees to sell the property to the prospective buyer. Remember, the seller can reject any offer.

Note that price is not the only term of the listing contract. For example, the listing contract may require that the sale be closed within 60 days after the contract date, and the buyer may want a delayed closing date six months from the contract. Also note that contracts that contain financing or other contingencies do not qualify the buyer as able until the contingency is met. For example, if a buyer cannot close because he cannot obtain the contingent financing, the agent is not due a commission.

The next test, and the more usual way in which a broker becomes legally entitled to a commission, is on the basis of acceptance. When a broker brings a buyer who is accepted by the seller, the broker is legally entitled to the commission. This acceptance could be on some price or terms other than the listed price in cash. For example, the listing contract may have specified $80,000 to be payable in cash. A broker may bring an offer to the seller of $78,500, and the offer may not be for payment in cash but may be subject to the assumption of the seller's existing mortgage by the buyer. If the seller accepts this offer, the broker is legally entitled to the commission on the basis of acceptance. The broker has brought the seller a buyer who is acceptable to the seller. Both tests are not required. This is an either–or situation. The broker earns a commission *either* on the basis of having brought a ready, willing, and able buyer *or* on the basis of having brought a buyer who is accepted by the seller.

In-House Sales

Commissions to be paid to sales associates in a real estate office are established by an agreement between the real estate firm and the associates. This is true whether the brokers are licensed with or without provisional status attached to their license. Under the usual agreement, sales associates can earn two commissions. One is a commission for listing the property. When a sales associate sells a property she has listed, the sales associate receives both the listing and the selling commission. At closing, the seller's commission is paid in full to the listing firm, which subsequently splits the fee among the respective parties. For example, assume a $6,000 total fee paid by a seller. A possible split of this might be as follows: Company A lists the property, and Company B finds a buyer. Company A gets $3,000, half of which goes to the brokerage firm and half to the listing agent; Company B receives the other half and gives 60% to the selling agent and retains 40% for the brokerage firm. If, however, Agent A with Company A lists and sells the property, Company A gets both parts of the commission, which is then split with Agent A according to Company A's commission split agreement. The listing company decides what split to offer to co-brokering companies. Each company determines what split it offers its agents. Commission splits cannot be set by multiple listing service (MLS), the National Association of REALTORS® (NAR), or any group of people such as firm principals. To do so constitutes an antitrust violation.

Co-Brokered Sales

When a property is sold as the result of cooperating efforts of two real estate firms, one of which is the listing firm and the other the selling firm, the commission agreed upon in the listing contract is paid to the listing broker by the property owner. The listing broker with the selling broker share this commission on a predetermined basis. The division of the commission to be received by the listing broker should be determined by agreement between the two cooperating brokers before the participation of the selling broker in the transaction.

The NAR requires board and association MLS participants to offer cooperation as follows.

MLS participants will be required to offer cooperation with accompanying compensation to other participants. This cooperation can take the form of offers to subagents, buyer agents or to both, at the listing broker's discretion. Listing brokers will still have the choice of offering subagency, of offering cooperation to buyer agents, or of making both offers. While all offers of cooperation must be accompanied by an offer of compensation, the listing broker may offer differing amounts to subagents and to buyer agents. As before, offers to particular brokers may be modified by advance, written communication to the other broker.

Now that MLS arrangements allow listing brokers to offer both subagency and buyer's agency, it is important that the position of the selling agent as agent for seller or agent for buyer be disclosed when the selling agent first contacts the listing agent for information or an appointment.

Co-Brokerage with an Out-of-State Broker

It is permissible for a broker to share a commission with a broker who is licensed in another state, as long as the out-of-state broker does *not* engage in activity that requires a real estate license while in North Carolina. For example, an out-of-state broker can refer a prospective buyer to a North Carolina broker and the North Carolina broker can pay a referral fee to the out-of-state broker if a sale results. The Real Estate License Law provides that an out-of-state broker cannot come into North Carolina and show the property, participate in negotiations, or conduct other activities that require a license. A nonresident may obtain a nonresident license in North Carolina by meeting the requirements set out in North Carolina General Statute (G.S.) 93A-9(a) (see Appendix C).

A limited broker's license (for commercial transactions only) may be issued to a nonresident who is licensed in another state or territory and who affiliates with a resident North Carolina broker. The North Carolina broker cannot be a provisional broker and must personally and actively supervise the nonresident broker to ensure compliance with North Carolina real estate law and rules. See North Carolina G.S. 93A-9(b) in Appendix C.

Earning Commission as a Buyer's Broker

Historically, the seller pays the brokerage fee to the listing broker, who then splits the fee with the agent who actually listed the property and with the cooperating broker if another company was involved in the sale. With the advent of buyer brokerage, however, the issue of a buyer's broker's compensation becomes a little more complex. A buyer's agent must have a buyer agency agreement, and this agreement controls how the buyer's agent is compensated.

The North Carolina Buyer Agency Agreement (see Figure 8.5, Exclusive Right to Represent Buyer) allows the agent to receive a **retainer fee.** This is *usually a small monetary compensation paid by the buyer up front for an agent's services.* A **success fee** or buyer's agent's compensation *may be received from the seller if the seller or seller's agent has offered compensation to the buyer's agent(s).* This agreement also provides for the buyer to directly compensate the buyer's broker.

Legal Payment to Expired or Inactive Broker

One of the basic requirements of License Law is that of requiring the broker to have an "active" licensing status at all times when engaging in real estate brokerage activities. In the event that license status is either expired or inactive, the broker must immediately cease all activities for which a license is required. This brings into question the compensation that may have been earned by a licensee during the time the license was active but compensation is being offered, or requested, after the inactive or expired status is achieved. Compensation may be paid to a broker whose license is on inactive or expired status (or perhaps a broker who is now deceased) ONLY IF the compensation is for work the broker licensee completed while the license was on active status AND the broker ceased brokerage activity when the license status changed to expired or inactive. For example, a broker licensee failed to complete the required continuing education classes before the June 10 deadline and now finds his license will be placed on inactive status on June 30. He has a closing scheduled for July 2. He asks another agent in his office to finish up the transaction and attend the closing. The firm will be allowed to compensate both the inactive as well as the active brokers. The inactive broker may be only compensated for work completed before the June 30 deadline, and the active broker will be compensated for work after that time. In the case of a referral fee, the compensation may be paid to the referring broker licensee, who is now on inactive or expired status, IF the license status was active on the date the referral was made. In other words, for this rule, the referral fee is earned the date of the referral and not the date of closing.

General Requirements for Agency Contracts (Sales and Rental Transactions)

According to North Carolina G.S. 93A-13 and Real Estate Commission rule A.0104(a), all agency agreements must be in writing from their inception with the possible exception of buyer agency agreements under certain conditions. Buyer agency agreements and tenant agency agreements are allowed to be oral until such time as the agent attempts to make her agreement exclusive or for a definite period of time as well as until such time as the agent attempts to present an offer on behalf of her buyer. At the point the agent attempts to make her agreement exclusive, or to present an offer on behalf of her buyer (tenant), the agency agreement must be reduced to writing. No exceptions. In the event that an agent wants to proceed with a nonexclusive buyer, or tenant, agency agreement in an oral format, it remains critical that the agent address all of the key elements that normally would have appeared in the written form.

Other types of agency agreements, such as exclusive listing agreements, must be in writing from the inception, and there is no allowance for them to be in an oral format. From the seller's perspective, any agreement to allow dual agency is addressed within the listing agreement. When a buyer enters into an oral buyer agency agreement, it is imperative the agent address the issue of dual agency permission. As long as the agent and buyer are operating legally under an oral nonexclusive buyer agency agreement, it is permissible to agree to allow oral dual agency. At such time as the buyer agency agreement must be reduced to writing, so too must any dual agency component of that agreement at the same time.

The general rule is that agency agreements must be for a specific period of time and are not allowed to have any automatic renewal or extension clauses contained within them. The basic premise is they must expire automatically without any requirement that the principal give notice of intent to terminate. In the case of an oral buyer agency agreement, the parties would not be allowed to stipulate a specific period of time without triggering the requirement the agreement be reduced to writing. The general interpretation is that these agreements are for a reasonable period of time and can be terminated at any time without prior notice. There is a notable exception within the property management agreements, however. Property management agreements are allowed to contain automatic renewal clauses as long as the principal is afforded the right to give proper notice to terminate the automatic renewal component.

Note that an agent having one type of agency agreement is not protected in cases in which an additional agency agreement is required. In the past few years, it has become increasingly common for sellers who have encountered difficulty in selling their homes to instruct the agent to attempt to rent the property as well as try to sell it. The seller further instructs the agent that if a tenant should enter a rental agreement, the agent is to provide property management services for the seller, in which case the agent would be paid a management commission. In this case, to be properly documented according to the Commission guidelines, the agent would be required to have a written property management agreement in addition to the written listing agreement.

It is also a requirement that all agency agreements shall contain the Commission-prescribed written language addressing nondiscrimination. The current wording to be contained in listing agreements is as follows: "THE BROKER SHALL CONDUCT ALL BROKERAGE ACTIVITIES IN REGARD TO THIS AGREEMENT WITHOUT RESPECT TO RACE, COLOR, RELIGION, SEX, NATIONAL ORIGIN, HANDICAP, OR FAMILIAL STATUS OF ANY PARTY OR PROSPECTIVE PARTY."

NOTE: The REALTOR® agency forms contain additional language regarding sexual orientation although that language is not part of the Commission requirement.

LISTING CONTRACTS AND PRACTICES

Definition and Purpose of Listing Contracts

A listing contract is a contract whereby the owner of property *employs* a real estate broker to find a buyer for his property. This contract creates an agency relationship in which the seller is the principal and the broker is the seller's special agent for this particular purpose. The listing agreement forms a special, or limited, agency relationship.

No transfer of interest in real property occurs under this contract. No title passes between the seller and the broker. Therefore, this contract does *not* fall under the Statute of Frauds in North Carolina. However, North Carolina G.S. 93A-13 and Real Estate Commission Rule A.0104(a) both require it to be in writing to be enforceable and require it to specify a time period. The written contract clearly spells out that the broker has been hired by the seller and sets forth all the terms and conditions of employment. The written listing contract substantially reduces lawsuits between brokers and property owners concerning matters of the broker's employment. Additionally, the Commission requires the insertion of the nondiscriminatory language clause presented earlier.

Types of Listing Contracts

Listing agreements vary from the "full-service" model in which agents are to provide a wide variety of necessary services to assist the seller completely in the sale of his property, to a more "limited services" model that varies from the basic insertion of the listing into the MLS, up to models that provide more service but not to the level of the full-service model. Last, in basic **protection agreements,** the seller enters an agreement to compensate the agent but is not obligated to an employment model.

Full-Service Listing Agreements

Three primary types of full-service listing models are used in the real estate industry. These are primarily based on who has the right to sell the property and earn compensation.

Open Listing

Under an **open listing,** *the seller lists a property with the assistance of one or more brokers. The broker generating the sale is entitled to the commission. If, however, the owner sells the property (not to a prospect generated by the broker), the owner owes no commission.*

There is no limit as to the number of firms that may accept an open listing. This type of listing is not beneficial to the owner or the broker. Usually, a broker cannot afford to spend advertising dollars and sales staff time on an open listing. The broker is competing with the owner and with every other broker who has an open listing on the property or who learns about the availability of the property and obtains an open listing. This type of listing also can lead to disputes among brokers about commissions and can present legal problems for the owner.

Exclusive Agency Listing

In an **exclusive agency** listing, *the property is listed exclusively with one broker.* If the broker effects a sale of the property, she is legally entitled to the commission agreed upon. Under this type of listing, however, *if the owner sells the property, the broker earns no commission.* In actual practice, when an agent is referring to an "exclusive listing," she generally is not referring to this type of listing but rather to the exclusive right to sell that follows. This type of listing is somewhat better than the open listing in that only one broker is involved, but that broker is still competing with the owner. The broker's advertising programs, including the office's "For Sale" sign on the property, may generate prospects for the owner.

Exclusive Right to Sell Listing

This is the best type of listing contract from the standpoint of both the broker and the seller. Under this listing contract, the property is listed with only one broker (exclusive). If the property is sold by anyone during the term of the listing contract, the broker is legally entitled to the commission. The seller is legally obligated to pay the broker's commission if the broker, the seller, or some third party effects a sale of the property during the term of the listing contract.

> **Test Tip!**
>
> The term "exclusive" listing is often used as an abbreviation for exclusive right to sell but should never be used to describe an exclusive agency.

> **Test Tip!**
>
> In an exclusive right to sell listing, the seller will owe the listing firm a commission *regardless* of who sells the property, even the seller.
>
> The exclusive right to sell listing contract benefits the owner because the broker is secure enough in the opportunity to earn a commission that she can afford to spend time and advertising dollars to effect a quick and satisfactory sale of the listed property. Also, with the agreement of the seller, the broker can put the listing in an MLS (see later discussion), providing significantly increased market exposure for the property. This type of listing is often referred to as an "exclusive listing."

Limited Service Listing Contracts

The limited service listing contracts vary widely with different brokers in providing services that may be limited to a singular act, such as insertion of the listing into the local MLS, to more involved services, which can allow for much more activity on the part of the broker that may be close to the services required under full-service agreements. More details about this type of agreement are provided later in this section.

Protection Agreement

In this arrangement, *a seller agrees to pay a fee to a broker for the sale to a specific buyer but does not list the property for sale to the general public.* These type agreements usually are utilized when dealing with a seller for a single transaction, such as a For Sale by Owner (FSBO). For example, a broker may have a client who is particularly interested in a specific type of home in the Mortgage Heights Subdivision, even though no such homes are currently on the market. A given owner may consent to have his property shown to this specific buyer, but only under established terms. Another common example is found in the commercial real estate environment in cases in which a seller has erected signage advertising a parcel of property with contact information followed by a statement, such as "brokers protected" or "call XYZ Corporation or your broker." Such language signifies a willingness for the seller to pay the broker a commission. It is wise for any broker to clarify exactly what the compensation amount and terms are to be before venturing too far into this type of situation. For an example of a common **protection agreement**, refer to the Unrepresented Seller Disclosure and Fee Agreement form in Appendix F.

Listing Contract Provisions

Figure 8.1 shows an Exclusive Right to Sell Listing Agreement. In this contract, the broker is promising to do certain things: to use his best efforts to procure a buyer; to take all actions considered appropriate to effect a satisfactory sale of the property, including advertising the property; and to provide the owner the benefit of the office staff's knowledge of financing and other real estate matters. Additionally, the broker promises to enter the listing in the MLS. The illustrated Exclusive Right to Sell Listing Agreement is broken down into numbered sections for reference to the discussion of the contract that follows.

The parties are identified at the top of the form.

Section 1 establishes the term of the contract, which provides for automatic termination of the agreement on a given date without prior notice by the principal to the agent.

Section 2 contains the property description. The street address and subdivision are included primarily for the purpose of enabling agents of the listing company to locate the property and to provide the same information to cooperating brokers acting as agents of the listing company. The additional descriptions identify the property by reference to recorded documents. These references eliminate any doubt as to the specific property listed.

Section 3 lists fixtures included in the transaction that will convey free of liens. Examples of fixtures that convey unless excluded are range/stove/oven, light fixtures, ceiling fans, drapery and curtain rods, outdoor plants and trees, and any object attached or affixed to the property. The "total circumstances test" (see Chapter 2) explains how to determine whether an item is a fixture. When the seller wishes to exclude a listed item or any item meeting the definition of a fixture, it must be entered as an exception in the space provided. The agent should

EXCLUSIVE RIGHT TO SELL LISTING AGREEMENT
[Consult "Guidelines" (Form 101G) for guidance in completing this form]

This EXCLUSIVE RIGHT TO SELL LISTING AGREEMENT ("Agreement") is entered into between _____ as Seller(s) ("Seller") of the property described below (the "Property"), and _____ as Listing Firm ("Firm"). The individual agent who signs this Agreement shall, on behalf of the Firm, be primarily responsible for ensuring that the Firm's duties hereunder are fulfilled; however, it is understood and agreed that other agents of the Firm may be assigned to fulfill such duties if deemed appropriate by the Firm. For purposes of this Agreement, the term "Firm," as the context may require, shall be deemed to include the individual agent who signs this Agreement and any other agents of the Firm.

In consideration for Firm's services and efforts to find a buyer for the Property, Firm is hereby granted the exclusive right to sell the Property on the terms and conditions set forth in this Agreement.

Seller represents that as of the Effective Date the Seller is not (or will not be, if the Property is currently listed) a party to a listing agreement with any other real estate firm regarding the Property. Seller also represents that Seller has received a copy of the "WORKING WITH REAL ESTATE AGENTS" brochure and has reviewed it with Firm.

1. **TERM OF AGREEMENT.**
    (a) **Term**. The term of this Agreement ("Term") shall begin on its Effective Date and shall end at midnight on its Expiration Date.
    (b) **Effective Date**. This Agreement shall become effective and the Seller and Firm's respective rights and obligations under this Agreement shall commence ("Effective Date") as follows (*check appropriate box*):
    ❑ The Effective Date shall be the date that this Agreement has been signed by both Seller and Firm
    ❑ The Property is currently listed for sale exclusively with another real estate firm. Seller represents that the current listing agreement expires on _____. The Effective Date of this Agreement shall commence immediately upon the expiration of the current listing agreement. (**NOTE**: According to Article 16 of the REALTORS® Code of Ethics: *"REALTORS® shall not engage in any practice or take any action inconsistent with exclusive representation or exclusive brokerage relationship agreements that other REALTORS® have with clients."*)
    (c) **Expiration Date**. This Agreement shall terminate at midnight on _____ ("Expiration Date").

2. **PROPERTY**. The Property that is the subject of this Agreement shall include all that real estate described below together with all appurtenances thereto including the improvements located thereon and the fixtures and personal property listed in Paragraphs 3 and 4 below.
    Street Address: _____
    City: _____ Zip _____
    County: _____, North Carolina

    NOTE: Governmental authority over taxes, zoning, school districts, utilities and mail delivery may differ from address shown. Legal Description: (Complete *ALL* applicable)

    - Plat Reference: Lot/Unit _____, Block/Section _____, Subdivision/Condominium _____, as shown on Plat Book/Slide _____ at Page(s) _____
    - The PIN/PID or other identification number of the Property is: _____
    - Other description: _____
    Some or all of the Property may be described in Deed Book _____ at Page _____

3. **FIXTURES AND EXCLUSIONS.**
    (a) **Specified Items:** Unless identified in subparagraph (d) below, the following items, including all related equipment and remote control devices, if any, are deemed fixtures and shall convey, included in the Purchase Price free of liens:

    - Alarm and security systems (attached) for security, fire, smoke, carbon monoxide or other toxins with all related access codes, sensors, cameras, dedicated monitors, hard drives, video recorders, power supplies and cables; doorbells/chimes
    - All stoves/ranges/ovens; built-in appliances; attached microwave oven; vent hood
    - Antennas; satellite dishes and receivers
    - Basketball goals and play equipment (permanently attached or in-ground)

    - Ceiling and wall-attached fans; light fixtures (including existing bulbs)
    - Fireplace insert; gas logs or starters; attached fireplace screens; wood or coal stoves
    - Floor coverings (attached)
    - Fuel tank(s) whether attached or buried and including any contents that have not been used, removed or resold to the fuel provider as of Settlement. **NOTE**: Seller's use, removal or resale of fuel in any fuel tank is subject to Seller's obligation under Paragraph 8(c) of the Offer to Purchase and

Page 1 of 10

Individual agent initials _____ Seller initials _____ _____

STANDARD FORM 101
Revised 7/2018
© 7/2018

FIGURE 8.1 Exclusive right to sell listing agreement.
Source: Used with permission of the North Carolina Association or REALTORS®

Contract (form 2-T) to provide working, existing utilities through the earlier of Closing or possession by Buyer.
- Garage door openers with all controls
- Generators that are permanently wired
- Invisible fencing with power supply, controls and receivers
- Landscape and outdoor trees and plants (except in moveable containers); raised garden; landscape and foundation lighting; outdoor sound systems; permanent irrigation systems and controls; rain barrels; landscape water features; address markers
- Mailboxes; mounted package and newspaper receptacles
- Mirrors attached to walls, ceilings, cabinets or doors; all bathroom wall mirrors
- Storage shed; utility building
- Swimming pool (excluding inflatable); spa; hot tub
- Solar electric and solar water heating systems
- Sump-pumps, radon fans and crawlspace ventilators; de-humidifiers that are permanently wired
- Surface-mounting brackets for television and speakers; recess-mounted speakers; mounted intercom system
- Water supply equipment, including filters, conditioning and softener systems; re-circulating pumps; well pumps and tanks
- Window/Door blinds and shades, curtain and drapery rods and brackets, door and window screens and combination doors, awnings and storm windows

(b) **Items Leased or Not Owned:** Any item which is leased or not owned by Seller, such as fuel tanks, antennas, satellite dishes and receivers, appliances, and alarm and security systems must be identified here and shall not convey: _____
_____
_____

(c) **Other Fixtures/Unspecified items:** Unless identified in subparagraph (d) below, any other item legally considered a fixture is included in the Purchase Price free of liens.

(d) **Other Items That Do Not Convey:** The following items shall not convey (*identify those items to be excluded under subparagraphs (a) and (c)*): _____
_____.
Seller shall repair any damage caused by removal of any items excluded above.

4. **PERSONAL PROPERTY.** The following personal property shall be transferred to Buyer at no value at Closing:
_____
_____

5. **HOME WARRANTY.** Seller ❑ agrees ❑ does not agree to obtain and pay for at settlement a one year home warranty for the Property at a cost not to exceed $_____. If Seller agrees to obtain and pay for a home warranty at any time, Firm hereby discloses that a fee of _____ will be offered to Firm by the person or entity through or from which any home warranty is obtained as compensation to Firm for its assistance in obtaining the home warranty, and Seller hereby consents to Firm's receipt of such fee.

6. **LISTING PRICE.** Seller lists the Property at a price of $_____ on the following terms: ❑ Cash ❑ FHA ❑ VA ❑ USDA ❑ Conventional ❑ Loan Assumption ❑ Seller Financing ❑ Other_____.
Seller agrees to sell the Property for the Listing Price or for any other price or on any other terms acceptable to Seller.

7. **FIRM'S COMPENSATION.**
   (a) **Fee**. Seller agrees to pay Firm a total fee of _____ % of the gross sales price of the Property, OR_____ ("Fee"), which shall include the amount of any compensation paid by Firm as set forth in paragraph 8 below to any other real estate firm, including individual agents and sole proprietors ("Cooperating Real Estate Firm").
   (b) **Fee Earned**. The Fee shall be deemed earned under any of the following circumstances:
      (i) If a ready, willing and able buyer is procured by Firm, a Cooperating Real Estate Firm, the Seller, or anyone else during the Term of this Agreement at the price and on the terms set forth herein, or at any price and upon any terms acceptable to the Seller;
      (ii) If the Property is sold, optioned, exchanged, conveyed or transferred, or the Seller agrees, during the Term of this Agreement or any renewal hereof, to sell, option, exchange, convey or transfer the Property at any price and upon any terms whatsoever; or
      (iii) If the circumstances set out in (i) or (ii) above have not occurred, and if, within _____ days after the Expiration Date ("Protection Period"), Seller either directly or indirectly sells, options, exchanges, conveys or transfers, or agrees to sell, option, exchange, convey or transfer the Property upon any terms whatsoever, to any person with whom Seller, Firm, or any Cooperating Real Estate Firm communicated regarding the Property during the Term of this Agreement or any renewal hereof, provided the names of such persons are delivered or postmarked to the Seller within 15 days after the Expiration Date. HOWEVER, Seller shall NOT be obligated to pay the Fee if a valid listing agreement is entered into between Seller and another real estate broker and the Property is subsequently sold, optioned, exchanged, conveyed or transferred during the Protection Period.

Page 2 of 10

Individual agent initials _____   Seller initials _____ _____

STANDARD FORM 101
Revised 7/2018
© 7/2018

FIGURE 8.1 (*Continued*)

(c) **Fee Due and Payable**. Once earned as set forth above, the Fee will be due and payable at the earlier of:
  (i) Closing on the Property;
  (ii) The Seller's failure to sell the Property (including but not limited to the Seller's refusal to sign an offer to purchase the Property at the price and terms stated herein or on other terms acceptable to the Seller, the Seller's default on an executed sales contract for the Property, or the Seller's agreement with a buyer to unreasonably modify or cancel an executed sales contract for the Property); or
  (iii) Seller's breach of this Agreement.

(d) **Transfer of Interest in Business Entity**. If Seller is a partnership, corporation or other business entity, and an interest in the partnership, corporation or other business entity is transferred, whether by merger, outright purchase or otherwise, in lieu of a sale of the Property, and applicable law does not prohibit the payment of a fee or commission in connection with such sale or transfer, the Fee shall be calculated on the fair market value of the Property, rather than the gross sales price, multiplied by the percentage of interest so transferred, and shall be paid by Seller at the time of the transfer.

(e) **Additional Compensation**. If additional compensation, incentive, bonus, rebate and/or other valuable consideration ("Additional Compensation") is offered to the Firm from any other party or person in connection with a sale of the Property, Seller will permit Firm to receive it in addition to the Fee. Firm shall timely disclose the promise or expectation of receiving any such Additional Compensation and confirm the disclosure in writing before Seller makes or accepts an offer to sell. (**NOTE:** NCAR Form #770 may be used to confirm the disclosure of any such Additional Compensation)

(f) **Attorney Fees and Costs**. If Firm is the prevailing party in any legal proceeding brought by Firm against Seller to recover any or all of the Fee, Firm shall be entitled to recover from Seller reasonable attorney fees and court costs incurred by Firm in connection with the proceeding.

8. **COOPERATION WITH/COMPENSATION TO OTHER FIRMS.** Firm has advised Seller of Firm's company policies regarding cooperation and the amount(s) of any compensation that will be offered to other brokers, including but not limited to, seller subagents, buyer agents or both, brokers who do or do not participate in a listing service and brokers who are or are not REALTORS®. Seller authorizes Firm to (*Check ALL applicable authorizations*):
  ❑ Cooperate with subagents representing the Seller and offer them the following compensation:_____% of the gross sales price or $_____; and/or,
  ❑ Cooperate with buyer agents representing the buyer and offer them the following compensation:_____% of the gross sales price or $_____; and/or,
  ❑ Cooperate with and compensate other Cooperating Real Estate Firms according to the Firm's attached policy.

Firm will promptly notify Seller if compensation offered to a Cooperating Real Estate Firm is different from that set forth above. Agents with Cooperating Real Estate Firms must orally disclose the nature of their relationship with a buyer (subagent or buyer agent) to Firm at the time of initial contact with Firm, and confirm that relationship in writing no later than the time an offer to purchase is submitted for the Seller's consideration. Seller should be careful about disclosing confidential information because agents representing buyers must disclose all relevant information to their clients.

9. **FIRM'S DUTIES.** Firm agrees to provide Seller the benefit of Firm's knowledge, experience and advice in the marketing and sale of the Property. Seller understands that Firm makes no representation or guarantee as to the sale of the Property, but Firm agrees to use its best efforts in good faith to find a buyer who is ready, willing and able to purchase the property. In accordance with the REALTORS® Code of Ethics, Firm shall, with Seller's approval, in response to inquiries from buyers or Cooperating Real Estate Firms, disclose the existence of offers on the Property. Where Seller authorizes disclosure, Firm shall also disclose whether offers were obtained by the individual agent who signs this Agreement, another agent of the Firm, or by a Cooperating Real Estate Firm. Seller acknowledges that real estate brokers are prohibited by N.C. Real Estate Commission rule from disclosing the price or other material terms contained in a party's offer to purchase, sell, lease, rent or option real property to a competing party without the express authority of the party making the offer.

Seller acknowledges that Firm is required by law to disclose to potential purchasers of the Property all material facts pertaining to the Property about which the Firm knows or reasonably should know, and that REALTORS® have an ethical responsibility to treat all parties to the transaction honestly. Seller further acknowledges that Firm is being retained solely as a real estate professional, and understands that other professional service providers are available to render advice or services to Seller, including but not limited to an attorney, insurance agent, tax advisor, surveyor, structural engineer, home inspector, environmental consultant, architect, or contractor. Although Firm may provide Seller the names of providers who claim to perform such services, Seller understands that Firm cannot guarantee the quality of service or level of expertise of any such provider. Seller agrees to pay the full amount due for all services directly to the service provider whether or not the transaction closes. Seller also agrees to indemnify and hold Firm harmless from and against any and all liability, claim, loss, damage, suit, or expense that Firm may incur either as a result of Seller's selection and use of any such provider or Seller's election not to have one or more of such services performed.

FIGURE 8.1 (*Continued*)

THE AGENT (FIRM) SHALL CONDUCT ALL BROKERAGE ACTIVITIES IN REGARD TO THIS AGREEMENT WITHOUT RESPECT TO THE RACE, COLOR, RELIGION, SEX, NATIONAL ORIGIN, HANDICAP OR FAMILIAL STATUS OF ANY PARTY OR PROSPECTIVE PARTY TO THE AGREEMENT. FURTHER, REALTORS® HAVE AN ETHICAL DUTY TO CONDUCT SUCH ACTIVITIES WITHOUT RESPECT TO THE SEXUAL ORIENTATION OR GENDER IDENTITY OF ANY PARTY OR PROSPECTIVE PARTY TO THIS AGREEMENT.

10. **MARKETING.**
    (a) **Commencement of Marketing.** The Firm is authorized to commence marketing the Property as described in subparagraph (b) below on the Effective Date OR, if selected ❑ on (insert date only if applicable) _____ ("Delayed Marketing Date").

> **NOTE:** If a Delayed Marketing Date is selected, Seller understands and acknowledges the following:
> - THE PROPERTY MAY NOT BE SHOWN BY ANY REAL ESTATE AGENT, INCLUDING FIRM'S AGENTS, PRIOR TO THE DELAYED MARKETING DATE.
> - FIRM IS OBLIGATED TO PRESENT TO SELLER ANY OFFERS ON THE PROPERTY THAT MAY BE SUBMITTED TO FIRM PRIOR TO THE DELAYED MARKETING DATE.
> - IT IS IN THE BEST INTEREST OF MOST SELLERS TO GET THE HIGHEST POSSIBLE PRICE ON THE BEST TERMS FOR THEIR PROPERTY, AND MAXIMIZING EXPOSURE OF THEIR PROPERTY ADVANCES THAT INTEREST. ACCEPTING AN OFFER ON THE PROPERTY BEFORE IT IS FULLY EXPOSED TO THE WIDEST GROUP OF POTENTIAL BUYERS MAY DENY SELLER THE BEST OPPORTUNITY TO ATTRACT OFFERS AT THE HIGHEST PRICE AND BEST TERMS.

(b) **Marketing Authorization.** Seller authorizes Firm (*Check ALL applicable sections*):
❑ **Signs.** To place "For Sale," "Under Contract," "Sale Pending," or other similar signs on the Property (where permitted by law and relevant covenants) and to remove other such signs.
❑ **Open Houses.** To conduct open houses of the Property at such times as Seller and Firm may subsequently agree.
❑ **Listing Service.** To submit pertinent information concerning the Property to any listing service of which Firm is a member or in which any of Firm's agents participate and to furnish to such listing service notice of all changes of information concerning the Property authorized in writing by Seller. Seller authorizes Firm, upon execution of a sales contract for the Property, to notify the listing service of the pending sale and the expiration date of any due diligence period, and upon closing of the sale, to disseminate sales information, including sales price, to the listing service, appraisers and real estate brokers.
❑ **Lock/Key Boxes.** The Seller ❑ does ❑ does not authorize Firm to place lock/key boxes on the Property.
❑ **Advertising Other Than On The Internet.** To advertise the Property in non-Internet media, and to permit other firms to advertise the Property in non-Internet media to the extent and in such manner as Firm may decide.
❑ **Internet Advertising.** To display information about the Property on the Internet either directly or through a program of any listing service of which the Firm is a member or in which any of Firm's agents participate. Seller further authorizes other firms who belong to any listing service of which the Firm is a member or in which any of Firm's agents participate to display information about the Property on the Internet in accordance with the listing service rules and regulations, and also authorizes any listing service of which the Firm is a member or in which any of Firm's agents participate to use, license or sell to others information about the Property entered into the listing service. Seller specifically authorizes the display of the address of the Property, automated estimates of the market value of the Property and third-party comments about the Property. If seller desires to limit or prohibit Internet advertising as set forth above, seller must complete an opt-out form in accordance with listing service rules.

> **NOTE:** NCAR Form #105 may be used to limit or prohibit Internet advertising and explains how such limitations may or may not be effective.

(c) **"Coming Soon" Advertising.** ❑ (Check only if applicable). If applicable, Firm is authorized to market the Property as "Coming Soon," commencing on the Effective Date, in any media Firm may in its discretion select, provided that any "Coming Soon" advertising shall be conducted in accordance with any restrictions and requirements of any listing service in which the Property will be included, a copy of which ❑ are ❑ are not attached to this Agreement.

(d) **Seller Acknowledgement.** Seller acknowledges and understands that while the marketing services selected above will facilitate the showing and sale of the Property, there are risks associated with allowing access to and disseminating information about the Property that are not within the reasonable control of the Firm, including but not limited to:
   (i) unauthorized use of a lock/key box,
   (ii) control of visitors during or after a showing or an open house, including the taking and use of photographs and videos of the Property

FIGURE 8.1 (*Continued*)

(iii) inappropriate use of information about the Property placed on the Internet or furnished to any listing service in which the Firm participates, and

(iv) information about the Property placed on the Internet by or through any listing service in which the Firm participates which is inaccurate or dated.

Seller therefore agrees to release and discharge Firm and Firm's agents from any and all claims, demands, rights and causes of action of whatsoever kind and nature not caused by Firm's negligence arising directly or indirectly out of any such marketing services.

> **WARNING**: IT MAY BE A CRIME UNDER FEDERAL AND STATE LAWS TO LISTEN TO OR RECORD AN ORAL COMMUNICATION THROUGH THE USE OF ANY ELECTRONIC, MECHANICAL, OR OTHER DEVICE WITHOUT THE CONSENT OF A PARTY TO THAT COMMUNICATION. If there is a video/audio/surveillance device(s) on the Property, Seller is advised: (i) that no audio surveillance device may be turned on during any showings, open houses, investigations, examinations or inspections of the Property; and (ii) that the placement of any video surveillance device should not violate a visitor's reasonable expectation of privacy.

11. **EARNEST MONEY**. Unless otherwise provided in the sales contract, any initial and additional earnest money deposits and any other earnest monies paid in connection with any transaction shall be held by the Firm, in escrow, until the consummation or termination of the transaction. Any earnest money forfeited by reason of the buyer's default under a sales contract shall be divided equally between the Firm and Seller. In no event shall the sum paid to the Firm because of a buyer's default be in excess of the fee that would have been due if the sale had closed as contemplated in the sales contract. In accordance with NC General Statutes Section 93A-12, if a dispute regarding the return or forfeiture of any earnest money deposit arises between Seller and the buyer, the escrow agent holding the deposit may deposit the disputed monies with the appropriate Clerk of Court following written notice to the parties. In the event of any such dispute, Seller directs Firm to disclose Seller's last known mailing address to the escrow agent upon request to enable the escrow agent to comply with the notice requirement of such law.

12. **SELLER REPRESENTATIONS**.

   (a) **Flood Hazard Disclosure/Insurance.** To the best of Seller's knowledge, the Property ❏ is ❏ is not located partly or entirely within a designated Special Flood Hazard Area. The Seller ❏ does ❏ does not currently maintain flood hazard insurance on the Property.

   (b) **Synthetic Stucco.** To the best of Seller's knowledge, the Property has not been clad previously (either in whole or in part) with an "exterior insulating and finishing system," commonly known as "EIFS" or "synthetic stucco", unless disclosed as follows: _____

   (c) **Owners' Association**. (Complete ONLY if the Property is subject to regulation and/or assessment by an owners' association.)

   (i) ❏ The Residential Property and Owner's Association Disclosure Statement is required: The name, address and telephone number of the president of the owners' association or the association manager is: _____
   _____
   Owners' association website address, if any: _____

   The name, address and telephone number of the president of the owners' association or the association manager is: _____
   _____
   Owners' association website address, if any: _____

   (ii) ❏ New Construction or the Residential Property and Owner's Association Disclosure Statement is NOT required:
   Seller agrees to promptly complete an Owners' Association Disclosure and Condominium Resale Statement Addendum (Standard Form 2A12-T) at **Seller's expense** and to attach it as an addendum to any contract for the sale of the Property.

   (iii) Seller authorizes and directs any owners' association or any management company of the owners' association to release to Firm true and accurate copies of the following items affecting the Property, including any amendments:
   - Seller's statement of account
   - master insurance policy showing the coverage provided and the deductible amount
   - Declaration and Restrictive Covenants
   - Rules and Regulations
   - Articles of Incorporation
   - Bylaws of the owners' association
   - current financial statement and budget of the owners' association
   - parking restrictions and information
   - architectural guidelines

   (d) **Termite Bond**. To the best of Seller's knowledge there ❏ is ❏ is not a termite bond on the Property. If there is a termite bond, it ❏ is ❏ is not transferable. If transferable, the transfer cost is $ _____, and the bonding company is: _____.

Page 5 of 10

Individual agent initials _____ Seller initials _____ _____

STANDARD FORM 101
Revised 7/2018
© 7/2018

FIGURE 8.1 (*Continued*)

(e) **Ownership**. Seller represents that Seller:
❑ has owned the Property for at least one year;
❑ has owned the Property for less than one year
❑ does not yet own the Property

If Seller does not yet own the Property, Seller agrees to promptly provide Firm information pertaining to Seller's acquisition of the Property, such as a copy of a sales contract or option for the Property, and to keep Firm timely informed of all developments pertaining to Seller's acquisition of the Property.

(f) **Receipt of Sample Forms**.
❑ Seller acknowledges receipt of a sample copy of an Offer to Purchase And Contract (form 2-T) or Offer to Purchase and Contract—New Construction (form 800-T), as may be appropriate for review purposes.
❑ Seller acknowledges receipt of a sample copy of a Professional Services Disclosure and Election form (form #760) for review purposes.

(g) **Current Liens**. Seller represents to the best of Seller's knowledge:
  (1) The Property ❑ is ❑ is not encumbered by a deed of trust or mortgage. *Complete any of the following where applicable:*
    (i) There is a first deed of trust or mortgage on the Property securing a loan held by:
      Lender Name: _____
      Approximate balance: $_____ Lender Phone#: _____
      Lender Address: _____
    (ii) There is a second deed of trust or mortgage on the Property securing a loan held by:
      Lender Name: _____
      Approximate balance: $_____ Lender Phone#: _____
      Lender Address: _____
    (iii) There is a deed of trust or mortgage on the Property securing an equity line of credit held by:
      Lender Name: _____
      Approximate balance: $_____ Lender Phone#: _____
      Lender Address: _____

  (2) Seller is current on all payments for the loans identified in numbered items (i), (ii) and (iii) above except as specified in (7) below.

  (3) Seller is not in default on any loan identified in numbered items (i), (ii) and (iii) above and has not received any notice(s) from the holder of any loan identified in numbered items (i), (ii) and (iii) above or from any other lien holder of any kind, regarding a default under the loan, threatened foreclosure, notice of foreclosure, or the filing of foreclosure except as specified in (7) below.

  (4) There are not any liens secured against the Property for Federal, State or local income taxes, unpaid real property taxes, unpaid condominium or homeowners' association fees, mechanics', laborers' or materialmen's liens, or other liens affecting the Property, and Seller has no knowledge of any matter that might result in a lien affecting the Property except as specified in (7) below.

  (5) There are not any judgments against Seller affecting the Property, and Seller has no knowledge of any matter that might result in a judgment that may potentially affect the Property except as specified in (7) below.

  (6) There are not any Uniform Commercial Code (UCC) fixture filings affecting the Property, and Seller has no knowledge of any matter that might result in a UCC fixture filing affecting the Property except as specified in (7) below.

  (7) Specify any information, including approximate balances, required by Seller representations (2) through (6) above

NOTE: Outstanding liens may affect Seller's net proceeds: _____
_____

(h) **Bankruptcy**. Seller currently:
  (1) ❑ is ❑ is not under bankruptcy protection under United States law.
  (2) ❑ is ❑ is not contemplating seeking bankruptcy protection during the term of this Agreement.

(i) **Access**. Seller represents that the Property has legal access to a public right of way. If access is by private road/easement/other, Seller further represents that there ❑ is ❑ is not an agreement regarding the maintenance of such private road/easement/other means of access. If applicable, Seller agrees to promptly provide Firm information pertaining to any such agreement.

(j) **Lease(s)**. To the best of Seller's knowledge, the Property ❑ is ❑ is not subject to any lease(s). If applicable:
  (i) Seller agrees to promptly provide Firm a copy of any such lease(s) or a written statement of the terms of any oral lease(s);
  (ii) If the Property is managed by someone other than Seller, the manager's name and contact information is as follows: _____.

Seller authorizes any such manager to release and disclose to Firm any relevant information about any leases(s) and to cooperate with Firm in the sale of the Property.

(k) **FHA Appraisal**. To the best of Seller's knowledge, an FHA appraisal ❑ has ❑ has not been performed on the Property within four months prior to the Effective Date. If applicable, Seller agrees to promptly provide Firm a copy of any such appraisal if available.

NOTE: Any such appraisal may or may not be binding on a buyer who intends to obtain FHA financing.

Individual agent initials _____ Seller initials _____ _____

STANDARD FORM 101
Revised 7/2018
© 7/2018

FIGURE 8.1 (*Continued*)

(l) **Special Assessments**. To the best of Seller's knowledge, there are no Proposed or Confirmed Special Assessments (as defined in the sample contract form provided to Seller) regarding the Property except as follows (Insert "none" or the identification of such assessments, if any): _____
_____

(m) **Manufactured (Mobile) Home**. Complete ONLY if there is a manufactured (mobile) home(s) on the Property that Seller intends to include as a part of the sale of the Property: VIN(s): _____ or ❑ VIN(s) unknown. Other description (*year, model, etc.*): _____

(n) **Fuel Tank/Fuel**: To the best of Seller's knowledge, there ❑ is ❑ is not a fuel tank(s) located on the Property. *If "yes" complete the following to the best of Seller's knowledge:*

Ownership of tank 1: ❑ owned ❑ leased. If leased, the name and contact information of tank lessor is: _____

Location of tank 1:	❑ above ground ❑ below ground
Type of fuel:	❑ oil ❑ propane ❑ gasoline and/or diesel ❑ other: _____
Refilling schedule:	❑ auto-refill (*insert frequency*): _____ ❑ other (*describe*): _____
Name and contact information of fuel vendor:	_____

Ownership of tank 2: ❑ owned ❑ leased If leased, the name and contact information of tank lessor is: _____

Location of tank 2:	❑ above ground ❑ below ground
Type of fuel:	❑ oil ❑ propane ❑ gasoline and/or diesel ❑ other: _____
Refilling schedule:	❑ auto-refill (*insert frequency*): _____ ❑ other (*describe*): _____
Name and contact information of fuel vendor:	_____

If, during the term of this Agreement, Seller becomes aware that any of the representations set forth in this paragraph 12 are incorrect or no longer accurate, Seller shall promptly notify Firm and cooperate with Firm in taking appropriate corrective action.

13. **SELLER'S DUTIES**. Seller agrees to cooperate with Firm in the marketing and sale of the Property, including but not limited to:
    (a) providing to Firm, in a timely manner, accurate information including but not limited to the following:
        (i) Residential Property and Owner's Association Disclosure Statement (unless exempt);
        (ii) Mineral and Oil and Gas Rights Mandatory Disclosure Statement (unless exempt); and
        (iii) Lead-Based Paint or Lead-Based Paint Hazard Addendum with respect to any residential dwelling built prior to 1978.
    (b) making the Property available for showing (including working, existing utilities) at reasonable times and upon reasonable notice;
    (c) providing Firm as soon as reasonably possible after the execution of this Agreement copies of the following documents (where relevant) in the possession of Seller:
        (1) restrictive covenants affecting the Property;
        (2) bylaws, articles of incorporation, rules and regulations, and other governing documents of the owners' association and/or the subdivision;
        (3) title insurance policies, attorney's opinions on title, surveys, covenants, deeds, notes and deeds of trust and easements relating to the Property.

Seller authorizes (1) any attorney presently or previously representing Seller to release and disclose any title insurance policy in such attorney's file to Firm, (2) the Property's title insurer or its agent to release and disclose all materials in the Property's title insurer's (or title insurer's agent's) file to Firm, and (3) the owners' association manager (or other authorized representative) to release and disclose copies of all documents referenced in subparagraphs (c)(1) and (c)(2) above. Seller acknowledges and understands that Firm is under no obligation to acquire any of the information referenced in this subparagraph (c) or to verify the accuracy of any such information that may be provided to Firm.

    (d) immediately referring to Firm all inquiries or offers it may receive regarding the Property; showing the Property only by appointment made by or through Firm; and conducting all negotiations through Firm;
    (e) executing and delivering at settlement a GENERAL WARRANTY DEED conveying fee simple marketable title to the Property, including legal access to a public right of way, free of all encumbrances except ad valorem taxes for the current year, utility easements, rights-of-way, and unviolated restrictive covenants, if any, and those encumbrances that the buyer agrees to assume in the sales contract.

Seller represents that the Seller has the right to convey the Property, and that there are currently no circumstances that would prohibit the Seller from conveying fee simple marketable title as set forth in the preceding sentence, except as follows *(insert N/A if not applicable)*: _____
_____

> **NOTE**: If any sale of the Property may be a "short sale," consideration should be given to attaching NCAR form 104 as an addendum to this Agreement.

Individual agent initials _____ Seller initials _____ _____

FIGURE 8.1 (*Continued*)

(f) providing Firm, in a timely manner, any information necessary (including any information omitted under Paragraph 12) to enable Firm to prepare an estimate of Seller's net proceeds at settlement. Seller acknowledges and understands that any such estimate is an approximation only and that Seller should verify the accuracy of the calculations.

(g) if required by N.C.G.S. §44A-11.1, timely designating a Lien Agent, and providing Firm as soon as reasonably possible a copy of the appointment of Lien Agent.

14. HOME INSPECTION: Seller is advised to obtain a home inspection for the purpose of evaluating the condition of the Property in order to enhance its marketability and to help reduce concerns of prospective buyers. Seller ❑ agrees ❑ does not agree to obtain and pay for a home inspection by a licensed NC Home Inspector within _____ days after the execution of this agreement.

❑ Seller acknowledges receipt of a copy of *Questions and Answers on: Home Inspections* by the NC Real Estate Commission.

15. PHOTOGRAPHS AND OTHER MATERIALS: Firm is specifically authorized to use, for any purposes whatsoever, any and all photographs, drawings, video, advertising copy or other information obtained by or provided to Firm pursuant to this Agreement (including but not limited to any information concerning the price and terms of the sale of the Property, the description of the Property and the length of time the Property is on the market) ("Materials"), both before and after the sale or, in the event there is not a sale, after this Agreement has expired. Seller shall not have or acquire any rights to use any of the Materials created by, on behalf of, or at the direction of Firm or an agent of Firm either during or after the Term of this Agreement without Firm's written consent. If Seller provides any Materials to Firm ("Seller Materials"), Seller represents that Seller owns the Seller Materials or otherwise has the legal right to provide the Seller Materials to Firm, and Seller grants to Firm and any listing service in which Firm or its agents participate a non-exclusive, perpetual license to use the Seller Materials, including the rights to display, reproduce, distribute or make derivative works from the Seller Materials. Seller agrees to indemnify and hold Firm and its agents harmless for any and all claims resulting from use of the Seller Materials under the terms of this license.

16. ADDITIONAL TERMS AND CONDITIONS. The following additional terms and conditions shall also be a part of this Agreement: _____
_____
_____

17. DUAL AGENCY. Seller understands that the potential for dual agency will arise if a buyer who has an agency relationship with Firm becomes interested in viewing the Property. Firm may represent more than one party in the same transaction only with the knowledge and informed consent of all parties for whom Firm acts.

(a) Disclosure of Information. In the event Firm serves as a dual agent, Seller agrees that without permission from the party about whom the information pertains, Firm shall not disclose to the other party the following information:

(1) that a party may agree to a price, terms, or any conditions of sale other than those offered;
(2) the motivation of a party for engaging in the transaction, unless disclosure is otherwise required by statute or rule; and
(3) any information about a party which that party has identified as confidential unless disclosure is otherwise required by statute or rule.

b) Firm's Role as Dual Agent. If Firm serves as agent for both Seller and a buyer in a transaction involving the Property, Firm shall make every reasonable effort to represent Seller and buyer in a balanced and fair manner. Firm shall also make every reasonable effort to encourage and effect communication and negotiation between Seller and buyer. Seller understands and acknowledges that:

(1) Prior to the time dual agency occurs, Firm will act as Seller's exclusive agent;
(2) In its separate representation of Seller and buyer, Firm may obtain information which, if disclosed, could harm the bargaining position of the party providing such information to Firm;
(3) Firm is required by law to disclose to Seller and buyer any known or reasonably ascertainable material facts.

Seller agrees Firm shall not be liable to Seller for (i) disclosing material facts required by law to be disclosed, and (ii) refusing or failing to disclose other information the law does not require to be disclosed which could harm or compromise one party's bargaining position but could benefit the other party.

(c) Seller's Role. Should Firm become a dual agent, Seller understands and acknowledges that:

(1) Seller has the responsibility of making Seller's own decisions as to what terms are to be included in any purchase and sale agreement with a buyer client of Firm;
(2) Seller is fully aware of and understands the implications and consequences of Firm's dual agency role as expressed herein to provide balanced and fair representation of Seller and buyer and to encourage and effect communication between them rather than as an advocate or exclusive agent or representative;
(3) Seller has determined that the benefits of dual agency outweigh any disadvantages or adverse consequences;
(4) Seller may seek independent legal counsel to assist Seller with the negotiation and preparation of a purchase and sale agreement or with any matter relating to the transaction which is the subject matter of a purchase and sale agreement.

Should Firm become a dual agent, Seller waives all claims, damages, losses, expenses or liabilities, other than for violations of the North Carolina Real Estate License Law and intentional wrongful acts, arising from Firm's role as a dual agent. Seller shall have a duty to

FIGURE 8.1 (*Continued*)

protect Seller's own interests and should read any purchase and sale agreement carefully to ensure that it accurately sets forth the terms which Seller wants included in said agreement.

(d) Authorization *(initial only ONE)*.

_____ _____ Seller authorizes the Firm to act as a dual agent, representing both the Seller and the buyer, subject to the terms and conditions set forth in Paragraph 17.

_____ _____ Seller desires exclusive representation at all times during this agreement and does NOT authorize Firm to act in the capacity of dual agent. *If Seller does not authorize Firm to act as a dual agent, the remainder of this paragraph shall not apply.*

(e) Designated Agent Option (*Initial only if applicable*).

_____ _____ Seller hereby authorizes the Firm to designate an individual agent(s) to represent the Seller. The individual designated agent(s) shall represent only the interests of the Seller to the extent permitted by law.

NOTE: When dual agency arises, an individual agent shall not practice designated agency and shall remain a dual agent if the individual agent has actually received confidential information concerning a buyer client of the Firm in connection with the transaction or if designated agency is otherwise prohibited by law.

18. **MEDIATION.** If a dispute arises out of or related to this Agreement or the breach thereof, and if the dispute cannot be settled through negotiation, the parties agree first to try in good faith to settle the dispute by mediation before resorting to arbitration, litigation, or some other dispute resolution procedure. If the need for mediation arises, the parties will choose a mutually acceptable mediator and will share the cost of mediation equally.

19. **WIRE FRAUD WARNING.**

IF SELLER'S PROCEEDS WILL BE WIRED, IT IS RECOMMENDED THAT SELLER PROVIDE WIRING INSTRUCTIONS AT CLOSING IN WRITING IN THE PRESENCE OF THE ATTORNEY. IF SELLER IS UNABLE TO ATTEND CLOSING, SELLER MAY BE REQUIRED TO SEND AN ORIGINAL NOTARIZED DIRECTIVE TO THE CLOSING ATTORNEY'S OFFICE CONTAINING THE WIRING INSTRUCTIONS. THIS MAY BE SENT WITH THE DEED, LIEN WAIVER AND TAX FORMS IF THOSE DOCUMENTS ARE BEING PREPARED FOR SELLER BY THE CLOSING ATTORNEY. AT A MINIMUM, SELLER SHOULD CALL THE CLOSING ATTORNEY'S OFFICE TO PROVIDE THE WIRE INSTRUCTIONS. THE WIRE INSTRUCTIONS SHOULD BE VERIFIED OVER THE TELEPHONE VIA A CALL TO SELLER INITIATED BY THE CLOSING ATTORNEY'S OFFICE TO ENSURE THAT THEY ARE NOT FROM A FRAUDULENT SOURCE.

SELLER SHOULD CALL THE CLOSING ATTORNEY'S OFFICE AT A NUMBER THAT IS INDEPENDENTLY OBTAINED. TO ENSURE THAT SELLER'S CONTACT IS LEGITIMATE, SELLER SHOULD NOT RELY ON A PHONE NUMBER IN AN EMAIL FROM THE CLOSING ATTORNEY'S OFFICE, SELLER'S REAL ESTATE AGENT OR ANYONE ELSE.

Seller acknowledges and understands that there are risks associated with wire transfers that are not within the reasonable control of Firm, and Seller hereby agrees to release and discharge Firm and Firm's agents from any and all claims, demands, rights and causes of action of whatsoever kind and nature not caused by gross negligence of Firm or Firm's agents arising directly or indirectly out of any wire transfer Seller sends or receives/was to receive in connection with any real estate transaction in which Firm represents Seller.

FIGURE 8.1 (*Continued*)

20. **ENTIRE AGREEMENT/CHANGES/TERMINATION.** This Agreement constitutes the entire agreement between Seller and Firm and there are no representations, inducements, or other provisions other than those expressed herein. This Agreement may be signed in multiple originals or counterparts, all of which together constitute one and the same instrument. All changes, additions, or deletions to this Agreement must be in writing and signed by both Seller and Firm. Seller acknowledges and understands that this Agreement constitutes a binding contract between Seller and Firm. Although Seller may at any time withdraw from the fiduciary relationship existing between Seller and Firm, the contract created by this Agreement may not be terminated by Seller or Firm prior to its Expiration Date without legally sufficient cause. Any such termination shall be by mutually-acceptable written agreement signed by both Seller and Firm. **Seller and Firm each acknowledge receipt of a signed copy of this Agreement.**

THE NORTH CAROLINA ASSOCIATION OF REALTORS®, INC. MAKES NO REPRESENTATION AS TO THE LEGAL VALIDITY OR ADEQUACY OF ANY PROVISION OF THIS FORM IN ANY SPECIFIC TRANSACTION.

Seller: _____   _____   _____
       Print Name   Signature   Date

Contact Information: _____ _____ _____ _____
        Home Work Cell   Email

Mailing Address: _____

Seller: _____   _____   _____
       Print Name   Signature   Date

Contact Information: _____ _____ _____ _____
        Home Work Cell   Email

Mailing Address: _____

Entity Seller: _____
(Name of LLC/Corporation/Partnership/Trust/etc.)

By: _____   Date: _____

Name: _____   Title: _____

Contact Information: _____ _____ _____ _____
        Home Work Cell   Email

Mailing Address: _____

Firm: _____   Phone: _____
  Print Real Estate Firm Name

By: _____   _____   _____
  Individual Agent Signature   Individual License Number   Date

Office: _____

Address: _____

Office Phone: _____   Fax: _____   Email: _____

STANDARD FORM 101
Revised 7/2018
© 7/2018

FIGURE 8.1 (*Continued*)

ensure that the exclusion also is entered in the appropriate space in the Offer to Purchase and Contract at the time the contract is executed.

Section 4 provides for the inclusion of any personal property in the sale of the real property. Because personal and real property definitions are the cause of many misunderstandings that arise in the world of practice, it is important to pay special attention to this section. NOTE: Freestanding appliances, with the exception of a range/stove/oven and draperies are examples of personal property often included here and in the contract. Other large expensive items of personal property, such as a riding lawn mower, may cause problems with the appraisal and are best handled through a separate sales agreement.

Section 5 establishes whether or not the seller will provide a one-year home warranty for the property.

Section 6 establishes the list price of the property and the type of financing the sellers will accept. Because few buyers have all the cash to purchase a home without a mortgage loan, most sellers need to allow for some type of loan contingency in the contract. Sellers need to understand that certain costs, conditions, and risks apply to some types of loan before they accept an Offer to Purchase and Contract with a loan contingency. For example, there are certain Department of Veterans Affairs (VA) and Federal Housing Administration (FHA) fees a buyer cannot pay and the seller will be asked to pay. Agents also need to be careful to point out the risks of owner financing due to the seller's inability to get a deficiency judgment in the case of foreclosure.

Section 7 is the essential part of the employment contract that spells out the compensation to the agent as well as the conditions under which the commission is earned. The meaning of the exclusive right to sell arrangement is reinforced in paragraph (b)(i), which indicates that a sale or an exchange effected by any person during the term of the listing entitles the agent to the full commission. Paragraph (b)(iii) is known as the **extender clause** that *provides for the full commission for any sale or exchange to registered prospects within the specified period after the termination of the contract*. In paragraph (e), Additional Compensation, the seller permits the firm to receive any additional compensation, such as an incentive, bonus, or rebate, from any other party or person in connection with a sale of the property provided the agent makes a timely disclosure of such arrangement and confirms the agreement in writing before the seller accepts an offer to sell.

Section 8 establishes the firm's ability to cooperate with other agents. The sellers can authorize the firm to cooperate and compensate subagents of the seller or exclusive buyer agents. One or both options can be selected.

Section 9 establishes the duties of the agent to use her best efforts and expertise to market the property, but it does not guarantee the sale. It also clearly states to the sellers that the agent is required to disclose all material facts that she knows or reasonably should know regarding the property. The section also outlines other professional services the seller may need to retain regarding the transaction (i.e., surveyor, attorney, or insurance agent). The language stipulated by fair housing rules is also presented in Section 9. It itemizes the agent's authority in marketing the property, such as being able to place a sign in the yard or enter the new listing in a listing service.

Section 10 addresses the marketing aspects of the transaction including permission to place signage and lock boxes on the property and the ability to host open houses as well as to enter the listing in the MLS and to provide pertinent data regarding the sale of the property to such service. This section also addresses whether the seller will permit Internet, as well as other than Internet, advertising forms to be utilized by the firm.

Section 11 permits that earnest money deposits are to be held in escrow by the firm and in the event that such earnest money shall be forfeited by reason of buyer default, the seller and the firm shall divide the monies equally as long as the firm's share shall not exceed the amount they would have received had there been no forfeiture.

Section 12 is perhaps the longest section and deals with representations by the seller. These representations, to the best of the seller's knowledge, include issues such as flood hazard disclosure and insurance, synthetic stucco, existence of an owners association, and termite bond. The seller also is asked to make representations regarding the length of his ownership of the property, whether the property serves as his primary residence, current liens on the property, bankruptcy or the contemplation of bankruptcy, existence of any leases, and VA or FHA appraisals as well as any special assessments.

Section 13 addresses the seller's duties to generally cooperate with the efforts of the firm in the marketing and sale of the property. These duties include providing to the firm copies of all relevant documents necessary to support the sale of the property as well as to disclose the existence of all inquiries or offers the seller may receive and to conduct all negotiations through the firm.

Section 14 advises the seller to obtain a home inspection before placing the home on the market for sale.

Section 15 gives the firm the specific authorization to use any and all photographs or other materials relevant to this property. The seller represents that any "Seller Materials" provided to the firm shall remain the property of the seller

Section 16 provides space to address any additional terms and conditions that are to be a part of this agreement.

Section 17 addresses the issue of dual agency and how the disclosure of information under such a relationship will be limited in some situations such as is shown in subsection (a). Additionally, the firm's and seller's role in dual agency is explained as well as permission to practice designated agency in certain circumstances.

Section 18 explains that if a dispute arises out of the agreement or the breach of the agreement, the sellers and the agents will seek a settlement through mediation. The parties can proceed to other dispute resolution options, such as arbitration or litigation, if the dispute is not settled in mediation. The cost of the mutually acceptable mediator will be split equally.

Section 19 indicates that this instrument contains the entire substance of the employment agreement between the owner and the agent.

The individual agent's license number is required below the signature line. The listing contract must be prepared with enough copies to provide each party with a copy. Commission rules mandate a specific expiration date. As a separate form (see Figure 8.2), the North Carolina Association of REALTORS® (NCAR) Exclusive Agency Agreement Renewal and/or Amendment provides for a renewal by the parties if they mutually agree and the property is not sold at the end of the initial listing period. This form also provides an easy way to amend the contract for price adjustments or other changes.

Brokerage Fee

Percentage of Final Sales Price

The most common commission arrangement found in listing contracts is for the commission to be a specified percentage of the final sales price of the property. Notice that this is not a percentage of the listed price (unless the listed price and final sales price are identical), but it is the price for which the property sells.

Flat Fee and Limited Service Agreements

Another form of commission arrangement is the **flat fee listing.** *The broker takes the listing based on a specified payment of money by the seller to the broker at the time of listing.* The broker is entitled to retain this fee for her marketing efforts. The broker's compensation, in this case, does not depend on the sale of the property. The amount of the flat fee is often substantially less than the broker normally would receive had the compensation been based on a percentage of the selling price. These contracts often are limited service contracts. The broker may contract to only advertise the property and put together a sales contract when buyer and seller agree on the terms. There may be several plans to choose from, each with specified services and fees. The seller has the sole responsibility for all aspects of the transaction other than those she contracted with the broker to do. In this type of arrangement, the agency is paid only for efforts and not for results, as is the case in the typical brokerage listing. In similar arrangements, however, the agency is paid the flat fee only at the conclusion of the sale. Although a broker may limit services by using a carefully worded listing contract, she cannot limit her duties under agency law and North Carolina Real Estate Law, Rules, and Regulations as they apply to the contracted services. Flat fee listing agreements are also commonly used to establish either a minimum commission amount, such as the case when the percentage method would yield less than required to profitably list the property or in cases involving very large amounts of money.

AGENCY AGREEMENT RENEWAL AND/OR AMENDMENT

This AGENCY AGREEMENT RENEWAL AND/OR AMENDMENT renews and/or amends the following agency agreement (referred to hereafter as the "Agency Agreement")

- ☐ NCAR Form #101 (Exclusive Right to Sell Listing Agreement) dated _____
- ☐ NCAR Form #103 (Exclusive Right to Sell Listing Agreement) dated _____
- ☐ NCAR Form #201 (Exclusive Buyer Agency Agreement) dated _____
- ☐ NCAR Form #203 (Non-Exclusive Buyer Agency Agreement) dated _____
- ☐ NCAR Form #601 (Exclusive Right to Sell Listing Agreement-Auction Sales) dated _____

Entered into by and between _____("Client")
and _____Real Estate Firm ("Firm").

Property Address/MLS# (if applicable): _____

Client and Firm agree that the Agency Agreement is hereby renewed and/or amended in the manner indicated below (***Fill in applicable blanks; enter "N/A" in any blank not used***):

Renewed and extended until midnight, _____, 20 _____. In the event that the term of the Agency Agreement has expired, Client and Firm specifically agree that this Agency Agreement Amendment and/or Renewal shall operate to revive the Agency Agreement for the agreed-upon period of time.

Price shall be changed from $_____ to $_____

Other amendments: _____
_____
_____
_____
_____
_____

All terms and conditions of the Agency Agreement not specifically amended herein shall remain the same.

Client and Firm each hereby acknowledge receipt of a signed copy of this document.

THE NORTH CAROLINA ASSOCIATION OF REALTORS®, INC. MAKES NO REPRESENTATION AS TO THE LEGAL VALIDITY OR ADEQUACY OF ANY PROVISION OF THIS FORM IN ANY SPECIFIC TRANSACTION.

Client: _____ Date: _____

Client: _____ Date: _____

Entity Client: _____
(Name of LLC/Corporation/Partnership/Trust/etc.)

By: _____ Date: _____

Name: _____ Title: _____

Firm (Firm Name): _____

By: _____ Date: _____
Authorized Representative

Page 1 of 1

North Carolina Association of REALTORS®, Inc

STANDARD FORM 710
Revised 7/2014
© 7/2018

FIGURE 8.2 Agency agreement renewal and/or amendment.
Source: Used with permission of North Carolina Association of REALTORS®

Net Listing

Another type of commission arrangement is the **net listing.** This is a situation in which *the seller, when listing the property, specifies a net amount of money he must receive from the sale.* All money received that is above the net amount the seller specified is designated as the broker's commission in effecting the sale. This type of commission arrangement is not recommended but is legal in North Carolina. The net listing is, at best, a very poor arrangement of commission schedule. It can lead to a great deal of dissatisfaction on the part of the owner if the property sells for substantially more than the owner anticipated, resulting in a disproportionate share of the proceeds for the broker. At the other extreme, sellers can request a net listing at a price that does not allow the broker to make any money.

When you consider the broker's responsibility to his principal, the owner, and look at the situation in light of the fact that one of the broker's responsibilities is to establish a fair market price for the property, it would seem the broker is fulfilling the responsibility in a much better and more professional manner by recommending a fair market price that would include a reasonable rate of commission established as a percentage of the sales price or at a reasonable flat fee.

Referral Fees

Brokers often pay a referral fee to other licensed brokers outside their locality when the other broker refers prospective buyers and sellers. Because real estate is a highly local market, the area of referral may be a nearby town or the other side of the country. A broker from another state may make a referral to a North Carolina broker. All that is necessary is that both brokers be duly licensed in their own states. At the current time, all 50 states allow the payment and collection of referral fees, although the individual requirements of each state may vary.

Duration of the Listing

North Carolina License Law Rule A.0104 specifies that all agency contracts, including the listing contract, be in writing and that they specify an automatic termination date. This means that the principal (owner) is not required to take any positive action to terminate the listing. Therefore, the agent is employed for a specific period of time unless the owner authorizes an extension. No automatic renewals are allowed.

Protection Period

Another negotiable item in the listing contract, the **override clause protection period,** *protects the agent for a period of time after expiration of the listing from sales to prospects the agent recruited.* A typical clause might specify that at the termination of the listing period, the agent will register with the seller prospects who were shown the property. A subsequent sale to any of these prospects within a specified period of time would require payment of the commission to the agent. This clause protects the agent from the seller's trying to strike a private deal with a buyer recruited by the agent's efforts to avoid payment of a commission. It is common that some listing agreements, such as those copyrighted by the NCAR, will terminate the override clauses in the event the property is listed with another REALTOR® or MLS member firm because the original listing broker still would be afforded the opportunity to sell the property and collect a commission.

Property Data Sheet

When the listing agent collects data on the subject property for dissemination to prospective buyers or other brokers through an MLS, she must take care to ensure that the data are complete and accurate. The agent has an affirmative duty to "discover and disclose" all material facts about the property. Although no specific format is required, the agent is responsible for proper disclosure. Furthermore, a subagent or a buyer's agent is not entitled to rely blindly on these data but has an affirmative duty to verify the information in making representations to her prospects. A disclaimer does not relieve an agent of responsibility or possible disciplinary action by the Real Estate Commission for failure to disclose.

Termination of Listing Contracts

Several factors have an influence on the termination of the listing contract. The first significant factor is Real Estate Commission Rule A.0104, which requires that all written listing contracts have an automatic termination date, with no action required by the seller. Any failure to abide by this provision, such as leaving the contract duration indefinite, would subject the agent to disciplinary action by the Real Estate Commission.

Unfortunately, some brokers have a mistaken concept on a second factor influencing the duration of a listing contract. Just as when one is hired by any employer, one is subject to being discharged or fired ("dehired" in a modern euphemism), and so it is with the listing contract. As you know, the listing contract is nothing more than an employment arrangement. Just as your present boss can fire you at almost any time, the seller-principal can terminate the listing contract at any time, regardless of how much time is left to run on the original agreement. If the sellers withdraw the agency authorization, the agent has no further right to proceed in representing them. The principal, however, may be liable to the agent for damages, which are up to the agent to prove. The seller cannot use this strategy to circumvent the agent's commission when the agent has done what he contracted to do, namely, find a ready, willing, and able buyer. Listings also can be terminated by the death of the listing agent; by destruction of the subject matter; or in the event the agent cannot otherwise, perhaps legally, perform. It is important to remember that the firm is the agent and the fact the individual who listed the property on behalf of the firm has deceased does not necessarily terminate the listing. As long as the firm has another person who possesses the necessary skills to carry out the terms of the listing, the agreement is not terminated. If, for example, one agent in the firm handled commercial transactions whereas the other agents all dealt with residential, the commercial listing might be terminated at the death of the person who listed the property because the firm does not have anyone else who can reasonably perform the necessary duties. A residential listing under similar circumstances could easily be handled by another member of the firm, and that listing might not be terminated. If the seller dies, the listing is terminated immediately. If the heirs wish for the same agent to continue to list the property, they would need to execute a new listing agreement showing them as the sellers. If the subject of the contract is destroyed, such as by fire, hurricane, or flood, the listing is considered to be terminated. A single practicing agent who loses her license, even for a brief period of time, would find the listing terminated. Certainly, the best way to terminate a listing is to simply sell the house and perform as the contract contemplated.

MULTIPLE LISTING SERVICE ARRANGEMENTS

The term *multiple listing* refers to an *organized method of placing listings in a pool of listings by member brokers*; it is not a type of listing. Multiple listing provides substantially increased market exposure for the listings placed in the pool. For this reason, a **multiple listing service (MLS)** is of significant benefit to brokers and sellers.

The listing broker is the agent of the property owner. The other member brokers participating to effect a sale of another broker's listing are either subagents of the listing broker or agents of the buyer.

A listing firm may offer cooperation and compensation to other MLS members who sell their properties. This offer may be made to subagents, buyer's agents, or both. Compensation may differ for subagents and buyer's agents. A cooperating broker acting as a subagent owes the same duties of agency to the seller as the listing firm does. A cooperating buyer's agent owes the duties of agency to the buyer. All agents should be especially careful to understand and adhere to the law of agency, because a violation of agency is a violation of the Real Estate License Law.

ANTITRUST LAW

The amount or rate of commission to be charged by or paid to a real estate broker is strictly a negotiable matter between the broker and the listing seller. It is a violation of federal law for any person or organization—either government or private—even to recommend a commission schedule to a broker or group of brokers. It is also illegal for two or more brokers to agree to charge certain rates of commission to listing sellers. These activities are "price fixing" and are acts in the restraint of trade in violation of the Sherman Antitrust Act.

Competing brokers cannot even be a party to a discussion of commission rates or the boycott of a competitor on the basis of his rates. Agents who are present in a room where such illegal activities are discussed might be held to be parties to a price-fixing conspiracy unless they take specific steps to disavow themselves from the discussion. For example, if an agent at a meeting, such as that of an MLS committee, were to say, "I think we ought to charge 10%," other members have a duty to protest that statement, leave the meeting, and report the discussion to the proper authorities to absolve themselves of complicity to the discussion. It also would be a direct violation for an MLS to exclude certain categories of business models, such as discount or limited services brokers, from participating as members.

LAWS AFFECTING SOLICITATION OF CLIENTS OR CUSTOMERS

Various state and federal laws affect the ability of the real estate agent to contact clients in addition to Code of Ethics violations of the NAR. Agents will need to be cognizant of these rules to make certain that violations do not occur.

Solicitation of Active Clients of Other Firms or Brokers

The attempt to solicit an active client of another REALTOR® member constitutes a violation of Article 16 of the REALTOR® Code of Ethics. Such violation may subject a REALTOR® member to disciplinary action by the local association. Additionally, such solicitation may constitute "tortious interference with contractual relations," commonly known as contract tampering, which could subject the agent and firm to civil litigation.

Federal and North Carolina Do Not Call Laws and Rules

Because of the unusually high volume of telephone solicitations, legislation was passed to allow consumers to seek protection from many of these calls by signing up on the **Do Not Call Registry**. This registry *allows consumers to block many of these unwelcome calls from solicitors where the purpose was to conduct commerce such as when the caller attempts to sell something, solicits investment in, or otherwise seeks to provide a service.*

A number of exempt calls are not affected by this legislation. Calls in which the recipient has given *express permission or invitation* to the caller are exempt,

> "You have to know the exceptions to the 'Do Not Call' rules. They are: charities, political campaigns, anyone with whom you previously did business within the last 18 months, a response to an inquiry within the last 90 days, a for sale by owner when you have a bona fide buyer."
>
> —Len Elder, DREI

such as when someone contacts another and asks that someone call them to discuss a situation further. Another situation, which affects real estate agents, is the case of a FSBO who has his personal house on the market and has a sign in the front yard that lists the seller's phone number as a means of contact. A potential buyer could certainly call that seller without regard for whether he is listed on the Do Not Call Registry, as the provision of the phone number was an open permission for an interested party to call and discuss the purchase of the house. A buyer's agent who has an interested buyer would also be allowed to call the seller to inquire whether the seller would be willing to work with him/her as a buyer's agent. If, however, the seller indicates that he is not interested in working with an agent, the call must end. The agent would not be permitted to ask whether the seller may be interested in listing the property for sale. This permission is interpreted as being rather narrow in focus. Likewise, a caller who has an *established business relationship* is allowed to call the person with whom he has the relationship during the period of their business dealings. For example, a seller who is registered on the Do Not Call Registry has listed his house for sale with an agent for 120 days. Certainly, during the time of the listing, the agent is allowed to call the seller without regard to the fact he is registered. There are additional periods of time in which such a call is considered exempt, and they are within *90 days of a caller making an inquiry into a product or service* and *18 months after the period of the business relationship has terminated*. Calls between people who have a *personal relationship* are also exempt. Exemptions also are allowed for nonprofit organizations, such as charities, political campaigns, and polling organizations.

The purpose of this legislation was to limit the number of situations in which a telephone solicitation call could be made. It was not intended to affect calls between friends and other types of calls in which there was no attempt at solicitation.

Telemarketers are required to search the registry at least every 31 days to update their lists of permitted numbers to call. Violations of this Act can incur penalties of up to $11,000 on the federal level. North Carolina has enacted legislation that essentially mirrors the federal act and imposes fines from $500 to $5,000.

"Junk Fax" Laws and Rules

These rules restrict unsolicited faxes in situations in which the recipient's permission has not been obtained. There is an exemption for an existing business relationship that has not been terminated. Such would be the case if an agent faxes an offer to purchase to her seller for her consideration. There is a requirement that there must be a prominent "opt-out" notice as the cover sheet of any fax. These laws do not recognize the same exemptions as the Do Not Call legislation, and senders would be wise to seek written permission before sending these faxes. Please note the permission letter cannot be faxed to the recipient.

"CAN-SPAM ACT"

Officially titled the "Controlling the Assault of Non-Solicited Pornography and Marketing Act" or the CAN-SPAM Act, this legislation seeks to regulate the practice of spamming by email. This act originally was passed to address the large number of emails in which the recipient would open an email only to discover that it contained pornography. This legislation requires the subject of the email to be presented in a manner in which the recipient knows the basic content before opening. The email must also contain the name and physical address of the sender as well as an prominent "opt-out" feature. It is thought that the CAN-SPAM Act has had limited impact on the real estate industry.

LISTING PROCEDURES

Impeccable listing procedures are essential to a successful real estate transaction. Major problems result from an improperly or sloppily listed property. The listing agent's fiduciary duty to his seller requires the agent to use due diligence in listing, pricing, and marketing the property to achieve an optimum outcome for the seller with the fewest possible risks or problems. An agent's duties to third parties require an accurate representation of the property being sold, including material facts. Because these duties are discussed in detail elsewhere, they are not presented here.

An agent with a firm that practices dual agency may find that he is also responsible to a buyer client of his firm who may want to purchase his listing. He may find himself in practical and public relations trouble in a dual agency situation, even if he has not actually violated any laws or Commission rules. The agent, therefore, needs to think ahead to a possible dual agency situation and thoroughly educate the seller-client at the time of listing about how to protect her own interest in a dual agency situation, including how to obtain information from outside professionals, if necessary. The seller should understand that any of the firm's buyer-clients will receive the buyer's version of the same briefing when the buyer signs a buyer agency agreement.

Preliminary Listing Procedures

1. At first substantial contact with seller, the agent must review with the seller the brochure *Working with Real Estate Agents* to make sure the seller adequately understands agency. The agent should ask but cannot require the seller to sign the perforated panel attached to the brochure to acknowledge explanation and receipt of the brochure. This acknowledgment is kept on file whether or not the seller lists the property with the agent. When and if the seller signs the listing contract, she should do so with informed consent.

2. The agent must educate the seller (client), as follows:
   - Discuss listing contract provisions and seller's and agent's duties and responsibilities under contract.

- Explain duties of seller and agent to third-party buyers and buyer-clients of the listing firm to disclose material fact and to provide a Residential Property and Owners' Association Disclosure Statement as well as a Lead-Based Paint or a Synthetic Stucco Disclosures when applicable.
- Discuss company's generic marketing plan, including frequency and types of advertising, such as Internet, newspapers, brochures, television, and radio, as applicable. Customize a plan for seller's property at some point during the listing process.
- Provide the seller with company's commission policy and additional fees, if any. Avoid suggesting that there are set commissions other than what each company sets for itself independently of all other companies.
- Explain the importance of proper pricing and how you will arrive at a suggested price range through a carefully prepared comparative market analysis (CMA). If property is unique and has few, if any, recent comparables, you may suggest an appraisal. Discuss CMAs and appraisals as a reflection of market value, not a setting of market value. Suggest that whatever the listing price, it should be reevaluated every four to six weeks until the property is sold.
- Give seller a sample copy of the NCAR Offer to Purchase and Contract. Review provisions with the seller and answer any questions.

3. The agent must sell himself and his company. If he cannot inspire confidence in this prelisting phase, he may not get the listing. If he does, he can proceed to the actual listing procedures. Educating the seller and selling himself and his company usually are accomplished at the same time. Properly educating the seller contributes greatly to the company's and the agent's image.

Final Listing Procedures

The following listing procedures may be followed by the agent as the individual situation requires:

1. The agent should inspect the property with the seller and should accurately complete a property data sheet and a "red flag" checklist of the property. She should note any physical defects and discuss repairs with the seller. The seller must decide what she is willing to repair and when. Ideally, repairs should be made before the property is marketed to help maximize the sales price. If the seller is unwilling to repair anything that will be required to be repaired by an appraisal, especially an FHA or VA or Rural Development appraisal, she needs to understand that the buyer may not be able to get a loan on a property with problems such as peeling paint, a leaking roof, rotten wood, broken glass, or safety hazards. Failure to do repairs may diminish the pool of buyers. The agent should determine what, if any, fixtures do not convey and what items

of personal property, if any, do convey and should include this information in the listing contract. The agent may assist the seller in completing the Residential Property and Owners' Association Disclosure Statement, but not do it for her. The agent should explain the difference between the seller's duties and the agent's duties. Although the seller can check "no representation," the agent has a legal obligation to disclose all material facts to buyers. The agent may explain the practical considerations of "no representation" to the seller and refer the seller to an attorney if she wants legal advice. Failure to fill out the form is not illegal, but it gives the buyer a three-day right of limited rescission. The agent should assist the seller in completing the Lead-Based Paint Disclosure, if applicable. This is a joint responsibility. The agent and the seller are legally liable for compliance. NOTE: Inspection and completion of these forms at this time identify factors that may affect the sale price of the property and, therefore, should be considered in the CMA.

2. The agent should carefully measure all structures according to the Real Estate Commission's *Residential Square Footage Guidelines* (see Appendix D). Accuracy and adherence to guidelines are imperative. NOTE: The agent may compare his measurements with the appraiser's measurements when the appraisal is done for the buyer before closing. Keep in mind the appraiser may utilize measurement standards that vary somewhat from those of the Commission. It is preferable to find mistakes before, rather than after, closing. The agent cannot rely on tax data, building plans, seller, or previous MLS listing information.

3. The broker can avoid many problems from the time of the listing through contract and closing if she gathers the following documents at the time of the listing:

    - Copies of deeds and title policies
    - Zoning restrictions
    - Restrictive/protective covenants
    - Transferable warranties

From these documents, the broker can verify information such as the dimensions and size of the lot, the legal description, and the seller's interest in the property. The local planning board should be able to answer questions about zoning and designated floodplains.

The agent should gently question the seller to determine whether other facts will affect the transaction. Occasionally, a seller forgets to tell the agent that she sold an interest in the property to his brother or sold a half-acre section off the back corner or gave an easement to a neighbor after purchasing the property. The seller may conveniently forget to mention a second mortgage, lien, or home equity line, which, when combined with the first mortgage balance, total more than the property is worth. In this case, the sale may fall through if the seller has no money to pay the difference and a compromise cannot be reached with the mortgage companies. If the agent is unaware of this fact until the closing, the attorney for the new "almost" buyer may discover it in the title search; in this case, agents, mortgage companies, attorneys, and other professionals, not to mention the buyer, may have expended a lot of effort for nothing. If any doubt exists about the seller's ability to convey clear title, the agent should consider obtaining a preliminary title search.

4. The agent can prepare and present a CMA. After obtaining and verifying all of the information on the seller's property, the listing agent can carefully prepare a CMA on the seller's property and an estimate of the seller's closing costs. The agent can also discuss with the seller any local market trends, such as sellers paying buyers' closing costs. With this information in hand, the agent is ready to advise the seller on an appropriate listing price and on the amount the seller can expect in terms of proceeds from the sale of the property.

5. The agent can assist the seller in determining the listing price, preferably within the range determined by the market analysis. Should the seller want to list at an unrealistically high price, the agent must decide whether to take the listing. Pricing objections can usually be overcome if the agent educates the seller about the disadvantages of listing too high. It has been proven through many studies that overpricing a house results in the sale taking much longer and in a lower sales price than would have been realized had the property been properly priced from the beginning.

6. The agent may prepare an estimated net proceeds sheet based on the listing price at the time of listing. See Figure 8.3 for a sample form designed for an area where it is customary for the seller to pay some or all of a buyer's closing costs. Any firm may design its own estimated net proceeds sheet reflecting general terms, conditions, and cost in its area. This sample form may be used for estimating either the seller's or buyer's cost or both if the seller is paying the buyer's closing costs. The agent would be wise to prepare a net proceeds estimate before presenting an offer and to emphasize that it is estimated. The estimate should be adjusted with each counteroffer.

7. A prudent broker will review the accuracy of the property data sheet completed at the inspection of the property with the seller. The broker will check the MLS computer printout with the property data sheet after information is entered into the computer.

8. The agent needs to use a well-drafted listing contract form, such as the Exclusive Right to Sell Listing Agreement shown in Figure 8.1. Other forms are acceptable as long as they meet the requirements of the Real Estate Commission. After all of these steps are complete and the agent is reasonably sure the seller understands what he is signing, the agent should have the seller sign the listing contract and any applicable addenda and disclosures. The agent should give the seller a copy of everything he signs.

SELLER'S ESTIMATED NET PROCEEDS

DATE _____

SELLERS _____

ADDRESS _____

SALES PRICE _____

SELLER'S CLOSING COSTS

$_____ DEED PREPARATION

$_____ EXCISE TAX

$_____ VA MANDATORY SELLER PAID CLOSING COSTS*

$_____ BROKERAGE SERVICES

$_____ 20___ REAL ESTATE TAXES

$_____ 1ST MORTGAGE PAYOFF

$_____ 2ND MORTGAGE PAYOFF

$_____ ADDITIONAL LIENS

$_____ INTEREST IN ARREARS

$_____ ONE-YEAR WARRANTY

$_____ LENDER'S INSPECTION FEE

$_____ TOTAL

BUYER'S CLOSING COSTS

$_____ SURVEY

$_____ TITLE INSURANCE

$_____ ATTORNEY'S FEES

$_____ RECORDING FEES

$_____ LOAN ORIGINATION FEE

$_____ APPRAISAL FEE

$_____ CREDIT REPORT

$_____ LENDER FEES*

$_____ TERMITE INSPECTION*

$_____ TOTAL   TOTAL BUYER CLOSING COSTS $ _____

BUYER'S PREPAIDS

$_____ INTERIM INTEREST
                    @ $ _____ PER DAY

$_____ 14-MO. HAZARD INS.

$_____ ___-MO. TAX ESCROW

$_____ TOTAL

*NOTE: ON VA LOANS, THE TERMITE INSPECTION AND CERTAIN LENDER FEES ARE PAID BY SELLER.

$_____ SALES PRICE

−_____ SELLER'S CLOSING COSTS

−_____ BUYER'S CLOSING COSTS AND/OR REPAIRS PAID BY SELLER (PUT -0- IF NOT APPLICABLE)

$_____ SELLER'S ESTIMATED NET PROCEEDS (THIS AMOUNT WILL BE REDUCED BY THE COSTS OF ANY REPAIRS SELLER MAKES PER REPAIR PROVISIONS OF THE CONTRACT, APPRAISAL, OR WDI REPORT.)

THE SELLER ACKNOWLEDGES THAT THIS IS ONLY AN ESTIMATE AND FINAL FIGURES MAY VARY.

SELLER _____ DATE _____ SELLER _____ DATE _____

FIGURE 8.3 Net proceeds sheet
Source: © 2019 OnCourse Learning

9. The agent should process the listing according to office procedures. The listing checklist is not all-inclusive, and not all items are necessary for every listing. For example, some sellers may choose not to offer a homeowner's warranty. The agent must include all items required by real estate law, rules, and regulations, such as listing contracts and signed acknowledgment from the *Working with Real Estate Agents* brochure.

10. The agent must implement the agreed-upon marketing plan.

11. The agent must maintain communication with the seller throughout the listing period. The agent should set appointments, offer feedback, discuss changes with the seller in price or market strategy, maintain a communication log, get any changes to the listing contract in writing, and refer to the listing contract when an offer to purchase is received. Items in the listing contract may be negotiated in or out of a sales contract, but reviewing the listing contract at this time prevents oversights.

BUYER AGENCY CONTRACTS

A buyer agency contract is an agreement between a prospective buyer and a broker in which the broker is contracted to act as the buyer's agent in the purchase of real estate.

Agency Disclosure and Nonexclusive Buyer Agency Agreement

A **nonexclusive buyer agency agreement** is one that retains a broker to act as the buyer's agent in the purchase of real estate but leaves the buyer free to enter into additional nonexclusive relationships with other brokers, to purchase real estate through a broker acting as a seller's agent or subagent, or to purchase real estate directly from an owner. It *establishes a buyer agency relationship but does not require the buyer to pay or assume the payment of a brokerage fee*. Under this type of agreement, the broker is entitled to a commission or success fee when the broker is the procuring cause of the purchase. The nonexclusive buyer agency agreements may be either oral or in writing. Oral nonexclusive buyer agency is allowed, provided it does not bind the buyer-client to a specific agent or company or to a definite period of time. As with other types of agency contracts involving the sale of real property, this nonexclusive buyer agency agreement must be reduced to writing before submitting the offer to purchase for the buyer (Figure 8.4).

Exclusive Buyer Agency Agreement

An **exclusive buyer agency contract** is one in which *the prospective buyer retains a broker as his exclusive agent*. Under this type of contract, the broker who is a party to the contract is the only real estate agent with whom the buyer can work in the purchase of a property as described in the agreement. Depending on the wording

NON-EXCLUSIVE BUYER AGENCY AGREEMENT

This NON-EXCLUSIVE BUYER AGENCY AGREEMENT ("Agreement") is entered into (Date) _____,
between _____ as Buyer(s) ("Buyer"),
and _____ ("Firm").
The individual agent who signs this Agreement shall, on behalf of the Firm, be primarily responsible for ensuring that the Firm's duties hereunder are fulfilled; however, it is understood and agreed that other agents of the Firm may be assigned to fulfill such duties if deemed appropriate by the Firm. For purposes of this Agreement, the term "Firm," as the context may require, shall be deemed to include the individual agent who signs this Agreement and any other agents of the Firm.

> The purpose of this form is to properly establish a written buyer agency relationship. The various forms of agency relationships are discussed in the "Working with Real Estate Agents" brochure, a copy of which Buyer has received and reviewed with the agent. Buyer's execution of this form confirms that Buyer has read and understands the contents of that brochure, and is making a decision to request buyer agency for the period of time set forth below. Buyer represents that, as of the commencement date of this Agreement, Buyer is not a party to an exclusive buyer representation agreement with any other real estate firm.

1. **PROPERTY.** Firm agrees to act as a non-exclusive buyer's agent representing Buyer in the acquisition of real property by **[Check all that apply]**: ❑ locating suitable real estate   ❑ showing the following specific property _____
_____

2. **DURATION OF AGENCY.** Firm's authority as Buyer's non-exclusive agent shall begin _____, and shall expire at midnight, _____.

3. **COMPENSATION OF FIRM.**
    (a) **Fee**. This agreement does not obligate Buyer to pay a brokerage fee or assure the payment of a brokerage fee to Firm. Buyer acknowledges and understands that Firm expects to receive and will seek a fee for Firm's services under an offer of compensation from a cooperating seller/listing firm in the amount of _____
_____ ("Fee")
(Insert dollar amount, percentage of purchase price, or other method of determining Firm's compensation for each type of property the Buyer may purchase, *such as resale, new construction, land/lot and/or unrepresented seller*. Do not insert N/A or a zero ($0)).
    (b) **Modification of Fee**. Provided, however, Firm may inform Buyer that the compensation offered is less than expected and, if Buyer is so informed prior to making an offer to purchase, Firm may seek a reasonable modification of the compensation terms herein and, if unable to reach such a modification, Firm may unilaterally terminate this Agreement.
    (c) **Additional Compensation**. If additional compensation, incentive, bonus, rebate and/or other valuable consideration ("Additional Compensation") is offered through the MLS or otherwise, Buyer will permit the Firm to receive it in addition to the Fee. Firm shall timely disclose the promise or expectation of receiving any such Additional Compensation and confirm the disclosure in writing before Buyer makes or accepts an offer to buy. (Note: NCAR Form #770 may be used to confirm the disclosure of any such Additional Compensation).
    (d) **When Compensation Earned**. The compensation shall be deemed earned if, during the term of this Agreement, Buyer, any assignee of Buyer or any person/legal entity acting on behalf of Buyer directly or indirectly enters into an agreement to purchase, option, and/or exchange property introduced to Buyer by Firm.

> **NOTE:** Buyer understands and acknowledges that there is the potential for a conflict of interest generated by a percentage of price based fee for representing Buyer. The amount, format or rate of real estate commission is not fixed by law, but is set by each broker individually, and may be negotiable between Buyer and Firm.

4. **ACKNOWLEDGMENTS OF RECEIPT.**
    ❑ Buyer acknowledges receipt of a sample copy of an Offer to Purchase and Contract for review purposes.
    ❑ Buyer acknowledges receipt of a copy of the brochure *Questions and Answers on: Home Inspections*.
    ❑ Buyer acknowledges receipt of a sample copy of a Professional Services Disclosure and Election form (form #760) for review purposes.

Page 1 of 4

North Carolina Association of REALTORS®, Inc.

Buyer initials _____ _____ Individual agent initials _____

STANDARD FORM 203
Revised 7/2018
© 7/2018

FIGURE 8.4 Agency disclosure and nonexclusive buyer agency agreement.

5. CONFIDENTIALITY OF OFFERS. Real estate brokers are prohibited by N.C. Real Estate Commission rule from disclosing the price or other material terms contained in a party's offer to purchase, sell, lease, rent or option real property to a competing party without the express authority of the party making the offer. However, sellers may elect not to treat the existence, terms, or conditions of any offers Buyer may make as confidential. Additionally, sellers may elect not to disclose or authorize seller's agent to disclose the existence of any other offer(s).

6. DISCLOSURE OF BUYER'S NAME/MAILING ADDRESS.
   (a) **Name**. Unless otherwise stated herein, Firm has Buyer's permission to disclose Buyer's name.
   (b) **Mailing Address**. In accordance with NC General Statutes Section 93A-12, if a dispute regarding the return or forfeiture of any earnest money deposit arises between Buyer and the seller of any real property Buyer may agree to purchase, the escrow agent holding the deposit may deposit the disputed monies with the appropriate Clerk of Court following written notice to the parties. In the event of any such dispute, Buyer directs Firm to disclose Buyer's last known mailing address to the escrow agent upon request to enable the escrow agent to comply with the notice requirement of such law.

7. DUAL AGENCY. Buyer understands that the potential for dual agency will arise if Buyer becomes interested in viewing property listed with Firm. Firm may represent more than one party in the same transaction only with the knowledge and informed consent of all parties for whom Firm acts.
   (a) **Disclosure of Information**. In the event Firm serves as a dual agent, Buyer agrees that without permission from the party about whom the information pertains, Firm shall not disclose to the other party the following information:
      (1) that a party may agree to a price, terms, or any conditions of sale other than those offered;
      (2) the motivation of a party for engaging in the transaction, unless disclosure is otherwise required by statute or rule; and
      (3) any information about a party which that party has identified as confidential unless disclosure is otherwise required by statute or rule.
   (b) **Firm's Role as Dual Agent**. If Firm serves as agent for both Buyer and a seller in a transaction, Firm shall make every reasonable effort to represent Buyer and seller in a balanced and fair manner. Firm shall also make every reasonable effort to encourage and effect communication and negotiation between Buyer and seller. Buyer understands and acknowledges that:
      (1) Prior to the time dual agency occurs, Firm will act as Buyer's exclusive agent;
      (2) In its separate representation of Buyer and seller, Firm may obtain information which, if disclosed, could harm the bargaining position of the party providing such information to Firm;
      (3) Firm is required by law to disclose to Buyer and seller any known or reasonably ascertainable material facts.

Buyer agrees Firm shall not be liable to Buyer for (i) disclosing material facts required by law to be disclosed, and (ii) refusing or failing to disclose other information the law does not require to be disclosed which could harm or compromise one party's bargaining position but could benefit the other party.

   (c) **Buyer's Role**. Should Firm become a dual agent, Buyer understands and acknowledges that:
      (1) Buyer has the responsibility of making Buyer's own decisions as to what terms are to be included in any purchase and sale agreement with a seller client of Firm;
      (2) Buyer is fully aware of and understands the implications and consequences of Firm's dual agency role as expressed herein to provide balanced and fair representation of Buyer and seller and to encourage and effect communication between them rather than as an advocate or exclusive agent or representative;
      (3) Buyer has determined that the benefits of dual agency outweigh any disadvantages or adverse consequences;
      (4) Buyer may seek independent legal counsel to assist Buyer with the negotiation and preparation of a purchase and sale agreement or with any matter relating to the transaction which is the subject matter of a purchase and sale agreement.

Should Firm become a dual agent, Buyer waives all claims, damages, losses, expenses or liabilities, other than for violations of the North Carolina Real Estate License Law and intentional wrongful acts, arising from Firm's role as a dual agent. Buyer shall have a duty to protect Buyer's own interests and should read any purchase and sale agreement carefully to ensure that it accurately sets forth the terms which Buyer wants included in said agreement.

   (d) **Authorization** *(initial only ONE)*.

   _____ _____ Buyer authorizes the Firm to act as a dual agent, representing both the Buyer and the seller, subject to the terms and conditions set forth in this paragraph.
   _____ _____ Buyer desires exclusive representation at all times during this agreement and does NOT authorize Firm to act in the capacity of dual agent. *If Buyer does not authorize Firm to act as a dual agent, the remainder of this paragraph shall not apply.*

FIGURE 8.4 *(Continued)*

(e) **Designated Agent Option** (*Initial only if applicable*).
_____ _____ Buyer hereby authorizes the Firm to designate an individual agent(s) to represent the Buyer. The individual designated agent(s) shall represent only the interests of the Buyer to the extent permitted by law.

NOTE: When dual agency arises, an individual agent shall not practice designated agency and shall remain a dual agent if the individual agent has actually received confidential information concerning a buyer client of the Firm in connection with the transaction or if designated agency is otherwise prohibited by law.

(f) **Dual Agency Compensation**. If the Firm acts as a dual agent (including designated agency), the total fee the Firm expects to receive for its services in representing Buyer and the seller shall be _____.
(Insert dollar amount, percentage of purchase price, or other method of determining Firm's compensation for each type of property such as resale, new construction and/or land/lot the Buyer may purchase.). THIS WILL IN NO WAY AFFECT OR MODIFY THE AMOUNT OF THE FEE SET FORTH IN PARAGRAPH 3 ABOVE THAT FIRM EXPECTS TO RECEIVE FOR ITS SERVICES IN REPRESENTING BUYER UNDER THIS AGREEMENT. In the event Buyer is interested in purchasing a property where the Firm's total fee is different from that described in this subparagraph (f), the Firm shall timely disclose the fee to Buyer and confirm it in writing before Buyer makes or accepts an offer to buy or sell any such property.

8. **NON-DISCRIMINATION. THE AGENT (FIRM) SHALL CONDUCT ALL BROKERAGE ACTIVITIES IN REGARD TO THIS AGREEMENT WITHOUT RESPECT TO THE RACE, COLOR, RELIGION, SEX, NATIONAL ORIGIN, HANDICAP OR FAMILIAL STATUS OF ANY PARTY OR PROSPECTIVE PARTY TO THE AGREEMENT. FURTHER, REALTORS® HAVE AN ETHICAL DUTY TO CONDUCT SUCH ACTIVITIES WITHOUT RESPECT TO THE SEXUAL ORIENTATION OR GENDER IDENTITY OF ANY PARTY OR PROSPECTIVE PARTY TO THIS AGREEMENT.**

9. **EXECUTION.** This Agreement may be signed in multiple originals or counterparts, all of which together constitute one and the same instrument.

10. **SURVEILLANCE; USE OF PHOTOGRAHS AND VIDEO**: Federal and State laws prohibit the interception of an oral communication through the use of any electronic, mechanical, or other device, whether or not recorded, without the consent of a party to that communication. However, video surveillance without consent is not illegal. Buyer is advised to be mindful of the fact that there could be surveillance/audio device(s) located on any property examined by Buyer and that Buyer or Buyer's representatives may be under surveillance during any such examination.

Unless a property owner has notified the public that photography and video recording is prohibited, it is permissible to photograph or video the interior of private property since the owner's permission to enter the property implies permission to do so. However, under no circumstances may Buyer take photographs or videos that intrude on a property owner's reasonable expectations of privacy. Buyer should only photograph or video things that are in "plain view". For example, taking a photo or video of the contents of a medicine cabinet or of financial records in a desk drawer would be impermissible In addition, any permitted photography or video should be used only in a manner related directly to Buyer's examination and purchase of a property. TAKING IMPERMISSIBLE PHOTOGRAPHS OR VIDEOS OR USING THEM FOR AN IMPERMISSIBLE PURPOSE COULD SUBJECT BUYER TO CIVIL LIABILITY.

11. **WIRE FRAUD WARNING:**

BEFORE SENDING ANY WIRE, BUYER SHOULD CALL THE CLOSING ATTORNEY'S OFFICE TO VERIFY THE INSTRUCTIONS. IF BUYER RECEIVES WIRING INSTRUCTIONS FOR A DIFFERENT BANK, BRANCH LOCATION, ACCOUNT NAME OR ACCOUNT NUMBER, THEY SHOULD BE PRESUMED FRAUDULENT. DO NOT SEND ANY FUNDS AND CONTACT THE CLOSING ATTORNEY'S OFFICE IMMEDIATELY.

BUYER SHOULD CALL THE CLOSING ATTORNEY'S OFFICE AT A NUMBER THAT IS INDEPENDENTLY OBTAINED. TO ENSURE THAT THE CONTACT IS LEGITIMATE, BUYER SHOULD NOT RELY ON A PHONE NUMBER IN AN EMAIL FROM THE CLOSING ATTORNEY'S OFFICE, BUYER'S REAL ESTATE AGENT OR ANYONE ELSE.

Buyer acknowledges and understands that there are risks associated with wire transfers that are not within the reasonable control of Firm, and Buyer hereby agrees to release and discharge Firm and Firm's agents from any and all claims, demands, rights and causes of action of whatsoever kind and nature not caused by gross negligence of Firm or Firm's agents arising directly or indirectly out of any wire transfer Buyer sends or receives/was to receive in connection with any real estate transaction in which Firm represents buyer.

Page 3 of 4

Buyer initials _____ _____ Individual agent initials _____

STANDARD FORM 203
Revised 7/2018
© 7/2018

FIGURE 8.4 (*Continued*)

THE NORTH CAROLINA ASSOCIATION OF REALTORS®, INC. MAKES NO REPRESENTATION AS TO THE LEGAL VALIDITY OR ADEQUACY OF ANY PROVISION OF THIS FORM IN ANY SPECIFIC TRANSACTION.

Buyer: _____ _____ _____
            Print Name   Signature   Date

Contact Information: _____ _____ _____ _____
                       Home   Work   Cell   Email

Mailing Address: _____

Buyer: _____ _____ _____
            Print Name   Signature   Date

Contact Information: _____ _____ _____ _____
                       Home   Work   Cell   Email

Mailing Address: _____

Entity Buyer: _____
        (Name of LLC/Corporation/Partnership/Trust/etc.)

By: _____ Date: _____

Name: _____ Title: _____

Contact Information: _____ _____ _____ _____
                     Home   Work   Cell   Email

Mailing Address: _____

Firm: _____ Phone: _____
      Print Real Estate Firm Name

By: _____ _____ _____
    Individual Agent Signature   Individual License Number   Date

Office: _____

Address: _____

Office Phone: _____ Fax: _____ Email_____

Page 4 of 4

STANDARD FORM 203
Revised 7/2018
© 7/2018

FIGURE 8.4 (*Continued*)

of the contract, the buyer also may be obligated to pay the broker compensation even if the buyer purchases a property from an owner without the assistance of a real estate agent.

Typical Provisions of a Buyer Agency Contract

When entering into a buyer agency agreement, all parties should be named on the contract and all parties should sign the contract. This includes *all* people who will be purchasing the property. The following list is a brief discussion of the typical provisions of a buyer agency contract. Reference is made to NCAR Standard Form 201, Exclusive Right to Represent Buyer (see Figure 8.5).

1. The type and general location of the property is described.
2. The effect of the agreement is to employ the broker as the buyer's exclusive agent and have him agree to conduct all negotiations through the firm.
3. A specific duration for the contract must be stated.
4. The amount and method of compensation are defined.
5. The agent is given permission to represent other buyers who may seek to buy and present offers for the same or similar property as the buyer seeks to purchase.
6. The agent's duties are described.
7. The firm has the right to disclose the buyer's name and mailing address.
8. Standard nondiscrimination language is included.
9. The buyer's duties are described.
10. The buyer is advised the agent cannot give professional advice outside of her field of expertise and cannot guarantee quality of service from any provider whose name the agent may provide to buyer. The buyer further agrees to pay for any authorized services and to hold agents harmless in regard to acts of contractors and quality of services provided by them. The buyer acknowledges that she received a sample copy of an Offer to Purchase and Contract and a copy of the pamphlet *Questions and Answers on: Home Inspections*.
11. The buyer has the right to purchase a home warranty if one is not provided by the seller.
12. Confidentiality of offers is addressed.
13. Additional provisions may be negotiated between buyer and agent.
14. Explanation of dual agency includes the firm's and buyer's role if the firm should become a dual agent. The buyer's consent to allow dual agency is addressed along with the consent to allow designated dual agency.
15. Parties agree to mediation first, if a dispute arises.
16. The entire agreement is contained herein.
17. The individual's license number is required below the signature line.

EXCLUSIVE BUYER AGENCY AGREEMENT
[Consult "Guidelines" (Form 201G) for guidance in completing this form]

This EXCLUSIVE BUYER AGENCY AGREEMENT ("Agreement") is entered into (Date)_____,
between_____ as Buyer(s) ("Buyer"),
and_____ ("Firm")
as the Buyer's exclusive agent to assist the Buyer in the acquisition of real property which may include any purchase, option and/or exchange on terms and conditions acceptable to Buyer. The individual agent who signs this Agreement on behalf of the Firm shall, on behalf of the Firm, be primarily responsible for ensuring that the Firm's duties hereunder are fulfilled; however, it is understood and agreed that other agents of the Firm may be assigned to fulfill such duties if deemed appropriate by the Firm. For purposes of this Agreement, the term "Firm," as the context may require, shall be deemed to include the individual agent who signs this Agreement and any other agents of the Firm.

Buyer represents that, as of the commencement date of this Agreement, the Buyer is not a party to a buyer representation agreement with any other real estate firm. Buyer has received a copy of the "WORKING WITH REAL ESTATE AGENTS" brochure and has reviewed it with Firm. Buyer further represents that Buyer has disclosed to Firm information about any properties of the type described in paragraph 1 below that Buyer has visited at any open houses or that Buyer has been shown by any other real estate firm.

1. **TYPE OF PROPERTY.** ❑ Residential (improved and unimproved) ❑ Commercial (improved and unimproved)
   ❑ Other _____
   (a) General Location: _____
   (b) Other: _____

2. **EFFECT OF AGREEMENT.** Buyer intends to acquire real property of the type described in paragraph 1. *By employing Firm as Buyer's exclusive agent, Buyer agrees to conduct all negotiations for such property through Firm, and to refer to Firm all inquiries received in any form from other real estate firms, prospective sellers or any other source, during the time this Agreement is in effect.*

3. **DURATION OF AGENCY.** Firm's authority as Buyer's exclusive agent shall begin _____, and subject to paragraph 4, shall expire at midnight, _____, or when Buyer acquires real property of the type described in paragraph 1, whichever occurs sooner.

4. **COMPENSATION OF FIRM.**
   (a) Firm acknowledges receipt of a non-refundable retainer fee in the amount of $_____ which ❑shall ❑ shall not be credited toward any compensation due Firm under this Agreement.
   (b) Buyer agrees that Firm's fee for services hereunder shall be in the amount of _____
   _____("Fee")
   (Insert dollar amount, percentage of purchase price, or other method of determining Firm's compensation for each type of property the Buyer may purchase, such as resale, new construction, land/lot and/or unrepresented seller. Do not insert N/A or a zero ($0)).
   (i) Firm shall seek the Fee from a cooperating listing firm (through the listing firm's offer of compensation in MLS or otherwise) or from the seller if there is no listing firm, and Buyer agrees that Firm shall be entitled to receive same in consideration for Firm's services hereunder.
   (ii) If Buyer purchases property where the compensation offered by the listing firm and/or seller is less than the Fee, or where no compensation is offered by either the listing firm or the seller, Buyer and Firm agree that Buyer will pay the difference between the Fee and the compensation offered unless prohibited by law. Firm will timely inform Buyer if the compensation offered is less than expected.
   (iii) If additional compensation, incentive, bonus, rebate and/or other valuable consideration *("Additional Compensation")* is offered through the MLS or otherwise, Buyer will permit the Firm to receive it in addition to the Fee. Firm shall timely disclose the promise or expectation of receiving any such Additional Compensation and confirm the disclosure in writing before Buyer makes or accepts an offer to buy. (Note: NCAR Form #770 may be used to confirm the disclosure of any such Additional Compensation)
   (c) The compensation shall be deemed earned under any of the following circumstances:
   (i) If, during the term of this Agreement, Buyer, any assignee of Buyer or any person/legal entity acting on behalf of Buyer directly or indirectly enters into an agreement to purchase, option, and/or exchange any property of the type described above regardless of the manner in which Buyer was introduced to the property; or
   (ii) If, within _____ days after expiration of this Agreement, Buyer enters into a contract to acquire property introduced to Buyer during the term of this Agreement by Firm or any third party, unless Buyer has entered into a valid buyer agency agreement with another real estate firm; or

North Carolina Association of REALTORS®, Inc.

Buyer initials _____ _____   Individual agent initials _____

STANDARD FORM 201
Revised 7/2018
© 7/2018

FIGURE 8.5 Exclusive right to represent buyer.

(iii) If, having entered into an enforceable contract to acquire property during the term of this Agreement, Buyer defaults under the terms of that contract.
(d) The compensation will be due and payable at closing or upon Buyer's default of any purchase agreement. If Buyer defaults, the total compensation that would have been due the Firm will be due and payable immediately in cash from the Buyer. No assignment of rights in real property obtained for Buyer or any assignee of Buyer or any person/legal entity acting on behalf of Buyer pursuant to this Agreement shall operate to defeat any of Firm rights under this Agreement.

> **NOTE:** Buyer understands and acknowledges that there is the potential for a conflict of interest generated by a percentage of price based fee for representing Buyer. The amount, format or rate of real estate commission is not fixed by law, but is set by each broker individually, and may be negotiable between Buyer and Firm.

(e) Attorney Fees and Costs. If Firm is the prevailing party in any legal proceeding brought by Firm against Buyer to recover the Fee, Firm shall be entitled to recover from Buyer reasonable attorney fees and court costs incurred by Firm in connection with the proceeding.

5. **OTHER POTENTIAL BUYERS.** Buyer understands that other prospective purchasers represented by Firm may seek property, submit offers, and contract to purchase property through Firm, including the same or similar property as Buyer seeks to purchase. Buyer acknowledges, understands and consents to such representation of other prospective purchasers by Firm through its agents.

6. **FIRM'S DUTIES.** During the term of this Agreement, Firm shall promote the interests of Buyer by: (a) performing the terms of this Agreement; (b) seeking property at a price and terms acceptable to Buyer; (c) presenting in a timely manner all written offers or counteroffers to and from Buyer; (d) disclosing to Buyer all material facts related to the property or concerning the transaction of which Firm has actual knowledge; and (e) accounting for in a timely manner all money and property received in which Buyer has or may have an interest. Unless otherwise provided by law or Buyer consents in writing to the release of the information, Firm shall maintain the confidentiality of all personal and financial information and other matters identified as confidential by Buyer, if that information is received from Buyer during the brokerage relationship. In satisfying these duties, Firm shall exercise ordinary care, comply with all applicable laws and regulations, and treat all prospective sellers honestly and not knowingly give them false information. In addition, Firm may show the same property to other buyers, represent other buyers, represent sellers relative to other properties, or provide assistance to a seller or prospective seller by performing ministerial acts that are not inconsistent with Firm's duties under this Agreement.

Upon closing of any sale of property not entered in a listing service of which Firm is a member, Buyer authorizes Firm to submit pertinent information concerning the property, including sales price, to such listing service.

7. **DISCLOSURE OF BUYER'S NAME/MAILING ADDRESS.**
(a) Unless otherwise stated in Paragraph 13 below, Firm has Buyer's permission to disclose Buyer's name.
(b) In accordance with NC General Statutes Section 93A-12, if a dispute regarding the return or forfeiture of any earnest money deposit arises between Buyer and the seller of any real property Buyer may agree to purchase, the escrow agent holding the deposit may deposit the disputed monies with the appropriate Clerk of Court following written notice to the parties. In the event of any such dispute, Buyer directs Firm to disclose Buyer's last known mailing address to the escrow agent upon request to enable the escrow agent to comply with the notice requirement of such law.

8. **NON-DISCRIMINATION. THE AGENT (FIRM) SHALL CONDUCT ALL BROKERAGE ACTIVITIES IN REGARD TO THIS AGREEMENT WITHOUT RESPECT TO THE RACE, COLOR, RELIGION, SEX, NATIONAL ORIGIN, HANDICAP OR FAMILIAL STATUS OF ANY PARTY OR PROSPECTIVE PARTY TO THE AGREEMENT. FURTHER, REALTORS® HAVE AN ETHICAL DUTY TO CONDUCT SUCH ACTIVITIES WITHOUT RESPECT TO THE SEXUAL ORIENTATION OR GENDER IDENTITY OF ANY PARTY OR PROSPECTIVE PARTY TO THIS AGREEMENT.**

9. **BUYER'S DUTIES.** Buyer agrees to cooperate with Firm in the acquisition of real property of the type described in paragraph 1, including but not limited to:
(a) working exclusively with Firm during the term of this Agreement;
(b) immediately referring to Firm information about any properties Buyer may have an interest in examining;
(c) complying with the reasonable requests of Firm to supply any pertinent financial or personal data needed to fulfill the terms of this Agreement;
(d) being available for reasonable periods of time to examine properties;
(e) examining properties only by appointments made by or through Firm and accompanied by an agent of Firm;
(f) conducting all negotiations and communications through Firm;
(g) conducting all due diligence on property in consultation with Firm; and

STANDARD FORM 201
Revised 7/2018
© 7/2018

FIGURE 8.5 (*Continued*)

(h) paying for all products and/or services required in the examination and evaluation of properties (examples: surveys, water/soil tests, title reports, property inspections, etc.).

10. **OTHER PROFESSIONAL ADVICE.** In addition to the services rendered to Buyer by the Firm under the terms of this Agreement, Buyer is advised to seek other professional advice in matters of law, taxation, financing, insurance, surveying, wood-destroying insect infestation, structural soundness, engineering, and other matters pertaining to any proposed transaction. Although Firm may provide Buyer the names of providers who claim to perform such services, Buyer understands that Firm cannot guarantee the quality of service or level of expertise of any such provider. Buyer agrees to pay the full amount due for all services directly to the service provider whether or not the transaction closes. Buyer also agrees to indemnify and hold Firm harmless from and against any and all liability, claim, loss, damage, suit, or expense that Firm may incur either as a result of Buyer's selection and use of any such provider or Buyer's election not to have one or more of such services performed.

- ❏ Buyer acknowledges receipt of a sample copy of an Offer to Purchase And Contract for review purposes.
- ❏ Buyer acknowledges receipt of a copy of the brochure *Questions and Answers on: Home Inspections*.
- ❏ Buyer acknowledges receipt of a sample copy of a Professional Services Disclosure and Election form (form #760) for review purposes.

11. **HOME WARRANTY.** The seller of any property Buyer may be interested in buying may or may not provide a home warranty as a part of any sale. If the seller does not provide a home warranty, Buyer may elect to purchase one. Buyer understands that although Firm will assist Buyer in identifying available home warranty products, Buyer must refer specific questions regarding coverage afforded by any such product to the provider thereof. If Firm assists Buyer in obtaining a home warranty, a fee of _____ will be offered to Firm by the person or entity through or from which any home warranty is obtained as compensation to Firm for its assistance in obtaining the home warranty, and Buyer hereby consents to Firm's receipt of such fee.

12. **CONFIDENTIALITY OF OFFERS.** Real estate brokers are prohibited by N.C. Real Estate Commission rule from disclosing the price or other material terms contained in a party's offer to purchase, sell, lease, rent or option real property to a competing party without the express authority of the party making the offer. However, sellers may elect not to treat the existence, terms, or conditions of any offers Buyer may make as confidential. Additionally, sellers may elect not to disclose or authorize seller's agent to disclose the existence of any other offer(s).

13. **ADDITIONAL PROVISIONS.** _____
_____

14. **DUAL AGENCY.** Buyer understands that the potential for dual agency will arise if Buyer becomes interested in viewing property listed with Firm. Firm may represent more than one party in the same transaction only with the knowledge and informed consent of all parties for whom Firm acts.

   (a) **Disclosure of Information.** In the event Firm serves as a dual agent, Buyer agrees that without permission from the party about whom the information pertains, Firm shall not disclose to the other party the following information:
   (1) that a party may agree to a price, terms, or any conditions of sale other than those offered;
   (2) the motivation of a party for engaging in the transaction, unless disclosure is otherwise required by statute or rule; and
   (3) any information about a party which that party has identified as confidential unless disclosure is otherwise required by statute or rule.

   (b) **Firm's Role as Dual Agent.** If Firm serves as agent for both Buyer and a seller in a transaction, Firm shall make every reasonable effort to represent Buyer and seller in a balanced and fair manner. Firm shall also make every reasonable effort to encourage and effect communication and negotiation between Buyer and seller. Buyer understands and acknowledges that:
   (1) Prior to the time dual agency occurs, Firm will act as Buyer's exclusive agent;
   (2) In its separate representation of Buyer and seller, Firm may obtain information which, if disclosed, could harm the bargaining position of the party providing such information to Firm;
   (3) Firm is required by law to disclose to Buyer and seller any known or reasonably ascertainable material facts.

Buyer agrees Firm shall not be liable to Buyer for (i) disclosing material facts required by law to be disclosed, and (ii) refusing or failing to disclose other information the law does not require to be disclosed which could harm or compromise one party's bargaining position but could benefit the other party.

Buyer initials _____ _____   Individual agent initials _____

STANDARD FORM 201
Revised 7/2018
© 7/2018

FIGURE 8.5 *(Continued)*

(c) **Buyer's Role**. Should Firm become a dual agent, Buyer understands and acknowledges that:
  (1) Buyer has the responsibility of making Buyer's own decisions as to what terms are to be included in any purchase and sale agreement with a seller client of Firm;
  (2) Buyer is fully aware of and understands the implications and consequences of Firm's dual agency role as expressed herein to provide balanced and fair representation of Buyer and seller and to encourage and effect communication between them rather than as an advocate or exclusive agent or representative;
  (3) Buyer has determined that the benefits of dual agency outweigh any disadvantages or adverse consequences;
  (4) Buyer may seek independent legal counsel to assist Buyer with the negotiation and preparation of a purchase and sale agreement or with any matter relating to the transaction which is the subject matter of a purchase and sale agreement.

Should Firm become a dual agent, Buyer waives all claims, damages, losses, expenses or liabilities, other than for violations of the North Carolina Real Estate License Law and intentional wrongful acts, arising from Firm's role as a dual agent. Buyer shall have a duty to protect Buyer's own interests and should read any purchase and sale agreement carefully to ensure that it accurately sets forth the terms which Buyer wants included in said agreement.

(d) **Authorization** (*initial only ONE*).

_____ _____ Buyer authorizes the Firm to act as a dual agent, representing both the Buyer and the seller, subject to the terms and conditions set forth in this Paragraph 14.

_____ _____ Buyer desires exclusive representation at all times during this agreement and does NOT authorize Firm to act in the capacity of dual agent. *If Buyer does not authorize Firm to act as a dual agent, the remainder of this paragraph shall not apply.*

(e) **Designated Agent Option** (*Initial only if applicable*).

_____ _____ Buyer hereby authorizes the Firm to designate an individual agent(s) to represent the Buyer, to the exclusion of any other individual agents associated with the Firm. The individual designated agent(s) shall represent only the interests of the Buyer to the extent permitted by law.

> **NOTE:** When dual agency arises, an individual agent shall not practice designated agency and shall remain a dual agent if the individual agent has actually received confidential information concerning a seller client of the Firm in connection with the transaction or if designated agency is otherwise prohibited by law.

(f) **Dual Agency Compensation**. If the Firm acts as a dual agent (including designated agency), the total fee the Firm expects to receive for its services in representing Buyer and the seller shall be _____.
(Insert dollar amount, percentage of purchase price, or other method of determining Firm's compensation for each type of property such as resale, new construction and/or land/lot the Buyer may purchase.). THIS WILL IN NO WAY AFFECT OR MODIFY THE AMOUNT OF THE FEE SET FORTH IN PARAGRAPH 4 ABOVE THAT FIRM EXPECTS TO RECEIVE FOR ITS SERVICES IN REPRESENTING BUYER UNDER THIS AGREEMENT. In the event Buyer is interested in purchasing a property where the Firm's total fee is different from that described in this subparagraph (f), the Firm shall timely disclose the fee to Buyer and confirm it in writing before Buyer makes or accepts an offer to buy or sell any such property.

15. **MEDIATION.** If a dispute arises out of or related to this Agreement or the breach thereof, and if the dispute cannot be settled through negotiation, the parties agree first to try in good faith to settle the dispute by mediation before resorting to arbitration, litigation, or some other dispute resolution procedure. If the need for mediation arises, the parties will choose a mutually acceptable mediator and will share the cost of mediation equally.

16. **ENTIRE AGREEMENT/CHANGES/TERMINATION.** This Agreement constitutes the entire agreement between Buyer and Firm relating to the subject thereof, and any prior agreements pertaining thereto, whether oral or written, have been merged and integrated into this Agreement. This Agreement may be signed in multiple originals or counterparts, all of which together constitute one and the same instrument. No modification of any of the terms of this Agreement shall be valid, binding upon the parties, or entitled to enforcement unless such modification has first been reduced to writing and signed by both Buyer and Firm. Buyer acknowledges and understands that this Agreement constitutes a binding contract between Buyer and Firm. Although Buyer may at

FIGURE 8.5 (*Continued*)

any time withdraw from the fiduciary relationship existing between Buyer and Firm, the contract created by this Agreement may not be terminated by Buyer or Firm prior to its Expiration Date without legally sufficient cause. Any such termination shall be by mutually-acceptable written agreement signed by both Buyer and Firm.

> **NOTE:** Buyer should consult with Firm before visiting any resale or new homes or contacting any other real estate firm representing sellers, to avoid the possibility of confusion over the brokerage relationship and misunderstandings about liability for compensation.

17. **SURVEILLANCE:** Buyer is advised to be mindful of the fact that there could be video/audio/surveillance device(s) located on any property examined by Buyer and that Buyer or Buyer's representatives may be under surveillance during any such examination. Federal and State laws prohibit the interception of an oral communication through the use of any electronic, mechanical, or other device, whether or not recorded, without the consent of a party to that communication. However, video surveillance without consent is not illegal.

18. **USE OF PHOTOGRAPHS AND VIDEO:** Unless a property owner has notified the public that photography and video recording is prohibited, it is permissible to photograph or video the interior of private property since the owner's permission to enter the property implies permission to do so. However, under no circumstances may Buyer take photographs or videos that intrude on a property owner's reasonable expectations of privacy.

Buyer should only photograph or video things that are in "plain view". For example, taking a photo or video of the contents of a medicine cabinet or of financial records in a desk drawer would be impermissible. In addition, any permitted photography or video should be used only in a manner related directly to Buyer's examination and purchase of a property. TAKING IMPERMISSIBLE PHOTOGRAPHS OR VIDEOS OR USING THEM FOR AN IMPERMISSIBLE PURPOSE COULD SUBJECT BUYER TO CIVIL LIABILITY.

19. **WIRE FRAUD WARNING:**

> **BEFORE SENDING ANY WIRE, BUYER SHOULD CALL THE CLOSING ATTORNEY'S OFFICE TO VERIFY THE INSTRUCTIONS. IF BUYER RECEIVES WIRING INSTRUCTIONS FOR A DIFFERENT BANK, BRANCH LOCATION, ACCOUNT NAME OR ACCOUNT NUMBER, THEY SHOULD BE PRESUMED FRAUDULENT. DO NOT SEND ANY FUNDS AND CONTACT THE CLOSING ATTORNEY'S OFFICE IMMEDIATELY.**
>
> **BUYER SHOULD CALL THE CLOSING ATTORNEY'S OFFICE AT A NUMBER THAT IS INDEPENDENTLY OBTAINED. TO ENSURE THAT THE CONTACT IS LEGITIMATE, BUYER SHOULD NOT RELY ON A PHONE NUMBER IN AN EMAIL FROM THE CLOSING ATTORNEY'S OFFICE, BUYER'S REAL ESTATE AGENT OR ANYONE ELSE.**
>
> Buyer acknowledges and understands that there are risks associated with wire transfers that are not within the reasonable control of Firm, and Buyer hereby agrees to release and discharge Firm and Firm's agents from any and all claims, demands, rights and causes of action of whatsoever kind and nature not caused by gross negligence of Firm or Firm's agents arising directly or indirectly out of any wire transfer Buyer sends or receives/was to receive in connection with any real estate transaction in which Firm represents buyer.

[THIS SPACE INTENTIONALLY LEFT BLANK]

Page 5 of 6

Buyer initials _____ _____   Individual agent initials _____

STANDARD FORM 201
Revised 7/2018
© 7/2018

FIGURE 8.5 (*Continued*)

Buyer and Firm each hereby acknowledge receipt of a signed copy of this Agreement.

THE NORTH CAROLINA ASSOCIATION OF REALTORS®, INC. MAKES NO REPRESENTATION AS TO THE LEGAL VALIDITY OR ADEQUACY OF ANY PROVISION OF THIS FORM IN ANY SPECIFIC TRANSACTION.

Buyer: _____   _____   _____
              Print Name   Signature   Date

Contact Information: _____   _____   _____   _____
              Home   Work   Cell   Email

Mailing Address: _____

Buyer: _____   _____   _____
              Print Name   Signature   Date

Contact Information: _____   _____   _____   _____
              Home   Work   Cell   Email

Mailing Address: _____

Entity Buyer: _____
        (Name of LLC/Corporation/Partnership/Trust/etc.)

By: _____   Date: _____

Name: _____   Title: _____

Contact Information: _____   _____   _____   _____
              Home   Work   Cell   Email

Mailing Address: _____

Firm: _____   Phone: _____
      Print Real Estate Firm Name

By: _____   _____   _____
     Individual Agent Signature   Individual License Number   Date

Office: _____

Address: _____

Office Phone: _____   Fax: _____   Email: _____

STANDARD FORM 201
Revised 7/2018
© 7/2018

FIGURE 8.5 (*Continued*)

WORKING WITH BUYERS

Unlike the listing agreement in which the agent is representing the seller's interest and for only one property, the agent's relationship with a buyer can take many forms and likely will involve several houses. For this reason, the agent must address the agency relationship with the buyer before engaging in showing any houses. In addition to the issues of representation, the agent also will need to address matters of compensation, who will be responsible for costs incurred by the agent, the ability of the agent to show other buyers the same properties that he will show the buyer, and many more important points. For these reasons, the agent will need to address these items up front before starting to work with any buyer.

Historically, all agents represented the seller and no one looked after the interests of the buyer. The problem that arose from this seller-agency-only approach was that many buyers thought the agent that had shown them the property was representing the buyer's interest. Many of these buyers complained they had told "their" agent personal information that, had they known the agent represented the seller's interest and that he was required to share such information with the seller as their principal, they would have never told the agent. Because of this confusion, buyer representation became a popular option in the mid-1990s. The problem is in many ways the same even with buyer agency capabilities. Because of the long historical pattern of seller agency, agents are still considered to represent the seller's interest when first encountering a buyer. Until and unless the buyer and the agent agree to engage in a relationship other than seller agency, the agent will remain a representative of the seller's interest. According to the rules of agency in North Carolina, the agent must disclose all material facts that he knows, or reasonably should know, to both parties. However, the agent must disclose all personal information about the third party to his principal but cannot disclose personal information about the principal to the third party. Because the agent is considered to represent the interests of the seller when first meeting with a buyer, the agent must "warn" the buyer not to disclose any personal information that he would not want the seller to know before the issue of agency representation is decided. The disclosure of material facts are not the same issue, as the agent would be required to disclose those regardless of who he represented in the transaction.

The point in the discussion during which the buyer will start to disclose any personal information that he would not want the seller to know is called *first substantial contact*. Certainly, an agent can engage in all types of conversation with a buyer about topics that are not considered personal to the degree the buyer would not want the seller to know without triggering the first substantial contact rule. Perhaps the safest way for an agent to handle this issue is to let the buyer know when discussions first begin to "not tell me anything you would not want the seller to know." Once the discussion begins to involve personal information about the buyer, the agent should stop the conversation and review the *Working with Real Estate Agents* brochure and secure the buyer's signature on the acknowledgment panel. After discussing the *Working with Real Estate Agents* brochure, the agent will want to discuss the various options in which the agent can work with the buyer. Companies are free to decide which agency models they wish to offer. Some companies represent buyers only. Others represent sellers only, whereas others will represent both buyers and sellers, even in the same transaction.

> The buyer's agent does NOT have to personally verify square footage before sharing data advertised by the listing agent.

The listing agent has the primary responsibility for the accuracy of any square footage advertised and the buyer agent is able to generally rely upon those representations. Only when the buyer agent has reason to suspect the advertised square footage is not correct does she have to verify.

Working with Buyers as a Seller Subagent

In the absence of a buyer agency agreement, the agent will represent the interests of the seller, and the buyer will be considered the third party or customer. The agent still will be required to disclose material facts to the buyer but now will be obligated to disclose all personal information the buyer shares with her seller. There is no separate contract agreement for seller subagency. The buyer will be asked to initial the "Disclosure of Seller Subagency" on the signature panel on the *Working with Real Estate Agents* brochure as the written evidence of this relationship. The subagent still will owe the buyer the requisite honesty and fairness in the transaction.

In the situation involving co-brokerage, any broker who is working with a buyer without a buyer agency agreement is considered to represent the interests of the seller. The question becomes this: "Will the seller permit co-brokerage with a seller subagent?" Because of the long-held concept that the principal is responsible for the actions of the agent, many firms and sellers do not wish to engage in seller subagency in co-brokerage transactions to limit liability. These are the types of questions the firm needs to address with their sellers at the time of the listing. Many firms have company policies that refuse to permit seller subagency with other firms. If a co-brokering agent is working with a buyer who will not agree to buyer agency and the seller refuses to allow co-brokerage with a seller subagent, the agent working with the buyer cannot show the home because there would be no agency alternative for her to practice.

PROCEDURES FOR BUYERS' AGENTS

Before entering into an exclusive or a nonexclusive buyer agency agreement (written or oral) with a prospective buyer, the agent must carefully explain to the buyer the agency options, duties, and relationships involved in each type of agency. North Carolina Real Estate Commission Rule A.0104(c) requires that all potential and actual clients and customers receive and the agent review with them the Commission's pamphlet *Working with Real Estate Agents* (see Figure 7.4).

Real Estate Commission Rule A.0104 also requires that every agreement for brokerage services in a transaction be in writing, provide for its existence for a definite period of time, and provide for termination without prior notice at the expiration of that time period. This rule applies to all agency agreements resulting in a real estate transaction. The oral buyer and dual agency may be express and nonexclusive until such time as the buyer or tenant wishes to contract for sale or lease of a property (i.e., a real estate transaction). Real Estate Commission Rule A.0104 applies to buyer agency agreements that seek to bind the buyer to exclusive representation or for a specific time period even if the agreement does not culminate in a transaction. It also requires that all brokerage service agreements contain the following provision: "THE BROKER SHALL CONDUCT ALL BROKERAGE ACTIVITIES IN REGARD TO THIS AGREEMENT WITHOUT RESPECT TO RACE, COLOR, RELIGION, SEX, NATIONAL ORIGIN, HANDICAP, OR FAMILIAL STATUS OF ANY PARTY OR PROSPECTIVE PARTY." This provision must be set forth in a clear and conspicuous manner that distinguishes it from other provisions in the contract.

The first step in any brokerage situation is explaining agency and having the prospect choose the type of agency he wants. If an agent subsequently is hired as a buyer's agent using a buyer agent agreement, the next step is to assist the buyer (client) to qualify for a loan, if financing is necessary. The agent not only should assist the buyer in determining the amount a buyer is qualified for but also help the buyer secure the best possible terms and conditions for a loan.

The successful buyer's agent will develop a thorough understanding of the buyer's needs and preferences to facilitate the buyer's search for a property. The agent's job entails much more than just showing properties. Although the listing agent may be held to a higher standard about material facts relating to the property, the buyer's agent also has the responsibility to discover and disclose material facts regarding a property and to verify information regarding the property. Before making an offer to purchase, the buyer's agent is expected to see that the buyer receives the North Carolina Residential Property and Owners' Association Disclosure Statement as well as any other relevant disclosures concerning such issues as lead-based paint and synthetic stucco. The buyer's agent may help the buyer obtain copies of any documents that restrict or limit the use of the property, such as restrictive/protective covenants and homeowners association bylaws. NCAR's Offer to Purchase and Contract (Standard Form No. 2T) advises the buyer to review these documents before signing an offer to purchase.

Once a property has been identified, the buyer's agent has the responsibility of preparing, presenting, and negotiating the offer to purchase. Part of this preparation may be to perform a CMA for the buyer. When conducting negotiations, the buyer's agent must remember his obligation to obtain the best price and terms possible for his buyer and not to disclose confidential information relating to the buyer.

Once an accepted contract is in place, the buyer's agent is expected to assist the buyer with preparations for the closing. This includes such activities as getting inspections performed, coordinating the closing with the attorney and the lender, performing a final walk-through inspection before closing, notifying the buyer of the amount of certified funds needed for closing, and confirming the accuracy of the closing statement.

Key Math Concepts Related to Agency

- Brokerage Commissions
- Estimating Net to Seller (after brokerage fee and other closing expenses are paid. Sales price needed to net "X" to seller)
- Profit/Loss on Sale of Real Estate; Percentage of Increase in Equity

Test Tip!

Math computations will use simple interest only . . . no compounding effect.

Brokerage Commissions

1. Sellmor Realty has listed a property for $250,000 at 6% commission and will keep half of that amount after splitting the fee with the selling company. If Sellmor agrees to pay the listing agent 60% of the listing half, how much will the listing agent receive?

2. Happy Homes Realty has listed a house for $210,000 with the seller agreeing to pay a 5% commission on the gross sales price. The company is to pay the local MLS a 5% fee, after which they are to pay the listing and sales agents collectively 70% of the remaining amount. How much money did Happy Homes get to keep in this transaction?

3. Sellsalot Realty has paid its agent $4,500 from the sale of a property where the firm received 3% after splitting the sales commission with the selling firm. If Sellsalot paid the agent 60% of the total it received, how much did the property sell for?

Estimating Net to Seller

1. Jo has agreed to sell her house and needs to "net" $329,000 from the sale after paying the brokerage firm a 6% commission. What will be the minimum amount she will need to sell the house for?

2. Taylor has recently listed his house for sale and agrees to pay the listing firm a 5% commission on the sales price. He will need $165,500 to pay off his existing mortgage and another $2,500 in miscellaneous costs. If he will have to spend $50,000 to purchase his new house, what will be the minimum amount he must sell his house for (round answer to whole dollar)?

Profit/Loss on Sale of Real Estate; Percentage of Increase in Equity

1. George recently sold his house for $360,000. If he had originally paid $300,000 for the house, what was his percentage of profit?

2. Ricardo purchased four lots for $30,000 each. He later subdivides the lots into a total of six lots and sells them for $25,000 each. What is his percentage of profit?

3. Johnson purchased a parcel of property for $200,000 that he sold four years later for $280,000. What was his average annual rate of profit?

4. Kirby recently sold his property for $300,000, which is 25% more than he had originally paid. How much did he originally pay for the home?

5. Marge purchased a home originally for $ 200,000. She later places the house on the market for sale at 20% more than she had originally paid. The house is later sold for 10% less that she was asking. What was the selling price?

6. Karen paid $165,000 for her home by paying $20,000 as a down payment. Assuming the property is now valued currently at $175,000, by what percentage has her equity increased?

7. Kim had originally purchased her home for $260,000. At the time of purchase she paid 20% down payment. If her property has now increased in value by 5%, by what percentage has her equity increased?

Solutions to Math Questions
Brokerage Commissions

1. $250,000 × 6% = $15,000 total sales commission
   $15,000 × 50% = $7,500 listing half of commission
   $7,500 × 60% = $4,500 listing broker share

2. $210,000 × 5% = $10,500 total sales commission
   $10,500 × 5% = $525 MLS share
   $10,500 − $525 = $9,975 commission after MLS share
   $9,975 × 70% = $6,982.50 listing and buyer broker share
   $9,975 − $6,982.50 = $2,992.50 firm share

3. 3% × 60% = 1.8% percent of sales price broker receives
   $4,500 ÷ 1.8% = $250,000 sales price

Estimating Net to Seller

1. 100% − 6% = 94% percent of sales price after commission
   $329,000 ÷ 94% = $350,000 minimum sales price
2. $165,500 + $2,500 + $50,000 = $218,000 sales price needed before commission
   100% − 5% = 95% percent of sales price $218,000 represents
   $218,000 ÷ 95% = $229,474 minimum sales price needed (rounded)

Profit/Loss on Sale of Real Estate

1. $360,000 − $300,000 = $60,000 amount of profit
   $60.000 ÷ $300,000 = 20% percentage of profit
2. $30,000 × 4 = $120,000 originally paid
   $25,000 × 6 = $150,000 total sales price
   $150,000 − $120,000 = $30,000 amount of profit
   $30,000 ÷ $120,000 = 25% percentage of profit
3. $280,000 − $200,000 = $80,000 amount of profit
   $80,000 ÷ $200,000 = 40% percentage of profit
   40% ÷ 4 = 10% average annual rate of profit
4. $300,000 ÷ 125% = $240,000 original purchase price
5. $200,000 × 20% = $40,000 amount of increase
   $200,000 + $40,000 = $240,000 asking price
   $240,000 × 10% + $24,000 amount of reduction in price
   $240,000 − $24,000 = $216,000 sales price
6. $20,000 was the original equity
   $175,000 − $165,000 + $10,000 amount of increase in equity
   $10,000 ÷ $20,000 = 50% increase in equity
7. 20% is the original equity
   5% is the amount of increase in equity
   5% ÷ 20% = 25% percentage of increase in equity

Summary of Important Points

1. A listing contract is one in which a property owner employs a broker to find a buyer for her property. The contract creates an agency relationship wherein the seller is the principal and the broker is the special, or limited, agent.

2. Even though the listing agent does not represent the buyer, the real estate agent must represent the property honestly, fairly, and accurately to all prospective buyers.
3. The three primary types of listing contracts are (1) open listing, (2) exclusive agency, and (3) exclusive right to sell.
4. Listing agreements are required to be in writing and to be for a definite period of time and also must contain the required fair housing language. These requirements are implemented by the North Carolina Real Estate Commission and not the Statute of Frauds.
5. A net listing is one in which the agent's commission will be all of the sales price in excess of a net amount to the seller. Net listings are legal in North Carolina but are strongly discouraged.
6. Buyer agency agreements may be oral ONLY if they are nonexclusive, and they must be reduced to writing at the time an offer is to be presented or at such time as the parties attempt to make the relationship exclusive or for a definite period of time.
7. A protection agreement is a compensation agreement between a seller and an agent but does not create a listing agreement.
8. MLS listings are typically exclusive right to sell agreements.
9. According to the North Carolina Real Estate Commission guidelines for computation of heated square footage, the area must be heated, finished, and accessible from other heated living area. Refer to Appendix D, Residential Square Footage Guidelines, for more details.
10. Heated square footage is calculated by the exterior dimensions of a house. The exterior walls are considered to be 6 inches thick. In an area that contains a sloped ceiling, at least 50% of the area must have at least 7 feet of ceiling height. Refer to Appendix D, Residential Square Footage Guidelines, for more specific details.
11. The North Carolina Residential Property and Owners' Association Disclosure form must be provided to residential purchasers no later than the initial offer to purchase being presented. Failure to provide this form will permit the buyer to withdraw up to three days from the date of delivery of the form or from the contract date, whichever date comes first. The Mineral and Oil and Gas Rights (MOG) disclosure must also be provided with the same rights of withdrawal even in cases of first sale never inhabited, lease with option to purchase where the lessee intends to occupy, and transfers between parties where the agreement is for no disclosure to be made.
12. The Do Not Call legislation prohibits agents from calling people who have registered their residential phone numbers on the National Do Not Call Registry unless the call is exempt. Agents may call registered persons if there is an existing business relationship or if there has been an existing business relationship within the past 18 months.

13. Be certain you understand the distinction between the primary forms of listing contracts and how and when the broker is entitled to a commission under each for-open listing, exclusive agency, and exclusive right to sell. *NOTE:* An agent can be "fired" during the listing period; that is, the seller can terminate the contract at any time before the agreed-to expiration date. Although the agent would have no authority to continue, the seller may be liable to the agent for damages.
14. The listing contract is simply an employment authority (not an interest in land) and therefore is *not* regulated by the Statute of Frauds. Real estate license laws and Commission rules require that the listing and all agency contracts be in writing.
15. At what point is the buyer "ready, willing, and able"? In theory, the agent has produced a ready, willing, and able buyer when he produces a buyer to buy the property at the listed price, terms, and conditions or such other price, terms, and conditions as was later contractually agreed upon. The current offer to purchase and contract form in use in North Carolina allows the buyer the ability to back out of the purchase agreement at any time before the due diligence date, so it is not likely that "ready, willing, and able" will exist before the due diligence date.
16. A common error is made in the calculation of heated square feet. The convention used is to take the *external* dimensions of the heated living area of the home, that is, only those portions you would live in during the winter. Exclude porch, garage, or unfinished basement. The only time you need to deal with the thickness of the walls is when you are forced to take the inside dimensions of an area (e.g., upstairs rooms) and calculate the external dimensions. The area occupied by stairs is included in the square footage for both the upper and lower levels. See Appendix D for a more in-depth discussion of calculating heated square footage.
17. An open listing is one in which the agent gets nothing if the property is sold by anyone else, such as the owner or another broker.
18. A net listing is one in which all the money above the amount specified by the seller that she wants to net, if any, goes to the broker.
19. In an exclusive agency listing and open listing, the owner does not pay a commission if he sells the property himself.
20. In an exclusive agency listing, the agency gets the commission if another broker sells the property.
21. In an exclusive right to sell listing agreement, the broker gets paid even if the owner sells the property himself.
22. Under Commission rule requirements for agency contracts, all agreements for brokerage services and for property owners associations must be in writing and signed by the parties. This writing must be from the inception of the agreement except as allowed in nonexclusive buyer agency agreements. These agreements shall be for a definite period of time, include the licensee's license number, and expire automatically without requirement of prior

notice except as allowed in an agreement between a landlord and broker, which can contain an automatic renewal clause as long as the agreement can be terminated by either party at the expiration of the term. Each agency agreement must contain the following provision: **"THE BROKER SHALL CONDUCT ALL BROKERAGE ACTIVITIES IN REGARD TO THIS AGREEMENT WITHOUT RESPECT TO RACE, COLOR, RELIGION, SEX, NATIONAL ORIGIN, HANDICAP, OR FAMILIAL STATUS OF ANY PARTY OR PROSPECTIVE PARTY."** This clause must be set forth in a manner that distinguishes it from the other provisions in the agreement.

23. According to North Carolina G.S. 93A-13, all contracts for broker services must be reduced to writing and signed by the party to be charged or some other person lawfully authorized by the party to sign.

24. According to rules for oral buyer agency agreements, agents are allowed to represent buyers under an oral buyer agency agreement in limited circumstances. The agreement must be nonexclusive and cannot be for a stipulated period of time, nor can it restrict the ability of the buyer to work with other agents. At such time as the agent attempts to bind the buyer for a specified period of time or limits the ability of the buyer to work with others, the agreement must be reduced to writing. Additionally, the agent cannot present an offer to purchase on behalf of his oral buyer client. The agency agreement must first be reduced to writing, whether it is exclusive or nonexclusive, before the agent can present such offer.

25. Antitrust regulations are designed to prohibit anticompetitive practices that will negatively affect open markets. The two primary practices that constitute antitrust are "price fixing" and "boycotting." "Price fixing" is the practice of two or more brokers/firms collaborating to set fees. As a result, firms/brokers should each establish their own fee structure and make certain not to recommend or suggest to others what the fees should be. "Boycotting" is the practice of a group of brokers/firms working in concert with each other to treat others in such a manner as to limit their ability to be competitive. An example would be when a group of brokers/ firms refuse to allow part-time or discount brokers from participating in organizations, such as an MLS, or refusing to show listings held by these part-time or discount brokers/firms.

26. According to "Do Not Call," "Junk Fax," and anti-spam (CAN-SPAM) laws and rules, telephone solicitors may not call people who have registered their personal phone number in the national "Do Not Call Registry" except under certain conditions. The purpose of this legislation was to prevent such telephone solicitors from contacting people at residential phone numbers to promote goods, investments, or services if the person has first registered his phone number with the Registry. The exemptions would include calls to consumers with the prior express permission of the consumer, to those

where an established business relationship exists between the caller and the consumer, by a tax-exempt organization, to someone with a "prior relationship" with the consumer, to a business number, by or on behalf of political parties or for polling or survey purposes, and for debt collection purposes.

27. Junk Fax rules prohibit the sending of unsolicited facsimile ("fax") transmissions without the prior express invitation of the receiving party. The fax must contain a clear "opt-out" notice on the cover sheet. Faxes may still be sent to people with whom the sender has a "prior or existing relationship." The CAN-SPAM legislation that attempts to limit the sending of email messages has no meaningful impact on real estate licensees.

28. Common Buyer Agency Contract provisions include the type of property to be purchased, effect and duration of the agreement, compensation, other potential buyers duties of the firm and the buyer, disclosure of the buyer's name and mailing address, statement of nondiscrimination, other professional advice, confidentiality of offers, and authorization of dual and designated agency.

Review Questions

Answers to the review questions are in the Answer Key at the back of the book.

1. The clause in a listing contract that protects the broker's commission entitlement beyond the listing term in the event of a sale of the property by the owner to a prospect who was shown the property by the listing firm or its agents is called a(n):
   A. forfeiture clause.
   B. extender clause.
   C. settlement clause.
   D. exclusive right clause.

2. Exclusive Right to Represent Buyer Agreements must have all of the following characteristics EXCEPT:
   A. being in writing.
   B. having a definite termination date.
   C. specifying provisions for an automatic renewal.
   D. incorporating conspicuously the commission prescribed "Description of Agent Duties and Relationships."

3. Which of the following clauses is required by the NC Real Estate Commission to be contained within every listing agreement?
   A. protection clause
   B. antitrust clause
   C. compensation clause
   D. antidiscrimination clause

4. Earnest money is:
   A. synonymous with consideration.
   B. typically held in a trust account.
   C. a minimum of $250.
   D. all of the above.

5. Samuel Seller lists his property with Exclusive Realty. Eventually Samuel convinces a co-worker, Wanda Wish, to purchase his home. In which situation would Samuel not owe a commission to Exclusive Realty?
   A. an open listing
   B. a percentage listing
   C. an exclusive right to sell listing
   D. a net listing

6. The type of listing agreement for which the seller will owe the listing agency a commission regardless of who sells the property is a(n):
   A. open listing.
   B. exclusive agency listing.
   C. exclusive right to sell listing.
   D. co-brokered listing.

7. All of the following will automatically terminate a residential listing agreement EXCEPT:
   A. expiration of the listing period.
   B. death of the seller.
   C. death of the listing broker who works at a large residential firm with many agents.
   D. sale of the house.

8. Which of the following would likely NOT constitute a violation of the Sherman Antitrust Act?
   A. a boycott of a discount brokerage's listings
   B. agreement with competitors to set commission rates
   C. refusal to place advertisements in a local paper that accepts ads from for sale by owners
   D. a firm's raising of its own commission rates

9. The primary difference between an open listing and an exclusive agency agreement would be:
   A. the seller retains the right to sell the property himself and is not liable for a commission.
   B. the seller can list with as many brokerages as he wishes in the open listing.
   C. the exclusive agency agreement stipulates the firm is the only one that can sell the property and be entitled to a commission regardless of who sells it, even the seller.
   D. the seller can sell it himself in the exclusive agency agreement but is not allowed to sell it himself in the open listing without being liable for the commission.

10. Which of the following is true regarding the Residential Property and Owners' Association Disclosure Statement?
    A. This form must be provided to the purchaser by a seller who is selling his own property without assistance from a real estate broker.
    B. In the event a seller does not provide the purchaser with this form by the date of the first offer, the transaction is automatically terminated by law.
    C. If the seller does not provide the purchaser with a copy of this form by the date of the offer, the buyer is automatically entitled to a refund of his earnest money deposit.
    D. This form is required to be provided by the seller in the sale of new construction that has been used as a model home but has not been occupied as a personal residence.

11. The rate of commission to be lawfully charged in a real estate transaction is set by:
    A. the local MLS.
    B. the Association of REALTORS®.
    C. the Sherman Antitrust Law.
    D. the firm and the seller.

12. Which is true of a valid listing agreement in North Carolina?
    A. it must contain a nondiscriminatory clause
    B. it may be oral up to presentation of the first offer
    C. it requires the seller to sell if a full price offer is made by a buyer
    D. it can contain an automatic renewal clause if both parties agree to it in writing

13. Steve Seller needs to receive $180,500 from the sale of his house after paying the broker a 5% commission. How much must the house sell for?
    A. $190,000
    B. $180,500
    C. $189,525
    D. $171,475

14. Angela wishes to net $25,000 from the sale of her house after paying off her loan of $121,900, miscellaneous costs of $3,500, and a commission of 6%. What should be the selling price of the property?
    A. $141,376
    B. $158,404
    C. $159,424
    D. $160,000

15. A property recently sold for $225,000 at a commission rate of 6%. If the firm collects a 6% franchise fee from the total commission and then pays the agent 55% of the remainder, how much did the agent make on this transaction?
    A. $8,235.00
    B. $7,425.00
    C. $6,979.50
    D. $5,710.00

16. Christy has sold a property, which was listed at a 5% commission rate with another firm, for $240,000. The listing firm agrees to a 50/50 commission split with the selling firm. Christy's company will charge a 5% franchise fee on all earned commissions and will then pay her 65% of the remainder. How much did Christy earn on this sale?
    A. $4,200
    B. $3,705
    C. $3,900
    D. $5,700

17. A broker's commission schedule calls for him to make 7% of the first $150,000 of sales price, 6% on the next $150,000, and 5% on the balance. What is the total commission on a sales price of $380,000?
    A. $19,000
    B. $22,000
    C. $23,500
    D. $27,000

18. An investor paid $150,000 for a property that he sold four years later for $210,000. What was his average annual rate of profit?
    A. 10%
    B. 4.5%
    C. 7.25%
    D. 40%

19. Buyer originally paid $150,000 for his house by paying $25,000 down. If the house is now valued at $160,000, by what percentage has his equity increased?
    A. 22%
    B. 40%
    C. 6.25%
    D. 5.0%

20. Lewis purchased a home two years ago for $120,000 by paying $30,000 as a down payment. Assuming that the value of the home has increased by 10%, by what percentage has his equity increased?
    A. 6.8%
    B. 31.8%
    C. 40.0%
    D. 46.7%

CHAPTER 9

BASIC CONTRACT LAW

KEY TERMS

accord and satisfaction
assignment
bilateral contract
breach of contract
compensatory damages
consideration
contractual capacity
counteroffer
duress
earnest money

executed contract
executory contracts
express contract
full performance
illusory offer
implied contract
land contracts
liquidated damages
mutual assent
negligent misrepresentation

novation
offeree
offeror
Parol Evidence Rule
ready, willing, and able
unilateral contract
valid contract
void contract
voidable contract

LEARNING OBJECTIVES

At the conclusion of this chapter, you should be able to:

1. Define basic contract terms, including express, implied, bilateral, unilateral, executed, executory, valid, void, and voidable contracts.
2. Define the essential elements of a contract, including mutual assent, consideration, capacity of the parties, and lawful objective.
3. Define the requirements for reality of consent to a contract.
4. Describe the contract law of auction sales.
5. Describe how contracts are discharged.
6. Describe the assignment of contracts.
7. List the rules for interpretation of contracts.
8. Describe contract remedies.

CHAPTER 9 Basic Contract Law

IN THIS CHAPTER

The real estate practice demands that all agents have a good working knowledge of contract law and how it affects the transaction. This knowledge will affect virtually every area of the real estate practice and will serve to keep the agent's risk for legal liability to a manageable level. Although the agent cannot engage in the unauthorized practice of law, it is essential to have a good understanding of the laws and their importance.

BASIC CONTRACT LAW

Basic Contract Terms and Classifications

> "There are four fundamental elements of a contract: mutual consent, competent parties, legal act and consideration."
> —Jim Fletemier

A contract is a legally enforceable agreement to do or not to do something. It states the price, terms, and conditions under which the parties agree to become contractually bound. The agreement must be with contractual intent between properly identified, legally competent parties to do some legal act of their own free will in exchange for **consideration.** A contract establishes the rights as well as the duties, or responsibilities, of the parties. Care should be taken to see that all contracts are valid and that no errors are introduced that make them voidable or void. Consideration refers to *anything of value offered as an inducement to contract, such as money, action, or forbearance, under the law.* The amount of the consideration is not the issue but simply rather that it exists.

Express Contracts

> "An express contract does not mean in writing. An express contract means the parties fully expressed and understood their intentions. An express contract can be written or oral."
> —Len Elder, DREI

An **express contract** is one in which the parties to the contract have definitely expressed *all the terms and conditions as agreed upon between them.* For most purposes, an express contract *can be either oral or written.* As you will see subsequently, however, certain types of contract must be in writing to be enforceable. A real estate listing contract and a real estate sales contract are examples of express contracts. All the terms and conditions of the contractual agreement are set forth in each of these contracts. The contracts are entered into expressly by the parties.

Implied Contracts

An **implied contract** is a contract that is implied from the *conduct and actions* of the parties. Implied contracts are enforced when the conduct of the parties clearly illustrates their intention to contract. A court implies a contract when a benefit has been received by one party at the expense of the other party. A court will require the recipient of the benefit to pay a reasonable compensation to the party rendering the benefit unless the benefit was actually a gift. An implied contract is created, for example, when one party orders merchandise from another party without stipulating the price to be paid for the merchandise. An implied contract to pay the reasonable value of the merchandise when delivered is created.

Bilateral and Unilateral Contracts

A **bilateral contract** is one that is *based on mutual exchange of promises or acts between the parties* at the time the contract is signed. It is a promise in exchange for the promise of another. The contract to purchase a home is bilateral in that the seller is promising to convey title to the buyer at the same time the buyer is promising to pay a certain price. If either party failed to perform what they promised, they would be liable for breach of contract.

Most listing contracts are bilateral in that the seller and the broker both promise something. The seller gives the broker the right to market the property during the listing period and promises a commission if the broker provides a **ready, willing, and able** buyer; that is, a buyer who is *ready to buy, willing to buy, and financially able to pay the asking price*. The broker promises to spend time and money marketing the property.

In contrast, a **unilateral contract** arises when *one party makes a promise to the other and the second party returns an action in response to the promise,* although he is not legally obligated to do so. It is a promise in exchange for the performance of another. The promise and acceptance are binding only if the other party actually performs the requested act. For example, your promise to a woodcutter to pay him a certain price for a cord of wood is a unilateral contract in that the woodcutter is not obligated to deliver the wood. If he does deliver, you are obligated to pay him the money. Unlike other listing contracts, the open listing contract is unilateral; the seller makes a promise to pay the broker if the broker sells the property, but the broker makes no promises. If the broker sells the property according to the terms offered in the open listing, the seller owes the broker a commission.

One way to determine if a contract is bilateral is by the use of the word "and," such as the buyer promises to buy the seller's house AND the seller promises to sell the buyer his house. In a unilateral contract, the key word is "if." IF you paint my house, I promise to pay you $1,500. The promise is based upon the fulfillment of the performance of the painter.

Executed and Executory Contracts

A contract that has been fully performed by the parties is called an **executed contract.** *All contracts that have not been fully performed* (because things still need *to be done* as required by the contract) *are* **executory contracts**. In essence, an executed contract has been completed or fulfilled and an executory contract is one that is pending. For example, a sales contract for a sale of real estate that has closed, is an executed bilateral contract, whereas before closing, the sales contract is executory.

Valid Contracts

A **valid contract** is a contract that is *binding and enforceable*. It is technically correct. The fact that a contract is valid doesn't necessarily mean the contract represents a good deal. The parties to a valid contract are legally obligated to abide by the terms and conditions of the contract. If a party to a valid contract defaults in the performance of obligations under the contract, the individual is subject to legal action by the other party or parties to the contract. In creating contracts, every effort should be made to ensure that a contract is valid.

> A valid contract simply means "good and enforceable" as opposed to whether it represents a good deal.

Voidable Contracts

A **voidable contract** *results from failure to meet some legal requirement* in negotiating the agreement. As a result, it is technically defective and is not enforceable by one or more of the parties. One of the parties may elect to avoid (or make void) the contract by stating this intention, or she may go ahead and consummate the agreement. For example, if a buyer contracted to purchase a house that was represented to be 2,000 square feet and later found that the actual size was only 1,800 square feet, the buyer could elect to avoid the contract or take the house anyway. Another example might be the purchase of a piece of real property by a minor. The contract is voidable at the discretion of the minor; however, the adult is bound to the contract pending the decision of the underage buyer.

The parties to a voidable contract are not required to set aside or avoid the contract, but they may voluntarily choose to fulfill their obligations under the contract and receive their benefits. At any time before complete performance of the contract, however, the disadvantaged party can elect to discontinue. Examples of conditions that result in the creation of voidable contracts are included in the subsequent discussion of requirements for contract validity.

Void Contracts

A **void contract** can be legally void or automatically void. A legally void contract is defective (voidable) and has been declared void. An automatically void contract, by comparison, is one that is *absolutely unenforceable and has no legal force or effect,* such as a contract to perform an unlawful act. The contract for an illegal purpose never was accorded legal status because you cannot have a contract to break the law; therefore, it cannot be breached. It was considered automatically void immediately.

In this instance, the term "legally void" can be misleading because the name might lead one to think it means illegal. Legally void simply means the contract does not meet the necessary criteria for a valid contract because of some defect, and the appropriate party now has voided it.

> "A contract is void if it does not meet all of the necessary elements. Contracts with minors are not void and they are not illegal. They are VOIDABLE by the minor because they lacked capacity. They are not voidable by the competent party."
> —Terry Wilson, DREI

Essential Elements of a Valid Contract

The objective in drawing up a contract is to create an agreement that is binding and enforceable. The essential elements required to create a valid enforceable contract follow.

Mutual Assent

To create a valid contract, the parties must enter into it voluntarily. The parties must be in **mutual assent** *(agree) to the terms and conditions in the contract.* If a person has entered into a written contract as evidenced by his signature on the contract, the individual is presumed to have assented to the terms and conditions of the contract. This must be of each party's own free will and not as the result of some duress.

The consent of the parties to enter into a contractual agreement must be a real consent. This is a consent that is based on the parties having an accurate knowledge of the terms and conditions of the contract. The failure of contract validity because of the lack of real and mutual consent by the parties results from the presence of mutual mistake, misrepresentation, fraud, undue influence, or duress (see the section "Requirements for Reality of Consent").

Offer and Acceptance

Each contract must contain an *offer* and an unconditional *acceptance* of the offer. An offer is the price, terms, and conditions under which the offeror agrees to become contractually bound. The *party making an offer* is the **offeror,** and the *party to whom the offer is made* is the **offeree.** Because an offer may be withdrawn any time before acceptance, it is very important that an offer be expeditiously presented. The contract is created at the time the unconditional acceptance of the offer is communicated to the offeror. The requirement of mutual assent, necessary for contract validity, is evidenced in the contract by the *unconditional* acceptance of an offer.

The offer must be definite and specific in its terms. If the offer is vague and indefinite and therefore subject to various interpretations, its acceptance will not result in the creation of a valid contract. For example, if an offer is made to a seller to purchase a house in the Executive Heights Subdivision without a specific property description, and the seller actually owns three houses in that subdivision, the *offer is vague and an acceptance will not result in the creation of a valid contract.* The offer must not be illusory and therefore not binding upon the offeror if accepted. For example, a person cannot offer to buy the seller's home in Security Estates only if the offeror decides to move to Security Estates. Here the offer is not binding upon the offeror; therefore, it is illusory, because the offeror has complete control over whether to move to Security Estates. The acceptance of an **illusory offer** does not result in the creation of a valid contract.

> "All of the following words are synonyms and mean the same thing on the test; consent, assent, mutual agreement and meeting of the minds."
> —Deb Cox

Acceptance must be absolutely identical with the terms of the offer. If the acceptance varies in any way from the offer as presented, it will not qualify as an acceptance and, instead, is actually a rejection of the offer and considered a counteroffer. Sometimes an offer specifies the manner in which the acceptance of the offer must be communicated to the offeror by the offeree. In the absence of any specific provision in this regard, the communication of acceptance should be made by the offeree in the same manner as the offer was made or in a customary manner. In the event that acceptance is by mail, the communication is effective and a contract is created at the time the acceptance is mailed by the offeree to the offeror or to the offeror's agent. This is known as the mailbox rule. Mailing it from the offeree to the offeree's agent does not constitute acceptance.

A contract for the sale of real property is a bilateral contract because it is based on the mutual promises of the seller to sell and of the buyer to buy. Therefore, the acceptance of the offer must be communicated to the offeror to create the contract. In presenting an offer to purchase real property, the broker should counsel the seller regarding all aspects of the offer. If the broker believes acceptance of a particular offer is not in the best interests of the seller, the broker should so advise the seller. If, however, the broker believes the offer is probably the best that can be obtained, the broker should urge the seller to accept. In either case, it is the seller's prerogative to accept or reject any offer. See Chapter 10 for additional coverage of offer and acceptance as it relates to real estate sales contracts.

Counteroffers

An offeree who is not happy with the terms proposed by an offerer may want to make a counteroffer.

 A **counteroffer** is actually a *rejection coupled with a new offer.*

In a typical real estate situation, a counteroffer reverses the roles of the buyer and seller. The seller becomes the new offeror, and the buyer would become the offeree. Three aspects are key to a counteroffer. First, the parties must understand that the original offer has been rejected, or killed, and therefore cannot be reinstituted by the rejecting party. Thus, if a seller rejects an offer, he or she has terminated this proposal, relieving the buyer from any further obligation at this point. Second, as indicated previously, if the party who has rejected the original offer (seller) has proposed a new offer in its place, he has reversed the roles of the offeror and the offeree. Finally, the party rejecting the offer must restore the offeror to his original position—that is, tender the return of any earnest money. The broker must then present the counteroffer to the prospective buyer for acceptance or rejection. In some real estate transactions, there are several offers and counteroffers before the buyer and seller reach an acceptable agreement.

Termination of Offers

Offers are terminated in the following ways: (1) by the expiration of a time limit specified by the offeror before acceptance, (2) by the death or insanity of the offeror or the offeree before acceptance, (3) by the revocation of the offer by the offeror before acceptance, (4) by the expiration of a "reasonable" period of time after the offer is made and before acceptance, (5) by the failure of the offeree to comply with the terms of the offer as to the specific manner in which the acceptance must be communicated, (6) by the expiration of a power of attorney when the offeror or the offeree is acting as attorney-in-fact under a power of attorney, and (7) by acceptance of the offer by the offeree. When the offer is accepted, a contract is created. Agents should remember that the list of ways that an offer is terminated is not identical to the list of how a contract would be terminated.

> **Test Tip!**
>
> Do not confuse those items that will terminate an offer with the items that will terminate a contract. They can be similar and often are used as answer choices within the same question.

Consideration

Consideration must be present in every contract for the contract to be valid and enforceable. Consideration is *anything of value,* such as money, or it consists of a promise in return for the performance of a specified act, as is the case in unilateral contracts. Unless there are mutual promises in a bilateral contract, the contract is not valid. For example, if one party promises to make a gift to another party, the contract will not be enforced because the one to receive the gift has furnished no consideration. There must be mutuality. Each party to the contract must do something or promise to do something. There are two exceptions to the general rule that mutual promises constitute consideration: a promise to fulfill a moral obligation and a promise to fulfill a legal obligation.

The consideration provided by one party does not have to be of equal value to the consideration provided by the other party. In other words, a contract does not have to be equally fair to both parties to be a "legal" contract. The amount and type of consideration is not relevant. Generally, a court will not inquire into whether the consideration is "sufficient" or "adequate" so long as there is some consideration from each party to support their agreement. For example, a house has a market value of $200,000. A buyer offers to buy the house from the seller for $150,000. Without making any effort to determine what the fair value of the property might be, the seller accepts the buyer's offer. Later, after learning that the house was worth much more than she contracted to sell it for, the seller attempts to terminate the agreement, citing lack of adequate consideration. The contract is binding because adequate consideration is not a contractual requirement.

Adequate consideration is more likely to be a factor in a case involving fraud. In this previous case, the buyer did not defraud the seller. She simply offered much less than the property was worth and the seller accepted the buyer's offer. By comparison, suppose the seller was convinced by her agent to accept this lower offer, to realize a quick sale, by the representation that $150,000 was all the property was worth. The question of adequate consideration would be an important issue in the seller's attempt to hold the agent liable for her misrepresentation.

Consideration is not the same thing as earnest money. **Earnest money** is *money the buyer deposits with the offer to purchase to show that the buyer is earnest, or sincere, in the intent to purchase the property.* Many buyers, sellers, real estate students, and new agents confuse these terms. An important difference is that consideration is necessary for contract validity; earnest money is not. It is simply good business practice to collect earnest money with an offer to purchase.

> "Earnest money and the due diligence fee are not consideration in a real estate purchase contract and are optional. The consideration is the purchase price being paid for the property. Therefore, an Offer to Purchase & Contract is valid and enforceable without these items."
> —Len Elder, DREI

Capacity of the Parties

The parties to a contract must have **contractual capacity**—that is, they must be *legally competent* to contract. Most people possess contractual capacity; therefore, this subject is discussed by pointing out the few conditions resulting in incompetency, which are age (minors) and mental competency. Minors are those who have not reached the age of majority as established by statutory law in each particular state. North Carolina specifies this age to be 18 years old.

If either party to a contract is mentally incompetent, the contract is voidable by the incompetent party and unenforceable against that party. In the case of minors, the contract is voidable at the option of the minor. The minor can hold an adult to a contract, but an adult cannot legally hold a minor to the contract. The contract is not legally enforceable against the minor. A minor may fulfill the terms of a contract. If he does (and does not take steps to terminate the contract after reaching the age of majority), the individual is said to have ratified the contract as an adult, and the contract will be binding. If a party to a contract is intoxicated or under the influence of drugs at the time of entering into the contract so that the person does not understand what is happening, the individual is considered temporarily mentally incompetent to contract; therefore, the contract will be unenforceable against that person. It is not sufficient for a party to state that he has a drinking or drug problem and therefore should be excused from performance in a contract. He would have to prove that he was so intoxicated at the time of contract that he could not understand, or comprehend, the quality of his actions.

Lawful Objective

The contract must be for a *legal purpose.* A contract for an illegal purpose is void. Examples of illegal contracts include contracts to sell a public office, contracts in restraint of trade, contracts to promote litigation or stifle prosecution, contracts that may be for a legal purpose on the surface when the only way they can be completed is to break the law, and contracts that restrain freedom to marry.

Requirements for Reality of Consent

A valid contract is based on the voluntary meeting of the minds, or mutual assent. Several factors can defeat this voluntary assent and therefore invalidate the contract.

Mutual Mistake

A mistake can be either a *mistake of fact* or a *mistake of law*. A mistake of a material fact can constitute grounds to nullify (rescind) a contract. This does not cover a misunderstanding of the law by one party or the other. However, if an incorrect property description has been used that identifies a property other than the one intended, the contract may be rescinded.

The key component regarding the concept of mistake of fact is that it must be "mutual." Not only do both parties have to make a mistake, they must be mistaken as to the same fact. It is not sufficient that one party stated he had made a mistake regarding some feature of a contract and the other stated she also made a mistake but regarding some other element of the contract. For example, both parties agreed to purchase a house but the written agreement contained an incorrect legal description. In this situation, both parties have made the same mistake. In the case of a mutual mistake of a material fact, either party can rescind the agreement.

A unilateral mistake would not have the same legal effect as the mutual mistake. A unilateral mistake is a mistake made by one but not both of the parties. Assuming there is no evidence of fraud, or misrepresentation, the mistaken party cannot avoid responsibility of the contract. In this case, the only way the mistaken party can be excused from contractual performance is if the other party agrees to release him from the obligation. Unlike a material mistake of fact, a mistake of *law* (e.g., as to the legal effect of a contract) by one or both parties will NOT excuse either party from performance.

Willful Misrepresentation or Fraud

Fraud is a willful misrepresentation of a material fact or the willful omission of a material fact by a party to a contract or the party's agent that effectively constitutes a false misrepresentation made for the purpose of inducing someone to enter into a contract to his detriment. If a party enters into a contract because of fraud, the defrauded party can avoid the contract. A false representation is deemed to be willful and fraudulent when the party making the representation knows it to be false or when the person making the false representation does not know whether the statement is true or untrue but without regard for its truth makes the statement anyway.

If a real estate broker, as agent of an owner of real property, commits an act of fraud, the injured party may rescind any contract entered into with the seller.

Also, the agent is liable to the buyer and the seller for damages incurred. See Chapter 7 for complete coverage of misrepresentation and fraud.

Negligent Misrepresentation

A **negligent misrepresentation** occurs as a result of *misconception as to the facts* on the part of the person making the unintentional misrepresentation. The person making the misrepresentation believes it to be true; however, a reasonable person in the same situation should have known it was not true. This is an unintentional misrepresentation but one in which the party "reasonably should have known" that there was an error. If a real estate broker makes the misrepresentation, the question becomes whether the broker was using reasonable skill, care, and due diligence. The fact that the party making the misrepresentation was acting in good faith is not a defense. A contracting party who has entered a contract in reliance upon a negligent misrepresentation of a material fact (important fact) and stands to be harmed as a result of the misrepresentation is legally entitled to rescind the contract. The contract is voidable by any party who relied upon the negligent misrepresentation to her detriment as a basis for entering the contract.

Innocent Misrepresentation

An innocent misrepresentation is an unintentional misstatement of material fact by a party (or his agent) when the party could not be expected to "reasonably have known" that it was false. Although the courts are less likely to rescind a contract or award damages for an innocent misrepresentation than one that is intentional or negligent, it is still a possibility, especially if a party is substantially harmed by the misrepresentation. Thus, contract law allows an injured party to avoid, or withdraw from, a contract they entered because of any type of misrepresentation be it willful, negligent, or innocent if the injured party was in fact harmed and reasonably relied on the misrepresentation. The Real Estate license law does not provide for disciplining a broker in cases of innocent misrepresentation because there was no way the agent could have reasonably known of the true facts. The license law, however, does hold the agent accountable for cases of willful or negligent misrepresentation.

Unfair and Deceptive Trade Practices

North Carolina General Statute (G.S.) 75-1.1 covers real estate agents and sellers who sell real estate on a regular basis. This statute, called the Unfair and Deceptive Trade Practices Act (see Chapter 7), can be the basis for invalidating a contract and awarding treble damages if the seller or her agent violates it. Proven fraud is an unfair and deceptive trade practice; however, it is not necessary to prove fraud to obtain legal relief under this act.

This statute does not prevent a party to a real estate contract injured by unfair and deceptive trade practices from taking additional legal actions under other laws.

Duress

The essential element of **duress** is that of *fear or threat.* One cannot be forced to sign a contract at gunpoint because this defeats the requirement for a voluntary meeting of the minds or reality of consent. Duress introduced in the negotiation of a contract renders it voidable, thereby allowing the threatened person to escape the contract if she takes a positive action to do so.

Undue Influence

Undue influence is any improper or wrongful influence by one person over another whereby the will of a person is overpowered so that he is induced to act or is prevented from acting of free will. Undue influence occurs when one person takes advantage of another person's lack of mental ability or when a person takes advantage of a special relationship that enables him to have an unusual influence over another person. Examples of such relationships are those between guardian and ward, legal advisor and client, or employer and employee. If a person is induced to enter a contract because undue influence is exerted, the individual can void the contract.

It is important for students to recognize the distinction between duress and undue influence.

Contract Law and Auction Sales

A special case in real estate is the transaction of a real estate auction. The auctioneer differs from the typical real estate agent in that the auctioneer has the capacity to bind the seller to the transaction. Although the real estate listing contract gives the agent strictly a limited or special agency and therefore empowers the agent to act only as a negotiator on behalf of the seller, an auctioneer actually accepts a bid (offer), something the agent should never consider doing.

Two types of auction represent two types of agreement between the auctioneer and the seller. In the first arrangement, the seller reserves the right to halt the bidding if the results do not appear to be satisfactory to her terms. This situation is known as an auction "With Reserve"; that is, the seller has reserved the right to reject all incoming bids. The seller should do so before the auction is completed and before the auctioneer has indicated an acceptance that would bind the seller anyway.

The second type of auction arrangement is "Without Reserve" or "Absolute"; that is, the seller holds no reservations and has indicated her acceptance of whatever bids are obtained. In either type of auction, "With Reserve" or "Without Reserve," the auctioneer binds the seller when he says "sold."

Even though the auctioneer has bound the seller to acceptance of a contract at the conclusion of the bidding, it is still necessary to formalize this agreement with a written document to comply with the Statute of Frauds. An auction is an example of a circumstance in which two or more documents may be used together to satisfy the Statute of Frauds requirement that all real estate contracts be in writing.

Performance Dates and Times

Contract law tends to interpret the indicated dates and times for performance in contracts as being "within a reasonable period of time" as opposed to being strict. The basic premise is that if the parties are working diligently and in good faith toward contract completion, they will be entitled to some reasonable period of time without being considered in breach of contract. The problem arises when the parties attempt to determine exactly what is reasonable because one party's interpretation is likely very different than another. Chapter 10 addresses the standard offer and contract form that is widely used in residential transactions in North Carolina. In that form, the parties are allowed a period of 14 days following the scheduled closing date to perform without being considered in breach. What is interesting is that the contract addresses exactly what period of time the parties have agreed to in advance as being reasonable.

If the parties wish to have the dates and times strictly interpreted, they should insert the phrase "time is of the essence." This creates a strict interpretation of the performance dates and does not allow any flexibility in the event the dates cannot be met. It is not a requirement that all of the dates and times within a contract be marked with "time is of the essence." On many occasions, there may be only one date that is to be strictly enforced, and the others will continue to be allowed flexibility, if needed.

Statute of Frauds

For most purposes, an oral contract is just as valid and enforceable as a written contract. The difficulty with oral contracts, however, lies in their leading to misunderstandings of the rights and obligations of the parties, and they may be extremely difficult to prove in a court proceeding if that should become necessary. A primary purpose of the Statute of Frauds is to "prevent fraudulent proof of an oral contract."

> Contracts involving the creation or conveyance of an interest in real property must be written to be enforceable.

"The statute of frauds requires certain types of contracts to be in writing in order to be enforceable. Remember DREAMOILS: Deeds, Restrictive Covenants, Easements, Assignments, Mortgages, Options, Installment Land Contracts, Leases for longer than 3 years, and Sales Contracts."
—Bill Gallagher, DREI

This requirement is created by the Statute of Frauds, which in North Carolina is G.S. 22-2. This statute was derived from an English statute by the same name. To prevent fraud in real estate contracts, this statute requires that they be written and contain all the elements essential for contract validity. Oral testimony does not suffice to create obligations under a contract involving transfer of title to real property. The statute does not require any particular form of writing. To be sufficient to satisfy the requirements of the statute, the writing can be a formal contract, a short memorandum, a receipt, and so on. The contract need not be in one document. Several documents can be put together to create the contract. The best form, however, is to have the entire contract in one document and signed by the parties. The written contract must contain the names of the parties, subject, terms and conditions, and signature of the party(ies) to be charged with performance.

Examples of real estate contracts falling under the Statute of Frauds are standard real estate sale or purchase, options, **land contracts** (also called *contracts for deed, installment contracts,* and *conditional sale contracts*), and contracts for the exchange of real estate. Lease contracts fall under the Statute of Frauds in North Carolina when the lease term will not be completed within three years of its making. Note that listing and other agency contracts do not convey an interest in real estate and are not required by the Statute of Frauds to be in writing. However, North Carolina G.S. 93A-13 and the Real Estate Commission rules require those contracts to be in writing.

With the exception of listing, buyer agency, and other agency-based contracts, literally all real estate contracts, except short-term leases of less than three years, must be in writing to be enforceable. As a reminder, if the contract has to be in writing, according to the Statute of Frauds, it will have to be recorded, under the Conner Act, to protect its interest.

Uniform Electronic Transaction Act

North Carolina has adopted a state version of the federal E-sign legislation named the Uniform Electronic Transaction Act (UETA) allowing contracts to be created by electronic means such as fax and email in addition to recognizing that an electronic signature is binding. For more details regarding electronic offers and acceptance, see Chapter 10.

Discharge of Contracts

Contracts are terminated by agreement of the parties, full performance, impossibility of performance, and operation of law.

Agreement of the Parties

A release is where each party specifically releases the other party from performance. The release must be agreed upon by both parties to be effective. It is, in essence, where both parties simply agree to call the whole thing off.

An **accord and satisfaction** is a *settlement agreement between the parties, often in the form of some compromise,* that annuls and discharges the original agreement. A situation may arise in which the buyer wants to get out of a purchase agreement, that is, default on the contract. A compromise is reached when the seller agrees to accept an amount of money as substitution for full performance of the buyer. This can be the earnest money or some other negotiable amount of money. If the contract specifies the amount of damages, the specified amount is called *liquidated damages*. The agent should not presume such an agreement unless clear, written intention of the parties is obtained, which would best be done in consultation with their respective attorneys. The North Carolina real estate license laws put a clear burden on the agent to make certain all requirements are met before disbursing trust or escrow funds.

A **novation** is *the substitution of a new contract for a prior contract.* There are two ways to create a novation. First, the parties to the original contract are changed. A new party to the contract agrees to satisfy a former contracting party's obligation to the second party in the previous contract. When the novation (new contract) is created, the old contract is discharged. Second, a novation is created when the same parties change the terms of the contract and void the old contract.

Under a Subsequent Modifying Agreement, as the name implies, some agreement modifies the earlier agreement. Often this is no more than an agreement to slightly alter some of the original terms to reflect changes in the contract.

> " 'Novation' is defined as the substitution of a new contract to replace an existing one. Remember 'Nova' the burst into a bright light of a star. Some people believe this is how new stars are formed."
> —Jim Hriso

Full Performance

The usual manner of terminating contracts is by **full performance.** When *all the terms of the contract have been fully performed by all parties,* the contract is executed and terminated.

Impossibility of Performance

The general rule is that even if a party to a contract is not able to perform obligations under the contract, the party is still not relieved of liability. The reasoning behind this is that the one who cannot perform should have provided for this possibility by a provision or contingency in the contract relieving him from liability.

There are exceptions to the general rule, however. One exception is in the case of a personal service contract. If a person contracts to render services to another person and those services cannot be rendered by someone else, the person obligated to render the service is relieved from liability in the event she dies or becomes incapacitated so that she cannot render the service. For example, the listing contract is a service contract. If the listing is with a one-broker firm and that broker dies, the listing contract is terminated. Generally, the death or incapacity of a seller or a buyer before closing does not terminate a real estate sales contract; such contracts survive death. Heirs can carry out the terms of the contract. A contingency in the contract could possibly terminate it, however. For example, the income of the one who died could be necessary to fulfill a loan contingency in the contract. In that case, the inability of the heirs to obtain the loan would terminate the contract. Another exception to the general rule occurs when the performance of an obligation under a contract becomes illegal as a result of a change in law after the contract was created. As a result, the obligated parties are relieved of responsibility.

Another common exception occurs in the case in which performance is impossible because of the destruction of the property. In the event the property should be destroyed, the question becomes whether the purchaser's intent still can be reasonably fulfilled. For example, a purchaser has agreed to purchase a house and 6 acres of land. Just before closing, the house burns to the ground. If the purchaser was buying the property as his residence, the destruction of the house would render the completion of the contract to be impossible for the seller to perform. If, by comparison, the land was zoned commercial or office-institutional and the buyer was purchasing the property to erect an office building, the buyer's intent can still be met. In this case, the buyer would have intended to have the structure removed to accommodate his new building; so the fact the house has burned down does not negatively affect his ability to have his reasonable expectations met. A well-drawn contract should indicate what would be the buyer's remedy for this situation. Suppose the seller, knowing the land was what the buyer really wanted instead of the house, told the buyer the sales price was the same even without the house. Most contracts would stipulate the buyer could back out, based on the impossibility of performance rule, or the buyer could go forward with the purchase and lay claim to any insurance proceeds paid in regards to the house.

Operation of Law

The term *operation of law* describes the manner in which the rights or liabilities of parties may be changed by the application of law without the act or cooperation of the parties affected. The following are examples of discharge of contracts by operation of law.

The time within which a legal action may be brought against a party to a contract by another party to the contract is limited by statute in every state. The statutes are called Statutes of Limitations. If a party to a contract fails to bring a lawsuit against a defaulting party to a contract within the statutory time period, the right of legal remedy is lost to the injured party by operation of law.

The bankruptcy of a party to a contract as established by the Federal Bankruptcy Act has the effect of terminating contracts because the bankruptcy law relieves the bankrupt party from liability under contracts to which she is a party as of the date of filing the bankruptcy petition with the federal court.

Breach of contract is defined as *failure, without legal excuse, to perform any promise that forms the whole or part of a contract.* The effect of the breach of contractual obligations by a party to a contract is to terminate the contract. The breach does not terminate the right to legal remedies against the defaulting party by the injured party, however.

Assignment of Contracts

A contract is assignable provided no prohibition against assignment is spelled out in the contract itself. **Assignment** refers to *the transfer of legal rights and obligations by one party to another.* The assignment of the contract, however, does not relieve the assignor of the responsibility for performance in the event the assignee fails to perform. An exception would be if the assignor has been released specifically by the other contracting party who accepts the assignee in place of the assignor. If that is not the case, the assignee is in the first position of responsibility and the assignor is in the second position of liability. A novation removes the liability of the assignor.

> A contract is generally assignable anytime it is not prohibited. Contract silence regarding such assignment is not considered a prohibition.

Time Is of the Essence

Time is of the essence, or simply "of the essence" means that contractual terms and dates must be strictly adhered to. A date that is shown as being time is of the essence is a drop-dead date in any language. There is to be no "grace period" or other leniency allowed. Because of this lack of flexibility, it is recommended that usage of these clauses be limited to those applications where it is essential for exact compliance. Time is of the essence clauses can be specific to one particular date and time or they can be more of a blanket coverage where every date and time throughout the contract is of the essence. Brokers in North Carolina will generally utilize NCAR/NCBA standardized forms, and it is the practice that all references to time is of the essence will be in bold for emphasis.

General Rules for Interpretation of Contracts

There are several rules and conventions for the interpretation of contracts in the event the writing of the contract is not sufficiently clear to all parties. The first convention involves the **Parol Evidence Rule.** This assumes that *the written words reflect the entire agreement and that oral statements that do not agree with the written words in the document are to be disregarded.* This rule enforces the concept that the written document embodies the entire agreement and will not be altered by any oral statements.

Contracts also will be interpreted in their entirety. It is common that a contractual agreement may involve several separate addenda, schedules, and so on, and they will all be interpreted as one whole agreement and no one element has to carry the weight of compliance with contract law. The important issue is whether collectively the contractual requirements have been met.

Contracts are assumed to be reasonable versus unreasonable. Therefore, a discrepancy of interpretation is resolved in favor of the most reasonable meaning. Words are to be construed in their ordinary sense in place of connoting any unusual meaning in a given word or phrase. Although linguists would argue that meaning is in people rather than words, ordinary meanings are given to words in their everyday context. It is this ordinary meaning that should be used in the interpretation of contracts.

Ambiguity will be construed most strongly against the preparer. If there is still ambiguity in the meaning of the document in the words that are chosen or in the way in which they are put together, the burden will fall on the person who constructed the document. It is not considered desirable to have someone benefit from creating the ambiguity. It is assumed that when someone put the document together, he should have taken care to make the meaning clear to all parties and, therefore, should have the document interpreted most seriously against himself rather than the other party in the event the meaning is ambiguous. Remember that real estate agents must not "construct/draft" contracts, which is the practice of law limited to attorneys. Therefore, agents should take care not to draft complex statements, but rather simply "fill in blanks" on standard forms, such as names, price, description of the property, and so on.

A final rule on the written word revolves around whether the words were printed or written. Written, as in handwritten, entries generally will be considered more in line with what the parties desired even in cases in which they conflict with the printed (preprinted) portions of a contract. In this case, the handwritten words are intended to modify the meaning of the printed form and, therefore, take precedence as they are considered to be more reflective of what the parties actually desired to have as the agreement.

Contract Remedies

In some situations, the parties simply are unable to work out an amicable solution to a contract disagreement and the legal process will have to provide the remedy. The question is how is justice best served, or even determined, in a real estate dispute? The following are the legal avenues that most likely will be utilized in the real estate lawsuit.

Money Damages

The injured party is entitled to receive *compensation for any financial loss caused by the breach as may be awarded by a court.* This is called **compensatory damages.** The general theory is the courts will try to restore the injured party to a financial position as near as possible to the position they would have had if the breach had not occurred. To prevail, the injured party will have to establish he suffered a loss because if no loss can be determined, the parties are considered to already be in the same financial position as they would have been if no breach had occurred.

Additionally, the court can award punitive damages if the breach of contract was willful, was malicious, and committed intentionally to do harm to the plaintiff. Such punitive damages are considered as punishment rather than a restoration of any measureable losses. In actuality, courts seldom award punitive damages in breach of contract cases.

If the amount of money for damages is agreed upon in the contract, this sum is referred to as **liquidated damages**. These liquidated damages are simply a pre-set amount of penalty in the event that a breach should occur. It represents both the minimum as well as the maximum that the parties will either receive or be liable to pay. This amount does not need to be the same amount as the earnest money in a real estate sales contract. Parties to a sales contract should be careful to establish a reasonable amount of money if liquidated damages clauses are sought as this will represent all of the money the seller will receive, regardless of his actual losses, and all that a buyer will be liable for.

Specific Performance

A second remedy is that of specific performance. This theory is used when there is no fair way to measure the monetary loss. The only fair remedy is to simply make the parties do what they originally contracted to do. As you learned in Chapter 1, every parcel of land has a unique value that cannot be substituted for any other commodity. Therefore, if one signals an intention to breach the contract to convey title to real property under a valid written contract, the legal remedy enforced by the courts probably will be to require the consummation of the specific contract as agreed. Monetary damages cannot substitute for the unique value of land in a given location. Therefore, the prospective purchaser may insist on title to the property in place of any other remedy. If factors such as the amount of land and the quality of title are misrepresented to the buyer to the extent that the value is affected, the buyer may sue for specific performance in addition to abatement. If the buyer wins, she may be able to enforce specific performance of the contract in addition to an abatement of the purchase price attributable to the difference between actual property value and the value of the misrepresented property.

Rescission

A final remedy is that of rescission of the contract by the injured party. In essence, a rescission renders the contract null and void, returning the parties to their original positions. The buyer's original position would be to have the refund of any money she advanced on behalf of the transaction. A buyer might request such a remedy in the event that the property proved to be different from what was represented, such as the size of a home, the number of acres in a tract of land, or a given zoning classification.

Summary of Important Points

1. A contract is an agreement between competent parties, upon legal consideration, to do or abstain from doing some legal act that is enforceable by law.
2. Bilateral contracts are based on mutual promises. Unilateral contracts are based on a promise by one party and an act by another party.
3. The requirements for contract validity are (1) competent parties, (2) mutual assent, (3) offer and acceptance, (4) consideration, and (5) legality of object.
4. An offer must not be indefinite or illusory.
5. An offer can be revoked by an offeror at any time before acceptance.
6. A contract is created by the unconditional acceptance of a valid offer. Acceptance of bilateral offers must be communicated. Communication of the acceptance of unilateral offers results from the performance of an act by the promisee.
7. Mutual assent is defeated and a contract made voidable by (1) misrepresentation, (2) fraud, (3) undue influence, or (4) duress.
8. Contracts are assignable in the absence of a specific prohibition against assignment in the contract.
9. A contract that transfers an interest in real property, including but not limited to sales contracts, must be in writing per the Statute of Frauds. The Real Estate Commission, not the Statute of Frauds, requires real estate agency contracts to be in writing. The only exception to this law is temporary oral buyer or oral dual agency. Even this type of agency agreement must be reduced to writing before submission of an Offer to Purchase and Contract.
10. Liquidated damages are the amount of money for damages agreed upon in the contract.
11. Compensatory damages are the compensation awarded by the court to the injured party for financial loss caused by a breach of contract by the defaulting party.
12. The Statute of Frauds requires the following types of contract to be in writing: contract to buy and sell real estate, options, land contracts, contracts for the exchange of real estate, and lease contracts exceeding three years.
13. The Statute of Frauds does not require the following types of contract to be in writing: agency contracts (listing, buyer agency, dual agency) and leases for three years or less.
14. Earnest money and consideration are not the same thing.

Review Questions

Answers to the review questions are in the Answer Key at the back of the book.

1. A contract in which mutual promises are exchanged at the time of signing (execution) is termed:
   A. multilateral.
   B. unilateral.
   C. bilateral.
   D. promissory.

2. Of the following statements regarding voidable contracts, which is NOT correct?
   A. A voidable contract can be voided by one or more parties.
   B. A voidable contract can be legally consummated by the parties.
   C. A voidable contract can never be consummated.
   D. A voidable contract results from failure to meet some legal requirement in negotiating the agreement.

3. For contracts in general, except for those of the sale of real property, the essential elements include all of the following EXCEPT:
   A. competent parties.
   B. offer and acceptance.
   C. legality of object.
   D. writing.

4. When are contracts considered to be assignable?
   A. ONLY when it is specifically stipulated in the contract that it is assignable.
   B. Contracts are always considered to be assignable.
   C. Anytime it is not prohibited.
   D. Contracts are never considered assignable.

5. Which of the following is the basis of duress?
   A. fear
   B. mistake
   C. indefiniteness
   D. illusion

6. A contract to sell real property may be terminated by each of the following EXCEPT:
   A. full performance.
   B. breach of contract.
   C. mutual agreement.
   D. death.

7. Which of the following has the effect of terminating contracts?
   A. consideration
   B. bankruptcy
   C. exercise
   D. assignment

8. In the event a seller defaults in his obligation to convey title to the property as agreed upon in a contract sale, which of the following remedies is available to the purchaser?
   A. suit for breach of contract
   B. suit for specific performance
   C. suit for compensatory damages
   D. all of the above

9. All of the following contracts are unilateral EXCEPT a(n):
   A. contract for the sale of real estate.
   B. open listing contract.
   C. option to purchase contract.
   D. contract to pay $1,000 if someone will paint your house.

10. A contract is automatically void if there is:
    A. duress.
    B. mutual mistake.
    C. willful misrepresentation.
    D. illegal purpose.

11. What type of real estate contract must be in writing per the Statute of Frauds?
    A. an Exclusive Right to Sell Listing agreement
    B. an Exclusive Right to Represent Buyer agreement
    C. an Offer to Purchase and Contract
    D. short-term rental agreements of less than three years

12. A substitution of a new contract for the former one is called a:
    A. commingling.
    B. revocation.
    C. reversion.
    D. novation.

13. A contract clause that stipulates the dates are to be strictly adhered to is the _____ clause.
    A. due diligence
    B. assignment
    C. time is of the essence
    D. expressed contract

14. Which of the following is not required to be in writing according to the Statute of Frauds?
    A. listing contract
    B. offer to purchase
    C. installment land contract
    D. leases for more than three years

15. A complete transfer of contractual rights and privileges is a(n):
    A. novation.
    B. specific performance.
    C. assignment.
    D. subsequent modifying agreement.

CHAPTER 10
SALES CONTRACTS AND RELATED PROCEDURES

KEY TERMS

contract for deed
due diligence fee
effective date
equitable title
installment land contracts
legal title
liquidated damages
offeree
offeror
option
optionee
optionor
right of first opportunity to purchase
right of first refusal

LEARNING OBJECTIVES

At the conclusion of this chapter, you should be able to:

1. Describe the essential and common provisions of the North Carolina Association of REALTORS®/North Carolina Bar Association (NCAR/NCBA) Offer to Purchase and Contract Form 2-T.
2. Describe the rights and obligations of the parties to a purchase contract.
3. Understand the due diligence process, including the rights and fees of the parties.
4. Describe the characteristics and requirements of the offer.
5. Define the characteristics and requirements of the counteroffer.
6. Describe the requirements for handling earnest money.
7. Understand the installment land contract (contract for deed) provisions, advantages, and disadvantages.
8. Understand the option to purchase and its requirements.
9. Understand the different "preemptive rights" to a contract.

IN THIS CHAPTER

The sales contract stipulates the written understanding and agreement between the buyer and the seller. It forms the basis of the relationship between these parties, and it must be clear as to avoid any misunderstanding. The North Carolina contract form uses a due diligence process that eliminates much of the confusion of past contract forms by implementing one date and time by which the buyer has to either withdraw from the agreement or proceed to the closing. This chapter will address the selection of the due diligence date as well as explore the role of the earnest money deposit and the due diligence fee. In addition to the traditional sales contract forms, it also introduces some of the more common, nontraditional type of sales contracts, such as the installment land contract and the option agreement.

INTRODUCTION

It often has been stated that the purchase of a home represents the largest single investment most consumers will ever make. Whether or not that remains true, there is no doubt that this purchase is an extremely important one for both the buyer as well as the seller. The cornerstone contract for the sale of real property is the sales contract. Although it is referred to by many different names in different areas, we will refer to it as the offer to purchase and contract of sale. As the name implies, this form actually has a dual personality in that it is both the offer to purchase, or sell, and the contract upon final acceptance of the offer. This contract stipulates the total agreement between the buyer and seller and provides guidance to both the lenders and the attorneys in addressing their roles in the completion of the transaction. It stipulates the price, terms, and conditions under which the purchaser will be contractually obligated to purchase the property. It is, therefore, a legal document and should be approached as such. Far too often, agents will complete these forms in a rather casual fashion that is insufficient as far as creating a complete understanding of the responsibilities of each party and does not provide proper guidance to the lender and attorney.

"Drafting" the Sales Contracts

A real estate broker is permitted to properly fill in the blanks of an offer to purchase and contract form that is designed for that purpose and prepared by an attorney. Normally, it is considered the unauthorized practice of law for a non attorney to prepare contract forms for another and for compensation, but this narrow exemption allows basic information to be inserted without being considered a violation. This is not to be broadly interpreted. This exemption is limited to providing only the information that is applicable to the blanks on the form. Brokers are not permitted to rewrite or create wording that alters the basic text of the forms. This is considered to be "drafting" of a contract form and is not permitted by state statutes and the North Carolina Real Estate Commission. See North Carolina General Statute (G.S.) 93A-6(a)(11), Commission rule 58A.0111, and G.S. 84-2.1 in Appendix C.

Even though a broker is permitted to fill in the blanks of an appropriate contract form, a broker will still be held responsible for the proper completion of the blanks. This includes not only the insertion of appropriate information but also the requirement to do so in an understandable, clear, and concise manner that protects the interests of the parties.

Importance of Appropriate Sales Contract Form (Including Sources)

One of the first steps that a broker must take is to determine which contract form will be recommended to the seller or buyer for use in a given transaction. It is often assumed the North Carolina Real Estate Commission (the Commission) has adopted numerous contract forms for use in real estate sales.

In reality, the Commission has not adopted any contract forms and does not dictate to the parties which forms they must use.

It is unrealistic to think that any preprinted contract form could possibly fulfill all the needs of the various real estate transactions the agent will encounter. Many preprinted forms are available today, including those for the sale of a single-family residential property, new construction, vacant land, commercial property, and more. In some cases, there will not be an appropriate preprinted form and the services of a competent attorney will need to be sought. A broker needs to utilize a form that is designed for the purpose that is appropriate to the type of transaction that he is brokering.

"If a buyer or seller want to make extensive revisions to a purchase contract the best approach for a real estate professional in North Carolina is to refer them to an attorney."
—Bill Gallagher, DREI

> Licensees can offer any preprinted sales contract form for use by the consumer as long as the form complies with the requirements of Rule 58A.0112. The licensee is NOT required to use an industry form.

In North Carolina, preprinted contract forms are mainly provided by two different industry leaders. The North Carolina Association of REALTORS® (NCAR) has joined forces with the North Carolina Bar Association (NCBA) to create a variety of industry forms for real estate transactions. The NCAR forms are available only to those members of that organization and are not to be utilized by the general public. NCAR forms are identified by the REALTOR® logo at the bottom of the contract page. Interestingly, the NCBA does provide the general public with the ability to purchase and use their forms. These NCBA forms contain the same text as the NCAR forms but without the REALTOR® logo. These NCBA forms are available from select printing firms contracted by the Bar Association.

As indicated earlier, there is no requirement these particular forms be the only ones allowed to be used.

The Joint Forms Committee (as the panel appointed by each of these organizations is called) has created the preprinted forms for the sale of single-family residential properties, the Offer to Purchase and Contract, Standard Form 2-T; for the sale of vacant lots and land, the Offer to Purchase and Contract–Vacant Lot/Land, Standard Form 12-T; and for the sale of new construction and commercial purpose properties. Samples of these forms can be accessed online at **www.ncrealtors.com.** More details regarding the offers to purchase for both residential and vacant land will be addressed later in this chapter.

The fact is that the North Carolina Real Estate Commission cannot require the parties to use any of these forms. Do not confuse the NCAR with the North Carolina Real Estate Commission. The Commission is a regulatory agency that adopts and enforces rules and regulations. The Commission regulates licensees, not buyers and sellers. Buyers and sellers are free to provide their own forms without restriction by the Commission. Agents, who are regulated by the Commission, are still required to properly fill in the blanks of any form the parties choose or, if she does not feel competent in a given situation, to refer the completion of the form to an attorney. From a pure contract law perspective, sales contracts are legally sufficient even if they only include the most minimal of information, such as names of the parties, description of property, terms and conditions of sale purchase, and proper signatures. Although this might comply with basic contract law, it would not be considered sufficient to properly address the wide variety of topics that a more complete contract would address. For this reason, the Commission has adopted Rule A.0112 (Figure 10.1), which requires that any preprinted form provided for use by a broker must contain 19 specific elements.

(a) A broker acting as an agent in a real estate transaction shall not use a preprinted offer or sales contract form unless the form describes or expressly requires the entry of the following information:

(1) the names of the buyer and seller;

(2) a legal description of the real property sufficient to identify and distinguish it from all other property;

(3) an itemization of any personal property to be included in the transaction;

(4) the purchase price and manner of payment;

(5) any portion of the purchase price that is to be paid by a promissory note, including the amount, interest rate, payment terms, whether or not the note is to be secured, and other material terms;

FIGURE 10.1 A.0112 Offers and Sales Contracts. (*Continued*)

(6) any portion of the purchase price that is to be paid by the assumption of an existing loan, including the amount of such loan, costs to be paid by the buyer or seller, the interest rate and number of discount points and a condition that the buyer must be able to qualify for the assumption of the loan and must make every reasonable effort to qualify for the assumption of the loan;

(7) the amount of earnest money, if any, the method of payment, the name of the broker or firm that will serve as escrow agent, an acknowledgment of earnest money receipt by the escrow agent, and the criteria for determining disposition of the earnest money, including disputed earnest money, consistent with Rule .0107 of this Subchapter;

(8) any loan that must be obtained by the buyer as a condition of the contract, including the amount and type of loan, interest rate and number of discount points, loan term, and who shall pay loan closing costs, and a condition that the buyer shall make every reasonable effort to obtain the loan;

(9) a general statement of the buyer's intended use of the property and a condition that such use must not be prohibited by private restriction or governmental regulation;

(10) the amount and purpose of any special assessment to which the property is subject and the responsibility of the parties for any unpaid charges;

(11) the date for closing and transfer of possession;

(12) the signatures of the buyer and seller;

(13) the date of offer and acceptance;

(14) a provision that title to the property must be delivered at closing by general warranty deed and must be fee simple marketable title, free of all encumbrances except ad valorem taxes for the current year, utility easements, and any other encumbrances approved by the buyer or a provision otherwise describing the estate to be conveyed with encumbrances, and the form of conveyance;

(15) the items to be prorated or adjusted at closing;

(16) who shall pay closing expenses;

(17) the buyer's right to inspect the property prior to closing and who shall pay for repairs and improvements, if any;

(18) a provision that the property shall at closing be in substantially the same condition as on the date of the offer (reasonable wear and tear excepted), or a description of the required property condition at closing: and

(19) a provision setting forth the identity of each real estate agent and firm involved in the transaction and disclosing the party each agent and firm represents.

(b) A broker acting as an agent in a real estate transaction shall not use a preprinted offer or sales contract form containing:

(1) any provision concerning the payment of a commission or compensation, including the forfeiture of earnest money, to any broker or firm; or

(2) any provision that attempts to disclaim the liability of a broker for his or her representations in connection with the transaction. A broker or anyone acting for or at the direction of the broker shall not insert or cause such provisions or terms to be inserted into any such preprinted form, even at the direction of the parties or their attorneys.

(c) The provisions of this rule shall apply only to preprinted offer and sales contract forms which a broker acting as an agent in a real estate transaction proposes for use by the buyer and seller. Nothing contained in this Rule shall be construed to prohibit the buyer and seller in a real estate transaction from altering, amending or deleting any provision in a form offer to purchase or contract nor shall this Rule be construed to limit the rights of the buyer and seller to draft their own offers or contracts or to have the same drafted by an attorney at law.

FIGURE 10.1
Source: With permission of North Carolina Association of REALTORS®

In addition to these 19 specific elements, there are two items that cannot be inserted by a broker in the form even if he has the permission of the parties or their attorney. The two items are (1) any provision concerning the payment, or forfeiture, of a commission; and (2) any provision that attempts to disclaim the liability of a broker in a transaction.

These restrictions apply only to those preprinted forms provided by a broker for use by the parties. Nothing prohibits the parties from producing their own forms or from having their attorneys prepare the contract for them. In the residential market, it is very common for larger builders to utilize their own contract forms for the sale of their new construction houses. These forms are not considered to be preprinted forms provided by the agent, so they do not have to comply with the Commission rules regarding the 19 specific elements and are typically slanted to favor the builder or seller.

THE OFFER TO PURCHASE AND CONTRACT

The Offer to Purchase and Contract, also referred to as Sales Contract, Purchase Contract, and Earnest Money Contract, as well as by other names, is the written agreement and understanding of the terms and conditions of the sale between the buyer and seller. Although the contract form can be provided by a number of sources, including industry standard preprinted forms, seller- or builder-supplied forms, attorney-drafted forms, and many others, this chapter will focus on the NCAR/NCBA Standard Form 2-T Offer to Purchase and Contract. This form is widely used, whether in the NCAR version available to REALTOR® members or the NCBA version available to their members as well as the general public. This form has the added advantage of closely following the 19 specific elements as required by the Commission. Following the coverage of Form 2-T, there will also be coverage of a similar form adopted by NCAR/NCBA that focuses on the sale of vacant lots/land.

The ability to use the array of industry-created forms does not relieve the broker from the responsibility to include all of the required data necessary to conclude the transaction. Additionally, **brokers are prohibited from including any clauses in the preprinted contract forms that are related to broker compensation or statements that** attempt to disclaim any liability on the part of the broker or firm.

Remember that brokers are not allowed to draft contract forms for each other, as that is considered the unauthorized practice of law. Brokers are allowed only to "fill in" blanks on preprinted contract forms that have been designed for that purpose, such as the NCAR/NCBA Offer to Purchase and Contract Standard Form (Figure 10.2). It is only permissible for a broker to add very simple, straightforward items to the offer to purchase. **A broker is prohibited against drafting contract language even in cases involving permission to do so from the client.** Any necessary provisions that are beyond the simple, straightforward standard should be referred to a competent attorney for proper assistance.

OFFER TO PURCHASE AND CONTRACT
[Consult "Guidelines" (Form 2G) for guidance in completing this form]

For valuable consideration, the receipt and legal sufficiency of which are hereby acknowledged, Buyer offers to purchase and Seller upon acceptance agrees to sell and convey the Property on the terms and conditions of this Offer To Purchase and Contract and any addendum or modification made in accordance with its terms (together the "Contract").

1. **TERMS AND DEFINITIONS**: The terms listed below shall have the respective meaning given them as set forth adjacent to each term.

   (a) "**Seller**": _____

   (b) "**Buyer**": _____

   (c) "**Property**": The Property shall include all that real estate described below together with all appurtenances thereto including the improvements located thereon and the fixtures and personal property listed in Paragraphs 2 and 3 below.

   > **NOTE**: If the Property will include a manufactured (mobile) home(s), Buyer and Seller should consider including the Manufactured (Mobile) Home provision in the Additional Provisions Addendum (Standard Form 2A11-T) with this offer.

   Street Address: _____
   City: _____ Zip: _____
   County: _____, North Carolina

   > **NOTE**: Governmental authority over taxes, zoning, school districts, utilities and mail delivery may differ from address shown.

   Legal Description: (Complete *ALL* applicable)
   Plat Reference: Lot/Unit_____, Block/Section _____, Subdivision/Condominium _____
   _____, as shown on Plat Book/Slide _____ at Page(s) _____
   The PIN/PID or other identification number of the Property is: _____
   Other description: _____
   Some or all of the Property may be described in Deed Book _____ at Page _____

   (d) "**Purchase Price**":

   $ _____ paid in U.S. Dollars upon the following terms:
   $ _____ BY DUE DILIGENCE FEE made payable and delivered to Seller by the Effective Date
   $ _____ BY INITIAL EARNEST MONEY DEPOSIT made payable and delivered to Escrow Agent named in Paragraph 1(f) by ❏ cash ❏ personal check ❏ official bank check ❏ wire transfer, ❏ electronic transfer, EITHER ❏ with this offer OR ❏ within five (5) days of the Effective Date of this Contract.
   $ _____ BY (ADDITIONAL) EARNEST MONEY DEPOSIT made payable and delivered to Escrow Agent named in Paragraph 1(f) by cash, official bank check, wire transfer or electronic transfer no later than 5 p.m. on _____, ***TIME BEING OF THE ESSENCE.***
   $ _____ BY ASSUMPTION of the unpaid principal balance and all obligations of Seller on the existing loan(s) secured by a deed of trust on the Property in accordance with the attached Loan Assumption Addendum (Standard Form 2A6-T).
   $ _____ BY SELLER FINANCING in accordance with the attached Seller Financing Addendum (Standard Form 2A5-T).
   $ _____ BY BUILDING DEPOSIT in accordance with the attached New Construction Addendum (Standard Form 2A3-T).
   $ _____ BALANCE of the Purchase Price in cash at Settlement (some or all of which may be paid with the proceeds of a new loan)

   Should Buyer fail to deliver either the Due Diligence Fee or any Initial Earnest Money Deposit by their due dates, or should any check or other funds paid by Buyer be dishonored, for any reason, by the institution upon which the payment is drawn, Buyer shall have one (1) banking day after written notice to deliver cash, official bank check, wire transfer or electronic transfer to the payee. In the event Buyer does not timely deliver the required funds, Seller shall have the right to terminate this Contract upon written notice to Buyer.

Page 1 of 13

This form jointly approved by:
North Carolina Bar Association
North Carolina Association of REALTORS®, Inc.

Buyer's initials _____ _____ Seller's initials _____ _____

STANDARD FORM 2-T
Revised 7/2018
© 7/2018

FIGURE 10.2 Offer to Purchase and Contract Form 2-T. (*Continued*)
Source: Used with permission of North Carolina Association of REALTORS®

(e) **"Earnest Money Deposit"**: The Initial Earnest Money Deposit, the Additional Earnest Money Deposit and any other earnest monies paid or required to be paid in connection with this transaction, collectively the "Earnest Money Deposit", shall be deposited and held in escrow by Escrow Agent until Closing, at which time it will be credited to Buyer, or until this Contract is otherwise terminated. In the event: (1) this offer is not accepted; or (2) a condition of any resulting contract is not satisfied, then the Earnest Money Deposit shall be refunded to Buyer. In the event of breach of this Contract by Seller, the Earnest Money Deposit shall be refunded to Buyer upon Buyer's request, but such return shall not affect any other remedies available to Buyer for such breach. In the event of breach of this Contract by Buyer, the Earnest Money Deposit shall be paid to Seller as liquidated damages and as Seller's sole and exclusive remedy for such breach, but without limiting Seller's rights under Paragraphs 4(d) and 4(e) for damage to the Property or Seller's right to retain the Due Diligence Fee. It is acknowledged by the parties that payment of the Earnest Money Deposit to Seller in the event of a breach of this Contract by Buyer is compensatory and not punitive, such amount being a reasonable estimation of the actual loss that Seller would incur as a result of such breach. The payment of the Earnest Money Deposit to Seller shall not constitute a penalty or forfeiture but actual compensation for Seller's anticipated loss, both parties acknowledging the difficulty determining Seller's actual damages for such breach. If legal proceedings are brought by Buyer or Seller against the other to recover the Earnest Money Deposit, the prevailing party in the proceeding shall be entitled to recover from the non-prevailing party reasonable attorney fees and court costs incurred in connection with the proceeding.

(f) **"Escrow Agent"** (insert name): _____

> **NOTE**: In the event of a dispute between Seller and Buyer over the disposition of the Earnest Money Deposit held in escrow, a licensed real estate broker ("Broker") is required by state law (and Escrow Agent, if not a Broker, hereby agrees) to retain the Earnest Money Deposit in the Escrow Agent's trust or escrow account until Escrow Agent has obtained a written release from the parties consenting to its disposition or until disbursement is ordered by a court of competent jurisdiction. Alternatively, if a Broker or an attorney licensed to practice law in North Carolina ("Attorney") is holding the Earnest Money Deposit, the Broker or Attorney may deposit the disputed monies with the appropriate clerk of court in accordance with the provisions of N.C.G.S. §93A-12.

THE PARTIES AGREE THAT A REAL ESTATE BROKERAGE FIRM ACTING AS ESCROW AGENT MAY PLACE THE EARNEST MONEY DEPOSIT IN AN INTEREST BEARING TRUST ACCOUNT AND THAT ANY INTEREST EARNED THEREON SHALL BE DISBURSED TO THE ESCROW AGENT MONTHLY IN CONSIDERATION OF THE EXPENSES INCURRED BY MAINTAINING SUCH ACCOUNT AND RECORDS ASSOCIATED THEREWITH.

(g) **"Effective Date"**: The date that: (1) the last one of Buyer and Seller has signed or initialed this offer or the final counteroffer, if any, and (2) such signing or initialing is communicated to the party making the offer or counteroffer, as the case may be. The parties acknowledge and agree that the initials lines at the bottom of each page of this Contract are merely evidence of their having reviewed the terms of each page, and that the complete execution of such initials lines shall not be a condition of the effectiveness of this Agreement.

(h) **"Due Diligence"**: Buyer's opportunity to investigate the Property and the transaction contemplated by this Contract, including but not necessarily limited to the matters described in Paragraph 4 below, to decide whether Buyer, in Buyer's sole discretion, will proceed with or terminate the transaction.

(i) **"Due Diligence Fee"**: A negotiated amount, if any, paid by Buyer to Seller with this Contract for Buyer's right to terminate the Contract for any reason or no reason during the Due Diligence Period. It shall be the property of Seller upon the Effective Date and shall be a credit to Buyer at Closing. The Due Diligence Fee shall be non-refundable except in the event of a material breach of this Contract by Seller, or if this Contract is terminated under Paragraph 8(n) or Paragraph 12, or as otherwise provided in any addendum hereto. Buyer and Seller each expressly waive any right that they may have to deny the right to conduct Due Diligence or to assert any defense as to the enforceability of this Contract based on the absence or alleged insufficiency of any Due Diligence Fee, it being the intent of the parties to create a legally binding contract for the purchase and sale of the Property without regard to the existence or amount of any Due Diligence Fee.

(j) **"Due Diligence Period"**: The period beginning on the Effective Date and extending through 5:00 p.m. on _____ _____***TIME BEING OF THE ESSENCE***.

(k) **"Settlement"**: The proper execution and delivery to the closing attorney of all documents necessary to complete the transaction contemplated by this Contract, including the deed, settlement statement, deed of trust and other loan or conveyance documents, and the closing attorney's receipt of all funds necessary to complete such transaction.

(l) **"Settlement Date":** The parties agree that Settlement will take place on _____ (the "Settlement Date"), unless otherwise agreed in writing, at a time and place designated by Buyer.

(m) **"Closing"**: The completion of the legal process which results in the transfer of title to the Property from Seller to Buyer, which

FIGURE 10.2 (*Continued*)

includes the following steps: (1) the Settlement (defined above); (2) the completion of a satisfactory title update to the Property following the Settlement; (3) the closing attorney's receipt of authorization to disburse all necessary funds; and (4) recordation in the appropriate county registry of the deed(s) and deed(s) of trust, if any, which shall take place as soon as reasonably possible for the closing attorney after Settlement. Upon Closing, the proceeds of sale shall be disbursed by the closing attorney in accordance with the settlement statement and the provisions of Chapter 45A of the North Carolina General Statutes. If the title update should reveal unexpected liens, encumbrances or other title defects, or if the closing attorney is not authorized to disburse all necessary funds, then the Closing shall be suspended and the Settlement deemed delayed under Paragraph 13 (Delay in Settlement/Closing).

> **WARNING**: The North Carolina State Bar has determined that the performance of most acts and services required for a closing constitutes the practice of law and must be performed only by an attorney licensed to practice law in North Carolina. State law prohibits unlicensed individuals or firms from rendering legal services or advice. Although non-attorney settlement agents may perform limited services in connection with a closing, they may not perform all the acts and services required to complete a closing. A closing involves significant legal issues that should be handled by an attorney. Accordingly it is the position of the North Carolina Bar Association and the North Carolina Association of REALTORS® that all buyers should hire an attorney licensed in North Carolina to perform a closing.

(n) **"Special Assessments"**: A charge against the Property by a governmental authority in addition to ad valorem taxes and recurring governmental service fees levied with such taxes, or by an owners' association in addition to any regular assessment (dues), either of which may be a lien against the Property. A Special Assessment may be either proposed or confirmed.

"Proposed Special Assessment": A Special Assessment that is under formal consideration but which has not been approved prior to Settlement.

"Confirmed Special Assessment": A Special Assessment that has been approved prior to Settlement whether payable in a lump sum or future installments.

> **NOTE:** Any Proposed and Confirmed Special Assessments must be identified by Seller in paragraph 7(c), and Buyer's and Seller's respective responsibilities for Proposed and Confirmed Special Assessments are addressed in paragraphs 6(a) and 8(k).

2. FIXTURES AND EXCLUSIONS:
(a) **Specified Items:** Unless identified in subparagraph (d) below, the following items, including all related equipment and remote control devices, if any, are deemed fixtures and shall convey, included in the Purchase Price free of liens:

- Alarm and security systems (attached) for security, fire, smoke, carbon monoxide or other toxins with all related access codes, sensors, cameras, dedicated monitors, hard drives, video recorders, power supplies and cables; doorbells/chimes
- All stoves/ranges/ovens; built-in appliances; attached microwave oven; vent hood
- Antennas; satellite dishes and receivers
- Basketball goals and play equipment (permanently attached or in-ground)
- Ceiling and wall-attached fans; light fixtures (including existing bulbs)
- Fireplace insert; gas logs or starters; attached fireplace screens; wood or coal stoves
- Floor coverings (attached)
- Fuel tank(s) whether attached or buried and including any contents that have not been used, removed or resold to the fuel provider as of Settlement. **NOTE:** Seller's use, removal or resale of fuel in any fuel tank is subject to Seller's obligation under Paragraph 8(c) to provide working, existing utilities through the earlier of Closing or possession by Buyer.
- Garage door openers with all controls
- Generators that are permanently wired
- Invisible fencing with power supply, controls and receivers
- Landscape and outdoor trees and plants (except in moveable containers); raised garden; landscape and foundation lighting; outdoor sound systems; permanent irrigation systems and controls; rain barrels; landscape water features; address markers
- Mailboxes; mounted package and newspaper receptacles
- Mirrors attached to walls, ceilings, cabinets or doors; all bathroom wall mirrors
- Storage shed; utility building
- Swimming pool (excluding inflatable); spa; hot tub
- Solar electric and solar water heating systems
- Sump-pumps, radon fans and crawlspace ventilators; de-humidifiers that are permanently wired
- Surface-mounting brackets for television and speakers; recess-mounted speakers; mounted intercom system
- Water supply equipment, including filters, conditioning and softener systems; re-circulating pumps; well pumps and tanks
- Window/Door blinds and shades, curtain and drapery rods and brackets, door and window screens and combination doors, awnings and storm windows

FIGURE 10.2 (*Continued*)

(b) **Items Leased or Not Owned:** Any item which is leased or not owned by Seller, such as fuel tanks, antennas, satellite dishes and receivers, appliances, and alarm and security systems must be identified here and shall not convey: _____
_____

(c) **Other Fixtures/Unspecified items:** Unless identified in subparagraph (d) below, any other item legally considered a fixture is included in the Purchase Price free of liens.

(d) **Other Items That Do Not Convey:** The following items shall not convey (*identify those items to be excluded under subparagraphs (a) and (c)*): _____
_____

Seller shall repair any damage caused by removal of any items excluded above.

3. **PERSONAL PROPERTY:** The following personal property shall be transferred to Buyer at no value at closing: _____
_____

> **NOTE:** Buyer is advised to consult with Buyer's lender to assure that the Personal Property items listed above can be included in this Contract.

4. **BUYER'S DUE DILIGENCE PROCESS:**

> **WARNING: BUYER IS STRONGLY ENCOURAGED TO CONDUCT DUE DILIGENCE DURING THE DUE DILIGENCE PERIOD.** If Buyer is not satisfied with the results or progress of Buyer's Due Diligence, Buyer should terminate this Contract, PRIOR TO THE EXPIRATION OF THE DUE DILIGENCE PERIOD, unless Buyer can obtain a written extension from Seller. SELLER IS NOT OBLIGATED TO GRANT AN EXTENSION. Although Buyer may continue to investigate the Property following the expiration of the Due Diligence Period, Buyer's failure to deliver a Termination Notice to Seller prior to the expiration of the Due Diligence Period will constitute a waiver by Buyer of any right to terminate this Contract based on any matter relating to Buyer's Due Diligence. Provided however, following the Due Diligence Period, Buyer may still exercise a right to terminate if Seller fails to materially comply with any of Seller's obligations under Paragraph 8 of this Contract or for any other reason permitted under the terms of this Contract or North Carolina law.

(a) **Loan**: Buyer, at Buyer's expense, shall be entitled to pursue qualification for and approval of the Loan if any.

> **NOTE**: Buyer's obligation to purchase the Property is not contingent on obtaining a Loan. Therefore, Buyer is advised to consult with Buyer's lender prior to signing this offer to assure that the Due Diligence Period allows sufficient time for the appraisal to be completed and for Buyer's lender to provide Buyer sufficient information to decide whether to proceed with or terminate the transaction.

(b) **Property Investigation**: Buyer or Buyer's agents or representatives, at Buyer's expense, shall be entitled to conduct all desired tests, surveys, appraisals, investigations, examinations and inspections of the Property as Buyer deems appropriate, including but NOT limited to the following:

(i) **Inspections**: Inspections to determine the condition of any improvements on the Property, the presence of unusual drainage conditions or evidence of excessive moisture adversely affecting any improvements on the Property, the presence of asbestos or existing environmental contamination, evidence of wood-destroying insects or damage therefrom, and the presence and level of radon gas on the Property.

(ii) **Review of Documents**: Review of the Declaration of Restrictive Covenants, Bylaws, Articles of Incorporation, Rules and Regulations, and other governing documents of any applicable owners' association and/or subdivision. If the Property is subject to regulation by an owners' association, it is recommended that Buyer review the completed Residential Property and Owners' Association Disclosure Statement provided by Seller prior to signing this offer. It is also recommended that the Buyer determine if the owners' association or its management company charges fees for providing information required by Buyer's lender or confirming restrictive covenant compliance.

(iii) **Insurance**: Investigation of the availability and cost of insurance for the Property.

(iv) **Appraisals**: An appraisal of the Property.

(v) **Survey**: A survey to determine whether the property is suitable for Buyer's intended use and the location of easements, setbacks, property boundaries and other issues which may or may not constitute title defects.

(vi) **Zoning and Governmental Regulation**: Investigation of current or proposed zoning or other governmental regulation that may affect Buyer's intended use of the Property, adjacent land uses, planned or proposed road construction, and school attendance zones.

FIGURE 10.2 (*Continued*)

(vii) **Flood Hazard**: Investigation of potential flood hazards on the Property, and/or any requirement to purchase flood insurance in order to obtain the Loan

(viii) **Utilities and Access**: Availability, quality, and obligations for maintenance of utilities including water, sewer, electric, gas, communication services, stormwater management, and means of access to the Property and amenities.

(ix) **Streets/Roads**: Investigation of the status of the street/road upon which the Property fronts as well as any other street/road used to access the Property, including: (1) whether any street(s)/road(s) are public or private, (2) whether any street(s)/road(s) designated as public are accepted for maintenance by the State of NC or any municipality, or (3) if private or not accepted for public maintenance, the consequences and responsibility for maintenance and the existence, terms and funding of any maintenance agreements.

(x) **Fuel Tank**: Inspections to determine the existence, type and ownership of any fuel tank located on the Property.

> **NOTE**: Buyer is advised to consult with the owner of any leased fuel tank regarding the terms under which Buyer may lease the tank and obtain fuel.

(c) **Repair/Improvement Negotiations/Agreement**: Buyer acknowledges and understands that unless the parties agree otherwise, THE PROPERTY IS BEING SOLD IN ITS CURRENT CONDITION. Buyer and Seller acknowledge and understand that they may, but are not required to, engage in negotiations for repairs/improvements to the Property. Buyer is advised to make any repair/improvement requests in sufficient time to allow repair/improvement negotiations to be concluded prior to the expiration of the Due Diligence Period. Any agreement that the parties may reach with respect to repairs/improvements shall be considered an obligation of the parties and is an addition to this Contract and as such, must be in writing and signed by the parties in accordance with Paragraph 20.

> **NOTE**: See Paragraph 8(c), Access to Property and Paragraph 8(m), Negotiated Repairs/Improvements.

(d) **Buyer's Obligation to Repair Damage**: Buyer shall, at Buyer's expense, promptly repair any damage to the Property resulting from any activities of Buyer and Buyer's agents and contractors, but Buyer shall not be responsible for any damage caused by accepted practices either approved by the N.C. Home Inspector Licensure Board or applicable to any other N.C. licensed professional performing reasonable appraisals, tests, surveys, examinations and inspections of the Property. This repair obligation shall survive any termination of this Contract.

(e) **Indemnity**: Buyer will indemnify and hold Seller harmless from all loss, damage, claims, suits or costs, which shall arise out of any contract, agreement, or injury to any person or property as a result of any activities of Buyer and Buyer's agents and contractors relating to the Property except for any loss, damage, claim, suit or cost arising out of pre-existing conditions of the Property and/or out of Seller's negligence or willful acts or omissions. This indemnity shall survive this Contract and any termination hereof.

(f) **Buyer's Right to Terminate:** Buyer shall have the right to terminate this Contract for any reason or no reason, by delivering to Seller written notice of termination (the "Termination Notice") during the Due Diligence Period (or any agreed-upon written extension of the Due Diligence Period), ***TIME BEING OF THE ESSENCE***. If Buyer timely delivers the Termination Notice, this Contract shall be terminated and the Earnest Money Deposit shall be refunded to Buyer.

(g) **CLOSING SHALL CONSTITUTE ACCEPTANCE OF THE PROPERTY IN ITS THEN EXISTING CONDITION UNLESS PROVISION IS OTHERWISE MADE IN WRITING.**

5. **BUYER REPRESENTATIONS**:

(a) **Loan**: Buyer ❑ does ❑ does not intend to obtain a new loan in order to purchase the Property. If Buyer is obtaining a new loan, Buyer intends to obtain a loan as follows: ❑ FHA ❑ VA (attach FHA/VA Financing Addendum) ❑ Conventional ❑ Other: _____ loan at a ❑ Fixed Rate ❑ Adjustable Rate in the principal amount of _____ plus any financed VA Funding Fee or FHA MIP for a term of _____ year(s), at an initial interest rate not to exceed _____ % per annum (the "Loan").

> **NOTE**: Buyer's obligations under this Contract are not conditioned upon obtaining or closing any loan.

> **NOTE:** If Buyer does not intend to obtain a new loan, Seller is advised, prior to signing this offer, to obtain documentation from Buyer which demonstrates that Buyer will be able to close on the Property without the necessity of obtaining a new loan.

(b) **Other Property**: Buyer ❑ does ❑ does not have to sell or lease other real property in order to qualify for a new loan or to complete the purchase.

> **NOTE**: This Contract is not conditioned upon the sale of Buyer's property unless a contingent sale addendum such as Standard Form 2A2-T is made a part of this Contract.

FIGURE 10.2 (*Continued*)

(c) **Performance of Buyer's Financial Obligations**: To the best of Buyer's knowledge, there are no other circumstances or conditions existing as of the date of this offer that would prohibit Buyer from performing Buyer's financial obligations in accordance with this Contract, except as may be specifically set forth herein.

(d) **Residential Property and Owners' Association Disclosure Statement** (*check only one*):
- ❏ Buyer has received a signed copy of the N.C. Residential Property and Owners' Association Disclosure Statement prior to the signing of this offer.
- ❏ Buyer has NOT received a signed copy of the N.C. Residential Property and Owners' Association Disclosure Statement prior to the signing of this offer and shall have the right to terminate or withdraw this Contract without penalty (including a refund of any Due Diligence Fee) prior to WHICHEVER OF THE FOLLOWING EVENTS OCCURS FIRST: (1) the end of the third calendar day following receipt of the Disclosure Statement; (2) the end of the third calendar day following the Effective Date; or (3) Settlement or occupancy by Buyer in the case of a sale or exchange.
- ❏ Exempt from N.C. Residential Property and Owners' Association Disclosure Statement because (SEE GUIDELINES):_____.

(e) **Mineral and Oil and Gas Rights Mandatory Disclosure Statement** (*check only one*):
- ❏ Buyer has received a signed copy of the N.C. Mineral and Oil and Gas Rights Mandatory Disclosure Statement prior to the signing of this offer.
- ❏ Buyer has NOT received a signed copy of the N.C. Mineral and Oil and Gas Rights Mandatory Disclosure Statement prior to the signing of this offer and shall have the right to terminate or withdraw this Contract without penalty (including a refund of any Due Diligence Fee) prior to WHICHEVER OF THE FOLLOWING EVENTS OCCURS FIRST: (1) the end of the third calendar day following receipt of the Disclosure Statement; (2) the end of the third calendar day following the Effective Date; or (3) Settlement or occupancy by Buyer in the case of a sale or exchange.
- ❏ Exempt from N.C. Mineral and Oil and Gas Rights Mandatory Disclosure Statement because (SEE GUIDELINES): _____.

Buyer's receipt of a Mineral and Oil and Gas Rights Mandatory Disclosure Statement does not modify or limit the obligations of Seller under Paragraph 8(g) of this Contract and shall not constitute the assumption or approval by Buyer of any severance of mineral and/or oil and gas rights, except as may be assumed or specifically approved by Buyer in writing.

> **NOTE**: The parties are advised to consult with a NC attorney prior to signing this Contract if severance of mineral and/or oil and gas rights has occurred or is intended.

6. BUYER OBLIGATIONS:
(a) **Responsibility for Proposed Special Assessments**: Buyer shall take title subject to all Proposed Special Assessments.

(b) **Responsibility for Certain Costs**: Buyer shall be responsible for all costs with respect to:
  (i) any loan obtained by Buyer, including charges by an owners association and/or management company as agent of an owners' association for providing information required by Buyer's lender;
  (ii) charges required by an owners' association declaration to be paid by Buyer for Buyer's future use and enjoyment of the Property, including, without limitation, working capital contributions, membership fees, or charges for Buyer's use of the common elements and/or services provided to Buyer, such as "move-in fees";
  (iii) determining restrictive covenant compliance;
  (iv) appraisal;
  (v) title search;
  (vi) title insurance;
  (vii) any fees charged by the closing attorney for the preparation of the Closing Disclosure, Seller Disclosure and any other settlement statement;
  (viii) recording the deed; and
  (ix) preparation and recording of all instruments required to secure the balance of the Purchase Price unpaid at Settlement.

(c) **Authorization to Disclose Information**: Buyer authorizes the Buyer's lender(s), the parties' real estate agent(s) and closing attorney: (1) to provide this Contract to any appraiser employed by Buyer or by Buyer's lender(s); and (2) to release and disclose any buyer's closing disclosure, settlement statement and/or disbursement summary, or any information therein, to the parties to this transaction, their real estate agent(s) and Buyer's lender(s).

7. SELLER REPRESENTATIONS:
(a) **Ownership**: Seller represents that Seller:
- ❏ has owned the Property for at least one year.

FIGURE 10.2 (*Continued*)

❑ has owned the Property for less than one year.
❑ does not yet own the Property.

(b) **Lead-Based Paint** (*check if applicable*):
❑ The Property is residential and was built prior to 1978 (Attach Lead-Based Paint or Lead-Based Paint Hazards Disclosure Addendum {Standard Form 2A9-T}).

(c) **Assessments**: To the best of Seller's knowledge there ❑ are ❑ are not any Proposed Special Assessments. If any Proposed Special Assessments, identify: _____

Seller warrants that there ❑ are ❑ are not any Confirmed Special Assessments. If any Confirmed Special Assessments, identify: _____

> **NOTE**: Buyer's and Seller's respective responsibilities for Proposed and Confirmed Special Assessments are addressed in paragraphs 6(a) and 8(k).

(d) **Owners' Association(s) and Dues**: Seller authorizes and directs any owners' association, any management company of the owners' association, any insurance company and any attorney who has previously represented the Seller to release to Buyer, Buyer's agents, representative, closing attorney or lender true and accurate copies of the following items affecting the Property, including any amendments:
- Seller's statement of account
- master insurance policy showing the coverage provided and the deductible amount
- Declaration and Restrictive Covenants
- Rules and Regulations
- Articles of Incorporation
- Bylaws of the owners' association
- current financial statement and budget of the owners' association
- parking restrictions and information
- architectural guidelines

❑ (specify name of association): _____whose regular assessments ("dues") are $_____ per_____. The name, address and telephone number of the president of the owners' association or the association manager is: _____
_____
Owners' association website address, if any: _____

❑ (specify name of association): _____whose regular assessments ("dues") are $_____ per_____. The name, address and telephone number of the president of the owners' association or the association manager is: _____
_____
Owners' association website address, if any_____

8. **SELLER OBLIGATIONS**:
(a) **Evidence of Title, Payoff Statement(s) and Non Foreign Status**:
(i) Seller agrees to use best efforts to provide to the closing attorney as soon as reasonably possible after the Effective Date, copies of all title information in possession of or available to Seller, including but not limited to: title insurance policies, attorney's opinions on title, surveys, covenants, deeds, notes and deeds of trust, leases, and easements relating to the Property.
(ii) Seller shall provide to the closing attorney all information needed to obtain a written payoff statement from any lender(s) regarding any security interest in the Property as soon as reasonably possible after the Effective Date, and Seller designates the closing attorney as Seller's agent with express authority to request and obtain on Seller's behalf payoff statements and/or short-pay statements from any such lender(s).
(iii) If Seller is not a foreign person as defined by the Foreign Investment in Real Property Tax Act, Seller shall also provide to the closing attorney a non-foreign status affidavit (pursuant to the Foreign Investment in Real Property Tax Act). In the event Seller shall not provide a non-foreign status affidavit, Seller acknowledges that there may be withholding as provided by the Internal Revenue Code.

(b) **Authorization to Disclose Information**: Seller authorizes: (i) any attorney presently or previously representing Seller to release and disclose any title insurance policy in such attorney's file to Buyer and both Buyer's and Seller's agents and attorneys; (ii) the Property's title insurer or its agent to release and disclose all materials in the Property's title insurer's (or title insurer's agent's) file to

FIGURE 10.2 (*Continued*)

Buyer and both Buyer's and Seller's agents and attorneys and (iii) the closing attorney to release and disclose any seller's closing disclosure, settlement statement and/or disbursement summary, or any information therein, to the parties to this transaction, their real estate agent(s) and Buyer's lender(s).

(c) **Access to Property**: Seller shall provide reasonable access to the Property (including working, existing utilities) through the earlier of Closing or possession by Buyer, including, but not limited to, allowing Buyer and/or Buyer's agents or representatives, an opportunity to (i) conduct Due Diligence, (ii) verify the satisfactory completion of negotiated repairs/improvements, and (iii) conduct a final walk-through inspection of the Property.

> **NOTE:** See WARNING in paragraph 4 above for limitation on Buyer's right to terminate this Contract as a result of Buyer's continued investigation of the Property following the expiration of the Due Diligence Period.

(d) **Removal of Seller's Property**: Seller shall remove, by the date possession is made available to Buyer, all personal property which is not a part of the purchase and all garbage and debris from the Property.

(e) **Affidavit and Indemnification Agreement**: Seller shall furnish at Settlement an affidavit(s) and indemnification agreement(s) in form satisfactory to Buyer and Buyer's title insurer, if any, executed by Seller and any person or entity who has performed or furnished labor, services, materials or rental equipment to the Property within 120 days prior to the date of Settlement and who may be entitled to claim a lien against the Property as described in N.C.G.S. §44A-8 verifying that each such person or entity has been paid in full and agreeing to indemnify Buyer, Buyer's lender(s) and Buyer's title insurer against all loss from any cause or claim arising therefrom.

(f) **Designation of Lien Agent, Payment and Satisfaction of Liens**: If required by N.C.G.S. §44A-11.1, Seller shall have designated a Lien Agent, and Seller shall deliver to Buyer as soon as reasonably possible a copy of the appointment of Lien Agent. All deeds of trust, deferred ad valorem taxes, liens and other charges against the Property, not assumed by Buyer, must be paid and satisfied by Seller prior to or at Settlement such that cancellation may be promptly obtained following Closing. Seller shall remain obligated to obtain any such cancellations following Closing.

(g) **Good Title, Legal Access**: Seller shall execute and deliver a GENERAL WARRANTY DEED for the Property in recordable form no later than Settlement, which shall convey fee simple marketable and insurable title, without exception for mechanics' liens, and free of any other liens, encumbrances or defects, including those which would be revealed by a current and accurate survey of the Property, except: ad valorem taxes for the current year (prorated through the date of Settlement); utility easements and unviolated covenants, conditions or restrictions that do not materially affect the value of the Property; and such other liens, encumbrances or defects as may be assumed or specifically approved by Buyer in writing. The Property must have legal access to a public right of way.

> **NOTE:** Buyer's failure to conduct a survey or examine title of the Property, prior to the expiration of the Due Diligence Period does not relieve the Seller of their obligation to deliver good title under this paragraph.

> **NOTE:** If any sale of the Property may be a "short sale," consideration should be given to attaching a Short Sale Addendum (Standard Form 2A14-T) as an addendum to this Contract.

(h) **Deed, Taxes and Fees**: Seller shall pay for preparation of a deed and all other documents necessary to perform Seller's obligations under this Contract, and for state and county excise taxes, and any deferred, discounted or rollback taxes, and local conveyance fees required by law. The deed is to be made to: _____
_____.

(i) **Agreement to Pay Buyer Expenses**: Seller shall pay at Settlement $_____ toward any of Buyer's expenses associated with the purchase of the Property, at the discretion of Buyer and/or lender, if any, including any FHA/VA lender and inspection costs that Buyer is not permitted to pay.

> **NOTE:** Parties should review the FHA/VA Addendum prior to entering an amount in Paragraph 8(i). Certain FHA/VA lender and inspection costs CANNOT be paid by Buyer at Settlement and the amount of these should be included in the blank above.

(j) **Owners' Association Fees/Charges**: Seller shall pay: (i) any fees required for confirming Seller's account payment information on owners' association dues or assessments for payment or proration; (ii) any fees imposed by an owners' association and/or a management company as agent of the owners' association in connection with the transaction contemplated by this Contract other than those fees required to be paid by Buyer under paragraph 6(b) above; and (iii) fees incurred by Seller in completing the Residential Property and Owners' Association Disclosure Statement, and resale or other certificates related to a proposed sale of the Property.

Page 8 of 13

STANDARD FORM 2-T
Revised 7/2018
© 7/2018

Buyer's Initials _____ _____   Seller's Initials _____ _____

FIGURE 10.2 (*Continued*)

(k) **Payment of Confirmed Special Assessments**: Seller shall pay, in full at Settlement, all Confirmed Special Assessments, whether payable in a lump sum or future installments, provided that the amount thereof can be reasonably determined or estimated. The payment of such estimated amount shall be the final payment between the Parties.

(l) **Late Listing Penalties**: All property tax late listing penalties, if any, shall be paid by Seller.

(m) **Negotiated Repairs/Improvements**: Negotiated repairs/improvements shall be made in a good and workmanlike manner and Buyer shall have the right to verify same prior to Settlement.

(n) **Seller's Failure to Comply or Breach**: If Seller fails to materially comply with any of Seller's obligations under this Paragraph 8 or Seller materially breaches this Contract, and Buyer elects to terminate this Contract as a result of such failure or breach, then the Earnest Money Deposit and the Due Diligence Fee shall be refunded to Buyer and Seller shall reimburse to Buyer the reasonable costs actually incurred by Buyer in connection with Buyer's Due Diligence without affecting any other remedies. If legal proceedings are brought by Buyer against Seller to recover the Earnest Money Deposit, the Due Diligence Fee and/or the reasonable costs actually incurred by Buyer in connection with Buyer's Due Diligence, the prevailing party in the proceeding shall be entitled to recover from the non-prevailing party reasonable attorney fees and court costs incurred in connection with the proceeding.

9. **PRORATIONS AND ADJUSTMENTS**: Unless otherwise provided, the following items shall be prorated through the date of Settlement and either adjusted between the parties or paid at Settlement:

(a) **Taxes on Real Property:** Ad valorem taxes and recurring governmental service fees levied with such taxes on real property shall be prorated on a calendar year basis;

(b) **Taxes on Personal Property:** Ad valorem taxes on personal property for the entire year shall be paid by Seller unless the personal property is conveyed to Buyer, in which case, the personal property taxes shall be prorated on a calendar year basis;

(c) **Rents**: Rents, if any, for the Property;

(d) **Dues**: Owners' association regular assessments (dues) and other like charges.

10. **HOME WARRANTY**: Select one of the following:
❑ No home warranty is to be provided by Seller.
❑ Buyer may obtain a one-year home warranty at a cost not to exceed $_____ which includes sales tax and Seller agrees to pay for it at Settlement.
❑ Seller has obtained and will provide a one-year home warranty from _____
at a cost of $ _____ which includes sales tax and will pay for it at Settlement.

NOTE: Home warranties typically have limitations on and conditions to coverage. Refer specific questions to the home warranty company.

11. **CONDITION OF PROPERTY AT CLOSING**: Buyer's obligation to complete the transaction contemplated by this Contract shall be contingent upon the Property being in substantially the same or better condition at Closing as on the date of this offer, reasonable wear and tear excepted.

12. **RISK OF LOSS**: The risk of loss or damage by fire or other casualty prior to Closing shall be upon Seller. If the improvements on the Property are destroyed or materially damaged prior to Closing, Buyer may terminate this Contract by written notice delivered to Seller or Seller's agent and the Earnest Money Deposit and any Due Diligence Fee shall be refunded to Buyer. In the event Buyer does NOT elect to terminate this Contract, Buyer shall be entitled to receive, in addition to the Property, any of Seller's insurance proceeds payable on account of the damage or destruction applicable to the Property being purchased. Seller is advised not to cancel existing insurance on the Property until after confirming recordation of the deed.

13. **DELAY IN SETTLEMENT/CLOSING**: Absent agreement to the contrary in this Contract or any subsequent modification thereto, if a party is unable to complete Settlement by the Settlement Date but intends to complete the transaction and is acting in good faith with reasonable diligence to proceed to Settlement ("Delaying Party"), and if the other party is ready, willing and able to complete Settlement on the Settlement Date ("Non-Delaying Party") then the Delaying Party shall give as much notice as possible to the Non-Delaying Party and closing attorney and shall be entitled to a delay in Settlement. If the parties fail to complete Settlement and Closing within fourteen (14) days of the Settlement Date (including any amended Settlement Date agreed to in writing by the parties) or to otherwise extend the Settlement Date by written agreement, then the Delaying Party shall be in breach and the Non-Delaying Party may terminate this Contract and shall be entitled to enforce any remedies available to such party under this Contract for the breach.

Buyer's Initials _____ _____ Seller's Initials _____ _____

STANDARD FORM 2-T
Revised 7/2018
© 7/2018

FIGURE 10.2 (*Continued*)

14. **POSSESSION**: Possession, including all means of access to the Property (keys, codes including security codes, garage door openers, electronic devices, etc.), shall be delivered upon Closing as defined in Paragraph 1(m) unless otherwise provided below:
   - ❑ A Buyer Possession Before Closing Agreement is attached (Standard Form 2A7-T)
   - ❑ A Seller Possession After Closing Agreement is attached (Standard Form 2A8-T)
   - ❑ Possession is subject to rights of tenant(s)

   NOTE: Consider attaching Additional Provisions Addendum (Form 2A11-T) or Vacation Rental Addendum (Form 2A13-T)

15. **ADDENDA:** CHECK ALL STANDARD ADDENDA THAT MAY BE A PART OF THIS CONTRACT, IF ANY, AND ATTACH HERETO. ITEMIZE ALL OTHER ADDENDA TO THIS CONTRACT, IF ANY, AND ATTACH HERETO.

   - ❑ Additional Provisions Addendum (Form 2A11-T)
   - ❑ Additional Signatures Addendum (Form 3-T)
   - ❑ Back-Up Contract Addendum (Form 2A1-T)
   - ❑ Contingent Sale Addendum (Form 2A2-T)
   - ❑ FHA/VA Financing Addendum (Form 2A4-T)
   - ❑ Lead-Based Paint Or Lead-Based Paint Hazard Addendum (Form 2A9-T)
   - ❑ Loan Assumption Addendum (Form 2A6-T)
   - ❑ New Construction Addendum (Form 2A3-T)
   - ❑ Owners' Association Disclosure And Condominium Resale Statement Addendum (Form 2A12-T)
   - ❑ Seller Financing Addendum (Form 2A5-T)
   - ❑ Short Sale Addendum (Form 2A14-T)
   - ❑ Vacation Rental Addendum (Form 2A13-T)

   ❑ Identify other attorney or party drafted addenda: _____

   NOTE: UNDER NORTH CAROLINA LAW, REAL ESTATE BROKERS ARE NOT PERMITTED TO DRAFT ADDENDA TO THIS CONTRACT.

16. **ASSIGNMENTS**: This Contract may not be assigned without the written consent of all parties except in connection with a tax-deferred exchange, but if assigned by agreement, then this Contract shall be binding on the assignee and assignee's heirs and successors.

17. **TAX-DEFERRED EXCHANGE**: In the event Buyer or Seller desires to effect a tax-deferred exchange in connection with the conveyance of the Property, Buyer and Seller agree to cooperate in effecting such exchange; provided, however, that the exchanging party shall be responsible for all additional costs associated with such exchange, and provided further, that a non-exchanging party shall not assume any additional liability with respect to such tax-deferred exchange. Buyer and Seller shall execute such additional documents, including assignment of this Contract in connection therewith, at no cost to the non-exchanging party, as shall be required to give effect to this provision.

18. **PARTIES**: This Contract shall be binding upon and shall inure to the benefit of Buyer and Seller and their respective heirs, successors and assigns. As used herein, words in the singular include the plural and the masculine includes the feminine and neuter genders, as appropriate.

19. **SURVIVAL:** If any provision herein contained which by its nature and effect is required to be observed, kept or performed after the Closing, it shall survive the Closing and remain binding upon and for the benefit of the parties hereto until fully observed, kept or performed.

20. **ENTIRE AGREEMENT**: This Contract contains the entire agreement of the parties and there are no representations, inducements or other provisions other than those expressed herein. All changes, additions or deletions hereto must be in writing and signed by all parties. Nothing contained herein shall alter any agreement between a REALTOR® or broker and Seller or Buyer as contained in any listing agreement, buyer agency agreement, or any other agency agreement between them.

21. **CONDUCT OF TRANSACTION**: The parties agree that any action between them relating to the transaction contemplated by this Contract may be conducted by electronic means, including the signing of this Contract by one or more of them and any notice or communication given in connection with this Contract. Any written notice or communication may be transmitted to any mailing address, e-mail address or fax number set forth in the "Notice Information" section below. Any notice or communication to be given to a party herein, and any fee, deposit or other payment to be delivered to a party herein, may be given to the party or to such party's agent. Seller and Buyer agree that the "Notice Information" and "Acknowledgment of Receipt of Monies" sections below shall not constitute a material part of this Contract, and that the addition or modification of any information therein shall not constitute a rejection of an offer or the creation of a counteroffer.

22. **EXECUTION**: This Contract may be signed in multiple originals or counterparts, all of which together constitute one and the same instrument.

FIGURE 10.2 (Continued)

23. COMPUTATION OF DAYS/TIME OF DAY: Unless otherwise provided, for purposes of this Contract, the term "days" shall mean consecutive calendar days, including Saturdays, Sundays, and holidays, whether federal, state, local or religious. For the purposes of calculating days, the count of "days" shall begin on the day following the day upon which any act or notice as provided in this Contract was required to be performed or made. Any reference to a date or time of day shall refer to the date and/or time of day in the State of North Carolina.

THE NORTH CAROLINA ASSOCIATION OF REALTORS®, INC. AND THE NORTH CAROLINA BAR ASSOCIATION MAKE NO REPRESENTATION AS TO THE LEGAL VALIDITY OR ADEQUACY OF ANY PROVISION OF THIS FORM IN ANY SPECIFIC TRANSACTION. IF YOU DO NOT UNDERSTAND THIS FORM OR FEEL THAT IT DOES NOT PROVIDE FOR YOUR LEGAL NEEDS, YOU SHOULD CONSULT A NORTH CAROLINA REAL ESTATE ATTORNEY BEFORE YOU SIGN IT.

This offer shall become a binding contract on the Effective Date. Unless specifically provided otherwise, Buyer's failure to timely deliver any fee, deposit or other payment provided for herein shall not prevent this offer from becoming a binding contract, provided that any such failure shall give Seller certain rights to terminate the contract as described herein or as otherwise permitted by law.

Date: _____ Date: _____

Buyer: _____ Seller: _____

Date: _____ Date: _____

Buyer: _____ Seller: _____

Entity Buyer: _____ Entity Seller: _____
(Name of LLC/Corporation/Partnership/Trust/etc.) (Name of LLC/Corporation/Partnership/Trust/etc.)

By: _____ By: _____

Name: _____ Name: _____

Title: _____ Title: _____

Date: _____ Date: _____

WIRE FRAUD WARNING

> TO BUYERS: BEFORE SENDING ANY WIRE, YOU SHOULD CALL THE CLOSING ATTORNEY'S OFFICE TO VERIFY THE INSTRUCTIONS. IF YOU RECEIVE WIRING INSTRUCTIONS FOR A DIFFERENT BANK, BRANCH LOCATION, ACCOUNT NAME OR ACCOUNT NUMBER, THEY SHOULD BE PRESUMED FRAUDULENT. DO NOT SEND ANY FUNDS AND CONTACT THE CLOSING ATTORNEY'S OFFICE IMMEDIATELY.
>
> TO SELLERS: IF YOUR PROCEEDS WILL BE WIRED, IT IS RECOMMENDED THAT YOU PROVIDE WIRING INSTRUCTIONS AT CLOSING IN WRITING IN THE PRESENCE OF THE ATTORNEY. IF YOU ARE UNABLE TO ATTEND CLOSING, YOU MAY BE REQUIRED TO SEND AN ORIGINAL NOTARIZED DIRECTIVE TO THE CLOSING ATTORNEY'S OFFICE CONTAINING THE WIRING INSTRUCTIONS. THIS MAY BE SENT WITH THE DEED, LIEN WAIVER AND TAX FORMS IF THOSE DOCUMENTS ARE BEING PREPARED FOR YOU BY THE CLOSING ATTORNEY. AT A MINIMUM, YOU SHOULD CALL THE CLOSING ATTORNEY'S OFFICE TO PROVIDE THE WIRE INSTRUCTIONS. THE WIRE INSTRUCTIONS SHOULD BE VERIFIED OVER THE TELEPHONE VIA A CALL TO YOU INITIATED BY THE CLOSING ATTORNEY'S OFFICE TO ENSURE THAT THEY ARE NOT FROM A FRAUDULENT SOURCE.
>
> WHETHER YOU ARE A BUYER OR A SELLER, YOU SHOULD CALL THE CLOSING ATTORNEY'S OFFICE AT A NUMBER THAT IS INDEPENDENTLY OBTAINED. TO ENSURE THAT YOUR CONTACT IS LEGITIMATE, YOU SHOULD NOT RELY ON A PHONE NUMBER IN AN EMAIL FROM THE CLOSING ATTORNEY'S OFFICE, YOUR REAL ESTATE AGENT OR ANYONE ELSE.

STANDARD FORM 2-T
Revised 7/2018
© 7/2018

FIGURE 10.2 (*Continued*)

The Offer to Purchase and Contract

NOTICE INFORMATION

NOTE: INSERT AT LEAST ONE ADDRESS AND/OR ELECTRONIC DELIVERY ADDRESS EACH PARTY AND AGENT APPROVES FOR THE RECEIPT OF ANY NOTICE CONTEMPLATED BY THIS CONTRACT. INSERT "N/A" FOR ANY WHICH ARE NOT APPROVED.

BUYER NOTICE ADDRESS:

Mailing Address: _____
_____

Buyer Fax#: _____

Buyer E-mail: _____

SELLER NOTICE ADDRESS:

Mailing Address: _____
_____

Seller Fax#: _____

Seller E-mail: _____

CONFIRMATION OF AGENCY/NOTICE ADDRESSES

Selling Firm Name: _____
Acting as ❑ Buyer's Agent ❑ Seller's (sub)Agent ❑ Dual Agent

Firm License #: _____

Mailing Address: _____
_____

Individual Selling Agent: _____
❑ Acting as a Designated Dual Agent (check only if applicable)

Selling Agent License #: _____

Selling Agent Phone #: _____

Selling Agent Fax # : _____

Selling Agent E-mail: _____

Listing Firm Name: _____
Acting as ❑ Seller's Agent ❑ Dual Agent

Firm License #: _____

Mailing Address: _____
_____

Individual Listing Agent: _____
❑ Acting as a Designated Dual Agent (check only if applicable)

Listing Agent License #: _____

Listing Agent Phone #: _____

Listing Agent Fax #: _____

Listing Agent E-mail: _____

[THIS SPACE INTENTIONALLY LEFT BLANK]

Page 12 of 13

STANDARD FORM 2-T
Revised 7/2018
© 7/2018

Buyer's Initials _____ _____   Seller's Initials _____ _____

FIGURE 10.2 (*Continued*)

ACKNOWLEDGMENT OF RECEIPT OF MONIES

Seller: _____ ("Seller")

Buyer: _____ ("Buyer")

Property Address: _____ ("Property")

- -

❑ **LISTING AGENT ACKNOWLEDGMENT OF RECEIPT OF DUE DILIGENCE FEE**
Paragraph 1(d) of the Offer to Purchase and Contract between Buyer and Seller for the sale of the Property provides for the payment to Seller of a Due Diligence Fee in the amount of $_____, receipt of which Listing Agent hereby acknowledges.

Date_____   Firm:_____

By:_____
(Signature)

_____
(Print name)

- -

❑ **SELLER ACKNOWLEDGMENT OF RECEIPT OF DUE DILIGENCE FEE**
Paragraph 1(d) of the Offer to Purchase and Contract between Buyer and Seller for the sale of the Property provides for the payment to Seller of a Due Diligence Fee in the amount of $_____, receipt of which Seller hereby acknowledges.

Date_____   Seller:_____
(Signature)

Date_____   Seller:_____
(Signature)

- -

❑ **ESCROW AGENT ACKNOWLEDGMENT OF RECEIPT OF INITIAL EARNEST MONEY DEPOSIT**
Paragraph 1(d) of the Offer to Purchase and Contract between Buyer and Seller for the sale of the Property provides for the payment to Escrow Agent of an Initial Earnest Money Deposit in the amount of $_____. Escrow Agent as identified in Paragraph 1(f) of the Offer to Purchase and Contract hereby acknowledges receipt of the Initial Earnest Money Deposit and agrees to hold and disburse the same in accordance with the terms of the Offer to Purchase and Contract.

Date_____   Firm:_____

By:_____
(Signature)

_____
(Print name)

- -

❑ **ESCROW AGENT ACKNOWLEDGMENT OF RECEIPT OF (ADDITIONAL) EARNEST MONEY DEPOSIT**
Paragraph 1(d) of the Offer to Purchase and Contract between Buyer and Seller for the sale of the Property provides for the payment to Escrow Agent of an (Additional) Earnest Money Deposit in the amount of $_____. Escrow Agent as identified in Paragraph 1(f) of the Offer to Purchase and Contract hereby acknowledges receipt of the (Additional) Earnest Money Deposit and agrees to hold and disburse the same in accordance with the terms of the Offer to Purchase and Contract.

Date: _____   Firm:_____

Time: _____ ❑ AM ❑ PM   By:_____
(Signature)

_____
(Print name)

Page 13 of 13

STANDARD FORM 2-T
Revised 7/2018
© 7/2018

FIGURE 10.2

The Offer to Purchase and Contract Standard Form 2-T

The Offer to Purchase and Contract Standard Form 2-T (OTPC) is a widely used industry standard form that is designed to be used for the sale of residential properties (see Figure 10.2). It is not an appropriate form for the sale of vacant lots/land, commercial properties, options, or installment sales contracts (contracts for deed) or for more complex transactions involving the sale of residential property. It is, however, an excellent form to use in the sale of most residential properties a broker will likely encounter. Brokers need to acquire a good working knowledge of the various terms and conditions used in the form as well as a good grasp of its layout.

The major sections, referred to as paragraphs, address the following (see Figure 10.3):

(a) A broker acting as an agent in a real estate transaction shall not use a pre-printed offer or sales contract form unless the form describes or expressly requires the entry of the following information:

(1) the names of the buyer and seller;
(2) a legal description of the real property sufficient to identify and distinguish it from all other property;
(3) an itemization of any personal property to be included in the transaction;
(4) the purchase price and manner of payment;
(5) any portion of the purchase price that is to be paid by a promissory note, including the amount, interest rate, payment terms, whether or not the note is to be secured, and other material terms;
(6) any portion of the purchase price that is to be paid by the assumption of an existing loan, including the amount of such loan, costs to be paid by the buyer or seller, the interest rate and number of discount points, and a condition that the buyer must be able to qualify for the assumption of the loan and must make every reasonable effort to qualify for the assumption of the loan;
(7) the amount of earnest money, if any, the method of payment, the name of the broker or firm that will serve as escrow agent, an acknowledgment of earnest money receipt by the escrow agent, and the criteria for determining disposition of the earnest money, including disputed earnest money, consistent with Rule 0.0107 of this Subchapter;
(8) any loan that must be obtained by the buyer as a condition of the contract, including the amount and type of loan, interest rate and number of discount points, loan term, and who shall pay loan closing costs, and a condition that the buyer shall make every reasonable effort to obtain the loan;
(9) a general statement of the buyer's intended use of the property and a condition that such use must not be prohibited by private restriction or governmental regulation;

(10) the amount and purpose of any special assessment to which the property is subject and the responsibility of the parties for any unpaid charges;

(11) the date for closing and transfer of possession;

(12) the signatures of the buyer and seller;

(13) the date of offer and acceptance;

(14) a provision that title to the property must be delivered at closing by general warranty deed and must be fee simple marketable title, free of all encumbrances except ad valorem taxes for the current year, utility easements, and any other encumbrances approved by the buyer or a provision otherwise describing the estate to be conveyed with encumbrances, and the form of conveyance;

(15) the items to be prorated or adjusted at closing;

(16) who shall pay closing expenses;

(17) the buyer's right to inspect the property prior to closing and who shall pay for repairs and improvements, if any;

(18) a provision that the property shall at closing be in substantially the same condition as on the date of the offer (reasonable wear and tear excepted), or a description of the required property condition at closing; and

(19) a provision setting forth the identity of each real estate agent and firm involved in the transaction and disclosing the party each agent and firm represents.

(b) A broker acting as an agent in a real estate transaction shall not use a preprinted offer or sales contract form containing:

(1) any provision concerning the payment of a commission or compensation, including the forfeiture of earnest money, to any broker or firm; or

(2) any provision that attempts to disclaim the liability of a broker for his representations in connection with the transaction.

A broker or anyone acting for or at the direction of the broker shall not insert or cause such provisions or terms to be inserted into any such preprinted form, even at the direction of the parties or their attorneys.

(c) The provisions of this rule shall apply only to preprinted offer and sales contract forms which a broker acting as an agent in a real estate transaction proposes for use by the buyer and seller. Nothing contained in this Rule shall be construed to prohibit the buyer and seller in a real estate transaction from altering, amending or deleting any provision in a form offer to purchase or contract nor shall this Rule be construed to limit the rights of the buyer and seller to draft their own offers or contracts or to have the same drafted by an attorney at law.

Source: With permission of North Carolina Association of REALTORS®

GUIDELINES FOR COMPLETING THE OFFER TO PURCHASE AND CONTRACT
(Form No. 2G)

INTRODUCTION: These guidelines are provided to assist Brokers and attorneys who are completing the Offer to Purchase and Contract form on behalf of Buyers and Sellers. The Offer to Purchase and Contract is the most important document in any real estate sale and it is imperative that it accurately reflects the entire agreement of Buyer and Seller. An improper contract may have substantial adverse effects on the rights and interests of the parties. These guidelines include general comments about contract completion as well as suggestions and explanations regarding selected contract provisions with which Brokers often have difficulty. However, situations will frequently arise that are not covered by these Guidelines. **All Paragraph numbers and Subparagraph numbers and letters used in these Guidelines correspond to the paragraph numbers and subparagraph numbers and letters used in the Offer to Purchase and Contract.** Brokers should always remember that a North Carolina real estate attorney should be consulted any time there is uncertainty regarding the proper completion of this important form.

USE OF FORM: The Offer to Purchase and Contract form is jointly approved by the NORTH CAROLINA ASSOCIATION OF REALTORS®, INC. and the NORTH CAROLINA BAR ASSOCIATION, as Form No. 2-T. The version of this form with the REALTOR® logo is produced by NCAR for use by its members, only as printed. The version of this form without the REALTOR® logo is produced for the NORTH CAROLINA BAR ASSOCIATION and may be used, only as printed, by attorneys and Brokers.

This form may be used in a variety of real estate sales transactions, but it was developed primarily for use in the sale of existing single-family residential properties. Do not use this form as a substitute for a lease-option agreement, lease-purchase agreement or installment land contract. Also, if the sale involves the construction (or completion of construction) of a new single-family dwelling, use the current standard New Construction Addendum (NCAR/NCBA Form 2A3-T) or consult a NC real estate attorney for an appropriate form.

GENERAL INSTRUCTIONS:
1. Type this form if possible; otherwise print or write legibly in ink.
2. Fill in all blank spaces. If any space is not used, enter "N/A" or "None" as appropriate.
3. Be precise. Avoid the use of abbreviations, acronyms, jargon, and other terminology that may not be clearly understood.
4. Every change, addition or deletion to an offer or contract must be initialed and should be dated by both Buyer and Seller.
5. If numerous changes are made or if the same item (such as the purchase price) is changed more than once, complete a new contract form to avoid possible confusion or disputes between the parties. If, *after the parties have entered into a valid contract*, you prepare a new form for the parties to sign because the existing contract contains so many changes that it is difficult to read, then do not discard the existing contract. Keep it with the new form.
6. Review with the parties all contract provisions. Advise the parties to consult their respective attorneys if they have any questions about the legal consequences of the contract or any particular provision.

---

1. **TERMS AND DEFINITIONS:**

    (a) **NAME(S) OF SELLER AND BUYER:** Fill in the complete name of each Seller. If husband and wife, show the names of both (John A. Doe and wife, Mary B. Doe). Do not use "Mr. and Mrs. John A. Doe," "Owner of Record," or last name only. In the majority of the situations, immediately upon death of the owner, the heirs or devisees under the will become the owner of the interest in the Property belonging to the deceased. All such heirs or devisees and their spouses should be named as Seller along with the executor or administrator (personal representative). BEFORE INSERTING THE SELLER'S NAME, YOU SHOULD OBTAIN COMPETENT LEGAL ADVICE FROM AN NC ATTORNEY.

    (b) **NAME(S) OF BUYER:** Fill in the complete name of each Buyer. Do not use "Mr. and Mrs. John A. Doe." If husband and wife, show the names of both (John A. Doe and wife, Mary B. Doe).

    (c) **PROPERTY/LEGAL DESCRIPTION:** Fill in street address of the Property if there is one (**NOT** the mailing address, which may be different from the street address). In addition to a street address, include a legal description sufficient to identify and distinguish the Property from all other property. Fill in all applicable blanks as completely as possible.

    (1) **Plat reference:** If the Property is a lot in a subdivision or a condominium unit, include the lot number or condominium unit number, the block or section number of the subdivision or condominium, the name of subdivision or condominium, and recording reference for the plat as recorded in the Register of Deeds office.

    (2) **PIN/PID or other identification number: CAUTION**: Although helpful, reference to a **PIN/PID** alone is generally not an adequate legal description.

This form jointly approved by:
North Carolina Bar Association
North Carolina Association of REALTORS®, Inc.

STANDARD FORM 2G
Revised 7/2017
© 7/2018

FIGURE 10.3 Guidelines for completing the Offer to Purchase and Contract Standard Form 2G. (*Continued*)
Source: Used with permission of North Carolina Association of REALTORS®

(3) **Other description:** A survey attached as an Exhibit or an abbreviated description such as 10+/- acres at the northeasterly quadrant of the intersection of Route 41 and Jackson Boulevard may be helpful. A copy of Seller's deed may be attached as an Exhibit. Do not attempt to complete a metes and bound description as an Exhibit. A North Carolina real estate attorney should be consulted if a metes and bounds description is necessary or if the information available is inadequate to clearly describe the Property.

(4) **Reference to a recorded deed:** If known, insert the book number and page number of Seller's deed as recorded in the office of the Register of Deeds office.

(d) **PURCHASE PRICE:**
 (1) **Purchase Price:** Insert the total amount of the purchase price in dollars on the first line.
 (2) **Due Diligence Fee:** If Buyer is paying Seller a Due Diligence fee, as defined in Paragraph 1(i), for the right to conduct Due Diligence during the Due Diligence Period as defined in Paragraph 1(j), insert the amount of the Due Diligence Fee on the second line.
 (3) **Initial Earnest Money Deposit:** Insert the amount of the Initial Earnest Money Deposit, if any, in dollars on the third line and check the appropriate box for method of payment. NOTE: Any Initial Earnest Money Deposit should be paid to the Escrow Agent designated in Paragraph 1(f) and delivered with the Contract.
 (4) **Additional Earnest Money Deposit:** If an Additional Earnest Money deposit is to be given at a later date, insert the amount of that deposit in dollars and the due date on the fourth line. Any Additional Earnest Money Deposit should be paid by one of the methods specified in paragraph 1(d) to the Escrow Agent designated in Paragraph 1(f) and delivered by the due date specified. **NOTE: A personal check is not** a specified method for payment of an Additional Earnest Money Deposit and may be rejected by the Seller. **NOTE: Time is "of the essence" with respect to the payment of any additional earnest money deposit**.
 (5) **Assumption of existing loan:** Insert the approximate principal amount of Seller's existing loan on the Property as of Settlement on the fifth line, and complete and attach the current standard Loan Assumption Addendum (NCBA/NCAR Form 2A6-T).
 (6) **Seller Financing:** Insert the dollar amount of the financing from Seller on the sixth line, and complete and attach the current standard Seller Financing Addendum (NCAR/NCBA Form 2A5-T).
 (7) **Building Deposit:** If Buyer is paying Seller a building deposit in connection with improvements to be constructed on the Property by Seller, insert the amount of the Building Deposit on the seventh line, and complete and attach the New Construction Addendum (Form 2A3-T).
 (8) **Balance of Purchase Price**: Insert the dollar amount of the balance due from Buyer on the eighth line. **NOTE: This amount should equal the purchase price minus any dollar amounts inserted in second through seventh lines. In the case of a counteroffer, which alters any figure in subparagraph (d), all altered figures must be initialed and should be dated by all parties. Care should be taken to be certain that the figures in the second through the eighth lines, when added, always equal the purchase price set forth in the first line.**

(f) **Escrow Agent:** Insert the name of the Escrow Agent designated to hold the Initial Earnest Money Deposit and/or the Additional Earnest Money Deposit, not the name of an individual Broker (unless it is to be held by a Broker who is a sole practitioner). Note that the name indicated here should also be indicated on the "Firm" line at the bottom of the form under the acknowledgment of receipt of the earnest money. **NOTE: Any earnest money check should be made payable to the designated Escrow Agent.**

(j) **Due Diligence Period:** Insert the date Buyer's rights to conduct Due Diligence, as defined in Paragraph 1(h), expires.

(k) **Settlement Date:** Insert the date upon which Settlement, as defined in Paragraph 1(k), is to occur. **NOTE: Closing, as defined in Paragraph 1(m), may or may not be completed on the same day Settlement occurs.**

(m) **Closing:** The residential real estate closing is a process typically including review and interpretation of the contract of sale, abstracting and certification of title and application for appropriate title insurance, preparation, review and interpretation of financial accountings and various legal documents, assuring compliance with mortgage lender loan instructions and recordation and cancellation of documents in accordance with law. According to the NC State Bar Rules of Professional Responsibility Authorized Practice Advisory Opinion (2002-1), a person who is not licensed to practice law in North Carolina and is not working under the direct supervision of an active member of the State Bar may not perform functions or services that constitute the practice of law. Under the express language of N.C. Gen. Stat. §§84-2.1 and 84-4, a non-lawyer who is not working under the direct supervision of an active member of the State Bar would be engaged in the unauthorized practice of law if he or she performs any of the following functions for one or more of the parties to a residential real estate transaction:

  (i) preparing or aiding in preparation of deeds, deeds of trust, lien waivers or affidavits, or other legal documents;
  (ii) abstracting or passing upon titles; or
  (iii) advising or giving an opinion upon the legal rights or obligations of any person, firm, or corporation.

Under the express language of N.C. Gen. Stat. § 84-4, it is unlawful for any person other than an active member of the State Bar to hold himself or herself out as competent or qualified to give legal advice or counsel or as furnishing any services that constitute the practice of law. Additionally, under N.C. Gen. Stat. § 84-5, a business entity, including a corporation or limited liability company,

FIGURE 10.3 (*Continued*)

may not provide or offer to provide legal services or the services of attorneys to its customers even if the services are performed by licensed attorneys employed by the entity.

Nonlawyers who undertake such responsibilities, and those who retain their services, should also be aware that (1) the North Carolina State Bar retains oversight authority concerning complaints about activities that constitute the unauthorized practice of law; (2) the North Carolina criminal justice system may prosecute instances of the unauthorized practice of law; and (3) that N.C. Gen. Stat. §84-10 provides a private cause of action to recover damages and attorneys' fees to any person who is damaged by the unauthorized practice of law against both the person who engages in unauthorized practice and anyone who knowingly aids and abets such person.

So long as a nonlawyer does not engage in any of the activities referenced above, or in other activities that likewise constitute the practice of law, a nonlawyer may:
(1) present and identify the documents necessary to complete a North Carolina residential real estate closing, direct the parties where to sign the documents, and ensure that the parties have properly executed the documents; or
(2) receive and disburse the closing funds.
Although these limited duties may be performed by nonlawyers, this does not mean that the nonlawyer is handling the closing. Additionally, nonlawyers may not advertise or represent to lenders, buyers/borrowers, or others in any manner that suggests that the nonlawyer will:
   (i) handle the "closing;"
   (ii) provide the legal services associated with a closing, such as providing title searches, title opinions, document preparation, or the services of a lawyer for the closing; or
   (iii) "represent" any party to the closing. The lawyer must be selected by the party for whom the legal services will be provided.
   (n) Special Assessments: Paragraph 1(n) excludes from the definition of "Special Assessments" ad valorem taxes on real property and recurring governmental service fees (such as annual solid waste, storm water management and similar fees) levied in connection with ad valorem taxes on real property.

2. **FIXTURES:**
   (a) Specified Items: Any item on the list in subparagraph (b) that is presently on the Property—including any related equipment and remote control devices—is considered a fixture and will be included in the sale unless the item is identified in subparagraphs (a) and/or (d). It is not necessary to cross out items that are listed in subparagraph (b) but are not on the Property.
   (b) Items Leased or Not Owned: Insert in the blank space in subparagraph (a) any item presently on the Property which may be considered a fixture but which is leased or not owned by Seller.
   (d) Insert in the blank space in subparagraph (d) any item on the Property which may be considered a fixture but which will not be included in the sale. If in doubt as to whether an item that the parties agree will be excluded from the sale is or is not a fixture, it is advisable to list the item to avoid a later dispute.

3. **PERSONAL PROPERTY:** List all items of personal property that are to be included in the sale. (EXAMPLES: Curtains, draperies, etc.; free standing appliances such as a refrigerator or a microwave oven; fireplace tools; window air conditioner; etc.) It is advisable to list any item included in the sale about which some dispute may arise. **NOTE: Care should be taken to ascertain that any personal property included in the sale is owned by Seller and is not merely rented or leased.**

4. **BUYER'S DUE DILIGENCE PROCESS:** The right of Buyer to conduct Due Diligence (defined in Paragraph 1(h)) is one of the most important elements of the Contract. Buyer is given the opportunity to investigate and examine all aspects of the Property and the transaction in order to decide whether to proceed with or terminate the transaction. If Buyer terminates the Contract prior to the expiration of the Due Diligence Period (defined in Paragraph 1(j)), Buyer may obtain a refund of the Earnest Money Deposit and any Additional Earnest Money Deposit paid prior to the expiration of the Due Diligence Period, but not any Due Diligence Fee. Buyer and Buyer's Broker should give careful consideration as to what types of Due Diligence should be performed during the Due Diligence Period and should heed the WARNING at the beginning of paragraph 4.

   (a) **Loan**: Buyer's Due Diligence should include investigating the availability of any desired or required financing. Buyer should understand that depending on the length of time Buyer and Seller agree that the Due Diligence Period will last, it is possible or even likely Buyer will not know with certainty that the loan will be approved prior to the end of the Due Diligence Period. In such case, Buyer should make a decision based on the information Buyer has from Buyer's lender at that time whether to terminate or proceed with the transaction. If Buyer terminates the contract, Buyer receives the Earnest Money Deposit back. If Buyer proceeds with the transaction and the lender does not ultimately approve the loan, Buyer would lose the Earnest Money Deposit if Buyer were unable to close without the loan. By making the loan qualification process a part of Buyer's Due Diligence, Buyer and Seller have the ability to fairly balance the risk that the Contract may not close due to Buyer's loan not

FIGURE 10.3 (*Continued*)

being approved by shifting that risk to Buyer at a mutually agreeable date. The date that the risk shifts to Buyer is the date that the Due Diligence Period expires.

(b) Property Investigation:
(ii) Review of Documents: Purchasers take title to property subject to the restrictive covenants and are bound to follow them, even if they did not actually know the property was subject to restrictive covenants. Once restrictions are properly imposed upon a property, they "run with the land" and are binding on the owner and all subsequent purchasers. No owner or purchaser can use the property for any purpose that violates the restrictions. During the Due Diligence Period, Buyer should review any document that may limit the use of the Property or govern the Property owner or obligate the Property owner to a financial payment other than the purchase price, taxes, and governmental assessments. If such documents are not available from either the listing Broker or Seller, then an attorney should be consulted by Buyer during the Due Diligence Period.

(iv) Appraisals: The Property being appraised at or equal to the Purchase Price is not a condition to Buyer's performance under the Contract except in transactions involving FHA/VA financing. If the appraised value of the Property is an important factor in determining whether a Buyer wishes to proceed with the purchase or whether necessary or desired financing is obtainable, Buyer should obtain and review an appraisal of the Property prior to the expiration of the Due Diligence Period.

(v) Survey: A survey of the Property can reveal important information about the Property, including setback lines and possible violations thereof, encroachments on to the Property or from the Property onto adjacent property, boundaries, the existence of utility, storm drainage and other easements which may prohibit construction of improvements within their areas, and many other important details about the physical nature of the Property. Lenders often tell buyers that they do not need a survey in order to close. That is because lenders are able to obtain title insurance coverage on their lenders' policies insuring against title defects which would be revealed by a survey. No such coverage is available to a buyer or borrower under an owners' policy of title insurance. In order to obtain title insurance coverage against defects which would be revealed by a current survey of the Property, Buyer should be encouraged to go to the expense of obtaining a new survey. Brokers should encourage a recalcitrant Buyer to consult with a North Carolina real estate attorney to understand the advantages of obtaining a new survey.

(vii) Flood Hazard: Buyer should determine whether the Property and/or any permanent improvements on the Property are wholly or partially located in a Special Flood Hazard Area and whether it is advisable for Buyer, or whether Buyer's lender may require Buyer, to obtain flood hazard insurance. A definition of the term "Special Flood Hazard Area" can be obtained from the website of the Federal Emergency Management Agency at www.fema.gov. Information about the state of North Carolina's Floodplain Mapping Program is available online at http://www.ncfloodmaps.com.

(e) Buyer's Obligation to Repair Damage: Buyer's obligation to repair damage under this Paragraph is not necessarily limited to circumstances where the damage is caused by the negligent or willful acts or omissions of Buyer or Buyer's agents and contractors. For example, assume that during an inspection of the exterior siding of a house located on the Property, Buyer's home inspector falls from his ladder, resulting in gouge marks in the siding. Assume further that the fall was caused by an unforeseen failure in the ladder rather than the inspector's negligence. Buyer should still be obligated to repair the damaged siding. On the other hand, Buyer should not be responsible for repairing pre-existing damage discovered during the inspection/investigation of the Property by Buyer and Buyer's agents and contractors. Using the example set forth above, if during his inspection, the inspector probes the siding with a screwdriver and discovers underlying wood rot on a portion of the siding, Buyer should not be obligated to repair the affected siding.

5. BUYER REPRESENTATIONS: Buyer Representations are statements of current facts that Seller may reasonably rely upon in deciding whether to enter into the Contract. Representations made "to the best of Buyer's knowledge" include only facts known to Buyer at the time the representation is made.
(a) Loan: Check the applicable box disclosing whether Buyer intends to obtain a loan in order to purchase the Property. If a Broker working with Buyer knows or reasonably should know under the circumstances that Buyer must obtain a loan in order to purchase the Property, it is a material fact under the real estate licensing law that must be disclosed by the Broker because it is a fact relating directly to the ability of Buyer to complete the transaction with Seller. If Buyer does in fact need a loan, check the boxes that best describe the type of loan; insert the desired or required interest rate, the principal amount of the loan, the term of the loan and the maximum interest rate acceptable to Buyer. **(NOTE: Buyer's obligations under the Contract are not conditioned upon Buyer being able to obtain the desired financing. Buyer should determine whether acceptable or necessary financing is available to Buyer prior to expiration of the Due Diligence Period. See Paragraph 4 above.)**

FIGURE 10.3 (*Continued*)

(b) **Other Property:** Check the box indicating whether Buyer does or does not have to sell or lease other real property in order to qualify for a new loan or to complete the purchase. If a Broker working with Buyer knows or reasonably should know under the circumstances that Buyer must sell other property in order to purchase the Property, it is a material fact under the real estate licensing law that must be disclosed by the Broker because it is a fact relating directly to the ability of Buyer to complete the transaction with Seller. If Buyer does need to sell in order to qualify for a new loan or to complete the purchase, consideration should be given to including and making a part of the Contract Contingent Sale Addendum (Form 2A2-T).

(d) **Property Disclosure:** Indicate the status of Buyer's receipt of the required N.C. Residential Property Disclosure Statement by checking the appropriate box. If the transaction is exempt from the N. C. Residential Property Disclosure Act, then enter one of the following: (1) Court Ordered Transfer; (2) Borrower to Lender Transfer; (3) Fiduciary Transfer; (4) Co-owner to Co-owner Transfer; (5) Within Family Transfer; (6) Spouse to Spouse Divorce Decree Transfer; (7) Tax Sale; (8) Governmental Transfer; (9) First Sale of Dwelling Never Inhabited; (10) Lease with Option to Purchase (where lessee occupies or intends to occupy the dwelling) **(Caution: See warning under "Use of Form")**; (11) Buyer and Seller Agreement; or (12) Property to be transferred consists of less than 1 or more than 4 residential units. ***See North Carolina General Statutes Section 47E-2 for a complete description of exemptions.***

(e) **Mineral and Oil and Gas Rights Mandatory Disclosure**: Indicate the status of Buyer's receipt of the required N.C. Mineral and Oil and Gas Rights Mandatory Disclosure Statement by checking the appropriate box. If the transaction is exempt from the N. C. Residential Property Disclosure Act, then enter one of the following: (1) Court Ordered Transfer; (2) Borrower to Lender Transfer; (3) Fiduciary Transfer; (4) Co-owner to Co-owner Transfer; (5) Within Family Transfer; (6) Spouse to Spouse Divorce Decree Transfer; (7) Tax Sale; (8) Governmental Transfer; or (9) Property to be transferred consists of less than 1 or more than 4 residential units. *See North Carolina General Statutes Section 47E-2 for a complete description of exemptions.*

7. **SELLER REPRESENTATIONS: Seller Representations are statements of current facts that Buyer may reasonably rely upon in deciding whether to enter into the Contract. Representations made "to the best of Seller's knowledge" include only facts known to Seller at the time the representation is made.**

   (a) **Ownership:** Check the applicable box disclosing how long Seller has owned the Property or whether Seller owns the Property at the time Seller executes the Contract. Seller's term of ownership may affect Buyer's ability to obtain mortgage financing. Some mortgage lenders require proof that the property is not being *flipped* from one purchaser at a lower price to another purchaser at a higher price within a short period of time. Any lender issues concerning Seller's term of ownership should be resolved during the Due Diligence Period.

   (b) **Lead-Based Paint**: If the Property is residential property built prior to 1978, the current standard Lead-Based Paint or Lead-Based Paint Hazard Addendum (NCAR/NCBA Form 2A9-T) must be attached

   (c) **Assessments:** Prior to accepting the Contract or making a counteroffer to Buyer, Seller should disclose any Proposed Special Assessments under consideration for the Property by any owners' association or municipal authority with the power to levy assessments, if any, of which Seller is aware. If Seller is unaware of any Proposed Special Assessments which are under such consideration and which may affect the Property, or if Seller is unable to obtain any information regarding same from any owners' association (or its managing agent) or municipal authority with the power to levy assessments, insert none. Pursuant to Paragraph 6(a) of the Contract, Buyer shall take title to the Property subject to any Proposed Special Assessments disclosed by Seller. Seller's representations in Paragraph 7(c) about *Confirmed Special Assessments* contain a warranty that the facts represented are accurate and may be relied on as such. A warranty may give rise to a claim by Buyer against Seller for breach of warranty in the event the facts warranted turn out to be untrue at the time they were made. Therefore, prior to accepting the Contract or making a counteroffer to Buyer, Seller should determine if there are any Confirmed Special Assessments, and to enter the amount of such Confirmed Special Assessment(s) If there are no Confirmed Special Assessments affecting the Property, enter "None". **(NOTE: Buyer should determine whether there are any Proposed or Confirmed Special Assessments prior to the expiration of the Due Diligence Period.)**

   (d) **Owners' Association(s) and Dues**: If the Property is subject to regulation by one or more owners' associations, the name, address and telephone number of the president of the association or the association manager and the association's web site address should be inserted in the blank spaces provided. The amount of the association's regular assessments (dues) should also be inserted in the blank space provided.

8. **SELLER OBLIGATIONS:** The Contract imposes numerous obligations upon Seller with respect to the transaction. If Seller fails to materially comply with such obligations or materially breaches the Contract, Buyer may terminate the Contract and receive a refund of any Earnest Money Deposit and Due Diligence Fee paid, obtain reimbursement from Seller for its reasonable costs incurred in conducting Due Diligence without affecting any other remedies available to Buyer.

   (e) **Affidavit and Indemnification Agreements (against Mechanics Liens)**: For Property for which a building or other permit has been issued on or after April 1, 2013, the Seller is required to have appointed a Lien Agent subject to the following two (2) exceptions: No lien Agent need be appointed when (1) the anticipated cost of the project permitted is expected to be under $30,000.00; or (2) if the improvements were made to a single family residence which is occupied by the Seller. The Designation of Lien Agent is made on the website LiensNC.com, where potential lien claimants may file a Notice to Lien Agent that they

STANDARD FORM 2G
Revised 7/2017
© 7/2018

FIGURE 10.3 (*Continued*)

are providing labor, services, material or rental equipment to the Property for which a lien may be claimed if they are not paid. A Closing Attorney will search the website for notices and will require lien waivers from each potential lien claimant who has filed such a Notice. Therefore to prevent delays in Closing, a Seller and Seller's Agent should promptly furnish to Buyer, the Buyer's Agent and the Buyer's Closing Attorney a copy of any Appointment of Lien Agent made by or on behalf of Seller (which may be printed off the LiensNC.com website). If a Seller fails to comply with the statutory requirement to designate a Lien Agent, it may not be possible to obtain title insurance on the Property and complete Closing in accordance with the Contract.

(h) **Deed, Taxes** and Fees: Insert the exact, legal name(s) of Buyer(s) as will appear in the deed. Buyer and Seller should note that using phrases such as "*as directed by Buyer*" or "*Buyer(s), or assigns*" may conflict with the restrictions on assignment of the Contract set forth in Paragraph 16. If the parties wish to permit assignment of the Contract, consultation with a North Carolina real estate attorney is recommended.

(i) **Agreement to Pay Buyer Expenses:** Insert the **fixed** dollar amount Seller will pay. This amount may also be expressed as a percentage of the purchase price. **Include in this amount any FHA/VA lender and inspection costs (seller mandated fees) that cannot be paid by Buyer.** Examples of Buyer's expenses associated with the purchase of the property may include, but are not limited to, discount points, loan origination fees, appraisal fees, attorney's fees, inspection fees and loan "pre-paids" (taxes, insurance, etc.). If Seller will not pay any such expenses, insert "0" in the blank. Note that Seller's payment of any such amount is subject to approval by Buyer's lender.

9. **TAXES ON REAL PROPERTY**: Paragraph 9(a) provides that ad valorem taxes on real property together with recurring governmental service fees levied with such taxes (such as annual solid waste, storm water management and similar fees) shall be prorated as of the date of Settlement on a calendar year basis.

10. **HOME WARRANTY**: If a home warranty is to be paid for by Seller, check one of the two boxes, insert maximum cost to be paid and identify warranty company if applicable. Note that the amount inserted includes the amount of any sales tax.

12. **RISK OF LOSS:** Since the risk of loss does not pass to Buyer until Closing occurs, Seller should consult with an attorney and Seller's insurance carrier before agreeing to allow Buyer to take possession at Settlement or any other time prior to the recordation of the deed. In the event of a casualty loss prior to the time the deed is recorded, the Buyer may be able to terminate the contract and obtain a refund of the Earnest Money Deposit and any Due Diligence Fee. Therefore Seller should be careful not to cancel Seller's existing hazard insurance policy until such time as the deed has been recorded and the net closing proceeds are available to Seller. A Buyer allowing Seller to remain in possession after Closing should also consult with Buyer's attorney and insurance carrier to determine that Buyer has adequate coverage in the event of a loss during the period of Seller's possession after Closing. Buyer should obtain hazard insurance coverage for the Property effective 12:01a.m. as of the date of Settlement.

13. **DELAY IN SETTLEMENT/CLOSING:** If either party anticipates a delay in Settlement and Closing, that party should try to negotiate a written extension from the other party prior to the expiration of the Due Diligence Period.

14. **POSSESSION:** The contract assumes possession will be delivered at Closing. "Closing" is defined in Paragraph 1(m) and requires that Settlement and all steps included in the process of Closing, including recording of the deed, be completed. Closing will not occur at the same time, and may not even occur on the same date as Settlement. In selecting the place and time of Settlement, Buyer should consider that completion of Closing, including recording, is necessary before possession may be delivered unless the parties otherwise agree. If possession by a certain date is critical, Settlement should be scheduled on a date and at a time that will allow sufficient time for Closing to be completed on or before that date. If the parties agree to transfer possession to Buyer prior to recording of the deed, then check the applicable box and attach a Buyer Possession Before Closing Agreement (NCAR/NCBA Form 2A7-T) or consult a NC real estate attorney for an appropriate agreement. If the parties agree to permit Seller to remain in possession after recording of the deed, then check the applicable box and attach a Seller Possession After Closing Agreement (NCAR/NBCA Form 2A8-T) or consult a NC real estate attorney for an appropriate agreement. Also consider Paragraph 12 of these guidelines, entitled "Risk of Loss." If the Property is being sold subject to an existing lease, check the applicable box and consider adding the Rental/Income/Investment Property provision in the Additional Provisions Addendum (form 2A11-T) or the Vacation Rental Addendum (form 2A13-T) to the Contract, as the case may be.

15. **OTHER PROVISIONS AND CONDITIONS:** Check any standard addenda that may be attached to the contract, and indicate by name any attorney or party drafted addenda to be attached. Any addenda referred to here should be properly identified, signed by the parties, and attached to each original of the contract. Any copy of the contract must always have all addenda attached. ***CAUTION:*** **UNDER NORTH CAROLINA LAW, REAL ESTATE BROKERS ARE NOT PERMITTED TO DRAFT ADDENDA TO THIS CONTRACT.**

FIGURE 10.3 (*Continued*)

17. TAX DEFERRED EXCHANGE: If either or both of the parties may be considering entering into a tax free exchange of like kind property in connection with the transaction, consultation with qualified attorneys or tax advisors is recommended.

20. ENTIRE AGREEMENT: The parties should make sure that all essential elements of the contemplated Contract are embodied in the Contract and all addenda attached thereto and made a part thereof.

22. EXECUTION: It is recommended that multiple originals or counterparts be executed and that each party receive an original or counterpart with original signatures. A fully executed copy of the complete contract and all addenda should be delivered to Buyer's prospective lender(s).

SIGNATURES AND DATES: All parties with an ownership interest (see Paragraph 1(a) where owner is deceased) must sign as Seller and all parties named as Buyer must sign as Buyer. *If Seller(s) is married, both the husband and wife always must sign the contract*. This is true even if the Property is owned by only one spouse. The non-owner spouse holds a potential "marital life estate" and a "right to dissent from the will" under North Carolina law and must sign the deed in order for the other spouse to convey clear title. The signature of the non-owner spouse on the contract will obligate that spouse to join in signing the deed. If the married Sellers have executed and recorded a pre-nuptial agreement, post-nuptial agreement, or a free trader agreement consult a North Carolina real estate attorney to determine who must sign. If a party (Buyer or Seller) is a corporation, limited liability company, partnership, limited partnership or other legal entity, a duly authorized officer, manager, general partner or other legal representative of such entity should sign on behalf of such party. If a party is a trust, the duly authorized trustee(s) of such trust should sign on behalf of such trust.

Indicate the dates that the parties actually sign the Offer to Purchase and Contract.

NOTICE INFORMATION: Insert the notice addresses for Buyer and Seller, including current mailing and e-mail addresses and fax numbers. Note that in accordance with Paragraph 21, the parties agree that any written notice or communication may be transmitted to any mailing address, e-mail address or fax number set forth in the contract which they select. Thus, it is very important that correct contact information be inserted. *At least one notice address for each party or their agent must be inserted.* If a party does not have an e-mail address or fax machine, or if a party does not desire written notice or communication to be transmitted to the party's e-mail address and/or fax machine, insert "N/A" or "None" in the relevant blank. REALTORS® representing a party to a transaction are reminded that if the other party to the transaction is exclusively represented, REALTORS® generally must conduct all dealings concerning the transaction with the other party's Broker and not the other party (see Standard of Practice 16-13 of the REALTOR® Code of Ethics).

Enter the names of the individual selling and listing Brokers, their respective individual license numbers and firm names and firm license numbers, and check the appropriate agency representation box for each. Note that this procedure is *confirmation* of a prior disclosure of the agency relationship and in no way should be considered as an initial disclosure of agency relationship. Signatures are not necessary. Also enter the notice addresses for the selling and listing Brokers, including current mailing and e-mail addresses and fax numbers.

ACKNOWLEDGMENT OF RECEIPT OF MONIES
LISTING AGENT ACKNOWLEDGMENT OF RECEIPT OF DUE DILIGENCE FEE: This section should be completed if the Offer to Purchase and Contract provides for payment of an Due Diligence Fee. If any Due Diligence Fee is delivered to the listing agent by whatever means, this section should be completed and signed by the individual listing agent or by some other authorized representative of the listing agent's Firm. If the Due Diligence Fee is delivered directly to the Seller rather than the listing agent, this section should not be completed.
SELLER ACKNOWLEDGMENT OF RECEIPT OF DUE DILIGENCE FEE: This section should be completed if the Offer to Purchase and Contract provides for payment of a Due Diligence Fee even if the listing agent has already acknowledged receipt of the Due Diligence Fee. When any Due Diligence Fee is delivered by whatever means to Seller, whether by the listing agent, selling agent, buyer or otherwise, this section should be completed and signed by Seller if possible.
ESCROW ACKNOWLEDGMENT OF INITIAL EARNEST MONEY DEPOSIT: This section should be completed if the Offer to Purchase and Contract provides for payment of an Initial Earnest Money Deposit. The "Firm" should be the same as the firm indicated as Escrow Agent in Paragraph 1(f). The individual signing for the firm serving as Escrow Agent on the "By:" line must be associated with that firm. The "Firm" may be a real estate brokerage firm, a law firm, or another entity. If the listing agent's firm will hold the Earnest Money Deposit, this usually will be the individual listing Broker. Although the contract states that the Earnest Money Acknowledgment section is not a material part of the Offer to Purchase and Contract, if the Escrow Agent named in Paragraph 1(f) of the contract is unable or unwilling to serve in such capacity, the Escrow Agent's name should be replaced with the name of a substitute Escrow Agent agreeable to Buyer and Seller, and the change initialed and dated by both parties.
ESCROW ACKNOWLEDGMENT OF (ADDITIONAL) EARNEST MONEY DEPOSIT: This section should be completed if the Offer to Purchase and Contract provides for payment of an Additional Earnest Money Deposit. The "Firm" should be the same as the firm indicated as Escrow Agent in Paragraph 1(f). The individual signing for the firm serving as Escrow Agent on the "By:" line must

FIGURE 10.3 (*Continued*)

be associated with that firm. The "Firm" may be a real estate brokerage firm, a law firm, or another entity. If the listing agent's firm will hold the Earnest Money Deposit, ~~Usually,~~ this usually will be the individual listing Broker. Although the contract states that the Earnest Money Acknowledgment section is not a material part of the Offer to Purchase and Contract, if the Escrow Agent named in Paragraph 1(f) of the contract is unable or unwilling to serve in such capacity, the Escrow Agent's name should be replaced with the name of a substitute Escrow Agent agreeable to Buyer and Seller, and the change initialed and dated by both parties.

STANDARD FORM 2G
Revised 7/2017
© 7/2018

FIGURE 10.3

1. **Terms and Definitions**: This section seeks to address, up front, the various important terms that will appear throughout the contract. Terms that use a capital letter as the first letter in the word indicate that the word is a proper noun or a defined term and should be used in the exact fashion as it is defined. The following are the primary terms and definitions that are addressed in this section:

    - **Seller:** The seller's full legal name should be inserted. Do not use nicknames. All persons possessing either an ownership or marital interest in the property being sold are to be included and will also need to sign as sellers at the end of the contract form.

    - **Buyer:** The buyer's full legal name should be inserted. Do not use nicknames. All buyers should be included in this space. Failure to include all buyers could result in the inability to require parties to sign documents later in the transaction. For example, the husband signs as the buyer but does not include the wife's name. The wife does not sign the contract as the buyer at the end of the contract as well. It is possible for the wife to refuse to sign necessary loan closing documents conveying marital rights, which could result in the property not being able to close.

    - **Property:** The legal description for the property is to be inserted in this section. The contract form provides for several different descriptions including address, plat book and page, Property Identification Number (PIN), and any other type of description that may be added.

    - **Purchase Price:** The purchase price is inserted along with a breakdown of the various components that will make up the purchase price, including the due diligence fee, earnest money deposit, the amount of any loan being assumed, seller financing, building deposit, and the balance that is to be paid in cash at the closing. The total of all of these blanks must equal the amount of the purchase price in the first blank in this section.

    - **Earnest Money Deposit:** The earnest money deposit is presented as either the "initial" earnest money deposit or as the "(ADDITIONAL)" earnest money deposit. Earnest money is desirable for the buyer to indicate *good faith* as a buyer but is not required to evidence consideration.

    - Initial earnest money is to be provided in one of two ways with the method indicated by checking the appropriate box. It can either be included at the time of the offer being presented to the seller or it can be delivered within five days of the effective date. The initial earnest money deposit can be paid by a personal check or some means of *immediately available funds* such as cash, official bank check, or wire transfer.

- There will be transactions where there is (ADDITIONAL) earnest money to be paid. Unlike the initial earnest money indicated above, these funds may ONLY be paid in *cash or immediately available funds*, making payment by personal check unacceptable. These funds may not truly be "additional" in the sense of adding to any amount in the "initial" earnest money section, but rather could simply indicate earnest money funds that will be paid at a later date (i.e., the contract shows $0). Initial earnest money deposit with this offer indicates there is to be $2,000 (ADDITIONAL) earnest money deposit to be paid by a certain date. Additional earnest money deposits are to be paid by the date indicated with "*time being of the essence.*"

- Regardless of the earnest money being "initial" or "additional," the contract indicates the earnest money shall be held in the escrow account of the party named in the blank in paragraph 1(a). The earnest money is held by the escrow agent until closing or termination of the contract. It will be applied to the purchase price at the closing. The buyer has the right to retain this earnest money should he terminate the contract agreement before the due diligence date. In the event of breach by the buyer, the earnest money shall serve as **liquidated damages** and will be the sole exclusive remedy for seller without limiting the seller's rights under paragraph 4(d) and 4(e). The earnest money shall serve as compensation for the seller's anticipated losses in the event of breach by the buyer given the difficulty in determining the extent of the seller's actual damages in such breach.

- **Escrow Agent:** The name of the escrow agent is inserted in the blank in 1(f). Traditionally, this is the listing firm, but it can be the buyer agency firm, the attorney, or any other party to whom the buyer and seller agree. The policy of how to handle the earnest money in the event of a dispute is also addressed. In the event of a dispute between the seller and buyer over the disposition of the funds held in escrow, the disputed funds are required to be held in the escrow account until such time as the escrow agent obtains a written release from the buyer and seller consenting to its disposition or until disbursement is ordered by a court of competent jurisdiction. North Carolina law (G.S. 93A-12) allows a licensed broker or attorney to deposit the disputed monies with the clerk of court in the county where the property is located after providing the buyer and seller with a minimum of 90 days' notice. After the money is delivered to the clerk of court under this law, the parties will have to handle any resolution through the court.

- The escrow agent is also given permission to place the earnest money in an interest-bearing account with the interest earned to be disbursed

- **Effective Date:** The effective date is the date of BOTH obtaining written acceptance and properly communicating the written acceptance to the offeror.

- **Due Diligence:** Due diligence is the ability of the buyer to inspect and investigate the entire property as well as to determine any other information he or she may determine is important.

- **Due Diligence Fee:** The due diligence fee serves as compensation to the seller for the buyer's right to conduct due diligence during the due diligence period. It is generally considered a *nonrefundable* deposit and shall be applied to the purchase price at closing. The buyer will not be entitled to a refund of the due diligence fee except in the event of seller breach, such as the inability to convey marketable title.

- **Due Diligence Period:** The period in which the buyer is provided with the opportunity to undertake due diligence with the right to terminate and receive a refund of her earnest money deposit. This period begins at the effective date and goes until 5 p.m., *time being of the essence*, of the date indicated in the blank.

- **Settlement:** Settlement is considered to be the process of both providing the necessary documentation to the closing attorney and executing all documents required to complete the transaction.

- **Settlement Date:** The settlement date is the date indicated for the settlement meeting to finalize the transaction. It will be at a place of the buyer's choosing unless otherwise stipulated.

- **Closing:** The date of recordation of the deed. In order to record the deed, the settlement, along with title update, has occurred as well as the necessary authorization to disburse funds. Typically, prorations and possession of the property will be as of the date of closing. The final disbursement of funds cannot be completed until closing has been achieved.

- **Special Assessments:** The proportionate share of the cost of some improvement typically by a municipality or owners association. These can be "proposed" or "confirmed."

- **Pending Special Assessment:** Any special assessment that is being considered but has not yet been confirmed.

- **Confirmed Special Assessment:** Any special assessment that has been approved, or adopted, prior to settlement. It is not relevant whether the assessment is payable or the work has commenced prior to the closing.

2. **Fixtures:** A fixture is defined as an item that was once personal property that has become real property by virtue of its attachment to the land or to an improvement such as a house. If an item is identified as a fixture, it is considered real property and conveys as part of the real property description. The primary test to determine whether an item is a fixture is the intent of the parties. By naming the items in this section, it establishes the party's intent for the items to be treated as a fixture unless specifically excepted. If a seller wants an item that is a fixture NOT to convey, that item must be written in on the blank line provided for that purpose.

   Agents do need to confirm that the fixture items are actually owned by the seller and are not leased or owned by another party.

3. **Personal Property:** The broker should list any items of personal property that are to be conveyed. Unlike the fixture section above where the items remain unless excepted, personal property will not be included unless named specifically in the contract.

4. **Buyer's Due Diligence Process:** The buyer is to undertake "due diligence" to obtain any needed loan; ascertain the condition of the property through inspections; review documents related to ownership and permitted uses of the property; investigate availability of insurance; obtain an appraisal; obtain a survey; and check into zoning and other governmental matters, potential flood hazards, and any other items that the buyer wishes to research. The buyer has the ability to research anything relevant to the property and negotiate any concerns he may have before the due diligence date (end of the due diligence period). It is very important to remember *the buyer may continue to undertake due diligence and attempt to negotiate all the way up to the closing.* He will be liable for the loss of his earnest money deposit (in addition to the due diligence fee) if he fails to perform anytime after the due diligence date unless the seller is in breach of contract. For this reason, most buyers will attempt to complete all items of due diligence before the due diligence date to retain their earnest money deposit. Buyers will have the right to terminate the agreement, for any reason or for no reason at all, anytime prior to 5:00 p.m. on the due diligence date. Closing shall constitute acceptance of the property in its then-existing condition unless otherwise agreed to by the parties in writing.

5. **Buyer Representations:** The buyer is asked to make a number of representations as to whether she will have to obtain financing to purchase the house, whether she has to sell or lease other property to purchase, and whether there is any reason or circumstances that will keep her from obtaining any necessary financing, as well as to disclose whether she has received a copy of the North Carolina Residential Property and Owners' Association Disclosure Statement prior to signing the offer.

6. **Buyer Obligations:** This section addresses the various expenses the buyer shall be responsible for paying, including owners association fees related to the transfer of ownership, proposed special assessments to be levied in the future, and certain closing-related costs, including the following:

    (a) **Owners Association Fees/Charges:** The buyer is to pay any fees charged to confirm his owners association account, including the normal association fees or assessments, and any transfer fee imposed by the association in conjunction with the buyer conveying the property to the seller.

    (b) **Responsibility for Proposed Special Assessments:** The buyer shall be responsible for all proposed special assessments that may be confirmed after the closing.

    (c) **Responsibility for Certain Costs:** This section indicates which costs the buyer shall be responsible for, including any costs incurred in order for the buyer to obtain a loan, appraisal, title search, title insurance, recordation of the deed, and loan-related documents.

7. **Seller Representations:** The seller makes a variety of representations to the buyer. They are as follows:

    (a) **Ownership:** The seller makes representations to whether he has owned the property for at least one year or less than one year or does not yet own the property. The length of time the seller has owned the property is relative to whether the buyer will be able to participate in some mortgage loan programs. These mortgage loan programs are discouraging the financing of properties that are being "flipped" and often require the seller to own the property for at least six months. The one-year term stipulated in this contract is more than most loan programs require and pads what most time concerns will be. The seller also is asked to indicate if they do not yet own the property. Sellers will sometimes attempt to sell properties they do not yet own, such as in the case of an option to purchase. If the seller can find a suitable buyer, he will then exercise his option to purchase and immediately re-sell to the buyer.

    (b) **Primary Residence:** The seller is asked to indicate if the property currently serves as her residence.

    (c) **Lead-Based Paint:** The seller is asked if the residential property was constructed before 1978 and, if so, will be required to attach a copy of the Lead-Based Paint or Lead-Based Paint Hazards Disclosure Addendum (NCAR 2A9-T).

    (d) **Assessments:** The seller represents "to the best of his knowledge" there are no proposed special assessments except as indicated. This does not mean there are no proposed special assessments currently being discussed, but rather the seller is stating he, "to the best of his knowledge," does not know of any.

(d) The Seller *warrants* there are no confirmed special assessments except as indicated in the blank. Note the seller is not merely stating there are no confirmed special assessments but is actually "warranting" there are none except as noted.

(e) **Owners Association(s) and Dues:** The seller authorizes the association, management company of the owners association, insurance company, and any attorney to release to the buyer accurate copies of information related to the master insurance policy, including the deductible, restrictive (protective) covenants, rules and regulations, bylaws, and articles of incorporation of the association, current financial statements and budget of the association, parking information, and architectural guidelines. The seller also is asked to provide the contact information for the president of the owners association and the website address for the association.

(f) **Oil and Gas Rights Disclosure:** This section includes a paragraph of text that is required to be reprinted verbatim along with three questions regarding the severing of oil and gas rights. The seller is asked to indicate if the oil and gas rights were severed from the property by a previous owner, although he can indicate *No Representation* as the answer. The seller is required to answer questions regarding if he has severed the oil and gas rights from the property or if he intends to sever the oil and gas rights prior to the closing. Unlike the first question about whether the previous owner has severed the rights, the seller is not allowed to answer *No Representation* to the last two questions. The parties are advised to consult with a North Carolina attorney prior to signing the agreement if the oil and gas rights have been severed or the seller intends to sever them prior to the closing.

8. **Seller Obligations:** This section lists a variety of items the seller will be contractually obligated to honor:

    (a) **Evidence of Title:** Seller promises to cooperate in providing copies of all title-related information that is available to him. This also includes the name of the title insurer, and the seller authorizes the release of her files.

    (b) **Access to Property/Walk-Through Inspection:** Seller agrees to provide reasonable access to the property prior to closing, or possession by the buyer. This agreement extends to the seller agreeing to provide working utilities so that the buyer may conduct desired inspections. The buyer is also allowed to conduct a final walk-through of the property prior to the closing.

    (c) **Removal of Seller's Property:** Seller is to remove all possessions, garbage, and debris prior to the buyer's possession.

(d) **Affidavit and Indemnification Agreement:** The seller is obligated to provide an affidavit and indemnification agreement executed by the seller and any person or entity who has provided labor or materials to the property within the prior 120 days. Note the 120 days is the period of time that is relevant to the ability of that person or entity to file a mechanics' lien against the property.

(e) **Designation of Lien Agent, Payment, and Satisfaction of Liens:** If the cost of the improvement is in excess of $30,000, the seller must designate a lien agent for the filing of potential mechanics' liens. Additionally, all liens such as property taxes, mortgages, and any other liens not assumed by the buyer shall be canceled as of closing.

(f) **Good Title, Legal Access:** Seller is obligated to deliver a General Warranty Deed that is capable of being recorded no later than settlement. The seller also stipulates the property has legal access to a public right of way. If the sale of this property constitutes a "short sale," the parties are urged to utilize a short sale addendum (NCAR form 2A14-T).

(g) **Deed, Excise Taxes:** The seller is obligated to pay for the deed preparation and any other documents as needed in order for the seller to perform her obligations. Revenue stamps are also paid for by the seller. The buyer is asked to indicate the name(s) in which the deed is to be made.

(h) **Agreement to Pay Buyer Expenses:** The seller indicates the amount, if any, he agrees to pay toward the buyer's closing-related expenses.

(i) **Payment of Confirmed Special Assessments:** The seller is obligated to pay all confirmed special assessments, if any.

(j) **Late Listing Penalties:** Any late listing penalties for property taxes are the responsibility of the seller.

(k) **Negotiated Repairs/Improvements:** The seller is obligated to complete all negotiated repairs in a good and workmanlike manner with the buyer retaining the right to verify the repairs prior to settlement.

(l) **Seller's Failure to Comply or Breach:** In the event of breach of contract by the seller, the buyer will be refunded the earnest money deposit in addition to any due diligence fees paid. The seller is also obligated to reimburse the buyer for any reasonable out-of-pocket expenses incurred by the buyer in connection with any due diligence. In the event the buyer initiates any legal proceedings against the seller for such breach, the prevailing party shall be entitled to recover reasonable attorney and court fees from the nonprevailing party.

9. **Prorations and Adjustments**: This section addresses the primary items that will likely be prorated in a residential transaction. These items are traditionally prorated through the date of the closing. The prorations items are as follows:

- Taxes on Real Property: Property taxes are prorated on a calendar year basis.

- Taxes on Personal Property: Personal property taxes are not prorated unless the property is conveyed to the buyer, in which case it will be prorated on a calendar year basis. If the personal property is not conveyed to the buyer, the bill will be paid totally by the seller.

- Rents: If the property is being rented, the rental income will be prorated.

- Dues: Typically owners association fees but could be any type of dues.

For more coverage on this topic, refer to Chapter 12, "Closing a Sales Transaction."

10. **Home Warranty**: The parties are asked to indicate if a home warranty is to be provided, and if so, who will obtain it and pay for it at settlement.

11. **Condition of Property at Closing**: Because there will be some period of time between the making of an offer and the actual closing, the contract stipulates the property is to be in substantially the same or better condition at the closing as it was on the date the offer was made.

12. **Risk of Loss**: The contract stipulates the seller will have the risk of loss prior to the closing even if the buyer acquires possession prior to the settlement. It also addresses the buyer's rights to terminate or to go forward with the settlement and lay claim to any relevant insurance proceeds from the seller.

13. **Delay in Settlement/Closing**: The contract allows a period of 14 days from the scheduled closing for the "delaying party" to be able to close without being considered in breach of contract. In the event the "delaying party" cannot close within 14 days, he will be considered in breach of contract unless the "non-delaying party" grants an extension. In the event of breach, the "non-delaying party" is allowed to enforce remedies available to him under this contract. If the buyer is in breach, the seller is entitled only to the earnest money deposit as liquidated damages and is not entitled to receive other relief. If the seller is the party in breach, the buyer is entitled to a refund of his due diligence fee and earnest money deposit and a reimbursement of his reasonable out-of-pocket expenses incurred in connection with his due diligence efforts in addition to attorney fees and court costs as applicable.

14. **Possession**: Possession shall be delivered at the closing unless otherwise agreed in writing, preferably using the Buyer, or Seller, Possession Before/After Closing addenda forms.

15. **Other Provisions and Conditions**: In this section of the contract, the parties are to indicate which of the listed preprinted standard addenda forms are being used as a part of this contract.

16. **Assignments**: In North Carolina, contracts are generally assignable unless expressly prohibited. This clause expressly prohibits such assignment of this contract unless the parties agree specifically in writing.

17. **Tax-Deferred Exchange**: This clause calls for the buyer and seller to generally cooperate with each other in the event this transaction is the subject of a tax-deferred exchange. The exchanging party is to be responsible for all additional costs of the exchange, and the nonexchanging party is not to incur any additional liability.

18. **Parties**: This contains fairly standard verbiage about the contract being binding upon the buyer and seller, heirs, successors, and assigns. It also addresses the usage of the terms in the masculine sense.

19. **Survival**: This does not refer to the concept of survivorship first mentioned in Chapter 2. This simply means that if any element of this contract cannot be completed by the closing, it shall survive the closing and still be enforceable as an element of this contract. For example, suppose a contract stipulates the seller is to retain possession for 30 days after the closing. This condition, by its very nature, cannot be completed by the settlement. This part of the agreement shall remain binding as an element of the contract upon both parties until its completion.

20. **Entire Agreement**: This contract represents all of whatever has been agreed to by the parties, and there are no "hidden" items that are not apparent in this form.

21. **Notice**: Any notice to either the buyer or the seller can also be given to their respective agents, and it shall be considered the same as communication given directly to that party. It also states that communication can be delivered to any mailing address, email, and fax number that is set forth in the "Notice Information" section later in this contract. For this reason, it is very important for agents to make certain the parties have provided ample information in this section as anything left blank, such as an email or fax number, is not considered an appropriate method of communication in this agreement.

22. **Execution**: Multiple copies containing original signatures or copies containing an original signature are permitted. Although multiple copies are allowed, please note that a contract exists if there is only one original to the agreement that has been fully completed and executed.

23. **Computation of Days**: This contains the recipe for how days are to be calculated. Unless otherwise stipulated, such as is the case with "banking days" contained earlier in this contract, days shall be considered calendar days without regard for weekends or holidays whether they shall be local, state, federal, or religious. The counting of days shall begin on the day after the named action.

24. **Signatures of the Parties**: Each party that is to perform must sign the offer to purchase and contract form. A married buyer can contract to purchase the property by himself, but it is advisable to have each of the married parties sign to avoid later issues such as the nonsigning party's refusal to sign a deed or deed of trust. All sellers who are shown as owners on the deed must sign, as well as any sellers who have marital rights in the property. It is always good for the agents to know the marital status of the parties to determine if additional signatures will be needed.

25. **Notice Information**: Information is requested that relates to the notice in paragraph 21. The parties will be wise to make certain that each has provided information that relates to all of the different means of communication as any means that are not indicated will not serve as an applicable method in which to communicate with the other party. This section also contains information regarding agency status as well as information about each agent, including her North Carolina real estate license number.

26. **Escrow Acknowledgment of Initial Earnest Money Deposit**: The escrow agent, typically the listing firm, will need to sign acknowledging receipt of the earnest money from the selling agent. Note that the escrow agent is a representative of the firm as opposed to only being considered the listing agent in the transaction. This does not have to be acknowledged by a licensee with the firm and can be signed by an office administrator who does not possess a license.

Commonly Used Standard Addenda Forms

The NCAR/NCBA Joint Forms Committee has adopted numerous addenda forms that will complement the Offer to Purchase and Contract form. These forms were designed with the idea of eliminating the need for agents to be tempted to write language that attempted to address many topics that the contract form did not address. Figure 10.4 shows a list of the nine most common addenda forms, and the text provides a brief explanation of the application of each. Sample copies of some of these forms can be found in Appendix F.

Back-Up Contract Addendum (2A1-T). The Back-Up Addendum is used when the property is already under contract and the new buyer wishes to solidify his

Commonly used standard addenda forms:

(1) Back-Up Contract Addendum (2A1-T)

(2) Contingent Sale Addendum (2A2-T)

(3) Federal Housing Administration/Department of Veterans Affairs Financing Addendum (2A4-T) Back-Up Contract Addendum (2A1-T)

(4) Buyer Possession before Closing Agreement (2A7-T)

(5) Seller Possession after Closing Agreement (2A8-T)

(6) Lead-Based Paint or Lead-Based Paint Hazards Addendum (2A9-T)

(7) Additional Provisions Addendum (2A11-T)

(8) Vacation Rental Addendum (2A13-T)

(9) Short Sale Addendum (2A14-T)

FIGURE 10.4 List of commonly used standard addenda forms.
Source: © 2019 OnCourse Learning

position if the primary contract should fall through. The back-up buyer has a binding contract to purchase the property only if the existing primary contract is terminated for any reason. The terms of this addendum call for it to terminate upon the closing of the primary contract or upon the passage of a stated date. The back-up buyer has the right to terminate this agreement at any time before being notified by the seller of the primary contract falling through and the back-up agreement being elevated to primary status. If the back-up buyer terminates his contract, he will be entitled to a refund of his earnest money deposit.

Contingent Sale Addendum (2A2-T). Buyers will often find a property they wish to purchase but will have to sell an existing property before they can close on it. In this case, the buyer will likely execute a Contingent Sale Addendum. As the name implies, the purchase will be contingent upon the sale of an existing property. This accommodates a buyer who has not yet entered into a contract of sale for her existing property as well as one whose house is currently under contract. In section 1. (a) the buyer is required to provide to the seller a copy of the contract for the buyer's property. The buyer is allowed to mark out confidential information such as the purchase price and her purchaser's name. If the buyer fails to provide the seller with a copy of a contract for the buyer's property by the expiration of the due diligence date, the contract agreement shall be null and void and the earnest money deposit shall be returned to the buyer.

In section 1. (b) the issue of the buyer's property currently being under contract is addressed. If there is a current contract for the buyer's house the closing of that property is to occur by the settlement date of the buyer's agreement with his seller. If the settlement does not occur by that date, the buyer is granted the right to terminate this contract within three days following the settlement date, *time being of the essence,* and the earnest money is to be returned to the buyer.

Federal Housing Administration/Department of Veterans Affairs (FHA/VA) Financing Addendum (2A4-T). An addendum that is required when a buyer is seeking to obtain FHA/VA financing, this form stipulates that a buyer can terminate the contract if the property does not appraise for the contract purchase price and the buyer is entitled to a refund of his earnest money. This is true even if the due diligence date has passed.

Buyer Possession before Closing Agreement Addendum (2A7-T). This addendum is to be used in those transactions in which the buyer is to take possession before the actual closing. It addresses issues of responsibilities for the buyer and seller, including utilities, insurance, pets, maintenance, and association fees. The Buyer Possession form is not to be used as a replacement for a lease agreement and is not to be used in situations involving possession for more than 14 days. This agreement will not prohibit a buyer from being able to terminate the contract by the due diligence date even if possession is granted before that time.

This form is also to be used in situations in which the deed will not be recorded until after the buyer wishes to take possession before closing, such as often occurs when the closing meeting is at the end of the day or week. Example: A closing meeting takes place late on a Friday, and the recordation cannot take place before Monday. The buyer wishes to go ahead and take possession for the weekend. This form should be executed by the parties before any possession by the buyer takes place.

Seller Possession after Closing Agreement Addendum (2A8-T). This addendum serves the same purpose as the Buyer Possession before Closing Agreement Addendum listed above with few differences. Because the seller would be addressing a period of time after closing, the concerns about the due diligence date are moot.

Lead-Based Paint or Lead-Based Paint Hazard Addendum (2A9-T). This is North Carolina's version of the federal lead-based paint and hazard addendum that must be given to the buyer before the first offer in the sale of houses built before 1978. It addresses whether the seller has knowledge of the existence of any lead-based paint or records pertaining to lead-based paint. It also gives the buyer a 10-day period in which to conduct an assessment to determine the existence of lead-based paint, although this right can be waived. Last, it also calls for the agent to acknowledge that she has informed the seller of her responsibilities under the law. This addendum, along with the Environmental Protection Agency pamphlet regarding lead-based paint hazards, will constitute notification to the buyer as required by law.

Additional Provisions Addendum (2A11-T). This addendum addresses four important aspects of the contract, including expiration of the offer by a certain date and time, modifications including the necessity of obtaining an Improvement Permit for a septic system from the local health department, rental and investment property details, and any agreed-upon repairs or improvements to be completed before the closing.

Vacation Rental Addendum (2A13-T). The Vacation Rental Addendum is to be used for any vacation rental property subject to the North Carolina Vacation Rental Act.

Short Sale Addendum (2A14-T). The Short Sale Addendum form is used in cases in which the sale does not produce enough money to pay off the existing mortgage and the seller's closing expenses and the seller is unable or unwilling to pay the difference. One of the most important aspects of this addendum is that it makes the contract contingent upon short sale approval even if it is after what has been stipulated as the due diligence date. If the short sale approval is not granted by the lender, the buyer would still be able to recoup his earnest money deposit. It also points out that any additional offers that appear must be presented to the lienholder by North Carolina law.

Form for Sale/Purchase of Vacant Lot/Land (2A12-T)

The NCAR/NCBA has also adopted a form similar to the Offer to Purchase and Contract form (Standard Form 2-T) called the Offer to Purchase and Contract–Vacant Lot/Land. As the name implies, it is designed for use in the sale of vacant lots and parcels of land where there is no relevant structure on the property. It is designed just like the standard offer to purchase but does not include fixtures, personal property, and any other items that would be addressed if there were a physical structure on the property. It does address the ability of the buyer to exercise due diligence in the same manner and with the same rights as in the offer to purchase and contract traditionally used for the purchase of a home as discussed previously in this chapter. In a variation from the standard offer to purchase agreement, the buyer is encouraged to investigate soil, utilities, and environmental matters to determine the suitability for the buyer's intended use as well as septic/sewage and water availability.

SALES CONTRACT PROCEDURES

Offer and Acceptance

To create a binding contract, there must be both offer and acceptance. Although this topic was covered in Chapter 9, "Basic Contract Law," it will be reviewed briefly here for convenience sake.

The Offer To Purchase

An offer is the price, terms, and conditions prepared by an offeror to an offeree. The party making the offer is the **offeror**, and the party receiving the offer is the **offeree**. Because the contract for the sale of real estate is required to be in writing according to the Statute of Frauds, the offer must be in writing as well. The only way to obtain a written contract is to couple a written offer with a written acceptance. A verbal offer cannot be combined with a written acceptance to achieve a written contract, nor can a written offer be combined with an oral acceptance to become a written contract. It is essential that both the offer and acceptance be in writing to create an enforceable agreement.

> **Test Tip!**
>
> The buyer and seller can each be considered the offeror or the offeree in a given transaction. In the event of a counteroffer, the roles of the offeror and the offeree will switch.

> "When an agent is acting as a dual agent in an offer and acceptance scenario, there is no need to communicate the acceptance back to the buyer. The contract becomes valid when the acceptance of the offer is signed, initialed, and communicated to the buyer and or their agent. Here the communication to the agent is immediate."
> —Steve Robinson

As mentioned previously, there is no such thing as a binding offer. The only way to make an offer binding is to accept it, at which point it becomes a contract. As a result, offers can be withdrawn, or revoked, at any time before acceptance. The offer is not considered to be revoked until such time as proper notice has been delivered to either the offeree or her agent. Even though the offeree may have already signed her acceptance to the document, the offeror can still revoke his offer before receiving actual communication of the offeree's written acceptance.

Example: Larry makes an offer to purchase Jean's house on October 1. Jean reviews the offer and signs her acceptance of the offer. She intends to mail the written acceptance of the offer to Larry the following day. Before she places it in the mail, she receives a call from Larry telling her that he has changed his mind and is withdrawing his offer. Jean protests that it is too late as she has already signed the offer and that it is ready to be mailed back and is therefore a binding contract. Jean is incorrect. Larry can revoke his offer as proper communication of the written acceptance has not yet occurred.

Acceptance of the Offer

> 🔑 To create a binding contract, it is essential that the offer must be properly accepted as noted earlier. This acceptance must be in writing to ensure compliance with the Statute of Frauds.

Oral acceptance will not result in a binding contract.

To constitute an acceptance, the following rules must be met:

- Acceptance must be identical with the terms of the offer.
- Offers must be accepted in writing by all parties to the contract. Until every signature is obtained and acceptance is communicated to the offeror, there is no acceptance even if there is an oral statement of intent to sign.
- Acceptance must comply with any reasonable requirement or restriction mandated by the offeror.

Example: An offer stated that it may be accepted only in writing and by being personally delivered to the offeror's place of business. Failure to comply with the reasonable restriction of delivery to the offeror's place of business will not constitute a valid acceptance.

A written acceptance that alters any of the terms of the offer will not constitute an acceptance and will be considered a counteroffer. Remember, a counteroffer is considered a rejection of the original offer coupled with a new offer. Once counteroffered, the original offer is terminated and cannot be revived without creation of a new offer.

Communication of Acceptance.

 Proper communication of the written acceptance is critical to create a contract.

An offer that has been accepted in writing but not communicated to the offeror is not considered an acceptance. A few rules of proper communication of acceptance are as follows:

- Communication of written acceptance can be delivered to the offeror or his agent if he has one.
- Communication of written acceptance to the offeree's agent will not constitute proper communication to the offeror unless the agent is a dual agent.
- Communication should be promptly delivered as the offeror retains the right of revocation prior to receiving proper notice of acceptance.
- Whereas the acceptance must be in writing, the communication of the written acceptance is not required to be in written form. Communication of written acceptance can be oral, visual, mailed, electronic, or even second-hand information. See the following examples:

Oral Communication. Example: Amy is a buyer who submits an offer through her agent, Allison, to Juan, who is the seller's listing agent. Upon presentation of the offer, the seller signs his acceptance to all of the terms of Amy's offer. Juan now calls Allison to inform her of the seller's written acceptance. Once the communication of written acceptance was communicated to Amy's agent, Allison, a contract was formed. Any future attempts by Amy to revoke her offer will be in vain as a valid contract has now been formed.

Visual Communication. Example: Bob, the selling agent, is in a dual agency capacity along with Roberta, the listing agent who works with him at his firm. Bob delivers a buyer's client offer to Roberta, who personally presents it to their seller client. The seller signs his acceptance to the offer in Roberta's presence. As soon as Roberta observes the seller sign, accepting the offer, a contract is formed. Although there was no oral statement or written communication directly to the buyer, once one of the dual agents visually observed the written acceptance, it constituted a valid communication to each of their respective parties and a contract was formed. Had there not been a dual agency situation in this case, there would not have been a contract until the acceptance had been communicated to Bob or his buyer client.

Mailbox Rule. The "mailbox rule" is interpreted as *effective when mailed*. Once a seller signs his written acceptance of an offer and places it in the mail to the offeror or the offeror's agent, communication of written acceptance has been achieved. This method creates challenges for the parties, as it is possible to have a binding contract, because of the legal communication of the written acceptance without the offeror or his agent having actual knowledge of the fact. It is extremely important to remember the mailbox rule does not apply to all aspects of offers and acceptance. The mailbox rule does apply to delivery of written acceptance, and communication will be considered effective when mailed. Revocation of an offer is not controlled by the mailbox rule and is not effective until actually received by the offeree.

Example: Bob Buyer mails a written offer to Susan Seller on Monday. Susan receives the offer on Tuesday and signs it but does not mail it back to Bob until Wednesday. Shortly after Bob mails his offer, he changes his mind about the purchase, and on Tuesday morning, Bob mails notice to Susan of his intent to revoke his offer. Susan does not receive the revocation letter from Bob until Thursday. In this case, we have a valid contract. Susan communicated her acceptance via the mailbox rule to Bob on Wednesday. Bob's revocation did not take effect until it was actually received by Susan on Thursday. Even though Bob had mailed his revocation the day before Susan mailed her acceptance, it did not take effect until it was actually received. Contract status was achieved on Wednesday as the communication was effective when mailed and not when received. If Bob had wanted to revoke his offer on Tuesday, he should have utilized a speedier means of communication, such as phone, email, or fax.

Electronic Communication. Acceptance can be achieved electronically by either fax or email. The original copy of the signed acceptance is faxed back to the offeror and is considered delivered at the time it is received by the receiving device. It is a valid contract at this point even though there is no form that contains both original signatures of the offeror and the offeree. Separate but related documents exist even though in two separate locations. Agents should endeavor to assemble both original documents in one location to solidify proof of contract.

An email may contain either an original signature or an electronic signature and be valid. Similar to the rule regarding faxes, the notice of acceptance is valid once received by the receiving recipient's server.

The advantage of electronic delivery of written acceptance is that notification is virtually instantaneous and leaves very little time for revocation by the offeror.

Submitting Offers to Sellers

> Every broker is legally and duty-bound to submit any and all offers to the seller for his consideration.

License law 93A-6 (13) stipulates the broker is to present all offers immediately, and Commission Rule A.0106 further refines that law to state that delivery should be accomplished immediately but in no case later than three days of the broker's receipt of an executed offer. Another way to better understand the presentation requirement is to realize that offers are considered material facts. Agents must disclose to transaction parties any and all material facts they know or reasonably should know. This would definitely include any offers in hand as well as other information, such as the likelihood of another offer in addition to both positive and negative information regarding an offer. For example, an offer might be presented along with information that the offeror may be willing to raise his initial offering price or that the offeror will have difficulty in obtaining a mortgage. Both scenarios involve information that is a material fact that must be disclosed to the broker's principal.

A broker is not permitted to independently either accept or reject any offers on behalf of his client, nor can he decide which offers will be presented. A broker is required to present all offers and to educate the seller on what is or is not being offered and otherwise inform the seller of all material facts so the seller can make the decision that is best for him.

One situation brokers will experience, particularly when they are working with a property that is in high demand, is multiple offers. Multiple offers on one property can pose a dilemma for buyers, sellers, and agents. Although the seller's agent must present all offers at the same time, the seller himself must decide how to deal with the offers. The requirement to present all offers at the same time only requires the broker to make the offeree aware of the fact there are multiple offers as practicality suggests the offers will then be presented individually. The broker should carefully explain to the client the requirements for presentation of multiple offers and proceed to explain each offer's contents, including the pros and cons of each, so that the offeree may make the decision that is best for him.

> "A licensee must have the seller's permission to reveal there ARE multiple offers. The permission of the offerors is required to disclose the terms and conditions of the offers to other prospective buyers. In both cases, if the listing agent tells one buyer, they must tell all buyers."
> —Terry Wilson, DREI

Real estate brokers may find themselves in a situation in which they have an offer in hand to present to the seller when they are informed that another broker has a client who will be making yet another offer that evening. The broker must treat the information about the potential offer as a material fact and present the possibility of its existence to the seller in addition to presenting the existing offer.

The offeree may decide to accept one of the multiple offers or reject them all. It is possible the seller may wish to make a counteroffer after rejecting a particular offer.

Negotiating multiple offers is a risk for both buyers and sellers. A seller's strategy may result in a higher price or in losing all the buyers. A buyer may end up paying too much for the property or being unable to obtain a loan because the property does not appraise for the contract price.

It is wise to deal with the potential of multiple offers before they materialize by educating buyers and sellers about multiple offers, the practical and ethical methods of handling them, and the advantages and risks to both parties.

The National Association of REALTORS® (NAR) publishes an excellent consumer brochure called *A Buyers' and Sellers' Guide to Multiple Offer Negotiations*, which can be downloaded by REALTORS® from the NAR website for use in informing their buyer and seller clients about multiple offers.

The requirement to present all offers extends to conditional "back-up" offers as well. Regardless of how the agent feels about back-up offers, they too must be presented to the seller along with the disclosure of their terms and conditions.

Handling Contract Modifications and Counteroffers

> It is important for a broker to understand the distinction between handling contract modifications and a counteroffer. In the case of a contract modification, a binding contract already exists and the parties wish to change the agreement in some way to reflect changes that are now desired.

Common examples of contract modifications include changes to the price, earnest money deposits, due diligence fees, due diligence date, scheduled closing date, or literally anything the parties feel is necessary. Brokers who are members of the NCAR typically will use the Agreement to Amend Contract (NCAR Form 330-T) to modify or amend the contract in most situations. If extensive modification is needed, it may be more practical to simply replace the original contract with one that is completely rewritten.

In the situation involving counteroffers, it is important to realize there has been no acceptance of an offer that would have resulted in a contract.

An original offer is often modified several times before the parties reach agreement. A broker should be careful in handling these counteroffers. A primary consideration to keep in mind is that once an offer has been changed in any manner, the offeror is relieved of obligation because the offer has been rejected (killed).

There are two primary methods of handling counteroffers. First, because the modification killed the original offer, a broker could use a new clean offer at any time in the process of negotiation. Whereas this would be the preferable format for clarity, it is often not practical. Therefore, brokers usually resort to the more common technique of striking out terms on the original document and inserting new terms in their place. When using this method of modification, certain standards of practice apply. All changes should be initialed and dated by all parties to the contract. Only one set of modifications should be included on a form. If a second or subsequent set of changes is to be proposed, a new form should be used. If extensive changes are made, a broker should consider starting with a new form. This is not a contract law requirement but rather a good business practice, as repeated corrections and changes on a contract form may lead to a contract that is far less than legible. It is far better to make certain that a clearly written and readable contract is achieved.

Acceptance of Counteroffers

> 🔑 Once a counteroffer has been received, it is up to the offeree to decide whether to accept or reject it, including to determine whether making another counteroffer is appropriate. If the intent is to accept, acceptance must be in writing and identical with the terms of the offer as any modification would result in another counteroffer.

The written acceptance can be accomplished by the offeree placing her initials beside each item that was countered and by inserting the date of the initialing. If the counteroffer was made by presenting a new offer to purchase form, the acceptance is made by having the offeree accept in writing just as an offer would be accepted that was not a counteroffer.

Once the counteroffer has been accepted in writing, that fact must be communicated to the offeror and or to her agent to constitute a contract. One of the many challenges with the counteroffer situation is to remember who is currently the offeror and who is the offeree as these roles switch positions with every counter. Notification of acceptance is not completed when the offeree only notifies her own agent. The notification must be communicated to the offeror or her agent.

Each counteroffer should be rejected by the offeree or withdrawn by the offeror before moving on to another counteroffer. A seller's agent should address outstanding counteroffers before allowing the seller to accept an offer from another party. The broker must be sure the outstanding counteroffer has not been accepted and communicated to another agent in the firm or to a seller's subagent from another company working with the buyer. If it has not been accepted, it can and should be withdrawn before accepting another offer.

If a seller receives a better offer after he has signed an offer—but before acceptance has been communicated to the buyer—the seller may be able to void his acceptance and accept the better offer. The broker should advise the seller to consult an attorney before accepting any other offer. Even though the broker may think there is no contract, he cannot give legal advice. Suppose the broker is a dual agent who does not fully understand dual agency (a horrible thought!). He may not realize that acceptance in his presence constitutes communication. If the seller accepts the second offer in this case, he could have two contracts to sell one property to two people. The interesting thing is that as difficult as it is to sell a house once, it is an amazingly simple task to inadvertently sell it twice!

A **Response to Buyer's Offer** (NCAR Form 340-T, Appendix F) may be preferable to a counteroffer. This is a rejection along with an offer to consider another offer from the offeror with suggested terms. It does not require the seller to accept the buyer's resulting offer even if it contains all of the modifications requested by the seller. It simply indicates the seller would be more inclined to accept an offer that included the indicated changes. It does not need to be withdrawn before accepting an offer from another party. The Response to Buyer's Offer is especially useful for handling multiple offers. The seller should not make a counteroffer to more than one person at a time; however, she can give a Response to Buyer's Offer to as many potential buyers as necessary. The seller can then choose from all offers that result.

All brokers should understand the following facts about offers and counteroffers:

- There is no such thing as a binding offer. To make any offer binding, it must be accepted, at which point it will become a contract.
- An expiration date in an offer does not preclude the offeror from withdrawing the offer before the expiration date. It means only that if the offer is not accepted or rejected by that time, it is automatically terminated.
- Changing any term in an offer is a rejection of the offer and thus makes it a counteroffer.
- Once the offeree rejects an offer, she cannot change her mind and accept it later. The offeror, however, can resubmit the same offer if she chooses.
- An offer with no specified expiration date terminates after a reasonable time period. It is best not to depend on this and to specifically terminate all offers that are not accepted within a reasonable time.
- An offer is terminated by the death or insanity of the offeror before the offer is accepted.
- An offer cannot be withdrawn after the communication of its acceptance because it would now be considered a contract. The parties can, however, terminate the resulting contract by mutual agreement.
- At every counteroffer, the role of the offeror and offeree will switch.

Electronically Submitted Offer and Acceptance

In today's business environment, it common for buyers and agents to submit offers electronically. Submitting offers and acceptance by either fax or email seems to be the norm for most transactions. Because of the federal e-sign legislation as well as North Carolina's Uniform Electronic Transaction Act, electronically submitted offers as well as acceptance can constitute compliance with the statute of frauds requirement for a written contract. As a bit of practical advice, agents should always make certain that any electronic submissions were received by the intended parties. Asking intended recipients to verify receipt could save disappointment in cases in which a party eagerly awaits an answer to her offer only to learn later the offer was never received and the house has now been sold to another buyer.

The same rules of electronic submission of offers apply to submission of revocation as well. If revocation is submitted by electronic means of delivery, it is recommended to follow up orally to ensure the notice has been received and to send written hard-copy evidence of revocation.

Offers can be made and transmitted by facsimile devices (fax). The acceptance can also be transmitted by fax. The faxed offer to purchase must be signed before faxing. The faxed copy of the signed offer the offeree receives is an indication that there is an original signature on an original document. If the offeree signs the faxed copy and faxes it back to the offeror, the signed faxed copy also indicates the presence of an original signature. Although the original signatures are on two different copies of the document, it still creates a valid contract. Because a copy with original signatures is needed for each company, the buyer, the seller, the mortgage company, and closing attorney, a good business practice is to follow up a faxed acceptance by obtaining original signatures on multiple copies of the contract. Each copy should be signed by the offeror and the offeree in a timely fashion. This is easily accomplished using express mail or delivery services.

The original signed offer can also be scanned into a computer and sent via email. The email can be printed, signed, scanned, and emailed back. This often makes a clearer copy than a copy that has been faxed to and from a buyer or seller. The important thing to remember is that original signatures must exist. Emailing an unsigned offer back and forth is like an oral agreement. If nothing is signed, it is not enforceable. With the advent and proliferation of e-signature programs whereby a document can be emailed, e-signed, and emailed back to the original source without downloading, signing, and scanning it, agents should ensure that any methods used to obtain signatures are secure and are legally acceptable.

"Remember a deposit is something you get back if you follow the rules. A fee is non-returnable; it is the price you paid to get something."
—Terry Wilson, DREI

Handling Earnest Money and Due Diligence Fee

The NCAR/NCBA Offer to Purchase and Contract Form 2-T addresses two different forms of monies. One is the due diligence fee and the other is earnest money deposit. Neither is required to create a binding contract, and agents may encounter transactions in which one, both, or neither is present. It is important to realize the function that each plays in the contract process.

Due diligence can be conducted up until the actual closing, although the buyer may not be entitled to a return of his earnest money deposit. The due diligence date is simply the last date the buyer can withdraw without penalty of losing his deposit, although he will not be entitled to a refund of the due diligence fee.

The **due diligence fee** is generally *nonrefundable unless there is a breach of contract by the seller. This fee is for the time period between the formation of the contract and the due diligence expiration date.* It compensates the seller for allowing the buyer time to conduct any due diligence the buyer feels is relevant. The buyer is allowed to terminate the contract for any reason or for no reason no later than 5:00 p.m. on the due diligence expiration date. Because the seller is losing potentially valuable marketing time waiting for the buyer's decision as to whether she will continue to pursue closing, this fee is intended to compensate the seller for her risk. The amount of any due diligence fee is negotiated between the parties and, in theory, is related to the amount of time the buyer has until the due diligence date or any other factors the seller feels are important. The due diligence fee check should be payable directly to the seller and should not be placed in the agent's escrow account unless it is received as cash. Its purpose is fulfilled upon the expiration of the due diligence period.

Both the earnest money deposit and due diligence fee are "good faith" monies to show the seller the seriousness of the buyer's offer. According to the NCAR/NCBA Offer to Purchase and Contract, the buyer can terminate the contract for any reason by delivering written notice of termination to the seller before 5:00 p.m. of the due diligence date and be entitled to a full refund of his earnest money. It is often stated that the buyer's earnest money "goes hard" at the expiration of the diligence period and the seller will be entitled to keep the earnest money should the buyer not perform in accordance with the contract. Note that in cases involving a breach of contract by the seller, the buyer would be entitled to a full refund of both the due diligence fee and the earnest money deposit. Note that the buyer's liability to the seller, in the event of buyer breach, is limited to the forfeiture of the earnest money as **liquidated damages**. It is very important for the seller and his agent to remember this liquidated damages clause, as it represents the entirety of what the seller is entitled to receive from the buyer regardless of the amount of any actual losses the seller may incur other than physical damage to the property caused by the buyer.

The offer to purchase and contract addresses the disposition of any earnest money deposits as well as due diligence fees. Agents will be bound to follow those instructions as well as to comply with Commission trust account guidelines.

There are potentially two main ways the agent will encounter earnest money deposits on a sales transaction. These are the initial earnest monies paid at the time of the offer or within five days of the effective date of the contract, whichever is indicated, or (Additional) earnest money that is payable to the escrow agent by some agreed-upon date, *time being of the essence*. If the initial earnest money deposit alternative is selected, the monies can be paid in the form of cash, personal check, official bank check, or wire transfer. Any (additional) earnest money deposits are required to be in the form of *immediately available funds*, and personal checks are not permitted as a source of funds. Typically, the earnest money is delivered at the time of the offer or within the five-day period. Form 2-T dictates the monies will be delivered to the named escrow agent for deposit into her trust or escrow account. Any agreed-upon recipient may serve as the escrow agent, including nonlicensees, such as an attorney or title insurance company. Most transactions will name one of the firms involved in the sale, usually the listing firm, as the agent into whose trust account the earnest money will be deposited, although this is primarily the result of tradition and custom as opposed to any rule requiring such.

If the contract provides for payment of a due diligence fee, it will not be treated as trust account or escrow funds but rather as monies paid directly to the seller by the buyer. The primary situation in which due diligence fees will be deposited in a firm's trust account is when the buyer paid the monies in the form of cash. In this case, the agent is to deposit the cash in his firm's trust account, and if a contract is reached, write the seller a check on the trust account for payment of the due diligence fee. Agents should be cautious about tendering the due diligence fee check with the offer for consideration by the seller, as the check is payable to the seller, and there is nothing to prevent a seller from cashing the check and rejecting the buyer's offer. The more prudent way to handle the transfer of due diligence funds is to hold the money until notice of acceptance of the contract has been given, at which time the agent should convey the check to the seller or his agent. Regardless of whom the broker represents or if there is a contract and monies are due to the seller—if a broker is still in possession of either an earnest money deposit or due diligence fee check and the buyer demands the return of these funds, the broker must comply with the instructions of the buyer.

Furnishing Copies of Offers and Contracts to Buyer and Seller

At the time of execution (but in no case later than 3 days), all parties must be provided with a copy of any instrument they signed. Thus, it is common practice for the offer to be prepared in six copies—one each for the prospective buyer, the selling agent, the listing agent, the seller, the mortgage company, and the closing attorney. Brokers are required to keep all instruments on file for three years for inspection by the Real Estate Commission at any time. This regulation applies to offers that are rejected or withdrawn, even if there is no further action on the offer. The offeree need not write "rejected" on the offer; the broker can simply do this and note the date.

Installment Land Contracts

> The **installment land contract** *is also referred to as a* **contract for deed**, *land contract, land sales contract, installment contract, and any number of other locally popular names.*

Although these types of contracts are somewhat rare in North Carolina, they do exist, especially in certain types of transactions, and they commonly are referred to by so many different names that agents will need to be aware of the characteristics of this type of agreement to be able to identify it when they are presented with such an arrangement. The installment land contract is a dual-personality contract in that it is a contract to convey title as well as the financing agreement all bundled in one. With this type of agreement, the seller will sell the property and finance the purchase but will not convey title until such time as the loan has been repaid in full or the buyer has repaid such amount as may be agreed between the parties. This is the opposite of typical seller financing in that the seller would normally convey title to the buyer upon purchase and take back a mortgage from the buyer, and then would have to foreclose to regain the collateral in the event of default. Because the title will stay with the seller, this type of agreement has many potential pitfalls that all of the parties should be aware of, as this type of contract is strongly slanted toward protection of the seller.

An installment land contract is sometimes used in situations in which the borrower may simply not be able to acquire financing any other way. The value may be too low, the down payment may be minimal, or the borrower's income and credit history may cause concern for a lender. By using this type of contract, the seller will not have to undergo the foreclosure process to regain the title, as he never conveyed it to the buyer. In case of default, the buyer would typically lose all of his down payment as well as everything he had paid into the property as well as the benefit of any increases in value due to inflation.

> "When dealing with a Contract for Deed (AKA Installment Land Contract) the parties must complete the terms of the contract (make all payments) before they get the deed."
> —Terry Wilson, DREI

Upon entering into a contract for deed, the buyer is said to have acquired equitable title and the seller will retain legal title. **Equitable title** is *a right in the property to have legal title conveyed once the terms of the agreement have been completed.* Once the buyer pays off the existing loan, the seller will then convey the title to the buyer by deed. **Legal title** is *the interest held by a party who owns real property.* Because the seller has never conveyed title to the buyer, she is considered to retain legal title under an installment land contract.

Because this agreement is for the conveyance of an interest in real property, it has to be in writing to be enforceable under the Statute of Frauds and therefore must be recorded to protect the buyer's interest. The question arises as to how to record the buyer's interest when the seller never conveyed title to the buyer. In cases such as this, the buyer will record the actual installment sales contract or a memorandum of the agreement so that there will be a publicly recorded document that outlines his interest.

There is no standard preprinted contract form for use in the installment land contract in North Carolina. These agreements will need to be drafted by an attorney or the parties themselves. It is never appropriate to use Form 2-T for the installment land contract sale or for a broker to draft such a contract.

If the installment land contract involves a one- to four-family dwelling, it will be governed by North Carolina G.S. Chapter 47H and must contain the following 17 required provisions:

1. Names and addresses of the parties.
2. Contract signing date.
3. Legal description of the property.
4. Sales price.

5. Charges or fees separate from the sales price.
6. Down payment.
7. Principal balance owed by the purchaser.
8. Amount and due date and number of installment payments.
9. Interest rate and method of determining the interest rate.
10. Conspicuous statement of any pending order or other matters of public record adversely affecting the property if the seller has actual knowledge of such.
11. Rights of purchaser to cure a default.
12. Obligations of each party and who is responsible for repairs, payment of taxes, hazard insurance premiums, flood insurance premiums, homeowner association dues, and any other charges.
13. Provision that purchaser has right to accelerate the payment or prepay payments without penalty unless the property is encumbered by a deed of trust that contains an acceleration clause that contains a prepayment penalty, in which case the purchaser will have to compensate the seller.
14. Description of conditions stating if the property includes water, sewer, septic, and electricity service and whether restrictive covenants prevent building or installing a dwelling. A copy of applicable restrictive covenants will also be made available to the purchaser before entering the contract.
15. Statement of taxes, homeowner association dues, and special assessments to be paid on the property, including the amounts that may be currently due. A reasonable estimate of the amounts of each may be given if the actual amount is not known at time of contract.
16. A statement of the amount of the lien as well as the amount and due date of any payments if the property is secured by any deed of trust or mortgage. There are exceptions to this rule if the seller is not a licensed general contractor or a licensed manufactured home dealer.
17. A conspicuous statement in not less than 14-point boldface type immediately above the purchaser's signature that the purchaser has the right to cancel this agreement anytime before midnight of the third business day following either execution or delivery of the contract, whichever is later. An example of this statement in its proper form is as follows.

THIS PROPERTY HAS EXISTING LIENS ON IT. IF THE SELLER FAILS TO MAKE TIMELY PAYMENTS TO THE LIEN HOLDER, THE LIEN HOLDER MAY FORECLOSE ON THE PROPERTY, EVEN IF YOU HAVE MADE ALL YOUR PAYMENTS.

The cited statute also requires a seller using an installment land contract to give a prospective buyer notice before contract execution if the seller as another lien (e.g., a mortgage) on the property and the consequences of a default by the seller. Additionally, the statute grants the buyer certain remedies she may pursue if the seller defaults on a lien on the property.

The *seller* is also required to record a copy of the contract or a "Memorandum of a Contract for Deed" within five business days after the contract has been signed and acknowledged by both the buyer and seller. This is to be recorded at the register of deeds office in the county where the property is located.

Advantages and Disadvantages

Advantages to Buyer

The installment land contract is often used in cases in which the buyer simply doesn't have any other real alternative to obtaining the necessary financing. Another advantage is that the buyer is entitled to claim normal tax advantages such as the deduction of mortgage interest on the payment of property taxes.

Disadvantages to Buyer

The buyer does not have the usual protections of the deed of trust foreclosure process in North Carolina (for more details, see Chapter 11, "Real Estate Financing"). As a result, the penalties for default are severe and the seller can declare the entire mortgage amount due if the buyer is in default of even one payment. The buyer does have the right to *equity of redemption* that would allow him to pay off the balance and retain the property. Another disadvantage can arise in cases in which the seller has an existing mortgage on the property. If the seller should default on that loan, the purchaser could find himself losing his property even if he is not late on any mortgage payments. The buyer does have the right to file a Request for Notice at the register of deeds office, in which case he would be notified if the seller is in default of his mortgage. Last, the buyer has a disadvantage in that he does not have legal title to the property. The public records will reflect the seller as the owner of record. It is for this reason that North Carolina G.S. 47H requires the seller to record the installment land contract or a memorandum of contract within five days of execution of contract.

Advantages to Seller

There are several advantages to the seller, including that she retains legal title to the property and if the buyer should default, foreclosure will not be required. In addition, the seller may be able to sell a property when the buyer had no real alternative way to finance the transaction.

Disadvantages to Seller

These types of transactions often involve buyers who have minimal, if any, down payment as well as marginal credit qualifications. In the event of default, the seller will still incur a time delay and the considerable legal expense to have the contract declared to be forfeited, thereby terminating the buyer's contractual interest.

OPTION TO PURCHASE REAL ESTATE

> 🔑 An **option** is *the right to purchase a specific piece of property for a specific price on stated terms and conditions for a specified period of time.*

It is as much the right not to buy it as it is to buy it. The purchaser, who receives the option rights, is called the **optionee** and the seller, who conveys the option rights to the buyer, is considered the **optionor**. It is an agreement that allows the optionee to tie up a piece of property but not be obligated to purchase it. This is commonly used to gain the buyer some time to do his due diligence, line up investors, research whether he can use it for his intended use, or perform any number of other tasks. The option contract requires the seller to sell if the buyer wishes to buy. It does not matter if the original terms are vastly different from what the property could currently bring in the marketplace.

The option agreement is required to be in writing under the Statute of Frauds and to be recorded under the Conner Act to protect the optionee's interest from third parties. The option agreement must be for a definite price and cannot be for an amount "to be determined" or "to be agreed upon at the option termination date." Those situations constitute an agreement to agree rather than a specific price being set. The option contract will also stipulate an option date by which time the optionee must either exercise her option to buy or lose the right to purchase. A well-drafted option agreement should specify the manner in which proper notice to exercise the option must be given. Normally, the optionee must deliver written notice of intent to exercise the option to purchase by the required date. Failure to timely exercise the option results in the loss of the opportunity to purchase the property on the terms stated in the option agreement. If the option is to be exercised, the optionee will be required to close the purchase within the number of days set forth within the purchase contract, which must either accompany or be contained within the option contract.

The optionee will pay an option fee to the optionor as consideration for this agreement. This amount is nonrefundable and needs to be addressed within the option contract as to whether it will apply to the purchase price if the option is exercised. Unlike any earnest money deposit that may be a part of this contract, the option fee will not be held in an escrow or trust account as it traditionally is paid to the optionor at the time of agreement and is the optionor's to keep, regardless of the outcome. It is often stated that if the optionee does not elect to purchase the property, he has "lost" his option fee. In reality, the fee was not lost, but rather the optionee got exactly what he paid for (i.e., the right to purchase the property without the obligation to do so).

There are currently no standard preprinted option contract forms available from the NCAR/NCBA Joint Forms Committee, as these agreements are considered too complex to allow agents to fill in the blanks of a preapproved form. The services of a competent attorney should be sought in the preparation of these agreements.

A variation of the option agreement is a lease with option to purchase. In these transactions, the tenant retains an option to purchase the property at some point in the future. Just as with the option contracts mentioned previously, there is no preprinted lease with option to purchase agreement for brokers to use in these transactions. An attorney must prepare these agreements. As an additional note, if the lease with option to purchase agreement involves property that will be used as the lessor's primary residence, it will be governed by North Carolina G.S. 43G.

Agreements for Preemptive Rights

Preemptive rights are those rights that give the buyer or tenant the first right to either purchase or lease a property. Not to be confused with the option agreement above, preemptive rights apply only if the owner or landlord decides to sell or lease.

Right of First Refusal

The **right of first refusal** is *an agreement that should the owner decide to sell or lease, she will offer it to the named party first.* There is no obligation for this owner ever to decide to sell, but rather an agreement that if she does, she will offer it to the recipient of the agreement first. This is unlike an option in which if the buyer decides to purchase, the seller would be obligated to sell. It is quite common that rights of first refusal will state that a particular buyer will have first rights of refusal. The property is offered for lease or sale to the public, and at such point a member of the public is willing to enter into a binding contract to purchase or lease the property, the "first" buyer will have the opportunity to match that party's offer. Should the first buyer be willing to match the second buyer's offer, she would have the right to purchase the property.

Right of First Opportunity to Purchase

These types of agreements are more commonly used in commercial lease transactions. In a **right of first opportunity to purchase**, *the owner agrees to give the lessee the first chance to purchase the property at a price determined in the future, if and when the owner decides to sell.* If the lessee does not buy the property at that price, the seller can then offer it to the public. It is usual for the seller to retain the right to sell the property for a price that falls within a certain percentage of the designated price without requiring him to offer it again to the original lessee. If the seller is unable to sell the property to another buyer during a stipulated time period, he must repeat the process by allowing the original lessee the first opportunity to purchase the property at a reduced price before offering it to anyone else. This is different from the right of first refusal in that the seller sets a designated price he is willing to accept, rather than waiting for an offer from a third party that the party holding the preemptive right may match. The owner must repeat the process of offering the original party the first opportunity to buy the property at a stated price every time he tries to sell the property until it is sold.

With the right of first refusal, the price for the property is established by what a third-party buyer/lessee is willing to pay.

Summary of Important Points

1. If a licensee proposes a preprinted sales contract form for use by the parties, it must contain the 19 specific items as required by North Carolina Real Estate Commission Rule A.0012.
2. The agent cannot insert any statement regarding the agent's compensation or reduction of liability in the preprinted contract even if she has permission from the seller and buyer.
3. The effective date is *the date of communication of written acceptance of an offer.*
4. Due diligence is the process of a buyer investigating the property to determine its physical conditions, value, compliance with legal issues such as zoning, and any other items deemed important to the buyer.
5. The due diligence fee is a nonrefundable, except in cases of breach of contract by the seller, fee paid as compensation to the seller for the buyer's right to investigate the property and withdraw for any reason before the end of the due diligence period.
6. There are no loan, appraisal, property inspection, or termite contingencies in the NCAR/NCBA Offer to Purchase and Contract Form.
7. If the purchaser fails to cancel before 5:00 p.m. on the due diligence date, he will forfeit his earnest money deposit as liquidated damages to the seller.
8. Liquidated damages are *preset outcomes in the event of breach of contract.* Typically liquidated damages are stated as a dollar amount and will represent the entirety of what the "injured" party will receive without regard for the amount of actual damages, if any, that were incurred. The injured party will not have to establish the amount of a loss, but rather simply prove that there was a breach.
9. Acceptance must be in writing and is effective at the point of communication to the offerer or her agent.
10. The mailbox rule is that notification is effective once mailed even if the recipient has no actual knowledge of its taking place. Not all items are controlled by this rule. Revocation, for example, is not effective until actually received.
11. The Uniform Electronic Transactions Act is a North Carolina law that allows contracts to be binding as the result of an electronically submitted offer and acceptance. It also recognizes an electronic signature as being binding.
12. Contract performance dates and times will generally be interpreted as "or within a reasonable amount of time" as long as the parties are genuinely working toward completion. If the parties wish for the dates and times to be strictly interpreted, they should insert the clause "time is of the essence."

13. The installment land contract (contract for deed) is a dual-personality contract that both conveys an interest in real property and is a financing instrument. The seller finances the purchase for the buyer but does not convey legal title (deed) until such time as the loan shall be paid in full. The buyer is said to have acquired equitable title until the loan balance is paid, at which time she will receive legal title.
14. An option is the right to purchase a specific parcel of property for a specific price, terms, and conditions for a specified period of time. It is the right not to buy it, as much as it is the right to buy it.
15. In an option agreement, the seller must sell if the buyer decides to buy according to the terms of the contract.
16. In an option, *the seller* is the optionor and *the buyer* is the optionee.
17. The right of first refusal is different from an option in that the seller is not required to sell or set a predetermined price. It simply means that should the seller decide to sell at some point in time and at some price, he has agreed to allow the buyer the first opportunity to buy the property before offering it to anyone else.

Review Questions

Answers to the review questions are in the Answer Key at the back of the book.

1. An agent proposes a preprinted sales contract form for use by the buyer and seller. The North Carolina Real Estate Commission prohibits the inclusion of which of the following in this contract form?
   A. loan contingency
   B. indefinite termination
   C. broker compensation
   D. liquidated damages

2. According to the NCAR/NCBA Standard Offer to Purchase and Contract form 2-T, if the seller is determined to be in breach of contract the day before the scheduled closing, which of the following is the seller liable to return to the buyer?
   A. due diligence fee, earnest money deposit, and reasonable expenses of purchase
   B. due diligence fee and earnest money deposit only
   C. earnest money deposit and expenses of purchase
   D. earnest money deposit only

3. The buyer has contracted for the purchase of the seller's home by utilizing the NCAR/NCBA Standard Offer to Purchase form 2-T. Two days after the due diligence date, the buyer informs the seller that the lender has rejected his mortgage application and he will be unable to purchase the home. The buyer is entitled to a refund of:
   A. earnest money deposit only.
   B. due diligence fee only.
   C. both earnest money deposit and due diligence fee.
   D. neither earnest money deposit or due diligence fee.

4. The buyer has contracted for the purchase of the seller's home by utilizing the NCAR/NCBA Standard Offer to Purchase and Contract form 2-T. Five days after the scheduled closing date, the buyer informs the seller he will be unable to complete the purchase of the home. The seller is entitled to retain or recover _____.
   A. earnest money deposit, due diligence fee, and reasonable attorney fees
   B. earnest money deposit and due diligence fee
   C. specific performance of the sale
   D. earnest money deposit, due diligence fee, and all reasonable expenses related to the purchase

5. A purchaser has submitted an offer to purchase that states the offer "shall remain open and in effect until 5:00 p.m. on Thursday, October 30." The offer further states the purchaser agrees not to withdraw the offer prior to that time. Late on Wednesday the 29th, the buyer informs the seller of his intent to withdraw the offer. This offer is:
   A. irrevocable until 5:00 p.m. on the 30th.
   B. revocable until such time as it becomes a contract regardless of what the offer states.
   C. irrevocable once the seller or his agent actually receives the signed offer.
   D. revocable until the seller or his agent actually receives the offer and even then not until 5:00 p.m on the 30th.

6. Under the installment sales contract (contract for deed), what interest best describes the buyer's rights in the property?
   A. constructive title
   B. fee simple title
   C. equitable title
   D. legal title

7. The effective date is considered to be the date in which:
   A. the buyer and seller have both signed the offer to purchase.
   B. the purchaser has completed due diligence and decides to finalize the purchase.
   C. the offeree has communicated notice of written acceptance to the offeror.
   D. the parties convey legal title to the property.

8. A buyer submits a written offer to purchase to the seller, who signs his acceptance without revision. The seller mails this agreement back to the buyer at his proper address. After it is mailed but before the buyer receives it, the seller faxes a notice to the buyer of his intent to revoke his signed agreement. Which of the following is correct?
   A. This became a contract as soon as the seller signed the agreement, so the seller cannot revoke it.
   B. This became a binding contract when the seller mailed the signed acceptance to the buyer, so the seller cannot revoke it.
   C. The seller can terminate this agreement since he communicated his intent to withdraw prior to the buyer receiving his signed document.
   D. The seller can terminate the agreement since the buyer has not communicated his notice of acceptance of the seller's acceptance of his offer.

9. Which of the following statements is correct in regards to the NCAR/NCBA Standard Offer to Purchase and Contract form 2-T?
   A. The scheduled closing date in the contract is time is of the essence.
   B. Proposed assessments are to be paid for by the seller if confirmed after the closing.
   C. In the event of buyer breach of contract the seller is limited to buyer's EMD as liquidated damages.
   D. The contract provides a period of 13 days from the scheduled closing date for the "delaying party" to be able to close without being considered a breach.

10. A buyer is informed by his lender five days after the due diligence date that his loan is not approved. Which of the following is true? The buyer can back out of the agreement:
    A. and get a refund of his earnest money deposit.
    B. and get a refund of his due diligence fee and his earnest money deposit.
    C. but will not be entitled to a refund of this earnest money deposit.
    D. and obtain a refund of his due diligence fee but not his earnest money deposit since his loan contingency has not been met.

11. Which of the following is correct concerning an installment land contract?
    A. The buyer receives legal title at closing.
    B. The seller retains equitable title at closing.
    C. The buyer conveys equitable title at closing.
    D. The buyer receives equitable title at closing.

12. An option contract:
    A. requires the buyer to buy if the seller decides to sell.
    B. states that if the seller decides to sell, the buyer will have the first right to purchase.
    C. requires the buyer to buy and the seller to sell.
    D. requires the seller to sell if the buyer decides to buy.

13. According to the Standard Offer to Purchase and Contract when is "closing"?
    A. at the attorney's office when documents are signed
    B. at delivery of the deed
    C. at distribution of the sale proceeds
    D. when the deed is recorded

14. Which of the following will NOT typically terminate an offer?
    A. acceptance
    B. counterfoffer
    C. death of offeror
    D. performance

15. Which of the following is NOT an allowed means of payment for an (Additional) earnest money deposit as indicated in paragraph 1(d) of the NCAR/NCBA Offer to Purchase and Contract form 2-T?
    A. cash
    B. personal check
    C. wire transfer
    D. official bank check

CHAPTER 11

REAL ESTATE FINANCING

KEY TERMS

- acceleration clause
- adjustable rate mortgage (ARM)
- alienation clause
- amortization
- arrears
- balloon payment
- beneficiary
- buydown loan
- certificate of reasonable value (CRV)
- conforming loans
- Consumer Financial Protection Bureau (CFPB)
- conventional loan
- deed in lieu of foreclosure
- deed of trust
- defaults
- defeasance clause
- deficiency judgment
- disintermediation
- due-on-sale clause
- Equal Credit Opportunity Act (ECOA)
- equity
- equity of redemption
- escrow account
- Federal Home Loan Mortgage Corporation (FHLMC), or Freddie Mac
- Federal Housing Administration (FHA)
- Federal National Mortgage Association (FNMA), or Fannie Mae
- FHA-insured loan
- foreclosure
- foreclosure under power of sale
- Government National Mortgage Association (GNMA), or Ginnie Mae
- graduated payment mortgage (GPM)
- grantor
- home equity mortgages
- hypothecation
- insured
- interest
- judicial foreclosure
- *Know Before You Owe*
- lien theory
- liquidity
- loan assumption
- loan cap
- loan-to-value (LTV) ratio
- loan underwriting
- mortgage
- mortgage banker
- mortgage broker
- mortgage insurance premium (MIP)
- mortgage note
- mortgagee
- mortgagor
- negative amortization
- negotiable note
- nonconforming loans
- nonjudicial foreclosure
- nonnegotiable note
- nonrecourse note
- open-end mortgage
- package mortgage
- periodic cap

power of sale clause
prepaid items
prepayment penalty
principal
private mortgage insurance (PMI)
promissory note
purchase money mortgage
real estate investment trusts (REITs)
Regulation Z
release of liability

reverse mortgage
right of assignment
savings and loan associations (S&Ls)
secondary mortgage market
statutory redemption period
strict foreclosure
subject to a loan
substitution of entitlement
term loan
title theory

trustee
trustor
Truth in Lending Simplification and Reform Act (TILSRA)
uninsured
upfront mortgage insurance premium (UFMIP)
usury
VA-guaranteed loan

LEARNING OBJECTIVES

At the conclusion of this chapter, you should be able to:

Section 1: Basic Finance Concepts, Terminology, and Calculations
1. Define the basic mortgage theories.
2. Define and describe the essential elements and common provisions of the mortgage note and the mortgage instrument (deed of trust).
3. Describe common note payment plans.
4. Describe the concepts of principal and interest, including calculations.
5. Define the rights of the parties in mortgage instruments.
6. Define three methods of sale of mortgaged property.
7. Describe the characteristics, major programs and payment plans, and qualification requirements of the following:
    a. Conventional mortgage loans
    b. Federal Housing Administration (FHA)-insured loans
    c. Department of Veterans Affairs (VA)-guaranteed loans
8. Describe the basic definitions, characteristics, and uses of other mortgage loans and payment methods.

Section 2: Primary Sources of Real Estate Finance
9. Describe common sources of financing.
10. Describe the major players in the secondary mortgage market.
11. Describe loan underwriting practices and procedures.
12. Define and describe mortgage legislation:
    a. Truth in Lending Simplification and Reform Act
    b. Equal Credit Opportunity Act

IN THIS CHAPTER

Section 1 of this chapter, "Basic Finance Concepts, Terminology, and Calculations" outlines financing instruments, such as mortgages, deeds of trust, and notes, and the various ways in which a real estate purchase can be financed. Knowledge of these financing methods is critical to real estate practitioners. Except in the unusual case of a cash sale, knowledge or lack of knowledge of the ways in which a sale can be financed may make the difference between a successful and an unsuccessful transaction. Section 2 of this chapter, "Primary Sources of Mortgage Funds," discusses major sources of real estate financing as well as the federal regulations of lending institutions and the secondary mortgage market.

SECTION 1: BASIC FINANCE CONCEPTS, TERMINOLOGY, AND CALCULATIONS

PRINCIPAL, INTEREST, TAXES, AND INSURANCE

Understanding the terms *interest* and *principal* is essential to understanding notes, mortgages, deeds of trust, and all real estate financing methods. **Interest** is the *money paid for using someone else's money*. The **principal** is the *amount of money on which interest is either paid or received*. In the case of an interest-bearing note, principal is the amount of money the lender has lent the borrower and on which the borrower will pay interest to the lender.

Simple interest is usually used for mortgage loan interest. This means the annual rate of interest is used to calculate payments even though payments normally are made monthly.

Mortgage loan interest almost always is calculated in **arrears**; that is, *a monthly payment due on the first of the month includes interest for using the money during the previous month*. Interest can also be calculated in advance; that is, a monthly payment due on the first of the month includes interest for the month in which the payment is due. When paying off or assuming a loan, one must know if the interest is paid in advance or in arrears to determine the amount of interest owed or to be prorated at closing. *Interest must be paid in arrears on all conforming loans, that is, loans sold in the secondary mortgage market. Mortgage interest that is being collected in advance tends to be the exception to the rule in today's real estate financing.*

The P&I payment is the part of the payment covering the principal and interest and is often referred to as the **debt service**. On a fixed-rate level payment loan, P&I stays constant for the life of the loan. In most cases, especially where the loan-to-value (LTV) ratio is more than 80%, mortgage companies require taxes and insurance to be escrowed; that is, one-twelfth of the annual taxes and insurance (T&I) are paid each month with the P&I payment. This combined payment is called **PITI** (principal, interest, taxes, and insurance). Taxes and insurance can, and do, change over the life of the loan; therefore, mortgage companies perform an annual escrow analysis and adjust the T&I accordingly for the following year.

Mortgage companies have good reason for requiring the funds to be escrowed to pay the taxes and insurance themselves. A property tax lien takes precedence over all other liens, even the mortgage lien.

> If the property is foreclosed for back taxes, the taxes are paid first.

The mortgage company will not get all of its money if the proceeds of the sale are not sufficient to cover the expenses of sale, property tax, and loan balance. If the homeowner/mortgagor does not keep the insurance in force and the property is destroyed, the mortgage company's collateral is destroyed. By collecting one-twelfth of the taxes and insurance monthly and paying these bills themselves, mortgage companies ensure their liens' priority and protection of their collateral. For the mortgage company to always have enough money in the account to pay the taxes and insurance when they become due, extra funds for taxes and insurance must be escrowed at closing and a one-year homeowner's insurance policy must be prepaid at closing (see Chapter 12, "Closing a Sales Transaction").

Amortization and Debt Service

Amortization is *the gradual reduction or extinguishing of a mortgage loan amount from the original amount of the loan to a zero balance through periodic payments,* which include both principal and interest.

Any agent should be able to determine the P&I payment for any given loan amount at any interest rate for any period of time. In the past, agents relied on amortization tables (Figure 11.1), which list factors per $1,000 of the loan amount at any interest rate and any time period. The agent only has to divide the loan amount by 1,000 to determine the number of units of $1,000 and multiply that number by the factor from the chart (see Figure 11.2). In this age of high technology, few agents use amortization tables.

In the beginning, most of the payment goes toward interest (see Figure 11.3). As each successive payment is made (Figure 11.4), a little more goes toward principal and a little less toward interest (see Figure 11.5). Toward the end of the loan term, most of the payment goes toward principal and only a little toward interest. To calculate the amount of interest paid for the life of the loan, see Figure 11.6.

Equity

Equity is the *difference between the market value of the property and what is owed on it.* If a homeowner pays $100,000 using a no-down-payment Department of

AMORTIZATION CHART (MONTHLY PAYMENTS PER $1,000 BORROWED)					
Annual interest rate	Years to fully amortize loan →	15	20	25	30
6.00		8.44	7.16	6.44	6.00
6.25		8.57	7.31	6.60	6.16
6.50		8.71	7.46	6.75	6.32
6.75		8.85	7.60	6.91	6.49
7.00		8.99	7.75	7.07	6.65
7.25		9.13	7.90	7.23	6.82
7.50		9.27	8.06	7.39	6.99
7.75		9.41	8.21	7.55	7.16
8.00		9.56	8.36	7.72	7.34
8.25		9.70	8.52	7.88	7.51
8.50		9.85	8.68	8.05	7.69
8.75		9.99	8.84	8.22	7.87
9.00		10.14	9.00	8.39	8.05
9.25		10.29	9.16	8.56	8.23
9.50		10.44	9.32	8.74	8.41
9.75		10.59	9.49	8.91	8.59
10.00		10.75	9.65	9.09	8.78

Note: This is an abbreviated amortization chart intended for example and learning purposes. Most real estate brokers find it easier to use a calculator to compute and compare payments and to solve other real estate math problems quickly.

FIGURE 11.1 An abbreviated amortization chart.

Source: © 2019 OnCourse Learning

Example: Assume a home purchase price of $87,500 with a conventional mortgage of 80% of the sales price at a rate of 8.5% for 30 years.

1. Amount of the loan: $87,500 × 80% = $70,000.
2. Figure 11.1 is given in a factor per $1,000; therefore, divide $70,000 by 1,000 = 70 units of 1,000.
3. Go to the 8.5% row. Read across to the 30-year column and find the figure of $7.69. This is the payment per month per $1,000 of the loan.
4. Multiply 70 × $7.69 = $538.30. This is the monthly payment of principal and interest to amortize (kill, pay off) a loan of $70,000 at 8.5% for 30 years.

FIGURE 11.2 Use of amortization chart.

Source: © 2019 OnCourse Learning

Veterans Affairs (VA) loan for a property valued at $100,000, he has no equity. If he uses a loan with a 5% down payment, he begins with equity of $5,000. As payments are made, the part of the payment applied to the principal reduces the amount owed, producing equity. Adding improvements that increase the market value of the property (without borrowing the money to pay for them) also adds

> *Example:* Use the data of Figure 11.2 to calculate how much of the payment (P&I) went to the interest portion (I) in the first month of the loan.
>
> 1. Interest (I) at any point is the principal (P) times the rate (R) times the period of time (T) you had the money, or:
>
>   I = P × R × T
>
> 2. In the example,
>
>   I = $70,000 × 8.5% × 1/12 of a year, or
>
> $$I = \frac{\$70,000 \times 0.085}{12} = \$495.83$$
>
> 3. Therefore, of the total payment of $538.30 in the first month, $495.83 went only to interest.

FIGURE 11.3 Interest paid per month.
Source: © 2019 OnCourse Learning

> Using the above data, how much did the first payment reduce the principal?
>
> 1. Calculate the P&I. $538.30
> 2. Subtract the amount that went to interest (I).   −495.83
> 3. The remainder went to principal (P). $ 42.47

FIGURE 11.4 Principal reduction.
Source: © 2019 OnCourse Learning

> Using the previous data, what is the loan balance after the first payment?
>
> 1. Calculate the amount that went to the principal (P). $ 42.47
> 2. Subtract this amount from the previous balance. $70,000.00
> 3. The remainder is the new balance on the loan. $70,000.00
>   −   42.47
> $69,957.53
>
> To calculate the balance on the loan after the second payment, repeat the steps in Figure 11.3 and Figure 11.4 using the new balance of $69,957.53.
>
> 1. $I = \dfrac{\$69,957.53 \times .085}{12}$ = $ 495.53
> 2. Monthly payment $ 538.30
> 3. Subtract the amount that went to interest (I)   −   495.53
> 4. The remainder went to principal (P) $ 42.77
> 5. Previous balance $69,957.53
> 6. Subtract amount that went to principal   −   42.77
> 7. The remainder is the new balance on the loan $69,914.76

FIGURE 11.5 Loan balance after first and second payments.
Source: © 2019 OnCourse Learning

Continuing to use the data from Figure 11.5, how much interest is paid over the life of the loan?

1. Calculate the monthly payment: $538.30.
2. Calculate the total number of months to be paid: 30 years is 12 months × 30 = 360 payments.
3. Multiply the monthly payment by the total number of months to be paid to calculate the total of the payments:

    $538.30 × 360 payments = $193,788 total payback
4. Subtract the amount borrowed from the total of the payback to calculate the amount that went to interest:

    $193,788
    − 70,000
    $123,788   total interest paid

FIGURE 11.6 Total Interest paid over the life of the loan.

equity. Most properties appreciate in value over time, thereby increasing equity. As the market value of the property goes up and the amount owed on it decreases, equity increases. When the loan is completely paid, the owner then has 100% equity in the property.

Usury

Usury is *interest charged in excess of the legal limit that is set by law*. For a transaction to constitute usury, there must be a loan with an agreement to pay a higher interest rate than the law allows. Both lender and borrower must understand that the money is to be paid back, and there must be a corrupt intent to charge more than the law allows. Usury laws vary by state and are frequently revised. If a rate appears usurious, the agent should advise his client to seek competent legal advice.

Discount Points and Yield

In making mortgage loans, lending institutions may charge *discount points* to increase the *yield* (profit) to the lender. In essence, discount points are simply a prepaid form of interest. Two aspects of discount points are important:

1. **Cost.** Each point charged by the lender costs somebody 1% of the loan amount and is paid at the time of loan closing.
2. **Effect.** The effect realized by the lender's charging points is to increase the effective interest rate. As a rule of thumb, each point charged will increase the loan's yield (effective interest rate) by one-eighth of a percentage point.

The following chart is helpful in illustrating this concept:
1 point = 1/8 of a percent increase in yield
2 points = 2/8 = 1/4 of a percent increase in yield
3 points = 3/8 of a percent increase in yield
4 points = 4/8 = 1/2 of a percent increase in yield

> **Test Tip!**
>
> Do not confuse the cost of discount points with the effect of points in regards to the yield. One point *costs* 1% of the loan amount but has the *effect* of one-eighth of 1% in the yield.

Lending institutions can charge discount points on conventional, Federal Housing Administration (FHA), or VA loans. Buyers or sellers can pay the points on all three types of loan, or they can choose a loan rate that requires no discount points. The buyer can negotiate with the lender any number of points to buy down the rate to a desirable rate, as long as she is paying the points. Each type of loan has limits on the amount of seller concessions; therefore, the total of points and other concessions paid by the seller for the buyer must not exceed those limits.

In the past, a buyer often paid points to buy down an interest rate. With the current low interest rates, many buyers opt for a "par" rate, the best rate they can get without discount points. Points are a "sunk cost." The borrower does not get them back when he sells or refinances. The borrower should look at the break-even point between a loan that has points and a par rate loan before making a choice. For example, the buyer could compare a $50,000 loan at 8.5% with no points and at 8% with 4 points. The following calculations show the effect to the borrower.

Points paid by borrower ($50,000 × 0.04)	= $2,000.00
Monthly principal and interest payment at 8.5% for 30 years	= 384.46
Monthly principal and interest payment at 8% for 30 years	= 366.88
Difference in payments	= 17.58 per month

Dividing the $2,000 paid in points by the monthly savings shows that it will take the borrower 113.76 months to save the $2,000 paid up front in points. That is approximately 9.5 years. Most loans are not held that long. Unless the borrower is reasonably sure of keeping the home that long or of selling it later under a loan assumption at the more advantageous 8% rate, the borrower may want to take the 8.5% loan with no points and invest the $2,000 elsewhere.

Loan Fees, Loan Values, and Loan-to-Value Ratio

Knowing the amount of PITI is an essential part of the prequalification process. If a buyer calls on a specific listing and absolutely wants only that property, then all the agent has to do is determine whether the prospective buyer qualifies for the PITI on that specific property. Most buyers, however, want to see a number of properties and need help in determining the amount of money a mortgage company is likely to lend them. If the agent determines the maximum amount of payment, including PITI, for which the client will qualify and the amount of money the client has for down payment and closing costs, he can calculate the maximum price the buyer can buy at the current interest rates.

Assisting the buyer in shopping for the best loan is one of the agent's most important duties. This does not mean referring buyer clients to a friend at XYZ Mortgage Company, unless XYZ Mortgage Company has the best loan types, rates, and closing costs.

The best loan for any buyer depends on a number of factors, including the amount of money she has for down payment and closing costs, his income and debt load, the length of time she intends to occupy the property, his credit score, and/or qualifications for a first-time home buyer program or for a no-down-payment loan, such as a VA or Rural Development (RD) loan.

Loan fees can vary greatly from one loan to another. The simple interest rate alone is not enough to determine the best loan. The annual percentage rate, a number that considers both the simple interest rate and closing costs, helps agents and clients compare loans more easily. A client planning to live in a property for 15 to 20 years or more may want to obtain the lowest interest rate possible even if he must pay more closing costs up front. A client knowing he is going to keep the property only two or three years may want to obtain a loan with a slightly higher interest rate with low or no closing costs. Some lenders offer loans with lender-funded closing costs, although at a slightly higher rate. An agent can calculate (or ask the mortgage banker to calculate) the break-even point between two loans.

Monthly principal and interest payment at 6.5% for 30 years, $2,500 closing costs	$632.07
Monthly principal and interest payment at 7% for 30 years, $0 closing costs	$665.30
Difference in monthly payments	$33.23

It will take more than 75 months before the borrower pays the extra $2,500 in closing costs. If she sells or refinances the property before 75 months, she will save with the higher interest loan.

Because a bank or other lending institution will not lend more than the appraised value of a property, *the loan value is always the lesser of the sales price or appraised value.* The loan amount is the loan value less the amount paid by the borrower as a down payment. Mortgage loans are generally classified according to their LTV.

Example: A buyer buys a home for $80,000. The appraised value of the home is also $80,000. If the buyer pays $16,000 as a down payment at closing, the LTV for this loan would be calculated as follows:

Loan Amount = $64,000 ($80,000 − $16,000)
Loan Value = $80,000
LTV = 80% ($64,000 ÷ $80,000)

If the borrower has 20% for a down payment, she may choose a conventional loan. There is usually no private mortgage insurance (PMI) with an 80% LTV ratio. This avoids the VA funding fee on VA loans and the mortgage insurance premium requirements of FHA. If she does not have 20% of the purchase price for a down payment, she can still go with a conventional loan. Most conventional loans require 5% down payment with that 5% coming from the borrower's own funds. RD loans and VA loans are usually the only no-down-payment loans; however, down-payment assistance is sometimes available for low- or moderate-income buyers, more often for first-time buyers. FHA loans are available with as little as 3% down payment and higher qualifying ratios than conventional loans.

MORTGAGE BASICS

In everyday language, we all refer to a "mortgage" as though it is one document that includes the obligation to pay back a loan on a property and also constitutes an encumbrance on the property. In actuality, a "mortgage" is two separate legal documents: a mortgage (promissory) note and a mortgage (or deed of trust). These documents are explained in this section.

The Mortgage Note (Promissory Note)

In making a mortgage loan, the lender requires the borrower to sign a **promissory note**, or bond (see Figure 11.7) The note, which must be in writing, provides evidence that a valid debt exists. The note contains a *promise that the borrower will be personally liable for paying the amount of money set forth* in the note and specifies the manner in which the debt is to be paid. Payment is typically in monthly installments of a stated amount commencing on a specified date. The note also states the annual rate of interest to be charged on the outstanding principal balance.

The note can be an interest-only note, on which interest is paid periodically until the note matures and the entire principal balance is paid at maturity. Construction notes are usually of this type. Or the note can be a single-payment loan that requires no payments on principal or interest until the note matures and the entire principal and interest is paid at maturity. This is seen more frequently in short-term notes. The note also can be an amortizing note, in which periodic payments are made on principal and interest until such time as the principal is completely paid. Most mortgage loans are of this type.

A **mortgage note** is *an IOU (promissory note) that is backed by a mortgage or a deed of trust pledging the property as collateral for the loan.* A valid mortgage note must contain a promise to pay a specified amount of money, must specify the terms of the repayment, and must be signed by the borrower. When the note is repaid, the mortgage or deed of trust is canceled. If the property is destroyed, condemned, or loses its value before the note is paid in full, the borrower is still responsible for paying the debt. If the lender forecloses on the property and the sale proceeds are insufficient to pay off the debt, the lender can get a deficiency judgment for the difference between the sale proceeds and what is actually owed

PROMISSORY NOTE

SATISFACTION: The debt evidenced by this Note has been satisfied in full this _____ day of _____, 19 ___.
Signed: _____

_____, N.C.
_____, 19 ___

$ _____

FOR VALUE RECEIVED the undersigned, jointly and severally, promise to pay to _____

_____ or order,

the principal sum of _____

DOLLARS ($ _____), with interest from _____, at the rate of _____ per cent (_____ %) per annum on the unpaid balance until paid or until default, both principal and interest payable in lawful money of the United States of America, at the office of _____

or at such place as the legal holder hereof may designate in writing. It is understood and agreed that additional amounts may be advanced by the holder hereof as provided in the instruments, if any, securing this Note and such advances will be added to the principal of this Note and will accrue interest at the above specified rate of interest from the date of advance until paid. The principal and interest shall be due and payable as follows:

If not sooner paid, the entire remaining indebtedness shall be due and payable on _____.

If payable in installments, each such installment shall, unless otherwise provided, be applied first to payment of interest then accrued and due on the unpaid principal balance, with the remainder applied to the unpaid principal.

Unless otherwise provided, this Note may be prepaid in full or in part at any time without penalty or premium. Partial prepayments shall be applied to installments due in reverse order of their maturity.

In the event of (a) default in payment of any installment of principal or interest hereof as the same becomes due and such default is not cured within ten (10) days from the due date, or (b) default under the terms of any instrument securing this Note, and such default is not cured within fifteen (15) days after written notice to maker, then in either such event the holder may without further notice, declare the remainder of the principal sum, together with all interest accrued thereon and, the prepayment premium, if any, at once due and payable. Failure to exercise this option shall not constitute a wavier of the right to exercise the same at any other time. The unpaid principal of this Note and any part thereof, accrued interest and all other sums due under this Note and the Deed of Trust, if any, shall bear interest at the rate of _____ per cent (_____ %) per annum after default until paid.

All parties to this Note, including maker and any sureties, endorsers, or guarantors hereby waive protest, presentment, notice of dishonor, and notice of acceleration of maturity and agree to continue to remain bound for the payment of principal, interest and all other sums due under this Note and the Deed of Trust notwithstanding any change or changes by way of release, surrender, exchange, modification or substitution of any security for this Note or by way of any extension or extensions of time for the payment of principal and interest; and all such parties waive all and every kind of notice of such change or changes and agree that the same may be made without notice or consent of any of them.

Upon default the holder of this Note may employ an attorney to enforce the holder's rights and remedies and the maker, principal, surety, guarantor and endorsers of this Note hereby agree to pay to the holder reasonable attorneys fees not exceeding a sum equal to fifteen percent (15%) of the outstanding balance owing on said Note, plus all other reasonable expenses incurred by the holder in exercising any of the holder's rights and remedies upon default. The rights and remedies of the holder as provided in this Note and any instrument securing this Note shall be cumulative and may be pursued singly, successively, or together against the property described in the Deed of Trust or any other funds, property or security held by the holder for payment or security, in the sole discretion of the holder. The failure to exercise any such right or remedy shall not be a waiver or release of such rights or remedies or the right to exercise any of them at another time.

This Note is to be governed and construed in accordance with the laws of the State of North Carolina.

This Note is given _____, and is secured by a _____ which is a _____ lien upon the property therein described.

IN TESTIMONY WHEREOF, each corporate maker has caused this instrument to be executed in its corporate name by its _____ President, attested by its _____ Secretary, and its corporate seal to be hereto affixed, all by order of its Board of Directors first duly given, the day and year first above written.

IN TESTIMONY WHEREOF, each individual maker has hereunto set his hand and adopted as his seal the word "SEAL" appearing beside his name, the day and year first above written.

(Corporate Name)
By: _____ President
ATTEST: _____ Secretary (Corporate Seal)

(Corporate Name)
By: _____ President
ATTEST: _____ Secretary (Corporate Seal)

USE BLACK INK ONLY

_____ (SEAL)
_____ (SEAL)
_____ (SEAL)
_____ (SEAL)
_____ (SEAL)
_____ (SEAL)

N.C. Bar Assoc. Form No. 4 © 1976, Revised © 1985 • Printed by Agreement with the N. C. Bar Assoc. — 1981 • James Williams & Co., Inc. • Box 127 • Yadkinville, NC 27055

Printed with permission by the North Carolina Bar Association.

FIGURE 11.7 A sample promissory note.

(for exceptions, see the sections "Deficiency Judgment" and "Nonrecourse Note"). This judgment would be a general lien allowing the lender to take action against other property belonging to the borrower.

Certain important items that are not essential to the validity of the note are often included in the note. These items are usually repeated in the mortgage or deed of trust. Nonessential items include acceleration clauses, prepayment penalty clauses, and due-on-sale clauses. An **acceleration clause** *provides the lender with the option of calling the entire loan due and payable at once if the buyer defaults or breaks the contract in any way.* Anything that violates the provisions of the note could trigger this clause. For example, the borrower could fail to make the payments or otherwise breach the contract by such actions as damaging the property, failing to make necessary repairs, or failing to maintain insurance.

A note may have a **prepayment penalty clause**, *which is a penalty in the event the mortgage is paid off faster than at the amortization rate stipulated.* This would include paying more for the monthly payment and would include loan payoffs, such as when the property is either sold or refinanced. Mortgage loans for personal residences rarely include such a clause. Government-backed loans (FHA, VA, and RD) and loans sold in the secondary mortgage market (conforming loans) do not allow prepayment penalties. North Carolina law prohibits prepayment penalties on first mortgage home loans with an original balance of $150,000 or less.

A lender frequently adds a **due-on-sale clause** (also called an **alienation clause**) to the note to *prevent a future purchaser from assuming the loan without the lender's permission.* A due-on-sale clause provides that if a buyer sells property to a new owner, the lender has the right to declare the entire note due and payable immediately. The lender does not have to declare the loan due and payable, however, and may allow the new owner to assume the loan at current market interest rates. In many ways, this due-on-sale clause is essentially a "nonassumption" clause because loans are generally assumable unless specifically prohibited in the loan agreement.

Negotiability of Note

Notes can either be negotiable or nonnegotiable. A **negotiable note** is a *written promise to pay a specified sum of money according to specified terms to the bearer or holder of the note.* The negotiable note will use such terms as "to bearer," "to holder," or "to a person or corporate or business entity, its heirs, successors, or assigns." It will not name an individual or entity as the payee, but rather it allows the payee to transfer its rights to receive payment to a third party. Most real estate notes are negotiable because mortgage lenders often sell their loans in the secondary mortgage markets. A **nonnegotiable note** is *a written promise to pay a specified sum of money according to specified terms to a particular individual or corporation,* thus limiting its ability to be sold in the secondary mortgage market.

Mortgage and Deed of Trust

Typically, a borrower's personal promise to pay a debt is not enough security for the large amount of money involved in a mortgage loan. Therefore, the lender requires the additional security of the property itself as collateral for the loan. When a *borrower pledges property as security for the loan without surrendering possession,* it is called **hypothecation**, and this is accomplished through the mortgage or deed of trust instrument. Therefore, every mortgage loan has two instruments: (1) the note (a personal IOU) and (2) the mortgage or deed of trust (a pledge of real property). Pledging the property does not require the borrower to give up possession unless the borrower **defaults**; that is, the borrower fails to make payments as scheduled or fails to fulfill other obligations as set forth in the mortgage or deed of trust.

The two main lending practices, or theories of financing, are (1) lien theory and (2) title theory.

Lien Theory

In **lien theory** (mortgage theory), *the loan constitutes a lien against the real property.* The **mortgage** is a two-party instrument between the lender and the borrower. *The borrower gives a piece of paper (mortgage) to the lender in return for the borrowed funds. The borrower who gives the mortgage is the* **mortgagor**. *The lender who receives the mortgage is the* **mortgagee**. The borrower (mortgagor) retains title to the property, but this title is encumbered by the lien created by the mortgage in favor of the lender (mortgagee). If the lender is not paid according to terms of the mortgage and note, the lender can execute the lien or foreclose on the mortgaged property. The mortgage creates a *specific lien* against the property. States that use mortgage theories are called lien theory states. Most states are lien theory states.

> **Test Tip!**
>
> North Carolina is a "title theory" state in regards to financing but a "pure race" state in regards to recordation. Make certain to use the correct theory with the correct topic in answering any test questions.

Title Theory

In **title theory** (granting theory), *a disinterested third party actually holds legal title to the property in security for the loan* through a **deed of trust** (see Figure 11.8). The deed of trust, which serves the same purpose as a mortgage in a lien theory state, is the legal instrument through which the buyer/borrower conveys legal title in the property to a neutral third party called the trustee. The buyer/

NORTH CAROLINA DEED OF TRUST

SATISFACTION: The debt secured by the within Deed of Trust together with the note(s) secured thereby has been satisfied in full.
This the _____ day of _____, 20___
Signed:_____
_____

Parcel Identifier No._____ Verified by _____ County on the ____ day of _____, 20__
By:_____

Mail/Box to: _____

This instrument was prepared by: _____

Brief description for the Index:_____

THIS DEED of TRUST made this _____ day of _____, 20____, by and between:

GRANTOR	TRUSTEE	BENEFICIARY

Enter in appropriate block for each party: name, address, and, if appropriate, character of entity, e.g. corporation or partnership.

The designation Grantor, Trustee, and Beneficiary as used herein shall include said parties, their heirs, successors, and assigns, and shall include singular, plural, masculine, feminine or neuter as required by context.

Page 1 of 5

Association Form No. 5 © Revised 7/2013
Printed by Agreement with the NC Bar Association

North Carolina Bar Association – NC Bar Form No. 5
North Carolina Association of Realtors®, Inc. – Standard Form 5

FIGURE 11.8 North Carolina deed of trust.
Source: This content is reproduced by permission of the North Carolina Bar Association.

WITNESSETH, That whereas the Grantor is indebted to the Beneficiary in the principal sum of _____ Dollars ($_____), as evidenced by a Promissory Note of even date herewith, the terms of which are incorporated herein by reference. The final due date for payments of said Promissory Note, if not sooner paid, is _____, 20__.

NOW, THEREFORE, as security for said indebtedness, advancements and other sums expended by Beneficiary pursuant to this Deed of Trust and costs of collection (including attorneys fees as provided in the Promissory Note) and other valuable consideration, the receipt of which is hereby acknowledged, the Grantor has bargained, sold, given and conveyed and does by these presents bargain, sell, give, grant and convey to said Trustee, his heirs, or successors, and assigns, all of that certain lot, parcel of land or condominium unit situated in the City of _____, _____ Township, _____ County, North Carolina, (the "Premises") and more particularly described as follows:

TO HAVE AND TO HOLD said Premises with all privileges and appurtenances thereunto belonging, to said Trustee, his heirs, successors, and assigns forever, upon the trusts, terms and conditions, and for the uses hereinafter set forth.

If the Grantor shall pay the Note secured hereby in accordance with its terms, together with interest thereon, and any renewals or extensions thereof in whole or in part, all other sums secured hereby and shall comply with all of the covenants, terms and conditions of this Deed of Trust, then this conveyance shall be null and void and may be canceled of record at the request and the expense of the Grantor.

If, however, there shall be any default (a) in the payment of any sums due under the Note, this Deed of Trust or any other instrument securing the Note and such default is not cured within ten (10) days from the due date, or (b) if there shall be default in any of the other covenants, terms or conditions of the Note secured hereby, or any failure or neglect to comply with the covenants, terms or conditions contained in this Deed of Trust or any other instrument securing the Note and such default is not cured within fifteen (15) days after written notice, then and in any of such events, without further notice, it shall be lawful for and the duty of the Trustee, upon request of the Beneficiary, to sell the land herein conveyed at public auction for cash, after having first giving such notice of hearing as to commencement of foreclosure proceedings and obtained such findings or leave of court as may then be required by law and giving such notice and advertising the time and place of such sale in such manner as may then be provided by law, and upon such and any resales and upon compliance with the law then relating to foreclosure proceedings under power of sale to convey title to the purchaser in as full and ample manner as the Trustee is empowered. The Trustee shall be authorized to retain an attorney to represent him in such proceedings.

The proceeds of the Sale shall after the Trustee retains his commission, together with reasonable attorneys fees incurred by the Trustee in such proceedings, be applied to the costs of sale, including, but not limited to, costs of collection, taxes, assessments, costs of recording, service fees and incidental expenditures, the amount due on the Note hereby secured and advancements and other sums expended by the Beneficiary according to the provisions hereof and otherwise as required by the then existing law relating to foreclosures. The Trustee's commission shall be five percent (5%) of the gross proceeds of the sale or the minimum sum of $_____ whichever is greater, for a completed foreclosure. In the event foreclosure is commenced, but not completed, the Grantor shall pay all expenses incurred by Trustee, including reasonable attorneys fees, and a partial commission computed on five per cent (5%) of the outstanding indebtedness or the above stated minimum sum, whichever is greater, in accordance with the following schedule, to-wit: one-fourth (¼) thereof before the Trustee issues a notice of hearing on the right to foreclosure; one-half (½) thereof after issuance of said notice, three-fourths (¾) thereof after such hearing; and the greater of the full commission or minimum sum after the initial sale.

And the said Grantor does hereby covenant and agree with the Trustee as follows:

1. INSURANCE. Grantor shall keep all improvements on said land, now or hereafter erected, constantly insured for the benefit of the Beneficiary against loss by fire, windstorm and such other casualties and contingencies, in such manner and in such companies and for such amounts, not less than that amount necessary to pay the sum secured by this Deed of Trust, and as may be satisfactory to the Beneficiary. Grantor shall purchase such insurance, pay all premiums therefor, and shall deliver to Beneficiary such policies along with evidence of premium payments as long as the Note secured hereby remains unpaid. If Grantor fails to purchase such insurance, pay premiums therefor or deliver said policies along with evidence of payment of premiums thereon, then Beneficiary, at his option, may purchase such insurance. Such amounts paid by Beneficiary shall be added to the principal of the Note secured by this Deed of Trust, and shall be due and payable upon demand of Beneficiary. All proceeds from any insurance so maintained shall at the option of Beneficiary be applied to the debt secured hereby and if payable in installments, applied in the inverse order of maturity of such installments or to the repair or reconstruction of any improvements located upon the Property.

Page 2 of 5

Association Form No. 5 © Revised 7/2013
Printed by Agreement with the NC Bar Association

North Carolina Bar Association – NC Bar Form No. 5
North Carolina Association of Realtors®, Inc. – Standard Form 5

FIGURE 11.8 (Continued)

2. TAXES, ASSESSMENTS, CHARGES. Grantor shall pay all taxes, assessments and charges as may be lawfully levied against said Premises within thirty (30) days after the same shall become due. In the event that Grantor fails to so pay all taxes, assessments and charges as herein required, then Beneficiary, at his option, may pay the same and the amounts so paid shall be added to the principal of the Note secured by this Deed of Trust, and shall be due and payable upon demand of Beneficiary.

3. ASSIGNMENTS OF RENTS AND PROFITS. Grantor assigns to Beneficiary, in the event of default, all rents and profits from the land and any improvements thereon, and authorizes Beneficiary to enter upon and take possession of such land and improvements, to rent same, at any reasonable rate of rent determined by Beneficiary, and after deducting from any such rents the cost of reletting and collection, to apply the remainder to the debt secured hereby.

4. PARTIAL RELEASE. Grantor shall not be entitled to the partial release of any of the above described property unless a specific provision providing therefor is included in this Deed of Trust. In the event a partial release provision is included in this Deed of Trust, Grantor must strictly comply with the terms thereof. Notwithstanding anything herein contained, Grantor shall not be entitled to any release of property unless Grantor is not in default and is in full compliance with all of the terms and provisions of the Note, this Deed of Trust, and any other instrument that may be securing said Note.

5. WASTE. The Grantor covenants that he will keep the Premises herein conveyed in as good order, repair and condition as they are now, reasonable wear and tear excepted, and will comply with all governmental requirements respecting the Premises or their use, and that he will not commit or permit any waste.

6. CONDEMNATION. In the event that any or all of the Premises shall be condemned and taken under the power of eminent domain, Grantor shall give immediate written notice to Beneficiary and Beneficiary shall have the right to receive and collect all damages awarded by reason of such taking, and the right to such damages hereby is assigned to Beneficiary who shall have the discretion to apply the amount so received, or any part thereof, to the indebtedness due hereunder and if payable in installments, applied in the inverse order of maturity of such installments, or to any alteration, repair or restoration of the Premises by Grantor.

7. WARRANTIES. Grantor covenants with Trustee and Beneficiary that he is seized of the Premises in fee simple, has the right to convey the same in fee simple, that title is marketable and free and clear of all encumbrances, and that he will warrant and defend the title against the lawful claims of all persons whomsoever, except for the exceptions hereinafter stated. Title to the property hereinabove described is subject to the following exceptions:

8. SUBSTITUTION OF TRUSTEE. Grantor and Trustee covenant and agree to and with Beneficiary that in case the said Trustee, or any successor trustee, shall die, become incapable of acting, renounce his trust, or for any reason the holder of the Note desires to replace said Trustee, then the holder may appoint, in writing, a trustee to take the place of the Trustee; and upon the probate and registration of the same, the trustee thus appointed shall succeed to all rights, powers and duties of the Trustee.

☐ **THE FOLLOWING PARAGRAPH, 9. SALE OF PREMISES, SHALL NOT APPLY UNLESS THE BLOCK TO THE LEFT MARGIN OF THIS SENTENCE IS MARKED AND/OR INITIALED.**

9. SALE OF PREMISES. Grantor agrees that if the Premises or any part thereof or interest therein is sold, assigned, transferred, conveyed or otherwise alienated by Grantor, whether voluntarily or involuntarily or by operation of law [other than: (i) the creation of a lien or other encumbrance subordinate to this Deed of Trust which does not relate to a transfer of rights of occupancy in the Premises; (ii) the creation of a purchase money security interest for household appliances; (iii) a transfer by devise, descent, or operation of law on the death of a joint tenant or tenant by the entirety; (iv) the grant of a leasehold interest of three (3) years or less not containing an option to purchase; (v) a transfer to a relative resulting from the death of a Grantor; (vi) a transfer where the spouse or children of the Grantor become the owner of the Premises; (vii) a transfer resulting from a decree of a dissolution of marriage, legal separation agreement, or from an incidental property settlement agreement, by which the spouse of the Grantor becomes an owner of the Premises; (viii) a transfer into an inter vivos trust in which the Grantor is and remains a beneficiary and which does not relate to a transfer of rights of occupancy in the Premises], without the prior written consent of Beneficiary, Beneficiary, at its own option, may declare the Note secured hereby and all other obligations hereunder to be forthwith due and payable. Any change in the legal or equitable title of the Premises or in the beneficial ownership of the Premises, including the sale, conveyance or disposition of a majority interest in the Grantor if a corporation or partnership, whether or not of record and whether or not for consideration, shall be deemed to be the transfer of an interest in the Premises.

10. ADVANCEMENTS. If Grantor shall fail to perform any of the covenants or obligations contained herein or in any other instrument given as additional security for the Note secured hereby, the Beneficiary may, but without obligation, make advances to perform such covenants or obligations, and all such sums so advanced shall be added to the principal sum, shall bear interest at the rate provided in the Note secured hereby for sums due after default and shall be due from Grantor on demand of the Beneficiary. No advancement or anything contained in this paragraph shall constitute a waiver by Beneficiary or prevent such failure to perform from constituting an event of default.

11. INDEMNITY. If any suit or proceeding be brought against the Trustee or Beneficiary or if any suit or proceeding be brought which may affect the value or title of the Premises, Grantor shall defend, indemnify and hold harmless and on demand reimburse Trustee or Beneficiary from any loss, cost, damage or expense and any sums expended by Trustee or Beneficiary shall bear interest as provided in the Note secured hereby for sums due after default and shall be due and payable on demand.

12. WAIVERS. Grantor waives all rights to require marshaling of assets by the Trustee or Beneficiary. No delay or omission of the Trustee or Beneficiary in the exercise of any right, power or remedy arising under the Note or this Deed of Trust shall be

Page 3 of 5

Association Form No. 5 © Revised 7/2013
Printed by Agreement with the NC Bar Association

North Carolina Bar Association – NC Bar Form No. 5
North Carolina Association of Realtors®, Inc. – Standard Form 5

FIGURE 11.8 (Continued)

deemed a waiver of any default or acquiescence therein or shall impair or waive the exercise of such right, power or remedy by Trustee or Beneficiary at any other time.

    13. CIVIL ACTION. In the event that the Trustee is named as a party to any civil action as Trustee in this Deed of Trust, the Trustee shall be entitled to employ an attorney at law, including himself if he is a licensed attorney, to represent him in said action and the reasonable attorney's fee of the Trustee in such action shall be paid by the Beneficiary and added to the principal of the Note secured by this Deed of Trust and bear interest at the rate provided in the Note for sums due after default.

    14. PRIOR LIENS. Default under the terms of any instrument secured by a lien to which this Deed of Trust is subordinate shall constitute default hereunder.

    15. OTHER TERMS.

IN WITNESS WHEREOF, the Grantor has duly executed the foregoing as of the day and year first above written.

_____(SEAL)
                (Entity Name)

By:_____(SEAL)
      Title:_____

By:_____(SEAL)
      Title:_____

By:_____(SEAL)
      Title:_____

State of North Carolina - County of _____

    I, the undersigned Notary Public of the County and State aforesaid, certify that _____ personally appeared before me this day and acknowledged the due execution of the foregoing instrument for the purposes therein expressed. Witness my hand and Notarial stamp or seal this _____ day of _____, 20__.

My Commission Expires:_____

                                Notary Public

State of North Carolina - County of _____

    I, the undersigned Notary Public of the County and State aforesaid, certify that _____ personally appeared before me this day and acknowledged the due execution of the foregoing instrument for the purposes therein expressed. Witness my hand and Notarial stamp or seal this _____ day of _____, 20__.

My Commission Expires:_____

                                Notary Public

State of North Carolina - County of _____

    I, the undersigned Notary Public of the County and State aforesaid, certify that _____ _____ personally came before me this day and acknowledged that _he is the _____ of _____, a North Carolina or _____ corporation/limited liability company/general partnership/limited partnership (strike through the inapplicable), and that by authority duly given and as the act of such entity, _he signed the foregoing instrument in its name on its behalf as its act and deed. Witness my hand and Notarial stamp or seal, this _____ day of _____, 20__.

Page 4 of 5

Association Form No. 5 © Revised 7/2013
Printed by Agreement with the NC Bar Association   North Carolina Bar Association – NC Bar Form No. 5
                                                         North Carolina Association of Realtors®, Inc. – Standard Form 5

My Commission Expires:_____

                                Notary Public

Page 5 of 5

Association Form No. 5 © Revised 7/2013
Printed by Agreement with the NC Bar Association   North Carolina Bar Association – NC Bar Form No. 5
                                                         North Carolina Association of Realtors®, Inc. – Standard Form 5

FIGURE 11.8 (*Continued*)

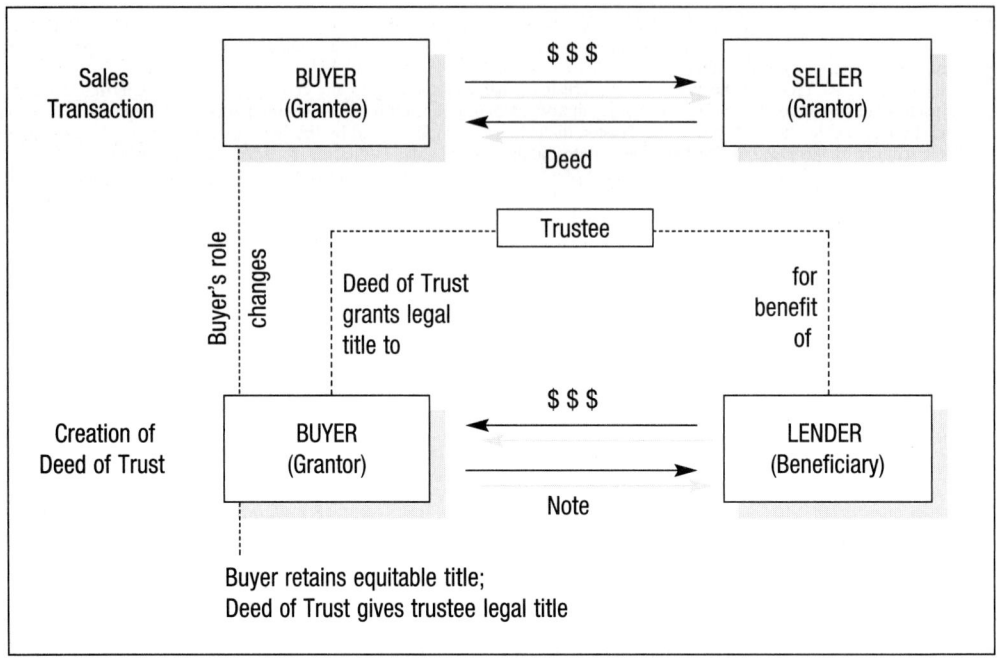

FIGURE 11.9 Relationships in a deed of trust transaction.

"Remember: BorrowOR, MortgagOR, TrustOR and GrantOR. When it comes to getting a loan the OR wants the money."
—Tim Terry, DREI

borrower retains equitable title in the property. This means that the buyer/borrower has the right to acquire legal title when the loan has been repaid. The **trustee**, who is usually an attorney, *holds the rights conveyed by the buyer/borrower in trust for the* **beneficiary**, who is the lender. The buyer/borrower, who is also called a **grantor** or **trustor**, signs a promissory note payable to the lender.

The lender then gives the buyer/borrower the money to buy the property (see Figure 11.9). If the buyer/borrower defaults on the promissory note, the beneficiary can ask the trustee who holds those rights conveyed by the buyer/borrower to begin foreclosure. *If the buyer/borrower lives up to the agreement he made with the beneficiary/lender by repaying the loan in full, the trustee will return all the rights conveyed.* This obligation on the part of the trustee is contained in a clause called the **defeasance clause**, which relates to the borrower's right to defeat, or pay off, the mortgage. It is the **power of sale clause** that gives the trustee the right to sell the property, without prior court approval being required, if the buyer defaults. Because legal title is conveyed, states that use deeds of trust are called title theory states. North Carolina is a title theory state. A deed of trust is a *specific lien* on the secured property.

One of the common misconceptions regarding real estate lending is the old saying of "it takes one to buy and two to sell." The question becomes is this statement really true or is it just a catchy phrase? There is no question that it really does only take one to buy but the question of how many to sell, or convey, is not quite as simple. It is important to remember that a deed of trust is a type of deed and deeds require all owners and marital rights interests to sign in order to convey. Even if one spouse were to sign the promissory note, if the lender would even allow it, there is still the requirement that both would have to sign the deed of trust. Remember, there are no marital rights for the promissory note, only the deed of trust. One spouse may be signing away their ownership rights and the other their marital rights, but it still takes two. Likewise if the couple is married, then there are two owners and clearly a requirement that both sign the document.

Mortgage or Deed of Trust—Essential Elements

For a mortgage or deed of trust to be legal and valid, it must contain the following essential elements:

1. The mortgage or deed of trust must be in writing, as required by the Statute of Frauds, because the mortgage or deed of trust pledges or conveys title to real property to secure payment of the note.
2. Because the mortgage or deed of trust is a contract, all parties must be identified and have contractual capacity.
3. There must be a valid debt to be secured by the mortgage or deed of trust. The existence of the valid debt is evidenced by the note.
4. To secure the debt in the mortgage or deed of trust, the mortgagor or trustor must have a valid interest in the property pledged or conveyed.
5. A legally acceptable description of the property must be included.
6. The mortgage or deed of trust must contain a mortgaging clause. In lien theory states, which use a mortgage form, the mortgaging clause is a statement demonstrating the mortgagor's intention to mortgage the property to the mortgagee. In title theory states, this clause takes the form of a deed of conveyance. The mortgaging clause in this case reads like the granting clause in a deed. This is not an absolute conveyance of title by the borrower; rather, it is a conditional conveyance made only to secure payment of the note.
7. The mortgage or deed of trust must contain a defeasance clause that defeats the lien and conveyance of title when the mortgage debt is fully satisfied.
8. The borrower must properly execute the mortgage or deed of trust. Only the borrower or grantor signs the document. The lender does not sign.
9. The mortgage or deed of trust must be delivered to and accepted by the mortgagee or trustee/beneficiary (lender).

"A Deed of Trust says to the lender, 'Trust me. I will repay the loan or you can take my deed.'"
—Terry Wilson, DREI

Clauses and Covenants

Examples of the various clauses and covenants included in a mortgage or deed of trust follow:

1. The note executed by the borrower, including acceleration, alienation, due-on-sale, and prepayment penalty clauses, is referenced in the mortgage or deed of trust.

2. The mortgage and the deed of trust require the borrower to pay all real property taxes and assessments on a timely basis, keep the buildings in a proper state of repair and preservation, and protect the buildings against loss by fire or other casualty with an insurance policy written in an amount at least 80% of the value of the structures. Many lenders also require insurance for 100% of the loan value minus the lot value.
3. Both documents provide the right of foreclosure to the lender if the borrower defaults.
4. In the mortgage form and the deed of trust form, a covenant specifies that the borrower must have a good and marketable title to the property that is being pledged to secure payment of the note.
5. The mortgage or deed of trust may contain an alienation or due-on-sale clause entitling the lender to declare the principal balance immediately due and payable if the borrower sells the property during the loan term. The clause makes the loan unassumable without the lender's permission. Permission to assume the mortgage at an interest rate prevailing at the time of assumption can be given at the discretion of the lender. The alienation clause can provide for release of the original borrower from liability if an assumption is permitted. This release is sometimes referred to as a *novation*.
6. The mortgage or deed of trust always provides for execution by the borrower.
7. The mortgage or deed of trust provides for *acknowledgment* by the borrower to make the document eligible for recording on the public record for the lender's protection.

Rights of Mortgage Borrowers

A borrower under a mortgage or deed of trust has the following rights:

1. The borrower has the right to possession of the property during the mortgage term as long as the borrower is not in default.
2. The defeasance clause gives the borrower the right to redeem the title or have the mortgage lien released at any time prior to default by paying the debt in full (i.e., to defeat the mortgage).
3. The borrower has the right of equity of redemption.

Equity of Redemption (Right of Redemption)

The *borrower has the right to pay off the loan and receive his title back any time before the final foreclosure sale.* This common law right is known as the **equity of redemption** or right of redemption. To be certain, foreclosure is not a necessity to utilize this right. For most borrowers, the equity of redemption is carried out by simply paying off the loan, whether by selling the property, refinancing, or just paying off the balance. In the event foreclosure becomes necessary, the borrower has the right to redeem his title any time prior to the final foreclosure action being completed. The equity of redemption period is strictly prior to final foreclosure sale as the final act of foreclosure terminates the borrower's equity of redemption.

After the sale of the property on the courthouse steps, a borrower has a different type of redemption right known as the statutory redemption period. The **statutory redemption period** *is strictly after the final foreclosure sale and is often referred to as the upset bid period.* In North Carolina, the highest bid on the courthouse steps must stand for a period of 10 days subject to an upset bid of at least 5% more than the highest bid with a minimum amount of $750. For example, if a house sold on the courthouse steps for $200,000, the minimum upset bid must be at least $210,000 and that bid would then be subject to an upset bid of at least 5% higher, that is $220,500. Finalization of the foreclosure sale after the end of the last 10-day upset bid period without an acceptable bid ends the statutory redemption period as well as the borrower's equity of redemption.

Rights of Lender

In lending funds to finance a mortgage, the lender has the following rights:

1. The lender has the right to transfer or to assign the mortgage note and mortgage or deed of trust. This enables the lender to sell the loan, if he so desires, and thereby free up the money invested. The **right of assignment** provides liquidity to the loan because the *lender can sell the loan at any time and obtain the money invested rather than wait for payment of the loan over an extended time.*
2. The lender has the right to foreclose on the property and to take possession of the property (after foreclosure) if the borrower defaults on loan payments.

Foreclosure

If the borrower does not make the payments as required or fails to fulfill other obligations as set forth in the mortgage or deed of trust, she is in default on the loan. The lender's ultimate power is to foreclose. **Foreclosure** is the *liquidation of title to the real property pledged to recover funds to pay off the debt.* This foreclosure right is what the lender utilizes to terminate the borrower's right of equity or redemption. The three types of foreclosure are *judicial, nonjudicial,* and strict.

Judicial Foreclosure. Judicial foreclosure, common in lien theory states, *requires the lender to bring a lawsuit against the borrower and obtain a judgment for the amount of debt the borrower owes.* When the judgment is obtained, the lender requests the court to issue an execution instructing the sheriff to take possession of the mortgaged property and sell it for cash to the highest bidder at a public auction. Because foreclosure in a judicial foreclosure state requires prior court approval as well as supervision, it generally takes much longer to conclude than it does in a nonjudicial state. Title is conveyed to the purchaser by a sheriff's deed or a trustee's deed.

Nonjudicial Foreclosure. Nonjudicial foreclosure, or **foreclosure under power of sale**, common in title theory states, *does not require the lender to bring a lawsuit against the defaulting borrower to obtain a judgment to foreclose*. It is, therefore, not court ordered. The North Carolina deed of trust form (Figure 11.8) has a power of sale clause that gives the trustee the right to foreclose after complying with all legal requirements for foreclosure. This type of foreclosure can generally be completed much more quickly than in the previous judicial foreclosure theory.

Nonjudicial foreclosure requires the mortgagee or trustee to file an abbreviated or summary court proceeding with a hearing before the clerk of the superior court. The sale of the property is advertised by posting a notice for a period of at least 15 days at the courthouse in the county where the property is located. The mortgagee or trustee must also advertise the sale in a newspaper published in the county in which the property is located at least once a week for a minimum of two consecutive weeks. The deed of trust may call for more stringent posting and advertising rules than required by state statutes. In both cases, the advertisement must describe the property and appoint a day and an hour for the sale to be held. Assuming the clerk of the court confirms the trustee's right to continue with the foreclosure, the sale is conducted by the trustee, who conveys the title to the new purchaser by a trustee's deed after the last 10-day upset period ends without a bid.

Strict Foreclosure. Under **strict foreclosure**, *the lender files a foreclosure petition with the court after the mortgagor is in default*. The court then issues a decree requiring the borrower to satisfy the mortgage debt within a stated period of time or lose his equitable right to redeem the title. Once this right is lost, the borrower cannot assert rights in the title, and the court awards legal title to the lender. The borrower forfeits all monies previously paid and has no right to surplus funds generated by the sale of the property. This type of foreclosure is not used in North Carolina, nor has it been in favor in the United States since the Great Depression.

Assignment. Lenders typically want the mortgage documents drafted where the loan and collateral is *for the benefit of the lenders and or his assigns*. By making the mortgage assignable, it will be payable either to the lender or whoever they decide to assign, or transfer, it to. This allows the lender to package the loan and sell it to investor groups thereby freeing up the money so that the lender can make new loans and thus new fees. Many lenders will primarily make their money by "manufacturing" new loans, selling them, and keeping the servicing contract. This will be discussed later in this chapter when the secondary market is explained.

Deed in Lieu of Foreclosure

In a measure sometimes called a friendly foreclosure but more formally a **deed in lieu of foreclosure**, *a borrower in default simply conveys the title to the property to the lender to avoid record of foreclosure.* Contrary to popular belief, the borrower cannot exercise this by simply handing the lender the keys. It can only be done by delivery and the voluntary acceptance of the deed by the lender. One disadvantage to the lender is that it does not eliminate other liens against the property. Furthermore, the lender loses the right to claim against mortgage insurance or guarantee programs such as FHA or VA as well as possible forfeiture of the ability to obtain a deficiency judgment against the borrower.

Distribution of Sale Proceeds

Proceeds of the mortgage or deed of trust foreclosure sale are distributed in the following order of priority:

1. All expenses of the sale are paid. These include court costs, trustee's fee, advertising fees, legal fees, accounting fees, and the like.
2. Any delinquent real or personal property tax liens and assessment liens are paid.
3. If there are no other lien holders with liens having priority over the lien of the mortgage or deed of trust, the lender is paid.
4. Any other creditors holding liens against the property are paid; however, creditors who are not secured by the foreclosed property are not paid from sale proceeds.
5. Any remaining monies (any surplus of equity) after items 1 through 4 have been satisfied are paid to the borrower.

Deficiency Judgment

The borrower in a mortgage loan is personally liable for payment of the note. Therefore, if the proceeds of a foreclosure sale are not sufficient to satisfy the balance due the lender, the lender can sue for a deficiency judgment on the note. A **deficiency judgment** is *a court order stating that the borrower still owes the lender money.* NOTE: North Carolina does not allow deficiency judgments when a seller forecloses on a purchase money mortgage (seller financing), as discussed later in this chapter.

Nonrecourse Note

One situation in which deficiency judgments are not available to the lender is in the case of a **nonrecourse note**. This type of note typically is used in mortgage loans secured by commercial property. Nonrecourse means *the borrower assumes no personal liability for paying the note;* therefore, the lender can look only to the property pledged in the mortgage to obtain the money owed in a case of default by the borrower.

Short Sale

The sharp and sustained decline in the real estate and general economy in the recent past caused a substantial decline in real estate values at the same time many people were losing their jobs. As more people needed for whatever reason to sell their house, many found that they were in the extremely difficult position of owing more money on their mortgage(s) than the property was worth. Such situations are commonly referred to as "underwater" or "upside down" or negative equity." The problem is the seller cannot sell his property and convey clear title without paying off the existing debt. In this situation, the seller may appeal to the lender for relief by allowing seller to sell the property for the price it is capable of bringing in the marketplace and by the lender accepting a reduced amount of money as the loan payoff. In other words, the owner may request the lender's approval of what is called a "short sale." At that point, the lender will essentially allow the property to be conveyed free from the old loan. Unfortunately, many borrowers fail to recognize that just because a lender agrees to a short sale, the lender has not necessarily relinquished its right to collect the amount of the loan that was not covered by the "short sale." It is extremely important for sellers to obtain competent legal advice concerning any future liability they might have to the lender before agreeing to a short sale.

Although different lenders have differing policies on how they handle the short sale process, there is much more in common than there are differences among these lenders. Generally a short sale application will be required along with a cover letter, a letter of hardship, supporting documentation as to the seller's finances, projections of the property's current value in the marketplace, and an estimate of proceeds using the U.S. Department of Housing and Urban Development (HUD)-1 form. In other words, the seller must "qualify" for a short sale on the lender's terms. It is very important for the real estate broker to recognize that his role is strictly that of a brokerage agent and not a legal or tax advisor. Agents are not allowed to negotiate revised loan terms or similar legal issues but are limited to more of a clerical role in assisting the process between the lender and the borrower. Numerous legal services in the marketplace will now assist the parties by handling the legal issues involved, thus hopefully reducing the agent's exposure to liability in these types of transactions.

SALES OF MORTGAGED PROPERTIES

Properties being sold often have loans secured by a mortgage or deed of trust. For the seller to give clear title to the buyer, these loans must be addressed. This can be done in several ways. The seller can pay off the existing loan with the proceeds from a cash sale. If the buyer has obtained new financing, the funds from the new loan provide cash to the seller to pay off the existing mortgage at closing. In both of these cases, the payoff of the loan cancels the mortgage or deed of trust and the seller has no further liability for the debt. Two other methods of addressing the existing loan are for the buyer to assume the loan or take title to the property "subject to" the lien of an existing loan.

There are three types of transactions in which the seller has an existing loan on the property that must be addressed at the closing:

1. Cash sale in which the existing loan is paid off
2. Loan assumption in which the seller's old loan is not paid off at the closing but rather is assumed by the purchaser
3. Taking title "subject to" an existing loan in which the old loan is not paid off at closing and the purchaser doesn't assume it either

Cash Sales

Technically, any transaction in which the seller receives all cash for the property at closing would qualify as a cash sale. The vast majority of these types of transactions will involve the purchaser obtaining financing to provide the seller with the necessary cash in which to purchase. The advantage to the seller of the cash sale is the former mortgage will be paid off at the closing, thus leaving the seller with no lingering liability from the old loan. It is not unusual for many parties to think that if the buyer has to obtain financing, the transaction is not really a cash sale. From the perspective of the seller receiving all of his money at the closing, it is a cash sale.

That is not the only type of cash sale that provides the seller all of his money at the closing. A cash sale can be as simple as the seller providing a deed and the buyer providing the cash. It is quite common for many parties to consider only this type of situation as a cash sale. Unfortunately, the simplicity of these cash transactions may cause an inexperienced real estate practitioner to make costly mistakes. No lender is involved in the transaction demanding an appraisal, a survey, a wood-destroying insect inspection, a structural inspection, deed recordation, payment of taxes or transfer fee, title search, and so on. Nonetheless, real estate practitioners have an obligation to make a reasonable effort to know and disclose to the buyer anything that might materially affect the value of the property and to safeguard the interests of their clients and be fair to the other party.

Loan Assumption

Although most conventional fixed-rate real estate loans are not assumable, some are, along with FHA-insured and VA-guaranteed loans (discussed later in this chapter). When a purchaser assumes the seller's existing loan, the purchaser assumes liability for the loan and personal liability for payment of the note. Therefore, purchasers who default in loan payments can lose their property as a result of a foreclosure sale and may be subject to a deficiency judgment obtained by the lender. In North Carolina, mortgage loans are generally assumable unless specifically prohibited. Therefore, a mortgage that does not state within the loan terms that the loan cannot be assumed is generally assumable (i.e., you can assume the loan unless it specifically states that you can't). However, a vast majority of mortgage loans today are not assumable. The clause that is utilized to prohibit the ability of a buyer to assume the seller's mortgage is the due-on-sale, or alienation, clause.

In a **loan assumption**, the *seller whose loan was assumed remains liable for the loan and payment of the note unless specifically released from liability by the lender.* If the purchaser defaults and the proceeds of a foreclosure sale are insufficient to pay off the loan, the seller whose loan was assumed may be subject to a deficiency judgment by the lender. The lender can foreclose against the current title holder and can sue the original borrower (or anyone who assumed the loan from the original borrower before the current defaulting borrower assumed it) for a deficiency judgment if the proceeds of the foreclosure sale do not satisfy the loan debt. The seller's agent has a responsibility to inform the seller of a property sold under a loan assumption about potential future liability and the benefits of a release of liability from the lender at the time of sale; however, the agent should refer his client to an attorney for legal advice, if necessary. Most loans made since the late 1980s require a release of liability as a condition of assumability.

Taking Title "Subject to" a Loan

If property is sold and title is conveyed subject to the lien of an existing loan (but that lien is not actually "assumed"), the lender can still foreclose against the property in the event of a default in loan payments. In taking title **subject to a loan**, *the new purchaser does not become liable for payment of the note.* Therefore, the lender cannot sue the purchaser for a deficiency judgment; she can obtain a deficiency judgment only against the seller, who remains personally liable for paying the debt as evidenced by the note. When purchasing a property using a wraparound mortgage or a land sales contract, a purchaser can take title or some degree of title "subject to" a loan backed by a mortgage or deed of trust. A buyer cannot purchase a mortgaged property financed after the late 1980s "subject to" the mortgage loan because most loans since that time have a due-on-sale clause or require a loan assumption with release of liability.

CATEGORIES OF RESIDENTIAL FIRST MORTGAGE LOANS

Most real estate transactions require new financing. The savings and loan problems and mortgage foreclosures in many areas of the country prompted mortgage lenders, the FHA, the VA, and PMI companies to tighten requirements for new financing. To help buyers choose the most advantageous method of new financing, today's real estate practitioner needs a thorough knowledge of real estate finance. Knowledge of down payments, closing cost regulations, amounts of allowable seller or third-party contributions, and methods of structuring the best possible payment plans is essential to a successful real estate transaction involving new financing.

This section discusses the various ways in which the buyer can finance the purchase of real property. The various types of loan that an individual can obtain from lending institutions are divided into two groups: (1) Conventional loans are loans in which there is no participation by an agency of the federal government, and (2) government loans are those in which the federal government participates, either by insuring the loan to protect the lender (e.g., FHA-insured loans) or by guaranteeing that the loan will be repaid (e.g., VA-guaranteed loans). The government also participates in loans through the RD and Farm Service Agency (FSA), a division of the U.S. Department of Agriculture (USDA). RD loans can be direct or guaranteed loans. The FSA makes direct loans.

Conventional Loans

A **conventional loan**, *one that has no participation by an agency of the federal government*, can be uninsured or insured. In the **uninsured** conventional loan, the borrower's *equity* in the property provides sufficient security for the lender to make the loan; therefore, insurance to protect the lender in case of the borrower's default is not required. In these cases, the borrower obtains a loan that does not exceed 80% of the property value and thus has an equity of at least 20%. An **insured** conventional loan typically is a conventional loan in which the borrower has a down payment of less than 20% and therefore borrows at least 80% of the property value. In these cases, *insuring repayment of the top portion of the loan to the lender is necessary in the event the borrower defaults.* The insurance is called **private mortgage insurance (PMI)**, and private insurance companies issue the policies. Today, PMI companies insure more mortgage loans than the FHA does. The premiums and features of PMI have grown more varied and complex in recent years.

The borrower pays the premium for the insurance. PMI is paid at closing, financed into the loan amount, or paid monthly. When the borrower's equity in the property reaches 20% of the current value, the borrower may request the lender to discontinue the insurance requirement. The lender must automatically do so at 78%.

Conventional loans are also referred to as "**conforming**" or "**nonconforming**." Conforming conventional mortgage loans are those that comply with Federal National Mortgage Association/Federal Home Loan Mortgage Corporation (FNMA/FHLMC) guidelines and are made using standardized loan forms.

Nonconforming conventional loans do not met these guidelines and standards. By making a conventional loan that is "conforming," the lender has the ability to sell the loan in the secondary market, thus freeing up funds for future loans. There will be a more detailed discussion of conforming/nonconforming as well as FNMA/FHLMC guidelines in the secondary market section that appears later in this chapter.

Another type of conventional mortgage loan is the "home equity loan" ("home equity line of credit" (HELOC)). In this type loan, the borrower will pledge his home as collateral to set up a line of credit that can be drawn against. Typically the lender will establish a maximum amount of loan that can be obtained using the HELOC; the borrower can borrow funds and later pay down the balance and later borrow again using the same mortgage. Unlike most mortgage loans, the borrower can pay the balance down to zero, but the mortgage loan still exists where the borrower can continue to borrow against the line of credit. These will often serve as a second mortgage and can result in foreclosure if the borrower becomes delinquent on the payments.

FHA-Insured Loans

Part of the mission of the **FHA**, created during the depression of the 1930s, *was to make home ownership available to more people, to improve housing construction standards, and to provide a more effective and stable method of financing homes.* It succeeded in this mission and provided the leadership to standardize procedures for qualifying buyers, appraising property, and evaluating construction. FHA has been an agency of HUD since 1968.

FHA does not make mortgage loans or supply the funds for FHA loans. Instead, the FHA insures loans on real property made by FHA-approved lenders. An **FHA-insured loan** *protects lenders against financial loss.* The buyer pays for this insurance protection by paying an **upfront mortgage insurance premium (UFMIP)** at closing and an annual **mortgage insurance premium (MIP)** prorated monthly and paid with the monthly mortgage payment. This insurance enables the FHA-approved lenders to provide financing when the **LTV ratio** is high. As explained earlier, LTV ratio *compares the loan amount to the property value.* With a high ratio, the borrower has to make only a small down payment. The amount of insurance protection to the lender is sufficient to protect the lender from financial loss in the event of a foreclosure sale because these loans are insured for 100% of the loan amount.

The most popular FHA program is the FHA 203(b) loan, which allows an owner-occupant to purchase a one- to four-family dwelling with an FHA-insured loan. FHA now offers a **reverse mortgage**, FHA 255, which is designed for senior citizens, age 62 or older, who need to access the equity in their home while continuing to occupy it. The FHA 255 provides a monthly income for the mortgagor and sometimes also pays debts or the existing mortgage. The mortgage loan does not have to be paid as long as the mortgagors continue to occupy the home. When their occupancy terminates, the property is sold and the mortgage loan is paid out of the proceeds. The FHA 245 graduated payment loan, the FHA 203(k) purchase and rehabilitation loan, and the FHA 234(c) condominium loan are also available when circumstances warrant. The FHA 245 is also used to purchase a one- to four-family owner-occupied dwelling; however, the 203(k) and 234(c) is used only to purchase a single-family owner-occupied unit.

FHA 203(b) Regular Loan Program

The FHA 203(b) regular loan program is the original and still the basic FHA program. It provides for insuring loans for the purchase or construction of one- to four-family dwellings. FHA does not set a maximum sales price, only a maximum loan amount. A buyer can purchase a home for more than the FHA maximum loan amount, but she must pay any amount above the maximum loan amount in cash. The maximum loan amount is based on *acquisition cost,* which is a combination of FHA-appraised value or sales price (whichever is lower) plus 100% of the buyer's closing costs the FHA will allow to be financed.

FHA Maximum Loan Amount

HUD or FHA sets basic loan limits for one- to four-family dwellings. Higher maximum loan limits are allowed in geographic regions designated as high-cost areas. For a more detailed listing of the maximum loan amounts for the various counties in North Carolina, refer to https://entp.hud.gov/idapp/html/hicost1.cfm. FHA guidelines require the purchaser to occupy a single-family dwelling or one unit of a two- to four-family dwelling.

FHA MIP

There are two phases of the FHA MIP: the upfront (or initial) premium (UFMIP) and the annual renewal premium (MIP). Currently, the UFMIP is set at 1.50% of the maximum FHA loan limits established for selected areas of North Carolina and is not affected by the term of the loan or the LTV ratio. Borrowers have a choice of paying the UFMIP in cash at closing or financing it into the loan. Most borrowers choose to finance it. Note that *the maximum loan amount for the area can be exceeded by the amount of the UFMIP if it is financed into the loan.*

Although the UFMIP charged on FHA loans is fixed at 1.50% for all FHA loans, the annual renewal premium varies based on the loan term and the LTV ratio. The annual premium ranges from 0 to 0.5% of the average unpaid principal balance.

FHA Loan Qualification

Under current FHA loan qualification guidelines, the monthly housing expenses composed of principal, interest, taxes, homeowner's insurance, MIP paid monthly, and homeowners association dues or assessments (if any) cannot exceed 31% of gross income.

The total housing expenses plus any of the borrower's recurring monthly debts that will extend for 10 months or more cannot exceed 43% of monthly gross income.

FHA Loan Assumption Policies

The HUD Reform Act of 1989 effectively stopped making new loans that allowed assumptions without a new buyer being able to give release of liability. For loans that originated after December 15, 1989, an assumption by a buyer wishing to occupy the property is allowed only after a complete buyer qualification. Furthermore, an assumption by a buyer looking to invest in the property is not allowed.

FHA Changes

Significant changes have taken place in the FHA home loan program since its inception. Real estate agents should understand these changes when selling properties purchased with FHA loans that originated under rules different from those currently in effect. When such a property is listed, the agent should obtain copies of the documents relating to the original sale to determine what rules apply to the present sale in the case of a loan assumption or a loan payoff. Rules for loan assumption qualification, release of liability, notification, and time of payoffs are important, and they differ according to when the loan was underwritten. Agents should remain current regarding FHA guidelines by looking to their broker-in-charge, the firm's training or loan processing department, a trade publication, or an FHA-approved lender.

Contract Requirements

When a sales contract contingent upon the buyer's obtaining an FHA-insured loan is created before an FHA appraisal and commitment to insure, the FHA requires that the contract contain the following wording:

> It is expressly agreed that, notwithstanding any other provisions of this contract, the purchaser shall not be obligated to complete the purchase of the property described herein or to incur any penalty by forfeiture of earnest money deposit or otherwise unless the seller has delivered to the purchaser a written statement issued by the Federal Housing Commissioner setting forth the appraised value of the property (exclusive of closing costs) of not less than $_____$, which statement seller hereby agrees to deliver to the purchaser promptly after such appraised value statement is made available to the seller. The purchaser shall, however, have the privilege and option of proceeding with the consummation of this contract without regard to the amount of the appraised valuation made by

the Federal Housing Commissioner. The appraised valuation is arrived at to determine the maximum mortgage the Department will insure. HUD does not warrant the value or the condition of the property. The purchaser should satisfy himself/herself that the price and the condition of the property are acceptable.

FHA loans, as well as all other loans and sales of residential property built before 1978, require a lead-based paint disclosure to be signed on or before the date of the contract of sale. FHA required disclosure long before the newer federal law requiring disclosure was enacted (see Chapter 6 and Appendix F, Lead-Based Paint or Lead-Based Paint Hazard Addendum form, for additional information).

FHA requires all FHA buyers to sign the form "For Your Protection: Get a Home Inspection," HUD Form 92564-Cn, before signing the offer to purchase. Failure to do so will require the Offer to Purchase and Contract to be re-executed. This form informs the buyer what FHA does and does not do for her, defines the difference between appraisals and home inspections, and explains what a home inspection is and why a buyer needs one. FHA treats the home inspection as an allowable closing cost when determining maximum loan amount and cash required to close.

> "The provisions in federal law which state that an FHA borrower or VA borrower has the right to cancel if the property does not appraise and have their funds returned to them is sometimes referred to as an 'Exculpatory Clause' or an 'Escape Clause.'"
> —Len Elder, DREI

VA-GUARANTEED LOAN PROGRAM

Whereas the FHA programs insure loans, the VA guarantees loans made through VA-approved lenders. Under a **VA-guaranteed loan**, the *VA guarantees repayment of the top portion of the loan to the lender* in the event the borrower defaults. Unlike the FHA, the VA does not set maximum loan amounts. The VA-guaranteed loan can be a 100% loan, which requires no down payment.

The loan amount can be 100% of the VA appraisal of the property set forth in the VA **certificate of reasonable value (CRV)** or 100% of the sales price, whichever is less.

The VA provides *this certificate, sometimes informally called the VA appraisal, to the lending institution as a basis for making the loan.* VA-guaranteed loans are available for the purchase or construction of one- to four-family dwellings. When obtaining the loan, the veteran must certify in writing that she will occupy the property being purchased. (If the veteran is on active duty, occupancy by the spouse will meet this requirement.) If the property is a multifamily dwelling (maximum of four units), the veteran must occupy one of the units.

Eligibility

For the borrower to be eligible for a VA-guaranteed loan, he must qualify as a veteran under VA requirements. If he is not on active duty, the veteran must have been discharged or released from duty under conditions other than dishonorable. The length of service required for eligibility depends on length and date of service and whether service was in war time or peace time. Members of the National Guard and reservists are also eligible for VA guaranteed loans if they meet the time requirements. In some cases, veterans' widows and widowers who have not remarried are eligible for a VA-guaranteed loan. An eligible veteran with full entitlement may be able to obtain a VA loan with no down payment, the loan amount not to exceed the FNMA loan limit, which changes each year. That limit for 2013 was $417,000.

Contract Requirements

If a contract of sale subject to the buyer's obtaining a VA-guaranteed loan is created before an appraisal and commitment by the VA, the VA requires that the contract contain the following statement:

> It is expressly agreed that, notwithstanding any other provisions of this contract, the purchaser shall not incur any penalty by forfeiture of earnest money or otherwise be obligated to complete the purchase of the property described herein, if the contract purchase price or cost exceeds the reasonable value of the property established by the Veterans Administration. The purchaser shall, however, have the privilege and option of proceeding with the consummation of this contract without regard to the amount of the reasonable value established by the Veterans Administration.

VA Funding Fee

To guarantee a VA loan, the VA charges a funding fee on all VA loans except those to a veteran who is receiving compensation for service-connected disabilities, a veteran who is receiving retirement pay in lieu of disability compensation, and a spouse of a veteran who died in service or from a service-connected disability. The fee is paid in cash or financed into the loan amount. If the funding fee is financed, the loan may exceed the VA appraisal by the amount of the funding fee. These fees vary, based on circumstances, between 0.5% for refinancing to 3.35% for a subsequent mortgage, although the typical amount for a no-down-payment first-time borrower is 2.15%.

Qualifying for VA Loans

The total housing expenses plus any recurring debts that extend for 10 months or more cannot exceed 41% of monthly gross income.

Restoration of Entitlement

When a veteran is discharged from the service, he receives a "certificate of eligibility." This certificate states the maximum guarantee in effect at the time the veteran is discharged. The maximum mortgage amount available without a down payment is tied to the conforming loan limit, which changes every year. If a veteran has used either full or partial entitlement in obtaining a VA loan, he can have that entitlement fully restored in one of the following ways:

1. The loan is paid in full, and the veteran has disposed of the property. The VA now grants a *one-time* exception to this rule; that is, a veteran can pay the loan in full *without* disposing of the property and get his entitlement back. This returned entitlement can be used only once. Any subsequent use requires disposing of both properties and having entitlement restored on the last VA loan.

2. A veteran purchaser who has as much remaining entitlement as the original veteran used to obtain the original loan and also satisfies the VA requirements for income, credit, and occupancy assumes the VA loan from the original veteran borrower. The assuming veteran must meet the same requirements as an original VA loan applicant and must agree to substitute her entitlement for that of the original veteran purchaser.

A mere release of liability by the lender and the VA does not in itself restore entitlement. A **release of liability** is a *procedure by which a mortgage holder agrees not to hold a borrower responsible for a mortgage on a property when another has assumed that borrower's loan and responsibility for it.* Anyone, veteran or nonveteran, owner-occupant or investor, can assume a VA loan and give a release of liability; however, only a qualified veteran, who intends to occupy the property, can give a **substitution of entitlement**. Other than the one-time exception in item 1, *simply paying the loan in full is not sufficient to restore the entitlement; the veteran must no longer own the property.*

If a veteran has a partial entitlement remaining, he may be able to buy a second property using the remaining entitlement. Lenders will usually lend up to four times the amount of any remaining entitlement.

History of Loan Guarantees

The loan guarantee the VA gives to lenders who make VA loans has steadily increased over the years from the lesser of $2,000 or 50% of the loan amount when the program was first initiated in 1944 to the present multilayered system.

Negotiability of VA Interest Rate

The interest rate is negotiable between the veteran and the lender. The VA allows veterans to pay discount points to obtain a lower interest rate. Sellers may also agree to pay discount points for the buyers to obtain a lower rate, but they are not required to do so.

OTHER ASPECTS OF FHA AND VA LOANS

Escrow Account

Both FHA and VA loans require that the borrower maintain an **escrow account** (also called an impound account) with the lending institution. The *borrower must pay an impound into this account each month to accumulate money to pay the annual real property tax bill and the annual homeowner's insurance policy premium.* In addition, if the loan is used to purchase a condominium apartment or a townhouse, *escrow deposits may include an amount to pay the property owner's assessment.* At closing, the borrower must put money into the account to get it started and provide a head start for accumulating the necessary funds. This includes two months' payments toward the next hazard insurance premium; several months toward the payment of the real property tax bill; and, if the loan is insured by the FHA, the equivalent of one month's FHA MIP. The number of months of property tax placed in escrow usually is determined by the lender, depending on the length of time since the last payment of taxes. These *insurance and tax monies deposited at the time of closing* are called **prepaid items** and are not considered a part of the borrower's actual closing costs; they are in excess of the closing costs.

Down Payment

If the VA CRV is less than the price the veteran is willing to pay for a home, the veteran can still obtain the VA loan and make a down payment for the difference between the loan amount and the purchase price. The FHA maximum loan amount is based on the sales price, the appraisal price, or the maximum FHA loan available in the area, whichever is less. The borrower must pay anything over the maximum loan amount as a down payment. In the case of a VA or FHA loan, the borrower cannot finance the down payment unless the loan for the down payment is secured by collateral other than the property and that loan is disclosed to the lender. If the down payment is a gift, he must have a gift letter stating that he is under no obligation to repay the money.

Miscellaneous

The maximum term of an FHA or VA loan is 30 years. Both types of loan are assumable, although with qualification after certain dates and at the interest rate at which the loan was originally created. Mortgages securing these loans cannot contain a due-on-sale or alienation clause as long as the purchaser meets the qualification requirements in effect at the time the loan was made and the loan is transferred in accordance with applicable regulations. In either an FHA or VA assumption, the difference between the loan amount assumed and the purchase price can be financed, although the loan payment on the amount financed must be considered in the qualification process on loan assumptions requiring release of liability. FHA and VA mortgages never require a **prepayment penalty**, *a charge for paying off the loan before the end of the mortgage term.*

RD AND FSA MORTGAGE LOANS

Whereas private mortgage lenders provide the funds for conventional, FHA, and VA loans, the government provides the funds for loans made through the USDA RD direct program and FSA. Through the Rural Housing Services Agency, RD provides subsidized and nonsubsidized no-down-payment loans for low- to moderate-income individuals or families for the purchase of a home in rural areas. Rural areas include not only open country but also communities with 20,000 or fewer people. The FSA, a separate USDA agency, makes loans to purchase and operate family-size farms. The agent working in rural areas may want to contact RD and FSA for information packets that describe these and other programs, such as grants for repair and rehabilitation and technical assistance grants to aid nonprofit organizations in "self-help" housing projects.

The purpose of these programs is to provide financing in designated rural areas to improve rural housing, develop community facilities, and maintain and create rural employment. RD provides loans for the purchase, repair, and rehabilitation of single- and multifamily residences. It also assists nonprofit groups in "self-help" housing projects. The RD direct loan is a 100% loan for a 33-year term with subsidized rates below other market loan rates.

In addition to the direct loan program, RD now has a nonsubsidized guaranteed program for borrowers who cannot qualify for any other loan. RD also has a hybrid loan, which combines the direct and guaranteed loans. One-half of the loan amount is subsidized by RD, and the other half is borrowed at the current rate from a lending institution. Designated lenders make 100% loans guaranteed by RD. These loans require no down payment and no private mortgage insurance and follow FHA guidelines for qualification ratios. There is no maximum loan amount; however, the income limits imposed by the program effectively limit the amount for which the borrower can qualify.

The FSA provides loans to purchase and operate family-size farms. Some FSA loans can be amortized over 40 years. Upper limits for qualifying income are established for each local area, and the loan payments are based on the buyer's ability to pay.

Types of Loans by Repayment Terms

In the early 1980s, there were more innovations in the types of loan than in the preceding 50 years. This was due to inflation and the accompanying increases in interest rates. Often these increases were radical and came about quickly. As a result, lending institutions, for their protection, shifted the burden resulting from rapid increases in interest rates from themselves to the borrowing public by introducing adjustable rate mortgages and graduated payment mortgages. Various types of repayment plans are discussed in this section, some of which are available with conventional, FHA, VA, and RD loans.

Fixed Rate—Level-Payment Plan

For this type of loan, the interest rate and the payment for principal and interest is fixed for the life of the loan. Each month the amounts allocated for each of principal and interest will change, and at the end of the mortgage term, the loan balance will be fully amortized to zero. During periods of low interest rates, this type of loan is very popular as it allows the borrower to obtain a large amount of money for a long repayment term without the risk of higher interest rates, which are likely over a 30-year term. Although many other loan types became popular during the past 30 years and remain popular today, the Fixed Rate—Level-Payment Plan is still the most widely used type of mortgage loan payment plan.

Adjustable (Variable) Interest Rate

The **adjustable rate mortgage (ARM)** is *a type of mortgage loan in which the lender has the right to alter, or adjust, the interest rate*. These adjustments are limited to terms established in making the original loan and are based on a variety of market indicators, with the *interest rate paid on* one-year treasury bills (T-Bills). The advantage of this type of mortgage is the flexibility of the loan to roll with the economic tide. In periods in which interest rates are increasing, the lender will receive a higher yield. In periods in which the rates are declining, the ARM interest rates will decrease. Certainly, over the period of a typical 30-year mortgage, one might reasonably expect rates to both increase and decrease. One advantage to the borrower is that the initial rate is typically lower than what might be encountered in the fixed-rate market. The disadvantage is that lenders will usually modify the monthly payment to reflect the interest rate adjustment, and this could dramatically increase the borrower's monthly mortgage payment.

In the ARM type of mortgage, the borrower should understand several important terms. The first is the index. There are several different indices on which the ARM is based, such as the cost of funds index, the LIBOR (London Interbank Offered Rate) rate, and perhaps the most popular, the T-Bill rate. Whichever method is being employed, the yearly average of its yield is obtained and referred to as the index. Once the index is determined, a profit mark-up, or margin, is added to the index to determine the new interest rate. Margins can certainly vary depending on a variety of market factors, but a typical margin on a good quality loan might be around 2.75%. To illustrate, if the T-Bills averaged 4.25% (index) and the margin was 2.75%, the resulting interest rate calculation would be 7%. To regulate how much the interest rate can adjust, the lender will utilize a cap. Caps are usually both a **periodic cap** (per adjustment period) as well as a life of the **loan cap**. It is quite normal for conventional ARM loans to utilize caps of two-sixths. The lower number will reflect the periodic cap of 2%, and the higher reflects the life of the loan cap (6%). This means that the loan interest rate, no matter what the market index and margin may be, cannot increase more than 2% in any one adjustment period or more than 6% over the life of the loan. The fact that in a prior period a lender did not use all of its ability to increase the interest rate at that time does not give it the ability to tack on *an extra increase in* a later period *beyond the maximum increase allowed for that period*. It is common for ARM loans to allow interest rates to decrease as well, and there is normally a minimum interest rate that will apply in case of extended low-interest rate periods. To stay on schedule with repayment, lenders will generally raise or lower the monthly payment to reflect changes in the interest rates. Failure to increase the payment at the time interest rates increase would result in **negative amortization** in which *the payment would not cover the amount due for interest*. The vast majority of ARM lenders do not allow negative amortization to exist in their loans.

Graduated Payment Plan

In the **graduated payment mortgage (GPM)**, the monthly payments are lower in the early years of the loan term. The *payments gradually increase at specified intervals until the payment amount is sufficient to amortize the loan over the remaining term*. The monthly payments are kept down in the early years by not requiring the borrower to pay all of the interest, the unpaid portion of which is added to the principal. This creates negative amortization. The purpose of this type of mortgage is to enable borrowers to achieve home ownership as a result of the lower initial monthly payments. An outstanding example of this type of mortgage loan is the FHA 245 GPM, which was briefly discussed earlier in this chapter.

Term Loan

The **term loan** (also called a "straight" loan) requires *the borrower to make interest-only payments for a specified term*. At the end of the term, the borrower is required to pay the entire principal balance. As a result, many homeowners lost their property through foreclosure in the 1900s before fully amortized home mortgage loans became prevalent. Interestingly, short-term home loans enjoyed a resurgence in popularity during the real estate boom period of early 2000s when real estate prices were escalating at an exceptionally high rate. Today, this type of home loan typically is used during the construction period of an improvement and infrequently is used in other situations involving home loans.

Growing Equity Mortgage

One popular type of repayment plan that results in paying off the loan much faster than would be normally scheduled is the growing equity mortgage. In this type of loan, the borrower will begin with monthly payments calculated at the fixed-rate mortgage level and then encounter prestipulated increases in monthly payments annually until the loan is fully amortized. In many ways, this type of loan simply factors in typical cost-of-living income increases that will go strictly to the principal allocation. Although this type of loan is similar in many ways to the graduated payment plans, the key distinction is that it does not involve negative amortization at any time. The same effect can be easily achieved with a standard amortized fixed-rate loan by simply making extra principal payments on a regular basis.

Buydown Loan

A **buydown loan** allows for either a *temporary or permanent* buydown of the interest rate. In the *temporary* version, the *lender allows the borrower to pay a lower interest rate in the early years of the loan.* The borrower agrees to this arrangement because the seller has agreed to pay the lender in advance for any shortfall that may result from the lower interest rate.

The seller, usually a builder, deposits the advance funds into a special escrow account with the lender. From this account, the lender withdraws the shortfall funds each month as the borrower makes the payments. A builder/seller may offer a 3/2/1 buydown plan to a buyer. Assume the current interest rate is 10%. A buyer/borrower would make payments based on 7% for the first year. The 3% shortfall is drawn from the account set up by the builder at the closing. The borrower makes payments at 8% the second year and 9% the third year. By the end of the third year, the account is depleted and the borrower then makes payments on the full 10% interest rate for the remaining life of the loan. There is no negative amortization.

The *permanent buydown* is used by borrowers in times of high interest rates. In return for paying discount points to the lender, *the borrower can permanently buy down the interest rate for the life of the loan.* Each discount point costs 1% of the loan amount and reduces the interest rate by 0.125%. For example, if the interest rate is 7% and a borrower pays 8 discount points, the interest rate will be 6% for the life of the loan. If the loan amount is $150,000, the cost to the borrower is $12,000 ($150,000 × 8% = $12,000).

Balloon Payment Plan (Partially Amortized)

Any *final loan payment that is substantially larger than any previous payment in order to satisfy the remaining principal and interest* is called a **balloon payment**. A typical balloon payment loan occurs when the payments are amortized over a long time, but the loan balance is due in full on a much sooner date. For example, a loan may have payments based on a 20-year amortization term but have a final due date in five years. If the balloon payment is to be a substantial amount, the note can provide for refinancing by the lender to provide the funds to the borrower in the event the borrower cannot otherwise make the payment. Do not confuse the balloon payment plan with the term loan. In the balloon payment plan, the borrower pays principal and interest, therefore amortizing the mortgage during the loan period, and then pays off the entire outstanding balance, whereas the term loan has the borrower paying interest only during the loan period with no amortization taking place.

TYPES OF LOANS BY PURPOSE OR SPECIAL FEATURE

Purchase Money Mortgages (Seller-Financed Loans)

Although any mortgage obtained in which to purchase a property is a **purchase money mortgage**, this term is most often used to describe traditional seller financing. In this situation, instead of the seller receiving all of the sales proceeds in cash, the seller will accept a promissory note from the buyer for all or part of the purchase price. The seller will still convey title to the buyer, but the buyer will execute a deed of trust to the seller for collateral. In the event of default, the seller will foreclose on the note. *Note that the seller will not be entitled to a deficiency judgment against the borrower in the event foreclosure proceeds to bring insufficient funds to pay off the mortgage debt.* The seller's sole remedy is the property itself.

Construction Loan

A construction loan is a form of interim, or temporary, short-term financing used to obtain the funds needed to create improvements on land. The applicant for a construction loan submits, for the lender's appraisal, the plans and specifications for the structure to be built and the property on which the construction is to take place. The lender makes the construction loan based on the value resulting from an appraisal of the property and the construction plans and specifications. Unlike more traditional forms of mortgage lending, the construction loan contract states that disbursements will be made as specified stages of construction are completed. These type of dispersements are referred to as draws. Interest is not charged until the money has been drawn or disbursed. Upon completion, the lender makes a final inspection and closes out the construction loan, which is paid off or converted to permanent, long-term financing. This situation is the most common use of a term loan and represents the riskiest of all mortgage loan types for the lender.

Often the lender requires the builder to be bonded for completion of the property. The bond is made payable to the lender in the event the builder goes bankrupt and is unable to complete the structure. In this way, the lender has the funds to complete the construction so as to have a valuable asset to sell and to recover the monies extended under the construction loan.

Open-End Mortgage

An **open-end mortgage** is *one that can be refinanced without rewriting the mortgage* and incurring closing costs. A credit ceiling is established. When the original mortgage has been paid down, the owner can draw additional funds up to the ceiling for purposes such as home improvements. This is not the typical residential mortgage. The currently popular **home equity mortgages** are considered to be in this category, however, because they are essentially an open-end line of credit secured by a second mortgage on the home.

Blanket Mortgage

In this form of mortgage, two or more parcels of real estate are pledged as security for payment of a mortgage debt. The blanket mortgage usually contains release clauses that provide for the release of certain parcels of property from the mortgage lien as the loan balance is reduced by a specified amount. The mortgage should always provide that sufficient property value is subject to the mortgage lien to secure the remaining principal balance at any given time.

The blanket mortgage with release clauses is typically used by real estate developers. In this way, the developer can obtain the release of certain parcels from the mortgage lien and convey a clear title to purchasers to generate a profit and provide the funds to make future mortgage payments on the developer's construction loans on properties that are being constructed or that haven't sold.

Package Mortgage

> "Don't confuse a blanket loan and a package loan. A blanket loan is a loan which encumbers more than one property. A package loan is a loan which is placed against both real and personal property."
> —Len Elder, DREI

This is a mortgage in which *personal property, in addition to real property, is pledged to secure payment of the mortgage loan.* The **package mortgage** is used frequently in the sale of furnished condominium units or resort properties and can include all furnishings in a unit. In this way, the buyer can obtain longer term financing for the furnishings and take advantage of interest deductions for the personal property as well as the real estate.

Bridge Loan

A bridge loan is a temporary, interim-type loan that is used to finance the period between the beginning of one loan and the ending of another. Typical examples might include a loan used by the purchaser to fund the purchase of a new home before the prior home is sold and that loan is paid off. It also is used fairly commonly with the interim construction loan and the acquisition of the permanent financing. Most bridge loans will involve the payment of interest only and often will not involve monthly payments but rather a singular payoff once the final process is completed.

TYPES OF LOANS BY MORTGAGE PRIORITIES

First (or Senior) Mortgage

A first mortgage may be the only mortgage or the mortgage that is higher in priority than all other mortgages on the same property. It gets its unique status from being the first mortgage to be recorded on a particular property. It is often referred to as the senior mortgage, although any mortgage that is higher in priority than another is technically a senior mortgage. Because of the priority of lien status, the first mortgage generally will involve a slightly lower interest rate than the subsequent mortgages.

Junior Mortgage

A junior mortgage is any mortgage recorded after the first mortgage. A junior mortgage may be a second or third mortgage. Note that a junior mortgage is always subordinate, or of a lesser degree of claim, to a mortgage recorded before it.

In the event of a foreclosure sale, the holder of the first mortgage has the first claim against the sale proceeds, and the first mortgage debt must be satisfied before the holder of the second mortgage is entitled to any money from the sale. The holder of a third mortgage is not entitled to any of the sale proceeds until the second mortgage is satisfied, and so on down the line of priorities. The priority is established by the time (date and hour) the mortgage is recorded on the public record in the county where the property is located. The more junior the mortgage, the higher the risk. Junior mortgages are usually for a shorter term and higher interest rate because of the greater risk.

Although the term "senior mortgage" has been used herein to describe a first mortgage loan, it is not limited in that regard. If there are three mortgage loans, the first is senior to the second and third mortgages, the second is junior to the first but senior to the third, and the third mortgage is junior to both the first and the second.

MORTGAGE PRIORITIES

Effect of Recordation

In North Carolina, to be effective against claims of third parties, all documents need to be recorded to establish a claim against a property. The Conner Act and the effect of the pure race system are discussed in Chapter 4. Although there are important exceptions, such as the real property tax lien, which always assumes the first priority (the tax collector has, in effect, already won the race to the courthouse), lenders are careful to preserve their position in the claims against the property subject to the mortgage. As a rule, the lender not only will insist on being in a first position but also will take care to ensure that no other claims upset this priority. This is particularly true in the case of a construction loan, in which the borrower might have had some work started on the property before closing the loan. Because the mechanic's lien dates from the first day the work was provided, the lender will want to clear all such possibilities so as not to interfere with her claim to the first lien holder priority.

Subordination of Mortgages

Mortgage priorities can be changed by agreement of the parties even after recording. For example, suppose a developer were to purchase land for the construction of new homes. The owner of the land may have taken a small down payment and agreed to release sections of the land as homes are built and sold. At this point, the landowner's mortgage on the sections is recorded in a first position priority. As discussed previously, no lender is going to agree to have her construction mortgage to the developer be placed secondary to the landowner or to anybody else. Therefore, as part of the land purchase negotiation, the developer can provide for the seller to move, or *subordinate*, the original lien and voluntarily place it behind the subsequent construction mortgage. In essence, a subordination simply means to make of a lesser degree of claim. Thus, the lender obtains the first position, and the landowner not only has a down payment but also has his land improved by the construction of the new home.

Releases

Recording a release of a mortgage, note, claim, or deed of trust is just as important as recording the original document. Failure to do so may cloud the title to the property. After the closing meeting, the attorney will need to record the new deed and deed of trust for the buyer and his lender as well as cancel the existing deed of trust. Generally, the seller's lender will not sign the paperwork allowing such a cancellation until after loan payoff has been received. It is quite normal that the complete cycle of deed recordation and deed of trust cancellation will take a period of at least a few days to complete.

THE ROLE OF THE FEDERAL RESERVE BANK

The Federal Reserve Bank (the Fed) is responsible for the nation's monetary policy. The president of the United States appoints the members of the Federal Reserve

Board of Governors, who serve 14-year terms. The president appoints one of the members to serve a four-year term as chair. The chair of the Federal Reserve Board holds one of the most powerful positions in the country. The activities of the Federal Reserve Board have a powerful influence on the real estate and security markets. Its most important influence derives from its control of monetary policy.

The Fed implements its monetary policies by controlling the money supply, influencing interest rates through its control of the discount rate, dictating cash reserve requirements for banks and other depository institutions, and controlling the amount of funds available in the banking system by its open market operations.

The Fed increases the money supply by creating money to buy U.S. Treasury Securities. It can move its large supplies of cash and government bonds in and out of the banking system at will. Buying government bonds for cash puts money into the banks, which then lend it to businesses, thereby stimulating a sluggish economy. Selling some of its supply of government bonds takes money from the banks in payment for the bonds, thereby reducing the amount the banks must lend and helping to slow an overheating economy. The Fed can also control the amount of money in circulation by increasing or decreasing the reserve requirements for depository institutions. These reserves consist of money each institution must keep on deposit with the Fed rather than lend to its customers. The higher the reserve requirement, the less money the bank has to lend. The lower the requirement, the more money the bank has to lend.

The Fed receives a lot of publicity when it raises or lowers the discount rate. Many real estate consumers think this automatically lowers mortgage interest rates. It does not. The discount rate is the rate the Fed charges its member institutions for money it lends them. It signals these institutions that an increase or decrease in interest rates is desired. The institutions are free to ignore the signal. They almost always heed the signal to increase their prime rate, the rate charged their best customers. Some may be a little slow to heed a signal to decrease their prime rate. Even if the prime rate decreases, long-term mortgage rates may not decrease accordingly. Short-term interest rates and long-term mortgage rates do not always increase or decrease in tandem.

A more detailed explanation of the use of these tools is beyond the scope of this text; however, agents should be aware of the effects the Fed's activities have on the real estate industry. The Fed has done an excellent job in the past few years of controlling inflation and keeping interest rates low and the economy sound. Those agents who have been in real estate for 20 years have seen firsthand that more people buy homes when wages and employment are high and interest rates are at an affordable rate rather than at 15% to 18%.

SECTION 2: PRIMARY SOURCES OF REAL ESTATE FINANCE

PRIMARY SOURCES OF MORTGAGE FUNDS

Within the lending industry, there are two different markets that must be understood. There is the primary market, where loans are actually made to consumers, and the secondary market, where loans are not made but rather where loans are sold within the financial world. The secondary market does not refer to second mortgage loans but rather the "market behind the scenes," which is where the primary lenders will sell their loans in order to obtain fresh supplies of funds with which to make new loans and earn additional fees.

The primary lenders are the providers of mortage loans. They process loan applications and make the decision to ultimately fund the mortage. They are effectively the "manufacturer" of the product and the secondary market is the distribution.

Savings and Loan Associations

Savings and loan associations (S&Ls) *lend money to construct housing, to purchase existing housing, and to effect improvements in existing housing.* As housing prices in some areas rose rapidly during the first five years of the twenty-first century, many buyers chose ARMs, interest-only, or 100% LTV mortgages in expectation of continually rising prices. As the bubble burst, interest rates increased on ARMs and many recent buyers found themselves with increasing payments on ARMs. In the case of the interest-only 100% LTV loans, owners not only had no equity in the beginning but also had a negative equity when the price of their homes fell. The right loan for the right buyer partially depends on how many risks the buyer can handle without being put in an untenable financial position. The agent should not give financial advice; however, she may point out the disadvantages of high-risk loans and advise the buyer to seek financial advice from a competent financial advisor. Traditionally, these organizations supplied more money for financing the purchase and construction of single-family dwellings than did any other type of lending institution; they continue to invest a large portion of their assets in residential real estate. Savings and loans are state-chartered or federally chartered; however, the practical difference has been blurred by passage of the Financial Institutions Reform, Recovery, and Enforcement Act in 1989. This Act, passed to curb the abuses and problems that led to the S&Ls' problems, affects all federally insured depository institutions. This legislation substituted (1) the Office of Thrift Supervision for the Federal Home Loan Bank Board and (2) the Savings Association Insurance Fund for the Federal Savings and Loan Insurance Corporation. The Federal Deposit Insurance Corporation (FDIC) now regulates and provides a safety net for both banks and S&Ls; however, the insuring funds are maintained separately. The primary purposes for which S&Ls exist are (1) to encourage thrift (hence the term *thrifts*) and (2) to provide financing for residential properties.

Savings Banks

Savings banks, formerly called mutual savings banks, are similar to S&Ls in that their main objectives are to encourage thrift and to provide financing for housing. These organizations exist primarily in the northeast portion of the United States and are chartered and regulated by the states in which they are located. Savings banks play a prominent role in financing housing in those states.

During the late 1970s and the 1980s, regulation changes allowed these institutions to branch out into other types of loans and to become more like commercial banks. These institutions currently differ from other depositor institutions primarily in form of ownership; they are depositor owned.

Commercial Banks

Commercial banks can be federally or state chartered. In both cases, commercial banks are sources of mortgage money for construction, purchase of existing housing, and home improvements. Their loan policies are usually more conservative than those of other types of lending institution.

Over the past few decades, commercial banks favored short-term loans to avoid committing valuable assets for a long time. In recent years, commercial banks have steadily increased their mortgage holdings, and it has become easier for commercial banks to sell their loans in the secondary mortgage market. This enables the banks to recoup their cash in a few months, so commercial banks now make many more long-term loans.

Commercial banks also continue to be a source of short-term loans for construction and home improvement projects. Additionally, many offer warehouse lines of credit to mortgage companies to fund loans until the mortgage company can accumulate the loans in large blocks to sell to investors. This is called a *warehouse line of credit* because the funds are held "in warehouse" until the large loan blocks are sold.

Mortgage Bankers and Mortgage Brokers

Mortgage bankers, also called mortgage companies, make mortgage loans for the construction of housing and the purchase of existing housing. They often specialize in FHA-insured loans and VA-guaranteed loans, although most also make conventional loans. A mortgage banker and a mortgage broker are quite different. Mortgage brokers generally work with and represent many lending institutions. They typically do not service mortgage loans.

> 🔑 A **mortgage banker** *makes and services mortgage loans.* A **mortgage broker** *brings together a lender and a borrower for a fee paid by the lending institution,* just as a real estate broker brings together a buyer and a seller of real property for a fee.

Life Insurance Companies

At one time, a number of life insurance companies were active in making loans directly to individual mortgage borrowers. Today they provide funds to mortgage banks and brokers to lend to individual borrowers and to provide funds primarily for the purchase or construction of large real estate projects, such as apartment complexes, office buildings, and shopping malls.

Credit Unions

Credit unions are an excellent source of mortgage money for their members. Usually, credit unions offer mortgage loans to their membership at an interest rate below the commercial rate at any given time. To be financially able to make long-term mortgage loans, the credit union must be of substantial size. A federal employees' credit union, a state employees credit union, and the credit union of a major industry are examples of large credit unions.

Real Estate Investment Trusts

Real estate investment trusts (REITs) *make loans secured by real property.* REITs are owned by stockholders and enjoy certain federal income tax advantages. They provide financing for large commercial projects such as second-home developments, apartment complexes, shopping malls, and office buildings. REITs invest in properties as owners and managers, known as equity REITs, or they choose to lend money on projects owned by others, known as mortgage REITs.

Individual Investors

Individuals also invest in mortgages. These individual investors usually are an excellent source for second mortgage loans. The seller of real property is definitely not to be overlooked as an individual investor. These sellers finance the sale of their properties by taking a regular second mortgage, taking a second mortgage in the form of a wraparound, taking a purchase money first mortgage, or financing by means of a contract for deed. In times of extremely high interest rates, a sale often cannot be made unless the seller provides a substantial part of the financing for the buyer.

Government Agencies

RD and the FSA have already been mentioned as sources of mortgage funds for certain qualified buyers. Community development funds are sometimes available for down payments and closing cost assistance. The North Carolina Housing Finance Agency sometimes provides down payment assistance and subsidized mortgage rates through local lenders and administers the Mortgage Credit Certificate Program, a federal program.

Employers

Many employers provide closing cost assistance for transferees. Some provide down payment assistance. A few provide loan assistance, especially in the form of bridge loans, until the employee's former home sells. As its name implies, a bridge loan is a loan made to bridge the time gap between the purchase of a new home and the selling of the old one when the new buyer is unable to sell the old home before closing on the new one. Often the old home is used as collateral for the bridge loan, which is repaid when the old home sells.

SECONDARY MORTGAGE MARKET

The primary mortgage market consists of lending institutions that make loans directly to borrowers. By contrast, the **secondary mortgage market** *buys and sometimes sells and services mortgages created in the primary mortgage market.* There must be an assignability feature, which allows the lender holding the mortgage to assign or sell the rights in the mortgage to another; thus, the money invested in the mortgage is freed without waiting for the borrower to repay the debt over the long mortgage term. Sale of the mortgage by the lender does not affect the borrower's rights or obligations. The mortgagor may not even be aware the mortgage has been sold; the original lending institution often continues to service the loan for the purchaser of the mortgage, and the mortgagor continues to make the necessary mortgage payments to the same lending institution that made the mortgage loan. If the purchaser of the mortgage prefers to service the mortgage, the original lender simply notifies the mortgagor to make payments to a different lender at a different address.

The secondary mortgage market benefits lending institutions and, in turn, the borrowing public by providing **liquidity** to mortgages. The mortgage is a liquid asset because *it can be readily converted to cash* by the lending institution selling the mortgage in the secondary market. Sale of the mortgage by the lender is especially beneficial in low-yield mortgages—those mortgages for which the lender receives a lesser return on her investment in terms of both discount and interest rate, expressed as an annual percentage rate. The lender gets the money out of these mortgages to reinvest in new mortgage loans at current higher yields. This provides stability in the supply of money for mortgage loans. Therefore, the secondary mortgage market benefits the borrowing public by enabling lending institutions to make money available for loans to qualified applicants.

Mortgage liquidity in the secondary market reduces the impact of disintermediation on lending institutions. **Disintermediation** is *the loss of funds available to lending institutions for making mortgage loans, caused by the withdrawal of funds by depositors for investment in higher-yield securities* in times of higher interest rates. Without the secondary mortgage market, disintermediation would result in funds available to lenders "drying up" to the extent that these loans would be practically unavailable. Some lending institutions limit their mortgage loans to their own assets rather than participating in the secondary mortgage market. For lenders that do participate in the secondary market, two types of markets are available: (1) the purchase and sale of mortgages between lending institutions and (2) the sale of mortgages by lending institutions to four organizations that provide a market for this purpose (FNMA, GNMA, and FHLMC), which are discussed on the following pages).

Activities among Lending Institutions

A major activity of the secondary mortgage market is the purchase and sale of mortgages by and among lending institutions. In this way, the market facilitates movement of capital from institutions that have funds to invest to lenders that do not have enough money for this purpose.

For example, at any time, the demand for mortgage loans may be low in a given locality. Institutions with funds available for making loans in those areas are unable to invest these funds in the local market by making primary mortgage loans. Their funds should be invested in mortgages where they can earn interest instead of being idle. At this same time, another part of the country may have a high demand for mortgage loans. A lender in that area may have a short supply of funds to lend to qualified loan applicants. The problems of both of these lending institutions can be solved if the institution whose funds are in short supply sells its mortgages on hand to a lender in another area that has a surplus of funds and a low demand for mortgage loans. As a result, the lender with otherwise idle funds has them invested in mortgages earning interest, as they should be, and the lender in short supply of money frees up capital invested in mortgages to meet the high demand for new mortgage loans in that area.

The direct sale of loans from investor to investor is legal and occurs relatively frequently, especially among small investors who sell to larger investors to make "pools." This "pooling" of mortgages allows investors to assemble a large body or mortgages in invest in and therefore diversify their investment risk. It is inevitable that some loans will result in losses no matter how thoroughly the loan was vetted. This way the risk is much more manageable for the investor. Much more likely are sales to organizations that buy and sell mortgages, as discussed in the following paragraphs.

Sale to Organizations

The organizations that actively participate in purchasing mortgages from financial institutions are FNMA, GNMA, and FHLMC. See Figure 11.10 for a summary of allowable mortgage purchases by these organizations.

ALLOWABLE MORTGAGE PURCHASES			
	VA	FHA	Conventional
FNMA	✓	✓	✓
GNMA	✓	✓	
FHLMC			✓

FIGURE 11.10 Allowable mortgage purchases.

Federal National Mortgage Association

The **FNMA** usually is referred to by its nickname, **Fannie Mae**. It is the oldest *secondary mortgage* institution and the largest holder of home mortgages. Fannie Mae was created in 1938 as a corporation completely owned by the federal government to provide a secondary market for residential mortgages. By 1968, it had evolved into a privately owned corporation and its stock was listed on the New York Stock Exchange. In 2008, FNMA reverted back to being a federally owned organization that purchases conventional as well as FHA and VA mortgage loans as part of a government bailout plan that placed FNMA and the FHLMC into a conservatorship to protect these entities from a catastrophic failure resulting from the great financial crisis that began in 2007.

Fannie Mae buys mortgages regularly. Mortgage bankers are major sellers of mortgages to Fannie Mae. S&Ls, savings banks, commercial banks, and life insurance companies also sell mortgages to Fannie Mae. Fannie Mae sells interest-bearing securities (bonds, notes, and debentures) to investors. These securities are backed by specific pools of mortgages purchased and held by Fannie Mae.

Government National Mortgage Association

The popular name for **GNMA** is taken from its acronym. Ginnie Mae was established in 1968, when Fannie Mae was fully converted to a private corporation. **Ginnie Mae**, an agency of HUD, *purchases mortgages to make capital available to lending institutions.* As a government agency, Ginnie Mae is limited to the purchase of VA-guaranteed and FHA-insured mortgages.

Ginnie Mae guarantees the "Ginnie Mae Pass-Through," a mortgage-backed security providing participation in a pool of FHA-insured or VA-guaranteed mortgages. The pass-throughs are originated by lending institutions, primarily mortgage bankers. Ginnie Mae guarantees these securities, making them highly secure investments for purchasers. The yield on each pass-through issue is guaranteed by the full faith and credit of the U.S. government; the pass-throughs are secured by the FHA-insured and VA-guaranteed loans; the lending institution originating the pass-through provides a guarantee as well. The government does not guarantee that investors in Ginnie Mae securities will make or not lose money on their investments. It only guarantees the loans backing the securities. When the interest rates change dramatically, the investor can make money or lose money.

Federal Home Loan Mortgage Corporation

Like the other organizations, the **FHLMC** has a nickname, **Freddie Mac**, and has seen dramatic changes within the last few years because of the lending crisis. Originally formed to provide a source for savings institutions to sell their conventional mortgages as an alternative to FNMA, FHLMC now operates, along with FNMA, as a government conservatorship under the newly formed Federal Housing Finance Agency. This move was necessitated by the financial crisis following the 2007–2008 sharp decline in the real estate and financial markets and the desire of the federal government to stabilize the financial markets as these two groups held almost half of all mortgage loans in America. This partnership created the need for literally a hundred billion dollars of funding commitments from the U.S. Department of the Treasury. It will be interesting to see what form this union takes on in the future.

Other Aspects of the Market

Primary lenders that wish to sell mortgages to Fannie Mae or Freddie Mac must use uniform loan documents that meet criteria established by FNMA and FHLMC. *Conventional loans processed on uniform loan forms and according to FNMA/FHLMC guidelines* are called "conventional conforming" loans, or just "**conforming loans**." For example, these organizations do not purchase mortgages that contain a prepayment penalty, an extra charge for paying off a mortgage sooner than specified in its terms. This requirement is particularly advantageous to individual borrowers when they are required to pay off their mortgage as a condition of a contract of sale. In some cases, prepayment penalties on nonconforming loans are extremely high and, therefore, pose a real hardship to sellers.

RESIDENTIAL LENDING PRACTICES AND PROCEDURES IN TRANSACTIONS SUBJECT TO TRUTH IN LENDING ACT/REAL ESTATE SETTLEMENT PROCEDURES ACT INTEGRATED DISCLOSURE

Loan Application Procedures

The overwhelming majority of home purchases involve some sort of financing to be obtained. Because mortgage loans are likely to be resold in the secondary market, there is a high degree of standardization that is utilized within the mortgage process. All mortgage loans will involve an application. Conforming loans will utilize the FNMA/FHLMC application form, and even lenders who do not plan to resell the loan will typically use this form as well because it keeps open the possibility for the mortgage to be sold within the secondary market at some point in the future. During the application process, detailed information will be gathered from the borrower, including income, expenses, credit history, and sources of funds to close. Such information will be required to be verified by third parties and may involve the submission of two years of past income tax returns as well as pay stubs, bank statements, and investment reports. The borrower will also need to provide a copy of the purchase agreement unless the application only involves refinancing. Typically, the lender will prepare a Loan Estimate (LE), which is an estimate of the various costs to obtain the mortgage loan. This document must be sent to the borrower within three days of loan application and allows an opportunity to compare different lenders offerings to obtain the best alternative. The only fee that a lender is allowed to charge the borrower before this time is the reasonable cost for a credit report. This breakdown will detail which of the closing costs cannot change at all and which can change without limit; it includes a group of items in which the costs, collectively, cannot exceed 10% of what is originally quoted. The figures that are provided within the LE will be duplicated on the Closing Disclosure closing form in such fashion as to allow comparison with the actual figures from the closing. In addition to the LE, the lender must also provide the borrower with a pamphlet that describes the various closing costs and other important details within three days of loan application.

In addition to the LE the lender will also be required to furnish the residential borrow with the booklet "**Know Before You Owe**," which is a brief guide to the mortgage loan process and will explain the loan process and what the borrower's rights and obligations will be. Just like the LE, this booklet must be provided to the borrower within three days of the loan application.

Most lenders will provide some assurance to the borrower that the interest rate being quoted will not change between the loan application and the closing. In the event the interest rate or loan product is changed, the lender will be required to issue a new LE. This is referred to as a "rate lock" and usually has a time limit on validity. As long as the borrower closes within the stipulated time period, the quoted interest rate will be the rate at the closing. If the borrower desires an interest rate lock for an extended period of time, such as involved in new construction, it is quite common for the lender to charge a fee for the lock.

Once all of the details regarding the application are collected and verified, including any appraisals, the package will be sent to an underwriting department for review. This review ensures compliance with the requirements that the lender, regulators, mortgage insurance companies, and secondary markets will impose. Once this review has been completed, the lender will either approve or reject the loan application. If the lender denies the loan application, the borrower must be informed in writing. Once the lender commits to the loan the borrower is allowed three days before the closing in which to review the loan documents. The loan will not be allowed to close prior to this three-day right of review. This topic will be discussed in further detail in Chapter 12.

Loan Underwriting

Loan underwriting is the *process by which an underwriter reviews loan documentation and evaluates a buyer's creditworthiness and the value of the property to be pledged as security for the payment of the note as well as to determine the ability of the loan to be sold within the secondary market.* The loan originator collects all the documentation and presents it to the underwriter, who may be an employee of the mortgage company, a private mortgage insurance company, or a government agency such as FHA, VA, RD, or FSA. These government agencies, except RD and FSA, allow approved lenders to underwrite the government loans they process. The result of this evaluation is an approval or a disapproval of the loan.

Borrower Analysis

When evaluating the loan applicant, the lending institution requires the applicant to have a stable and effective income, sufficient to enable the borrower to make the loan payments and to continue to meet other recurring financial obligations. The effective income may be a combination of an applicant's and a co-applicant's income (e.g., husband and wife).

The applicant must also have a satisfactory credit history. The applicant is required to furnish credit information covering at least the two-year period immediately preceding the date of the application. If the applicant's credit history is unsatisfactory, the application may be denied regardless of the amount and quality of the applicant's income in relation to the loan payments.

The applicant's assets are also taken into consideration by the lending institution. If the applicant's income is borderline in relation to the mortgage payment required, but the individual has sufficient good-quality assets, the existence of these assets may make the difference between approval and disapproval of the loan application.

Lenders will want to determine whether the borrower makes adequate income to be able to afford to repay the loan. Most lenders will want to analyze not only the monthly costs of the loan and its related expenses such as PITI plus monthly PMI costs as well as any homeowners association fees (Housing Expenses) but also examine the monthly debts the borrower is obligated for (Total Recurring Debts). It is common for lenders to count only those monthly debts that have at least a given number of payments remaining, such as 6 months for conventional and 10 months for FHA. This adequacy of income is generally stated in terms of a ratio for both housing expenses followed by total recurring debts. For example a conventional loan will typically be considered by a ratio of 28%/36%, which translates as housing expenses are not to exceed 28% of monthly gross income and housing expenses plus monthly recurring debts that are counted are not to exceed 36%.

> **Test Tip!**
>
> Typical Loan Qualification Ratios
> Conventional 28%/36%
> FHA 31%/43%
> VA 41% total monthly expenses

Property Analysis

The lender hires a state-licensed or state-certified appraiser to estimate the value of the property, that is, to appraise the property according to the appraisal standards made known by federal regulators. The primary purpose of the appraisal is to assure the lender that the value of the property is such that the property will sell for a price that will cover the loan amount and the lender's costs should the borrower default and the lender needs to foreclose.

The appraiser is not a home inspector; however, he does inspect and analyze the property, taking into account all factors that have a bearing on its value (for details, see Chapter 13, "Real Property Valuation"). The appraiser then submits a report of value, noting observed conditions. The lender will most likely require that rotten wood, peeling paint, broken glass, a worn-out roof, and safety hazards be corrected. Anything of this nature on the appraisal (and findings on the wood-destroying insect report) usually needs to be corrected and re-inspected before closing the loan.

NOTE: A buyer should not rely on the appraisal as an inspection. He should be advised to inspect the property himself and hire a licensed home inspector.

The loan amount is based on the appraised value or sales price, whichever is lower. The lender determines the loan amount by multiplying the lesser of the sales or appraised value by the percentage indicated by the desired LTV ratio. For example, if the contract sales price is $102,000, the appraised value is $100,000, and the LTV ratio is 95%, the lender will lend $95,000. The seller could reduce the sales price to the appraised value, the buyer could pay a $7,000 down payment, or the parties could cancel the contract provided it was contingent upon the buyer obtaining a loan of more than $95,000 or provided the contract's due diligence period had not expired.

The lender wants to be assured of the property's value and condition; he also wants to be assured that the title to the property is clear when the loan is made and that his mortgage is the first mortgage. He gets this assurance by having an attorney search the title, give an attorney's opinion of title, and obtain a title insurance policy. The attorney does a preliminary search before closing and a final search just before recording the documents. This ensures that nothing happened to cloud the title between the initial search and the closing and recording of the deed and financing instruments.

Loan Analysis

After the lender completes his analysis of both the borrower as well as the property, she will also need to analyze the mortgage itself to determine whether it meets the criteria necessary for the financial goals of the lender as well as to determine its ability to be sold within the secondary marketplace. The interest rate being charged along with any applicable discount points will be analyzed to determine whether the yield is consistent with what the market will demand of a borrower with the credit score, down payment, income, and expenses of the borrower. The loan term will be compared along with the economic life expectancy indicated in the appraisal to make certain the duration of the mortgage is less than the estimated life of the property. The amount of the loan relative to the appraised value, or purchase price, whichever is less, will be analyzed to make certain there is sufficient equity in the property to reduce lender risk in the event foreclosure shall become necessary. If the LTV exceeds 80% for a conventional loan, the lender will need to make certain that PMI is purchased. The LTV is less important in this regard for both an FHA as well as a VA loan because they are always government-insured or guaranteed.

Loan Commitment and Closing

Once the lender completes the analysis of the borrower, the property, and the loan, the decision is made on whether to fund the mortgage. If the applicable PMI, FHA, and VA insurance and guaranty program is in agreement with the loan, the lender will proceed to the closing process.

FINANCING LEGISLATION

Dodd-Frank Wall Street Reform and Consumer Protection Act

The United States suffered through a financial crisis and recession beginning in 2007 that many people feel was the direct result of abuses of the financial industry, including the mortgage market. This economic downturn resulted in massive loss of wealth, record high foreclosures, business and bank failures, high unemployment, and the necessity of bank and business bailouts by the taxpayers. As a result of these conditions, Congress passed the Dodd-Frank Wall Street Reform and Consumer Protection Act in July of 2010 (the Dodd-Frank Act). This act is the largest financial reform legislation since the Great Depression and establishes a new agency, the Bureau of Consumer Financial Protection, although it is referred to as the **Consumer Financial Protection Bureau (CFPB)**.

The major elements addressed by the Dodd-Frank Act are as follows:

- Bank capital requirements
- Minimum mortgage origination standards
- Mortgage broker compensation
- Sale of mortgage loans

- Establishment of the CFPB
- Establishment of the Financial Stability Oversight Council
- FDIC standards
- Federal Reserve emergency lending powers
- Regulation of banks' abilities in certain investments
- Regulation of "derivatives" and "hedge funds" and private equity funds
- Liquidation of failing banks
- Control over publicly traded financial services companies, including disclosures relating to executive compensation
- Regulation of credit rating firms

Consumer Financial Protection Bureau

The CFPB was established to prevent abuses by lenders, including predatory lending and inappropriate fees, as well as to incorporate federal regulations pertaining to consumers into one overall agency. The CFPB has broad authority to implement necessary rules for *consumer* protection in financial products. In addition, many of the consumer financial protection responsibilities of many federal agencies were transferred to the CFPB, enabling the agency to respond quickly to any questionable business practices without the necessity of Congress having to pass legislation. These agencies include the following:

- Office of the Comptroller of the Currency
- Office of Thrift Supervision (abolished)
- Federal Reserve Board
- FDIC
- National Credit Union Administration
- HUD
- Federal Trade Commission

The CFPB has responsibility for the rules of the Truth in Lending Act (TILA), Real Estate Settle Procedures Act (RESPA), the Fair Credit Reporting Act (FCRA), and the Equal Credit Opportunity Act (ECOA). Part of this responsibility was to help reduce the confusion and duplication caused by the TILA and RESPA.

Truth in Lending Act

> **The Truth in Lending Act** is a part of the Federal Consumer Credit Protection Act, which became effective July 1, 1969. It was subsequently amended to be known as the Truth in Lending Simplification and Reform Act (TILSRA) of 1980 but is still commonly referred to as simply the Truth in Lending Act.

> " 'Trigger terms' in a real estate ad that require the disclosure of APR occur when you mention a specific number in regard to the financing, such as the amount of down payment, payment, or interest rate. Disclose a number and you need to disclose the APR."
>
> —Jim Hriso

TILA empowered the Federal Reserve Board to adopt regulations known as Regulation Z. The law and regulations *require four chief disclosures in connection with residential mortgage loans and personal consumer loans under $53,000 (2013 level). These are annual percentage rate, finance charge, amount financed, and total of payments. The Federal Reserve Board implemented these regulations by establishing Regulation Z.* In 2010, the responsibility for enforcement of TILA and Regulation Z was assumed by the Consumer Protection Financial Bureau (CPFB) pursuant to the Dodd-Frank Act, discussed previously.

> **Test Tip!**
>
> In general, whenever you name a number (i.e., a **financial number** such as the interest rate as opposed to the number of bedrooms) in an advertisement, including financing information, you likely have triggered a full disclosure under Regulation Z of the TILA.

Regulation Z does not regulate interest rates, but instead *provides specific consumer protections in mortgage loans for residential real estate.* All real estate loans for personal, family, or household purposes are covered by Regulation Z. The regulation does not apply to commercial or agricultural loans. Regulation Z also standardizes the procedures in residential loan transactions. It requires that the borrower be fully informed of all aspects of the loan transaction. In addition, the regulation applies to the advertisement of credit terms for residential real estate. The rules require that any person, company, or institution engaged in regularly extending credit for mortgage purposes as well as companies or individuals who extend credit to others more than five times in a year, excepting loans made to family members, are considered arrangers of credit and must comply with Regulation Z. Real estate brokers and mortgage brokers are not typically considered arrangers of credit and are not generally affected unless they are actually lending money themselves or place advertising containing credit terms for a real estate loan. The specific requirements of Regulation Z are discussed in the following paragraphs.

Disclosure

In recent years, several important changes were brought to the real estate lending industry in the form of the LE. The purpose of the LE is to allow consumers to shop and compare the cost of the credit being sought and must be delivered within three business days of loan application. Hopefully, the LE will eliminate much of the confusion that had been common under the previous practice of the preliminary TILA and RESPA forms. These points are discussed further at the end of Chapter 12.

Loan application is further defined as the lender's receipt of the following six pieces of information from the borrower: (1) legal name; (2) statement of gross income; (3) Social Security number to allow a credit report to be obtained; (4) property address; (5) estimate of property value; and (6) the amount of the mortgage loan requested. Once these six items are obtained, it is considered a loan application even absent any "formal" document being signed by the consumer.

Lenders may not charge the consumer any fees before providing the LE other than a reasonable amount to cover the actual cost of a credit report. Lenders are not allowed to even obtain a credit card number or a check from the consumer for any other items even if the agreement is that these will not be cashed until the consumer has decided to actually obtain the loan.

Lenders will be bound to the accuracy of the LE. Brokers will not have liability for the LE contents and actually never see the LE provided by the lender to the consumer. Once provided, the LE may not be revised by the lender unless one of the following has changed: (1) a prepayment penalty has been added; (2) the loan product itself is changed, such as a fixed rate to an adjustable; and (3) the APR increases by more than 0.125% for a fixed rate loan or 0.25% for an adjustable rate loan.

Lenders must break down the closing-related costs into what previously has been called "tolerance limits," although they are now referred to as "permissible variations." These categories are based on the following three theories: (1) no variation allowed for items, such as (a) fees paid to the lender, (b) lender-required services for which the borrower may not shop, and (c) transfer taxes, which in North Carolina are typically paid by the seller and therefore will not affect the buyer; (2) 10% variation allowed in which the cumulative costs cannot exceed the total estimate provided within the LE by more than 10% without penalty to the lender; and (3) services that the borrower may shop in which case the lender is not responsible for any differences between the amount the lender provided in the LE and the actual amount paid by the borrower.

If the borrower is refinancing or obtaining a second mortgage loan and is pledging a principal residence already owned as security for such loan, the disclosure statement must provide for a right of rescission for the loan transaction. The right to rescind, or cancel, the loan must be exercised by the borrower before midnight of the third business day following the date the transaction was closed. The three-day right of rescission does not apply when the loan is to finance the purchase of a new home or the construction of a dwelling to be used as a principal residence.

Advertising

Regulation Z also applies to advertising the credit terms available for the purchase of a home. The only specific thing that can be stated in the advertisement without making a full disclosure is the annual percentage rate spelled out in full, that is, not abbreviated as APR. If any other credit terms (trigger terms), such as the down payment, monthly payment, dollar amount of finance charge, number of payments, or repayment period, are included in the advertisement, a full disclosure must be provided. For example, an advertisement mentioning a specific down payment *triggers* the requirement to make a complete disclosure of all of the following credit terms: the cash price of the property, the APR, the amount of down payment, the amount of each payment, the date each payment is due, and the total number of payments over the mortgage term. If the annual percentage rate is not a fixed rate but is a variable rate, the ad must specify the rate to be a variable or adjustable rate. General statements regarding the financing can be made without a full disclosure. Such statements as "good financing available," "FHA financing available," and "loan assumption available" are satisfactory for this purpose. Real estate agents must take special care not to violate the advertising requirements of Regulation Z. An interesting way to determine whether a full disclosure is mandated (as stated earlier) is that whenever you advertise a number (related to finance as opposed to the number of bedrooms or baths), you will likely have triggered this rule.

Penalties

A violator of Regulation Z is subject to criminal liability and punishment by fine up to $5,000, imprisonment for up to one year, or both. In the event the borrower has suffered a financial loss as a result of the violation, the borrower can sue the violator under civil law in federal court for damages.

Fair Credit Reporting Act

The purpose of the FCRA is to ensure that consumer credit reporting agencies use reasonable procedures to collect and evaluate relevant consumer credit information fairly and impartially and use this information properly and with respect for the consumer's privacy rights. The rationales underlying this act are that fair and accurate credit reporting is essential to the banking system and that unfair methods of reporting credit erode public confidence essential to the operation of the banking system.

A consumer report is a credit reporting agency's communication of information (in any manner) about the consumer's credit, reputation, lifestyle, or personal characteristics for the actual or intended purpose of partially or completely determining a consumer's eligibility for employment, credit, insurance, or other purposes authorized by the act.

Several items addressed by the FCRA are as follows:

1. Permissible uses of reports
2. Requirements pertaining to information in reports
3. Disclosure of information to consumers

4. Procedure for disputing the report's accuracy
5. Consumer report user requirements
6. Civil liability for willful or negligent noncompliance with the act
7. Penalties for unauthorized disclosure by consumer credit reporting agencies

People have the right to check their consumer reports and to force credit bureaus to correct mistakes in them. There is no charge for this check to the individual who has been denied credit based on information contained in the report. Credit reporting agencies must now provide one free credit report per year to anyone who requests his own report, even if the person requesting the report has not been denied credit. Otherwise, there is usually a service fee. Bankruptcies remain on a credit report for 10 years, but other information must be removed after 7 years. The FCRA is available at http://www.ftc.gov/os/statutes/ 031224fcra.pdf.

The Equal Credit Opportunity Act

Congress enacted and amended the **ECOA** in the mid-1970s. Its purpose is to *prevent discrimination in the loan process* on the part of lending institutions. The act requires financial institutions engaged in making loans to do so on an equal basis to all creditworthy customers without regard for discriminatory factors. The ECOA is implemented by Regulation B of the Federal Reserve Board.

Requirements of ECOA

The ECOA makes it unlawful for a creditor to discriminate against a loan applicant in any aspect of a credit transaction as follows:

1. On the basis of race, color, religion, sex, national origin, marital status, or age (unless the applicant is a minor because a minor does not have the capacity to contract);
2. Because part of the applicant's income is derived from a public assistance program; or
3. Because the applicant has, in good faith, exercised any right under the Federal Consumer Credit Protection Act, of which TILA (Regulation Z) is a part.

> "A Deed of Trust is used to secure payment of the Promissory Note (IOU). It is not a type of deed used to convey ownership of property; it is a lending instrument."
> —Jim Hriso

North Carolina Lending Acts

North Carolina has been proactive in the pursuit of lending legislation in the wake of the financial crisis. North Carolina is generally credited as being the first state to enact a predatory lending act to create restrictions and limits as well as to prohibit unfair and deceptive trade practices in the making of certain high-cost loans. In addition, North Carolina also passed legislation that makes mortgage loan fraud a felony.

Key Finance Math Concepts

Many of these concepts were introduced in the first part of this chapter to better illustrate the important real estate terminology that is associated with these problems. Students should be prepared for the following categories of math problems when preparing for the examination.

- Simple interest calculations, including determining the amount of interest paid over the life of a fixed-rate loan.
- Calculation of monthly P&I using *factors*
- Calculation of mortgage principal balance after *one* monthly payment
- Calculation of loan origination fees and discount points
- Application of LTV ratios
- Determining yield on mortgage loans using *rule of thumb* values

Simple interest calculations

1. Robert has obtained a mortgage that has an outstanding loan balance of $168,425 at 6% interest. What is the amount of interest that he will owe this month?

2. Denise has obtained a 30-year mortgage loan of $149,600 at 5% interest. Her monthly P&I payment is $803.09. What will be the total amount of interest she will pay over the life of this mortgage loan if she keeps it for the entire term?

Calculation of monthly P&I using factors

3. Kent is considering obtaining a mortgage loan of $219,500 at 5.75% interest for a term of 30 years. The lender tells Kent this loan has a P&I factor of $5.84 per month per $1,000 borrowed. What will be Kent's monthly P&I payment for this loan?

Calculation of mortgage principal balance after one payment

4. David has obtained a new mortgage loan of $235,700 at 5.5% interest for 30 years. His monthly P&I payment is $1,338.28. What will be the outstanding loan balance on this mortgage after the first monthly payment?

5. Angela has just obtained a 30-year mortgage loan of $179,500 at 5% interest. Her PITI payment is $1,213.59 per month of which $250.00 is allocated to taxes and insurance. What will be the outstanding loan balance remaining on her mortgage after the first monthly payment?

Calculation of loan origination fees and discount points

6. John has just purchased a home for $319,900 and has obtained a new mortgage loan of $255,900 at 5.25% interest. The lender charged John 1.5 discount

points for making this loan. What was the total amount the lender charged John for discount points?

Application of LTV ratios

7. A purchaser has recently bought a house for $325,000 and desires to obtain an 80% LTV mortgage. What would be the loan amount for this purchase?

8. Rhonda is purchasing a home for $279,500 and is applying for a 90% mortgage loan from the lender. The property has now been appraised and the appraisal was for $278,800. What is the amount of the mortgage the lender is willing to make?

Yield on mortgage loans using rule of thumb values

9. A lender has quoted a willingness to make a borrower a mortgage loan for a 6.375% interest rate. If the borrower is willing to pay 2 discount points, at what interest rate would the lender be willing to make the loan?

10. A property has just been sold for $189,900 in which the appraisal indicates an appraised value of $187,500. The lender agrees to make a 90% LTV mortgage at 5.625% with 1 point collected for the loan origination fee. Assuming the investor demands an 6.25% yield, what would be the total amount collected for all types of points at the closing?

Solutions to Problems

Simple interest calculations

1. $168,425 × 6% = $10,105.50 annualized interest due
   $10,105.50 ÷ 12 = $842.13 interest due for this month

2. $803.09 × 360 = $289,112.40 total P&I paid over 30 years (360 months)
   $289,112.40 − $149,600 = $139,512.40 total interest paid over 30-year term

Calculation of monthly P&I using *factors*

3. $219,500 ÷ $1,000 = 219.5 number of $1,000 increments
   $5.84 × 219.5 = $1,281.88 monthly P&I payment

Calculation of mortgage principal balance after one payment

4. $235,700 × 5.5% = $12,963.50 annualized interest
   $12,963.50 ÷ 12 = $1,080.29 interest due first month
   $1,338.28 − $1,080.29 = $257.99 principal allocation the first month
   $235,700 − $257.99 = $235,442.01 loan balance after first monthly payment

5. $1,213.59 − $250.00 = $963.59 P&I payment per month
   $179,500 × 5% = $8,975 annualized interest due

$8,975 \div 12 = \$747.92$ interest due first month
$963.59 - \$747.92 = \$215.67$ principal allocation first month
$179,500 - \$215.67 = \$179,284.33$ loan balance after first monthly payment

Calculation of loan origination fees and discount points

6. $\$255,900 \times 1.5\% = \$3,838.50$ cost of 1.5 discount points

Application of LTV ratios

7. $\$325,000 \times 80\% = \$260,000$ loan amount
8. $\$278,800 \times 90\% = \$250,920$ loan amount

Yield on mortgage loans using *rule of thumb* values

9. 2 points = 2/8% or 1/4% effect of 2 points on mortgage yield
   6 3/8% − 2/8% = 6 1/8% interest rate
10. $\$187,500 \times 90\% = \$168,750$ loan amount
    6.25 − 5.625 = .625 or 5/8% or 5 discount points
    5 + 1 = 6 points collected
    $\$168,750 \times 6\% = \$10,125$ total of all points collected

Summary of Important Points

1. The purpose of a mortgage or deed of trust is to secure the payment of a promissory note. The promissory note is evidence of the debt (IOU), whereas the mortgage or deed of trust conveys collateral.
2. Two legal theories regarding a mortgage or deed of trust are the lien theory and the title theory. North Carolina is a *title theory* state.
3. The requirements for a valid mortgage or deed of trust are (1) written document, (2) competent parties, (3) valid debt, (4) valid interest, (5) description, (6) mortgaging clause, (7) defeasance clause, (8) execution by borrower, and (9) delivery to and acceptance by lender or trustee.
4. The lender's rights are (1) possession upon default, (2) foreclosure, and (3) assignment of the finance instruments.
5. The borrower's rights are (1) possession prior to default, (2) ability to defeat the lien by paying debt in full prior to default, and (3) right or equity of redemption.
6. There are two types of foreclosure: judicial and nonjudicial (or power of sale). Foreclosure sale proceeds are distributed in a special order of priority.

The funds are used to pay (1) costs of foreclosure, (2) unpaid property taxes and assessments, (3) liens in order of priority, and (4) the borrower. If the sale proceeds available to the lender are insufficient to satisfy the debt, the lender can sue for a deficiency judgment. Sellers who finance their own property with a purchase money deed of trust are not permitted a deficiency judgment in North Carolina.

7. A buyer assuming a seller's mortgage assumes liability on the mortgage and the note. The seller remains liable on the note unless specifically released by a mortgage clause or by the lender. A buyer taking title "subject to" an existing mortgage has no personal liability on the note to the lender.

8. A fully amortizing mortgage requires payments of principal and interest that will satisfy the debt completely over the mortgage term.

9. Various types of mortgages include balloon, open-end, graduated payment, adjustable rate, wraparound, package, blanket, construction, reverse, and junior.

10. Construction loans typically represent the greatest risk of all mortgage loans for the lender. They are an example of a term loan and are usually made by a commercial bank.

11. Junior mortgages are lower in priority than a *senior* mortgage and typically are for a shorter period of time and a higher interest rate.

12. The major sources of residential financing are S&Ls, savings banks, commercial banks, and mortgage bankers.

13. The methods of financing are insured and uninsured conventional mortgage loans, FHA-insured loans, VA-guaranteed loans, RD, and FSA loans, and various types of seller financing.

14. Conventional loans are not required to be insured if the loan amount does not exceed 80% of the property value. Most conventional insured loans are 90% and 95% loans. The insurance is called PMI. The premium is paid by the borrower.

15. FHA-insured and VA-guaranteed loans are made by qualified lending institutions to buyers who are going to occupy the property. Rates on both of these loans can be negotiated between lender and borrower. Either a borrower or a seller may pay the discount points, if any, on VA, FHA, or conventional loans.

16. The FHA programs include 203(b), 203(k), 245, and 234(c). The FHA insurance is called MIP and protects the lender and the purchaser of the loan (that is, the secondary mortgage market) from a financial loss in the event of a foreclosure. The premium is paid by the borrower. The loan amount is a percentage of the acquisition cost as established by the FHA. The interest rate is set by the lender, not the FHA.

17. VA loans are guaranteed. VA loans can be made up to 100% of the property value established by a VA appraisal and stated in the CRV, which is issued by the VA. The interest rate is established by the lender and not the VA.

A borrower must be an eligible veteran (with some minor exceptions) to obtain a VA loan, but a non-veteran is allowed to assume a VA loan.

18. FHA-insured and VA-guaranteed loans require escrow accounts, are for 30-year maximum terms, are assumable with qualification, and do not impose a prepayment penalty. VA-guaranteed loans made after March 1, 1988, require the purchaser wishing to assume the loan to qualify, be approved by the VA, and pay a 0.5% assumption fee. The down payment can be borrowed if secured by other collateral. FHA-insured loans originated after December 15, 1989, require qualification to assume.

19. Mortgage bankers can actually loan the borrower their own money or money from other sources and may or may not sell the loan in the secondary market after it is closed. Mortgage brokers do not actually loan out their own money, but rather put lenders and borrowers together, for which they earn a fee.

20. Federal laws that regulate lending institutions in making consumer loans include the Dodd-Frank Act, TILA, and ECOA.

21. In the primary mortgage market, lending institutions make loans directly to individual borrowers. In the secondary market, mortgages that originated in the primary market are bought and sold. The secondary market consists of the purchase and sale of mortgages among lenders, as well as the sale of mortgages by lenders to Fannie Mae, Ginnie Mae, and Freddie Mac. The market provides liquidity to mortgages, thereby reducing the effect of disintermediation for the benefit of lending institutions and borrowers as well.

22. Fannie Mae purchases VA, FHA, and conventional mortgages. Ginnie Mae purchases only government mortgages. Freddie Mac purchases only conventional mortgages.

Review Questions

Answers to the review questions are in the Answer Key at the back of the book.

1. All of the following statements are applicable to real estate promissory notes EXCEPT:
   A. They must be written.
   B. The borrower is personally liable for payment.
   C. They must provide evidence of a valid debt.
   D. They must be executed by the lender.

2. Which of the following statements concerning a mortgage is correct?
   A. The purpose of a mortgage is to secure the payment of a promissory note.
   B. The delivery of a mortgage is a conditional conveyance of title.
   C. A mortgage is a three-party instrument.
   D. The mortgage lender is called the mortgagor.

3. Which of the following is not a right given to lenders by a deed of trust?
   A. assignment
   B. possession after default
   C. foreclosure
   D. equity of redemption

4. The clause that makes a mortgage unassumable is which of the following?
   A. defeasance
   B. alienation
   C. mortgaging
   D. prepayment

5. Which of the following gives a borrower the right to pay a debt in full and remove the mortgage lien at any time after default and prior to foreclosure?
   A. defeasance
   B. prepayment
   C. equity of redemption
   D. foreclosure

6. A deed in lieu of foreclosure conveys a title to which of the following?
   A. lender
   B. borrower
   C. trustee
   D. mortgagor

7. Which of the following is paid first from the proceeds of a foreclosure sale?
   A. mortgage debt
   B. real property taxes
   C. mortgagee's equity
   D. sale expenses

8. A deficiency judgment is available to which of the following?
   A. mortgagee
   B. mortgagor
   C. trustee
   D. trustor

9. A buyer assumed the seller's mortgage without the seller's obtaining release of liability. The buyer subsequently defaulted. Which of the following statements is correct?
   A. Only the buyer is personally liable for payment of the note.
   B. Only the seller is personally liable for payment of the note.
   C. Both the buyer and the seller are personally responsible for payment of the note.
   D. Neither the buyer nor the seller is personally responsible.

10. The type of mortgage requiring the borrower to pay only interest during the mortgage term is which of the following?
    A. balloon
    B. open-end
    C. term
    D. closed

11. What is the amount of interest paid on an amortizing mortgage at an annual rate of 12% for a month in which the principal balance is $73,000?
    A. $600
    B. $730
    C. $876
    D. $1,369

12. Which of the following is a mortgage that is not on a fully amortizing basis and therefore requires a larger final payment?
    A. graduated mortgage
    B. balloon mortgage
    C. open-end mortgage
    D. flexible mortgage

13. Which of the following statements regarding adjustable rate mortgages (ARMs) is correct?
    A. The interest rate changes according to changes in a selected index.
    B. Adjustable rate mortgages always contain a due-on-sale clause and a prepayment penalty.
    C. All adjustable rate mortgages have a conversion feature that allows them to be converted to a fixed rate.
    D. None of the above.

14. Which of the following are NOT considered to be one of the six elements of a loan application?
    A. marital status
    B. Social Security number of the applicant
    C. property address
    D. estimate of property value

15. Which of the following is a mortgage in which two or more parcels of land are pledged?
    A. blanket
    B. package
    C. all-inclusive
    D. junior

16. Which of the following is a mortgage that is subordinate to another?
    A. leasehold
    B. blanket
    C. junior
    D. participation

17. The priority of mortgages in relation to one another is based on which of the following?
    A. time of execution
    B. time of recording
    C. time of delivery
    D. time of acknowledgment

18. Which of the following is a mortgage given by the buyer to the seller to secure payment of part of the purchase price?
    A. purchase money mortgage
    B. earnest money mortgage
    C. participation mortgage
    D. graduated payment mortgage

19. Insurance for the protection of lending institutions making conventional loans is:
    A. mutual mortgage insurance
    B. conventional mortgage insurance
    C. institutional insurance
    D. private mortgage insurance

20. What is the purpose of FHA programs?
    A. making housing loans
    B. guaranteeing housing loans
    C. purchasing housing loans
    D. insuring housing loans

21. The FHA bases its commitment on a percentage of which of the following?
    A. certificate of reasonable value (CRV)
    B. purchase price
    C. selling price
    D. acquisition cost or appraisal value, whichever is less

22. A property has recently sold for $173,000, and the appraisal indicates an appraised value of $172,000. The lender agrees to make an 80% LTV loan at 5 ¾% interest. Assuming the investor demands a 6 3/8% yield, what would be the total amount collected for points at the closing?
    A. $8,328
    B. $8,256
    C. $6,940
    D. $6,880

23. The major benefit of the secondary mortgage market is to reduce the effect of which of the following?
    A. amortization
    B. liquidity
    C. disintermediation
    D. expensive settlement charges

24. Which of the following statements about VA loans is (are) correct?
    A. The repayment of a percentage of VA loans in the event of borrower default is insured to the lender.
    B. VA loans are for 100% of the lesser of property value established by the VA or the sales price.
    C. A veteran cannot use his VA loan entitlement more than once.
    D. A non-veteran may not assume a VA loan.

25. All of the following statements about FHA and VA loans are correct EXCEPT:
    A. They are assumable.
    B. They require a prepayment penalty.
    C. The maximum term is 30 years.
    D. They require an escrow account.

26. Which of the following statements about discount points is correct?
    A. Each point charged increases the lender's yield on the loan by 1 percentage point.
    B. Each point charged by the lender costs 1/8% of the loan amount.
    C. Points must be paid by buyer on conventional loans.
    D. Discount points are a form of prepaid interest.

27. All of the following statements about Regulation Z are correct EXCEPT:
    A. It applies to commercial mortgage loans.
    B. It requires lenders to furnish a disclosure statement to the borrower.
    C. It provides for a three-day right of rescission when a residence already owned is being pledged as security for a new mortgage.
    D. It regulates the advertising of credit terms of the property offered for sale.

28. ECOA requires lenders to make consumer loans without regard to all of the following EXCEPT:
    A. age
    B. occupation
    C. sex
    D. marital status

29. The activity of lending institutions making mortgage loans directly to individual borrowers is:
    A. secondary mortgage market
    B. money market
    C. institutional market
    D. primary mortgage market

30. Which of the following is a government-owned corporation that purchases mortgages?
    A. Fannie Mae
    B. Ginnie Mae
    C. Freddie Mac
    D. Consumer Financial Protection Bureau

31. Harold has purchased a property for $118,000 and plans to obtain an 85% LTV mortgage. The cost to amortize the loan, per $1,000, is $6.16. What will Harold's monthly P&I cost?

    A. $513.33
    B. $616.00
    C. $617.85
    D. $726.88

32. A borrower has obtained a loan of $184,300 at 5.75% interest for 30 years. If his monthly P&I payment is $1,075.52, what would be the outstanding loan balance after the first monthly payment?

    A. $183,807.58
    B. $184,107.58
    C. $183,224.48
    D. $183,416.90

33. Roger has closed on a house that he purchased for $195,000 by obtaining an 80% LTV mortgage at 5.5% interest for 30 years. His monthly debt service payment is $885.75. What will be the total amount Roger will pay for interest over the term of the loan?

    A. $123,870
    B. $162,870
    C. $257,400
    D. $292,298

34. What is the LTV ratio where the purchase price is $193,750, the appraised value is $182,350, and the loan amount is $155,000?

    A. 75%
    B. 80%
    C. 85%
    D. 94%

CHAPTER 12

CLOSING A SALES TRANSACTION

KEY TERMS

Closing Disclosure (CD)
credit
debit
double entry
interim interest

Loan Estimate (LE)
prorating
Real Estate Settlement
    Procedures Act (RESPA)
settlement

single entry
Truth in Lending Act (TILA)
TILA/RESPA Integrated
    Disclosure (TRID)

LEARNING OBJECTIVES

At the conclusion of this chapter, you should be able to:

1. List the preliminaries to closing.
2. List the items required at the closing.
3. Describe the process of the closing meeting.
4. Describe the placement of items as debits and credits in the closing statement.
5. Describe the provisions of the Real Estate Settlement Procedures Act.
6. Calculate the balance due from the buyer to the seller in a closing statement.

IN THIS CHAPTER

Closing is the consummation of the sales effort that began when the broker obtained a written listing agreement. This event is given different names, such as settlement and the closing of escrow. At the closing, the buyer receives a deed and the seller receives payment for the property. In North Carolina, the predominant practice is to assemble the parties for a closing meeting where all the paperwork is signed. In addition, this chapter will introduce the traditional ways of handling the closing process and who will be charged for the various expenses. The federal requirements for

closing forms will also be addressed. The chapter will introduce the North Carolina Closing Core Worksheet, which is the form designed to be used on the classroom and state exams.

PRECLOSING PROCEDURES

Closing is the consummation of the sales effort that began when the broker first obtained a listing all the way through the contracting for sale and the undertaking of due diligence to better understand the important aspects of the property. Although known by various names, including settlement and even escrow in some states, we will utilize "settlement" as the predominant name in these pages. **Settlement** refers to *the preparation and delivery of document as well as collection of funds necessary to finalize the transaction.* **Closing** is *the multistep process of undertaking due diligence relative to the title, the preparation of documents, the conveyance of the deed, and the collection and disbursement of funds.* After these steps have been completed, closing involves the *proper registration of the deed and related mortgage documents along with the clearing of the prior mortgage and liens to make certain the seller has no lingering legal issues to the property.* In many states, this process is completed by an escrow agent and the buyer and seller do not actually attend a meeting to complete the necessary documents. In North Carolina, the predominate method is to use the closing or settlement meeting process in which the parties or their representative meet to complete all the necessary paperwork. It is this process that we will concentrate on for this chapter.

SELECTING AND PROVIDING INFORMATION TO CLOSING ATTORNEY

One of the first steps involved in the closing process is to select the attorney who will provide the relevant services. It is the buyer's responsibility to select the desired attorney, although many will not know which attorney to use. In most cases, it will probably be the real estate broker working with the buyer who will assist the buyer in selecting who will provide legal services. In some instances, especially involving new construction builders, the seller may insist on naming the closing attorney, especially if they are paying the closing costs. Remember that the lender has the right to insist on the attorney being someone who is on their "approved list," although most attorneys who specialize in real estate closings will likely be on most lenders' approved list or can be included on it with some degree of education about that particular lender's policies about how they wish the closing process to be carried out. Lenders can certainly maintain an approved list of attorneys as long as it is not unduly restrictive to be included on the list.

Once the attorney has been selected, the broker will likely be more in contact with the administrative staff than the actual closing attorney before the closing meeting. There will need to be some understanding as to who is to provide what services, such as ordering the termite and pest control report, and who will be preparing the deed. If the deed is to be prepared by another attorney, the broker will need to make certain that it is delivered to the closing attorney for it to be reviewed as part of the title process. The agent will need to provide a copy of the Offer to Purchase and Contract (OPC) to the closing attorney so that information such as who the grantee in the deed is to be made out to, as well as the seller's name, can be determined. The broker may also be requested to provide a copy of the seller's title insurance policy, and he will also need to disclose to the attorney if there are any changes in marital status, including marriage, legal separation, divorce, or death.

Buyer's Due Diligence Process

The buyer's due diligence period is typically described as that time between the effective date and 5:00 p.m. of the due diligence date. The philosophy of the North Carolina Association of REALTORS®/North Carolina Bar Association (NCAR/NCBA) Standard Form 2-T OPC is to allow the buyer to investigate anything that is important to the buyer relative to the property being purchased. During this time, the buyer can have the property appraised, inspected, surveyed, and checked to determine the suitability for a septic system, can determine whether there are any zoning or restrictive covenant issues of concern, can determine the ability to obtain insurance, and can look into any other items the buyer feels are important. During this time period, the buyer is also to use his efforts to obtain necessary financing. The important thing to remember is that although the OPC stipulates the buyer has until 5:00 p.m. of the due diligence date to explore these areas of concern, the reality is the buyer actually has until the actual closing itself to undertake due diligence.

Perhaps the confusion stems from the fact the buyer can withdraw for any reason, including no reason at all, at any time before the 5:00 p.m. deadline. In reality, the buyer can withdraw for any reason whatsoever after 5:00 p.m. of the due diligence date with the only difference being the loss of his earnest money deposit as liquidated damages. This liquidated damages clause means the buyer has a certain liability to the seller in the event that she does not follow through and perform according to the terms of the contract. Once the 5:00 p.m. deadline has passed, the only way the seller will be liable for return of the buyer's earnest money deposit will be if the seller is unable to convey good and marketable title to the property unless there is an additional clause contained in some other addendum that will require the seller to refund the deposit, such as the provisions contained in the Short Sale Addendum or the Contingent Sale Addendum.

One of the biggest areas of concern of buyer's due diligence is the title search process and the determination of whether the seller can convey clear title to the property. This act of due diligence has not typically been undertaken until just prior to the actual closing and therefore usually after the 5:00 p.m. due diligence deadline has passed. One reason this was not undertaken prior to the 5:00 p.m. deadline like most of the other areas of due diligence is the buyer was not at risk for loss of his earnest money in the event the seller cannot convey clear title.

Given the October 3, 2015, implementation date for delivery of the buyer's closing disclosures (details to follow) it is interesting to see how these new rules have affected the parties' selection of the due diligence date given that attorneys will need to complete all title work in plenty of time to accommodate the lender's having time to review and send out final disclosures to the buyers at least three to six business days before any closing can occur.

Buyer's Loan

The current OPC no longer stipulates a loan contingency. If the buyer needs to obtain financing and the financing is not obtained before the 5:00 p.m. deadline on the due diligence date, the earnest money will be at risk for forfeiture to the seller. Ideally the buyer would want to obtain any necessary financing before the due diligence deadline, but there is always the possibility that any loan approval could be withdrawn by the lender before the actual funding as part of the closing process. For many buyers, the period of time that will be needed to obtain the financing will play the primary role in determining how they will negotiate the duration of the due diligence period. If the buyer cannot obtain the financing within the due diligence period, he will likely try to negotiate an extension with the seller for more time. The seller is under no obligation to agree to any such extension but would incur the risk that the buyer may simply ask out of the contract and leave the seller back to the proverbial "square one," having to start the sales process all over again. The wise buyer agent will insist on the buyer beginning the loan application process early on in the buying process, even perhaps before starting to look for any properties. As the housing market improves, buyers may very well find themselves wanting to purchase a property where the seller is not willing to give the buyer enough time to obtain financing before the passage of the due diligence date. In this case, the seller would be entitled to retain the buyer's earnest money deposit if the buyer is unable to secure the needed financing in order to close.

Appraisal

There is no appraisal contingency contained within the OPC; therefore, any desired appraisal should be obtained before the expiration of the due diligence period. If the property does not appraise after the due diligence period, the buyer would forfeit his earnest money deposit in the event that she does not conclude the purchase.

Property Survey

The property survey is obtained to establish the location of the property boundaries as well as the location of any improvements on the property. As a result, the survey will typically show any encroachments relative to the property. It is advisable to obtain the survey before the expiration of the due diligence period; however, if the survey should indicate title problems such as encroachments, it may be possible for the buyer to retain his earnest money deposit as the contract is contingent upon the seller conveying a good and marketable title to the property.

Property Insurance

The buyer is wise to determine the insurability, as well as cost of such insurance, prior to the end of the due diligence period even though the insurance may not be purchased until the time of closing. The buyer and seller need to make certain that the coverage is in effect at the time of closing. The seller's policy should only be canceled after it can be ascertained the closing has completed and the buyer has his coverage in effect. If the seller is to retain possession after the closing, he should notify his insurance agent to make certain he is properly covered and he may be required to convert to a "renter's" type policy while he remains in possession. Typically the lender will establish the minimum requirements for insurance the borrower will have to obtain; will require the policy to be in effect, along with a receipt showing the policy has been paid for; and will require that a copy of the insurance be included with the loan documents by the closing attorney. In situations involving owner-occupied dwellings, the insurance will typically be a homeowner's policy. In cases involving non-owner-occupied properties, such as rentals, the coverage will be a variation of fire and liability such as an owner/landlord policy. In addition to hazard insurance, the property owner will be required by the lender to obtain a flood insurance certification and to obtain a flood insurance policy in the case in which the property is located within a designated floodplain.

Inspections

It is perhaps the area of inspections that most parties associate with doing due diligence. There are many different areas of inspection that buyers will want to undertake before the due diligence date. Although these inspections can continue to be completed up to the actual closing, the buyer would forfeit her earnest money deposit to the seller if she were to back out of the contract after 5:00 p.m. of the due diligence date.

North Carolina is a state that has a notable presence of termites and other wood-destroying organisms. It is advised, if not actually required by the lender, that a buyer contract with a licensed pest control operator to inspect the buildings for the infestation of wood-destroying insects. Many lenders will require evidence of a termite inspection within a specified number of days before the closing.

This is important as the buyer would want to obtain a termite report before the due diligence date, yet may be required to have a reinspection in cases in which the actual closing date is scheduled many days beyond the actual inspection date.

It is highly recommended to have the building inspected by a licensed home inspector before the due diligence date. The home inspector can provide expertise on many inspection matters that are beyond the expertise of real estate brokers. As a matter of risk management, the broker should refer inquiries about inspection-related matters to a licensed professional rather than attempt to make representations that she will later regret should problems arise.

There are many items that only a physical inspection can disclose to a buyer. For example, there may be tenants living in the property who have not been disclosed. Remember that a lease that can be completed in less than three years of its making will not be required to be in writing or recorded; therefore, it would not be discovered in the title search process. It may be that the existence of encroachments and easements are observed and the buyer may wish to obtain a property survey to determine for certain whether there is a problem.

The buyer should also check to determine whether there is evidence of recent construction or any modifications to the property since it was originally contracted. In the case of recent construction within the past 120 days, it may be necessary to obtain lien releases to protect the buyer from mechanics' lien claims filed by unpaid contractors and suppliers. Remember that mechanics' liens are liens against the property and not against the prior owner who actually may have been the person who ordered the work. In the case of observed modifications to the property that have been made since original construction, it is wise to determine whether the proper building permits and inspections were obtained. It is entirely possible that a permit and inspection may be required for work that was completed years earlier to protect the buyer from possible problems later on. In the situation in which it appears that an additional bedroom or bathroom was added or in which a previously unfinished basement was modified, it will be necessary to obtain evidence of the required permits as the house may now exceed the septic capacity for which the property was approved.

Septic/Sewer System

It is important to know whether the property is served by a municipal or county sewage system or if a private system will be required. In the event that a private system will be required, such as when purchasing vacant land, it will be important to secure the necessary permits to allow installation of the system that will accommodate the desired numbers of bedrooms. Before such a permit is issued, it will be necessary to secure a percolation, or "perc," test, as it is commonly called, from the local health department. In reality, the term "perc" is technically obsolete as the modern test actually involves a soil analysis and is called a soil suitability test. Such permits are issued and are good for construction within a designated number of years even if the requirements should later change. If the purchase involves existing construction, it will be important to understand that the permit was sufficient for the number of bedrooms the house contains. This will be very important in situations in which it appears the number of bedrooms, or bathrooms, has changed since original construction.

Certainly, there can be any number of tests the buyer will want to consider as part of his due diligence. Depending on the age and location of the property, the buyer may wish to consider testing for environmental concerns such as lead-based paint, radon, asbestos, and mold contamination.

Resolution of Repair-Related Issues

Once the physical inspections have been completed, it may be necessary for the buyer to negotiate with the seller regarding repairs and improvements. According to the OPC, the buyer is free to negotiate the repair of anything that he wishes and to whatever "standard" of acceptability he desires. Such negotiations should be completed before the due diligence date, although the actual repair work may not be completed until after that time. In the event the work is completed after the due diligence date, the work is to be completed in a good and professional manner.

Review of Restrictive Covenants and Homeowners Association Documents

One of the important things to remember in the purchase of any home is the necessity to review the rules of owning such a home as imposed by private restrictive covenants and rules and regulations of any applicable homeowners association. This is especially important to discover before the passage of the due diligence period as the buyer may have desires to use the property in such a way as is not permitted by either of these sets of rules. For example, the buyer may want to construct a fence around the boundary of the property after the purchase only to find that such a fence is not allowed. It is essential to note that any property use the buyer wishes to make that is different from the current property use or those of any of the surrounding properties should absolutely be checked to determine its legality before passage of the due diligence period.

Other Matters of Interest

Additionally, the buyer will want to research current zoning maps to determine what is permitted for adjoining lands. She will also want to inquire about road widening and extension projects that will affect her future enjoyment. It will also be important to determine whether the roads are publicly or privately maintained. If they are privately maintained, the buyer should ascertain whether there are appropriate road maintenance agreements in place and who will bear the cost of maintenance (usually shared by the homeowners in the subdivision).

Other Preclosing Matters

Most of the previous items of due diligence are things the buyer will want to complete before the due diligence date as to avoid loss of the earnest money deposit. Many other items important to the due diligence process may, or may not, be completed, before the due diligence date. These items do not cause concern about the loss of earnest money as the seller has promised to convey good and marketable title. These important elements of due diligence will involve a title search by the closing attorney to determine whether the seller possesses good and marketable title, including a review of mechanics' liens as well as Uniform Commercial Code (UCC) filings. Title searches are conducted to determine whether the seller has the right to convey title, and they include reviews to determine whether there are any missing signatures, if the past deeds have been properly notarized, and if past liens such as mortgages have been properly canceled. In the event that title defects are discovered, it will become necessary for the attorney to clear these issues to the satisfaction of the buyer as well as the lender and the title insurance company. Title insurance companies will not issue any policy until they are completely satisfied as to the quality of any title they are asked to insure. The attorney will need to complete this title work in plenty of time to allow the lender to review and prepare necessary documents to send them to the buyer in plenty of time as required by **Truth in Lending Act (TILA)/Real Estate Settlement Procedures Act (RESPA) Integrated Disclosure (TRID)** rules. This will be at least six business days, although most lenders will typically require a few days longer for their own purposes.

In the event that title defects are discovered, it will become necessary for the attorney to clear these issues to the satisfaction of the buyer as well as the lender and title insurance company. Title insurance companies will not issue any policy until they are completely satisfied as to the quality of any title they are asked to insure.

Once all of these steps are completed, the closing attorney will complete the paperwork, including the final closing statement. The parties are allowed to review the closing statement one day before the closing meeting. In the event the closing attorney does not have complete information for the closing statement, he would be required to disclose to the buyer what information he does have at that time. This right to review the closing statement is often not addressed by any of the parties. The agent working with the buyer will need to obtain the final amount due from the buyer in order to close. Closing attorneys will require this amount to be paid in the form of certified funds, money orders, official bank checks, funds drawn on another attorney's or broker's trust account, or any other such source of immediately available funds. It is possible that some limited amount of funds paid by personal check may be permitted, but this should always be addressed with the closing attorney beforehand.

One of the things that brokers and buyers will need to keep in mind, in the selection of the due diligence date, is that lenders will likely require all paperwork, including title searches, to be delivered to the lender for review perhaps as early as 10–14 days before the anticipated closing. For this reason, buyers need to understand that if they order title work from an attorney and then later back out by the due diligence date, they will still be liable for the attorney fees incurred. It may be that the selection of the due diligence date will need to be perhaps two weeks before the closing in many cases.

The broker will need to discuss with the closing attorney how the earnest money deposit is to be handled. Some attorneys will want to have the deposit handed over to them for final disbursement. The North Carolina Real Estate Commission allows the broker to turn this deposit over to the closing attorney up to 10 days prior to the scheduled closing. Some closing attorneys allow the broker holding the buyer's earnest money in their trust account to retain the earnest money, and the attorney will deduct this amount from the commission that would normally be disbursed to the firm. The firm would then withdraw the earnest money as part of its earned commission after the closing is completed.

The agent working with the buyer will need to obtain the final amount due from the buyer in order to close. Closing attorneys will require this amount to be paid in the form of certified funds, money orders, official bank checks, funds drawn on another attorney's or broker's trust account, or any other such source of immediately available funds. It is possible that some limited amount of funds paid by personal check may be permitted, but this should always be addressed with the closing attorney beforehand.

CLOSING PROCEDURES

There is often some degree of confusion over the use of terminology involving closing, settlement, and the closing meeting. In many ways, the terms "closing" and "settlement" are often used interchangeably by the parties to the transaction, but there is some distinction to be made between the two. Perhaps it is useful to describe the settlement process as the overall multistep process that includes everything from the time the closing attorney receives the title search request, to the lender preparing documents, to the attorney obtaining all of the necessary associated documents and items, conducting the actual closing meeting, recording documents, disbursing of funds, delivering the keys, and doing anything else necessary to finalize the transaction. The settlement meeting is the actual meeting of the parties to execute the necessary documents and review the overall finalizing of the transaction. Two primary functions are accomplished at this meeting. The deed is delivered from the seller to the buyer, and the buyer's mortgage loan documents are executed. In reality, the majority of the paperwork and time is spent finalizing the buyer's loan. Many people actually consider this meeting to be the actual closing, but in North Carolina, the Good Funds Settlement Act, as well as the OPC, define **closing as the act of recordation of the deed**. For this reason, it is entirely possible for the settlement meeting to be held on one day and the actual recordation to occur the following day or week. Most closing attorneys will work diligently to conduct the settlement meeting and execute the recordation on the same day to avoid problems. It is important to remember that title, and possible possession, does not pass until recordation (closing), and the parties will need to be diligent in making certain the proper insurances are maintained until everything is finalized.

Closing Methods and Procedures

There are two predominant methods of closing used throughout the country, the escrow method and the settlement meeting method. Although both are legal methods to use in North Carolina, the settlement meeting method is more common. In the escrow method, the buyer and seller do not attend the closing, but rather all paperwork and filing is completed by an escrow agent, often working with the title insurance company. The parties will execute all documents and deliver them back to the escrow agent, who will record the deed, pay off the existing mortgage, and otherwise accomplish everything the settlement meeting method will achieve.

The settlement meeting method is used more frequently in this state and involves an actual meeting of the parties with the closing attorney. This meeting will generally take place at the buyer's closing attorney's office, although it can occur at any mutually agreeable location. It is quite common for the seller to execute the deed, review the closing statement, and deliver the keys in advance of the actual meeting, leaving only the buyer and her agent to meet with the attorney. Once the seller delivers the signed deed and reviews her relevant items on the closing statement, there is nothing that really requires her to attend the remainder of the meeting because the disbursement of funds cannot occur until after the deed has been recorded. As a result, most closing meetings will be attended only by the buyer and her agent, although the lender may desire to have a representative attend, and occasionally the seller's agent will attend in the event that issues affecting the seller arise.

The buyer will be required to sign a substantial amount of paperwork that is related to obtaining the mortgage. After all paperwork has been signed, there will be a review of the closing statement items that pertain to the buyer and delivery by the buyer to the closing attorney of the necessary funds in order to close. Any funds the buyer will need to provide will be paid by certified check although the Good Funds Settlement Act of North Carolina does allow a modest amount of monies to be paid by personal check.

Procedures after the Settlement Meeting

The closing meeting does not represent the end of the transfer or title issues. The title insurance company will wish to review all of the pertinent documents relating to the title before insuring the quality of the title. Additionally, the title search of all ownership interests and liens is generally reviewed several days before the actual closing. It will be important for the closing attorney to review the public record to make certain that no unknown transfers of title or new lien filings have occurred since the original title search was completed. This updating of the review of public record will take place at the time of recordation of the deed. In the event that something questionable is discovered, the attorney will not record the deed, hence delaying the conveyance of title until these new issues can be satisfactorily addressed. It is often stated that the seller's old mortgage will be canceled before the buyer's new deed is recorded, but often the attorney will not be able to cancel it until the seller's lender receives the payoff of the seller's loan and delivers evidence of the cancellation of the seller's old loan. This would likely be several days after the buyer's deed is recorded. Once the buyer's deed is recorded, the deed of trust, conveying the title as collateral for the loan, will be recorded immediately. It is important for the closing attorney to have the documents recorded in the appropriate order as the buyer cannot convey title as collateral until he actually has a title to convey.

According to the North Carolina Good Funds Settlement Act, the closing attorney cannot disburse the funds until after the deed has been recorded and the funds are determined to be "good and collected." According to this act, the funds are considered good and collected when they are paid in the form of official or certified bank funds, checks drawn on an attorney's or real estate firm's trust account, checks from a Federal Deposit Insurance Corporation–insured bank, and checks from a local, state, or federal governmental agency. For this reason, closing attorneys will require the buyer to pay monies due in one or more of these appropriate forms. Once the deed recordation has taken place, the monies can then be disbursed.

It is quite common for attorneys to disburse the earned sales commission to the firm by advising the broker holding the earnest money to keep those funds and by deducting the amount of the earnest money deposit from the total sales commission due. The reason is simply one of efficiency for both the attorney as well as the escrow agent firm (usually the listing firm), as the firm does not have to go through the trouble of issuing a check for the earnest money and the attorney doesn't have to deal with the subsequent deposit of money into her trust account and having to determine whether the check from the broker has cleared before disbursing funds.

The closing attorney will also report the transaction to the Internal Revenue Service by filing the required Form 1099-S. This filing will include the name of the parties, social security number, and sales price.

Real Estate Settlement Procedures Act

The **Real Estate Settlement Procedures Act (RESPA)** was originally enacted in 1974 to provide assistance to buyers regarding the obtaining of a mortgage loan when purchasing a residential property. The original version of this legislation required lenders to provide a good faith estimate of the closing costs within three business days of the loan application as well as provide an informational pamphlet that explained the various costs and the borrower's rights. These costs were based on the lender's knowledge of the approximate costs for various services and products that would be required in order to close. Federally backed mortgage loans are those that are made, or guaranteed, by a federally insured bank or are owner-occupied residential one- to four-family home loans that will be sold within the secondary mortgage market. RESPA regulations do not apply to sales transactions that include loans for commercial, business, or agricultural purposes, including loans for rental purposes, as they are considered business related. *As a practical matter, federally related mortgages are virtually any mortgage loan made by an institutional lender that does not include owner financing and cash transactions.*

The original RESPA regulations of 1974 served consumers reasonably well for many years by allowing the borrower to "shop" various lenders and compare interest rates as well as costs incurred to obtain financing. The idea was that borrowers would be armed with key information that would allow comparisons and therefore be able to obtain the best loan possible to satisfy their needs.

SUMMARY OF RESPA REQUIREMENTS

- Loan Application. A loan application is that point in which the lender obtains the borrower's:

    1. name;
    2. monthly income;
    3. social security number, which allows the credit report to be obtained;
    4. address of the property to be pledged as collateral;
    5. estimated value of the property; and
    6. the requested loan amount.

- Information Booklet. Lenders are required to provide borrowers, within three business days of loan application, an informational pamphlet *"Know Before You Owe"* that is designed to provide basic guidance on the process of shopping for a house, the loan process, and closing.
- TILA/RESPA Integrated Disclosure (TRID). For the past few decades there was a practice or requiring disclosures from both the TILA as well as RESPA.

Unfortunately, the result was confusion over the way that certain financial information was required to be reported in addition to too much duplication. To streamline the process the Dodd-Frank legislation sought to combine elements from each in such a way as to make things easier for the consumer to understand. The result is now called TRID to illustrate how the previous duplication from TILA and RESPA could be combined into one form called the **Loan Estimate (LE)**. There is still a requirement for a final **Closing Disclosure (CD)** that will take place on the required federal closing document, the CD.

- Yield Spread Premiums. In the event the mortgage is originated by a mortgage broker, as opposed to directly by the lender, the existence of any "yield spread premium" must be disclosed to the borrower as a credit for the amount of any fees paid for making the loan at the "above-market rate" terms the borrower was otherwise reasonably entitled to.

- CD. To provide more privacy for the buyer and the seller, there are now separate closing documents: the Closing Disclosure for Sellers (Figure 12.1) and the Closing Disclosure for Buyers (Figure 12.2). Closing attorneys are now required to use these forms for all applicable federally related loans.

- Amount of reserves for escrow accounts. The lender is limited to collecting only an amount necessary to fund the actual amount charged (one-twelfth per month) for escrow requirements such as property taxes and insurance premiums. There is a limited exception to this rule that allows lenders to collect an amount up to one-sixth of the expected disbursement to provide an adequate "cushion" to maintain the account.

- Disclosure of Loan Servicing. Lenders are required to disclose to the borrower if they have the right to transfer the servicing of the loan and the likelihood of such transfer. In the event the servicing is ultimately transferred, the borrower must actually be notified by the lender.

- Kickbacks for Referrals. One of the original concerns of RESPA regulations was the practice of charging referral fees for closing-related services. In reality, these kickbacks provided nothing of value to the transaction and only served to increase the cost to the consumer. The thinking is that the real estate agent is paid sufficiently in the form of the sales commission and that this fee already compensates the agent for providing referrals for the various service providers necessary to close the transaction. For this reason, kickbacks for closing-related referrals, such as from attorneys, appraisers, inspectors, and real estate brokers, are strictly prohibited under RESPA regulations. Therefore, real estate brokers cannot accept, nor can service providers pay to brokers, referral fees for closing-related services. It should be noted that real estate agents can legally pay and accept referral fees for brokerage services such as a listing or a buyer referral, as those fees would not increase the amount ultimately paid by the consumer.

Closing Disclosure

Closing Information
Date Issued
Closing Date
Disbursement Date
Settlement Agent
File #
Property

Sale Price

Transaction Information
Borrower

Seller

Summaries of Transactions

SELLER'S TRANSACTION

Due to Seller at Closing
01 Sale Price of Property
02 Sale Price of Any Personal Property Included in Sale
03
04
05
06
07
08

Adjustments for Items Paid by Seller in Advance
09 City/Town Taxes   to
10 County Taxes   to
11 Assessments   to
12
13
14
15
16

Due from Seller at Closing
01 Excess Deposit
02 Closing Costs Paid at Closing (J)
03 Existing Loan(s) Assumed or Taken Subject to
04 Payoff of First Mortgage Loan
05 Payoff of Second Mortgage Loan
06
07
08 Seller Credit
09
10
11
12
13

Adjustments for Items Unpaid by Seller
14 City/Town Taxes   to
15 County Taxes   to
16 Assessments   to
17
18
19

CALCULATION
Total Due to Seller at Closing
Total Due from Seller at Closing
Cash ☐ From ☐ To Seller

Contact Information

REAL ESTATE BROKER (B)
Name
Address

__ License ID
Contact
Contact __ License ID
Email
Phone

REAL ESTATE BROKER (S)
Name
Address

__ License ID
Contact
Contact __ License ID
Email
Phone

SETTLEMENT AGENT
Name
Address

__ License ID
Contact
Contact __ License ID
Email
Phone

Questions? If you have questions about the loan terms or costs on this form, use the contact information above. To get more information or make a complaint, contact the Consumer Financial Protection Bureau at **www.consumerfinance.gov/mortgage-closing**

CLOSING DISCLOSURE

FIGURE 12.1 Closing Disclosure for sellers.

Closing Cost Details

Loan Costs

		Seller-Paid	
		At Closing	Before Closing
A. Origination Charges			
01	% of Loan Amount (Points)		
02			
03			
04			
05			
06			
07			
08			
B. Services Borrower Did Not Shop For			
01			
02			
03			
04			
05			
06			
07			
08			
C. Services Borrower Did Shop For			
01			
02			
03			
04			
05			
06			
07			
08			

Other Costs

		At Closing	Before Closing
E. Taxes and Other Government Fees			
01	Recording Fees Deed: Mortgage:		
02			
F. Prepaids			
01	Homeowner's Insurance Premium (mo.)		
02	Mortgage Insurance Premium (mo.)		
03	Prepaid Interest (per day from to)		
04	Property Taxes (mo.)		
05			
G. Initial Escrow Payment at Closing			
01	Homeowner's Insurance per month for mo.		
02	Mortgage Insurance per month for mo.		
03	Property Taxes per month for mo.		
04			
05			
06			
07			
08	Aggregate Adjustment		
H. Other			
01			
02			
03			
04			
05			
06			
07			
08			
09			
10			
11			
12			
13			
J. TOTAL CLOSING COSTS			

FIGURE 12.1 (*Continued.*)

Closing Disclosure

This form is a statement of final loan terms and closing costs. Compare this document with your Loan Estimate.

Closing Information
Date Issued: 4/15/2013
Closing Date: 4/15/2013
Disbursement Date: 4/15/2013
Settlement Agent: Epsilon Title Co.
File #: 12-3456
Property: 456 Somewhere Ave
Anytown, ST 12345
Sale Price: $180,000

Transaction Information
Borrower: Michael Jones and Mary Stone
123 Anywhere Street
Anytown, ST 12345
Seller: Steve Cole and Amy Doe
321 Somewhere Drive
Anytown, ST 12345
Lender: Ficus Bank

Loan Information
Loan Term: 30 years
Purpose: Purchase
Product: Fixed Rate
Loan Type: ☒ Conventional ☐ FHA ☐ VA ☐ _____
Loan ID #: 123456789
MIC #: 000654321

Loan Terms

		Can this amount increase after closing?
Loan Amount	$162,000	NO
Interest Rate	3.875%	NO
Monthly Principal & Interest *See Projected Payments below for your Estimated Total Monthly Payment*	$761.78	NO
		Does the loan have these features?
Prepayment Penalty		YES • As high as **$3,240** if you pay off the loan during the first 2 years
Balloon Payment		NO

Projected Payments

Payment Calculation	Years 1-7	Years 8-30
Principal & Interest	$761.78	$761.78
Mortgage Insurance	+ 82.35	+ —
Estimated Escrow *Amount can increase over time*	+ 206.13	+ 206.13
Estimated Total Monthly Payment	**$1,050.26**	**$967.91**

| Estimated Taxes, Insurance & Assessments
Amount can increase over time
See page 4 for details | $356.13
a month | **This estimate includes**
☒ Property Taxes
☒ Homeowner's Insurance
☒ Other: Homeowner's Association Dues
See Escrow Account on page 4 for details. You must pay for other property costs separately. | **In escrow?**
YES
YES
NO |

Costs at Closing

Closing Costs	$9,712.10	Includes $4,694.05 in Loan Costs + $5,018.05 in Other Costs – $0 in Lender Credits. *See page 2 for details.*
Cash to Close	$14,147.26	Includes Closing Costs. *See Calculating Cash to Close on page 3 for details.*

FIGURE 12.2 Closing Disclosure for buyers.

Closing Cost Details

Loan Costs

		Borrower-Paid		Seller-Paid		Paid by Others
		At Closing	Before Closing	At Closing	Before Closing	
A. Origination Charges		**$1,802.00**				
01 0.25 % of Loan Amount (Points)		$405.00				
02 Application Fee		$300.00				
03 Underwriting Fee		$1,097.00				
04						
05						
06						
07						
08						
B. Services Borrower Did Not Shop For		**$236.55**				$405.00
01 Appraisal Fee	to John Smith Appraisers Inc.					
02 Credit Report Fee	to Information Inc.		$29.80			
03 Flood Determination Fee	to Info Co.	$20.00				
04 Flood Monitoring Fee	to Info Co.	$31.75				
05 Tax Monitoring Fee	to Info Co.	$75.00				
06 Tax Status Research Fee	to Info Co.	$80.00				
07						
08						
09						
10						
C. Services Borrower Did Shop For		**$2,655.50**				
01 Pest Inspection Fee	to Pests Co.	$120.50				
02 Survey Fee	to Surveys Co.	$85.00				
03 Title – Insurance Binder	to Epsilon Title Co.	$650.00				
04 Title – Lender's Title Insurance	to Epsilon Title Co.	$500.00				
05 Title – Settlement Agent Fee	to Epsilon Title Co.	$500.00				
06 Title – Title Search	to Epsilon Title Co.	$800.00				
07						
08						
D. TOTAL LOAN COSTS (Borrower-Paid)		**$4,694.05**				
Loan Costs Subtotals (A + B + C)		$4,664.25	$29.80			

Other Costs

		Borrower-Paid		Seller-Paid		Paid by Others
		At Closing	Before Closing	At Closing	Before Closing	
E. Taxes and Other Government Fees		**$85.00**				
01 Recording Fees Deed: $40.00 Mortgage: $45.00		$85.00				
02 Transfer Tax	to Any State			$950.00		
F. Prepaids		**$2,120.80**				
01 Homeowner's Insurance Premium (12 mo.) to Insurance Co.		$1,209.96				
02 Mortgage Insurance Premium (mo.)						
03 Prepaid Interest ($17.44 per day from 4/15/13 to 5/1/13)		$279.04				
04 Property Taxes (6 mo.) to Any County USA		$631.80				
05						
G. Initial Escrow Payment at Closing		**$412.25**				
01 Homeowner's Insurance $100.83 per month for 2 mo.		$201.66				
02 Mortgage Insurance per month for mo.						
03 Property Taxes $105.30 per month for 2 mo.		$210.60				
04						
05						
06						
07						
08 Aggregate Adjustment		− 0.01				
H. Other		**$2,400.00**				
01 HOA Capital Contribution	to HOA Acre Inc.	$500.00				
02 HOA Processing Fee	to HOA Acre Inc.	$150.00				
03 Home Inspection Fee	to Engineers Inc.	$750.00			$750.00	
04 Home Warranty Fee	to XYZ Warranty Inc.			$450.00		
05 Real Estate Commission	to Alpha Real Estate Broker			$5,700.00		
06 Real Estate Commission	to Omega Real Estate Broker			$5,700.00		
07 Title – Owner's Title Insurance (optional) to Epsilon Title Co.		$1,000.00				
08						
I. TOTAL OTHER COSTS (Borrower-Paid)		**$5,018.05**				
Other Costs Subtotals (E + F + G + H)		$5,018.05				
J. TOTAL CLOSING COSTS (Borrower-Paid)		**$9,712.10**				
Closing Costs Subtotals (D + I)		$9,682.30	$29.80	$12,800.00	$750.00	$405.00
Lender Credits						

CLOSING DISCLOSURE

FIGURE 12.2 (Continued.)

Calculating Cash to Close

Use this table to see what has changed from your Loan Estimate.

	Loan Estimate	Final	Did this change?	
Total Closing Costs (J)	$8,054.00	$9,712.10	YES	• See **Total Loan Costs (D)** and **Total Other Costs (I)**
Closing Costs Paid Before Closing	$0	− $29.80	YES	• You paid these Closing Costs **before closing**
Closing Costs Financed (Paid from your Loan Amount)	$0	$0	NO	
Down Payment/Funds from Borrower	$18,000.00	$18,000.00	NO	
Deposit	− $10,000.00	− $10,000.00	NO	
Funds for Borrower	$0	$0	NO	
Seller Credits	$0	− $2,500.00	YES	• See Seller Credits in **Section L**
Adjustments and Other Credits	$0	− $1,035.04	YES	• See details in **Sections K and L**
Cash to Close	$16,054.00	$14,147.26		

Summaries of Transactions

Use this table to see a summary of your transaction.

BORROWER'S TRANSACTION

K. Due from Borrower at Closing		$189,762.30
01 Sale Price of Property		$180,000.00
02 Sale Price of Any Personal Property Included in Sale		
03 Closing Costs Paid at Closing (J)		$9,682.30
04		
Adjustments		
05		
06		
07		
Adjustments for Items Paid by Seller in Advance		
08 City/Town Taxes	to	
09 County Taxes	to	
10 Assessments	to	
11 HOA Dues 4/15/13	to 4/30/13	$80.00
12		
13		
14		
15		

L. Paid Already by or on Behalf of Borrower at Closing	$175,615.04
01 Deposit	$10,000.00
02 Loan Amount	$162,000.00
03 Existing Loan(s) Assumed or Taken Subject to	
04	
05 Seller Credit	$2,500.00
Other Credits	
06 Rebate from Epsilon Title Co.	$750.00
07	
Adjustments	
08	
09	
10	
11	
Adjustments for Items Unpaid by Seller	
12 City/Town Taxes 1/1/13 to 4/14/13	$365.04
13 County Taxes to	
14 Assessments to	
15	
16	
17	

CALCULATION	
Total Due from Borrower at Closing (K)	$189,762.30
Total Paid Already by or on Behalf of Borrower at Closing (L)	− $175,615.04
Cash to Close ☒ From ☐ To Borrower	**$14,147.26**

SELLER'S TRANSACTION

M. Due to Seller at Closing		$180,080.00
01 Sale Price of Property		$180,000.00
02 Sale Price of Any Personal Property Included in Sale		
03		
04		
05		
06		
07		
08		
Adjustments for Items Paid by Seller in Advance		
09 City/Town Taxes	to	
10 County Taxes	to	
11 Assessments	to	
12 HOA Dues 4/15/13	to 4/30/13	$80.00
13		
14		
15		
16		

N. Due from Seller at Closing	$115,665.04
01 Excess Deposit	
02 Closing Costs Paid at Closing (J)	$12,800.00
03 Existing Loan(s) Assumed or Taken Subject to	
04 Payoff of First Mortgage Loan	$100,000.00
05 Payoff of Second Mortgage Loan	
06	
07	
08 Seller Credit	$2,500.00
09	
10	
11	
12	
13	
Adjustments for Items Unpaid by Seller	
14 City/Town Taxes 1/1/13 to 4/14/13	$365.04
15 County Taxes to	
16 Assessments to	
17	
18	
19	

CALCULATION	
Total Due to Seller at Closing (M)	$180,080.00
Total Due from Seller at Closing (N)	− $115,665.04
Cash ☐ From ☒ To Seller	**$64,414.96**

CLOSING DISCLOSURE

FIGURE 12.2 (*Continued.*)

Additional Information About This Loan

Loan Disclosures

Assumption
If you sell or transfer this property to another person, your lender
☐ will allow, under certain conditions, this person to assume this loan on the original terms.
☒ will not allow assumption of this loan on the original terms.

Demand Feature
Your loan
☐ has a demand feature, which permits your lender to require early repayment of the loan. You should review your note for details.
☒ does not have a demand feature.

Late Payment
If your payment is more than 15 days late, your lender will charge a late fee of 5% of the monthly principal and interest payment.

Negative Amortization (Increase in Loan Amount)
Under your loan terms, you
☐ are scheduled to make monthly payments that do not pay all of the interest due that month. As a result, your loan amount will increase (negatively amortize), and your loan amount will likely become larger than your original loan amount. Increases in your loan amount lower the equity you have in this property.
☐ may have monthly payments that do not pay all of the interest due that month. If you do, your loan amount will increase (negatively amortize), and, as a result, your loan amount may become larger than your original loan amount. Increases in your loan amount lower the equity you have in this property.
☒ do not have a negative amortization feature.

Partial Payments
Your lender
☒ may accept payments that are less than the full amount due (partial payments) and apply them to your loan.
☐ may hold them in a separate account until you pay the rest of the payment, and then apply the full payment to your loan.
☐ does not accept any partial payments.
If this loan is sold, your new lender may have a different policy.

Security Interest
You are granting a security interest in
456 Somewhere Ave., Anytown, ST 12345

You may lose this property if you do not make your payments or satisfy other obligations for this loan.

Escrow Account
For now, your loan
☒ will have an escrow account (also called an "impound" or "trust" account) to pay the property costs listed below. Without an escrow account, you would pay them directly, possibly in one or two large payments a year. Your lender may be liable for penalties and interest for failing to make a payment.

Escrow		
Escrowed Property Costs over Year 1	$2,473.56	Estimated total amount over year 1 for your escrowed property costs: *Homeowner's Insurance Property Taxes*
Non-Escrowed Property Costs over Year 1	$1,800.00	Estimated total amount over year 1 for your non-escrowed property costs: *Homeowner's Association Dues* You may have other property costs.
Initial Escrow Payment	$412.25	A cushion for the escrow account you pay at closing. See Section G on page 2.
Monthly Escrow Payment	$206.13	The amount included in your total monthly payment.

☐ will not have an escrow account because ☐ you declined it ☐ your lender does not offer one. You must directly pay your property costs, such as taxes and homeowner's insurance. Contact your lender to ask if your loan can have an escrow account.

No Escrow		
Estimated Property Costs over Year 1		Estimated total amount over year 1. You must pay these costs directly, possibly in one or two large payments a year.
Escrow Waiver Fee		

In the future,
Your property costs may change and, as a result, your escrow payment may change. You may be able to cancel your escrow account, but if you do, you must pay your property costs directly. If you fail to pay your property taxes, your state or local government may (1) impose fines and penalties or (2) place a tax lien on this property. If you fail to pay any of your property costs, your lender may (1) add the amounts to your loan balance, (2) add an escrow account to your loan, or (3) require you to pay for property insurance that the lender buys on your behalf, which likely would cost more and provide fewer benefits than what you could buy on your own.

FIGURE 12.2 (*Continued.*)

Loan Calculations

Total of Payments. Total you will have paid after you make all payments of principal, interest, mortgage insurance, and loan costs, as scheduled.	$285,803.36
Finance Charge. The dollar amount the loan will cost you.	$118,830.27
Amount Financed. The loan amount available after paying your upfront finance charge.	$162,000.00
Annual Percentage Rate (APR). Your costs over the loan term expressed as a rate. This is not your interest rate.	4.174%
Total Interest Percentage (TIP). The total amount of interest that you will pay over the loan term as a percentage of your loan amount.	69.46%

Questions? If you have questions about the loan terms or costs on this form, use the contact information below. To get more information or make a complaint, contact the Consumer Financial Protection Bureau at www.consumerfinance.gov/mortgage-closing

Other Disclosures

Appraisal
If the property was appraised for your loan, your lender is required to give you a copy at no additional cost at least 3 days before closing. If you have not yet received it, please contact your lender at the information listed below.

Contract Details
See your note and security instrument for information about
- what happens if you fail to make your payments,
- what is a default on the loan,
- situations in which your lender can require early repayment of the loan, and
- the rules for making payments before they are due.

Liability after Foreclosure
If your lender forecloses on this property and the foreclosure does not cover the amount of unpaid balance on this loan,
- ☒ state law may protect you from liability for the unpaid balance. If you refinance or take on any additional debt on this property, you may lose this protection and have to pay any debt remaining even after foreclosure. You may want to consult a lawyer for more information.
- ☐ state law does not protect you from liability for the unpaid balance.

Refinance
Refinancing this loan will depend on your future financial situation, the property value, and market conditions. You may not be able to refinance this loan.

Tax Deductions
If you borrow more than this property is worth, the interest on the loan amount above this property's fair market value is not deductible from your federal income taxes. You should consult a tax advisor for more information.

Contact Information

	Lender	Mortgage Broker	Real Estate Broker (B)	Real Estate Broker (S)	Settlement Agent
Name	Ficus Bank		Omega Real Estate Broker Inc.	Alpha Real Estate Broker Co.	Epsilon Title Co.
Address	4321 Random Blvd. Somecity, ST 12340		789 Local Lane Sometown, ST 12345	987 Suburb Ct. Someplace, ST 12340	123 Commerce Pl. Somecity, ST 12344
NMLS ID					
ST License ID			Z765416	Z61456	Z61616
Contact	Joe Smith		Samuel Green	Joseph Cain	Sarah Arnold
Contact NMLS ID	12345				
Contact ST License ID			P16415	P51461	PT1234
Email	joesmith@ficusbank.com		sam@omegare.biz	joe@alphare.biz	sarah@epsilontitle.com
Phone	123-456-7890		123-555-1717	321-555-7171	987-555-4321

Confirm Receipt

By signing, you are only confirming that you have received this form. You do not have to accept this loan because you have signed or received this form.

_____   _____   _____   _____
Applicant Signature   Date   Co-Applicant Signature   Date

CLOSING DISCLOSURE

FIGURE 12.2 (*Continued.*)

There is a limited exception for "Controlled or Affiliated Business Arrangements" that are common especially within larger brokerage firms. Note that the rules regarding such arrangements are quite complex and are beyond the limited coverage provided within this text. An example of this arrangement would be where the real estate brokerage firm also owns an affiliated mortgage company, title insurance company, and perhaps an inspection company. RESPA regulations allow such "one-stop shopping" without violation as long as (1) such affiliated arrangements are disclosed and a written estimate of the provider's fees are disclosed, (2) the consumer is not required to use such services, and (3) the only "thing of value" received by the referring person is the potential profit earned on his ownership interest in the affiliated firm.

In situations involving an apparent affiliation of a service provider who pays the firm compensation for using company-owned space, there can be a violation under RESPA. If the amount of rent exceeds the fair amount due for such space, it will likely be considered a kickback for referrals and the firm would find itself at risk for RESPA violations.

Penalties for RESPA Violations

The penalties for violations of RESPA requirements are severe and include both criminal as well as civil liability. Fines can be levied for up to $10,000 per violation in addition to imprisonment of up to one year. The law also permits civil lawsuits, including class action lawsuits, and may award monetary damages up to three times the amount of the overcharge, plus court costs and attorney fees. A violation of RESPA is also a violation of General Statute (G.S.) 93A-6(a)(10) prohibiting "improper, fraudulent, or dishonest dealing."

The Loan Estimate

 The form provides on the first page:
- The loan amount;
- The interest rate;
- If there is any prepayment or balloon payment allowed;
- The monthly principal and interest payment;
- Projected real property taxes and homeowners insurance;
- Estimated closing costs;
- Estimated cash needed in order to close.

The purpose of the LE (Figure 12.3) is to provide an easy comparison of loan costs and terms in such a form that will allow the borrower to shop and compare the

TowneBank Mortgage
600 22nd St Suite 300
Virginia Beach, VA 23451

Save this Loan Estimate to compare with your Closing Disclosure.

Loan Estimate

DATE ISSUED 09/14/2015
APPLICANTS TEST FAIRLEY

PROPERTY 123 MANGUM STREET
RALEIGH, NC 27615
SALE PRICE $250,000.00

LOAN TERM 30 years
PURPOSE Purchase
PRODUCT Fixed Rate
LOAN TYPE [X] Conventional [ ] FHA [ ] VA [ ] ____
LOAN ID # 000094054
RATE LOCK [X] NO [ ] YES, until

Before closing, your interest rate, points, and lender credits can change unless you lock the interest rate. All other estimated closing costs expire on **09/28/2015** at 5:00pm EDT

Loan Terms

		Can this amount increase after closing?
Loan Amount	$225,000	NO
Interest Rate	6%	NO
Monthly Principal & Interest *See Projected Payments below for your Estimated Total Monthly Payment*	$1,348.99	NO

	Does the loan have these features?
Prepayment Penalty	NO
Balloon Payment	NO

Projected Payments

Payment Calculation	Years 1 - 30
Principal & Interest	$1,348.99
Mortgage Insurance	+ 0
Estimated Escrow *Amount can increase over time*	+ $320
Estimated Total Monthly Payment	$1,668

Estimated Taxes, Insurance & Assessments *Amount can increase over time*	$320 a month	This estimate includes [X] Property Taxes [X] Homeowner's Insurance [ ] Other: *See Section G on page 2 for escrowed property costs. You must pay for other property costs separately.*	In escrow? YES YES

Costs at Closing

Estimated Closing Costs	$13,893	Includes $10,545 in Loan Costs + $3,348 in Other Costs - $0 in Lender Credits. *See page 2 for details.*
Estimated Cash to Close	$35,285	Includes Closing Costs. *See Calculating Cash to Close on page 2 for details.*

Visit www.consumerfinance.gov/mortgage-estimate for general information and tools.

LOAN ESTIMATE
LOANEST -1rev (3/15)r

FIGURE 12.3 Loan Estimate.

Closing Cost Details

Loan Costs

A. Origination Charges	$6,750
2 % of Loan Amount (Points)	$4,500
Origination Fee	$2,250

B. Services You Cannot Shop For	$2,645
Appraisal Fee	$300
Credit Report Fee	$65
Flood Certification	$30
Mortgage Insurance Premium	$2,250

C. Services You Can Shop For	$1,150
Title - Lenders Coverage Premium	$600
Title - Settlement Fee	$550

D. TOTAL LOAN COSTS (A +B +C)	$10,545

Other Costs

E. Taxes and Other Government Fees	$45
Recording Fees and Other Taxes	$45
Transfer Taxes	

F. Prepaids	$1,704
Homeowner's Insurance Premium (12 months)	$954
Mortgage Insurance Premium (12 months)	
Prepaid Interest ($37.50 for 20 days @ 6%)	$750
Property Taxes (months)	

G. Initial Escrow Payment at Closing				$1,359
Homeowner's Insurance	$79.50	per month for	2 mo.	$159
Mortgage Insurance		per month for	mo.	
Property Taxes		per month for	mo.	
County Property Taxes	$240.00	per month for	5 mo.	$1,200

H. Other	$240
Pest Inspection Fee	$65
Survey Fee	$175

I. TOTAL OTHER COSTS (E + F + G + H)	$3,348

J. TOTAL CLOSING COSTS	$13,893
D + I	$13,893
Lender Credits	

Calculating Cash to Close

Total Closing Costs (J)	$13,893
Closing Costs Financed (Paid from your Loan Amount)	$0
Down Payment/Funds from Borrower	$25,000
Deposit	$-2,500
Funds for Borrower	$0
Seller Credits	$0
Adjustments and Other Credits	$-1,108
Estimated Cash to Close	$35,285

LOAN ESTIMATE
LOANEST -2rev (3/15)

FIGURE 12.3 (Continued.)

Additional Information About This Loan

LENDER TowneBank Mortgage
NMLS/__ LICENSE ID 512138
LOAN OFFICER
NMLS/__ LICENSE ID
EMAIL
PHONE

MORTGAGE BROKER
NMLS/__ LICENSE ID
LOAN OFFICER
NMLS/__ LICENSE ID
EMAIL
PHONE

Comparisons
Use these measures to compare this loan with other loans.

In 5 Years	$92,234	Total you will have paid in principal, interest, mortgage insurance and loan costs.
	$15,628	Principal you will have paid off.
Annual Percentage Rate (APR)	6.345%	Your costs over the loan term expressed as a rate. This is not your interest rate.
Total Interest Percentage (TIP)	116.171%	The total amount of interest that you will pay over the loan term as a percentage of your loan amount.

Other Considerations

Appraisal — We may order an appraisal to determine the property's value and charge you for this appraisal. We will promptly give you a copy of any appraisal, even if your loan does not close. You can pay for an additional appraisal for your own use at your own cost.

Assumption — If you sell or transfer this property to another person, we
☐ will allow, under certain conditions, this person to assume this loan on the original terms.
☒ will not allow assumption of this loan on the original terms.

Homeowner's Insurance — This loan requires homeowner's insurance on the property, which you may obtain from a company of your choice that we find acceptable.

Late Payment — If your payment is more than *15* days late, we will charge a late fee of *4% of the principal & interest*.

Refinance — Refinancing this loan will depend on your future financial situation, the property value, and market conditions. You may not be able to refinance this loan.

Servicing — We intend
☐ to service your loan. If so, you will make your payments to us.
☒ to transfer servicing of your loan.

Confirm Receipt

By signing, you are only confirming that you have received this form. You do not have to accept this loan because you have signed or received this form.

_____   _____
TEST FAIRLEY   Date

LOAN ESTIMATE
LOANEST -3rev (3/15)r3

FIGURE 12.3 (*Continued.*)

costs of obtaining the loan from various lenders. By standardizing this form it allows the borrower to compare forms from all federally related lenders in such a way to better enhance understanding. Borrowers are required to be provided the LE within three business days of the loan application.

Permissible Variations

Originally referred to for many years as "tolerance limits," the permissible variations impose limits on various costs associated with obtaining a loan. Lenders are required to insert in the LE mortgage-related costs into three basic groups:

- No Tolerance—These fees are totally within the control of the lender and cannot be altered before the closing. Examples include loan origination fees, discount points, interest rates once locked in, and transfer taxes.
- 10% Tolerance—This is a group of fees that cannot change more than 10% in aggregate. In other words, it is possible that any particular fee in this group may change more than 10%, but the collective total cannot alter by more than that amount; otherwise, the lender must reimburse the borrower at the closing for the amount exceeding 10%. These fees include such items as any required services for which the lender selects or recommends, title insurance fees, and government recording fees. The borrower may or may not choose to use the services of the recommended provider, but the 10% tolerance rules only apply should the borrower use the named provider.
- Unlimited Tolerance—These fees can change by any amount without any repercussions upon the lender. These fees include items or services that the borrower obtains on his own, such a homeowner's insurance, or required services in which the borrower selects his own provider instead of utilizing the services recommended by the lender. For example, the lender may have quoted attorney fees that are available within the marketplace. The borrower decides to use his attorney's services instead of those quoted by the lender. The lender will suffer no financial consequences should the borrower's attorney charge higher fees than those quoted by the lender's attorney selection. Regardless, the lender does have the right of final approval as to the selection of the service provider to ensure the quality of the closing.

The Closing Disclosures

To alleviate concerns of privacy violations under the federal Gramm-Leach-Bliley Act, there is now two separate CD forms. One is for the borrower/buyer (five pages; Figure 12.2) and the other is for the sellers (two pages; Figure 12.1). The lender is held responsible for the accuracy of these closing statements with, as mentioned earlier in the chapter, substantial liability for the accuracy of the statement regardless of who prepared it. As a result, most major lenders will require they prepare the forms for the attorneys and will not allow any changes to be made unless resubmitted to the lender. Because of this concern it is likely there will be numerous cases of delay due to having to wait for a response from the lender.

In one of the largest impacts for brokers and consumers is the requirement that lenders MUST provide the borrower with a completed borrower CD three business days before closing. The delivery of the CD can be either by personal delivery (i.e., hand delivery) or any other method (i.e., U.S. Mail, fax, email).

If the borrower CD is delivered by any other means than personal delivery, the lender must add three more business days for delivery. There is likely to be relatively few "personal" deliveries of these forms although some small lenders may utilize that capability. It is unlikely larger lenders will provide "personal delivery" of the CD. As a result most lenders will reference the fact they need six business days in which to deliver the CD before the closing can legally occur. In somewhat of a twist to North Carolina's definition of a "business day," TRID rules consider the business day to be any day other than Sunday because the mail is delivered each of the other six days. Of course, this would not include the currently recognized 10 federal public holidays as the mail is not delivered on those days.

It is likely that most lenders will impose their own "practical" number of days that exceed even the six-day rule to provide them enough time to review and send these documents to the borrower within the required time frame.

Many brokers and consumers express concern that even minimal modifications to the CD will require a "resetting of the clock" and delay the closing. In reality there are relatively few instances in which the three-day/six-day rule will have to be reset. These instances are (1) The APR (annual percentage rate) increases by more than 0.125% for fixed-rate loans or 0.25% for adjustable loans. A decrease in APR will not require a new three-day period to begin, and (2) a prepayment penalty is added. Note that prepayment penalties are generally not allowed in North Carolina, and (3) there is a change in the basic loan product, such as when the borrower is switching from a fixed rate to an adjustable rate or to an interest-only payment loan.

CLOSING STATEMENT (WITH LE AND CD WORKSHEET)

The following section provides an example of a typical closing scenario utilizing the LE (Figure 12.3), and CD (Figure 12.5) forms. Although they are being provided primarily for illustration purposes, students will benefit from practicing these entries and prorations for testing purposes. Proration solutions are provided in Figure 12.6.

Settlement Statement Entries and Calculations

The closing statement is simply an accounting of all funds that are handled in regards to the transfer of title and the finalization of the mortgage loan. Although

> "You will not have to complete a Closing Disclosure Worksheet for either the Superior final examination or the North Carolina Real Estate Licensing Examination. You should understand basic concepts and you should be able to make calculations that are required to determine buyer and seller net amounts."
> —Bill Gallagher, DREI

> Fairley purchased a home from Victoria utilizing the standard Offer to Purchase and Contract from NCAR/NCBA. Use the 360-day/year and 30-day month for all calculations. The relevant facts are as follows:
>
> - Closing date- April 11 (not a leap year)
> - Sales price- $250,000
> - Earnest money deposit- $2,500
> - Due Diligence fee- $300 (paid at time of the offer acceptance)
> - Financing- $225,000 new conventional mortgage, interest rate of 6%, 1% loan origination fee, and 2 discount points to be paid by buyer
> - Prepaid interim interest- prepaid interim interest for April to be collected at closing
> - Loan payoff- $119,250
> - Appraisal fee- $300 (paid as loan application)
> - Credit report- $65 (paid as loan application)
> - Private mortgage insurance premium- $2,250
> - Real property taxes- $2,880 for the year based upon last year's bill. Taxes for the year have not yet been paid and will be prorated at closing.
> - Buyer's homeowners insurance premium (1st year)- $954
> - Loan escrow account deposits required by lender- five (5) months of real property taxes, and two (2) months of homeowners insurance premiums and two (2) months of private mortgage insurance premiums based upon a monthly renewal amount of $52
> - Attorney fees- $550
> - Survey- $175
> - Flood certification fee- $30
> - Pest inspection- $65
> - Deed preparation fee- $75
> - Preparation of quitclaim deed for title defect- $70
> - Recording fees: Deed- $20
>   Mortgage- $25
>   Quitclaim deed for title defect- $20
> - Revenue stamps- Use state rate
> - Title insurance- $600
> - Commission- 6%
> - Carpet cleaning bill- $175 (use page 2 for seller)

FIGURE 12.4 Sample closing practice problem.
Source: © 2019 OnCourse Learning

the closing statement may appear to be rather intimidating at first glance, it really is, with minor exceptions, a fairly straightforward form that states the name of the item to be entered on a respective line. The CD, as mentioned previously, is the form that is required by RESPA regulations when closing a residential sales transaction with a federally related mortgage.

A closing statement is made up of a variety of entries called debits and credits. A **debit** is *an amount, or charge, that a person pays, and a* **credit** *is simply an amount, or charge that one receives.* A simple way to remember this is to think

Closing Cost Details

Loan Costs		Borrower-Paid		Seller-Paid		Paid by Others
		At Closing	Before Closing	At Closing	Before Closing	
A. Origination Charges		$ 6,750.00				
01 % of Loan Amount (Points)	to ABC Lender	$ 2,250.00				
02 2% Loan Discount Points	to ABC Lender	$ 4,500.00				
03						
04						
05						
06						
07						
08						
B. Services Borrower Did Not Shop For		$ 1,545.00				
01 Appraisal Fee			$ 300.00			
02 Credit Report Fee			$ 65.00			
03 Flood Certification Fee	to ABC Lender	$ 30.00				
04 Title - Closing Fee	to Law Offices of Good Attorne	$ 550.00				
05 Title - Lender's Title Insurance	to Law Offices of Good Attorne	$ 600.00				
06						
07						
08						
09						
10						
C. Services Borrower Did Shop For						
01						
02						
03						
04						
05						
06						
07						
08						
D. TOTAL LOAN COSTS (Borrower-Paid)		$ 8,295.00				
Loan Costs Subtotals (A + B + C)		$ 7,930.00	$ 365.00			

Other Costs						
E. Taxes and Other Government Fees		$ 45.00				
01 Recording Fees	Deed: Mortgage:	$ 45.00		$ 20.00		
02 Revenue Stamps	to Register of Deeds			$ 500.00		
F. Prepaids		$ 3,954.00				
01 Homeowner's Insurance Premium	to Homeowner's Insurance Com (mo.)	$ 954.00				
02 Mortgage Insurance Premium	to MIP Company (mo.)	$ 2,250.00				
03 Prepaid Interest	$37.5 per day from 04/11/15 to 05/01/15	$ 750.00				
04 Property Taxes	(mo.)					
05						
G. Initial Escrow Payment at Closing		$ 1,463.00				
01 Homeowner's Insurance	$79.50 per month for 2 mo.	$ 159.00				
02 Mortgage Insurance	$52.00 per month for 2 mo.	$ 104.00				
03 Property Taxes	$240.00 per month for 5 mo.	$ 1,200.00				
04						
05						
06						
07						
08 Aggregate Adjustment						
H. Other		$ 240.00				
01 Commission	to Listing Agent Company			$ 7,500.00		
02 Commission	to Selling Agent Company			$ 7,500.00		
03 Deed Preparation Fee	to Law Offices of Good Attorne			$ 75.00		
04 Pest Inspection	to Pest Inspection Company	$ 65.00				
05 Quitclaim Deed Preparation Fee	to Law Offices of Good Attorne			$ 70.00		
06 Survey	to Surveying Company	$ 175.00				
07						
08						
I. TOTAL OTHER COSTS (Borrower-Paid)		$ 5,702.00				
Other Costs Subtotals (E + F + G + H)		$ 5,702.00				
J. TOTAL CLOSING COSTS (Borrower-Paid)		$ 13,997.00				
Closing Costs Subtotals (D + I)		$ 13,632.00	$ 365.00	$ 15,665.00		
Lender Credits						

CLOSING DISCLOSURE

FIGURE 12.5 Closing practice problem solution.
Source: © 2019 OnCourse Learning

Calculating Cash to Close

Use this table to see what has changed from your Loan Estimate.

	Loan Estimate	Final	Did this change?
Total Closing Costs (J)	$0	$ 13,997.00	YES
Closing Costs Paid Before Closing	$0	$ -365.00	YES
Closing Costs Financed (Paid from your Loan Amount)	$0	$0	NO
Down Payment/Funds from Borrower	$0	$ 25,000.00	YES
Deposit	$0	$ -2,500.00	YES
Funds for Borrower	$0	$0	YES
Seller Credits	$0	$ -300.00	YES
Adjustments and Other Credits	$0	$ -808.00	YES
Cash to Close	$0	$ 35,024.00	

Summaries of Transactions

Use this table to see a summary of your transaction.

BORROWER'S TRANSACTION

K. Due from Borrower at Closing — $ 263,632.00
- 01 Sale Price of Property — $ 250,000.00
- 02 Sale Price of Any Personal Property Included in Sale
- 03 Closing Costs Paid at Closing (J) — $ 13,632.00
- 04

Adjustments
- 05
- 06
- 07

Adjustments for Items Paid by Seller in Advance
- 08 City/Town Taxes
- 09 County Taxes
- 10 Assessments
- 11
- 12
- 13
- 14
- 15

L. Paid Already by or on Behalf of Borrower at Closing — $ 228,608.00
- 01 Deposit — $ 2,500.00
- 02 Loan Amount — $ 225,000.00
- 03 Existing Loan(s) Assumed or Taken Subject to
- 04
- 05 Due Diligence — $ 300.00

Other Credits
- 06
- 07

Adjustments
- 08
- 09
- 10
- 11

Adjustments for Items Unpaid by Seller
- 12 City/Town Taxes
- 13 County Taxes 01/15/15 to 04/12/15 — $ 808.00
- 14 Assessments
- 15
- 16
- 17

CALCULATION
- Total Due from Borrower at Closing (K) — $ 263,632.00
- Total Paid Already by or on Behalf of Borrower at Closing (L) — - $ 228,608.00
- Cash to Close [X] From [ ] To Borrower — $ 35,024.00

SELLER'S TRANSACTION

M. Due to Seller at Closing — $ 250,000.00
- 01 Sale Price of Property — $ 250,000.00
- 02 Sale Price of Any Personal Property Included in Sale
- 03
- 04
- 05
- 06
- 07
- 08

Adjustments for Items Paid by Seller in Advance
- 09 City/Town Taxes
- 10 County Taxes
- 11 Assessments
- 12
- 13
- 14
- 15
- 16

N. Due from Seller at Closing — $ 136,198.00
- 01 Excess Deposit
- 02 Closing Costs Paid at Closing (J) — $ 15,665.00
- 03 Existing Loan(s) Assumed or Taken Subject to
- 04 Payoff of First Mortgage Loan — $ 119,250.00
- 05 Payoff of Second Mortgage Loan
- 06 Carpet Cleaning Bill — $ 175.00
- 07
- 08 Due Diligence — $ 300.00
- 09
- 10
- 11
- 12
- 13

Adjustments for Items Unpaid by Seller
- 14 City/Town Taxes
- 15 County Taxes 01/15/15 to 04/12/15 — $ 808.00
- 16 Assessments
- 17
- 18
- 19

CALCULATION
- Total Due to Seller at Closing (M) — $ 250,000.00
- Total Due from Seller at Closing (N) — - $ 136,198.00
- Cash [ ] From [X] To Seller — $ 113,802.00

CLOSING DISCLOSURE

FIGURE 12.5 (Continued.)

Prepaid Interim Interest

$225,000 × 6% = $13,500.00 interest per year
$13,500/360 = $37.50 interest per day
$37.50 × 20 days* = $750.00 debit buyer

*4/11 – 30 = 19 days + 1 (11th) = 20 days

Loan Origination Fee

$225,000.00 × 1% = $2,250.00 loan origination fee

Discount Points

$225,000.00 × 2% = $4,500.00 discount points

Real Property Taxes

$2,880.00/360 = $8.00 taxes per day
$8.00 × 101 days* = $808.00 debit seller, credit buyer

*1/1 – 4/11 = 30 days (Jan) + 30 days (Feb) × 30 days (Mar) + 11 days (Apr) = 101 days

Escrows

Real Property Taxes

$2,880.00/12 = $240.00 taxes per month
$240.00 × 5 = $1,200.00 five months – taxes

Homeowners insurance

$954.00/12 = $79.50 homeowners insurance per month
$79.50 × 2 = $159.00 2 months homeowners insurance

Private Mortgage Insurance

$52 × 2 = $104.00 2 months private mortgage insurance

Commission

$250,000.00 × 6% = $15,000.00 sales commission

FIGURE 12.6 Computation of prorated/prepaid/escrow items (from Figure 12.4).
Source: © 2019 OnCourse Learning

that it is the debit who pays and credit who receives. Additionally, the closing statement is made up of single- and double-entry items. A **single entry** *appears on only the buyer's or seller's side of the statement,* whereas a **double entry** *appears on both the buyer's and the seller's sides.* An easy way to remember this would be to say that if the buyer pays an amount to someone other than the seller, it would be a single-entry item, as would be the case if the seller paid someone other than the buyer. This is especially prevalent regarding many of the services paid at closing that are unique to either the buyer or the seller. You will observe that the vast majority of single-entry items are debits to the buyer, with the single-entry debits to the seller being primarily limited to deed preparation, revenue (excise or transfer) stamps, and sales commission. A limited number of single-entry credits will appear on the buyer's side, such as loan proceeds, earnest money deposit, and the amount the buyer will have to bring to the transaction to close. There will be no single-entry credits to the seller. The majority of these single entry debits will appear on page 2 of the CD and will provide a column for both items paid at the closing as well as those paid before closing. With double-entry items, the buyer pays the seller or the seller pays the buyer. A good example would be the purchase price of $250,000, which would appear as a debit to the buyer and a credit to the seller as the buyer pays it and the seller receives it. Other ways to look at the debits and credits are based on increases and decreases in monies paid or received. A debit to the buyer *increases* the amount of money that a buyer would have to bring to the transaction to close. Alternatively, a credit to the seller *increases* the amount the seller will take home. The opposite of each of these is also true as a credit to the buyer *decreases* the amount the buyer will have to bring to the transaction and *increases* the amount the seller will take home. Again, a simple review of the purchase price illustrates this point. The $250,000 purchase price would appear as a debit to the buyer, as the buyer must pay it and it increases the amount the buyer must pay in order to close, as well as a credit to the seller as the seller will receive it. This increases the amount of money the seller will take home.

The closing statement will address all of the relevant items to the closing and show them as a variety of debits and credits as well as both single and double entries. The following discusses the primary entries that will appear in most residential closings.

> **Test Tip!**
>
> You debit the party who pays for the item and you credit the party who receives it!

Sales Price

The sales price indicates the amount paid for the property by the buyer to the seller. It is paid by the buyer to the seller and therefore increases the amount the buyer must bring to the transaction to close, as well as increases the amount the seller will take home. It is a double-entry item and will appear as a *debit to the buyer* and a *credit to the seller*.

Earnest Money Deposit

The earnest money deposit is typically held in the listing broker's trust or escrow account and is given to the closing attorney, who will disburse it to the parties at the closing. NOTE: Although most attorneys will have the escrow agent retain this deposit in his trust account and deduct it from the sales commission paid to the listing firm, it is perhaps easiest to initially account for this entry by assuming the monies are paid to the closing attorney for disbursement. This earnest money deposit will reduce the amount the buyer must bring to the transaction to close, as it has already been paid at the time of the initial purchase agreement and is applied to the purchase price at closing. It is a single-entry item and will appear as a *credit to the buyer*.

Due Diligence Fee

The due diligence fee is a fee that is addressed in the NCAR/NCBA OPC form and may or may not be a item within a closing statement. The OPC dictates that any due diligence fee is to be credited to the buyer at the closing and debited to the seller, as this fee was paid directly from the buyer to the seller at the point of contract and therefore reduces the amount the buyer will need to bring to the transaction and reduces the amount the seller will receive at the closing. It will appear as a *debit to the seller* and a *credit to the buyer*.

New First Mortgage Loan

It is most likely that buyers will have to obtain some type of financing to purchase the property. As far as the closing statement is concerned, it does not matter whether it is a first or second mortgage, as the entry is the same. The mortgage is a single-entry item, as the lender is paying the money and giving it to the buyer. It therefore reduces the amount the buyer has to pay to close but has no direct bearing on the seller's proceeds. It represents a *credit to the buyer*.

Loan Payoff

The seller may have an unpaid balance that is due on his mortgage and will have to be paid off at the closing to convey the title free of liens as stipulated in the sales contract. The loan payoff is obtained from the seller's mortgage company by the closing attorney as part of the closing preparation and usually will be presented as the principal balance due as well as any accrued interest since the last payment. The loan payoff is a *debit to the seller*, as it reduces the amount due to the seller at closing. It is a single-entry item that has no bearing on the buyer's proceeds and therefore does not appear on the buyer's side of the closing statement.

Loan Fees

Loan fees are an assortment of the various fees that are incurred to obtain the mortgage loan. These include such items as the loan origination fee, discount points, and any fees required by a given lender. These are all *debited (added) to the buyer*, as the buyer will pay these fees to the lender and therefore increase the amount of money she will have to bring to the transaction to close. These are single-entry items and do not appear on the seller's side unless the seller has contractually agreed to pay them as a condition of the purchase agreement.

Attorney Fees

Attorney fees are the fees charged by an attorney to provide legal services to close the transaction *with the exception of deed preparation fees, which are paid traditionally by the seller*. These fees may appear as a lump sum amount—as total cost of providing the overall package of closing-related services—or they may appear as an itemized list. Typical services would include conducting the title search, preparing documents (with the exception of deed preparation), conducting the closing meeting, recording the documents (but not the actual recording fees), and distributing funds. Either method is common and tends to be related to local practice. Regardless of whether a lump sum or an itemized list is used, these fees will appear as a *debit to the buyer* and do not appear on the seller's side, as they are a single-entry item.

Title Insurance

Title insurance is required by the lender and provides protection in the event of title problems in the future. The amount paid for this insurance may be presented as a lump sum amount or separated and presented as the borrower's policy and the lender's policy. Regardless, the total due for title insurance will be a *debit to the buyer* and is a single-entry item only, so it does not appear on the seller's side of the closing statement.

Appraisal Fees

The lender will require an appraisal before consenting to make the loan, and the buyer will typically be required to pay this up front at the time of loan application. Along with the *credit report*, which is handled in a similar fashion, this fee will appear somewhat differently on most closing statements. Although it would normally appear as a debit to the buyer, it will *appear as "paid before closing,"* as it is one of the few closing-related fees that will be paid early in the transaction. If it is being collected at closing, it would appear as a *debit to the buyer*. It will not appear on the seller's side, as it is a single-entry item.

Credit Report

The lender will also want to determine the borrower's creditworthiness and will order a credit report early in the transaction. Similar to the appraisal described earlier, the lender will normally collect this fee at the point of loan application, and it will therefore *appear as a Paid before Closing item unless it is being collected at the closing, in which case it would appear as a debit to the buyer*. Like the appraisal fee, it represents a single-entry item and does not appear on the seller's side.

Survey

The borrower may or may not be required to obtain a property survey as a condition of closing. Nevertheless, it may be beneficial for the buyer to acquire a survey, as it would indicate the existence of any encroachments relating to the property. The survey cost is paid by the buyer and would be a single-entry *debit to the buyer* and would not appear on the seller's side.

Homeowner's Insurance Policy

As a condition for obtaining the loan, the lender will require the purchaser to insure the property. The lender will require certain levels and types of coverage to be obtained, and the buyer will typically purchase this policy from his own insurance company. The lender will require proof of the policy being obtained and paid for before finalizing the closing. The policy is paid for by the buyer and is a single-entry item and does not appear on the seller's side. It will be a *debit to the buyer*. This entry is for the initial purchase of the homeowner's policy. It is very likely the lender will require escrows to be maintained to provide for the purchase of the following year's policy once the original expires. These escrows, or reserves, will appear elsewhere on the closing statement.

Deed Preparation

Deed preparation is not considered a part of the attorney fees mentioned earlier and are considered to be a seller's expense. These will appear as a *debit to the seller* and will not appear on the buyer's side.

Excise Tax

These fees are also known by the names revenue and transfer stamps. These are not really stamps at all, but rather a fee charged on the transfer of real property. The amount due is related to the purchase price, and the fee is $1.00 per $500 of sales price or any portion thereof. These fees are traditionally paid by the seller and will be a single-entry *debit to the seller*.

Recording Fees

Recording fees are paid at the time of recording various documents and, depending on the document, may be charged to either the buyer or the seller. Fees related to transfer of title or acquisition of a mortgage loan, such as recording of the deed of conveyance and the deed of trust, are paid by the buyer and appear as a *debit to the buyer*. The seller would be required to pay any recording fees necessary to clear the title. If there are fees charged to cancel, or release, the prior mortgage or if the seller has to record a quitclaim deed to correct a prior title defect, these would be paid for by the seller and appear as a *debit to the seller*.

Sales Commission

The sales commission typically is paid by the seller to the listing company in accordance with the original listing agreement. It is rather common for closing attorneys to split the commission between the listing and selling companies, but whether paid to one firm or two, these fees would appear as a *debit to the seller* as a single-entry item.

Prepaid Interim Interest

In transactions involving the buyer acquiring a new first mortgage, the lender will require the collection of interim interest. For a more detailed explanation of this entry, see the section "Prorations and Prepaids." Prepaid interim interest is paid by the buyer and appears as a single-entry item and a *debit to the buyer*.

Reserves and Escrows Required by Lender

It is common for lenders to require the buyer to establish a reserve, or escrow, account to pay for property taxes, homeowner's insurance, and mortgage insurance in future years. In many ways, this is a forced savings account that ensures there will be monies on hand to pay the related expenses when they become due. They will appear as *debits to the buyer* and are single-entry items.

Prorations

Several items must be split between the parties at the closing. Typical items would include property taxes, homeowner association dues, and rents from income-producing properties. These would be double-entry items and can appear as debits or credits to either party depending upon the details of a particular transaction or type of proration. More in-depth coverage of the proration process follows in this chapter.

Other Fees

A wide range of fees potentially can appear on a given closing statement. Because the intent of a prelicensing course is to introduce the basics of a given topic, coverage is limited to those charges appearing above. There will be additional and more in-depth coverage of various closing expenses contained within the broker postlicensing courses in North Carolina.

Prorations and Prepaids

It is common for a closing statement to contain several items, such as property taxes and homeowners association fees, that will have to be divided to ensure that each party pays only their respective share. Some of these items will already have been paid by the seller, and others will not be paid until the closing or perhaps even after. Although prorations may appear difficult to the beginning practitioner, note that you likely have been **prorating** most of your life. Suppose you go out to lunch with friends, and when the bill comes, each person pays her respective share. Even if you are dividing the bill equally, it still represents a proration of the amount due. The practice of real estate prorations is no different.

Regardless of the item to be prorated, the agent will have to address two basic considerations:

- Who owes whom?
- How much?

The answer to the question of who owes whom will establish who is debited and who is credited. If, for example, the buyer owes the seller, the entry would appear as a debit to the buyer and a credit to the seller. Conversely, if the seller owes the buyer, it would appear as a debit to the seller and a credit to the buyer. Once the issue of who owes whom is addressed, it becomes a simple matter of determining the amount due for the period in question. There are numerous ways to prorate the amount due, and the only rule is to make certain that everyone at the closing is in agreement with the method that will be used. It is even permissible to use more than one basic approach of prorating as long as everyone is in agreement. The two main methods in use today are the 30-day month/360-day year method and the 365-day year/actual days in the month method. A basic review as follows.

30-Day Month/360-Day Year Method

This method is also commonly referred to as the "banker's method" and is the method used on the North Carolina real estate license examination. *With this method, every month is treated equally, with all being considered to have 30 days regardless of the actual days that are contained in any given month.* There will be no special treatment for months that contain 28 or 31 days. With this method, the annual cost is divided by 360 days or the monthly cost is divided by 30 days to determine the daily rate.

365-Day Year/Actual Days in the Month Method

As the name implies, the daily cost factor is determined by dividing the annual cost by 365 days and the monthly cost will be determined by dividing by the actual number of days that particular month contains. There will need to be a determination if the closing year represents a leap year or not, as that will affect the daily factor for the month of February. It is more likely that the closings encountered in the actual practice of real estate will involve this method. The closing attorney will dictate to the agent which method is being utilized at the closing.

The decision as to which method to utilize will affect the final amount to be entered into the closing statement. The daily rate could be altered by a few cents per day, but when multiplied by several hundred days, as is common in an actual closing statement, the answer will probably vary only a few dollars from the answer calculated through the other method. Again, the main thing to remember is that the attorney will establish the "ground rules" for the closing proration method and this is generally a nonissue. The seller *generally is considered to own the property on the day of closing for proration purposes.*

It is appropriate to be concerned about which method to use when calculating the answers for the final or state exam, however. Some instructors teach students to round off to the nearest 2 decimals, and others use 3 decimals as the rule. The reality is the North Carolina real estate license exam typically uses amounts that will round off evenly, and this tends to be a nonissue. Remember, **the state exam is more interested in the student calculating the entry correctly than it is in trying to confuse you with an answer that is a few cents off**. For more details about this, refer to the next section, "Real Property Taxes," regarding the practical computation of the North Carolina CD Core worksheet.

The following items will represent the traditional proration entries:

- Real property taxes
- Homeowners association fees
- Rental income
- Mortgage interest

The seller will be considered to be responsible for the day of closing, and all daily rates will be considered rounded to three decimal places. The 30-day month/360-day year method will be utilized for all of the included calculations.

Real Property Taxes

One of the most challenging entries that will involve prorating is that of property taxes. Property taxes in North Carolina are prorated on a calendar year basis even though the fiscal year is from July 1 through June 30 of the following year. The property tax rate will be established after the annual budget is adopted, and the tax bill must be mailed out; therefore, taxes are payable by September 1. Because of advances in technology, the tax bill may be delivered soon after July 1, well before September 1. One of the first questions that must be addressed by parties is to ask if the tax bill has been paid. Obviously, taxes will not have been paid if the closing is before July 1 because the tax amount due has not been determined. After July 1, it must be determined if the taxes have already been paid by the seller. The lender will dictate to the closing attorney how to handle the issue of property taxes on the closing statement. Generally, the lender will require that if the tax bill can be paid off at the closing, it will be paid off at the closing. If the tax bill has not yet been calculated, such as is the case before July 1, the amount that will be prorated is a best-guess estimate based on the prior year's bill and the closing attorney's best estimate as to whether the tax rate is the same as before or has been, or is likely to be, increased. The challenge for the real estate student is to calculate the entry based on the information contained within the closing statement problem, which may vary slightly from what might have been done in actual practice. To address this, we will explore the four different ways the information may be presented followed by some basic assumptions about the taxes due.

- Taxes have not been paid—Taxes not yet payable
- Taxes have not been paid—Taxes payable (paid at closing)
- Taxes have already been paid by the seller

NOTE: All of the following prorations will be calculated by using the 30-day month/360-day year method. Assume the property tax bill for the year is $1,980. To determine the daily tax rate, you would need to divide the $1,980 by 360 days: $1,980 ÷ 360 = $5.50 per day.

> There are three primary ways for property taxes to appear on the closing statement: (1) buyer owes the seller, (2) seller owes the buyer, and (3) monies will be collected from each and taxes paid off at the closing. Make certain you are familiar with each scenario and how it will be presented and entered on the closing worksheet.

Taxes Have Not Been Paid—Taxes Not Yet Payable

This is the case when the closing is held prior to the computation of the annual taxes and is typically estimated based on the prior year's tax bill. To calculate the correct entry, we need to ask ourselves two main questions that deal with any proration entry: Who owes whom and how much? Because the buyer will own the property once the tax bill is due and paid, the seller will owe the buyer for the number of days the seller owned the property. Let's assume the closing is to be held on April 11. The seller is responsible for the period from January 1 until and including April 11.

First, calculate the number of days the seller actually owned the property.

January	30 days
February	30 days
March	30 days
April	11 days
Total	101 days

Next, multiply the daily rate ($5.50) times the number of days (101) the seller owes the buyer:

$$\$5.50 \times 101 = \$555.50$$

Because the seller owes the buyer, the resulting entry will appear as a debit to the seller and a credit to the buyer.

Taxes Have Not Been Paid—Taxes Payable (Paid at Closing)

It is far more likely that if the tax lien can be cleared off the title at closing, the lender will require it be paid. The closing attorney will collect from both the buyer and the seller their respective share of the annual tax bill. Assuming the closing is being held on August 20, what would be the correct amount collected for taxes?

First, calculate the number of days each party is responsible for.

Seller

January	30 days
February	30 days
March	30 days
April	30 days
May	30 days
June	30 days
July	30 days
August	20 days
Total	230 days

If we assume there are 360 days in the year and the seller is responsible for 230 days, the buyer would be responsible for the remaining 130 days (360 – 230 = 130).

Next, multiply the number of days each party is responsible for times the daily rate ($5.50):

$$\text{Seller: } \$5.50 \times 230 = \$1,265.00$$

$$\text{Buyer: } \$5.50 \times 130 = \$715.00$$

Each of these amounts would appear as a single-entry debit to the appropriate party. Note that the North Carolina CD Core worksheet does not have a preprinted reference for entering a debit to both the buyer and seller for unpaid property taxes. The closing narrative, in these cases, will instruct the student on how to make the appropriate entry. Typically you will be instructed to enter an amount for the buyer and the seller on page 1 on the CD Core worksheet.

Taxes Have Already Been Paid by the Seller

Once the property tax bills are mailed, it is possible the seller may have already paid the bill for the entire year. In this case, the buyer will owe the seller for the number of days the buyer will actually own the property; thus, the resulting entry will appear as a debit to the buyer and a credit to the seller. Again, we assume the seller will own the property for the day of closing. How would the closing entry appear if the closing was held on November 23?

First, calculate the number of days the buyer will be responsible for paying to the seller:

November: 7 days

December: 30 days

Total 37 days

Remember that the buyer will be responsible only for the days *after* the closing on November 23. The seller owned the property for 23 days in November, and the buyer owned it for only the last 7. It is a common error for students to mistakenly calculate 23 days for November and 30 for December. Next, multiply the daily times the number of days the buyer is responsible for:

$$\$5.50 \times 37 = \$203.50$$

The resulting entry would be to debit the buyer and credit the seller for $233.50.

Homeowners Association Fees

The increasing presence of homeowners associations has made the prorating of the resulting fees a common closing statement entry. These fees can be collected annually, semi-annually, quarterly, or monthly. Generally, they are billed and are to be paid in advance of the payment period. Because there are so many different payment period options, we will limit our discussion to an annual payment, based on a calendar year, to be paid in advance.

Assume the annual homeowners association fees are $432 for the year and have been paid in advance by the seller. The closing is scheduled for September 12. How would the resulting entry appear on the closing statement?

We begin by calculating the daily rate:

$$\$432 \div 360 \text{ days} = \$1.20 \text{ per day}$$

Next, calculate the number of days the buyer would be responsible for payment to the seller:

September: 18 days
October: 30 days
November: 30 days
December: 30 days
Total 108 days

Now, simply multiply the daily rate ($1.20) times the number of days the buyer owes the seller:

$$\$1.20 \times 108 \text{ days} = \$129.60$$

Because the buyer owes the seller, the resulting entry would appear as a debit to the buyer and a credit to the seller. Again, note that the buyer is responsible for only the remaining 18 days in September as the seller owned the property for the first 12 days.

Rental Income

In transactions involving the sale of income-producing properties, the buyer and seller will need to prorate the rental income for the current rental period. In the vast majority of residential situations, the rents are due and payable in advance at the first of the month. Because the seller will have already collected the rents due for the current month, he will owe the buyer for the number of days the buyer will actually own the property. Assume the monthly rent is $1,320 and the closing is to be conducted on the 19th of the month.

Again, start by calculating the daily rate for the monthly rent:

$$\$1{,}320 \div 30 \text{ days} = \$44 \text{ per day}$$

Next, determine how many days the buyer will actually own the property:

$$30 \text{ days} - 19 \text{ days} = 11 \text{ days}$$

The seller will owe the buyer the rental income due for the remaining 11 days in the month:

$$\$44 \times 11 = \$484.00$$

Because the seller owes the buyer, the resulting entry will appear as a debit to the seller and a credit to the buyer. The proration of rental income is especially tricky. Generally, when the seller owes the buyer, in other proration situations, it will be for the number of days the seller will actually own the property. *In rental income transactions, the seller owes the buyer for the number of days the buyer will actually own the property and therefore be entitled to the rent.* You are not prorating a bill to be paid, but rather income that has been received where the seller is not entitled to keep all of it. In this case, the seller has received all 30 days' worth of rental income but is entitled to retain only 19 days of rent; the buyer is to receive 11 days.

In situations in which the tenant has not yet paid the current month's rent, it will become necessary for the parties to come to some understanding of how to handle the unpaid rent. Generally, the parties will make every effort to get the tenant to pay the rent so that it can be handled appropriately at the closing. If this cannot happen, it may well be that the rent income will not be prorated at the closing, but rather some agreement will be reached as to how to handle the monies once they are paid. You generally will not prorate monies that do not exist at the time of closing but *may* be paid at a later date.

Mortgage Interest

Residential mortgage interest is calculated on a monthly basis with the payment being due the first of each month. Interest is generally calculated in *arrears,* which means each month's payment includes interest for the previous month. For example, a March 1 payment will include interest due for February, April 1 will include interest for March, May 1 will include interest for April, and so on. The method for calculating when interest is due is important, as the interest will have to be accounted for at closing. There will be two primary situations in which mortgage interest will be calculated at the closing: **interim interest** on a new loan and a *loan assumption.*

It is perhaps inaccurate to describe prepaid *interim interest* as a proration. It is being treated as such here simply because it involves the calculation of a daily rate and the number of days that must be paid; hence, it is a sort of proration. When a buyer obtains a new mortgage loan, the lender will calculate interest in arrears, which, as indicated earlier, means that interest due in any particular month is not paid until after it is earned by the lender. The first mortgage payment will not be due until the first day of the month following the next month after the closing. For example, if closing is held on May 15, the first payment will not be due until July 1, which would include interest due for the month of June. As a second example, if the closing were to be held on September 28, the first payment would not be due until the first of November, which would include interest due for October. The "problem" is there is no payment to be paid on the first of the following month, which would have included interest for the month of closing. As a result, even though interest is calculated in arrears, the interest due for the month of closing will be collected in advance. To quote the previous examples, interest due for May would be paid in advance at the closing and no payment would be paid on June 1. The July 1 payment would include interest for June, the August payment would include interest for July, and so forth. In the second example, the interest due for September would be collected in advance at the closing with no payment being scheduled for October 1, which normally would have been when the September interest would have been paid.

To calculate the interim interest using the above closing dates, use a loan amount of $165,000 at 6% interest. Because the resulting amount due is to be paid by the buyer to the lender and does not involve the seller at all, it will appear as a debit to the buyer and will not appear on the seller's side at all.

First, calculate the interest due as a daily rate:

$$\$165{,}000 \times 6\% = \$9{,}900 \text{ interest per year}$$

$$\$9{,}900 \div 360 = \$27.50 \text{ interest per day}$$

Next, calculate the number of days the lender will charge the buyer interest on the loan. NOTE: The lender will collect interest for the day of closing from the buyer. This will likely be the only time that you will need to charge the buyer for the day of closing, as the seller has nothing to do with the buyer's new loan and therefore is not held responsible for the day of closing.

Because the closing is to be held on May 15, the lender will actually collect 16 days of interest, as the buyer is responsible not only for the remaining 15 days but also for the day of closing (the 15th).

$$\$27.50 \times 16 = \$440.00$$

This amount will appear as a debit to the buyer only.

In the second example in which closing is conducted on September 28, you would need to collect three days of interim mortgage interest. This would represent interest for September 28, 29, and 30.

$$\$27.50 \times 3 = 82.50$$

Again, this will appear as a debit to the buyer only.

In today's real estate world, *loan assumptions* are rare but may reappear in the future depending on economic conditions. In a loan assumption, the interest will be calculated in arrears, which would mean the seller will owe the buyer for the number of days the seller actually owned the property. Unlike the interim interest calculation just illustrated, the seller will be charged for the day of closing. Hence, if closing is to be held on the 8th of the month, the seller would owe the buyer 8 days of interest, but if the closing is conducted on the 25th of the month, the seller would owe the buyer 25 days of interest, and so on. Using the same daily rate as before, the respective calculations would appear as follows:

$$\$27.50 \times 8 = \$220.00$$

$$\$27.50 \times 25 = \$687.50$$

In each case, the resulting entry would appear as a debit to the seller and a credit to the buyer.

Practice Settlement Statement Entries and Calculations

For tips on solving the following problems, see Figure 12.7.

1. Trey has entered into a contract for the purchase of a home. He has agreed to pay $192,500 and closing is scheduled for April 11. The buyer has paid $3,000 in the form of an earnest money deposit and an additional $250 for the due diligence fee. He is to obtain an 80% LTV mortgage at 5.25% for 30 years. The lender has agreed to make this loan and is charging him 1% loan origination fee with 2 discount points. The buyer will be responsible for the payment of interim interest at the closing. Other fees incurred at the closing include: attorney fees = $1,200, deed preparation = $85, title insurance = $385, and recording fees = $$65. Annual property taxes are estimated to be $1,800 and the first year homeowner's insurance premium will be $864. The lender is requiring the buyer to place five months of taxes and two months of insurance into escrow at closing. How much money will the buyer have to bring to the closing?

2. A seller has recently contracted to sell her home for $175,000 and has agreed to pay the broker a 6% sales commission. A lender has agreed to loan the purchaser $140,000 with one discount point that will be paid for by the seller. The outstanding loan balance on the seller's mortgage is $62,850 as of the November 10 closing date. Real property taxes are $720 for the year and

- Make certain the deed, stamps, and commission on page 2 are in the seller's column.
- Calculate the loan origination fee and discount points on the loan amount—not the sales price.
- Do not let simple mistakes derail your confidence when working your first couple of settlement problems. It is the rare student who does not make errors on the first few problems.
- Make certain to practice a variety of closing-related scenarios in your sample problems. You will minimally want to practice closing narratives that present property taxes in at least three ways: taxes not yet payable at the time of closing, unpaid taxes where collected and paid at the closing, and taxes that have already been paid prior to the closing. The closing narratives in this chapter, including the questions contained at the end of the chapter, present each of these scenarios.
- As you gain practice and confidence, there will be other entries that will appear as challenges to you. Do not panic. Remember, the buyer will typically pay associated loan acquisition costs such as loan application fees, flood certification fees, mortgage insurance premiums, etc.
- A wide variety of closing-related entries can be presented in a given closing narrative that are beyond the scope of the Pre-Licensing course. The Contracts and Closing Post-Licensing course will explore many of the entries in greater depth.
- The narratives contained in this text are designed to challenge the student and ultimately build confidence in your ability to handle closing problems. When confronted with these new entries, try to rationalize how they should be entered based upon the other entries that you have made.
- Remember the old saying—practice makes perfect! Many errors that are made on the first closing problems quickly become an issue of the past with minimal practice.

FIGURE 12.7 Important tips for closing worksheet problems.
Source: © 2019 OnCourse Learning

have been paid previously by the seller. The seller has also agreed to pay $90 for deed preparation in addition to revenue stamps at the current state rate. In addition the seller has agreed to pay $200 in miscellaneous costs for the buyer. How much will the seller "net" at the closing?

Solutions to Practice Settlement Statement Entries and Calculations

1.

ITEM	BUYER DEBIT	BUYER CREDIT
Sales Price	$192,500	
Earnest Money Due		$3,000
Due Diligence Fee		$250
New Loan		$154,000
Loan Origination Fee	$1,540	
Discount Points	$3,080	
Interim Insurance	$449.20	

ITEM	BUYER DEBIT	BUYER CREDIT
Attorney Fee	$1,200	
Title Insurance	$385	
Recording Fee	$65	
Property Taxes	$505	
Homeowners Insurance	$864	
Escrow for Taxes	$750	
Escrow for Insurance	$144	
Subtotals	$201,482.20	$157,250.00
Due from Buyer		$44,232.20
Totals	$201,482.20	$201,482.20

Prepaid interim interest

$154,000 \times 0.0525 = \$8,085$ annualized interest

$8,085 \div 360 = \$22.46$ interest per day

$22.46 \times 20 = \$449.20$ debit to buyer for 20 days

Property Taxes

$1,800 \div 360 = \$5$ property taxes per day

$5 \times 101 = \$505$ debit to buyer for 101 days

Escrows for Taxes and Insurance

$1,800 \div 12 = \$150$ property taxes per month

$150 \times 5 = \$750$ debit to buyer

$864 \div 12 = \$72$ insurance per month

$72 \times 2 = \$144$ debit to buyer

2.

ITEM	SELLER DEBIT	SELLER CREDIT
Sales Price		$175,000
Commission	$10,500	
Discount Points	$1,400	
Loan Payoff	$62,850	
Property Taxes		$100
Deed Preparation	$90	
Revenue Stamps	$350	
Miscellaneous Cost	$200	
Subtotals	$75,390	$175,100
Balance Due/Seller	$99,710	
Totals	$175,100	$175,100

Property Taxes

$720 ÷ 360 = $2 property taxes per day

$2 × 50 = $100 credit to seller for 50 days

> ### Test Tip!
> Review Figure 12.7 Important Tips for Closing Worksheet Problems.

Broker's Responsibilities Relating to Settlement Statements

The fact that closing statements are prepared by the lenders with input from the closing attorney does not relieve the broker from all responsibilities regarding the accuracy of these forms. Far too many brokers are willing to accept the closing statements provided by the attorney as always being correct and experience will teach otherwise. G.S. 93A-6 (a)(14) requires brokers to furnish both the buyer and seller with a detailed and accurate closing statement. Note that the law only requires the broker to provide the parties with a detailed and accurate settlement statement but not necessarily one actually prepared by the broker. It is rare that the real estate broker will personally prepare a closing statement in today's practice. It is most likely the statement will be prepared by the combination of the lender and attorney.

The broker, however, is held to a standard that he will be responsible for the entries about which he has *direct knowledge*. Items such as the correct sales price, earnest money deposits, due diligence fees, commissions, excise stamps, interim interest, and a general review of the correctness of prorations and making certain the correct party is charged are all responsibilities of the broker. Generally the broker will not be held liable for amounts supplied by the attorney from third-party suppliers, as it is reasonable to assume these figures are correct unless there is evidence of *red flags*. In addition, the broker will need to determine that any *bottom-line* figures are correct.

Summary of Important Points

1. The settlement meeting is used in North Carolina to bring all parties together to execute the required documents transferring title to the buyer. Settlement of the real estate transaction is the culmination of all of the agent's efforts. The buyer acquires title to a valuable asset, and the seller receives compensation out of which she pays her expenses of the sale.

2. The real estate broker is generally responsible for the accuracy of the settlement statement, even though this document is usually prepared by another party, such as an attorney. The broker will not typically be held responsible

for amounts due to or from third parties where the broker would not typically have any direct knowledge of there being an error such as the amount of attorney fees (in the absence of any red flags). The broker is also held accountable for the immediate delivery of the statement to all parties.

3. The real estate broker is responsible for the coordination of all details of the settlement meeting, although an attorney usually conducts the meeting and prepares all of the documents.
4. Preliminaries to settlement include property inspections; title examination; and drafting of documents, including the deed, financing instruments, and the closing statement.
5. The seller is responsible for preparing the deed, clearing any title defects, and providing receipts for the payment of taxes and utilities.
6. The buyer is responsible for title examination and insurance, hazard insurance, preparation of the financing instruments (promissory note and deed of trust), wood-destroying insect (termite) inspection (unless a Department of Veterans Affairs loan is used), and final inspection of the property.
7. The settlement statement itemizes the expenses and credits for the buyer and the seller. A debit is a cost or expense to a party. A credit is income or something received by a party. The buyer's totals will be different from the seller's totals.
8. Prorating is the method of dividing expenses fairly between the buyer and the seller according to their respective responsibilities. The 360-day-year method is used for study and exam purposes. Annual expenses are divided by 360 and multiplied by the number of days used by a given party to calculate that person's expenses. All months are presumed to have 30 days for study and exam purposes.
9. Prorated entries include real property taxes (but not personal property taxes), homeowners association fees, rents, and interest on an assumed loan. These items include a debit to one party and a corresponding credit to the other for their respective shares of the expense.
10. Not all double-entry items are prorated. Double-entry items not prorated include the purchase price, due diligence fee, a purchase money mortgage, an assumed mortgage, tenant security deposits, and the escrow account on an assumed loan.
11. Not all items on the settlement statement are double entry. Single-entry debits to the buyer include the cost of a new hazard insurance policy, title examination, title insurance, preparation of the financing instruments, recording fees, loan origination fees, credit report, and property survey. Termite inspections, well/water and septic/sewer reports, and discount points are also typically paid for by the buyer, although these can be paid by the seller if contractually agreed.

12. Single-entry credits to the buyer include earnest money and a new mortgage.
13. There are no single-entry credits to the seller.
14. Single-entry debits to the seller include payoff of an existing mortgage, excise tax, preparation of the deed, any delinquent (versus arrears) property taxes, soil/site evaluation, utility bills, and the broker's fee.
15. A useful check on the accuracy of the settlement statement is to assume you are the attorney handling the collection and disbursement of funds from your trust account. You want to be certain the cash you take in is identical to the amount that is paid out. Funds received into your account include the buyer's earnest money, a new mortgage, and the balance due from the buyer. Funds disbursed include payments to third parties, such as insurance, inspections, loan fees, recording fees, credit report, survey, broker's fee, and balance due to the seller.
16. RESPA rules are enforced by the Consumer Financial Protection Bureau.
17. The booklet *Know before You Owe* must be provided to the borrower within three days of the loan application.
18. The LE must also be provided to the borrower within three days of the loan application. In all TRID-related mortgages the buyer CD form is required to be used as the closing statement.
19. RESPA prohibits a kickback or referral fee payment to any settlement service provider.
20. Real estate agents are allowed to pay or receive referral fees to or from another agent.
21. Loan servicers must disclose to the borrower if they have the right to transfer the servicing of the borrower's loan.
22. RESPA considers a loan application to be at the point the lender obtains the borrower's (1) name, (2) monthly income, (3) social security number, which allows the credit report to be obtained, (4) address of the property pledged as collateral, (5) estimated value of the property, and (6) and the requested loan amount. Loan application is not considered to only occur upon the buyer signing a written application form. Once these six items are obtained the three-day disclosure period begins.
23. The LE contains "permissible variations" of up to 10% for one group of costs. Remember that individual items within this group may exceed 10% of the original estimate as long as the collective total of this section does not exceed 10% of the original estimate. Any amount *exceeding* this 10% figure is to be paid by the lender.
24. The CD must be provided to the buyer at least three days before the actual closing. This right cannot be waived. In order to meet this requirement the lender will be required to send the CD for review at least six days before the closing, unless being hand delivered, for the buyer to receive it before the three-day period is violated.

Review Questions

Answers to the review questions are in the Answer Key at the back of the book.

1. The cost of recording the deed would appear as a _____ on the closing statement?
   A. debit to the buyer
   B. debit to the seller
   C. credit to the buyer
   D. credit to the seller

2. The amount of the earnest money deposit appears in:
   A. buyer's closing statement as a credit.
   B. seller's closing statement as a debit.
   C. buyer's closing statement as a debit.
   D. seller's closing statement as a credit.

3. If property were listed for sale at $130,000 and sold for $128,500, a 6% broker's fee would appear in the seller's statement as a:
   A. credit of $7,800.
   B. debit of $7,710.
   C. credit of $7,710.
   D. debit of $7,800.

4. The cost of preparing a deed appears as a:
   A. debit in the buyer's statement.
   B. credit in the seller's statement.
   C. credit in the buyer's statement.
   D. debit in the seller's statement.

5. The day of closing is typically:
   A. charged to the seller.
   B. charged to the buyer.
   C. split equally between the buyer and seller.
   D. it depends on the type of loan.

6. In a real estate transaction, the buyer obtained a loan in the amount of $160,000. The lending institution charged 1 discount point, which the buyer agreed to pay. The cost of this point appears as a:
   A. credit to the buyer's statement of $1,600.
   B. debit to the seller's statement of $1,600.
   C. debit to the buyer's statement of $1,600.
   D. credit to the seller's statement of $1,600.

7. A buyer purchased a rental property and closed the transaction on July 20. The tenant had paid rent for the month of July in the amount of $600 on July 1. The rent should be shown as:
   A. $200 debit to buyer and credit to seller.
   B. $400 debit to buyer and credit to seller.
   C. $200 debit to seller and credit to buyer.
   D. $400 debit to buyer and credit to seller.

8. The cost of the due diligence fee appears as a:
   A. credit to the seller and debit to the buyer.
   B. debit to the buyer and a credit to the seller.
   C. credit to the buyer and a debit to the seller.
   D. debit to the seller.

9. A property sold for $151,050. The excise tax on the transaction will appear on the closing worksheet as a:
   A. $151.50 credit to the seller.
   B. $152.00 debit to the seller.
   C. $302.00 debit to the seller.
   D. $303.00 debit to the seller.

10. Provided nothing is written into the contract to the contrary, a wood-destroying insect report will appear on the closing statement as a:
    A. debit to buyer, credit to seller.
    B. credit to buyer, debit to seller.
    C. credit to seller only.
    D. debit to buyer only.

11. In a residential federally backed mortgage loan for the purchase of a property transaction, RESPA requires all of the following EXCEPT:
    A. use of the Closing Disclosure (CD).
    B. a three-day right of rescission.
    C. a good faith estimate.
    D. the providing of the informational booklet *Know Before You Owe*.

12. Which expenses are typically prorated between the buyer and the seller on the closing statement?
    A. private mortgage insurance
    B. interim interest
    C. commission to agent
    D. real property taxes

13. Which item is ALWAYS a single-sided entry?
    A. assumed mortgage
    B. sales price
    C. new first mortgage
    D. rental income

14. In North Carolina, the closing meeting is typically held at the:
    A. listing agent's office.
    B. selling agent's office.
    C. attorney's office.
    D. courthouse.

15. According to TRID, which of the following items would NOT be considered a required element of a loan application?
    A. borrower's monthly income
    B. borrower's Social Security number
    C. purchase price
    D. estimated value of the property

16. It is a requirement of TRID that the Loan Estimate be given to the borrower no later than three business days of the:
    A. date of loan application.
    B. date of loan acceptance.
    C. due diligence date.
    D. date of closing.

17. Rico is obtaining a mortgage of $243,250 at 5.25% interest rate with settlement to be conducted on June 26th. How will the resulting entry for the interim interest appear on a closing worksheet?
    A. $141.88 debit – buyer
    B. $177.37 debit – buyer
    C. $886.75 credit – buyer
    D. $922.22 credit – buyer

18. A duplex is being rented for $600 per unit and is being sold to an investor with closing to be on the 22nd of September. How will the resulting entry appear on the closing worksheet?
    A. $160 debit – seller, credit – buyer
    B. $160 debit – buyer, credit – seller
    C. $320 debit – seller, credit – buyer
    D. $320 credit – seller, debit – buyer

19. A property is being sold with settlement set for March 19. Property taxes for the year are estimated to be $864. How will the resulting entry appear on the settlement worksheet?
    A. $674.40 debit – seller, credit – buyer
    B. $674.40 debit – buyer, credit – seller
    C. $189.60 debit – seller, credit – buyer
    D. $189.60 debit – buyer, credit – seller

20. Fairley is selling her house to Marian with settlement to be conducted on October 21. The annual HOA assessment, based upon the calendar year, was levied on the property for $360 and was paid in January. How will the resulting entry appear on the closing worksheet?
    A. $291.00 debit – buyer, credit – seller
    B. $291.00 credit – buyer, debit – seller
    C. $69.00 credit – buyer, debit – seller
    D. $69.00 debit – buyer, credit – seller

21. Linda is selling her house to Heather with settlement scheduled for November 27th. Property taxes for the year are $594 and have not yet been paid. The lender is requiring the taxes to be paid at the settlement. How will the resulting entry appear of a settlement worksheet?
    A. $539.55 debit – seller, credit – buyer
    B. $54.45 debit – buyer, credit – seller
    C. $539.55 debit – seller and $54.45 debit – buyer
    D. $54.45 debit – seller, credit – buyer

22. Matt is obtaining a mortgage loan of $178,000 at 5.5% interest. Settlement is to occur on the 27th day of the month. How will the interim interest appear on the settlement worksheet?
    A. $734.13 debit – buyer
    B. $706.94 debit – buyer
    C. $108.76 debit – buyer
    D. $81.57 debit – buyer

23. Gene has agreed to sell his property to Amy with settlement to be on December 11. Property taxes of $810 for the year have already been paid. How will the resulting entry appear on the settlement worksheet?
    A. $767.25 debit – buyer, credit – seller
    B. $24.75 debit – buyer, credit – seller
    C. $24.75 credit – seller, debit – buyer
    D. $42.75 debit – buyer, credit – seller

24. Ashley contracts to purchase August's home for $250,000 with settlement set for October 21. The lender agrees to make her a 80% LTV mortgage at 5.5% interest with 1% loan origination fee and 1.5 discount points. In addition, interim interest to the end of the month must be collected. Property taxes are $2,750 for the year and the lender requires these to be paid off at the settlement. At settlement the following items must be paid by the party who would traditionally pay them: attorney fees – $950; survey – $450; deed preparation – $90; title insurance – $500; termite report – $75; commission – 6%; revenue stamps – use state rate. The buyer has paid $475 for the appraisal and $75 for the credit report at the time of the loan application. In addition the buyer has paid $2,500 in earnest money deposit and $200 in the form of the due diligence fee. How much money will Ashley need to bring to the settlement in order to close? (Round all proration entries to the nearest whole dollar amount.)
    A. $52,357
    B. $55,108
    C. $55,308
    D. $56,358

25. Danette has agreed to sell her house to Thomas for $319,000 and settlement to be scheduled for April 23. Thomas paid earnest money of $3,000 and an additional $1,000 as a due diligence fee with the offer. The balance due at closing on Danette's mortgage is $191,415. Terms of the agreement are for the annual property taxes of $4,032 to be prorated along with the monthly homeowners association fees of $48 that have already been paid by the seller.
In addition to the above items, the settlement attorney will collect deed preparation fees of $80, recording fees $40, revenue stamps using the state rate, and the sales commission of 5%. What will be the amount the seller will receive at the settlement? (Enter all proration entries to the nearest whole dollar amount.)

A. $108,662
B. $109,938
C. $110,663
D. $111,194

CHAPTER 13

REAL PROPERTY VALUATION

KEY TERMS

anticipation
appraisal
broker price opinion (BPO)
capitalization
capitalization formula
cash flow
chronological age
comparable
comparative market analysis (CMA)
competition
conformity
contribution
cost
cost approach
curable
debt service
demand
depreciation
economic obsolescence
effective age
effective demand
functional obsolescence
gross effective income
income (capitalization) approach
incurable
market value
net operating income (NOI)
operating expenses
physical deterioration
potential gross income
price
probable sales price
quantity survey method
replacement cost
replacement reserve
reproduction cost
scarcity
square-foot method
substitution
supply and demand
transferability
unit-in-place method
utility
value
value in use

LEARNING OBJECTIVES

At the conclusion of this chapter, you should be able to:

1. Define the basic terminology of valuation.
2. Define the basic concepts of value, including appraisal, evaluation, valuation, value in use, and market value.
3. Describe the forces and factors that affect value.
4. Describe the economic principles of value.
5. Define the basic terminology of appraisal methodology.

6. Describe the general use and procedures of the direct sales comparison (market data) approach. Make simple adjustments to comparable properties to derive an indication of a subject property's value.
7. Describe the general use and procedures of the cost approach.
8. Describe the general use and procedures of the income approach.
9. Understand the laws and rules governing the performance of broker price opinions and comparative market analysis by brokers.
10. Understand how to properly perform broker price opinion/comparative market analysis (BPO/CMA) of a single-family residential property.

IN THIS CHAPTER

Real estate practitioners must have a good working knowledge of the principles of establishing the probable sales price of a given property. The Real Estate Commission holds an agent responsible for estimating the probable selling price of a property being listed and properly advising an owner of this estimate. If an agent recommends a listing price too low, the result will be a loss of money for the seller. In a similar fashion, when an agent attempts to obtain a listing by telling the owner the property should sell for far more than its probable selling price, this is misrepresentation. In any event, the agent should be able to demonstrate the data and process by which she reached a conclusion as to the probable selling price. This chapter discusses the principle of valuation and demonstrates the three primary approaches used by appraisers to reach a conclusion of property value as well as discusses the law and rules governing broker price opinions (BPOs) and comparative market analyses (CMAs) by brokers. In addition to estimating a property's probable selling price for their sellers and buyers, real estate agents also need a good basic understanding of the process professional appraisers use in appraising real estate for sale or lease transactions.

Test Tip!

Students will be tested on the state exam on several areas of valuation calculations, including the following:

- Sales comparison approach and comparative market analysis
- Cost approach
- Income approach including income capitalization and gross rent multiplier

APPRAISER REGULATION

In 1989, in the aftermath of the savings and loan crisis, Congress passed the Financial Institutions Reform, Recovery, and Enforcement Act (FIRREA). One of the effects of this act was to establish a regulatory system for real estate appraisers performing appraisals of property connected with federally related transactions. This includes the majority of real estate loans. The result of these regulated appraisals means that the appraiser must adhere to the standards and qualifications established under this act.

Licensure and Certification

The North Carolina Appraisal Board operates a mandatory licensing program, which enables real estate appraisers to become state licensed to perform appraisals. An appraisal license or certification is required to perform appraisals in North Carolina.

BASIC APPRAISAL CONCEPTS

Definition of Appraisal

An **appraisal** is, quite simply, *an estimate of value*. It does not set the value nor does it determine value. The term *appraisal* is also used to refer to the *act of estimating value*. Although this term can apply to any estimate of value, in real estate, it is generally used only in reference to a formal, written estimate of value performed by a professional appraiser. The North Carolina Appraisers Act, North Carolina General Statute (G.S.) Chapter 93E, defines an appraisal as "an analysis, opinion, or conclusion as to the value of identified real estate or specified interests therein performed for compensation or other valuable consideration." To form an appraisal for another, for compensation, requires a North Carolina appraisal license although a real estate license is not required.

Broker Price Opinion/Comparative Market Analysis

The terms **broker price opinion (BPO)** and **comparative market analysis (CMA)** are not to be confused with "appraisal." According to G.S. 93A-82 of the North Carolina Licensing Law and G.S. 93E-1-4(7c) of the North Carolina Appraisers Act, the definitions of CMAs and BPOs are identical; they are defined as "the analysis of sales of similar recently sold properties in order to derive an indication of the **probable sales price** of a particular property *by a licensed real estate broker.*"

Effective October 1, 2012, there were major changes to both the Real Estate Law and the Appraisers Act. These changes are summarized as follows:

- A BPO and CMA are considered to have exactly the same meaning.
- Only an active "nonprovisional" broker licensee may perform a CMA/BPO *for a fee*.
- A CMA/BPO may NOT estimate the value of a property but rather must estimate the probable sales or leasing price only.
- If a CMA/BPO does estimate the "value" or "worth" of a property, it shall be legally considered an "appraisal," which may only be completed by a properly licensed appraiser.
- The CMA/BPO should specifically state that it is not an appraisal.
- Any CMA/BPO that is completed for a fee must comply with Article 6 of the Real Estate License Law and the rules of the North Carolina Real Estate Commission.

For more complete coverage regarding BPOs/CMAs, refer to the end of this chapter.

Value, Price, and Cost

The terms *value, price,* and *cost* do not have the same meaning. **Value** results from *the anticipation of future benefits resulting from ownership of a particular property.* **Cost** is a *measure of expenditures of labor and materials made some time in the past.* Therefore, value is based on the future, whereas cost is based on the past.

Price is *the amount of money paid for a property.* Price may be more than or less than value or cost. Under normal market conditions, however, price is generally in line with value because the owner usually does not want to accept a price substantially less than value, nor does a purchaser want to pay an amount significantly in excess of value. The more knowledgeable buyers and sellers are about property value, the more closely related price and value will be.

Value is also referred to as **market value**. An appraiser estimates market value. *Price* and *market price* are used interchangeably.

A simple way to compare the meaning of these terms is to think of them this way: value is what something is actually worth, cost is what you have invested in the property, and price is what the marketplace will currently pay for the property.

Market Value

The determination of "market value" of a property tends to be the goal of most valuation efforts. The question of what a property is worth is typically at the forefront of the seller's mind whether he is buying, selling, seeking to refinance, challenging an assessed value, or any number of other potential reasons. In reality, the market value is subject to many factors that can affect what any property has sold for, such as the following: What was the buyer's or the seller's motivation? Was the property placed on the market for sale at too low of a price due to seller ignorance? Was the property not advertised in a *normal* fashion? Was the transaction a result of a job transfer, separation, or divorce, or a potential foreclosure? For these reasons, and many others, the market value is not as easy to determine as many make it out to be.

The Uniform Residential Appraisal Report (URAR), promulgated by Fannie Mae and Freddie Mac (2005 edition), provides one of the more easily followed definitions of market value: "The most probable price that a property should bring in a competitive and open market under all conditions requisite to a fair sale, the buyer and seller, each acting prudently, knowledgeably and assuming the price is not affected by undue stimulus."

Implicit in this definition is consummation of a sale as of a specified date and the passing of title from seller to buyer under all of the following conditions:

- Buyer and seller are typically motivated.
- Both parties are well informed or well advised and each is acting in what she considers to be her own best interest.
- A reasonable time is allowed for exposure in the open market.
- Payment is made in terms of cash in U.S. dollars or in terms of financial arrangements comparable thereto.
- The price represents the normal consideration for the property sold unaffected by special or creative financing or sales concessions granted by anyone associated with the sale.

The term *market value* is more suitable for appraisers, but real estate agents will rely on some of the same principles in seeking to determine the "probable sales price" when completing the CMA/BPO.

Value in Use and Value in Exchange

Value in use is *a special value to a person, usually the owner of a property. In this sense, the property takes on either a subjective or an objective value to the owner.* Subjective value may stem from pride of ownership and probably is not reflected by the general public. An owner often believes her property is worth more than its market value. The property's objective value to the owner may be an income from a use of the property for which there is little or no competitive market demand. In this case, the value in use may be greater than its value in exchange (the amount the owner could receive for it in money or other commodities).

Valuation versus Evaluation

There is a significant difference between the concepts of valuation and evaluation. Valuation, or appraisal, is the subject of this section and is concerned with *estimating what the average buyer would pay for a property, or its fair market value.*

Evaluation is concerned with the economic feasibility of a project and can be considered in two areas: economic feasibility and land use.

An economic feasibility study might be concerned with the "workability" of a project, such as the development of a residential subdivision, office project, or shopping center. Before committing to the project, the developers would want to study the *absorption rate of the market*, that is, the **effective demand** by the public. Before financing a commercial project, a lender might require the developer to obtain a certain percentage of "rental achievements," that is, commitments for lease of a certain portion of the project.

A land utilization study determines the best current use of a given property. Often, existing homes on a property could be best adapted to commercial uses. For vacant land, one would want to determine whether the land would best be developed for a residential subdivision or for commercial purposes.

Additional Concepts of Value

For a property to have value, it must have certain legal and economic characteristics. The characteristics are (1) demand, (2) utility, (3) scarcity, and (4) transferability. A popular way to recall these concepts is by remembering the acronym DUST.

Demand

Demand is *a desire or need for a property that is coupled with the financial ability to satisfy the need.* In times of excessively high interest rates, many people with a strong desire and substantial need for housing are priced out of the mortgage market; therefore, the demand for property is not an effective demand because individuals who want to buy do not have the financial ability to satisfy the demand. In creating housing or other types of property, such as office buildings, shopping malls, and hotels, a developer must take into consideration not only the need for these types of property but also the financial ability of prospective tenants or purchasers to satisfy their needs.

Utility

Utility is *the ability to satisfy a need.* The property must be useful. It must be possible to use or adapt the property for some legal purpose. If the property cannot be put to some beneficial use and cannot fill a need of some kind, it does not have value.

Scarcity

The degree of **scarcity** is *based on the supply of the property in relation to the effective demand for the property.* The more abundant the supply of property in comparison to the effective demand for the property at any given time, the lower the value. Conversely, the fewer properties available on the market in comparison to the effective demand or bidding for these properties at any given time, the greater the value of the properties.

Transferability

Transferability is a legal concept that must be present for a property to have value. Transferability is what *makes it possible for the owner to transfer the ownership interests to a prospective buyer*. These ownership interests include all of those expressed in the "bundle of rights" theory previously discussed.

Forces and Factors Influencing Value

The forces that affect real property value are (1) social, (2) economic, (3) governmental, and (4) physical.

Social Ideas and Standards

Social forces include rates of marriage, birth, divorce, and death; the rate of population growth or decline; and public attitudes toward such things as education, cultural activities, and recreation.

Economic Forces

Economic forces include employment levels, income levels, availability of credit, interest rates, price levels, and the amount of real property taxes.

Government Activities

Governmental forces include regulations such as zoning laws, building codes, fire regulations, city or county planning, and regulations designed to promote or retard growth and development.

Physical Forces

Physical forces are both natural and artificial. Natural forces include topography, soil conditions, mineral resources, size, shape, climate, and location. Artificial factors include utilities, proximity to streets and highways, availability of public transportation, and access.

Basic Economic Principles of Value

Supply and Demand

The economic principle of **supply and demand** is applicable to the real estate industry just as it is applicable to other economic activities in the free enterprise system. This principle states that *the greater the supply of any commodity in* *comparison with the demand for that commodity, the lower the value (high supply, low demand = lower value). Conversely, the smaller the supply and the greater the demand, the higher the value (low supply, high demand = higher value).* Therefore, factors that influence the demand and supply of real estate also affect property values—either beneficially or adversely.

> ### Test Tip!
>
> Students will need to be familiar with all of the economic principles of value.

Anticipation

The principle of **anticipation** provides that *property value is based on the anticipation of the future benefits of ownership.* This is also stated as the present value of future income. To put it another way, how much would someone pay today for the rights and benefits of ownership for the future? The future, not the past, is important in estimating the value of property. Changes in the expected demand for property can result from the creation of various improvements in an area, such as schools, shopping centers, and freeways. Therefore, real estate practitioners must be aware of plans for development in their local market area. There may be changes that will adversely affect the expected demand for property, resulting from such things as changes in surrounding land use patterns. Changes that cause an increase in demand will increase property values, whereas changes that cause a reduction in demand will cause depreciation.

Substitution

The principle of **substitution** provides that *the highest value of a property has a tendency to be established by the cost of purchasing or constructing another property of equal utility and desirability, provided the substitution can be made without unusual delay.* Therefore, if two properties are on the market, each having the same degree of desirability and utility, and one is priced at $100,000 and the other is priced at $95,000, a buyer would substitute the $95,000 property instead of purchasing the $100,000 property. Simply put, given a choice, the purchaser will typically choose the lesser priced alternative given the same amenities, similar benefits, equal utility and desirability, and opportunity to purchase with no undue delay. Substitution is the foundation of the direct sales comparison approach to valuation.

Conformity

Conformity results from the *homogeneous or compatible uses of land within a given area.* Therefore, properties in a given area will tend to be of similar size, style, age, construction, and quality. Adherence to the principle of conformity will result in maximizing property values. Failure to adhere to the principle will result in inharmonious and incompatible uses of land within the area, with the consequence of depreciating property values. In residential subdivisions, conformity is achieved through the use of restrictive covenants. In other areas, conformity is accomplished through zoning laws and subdivision ordinances.

Contribution

The principle of **contribution** states that *various elements of a property add value to the entire property.* Simply put, the worth of something is relative to what it adds to overall value. For example, if a typical buyer would pay $5,500 more for a property with a garage than for the same property without a garage, the contribution is that the element adds a value of $5,500 by itself.

This principle is used in the direct sales comparison approach to the value estimate in making adjustments to comparable properties to compare them to the subject property (the property that is the subject of the appraisal). For example, a subject property may have a fireplace, whereas a **comparable** does not. A comparable *is a recently sold property that is compared to the subject property (the property being valued) to determine the value of the subject property.* In making the appraisal, one must estimate the value increase resulting from the presence of the fireplace in the subject property compared with the loss in value resulting from the absence of the fireplace in the comparable.

The principle of contribution also applies to decisions regarding expenditures to modernize or improve a property. For example, will the addition of a garage or carport increase the value of a home sufficiently to cover the cost of constructing the improvement? This principle also applies to improving an investment property. For example, will the cost of improving the property by installing an elevator in a four-story office building be offset by the increase in rental income resulting from the installation of the elevator? In other words, does the elevator make a sufficient contribution to value in the form of additional property income to offset the cost associated with creating the improvement? The economic principle of contribution is an excellent example of cost versus value.

Competition

The principle of **competition** states that *when the net profit generated by a property is excessive, the result is to create very strong competition.* For example, if a growth area contains only one or two properties of a certain type, such as one or two apartment complexes or office buildings, these properties will produce excess profits from rental income. The result is to attract a number of competitors eager to participate in the profits. Increased competition will cause a reduction in excess profits as the supply of competing services increases until excess profits are finally eliminated, thereby lowering property values.

Change

The economic principle of change indicates that all properties undergo a life cycle, and it is important to realize where a given property is on the cycle to establish value. For example, a growth cycle occurs when a developer creates a new subdivision and builds new houses with the latest in architectural styling and features. Next is the stabilization phase when these properties are occupied by the owners and used in such a way as to maintain the property values. The next phase is decline, when you start to see a higher incidence of nonowner occupancy coupled with a general sense of "dated" architecture, and when the house no longer has the latest in styling and features, along with an increased amount of deferred maintenance. Finally, you see the renewal phase when these houses are either renovated to make them more current in styling and features or the houses are torn down to be rebuilt as more modern housing or to make way for another use such as commercial.

Highest and Best Use

The principle of highest and best use is that use which will give the owner the highest net rate of return or profitability. This is a classic case of a prospective purchaser analyzing a property based not so much on how it is currently being used, but rather how it could be used to be more profitable. This is very often the case when someone sees a rather modest house on the market for $500,000 and "the value is in the land" is being emphasized. Essentially, the seller is saying that the highest and best use is not for residential purposes but rather for commercial or office-institutional use. In theory, there is only one highest and best use at any given time. Certainly, over time, what constitutes the highest and best use will change such as from agricultural land to residential housing to office or commercial to major commercial or industrial.

THE VALUATION PROCESS

An appraisal is an estimate of property value based on factual data. In estimating property value, an organized and systematic program must be followed. The orderly progression of the appraisal process includes the following steps, listed in chronological order:

1. Define the appraisal problem. This includes the determination of the purpose of the appraisal and the type of value to be estimated.
2. Obtain a complete and accurate description of the property that is the subject of the appraisal. The appraisal report must contain a legal description of the property to locate and identify the property precisely. The identification must specify the limits of the area in the appraisal.
3. Inspect the surrounding area and the property to be appraised.
4. Determine the specific data required as the basis for the value estimate. Establish a separate estimate of land value, and perform a highest and best use analysis.

5. Analyze the data and arrive at a value estimate by three appraisal methods: market data, cost, and income.
6. Reconcile the results obtained by the three methods, thereby arriving at a value estimate.
7. Prepare the appraisal report.

APPROACHES TO VALUE

Sales Comparison (Market Data) Approach

> 🔑 The sales comparison, or market data, approach to appraising is used when the appraiser has sufficient sales activity to make a comparison. Therefore, it is the primary method used when valuing single-family houses and is always the choice when appraising vacant land (see Figure 13.1).

The basic premise behind the sales comparison method is that the best way to determine what something is worth is to compare it with similar properties that are selling in the marketplace. The issue is that similar will not mean identical, so the appraiser must make adjustments for the similar sales to determine what the property being appraised is worth. The adjustments for the comparables are based on the theory of contribution, meaning the amount something is worth relative to what it contributes to the overall value. To present a more complete illustration of this process, the following terms and guidelines will be employed.

> **Test Tip!**
>
> The sales comparison method is especially important for students to understand for testing purposes.

---

1. The direct sales comparison approach
   Compares subject property to similar properties sold recently
2. The cost approach
   Theoretically rebuilds the structure anew and then adjusts it to its present condition
3. The income method
   Applies the capitalization formula to the income (rent) produced

---

FIGURE 13.1 Approaches to value (appraisal methods).
Source: © 2019 OnCourse Learning

Key Points about Sales Comparison Approach

- Subject—The subject is the property being appraised.
- Comparable—Commonly referred to as comps. Comparables are similar properties that have been sold in the marketplace. Preferably they have been sold in the past six months and located reasonably close to the subject although that will not always be practical in some markets.
- Three to four comps are generally sufficient. More comparables can be employed but never less than three.
- Comparables should be verified, closed out, sales prices. Asking prices are not to be used as those properties will typically sell for full price or less.
- You only adjust the comparables, never the subject.

Comparables should be as similar as possible in all respects to subject property. They may be found in real estate office files of closed sales, in the closed sales data of a multiple listing service, and from other appraisers. The more recent the date of sale of the comparable, the more valuable the comparable is to the appraisal process. Also of great importance is the degree of similarity of the physical characteristics of the comparable to the subject property and the location of the comparable. It often has been stated that the best comparable consists of the identical house next door to the subject. The further from this ideal the appraiser finds himself, the more adjustments that must be made to the comps. The credibility of the end result to the appraisal will start with the quality of the comparable selected.

Real estate agents will generally utilize sales comparison techniques in completing a CMA. NOTE: For a more complete explanation of CMAs and BPOs, please refer to the end of this sales comparison section.

Let's look at the sales comparison approach portion of the appraisal process:

1. Collect all pertinent information for subject property by inspecting the property and acquiring necessary documents, such as deeds, surveys, and legal descriptions.
2. Enter information pertaining to subject property on a CMA Worksheet (see Figure 13.2 for an example). An appraiser would enter the information into the URAR in the Sales Comparison Approach Section (see Figure 13.3). Enter the information obtained from your inspection with the homeowner, and proceed down the subject columns, entering all pertinent facts and amenities of the subject. No sales price or price per square foot can be entered at this time because that has not been determined.
3. Identify possible comparables from MLS data, real estate company files, or appraisers. Comparables must be actual verified closed sales.

Date: 12-9-CY	Subject Property	Comparable 1		Comparable 2		Comparable 3	
Address	524 Amortization Dr.	602 Amortization Dr.		301 Acceleration Circle		12 Redemption Lane	
Sales Price		$192,000		$185,500		$182,500	
			Adjustment		Adjustment		Adjustment
Sale Date		11-10-CY	+$400	10-20-CY	+ $800	6-11-CY	+$2,300
Location	Good	Good	0	Good	0	Fair	+ 1,000
Lot Size	150 × 175 (26,250 sq. ft.)	140 × 170 (23,800)	+ 500	150 × 170 (25,500)	0	125 × 150 (18,750)	+ 1,500
Age	5	6	0	7	0	8	0
Condition	Good	Good	0	Fair	+ 1,000	Fair	+ 1,000
Square Footage	1,800	1,900	$-4,000	1,800	0	1,650	+$6,000
Bathrooms	2½	3	− 1,000	2½	0	2	+1,000
Style	Ranch	Ranch	0	Ranch	0	Ranch	0
Construction	Frame	Brick & Frame	0	Frame	0	Frame	0
Air Conditioning	Central	Central	0	Central	0	None	+$2,000
Garage	Garage-2 Car	Garage-2 Car	0	Garage-2 Car	0	Carport-1 Car	+ 3,500
Driveway	Paved	Paved	0	Gravel	+ 1,000	Gravel	+ 1,000
TOTAL ADJUSTMENT			− 4,100		+ 2,800		+19,300
ADJUSTED PRICE			$187,900		$188,300		$201,800

Reconciliation Process

Comparable 1 $187,900 × 35% = $65,765
Comparable 2 $188,300 × 40% = $75,320
Comparable 3 $201,800 × 25% = $50,450

(Not all three properties are given the same importance. The appraiser has assigned the most weight to Comparable 2 since he believes it is most similar to the subject; Comparable 3, with the largest adjustment, is deemed to be at least similar and is assigned the least weight.)

Weighted Average = $191,535 rounded to $191,600 indicated value of subject property

FIGURE 13.2 Sales comparison (market data) approach.

Source: © 2019 OnCourse Learning

4. Choose most suitable comparables by evaluating each possible comparable according to the following criteria:
   - Location
   - Size
   - Age
   - Lot/land value
   - Design
   - Type and quality of construction
   - Similarity of physical characteristics and amenities
   - Date of sale
   - Verified sales price
   - Seller concessions
   - Seller motivation
   - Method of financing used by purchaser
   - Terms and conditions of sale

Uniform Residential Appraisal Report

File #

The purpose of this summary appraisal report is to provide the lender/client with an accurate, and adequately supported, opinion of the market value of the subject property.

SUBJECT

Property Address | City | State | Zip Code

Borrower | Owner of Public Record | County

Legal Description

Assessor's Parcel # | Tax Year | R.E. Taxes $

Neighborhood Name | Map Reference | Census Tract

Occupant ☐ Owner ☐ Tenant ☐ Vacant | Special Assessments $ | ☐ PUD | HOA $ | ☐ per year ☐ per month

Property Rights Appraised ☐ Fee Simple ☐ Leasehold ☐ Other (describe)

Assignment Type ☐ Purchase Transaction ☐ Refinance Transaction ☐ Other (describe)

Lender/Client | Address

Is the subject property currently offered for sale or has it been offered for sale in the twelve months prior to the effective date of this appraisal? ☐ Yes ☐ No

Report data source(s) used, offering price(s), and date(s).

CONTRACT

I ☐ did ☐ did not analyze the contract for sale for the subject purchase transaction. Explain the results of the analysis of the contract for sale or why the analysis was not performed.

Contract Price $ | Date of Contract | Is the property seller the owner of public record? ☐ Yes ☐ No | Data Source(s)

Is there any financial assistance (loan charges, sale concessions, gift or downpayment assistance, etc.) to be paid by any party on behalf of the borrower? ☐ Yes ☐ No

If Yes, report the total dollar amount and describe the items to be paid.

NEIGHBORHOOD

Note: Race and the racial composition of the neighborhood are not appraisal factors.

Neighborhood Characteristics	One-Unit Housing Trends	One-Unit Housing		Present Land Use %	
Location ☐ Urban ☐ Suburban ☐ Rural	Property Values ☐ Increasing ☐ Stable ☐ Declining	PRICE	AGE	One-Unit	%
Built-Up ☐ Over 75% ☐ 25–75% ☐ Under 25%	Demand/Supply ☐ Shortage ☐ In Balance ☐ Over Supply	$ (000)	(yrs)	2-4 Unit	%
Growth ☐ Rapid ☐ Stable ☐ Slow	Marketing Time ☐ Under 3 mths ☐ 3–6 mths ☐ Over 6 mths	Low		Multi-Family	%
Neighborhood Boundaries		High		Commercial	%
		Pred.		Other	%

Neighborhood Description

Market Conditions (including support for the above conclusions)

SITE

Dimensions | Area | Shape | View

Specific Zoning Classification | Zoning Description

Zoning Compliance ☐ Legal ☐ Legal Nonconforming (Grandfathered Use) ☐ No Zoning ☐ Illegal (describe)

Is the highest and best use of the subject property as improved (or as proposed per plans and specifications) the present use? ☐ Yes ☐ No If No, describe

Utilities	Public	Other (describe)		Public	Other (describe)	Off-site Improvements—Type	Public	Private
Electricity	☐	☐	Water	☐	☐	Street	☐	☐
Gas	☐	☐	Sanitary Sewer	☐	☐	Alley	☐	☐

FEMA Special Flood Hazard Area ☐ Yes ☐ No | FEMA Flood Zone | FEMA Map # | FEMA Map Date

Are the utilities and off-site improvements typical for the market area? ☐ Yes ☐ No If No, describe

Are there any adverse site conditions or external factors (easements, encroachments, environmental conditions, land uses, etc.)? ☐ Yes ☐ No If Yes, describe

IMPROVEMENTS

General Description		Foundation		Exterior Description	materials/condition	Interior	materials/condition
Units ☐ One ☐ One with Accessory Unit		☐ Concrete Slab ☐ Crawl Space		Foundation Walls		Floors	
# of Stories		☐ Full Basement ☐ Partial Basement		Exterior Walls		Walls	
Type ☐ Det. ☐ Att. ☐ S-Det./End Unit		Basement Area	sq. ft.	Roof Surface		Trim/Finish	
☐ Existing ☐ Proposed ☐ Under Const.		Basement Finish	%	Gutters & Downspouts		Bath Floor	
Design (Style)		☐ Outside Entry/Exit ☐ Sump Pump		Window Type		Bath Wainscot	
Year Built		Evidence of ☐ Infestation		Storm Sash/Insulated		Car Storage ☐ None	
Effective Age (Yrs)		☐ Dampness ☐ Settlement		Screens		☐ Driveway # of Cars	
Attic	☐ None	Heating ☐ FWA ☐ HWBB ☐ Radiant		Amenities	☐ Woodstove(s) #	Driveway Surface	
☐ Drop Stair	☐ Stairs	☐ Other	Fuel	☐ Fireplace(s) #	☐ Fence	☐ Garage # of Cars	
☐ Floor	☐ Scuttle	Cooling ☐ Central Air Conditioning		☐ Patio/Deck	☐ Porch	☐ Carport # of Cars	
☐ Finished	☐ Heated	☐ Individual	☐ Other	☐ Pool	☐ Other	☐ Att. ☐ Det. ☐ Built-in	

Appliances ☐ Refrigerator ☐ Range/Oven ☐ Dishwasher ☐ Disposal ☐ Microwave ☐ Washer/Dryer ☐ Other (describe)

Finished area **above** grade contains: | Rooms | Bedrooms | Bath(s) | Square Feet of Gross Living Area Above Grade

Additional features (special energy efficient items, etc.)

Describe the condition of the property (including needed repairs, deterioration, renovations, remodeling, etc.).

Are there any physical deficiencies or adverse conditions that affect the livability, soundness, or structural integrity of the property? ☐ Yes ☐ No If Yes, describe

Does the property generally conform to the neighborhood (functional utility, style, condition, use, construction, etc.)? ☐ Yes ☐ No If No, describe

Freddie Mac Form 70 March 2005 | Page 1 of 6 | Fannie Mae Form 1004 March 2005

FIGURE 13.3 Uniform residential appraisal report.

Source: www.efanniemae.com

Uniform Residential Appraisal Report

File #

There are _____ comparable properties currently offered for sale in the subject neighborhood ranging in price from $ _____ to $ _____.
There are _____ comparable sales in the subject neighborhood within the past twelve months ranging in sale price from $ _____ to $ _____.

FEATURE	SUBJECT	COMPARABLE SALE # 1		COMPARABLE SALE # 2		COMPARABLE SALE # 3	
Address							
Proximity to Subject							
Sale Price	$		$		$		$
Sale Price/Gross Liv. Area	$ sq. ft.	$ sq. ft.		$ sq. ft.		$ sq. ft.	
Data Source(s)							
Verification Source(s)							
VALUE ADJUSTMENTS	DESCRIPTION	DESCRIPTION	+(-) $ Adjustment	DESCRIPTION	+(-) $ Adjustment	DESCRIPTION	+(-) $ Adjustment
Sale or Financing Concessions							
Date of Sale/Time							
Location							
Leasehold/Fee Simple							
Site							
View							
Design (Style)							
Quality of Construction							
Actual Age							
Condition							
Above Grade Room Count	Total Bdrms. Baths	Total Bdrms. Baths		Total Bdrms. Baths		Total Bdrms. Baths	
Gross Living Area	sq. ft.	sq. ft.		sq. ft.		sq. ft.	
Basement & Finished Rooms Below Grade							
Functional Utility							
Heating/Cooling							
Energy Efficient Items							
Garage/Carport							
Porch/Patio/Deck							
Net Adjustment (Total)		☐ + ☐ -	$	☐ + ☐ -	$	☐ + ☐ -	$
Adjusted Sale Price of Comparables		Net Adj. % Gross Adj. %	$	Net Adj. % Gross Adj. %	$	Net Adj. % Gross Adj. %	$

I ☐ did ☐ did not research the sale or transfer history of the subject property and comparable sales. If not, explain

My research ☐ did ☐ did not reveal any prior sales or transfers of the subject property for the three years prior to the effective date of this appraisal.
Data source(s)
My research ☐ did ☐ did not reveal any prior sales or transfers of the comparable sales for the year prior to the date of sale of the comparable sale.
Data source(s)
Report the results of the research and analysis of the prior sale or transfer history of the subject property and comparable sales (report additional prior sales on page 3).

ITEM	SUBJECT	COMPARABLE SALE # 1	COMPARABLE SALE # 2	COMPARABLE SALE # 3
Date of Prior Sale/Transfer				
Price of Prior Sale/Transfer				
Data Source(s)				
Effective Date of Data Source(s)				

Analysis of prior sale or transfer history of the subject property and comparable sales

Summary of Sales Comparison Approach

Indicated Value by Sales Comparison Approach $

Indicated Value by: Sales Comparison Approach $ _____ Cost Approach (if developed) $ _____ Income Approach (if developed) $ _____

This appraisal is made ☐ "as is", ☐ subject to completion per plans and specifications on the basis of a hypothetical condition that the improvements have been completed, ☐ subject to the following repairs or alterations on the basis of a hypothetical condition that the repairs or alterations have been completed, or ☐ subject to the following required inspection based on the extraordinary assumption that the condition or deficiency does not require alteration or repair:

Based on a complete visual inspection of the interior and exterior areas of the subject property, defined scope of work, statement of assumptions and limiting conditions, and appraiser's certification, my (our) opinion of the market value, as defined, of the real property that is the subject of this report is $ _____, as of _____, which is the date of inspection and the effective date of this appraisal.

Freddie Mac Form 70 March 2005   Page 2 of 6   Fannie Mae Form 1004 March 2005

FIGURE 13.3 (*Continued*)

Uniform Residential Appraisal Report   File

ADDITIONAL COMMENTS

COST APPROACH TO VALUE (not required by Fannie Mae)

Provide adequate information for the lender/client to replicate the below cost figures and calculations.
Support for the opinion of site value (summary of comparable land sales or other methods for estimating site value)

ESTIMATED ☐ REPRODUCTION OR ☐ REPLACEMENT COST NEW	OPINION OF SITE VALUE .... = $
Source of cost data	Dwelling Sq. Ft. @ $ .... = $
Quality rating from cost service Effective date of cost data	Sq. Ft. @ $ .... = $
Comments on Cost Approach (gross living area calculations, depreciation, etc.)	Garage/Carport Sq. Ft. @ $ .... = $
	Total Estimate of Cost-New .... = $
	Less Physical Functional External
	Depreciation =$( )
	Depreciated Cost of Improvements............................. = $
	"As-is" Value of Site Improvements............................. = $
Estimated Remaining Economic Life (HUD and VA only) Years	Indicated Value By Cost Approach .... = $

INCOME APPROACH TO VALUE (not required by Fannie Mae)

Estimated Monthly Market Rent $ X Gross Rent Multiplier   = $ Indicated Value by Income Approach
Summary of Income Approach (including support for market rent and GRM)

PROJECT INFORMATION FOR PUDs (if applicable)

Is the developer/builder in control of the Homeowners' Association (HOA)? ☐ Yes ☐ No   Unit type(s) ☐ Detached ☐ Attached
Provide the following information for PUDs ONLY if the developer/builder is in control of the HOA and the subject property is an attached dwelling unit.
Legal name of project
Total number of phases   Total number of units   Total number of units sold
Total number of units rented   Total number of units for sale   Data source(s)
Was the project created by the conversion of an existing building(s) into a PUD? ☐ Yes ☐ No   If Yes, date of conversion
Does the project contain any multi-dwelling units? ☐ Yes ☐ No   Data source(s)
Are the units, common elements, and recreation facilities complete? ☐ Yes ☐ No   If No, describe the status of completion.

Are the common elements leased to or by the Homeowners' Association? ☐ Yes ☐ No   If Yes, describe the rental terms and options.

Describe common elements and recreational facilities

Freddie Mac Form 70   March 2005   Page 3 of 6   Fannie Mae Form 1004   March 2005

FIGURE 13.3 (*Continued*)

Uniform Residential Appraisal Report

File #

This report form is designed to report an appraisal of a one-unit property or a one-unit property with an accessory unit; including a unit in a planned unit development (PUD). This report form is not designed to report an appraisal of a manufactured home or a unit in a condominium or cooperative project.

This appraisal report is subject to the following scope of work, intended use, intended user, definition of market value, statement of assumptions and limiting conditions, and certifications. Modifications, additions, or deletions to the intended use, intended user, definition of market value, or assumptions and limiting conditions are not permitted. The appraiser may expand the scope of work to include any additional research or analysis necessary based on the complexity of this appraisal assignment. Modifications or deletions to the certifications are also not permitted. However, additional certifications that do not constitute material alterations to this appraisal report, such as those required by law or those related to the appraiser's continuing education or membership in an appraisal organization, are permitted.

SCOPE OF WORK: The scope of work for this appraisal is defined by the complexity of this appraisal assignment and the reporting requirements of this appraisal report form, including the following definition of market value, statement of assumptions and limiting conditions, and certifications. The appraiser must, at a minimum: (1) perform a complete visual inspection of the interior and exterior areas of the subject property, (2) inspect the neighborhood, (3) inspect each of the comparable sales from at least the street, (4) research, verify, and analyze data from reliable public and/or private sources, and (5) report his or her analysis, opinions, and conclusions in this appraisal report.

INTENDED USE: The intended use of this appraisal report is for the lender/client to evaluate the property that is the subject of this appraisal for a mortgage finance transaction.

INTENDED USER: The intended user of this appraisal report is the lender/client.

DEFINITION OF MARKET VALUE: The most probable price which a property should bring in a competitive and open market under all conditions requisite to a fair sale, the buyer and seller, each acting prudently, knowledgeably and assuming the price is not affected by undue stimulus. Implicit in this definition is the consummation of a sale as of a specified date and the passing of title from seller to buyer under conditions whereby: (1) buyer and seller are typically motivated; (2) both parties are well informed or well advised, and each acting in what he or she considers his or her own best interest; (3) a reasonable time is allowed for exposure in the open market; (4) payment is made in terms of cash in U. S. dollars or in terms of financial arrangements comparable thereto; and (5) the price represents the normal consideration for the property sold unaffected by special or creative financing or sales concessions* granted by anyone associated with the sale.

*Adjustments to the comparables must be made for special or creative financing or sales concessions. No adjustments are necessary for those costs which are normally paid by sellers as a result of tradition or law in a market area; these costs are readily identifiable since the seller pays these costs in virtually all sales transactions. Special or creative financing adjustments can be made to the comparable property by comparisons to financing terms offered by a third party institutional lender that is not already involved in the property or transaction. Any adjustment should not be calculated on a mechanical dollar for dollar cost of the financing or concession but the dollar amount of any adjustment should approximate the market's reaction to the financing or concessions based on the appraiser's judgment.

STATEMENT OF ASSUMPTIONS AND LIMITING CONDITIONS: The appraiser's certification in this report is subject to the following assumptions and limiting conditions:

1. The appraiser will not be responsible for matters of a legal nature that affect either the property being appraised or the title to it, except for information that he or she became aware of during the research involved in performing this appraisal. The appraiser assumes that the title is good and marketable and will not render any opinions about the title.

2. The appraiser has provided a sketch in this appraisal report to show the approximate dimensions of the improvements. The sketch is included only to assist the reader in visualizing the property and understanding the appraiser's determination of its size.

3. The appraiser has examined the available flood maps that are provided by the Federal Emergency Management Agency (or other data sources) and has noted in this appraisal report whether any portion of the subject site is located in an identified Special Flood Hazard Area. Because the appraiser is not a surveyor, he or she makes no guarantees, express or implied, regarding this determination.

4. The appraiser will not give testimony or appear in court because he or she made an appraisal of the property in question, unless specific arrangements to do so have been made beforehand, or as otherwise required by law.

5. The appraiser has noted in this appraisal report any adverse conditions (such as needed repairs, deterioration, the presence of hazardous wastes, toxic substances, etc.) observed during the inspection of the subject property or that he or she became aware of during the research involved in performing this appraisal. Unless otherwise stated in this appraisal report, the appraiser has no knowledge of any hidden or unapparent physical deficiencies or adverse conditions of the property (such as, but not limited to, needed repairs, deterioration, the presence of hazardous wastes, toxic substances, adverse environmental conditions, etc.) that would make the property less valuable, and has assumed that there are no such conditions and makes no guarantees or warranties, express or implied. The appraiser will not be responsible for any such conditions that do exist or for any engineering or testing that might be required to discover whether such conditions exist. Because the appraiser is not an expert in the field of environmental hazards, this appraisal report must not be considered as an environmental assessment of the property.

6. The appraiser has based his or her appraisal report and valuation conclusion for an appraisal that is subject to satisfactory completion, repairs, or alterations on the assumption that the completion, repairs, or alterations of the subject property will be performed in a professional manner.

Freddie Mac Form 70   March 2005   Page 4 of 6   Fannie Mae Form 1004   March 2005

FIGURE 13.3 (*Continued*)

Uniform Residential Appraisal Report File #

APPRAISER'S CERTIFICATION: The Appraiser certifies and agrees that:

1. I have, at a minimum, developed and reported this appraisal in accordance with the scope of work requirements stated in this appraisal report.

2. I performed a complete visual inspection of the interior and exterior areas of the subject property. I reported the condition of the improvements in factual, specific terms. I identified and reported the physical deficiencies that could affect the livability, soundness, or structural integrity of the property.

3. I performed this appraisal in accordance with the requirements of the Uniform Standards of Professional Appraisal Practice that were adopted and promulgated by the Appraisal Standards Board of The Appraisal Foundation and that were in place at the time this appraisal report was prepared.

4. I developed my opinion of the market value of the real property that is the subject of this report based on the sales comparison approach to value. I have adequate comparable market data to develop a reliable sales comparison approach for this appraisal assignment. I further certify that I considered the cost and income approaches to value but did not develop them, unless otherwise indicated in this report.

5. I researched, verified, analyzed, and reported on any current agreement for sale for the subject property, any offering for sale of the subject property in the twelve months prior to the effective date of this appraisal, and the prior sales of the subject property for a minimum of three years prior to the effective date of this appraisal, unless otherwise indicated in this report.

6. I researched, verified, analyzed, and reported on the prior sales of the comparable sales for a minimum of one year prior to the date of sale of the comparable sale, unless otherwise indicated in this report.

7. I selected and used comparable sales that are locationally, physically, and functionally the most similar to the subject property.

8. I have not used comparable sales that were the result of combining a land sale with the contract purchase price of a home that has been built or will be built on the land.

9. I have reported adjustments to the comparable sales that reflect the market's reaction to the differences between the subject property and the comparable sales.

10. I verified, from a disinterested source, all information in this report that was provided by parties who have a financial interest in the sale or financing of the subject property.

11. I have knowledge and experience in appraising this type of property in this market area.

12. I am aware of, and have access to, the necessary and appropriate public and private data sources, such as multiple listing services, tax assessment records, public land records and other such data sources for the area in which the property is located.

13. I obtained the information, estimates, and opinions furnished by other parties and expressed in this appraisal report from reliable sources that I believe to be true and correct.

14. I have taken into consideration the factors that have an impact on value with respect to the subject neighborhood, subject property, and the proximity of the subject property to adverse influences in the development of my opinion of market value. I have noted in this appraisal report any adverse conditions (such as, but not limited to, needed repairs, deterioration, the presence of hazardous wastes, toxic substances, adverse environmental conditions, etc.) observed during the inspection of the subject property or that I became aware of during the research involved in performing this appraisal. I have considered these adverse conditions in my analysis of the property value, and have reported on the effect of the conditions on the value and marketability of the subject property.

15. I have not knowingly withheld any significant information from this appraisal report and, to the best of my knowledge, all statements and information in this appraisal report are true and correct.

16. I stated in this appraisal report my own personal, unbiased, and professional analysis, opinions, and conclusions, which are subject only to the assumptions and limiting conditions in this appraisal report.

17. I have no present or prospective interest in the property that is the subject of this report, and I have no present or prospective personal interest or bias with respect to the participants in the transaction. I did not base, either partially or completely, my analysis and/or opinion of market value in this appraisal report on the race, color, religion, sex, age, marital status, handicap, familial status, or national origin of either the prospective owners or occupants of the subject property or of the present owners or occupants of the properties in the vicinity of the subject property or on any other basis prohibited by law.

18. My employment and/or compensation for performing this appraisal or any future or anticipated appraisals was not conditioned on any agreement or understanding, written or otherwise, that I would report (or present analysis supporting) a predetermined specific value, a predetermined minimum value, a range or direction in value, a value that favors the cause of any party, or the attainment of a specific result or occurrence of a specific subsequent event (such as approval of a pending mortgage loan application).

19. I personally prepared all conclusions and opinions about the real estate that were set forth in this appraisal report. If I relied on significant real property appraisal assistance from any individual or individuals in the performance of this appraisal or the preparation of this appraisal report, I have named such individual(s) and disclosed the specific tasks performed in this appraisal report. I certify that any individual so named is qualified to perform the tasks. I have not authorized anyone to make a change to any item in this appraisal report; therefore, any change made to this appraisal is unauthorized and I will take no responsibility for it.

20. I identified the lender/client in this appraisal report who is the individual, organization, or agent for the organization that ordered and will receive this appraisal report.

Freddie Mac Form 70 March 2005   Fannie Mae Form 1004 March 2005

FIGURE 13.3 (*Continued*)

Uniform Residential Appraisal Report

File #

21. The lender/client may disclose or distribute this appraisal report to: the borrower; another lender at the request of the borrower; the mortgagee or its successors and assigns; mortgage insurers; government sponsored enterprises; other secondary market participants; data collection or reporting services; professional appraisal organizations; any department, agency, or instrumentality of the United States; and any state, the District of Columbia, or other jurisdictions; without having to obtain the appraiser's or supervisory appraiser's (if applicable) consent. Such consent must be obtained before this appraisal report may be disclosed or distributed to any other party (including, but not limited to, the public through advertising, public relations, news, sales, or other media).

22. I am aware that any disclosure or distribution of this appraisal report by me or the lender/client may be subject to certain laws and regulations. Further, I am also subject to the provisions of the Uniform Standards of Professional Appraisal Practice that pertain to disclosure or distribution by me.

23. The borrower, another lender at the request of the borrower, the mortgagee or its successors and assigns, mortgage insurers, government sponsored enterprises, and other secondary market participants may rely on this appraisal report as part of any mortgage finance transaction that involves any one or more of these parties.

24. If this appraisal report was transmitted as an "electronic record" containing my "electronic signature," as those terms are defined in applicable federal and/or state laws (excluding audio and video recordings), or a facsimile transmission of this appraisal report containing a copy or representation of my signature, the appraisal report shall be as effective, enforceable and valid as if a paper version of this appraisal report were delivered containing my original hand written signature.

25. Any intentional or negligent misrepresentation(s) contained in this appraisal report may result in civil liability and/or criminal penalties including, but not limited to, fine or imprisonment or both under the provisions of Title 18, United States Code, Section 1001, et seq., or similar state laws.

SUPERVISORY APPRAISER'S CERTIFICATION: The Supervisory Appraiser certifies and agrees that:

1. I directly supervised the appraiser for this appraisal assignment, have read the appraisal report, and agree with the appraiser's analysis, opinions, statements, conclusions, and the appraiser's certification.

2. I accept full responsibility for the contents of this appraisal report including, but not limited to, the appraiser's analysis, opinions, statements, conclusions, and the appraiser's certification.

3. The appraiser identified in this appraisal report is either a sub-contractor or an employee of the supervisory appraiser (or the appraisal firm), is qualified to perform this appraisal, and is acceptable to perform this appraisal under the applicable state law.

4. This appraisal report complies with the Uniform Standards of Professional Appraisal Practice that were adopted and promulgated by the Appraisal Standards Board of The Appraisal Foundation and that were in place at the time this appraisal report was prepared.

5. If this appraisal report was transmitted as an "electronic record" containing my "electronic signature," as those terms are defined in applicable federal and/or state laws (excluding audio and video recordings), or a facsimile transmission of this appraisal report containing a copy or representation of my signature, the appraisal report shall be as effective, enforceable and valid as if a paper version of this appraisal report were delivered containing my original hand written signature.

APPRAISER

Signature _____
Name _____
Company Name _____
Company Address _____

Telephone Number _____
Email Address _____
Date of Signature and Report _____
Effective Date of Appraisal _____
State Certification # _____
or State License # _____
or Other (describe) _____ State # _____
State _____
Expiration Date of Certification or License _____

ADDRESS OF PROPERTY APPRAISED
_____
_____

APPRAISED VALUE OF SUBJECT PROPERTY $ _____
LENDER/CLIENT
Name _____
Company Name _____
Company Address _____
_____
Email Address _____

SUPERVISORY APPRAISER (ONLY IF REQUIRED)

Signature _____
Name _____
Company Name _____
Company Address _____

Telephone Number _____
Email Address _____
Date of Signature _____
State Certification # _____
or State License # _____
State _____
Expiration Date of Certification or License _____

SUBJECT PROPERTY

☐ Did not inspect subject property
☐ Did inspect exterior of subject property from street
  Date of Inspection _____
☐ Did inspect interior and exterior of subject property
  Date of Inspection _____

COMPARABLE SALES

☐ Did not inspect exterior of comparable sales from street
☐ Did inspect exterior of comparable sales from street
  Date of Inspection _____

Freddie Mac Form 70   March 2005   Fannie Mae Form 1004   March 2005

FIGURE 13.3 (*Continued*)

Location, size, and age: These criteria can skew an appraisal if there are large differences. Location should be as close to the subject property as possible, preferably in the same subdivision and ideally on the same street. If no comparable exists in the subdivision or in the immediate vicinity of the subject, it is permissible to go to the closest subdivisions that are similar in price, style, amenity, and so on. It is preferable to compare county property to county property and city property to city property. Other factors that can be used to determine similar locations are school districts; proximity to shopping, churches, and other amenities; commuting distances to major employment areas; and so on.

Large size differences can be especially problematic: The smaller the size difference, the more accurate the results. The difference should be kept under 5% either way if possible. If size differences are small and there are no additional electrical, heating, and plumbing requirements necessary, the cost per square foot for the difference will probably be less than the total cost per square foot to build the entire structure.

For example, if two nearly identical houses have a 50-square-foot difference and the smaller house sells for $100 per square foot, the extra 50 square feet in the larger house may be worth only $50 per square foot. The amount per square foot differs for location, age, quality, and presence or absence of amenities.

Age: Age difference, if significant, can affect the accuracy of an appraisal; therefore, it is best to compare properties of approximately the same age. Effective age, not actual age, is the standard used for determining value; however, chronological age is the proper one to enter on listings, MLS data, and so on. Both chronological age and effective age are noted on the appraisal. A 5-year-old home should not usually be compared with a 50-year-old home unless the 50-year-old home has been modernized to have a much younger effective age.

Lot/land value: Lots in different subdivisions can differ in price. Additional acreage, such as pastureland, may be of considerable value. Small differences in lot size in the same neighborhood usually require no adjustment.

Design: When possible, two-story homes should be compared to two-story homes, ranch homes to ranch homes, farmhouses to farmhouses, and contemporary homes to contemporary homes.

Type and quality of construction: Differences in types of construction vary from area to area. When possible, comparisons should be made between homes of like construction. A basic "spec" house built to minimum code is probably not worth as much as a custom-built house with hardwood floors, ceramic tile, an architectural roof, and upgraded appliances.

Similarity of physical characteristics and amenities: If one home has a pool, a hot tub, a large wired workshop, 10-foot ceilings, and a four-car garage, it may not be a good comparable for a similarly sized and aged home in the same neighborhood with a two-car garage, 8-foot ceilings, and none of the other amenities. The relatively recent increase in the demand for more and better car storage makes the number of garages, especially on higher-priced homes, an important amenity to consider. While an adjustment can easily be made for the difference between a one- and two-car garage, a home with a carport is not a good comparable for a house with a four-car garage.

Date of sale: In an appreciating market, the comparable's sold price must be adjusted upward because its value would have increased from the time of the sale until the present. In a depreciating market, the comparable's price would need to be adjusted downward (see Figure 13.4).

Seller concessions: If a seller sells his property and pays $4,000 of the buyer's closing costs, the seller is actually receiving $4,000 less for his home, and the price must be adjusted accordingly. In the past, appraisers were required to adjust for seller concessions, but they are no longer required to do so unless the concessions are excessive. In markets in which seller concessions are the norm, they should be considered in the CMA and the listing process.

Seller motivation: A distress sale may take place when a seller sells her home for significantly less than market value because she was facing foreclosure, bankruptcy, or divorce. This sale should not be used in a CMA/appraisal. If she sells for a reduced price to a relative or friend in a transaction that is not an arm's-length transaction, that sale should not be used either.

Method of financing used by purchaser: The price may be affected positively or negatively by the type of financing. Properties sold with owner financing or as a loan assumption with a rate considerably below current market rates are sometimes sold at a premium price. Differences in financing between Department of Veterans Affairs (VA), Federal Housing Administration (FHA), and conventional loans are not as important now as in the past because government loans no longer require sellers to pay points and similar but not identical seller concessions are allowed on all types of loan.

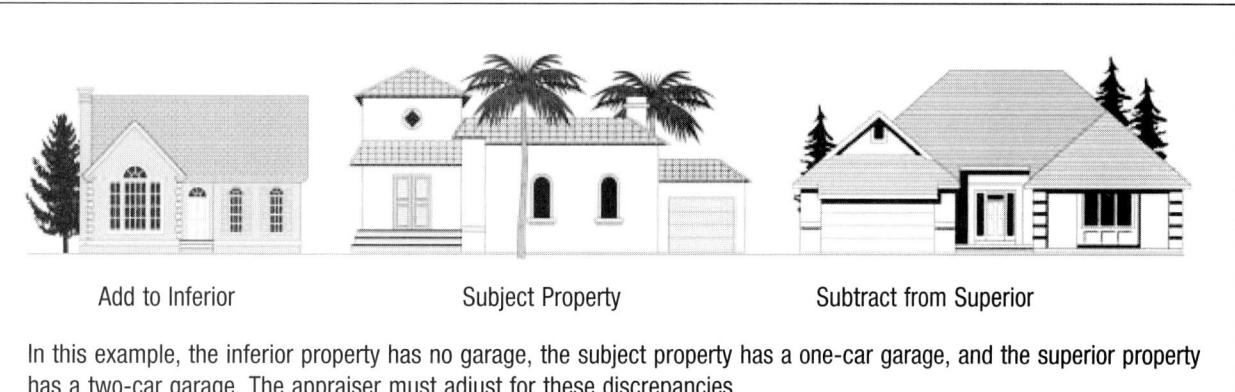

In this example, the inferior property has no garage, the subject property has a one-car garage, and the superior property has a two-car garage. The appraiser must adjust for these discrepancies.

FIGURE 13.4 When adjusting comparables to the subject property, an appraiser must add to inferior properties and subtract from superior comparables to arrive at an adjusted comparison.

Source: © 2019 OnCourse Learning

5. **Enter data on comps.** On the CMA worksheet, enter data in the blanks one at a time for the three to six most comparable properties to subject.
6. **Make adjustments to comparable sales prices.**

To understand the process of the direct sales comparison approach, refer to Figure 13.2. An important point to understand before using the chart is that the data values are the result of careful analysis of records maintained by the broker or appraiser. For example, a value of $3,500 for the difference between a two-car garage and a one-car carport is not an arbitrary number pulled from the air; rather, it is the result of carefully paired sales analysis data kept in the broker's files. The paired sales analysis is the process of comparing similar comparables in such a manner as to determine how much the particular feature adds, or subtracts, from the value of the home. This is the basis for making the adjustments to the comparables. For example, suppose Sale A sold for $260,000 with a two-car garage; Sale B sold for $259,000 and also has a two-car garage; and Sale C sold for $265,000 and has a three-car garage. This information assumes that if all information is current and there are no other differences between the properties, a three-car garage has a premium of between $5,000–$6,000. Nor is the number for the cost of building an element because, as explained earlier in the chapter, cost is not the same as value. To arrive at the proper value of an element, an agent must constantly abstract or reflect from the marketplace what the average buyer will pay for the element.

All of the data used in making the adjustments between the comparable properties and the subject property must be laid out in an orderly, detailed, and accurate manner, as illustrated in Figure 13.2. The comparison sets forth all of the property and nonproperty characteristics (such as location, physical characteristics, land or lot size, amenities, and condition) used in the value estimate.

Plus and minus adjustments are made to reconcile the differences and to arrive at a value estimate for the subject property on the basis of the price for which each comparable was sold. You always adjust the comparable, never the subject property (see Figure 13.4). Because you are trying to estimate the value of the subject property, it does not yet have a value to be adjusted.

First, an adjustment for the time of sale is made using an annual appreciation rate of 2.5%, also derived from paired sales analysis data for the area. The sales price of the comparable is multiplied by the appreciation rate and divided by 12 to get a monthly appreciation, which is then multiplied by the number of months since the sale of that comparable.

Study the following example:

Sales price × 2.5% = Annual appreciation ÷ 12 = Monthly appreciation × Number of months = Appreciation adjustment

Comparable 1: $192,000 × 2.5% = $4,800/12 = $400 × 1 = $400

Comparable 2: $185,500 × 2.5% = $4,637.50/12 = $386.46 × 2 = $772.92 rounded to $800

Comparable 3: $182,500 × 2.5% = $4,562.50/12 = $380.21 × 6 = $2,281.26 rounded to $2,300

A plus adjustment to a comparable is made when the comparable is deficient in a particular respect when compared with the subject property. This is illustrated in Figure 13.2. The lot size adjustment of +$500 in Comparable 1 is made because of the smaller lot size of Comparable 1 in comparison to the lot size of the subject property. The adjustment indicates that Comparable 1 would have sold for $500 more had its lot size been as large as the subject property.

A minus adjustment to a comparable is made when it contains a specific feature that the subject property does not contain. For example, an adjustment of −$1,000 is made to Comparable 1 because it has three bathrooms instead of two and a half, as does the subject property. Therefore, if Comparable 1 had the same number of bathrooms as the subject property, it would have sold for $1,000 less than it did.

Paired sales analysis data reveal that a gravel driveway is considered inferior to a paved driveway in the amount of $1,000. The subject has a paved driveway, as does Comparable 1; therefore, no adjustment is made to Comparable 1. Comparables 2 and 3 have gravel driveways that are inferior. If these comparable driveways were paved, the homes would have sold for $1,000 more than their actual sales price. Comparables 2 and 3 are inferior; therefore, $1,000 is added to their sales prices.

Reconciliation

After all adjustments, the net adjustment amount for each comparable is calculated and the result is applied to the price for which the comparable sold to arrive at an adjusted price. The adjusted price is an estimate of the price for which the comparable would have sold if all factors had been the same as the subject property. The adjusted prices of the comparables are reconciled to arrive at an indicated market value for the subject property. This *reconciliation* is a weighted average of the adjusted sales price of the comparable to determine a single reliable estimate of value for the property being appraised (the subject property). In Figure 13.2, Comparable 2 is given the greatest weight (40%) because it requires the fewest adjustments and although this cannot be determined from the illustration, it is located in the same subdivision as the subject property. Comparable 1 has slightly less similarity to the subject property than Comparable 2 and is only given a weight of 35%. Comparable 3 is given the least weight (25%) because it is located in a different subdivision and is least similar to the subject property. Note that the assigned percentage must equal 100% no matter how many comparables are used.

The Cost Approach

The **cost approach** is the primary method for estimating value when there are not sufficient comparables and when it does not involve an income-producing property. It is mainly a method used when attempting to value a specialty type building, such as churches, schools, factories, hospitals, and various public use properties. The cost approach is based on the theory that no one will pay more for a property than they will spend to build it for themselves (see the section "Basic Economic Principles of Value") and, as such, generally this approach sets the upper limits of value.

The procedure for estimating value by the cost approach is as follows:

1. Estimate construction costs to replace or reproduce the improvements.
2. Estimate total accrued depreciation of improvements.
3. Subtract depreciation of improvements from construction costs to determine the value of improvements.
4. Estimate the value of land using direct sales comparison approach.
5. Add the lot value to the value of the improvements to get the appraised value.
6. Find the total, which represents the appraised value provided by the cost approach.

Estimating Replacement/Reproduction Cost

The first step in the cost approach is to estimate the cost to rebuild the improvements by using either the reproduction or replacement cost method. The **reproduction cost** is that *cost to rebuild an exact duplicate of the property when new.* The difficulty of this method is that for older properties many of the materials, building techniques, and skills simply are not available. As such, this method will generally be much higher than that of the replacement cost and quite often it is not practical to use in estimating the cost to build. The **replacement cost** is that *cost to rebuild using today's modern building materials and construction techniques.* It is clearly the more practical of the two methods and is the more commonly used by the real estate practitioner. As a quick comparison of these two methods, an appraiser is analyzing the cost to build an older home that has real plaster walls and ceilings. The cost to rebuild using real plaster walls and ceilings is likely quite prohibitive simply because there aren't many houses constructed by this method because the building techniques are so costly and plaster craftsmen are hard to find. By comparison, the replacement cost method would estimate the cost to rebuild using drywall, which does not require costly building techniques and uses relatively easy to find drywall installers.

Once the decision has been reached as to whether to utilize the reproduction, or replacement, cost method, the appraisers will use one of the three primary methods to determine the cost to build. Any of these three can be used with either the reproduction or replacement cost theory. The three primary methods of estimating the cost to build are the quantity survey method, unit-in-place method, and square-foot method.

- **Quantity survey method.** This method is generally considered the most accurate but most complex and time-consuming method of the three. The quantity survey method is likely too involved for the typical real estate agent and is rarely used by appraisers. This method is most often utilized by construction estimators where they literally *break down the task into an in-depth materials cost and then add in the costs of labor, permits, overhead, taxes, and profit.*
- **Unit-in-place method.** The unit-in-place method *breaks the costs into an estimate for various units.* Similar to the quantity survey method discussed previously, the unit-in-place method is likely too involved for the typical real estate agent and is rarely used by appraisers.
- **Square-foot method.** This is the simplest and most popular, but least accurate of the three methods. Even though it may be the least accurate of the three, it is likely still accurate enough for what is needed to reasonably estimate the cost to build. In this method, you would simply *determine what similar properties are costing per square foot to construct and then multiply this cost by the number of square feet within the improvements.*

Estimating Depreciation

The next step in the cost approach is to subtract the depreciation from the cost to build. Unlike the concept of depreciation being a "paper loss," as demonstrated in Chapter 17, consider **depreciation** as *an actual loss of value from any cause.* Depreciation methods break down costs into three subgroups, just as the previously described cost to build methods do. The three methods are the age/life (straight-line) method, market abstraction method, and breakdown method.

Age/Life (Straight-Line) Method. In many ways, the age/life method has some things in common with the square-foot method of estimating the cost to build. Both are simple to use but are considered to give the least accurate results. The age/life method establishes the life expectancy of the improvements and then compares the age of the properties to determine depreciation. In this method, the appraiser will first make a determination of a property's physical as well as economic or useful life expectancy. Physical life is the period of time the property may exist although not necessarily profitably. Economic life is simply that period of time in which the property is estimated to be used economically. The physical life will always be longer than the economic life, similar to how long a person may live versus the period in which they may be economically employable. Certainly, it is common for buildings to undergo renovations that will greatly extend their economic or useful life expectancy. It is quite common that buildings will be utilized for far longer than their original estimated economic life. Most lenders will base their loan term on a property's estimated economic life by not loaning more than two-thirds to three-quarters of the remaining economic life. Hence, a property with a 30-year loan likely will have at least 40–45 years of economic life remaining at the time of the loan being made.

Note that where life may mean life, age does not necessarily mean age. It is essential to know the difference between chronological age and effective age. **Chronological age** is the *actual age of the property*. The problem with using chronological age is that the property may, or may not, have been properly maintained to the extent that it is possible that the house may be the equivalent of a house much younger than its actual age or perhaps much older than its actual age. Therefore, it is more useful to utilize the effective age of a property. The **effective age** is *the age that the property appears to be based on its condition*. Hence, if a property was carefully maintained, it would be of an age less than its actual age. Conversely, if a property had not been properly maintained and had extensive wear and tear, it might be considered to be of an age much older than its actual age. For these reasons, the appraiser will be more interested in the effective age of a property.

For example, a building has an estimated cost to build of $160,000 and has an economic, or useful, life of 40 years. The appraiser estimates that the building has an effective age of only 8 years even though the building is actually several years older. Based on the $160,000 cost to build divided by the 40-year economic life, the appraiser would estimate the building is depreciating at a rate of $4,000 per year ($160,000 ÷ 40 = $4,000). Because the building is estimated to have an 8-year effective age, you would multiply the $4,000 depreciation per year times 8 years to come up with $32,000 total depreciation. Therefore, $160,000 − $32,000 = $128,000 depreciated value under the age/life method.

> "Depreciation as it is used here is an appraiser's opinion as to the approximate decrease in value the structure has suffered. This is completely different from the IRS calculation of depreciation for tax purposes on investment property, which is a mathematical tax formula."
> —Bill Gallagher, DREI

Market Abstraction Method. The market abstraction method is a more objective and analytical method of determining depreciation than is the age/life (straight-line) method. The market abstraction method assumes that replacement costs of comparable properties minus their sales prices approximate the cumulative depreciation. It applies the cost approach to comparable sales in an area by estimating the cost of improvements and adding that estimate to the values for the site and site improvements to arrive at the replacement cost of the comparable, as if it were newly built at the time of the estimate. To use this method, subtract the sales price of the comparable from the previous estimate to determine the cumulative depreciation. Divide the cumulative depreciation by the age in years of the comparable to find the annual depreciation rate. If this procedure is applied to several properties in the same neighborhood with similar results, it likely reflects the actual depreciation rate.

Breakdown Method. This method breaks down depreciation into three basic causes (see Figure 13.5): (1) **physical deterioration,** (2) **functional obsolescence,** and (3) **economic obsolescence.** The first two, physical deterioration and functional obsolescence, result from factors ONLY within the property itself. The third method, economic obsolescence, is from factors ONLY outside the property itself. Note that physical deterioration results from the degradation of the physical features of the property, whereas the other two result from obsolescence, or the making of something obsolete or out of date. Certainly, factors can be obsolete but yet in very good, if not new, condition. Some building designs actually build in an element of obsolescence, such as restaurants that are built to reflect a much older style of building and materials.

> Curable versus incurable does not relate to whether an item can be corrected (cured) but rather to the economic feasibility of such correction.

Let us now discuss the concept of curable and incurable. Not to be confused with whether an item can be "cured" or fixed, the concept of curable/incurable simply relates to the economic feasibility of fixing the problem. An item that is **curable** *is economically worthwhile to repair*. The cost to repair, and perhaps more, can be recouped from the increase in value. For example, if a house costs $2,500 to paint and results in an increase in value of at least $2,500 or more, the issue of whether to paint would be considered curable. **Incurable** items are those for which *the cost to fix will not be recouped from an increase in value*. The resulting increase in value, if any, would be less than the cost incurred to fix. Indeed, it is not uncommon that it is economically better to leave the problem than it would be to fix, simply because the loss in value is less than the loss incurred in fixing the problem. A common example might be where a three-bedroom house has

---

Physical Deterioration

Curable	Incurable*
Roof leak	Severe foundation problems
Outdated paint	Deteriorated floor joists

Functional Obsolescence

Curable	Incurable*
Outdated appliances	No interior plumbing
Exposed wiring	7-foot-high ceilings

Economic Obsolescence

Curable**	Incurable
	Four-lane highway in place of two-lane country road
	Zoning change from residential to commercial

*These are listed as incurable based on the cost to correct the problem. All items listed can be cured, but the cost of repair may exceed the value of the home.

**Generally, economic obsolescence is seen as incurable only. Typically, it is beyond the homeowner's control to correct the problem.

FIGURE 13.5 Three causes of depreciation.
Source: © 2019 OnCourse Learning

only one bath, which likely impairs its value. The cost to build a second bathroom would likely be much higher than the value of the house would be increased. As a result, the one-bath example would be considered incurable.

Physical Deterioration. As the name implies, this is simply a situation in which *the property has deteriorated in some physical manner.*

Common obvious examples would be for items that need repairing, such as a house that needs painting, rusted out gutters, a loose handrail, or any deferred maintenance. But many examples of physical deterioration are not as obvious such as wear and tear from routine use where the item does not need immediate attention but the shortened life expectancy until the item must be replaced must be considered (i.e., a 10-year-old roof that might only be expected to last 25 years). Some degree of loss of value must be factored in. Physical deterioration items can be considered either curable or incurable.

Functional Obsolescence. *This occurs quite literally when the property is obsolete. The building features and design are not up to modern standards.*

Examples might be design-related; for example, a house has four bedrooms and only one bath, or even a poorly designed floor plan or low ceiling height. Other examples might be related to the features within the house such as a lack of central heating and air conditioning, and inadequate electrical, plumbing, insulation, windows, and so on. Not all issues of functional obsolescence are related to inadequacy. Other examples might include situations in which rooms are literally too large for the scale of the house or spaces that are special use to the current owner but would have very limited appeal in the marketplace. Functional obsolescence can be either curable or incurable. Again, the issue is whether it is economically feasible to correct the problem or not.

> "Functional obsolescence is a type of decrease in value due to factors within the property. Economic obsolescence is always caused by outside factors in the neighborhood or area where the property is located."
> —Len Elder, DREI

Economic Obsolescence. Economic obsolescence is always related to factors outside the property itself. Whereas both physical deterioration and functional obsolescence are always related to issues involving the property itself, *economic obsolescence is strictly related to the surrounding areas and its influence on the desirability of the property being valued.* Common examples include the impact of roadways, airports, railroads, farming, and other commercial uses nearby and the resulting noise, lighting, odors, and traffic that will ensue. Other examples would include changes in zoning, growth patterns, and other economic factors adversely affecting the property. Determining economic obsolescence is different from the other two methods not only in that it is based on factors outside the property itself but also that it is always incurable, as the cost to correct the issue will always exceed the increase in property value.

Estimating Land Value. The next step in the cost approach is to estimate the value of the land as though it were vacant and at its highest and best use. The land value is always estimated by utilizing the direct sales comparison (market data approach) and involves the comparison of comparable parcels of land. In cases of residential houses within an established neighborhood where there are no recent comparable sales of lots to be utilized, appraisers will often take the median sales price of houses within the subdivision and use approximately 20% of that value for the land value.

Estimate of Value. The estimate of land value is added to the depreciated cost estimate to derive the estimate of value for the property. The various steps and calculations employed in the cost approach are illustrated by the example of the cost approach calculations in Figure 13.6.

The Income Approach

The **income approach**, or **income capitalization approach**, is *the primary method used to estimate the present value of properties that produce rental income.* **Capitalization** is *the process of converting net operating income into an indication of value.* Properties included in this category are apartment complexes, single-family rental houses, office buildings, shopping malls, parking garages, leased industrial plants, and individual properties occupied by commercial tenants. In many ways, the appraiser is appraising the value of the property for its investment potential as much as anything.

The value of the property is estimated by capitalizing **net operating income (NOI)** into an indication of present value by the application of a capitalization,

Replacement or reproduction cost:		
21,000 sq. ft. @ $52.50 per sq. ft.		$1,102,500
Less structure depreciation:		
Physical deterioration	$33,075	
Functional obsolescence	44,100	
Economic obsolescence	-0-	− 77,175
Depreciated value of structure		$1,025,325
Depreciated value of other improvements:		
Retaining walls	$10,000	
Paved drive and parking	15,000	
Exterior lighting	2,000	
Fencing	1,500	28,500
Depreciated value of all improvements		$1,053,825
Land value by direct sales comparison		253,000
Total property value		$1,306,825

FIGURE 13.6 Cost approach calculations.
Source: © 2019 OnCourse Learning

or cap rate. This procedure is illustrated in Figure 13.7. It shows an operating statement and the capitalization of the net annual income into an indication of value by applying the capitalization formula following the statement. A complete explanation of the income approach is presented by the analysis of the operating statement and the example of the application of the formula.

Analysis of Operating Statement

Income. An apartment complex has a **potential gross income** of $1,350,000. This is *the income that would be produced if every apartment were rented 100% of the time at $450/month for 12 months.* It is not realistic to expect any rental property to be occupied 100% of the time on a continuing basis. Therefore, the potential gross income must be reduced by an allowance for vacancies that will inevitably occur and losses due to some tenants' failing to pay their rent or paying with checks that are not collectible. Note that a vacancy allowance does not necessarily mean the property is vacant, only that the scheduled income is not received. In the example, it is anticipated that vacancy and credit losses will amount to 6% of gross potential income, or $81,000 per year.

250-unit apartment complex with rent schedule of $450 per month per unit

Potential gross income: 250 × $450 × 12		$1,350,000
Less vacancy and credit losses (6%)		− 81,000
Plus other income		+ 25,000
Gross effective income		$1,294,000
Less expenses		
Fixed expenses:		
Property insurance	$ 24,500	
Property taxes	95,300	
Licenses and permits	1,200	$ 121,000
Operating expenses:		
Maintenance	$106,000	
Utilities	103,200	
Supplies	16,000	
Advertising	7,500	
Legal and accounting	15,000	
Wages and salaries	90,000	
Property management	64,700	402,400
Replacement reserve	$ 25,000	25,000
Total expenses		$ (548,400)
Net operating income		$ 745,600

FIGURE 13.7 Operating statement.
Source: © 2019 OnCourse Learning

This apartment complex has other income generated by vending machines and laundry facilities used by the tenants. This income is projected to be $25,000 per year. With the addition of other income, the **gross effective income** equals *potential gross income minus vacancy and credit losses plus other income.* This gross effective income is the amount of money the apartment complex can realistically expect to generate in a 12-month period.

Expenses. To arrive at net income, which is the basis for calculating the value estimate in the income approach, various expenses must be subtracted from gross income. These expenses include fixed expenses, operating expenses, and the expense of replacement reserve.

Fixed Expenses. These expenses do not fluctuate with the operating level of the complex. The fixed expenses remain essentially the same whether the occupancy rate is 95% or 75%. Here is an example of calculating fixed expenses: There is an expense of $24,500 in the form of an annual premium for a hazard insurance policy to protect against financial loss caused by fire or other casualty. Real property taxes are one of the largest expense items and amount to $95,300. The $1,200 cost for licenses and permits represents fees paid to local governments as required for the operation of vending machines and other income-producing facilities. The fixed expenses total $121,000 and are 9.35% of gross effective income.

Operating Expenses. Operating expenses, or *the costs of operating a property held as an investment,* generally fluctuate with the operating level or occupancy level of the property. As in the case of the apartment complex, maintenance is a major operating expense, amounting to $106,000. This operating expense varies with the level of operation and is related, to a large degree, to the age and condition of the property when purchased. Older properties naturally require a higher level of expenditures for maintenance than newer properties. The maintenance covers not only the cost of repair and maintenance to the structures but also the maintenance of grounds and parking areas. The cost of utilities for the common areas and the cost of wages and salaries paid to employees follow maintenance costs as the next two largest expenses. Operating expenses do not include debt service, depreciation, or the cost of capital improvements.

Here is an example of operating expenses: The property manager's fee of $64,700 is a percentage of the gross effective income. The property management fee in this example is 5% of gross effective income. The small expense items of legal and accounting fees, advertising, and supplies round out the operating expenses, which total $402,400, or 31.09% of gross effective income. Operating expenses represent the largest group in the three types of expense.

> **Test Tip!**
>
> Operating expenses include all expenses except three: principal and interest, depreciation, and capital improvements. To obtain NOI, you should subtract only the operating expenses from income that is actually collected.

Replacement Reserve. This expense item of $25,000 represents a **replacement reserve**, which is *an amount of money that is set aside each year to replace short-lived equipment,* such as hot water heaters, ranges and ovens, dishwashers, and disposals. Setting aside an amount of money for this purpose each year enables the project to avoid the impact of a substantial expenditure in any given year when a number of short-lived items must be replaced.

Total Expenses and Net Income. The total of the three types of expenses (fixed expenses, operating expenses, and the expense of replacement reserve) in Figure 13.7 amounts to $548,400, which represents 42.38% of gross effective income. **Debt service** *(mortgage principal and interest payments)* is not included in the list of operating expenses for appraisal purposes. For this purpose, debt service is considered a personal obligation of the property owner. In this way, the appraisal process puts all comparable properties on the same basis by eliminating an item that varies substantially from one property to another. Outside the appraisal process, debt service would be deducted from gross effective income to arrive at cash flow. **Cash flow** is *the amount of money the owner actually receives in a given year prior to the subtraction of the income tax liability for the property.* When calculating net taxable income before depreciation, the payment of mortgage interest but not principal is deductible.

NOI. NOI is derived by subtracting total expenses from effective gross income. The NOI of $745,600 represents a return of 12% on an investment of $6,213,333, as illustrated by the application of the capitalization formula in Figure 13.8.

The final step in estimating property value by the income approach is the application of the **capitalization formula**. This involves the simple process of *dividing NOI by a capitalization rate.* The difficulty lies in arriving at the proper capitalization (cap) rate. A number of rather complex methods for establishing this rate are beyond the scope of this text and are not covered in prelicensing real estate examinations. In essence, however, the appropriate rate is that rate of return investors in comparable properties are achieving on investments in the same locality at the time of the appraisal. The rate of return on any investment includes a consideration of the risk factor. The greater the risk of loss

$$I = R \times V \qquad \text{Income} = \text{Rate} \times \text{Value} \qquad \text{Value} = \frac{\text{Income}}{\text{Rate}}$$

Given: Income = $745,600
Rate = 12%

Value: $\dfrac{\$745{,}600}{12\%}$ = Value = $6,213,333

FIGURE 13.8 Capitalization formula.
Source: © 2019 OnCourse Learning

taken by the investor, the higher potential rate of return the investor is entitled to expect.

In the application of the capitalization formula to the apartment complex, a rate of 12% was adopted as the appropriate rate for this investment in this area at this time. By dividing the NOI of $745,600 by 0.12, a value estimate of $6,213,333 (typically rounded to $6,213,000) is indicated. In other words, if an investor paid this price for the apartment complex and continued to realize a NOI of $745,600, the investor would realize a return of 12% before deductions for debt service and income tax. The investor's federal income tax may be reduced as a result of the deduction for depreciation, interest on debt services, property tax, and other expenses.

The importance of the selection of a proper capitalization rate cannot be overemphasized. Even a slight variation in this rate results in a substantial change in the value estimate. For example, if a 13% rate had been used in the foregoing example, the value estimate would be $5,735,385, which represents a reduction of indicated value of $477,949, or 7.69% of the original estimate. The higher the capitalization rate, the lower the value estimate; and, conversely, the lower the rate, the higher the resulting value estimate. Other examples of the application of the capitalization formula are found in Appendix B, Real Estate Math.

Gross Rent Multiplier

Gross rent multipliers are a type of income approach to estimating value that may be used to estimate the value of property producing rental income. There is a degree of unreliability in the use of this method because calculations are based on gross income rather than net income. If the property has been managed efficiently, the gross income will provide a reliable basis for calculating an estimate of value. If expenses are out of line, however, gross income will not fairly reflect property value.

Gross rent multipliers are calculated by dividing the monthly or annual gross income of a property into the price for which it was sold. It does not matter whether gross annual or gross monthly income is used as long as one or the other is used consistently. The accompanying illustration (see Figure 13.9) provides examples of calculating gross income multipliers on a monthly and an annual basis. As you can see, a much lower multiplier results from the calculations based on annual income.

In estimating the value of an income property, gross rental incomes can be established for comparable income properties that have been sold recently. An average of the gross rent multipliers can be used as a multiplier for the gross monthly or annual income produced by a property under consideration to provide an indication of property value. For example, if the property being considered produced a gross monthly income of $99,000, this would be multiplied by the average gross rent multiplier of 58, as shown in Figure 13.10. This multiplication ($99,000 × 58) provides a value indication of $5,742,000. This indicated value is as reliable as the gross monthly incomes and prices used in calculating the average gross rent multiplier.

RECONCILIATION AND APPRAISAL REPORT

When making an appraisal, a professional appraiser uses the most relevant approach to the value estimate as the primary appraisal method. Which method is most relevant depends on the type of property that is the subject of appraisal. For example, in estimating the value of a single-family owner-occupied dwelling,

COMPARABLE	PRICE	MONTHLY GROSS	GRM	ANNUAL GROSS	GRM
No. 1	$621,300	$5,350	116	$64,200	9.7
No. 2	$586,500	$4,890	120	$58,680	10.0
No. 3	$512,500	$4,135	124	$49,620	10.3
No. 4	$606,000	$5,135	118	$61,620	9.8
No. 5	$725,000	$5,945	122	$71,340	10.2
No. 6	$658,800	$5,490	120	$65,880	10.0
Average GRM					10.0

FIGURE 13.9 Calculating gross rent multipliers (GRMs).
Source: © 2019 OnCourse Learning

A. $\dfrac{\text{Comparable's sales price}}{\text{Rent}} = \text{GRM}$

B. Subject's rent × GRM = Estimate of subject's value

FIGURE 13.10 Application of gross rent multiplier (GRM).
Source: © 2019 OnCourse Learning

the most relevant method is the direct sales comparison, or market data approach. The qualified appraiser also estimates the value of the property by each of the other two methods. In the case of the single-family dwelling, the appraiser treats the property as though it were rental property and estimates the value using the income approach. Finally, the appraiser arrives at a value estimate by the cost approach.

As a practical matter, the results obtained by these three methods are not identical. There must be a reconciliation of the three approaches. In the reconciliation process, three factors are taken into consideration: the relevancy of each method to the subject property, the reliability of the data on which each estimate is based, and the strong and weak points of each method. After these considerations, the greatest weight should be given to the estimate resulting from the most appropriate or relevant method for the type of property that is the subject of the appraisal. For example, if the property is an office building, the most relevant approach and the one to receive the greatest weight would be the income approach. Even though the results obtained by the different approaches are not exactly the same, they should be reasonably close. Therefore, each approach provides a check on the other two. If the result by one method is considerably out of line with the others, this indicates some calculation error or some error in the data used as a basis.

The final step in the appraisal process is the preparation of the appraisal report. A sample URAR is shown in Figure 13.3. The report contains the appraiser's opinion of value based on the observation of the results obtained by the three methods and the appraiser's reasons for adopting the final estimate of value. The appraisal report may be either a narrative or a form. The narrative report provides all the factual data about the property and the elements of judgment used by the appraiser in arriving at the estimate of value. When a standard form is used to report the various property data and the appraisal method employed, it is called a form report. A form report does not contain narrative information, as the narrative report does, but rather it simply sets forth various facts and figures used in the appraisal process and the reconciliation of the final estimate of market value.

BROKER PRICE OPINION/COMPARATIVE MARKET ANALYSIS

NOTE: The following discussion will address the BPO/CMA by simply referring to it as a CMA.

The ability of a real estate broker to complete a CMA was addressed in the North Carolina Appraisers Act (G.S. Chapter 93A) effective in 1991. The Appraisers Act defined both an appraisal as well as a CMA. Whereas the appraisal was an *"analysis, opinion, or conclusion as to the value . . . for compensation"* the CMA was defined as *"the analysis of sales of similar recently sold properties in order to derive an indication of the probable sales price of a particular property by a licensed real estate broker."* The Appraisers Act specifically exempted a CMA from requiring an appraisal license only when it was performed by a real estate broker on behalf of an *actual or prospective* brokerage client or when it involved an employee relocation program. This law did not restrict the type of license the broker could possess (i.e., provisional or nonprovisional), and it required the CMA to be performed by using the methodology of the sales comparison method. In reality, many brokers performed CMAs without regard for the limitations imposed by this law such as stating the final conclusion as the "market value" or "worth" of the property. Although many brokers are of the opinion that recent law changes have made such labeling to be illegal, the fact is that it was never permitted since the introduction of the Appraisers Act in 1991.

Because of the economic downturn in recent years, many lenders utilized the services of broker licensees to complete CMAs for the purpose of determining whether to pursue foreclosure or short sale situations. The problem was the brokers were not allowed to complete these assignments for compensation as they were not for an actual or prospective brokerage client and there was no commission to be paid or earned from such efforts. North Carolina adopted several changes to the Appraisers Act effective October 1, 2012, thus requiring the North Carolina Real Estate Commission to adopt a number of rule changes to allow brokers to complete CMAs for a fee without regard to whether it is for an actual or prospective brokerage client under certain conditions.

Key Elements of the Appraisers Act Revision

- CMA and BPO are considered identical.
- A CMA may be performed for a fee and for someone that is not an actual or prospective brokerage client only when it is being completed by a nonprovisional broker. A provisional broker is not considered to possess sufficient experience and has not likely been given enough instruction to allow them to complete CMAs for anyone who is not an actual or prospective brokerage client.
- A broker may NOT prepare a CMA for any existing or potential lienholder where the purpose is for originating any mortgage loan including an equity line of credit.
- Any CMA that estimates the "value" or "worth" of a property is considered to be an appraisal and will be considered as a violation of the Appraisal Act and License Law. Brokers may estimate only the "probable sales price" or "probable leasing price."
- A broker is now permitted to utilize the income approach methodology where appropriate.
- The CMA must be in writing.

- The broker can accept a CMA assignment only if the broker has knowledge of the real estate market and direct access to sales or leasing information as well as brokerage or appraisal experience in the same geographical area as the assignment.
- The broker MUST personally inspect both the exterior as well as the interior of the property unless this requirement is waived by the client for whom the CMA is being performed.
- If the assignment is for a residential property, the CMA should utilize the "sales comparison" methodology. If it is being performed on a residential rental property, the gross rent multiplier method may be used.
- If the assignment is for an income property, such as for a more than five-unit residential or other commercial property, the broker should use both the sales comparison as well as the income capitalization methodology.

Standards for CMA/BPO

A broker can accept a CMA assignment only when he is qualified to undertake such assignment. This generally means the broker has knowledge of the real estate market in the area the property is located in as well as access to sufficient data to research the past sales prices of similar properties. The broker must complete this assignment in a competent manner and must exercise "objective and independent judgment." The broker must have inspected both the exterior and interior of the property unless he has had this obligation waived. The broker should never suggest waiver to the client. Certainly, the broker is to utilize the appropriate methodology for any assignment and may now use either sales comparison or income approaches to determine the probable sales price.

> "A real estate licensee may never call any property pricing activity an "appraisal" or a "estimate of value." Licensees are permitted to perform a CMA or broker price opinion and may charge separately for them. A provisional broker may perform them but cannot charge for that service."
> —Jim Fletemier

Summary of Important Points

1. Value in exchange is the amount of money a typical buyer will give in exchange for a property. Value in exchange is market value.
2. For a property to have value, it must possess the characteristics of utility, scarcity, and transferability, and there must be an effective demand.
3. Value, price, and cost are not the same.
4. Market value is the highest price, in terms of money, that a property will bring assuming all parties are fully informed, act intelligently, and neither is under any undue compulsion to act.
5. A BPO or CMA is defined by the North Carolina Appraisers Act (G.S. Chapter 93E) as "the analysis of sales of similar sold properties in order to derive an indication of the probable sales price of a particular property by a licensed real estate broker."

6. The basic economic principles are highest and best use, substitution, supply and demand, conformity, anticipation, contribution, competition, and change.
7. Depreciation is the loss in value from any cause. In structures (land does not depreciate), the causes of depreciation are physical deterioration, functional obsolescence, and economic obsolescence.
8. An appraisal is an estimate (not a determination) of value based on factual data. It is good for one day, that is, the day of the appraisal.
9. The direct sales comparison approach (market data approach) to value is the most relevant appraisal method for estimating the value of single-family owner-occupied dwellings and of vacant land. When one reconciles the three approaches on single-family owner-occupied dwellings, this approach should be heavily weighted.
10. The income approach, or appraisal by capitalization, is the most appropriate appraisal method for estimating the value of property that produces rental income. NOI equals potential gross income minus vacancy and credit losses and expenses. Value is derived by dividing the NOI by the capitalization rate. The higher the capitalization rate, the lower the value estimate; the lower the rate, the higher the estimate.
11. The cost approach is the primary appraisal method for estimating the value of property that is not income producing and does not have sufficient comparable activity with which to compare.
12. A gross rent multiplier may be appropriate for estimating the value of rental property. The gross rent multiplier equals the selling price divided by the monthly or annual gross income. Conversely, the value of a property is derived by multiplying the gross rent by the gross rent multiplier.
13. An appraisal report provides a value estimate based on a reconciliation of the estimates obtained by all three approaches. Reconciliation is the process of weighted evaluation of the estimates derived from the three approaches to determine a single reliable estimate of value.
14. Real estate practitioners have a very important duty in the task of estimating the proper value of a property. Inherent in the practitioner's representation as an expert in the marketing of property is his duty to know the effect of the forces that affect value in his locality. Therefore, when estimating a value, the practitioner has a clear duty to be accurate and should be able to demonstrate sound data upon which his value estimate is based.
15. Contribution is the principle used in the direct sales comparison approach that states that various elements of a property add value to the entire property. In the direct sales comparison approach, one must estimate the value an element adds to the overall value.

16. In the sales comparison approach, always adjust the comparable. If the comparable is superior, subtract the amount from the sold price; if the comparable is inferior, add to the sold price.
17. The one and only use of land that will preserve its utility and yield the optimal income forms the highest and best *present* value of the land (this may change over time).
18. The CMA is allowed to estimate only the "probable sales price" or "probable leasing price" of a property. Any estimate that stipulates the "value" or "worth" shall be considered an appraisal.
19. Only "nonprovisional" broker licensees are permitted to complete a BPO/CMA for someone who is not considered an actual or prospective brokerage client.
20. A BPO/CMA is allowed to indicate only the "probable sales (leasing) price" and may NOT show the results as either "value" or "worth." Any valuation report that indicates the "value" or "worth" of a property shall be considered an appraisal and may only be completed by a licensed appraiser.
21. A BPO/CMA may be completed for compensation only by a "nonprovisional" broker licensee. It is important to note the North Carolina Real Estate Commission does NOT consider a "provisional broker" who completes a CMA/BPO for an actual or prospective brokerage client to be in violation if the only compensation will be that of an earned brokerage commission.
22. A broker may not prepare a BPO/CMA for a lienholder when the report is to be used as the basis for originating a first or second mortgage loan or home equity line of credit.

Review Questions

Answers to the review questions are in the Answer Key at the back of the book.

1. The basis of market value is most typically which of the following?
   A. value in use
   B. book value
   C. subjective value
   D. value in exchange

2. All of the following characteristics must be present for a property to have value EXCEPT:
   A. utility.
   B. obsolescence.
   C. transferability.
   D. effective demand.

3. Value is most closely related to which of the following?
   A. price
   B. competition
   C. cost
   D. supply

4. Adherence to the principle of conformity causes which of the following?
   A. depreciation
   B. minimizing value
   C. maximizing value
   D. competition

5. The first step in the appraisal process is to:
   A. define the appraisal problem.
   B. obtain a complete and accurate description of subject property.
   C. determine data required for estimate of value.
   D. prepare the appraisal report.

6. Physical deterioration is caused by:
   A. poor floorplan.
   B. outdated heating system.
   C. unrepaired damage.
   D. no central heating and cooling.

7. Functional obsolescence results from:
   A. faulty design and inefficient use of space.
   B. changes in the surrounding land use patterns.
   C. house on a busy street.
   D. a broken furnace.

8. Which cause of depreciation is not curable by a property owner?
   A. economic obsolescence
   B. functional obsolescence
   C. competitive obsolescence
   D. physical deterioration

9. Which economic principle is used in making adjustments to comparables in an appraisal by the direct sales comparison approach?
   A. competition
   B. change
   C. contribution
   D. conformity

10. An appraisal is which of the following?
    A. estimate of value
    B. appropriation of value
    C. correlation of value
    D. determination of value

11. All of the following are approaches to value EXCEPT:
    A. cost approach.
    B. contribution approach.
    C. income approach.
    D. direct sales comparison approach.

12. Which of the following is the primary appraisal method for estimating the value of vacant land?
    A. cost approach
    B. direct sales comparison approach
    C. income approach
    D. appraisal by capitalization

13. All of the following are important data in the selection of comparables for an owner-occupied single-family house EXCEPT:
    A. size.
    B. income.
    C. location.
    D. condition.

14. Which of the following is the income used as a basis for estimating value by the capitalization formula?
    A. monthly net operating income
    B. annual gross effective income
    C. monthly gross effective income
    D. annual net operating income

15. If the potential gross income is $580,000, the net operating income is $480,000, and the capitalization rate is 11%, which of the following will be the estimate of property value?
    A. $2,290,000
    B. $2,990,000
    C. $4,363,636
    D. $5,280,000

16. All the following are deductible from gross effective income to arrive at net operating income for appraisal purposes EXCEPT:
    A. maintenance.
    B. legal fees.
    C. replacement reserve.
    D. debt service.

17. In the income approach, which of the following is deducted from gross potential income to calculate gross effective income?
    A. fixed expenses
    B. vacancy rate
    C. other income
    D. replacement reserve

18. The cost approach is the primary method for appraisal of a:
    A. shopping mall.
    B. courthouse.
    C. parking lot.
    D. condominium.

19. All the following are methods used for estimating replacement cost EXCEPT:
    A. quantity survey.
    B. square-foot.
    C. unit-in-place.
    D. quality survey.

20. Which of the following is described as the cost of constructing a building of comparable utility using modern techniques and materials?
    A. reproduction cost
    B. operating cost
    C. unit cost
    D. replacement cost

21. A CMA may be legally prepared for compensation by:
    A. a provisional broker who is preparing the report for a lender who is using it to make a final determination of whether to approve a short sale request for another broker.
    B. a broker who is undertaking a project that will require the use of the cost approach.
    C. a provisional broker who is preparing it for a prospective listing brokerage client.
    D. a broker who is preparing the report for a lender who is utilizing it for the purpose of a home equity line of credit.

22. An appraisal is considered accurate for:
    A. 1 day.
    B. 30 days.
    C. 90 days.
    D. 180 days.

23. The foundation of the direct sales comparison approach is:
    A. conformity.
    B. anticipation.
    C. contribution.
    D. substitution.

24. The economic principle of supply and demand states that:
    A. high supply and low demand = higher value
    B. low supply and high demand = lower value
    C. high supply and low demand = lower value
    D. none of the above

25. All of the following are true about the principle of highest and best use EXCEPT:
    A. it must be possible.
    B. it must be legal.
    C. there is only one highest and best use of a given property at a given time.
    D. it is highly speculative.

26. Which is a curable form of obsolescence?
    A. changes in zoning
    B. unrepaired roof damage
    C. population shifts
    D. All of the above are curable by the property owner.

27. Which economic principle results in maximizing property value?
    A. supply and demand
    B. substitution
    C. conformity
    D. competition

28. The principle of highest and best use for a property:
    A. remains the same for the entire life of the property.
    B. may change with time.
    C. requires that present use is the same as future use.
    D. is used to calculate depreciation.

29. The value of a half bath is $1,500. The comparable has a half bath, but the subject property does not. Which is correct?
    A. Subtract $1,500 from the subject.
    B. Subtract $1,500 from the comparable.
    C. Add $1,500 to the subject.
    D. Add $1,500 to the comparable.

30. An appraisal prepared by an appraiser is completed on which form?
    A. competitive market analysis
    B. Uniform Residential Appraisal Report
    C. comparative market analysis
    D. any of the above

31. An appraiser is valuing a subject property with 1,650 square feet, 2 baths, a fireplace, and a one-car garage. He has located 3 comps with the following facts: Comparable #1 sold for $159,000 and contains 1,550 square feet, 1½ baths, no fireplace, and a one-car garage. Comparable #2 sold for $160,000 and contains 1,600 square feet, 2 baths, a fireplace, but no garage. Comparable #3 sold for $175,000 and contains 1,725 square feet, 2½ baths, a fireplace, and a one-car garage. Assume that construction costs are $50 per square foot, the value of a full bath is $2,500 and a half bath is $1,500, a fireplace is $3,000, and a single-car garage is $7,000. The appraiser notes that properties in the area have appreciated 2% since the time of the sale. What is the indicated value range of the subject property?
    A. $167,700–$173,250
    B. $171,180–$173,250
    C. $171,680–$173,250
    D. $167,900–$173,250

32. An appraiser has been asked to appraise a house containing 1,750 square feet, 2½ baths, and a two-car garage. A comparable property sold four months ago for $180,000. It contained 1,675 square feet, 3 baths, and a one-car garage. Assume construction costs to be $70 per square foot, a full bath to be $2,500 and a half bath to be $1,400, a one-car garage to be $8,000, and a two-car garage to be $14,000, and appreciation to be 2% since the time of the sale of the comparable. What would be the value of the subject property?

A. $193,450
B. $193,750
C. $183,250
D. $182,950

33. The result of a CMA performed by a broker on a property being listed is called the:

A. probable sales price.
B. appraisal.
C. estimated value.
D. projected value.

CHAPTER 14
PROPERTY INSURANCE

KEY TERMS

co-insurance clause
condition
endorsement
exclusion

homeowner's policy
insurable interest
liability insurance

package policy
peril
property (or hazard) insurance

LEARNING OBJECTIVES

At the conclusion of this chapter, you should be able to:

1. Define the basic concepts and terminology of insurance.
2. Describe the various types of homeowner's insurance policies.
3. Describe co-insurance.

IN THIS CHAPTER

The practice of real estate brokerage requires agents to possess a very basic working knowledge of the common terms and concepts involving homeowner's insurance policies in addition to basic flood insurance. Although specific questions and details regarding the insurance needs of a customer are to be obtained from a licensed insurance professional, it is imperative the real estate broker be able to understand at least the basic concepts and terms involved.

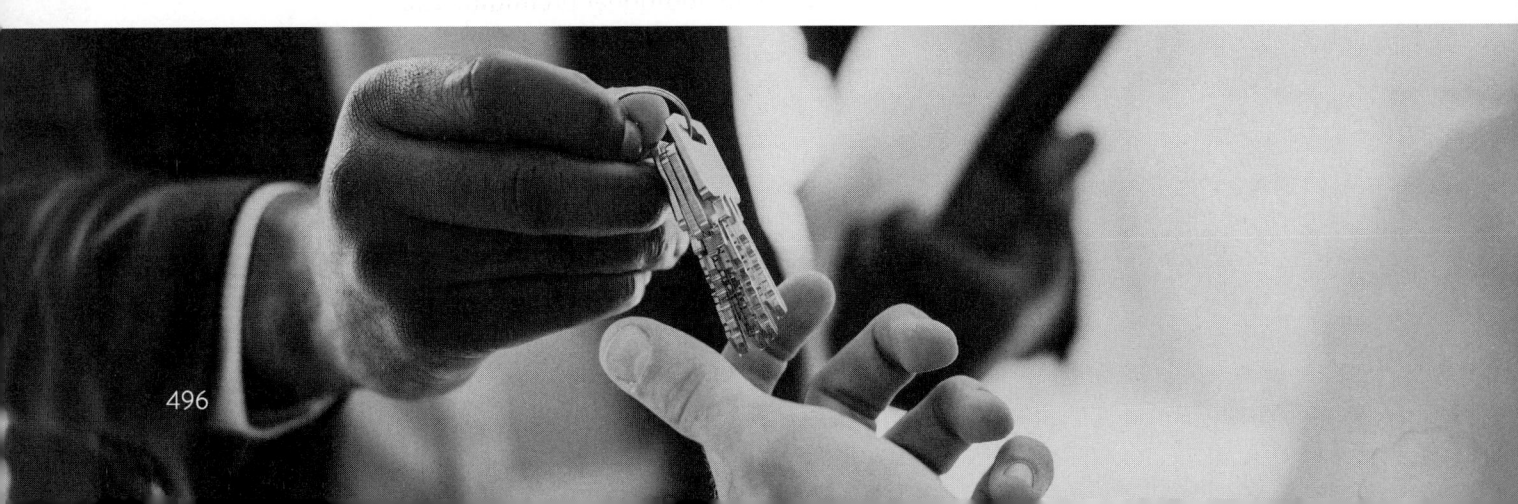

PROPERTY INSURANCE BASICS

Basic Concepts and Terminology

Before reviewing different property insurance policies and clauses, it is important to define some basic terminology:

1. The **insurer** is the insurance company that provides the insurance coverage to the owner of the property or other parties who may have an insurable interest in the property.
2. The **insured** is the person who benefits from the insurance coverage provided by the insurer. The insured must have an insurable interest in the property.
3. Insurance that *provides coverage to the basic structure of the property* (i.e., to the home itself or to other improvements) is called **property (or hazard) insurance.** The basic type of structural coverage begins with fire protection.
4. An insurance **peril** is *an insured hazard or risk of loss.* The first peril insured against is that of fire.
5. In addition to insuring against the peril of fire, a property owner should consider purchasing **liability insurance,** which *provides coverage for the financial claims of others.*
6. A **package policy** *combines insurance coverage for the two major elements of property and liability.* Additionally, for an income-producing property such as an apartment building, a package policy can include coverage for loss of income in the event that a fire or another peril renders the property unfit to produce its normal rental income for a period of time.

Standardized Homeowner's Insurance

Most fire insurance policies in the United States are based on the New York standard policy form as revised in 1943. The fire insurance policy indemnifies the insured against loss caused by fire. If the insured wishes to provide protection against losses resulting from other hazards, she must obtain an extended coverage endorsement to the fire policy. This endorsement, which is in the form of a rider attached to the fire policy, requires the payment of an additional premium. The extended coverage endorsement usually includes coverage from losses resulting from hail, explosion, windstorm, aircraft, civil commotion, vehicles, and smoke. A policy may have qualifications, exclusions, or conditions limiting coverage of some of these perils. One should check closely the details of the policy.

A package insurance policy is available to homeowners. This form of policy, called a **homeowner's policy,** *provides coverage for the structure and contents* (property insurance). This package policy is made up of a variety of insured perils that are considered beneficial to the homeowner and are not limited to just the property in question. The homeowner's policy also *provides coverage against a variety of hazards,* such as loss caused by fire, windstorm, hail, dust, waves, surface waters, freezing of plumbing, vandalism, and industrial smoke. Damage from dust or water are covered when either or both are forced in by wind or when the structure is damaged so that dust or water can enter through an opening caused by the damage and then damage the home's contents. The policy covers not only damage to the structure but also damage to the contents. Additionally, the homeowner's policy provides personal financial liability coverage to the policyholder. This protects the policyholder against liability for personal injury and property damage that he caused.

Homeowner's policies are identified as HO-2, -3, -4, and -6. HO-4 is a tenant's policy (for renters to cover their personal property), and HO-6 is designed for condominiums and cooperatives. HO-2 and HO-3 cover owners of single-family dwellings. Few, if any, North Carolina insurance companies write HO-1 and HO-5 policies anymore. HO-3 with full replacement coverage is now used widely. This coverage is usually marketed to owners of expensive properties. Every hazard insurance policy must contain a description of the insured property. The street address is usually adequate; however, some insurers require a full legal description.

Common Homeowner's Insurance Policies

- HO-1 = Basic Form. Not likely to be encountered.
- HO-2 = Broad Form. Covers more than the basic form. Named peril policy.
- HO-3 = All risk form. Most popular form. All risk for real property. Named peril for personal.
- HO-4 = Renter's or Tenant's Policy. Does not cover the structure.
- HO-6 = Condominium Policy. Mainly covers the contents and the interior of the unit as well.

Standard Form (HO-3) Policy

Agreement to Insure

This introductory part of the policy establishes the contractual relationship between the insurer and the insured. In essence, the insurer agrees to provide financial reimbursement to the insured, provided the latter provides timely payments and acts in good faith with the insurance provider. The insurer sets forth restrictions in its part of the contract, and the insured agrees to abstain from deceptive practices.

Declaration Page

The declaration page begins to spell out the details of the policy.

Period of coverage. The period of coverage is identified, usually starting at 12:01 a.m. Eastern Standard Time on a named date. Because this provision is an illustration of the specific nature of the policy, it is essential to pay close attention to detail. Obviously, no closing will proceed until verification that the policy is in effect.

Property description. The type and construction of the property affects the insurance rating. Because the main peril is the risk of fire, the property structure and fire protection are primary considerations in establishing the rating.

Coverage. The coverage section describes the real property improvement that is insured. Coverage of the personal property contents is usually described as a percentage of the structure. Therefore, if the structure were insured at $100,000 with a 50% personal property coverage, the contents would be covered up to a value of $50,000; however, there are some personal property exceptions. Other aspects of coverage include outside living expenses if the structure is made uninhabitable. Loss of income is also covered in income-producing property. The total amount of the coverage is specified as the insurer's limit of liability. The standard deductible is $250; however, a $100 deductible is available with a higher premium.

Endorsements. Endorsements (additions to the general policy that increase the number of perils or items covered by the policy) are disclosed on the declaration page. These are often referred to as a "rider."

Names. The premium payment is specified in this section, as are the names of the insurance agent and the mortgagee (lender). The lender clearly has an interest in the property as collateral for the home mortgage. In the event of a loss, the lender would have a claim on the insurance policy along with the homeowner.

Standardized Policy Provisions

This part of the policy contains all the details of the policy. If it is an HO-2 (i.e., a "named peril" policy [also called broad form]), all of the covered perils insured against are itemized here. If the policy is an HO-3 (formerly called an "all-risk" form), those perils not covered are itemized. This policy is now referred to as "risk of direct physical loss," but it still functions the same way. It covers all perils except the itemized exclusions. The real and personal property covered, conditions, exclusions, and endorsements are also included here.

Definitions

Other definitions that apply to insurance policies include the following:

1. A **condition** *limits the coverage of a specified property.* For example, if several people have a financial interest in the property, a condition limits any one person's insurance claim to the amount of her financial interest in the property. Personal property such as boats, golf carts, and personal computers may be limited to a minimal value as a condition of the policy. Thus, certain items need additional special policies or riders to provide full insurance value.

2. An **exclusion** is *something that is not covered for loss.* A "risk of direct physical loss" policy clearly defines perils that are not insured. Examples include losses resulting from earthquake, nuclear hazard, flood, or acts of war.

3. An **endorsement** *adds coverage for specified items or perils that are not covered under other provisions of the policy.* For example, works of art, collectibles, and personal computers used in the home for business may have great value but are not insured under the basic policy. Therefore, it is important to add coverage for these items, with either a special policy or an endorsement to the master policy for the property. Insurance companies may require an appraisal before adding these items, depending on the value limits set by the individual company.

SELECT LEGAL ISSUES

Insurable Interest

The insured must have a *legitimate financial interest,* known as an **insurable interest**, *in the property to be eligible for insurance coverage of any type.* In the absence of an insurable interest, the policy is void. Examples of persons having an insurable interest include owner, part owner, trustee, receiver, life tenant, mortgagor, and mortgagee.

Co-Insurance

Insurance policies usually contain a **co-insurance clause**. This clause requires the *property owner to insure the property for at least 80% of its value.* Some policies require 90% or 100%, but 80% is the typical requirement in policies insuring an owner-occupied residence. If the coverage is for less than 80% of value, the policy will pay only a part of the loss in proportion to the percentage of value insured by the policy owner. For example, if a structure is worth $100,000, the co-insurance clause is 80%, and the insurance carried is $60,000, in the event of a partial loss

($30,000), the company's liability is only $22,500. The amount of the insurance company's liability is calculated by using the following formula:

Insurance carried ÷ Insurance required × Loss = Company's limit of liability

$60,000 ÷ $80,000 × $30,000 = $22,500

If there is a loss of $80,000 or more (insurance required), the insurance company's liability is the amount of insurance carried. This is illustrated by the following example:

Value of structure $100,000

Insurance required (80%) $80,000

Insurance policy amount $60,000

Loss $90,000

Insurance carried ÷ Insurance required × Loss = Company's limit of liability

$60,000 ÷ $80,000 × $90,000 = $67,500

Insurance company's liability = $60,000

Because the loss equals or exceeds the amount of insurance required by the co-insurance clause, the insurance company will pay the policy amount even though the requirement of the co-insurance clause is not met. However, in no event will the policy pay an amount in excess of the amount of coverage specified in the policy.

Unoccupied Building Exclusion

A general concept of insurance risk is that a building left empty, without occupants to look after it, is at more risk than one that is constantly occupied. This is reflected in the fact that most policies lapse after a given period of time if the owners are not present. A building is considered *vacant* when the owners have moved out and have removed their personal property, such as furniture and household contents. Additionally, a property is considered *unoccupied* when the owner's property is still present but nobody has been physically present in the building for a stated period. Typically, when a building is vacant or unoccupied for the period specified by a policy, the policy ceases to cover all or certain perils.

The real estate practitioner should be aware of these limitations of policies, especially when taking a listing for an owner who is moving out of the home immediately. The listing agent should urge the owner to contact his insurance agent to be sure there is no lapse in coverage at this time.

Interpretation of Policies

Although many policies now use plain language to assist the public in understanding the concepts contained in the policy, there is still room for misinterpretation based on certain blanket assumptions of the insured. Perhaps the best rule is to avoid making assumptions about areas that are not explained in detail by the insurer. A general rule of contracts is that the one who constructs the agreement (in this case, the insurer) has the burden in the event of an ambiguous phrase. Simple misunderstandings of clear terminology, however, will not work in favor of the insured. For example, not all kinds of personal property are covered under a homeowner's policy. A condition may limit the amount of coverage, such as by setting a low upper limit on a boat stored at the home. Additionally, there are exclusions for a number of items, such as currency, artwork, and collectibles. Of interest to real estate practitioners is the potential exclusion of any business activities that take place at a home residence, such as meeting customers, or the use of hardware, such as a personal computer for real estate work at home. Just as practitioners should not offer advice to others about insurance concerns, they probably should seek insurance advice to ensure that they are not exposed to uncovered liability in the use of their residence for business activities.

Co-Owners

A hazard insurance policy covers only the person named as the insured in the policy and only to the extent of her interest. For example, if the title is held by two parties as tenants in common and the policy is in the name of only one of them and a loss occurs, the policy will pay only the person named as the insured. If the co-tenant named in the policy owned one-half interest in the property, the insurance company would pay up to one-half the face amount of the policy but no more than the loss sustained by the tenant in common owning the one-half interest. This is also important in the case of a married couple holding the title as joint tenants or by the entireties. If the policy names only one of them as the insured and that spouse dies, the surviving spouse receives title to the deceased spouse's half interest and becomes the sole owner of the entire property; because the insurance policy did not include the surviving spouse's name as an insured, he would have no insurance protection in the event of a loss resulting from an insured hazard. Any time ownership in property is changed, the insurance coverage should also be changed to provide adequate protection for any owner or owners.

Mortgagee's Insurable Interest

As previously stated, a mortgagee is an individual, a group of individuals, or an insurable organization that has an interest in a property. The mortgagee usually requires, in the mortgage, that the borrower maintain adequate hazard insurance coverage on the property. In this case, the policy is issued in the names of the mortgagee and the mortgagor. The policy protects the mortgagee up to the amount of principal balance owed within the coverage limits provided by the policy. In the event of a partial loss, the insurance company pays the mortgagor so she can make the appropriate repairs. In the event of a total loss, the mortgagee is paid first—up to the amount of the outstanding mortgage debt—with any surplus going to the mortgagor. NOTE: North Carolina uses a deed of trust rather than a mortgage. Therefore, mortgagor and mortgagee are not the precise terms for the borrower and lender. However, these are the terms commonly used in reference to insurance loss payee clauses.

Assignment

Insurance policies are generally assignable with the written consent of the insurance company. A seller sometimes assigns his interest in a hazard insurance policy to a buyer of the property as of the date of closing, with the premium being prorated between buyer and seller. This is more likely to occur with purchases using loan assumptions than with purchases using new loans. The assignment is not valid, however, unless the written consent of the insurer is obtained. The insurance company typically provides evidence of consent by issuing an endorsement to the policy, changing the name of the insured.

Flood Insurance

The risk of water damage can either be from "falling water," such as a leak or overflow within a property, and "rising water," which is considered a flood. Unlike the damages caused by falling water, which is typically covered within a homeowner's policy, the risk of flood is NOT covered by a homeowner's insurance policy. In many high-risk areas the risk of loss by flood can be twice that of fire. Because structures located in these high-risk flood hazard areas have a significant risk of flood damage during the normal course of a 30-year mortgage, Congress enacted the National Flood Insurance Program (NFIP) to be carried out by the Federal Emergency Management Agency (FEMA) to mitigate flood losses nationwide.

The NFIP works with local communities and the federal government to adopt and enforce a flood area management plan to reduce the risks from flooding. These agreements are the basis for the federal government's provision of flood insurance. Even though the government stands behind this program, the insurance itself is purchased through private insurance companies. If this cooperative agreement did not exist, it is likely that privately owned insurance companies could not afford the risks of large-scale flooding. For this reason, this program allows homeowners to purchase affordable flood insurance that otherwise would perhaps not be available.

In areas designated as flood hazard areas by FEMA, flood insurance will be required when obtaining any federally related mortgage loan. A review of FEMA flood maps and surveys of the property are reviewed before the mortgage being obtained to determine whether flood insurance will be required. Any structure that has a 1% chance of being flooded in a given year will be required to be covered by the insurance. This 1% rule is what many people refer to as the 100-year flood rule. Homeowners need to be aware these FEMA maps are not always up to date, and if there are concerns, then appropriate experts should be sought for advice. Frequently, new construction, grading, and paving can alter the flood patterns so that areas that have not historically been prone to floods can now be susceptible. Brokers should keep in mind that a property's location within a designated flood hazard area is a material fact that must be disclosed.

Insurability Issues

Insurance companies are asked to provide an affordable cost policy on properties that may expose them to excessive losses, which poses risk. For this reason, insurance underwriters are utilizing a database called the Comprehensive Loss Underwriting Exchange (CLUE) commonly referred to as the CLUE report. This insurance industry database provides valuable information on property addresses and owners to determine the history of claims associated with either. These reports address losses within the past seven years and allow the underwriters to determine whether the property, or the owner, is an acceptable insurance risk and if additional premiums may be required.

Residential Sales Transaction Concerns

Unoccupied Building Exclusion

A general concept of insurance risk is that a building left empty, without occupants to look after it, is at more risk than one that is constantly occupied. This is reflected in the fact that most policies lapse after a given period of time if the owners are not present. A building is considered *vacant* when the owners have moved out and have removed their personal property, such as furniture and household contents. Additionally, a property is considered *unoccupied* when the owner's property is still present but nobody has been physically present in the building for a stated period. Typically, when a building is vacant or unoccupied for the period specified by a policy, the policy ceases to cover all or certain perils.

The real estate practitioner should be aware of these limitations of policies, especially when taking a listing for an owner who is moving out of the home immediately. The listing agent should urge the owner to contact his insurance agent to ensure that there is no lapse in coverage at this time.

Early or Late Possession by Parties

In the event of early or late possession by the buyer or seller, the typical homeowner's policy will not be sufficient. If the seller retains possession after the closing the property is no longer considered "owner occupied." The seller should contact her insurance professional who will likely provide her with some type of renter's insurance because she no longer owns the property.

If the buyer is to take early possession of the property before the closing, or allows the seller to retain possession after, he will need to contact his insurance professional. He will likely provide them with renter's insurance before the closing and some type of landlord liability policy for cases in which the seller remains in possession after the closing.

Risk of Loss before Recordation/Closing

Sellers and brokers should both remember the risk of loss provision in the Standard OTP 2-T, which states the seller shall retain the risk of loss before the closing (recordation of the deed). The parties should always ascertain the new deed has been properly recorded before canceling the seller's policy.

Test Tip!

Students should be able to define the following terms:

1. **Endorsement.** An endorsement is something that is added to a basic policy—that is, another peril (source of loss) or item is covered. For example, the peril of earthquake is not covered by ordinary policies, but an endorsement to a policy can provide this protection. Likewise, valuable antiques not covered by an ordinary policy can be covered by an endorsement to the policy.
2. **Condition.** A condition limits the protection of a policy for special risk peril. Examples include the coverage of computer hardware used for business purposes at home or a boat on someone's property. Although one might be tempted to assume these items are covered as personal property, the condition might limit such coverage to a minimal amount, such as $100 to $500, that is far below the item's actual value.
3. **Co-insurance.** NOTE: The following math is used to explain the concept and is not a part of the examination. Co-insurance is a concept greatly misunderstood by average clients. When they see a typical policy with an 80% co-insurance clause, they think they can recover 80% of a given loss. As you now know by studying the examples in this chapter, this is not correct. Co-insurance is simply a penalty clause requiring owners to carry a minimum amount, usually 80%, of the value and penalizing them proportionally if they do not. For example, because fire statistics indicate that the worst fire loss an average homeowner might expect is one-third of the structure's value, the owner might try to squeeze pennies by buying only 40% coverage. Referring to the formulas in the section "Co-Insurance," you see that if the home value was $100,000, the insurance purchased was $40,000, and the loss was for $20,000, the owner would be paid only $10,000. Even though the owner had $40,000 "coverage," the loss is only half covered.

What if the $100,000 home was covered with a $100,000 policy and an 80% co-insurance policy? In the event of a total loss, the owner would be paid the full $100,000 (not $80,000 or $125,000).

Summary of Important Points

1. The valuable asset of real property is subject to many risk factors and potential losses. A source of loss is called a peril. Homeowner's policies are package policies providing coverage for a number of perils to the structure, known as property insurance, as well as the financial claims of others, known as liability insurance.
2. A fire insurance policy indemnifies the insured against loss by fire. Protection from losses from other hazards is obtained by an extended coverage endorsement.
3. Package policies, or homeowner's policies, provide all usual protections in one policy. These policies are available to homeowners and renters.
4. To be eligible for insurance, an applicant must have an insurable interest in the property. People who have an insurable interest include owner, part owner, trustee, receiver, life tenant, mortgagor, and mortgagee.
5. Every hazard insurance policy contains a co-insurance clause requiring the property owner to insure for at least 80% of the property value. In the event of a partial loss when the coverage is for less than 80% of value, the policy pays only part of the loss. When the loss equals or exceeds the amount of coverage required by the co-insurance clause, however, the insurance company pays the policy amount even though the requirement of the co-insurance clause is not met.
6. Insurance policies are usually assignable with the written consent of the insurance company. The consent is evidenced by an endorsement to the policy.
7. Flood insurance is required in areas designated as flood hazard areas by FEMA. Other land use restrictions often apply in these areas.

Review Questions

Answers to the review questions are in the Answer Key at the back of the book.

1. A homeowner's insurance policy includes coverage for:
   A. structure and contents only.
   B. personal liability only.
   C. both structure/contents and personal liability.
   D. neither structure/contents nor personal liability.

2. The type of homeowner's insurance policy that is known as "all risk" is:
   A. HO-2.
   B. HO-3.
   C. HO-4.
   D. HO-6.

3. The clause within a homeowner's insurance policy that penalizes the policyholder for underinsuring the property is:
   A. exclusion.
   B. subrogation.
   C. condition.
   D. co-insurance.

4. An insured hazard or risk is known as:
   A. endorsement.
   B. liability.
   C. peril.
   D. condition.

5. The type of homeowner's insurance that is known as "renter's insurance" is:
   A. HO-2.
   B. HO-3.
   C. HO-4.
   D. HO-6.

6. Flood insurance policies are typically:
   A. purchased from private insurance companies.
   B. purchased from the federal government.
   C. purchased from FEMA.
   D. part of the homeowner's insurance policy.

7. The type of homeowner's insurance policy that is associated with ownership of a condominium is:
   A. HO-2.
   B. HO-3.
   C. HO-4.
   D. HO-6.

8. If a seller sells his/her house and retains possession for 30 days after the closing, they will most likely be:
   A. required to purchase a HO-4 policy.
   B. allowed to retain their previous homeowner's policy.
   C. covered under the buyer's new insurance policy.
   D. required to purchase some type of property damage policy.

CHAPTER 15
LANDLORD AND TENANT

KEY TERMS

breach of condition
constructive eviction
estate at sufferance
estate at will
estate for years
estate from period to period
fit premises
full-service leases
graduated lease

gross lease
ground (land) lease
index lease
landlord
lease
lessee
lessor
net lease
North Carolina Residential Rental Agreements Act

North Carolina Tenant Security Deposit Act
percentage leases
periodic tenancy
residential eviction remedies
retaliatory eviction statute
sale and leaseback
tenant

LEARNING OBJECTIVES

At the conclusion of this chapter, you should be able to:

1. Describe the basic concepts and terminology of the relationship between landlord and tenant.
2. List and define the nonfreehold estates.
3. List the essential provisions of the North Carolina Residential Rental Agreements Act.
4. List the essential provisions of the North Carolina Tenant Security Deposit Act.
5. List the types and characteristics of leases.
6. Describe the essential and common provisions of leases.
7. Describe the application of the Statute of Frauds to leases.
8. Define the rights of the parties to a lease.
9. Describe the requirements for recording leases.

IN THIS CHAPTER

The predominant practice of residential real estate will focus on the sale of property, but brokers will need to acquire a working knowledge of the rental aspect of brokerage as well. North Carolina has created detailed guidelines for the rental operations of residential real estate in Chapter 42 of the General Statutes, which provides the foundation for what every practicing broker will need to know. Of particular importance are the North Carolina Residential Rental Agreements Act and the Tenant Security Deposit Act. In addition to the Residential Rental Contract, this chapter will address the Vacation Rental Act, nonfreehold estates, types of leases, and common lease provisions.

DEFINITIONS

A **lease** *is a contract whereby a landlord gives a tenant the right to use and possess property for a specified period of time in exchange for rent.* The verbs "lease," "let," and "demise" all describe the conveyance of a possessory interest in property by a lease. Because a lease is both a contract and a conveyance, it creates two sets of rights and duties between the parties. For example, *the landlord grants the tenant the exclusive right of possession in the lease, which is a nonfreehold estate, or leasehold interest.* At the same time, the landlord retains ownership of the property and the right to be paid rent by the lessees. As a result, the lease creates an interest in the property for both parties as well as contractual rights for both parties. The *owner of the property* is the **landlord**, the *one who gives the lease,* who is also known as the **lessor**. The *one who receives the lease* is the **lessee**, or **tenant**. If the original tenant (lessee) subleases the property, she becomes the sublessor. The tenant to whom she subleases is the sublessee.

As introduced in Chapter 2, a leasehold estate is also known as a *nonfreehold* or *less than freehold estate.* The landlord, of course, retains title to the property and has a freehold estate. Therefore, in the creation of a lease, both freehold and nonfreehold estates exist at the same time as one party owns the property and the other leases it. *The landlord owns the property (freehold) but has handed over possession to the tenant (nonfreehold).*

ESTATES AND CONTRACTS

In the creation of a rental estate, two concepts are involved. The first, that of estates, was just discussed. As outlined in Chapter 2, estates can vary widely in the quantity and quality of interest in real property. The landlord maintains the highest quantity of interest by holding title to the land. He has, however, temporarily diminished his bundle of rights by giving the tenant the right of possession of the property, essentially to the landlord's exclusion. The right of possession reverts to the landlord/owner at the end of the lease; however, during the lease period, the tenant's right of possession creates an encumbrance.

The second concept is that of contract law, which establishes the rights and the duties of the parties. As we will see in the examination of the **North Carolina Residential Rental Agreements Act**, the duty of each party is related to the other party's performance.

THE RESIDENTIAL RENTAL AGREEMENTS ACT

In the creation of the rental or leasehold estate, the roles of the two parties are defined in the North Carolina Residential Rental Agreements Act. As indicated by the word *residential,* the act applies only to residential property. It does not regulate commercial property or transient-type quarters. This rule is not limited to real estate licensees and property managers but is applicable to all private property owners renting residential properties.

Obligations of Landlord and Tenant

An important statutory provision is that the duties of landlord and tenant are mutually dependent. If one party fails to fulfill her duties, the other party is excused from his respective responsibility. The concept of **constructive eviction** provides *a remedy for the tenant in the event the landlord fails to perform her duty,* such as that of maintaining the heating system. If the owner fails to do so, the tenant is excused from the lease, regardless of the remaining term. In a like manner, if the tenant fails to pay rent, the landlord is not required to allow the tenant to remain in the premises. The manner of eviction, however, is carefully regulated.

> In the event of constructive eviction, the tenant is never allowed to withhold rent and remain in possession of the property.

Landlord's Statutory Duties

"Since July 2014 it has also been mandatory to have carbon monoxide detectors in all rental units with either an attached garage or a fossil fuel burning appliance."
—Melea Lemon, DREI

The landlord's major duty is to provide **fit premises**, that is, *fit for human habitation.* The landlord cannot waive this duty or excuse himself in any way. The landlord must comply with building codes; maintain and repair common areas; repair utilities such as heat, plumbing, and electrical; and repair appliances provided on the premises. Generally, the landlord must do whatever is needed to make and keep the unit habitable. These duties come under the "Warranty of Habitability."

Smoke detectors and carbon monoxide alarms must be provided in all rental properties. The act requires the placement of at least one operable smoke alarm in each rental unit and at least one operable carbon monoxide alarm per rental unit per level. The act further requires all landlords to repair or replace any alarm within 15 days of being notified of inoperability. New batteries are the landlord's responsibility when property is initially rented by a new tenant. Thereafter, replacement batteries are the tenant's responsibility. Minimum standards for the batteries are they must be at least a 10-year lithium battery as to limit the short life of traditional batteries.

Tenant's Statutory Duties

The tenant's primary duties are to maintain the individual living unit, including keeping the unit safe and clean; properly disposing of trash; keeping plumbing fixtures clean; and being financially responsible for any destruction, defacement, or damage.

Tenant Remedies for Breach by Landlord

If a landlord fails to provide a habitable rental unit, a tenant can bring action against the landlord for damages, including the recovery of rent paid while the unit was uninhabitable. The courts can also require the landlord to correct defects in the property.

A tenant may not, however, remain in the property and unilaterally withhold rent without a court order. In the event of constructive eviction by the landlord, the tenant is excused from completing the lease term. **Constructive eviction** is deemed to have occurred if the *landlord breaks his duty to provide fit and habitable premises and fails to remedy the problem within a reasonable length of time after being notified of the problem by the tenant.* For example, the landlord fails to maintain the property in that the roof leaks during periods of rain. The leakage is sufficiently severe to deprive the tenant of reasonable occupancy of the premises. As a result, the tenant has to vacate. The landlord has not legally evicted the tenant but rather has caused the tenant to be deprived of reasonable occupancy by failure to provide fit and habitable premises.

Application of the Law of Negligence

North Carolina law has traditionally applied the Law of Negligence differently to the occupied premises and common areas. The landlord is responsible for maintaining the common areas and is, therefore, potentially liable for injury occurring in these areas to a tenant, a tenant's family, and guests. The landlord's liability increases if it can be shown that he knew about the hazard that caused the injury and failed to correct it and if no negligence is shown on the part of the injured party.

In the past, the landlord was not usually held liable for injury occurring within the leased area itself because the tenant was responsible for that area. Because the North Carolina Residential Rental Agreements Act now holds the landlord responsible for keeping the premises safe and habitable, the landlord may face more liability in that area in the future. Although a violation of the act does not create liability, it could possibly be used as evidence of liability, especially absent negligence on the part of the tenant.

RETALIATORY EVICTION

The **retaliatory eviction statute** *protects tenants in asserting their rights,* such as requesting repairs or participating in a tenants union or filing a complaint against the landlord. The statute provides an *automatic defense* from eviction for up to one year from any such event. This does not mean the tenant cannot be evicted or that the landlord is prohibited from altering the lease terms during the year. It simply means that any action by the landlord is subject to review to determine whether a retaliatory motive exists. For example, the landlord informs the tenant of a rental increase at the end of the current lease, but within one year of a protected tenant activity. If the projected rental rate is in line with other similar rental properties in the area, the landlord can impose the change in rent.

NORTH CAROLINA TENANT SECURITY DEPOSIT ACT

"Neither the Residential Rental Agreements Act, the North Carolina Tenant Security Deposit Act nor the Vacation Rental Act are limited to licensees and property managers. These statutes apply to private owners and non-licensees as well."
—Derrin Dunzweiler

The **North Carolina Tenant Security Deposit Act** *sets limitations on the holding of security deposits by the landlord.* Similar to the Residential Rental Agreements Act, this act *applies only to residential property* and is applicable to all private property owners renting or leasing their own properties. When collecting the money, the private landlord has two choices of what to do with the funds. The landlord can place the funds in a North Carolina bank trust account, in which case the landlord must notify the tenant of the bank's location. Alternatively, the landlord can guarantee the return of the funds with a performance bond and notifies the tenant of the bonding company's name. NOTE: Real estate agents can use only the trust account method. There are strict accounting rules (Rule A.0116 and A.0117) for the operation of trust accounts. Agents cannot use the bond option in their fiduciary capacity.

Permitted uses of the deposit are limited to damage to the unit, nonfulfillment of the rental period, unpaid rent, court costs of eviction, and costs of re-rental if the tenant breaches the lease. The landlord must account for or refund the deposit within 30 days of the end of the lease. If this is not possible, an interim accounting within 30 days with a final accounting within 60 days is allowed.

Permitted Uses of Tenant Security Deposits

 Following are permitted uses of tenant security deposits:
- Nonpayment of rent, including costs for services provided by landlord
- Damages to the property that exceed "normal wear and tear," including damage to smoke and carbon monoxide alarms

- Nonfulfillment of the rental period (future rent due)
- Unpaid bills that become a lien against the property
- Cost of re-renting the property after tenant breach
- Costs of removal and storage of tenant's property after eviction
- Costs of court
- Late fees for rents due more than five days
- Permitted complaint filing fees or court appearance fees

Amounts that can be collected for security deposit are related to the period of the lease. If the tenancy is weekly, the maximum deposit is two weeks' rent; if the tenancy is monthly, a month and a half's rent; and if the tenancy is greater than a month, two months' rent. This act also allows the landlord to require a *reasonable nonrefundable* pet deposit for pets kept on the premises by the tenant.

Maximum Amounts for Security Deposits

 Following are maximum allowable security deposits:

- Week-to-week: 2 weeks' rent
- Month-to-month: 1.5 months' rent
- More than month-to-month: 2 months' rent

The landlord is allowed to collect a reasonable fee for pets that are kept by the tenants. This fee is totally separate from the security deposit amounts shown above and is nonrefundable. It is important for the landlord to understand they cannot collect a pet fee for a service animal, such as a sight assistance dog. Such animals are not considered as pets nor can the landlord prohibit the tenant from possessing such an animal in the event the policy is not to allow pets. The pet fee is only for the ability to own a pet. The fee does not include any remedy for the landlord in the event the pet causes damages. Those damages must be collected only from the security deposit or additional legal action if the deposit amount has been exceeded.

Frequent disputes arise over what is "normal" wear and tear and what is damage not resulting from "normal" wear and tear. Damage caused by everyday activities of reasonably careful people is probably normal wear and tear. Dirt and dust on walls and windows, worn or dirty carpet due to normal foot traffic or age, age-related repairs to appliances, and worn or frayed window treatments are examples of normal wear and tear. Examples of damage beyond ordinary wear and tear include anything broken by force; crayon, nail polish, motor oil, and other stains on carpets, walls, trim, or fixtures; burns or large holes on walls, carpets, countertops, and so on; extremely filthy premises or appliances; and fixtures requiring extraordinary cleaning.

Typical Examples of Normal Wear and Tear

According to the North Carolina Real Estate Commission's consumer pamphlet *North Carolina Real Estate Manual*, normal wear and tear includes the following:

- Worn or dirty carpeting
- Faded or cracked paint
- Dirty windows
- Dirty walls
- Frayed or broken curtain or blind strings
- Leaking faucets or toilets
- Small nail holes in walls (from hanging pictures)
- Worn lavatory basin
- Burned-out range heating elements

Common Examples of "Other Damage"

Following are examples of "other damage," from the *North Carolina Real Estate Manual*:

- Crayon marks on walls
- Large holes in walls
- Broken windows
- Burned spots or stains on carpeting
- Bizarre or unauthorized paint colors
- Broken counter tops
- Filthy appliances (such as ovens or refrigerators) requiring extraordinary cleaning
- Exceptionally filthy premises (in general) requiring extraordinary cleaning

Time spent with tenants upon renting, explaining what is expected of them, including a written explanation of expectations and a properly completed property condition report, greatly reduces the possibility of misunderstandings.

Test Tip!

Do not confuse the maximum amount of deposit allowed with the minimum notice period required to terminate a lease.

Limits on Late Payment Fees

Landlords are allowed to collect late payment fees in the event the tenant is more than five days late in paying rents due. For monthly rents due, the late fees cannot exceed $15 or 5% of the monthly rent, whichever is greater. For weekly rentals, the fee cannot exceed $4 or 5% of the rent due, whichever is greater.

Late fees may be imposed only once for each rent payment due.

RESIDENTIAL EVICTION REMEDIES

Residential eviction (or *judicial eviction*) **remedies** prohibit peaceable self-help, which includes acts such as locking tenants out or shutting off their utilities. Furthermore, the distress or distraint of chattel (personal property) is prohibited. Therefore, the landlord cannot seize the tenant's furniture, cut off the electricity, or put padlocks on the unit. His only remedy is to seek judicial eviction, which is also known as *summary ejectment* or *actual eviction*. Seizure of the tenant's personal property is not allowed as a remedy for the nonpayment of rent and any statement within the residential lease agreement attempting to override this rule will be considered null and void. North Carolina does have rules pertaining to property that has been abandoned by a tenant upon termination, but they are beyond the scope of this course.

> "There are two types of evictions. When a tenant breaches a lease, it is an actual eviction. When the landlord breaches the lease, it is a constructive eviction."
> —Len Elder, DREI

DISCRIMINATION AND SEXUAL HARASSMENT

Federal and state laws prohibit discrimination against tenants based on race, color, religion, sex, handicap, familial status, or national origin. See Chapter 16, Property Management, for a detailed discussion on this topic.

North Carolina law also prohibits sexual harassment of a lessee or prospective tenant (N.C. General Statute 14-395) by a lessor or lessor's agent. **Sexual harassment** is defined as *unsolicited overt requests or demands for sexual acts when submission to such conduct is made a term of execution or continuation of a lease* agreement or submission or rejection of such conduct is used to determine whether rights under the lease are accorded.

RIGHTS OF TENANTS IN PUBLIC HOUSING

Real estate practitioners are expected to have special expertise and training in all dealings with their clients and the general public. Therefore, agents need to know that North Carolina has legal precedent for establishing the concept that special rules or interpretations apply to tenants of public housing. In this type of housing, tenants are assumed to have a special entitlement to continued occupancy, which may not be suddenly terminated, especially if they have personal circumstances beyond their control. They are entitled to due process under federal and state constitutions.

VACATION RENTAL ACT

Most of the original rental legislation and rules were based on traditional residential situations such as a tenant renting a property for a period of one year or perhaps month to month. In these cases, the tenant would likely provide utilities in his own name and would otherwise be treated as a long-term occupant. The landlord was required to provide fit and habitable premises and return the tenant's security deposit within 30 days of the end of the lease. The problem with that theory is that vacation rentals don't fit neatly within the confines of such rental legislation. The law that required landlords to provide fit and habitable properties exempted short-term, transient-type occupancy, such as the vacation rental, from its requirements. Landlords were likely to provide the utilities, and the furnishings, for the vacation rentals and complained that they were required to return a tenant's security deposit within 30 days, which might be before the bills were delivered to the landlord. Eviction rules that applied to more traditional, longer term rentals, did not work well for vacation rentals, which were often for only a few days. Last, traditional longer term rental legislation didn't address what happens in the case in which an area declares a mandatory evacuation because of a hurricane warning. Does the landlord have to rebate a tenant for the rent for the period he was required by law enforcement to vacate? Because of these types of concerns, it became apparent that the standard rental legislation needed to be expanded to address the unique needs of the vacation rental market.

Purpose

The Vacation Rental Act became effective January 1, 2000. Similar to the Residential Rental Agreements Act and the North Carolina Tenant Security Deposit Act, the Vacation Rental Act of North Carolina does not apply only to licensees or property managers. It applies to any landlord or agent who rents property used only for vacation, recreation, or leisure for time periods of fewer than 90 days, but specifically exempts hotels, motels, and certain other lodgings regulated by other North Carolina Statutes. The act does not apply to rentals for business purposes or for short-term temporary residences for individuals with no other permanent resident to which they plan to return at some point after the rental.

Must Be in Writing

The act requires all vacation rental agreements to be in writing. Otherwise, such agreements are not enforceable. A tenant must accept a vacation rental agreement in one of the following ways:

1. By signing the agreement
2. By paying the landlord or broker a part of the consideration or security deposit AFTER the tenant receives a copy of the written agreement

> "Ordinarily, the statute of frauds only requires leases that are longer than 3 years to be in writing. The North Carolina Vacation Rental Act requires all vacation rental leases that are shorter than 90 days to be in writing."
> —Len Elder, DREI

3. By taking possession of the property AFTER receiving a copy of the agreement. As with most real estate–related issues, the general statutes put a greater burden on a broker acting as agent for a principal than an owner or landlord acting for herself. A landlord renting his own property cannot enforce his contract with a tenant if the agreement is not in writing, but the landlord is not subject to the penalties of G.S. 75-1.1 for an unfair trade practice due to his failure to get the agreement in writing. However, the broker acting as a landlord's agent may be guilty of an unfair trade practice under G.S. 75-1.1 by failing to obtain a written agreement for a vacation rental. These penalties can be steep, including treble damages or a civil penalty, as well as attorney fees.

Procedures for Rents and Deposits

The Vacation Rental Act requires tenant security deposits to be held in a trust account, mostly in accordance with the Tenant Security Deposit Act, but with minor modifications for the special circumstances of vacation rentals only. Under the act, the landlord/agent may collect advance payments from the tenant and deposit such payments in a trust account. The landlord/agent may then withdraw/disburse from the trust account an amount not to exceed 50% of the gross rent before occupancy. This does not include 50% of other fees, such as security deposits.

The landlord does not have the option of having a bond rather than depositing monies into an escrow account. The landlord/agent has 45 rather than 30 days to account for deposit monies after the end of a vacation rental. In addition to permitted uses of the security deposit under the Tenant Security Deposit Act, the Vacation Rental Act specifically allows security deposits to be used to pay long-distance phone calls or cable charges that are a tenant's obligation.

Under the act, a landlord/agent may charge reasonable fees to a tenant for making, transferring, or canceling the tenancy, provided such fees are included in the agreement and reasonably approximate the actual cost of such services. No other fees may be charged.

A landlord who cannot make the property available to a tenant in a fit and habitable condition must substitute a reasonably comparable property or refund the tenant's payment.

Tenant Protection When Property Is Sold

The act provides some protection for tenants who have vacation rental agreements. Landlords voluntarily selling or transferring property covered under the Vacation Rental Act must disclose to purchasers or grantees the existence of any leases ending within 180 days after transfer of title to the grantee. The grantee takes the property subject to these rental agreements. After the sale,

> "The Vacation Rental Act changes the standard time for the return and accounting for a security deposit from 30 days (on other rentals) to 45 days on vacation rentals."
> —Terry Wilson, DREI

> "Typically a new owner must honor all existing leases. On vacation rentals the new owner must only honor leases and reservations for the next 180 days after purchase."
> —Jack Marinello, DREI

the landlords/sellers must also inform tenants of their rights under the act. Tenants not protected by the act, such as those whose tenancy ends beyond the 180-day period or those whose tenancy is terminated by an involuntary transfer, are entitled to a refund of monies already paid minus some allowable deductions.

Within 10 days after transfer of property covered by the act, the buyer or her agent must notify each tenant of the property transfer in writing and inform each tenant as to whether she still has the right to occupy the property or to have any payments refunded. The new owner has no obligation to honor vacation rentals beginning after 180 days of property transfer but may do so voluntarily.

Expedited Eviction

The act provides for expedited eviction procedures for tenants in vacation rentals under tenancies for 30 days or less when such tenants have breached the agreement. Examples of breaches of the agreement include destroying property, exhibiting loud and disruptive behavior, and holding over beyond the end of the agreement. The landlord/agent must give the tenant a minimum of a four-hour notice to vacate the premises after a breach. Oral notice is allowed, but written notice is easier to document. The process moves rapidly. The case must be heard 12 to 48 hours after complaint is served and tenant is summoned. If the magistrate orders the tenant to vacate, the tenant must do so at the time set by court but no more than eight hours after the service of the order.

This expedited eviction procedure must not be abused. The act imposes severe penalties for landlords/agents who act in bad faith without sufficient grounds or without a written agreement. Such penalties include civil penalties, treble damages, and possible criminal prosecution.

Landlord and Tenant Duties

Landlord and tenant duties imposed by the Vacation Rental Act are essentially the same as landlord and tenant duties for other rental properties. The landlord must make a reasonable effort to provide safe, habitable, and fit premises and keep property repaired. The tenant must not do anything to purposely damage or destroy the property.

Mandatory Evacuation

The act entitles a tenant forced to evacuate a vacation rental by proper state or local authorities to a prorated refund unless the landlord/agent has offered the North Carolina Department of Insurance approved "interruption insurance" covering this possible risk to the tenant at a cost of 8% or less of the total rental amount charged to the tenant. The act also requires tenants to comply with a mandatory evacuation order by state and local government.

Payment of Commissions to Travel Agents

In response to requests from vacation rental agents and firms, North Carolina now permits the payment of commissions to unlicensed travel agents who arrange the rental of vacation properties. This request was in response to agents who were having difficulty competing with other states who allowed such practice. The travel agent must only introduce the tenant to the property manager who will handle the details of the lease. Such commissions can only be earned by travel agents who are handling these arrangements within the normal practice of their duties, and they cannot be paid the commission until after the lease term is completed.

"The payment of referral fees to travel agents is the ONLY exception in North Carolina law for the payment of compensation to a non-licensee."

—Deb Cox

NONFREEHOLD ESTATES

Estate for Years

The *lease creating an* **estate for years** *must be for a definite period of time.* The term "years" is a bit misleading as it means "period" rather than referencing calendar terminology. If there is any indefiniteness or vagueness regarding this matter, the contract will not create a lease in the form of an estate for years but will create a periodic tenancy or estate from year to year. A definite time period creates a lease in the form of an estate for years, even though the period may be for only six months, three months, or even less. Because of the definite period of time, the estate for years lease will expire automatically and does not require any notice to terminate. In situations in which the lease term expires and the tenant continues to pay rent, and the landlord continues to accept the rent payments, this lease will automatically renew for another fixed term. Because of this feature, most estate leases for years will stipulate they convert to an estate from period to period at the end of the fixed term to keep from converting to another fixed term should the tenant continue to pay rent.

> An ownership and a leasehold interest may coexist on a piece of property at the same time (i.e., landlord = ownership, tenant = leasehold).

Test Tip!

The term "years" simply denotes a specific period of time without regard to whether or not it involves an actual year.

Estate from Period to Period

An **estate from period to period** is commonly known as a **periodic tenancy** (and is also referred to as an *estate from year to year, month to month, or week to week*) and *is for an indefinite period of time*. An example of an estate from period to period is the typical residential lease. Its key feature is that *it automatically renews itself at the end of the period unless one party gives notice to the other during a prescribed time at the end of the estate*. The statutory notice for an estate from year to year, if none is stated in the lease, is one month. For example, if the required notice period is one month and the parties entered the last 30 days of the lease without notifying the other of any change, a new lease would automatically be created for another period at the same terms. A lease can specify a longer notice.

The first two estates are essentially opposite in terms of what happens at the end of their original lease period. The estate for years terminates, and the estate from period to period renews itself.

Estate at Will

In the **estate at will**, the duration of the *term is completely unknown* at the time the estate is created. This is because the estate at will *may be terminated by either party at will, by simply giving the other party notice*. For example, the owners of a property in Asheville might allow college students to occupy their home while they spend a portion of the winter in Florida. Both profit in that the owners have their home looked after in their absence, and the students have a place to stay for an indefinite period of time. Either party can terminate the arrangement, however, by simply providing notice to the other. The period of notice is instantaneous. In a residential property, the notice need be only a few days; in a vacation property, a few hours. If the tenant decides to vacate, he must inform the landlord of his decision as he does have some obligation to protect the owner's property. He cannot simply vacate without some degree of notice. If rent is paid and accepted, this type of tenancy is converted to a periodic tenancy. The key point is that in an estate for will the occupant is in possession with permission.

Because the law provides that the land should be productive, the tenant at will does have some rights protected. If crops were planted, the tenant would still have the right to harvest the crops planted during the tenancy, even if the lease was terminated.

Estate at Sufferance

An **estate at sufferance** is used to describe *someone who had originally been in lawful possession of another's property but whose right to possession was terminated*. This is someone who originally had permission to possess the property but no longer has permission to do so. The only reason the tenant is still in possession is that she has not yet been evicted. This could occur upon termination of any of the three previously discussed leasehold estates. The term is used to make a distinction between the tenant at sufferance who was originally in lawful possession of the property and someone who was on the property illegally from the beginning (trespasser). The estate at sufferance continues until such time that the property owner brings a legal action to evict the person wrongfully holding over or until the one holding over vacates voluntarily. During this period, the occupier is called a *tenant at sufferance* or *holdover tenant*. It is possible that a tenant still qualifies as a tenant at sufferance but continues to pay rent and seemingly has permission from the landlord to remain in possession. For example, a commercial tenant is at the end of her lease term, but her new building is not quite finished and ready for occupancy. Additionally, the landlord has not yet found a new tenant for this space. In this situation, the landlord can allow the tenant to remain as a tenant at sufferance, or a holdover tenant, until the new space is ready for occupancy and the tenant will continue to pay rent. The landlord will generally put such an agreement in writing stipulating that the tenant can continue to remain and pay rent but that she is considered a holdover tenant and eviction proceedings can be initiated at any time.

TYPES OF LEASES

Two primary classes of leases are based on the arrangement of paying the expenses of the rental property. A **gross lease** is one in which *the owner (lessor) pays all costs of operating and maintaining the property in addition to real property taxes and insurance.* A **net lease** means the *tenant (lessee) pays expenses, such as taxes, assessments, maintenance, insurance, and utilities.* Some use terms such as *net, double net,* or even *triple net,* but the two major classifications, gross and net, are more appropriate. Most residential leases are gross leases, whereas a commercial lease is often a net lease.

> "Estate at Sufferance occurs when the renter will not leave. The landlord 'suffers' because they must now evict the tenant who is in possession beyond the end of their lease term."
> —Jim Hriso

Fixed Rental (Flat or Gross)

A fixed rental lease, also known as a flat or gross lease, is one in which the rent does not change during the lease term. The landlord will collect a certain amount of rent and will be responsible for the expenses. The amount the landlord will actually get to keep each month is therefore uncertain. Because the North Carolina Residential Rental Agreements Act makes the landlord responsible for maintenance of the property, the gross lease is the most popular in residential tenancies.

Net

In a net lease, the lessee agrees to pay, in addition to the fixed rental, specified costs and expenses associated with the property. These costs and expenses may include such things as real estate taxes and assessments, maintenance, insurance, and utilities. As a result of these payments by the lessee, the rental income is a net income to the lessor.

In comparison with the gross lease, in the net lease, the landlord knows exactly how much money he will net in any given month, whereas the tenant does not know exactly how much he may have to pay for expenses in any given month. In the gross lease the tenant knows exactly how much he will have to pay each month, and it is the landlord who does not know how much he will net in a given month.

Percentage

Many commercial leases are **percentage leases**. The rent in a percentage lease includes a fairly low fixed amount of rent per month plus an additional monthly rent that is a percentage of the lessee's gross sales. The majority of commercial leases are percentage leases in cases in which the lessee is using the property to conduct a retail business. This is especially true of shopping malls. The percentage lease *provides the lessor with a guaranteed monthly rental plus the opportunity to participate in the sales volume of the lessee on a percentage basis.* The disadvantage of this type of lease is that the landlord also shares the risk of loss with the tenant.

Graduated

A **graduated lease** is one in which *the rental amount changes from period to period over the lease term.* The change in rental amount is specified in the lease contract. For example, a lease may be at $300 per month for the first year, $350 per month the second year, and $400 per month the third year. Both the landlord and the tenant know exactly when the increase will occur and how much it will be.

Index

An **index lease** is one in which *the rental amount is changed in proportion to changes in the Consumer Price Index* (CPI) published by the U.S. Department of Labor or other similar index. The lease specifies a percentage change in relation to the number of points the CPI changes annually. This type of lease is very common in office building rentals, although it is used in many different settings.

Full Service

Full-service leases are common in large multitenant office buildings and shopping centers. Under a full-service lease, the landlord provides all utilities and maintenance, and each *tenant pays a portion of the overall operating expenses* for the building and common areas in accordance with how many square feet they lease in addition to a base rent.

Ground

The **ground (land) lease** is a *lease of unimproved land.* It normally contains a provision that a building will be constructed on the land by the lessee. The lease should always contain a provision as to the disposition of the improvements on the land constructed by the lessee at the end of the lease term. In the absence of a provision as to the disposition of the improvements at the end of the lease term, the improvements automatically belong to the lessor as owner of the land. The ground lease is a long-term lease because the lessee must have sufficient time to recoup costs and earn a profit during the term of the lease. The advantage to the tenant is that land costs cannot be depreciated so the tax advantages may outweigh the risks of having to leave the building to the landlord at the end of the lease.

> "In a ground lease the tenant usually has the right to make improvements but does not obtain the rights to minerals, oil and gas."
> —Jim Fletemier

Mineral

The lessee under a mineral lease has the right to search for and mine minerals during the lease period. Like other parts of the bundle of rights in real property, mineral rights can be severed from other rights in land. A mineral lease must be in writing, regardless of the duration, to comply with the North Carolina Statute of Frauds.

Sale and Leaseback

A **sale and leaseback** is a transaction *wherein a property owner sells a property to an investor and the investor agrees to immediately lease the property back to the tenant.* The tenant, usually commercial, will essentially build a building to his specifications on land located where she wants it to be. The advantage to the tenant is that she can free up capital to further expand the business. Additionally, lease payments are fully deductible as a business expense.

COMMON LEASE PROVISIONS

Essential Provisions

The following are essential lease provisions:

1. **Mutual agreement.** There must be mutual agreement to the terms of the contract by parties who have the legal capacity to contract.
2. **Legal description.** The land must be identified clearly. A legal description is best, but usually a street address will suffice for a single-family dwelling.
3. **Terms and conditions.** All essential aspects of the agreement (rent, occupancy dates, terms, and so on) must be set forth.
4. **Consideration.** All valid lease contracts must be supported by legal consideration.
5. **Legal purpose.** The lease must contemplate a lawful objective.

Other Provisions

In addition to the essential elements of a valid lease, many provisions are often found in lease contracts. The following is a discussion of some of the more common provisions.

- **Tenant's use.** A lessor may wish to restrict the use of a rental unit (e.g., residential use only), or a lessee may want to make a specific use a condition of the lease (e.g., that a permit can be obtained to sell alcoholic beverages on the premises).
- **Environmental matters.** Provisions can prohibit the use, storage, or discharge of hazardous substances on the rented premises.
- **Fixtures.** If the lessee intends to add fixtures to the premises, a provision should address the issue of removal of these fixtures and the return of the premises to its original condition.
- **Repairs (nonresidential property).** Responsibility for repairs on commercial or industrial property depends on the type of property and specific lease provisions. Therefore, upkeep and repair responsibilities of the lessor and lessee should be carefully addressed in any such lease. Residential leases, in North Carolina, do not need to contain a clause stipulating who is to pay for repairs because the Residential Rental Agreements Act requires the landlord to accept responsibility.
- **Upfitting improvements.** *Upfitting* involves improvements to a commercial property at the lessor's expense to obtain or retain a tenant. An example would be when a tenant agrees to lease an office space and requires the landlord to renovate the space to meet the tenant's requirements as a condition of the lease.
- **Assignments and subleases.** A lease provision can restrict or prohibit a lessee's right to *assign* or *sublease* the premises. *Assignment* is the total transfer of the lessee's rights and obligations remaining in the lease. In an assignment, the original tenant is not returning to regain possession of the leased premises. The original tenant is referred to as the assignor and the new tenant is referred to as the assignee. In the assignment, the new tenant (assignee) will pay his rent directly to the landlord. In the event that he does not pay, the original tenant (assignor) will be held "secondarily" liable. This is similar to being a co-signor on a note. In North Carolina, a lease is generally assignable any time that it is not prohibited. In the event the lease is silent regarding such assignment, the rule is that it will be allowed since it was not prohibited.
- **Default.** A well-drafted lease provides for legal remedies by the lessor and the lessee in the event of default. The most common forms of default would include the nonpayment of rent, damage to the property exceeding ordinary wear and tear, and nonfulfillment of the lease term.

> ### Test Tip!
>
> Students should be aware of the difference between an assignment of a lease and a sublease. A prohibition against an assignment will in no way affect the ability to sublease and any prohibition against subleasing will in no way affect the ability to assign. If the landlord wishes to prohibit assignments as well as subleasing, *both* must be specifically stated in the lease.

- A sublease (also referred to as sublet or a sandwich lease) is the partial transfer of remaining lease rights and obligations. Unlike in an assignment, the original tenant will be returning to regain possession even if it is on the final day of the lease and would be largely symbolic. The original tenant is referred to as the sublessor and the new tenant is the sublessee. In the sublease, the new tenant (sublessee) pays her rent directly to the original tenant (sublessor) who in turn continues to pay the landlord. A sublease does not relieve the original lessee of her liability under the terms of the original lease. The sublessor is liable for payment to the landlord regardless of whether the sublessee has paid her the rent or not. The sublessor is not limited to leasing the property for the stated rent in his lease. Sublessors may lease the property to the sublessee for more than they are paying the landlord or for less.

- Very similar in theory to the assignment mentioned previously, the original tenant may sublease the property any time that it is not prohibited. Silence in the lease does not constitute a prohibition and subleasing will be permitted. Remember that a prohibition against an assignment in no way prohibits subleasing and a prohibition against subleasing in no way prohibits an assignment. If the landlord wished to prohibit both, he must specifically stipulate in the lease that neither will be allowed.

- **Renewal of lease.** Unless there is an express provision for renewal of the lease, a lessee does not have an implied right to renew her lease. The fact that a landlord has renewed the lease in the past in no way places him under an obligation to do so in the future.
- **Option to purchase/right of first refusal.** A lease provision giving the tenant an *option to purchase* should specify a purchase price, the type of conveyance to be made by the grantor/lessor, and the time and manner in which the lessee must exercise his option. A lease may also contain a provision for *right of first refusal,* whereby the tenant has the right to the first opportunity to purchase the property in the event the lessor decides to sell. The primary difference between the two is that in an option agreement the landlord would be required to sell if the tenant wished to purchase and the right of first refusal does not obligate the landlord to ever agree to sell.

- **Landlord's right to enter premises.** Often provisions are used that give the landlord the right to enter the premises during the lease term to inspect the property, make necessary repairs, respond to an emergency, or show the premises to prospective buyers or tenants. Landlords must be careful to understand that just because they own the property, it does not mean they have the rights of re-entry. Lease contracts give the tenant the rights of possession and a landlord can be arrested for trespassing on her own property if she were to enter the premises without consent from the tenant.

Figure 15.1 reproduces pages 1 to 7 of NCAR's Residential Rental Contract. Following this figure is a summary of some of the major aspects included on this form. The names of the landlord (lessor) and tenant(s) (lessees) appear at the top of the form.

- The duration of the initial term of the contract is given. The period of the contract and specific starting and ending dates are given.
- The due dates of the first and subsequent rental payments are set forth.
- The amount of rent and the period for paying rent (yearly, monthly, weekly) are specified.
- Late payment fees are specified.
- The amount of security deposit and the name of the bank that will hold the deposit are specified.
- The tenant's responsibility to pay for returned check fees for each check of the tenant that is returned for insufficient funds is specified.
- Number and type of pets, if allowed, and the nonrefundable pet deposit are specified.
- Permitted occupants in addition to tenant are named.

1. This paragraph describes what is to happen at the end of this initial term. The lessor or lessee can give notice to terminate. If notice is not given, the initial term is then modified to a shorter period-to-period tenancy.
2. This paragraph informs the tenant when the first and subsequent rental payments will be due and that the tenant shall pay the rent on those dates without notice, demand, or deduction.
3. This paragraph informs the tenant that a late payment fee will be due if rent is not paid by midnight on the fifth day after it is due. The tenant is also responsible for paying the returned check fees for each check of the tenant that is returned for insufficient funds.
4. The lease clearly explains how the tenant security deposit must be handled and how and when it may be used or disbursed as dictated by the North Carolina Tenant Security Deposit Act. The amount of the deposit must be within the statutory limits. A real estate agent must handle such funds through his agency trust account and inform the tenant of the location of the depository

RESIDENTIAL RENTAL CONTRACT

RESIDENT: _____("Tenant")

OWNER: _____("Landlord")

REAL ESTATE MANAGEMENT FIRM: _____("Agent")

PREMISES: City:_____ County: _____ State of North Carolina
  ❑ Street Address:_____ Zip Code:_____
  ❑ Apartment Complex:_____Apartment No. _____
  ❑ Other Description (Room, portion of above address, etc.):_____
_____

INITIAL TERM: Beginning Date of Lease: _____ Ending Date of Lease: _____

RENT: $ _____ PAYMENT PERIOD: ❑ monthly ❑ weekly ❑ yearly ❑ other:_____

LATE PAYMENT FEE: $_____ OR _____% of rental payment, whichever is greater
(State law provides that the late fee may not exceed $15.00 or five percent (5%) of the rental payment, whichever is greater.)
RETURNED CHECK FEE: $ _____ *(The maximum processing fee allowed under State law is $25.00.)*
SECURITY DEPOSIT: $ _____ to be deposited with: (check one) ❑ Landlord ❑ Agent
LOCATION OF DEPOSIT: (insert name of bank): _____
BANK ADDRESS: _____

FEES FOR COMPLAINT FOR SUMMARY EJECTMENT AND/OR MONEY OWED (See paragraph 17) (NOTE: Landlord may charge and retain only one of the following fees in addition to any court costs):
- COMPLAINT-FILING FEE: $_____ OR _____% of rental payment, whichever is greater *(Fee may not exceed $15.00 or five percent (5%) of the rental payment, whichever is greater.)*
- COURT APPEARANCE FEE: _____% of rental payment *(Fee may not exceed ten percent (10%) of the rental payment.)*
- SECOND TRIAL FEE: _____% of rental payment *(Fee may not exceed twelve percent (12%) of the rental payment.)*

PERMITTED OCCUPANTS (in addition to Tenant):_____
_____

CONTACT PERSON IN EVENT OF DEATH OR EMERGENCY OF TENANT (name and contact information):_____
_____

  IN CONSIDERATION of the promises contained in this Agreement, Landlord, by and through Agent, hereby agrees to lease the Premises to Tenant on the following terms and conditions:

  1. Termination and Renewal:
  (a) **Termination at End of Initial Term**. EITHER LANDLORD OR TENANT MAY TERMINATE THE TENANCY AT THE EXPIRATION OF THE INITIAL TERM BY GIVING WRITTEN NOTICE TO THE OTHER AT LEAST _____ DAYS PRIOR TO THE EXPIRATION DATE OF THE INITIAL TERM.
  (b) **Renewal**. IN THE EVENT SUCH WRITTEN NOTICE IS NOT GIVEN OR IF THE TENANT HOLDS OVER BEYOND THE INITIAL TERM, THE TENANCY SHALL AUTOMATICALLY BECOME A _____ (PERIOD) TO _____ (PERIOD) TENANCY UPON THE SAME TERMS AND CONDITIONS CONTAINED HEREIN.
  (c) **Termination at End of Renewal Term**. IF THE TENANCY IS RENEWED ON A CALENDAR MONTH-TO-MONTH BASIS, IT MAY THEREAFTER BE TERMINATED BY EITHER LANDLORD OR TENANT GIVING THE OTHER WRITTEN NOTICE, WITH THE TERMINATION TO BE EFFECTIVE ON THE LAST DAY OF THE CALENDAR MONTH FOLLOWING THE CALENDAR MONTH DURING WHICH THE NOTICE IS GIVEN. IF THE TENANCY IS RENEWED ON ANYTHING OTHER THAN A CALENDAR MONTH-TO-MONTH BASIS, THE TENANCY MAY BE TERMINATED BY EITHER LANDLORD OR TENANT GIVING THE OTHER _____ DAYS WRITTEN NOTICE PRIOR TO THE LAST DAY OF THE FINAL PERIOD OF THE TENANCY, WITH THE TERMINATION TO BE EFFECTIVE ON THE LAST DAY OF THE FINAL PERIOD OF THE TENANCY.

North Carolina Association of REALTORS®, Inc.

Tenant Initials _____ _____

STANDARD FORM 410-T
Revised 8/2018
© 8/2018

FIGURE 15.1 Residential rental contract.

(**NOTE:** State and Federal law permit early termination of leases under certain circumstances by members of the United States Armed Forces. For information, see *Questions and Answers on: North Carolina Military Personnel Residential Lease Termination*, available on the website of the NC Real Estate Commission at www.ncrec.gov).

2. **Rent:** Tenant shall pay the Rent, without notice, demand or deduction, to Landlord or as Landlord directs. The first Rent payment, which shall be prorated if the Initial Term commences on a day other than the first day of the Payment Period, shall be due on _____ (date). Thereafter, all rentals shall be paid in advance on or before the **FIRST** day of each subsequent Payment Period for the duration of the tenancy. Rentals not paid on or before the first day of the Payment Period will be considered late, and any such non-payment will constitute a breach of this Agreement.

3. **Late Payment Fees and Returned Check Fees:** Tenant shall pay the Late Payment Fee if any rental payment is five (5) days or more late. *This late payment fee shall be due immediately without demand therefor and shall be added to and paid with the late rental payment. Tenant also agrees to pay the Returned Check Fee for each check of Tenant that is returned by the financial institution because of insufficient funds or because the Tenant did not have an account at the financial institution.*

4. **Tenant Security Deposit:** The Security Deposit shall be administered in accordance with the North Carolina Tenant Security Deposit Act (N.C.G.S. § 42-50 et. seq.). IT MAY, IN THE DISCRETION OF EITHER THE LANDLORD OR THE AGENT, BE DEPOSITED IN AN INTEREST-BEARING ACCOUNT WITH THE BANK OR SAVINGS INSTITUTION NAMED ABOVE. ANY INTEREST EARNED UPON THE TENANT SECURITY DEPOSIT SHALL ACCRUE FOR THE BENEFIT OF, AND SHALL BE PAID TO, THE LANDLORD, OR AS THE LANDLORD DIRECTS. SUCH INTEREST, IF ANY, MAY BE WITHDRAWN BY LANDLORD OR AGENT FROM SUCH ACCOUNT AS IT ACCRUES AS OFTEN AS IS PERMITTED BY THE TERMS OF THE ACCOUNT.

Upon any termination of the tenancy herein created, the Landlord may deduct from the Tenant Security Deposit amounts permitted under the Tenant Security Deposit Act. If there is more than one person listed above as Tenant, Agent may, in Agent's discretion, pay any balance of the Tenant Security Deposit to any such person, and the other person(s) agree to hold Agent harmless for such action. If the Tenant's address is unknown to the Landlord, the Landlord may deduct any permitted amounts and shall then hold the balance of the Tenant Security Deposit for the Tenant's collection.

If the Landlord removes Agent or Agent resigns, the Tenant agrees that Agent may transfer any Tenant Security Deposit held by Agent hereunder to the Landlord or the Landlord's designee and thereafter notify the Tenant by mail of such transfer and of the transferee's name and address. The Tenant agrees that such action by Agent shall relieve Agent of further liability with respect to the Tenant Security Deposit. If Landlord's interest in the Premises terminates (whether by sale, assignment, death, appointment of receiver or otherwise), Agent shall transfer the Tenant Security Deposit in accordance with the provisions of North Carolina General Statutes § 42-54.

5. **Tenant's Obligations:** Unless otherwise agreed upon, the Tenant shall:
(a) use the Premises for residential purposes only and in a manner so as not to disturb the other tenants;
(b) not use the Premises for any unlawful or immoral purposes or occupy them in such a way as to constitute a nuisance;
(c) not engage in, or permit any member of Tenant's household or any guest to engage in, criminal activity on or in the immediate vicinity of any portion of the Premises;
(d) keep the Premises, including but not limited to all plumbing fixtures, facilities and appliances, in a clean and safe condition;
(e) cause no unsafe or unsanitary condition in the common areas and remainder of the Premises used by him;
(f) comply with any and all obligations imposed upon tenants by applicable building and housing codes;
(g) dispose of all ashes, rubbish, garbage, and other waste in a clean and safe manner and comply with all applicable ordinances concerning garbage collection, waste and other refuse;
(h) use in a proper and reasonable manner all electrical, plumbing, sanitary, heating, ventilating, air conditioning, and other facilities and appliances, if any, furnished as a part of the Premises;
(i) not deliberately or negligently destroy, deface, damage or remove any part of the Premises (including all facilities, appliances or fixtures) or permit any person, known or unknown to the Tenant, to do so;
(j) pay the costs of all utility services to the Premises which are billed directly to the Tenant and not included as a part of the rentals, including, but not limited to, water, electric, telephone, and gas services;
(k) conduct himself and require all other persons on the Premises with his consent to conduct themselves in a reasonable manner and so as not to disturb other tenants' peaceful enjoyment of the Premises;
(l) not abandon or vacate the Premises during the Initial Term or any renewals or extensions thereof. Tenant shall be deemed to have abandoned or vacated the Premises if Tenant removes substantially all of his possessions from the Premises;
(m) not smoke cigarettes, cigars, pipes or any other tobacco or lighted product of any kind in any interior portion of the Premises, including any detached structures, and to pay the cost of any abatement, cleaning, ductwork replacement that may be necessary as a result of Tenant's failure to comply with this obligation; and

Page 2 of 8

STANDARD FORM 410-T
Revised 8/2018
© 8/2018

Tenant Initials _____ _____

FIGURE 15.1 (*Continued*)

(n)_____
_____
_____

6. **Landlord's Obligations:** Unless otherwise agreed upon, the Landlord shall:

(a) comply with the applicable building and housing codes to the extent required by such building and housing codes;

(b) make all repairs to the Premises as may be necessary to keep the Premises in a fit and habitable condition; provided, however, in accordance with paragraph 11, the Tenant shall be liable to the Landlord for any repairs necessitated by the Tenant's intentional or negligent misuse of the Premises;

(c) keep all common areas, if any, used in conjunction with the Premises in a clean and safe condition;

(d) promptly repair all facilities and appliances, if any, as may be furnished by the Landlord as part of the Premises, including electrical, plumbing, sanitary, heating, ventilating, and air conditioning systems, provided that the Landlord, except in emergency situations, actually receives notification from the Tenant in writing of the needed repairs; and

(e) within a reasonable period of time based upon the severity of the condition, repair or remedy any imminently dangerous condition on the Premises after acquiring actual knowledge or receiving notice of the condition. Notwithstanding Landlord's repair or remedy of any imminently dangerous condition, Landlord may recover from Tenant the actual and reasonable costs of repairs that are the fault of Tenant.

7. **Utility Bills/Service Contracts:** Landlord and Tenant agree that utility bills and service contracts ("Service Obligations") for the Premises shall be paid by the party indicated below as to each Service Obligation. The party agreeing to be responsible for payment of a Service Obligation agrees to timely pay the applicable Service Obligation, including any metering, hook-up fees or other miscellaneous charges associated with establishing, installing and maintaining such utility or contract in that party's name. Within thirty (30) days of the Beginning Date of this Lease, Tenant shall provide Landlord with a copy of any requested information about any Service Obligation for which Tenant has agreed to be responsible. Any Service Obligation not designated below shall be the responsibility of Tenant unless the parties agree otherwise in writing.

Service obligation	Landlord	Tenant	N/A
Sewer/Septic	❏	❏	❏
Water	❏	❏	❏
Electric	❏	❏	❏
Gas	❏	❏	❏
Telephone	❏	❏	❏
Security System	❏	❏	❏
Trash disposal/dumpster	❏	❏	❏
Landscaping	❏	❏	❏
Lawn Maintenance	❏	❏	❏
	❏	❏	❏
	❏	❏	❏
	❏	❏	❏

8. **Smoke and Carbon Monoxide Alarms:** Pursuant to North Carolina General Statutes § 42-42, the Landlord shall provide operable smoke alarms, either battery-operated or electrical. If the Premises has a fossil-fuel burning heater, appliance, or fireplace, or an attached garage, the Landlord shall provide and install a minimum of one operable carbon monoxide alarm per level in the

Tenant Initials _____ _____

FIGURE 15.1 (*Continued*)

Premises, either battery operated or electrical. The Tenant shall notify the Landlord, in writing, of the need for replacement of or repairs to a smoke or carbon monoxide alarm. The Landlord shall replace or repair the smoke or carbon monoxide alarm within 15 days of receipt of notification if the Landlord is notified of needed replacement or repairs in writing by the Tenant. The Landlord shall ensure that a smoke or carbon monoxide alarm is operable and in good repair at the beginning of the Initial Term of the Tenancy. The Landlord shall place new batteries in any battery-operated smoke or carbon monoxide alarms at the beginning of the Initial Term of the tenancy **and the Tenant shall replace the batteries as needed during the tenancy**, except where the smoke alarm is a tamper-resistant, 10-year lithium battery smoke alarm.

9. **Rules and Regulations:**

   (a) **Landlord Rules and Regulations:** The Tenant, his family, servants, guests and agents shall comply with and abide by all the Landlord's existing rules and regulations and such future reasonable rules and regulations as the Landlord may, at Landlord's discretion, from time to time, adopt governing the use and occupancy of the Premises and any common areas used in connection with them (the "Rules and Regulations"). Landlord reserves the right to make changes to the existing Rules and Regulations and to adopt additional reasonable rules and regulations from time to time; provided however, such changes and additions shall not alter the essential terms of this lease or any substantive rights granted hereunder and shall not become effective until thirty (30) days' written notice thereof shall have been furnished to Tenant. A copy of the existing Rules and Regulations are attached hereto and the Tenant acknowledges that he has read them. The Rules and Regulations shall be deemed to be a part of this lease giving to the Landlord all the rights and remedies herein provided.

   (b) ❑ (*check if applicable*) **Owner Association Rules and Regulations:** The Premises are subject to regulation by the following owners/condo association:
   - Name of association:____ _____
   - Name of association property manager:_____
   - Property manager address and phone number:_____
   - Association website address, if any: _____

   Tenant agrees to abide by any applicable owners' association regulations as they now exist or may be amended.

10. **Right of Entry:** Landlord hereby reserves the right to Landlord, Agent and their respective agents and representatives to enter the Premises during reasonable hours for the purpose of (1) inspecting the Premises and the Tenant's compliance with the terms of this lease; (2) making such repairs, alterations, improvements or additions thereto as they may deem appropriate; (3) showing the Premises to prospective purchasers or tenants; and (4) displaying "For Sale" or "For Rent" signs in a reasonable manner upon the Premises. Tenant acknowledges and understands that in the case of an emergency, the Landlord, Agent and their agents and representatives may need to enter the Premises at any hour to cause repairs to be made to preserve or prevent further damage from occurring to the Premises, and the Tenant agrees to cooperate reasonably with them in the event of any such emergency.

11. **Damages:** Tenant shall be responsible for all damage, defacement, or removal of any property inside a dwelling unit in the Tenant's exclusive control unless the damage, defacement or removal was due to ordinary wear and tear, acts of the Landlord or the Landlord's agent, defective products supplied or repairs authorized by the Landlord, acts of third parties not invitees of the Tenant, or natural forces. Tenant agrees to pay Landlord for the cost of repairing any damage for which Tenant is responsible upon receipt of Landlord's demand therefor, and to pay the Rent during the period the Premises may not be habitable as a result of any such damage. Such damage may include but is not limited to window panes or screens damaged by Tenant, filthy ovens, refrigerators, kitchen floors, cabinets or bathrooms, drink stains on carpet, and unauthorized paint colors.

12. **Pets:** Tenant agrees not to keep or allow anywhere on or about the Premises any animals or pets of any kind, whether on a temporary basis or otherwise and whether belonging to the Tenant or anybody else, including but not limited to, dogs, cats, birds, rodents, reptiles or marine animals, unless permitted under the terms of a Pet Addendum attached to this Agreement. Tenant shall be subject to a fine of $_____ for any violation of this paragraph or of the terms of any Pet Addendum that may be a part of this Agreement, and Tenant agrees to pay any such fine upon receipt of Landlord's demand therefore.

13. **Alterations**: The Tenant shall not paint, mark, drive nails or screws into, or otherwise deface or alter walls, ceilings, floors, windows, cabinets, woodwork, stone, ironwork or any other part of the Premises, decorate the Premises, change or remove any existing locks or add any additional locks, or make any alterations, additions, or improvements in, to, on or about the Premises without the Landlord's prior written consent and then only in a workmanlike manner using materials and contractors approved by the Landlord. All such work shall be done at the Tenant's expense and at such times and in such manner as the Landlord may approve, and keys for any changed or additional locks shall immediately be provided to the Landlord. All alterations, additions, and improvements upon the Premises, made by either the Landlord or Tenant, shall become the property of the Landlord and shall remain upon and become a part of the Premises at the end of the tenancy hereby created.

Tenant Initials _____ _____

FIGURE 15.1 (*Continued*)

14. **Occupants:** The Tenant shall not allow or permit the Premises to be occupied or used as a residence by any person other than Tenant and the Permitted Occupants. Tenant shall be subject to a fine of $ _____ for any violation of this paragraph, and Tenant agrees to pay any such fine upon receipt of Landlord's demand therefor.

15. **Rental Application:** In the event the Tenant has submitted a Rental Application in connection with this lease, Tenant acknowledges that the Landlord has relied upon the Application as an inducement for entering into this Lease and Tenant warrants to Landlord that the facts stated in the Application are true to the best of Tenant's knowledge. If any facts stated in the Rental Application prove to be untrue, the Landlord shall have the right to terminate the tenancy and to collect from Tenant any damages resulting therefrom.

16. **Tenant's Duties Upon Termination:** Upon any termination of the Tenancy created hereby, whether by the Landlord or the Tenant and whether for breach or otherwise, the Tenant shall: (1) pay all utility bills due for services to the Premises for which he is responsible and have all such utility services discontinued; (2) vacate the Premises removing there from all Tenant's personal property of whatever nature; (3) properly sweep and clean the Premises, including plumbing fixtures, refrigerators, stoves and sinks, removing there from all rubbish, trash, garbage and refuse; (4) make such repairs and perform such other acts as are necessary to return the Premises, and any appliances or fixtures furnished in connection therewith, in the same condition as when Tenant took possession of the Premises; provided, however, Tenant shall not be responsible for ordinary wear and tear or for repairs required by law or by paragraph 6 above to be performed by Landlord; (5) fasten and lock all doors and windows; (6) return to the Landlord any and all keys, other access devices, parking and pool passes, garage door openers and other similar items to the Premises and any amenities; (7) restore the level of fuel in any fuel tank used by the Tenant to its level as of the Beginning Date of the Tenancy; and (8) notify the Landlord of the address to which the balance of the Security Deposit may be returned. If the Tenant fails to sweep out and clean the Premises, appliances and fixtures as herein provided, Tenant shall become liable, without notice or demand, to the Landlord for the actual costs of cleaning (over and above ordinary wear and tear), which may be deducted from the Security Deposit as provided in paragraph 4 above.

In the event Tenant desires to terminate the Tenancy prior to the end of its term then in effect, Tenant acknowledges and understands that the Landlord will use reasonable efforts to re-rent the Premises, but that the Tenant shall remain responsible for the performance of all the Tenant's obligations under this Agreement until such time as the Landlord may be able to re-rent the Premises, unless the Landlord and the Tenant agree otherwise in writing.

17. **Tenant's Breach:**
   (a) **Events Constituting Breach:** It shall constitute a breach of this Agreement if Tenant fails to:
      (i) pay the full amount of rent herein reserved as and when it shall become due hereunder; or
      (ii) perform any other promise, duty or obligation herein agreed to by him or imposed upon him by law and such failure shall continue for a period of five (5) days from the date the Landlord provides Tenant with written notice of such failure.

In either of such events and as often as either of them may occur, the Landlord, in addition to all other rights and remedies provided by law, may, at its option and with or without notice to Tenant, either terminate this lease or terminate the Tenant's right to possession of the Premises without terminating this lease.

   (b) **Landlord's Right to Possession:** Regardless of whether Landlord terminates this lease or only terminates the Tenant's right of possession without terminating this lease, Landlord shall be immediately entitled to possession of the Premises and the Tenant shall peacefully surrender possession of the Premises to Landlord immediately upon Landlord's demand. In the event Tenant shall fail or refuse to surrender possession of the Premises, Landlord shall, in compliance with Article 2A of Chapter 42 of the General Statutes of North Carolina, reenter and retake possession of the Premises only through a summary ejectment proceeding.

   (c) **Fees/Costs of Summary Ejectment Proceeding:** If a summary ejectment proceeding is instituted against Tenant, Landlord shall be entitled to recover from Tenant the following fees/costs in accordance with NC General Statutes §42-46: (i) filing fees charged by the court, (ii) costs for service of process, (iii) the relevant Complaint-Filing Fee, Court Appearance Fee or Second Trial Fee, and, (iv) reasonable attorneys' fees actually incurred not to exceed fifteen percent (15%) of the amount owed by Tenant, or fifteen percent (15%) of the monthly rent stated in this Agreement if the summary ejectment proceeding is based on a default other than the nonpayment of rent.

   (d) **Acceptance of Partial Rent:** Tenant acknowledges and understands that Landlord's acceptance of partial rent or partial housing subsidy will not waive Tenant's breach of this Agreement or limit Landlord's rights to evict Tenant through a summary ejectment proceeding, whether filed before or after Landlord's acceptance of any such partial rent or partial housing subsidy.

   (e) **Termination of Lease:** In the event Landlord terminates this lease, all further rights and duties hereunder shall terminate and Landlord shall be entitled to collect from Tenant all accrued but unpaid rents and any damages resulting from the Tenant's breach, including but not limited to damages for Tenant's continued occupancy of the Premises following the Landlord's termination.

Page 5 of 8

STANDARD FORM 410-T
Revised 8/2018
© 8/2018

Tenant Initials _____ _____

FIGURE 15.1 (*Continued*)

(f) **Termination of Tenant's Right of Possession:** In the event Landlord terminates the Tenant's right of possession without terminating this lease, Tenant shall remain liable for the full performance of all the covenants hereof, and Landlord shall use reasonable efforts to re-let the Premises on Tenant's behalf. Any such rentals reserved from such re-letting shall be applied first to the costs of re-letting the Premises and then to the rentals due hereunder. In the event the rentals from such re-letting are insufficient to pay the rentals due hereunder in full, Tenant shall be liable to the Landlord for any deficiency. In the event Landlord institutes a legal action against the Tenant to enforce the lease or to recover any sums due hereunder, Tenant agrees to pay Landlord reasonable attorney's fees in addition to all other damages.

18. **Landlord's Default; Limitation of Remedies and Damages**: Until the Tenant notifies the Landlord in writing of an alleged default and affords the Landlord a reasonable time within which to cure, no default by the Landlord in the performance of any of the promises or obligations herein agreed to by him or imposed upon him by law shall constitute a material breach of this lease and the Tenant shall have no right to terminate this lease for any such default or suspend his performance hereunder. In no event and regardless of their duration shall any defective condition of or failure to repair, maintain, or provide any area, fixture or facility used in connection with recreation or recreational activities, including but not limited to swimming pools, club houses, and tennis courts, constitute a material breach of this lease and the Tenant shall have no right to terminate this lease or to suspend his performance hereunder. In any legal action instituted by the Tenant against the Landlord, the Tenant's damages shall be limited to the difference, if any, between the rent reserved in this lease and the reasonable rental value of the Premises, taking into account the Landlord's breach or breaches, and in no event, except in the case of the Landlord's willful or wanton negligence, shall the Tenant collect any consequential or secondary damages resulting from the breach or breaches, including but not limited to the following items: damage or destruction of furniture or other personal property of any kind located in or about the Premises, moving expenses, storage expenses, alternative interim housing expenses, and expenses of locating and procuring alternative housing.

19. **Bankruptcy:** If any bankruptcy or insolvency proceedings are filed by or against the Tenant or if the Tenant makes any assignment for the benefit of creditors, the Landlord may, at his option, immediately terminate this Tenancy, and reenter and repossess the Premises, subject to the provisions of the Bankruptcy Code (11 USC Section 101, et. seq.) and the order of any court having jurisdiction thereunder.

20. **Tenant's Insurance; Release and Indemnity Provisions:**
(a) **Personal Property Insurance** (*Tenant initial if applicable**):
_____ _____ Tenant shall be required to obtain and maintain throughout the term of the tenancy a renter's insurance policy, which policy shall, without cost to Landlord or Agent, name Landlord and Agent as an additional insured, and to promptly provide Landlord evidence of such insurance upon Landlord's request. In addition to coverage for damage or loss to Tenant's personal property in such amount as Tenant may determine, the policy shall include coverage for bodily injury and property damage for which Tenant may be liable in the amount of _____.
*If not initialed, Tenant shall not be required to obtain a renter's insurance policy
(b) Whether or not Tenant is required to obtain a renter's insurance policy, Tenant shall be solely responsible for insuring any of his personal property located or stored upon the Premises upon the risks of damage, destruction, or loss resulting from theft, fire, storm and all other hazards and casualties. Regardless of whether the Tenant secures such insurance, the Landlord and his agents shall not be liable for any damage to, or destruction or loss of, any of the Tenant's personal property located or stored upon the Premises regardless of the cause or causes of such damage, destruction, or loss, unless such loss or destruction is attributable to the intentional acts or willful or wanton negligence of the Landlord.
(c) The Tenant agrees to release and indemnify the Landlord and his agents from and against liability for injury to the person of the Tenant or to any members of his household resulting from any cause whatsoever except only such personal injury caused by the negligent, or intentional acts of the Landlord or his agents.

21. **Agent:** The Landlord and the Tenant acknowledge that the Landlord may, from time to time in his discretion, engage a third party ("the Agent") to manage, supervise and operate the Premises or the complex, if any, of which they are a part. If such an Agent is managing, supervising and operating the Premises at the time this lease is executed, his name will be shown as "Agent" on the first page hereof. With respect to any Agent engaged pursuant to this paragraph, the Landlord and the Tenant hereby agree that: (1) Agent acts for and represents Landlord in this transaction; (2) Agent shall have only such authority as provided in the management contract existing between the Landlord and Agent; (3) Agent may perform without objection from the Tenant, any obligation or exercise any right of the Landlord imposed or given herein or by law and such performance shall be valid and binding, if authorized by the Landlord, as if performed by the Landlord; (4) the Tenant shall pay all rents to the Agent if directed to do so by the Landlord; (5) except as otherwise provided by law, the Agent shall not be liable to the Tenant for the nonperformance of the obligations or promises of the Landlord contained herein; (6) nothing contained herein shall modify the management contract existing between the Landlord and the Agent; however, the Landlord and the Agent may from time to time modify the management agreement in any manner which they deem appropriate; (7) the Landlord, may, in his discretion and in accordance with any management agreement, remove without replacing or remove and replace any agent engaged to manage, supervise and operate the Premises.

Page 6 of 8

Tenant Initials _____ _____

STANDARD FORM 410-T
Revised 8/2018
© 8/2018

FIGURE 15.1 (*Continued*)

22. **Form**: The Landlord and Tenant hereby acknowledge that their agreement is evidenced by this form contract which may contain some minor inaccuracies when applied to the particular factual setting of the parties. The Landlord and Tenant agree that the courts shall liberally and broadly interpret this lease, ignoring minor inconsistencies and inaccuracies, and that the courts shall apply the lease to determine all disputes between the parties in the manner which most effectuates their intent as expressed herein. The following rules of construction shall apply: (1) handwritten and typed additions or alterations shall control over the preprinted language when there is an inconsistency between them; (2) the lease shall not be strictly construed against either the Landlord or the Tenant; (3) paragraph headings are used only for convenience of reference and shall not be considered as a substantive part of this lease; (4) words in the singular shall include the plural and the masculine shall include the feminine and neuter genders, as appropriate; and (5) the invalidity of one or more provisions of this lease shall not affect the validity of any other provisions hereof and this lease shall be construed and enforced as if such invalid provision(s) were not included.

23. **Amendment of Laws:** In the event that subsequent to the execution of this lease any state statute regulating or affecting any duty or obligation imposed upon the Landlord pursuant to this lease is enacted, amended, or repealed, the Landlord may, at his option, elect to perform in accordance with such statute, amendment, or act of repeal in lieu of complying with the analogous provision of this lease.

24. **Eminent Domain and Casualties:** The Landlord shall have the option to terminate this lease if the Premises, or any part thereof, are condemned or sold in lieu of condemnation or damaged by fire or other casualty.

25. **Assignment:** The Tenant shall not assign this lease or sublet the Premises in whole or part.

26. **Waiver:** No waiver of any breach of any obligation or promise contained herein shall be regarded as a waiver of any future breach of the same or any other obligation or promise.

27. **Joint and Several Liability:** If there are multiple persons listed as Tenant, their obligations under this Agreement shall be joint and several.

28. **Other Terms and Conditions:**
   (a) If there is an Agent involved in this transaction, Agent hereby discloses to Tenant that Agent is acting for and represents Landlord.
   (b) Itemize all addenda to this Contract and attach hereto:
   ❑ Disclosure of Information on Lead-Based Paint and Lead-Based Paint Hazards (form 430-T) (if Premises built prior to 1978)
   ❑ Maintenance Addendum (form 440-T)
   ❑ Pet Addendum (form 442-T)
   ❑ OTHER: _____
   _____

   (c) The following additional terms and conditions shall also be a part of this lease: _____
   _____
   _____
   _____
   _____

29. **Inspection of Premises:** Within _____ days of occupying the Premises, Tenant has the right to inspect the Premises and complete a Move-in Inspection Form.

30. **Tenant Information:** Tenant acknowledges and understands that during or after the term of this Agreement, the Landlord may provide information about Tenant or relating to the Tenancy in accordance with applicable laws, including but not limited to providing such information to a credit reporting agency.

31. **Execution; Counterparts:** When Tenant signs this lease, he acknowledges he has read and agrees to the provisions of this lease. This lease is executed in_____ (number) counterparts with an executed counterpart being retained by each party.

32. **Entire Agreement:** This Agreement contains the entire agreement of the parties and there are no representations, inducements or other provisions other than those expressed in writing. All changes, additions or deletions hereto must be in writing and signed by all parties.

STANDARD FORM 410-T
Revised 8/2018
© 8/2018

Tenant Initials _____ _____

FIGURE 15.1 (*Continued*)

33. **Use of Electronic Means; Notice.** The parties agree that electronic means may be used to sign this Agreement or to make any modifications the parties may agree to, and that any written notice, communication or documents may be transmitted electronically to any e-mail address, cell phone number or fax number used by the parties to communicate during the course of this Agreement. Any notices required or authorized to be given hereunder or pursuant to applicable law may also be mailed or hand delivered to the Tenant at the address of the Premises and to the Landlord at the address of the Agent.

THE NORTH CAROLINA ASSOCIATION OF REALTORS®, INC. MAKES NO REPRESENTATION AS TO THE LEGAL VALIDITY OR ADEQUACY OF ANY PROVISION OF THIS FORM IN ANY SPECIFIC TRANSACTION.

LANDLORD: _____

LANDLORD: _____

BY: AGENT: _____
               [Name of real estate firm]

By: _____ Individual license # _____ Date: _____
    [Signature of authorized representative]

Address: _____

Telephone: _____ Fax: _____ E-mail: _____

TENANT: _____ Date: _____
    [Tenant signature]
Contact information: _____ _____ _____ _____
                       Home   Work   Cell   Email

TENANT: _____ Date: _____
    [Tenant signature]
Contact information: _____ _____ _____ _____
                       Home   Work   Cell   Email

TENANT: _____ Date: _____
    [Tenant signature]
Contact information: _____ _____ _____ _____
                       Home   Work   Cell   Email

TENANT: _____ Date: _____
    [Tenant signature]
Contact information: _____ _____ _____ _____
                       Home   Work   Cell   Email

STANDARD FORM 410-T
Revised 8/2018
© 8/2018

FIGURE 15.1 (*Continued*)

where the security deposit is held in trust. Accounting procedures are strictly regulated by Rule A.0107 of the Real Estate Commission. Although private (non–real estate agent) landlords have the option of guaranteeing the return of these funds with an insurance bond, the property management agent *cannot* use this option in her fiduciary capacity. In no case could a landlord simply place the funds in her own pocket without complying with one or the other of these alternatives, namely a trust or escrow account in an insured North Carolina bank or savings and loan or post a bond. An interest-bearing trust account is also provided for in compliance with the North Carolina Real Estate Commission Rules. Notice that this clause is set forth prominently in all capital letters, in compliance with Rule A.0107 requiring such terms to be "set forth in a conspicuous manner."

5. The tenant's obligations include using the premises for lawful residential purposes, refraining from disturbing other tenants or creating a nuisance, keeping the premises clean, safe, and sanitary, disposing of all waste in compliance with all ordinances, using all systems and appliances properly and safely, avoiding defacing or destroying the property, paying all utility bills billed directly to him, and remaining in property for the lease term.

6. The landlord's obligations include complying with building and housing codes, providing and maintaining fit and habitable premises by making appropriate repairs, maintaining safe and clean premises, and promptly repairing all systems and appliances after receiving actual written notification from tenant.

7. This section addresses the utility bills/service contracts and includes a chart that indicates which party agrees to pay which service obligation.

8. The landlord will provide operable smoke detectors. It is the landlord's responsibility to install new batteries in the smoke detector at the beginning of the lease term. It is the tenant's responsibility to replace smoke detector batteries during the lease term.

9. The tenant agrees to comply with reasonable rules and regulations as established by the landlord through his agent.

10. The landlord may enter the property for the purpose of inspecting the premises and the tenant's compliance with the terms of the rental contract or for the purpose of making repairs or improvements to the property. The landlord must exercise this right at reasonable times. If this right was not given in the lease, the landlord would not have the right to enter. NOTE: The Property Management Contract in Chapter 16 states that the landlord or agent will not enter property without making an appointment with the tenant.

11. Tenant's responsibility for damages and restitution for damages beyond normal wear and tear are set forth.

12. Pets are not allowed by landlords due to the increased risk of damage and cleaning costs. It should be noted that some landlords will agree to allow pets, subject to an additional fee. This fee should not be confused with the security deposit. Because the fee is a nonrefundable cost to the tenant, it is paid directly to the landlord and not held in the trust account.
13. Alterations to the property are to be done only with the landlord's written consent and at tenant's expense.
14. Only the tenant and the named occupants can use the premises as a residence.
15. The tenant warrants the truth of facts provided on rental application.
16. Tenant's duties upon termination are set forth. The tenant must leave property cleaned, swept, and in same condition as when he took possession. Tenant shall not be responsible for normal wear and tear. He must also remove all personal property, secure doors and windows, disconnect utility service, and pay utility bills. Finally, he must return keys and provide the landlord an address where the security deposit may be returned if there are no damages or other legitimate reasons for keeping the security deposit.
17. The landlord has the right to possess the rental property in the event of tenant default. However, the landlord may only do this through a summary ejectment proceeding if the tenant does not surrender possession voluntarily.
18. The tenant must notify the landlord in writing of alleged default by the landlord and give the landlord a reasonable time to correct default. Absent willful negligence, the tenant is prohibited from collecting secondary or consequential damages.
19. The landlord has the right to terminate the tenancy subject to provisions of the bankruptcy code.
20. It is the tenant's responsibility to insure her personal property, and the landlord is released of liability for injury of the tenant and other occupants unless such injury is caused by landlord's or her agent's negligence.
21. The landlord can engage an agent to manage the property.
22. Both the landlord and the tenant acknowledge that their agreement is evidenced by the contract they are signing. They both also acknowledge that there may be minor inaccuracies in the form.
23. The landlord is given the authority to comply with changes in laws or statutes that occur after execution of the lease.
24. The landlord has the option to terminate the lease in the event of condemnation or damage by fire or other casualties.
25. This paragraph prevents assignment or subletting of the lease by the tenant. If the lessor does not want the lease to be assigned or sublet, both must be

specified as they are in this lease form. If a lease is assigned, the remaining term of the lease is transferred without reversion of interest to the original lessee. If a lease is sublet, a part of the lease term is transferred, with a reversion of the remaining term to the original lessee.

26. A waiver of any breach of this contract cannot be construed as a waiver of any future breaches.
27. If multiple persons are shown as the tenant they will each be held jointly (collectively) and severally (individually) liable for performance.
28. This paragraph itemizes addenda, any additional provisions, and provides for lead-based paint disclosure and disclosure that the agent represents the landlord.
29. The tenant acknowledges having inspected the property or having the right to inspect before occupancy.
30. Required notices are to be sent to tenant at the property address and to the landlord at address where rental payment is delivered.
31. A counterpart is an original copy of the document. Typically, three originals are made—one for the tenant, another for the agent, and one for the landlord/owner. The tenants execute their signatures, and the agent can sign on behalf of the landlord under the authority granted her by the property management contract.
32. This document represents the entire agreement between the parties.

Landlord's Implied Covenant of Quiet Enjoyment

In a lease, the covenant of quiet enjoyment is a promise that the lessee will not be disturbed in his use of the property because of a defect in the lessor's title. Every lease implies such a covenant, even if it is not directly expressed in the lease. This covenant protects the tenant only against claims arising from the landlord, the landlord's agents, or someone whose title is superior to that of the landlord. An actual or constructive eviction of the tenant by any of the previously named parties breaches this covenant. Quiet enjoyment is not, as the name would imply, related to the noise level created by the tenants.

Termination of Leases

Leases are terminated in many ways. One primary consideration is that the duties of landlord and tenant are mutually dependent. Thus, if one party fails his responsibility, the other party is relieved of her duty.

Expiration of lease term. As previously noted, a lease creating an estate for years automatically terminates upon the expiration of the lease term. No notice is required by the lessor to the lessee or vice versa.

Agreement of the parties. A lease, as other executory contracts, can be terminated by the mutual agreement of the parties. The release by each party of the other provides the consideration for the agreement to terminate.

Breach of condition. *If lessor or lessee fails to live up to his respective duties,* the lease can be terminated by **breach of condition**. The lessee has the primary duty to pay the rent promptly as well as maintain the individual unit and conform to the specified use. The lessor has the duty to maintain the utilities and common areas of the property. If the tenant fails to pay the rent or the landlord fails to provide heat, the rental contract is breached.

Condemnation. A lease can be terminated by condemnation under the power of eminent domain. If the entire property is condemned, the lessee is entitled to compensation from the lessor for the remaining value of her leasehold interest. If only a part of the leased property is condemned, the lease will provide a lessee with the option to terminate the lease or remain in possession of the remainder of the premises at a reduced rent.

Judicial eviction (actual eviction, summary ejectment). When the lessee fails to adhere to the conditions of the lease, the lessor has the right to evict the tenant. In the event the lessee fails to surrender possession upon demand, the lessor can resort to legal action to evict the tenant after giving the tenant sufficient notice before filing the suit. If the lessee does not surrender possession voluntarily after the court awarded the lessor a judgment for possession, the lessee can be forcibly removed by an officer of the court.

Constructive eviction. Constructive eviction results from some action or inaction by the lessor that renders the premises unfit for habitation. The North Carolina Residential Rental Agreements Act obligates the lessor to provide heat, water, and electricity. If the lessor fails to do so through personal fault or negligence, the lessee is entitled to abandon the premises, terminate the lease, and sue for damages.

Application of the Statute of Frauds

The North Carolina Statute of Frauds requires certain contracts to be in writing to be effective. The Statute of Frauds requires any lease contract that cannot be completed or fulfilled within three years of the date of its making must be in writing to be enforceable. Notice that the lease term can be for less than three years.

Recordation of Leases

In North Carolina, the Conner Act requires a lease that extends for a period of *more* than three years from the date of making to be recorded to be enforceable against third parties. When a lease required by the statute to be in writing is not recorded, a purchaser of the property is not required to honor the full term of the lease. If, however, the lease is of short duration and, therefore, is not in writing, the fact that the lessee is in possession of the property at the time of a sale by the lessor will protect the lessee and thereby require the purchaser to honor the lease for the remainder of the term.

The best way to remember this is that if a contract (lease) has to be in writing under the Statute of Frauds (as opposed to the North Carolina Real Estate Commission), it also must be recorded to protect that right.

Summary of Important Points

1. A landlord is the lessor who retains a freehold estate (ownership) while conveying a nonfreehold estate (possession) to the tenant or lessee.

2. A rental interest involves the concepts of contracts and estates. Landlord and tenant statutes of the state clearly establish the duties and rights of both parties. A leasehold interest results from the conveyance of an estate (nonfreehold) by the landlord (lessor) to the tenant (lessee). The landlord retains title in the estate (freehold); thus, freehold and nonfreehold estates exist at the same time.

3. Landlords' and tenants' duties are mutually dependent; failure of one party to perform a duty excuses the other from his obligations. Failure of the landlord's duty constitutes constructive eviction. The tenant's failure to pay the rent is default and subjects the tenant to eviction (ejectment).

4. The North Carolina Residential Rental Agreements Act requires the landlord to maintain "fit and habitable premises" by maintaining the common areas, plumbing, heating and cooling systems, and any appliances provided.

    The landlord is required to provide a properly installed smoke detector. If it is battery-operated, the landlord must provide new batteries at the beginning of each tenancy.

    As of December 6, 1996, lead-based paint disclosure is required (see Chapter 6). The tenant must maintain the individual dwelling unit, complying with building codes, being responsible for damage, and properly disposing of trash.

5. The North Carolina Tenant Security Deposit Act requires landlords to account for tenants' funds by depositing the funds in an insured trust account or guaranteeing the return of the funds with an insurance bond. The tenant must be notified which of these mechanisms the landlord is using. Maximum limits for the amount of funds that can be held are set and are related to the rental period. Funds must be accounted for or returned within 30 days of the termination of the lease. Note that where this act permits the use of a bond to the general public, the North Carolina Real Estate

Commission does not allow licensees to use the bond alternative but rather requires licensees to deposit the monies in a trust or escrow account as per their rules.

6. The retaliatory eviction doctrine protects the tenant from ejectment by the landlord if the tenant asserts her rights in good faith.

7. Residential eviction remedies prohibit the landlord from physically barring the tenant from the unit (peaceable self-help) as well as from seizing the tenant's personal property.

8. A tenant cannot unilaterally withhold rent but can seek court action for a refund or be excused from the lease if the landlord breaches his duty.

9. There are four primary types of lease: (1) An estate for years is for a fixed period of time, (2) an estate from period to period automatically renews itself in the absence of notice by either party within a prescribed period, (3) an estate at will is for an indefinite or undetermined period of time, and (4) an estate at sufferance arises when a tenant is still in possession of the premises after the legal rental period has expired.

10. The two primary classifications of leases are a gross lease, in which the owner pays all of the expenses of the property, and a net lease, in which the tenant pays some or all of the expenses. Types of lease based on the payment arrangement include percentage, flat, graduated, indexed, escalated, sale and leaseback, and mineral. A ground lease is for the rental of the land alone, which can be improved by the tenant.

11. Termination of leases can occur by (1) breach of condition, (2) expiration of the rental term, (3) mutual agreement, and (4) condemnation of the property.

12. Actual eviction (summary ejectment) occurs when the lessee fails to adhere to conditions of the lease. Constructive eviction results from action or inaction of the lessor that renders the premises uninhabitable.

13. A lease contract that extends for more than three years from the date of making is required to be in writing by the Statute of Frauds and to be recorded by the Conner Act to be enforceable.

14. The Vacation Rental Act provides for fees to be paid to travel agents by real estate agents under specific circumstances.

15. In a gross lease, typically residential, the landlord pays the expenses of the property. A net lease, in which the tenant pays some or all of the expenses, is more typical of commercial leases. (Think of gross income, from which you must pay expenses or deductions, versus net income, which is pure profit.)

16. *For lease terminology,* refer to the text discussion of how leases are terminated. The lessor (landlord) is promising the sanctity of the tenant's use of the premises (covenant of quiet enjoyment). The concept of constructive

eviction provides that when the lessor breaches this duty, the lessee (tenant) is excused from the lease, that is, fulfillment of the rental period.

17. The North Carolina Residential Rental Agreements Act does not protect transient occupancy or commercial quarters.

18. Constructive eviction literally means "effective eviction" in the sense that the tenant is not actually being evicted, but rather is being deprived of reasonable use of the property. This is very often due to the failure of the landlord to keep the property "fit and habitable," and the tenant has to vacate due to the property condition.

19. The covenant of quiet enjoyment agreement is not based on noise but rather on the fact the tenant is conveyed "peaceable possession" and has the right to be in possession without someone stating they have a higher right of claim to the property. For example, a tenant has a lease and now is being notified the lender is foreclosing on the property. The mortgage, which was recorded before the lease, can now be foreclosed upon and cause the tenant to lose his right of possession, thus violating the tenant's right to peaceable possession.

20. *The various types of leasehold tenancies* include estate for years, estate from year to year, or periodic estates, estate at will, and estate at sufferance.

21. The Tenant Security Deposit Act stipulates how much deposit can be charged as well as the permitted uses, and the proper handling of the monies in a residential lease. Permitted uses include the following: (1) nonpayment of rent, (2) damage beyond reasonable wear and tear, (3) damages from the nonfulfillment of the rental period, (4) unpaid bills that become a lien against the property, (5) the cost of re-renting the property if there was a breach of contract by the tenant, (6) the costs of removal and storage of the tenant's property in the case of eviction, (7) court costs, (8) late fees, and (9) filing fees and costs of court.

22. *The various types of leases include* a fixed lease, which is most commonly used in residential leases; various commercial leases, such as percentage, net, graduated, index, and full-service leases; and special circumstance leases, such as a ground, or land, lease.

23. Assignments are the total transfer of lease rights and obligations, whereas subleases are the partial transfer of lease rights and obligations. In an assignment, the new tenant (assignee) pays the rent directly to the landlord and the original tenant (assignor) is held secondarily liable for the rent unless he is able to obtain a release from the landlord. The original tenant will not regain possession of the property. In a sublease, the original tenant (sublessor) only conveys a portion of the remaining lease term to the new tenant (sublessee) and will regain possession of the property. In the sublease, the sublessee will pay rent directly to the sublessor who remains primarily liable to the landlord for the rent. A lease can generally be assigned, or subleased, unless specifically prohibited in the contract, although a prohibition against

assignment will not prohibit any rights of subleasing and any prohibition of subleasing will not prohibit the right to assign. If the landlord does not wish for the tenant to either be able to assign, nor sublet, he must specifically prohibit each in the agreement. A sublease is also referred to as a sublet or a sandwich lease.

24. The Statute of Frauds stipulates any lease that cannot be fulfilled within three years of the date of its making must be in writing to be enforceable. Remember that if a lease must be writing under the Statute of Frauds, it also will be required to be recorded to protect that interest according to the Conner Act.

Review Questions

Answers to the review questions are found in the Answer Key at the back of the book.

1. In the creation of a nonfreehold estate:
   A. the landlord retains a freehold estate.
   B. a freehold and nonfreehold estate exist at the same time.
   C. the tenant has a nonfreehold estate.
   D. all of the above.

2. If the landlord fails to perform her duty, the tenant can do all of the following EXCEPT:
   A. abandon the premises.
   B. decide by himself to refuse to pay rent.
   C. terminate the lease.
   D. sue for damages.

3. All of the following are duties of the landlord EXCEPT:
   A. complying with building codes.
   B. being responsible for destruction or defacement caused by the tenant.
   C. repairing utilities and appliances.
   D. maintaining the common areas.

4. Jane Smith signed a lease for one year at a rent of $200 per month. She wanted to keep a small kitten in the apartment, but the landlord automatically assumed there would be some degree of damage by the pet for which he wanted to assess an additional fee of $100. What is the maximum security deposit he could collect from Jane?
   A. $200
   B. $300
   C. $400
   D. $500

5. Larry Landlord is a private citizen, non–real estate agent renting his own apartments without the help of a broker. He has received $1,000 in security deposits from his tenants. Which of the following is true?
   A. He must deposit these funds in a trust account.
   B. He could spend $200 of the funds on a personal vacation after guaranteeing return of the money with a performance bond.
   C. He can deposit these funds in his personal account without a bond.
   D. He must provide a bond no matter where he deposits the money or what he does with it.

6. A tenant has a fixed term lease for a 1-year period. What is the minimum period of time that he must be given notice to vacate by the landlord if it is not stipulated in the lease terms?
   A. one week
   B. one month
   C. one and a half months
   D. two months

7. All of the following statements regarding an estate for years are correct EXCEPT:
   A. The duration of the estate must be definite.
   B. The duration of the estate must be at least one year.
   C. The estate automatically terminates without notice.
   D. The contract creating an estate for years is, in some cases, required to be in writing in order to be valid.

8. Which is an estate that automatically renews itself for consecutive periods?
   A. estate at will
   B. life estate
   C. estate from year to year
   D. estate for years

9. After the termination of a lease, a tenant continued in possession of the property without permission of the property owner. The tenant's status is:
   A. tenant at will.
   B. lessee.
   C. trespasser.
   D. tenant at sufferance.

10. All of the following are essential elements of a valid lease EXCEPT:
    A. the parties must have the legal capacity to contract.
    B. the property must be clearly identified.
    C. provision must be made for automatic renewal.
    D. all essential aspects of the agreement (rent, occupancy dates, and so on) must be set forth.

11. In which type of lease does the lessee agree to pay an increasing rental fee as sales in the demised property increase?
    A. escalated
    B. percentage
    C. ground
    D. none of the above

12. A lease contract provides for which of the following?
    A. a freehold estate for the lessee
    B. a nonfreehold estate for the lessor
    C. a freehold estate for the tenant
    D. a leasehold estate for the lessee

13. Which of the following is NOT a correct statement regarding the real property and contractual rights of the lessor and lessee as created by a residential lease contract?
    A. The lessee has the exclusive right to possession and control of the leased premises during the term of the lease.
    B. The lessor retains the title to the leased premises during the term of the lease and has the right to regain possession upon the termination of the lease.
    C. The lessor has the right to enter the property at any time during the term of the lease.
    D. The landlord must provide premises fit for human habitation.

14. All of the following are typical provisions of lease contracts for an estate for years EXCEPT:
    A. provision for a term of indefinite duration.
    B. right of first refusal.
    C. right to make alterations.
    D. option to renew.

15. Which of the following is a lease in which the rental amount is changed a specified percentage of the change in the Consumer Price Index?
    A. percentage
    B. index
    C. escalated
    D. graduated

16. A transaction in which a property owner sells the property and leases it from the purchaser is described as which of the following?
    A. option to renew
    B. sale and leaseback
    C. ground lease
    D. sublease

17. A lease is terminated by each of the following EXCEPT:
    A. constructive eviction.
    B. condemnation.
    C. breach of condition.
    D. right of first refusal.

18. Tina Tenant rents an apartment from Larry Landlord. Larry refuses to repair the heating and plumbing; therefore, Tina has no heat or water. Tina can legally:
    A. remain in the apartment and refuse to pay rent.
    B. move out of the apartment and refuse to pay rent.
    C. hire a contractor to make repairs and automatically deduct the amount from the following month's rent.
    D. remain in the unit for the remainder of the lease term and with no rent due.

19. If a tenant pays rent as well as maintenance, utilities, taxes, and insurance, the lease is a:
    A. net lease.
    B. gross lease.
    C. ground lease.
    D. flat lease.

20. Randy Renter starts a tenants' union to try to improve the maintenance of the apartment complex where he lives. Oscar Owner immediately gives Randy notice to move out. Randy has protection from eviction for one year under the statutory provision of:
    A. self-help.
    B. retaliatory eviction.
    C. constructive eviction.
    D. negligence.

21. _____ is considered to have occurred if the landlord breaches his duty to provide fit and habitable premises and fails to remedy the problem within a reasonable period of time after being properly notified of the problem by the tenant.
    A. Retaliatory eviction
    B. Judicial eviction
    C. Constructive eviction
    D. Expedited eviction

22. The Vacation Rental Act allows "acceptance" of the rental agreement to occur in all of the following ways EXCEPT:
    A. signing the agreement.
    B. paying the landlord part of the consideration or security deposit AFTER tenant receives copy of the written agreement.
    C. by taking possession AFTER receiving a copy of the agreement.
    D. by oral agreement.

23. Which estate affords the tenant the most security?
    A. estate at will
    B. estate from year to year
    C. estate at sufferance
    D. freehold estate

CHAPTER 16
PROPERTY MANAGEMENT

KEY TERMS

management plan
management proposal
operating budget
property management
property management agreement
property management report
property manager
resident manager

LEARNING OBJECTIVES

At the conclusion of this chapter, you should be able to:

1. Define the owner–property manager relationship.
2. Describe the principal functions of property managers.

IN THIS CHAPTER

This chapter discusses the fiduciary duty of the real estate agent in the specialized field of property management and identifies his or her duty of agency in this area. The math computations shown in this chapter are for illustration purposes only. There are no math computations in the current state outline for this chapter.

THE OWNER–PROPERTY MANAGER RELATIONSHIP

Purposes of Property Management

The basic purpose of **property management** is *to represent the owner or principal in much the same manner as the listing and selling agents represent the owner/seller of a property.* Inherent in this relationship is the fiduciary duty of agency that binds the agent to absolute fidelity to the owner's best interests.

A **property manager** is usually *a special (limited) agent (broker)*; however, a property manager of a large shopping center, office complex, or apartment building who has been given the authority to act in place of the owner and perform a wide variety of activities can be a general agent. In the owner–property manager relationship, the agent essentially stands in the place of the owners to perform the duties of an efficient business operation that the owners cannot or do not wish to perform for themselves. The owners may have many reasons for transferring their duties to the agent, such as that of owning multiple properties in various locations. Each property is a serious business investment that represents considerable potential advantages to the owners. It is often altogether fitting that the owners seek the skills of the real estate professional to gain the maximum advantage of their property. By virtue of her special training and experience, the agent offers the owners expertise that they may not possess.

> Property managers are generally compensated based on the amount of rents actually collected.

Types of Property Requiring Management

Many types of property can benefit from real estate management services of the broker. Residential property can include apartments, condominiums, single-family homes, and vacation property. Retail or commercial property can include offices, small retail stores, office condominiums, and large shopping malls. Industrial property is another specialization that can include industrial parks.

PROPERTY MANAGEMENT FEE

All fees and rates of compensation between agents and principals are strictly negotiable between the parties. It is a violation of federal antitrust laws for competitors even to discuss such things as rates of compensation or the boycotting of another competitor based on a rate of compensation. Therefore, if any group of agents were to try to establish a "going rate" for property management (or anything else), they would be in serious trouble with the law. All agents who are parties to such conversations can be held liable.

Compensation negotiated between the principal and agent can take any number of forms. Often, this form is that of a percentage of the rents actually collected, but the establishment of a flat fee or minimum fee is often added to the formula of compensation. Real estate agents should be able to calculate the total compensation due, given the formula or combination of formulas established by the parties. For example, Darby Apartments consists of eight units that rent for $325 per month and six units that rent for $275. The manager's fee is 10% of the gross monthly rents collected. During the month of March, two of the $325 units were vacant as was one of the $275 units. The manager's fee would be calculated as follows:

$$6 \times \$325 \times 10\% = \$195.00$$
$$5 \times \$275 \times 10\% = \$137.50$$
$$\$195 + \$137.50 = \$332.50$$

If a unit were rented for only a portion of the month, the rent and fee would be prorated according to the days actually used. For example, if one of the vacant $325 units were rented only for the last 10 days of the month, this calculation would be as follows:

$$\$325 \div 30 \times 10 \text{ days} \times 10\% = \$10.83 \text{ manager's fee}$$

Travel Agent Referral Fees in Vacation Rentals

A real estate agent may pay or promise to pay a travel agent a consideration under specific circumstances. According to Rule A.0109(e), this consideration may be made if the travel agent introduces the tenant to the agent in the normal course of the travel agent's business, if the travel agent has not engaged in an activity requiring a real estate license, and if the travel agent has not received money in connection with the vacation rental. This is a major revision in state law that in the past has allowed only the real estate agent to offer consideration or referral fees to other licensed real estate agents (in or out of North Carolina). The payment of any consideration or referral fee may be disbursed only after the conclusion of the rental period. The agent also must retain records of these payments for three years, including the details of the transaction, such as the tenant's name, the travel agent's name, the amount paid to the travel agent, and the dates of tenancy.

AGENCY RELATIONSHIP IN RENTALS

The point at which all agency agreements, including those with landlords and tenants, must be in writing depends on who the party is to the agreement. Agency agreements, with or without dual agency authorization, with property owners must be in writing from the beginning of any relationship between an agent and a property owner, whether the property owner's role is that of a seller or a lessor/landlord. Unlike an agency agreement with an owner/seller, which must be for a definite period and must expire on the stated date, agency agreements with lessors/landlords can contain an automatic renewal provided the landlord can end the agreement with notice at the end of the initial contract period or any subsequent renewal period.

If an agency relationship is to exist between an agent and a tenant, such agreement must be expressed from the beginning of the relationship and be committed to writing before the tenant makes an offer to rent or lease real estate to another. If the agreement seeks to bind the prospective tenant for a specific time period or restrict the tenant from working independently or with other agents, that fact must be in writing from the beginning of the relationship.

Undisclosed dual agency is prohibited in landlord–tenant transactions as well as sales transactions. If this permission is not given by either or both parties from the outset of the agency relationship and the need for dual agency later arises, permission must be obtained from both parties before dual agency can be initiated. Agents working with landlords or tenants are not required to provide the *Working with Real Estate Agents* brochure; however, it is a good practice to do so. Although an agent is not required to give the tenant written notice that he is working as the landlord's agent, he should inform potential commercial and residential tenants that he represents the property owner and that the tenants should not tell the agent anything they do not want the property owner to know.

When they have entered a dual agency situation, agents are required by Rule A.0104(i) to disclose this relationship to all parties. This means that in the landlord–tenant situation, the dual agency must have been authorized in writing by the landlord and expressly authorized by the tenant, either orally or in writing. Such an express oral authorization by the tenant must be committed to writing before an offer to rent or lease is made.

Property Management Contracts

The property manager's authority arises in basically the same way as the listing agent's authority, namely, through a clear employment agreement. Like the listing contract, the property management contract is with a broker or brokerage firm. Figure 16.1 illustrates the standard form adopted by the North Carolina Association of REALTORS®. This particular form is copyrighted for use by members only but serves as a good illustration of an appropriate form. The **property management agreement** should set out the following items, starting with the inception date and names of the parties:

1. The property location is identified. Note that an informal reference (street address) is usually sufficient for the property management agreement.
2. The duration of the agency agreement between the owner and real estate agent is defined.
3. The agent's fee is established.
4. The handling of other fees, including processing tenant rental applications, late payment fees, and returned checks is discussed.
5. The agent's authority and responsibilities are spelled out in specific areas. Even though the agent is given more decision-making authority in this agreement than in the case of listing a property for sale, the agent is still considered a *special (limited) agent*. A property manager of a large complex who has vast authority to perform a wide variety of functions may be a general agent. Details of the agent's promises to the owner are identified. The Real Estate Commission holds that

"Listing agreements, buyer agency agreements, and property management agreements are service contracts. 'I hired you and your firm to do something. I want YOU to provide service.' Offers to purchase and lease agreements are performance agreements. 'I don't care who performs as long as somebody buys the property, sells the property, or rents the property.' Therefore service contracts terminate with the death of the parties. Performance contracts continue and begin obligation of the estate."

–Terry Wilson, DREI

EXCLUSIVE PROPERTY MANAGEMENT AGREEMENT
Long-term Rental Property

This Exclusive Property Management Agreement is entered into by and between _____ ("Owner") and _____ ("Agent").

IN CONSIDERATION of the mutual covenants and promises set forth herein, Owner hereby contracts with Agent, and Agent hereby contracts with Owner, to lease and manage the property described below, as well as any other property Owner and Agent may from time to time agree in writing will be subject to this Agreement (the "Property"), in accordance with all applicable laws and regulations, upon the terms and conditions contained herein.

1. Property. City:_____ County:_____, NC
Street Address:_____ Zip Code:_____
Other Description:_____

❏ **MULTIPLE PARCELS** (*check if applicable*). Additional parcels of real property are the subject of this Agreement, as described in the attached Multi-Parcel Addendum. The term "Property" as used herein shall be deemed to refer to all such parcels unless specifically indicated otherwise.

2. Duration of Agreement. This Agreement shall be binding when it has been signed and dated below by Owner and Agent. It shall become effective on _____ ("Effective Date") and shall be for an initial term of _____. NOT LESS THAN _____ DAYS PRIOR TO THE CONCLUSION OF THE INITIAL TERM, EITHER PARTY MAY NOTIFY THE OTHER PARTY IN WRITING OF ITS DESIRE TO TERMINATE THIS AGREEMENT, IN WHICH CASE IT SHALL TERMINATE AT THE CONCLUSION OF THE INITIAL TERM. IF NOT SO TERMINATED, THIS AGREEMENT SHALL AUTOMATICALLY RENEW FOR SUCCESSIVE TERMS OF _____ EACH UNLESS EITHER PARTY GIVES THE OTHER PARTY WRITTEN NOTICE OF ITS DESIRE TO TERMINATE THIS AGREEMENT AT LEAST _____ DAYS PRIOR TO THE CONCLUSION OF ANY SUCH RENEWAL TERM, IN WHICH CASE THIS AGREEMENT SHALL TERMINATE AT THE CONCLUSION OF SUCH TERM.

3. Agent's Fees. For services performed hereunder, Owner shall compensate Agent in the following manner:
  ❏ A fee ("Fee") equal to the greater of:
   (i) _____ percent (___%) of total gross rental income received on all rental agreements, or
   (ii) $_____ per month for each month of the Initial Term or any renewal term of this Agreement.
  ❏ Other (*describe method of compensation*): _____.

❏ (*Check if applicable*) Agent may from time to time provide services for Owner or arrange services for Owner from third-party vendors, including but not limited to services relating to maintenance, repair and/or improvements to the Property. Owner agrees that Owner shall compensate Agent for the provision or arrangement of any such services in the following manner: _____.

Note: No fees may be deducted from any tenant security deposit until the termination of the tenancy. Thereafter, any fees due Agent from Owner may be deducted from any portion of the security deposit due to Owner.

4. Early Termination Fee: IF, PRIOR TO THE END OF THE INITIAL TERM OR ANY RENEWAL TERM OF THIS AGREEMENT, (I) OWNER TERMINATES THIS AGREEMENT WITHOUT LEGALLY SUFFICIENT CAUSE OR (II) AGENT TERMINATES THIS AGREEMENT FOR LEGALLY SUFFICIENT CAUSE, OWNER SHALL PAY AGENT AN AMOUNT EQUAL TO THE FEE AGENT WOULD HAVE BEEN ENTITLED TO RECEIVE DURING THE BALANCE OF THE THEN-EXISTING TERM OF THIS AGREEMENT, TAKING INTO ACCOUNT ANY RENTAL AGREEMENTS IN EFFECT AT THE TIME OF SUCH TERMINATION.

5. Other Fees: Agent may charge tenants reasonable administrative fees permitted by law and retain any such fees, including but not limited to, fees to cover the costs of processing tenant rental applications. If, in Agent's discretion, tenant leases provide for late payment fees and/or returned check fees, such fees, when collected by Agent, shall belong to _____ (Owner or Agent). Fees for purposes covered under the Tenant Security Deposit Act will be collected, held and disbursed in accordance with the Act and paragraphs 10, 17, and 21 of this Agreement.

Page 1 of 8
North Carolina Association of REALTORS®, Inc.

STANDARD FORM 401
Revised 7/2018
©7/2018

Owner Initials _____ _____   Agent Initials _____ _____

FIGURE 16.1 Exclusive property management agreement.

6. **Authority and Responsibilities of Agent:** During the time this Agreement is in effect, Agent shall:
   (a) Manage the Property to the best of Agent's ability, devoting thereto such time and attention as may be necessary;
   (b) OFFER THE PROPERTY FOR RENT IN COMPLIANCE WITH ALL APPLICABLE FEDERAL AND STATE LAWS, REGULATIONS AND ETHICAL DUTIES, INCLUDING BUT NOT LIMITED TO, THOSE PROHIBITING DISCRIMINATION ON THE BASIS OF RACE, COLOR, RELIGION, SEX, NATIONAL ORIGIN, HANDICAP, FAMILIAL STATUS, SEXUAL ORIENTATION OR GENDER IDENTITY IN THE LEASING OF THE PROPERTY; USE AGENT'S BEST EFFORTS TO SOLICIT, SECURE AND MAINTAIN TENANTS, INCLUDING THE AUTHORITY TO NEGOTIATE, EXECUTE, EXTEND AND RENEW LEASES IN OWNER'S NAME FOR TERMS NOT IN EXCESS OF _____;
   (c) Collect all rentals and other charges and amounts due under tenant leases and give receipts for amounts so collected;
   (d) Deliver to Owner within 45 days following the date of execution of any rental agreement an accounting which sets forth the name of the tenant, the rental rate and rents collected, and promptly provide a copy of any rental agreement to Owner upon reasonable request;
   (e) Provide Owner monthly statements of all monies received and disbursed in connection with Agent's management of the Property, and remit to Owner rental proceeds collected, less any deductions authorized hereunder; provided: (1) this shall not constitute a guarantee by Agent for rental payments that Agent is unable to collect in the exercise of reasonable diligence; (2) if, pursuant to this Agreement or required by law, Agent either has refunded or will refund in whole or in part any rental payments made by a tenant and previously remitted to Owner, Owner agrees to return same to Agent promptly upon Agent's demand; and (3) any rents pre-paid by a tenant shall be held in trust by Agent and disbursed to Owner as and when they become due under the terms of the tenant's lease;
   (f) Make arrangements on Owner's behalf for any repairs which, in Agent's opinion, may be necessary to preserve, maintain and protect the Property; provided, Agent may not make arrangements for any repairs that exceed $_____ without prior approval of Owner, except that in the case of an emergency, Agent may, without prior approval, make arrangements for whatever expenditures on behalf of Owner that are reasonably necessary to preserve the Property or prevent further damage from occurring;
   (g) Answer tenant requests and complaints and perform the duties imposed upon Owner by tenant leases or any local, state or federal law or regulations, including the authority to purchase such supplies and hire such labor as may be necessary in Agent's opinion to accomplish any necessary repairs;
   (h) Retain such amounts from Owner's rental proceeds as may be necessary from time to time to pay expenses associated with the management and operation of the Property for which Owner is responsible hereunder. Agent will establish and maintain a fund on Owner's behalf in the amount of $_____ from which expenses may be paid, but Owner acknowledges and understands that Agent may from time to time retain additional amounts as Agent notifies Owner in advance in writing are reasonably necessary; Negotiate partial refunds with tenants if, in Agent's reasonable opinion, the tenant's use and enjoyment of the Property has been or will be materially and adversely affected as a result of a defect in the condition of the Property (such as a repair to the electrical, plumbing, sanitary, heating or ventilating facilities or a major appliance that cannot be made reasonably and promptly);
   (i) Institute and prosecute such proceedings in small claims court as may be necessary and advisable, in Agent's opinion, to recover rents due the Owner from tenants or to evict tenants and regain possession, including the authority, in Agent's discretion, to settle, compromise and release any and all such small claims proceedings; provided, that with respect to any such small claims proceeding, Agent shall have actual knowledge of the facts alleged in the complaint; and
   (j) _____
   _____
   _____
   _____

7. **Cooperation With/Compensation To Other Agents:** Agent has advised Owner of Agent's company policies regarding cooperation and the amount(s) of any compensation, if any, that will be offered to subagents, tenant agents or both. Owner authorizes Agent to (*Check ALL applicable authorizations*):
   ❑ Cooperate with subagents representing only the Owner and offer them the following compensation: _____

   ❑ Cooperate with tenant agents representing only the tenant and offer them the following compensation: _____

   ❑ Cooperate with and compensate agents from other firms according to the attached company policy.

Agent will promptly notify Owner if Agent offers compensation to a cooperating agent(s) that is different from that set forth above.

FIGURE 16.1 (*Continued*)

8. **Marketing.** Owner authorizes Agent to advertise the Property in such manner as may be appropriate in Agent's opinion, including the authority to: (*Check ALL applicable sections*)
   - ☐ place "For Rent" signs on the Property (where permitted by law and relevant covenants) and to remove other such signs.
   - ☐ submit pertinent information concerning the Property to any listing service of which Agent is a member or in which any of Agent's associates participates and to furnish to such listing service notice of all changes of information concerning the Property authorized in writing by Owner. Owner authorizes Agent, upon execution of a rental contract for the Property, to notify the listing service of the rental, and to disseminate rental information, including rental price, to the listing service, appraisers and real estate brokers.
   - ☐ advertise the Property in non-Internet media, and to permit other firms to advertise the Property in non-Internet media to the extent and in such manner as Agent may decide.
   - ☐ display information about the Property on the Internet either directly or through a program of any listing service of which the Agent is a member or in which any of Agent's associates participates, and to authorize other firms who belong to any listing service of which the Agent is a member or in which any of Agent's associates participates to display information about the Property on the Internet in accordance with the listing service rules and regulations. Owner also authorizes any listing service of which Agent is a member or in which any of Agent's associates participates to use, license or sell to others information about the Property entered into the listing service. Owner specifically authorizes the display of the address of the Property, automated estimates of the market value of the Property and third-party comments about the Property. If Owner desires to limit or prohibit Internet advertising as set forth above, Owner must complete an opt-out form in accordance with listing service rules.

   (**NOTE**: NCAR Form #105 may be used to limit or prohibit Internet advertising and explains how such limitations may or may not be effective.)

9. **Responsibilities of Owner:** During the time this Agreement is in effect, Owner shall:
   (a) Be responsible for all costs and expenses associated with the maintenance and operation of the Property in accordance with the requirements of: (i) NC General Statutes Section 42-42, including but not limited to the placement of new batteries in a battery-operated smoke or carbon monoxide alarm at the beginning of a tenancy, (ii) any other local, state or federal law or regulations and (iii) tenant leases, and advance to Agent such sums as may be necessary from time to time to pay such costs and expenses;
   (b) Provide funds to Agent promptly upon Agent's request for any cost or expense for which Owner is responsible that Agent, in Agent's discretion, incurs on Owner's behalf, including but not limited to, the costs of advertising, emergency maintenance and repairs, utilities, property taxes, owners' association dues and assessments, court costs and attorney's fees; and further, pay interest at the rate of _____percent (%) per year on the amount of any outstanding balance thereof not paid to Agent within _____ days of Agent's written request therefore;
   (c) NOT TAKE ANY ACTION OR ADOPT ANY POLICY THE EFFECT OF WHICH WOULD BE TO PREVENT AGENT FROM OFFERING THE PROPERTY FOR RENT IN COMPLIANCE WITH ALL APPLICABLE FEDERAL AND STATE LAWS, REGULATIONS AND ETHICAL DUTIES, INCLUDING BUT NOT LIMITED TO, THOSE PROHIBITING DISCRIMINATION ON THE BASIS OF RACE, COLOR, RELIGION, SEX, NATIONAL ORIGIN, HANDICAP, FAMILIAL STATUS, SEXUAL ORIENTATION OR GENDER IDENTITY IN THE LEASING OF THE PROPERTY;
   (d) Carry, at Owner's expense, public liability insurance against any and all claims or demands whatever arising out of, or in any way connected with, the operation, leasing and maintenance of the Property, including property damage and personal injury, in the amount of not less than $_____, which policy shall, without cost to Agent, name Agent as an additional insured as its interest may appear, and provide at least annually a copy of such insurance policy or policies to Agent upon Agent's request;
   (Name of insurance agent:_____; telephone no.:_____)
   (e) Indemnify and hold Agent harmless to the extent allowable by law from any and all costs, expenses, attorneys' fees, suits, liabilities, damages or claims for damages, including but not limited to, those arising out of any injury or death to any person or loss or damage to any property of any kind whatsoever and to whomsoever belonging, including Owner, in any way relating to the management of the Property by Agent or the performance or exercise of any duty, obligation or authority set forth herein or hereafter granted to Agent, or arising out of a tenant's breach of any lease for the Property, except to the extent that such may be the result of gross negligence or willful or intentional misconduct by Agent;
   (f) Be responsible for timely payment of all property taxes, mortgage payments, governmental or owners' association assessments associated with the Property, and any other expenses which could become a lien against the Property, and for promptly notifying Agent in the event that Owner receives any notice(s) from the holder of any loan or from any other lien holder of any kind, regarding a default in payment, threatened foreclosure or the filing of a foreclosure proceeding; and

FIGURE 16.1 (*Continued*)

(g) _____
_____
_____
_____
_____
_____
_____

10. **Tenant Security Deposits.** Agent may, in Agent's discretion, require tenants to make security deposits in an amount permitted by law to secure tenants' lease obligations (such security deposits shall hereinafter be referred to as "Tenant Security Deposits"). If the Agent requires Tenant Security Deposits, they shall be placed in a trust account in Agent's name in a North Carolina bank or savings and loan association. Upon the commencement of this Agreement, Owner shall deliver to Agent a list of any current tenants who previously made Tenant Security Deposits under existing leases and the amounts thereof. Simultaneously therewith, any such Tenant Security Deposits shall be placed in a trust account in Agent's name in a North Carolina bank or savings and loan association, and shall thereafter be administered in accordance with this Agreement.

11. **Pets.** Tenants *(check one of the following)* ❑ shall not be allowed to bring Pets onto the Property ❑ shall be allowed to bring pets onto the Property in accordance with Agent's company policy, a copy of which shall be provided to Owner and made a part of any rental agreement. Owner acknowledges and understands that whether or not pets are allowed, a person who has a demonstrated need for an assistance animal which alleviates one or more of the identified symptoms or effects of an existing disability has the legal right to be accompanied by an assistance animal in the Property, that no pet fee may be charged to such person, but that such person would be liable for any damage done by the assistance animal to the Property.

12. **Smoking.** Smoking cigarettes, cigars, pipes or any other tobacco or lighted product of any kind shall be:
❑ prohibited in any interior portion of the Premises, including any detached structures
❑ permitted on the Premises
❑ prohibited or permitted in accordance with Agent's company policy, a copy of which is attached hereto

13. **Owner/Condo Association** ❑ *(check if applicable)*.
- Name of association: _____
- Name of association property manager: _____
- Property manager address and phone number: _____
- Association website address, if any: _____

❑ Owner ❑ Agent *(check one)* will pay regular association dues to the association. If Agent is to pay, Owner will remain responsible for the amount of such payment in accordance with Paragraph 9 of this Agreement.

14. **Sewage Disposal.** Owner represents that the Property is served by *(check one)*: ❑ public sewer ❑ septic tank. If served by a septic tank, Owner understands and acknowledges that occupancy will be limited to the number of bedrooms permitted by the septic permit.

15. **Occupancy Limits.** Owner understands and acknowledges that whether the Property is served by public sewer or septic system, occupancy of the Property shall generally be limited to two persons per bedroom, but that other factors, including local occupancy limits and State and Federal Fair Housing laws, may affect maximum occupancy of the Property.

16. **Service Contracts.** Owner represents that the service contracts identified below are in existence as of the Effective Date of this Agreement. Owner acknowledges and understands that Agent's agreement to be responsible for payment of any such contract does not relieve Owner of responsibility for the amount of any such payment in accordance with Paragraph 9 of this Agreement.

[THIS SPACE INTENTIONALLY LEFT BLANK]

Owner Initials _____ _____ Agent Initials _____ _____

FIGURE 16.1 *(Continued)*

Service contract (*insert provider name and contact information in blank*)	Owner pays	Agent pays	N/A
Home warranty: _____	☐	☐	☐
Pest Control: _____	☐	☐	☐
HVAC: _____	☐	☐	☐
Lawn Service: _____	☐	☐	☐
	☐	☐	☐
	☐	☐	☐
	☐	☐	☐

17. **Trust Account Interest.** Agent may, in Agent's discretion, place gross receipts and collections, including Tenant Security Deposits, in an interest bearing trust account in the name of Agent in an insured bank or savings and loan association in North Carolina. Interest on any such amounts shall belong to _____(Owner or Agent), except that with respect to any Tenant Security Deposits, tenant leases shall specify, in Agent's discretion, whether such interest shall be payable to Owner or to the tenant. If the lease provides that such interest is payable to the tenant, Agent shall account for the interest in the manner set forth in such lease. If the lease provides that such interest is payable to Owner or as Owner directs, then such interest shall be paid to Owner or Agent as set forth above. Agent may remove any interest payable to Agent from the account at all times and with such frequency as is permitted under the terms of the account and as the law may require.

18. **Entry by Owner.** Owner agrees that neither Owner nor any third party acting at Owner's direction, shall enter the Property for any purpose whatsoever during any time that it is occupied by a tenant in the absence of reasonable notice to Agent or tenant and scheduling by Agent or tenant of an appropriate time for any such entry.

19. **Lead-Based Paint/Hazard Disclosure.** If the Property was built prior to 1978, Landlord understands that Landlord is required under 42 U.S.C. 4852(d) to disclose information about lead-based paint and lead-based paint hazards, and that Agent is required to ensure Landlord's compliance with said law. Landlord agrees to complete and sign a "Disclosure Of Information On Lead-Based Paint And Lead-Based Paint Hazards" form (NCAR form #430-T), photocopies of which will be provided by Agent to prospective tenants. In the alternative, Landlord authorizes Agent, in Agent's discretion, to fulfill Landlord's disclosure obligations by completing and signing said form on Landlord's behalf based on information provided by Landlord to Agent.

20. **Tenant Information.** Owner acknowledges and understands: (i) that state and federal laws regulate the maintenance and disposal of certain personal information of consumers, such as social security numbers, drivers' license numbers, account numbers and other numbers that may be used to access a person's financial resources, and (ii) that contractual limitations with third-party providers of credit reports or other background information relating to prospective tenants may limit or prohibit Agent's dissemination of such reports/information. Owner agrees that Agent shall not be required to disclose any such information to Owner about a tenant or prospective tenant, and that if Agent does disclose any such information to Owner, Owner will indemnify and hold Agent harmless from any and all costs, expenses, attorneys' fees, suits, liabilities, damages or claims for damages as set forth in paragraph 9(e) of this Agreement as a result of the disclosure of any such information to or by Owner.

21. **Duties on Termination.** Upon termination of this Agreement by either party, each shall take such steps as are necessary to settle all accounts between them, including, but not limited to, the following:
   (a) Agent shall promptly render to Owner all rents then on hand after having deducted therefrom any Agent's fees then due and amounts sufficient to cover all other outstanding expenditures of Agent incurred in connection with operating the Property;
   (b) Agent shall transfer any security deposits held by Agent to Owner or such other person or entity as Owner may designate in writing; provided, Owner understands and acknowledges that the Tenant Security Deposit Act requires Owner to either deposit any such deposits in a trust account with a licensed and insured bank or savings institution located in North Carolina, or furnish a bond from an insurance company licensed to do business in North Carolina; and provided further, Owner shall be responsible for any out-of-pocket transfer costs incurred by Agent;

FIGURE 16.1 (*Continued*)

(c) Owner shall promptly pay to Agent any fees or amounts due the Agent under the Agreement or any current rental agreement and shall reimburse Agent for any expenditures made and outstanding at the time of termination;
(d) Agent shall deliver to Owner copies of all tenant leases and other instruments entered into on behalf of Owner (Agent may retain copies of such leases and instruments for Agent's records); and
(e) Owner shall notify all current tenants of the termination of this Agreement and transfer of any advance rents and security deposits to Owner.

22. **Sale of Property.** In the event Owner desires to sell the Property through Owner's own efforts or those of a firm other than Agent, Owner shall: (a) promptly notify Agent that the Property is for sale and, if applicable, disclose to Agent the name of the listing firm; and (b) promptly notify Agent if the Property goes under contract and disclose to Agent the agreed-upon closing date.

23. **Entire Agreement; Modification.** This Agreement contains the entire agreement of the parties and supersedes all prior written and oral proposals, understandings, agreements and representations, all of which are merged herein. No modification of this Agreement shall be effective unless it is in writing and executed by all parties hereto.

24. **Non-Waiver of Default.** The failure of either party to insist, in any one or more instances, on the performance of any term or condition of this Agreement shall not be construed as a waiver or relinquishment of any rights granted hereunder or of the future performance of any such term or condition, and the obligations of the non-performing party with respect thereto shall continue in full force and effect.

25. **Governing Law; Venue.** The parties agree that this Agreement shall be governed by and construed in accordance with the laws of the State of North Carolina, and that in the event of a dispute, any legal action may only be instituted in the county where the Property is located.

26. **Relationship of Parties.** Although Owner and Agent agree that they will actively and materially participate with each other on a regular basis in fulfilling their respective obligations hereunder, the parties intend for their relationship to be that of independent contractors, and nothing contained in this Agreement shall be construed to create a partnership or joint venture of any kind.

27. **Exclusivity.** Owner agrees that Agent shall be the exclusive rental agent for the Property, and that no other party, including Owner, shall offer the Property for rent during the time this Agreement is in effect. Any rent nevertheless received by Owner or any third party will be transferred to Agent and thereafter accounted for as if originally received by Agent, including the deduction therefrom of any fee due Agent hereunder.

28. **Default.** If either party defaults in the performance of any of its obligations hereunder, in addition to any other remedies provided herein or by applicable law, the non-defaulting party shall have the right to terminate this Agreement if, within thirty days after providing the defaulting party with written notice of the default and the intent to terminate, the default remains uncured. Notwithstanding the foregoing, Agent shall have the right to terminate this Agreement immediately on written notice in the event Owner seeks bankruptcy protection, or the Property becomes subject to a foreclosure proceeding, or Owner fails to promptly pay for any costs associated with Owner's obligations under NC General Statutes Section 42-42 or to advance to Agent such sums as may be necessary to pay such costs.

29. **Costs in Event of Default.** If legal proceedings are brought by a party to enforce the terms, conditions or provisions of this Agreement, the prevailing party shall be entitled to recover all expenses (including, but not limited to, reasonable attorney fees, legal expenses and reasonable costs of collection) paid or incurred by such prevailing party in endeavoring to enforce the terms, conditions, or provisions of this Agreement and/or collect any amount owing in accordance with this Agreement.

30. **Authority to Enter into Agreement; Principal Contact.** Owner represents and warrants to Agent that Owner has full authority to enter into this Agreement, and that there is no other party with an interest in the Property whose joinder in this Agreement is necessary. Either _____ or _____ shall serve as Owner's principal contact for purposes of making all decisions and receiving all notices and rental payments contemplated by this Agreement, and all persons signing this Agreement as Owner hereby appoint either of said persons as Owner's agent and attorney-in-fact for the purposes set forth in this section.

31. **Use of Electronic Means; Notice.** The parties agree that electronic means may be used to sign this Agreement or to make any modifications the parties may agree to, and that any written notice, communication or documents may be transmitted to any mailing address, e-mail address, cell phone number or fax number used by the parties to communicate during the course of this Agreement. Either party may change the address to which any notice or documents should be sent by written notification to the other party in a manner permitted by this paragraph.

Page 6 of 8

Owner Initials _____ _____   Agent Initials _____ _____

STANDARD FORM 401
Revised 7/2018
©7/2018

FIGURE 16.1 (*Continued*)

32. **Binding Nature of Agreement.** This Agreement shall be binding upon and inure to the benefit of the heirs, legal and personal representatives, successors and permitted assigns of the parties.

33. **Assignments by Agent; Change of Ownership.** Owner agrees that at any time during the term of this Agreement, Agent may either assign Agent's rights and responsibilities hereunder to another real estate agency, or transfer to another person or entity all or part of the ownership of Agent's real estate agency, and that in the event of any such assignment or transfer, this Agreement shall continue in full force and effect; provided, that any assignee or transferee must be licensed to engage in the business of real estate brokerage in the State of North Carolina, and provided further that Agent promptly notifies Owner of such assignment or transfer. In the event of any such assignment or transfer, Owner may, in addition to all other termination rights hereunder, for a period of sixty (60) days' following the effective date of any such assignment or transfer, terminate this Agreement without cause on sixty (60) days' prior written notice to the assignee or transferee of Owner's intent to terminate this Agreement.

34. **Other Professional Services.** Owner acknowledges that Agent is being retained solely as a real estate professional, and understands that other professional service providers are available to render advice or services to Owner at Owner's expense, including but not limited to an attorney, insurance agent, tax advisor, engineer, home inspector, environmental consultant, architect, or contractor. If Agent procures any such services at the request of Owner, Owner agrees that Agent shall incur no liability or responsibility in connection therewith.

35. **Addenda.** Any addenda to this Agreement are described in the following space and attached hereto: _____
_____
_____
_____.

The parties agree that any such addenda shall constitute an integral part of this Agreement. In the event of a conflict between this Agreement and any such addenda, the terms of such addenda shall control.

36 .**Other.** _____
_____
_____
_____

[THIS SPACE INTENTIONALLY LEFT BLANK]

FIGURE 16.1 (*Continued*)

THE AGENT SHALL CONDUCT ALL BROKERAGE ACTIVITIES IN REGARD TO THIS AGREEMENT WITHOUT RESPECT TO THE RACE, COLOR, RELIGION, SEX, NATIONAL ORIGIN, HANDICAP OR FAMILIAL STATUS OF ANY PARTY OR PROSPECTIVE PARTY TO THE AGREEMENT. FURTHER, REALTORS® HAVE AN ETHICAL DUTY TO CONDUCT SUCH ACTIVITIES WITHOUT RESPECT TO THE SEXUAL ORIENTATION OR GENDER IDENTITY OF ANY PARTY OR PROSPECTIVE PARTY TO THIS AGREEMENT.

THE NORTH CAROLINA ASSOCIATION OF REALTORS®, INC. MAKES NO REPRESENTATION AS TO THE LEGAL VALIDITY OR ADEQUACY OF ANY PROVISION OF THIS FORM IN ANY SPECIFIC TRANSACTION.

OWNER:

_____(SEAL)   DATE:_____

_____(SEAL)   DATE:_____

_____(SEAL)   DATE:_____

_____(SEAL)   DATE:_____

AGENT: _____
          [Name of real estate firm]

BY:_____ Individual license #_____ DATE:_____
     [Authorized Representative]
Address:_____

Telephone:_____ Fax:_____ E-mail:_____

Owner:_____

Address:_____

Contact information: _____ _____ _____ _____
                      Home   Work   Cell   Email

Owner:_____

Address:_____

Contact information: _____ _____ _____ _____
                      Home   Work   Cell   Email

Owner:_____

Address:_____

Contact information: _____ _____ _____ _____
                      Home   Work   Cell   Email

Owner:_____

Address:_____

Contact information: _____ _____ _____ _____
                      Home   Work   Cell   Email

Page 8 of 8

STANDARD FORM 401
Revised 7/2018
©7/2018

FIGURE 16.1 (*Continued*)

failure to perform the duties identified under this agreement constitutes *breach of agency,* a serious infraction of the license law.

6. Terms under which other agents may be compensated are authorized.
7. Methods of marketing are authorized.
8. The owner's covenants are defined, including the owner's agreement to pay for authorized services, to allow agent to offer property without discrimination, to maintain a specified amount of liability insurance, and to hold the agent harmless if allowable by law from any claim resulting from managing property other than those claims resulting from agent's gross negligence or deliberate misconduct.
9. The handling of security deposits by the agent is specified in accordance with both license law and state law.
10. This paragraph authorizes the agent to put rental and tenant security deposits in an interest-bearing trust account.
11. Reasonable notice must be provided to the tenant before the owner or agent may enter the premises.
12. If the property was built before 1978, the owner is required to disclose information about lead-based paint and lead-based paint hazards. It is the agent's responsibility to ensure the owner's compliance with this requirement.
13. This paragraph provides for the agent's and the owner's duties to settle all accounts between them upon termination of the contract.
14. If the owner wishes to sell the property, the owner is required to notify the agent promptly of such intention. The owner is further required to notify the agent promptly if the property is put under contract.
15. The owner and the agent agree that the entire scope of their agreement has been defined as well as possible in this form as constructed and agree to standard rules of interpretation.
16. Nonwaiver of default.
17. Any legal action instituted under the rental agreement will be heard only in the county in which the property is located.
18. The owner and agent agree to work with each other in an independent contractor relationship. Their relationship shall not be construed as a partnership or a joint venture.
19. The owner agrees that the agent will act as the exclusive rental agent for the property.
20. In the event of default by either party, in addition to other remedies available by law, the nondefaulting party may terminate the contract.
21. In the event of a default, all expenses related to the default shall be repaid to the prevailing party.

22. The owner warrants to the agent that he has the authority to enter into this property management contract. The owner also warrants that there is no other party with an interest in the property who would be required to sign the contract.
23. Any notices required by either party shall be in writing and shall be sent via certified mail.
24. The contract shall be binding upon heirs, legal and personal representatives, successors, and permitted assigns of the parties.
25. The agent may assign her rights and responsibilities under the contract at any time to an entity licensed to engage in real estate brokerage in North Carolina. The owner, however, may terminate the contract without cause with 60 days' written notice.
26. The owner acknowledges that the agent is being retained solely for real estate services and should not be relied on for professional advice outside this area.
27. This paragraph lists any addenda attached to the contract.

Duties of the Property Manager

Property management is one of a number of specializations within the real estate industry. A property manager is a licensed real estate broker or brokerage firm that manages properties for owners as an agent. In acting as an agent, the property manager is a fiduciary and, therefore, owes all of the obligations imposed by the law of agency to each owner/principal. Additionally, because the property manager acts as an agent in renting, leasing, and perhaps selling the property, the property manager must have a real estate broker's license.

Any employee of the broker (property manager) who assists in any aspect of the property management process that requires negotiating rental or lease agreements or the amount of rents or security deposits must have a real estate broker's license, although the license may have provisional status attached to it. The property manager needs comprehensive specialized training to be able to satisfactorily perform the functions accepted under the typical contract with the property owner). In contrast to a property manager, a **resident manager** is *a person who may or may not actually live on the premises who is a salaried employee of the owner*. This person is required to have a real estate license unless he is employed by a corporation that owns the property or is a partner with an ownership interest in the entity that owns the property, if the owner is an entity other than a corporation.

According to North Carolina General Statute (G.S.) 93A-2 (c) (6), there is an exception made for W-2 employees of licensed brokers (property managers) to do certain tasks associated with renting or leasing the unit. These tasks, however, do not include listing, buying, renting, leasing, or auctioning real estate or offering to list, sell, buy, rent, lease, or auction real estate for compensation for others. Although a W-2 employee may not auction or offer to auction, he is not prohibited from being the crier at an auction. Only real estate licensees may auction or offer to auction, and they also must be licensed as an auctioneer. Referring a potential client or customer to a licensee for compensation is strictly prohibited.

The W-2 employee of a broker may perform certain ministerial tasks as outlined in North Carolina G.S. 93-A-2 under the supervision of the employing broker (See North Carolina General Statutes for details). Expert management is often necessary for income property to be a profitable investment. Competent management can provide a comprehensive, orderly program, on a continuing basis, of analyzing all of the investment aspects of a property to ensure a financially successful project.

PRINCIPAL FUNCTIONS OF PROPERTY MANAGERS

Renting space, collecting rents, and paying expenses are important basic functions of property managers; however, their functions and responsibilities exceed these activities to a considerable extent. In essence, a property manager's basic responsibilities are to produce the best possible net operating income from the property and to maintain and increase the value of the principal's investment.

The property manager may perform all of these duties, but it is not uncommon for duties such as marketing, executing leases, collecting rents, maintaining property, enforcing rules, performing a landlord's legal duties, and instituting legal actions to be delegated to an affiliated leasing agent. Remember that any person engaged in negotiating terms of a rental agreement or lease must have a real estate license. Even when some duties are assigned to a leasing agent, the property manager normally does not delegate responsibility for the management plan, the preparation of income/expense reports, record maintenance, and the handling of monies collected.

Preparing the Management Plan

Before entering into a management agreement with a property owner, the property manager must formulate a long-range plan to be followed in managing the property. The **management plan** is included in the **management proposal** submitted to the owner, along with a proposed management agreement. The formulation of the management plan includes the following steps:

1. **Analysis of the owner's objectives.** A determination of the owner's objective(s) in ownership of the property must be made. The property manager must be satisfied that these objectives are realistic. The owner's primary objective may be income, capital appreciation, or a tax shelter provided by depreciation. The Tax Reform Act of 1986 has limited the previous generous benefits in this area, but there are still significant tax advantages to the investor.

2. **Establishment of a rental schedule.** Several steps are involved in the formulation of a proper rental schedule that will provide the best income for

the owner. First, one must evaluate the national, regional, and local trends for the particular type of property. For example, if one were to evaluate the market for office space, it would be important to note that there has been a general oversupply of such property on a national and regional scale. A careful local analysis is also essential to evaluate how this trend might affect the specific property and its unique location. Next, one needs to prepare an analysis of comparable properties that are currently available for rent, just as one would identify comparable sales for listing a property. Finally, one should prepare an operating budget in advance, reflecting a realistic analysis of the projected income and expenses.

3. **Property analysis.** The property analysis covers a survey of the economic and physical aspects of the property. The economic aspects are data on previous duration of leases, vacancy and credit losses, rent schedules, and operating costs. The analysis of the physical aspects includes the determination of the condition of the property, necessary repairs, and necessary or appropriate capital expenditures.

4. **Preparation of budgets.** The last step in the formulation of a management plan is to establish an operating budget. The **operating budget** is *an annual budget and includes only those items of income and expense expected during a particular budget year* (see Figure 16.2).

Marketing and Renting the Property

The property manager needs to establish an effective advertising schedule to attract qualified tenants. This program must take into consideration many forms of advertising and other contacts to keep the recruitment of tenants as an ongoing process. In general, the manager strives to keep the vacancy rate low, because vacant property means loss of income not only to the owner but also to the manager if she is paid a percentage of the rents collected. A vacancy rate that is too low or nonexistent, however, may well be an indication of a rental schedule that is below market value. Therefore, a vacancy factor of about 3% is often taken as a favorable reflection of appropriate market rent as well as the marketing plan. A vacancy rate of 3% means the property is vacant 3% of the time. Conversely, an occupancy rate of 97% means the property is occupied 97% of the time. A property with a vacancy rate of 3% and an occupancy rate of 97% is vacant an average of 11 days per year and occupied an average of 354 days per year.

Qualifying and Selecting Tenants

Once a prospect has responded to the marketing efforts of the management company, the task of qualifying the tenant becomes very important. The prudent owner or manager will want to obtain a credit report as well as a criminal background check on all prospective tenants. In addition, the tenant's income will

"Refusing to rent or qualify tenants on the basis of criminal background, credit score, employment and income is acceptable if done in a non-discriminatory fashion and is not a violation of fair housing."
—Jack Marinello, DREI

Property:

Happy Hills Apartments

150 Childers Lane

Anywhere, NC

Income:		
Scheduled Gross Rental Income	$878,400	
24 Units @ $850/mo = $244,800		
66 Units @ $800/mo = $633,600		
Less Vacancy and Collection Losses (6%)	−52,704	
Plus Other Income (Vending, Laundry)	+6,500	
Effective Gross Income	$832,196	$832,196
Expenses:		
Management Fee	$83,220	
Maintenance Personnel	$30,000	
Ad valorem Property Taxes	$78,000	
Insurance Premiums	$14,900	
Electricity—offices & common areas	$7,200	
Water & Sewer	$43,200	
Advertising	$6,500	
Maintenance and Repair	$25,000	
Legal	$3,500	
Total Operating Expenses	$291,520	−$291,520
Net Operating Income		**$540,676**
Debt Service (principle & interest)		−377,450
Capital Expenditures		−28,000
Before Tax Cash Flow (to Property Owner)		**$135,226**

FIGURE 16.2 Sample annual operating budget.
Source: © 2019 OnCourse Learning

need to be verified to ascertain his ability to pay the required rent. It is preferable to also obtain references from prior landlords to determine the prospective tenant's history of paying rent. All of these steps will be used to help to establish the tenant's capability and "track record" of being able to fulfill his rental obligations. Certainly, checking these issues beforehand is extremely important to the decision of whether to rent to any prospective tenant. This process is similar to what mortgage lenders do when analyzing a borrower's capability to pay the monthly payments. Information that the owner or manager cannot consider in selecting a tenant includes race, color, religion, sex, national origin, handicap, or familial status. These are classes protected by fair housing legislations. For more detailed information, consult Chapter 17. The manager should also take steps to ensure that the space is suitable for the tenants' needs. Often, in the quest for increased occupancy, landlords and managers will rent properties to tenants that are not particularly well suited to the space being considered. The size and configuration of the space should be carefully considered as well as the length of time the tenant, and landlord, are willing to enter into a lease agreement. Many landlords will not be interested in short-term rentals due to the turnover cost of having to re-lease the property as well as the clean-up costs involved. The best situation is when a well-qualified tenant finds a property that meets his needs as far as rental terms, size, and layout as well as its availability for his use for the desired period of time.

Collecting Rents and Security Deposits

Perhaps the most important single function of the manager is the faithful accounting of all funds that come into her possession. North Carolina has three major statutes that affect the handling of funds of others in the agent's fiduciary role. The Real Estate License Law and the Rules of the Real Estate Commission enforce strict duties of accounting and the operation of trust accounts. The North Carolina Residential Rental Agreements Act, addressed in Chapter 15, influences the relationship of the manager to tenants in residential property, such as that in the management of apartment buildings. The North Carolina Tenant Security Deposit Act (see Chapter 15) specifically addresses the amounts, handling, accounting, and refund of funds belonging to tenants.

Instituting Legal Actions

The real estate agent is not authorized to engage in actions that constitute the practice of law. Examples of such activities include giving legal advice or opinion, drafting contracts, and attempting to provide legal representation for another person. Just as the agent can institute legal action on his own behalf as a private citizen, the agent is authorized to file complaints and seek appropriate legal actions for the owner. These actions include the collection of rents and instituting proceedings for eviction.

Maintaining the Property

The property manager is the trustee for the owner, who has placed a great deal of trust in and responsibility upon the agent to take proper care of a substantial financial asset. Upkeep of the property to maintain and increase its value is an ongoing task. The manager should have a schedule for daily routine attention as well as long-range plans for items such as painting and major repairs such as reroofing. If repairs and maintenance are not kept up appropriately, the attractiveness to tenants and subsequent rental income will suffer. It is an excellent practice to make use of a property condition checklist that will be used upon initial move-in by the tenant as well as for periodic inspections and for use during the move-out inspection. Most property managers do not make debt service payments for the owner, because debt service is not considered an operating expense.

Property managers should consult the property owners to determine that the appropriate types and amount of insurance are maintained on the property. Insurance protects the property adequately from fire and other hazards and protects the owner and the agent from liability. The property management contract should designate the person responsible for maintaining the insurance coverage.

Performing the Landlord's Duties

Upon signing the property management agreement, the landlord has essentially delegated her statutory duties to the real estate agent. Failure to perform these duties properly is a specific example of the breach of the duty of agency as defined by the Real Estate Commission, and it subjects the agent to serious penalties. In the case of residential property, the Residential Rental Agreements Act specifically requires the owner to maintain "fit premises." The owner and the agent are required to do all that is necessary to provide and maintain property so it is fit for human habitation. Individual leases may require other specific items of performance by the agent, such as certain services or maintenance. Failure to provide all such services as called for would breach the lease as well as the fiduciary agency duty.

A smoke detector law requires landlords and their agents to provide properly installed smoke detectors in all residential rental properties in North Carolina. Landlords and their agents are further required to install new batteries when a new tenant moves in and to repair inoperative smoke detectors when notified of the inoperative condition of the detector in writing by the tenant. The tenant shall be responsible for the periodic replacement of the batteries as needed during the period of tenancy.

"A property manager has a 30-day reporting requirement to the owner, but has 45 days to deliver copies of documents and leases to the owner. This is the ONLY exception to the general rule that a licensee must provide all documents to a client immediately, but never later than 5 days."
—Steve Robinson

Maintaining Records and Reporting to the Owner

Included in the agent's covenants is a requirement that the property manager provide a *periodic (monthly) accounting of all funds received and disbursed*. This accounting is called a **property management report**. It contains detailed information of all receipts and expenditures for the period covered (plus the year-to-date) and relates each item to the operating budget for the period.

Americans with Disabilities Act and Fair Housing Laws

"The Americans with Disabilities Act (ADA) also requires all employers who employ more than 15 people to make reasonable accommodations to any employee who has a handicap or disability."
—Melea Lemon, DREI

Property managers will need to keep themselves informed as to the Americans with Disabilities Act (ADA) and other fair housing laws. The ADA attempts to make certain that all places of public accommodation will be reasonably accessible to all people whether or not they have a handicapped condition. In older properties, the manager may have to assist the owner in creating a plan to retro-fit certain aspects of the building to remove barriers that can limit, as well as to construct features that can enable, public accessibility to all areas of the property. These areas of modification are undertaken in cases in which the changes can be made reasonably and are economically practical. For more details visit www.ada.gov.

Math Concepts for this Chapter

Commission earned on property management transaction:

1. Danny is the property manager for Tarheel Apartments. There are 10 units in the building that rent for $750 each per month. One of the units was vacant for 15 days last month. If Danny's management fee is 10% and he is only paid when properties are occupied, what amount did he earn last month?

   Solution:
   $750 × 9 = $6,750 rents due for 9 units
   $750 ÷ 2 = $375 rents due for half month (15 days)
   $6,750 + $375 = $7,125 total rents paid
   $7,125 × 10% = $712.50 management fee earned

Summary of Important Points

1. Property managers are agents entrusted with the fiduciary duty of managing property for others and, therefore, must have a real estate broker's license.
2. The property manager's basic responsibilities are to produce the best possible net operating income from the property and to maintain and increase the value of the principal's investment.
3. The property manager fulfills his basic responsibilities by formulating a management plan, soliciting tenants, leasing space, collecting rent, hiring and training employees, maintaining good tenant relations, providing for adequate maintenance, protecting tenants, maintaining adequate insurance, keeping adequate records, and auditing and paying bills.
4. The management proposal contains performance commitments on the part of the property manager, if employed by the owner.
5. A primary function of the property manager is that of accounting for all funds received on behalf of the principal. Several state regulations, including the Residential Rental Agreements Act, the Tenant Security Deposit Act, and the North Carolina Real Estate License Law, govern this accounting process.
6. The management agreement is an employment contract in which a property manager is employed by a property owner to act as her agent. Like the listing agreement, it establishes the agency relationship. The property

manager is responsible for fulfilling the owner's obligations, and failure to perform the duties properly is deemed a breach of the agency duty.

7. The property management report is a periodic accounting provided by a property manager to the property owner.

8. Properties that may require management are condominiums, cooperatives, apartments, single-family rental houses, mobile home parks, office buildings, shopping malls, and industrial property.

9. Agency agreements with owners/landlords must be in writing from the point of inception.

10. Agency agreements with tenants can be oral but must be converted to writing before making offer to rent or lease.

Review Questions

Answers to the review questions are in the Answer Key at the back of the book.

1. All of the following statements about property management are correct EXCEPT:
   A. property management is a specialized field within the real estate industry.
   B. a property manager acts as an agent of the property owner.
   C. the terms property manager and resident manager have the same meaning.
   D. a property manager is a fiduciary.

2. The property management agreement is different from that of a listing agreement in which of the following ways?
   A. property management contracts do not have to be in writing from the inception of the agreement
   B. dual agency is NOT allowed in a property management agreement
   C. property management contracts do NOT have to automatically expire at the end of the agreement
   D. property management agreements do NOT have to have to contain anti discrimination language

3. A budget based on forecast income and anticipated expenses over a period of years is called a(n):
   A. stabilized budget.
   B. projected budget.
   C. anticipated budget.
   D. operating budget.

4. Which of the following creates an agency relationship between a property manager and the property owner?
   A. management proposal
   B. management report
   C. management agreement
   D. management plan

5. A nonlicensed, salaried employee working for a licensed real estate broker who is contracted to manage property for a property owner can perform all of the following activities without a real estate license EXCEPT:
   A. marketing.
   B. showing properties.
   C. negotiating terms of a lease.
   D. instituting legal actions.

6. Failure of the broker to perform duties under the property management agreement:
   A. is a breach of the duty of agency.
   B. would make the broker liable to the owner, but not to the Real Estate Commission.
   C. would make the broker liable to the Real Estate Commission, but not to the owner.
   D. none of the above.

7. Agency agreements must be in writing from the time of inception with a:
   A. licensee.
   B. lessor.
   C. lessee.
   D. lien holder.

8. With a tenant, oral agency must be converted to a written format prior to:
   A. the beginning of the lease term.
   B. first substantial contact.
   C. submitting an offer to purchase.
   D. submitting an offer to lease or rent.

9. Acme Property Management has contracted to manage a eight-unit apartment building for a 9% management fee on all rents collected. The units each rent for $850 per month. Currently there are six units that are fully rented, one that was rented for 18 days and one that was occupied but the tenant failed to pay the monthly rent. How much management fee is Acme entitled to this month?
   A. $612
   B. $581
   C. $505
   D. $490

10. A property management company has agreed to manage the Happy Hills apartments. Happy Hills consists of six units that each rent for $950 per month. Last month one of the units was vacant. If the management fee was 8% what amount did the management company earn?
   A. $190
   B. $380
   C. $456
   D. $4,560

CHAPTER 17
FAIR HOUSING

KEY TERMS

Americans with Disabilities Act
blockbusting
brokerage
Civil Rights Act of 1866
civil suit
disability
discriminatory advertising
Federal Fair Housing Act of 1968
Federal Fair Housing Amendments Act of 1988
North Carolina Fair Housing Act of 1983
North Carolina Human Relations Commission
redlining
steering

LEARNING OBJECTIVES

At the conclusion of this chapter, you should be able to:

1. Describe the provisions of the Federal Fair Housing Act of 1968 as amended in 1988, including the criteria upon which discrimination is prohibited, definitions of terminology, exemptions, and provisions for enforcement.
2. Describe the provisions of the North Carolina Fair Housing Act of 1983, including unlawful discriminatory practices, exemptions, enforcement, and penalties.
3. Describe the provisions of the Civil Rights Act of 1866, including prohibitions and enforcement.

IN THIS CHAPTER

This chapter discusses the federal laws that prohibit discrimination in housing, as well as the North Carolina Fair Housing Act of 1983. Of major importance is the Federal Fair Housing Act of 1968 (Title VIII of the 1968 Civil Rights Act), as amended. The other significant federal law is the Civil Rights Act of 1866. The 1968 Act applies specifically to housing, whereas the 1866 law prohibits all discrimination

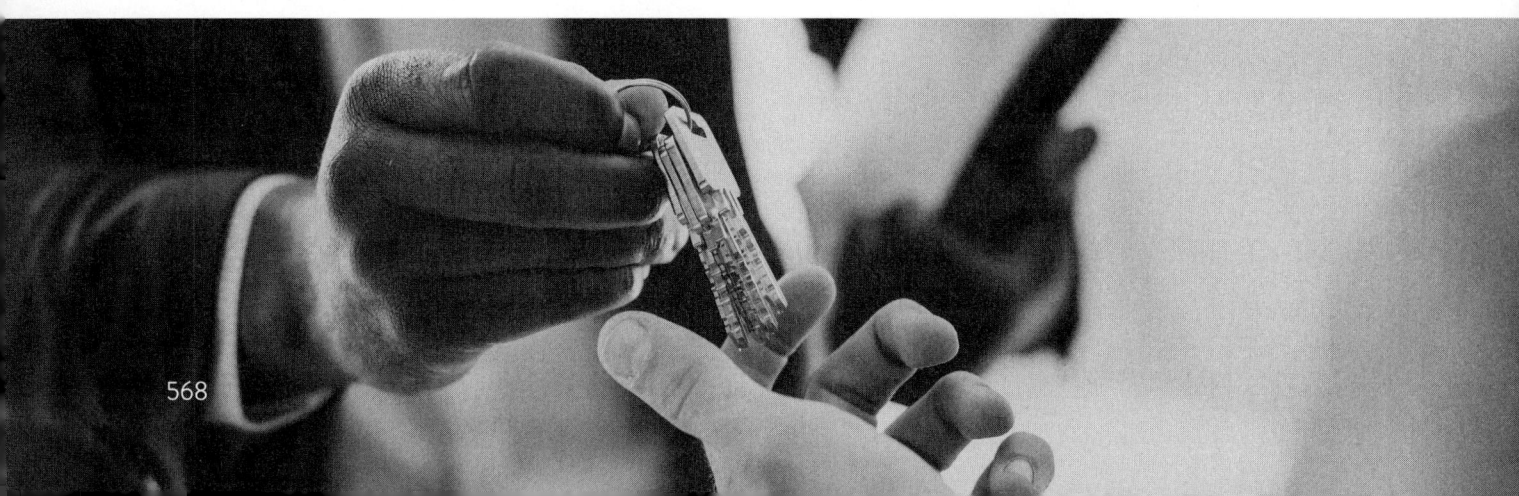

based on race in housing and in any other situation. The North Carolina Act is similar to Title VIII of the 1968 Civil Rights Act but has significantly different exemptions.

FEDERAL FAIR HOUSING ACT

Originally enacted by Congress as Title VIII of the Civil Rights Act of 1968, the **Federal Fair Housing Act of 1968** (Figure 17.1) *prohibited discrimination in housing on the basis of race, color, religion, or national origin.* An amendment in the Housing and Community Development Act of 1974 added the prohibition against discrimination on the basis of sex. The **Federal Fair Housing Amendments Act of 1988** added *provisions to prevent discrimination based on both mental and physical handicaps or familial status.* The addition of the "handicapped" category requires landlords to allow people with disabilities to make reasonable modifications to an apartment, at the tenant's expense, to accommodate their special needs. For example, a tenant must be allowed to install a ramp or widen doors to accommodate a wheelchair or install grab bars in a bathroom. At the end of the tenancy, the tenant must return the premises to their original condition, also at his own expense. The "familial status" category prevents landlords from recruiting for "Adults Only" in most circumstances. Provisions do exist, however, for elderly housing.

As the law presently exists, it is illegal to discriminate on the basis of race, color, religion, sex, national origin, handicap, or familial status in the sale or rental of housing or residential lots, in the advertising of the sale or rental of housing, in the financing of housing, and in the provision of real estate brokerage services.

> "There are seven different protected class categories. Think FReSHCoRN. Familial status, race, sex (gender), handicapped, color, religion or creed, and national origin."
> –Bill Gallaher, DREI

Definitions

The Federal Fair Housing Act as amended in 1988 contains definitions of certain terms, as follows:

> *Dwelling*—"Any building, structure, or portion thereof which is occupied as, or designed or intended for occupancy as, a residence by one or more families, and any vacant land which is offered for sale or lease for the construction or location thereon of any such building, structure or portion thereof."
>
> *Elderly Housing*—Housing in which 80% of the units are occupied by at least one person aged 55 or older.
>
> *Familial Status*—"Includes children under age 18; pregnant women; or persons with, or in the process of obtaining, custody of children."

> "'Familial status' doesn't mean 'families' or 'married couples.' It protects custodial parent with children under the age of 18. Familial status makes it illegal to restrict or prohibit the presence of children."
> –Jim Hriso

CHAPTER 17 Fair Housing

FIGURE 17.1 Poster for equal housing opportunity.
Source: www.HUD.gov

Handicap—Any physical or mental impairment that limits one or more of the essential functions of life.

Person—"Includes one or more individuals, corporations, partnerships, associations, labor organizations, legal representatives, mutual companies, joint stock companies, trusts, unincorporated organizations, trustees, trustees in bankruptcy, receivers, and fiduciaries."

To Rent—"Includes to lease, to sublease, to let, and otherwise to grant for a consideration the right to occupy premises not owned by the occupant."

The following discussion addresses specific acts prohibited in each category.

Blockbusting

The Fair Housing Act of 1968 specifically makes **blockbusting** (also known as *panic peddling*) illegal and defines the practice as *"for profit, to induce or attempt to induce any person to sell or rent any dwelling by representations regarding the entry or prospective entry into the neighborhood of a person or persons of a particular race, color, religion, sex, national origin, handicap, or familial status."* Blockbusting describes the practice of real estate agents attempting to induce owners to list property for sale or rent by telling them that people of a particular race, color, religion, sex, national origin, handicap, or familial status are moving into the area.

Steering

Steering *is the directing of prospective purchasers or tenants, especially minority purchasers or tenants, toward or away from specific neighborhoods because they belong to a protected class under the Fair Housing Act (i.e., because of their race, color, religion, sex, handicap, national origin, or familial status).* The prohibition against steering falls under the general prohibition of refusing to sell, rent, or negotiate the sale or rental of housing or residential lots. Examples of steering include a real estate agent (1) showing a white prospect properties located in areas populated only by white people, (2) showing black prospects properties only in integrated areas or areas populated only by blacks, (3) showing Polish prospects properties in areas populated only by Poles, and (4) showing tenants with disabilities only units in buildings already housing tenants with disabilities.

Advertising

Additionally the Fair Housing Act of 1968 specifies that it is illegal "to make, print, or publish, or cause to be made, printed, or published *any notice, statement, or advertisement, with respect to the sale or rental of a dwelling that indicates any preference, limitation, or discrimination based on race, color, religion, sex, national origin, handicap or familial status, or an intention to make any such preference, limitation, or discrimination.*" Examples of **discriminatory advertising** are (1) an advertisement for the sale of condominium units or rental apartments that contains pictures showing owners or tenants on the property who are of only one race, (2) an advertisement stating that the owner prefers tenants who are male college students, (3) a "For Sale" sign that specifies "No Puerto Ricans," (4) an apartment advertisement stating "Adults Only."

Prohibited Acts

This category contains a limited number of exemptions for owners in renting or selling their own property. These exemptions are examined subsequently in the chapter. In the absence of an exemption, the following specific acts are prohibited:

1. Refusing to sell or rent housing or refusing to negotiate the sale or rental of residential lots on the basis of discrimination because of race, color, religion, sex, national origin, handicap, or familial status. This includes representing to any person on discriminatory grounds "that any dwelling is not available for inspection, sale, or rental when such dwelling is in fact available." Also, it is illegal "to refuse to sell or rent after the making of a bona fide offer, or to refuse to negotiate for the sale or rental of, or otherwise make unavailable or deny, a dwelling to a person" because of race, color, religion, sex, national origin, handicap, or familial status.

    Examples of violations of these prohibited acts are (1) advising a prospective buyer that a house has been sold when it has not, because of the prospect's national origin; (2) refusing to accept an offer to purchase because the offeror is a member of a particular religious faith; (3) telling a rental applicant that an apartment is not available for inspection because the applicant is a female (or male) when the apartment is actually vacant and available for inspection; (4) refusing to rent to a person confined to a wheelchair or refusing to make reasonable modifications (at the tenant's expense) to an apartment to accommodate a wheelchair; and (5) refusing to rent to a family with children.

2. The act makes it illegal "to discriminate against any person in the terms, conditions, or privileges of sale or rental of a dwelling, or in the provision of services or facilities in connection therewith, because of race, color, religion, sex, national origin, handicap or familial status."

    Examples of prohibited acts in this category are as follows: (1) The manager of an apartment complex routinely requires tenants to have a security deposit in an amount equivalent to one month's rent unless the rental applicant is black, in which case a deposit equivalent to two months' rent is required. (2) The manager of an apartment complex restricts use of the complex swimming pool to white tenants only. (3) The owner of a condominium will include in the purchase of a condominium apartment a share of stock and membership in a nearby country club, provided the purchaser is not from Israel. (4) A landlord charges a larger deposit to a couple with young children. (5) A landlord charges a higher rent to a person in a wheelchair.

Illegal Financing

Redlining describes violations of the Fair Housing Act by lending institutions. The term is based on the theory that some lending institutions, before the enactment of the Fair Housing Act, may have circled certain areas on the map with a red line and refused to make loans to people who wanted to buy property in the areas circled.

The act prohibits lending institutions from refusing to make loans to purchase, construct, or repair a dwelling by discriminating on the basis of race, color, religion, sex, national origin, handicap, or familial status. In the past, areas were redlined because they were highly integrated or populated by minorities. Today, however, the Fair Housing Act does not limit the prohibition against financial discrimination to the refusal to make loans because of the character of the neighborhood in which the property is located. The prohibition against discrimination also applies to individuals by making it illegal "to deny a loan or other financial assistance to a person applying therefore for the purpose of purchasing, constructing, improving, repairing, or maintaining a dwelling" or "to discriminate against him in fixing the amount, interest rate, duration, or other terms or conditions of such loan or other financial assistance."

Real Estate Brokerage Services

The Federal Fair Housing Act as amended in 1988 prohibits discrimination in the provision of **brokerage** services (designed to *bring buyers and sellers together to negotiate terms of a real estate sale*) and states that:

> it shall be unlawful to deny any person access to or membership or participation in any multiple listing service, real estate brokers' organization, or other service, organization, or facility relating to the business of selling or renting dwellings, or to discriminate against him in the terms or conditions of such access, membership or participation on account of race, color, religion, sex, national origin, handicap, or familial status.

This provision of the Fair Housing Law makes the denial of membership or the imposition of special terms or conditions of membership in any real estate organization on discriminatory grounds illegal. Additionally, the refusal of a multiple listing service to accept a property for inclusion in the service or the refusal of a member broker to place a listing in the service on discriminatory grounds is illegal. The act requires real estate organizations and real estate agents to provide their services without discrimination.

Exemptions

The Fair Housing Law provides exemptions to property owners under certain conditions. None of these exemptions is available, however, if either of the following has occurred:

1. Discriminatory advertising has been used.
2. The services of a real estate licensee or the services of any person in the business of selling or renting dwellings are used. (Additionally, North Carolina licensing provisions prohibit licensees from discriminatory practices in their personal dealings, even when they are acting for themselves and not as an agent for others.)

For the purpose of this act, a person is deemed to be in the business of selling or renting dwellings if the individual has, within the preceding 12 months, participated as principal in three or more transactions involving the sale or rental of any dwelling or any interest therein; the person has, within the preceding 12 months, participated as agent, other than in the sale of one's personal residence, in providing sales or rental facilities or sales or rental services in two or more transactions involving the sale or rental of any dwelling or any interest therein; or the individual is the owner of any dwelling designed or intended for occupancy by, or occupied by, five or more families.

In the absence of either of the preceding occurrences, exemptions from the Fair Housing Act are available as follows:

1. An owner who does not own more than three single-family dwellings at one time is exempt. Unless the owner was living in or was the most recent occupant of the house sold, she is limited to only one exemption in any 24-month period.
2. An owner of an apartment building containing no more than four apartments is exempt in the rental of the apartments, provided the owner occupies one of the apartments as a personal residence.
3. Religious organizations are exempt as regards properties owned and operated for the benefit of their members only and not for commercial purposes, provided membership in the organization is not restricted on account of race, color, sex, national origin, handicap, or familial status.
4. A private club not open to the public is exempt as regards properties owned by the club to provide lodging for the benefit of the members and not for commercial purposes, provided membership in the organization is not

restricted on account of race, color, religion, sex, national origin, handicap, or familial status.

5. In certain cases involving housing for the elderly, there is a limited exemption permitting discrimination based on familial status.

Enforcement

The Fair Housing Act is enforced in three ways:

1. By administrative procedure through the Office of Equal Opportunity of the Department of Housing and Urban Development (HUD), HUD can act on its own information and initiative, and it must act in response to complaints filed up to one year after an alleged discrimination. If a state or local law where the property is located is substantially equivalent, HUD must refer the complaint to the state or to local authorities. In North Carolina, complaints are referred to the **North Carolina Human Relations Commission** (NCHRC) unless there is a local equivalent fair housing agency. Complaints must be in writing and state the facts upon which an alleged violation is based. If HUD or the equivalent state or local organization is unable to obtain a voluntary conciliation and the appropriate one of these organizations determines that there are reasonable grounds for complaint, a charge will be filed and the case will be referred to an administrative law judge (ALJ), unless either party elects to have the case tried in a civil court. The ALJ may make a recommendation to the NCHRC. Three commissioners then determine whether to impose a civil penalty of up to $10,000 for a first offense, $25,000 if there has been another violation within five years, and $50,000 if there have been two or more violations in seven years. An individual can be fined $25,000 or $50,000 without limitation of time periods if he engages in multiple discriminatory practices.

2. The aggrieved party, with or without filing a complaint to HUD, can bring a **civil suit** in federal district court within two years of the alleged violation of the Act. A civil suit is *an action in a court of equity that seeks financial compensation for loss caused by another.* If the aggrieved party wins the case, the court can issue an injunction against the violator and award actual damages and punitive damages with no limitation by the statute.

3. The Department of Justice can file a civil suit in any appropriate U.S. District Court where the attorney general has reasonable cause to believe that any person or group is engaged in a pattern of violation of the act and, as such, raises an issue of general public importance. The court can issue an injunction or a restraining order against the person responsible and impose fines of up to $50,000 to "vindicate the public interest." A first-time fine of $50,000 may be imposed where a "pattern of practice" of discrimination is discovered.

NORTH CAROLINA FAIR HOUSING ACT

Unlawful Discrimination

The **North Carolina Fair Housing Act of 1983** is similar to the Federal Fair Housing Act of 1968. The *prohibitions of discrimination in housing are virtually identical to those of the federal act.* Therefore, any violation of these provisions subjects the individual to both state and federal penalties. The NCHRC and equivalent local agencies now handle fair housing complaints within North Carolina.

Exemptions

Although the prohibited discrimination acts are essentially identical in the federal and state fair housing laws, the North Carolina Fair Housing Act has several very different exemptions.

1. Whereas the federal law provides an exemption for a private owner selling his own home without the participation of a real estate broker, the state act does not provide any such consideration. Therefore, the North Carolina law is more restrictive than the federal law on this point. In a for sale by owner (FSBO) transaction, the owner does *not* have the right to turn away a minority applicant. The state does, however, provide an exemption for the rental of rooms in a home (not a boarding house) occupied by the owner.
2. The federal act provides exemptions for the owner of a rental unit of four families or fewer if the owner occupies one of the units. The state act broadens this exemption to include the case in which the owner or a member of the owner's family occupies one of the units.
3. The state law also makes a provision for the rental of rooms in a single-sex dormitory, an issue that is not addressed in the federal law.

Enforcement and Penalties

The North Carolina statute also includes provisions for the enforcement of the law that are different from the enforcement provisions of the federal law. The primary agency is the NCHRC. Any person who believes she has been discriminated against in a housing matter can file a complaint with this commission or an equivalent local enforcement agency. The commission or local agency must then investigate the situation and try to effect voluntary compliance with the law through negotiation and persuasion. If this action is not effective in gaining voluntary compliance, the commission or local agency must either initiate a lawsuit in a state court on behalf of the complainant or advise the aggrieved party of her right to start a private lawsuit. The individual has this latter right even if the commission or local agency does not find merit in the case through its own proceedings.

The NCHRC is certified as a "substantially equivalent agency" to HUD as defined in the federal statute. Thus, the Commission enforces the 1968 Fair Housing Act and the 1988 amendments to it as well as the North Carolina law.

FEDERAL CIVIL RIGHTS ACT OF 1866

The first significant statute affecting equal housing opportunity was the **Civil Rights Act of 1866**. Far from being an obsolete law, this statute has had a major impact on fair housing concepts, interestingly through a landmark case in 1968, the same year the Federal Fair Housing Act became law. In the case of *Jones* v. *Alfred H. Mayer Company,* the plaintiff was denied an apartment because of his race. The U.S. Supreme Court applied the Civil Rights Act of 1866 to prohibit racially based discrimination in housing, notwithstanding the exemptions written into the Fair Housing Act of 1968. The ruling provides an interesting interplay between the two acts. Although the 1968 statute has a number of exemptions, the 1866 law has no exemptions and, among other things, contains the blanket statement that all citizens have the same right to inherit, buy, sell, or lease all real and personal property. The basic interpretation of this statute is that *it prohibits all racial discrimination.* The exemptions provided for in the 1968 law *cannot* be used to enforce any racial discrimination.

> ### Test Tip!
> There are no exemptions to the Civil Rights Act of 1866. The exemptions applicable to the 1968 Act do not apply to the 1866 Act or to the sale of a personal residence under the state Act of 1983.

ADDITIONAL REGULATION OF FAIR HOUSING IN NORTH CAROLINA

In addition to the two federal and one state Fair Housing Acts, real estate brokers have several other regulations to comply with in their brokerage practice:

1. Regulations of the North Carolina Real Estate Commission prohibit licensees from engaging in discriminatory practices in their personal transactions, that is, when not acting as an agent or a fiduciary. Even though a private individual (nonlicensee) still has a few limited exemptions to the laws, licensees are held to a higher standard of conduct. Thus, one who practices any form of discrimination on a personal level is disqualified from holding a certificate of public trust, in this case, a real estate license.

2. The following provision must be included in all written agency contracts, highlighted, as in boldface type:

   THE AGENT (FIRM) SHALL CONDUCT ALL BROKERAGE ACTIVITIES IN REGARD TO THIS AGREEMENT WITHOUT RESPECT TO THE RACE, COLOR, RELIGION, SEX, NATIONAL ORIGIN, HANDICAP OR FAMILIAL STATUS OF ANY PARTY OR PROSPECTIVE PARTY TO THE AGREEMENT. FURTHER, REALTORS HAVE AN ETHICAL DUTY TO CONDUCT SUCH ACTIVITIES WITHOUT RESPECT TO THE SEXUAL ORIENTATION OR GENDER IDENTITY OF ANY PARTY OR PROSPECTIVE PARTY TO THIS AGREEMENT.

3. The Real Estate Commission's Rule A.1601 makes brokers who violate the state Fair Housing Act subject to disciplinary action by the Commission.
4. Additionally, REALTORS® (remember, not all brokers are REALTORS®) are bound to a commitment to fair housing and equal opportunity through Article 10 of their Code of Ethics.

Thus, federal law, state law, and the Real Estate Licensing Commission require a real estate licensee practicing in North Carolina to practice fair housing. The REALTORS® Code of Ethics further requires REALTORS® to practice fair housing.

EQUAL HOUSING OPPORTUNITY TODAY

When the concept of fair housing is discussed, many people have the idea that the issue has long been resolved through actions such as the civil rights movement of the 1960s. Despite the intention of the 1866 and the 1968 Civil Rights Acts to provide equal housing opportunity for all citizens, this goal has not been achieved in practice. Many proposals have been developed to correct this situation. One means of enforcing the law is through an organized program of testing by civil rights groups. In 1968 the Johnson administration supported a Fair Housing Initiatives Program to provide funding of testers. The National Association of REALTORS® negotiated an agreement with HUD to ensure that funded testing is objective, reliable, and controlled and then provided its endorsement to the program. The program is ongoing.

AMERICANS WITH DISABILITIES ACT

The **Americans with Disabilities Act,** which took effect on January 26, 1992, specifically *protects the rights of individuals with disabilities.* **Disability** is defined in U.S. Code 42, Sec. 12101, as a *physical or mental impairment that substantially limits one or more of the major life activities of a person.* Under this law, individuals with disabilities cannot be denied access to public transportation, any commercial facility, or public accommodation. This act covers employers who have

15 or more employees. It also applies to all local and state governments. Public accommodations are defined as private businesses that affect commerce and trade, such as inns, banks, places of education, and daycare centers. Commercial facilities are those intended for nonresidential use, such as factories.

To comply with this law, public accommodations and commercial facilities are to be designed, constructed, and altered to meet the accessibility standards of the new law if readily achievable. "Readily achievable" means able to be carried out without undue difficulty or expense. Examples of barriers to be removed or alterations to be made include placing ramps, lowering telephones, widening doors, installing grab bars in toilet stalls, and adding raised letters on elevator controls. Commercial facilities are not required to remove barriers in existing facilities.

As of March 13, 1991, all newly constructed public accommodations and commercial facilities must be readily accessible and usable by individuals with disabilities. The Americans with Disabilities Act is enforced by the U.S. attorney general. Punishment for violating this law includes injunctions against operation of a business, a fine of up to $50,000 for the first offense, and a fine of $100,000 for subsequent offenses. Be aware that individuals with AIDS, alcoholism, or mental illness are included in the category of people with a mental or physical disability that impairs one or more of their life functions.

SEXUAL HARASSMENT

It is a violation of North Carolina law for a lessor or his agent to sexually harass a tenant or prospective tenant. The landlord or his agent is prohibited from making unsolicited overt requests for sexual acts when submission to such conduct is a term of the execution or continuation of a lease or the according of tenant's rights under the lease.

Summary of Important Points

1. The Federal Fair Housing Act of 1968, as amended, prohibits discrimination in housing because of race, color, religion, sex, national origin, mental or physical handicap, or familial status (family members under 18 years of age, pregnant women, or persons with or in the process of obtaining custody of children).
2. Discrimination is prohibited in the selling or renting of housing, in advertising the sale or rental of housing, in the financing of housing, and in providing real estate brokerage services. The Federal Fair Housing Act of 1968 also makes blockbusting illegal.
3. Four exemptions are provided to owners by the 1968 Federal Fair Housing Act in selling or renting housing: to owners who do not own more than three houses, owners of apartment buildings in which there are not more than

four apartments where the owner occupies one of the apartments, religious organizations as regards properties used for the benefit of members only, and private clubs as regards lodging used for the benefit of members only.

4. Owners' exemptions are not available if the owner used discriminatory advertising or the services of a real estate broker. Additionally, North Carolina real estate licensees are prohibited from discriminatory practices in their personal affairs.

5. Title VIII of the 1968 Civil Rights Act, referred to as the Fair Housing Act, was amended significantly in 1988. It is now enforced through the office of Equal Opportunity of HUD by referring complaints to the NCHRC. The NCHRC first attempts voluntary conciliation and if necessary, refers the case to an ALJ, who can impose financial penalties of $10,000 to $50,000. Fair Housing violations may result in a civil suit in federal court or a lawsuit in federal court brought by the U.S. attorney general. Penalties of up to $50,000 may be imposed for the first offense if there is shown to be a pattern of discrimination.

6. North Carolina has its own Fair Housing Act, which is similar to the federal act in its prohibitions of discrimination. The exemptions are different in that there is no exemption for the sale of a home by a private owner, and the exemption for an apartment building with four or fewer units is extended to include a unit occupied by an owner or a member of the owner's family.

7. North Carolina has its own Fair Housing Act enforcement agency, the NCHRC. This agency is recognized as being "substantially equivalent" to HUD and its federal enforcement procedures. The NCHRC is authorized to investigate complaints and initiate a lawsuit in a state court or advise the party of the right to do so alone. Several larger cities and counties also have local fair housing enforcement agencies recognized by HUD as "substantially equivalent."

8. The Civil Rights Act of 1866 prohibits discrimination only on the basis of race. The prohibition is not limited to housing but includes all real estate and personal property transactions. The act can be enforced only by civil suit in federal court.

9. Real estate agents have additional restrictions imposed on them by the NCHRC, as do REALTORS® by the REALTORS® Code of Ethics.

10. *Blockbusting* (also known as *panic peddling*) is inducing or attempting to induce, for profit, any person to sell or rent any dwelling by representations regarding the entry or prospective entry into the neighborhood of a person or persons of a particular race, color, religion, sex, national origin, handicap, or familial status.

11. *Steering* is directing prospective purchasers or tenants, especially minority purchasers or tenants, toward or away from specific neighborhoods

> "The Housing for Older Persons Act (HOPA) did not create the protected class of age. Age is never a protected class in fair housing. HOPA allows certain age restricted communities who 1) hold themselves out as such and 2) qualify in certain ways and 3) verify residents' ages to be exempted from familial status and therefore prohibit children."
>
> –Len Elder, DREI

because they belong to a protected class under the Fair Housing Act (i.e., because of their race, color, religion, sex, handicap, national origin, or familial status). The prohibition against steering falls under the general prohibition of refusing to sell, rent, or negotiate the sale or rental of housing or residential lots.

12. *Redlining* is the practice of circling areas on a map with a red line and refusing to make loans to people who want to buy property in the areas circled.

13. The Federal Fair Housing Act's prohibitions also apply to individuals. Therefore, it is illegal to deny a loan or other financial assistance to a person applying for the purpose of purchasing, constructing, improving, repairing, or maintaining a dwelling or to discriminate against a person in fixing the amount, interest rate, duration, or other terms or conditions of such a loan or other financial assistance by discriminating on the basis of race, color, religion, sex, national origin, handicap, or familial status.

14. The North Carolina Fair Housing Act contains discrimination prohibitions that are virtually identical to those of the federal act. However, some of the exemptions are different.

15. The state act does not provide an exemption for a private owner selling her own home without the participation of a real estate broker, as in the federal law. In a North Carolina FSBO, the owner does not have the right to turn away a minority applicant. (An exception is rental of rooms in a home occupied by the owner, but this exception does not include boarding houses.)

16. The state act broadens the federal exemption for owners of rental units of four families or fewer (if the owner occupies one of the units) to include the case in which a member of the owner's family is the occupant.

17. The state act also makes a provision for the rental of rooms in a single-sex dormitory, an issue that is not addressed in the federal law.

Review Questions

Answers to the review questions are in the Answer Key at the back of the book.

1. Sam Seller refused to accept an offer to purchase his home from Juan Alvarado because Sam considered the $50 deposit insufficient. As to Sam's refusal, which of the following is correct?
    A. Sam is in violation of the Fair Housing Law because he discriminated on the basis of national origin.
    B. Since Sam refused the offer for financial reasons, he is not in violation of the 1968 Act.
    C. Sam is in violation of the Civil Rights Act of 1866.
    D. Sam is in violation of the North Carolina Fair Housing Act of 1983.

2. Which of the following is not a basis of discrimination prohibited by the 1968 Federal Fair Housing Act and/or the 1988 amendments?
   A. race
   B. sex
   C. occupation
   D. religion

3. Larry Landlord refused to rent one of five apartments in his building to Barbara Barrister, a black attorney. Which of the following statements about Larry's refusal is NOT correct?
   A. If Larry's refusal to rent to Barbara was because she is an attorney, he is not in violation of the 1968 Act.
   B. If Larry's refusal to rent to Barbara was because she is female, Larry is in violation of the 1968 Act amended in 1974.
   C. If Larry's refusal to rent to Barbara was because she is black, he is in violation of the 1968 Act and the Civil Rights Act of 1866.
   D. Larry is not in violation because his property contains more than four units.

4. Seller's Town Multiple Listing Service refuses to accept a listing of a property because the owner is from the former Soviet Union. Which of the following is correct?
   A. A multiple listing service (MLS) does not come under the Act because it is a private nonprofit organization.
   B. The Act does not prohibit discrimination against Russians.
   C. The listing broker's membership in the MLS may be terminated for taking the listing.
   D. The MLS is in violation of the 1968 Act for denying access to the service because of the owner's national origin.

5. A property manager refuses to rent an office because the rental applicant is black. The applicant has legal recourse under the:
   A. Federal Fair Housing Act of 1968.
   B. Civil Rights Act of 1866.
   C. North Carolina Fair Housing Act of 1983.
   D. North Carolina Residential Rental Agreements Act.

6. In an advertisement offering her only house for sale, the owner states that she will give preference to cash buyers who are female and Roman Catholic. The owner subsequently refused a cash offer because the buyer was a male Presbyterian. Which of the following is correct?
   A. Since the seller owned only one house, she is exempt from the 1968 Act.
   B. Since the advertisement stated a preference, but not an outright limitation, it is not discriminatory.
   C. Since the North Carolina Fair Housing Act has no exemptions for an owner selling her own home, the seller has violated state law.
   D. The seller is allowed one "exempt" sale every three years assuming she has not used it before.

7. A real estate agent showed white prospects houses in all-white areas only. This discriminatory practice is called:
   A. redlining.
   B. blockbusting.
   C. steering.
   D. directing.

8. Which of the following is exempt from the provisions of the 1968 Act?
   A. an owner of four houses
   B. an owner occupying one of four apartments in his or her building
   C. a religious organization renting 1 of 16 apartments it owns and operates for commercial purposes
   D. an owner listing a residential lot for sale with a real estate broker

9. A resident of Raleigh decided to sell her home by herself without listing it with a real estate company. There was no discriminatory advertising. When an African American buyer asked to see the home, the owner refused. The owner:
   A. is in violation of the federal Fair Housing Act of 1968.
   B. is in violation of the North Carolina Fair Housing Act of 1983.
   C. is not in violation of the Civil Rights Act of 1866.
   D. is not in violation of any of the Fair Housing Acts.

10. The term familial status applies to:
    A. families with children under the age of 18.
    B. same sex couples living together.
    C. two different sets of families sharing the same household.
    D. restrictions on the number of people living in the rental unit.

11. The practice of using discriminatory lending practices to avoid making loans to persons located in areas occupied primarily by minorities is:
    A. blockbusting.
    B. steering.
    C. redlining.
    D. panic peddling.

12. The owner of a FSBO (for sale by owner) availed herself of the exemption provided by the 1968 Act and refused to accept a purchase offer because the offeror was white. The offeror can do all of the following EXCEPT:
    A. pursue a lawsuit under the 1866 law.
    B. seek legal action under the 1968 law.
    C. seek legal action under the North Carolina Fair Housing Act.
    D. file a complaint with the North Carolina Human Relations Commission.

13. Jane Smith rented a room in her own private home but refused African American tenants. Jane is in violation of:
    A. the Federal Fair Housing Act of 1968.
    B. the North Carolina Fair Housing Act of 1983.
    C. the Civil Rights Act of 1866.
    D. There is no violation in this example.

14. An apartment complex refused to rent to a couple that had two small children because there was no available unit in the "children" buildings but several units were in the "no children" buildings. Which of the following statements are true?
    A. This is not discriminatory because the apartment complex does not refuse to rent to couples with children.
    B. This is an example of steering.
    C. The apartment complex is allowed to stipulate that certain buildings are for children and others are not.
    D. As long as the apartment complex does not advertise this practice, it is legal.

15. A person confined to a wheelchair requested that an apartment be modified to meet his physical needs. Which of the following is true?

    A. The owner must make appropriate modifications at the owner's expense.
    B. At the end of the tenancy, the disabled tenant can be required to pay for returning the premises to their original condition.
    C. The owner can refuse to rent to this tenant.
    D. The owner is never allowed to charge the disabled tenant a deposit for returning the modifications to their original state upon termination of the lease.

CHAPTER 18

FEDERAL INCOME TAXATION OF HOME OWNERSHIP/SALE

KEY TERMS

acquisition debt
adjusted basis
amount realized
basis

boot
capital gain
capital improvement
capital loss

costs of acquisition
equity debt
installment sale
tax-deductible expense

LEARNING OBJECTIVES

At the conclusion of this chapter, you should be able to:

1. Define and list examples of income tax deduction benefits of home ownership.
2. Define, and be able to calculate, basis, adjusted basis, amount realized, and gain realized in the sale of a personal residence.

IN THIS CHAPTER

Real estate licensees should have a basic understanding of the federal income tax laws that affect real property. Real estate brokers are not authorized to give tax advice to others. Tax advice should be given only by competent professional tax counsel familiar with the taxpayer's position. Real estate brokers should recommend that buyers and sellers seek such counsel when appropriate. This chapter primarily discusses federal tax implications related to a principal residence.

Tax Deductions For Homeowners

Home ownership provides two **tax-deductible expenses:** *real property taxes paid to the local taxing authority* and *mortgage interest (not principal)*. This includes discount points for obtaining a purchase or refinance loan (see page 444 for rules on discount point exemptions).

People who do not own real property often find it advantageous to use the allowable standard deduction when calculating taxes, especially because allowable deductions have decreased, whereas the standard deduction has increased. Homeowners, however, may find that the allowable deductions for property taxes and mortgage interest, along with other deductible expenses, provide greater tax relief than does the standard deduction.

> ### Test Tip!
>
> Homeownership allows the deduction of mortgage interest and property taxes. Caution: Do not confuse an answer containing property taxes and *interest* with property taxes and *insurance*.

Real Property Taxes

The taxes on real property are deductible for income tax purposes, but the deductions must be documented. They must be deducted from taxes for the year during which the homeowner or mortgage company actually paid them to the taxing authority. Assessments are not deductible when paid; however, they may be itemized to claim as additions to the **basis** *(i.e., the original cost of the property plus material improvements that increase its value)* when the property is sold.

Mortgage Interest

The mortgage interest deduction for a personal residence is often a major advantage of homeownership. The tax savings depend on the amount of interest paid, the taxpayer's tax bracket, the amount of the minimum standard deduction, and the number of other itemized deductions the taxpayer claims. Recent trends toward lower interest rates and higher standard deductions have reduced or eliminated some tax savings, especially for owners of modestly priced homes financed at low interest rates.

Debt that generates "qualified residence interest" must be either acquisition debt or home equity debt. Both must be secured by the property. Acquisition debt is the debt incurred in the purchase of a personal residence. Interest generated by the first $1,000,000 of acquisition debt is deductible as mortgage interest. Equity debt is all debt secured by a qualified residence to the extent it does not exceed the fair market value of the residence reduced by the acquisition debt. Interest generated by the first $100,000 of home equity debt is deductible as mortgage interest. See page 446 for a discussion of deductibility of discount points for the purchase or refinance of a home.

Purchasers will often be charged discount points when obtaining a mortgage loan. Discount points are prepaid mortgage interest and are therefore deductible. The question is when. Discount points paid to lower the interest rate when purchasing a home are deductible in the year in which paid. When discount points are paid in the refinancing of a mortgage, they are not fully deductible in the year in which paid but rather must be spread out over the term of the loan. For example, a person refinances her home and incurs $1,500 in discount points on the new 30-year mortgage. Instead of being able to write off the entire $1,500 sum in that tax year, she can write off only $50 per year ($1,500 ÷ 30 = $50). This limitation on the amount of deduction per year makes the payment of discount points on refinance loans less attractive than when acquiring the home originally.

> **Test Tip!**
>
> Discount points are generally deductible in the year in which paid unless involving refinancing or investment loans.

One other form of potential mortgage interest is the payment of the loan origination fee (LOF) at the closing. Although current tax rules make the deductibility of the LOF similar to that of discount points, agents should always tell the client to seek competent tax advice in this matter as the rules are complex and these fees may, or may not, be deductible in any given scenario.

SALE OF A PERSONAL RESIDENCE BASIS

The tax deductibility of property taxes and mortgage interest allows an annual benefit of homeownership. There is another component of income taxation as regards the homeowner and that is the profit, or loss, that is incurred when the property is sold. The taxpayer will need to calculate *the profit,* or **capital gain**, *from the sale of the property* to determine whether there is any tax liability. One advantage of personal residence-related capital gains is the existence of generous exemptions, covered later in this chapter, which will eliminate the majority of those transactions from any tax liability at all. Unfortunately, as the recent economic downturn has illustrated, it is possible for the homeowner to incur *losses on the sale of his home.* The losses, known as **capital losses** are not deductible as the basic premise seems to be that if the tax laws are not going to tax you on your profits, in many cases they will not allow you a write-off in the event of a loss. Please note that capital losses incurred on the sale of investment properties can be deductible for tax purposes. Capital gains can be either long term or short term. The difference is based on the period of time the property was held. Sales for property that was held 12 months or less are considered short-term capital gains and are taxed at the same rate as the taxpayer's ordinary income. If the asset was held for more than 12 months, it would qualify for reduced tax rates, which currently do not exceed 15%, which is far less than a taxpayer's typical tax rate.

To calculate the profit, or capital gain, from the sale of the property, the taxpayer will need to determine how much he had invested in the property subtracted from how much he sold it for after accounting for allowable expenses of sale. It is common to hear someone say that the way to calculate profits is to simply take what you sold it for minus what you paid for it. In the calculation of capital gains perhaps it is better to say what was your "net sales price," that is, sales price minus allowable expenses of sale, and subtract what you have in it. What you have invested in it is likely the purchase price plus allowable "costs of acquisition" plus the cost of any capital improvements that may have been added since the original date of purchase. Capital improvements are those *items that are permanent and will increase the value of the property*. Capital improvements should not be confused with costs for repairs and maintenance, which are not allowed to be considered. For example the replacement of a couple of loose shingles is likely a repair, whereas the replacement of the roof would be a capital improvement. The replacement of a burned out hot water heater element will constitute a repair, whereas the replacement of the hot water heater would qualify as a capital improvement.

The definitions of basic terms listed below should help you understand the capital gain computation process.

- **Basis** (also known as *tax*, *cost*, or *original basis*)—This is the *amount originally paid for the property*. In most cases, it is simply the purchase price. It is very important for students to understand the meaning of "basis."
- **Adjusted basis**—The adjusted basis is the *original basis adjusted to add allowable costs of acquisition as well as the cost of capital improvements*. Not all closing costs will qualify as an allowable cost of acquisition as shown in the list below.
- **Amount Realized**—The amount realized is the *sales price minus allowable expenses of sale*.
- **Costs of Acquisition**—These are the allowable closing costs that are incurred as a result of purchasing and acquiring title to the property. For a more complete list of allowable costs refer to the section "Effect of Purchase and Sale" later in this chapter.

Using this new terminology, the formula to determine the amount of capital gain is as follows:

$$\text{Amount Realized} - \text{Adjusted Basis} = \text{Capital Gain}$$

As mentioned previously, the adjusted basis is essentially the original cost of the property plus the allowable costs of acquisition plus the cost of any capital improvements that increase its value. It is to the homeowner's advantage to have as large a basis as possible to minimize the tax gain realized when the property is eventually sold. Alternatively, the gain is minimized by deduction of certain items from the sales price. The application of these adjustments is discussed in the next section.

Effect of Purchase and Sale

There are certain expenses for both buyer and seller in the purchase and sale of a personal residence. The following list gives examples of these expenses and their application by the buyer or the seller in calculating taxable gain. You do not need to remember all of these examples. Rather, you should understand the principle that when the cost is paid by the owner in acquiring the property, the cost is included in the basis; when the cost is incurred in selling the property, the cost is deducted from the gross sales price.

1. The premium paid for a title insurance policy is subtracted from the selling price when paid by the seller. It is added to the buyer's basis when paid by the buyer.
2. Transfer taxes (ordinarily paid by the seller) are deducted by the seller from the selling price. When the tax is paid by the buyer, however, the amount is added to the buyer's basis.
3. The attorney fees paid by the seller are deductible from the selling price. Attorney fees paid by the buyer are added to the buyer's basis.
4. When the seller pays the attorney fee for the preparation of a deed, this fee is deducted by the seller from the selling price. When the fee for drawing up the deed is paid by the buyer, it is added to the buyer's basis.
5. The buyer's closing costs that are allocable to purchasing the property are added to the buyer's basis, but expenses of borrowing the purchase price may not be added to the buyer's basis. Examples of expenses involved with obtaining the loan include appraisal fees, mortgage insurance premiums, charges by the lender's attorney, and credit report cost.
6. Discount points charged by lending institutions are deducted from the selling price when paid by the seller to enable the buyer to obtain a loan. These points are not deductible as interest by the seller.

Until recently, if the property's seller paid the points for the buyer, the buyer could not deduct the points as interest because they were not paid directly by the buyer. The Internal Revenue Service (IRS) has now stated that points paid by the seller for the buyer must be treated as paid directly by the buyer from funds not borrowed for this purpose. The buyer (taxpayer), however, will reduce the basis of the new residence by an amount equal to points paid by the seller.

Discount points paid by the buyer to purchase a home are deductible as interest by the buyer for the year in which the points are paid. In 1986, the IRS ruled that discount points paid by the buyer to refinance an existing loan would need to be spread over the term of the loan. The essential difference is that if the buyer paid $2,000 in points for a new home, he could deduct all $2,000 in the year paid. If the buyer refinanced his present loan for 20 years, however, he could deduct only $100 per year. If the mortgage loan was not obtained to purchase or improve a principal residence, deduction of the discount points as interest must be spread over the life of the loan. For example, if a borrower paid $2,000 in discount points to obtain a 20-year conventional loan to purchase an apartment building, the discount points would be deductible at the rate of $100 per year for 20 years.

7. When the borrower pays a loan origination fee or loan processing fee, typically 1% of the amount of the loan, the fee is not deductible as interest because the fee is for loan services and not for the use of the money borrowed. Also, the borrower cannot add the cost of a loan origination or processing fee to the basis of the property because this is an expense of borrowing the purchase price rather than a cost of obtaining the property. Loan origination fees paid by the seller are a selling expense and are deducted from the sales price in arriving at the amount realized.

8. Other expense items, such as surveys, escrow fees, title abstracts, recording fees, and advertising costs, are added to the buyer's basis when paid by the buyer or subtracted from the selling price when paid by the seller.

9. The real estate commission paid by the seller is deducted from the selling price. The commission paid is not deductible from ordinary income by the seller.

10. Fix-up expenses, even if necessary for the sale, are no longer deductible.

11. The distance requirement for deduction of job-related moving expenses is that the new job location be 50 miles farther from the former residence than the old job location. For example, the distance from the transferee's former residence to his old job was 5 miles. The distance from his former residence to his new job must be at least 55 miles for him to be able to deduct job-related moving expenses. Moving expenses are treated as income adjustments. Therefore, moving expenses that are not paid for or reimbursed by

an employer are subtracted from income, a benefit for those who do not itemize deductions. In essence, only deductions for moving household and personal goods and traveling expenses, such as lodging during the trip from the old to the new location, are allowed.

12. A financial penalty (prepayment penalty) required by a lender for early pay-off of a mortgage loan is deductible as interest by the borrower for the year in which the prepayment penalty is paid.

13. Most of the noted expenses pertaining to the purchase of a residence are added to the basis of the new home. Most of the expenses of the sale of a residence are used to reduce the amount realized on the sale. Notable exceptions are costs associated with the mortgage loan, discount points paid by the buyer, prepayment penalties, fix-up expenses, and job-related moving expenses. See items 5, 6, 7, 10, and 11 in this list for the tax treatment of these exceptions.

Computing Taxable Gain

When computing the gain or loss in the sale of a principal residence, the first step is to establish the owner's **tax basis**, or **basis**, in the property which is *typically the original purchase price plus any costs incurred in acquiring the property (other than those incurred in arranging financing)*. Next, you need to calculate the seller's adjusted basis. The **adjusted basis** consists of the tax basis *plus the costs of any capital improvements (not repairs) made during ownership*. At this point, the sales price of the property is determined and allowable costs of sale, such as the sales commission, costs of deed preparation, and transfer taxes, are subtracted to determine the "net" sales price or, more correctly, the amount realized. Again, the formula for capital gain is Amount Realized − Adjusted Basis = Capital Gain.

> **Example:** Michael Browne purchased a home 15 years ago for $185,000. At the time of purchase, he incurred costs of acquisition of $2,800. Since that time, he has spent $5,500 repainting the house and another $6,500 in replacing the heating system. He now sells the house for $650,000 and pays $42,000 in commissions and allowable closing-related expenses.

Questions:

1. What is the original cost basis for the property?
2. What is the amount of the adjusted basis?
3. How much is the amount realized?
4. What is the amount of capital gain on the sale?

Solution:

$185,000   Original cost basis (purchase price)
+ 2,800   Cost of acquisition

+ 6,500	Capital improvements*
= $194,300	Adjusted basis
$650,000	Sales price
−42,000	Allowable closing-related expenses
= $608,000	Amount realized
$608,000	Amount realized
−194,300	Adjusted basis
= $413,700	Capital gain

*The $5,500 for painting is for repairs maintenance and does not qualify as a capital improvement.

Answers:

1. $185,000 original cost basis
2. $194,300 adjusted basis
3. $608,000 amount realized
4. $413,700 capital gain

Depending on the marital status of the seller, she may, or may not, owe capital gains taxes on this sale. If she is married and filing jointly, there would be no taxes owed as $413,700 is less than the $500,000 exclusion and ownership and occupancy are both more than two years. If she is single, she would be taxed on the amount of capital gain in excess of $250,000, or $163,700 ($413,700 − 250,000 = $163,700).

RULES FOR TAXATION OF CAPITAL GAIN

New capital gains tax rules have been in place since 1997. Taxpayers who took advantage of the prior rules are now eligible to take advantage of the new rules without regard to their past capital gains tax history. Unlike earlier rules, which required taxpayers to keep records over long periods of time, as well as purchasing a more expensive house just to avoid potentially costly capital gains tax bills from the government, the new rules are quite simple and far less restraining. The new rules for personal residences allow capital gains of $250,000 or less to be excluded from taxation for a single taxpayer ($500,000 for a married couple filing jointly) if certain requirements are met. Such rules greatly simplify the record keeping and tax computation process. If the amount of capital gain exceeds the exemption amount, the taxpayer(s) would pay taxes on the amount in excess of the exemption.

The new rules require the seller(s) to own AND occupy the residence for any two of the previous five years. There is no limit to the number of times this exclusion can be used as long as it involves a primary residence and both the two-year ownership and occupancy rules have been met.

The ownership requirement mandates the property must be owned for a period of at least two years. In the case involving a married couple, only one of the two is required to actually own the property for the two-year period for both of them to qualify.

The occupancy rule allows for some degree of flexibility in that, unlike ownership, the taxpayer may drift in and out of occupancy. For example, a taxpayer may occupy the property for a period of 12 months, move away for a year, and then return and occupy the property for another year and be able to qualify for the exemption. Occupancy is not limited to ownership periods only. Occupancy can be a combination of renting as well as owning. A taxpayer may rent a house for 12 months and later purchase it from the landlord and continue to reside there for another year. After that time, he moves away and rents the house to a tenant for the next two years at which time he sells the house. In this situation, the taxpayer has owned the property for three years and has personally occupied it for at least two years. In this case, the house was occupied for one year by the owner as a tenant and the other year as the owner. Again, occupancy is not restricted to whether or not the taxpayer actually owned the property to qualify. The occupancy need not be continuous as this illustration shows. All that is necessary is to able to show occupancy, as a tenant or the owner, for at least 730 days within the past five years (365 days a year × 2 = 730 days).

Note that, for a married couple filing jointly, BOTH must meet the occupancy requirements, but only one of the two will be required to meet the two-year ownership rule. As a result, this exclusion can be used only once in a two-year period and is not available for vacation and second homes.

In the event of death of one of the married spouses, the question might be asked if the surviving spouse is entitled to the $500,000 exemption that is accorded to a married couple or if they would be reduced to the $250,000 limit for a single taxpayer. As is so often the case in tax situations, the answer is "it depends." Assuming the couple qualified for the $500,000 exemption to begin with, the surviving spouse is entitled to that same amount if he sells the property within the same tax year as the death occurred. If the property is sold after the year of the death, the surviving spouse would retreat to the $250,000 limit. This creates a difficult challenge if the spouse died rather late in the calendar year, as the surviving spouse may not have time in which to sell the property. It is possible that if the surviving spouse later remarries, the new couple could later qualify for the $500,000 amount after they meet the "2 out of 5" rule.

The following examples illustrate the various options of two single taxpayers/homeowners who marry.

1. If neither has used the exclusion, each can exclude up to $250,000 from the sale of the respective house owned at the time of the marriage, providing the other requirements are met. If they qualify for these exclusions, they can use them whether filing a single or joint return. The provision of one sale every two years does not apply in this instance.

2. If one spouse has already used the $250,000 exclusion within the two years before the marriage, the other newly married taxpayer can still use the $250,000 exclusion.
3. After two years have passed since either used their exclusions, the couple can file a joint return and exclude the $500,000 gain on the property for which they both meet the use test.

Taxpayers who maintain an office in their homes cannot exclude that part of the gain attributable to the home office. They must pay capital gains tax on the part of the gain and recapture tax on any depreciation taken. If the taxpayer has ceased using the home office and returned the space to residential use two years before the date the property is sold, he can include the capital gain from the office portion in the exclusion. All of the gain except that resulting from depreciation after May 6, 1997, qualifies for the exclusion, provided the gain does not exceed the $250,000/$500,000 limit. Capital gain from the recapture of depreciation taken after May 6, 1997, is subject to a recapture tax not to exceed 25%. All other capital gain is taxed according to the taxpayer's tax bracket not to exceed 15%.

This capital gains rule has many attractive advantages for the taxpayers. No longer are they required to purchase another, more expensive, home to be entitled to favorable tax benefits. Now they can downsize, rent, or relocate to a less expensive locale without incurring major tax ramifications in the process.

Reporting Features

Sale of a primary residence after May 6, 1997, at or below the exclusion amount does not require the real estate closing agent to notify the IRS using a Form 1099S. Revenue Procedure 98-20, however, requires the seller to provide the closing agent with certain assurances before January 31 of the year immediately following the year the property is sold or exchanged. The seller must certify that seller and spouse, if applicable, have met ownership, occupancy, and use requirements for the exclusion; that no part of the residence has been used for rental or business after May 6, 1997; and that the gain does not exceed the limit of $250,000/$500,000, whichever one applies. The certification must include a separate assurance for each requirement.

SPECIAL RULES THAT MAY APPLY TO SOME RESIDENTIAL TRANSACTIONS

Installment Sales

An **installment sale** is *any sale that involves the seller financing a portion of the sales price and receiving monies in two or more tax years*. In situations in which the seller is subjected to paying capital gains taxes, she would pay only taxes on the portion of each year's payments that are representative of the amount of capital gains, For example, a seller has sold, and financed, a property for $100,000 of which $25,000 is calculated as capital gain, or 25%. As the buyer makes mortgage payments each year, the seller will need to separate the amount paid into what is representative of interest and what was allocated to the principal. The seller will be required to pay taxes on the earned interest and that portion has no bearing on the capital gain. For the portion that is representative of the repayment of principal, the seller will be required to treat 25% of this amount as capital gain. The other 75% does not represent profit and is not taxed.

Like-Kind Exchange

A like-kind exchange is referred to by several different names, including tax deferred exchange and as a tax-free exchange. Although it is a fairly popular way to refer to this, there is indeed nothing that is "tax free" about such an exchange. It merely defers any taxes until a later time and is, as such, a tax deferral and not a tax evasion, which is illegal. A like-kind exchange is not so much an actual exchange as it really involves the sale of a property in which case the proceeds are kept by an approved "intermediary" who holds the monies until such time as the seller purchases another property in accordance with the tax rules. The advantage is that taxes can literally be deferred indefinitely, which allows the investor to reinvest in more properties for which, hopefully, even more profits will be attained. Ultimately, the acquired property will be sold and there will be no exchange, at which time the investor will be taxed on the accumulated profits.

It is *unlikely that the two properties being exchanged will be worth exactly the same amount. Typically, there will need to be the payment of cash, or other personal property, to make up for the shortage. This cash, or personal property, is referred to as* boot. The person receiving the boot will be taxed on the value of the boot at the time of the sale.

The like-kind exchange rule does not apply to the sale of a personal residence but rather to investment properties. Like-kind only refers to the fact that both properties, the one sold as well as the property being acquired, must be held for productive use in a trade or business or held for investment. Deadlines are enforced strictly and failure to comply will result in unfavorable tax consequences.

Vacation Homes

It is a common component of the American dream to one day own a vacation home in some location far removed from everyday life. For those fortunate enough to acquire such a property, it is quite common that the owners will resort to renting it out during the periods when it is not occupied by the owner. The question arises as to the tax deductibility of such an "investment." The basic rule is that if the property is used only by tenants and is simply an income-producing investment that just happens to be in a vacation area, the expenses of operation are fully deductible. If the owner personally uses the property for more than 14 days per year, or more than 10% of the number of days in which the property is being rented, whichever is greater, some deductions will not be allowed.

Home Office

In today's world, it is becoming increasingly common that people are working directly from their homes. Companies are seeing the benefits of hiring workers who can work from their homes without the firm needing to furnish large expensive office spaces. The practice is more common for jobs involving technology for which there is no need to work from some big office space. The question is whether the taxpayer should write off that portion of the home that is occupied by the office space. This is definitely one area that competent tax advice should be secured, because it may be more beneficial from a tax perspective to avoid using this benefit. Again, tax advice should be sought to determine what is best for each individual taxpayer. To qualify as a home office deduction, the IRS institutes a few basic guidelines. The home office must be used exclusively for business purposes and be the principal place of business. It must be an area where clients and customers are met in the normal practice of business OR be contained within an entirely separate structure on the property. For example, a taxpayer may have opened a beauty salon within his home. The space may be an addition to the home that has a separate entrance for customers to enter. In this case, the space would be outfitted with chairs and sinks that make it specific to the beauty shop business and likely would qualify easily as a home office.

Summary of Important Points

1. There are definite tax advantages in the ownership of real property. A primary advantage is the deduction allowance for mortgage interest paid. Although the major portion of the payment on a mortgage loan in the early years goes to interest, the deductibility of this amount results in a lower effective interest rate than most people realize.
2. Real estate practitioners must refrain from giving tax advice.
3. A homeowner's real estate property taxes and mortgage interest are deductible expenses in calculating federal income tax liability.
4. Losses incurred in the sale of a home are not tax deductible.
5. The $250,000 exclusion for single taxpayers and the $500,000 exclusion for married taxpayers filing jointly is available to taxpayers of all ages. This exclusion can be used repeatedly as long as the ownership, use, and one-sale-in-two-years requirements are met.
6. Previous use of the over-55 exclusion (before May 1997) does not affect the ability of the homeowner to use the new (after June 1997) exclusions.

7. Fix-up expenses are no longer deductible under any circumstances.
8. A buyer's closing costs and improvements are allowable adjustments to the basis of a personal residence.
9. A seller's closing costs are subtracted from the sale price to obtain the amount realized. Improvements are added to basis of old home to obtain the adjusted basis.
10. Gain equals the amount realized minus the adjusted basis.

Review Questions

Answers to the review questions are in the Answer Key at the back of the book.

1. Which of the following is a tax-deductible expense resulting from home ownership?
    A. operating expenses
    B. depreciation
    C. mortgage interest
    D. energy usage

2. Discount points paid by a borrower to obtain a conventional mortgage loan to purchase a principal residence:
    A. do not increase the yield on the mortgage.
    B. are not deductible by the borrower as interest.
    C. are not deductible at all.
    D. are deductible in the year paid.

3. With regard to a real estate commission paid by a seller, which of the following is NOT correct?
    A. The commission can be deducted from the selling price as a selling expense in calculating the amount realized in the sale of a principal residence.
    B. The commission paid can be deducted as a moving expense by the seller when itemizing tax-deductible expenses.
    C. The commission is not deductible under any circumstance.
    D. The commission deducted as a moving expense is subject to a cap.

Questions 4 and 5 are based on the following information:

- Selling price of home: $150,000
- Selling expenses of home: $10,000
- Basis of home: $80,000
- Closing costs of home when it was purchased: $5,000
- Improvements to home: $20,000

4. Adjusted basis of old home is:
    A. $75,000.
    B. $85,000.
    C. $100,000.
    D. $105,000.

5. Gain realized from old home is:
    A. $35,000.
    B. $40,000.
    C. $50,000.
    D. $70,000.

6. All of the following are considered sales under the capital gain exemption provision EXCEPT:
   A. exchange of a principal residence for another principal residence.
   B. foreclosure or repossession of a principal residence.
   C. destruction or condemnation of a principal residence.
   D. sale of a remainder interest to a related party while reserving a life estate for the grantor.

7. All of the following are true of the capital gain exemption EXCEPT:
   A. ownership and use period must be simultaneous.
   B. a partial exclusion can sometimes be used if sale of residence results from a job transfer or health reasons.
   C. a married couple can use the $500,000 joint exemption if only one of them owns the residence and both meet the occupancy requirement.
   D. taxpayers who currently maintain an office in their home must pay capital gains tax on that part of the gain attributable to the office.

8. The sales price minus allowable expenses of sale is known as the:
   A. adjusted basis.
   B. amount realized.
   C. capital gain.
   D. net sales price.

9. For an interest on a debt to be considered "qualified residence interest" for tax deduction purposes, it can be all of the following EXCEPT:
   A. acquisition debt from the purchase of a personal residence.
   B. equity debt secured by the property to the extent that the sum of acquisition and equity debt does not exceed fair market value of the property.
   C. interest generated by the first $100,000 of equity debt.
   D. interest generated by the first $2,000,000 of acquisition debt.

10. Which of the following is NOT true about the capital gain exemption in the sale of a primary residence?
    A. A married couple meeting the ownership, residency, and time requirements can exclude up to a $500,000 gain on a joint tax return.
    B. A single individual meeting the ownership, residency, and time requirements can exclude up to a $250,000 gain on his individual tax return.
    C. A husband and/or wife can use the exclusion only once in a lifetime; use by either husband or wife eliminates future exemptions.
    D. A partial exclusion can sometimes be used if early sale of the residence is the result of a job transfer or is for health reasons.

CHAPTER 19
BASIC CONSTRUCTION

KEY TERMS

Cape Cod
certificate of occupancy
concrete slab
fascia
flashing
footing
foundation vents
framing
frieze board
gable roof
girder
headers
hip roof
HVAC (heating, ventilation, and air conditioning)
insulation
joist
North Carolina Uniform Residential Building Code
on center
piers
rafter
ranch style
R-factor
ridge board
sheathing
sill
soffit
studs
truss
Tudor style
vapor barrier
Victorian
weather stripping
weepholes

LEARNING OBJECTIVES

At the conclusion of this chapter, you should be able to:

1. List the primary styles of residential architecture.
2. Describe the major components of residential construction, including foundation systems, framing, walls, ceiling and roof, windows, insulation, interior finishes, and heating/cooling systems.
3. Describe government regulation of residential construction.

IN THIS CHAPTER

This chapter provides basic information about the principles, terminology, and methods of residential construction. The chapter gives an overview of the construction process from the foundation to the roof. Also included is common terminology used in residential construction. The material in this chapter is confined to wood-frame and masonry construction, the two most common types of residential construction in North Carolina.

ARCHITECTURAL TYPES AND STYLES

The four basic types of home are one-story ranch, one-and-a-half-story, two-story, and split-level. Homes of two-and-a-half and three stories are available, but these homes typically are very large and expensive and thus are not as common as the others.

The popularity of a particular type and style of construction varies from person to person and region to region and ultimately is a matter of functionality, affordability, and taste.

> 🔑 The ranch style tends to be generally the most expensive to build per square foot.

A one-and-a-half-story **Cape Cod** typically provides future expansion space on the upper level for a growing family. The traditional two-story is quite popular, as it can be built in a variety of styles to suit almost anyone's taste. Its extra space is perfect for a growing family or a family that needs extra room for any reason. The split-level, not as popular as the other types of construction, takes advantage of the terrain by having the lower level partially below ground, similar to a basement. One disadvantage to this type of construction is that stairs are required to get from one level to another. In some cases, as many as two or three sets of stairs are required. This typically is a disadvantage for older homeowners who do not desire to use stairs to access all areas of the house.

Many modern styles of housing take advantage of high and open ceilings, lofts, or balconies. A variety of styles exists in this category to suit modern tastes. A renaissance of **Victorian** architecture has occurred, and these new homes take advantage of factory-built molded trim and exterior detailing in an attempt to keep costs down and make the homes more affordable.

Of course, in any type or style of construction, the floor plan must provide functional utility. Good design increases the comfort and resale potential of any home. Good design includes a modern heating and cooling system, adequate closets and storage space, access to a bathroom for every bedroom, living and sleeping areas of sufficient size, and the proper placement and size of windows to provide

> "No one is going to give you home drawings on an exam and expect you to identify the type of home, type of roof, or label construction items in a diagram. You do have to understand basic vocabulary and the function of some of the construction components."
> –Bill Gallagher, DREI

FIGURE 19.1 Architectural styles.

adequate light and ventilation. The grouping of bedroom and bathroom areas so as to provide privacy is also important. The kitchen should be designed to provide an efficient, attractive work area, and it should be located near a utility, rear, or side entrance, for access to the outside. The traditional living room and living room/den arrangement is sometimes replaced by the "great room" (one large room that is used for both entertaining and daily family activities). Modern design may include an attached two-car garage, wood deck and/or patio, and a great room.

LOCATION ON SITE

The location of the house on the building site can have a significant effect on value. Land use regulations and local covenants usually mandate a setback from the street and side and rear property lines. A location that takes advantage of views, privacy, terrain, and ease of access adds to the value and enjoyment of the home.

FOUNDATIONS

Footings

Arguably the most important foundation building block is the **footing**. The footing is *the concrete base below the frost line that supports the foundation of the structure.* This is to avoid the shifting that can be caused when the ground freezes. Trenches are dug for the footings, which must rest on undisturbed soil. *Grade stakes* are then placed in the trenches to *measure and verify proper elevation and thickness of the footing* before pouring the concrete. Once this is complete, the footing can be poured. Footings are composed of cast-in-place concrete. When constructing footings, reinforcement rods, commonly known as *rebar*, should be *placed in the concrete to aid in temperature control and to strengthen the footing.* This is especially important in areas with unstable soil or a high water table and in coastal regions.

The width of the footing is twice the width of the foundation wall. The depth of the footing is usually a minimum of 8 inches (for one- and two-story homes); it should be the same thickness as the foundation wall. If the wall is wider, the footing must be thicker. Footings for masonry fireplaces must be a minimum of 12 inches thick. The purpose of the footing is to support the foundation wall and, subsequently, the entire weight load of the structure. The footings must provide an adequate base for the structure to prevent settling of the house.

> 🔑 Students need to be able to differentiate between a "footing," "foundation wall," and a "pier."

Foundation Walls

Foundation walls in North Carolina generally are composed of poured concrete, masonry block, or brick. The most common type of foundation wall is made with masonry block and brick. The masonry block forms the back half of the wall and is covered with a brick veneer on the front. Vertical masonry **piers** are *built inside the foundation walls to provide additional support for the house.* If only masonry block is used in the foundation wall, the exterior portions of the blocks are faced with a smooth mortar finish known as *parging*. The parged walls are painted to improve the appearance of the foundation. In some instances, foundation walls are covered with stucco to improve the appearance and to hide the masonry block.

In level terrain, the foundation may be a *concrete slab* instead of a foundation wall. The **concrete slab** is poured directly on the ground and eliminates the crawl space or basement. The slab provides the floor of the dwelling and the support for the exterior and interior walls. The concrete slab method is less expensive than the foundation wall system or basement, but it is not practical in all building situations. The foundation wall with crawl space is widely used throughout

North Carolina. Basements, although popular, are expensive to construct and are seldom used in the eastern and coastal regions of the state because of a high water table. Moisture control is a serious problem that must be addressed in any foundation system. First, grading of the soil must ensure that surface water is directed away from the foundation and that proper drainage is provided. Footing drain tile is used below grade around all concrete or masonry foundations enclosing habitable or usable space. Additionally, crawl spaces under homes must be properly graded to ensure positive drainage.

Equally important, **foundation vents** must be installed in foundation walls to properly ventilate the crawl space underneath the house. Adequate vents and sometimes a **vapor barrier** are necessary to allow the crawl space and wood members of the floor system to remain dry and free from unnecessary moisture damage. Termite treatment is applied after the foundation is complete and before the vapor barrier installation. In the case of a concrete basement floor or slab, termite treatment and vapor barrier are applied before pouring the concrete. As additional termite preventive measures, all woody debris should be removed from under the foundation and all wood in direct contact with the ground or a concrete slab should be pressure treated.

FRAMING

Framing refers to the wooden skeleton of the home. Framing members are lumber with a nominal *thickness* of 2 inches. For example, a 2 × 4 is a piece of lumber theoretically 2 inches thick by 4 inches wide. It is actually slightly smaller. Wall **studs** are commonly 2 × 4s; 2 × 8s, 2 × 10s, or 2 × 12s are commonly used for **joists** for floor and ceiling framing. Usually, 2 × 6s or 2 × 8s are used as **rafters** in the roof system (see Figures 19.2 and 19.3).

Flooring

The top of the foundation wall is finished off with a course of solid masonry. On top of this course of solid masonry rests the foundation **sill**. The sill is usually made up of pressure-treated 2 × 6s or 2 × 8s. In the event pressure-treated lumber is not used for the sill, metal **flashing** must be placed between the foundation wall and wooden member. The wooden sill is fastened to the foundation wall by anchor bolts or nails. The sill is the first wooden member of the house and is used as the nailing surface for the floor system.

The box sill, or banding, rests on the sill plate and is the same size wood member as the floor joists (2" × 8", 2" × 10", or 2" × 12"). The banding runs around the top of the foundation wall, attached to the sill plate.

The floor joists span the distance between the foundation walls and the **girder** and provide support for the subfloor. The girder is either a steel beam or several wooden members fastened together (usually 2 × 10s, 2 × 12s, or larger) that spans

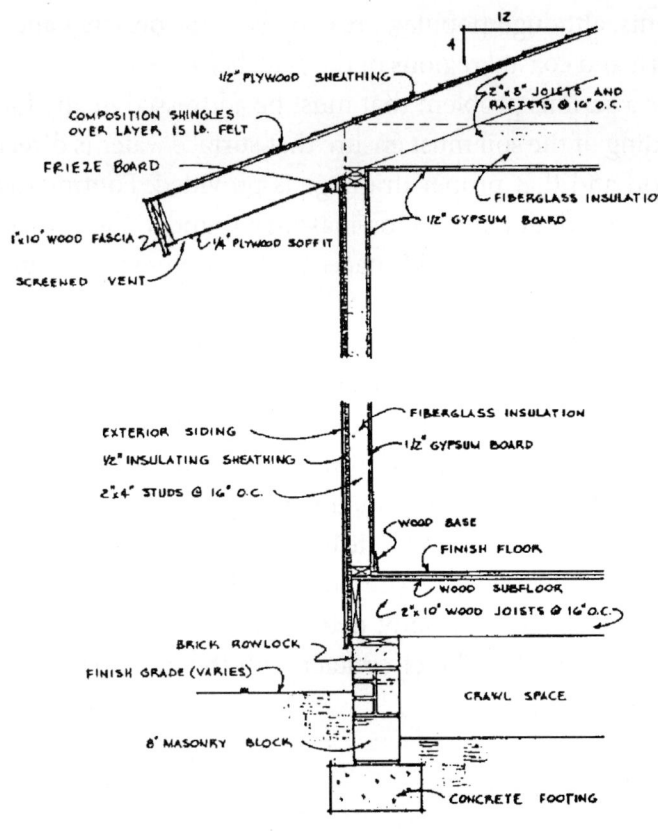

FIGURE 19.2 Typical wall section.
Source: Copyright © 2003 by Home Planners, LLC, Tucson, AZ

the distance from one side of the foundation to the other. The joists rest on the girder for support. Typical framing places wooden members at 16 inches **on center**. The 16-inch spacing of framing members depends primarily on strength considerations for lumber sizing. Additionally, covering materials such as plywood, **sheathing**, and wallboard are made in 4-foot widths. The 16-inch spacing, therefore, provides a uniform nailing pattern of four rows for each piece of covering material.

Depending on the area to be spanned, the joists are doubled or even tripled to support the load. *Bridging* provides support and "stiffening" to the joists to prevent lateral movement of the joists. Bridging is usually constructed in one of two ways. One type of bridging is solid bridging, which uses the same size wooden member as the joists. This type of bridging forms a "solid" bridge between the joists. Cross-bridging uses 1 × 4s or 2 × 4s placed in an pattern between the joists.

Some modern construction methods use wooden floor **trusses** in place of single floor joists. A truss is a support member constructed in a factory by nailing a number of smaller members (2 × 4s or 2 × 6s) together in a number of triangular patterns to provide maximum strength.

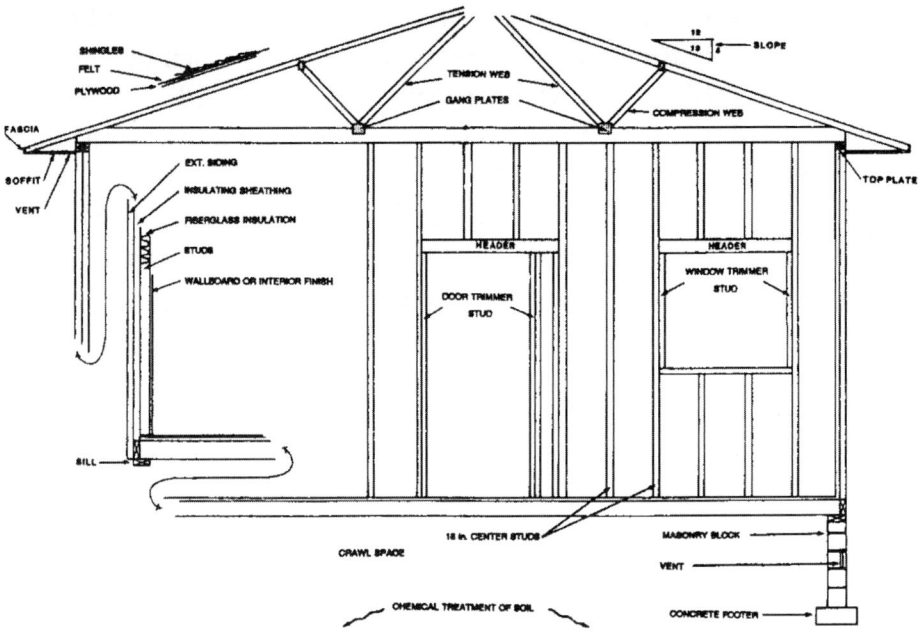

FIGURE 19.3 Roof section using truss system.
Source: Copyright © 2003 by Home Planners, LLC, Tucson, AZ

A plywood or particle board subflooring rests directly on top of the joists. Quality construction practice sees this subfloor glued and fastened with nails or shank screws to prevent nail popping and squeaky floors. Finish flooring rests on top of the subflooring. Typical finish flooring includes hardwood, tile, carpet, and vinyl.

Walls

The floor system usually serves as a stage or platform for the wall system. The walls are usually built of 2 × 4 studs, 16 inches on center. A stud is simply the vertical framing member of a house and is most likely wood; metal studs are used in some applications, but they are more common in commercial installations. Less common is a wall system of 2 × 6s at 16 or 24 inches on center. A horizontal base plate, also called a sole plate, serves as the foundation for the wall system. A double top plate ties the walls together to provide additional support for the ceiling and roof system. Exterior and interior walls are framed in a rough carpentry skeleton. Openings in the wall for doors and windows must be reinforced to pick up the missing support for the vertical load. This is done with 2 × 8s, 2 × 10s, or 2 × 12s, known as **headers**, on end, over the top of the opening. Headers should form a solid wood bridge over the opening and extend to the bottom of the top plate. The type of framing described above is known as *platform framing* because the framing of the structure rests on a subfloor platform. Platform framing is the most common type of framing used in residential construction (see Figure 19.2).

An alternative to platform framing is *balloon framing*. This method uses a single system of wall studs that runs from the foundation through the first and second floors to the ceiling support. This method is rarely used in residential construction. A third type of framing is *post-and-beam framing*. These members are much larger than ordinary studs and may be 4 or 6 inches square. The larger posts can be placed several feet apart instead of 16 or 24 inches on center. Like balloon framing, this type of framing is seldom used in residential construction.

Plumbing, electrical, and heating and cooling systems are run through the walls, floors, and ceilings before they are covered up. Inspections by the local building inspector must be made before any of these systems can be covered with insulation and wallboard. A vapor barrier is applied to the warm (inside) wall on exterior walls. The vapor barrier is important in preventing the warm interior air from mixing with the cold exterior air and forming condensation within the wall.

Ceiling Framing and Roof

The ceiling joists rest on the top plate of the wall. These joists should be placed directly over the vertical studs for maximum bearing strength. The joists span the structure between the outer walls. In traditional framing, these joists are usually 2 × 8s, and the inner walls are important in helping to bear the load of the roof. This is different in the contemporary use of roof truss systems, in which the truss carries the load-bearing function to the outer walls. This feature provides freedom of placement of the inner walls. Because a roof truss is made up of a number of smaller members (usually 2 × 4s), the attic space is almost completely lost (see Figure 19.3).

The **ridge board** is the *highest part of the framing and forms top line of the roof.* Rafters are the long wooden members that are fastened to the ends of the ceiling joists; they form the gables of the roof. Rafters are usually 2 × 6s or 2 × 8s. The rafters are fastened to the ridge at the peak of the gable.

Contemporary residential construction sees roof styles in two varieties. These are the traditional **gable roof** and the **hip roof**. Some homes even employ both styles to create a distinctive roofline. The gable roof is the most popular roof style in North Carolina. In years past, the gambrel and mansard roof styles were sometimes used, but these styles were never as popular or as functional as the gable or hip. As a result, the mansard and gambrel are rarely used on houses, but they are sometimes found on barns, stables, and other types of nonresidential structure. (The gambrel roof actually resembles a barn.) Two other roof types—seldom found on homes but sometimes used on outbuildings or additions such as utility rooms or porches—are the *shed roof* (which resembles one side of a gable roof) and the *flat roof*. Figure 19.4 shows the four roof styles: gable, hip, gambrel, and mansard.

The part of the roof that extends beyond the exterior wall and forms the connection between the roof and the exterior walls is known as the *eave*, or overhang.

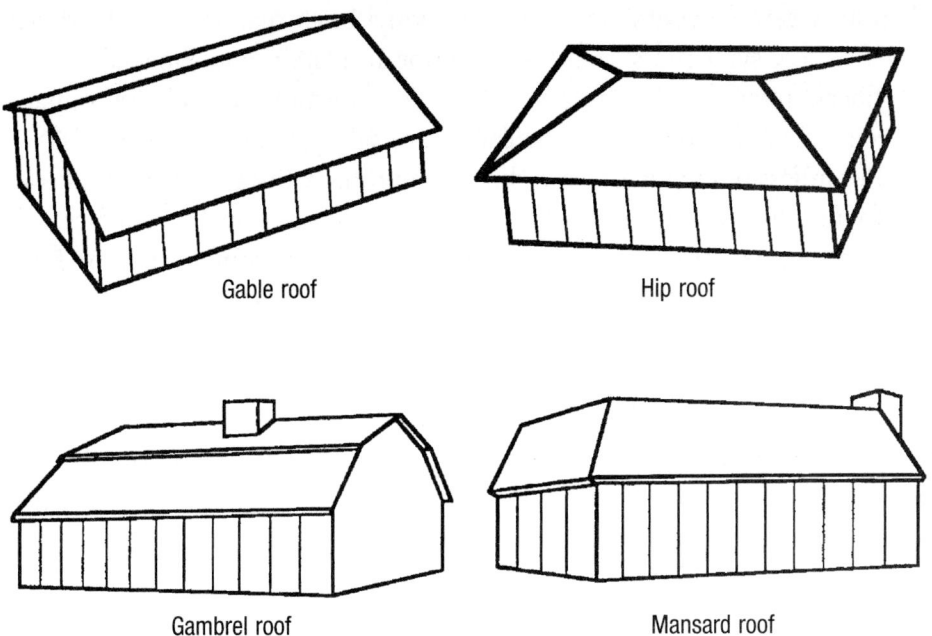

FIGURE 19.4 Roof styles.
Source: Copyright © 2003 by Home Planners, LLC, Tucson, AZ

The roof should extend at least 6 inches beyond the exterior of the structure. Common construction practices see a 12-inch overhang on the front and rear, with a 6-inch overhang on the side. The larger the overhang, the more protection there is from sun and rain for the exterior walls, windows, and doors.

The overhang is made up of three components: the soffit, the fascia, and the frieze board. The **soffit** is the *area under the eave*. This is made of wood, aluminum, or vinyl (depending on the type of siding). The area of *material facing the outer edge of the soffit* is the **fascia**. The fascia is typically a 1 × 6 or 1 × 8. If guttering is installed on the roof, it is fastened to the fascia. The third component of the eave is the **frieze board**. This is a *wooden member* (usually a 2 4, 2 6, or 2 8) that is *fastened directly under the soffit* against the top of the wall. The function of the frieze board is both decorative and functional. The frieze board prevents wind and moisture from penetrating the junction of the soffit and sheathing. Depending on the style of the home, additional trim boards are sometimes fastened on and around the frieze board to give the house the desired look.

EXTERIOR WALLS

The exterior wall of a house is covered with a sheathing material. This material is usually plywood or particleboard. The purpose of the sheathing is to strengthen the wall and add some insulation protection. An insulating "house wrap" is sometimes applied over this sheathing to increase the **R-factor** (*resistance to heat transfer*) of the walls. Upon this material, the exterior siding is applied.

There are several types of siding: aluminum, vinyl, brick, manufactured hardboard masonite, stucco, synthetic stucco (i.e., Exterior Insulation and Finishing System [EIFS]), fiber-cement board, and wood. Each type has advantages and disadvantages, and for every person who likes a particular type of siding, there is someone else who doesn't. Regardless of the type, siding should be properly installed to prevent water damage to the house and to give the house a first-rate, professional appearance.

In brick construction, builders typically install sheathing paper or house wrap, which seals the home from the intrusion of moisture through the brick. A small gap exists between the brick veneer walls and the interior sheathing. This is necessary to allow any moisture that seeps through the brick mortar to run down the back of the masonry wall and out through the weepholes at the bottom of the wall. **Weepholes** are *small holes in the bottom course of brick that allow any moisture on the inside of the wall an avenue to the exterior* and also allow ventilation into this area to keep the inside of the wall dry.

WINDOWS

Windows fall into three general classes: *sliding*, *swinging*, and *fixed*. Although there are other classes, they are not as common. Windows manufactured today are made from wood, metals such as aluminum, and even some composite materials. Whereas older windows were a single pane of glass, contemporary windows use a thermal insulating design with a double- or triple-glass pane. A small air space is sandwiched between the glass panes. This design provides excellent insulation and efficiency of heating and cooling, because windows make up a large portion of the wall and even roof surface area (in the case of skylights). Additionally, single-pane windows produce interior condensation in cold weather, which can damage woodwork and interior finishes. These antiquated single-pane windows require an exterior glass unit (storm window) to provide proper insulation in summer and winter.

The major parts of a window framework are labeled in the same way as the parts of a door opening. For example, the sill is the bottom or base part, the jamb is the side, and the header is the top of the opening.

The sash is the glass panel unit that slides up and down. In the past, glass manufacturers were able to make only small glass panes for windows. These windows were held together with wood strips known as mullions or grills. Today, many windows have nonfunctional mullions or grills added as decorative strips to simulate a multiple pane appearance. The stile is the side part of the sash; the top and bottom portions of the sash are known as rails.

Sliding Windows

Vertical Sliding (Double-Hung)

The most common type of window used in residential construction is vertical sliding, known as a *double-hung window* (see Figure 19.5). These

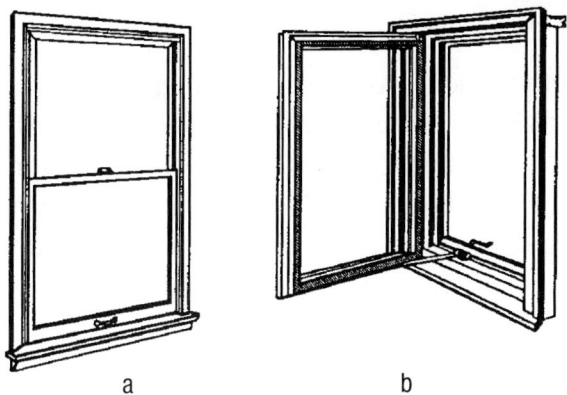

FIGURE 19.5 (a) Double-hung window and (b) casement window.
Source: Copyright © 2003 by Home Planners, LLC, Tucson, AZ

windows are composed of two glass pane units, or sashes, that vertically slide by each other. In older construction, the weight of the heavy window unit was supported or balanced by a rope-(sash cord)-and-pulley system in the wall. Lighter modern systems are governed entirely by the friction of the unit sliding in its track.

Horizontal Sliding

Horizontal sliding windows are often found in modern homes, sometimes in a bedroom. These units often have two sashes that slide by each other horizontally. In the case of a three-sash unit, the central portion is usually fixed, with only two sliding sashes. These windows are nearly identical in construction and composition to the double-hung vertical window described previously, except for the manner in which they open.

Swinging Windows

The *casement window* has a sash hinged on one side, and it swings outward (see Figure 19.5). The swinging mechanism is usually a geared crank system with an operating handle on the interior sill. Latches are often used to lock this type of window for a weather-tight seal.

Older homes sometimes have jalousie, hopper, or awning windows. All of these windows swing inward or outward and, as a result, have limitations because they interfere with living space. Typically, these windows do not insulate well, and as technology and energy efficiency have improved window construction and insulating requirements, the jalousie, hopper, and awning windows have become a thing of the past. The only swinging window that seems to have improved and kept pace with technological and architectural improvements is the casement window.

Fixed Windows

Fixed windows do not have movable sections. As air conditioning and ventilation systems have evolved, there is less need to have windows that can open. The common types of fixed window include picture, bay, bow, and Palladian. In some window assemblies, a fixed window may be a center section with some form of movable or openable window on either side. These windows are designed to allow maximum lighting and are strategically placed for maximum functionality and aesthetic appeal.

DOORS

Doors, like windows, come in many shapes and styles. However, there are only two classes, interior and exterior. Doors can be made of wood, steel, aluminum, composite materials, and glass. Maximum insulation is desired in exterior doors, which are usually composed of solid wood or steel with a high-insulating core.

All doors and windows must be tightly sealed to prevent the movement of air around them. A high-quality door coupled with proper installation is essential for maintaining proper energy efficiency. External caulking around windows and doors helps complete the tight seal, as does **weather stripping** in the doorframes. When you consider the large area of walls that doors and windows occupy in a typical home, you can see why it is extremely important that they be properly installed; even tiny cracks and leaks can result in significant heating and cooling bills.

Common types of exterior door include the flush door, which is one continuous smooth unit, and the panel door, which is composed of several recessed or raised panels that may include glass. The sliding glass door unit is popular and is used for access to patios, decks, and porches. The glass door often has one fixed panel and one panel that slides on a track or rollers. French doors have become popular high-style decorative units that open onto patios, decks, and porches.

Interior doors are usually made of wood or a composite material. These doors differ from their exterior counterparts in that they usually do not have a solid core and are not designed for energy efficiency. Their main function is decoration and privacy. Interior doors can be flush, have panels, and even be glass (French doors).

ROOFING

Once the structural skeleton of the roof system is in place, it is covered with plywood or particleboard *sheathing (decking)*. On top of this, roofing paper is applied to aid in weather-proofing the structure. On top of the roofing paper, shingles are applied. Most construction uses the fiberglass shingle, but tile and wood shingles also are used.

INSULATION

The primary purpose of **insulation** is to *resist the flow of heat from one area to another*. It provides the double benefit of preventing heat loss in the winter and protecting against heat load in the summer. The areas of the home that must be insulated are the ceiling, walls, and floor. Insulation is rated in an R-factor. The larger the R-factor, the greater the degree of insulation. The North Carolina Residential Building Code requires installation of insulation with an R-factor of 13 in walls. R-30 is required in ceilings; R-19, in floors. Higher values are required in the colder northwestern portion of North Carolina (R-18 for walls and R-38 for ceilings). Homes built to superior energy-efficient standards should exceed these minimum requirements. Local utility companies usually offer discount rates to homes meeting their energy-efficient standards. Additionally, they sometimes offer low-cost loan programs to homeowners to improve the insulating value of their homes.

A common form of insulation is that of fiberglass sold in 15.5-inch-wide rolls, designed to fit in the space between framing members, such as joists and studs. Unfaced rolls (without paper covering) and loose blown-in insulation can be added on top of existing attic insulation to improve the energy efficiency of homes. As previously discussed, exterior sheathings and house wrapping material can also provide a high degree of insulating value.

Insulation also provides a degree of soundproofing between adjacent floors and walls of townhouses, condominiums, and apartments. Air leaking into or out of a home can significantly affect heat loss or gain. Therefore, careful attention should be paid to caulking around openings for plumbing and wiring and weather-stripping around windows and doors.

Moisture Control

Normal household activities such as cooking, showering, and laundering create water vapor. Condensation from vapor that passes through interior wall surfaces can cause damage to the structure. For this reason, a vapor barrier (which may be made of plastic film, foil, or crafted paper) should be installed on the inside wall side of the insulation.

As in the crawl space below the house, proper ventilation of the attic space is important. This is accomplished through the use of vents to allow the free movement of air in the attic, which keeps moisture from forming, thereby rotting the wood. The ventilation also aids in removing unwanted heat from the attic, allowing air conditioners to work more efficiently in cooling the home. Roof vents come in many shapes and styles. Older homes usually have gable vents at the peak on each end of the house. Newer homes often use a single-piece ridge vent that is installed along the ridgeline. Intake vents are placed in the soffit or overhang of the roof. These vents allow air to travel from the outside, through the soffit vents, through the attic, and outside through the ridge vent.

HEATING/AIR CONDITIONING SYSTEMS

HVAC is an acronym for *heating, ventilation, and air conditioning*. A wide variety of heating and cooling systems is available for residential construction. Older structures relied on heating systems such as fireplaces, electric baseboard heaters, and oil furnaces. Unfortunately, these systems were rather inefficient and in some instances, costly to operate. In recent years, there has been interest in relatively efficient fireplace inserts rather than traditional fireplaces. Although picturesque, a masonry fireplace by itself is an inefficient heating structure. It serves largely to exhaust air (and subsequently heat) from the house.

The only truly efficient heating system is a central unit. Older systems relied heavily on the convection of heated air to circulate and warm the house. Today's heating and cooling systems use a central blower to distribute the heated or cooled air throughout the house. Each room is required to have an air duct, and return ducts to the main unit must be centrally located for maximum efficiency. These modern systems come in a variety of sizes and capabilities to suit a particular home and can be powered by gas or electricity.

The makeup of these systems is largely one of convenience, cost, and individual preference. Efficiency and operating costs should also be top priorities for builders and homeowners. Which system (gas or electric) is the most efficient and has the lowest installation and operating costs is an ongoing debate.

Gas forced-air furnaces are popular among many homeowners because of their relatively low cost, their high efficiency, and the warm, cozy environment they create when the heat comes on. Electric furnaces are popular for the same reasons, but rising utility costs over the past several years have made the electric furnace less economical than in the past.

Another popular heating and cooling system, especially in areas with mild climates, is the heat pump. The heat pump extracts heat from the outside, even in moderately cold weather, and transfers the heat into the home. The cycle is reversed in the summer to extract heat from the interior and produce air conditioning. A limitation of the heat pump is that it can operate efficiently only in moderate climates. In climates that have cold winters, a separate furnace, fireplace, or wood stove is necessary to provide the heat when the outside temperature drops significantly below freezing. Another drawback to the heat pump is that the heat coming out of the vent feels cooler than that generated by a furnace. For this reason, homeowners sometimes have a backup heating system to maintain a comfortable living environment.

Air conditioning systems usually are powered by electricity. As previously discussed, the heat pump is the only heating and cooling system that is built into the same unit. Furnaces typically are located in the utility room, basement, or garage, while the air conditioning unit is placed outside the house, which is necessary for proper operation and efficiency.

Advances in technology have integrated the heating, cooling, and ventilation controls into a central thermostat, eliminating the need for separate controls. A further advance is the development of "smart houses," which use a central computer to automate the entire operating infrastructure of the house. With these state-of-the-art systems, you can adjust the controls of the heating and cooling system, activate the lawn sprinkler, draw a bath, or program a security system—all by telephone or computer modem link. These systems are extremely expensive but offer tremendous savings in efficiency and productivity for homeowners.

Finally, when designing, replacing, or installing a new HVAC system, builders and homeowners should ensure that the system meets the requirements of the home. Modern practice often sees duplicate systems installed in homes of two or more stories. Although individual furnaces, heat pumps, and air conditioners are designed to adequately heat or cool a specific size home, these systems are often underpowered or overworked to accomplish the task. The net result is a system that does not operate at peak efficiency and ultimately breaks down sooner than desired. With the installation of dual systems (one for the upstairs and one for the downstairs), the entire system can operate more efficiently, saving the homeowner considerable money in the long run. HVAC systems are expensive, so it makes sense for homeowners to carefully research any such expenditure to ensure that they are getting what they want and need in a heating and cooling system.

Solar Heat

Much attention has been given to solar heat in recent years. The two main types of solar heating are passive and active.

Passive solar heating simply takes advantage of exposure to the sun. Direct exposure heats a given area during the day. Indirect exposure involves heating water units or masonry surfaces to "give off" heat during the night. To be able to incorporate passive solar heating, a home must be situated so the front or rear of the house faces south, and the southern exposure should incorporate sufficient windows to allow the sun's rays to penetrate the home.

Active solar heating involves a more sophisticated method of collecting, storing, and distributing heat. The system starts with a collection panel(s), with a glass front, water tubing, and black flat plates. The glass is useful in allowing the solar energy to enter but preventing its escape. The black plates absorb the heat energy for transmission to the water tubing. The heated water is pumped to a storage tank for later distribution throughout the home. A heat exchange system provides for distribution of the heat from the circulated water.

Unfortunately, solar systems typically cannot provide more than 50–60% of the heating needed for a home. Thus, auxiliary systems (such as a furnace or heat pump) are usually needed.

ELECTRICAL SYSTEMS

Like the HVAC system, the electrical system in a house serves a critical purpose. Care should be taken to ascertain the proper design, scope, and layout of electrical outlets and components and to ensure the system is adequate to handle the current and future requirements. Modern construction requires a 110/220 volt wiring system with a capacity of approximately 200 amps, fitted with circuit breakers. The electrical box and panel should be located in a utility room, basement, or garage for ease of access to reset circuit breakers and to perform maintenance.

The home should be wired with sufficient electrical wall receptacles for the use of the household. Utility areas such as garages and bathrooms require the installation of dedicated breakers to prevent accidental electrical shock. Additionally, the installation of smoke detectors outside sleeping areas is required to warn occupants of fire danger. These systems must be wired into the house's electrical current and have a battery backup. The smoke detector must have a visible warning light or be designed to give off a warning signal of 85 db at 10 feet. This is a requirement for all new residential construction, as outlined in the North Carolina residential building code.

PLUMBING SYSTEMS

The adequacy and quality of the plumbing system are important facets in the quality of residential construction. Common construction practice uses copper, brass, cast iron, galvanized steel, chlorinated polyvinyl chloride, or polybutylene plastic pipe for water distribution systems. Each bathroom should be vented to the exterior by the use of a metal pipe that is run through the roof. The venting of sink traps is also required. All water fixtures should have separate cutoffs so a repair can be made without shutting down the entire system. Like the HVAC and electrical systems, the plumbing system should be designed for maximum efficiency and functional utility. Hot water heaters should be well insulated and large enough to accommodate the demands placed upon them. Typically, single-family homes require at least a 50-gallon water heater. A large home or a larger family may require a bigger water heater or multiple water heaters.

GOVERNMENT REGULATION

North Carolina Uniform Residential Building Code

North Carolina enforces a statewide residential building code that is designed to ensure uniformity, safety, sanitation, and high-quality construction of residential homes. The **North Carolina Uniform Residential Building Code** is based on the International Residential Code for One- and Two-Family Dwellings (as amended for North Carolina). The provisions of the International Code are compatible with the codes of the Building Officials Code Administrators International, Inc.; the International Conference of Building Officials; and the Southern Building Code Congress International, Inc.

Each local government, county, or city has a building inspections department that enforces the local adaptations of the building code. Before any construction can begin, the builder must submit appropriate construction information to obtain a **building permit**. The building permit is obtained to determine whether the proposed use is allowed under existing zoning rules and will initiate the process for determining whether the construction is completed according to applicable building codes. The inspection officer must then approve each stage of the construction before the next stage is allowed to begin. At the satisfactory completion of the construction and inspection process, a **certificate of occupancy** is issued. Typically, one cannot obtain permanent utility services for a home until the certificate of occupancy is issued.

FHA/VA Minimum Standards

Homes built to be sold to buyers using a Federal Housing Administration (FHA)-insured or Department of Veterans Affairs (VA)-guaranteed loan do not need to be built under FHA or VA supervision or need a 10-year warranty. FHA requires a building certificate for any home under one year old. VA requires a builder to be on its approved builder's list before the new homes can be financed with a VA loan. All new construction requires a certificate of occupancy by the local building inspector. Such a certificate is issued only after all required inspections have been completed.

Contractor Licensing

To obtain a *contractor's license*, an applicant must pass an examination. The examination tests state building codes, contract law, worker's compensation laws, blueprint reading/estimating, and Occupational Safety and Health Administration laws and regulations. In addition to passing an exam, an applicant must have a net worth of $17,000 to $150,000 depending on the classification of license requested. Property managers, who oversee renovations or improvements to apartment complexes or commercial properties that exceed $30,000 must also have a general contractor's license.

The Contractor's Licensing Board falls under the North Carolina Department of Insurance and is a separate entity not related to the Real Estate Commission.

Summary of Important Points

1. Wood-frame construction is the most popular method for residential building because it offers flexibility of design, is less expensive, is easy to insulate, and can be built relatively quickly.
2. A variety of styles are found in residential construction, including the single-story ranch, two-story contemporary, and one-and-a-half-story Cape Cod. Colonial, French provincial, and Victorian styles are also found.
3. Foundation systems provide the proper support for a structure as well as control drainage and moisture.
4. The foundation footing must be carefully placed in firm, undisturbed soil or on solid rock. The footing must be below the frost line and should have a drainage system to carry groundwater away from the foundation.
5. Foundation walls are commonly made of poured concrete, masonry block, or brick. A smooth mortar exterior surfacing is known as parging.
6. The best protection against wood-destroying insects is chemical treatment of the soil. Termite treatment is applied after the foundation is complete and before the vapor barrier installation. In the case of a concrete slab, treatment and vapor barrier are applied before pouring the concrete.
7. The crawl space of a home must provide for adequate ventilation and waterproofing. Moisture buildup can cause major damage to wooden structural members. A vapor barrier can be installed in a crawl spaces and under concrete slabs.
8. Framing is the wooden skeleton of a structure. Framing is done with lumber of a nominal 4-inch width and 2-inch thickness based on the function of the component system. Framing is usually on 16-inch centers. This provides a uniform nailing pattern of four rows, because most structural covering materials are in 4-foot widths.
9. The floor system starts with a pressure-treated wood member, the sill plate (2" × 6"), nailed to the foundation system, which is usually 8 inches wide. Wood joists (2" × 8", 2" × 10", or 2" × 12") support the subfloor material, which is commonly plywood sheets. Bridging is a system of bracing between the floor joists to add strength and prevent lateral movement of the floor support structure.
10. Finish floor systems consist of components such as hardwood, tile, linoleum, and carpet.
11. Wall framing is almost exclusively 2" × 4" studs placed 16 inches on center. Other methods include 2" × 6" studs 24 inches on center or larger post-and-beam framing of 4- or 6-inch square studs, which are spaced several feet apart.

12. The most common wall framing system is the platform method. This consists of a 2" × 4" base plate, an 8-foot 2" × 4" stud, and a double top plate. This system sits on top of the floor system, which serves as the platform for the wall. An alternative method is balloon framing, in which wall studs run from the foundation to the roof system of a two-story structure.
13. A truss is a number of wooden members nailed together into one framework. Trusses can be used for floor and roof framing.
14. A truss shifts the weight-bearing function to the outer walls. This provides freedom of placement of inner walls, which are usually non-weight-bearing because they are not required to support the roof.
15. The roof structural skeleton is usually built with 2" × 8" ceiling joists and 2"× 6" or 2" × 8" rafters. Contemporary roof construction can also use 2" × 4" trusses in place of conventional framing lumber.
16. The roof skeleton is usually covered with plywood, a felt paper underlayment, and shingles. Shingles are commonly made of asphalt or fiberglass.
17. Common roof types on residential property are gable, and hip. Mansard and gambrel are used much less frequently.
18. Exterior walls are usually covered with a sheathing material such as plywood, particleboard, or various brands of insulating sheathing. The final exterior siding or veneer is placed on top of the sheathing.
19. Insulation should be placed in floors, walls, and ceilings. The higher the R-factor number, the greater the resistance to heat flow and, therefore, the greater the insulating effect. A particularly effective place for insulation is the ceiling. This not only protects against heat loss in the winter but also insulates against heat load in the summer.
20. Windows fall into three general classes: sliding, swinging, and fixed. Windows are usually made of wood, metal, aluminum, or composite materials. Most construction uses double-pane glass windows to improve the energy efficiency of the home and to meet the state building code.
21. HVAC is an acronym for heating, ventilation, and air conditioning. Some systems use fuel oil or natural gas for energy, while heat pump systems use electricity.
22. Today's heating and cooling systems use a central blower to distribute the heated or cooled air throughout the house. Each room has an air duct, and return ducts are centrally located to maximize efficiency.
23. The heat pump is a modern system that cools in the summer as well as heats in the winter.
24. Air conditioning is typically a central forced-air system powered by electricity, but it can also be powered by gas or oil. Room air conditioning is often provided by window units.
25. A sill is a wooden member of the frame that is attached to the foundation.

26. Piers are vertical masonry structures placed inside foundation walls to support the subflooring.
27. Passive solar systems merely collect heat by placement of the building for the best exposure to the sun. Active systems are more complex in that they move the heat to other parts of the house.
28. Government regulation of home construction is evidenced in the residential building code, modified by city or county codes; minimum U.S. Department of Housing and Urban Development standards for projects under their financing programs; and the licensing requirements of contractors.

Review Questions

Answers to the review questions are in the Answer Key at the back of the book.

1. The most common type of residential construction is which of the following?
   A. wood-frame
   B. solid brick
   C. prefabricated
   D. structural steel

2. The most expensive style of home to build per square foot is usually a:
   A. one-and-a-half-story home.
   B. one-story ranch.
   C. two-story home.
   D. split-level home.

3. The supporting wall system members are which of the following?
   A. joists
   B. studs
   C. rafters
   D. wallboard

4. Soffit and fascia are found in which structural system?
   A. foundation
   B. wall
   C. floor
   D. roof

5. The best form of termite protection is:
   A. mechanical barriers.
   B. chemical treatment.
   C. concrete foundations.
   D. slab construction.

6. A soffit vent is found in the:
   A. crawl space.
   B. roof overhang.
   C. wall.
   D. ceiling.

7. A result of modern construction methods using truss systems is:
   A. greater attic space.
   B. dependence on inner walls for load bearing.
   C. less dependence on outer walls for load bearing.
   D. freedom of inner wall placement.

8. The structural member used to take up the support function over openings for windows or doors is a:
   A. header.
   B. footing.
   C. jamb.
   D. joist.

9. In reference to insulation:
   A. the greater the R-factor value, the lesser the insulation.
   B. insulation should be placed only in the walls.
   C. building codes do not typically stipulate the level of insulation to be used.
   D. in many older homes there may not be any insulation present.

10. Members of the wall system include all of the following EXCEPT:
    A. sole plate.
    B. joist.
    C. stud.
    D. double top plate.

11. Piers are used to:
    A. form roof components.
    B. support floor systems.
    C. provide ventilation.
    D. prevent erosion.

12. The metal work used to divert water intrusion when joining a vertical to a horizontal surface is:
    A. flashing.
    B. sheathing.
    C. pitch.
    D. fascia.

13. Before construction is allowed to begin, the acquisition of a _____ is required.
    A. certificate of occupancy
    B. NC Uniform Residential Building Code
    C. NC Residential Property and Owners Disclosure Statement
    D. building permit

14. Which of the following are exempt from the building contractor licensing requirement?
    A. REALTORS®
    B. owner-developers
    C. projects of more than $125,000
    D. projects of less than $30,000

15. A wooden member of the frame that is attached to the foundation is a:
    A. stoop.
    B. pier.
    C. ridge board.
    D. sill.

16. Vertical masonry structures placed inside the foundation walls to support the subflooring are:
    A. headers.
    B. sills.
    C. piers.
    D. joists.

17. What is the average height of a residential ceiling?
    A. 7 feet
    B. 8 feet
    C. 9 feet
    D. 10 feet

18. What is the lowest concrete part of a house?
    A. slab
    B. foundation
    C. sill
    D. footing

19. What is the overhang of the roof called?
    A. eave
    B. soffit
    C. fascia
    D. pitch

20. The type of roof system that allows a house to be built free of interior load bearing walls is a:
    A. rafter.
    B. gambrel.
    C. gable.
    D. truss.

21. The angle or slope of a roof is the:
    A. shed.
    B. gambrel.
    C. pitch.
    D. bridging.

22. The type of heating system that utilizes a duct-work and blower is:
    A. gravity warm air.
    B. space heating.
    C. passive heating.
    D. forced warm air.

23. The lowest horizontal framing member of a house is the:
    A. joist.
    B. sill.
    C. stud.
    D. fascia.

24. The most external part of the exterior wall system is the:
    A. siding.
    B. sheathing.
    C. stud.
    D. flashing.

25. The material that is attached directly to the exterior of the external studs of a house is the:
    A. siding.
    B. gypsum board.
    C. wrapping.
    D. sheathing.

CHAPTER 20

BASIC REAL ESTATE INVESTMENT

KEY TERMS

appreciation
cash flow
leverage

liquidity
return on investment

LEARNING OBJECTIVE

At the conclusion of this chapter, you should be able to:

1. Define equity, leverage, cash flow, and appreciation.

IN THIS CHAPTER

This chapter will address some of the more basic forms of investment terminology as well as illustrate some of the more common ways to analyze a potential investment. As with any new topic, a little knowledge can be a dangerous thing. Real estate practitioners need to be aware that coverage of such an involved topic as investments in a fundamentals text is clearly introductory and is not a substitute for more detailed and professional analysis. Providing investment, legal, or tax advice without possessing the required competence is to be avoided.

BASIC REAL ESTATE INVESTMENT

Real estate investing is a multidimensional topic with a wide variety of directions that an investor can take. Many people consider the purchase of their home to be the largest single investment of their lives. Others consider home buying an investment only when they purchase an income-providing property. Yet others consider real estate investments as the purchase of a property in which the investor is also the end user, such as purchasing a property to be used in one's own business. Still others might consider investing as a much larger scale purchase with other investors whom they may not know or have anything in common with other than the purchase on a common investment. Regardless of one's view of real estate investing, it is clear that the real estate professional would be wise to obtain at least a working knowledge of real estate investing.

Investing versus Speculation

Certainly, real estate investing means different things to different people. One investor's goals might consist of the short-term, quick profit that is realized in "flipping" properties. Flipping is the process of purchasing a property and then quickly marketing it for a higher price with the idea of making an attractive profit. Such action can certainly result in a quick, hopefully sizeable, profit. Another person may acquire a parcel of land and simply wait for development to spread until he is able to sell the land for much more than was originally paid.

The author considers "flipping" property to be speculative rather than investing. If land or property is acquired only to make a profit by buying it and then selling it later for more than was originally paid, that is considered speculating or speculation.

As used within this chapter, real estate investing is the process of purchasing a property and operating it to allow revenue and profit to grow over time and therefore lead to an increase in the value of the investment.

There are many advantages to investing in real estate. Real estate has proven over time to increase in value at least at the rate of inflation. Historically, *mortgage lenders have been willing to loan the majority of the purchase price for real estate and allow the investor to purchase property by paying a modest down payment.*

This concept is known as **leverage** and not only allows the investor to make a much larger investment than if she had to pay in all cash but also allows a higher rate of return on the amount of money that was invested. Another potential advantage is that of cash flow. **Cash flow** refers to the *amount of readily spendable cash that remains after all operating expenses and debt service obligations have been paid.* In addition, tax laws have generally been quite favorable to the real estate investment community. Whereas the homeowner can declare tax deductions for mortgage interest and property taxes, the investment property tax rules allow the investor to deduct depreciation, maintenance, management fees, and all other business-related expenses of the investment. Additionally, upon the sale of the investment, capital gains tax rates are lower than the ordinary tax rates. Unlike the rules regarding a personal residence, an investor has the ability to utilize strategies, such as the 1031 tax-deferred exchange rules on the sale of investment properties, that will allow her to defer the payment of taxes to maximize the amount of capital available for further investing.

Certainly, there are disadvantages to real estate investing as well. Real estate investments tend to be larger investments than many other investment opportunities that are readily available to the investor, such as stock and bonds. This larger size often limits participants to only those who have already amassed the financial ability to secure such an investment. Another disadvantage is the lack of liquidity. **Liquidity** is the *ability to quickly convert the investment to cash should that be necessary*. Real estate investments are not the easiest and quickest to dispose of if a sale needs to be made and the costs to both acquire and sell can be considerable. Real estate investments can easily require investors to have to make additional cash transfusions if expenses exceed the revenues, thereby making adequate cash reserves not so much a luxury but rather a necessity. There can be high levels of risk, ranging from being responsible for the expenses to the risk of someone being injured on the property. Despite many noninvestors' opinions that real estate investing is the sure path to riches, the reality is that the road to riches can be a risky path to take.

Basic Concepts

The purchase of any real estate investment should be made only after a careful analysis of four basic areas: *cash flow, equity and equity build-up,* including the *potential for appreciation,* and *tax-related benefits.*

Cash Flow: It can be said that all investment properties have cash flow, but that it's not always positive.

For this reason, the astute investor will need to carefully analyze the projected income and expenses related to any potential investment.

One such analysis is that of cash flow, which is simply the amount of readily spendable cash remaining after operating expenses (e.g., maintenance, supplies, utilities, taxes, insurance, management fees) and debt service obligations have been paid. It is quite common that many investment opportunities will not have positive cash flow in the early stages of ownership and there will likely be periods of time when inevitable unexpected costs will place the investor in situations of negative cash flow. For this reason, investors will find it beneficial to retain adequate reserves to get them through these periods of time.

Equity and Equity Build-Up: The concept of equity is traditionally defined as the difference between what the property is worth minus what is currently owed. Equity is created by three separate methods, including (1) the ability to purchase a property for less than it is worth, (2) the amount of the down payment, and (3) the gradual reduction of loan balance through amortization.

The ability to purchase the property for less than market value creates an immediate form of equity to the investor. This very well may prove to be an attraction to the investor who may be weighing other concerns about a particular real estate investment. One of the advantages is that if the property can be purchased for less than its actual value, the investor will not have to depend on appreciation in order to recoup the initial investment should a sale become necessary if the investment does not work out. Additionally, by purchasing the property for less than market value, the resulting loan amount would normally be less, which will create a lower monthly mortgage payment.

Another form of equity will result from the amount of cash invested in a particular transaction. If an investor paid all cash for a property, the result would be 100% equity for the investor.

Whereas this might be attractive in that no loan costs would help to maximize cash flow, it would not provide as many tax benefits, and the investor would be limited to purchasing only as much investment opportunity as he would have the cash to pay for.

For this reason, many investors would prefer to leverage the purchase of the property. *Simply put, leverage is the concept of utilizing a smaller amount of his own money and borrowing the majority of the purchase price from the mortgage lender.* By wisely financing the property with someone else's money, the investor can limit his own risk as well as make a much larger investment than he could if he tried to use all cash. As a result, the rate of return for the investment would be calculated on the actual amount invested but the profit would be generated by the entire value of the property.

Example: An investor purchases a duplex for $150,000 by paying all cash. Four years later, he sells the duplex for $180,000, which would generate a return of 20% on his initial investment. ($180,000 - $150,000 = $30,000 profit ÷ $150,000 purchase price). Now suppose this investor had been able to leverage this purchase by paying 20% down and borrowing the remainder. In this situation, the rate of return would be 100% based on the initial investment ($150,000 × 20% = $30,000 initial investment; $30,000 profit ÷ $30,000 down payment = 100% rate of return).

The overuse of leverage can be a major cause of concern in any investment as the more money borrowed will reflect a higher monthly mortgage and therefore diminish cash flow. During periods of low, or no revenues, and higher expenses, the highly leveraged investor will find himself in a very risky situation.

One other way that equity is calculated is through equity build-up. As the mortgage payments are made each month, the portion allocated to principal after interest has been paid will also serve to increase the equity. Unlike cash flow, which was mentioned earlier, the equity build-up does not reflect readily spendable cash and will be realized by the investor only upon the refinance or ultimate sale of the property.

Appreciation: The third method of increasing equity is that created by the appreciation of the property. This is *caused by a combination of inflation as well as market demand for a certain type, and location, of a property.*

As we have seen over the past few years, appreciation is not certain, but over the longer term, this has been a staple for much of the real estate industry.

The investor achieves maximum equity build-up through a combination of purchasing the property for less than fair market value, the gradual reduction in loan balance by amortization, and appreciation. Although the individual investor cannot control the rate of inflation, she can benefit from selecting investment properties in an area ripe for appreciation coupled with attractive financing and good management practices.

Tax-Related Benefits: The final section of the investment analysis is to determine the tax-related benefits of ownership. The tax benefits of an investment property exceed those of the personal residence. The investor not only can write off the property taxes and mortgage interest as with a personal residence, but also can deduct operating expenses, such as repair and maintenance costs, utilities, supplies, mileage, management fees, professional fees, and depreciation, as well as any other reasonable expenses for the continued efficient operation of the investment. In reality, these tax benefits can be considerable and can increase the rate of return on investment.

Summary of Important Points

1. The fastest way to increase equity is to (1) buy the property below market value, (2) pay a down payment, and (3) benefit from maximum appreciation.
2. Leverage is the process of utilizing a smaller amount of the investor's money and a larger amount of someone else's money in order to purchase an investment.
3. Excessive leverage greatly increases the investor's risk of negative cash flow.

Review Questions

Answers to the review questions are in the Answer Key at the back of the book.

1. The term "leverage" refers to:
   A. the use of a small amount of the investor's money and a larger amount of someone else's money to acquire a property.
   B. hedging potential liability by investing with other "like minded" investors.
   C. increasing your liquidity.
   D. utilizing managing partners to control the day-to-day operations.

2. The term "cash flow" refers to the amount of readily spendable cash remaining after all operating expenses and which of the following have been paid?
   A. no other expenses
   B. depreciation
   C. mortgage debt service
   D. capital improvement

3. The term "liquidity" refers to:
   A. the ability to convert the investment to cash in a short period of time.
   B. the maximization of cash flow.
   C. a situation in which the tax benefits flow through to the investors.
   D. using other people's money to purchase an investment.

4. Equity build-up is the result of
   A. ability to purchase property for less than it is worth.
   B. amount of down payment.
   C. gradual reduction of loan balance through amortization.
   D. all of the above.

5. The ability to convert an investment to cash quickly is:
   A. cash flow.
   B. appreciation.
   C. liquidity.
   D. leverage.

APPENDICES

Appendix A: Exam Preparation Tips and Strategies and Practice National and State Examinations	p. 628
Appendix B: Real Estate Math	p. 666
Appendix C: North Carolina Real Estate License Law, North Carolina Real Estate Commission Rules, and License Law and Rule Comments	p. 696
Chapter 93A: North Carolina Real Estate License Law	p. 697
Chapter 58A: North Carolina Real Estate Commission Rules	p. 738
License Law and Rule Comments	p. 835
Appendix D: Residential Square Footage Guidelines	p. 857
Appendix E: Safety Issues for Real Estate Brokers	p. 885
Appendix F: Real Estate Forms and Addenda	p. 889

APPENDIX A: EXAM PREPARATION TIPS AND STRATEGIES AND PRACTICE NATIONAL AND STATE EXAMINATIONS

EXAM PREPARATION

Mental Preparation

- It is entirely normal to feel stress in the preparation for, and during the actual taking of, the exam. Most adult learners have been away from the academic environment, and therefore testing, for quite a while.
- A reasonably rested mind and body is better prepared for the exam than one that is worn out from pulling the proverbial "all-nighter."
- It is not likely that you will ever know everything about the subject and be totally prepared for every conceivable way the question can be presented. That is normal and perfectly fine.
- Remember, there are really only two scores given. Those that score 71% and above and those that score below 71%. Note that 71% is the minimum score to pass the National section. The State section requires 29 correct out of 40 or 72.5%.
- There is no real benefit to being stressed about scoring 100% on the test. In many ways you are better served by being adequately prepared to score comfortably above 71% in each section.
- It is perfectly okay to miss a question. The truth is that very few test takers ever score that elusive 100%. One way to think about it is to give yourself permission to miss three or four questions on each of the National and State portions of the exam. The last thing you want to do during a test is to allow any one question to rattle your nerves to the extent that it causes you to miss another question, or two, as a result.

General Test Strategies

- Read each test question and answer carefully.
- You have always heard that your first answer is most likely the correct one. If you have ever been in a position to grade tests, you know this is very true. Test takers who repeatedly change answers are typically reflecting a lack of confidence rather than improving their score.
- A well-written test question provides good quality answers. The answer choices will contain the correct answer and "distractors," which are likely answer choices that will appear as legitimate alternatives to the correct answer.
- When multiple parties are involved in a question, make certain that you have the correct person in mind when answering the question.

APPENDIX A Exam Preparation Tips and Strategies and Practice National and State Examinations

- If it seems as though there are at least two correct answers, the issue is likely in the question itself. Very often when test takers have the answer choices narrowed down to two, it will prove useful to re-read the question and see if it is more specific than you have originally realized.

- It may prove helpful to eliminate any known incorrect answers before making your final selection.

- It is worth mentioning again, you only need to score 71% correct in order to pass the National, 72.5% for the State, section of the examination. Do not worry excessively about any one question. No one question should ever be allowed to make you anxious and cause you to miss other questions. Remember, there are questions that are "test-driven" on both sections of your exam. It is entirely possible the question causing you the most stress may not even be counted toward your final score.

- The most difficult question on the test counts exactly the same as the easiest.

- It is very common for test takers to be on guard for the proverbial "trick" question. In reality most so-called trick questions are nothing more than a student's lack of reading the question carefully or not being well prepared to differentiate the actual correct answer from other good distractors.

- One important change to exam questions is an honest effort to be more straight-forward than many of the types of questions used in the past. (Whether any particular question can be agreed upon as straight-forward may be a matter of interpretation.) Please note that the intent is to eliminate all of the former "Roman numeral I and II formats" with I only, II only, both I and II, and neither I nor II. The current format utilizes questions with A, B, C, and D choice formats. That is true for both theory as well as math questions.

Specific Test Preparation Strategies

- Make certain to include some variety in your test preparation by working on both subject matter content as well as practicing sample test questions. At some point, your strategy has to move from just making your brain a garage for stored facts to being able to apply that information to the actual test questions.

- There is no real benefit from being overly prepared in any one subject area. The actual test contains questions that are spread over all of the chapters and subject areas and the number of questions that can be assigned to any of the areas is quite limited. Certainly there are some areas, i.e., License Law and Commission Rules and Regulations, in which the coverage is more detailed and contains many more questions, but this is the exception rather than the rule.

- Determine if your real estate school will allow you to continue to audit classes, perhaps at no charge, up until the date that you actually take the exam. Many schools will allow their former students to do this, not only as a service to the student but as a potential boost to their own passing rates. This is especially true if there were specific classes that you may have missed during the time you took your course.
- Don't leave out the glossary as a good source of potential test question information. Any good test will demand a good understanding of the language of the subject matter.
- Specific "Problem Topics" are not available from the testing firm that indicate items from the National portion of the exam with which students are having difficulty.
- Specific "Problem Topics" for the State portion of the exam are available and are located at the end of this Appendix A.

Math Preparation Strategies

- Math is an area that often creates stress for test takers. You may likely find the math contained in the National portion is easier than you anticipate. I find that the biggest detriment to the student and math is not so much the difficulty of the question but rather potential non-exposure to the type of questions in the course prep. Effective April 1, 2019, many of the historically most difficult math questions for students will no longer be tested on the exam.
- Math questions will contain four answers from which to choose. These will typically be the correct answer and the three most common ways to miss the question.
- Math questions can often be worked backwards, from the provided answers, in order to provide the solution.
- Try "visualizing" the approximate answer. This helps especially when you might have worked a question backwards in such a way that you divided when you actually needed to multiply.
- As with the advice stated previously, there is no real benefit to being overly prepared in any one section of the math. For example, although an "area" question might be stated in many different ways, the reality is you will likely only encounter one or two at the most. The same goes for many other sections of the math.
- Should you start with the math? This is a common question but not one that we typically hear from someone who is actually reasonably prepared for and confident in the math. The answer is to start with question 1 and proceed in the order of the questions. This will also prove to enhance your confidence in taking the test itself.

- Effective April 1, 2019, the plan is to no longer have any math questions contained within the State portion of the exam. All math questions will be contained within the National portion of the exam.
- Current guidelines call for only about 13 math questions on the National portion of the exam. Historically there were as many as 20 or 21. Please remember that many of your well-intentioned friends in the real estate world may mean well when they tell you how difficult the math questions are, but that was a different day and time as far as math and the exam.

The Actual Test Itself

- Your exam will actually provide a tutorial in order to make you familiar with the test process. The time spent on the tutorial section does not count towards the four hours that you are allotted.
- You will be allowed to "mark" a question and then return to it at a later point. Make absolutely certain that you have returned to answer any question that you may have marked in this fashion.
- You have been told that your exam will contain 100 questions on the National section and 40 on the State section. In reality, both sections will contain approximately 5 questions that are being "analyzed" to determine their suitability for future examinations. These questions will not be scored as a part of your testing.
- Take a deep breath and then begin your exam. Remember that this is only a test and not an indicator of whether you are smart, are a good person, or whether you will be a good real estate agent. Certainly it is disappointing not to pass, but it is really just a test. You can always go back and take just the section you did not pass next time.
- Good luck!

PRACTICE EXAMINATIONS

The following practice exams are in the format in which the National and State sections of the exam will be presented. This National section test consists totally of theory questions. For more preparation for math-related questions, refer to the math section of the appendix and to questions contained within the end-of-chapter quizzes.

SAMPLE NATIONAL SECTION PRACTICE EXAM

This section consists of 100 questions that are not specific to North Carolina. The answers are provided in the Answer Key following the appendix. For a more complete listing of the subject areas that comprise each section, refer to the North Carolina

Real Estate Commission booklet Real Estate Licensing in North Carolina *that is available in print from as well as online at www.ncrec.gov.*

Agency Relationships and Contracts

1. Which of the following would terminate a residential sales agreement?

    A. death of the seller
    B. legal declaration of insanity of the seller
    C. the sale of the property
    D. an assignment

2. Which of the following statements is NOT correct?

    A. A principal is responsible for acts of his agent while engaged in activities concerning the agency.
    B. An agent is in a fiduciary relationship to her principal.
    C. The agent has no duties to third parties in a transaction.
    D. The principal owes cooperation to the agent.

3. On the broker's recommendation, a seller accepted an offer that was 8% below the listed price. The broker did not disclose to the listing seller that the buyer was the broker's brother-in-law. Which of the following is correct?

    A. The broker violated his obligations as agent of the seller.
    B. The fact that the buyer is related to the broker does not need to be divulged to the seller.
    C. The broker would only be obligated to disclose this relationship if the buyer had hired the broker as a buyer agent
    D. There is no violation since the seller was in agreement with the terms of the buyer's offer.

4. An agent's responsibilities and duties to a third person include:

    A. not to disclose personal information regarding the third party.
    B. disclosure of all material facts the agent knows or reasonably should know.
    C. disclosure of personal information about the principal.
    D. obedience to the lawful instructions of the third party.

5. An agent, based upon statements made by the seller, tells her buyer that all mechanical systems are in "good working order." The agent did not personally verify this information. The buyer decided not to have the property inspected since the seller had indicated they were selling "as is." After the closing, the furnace is found to be defective and must be replaced.

A. The agent is not liable because the buyer opted to not have it inspected.
B. The agent is not liable since he relied upon representation made by the seller.
C. The agent is guilty of an innocent omission of material fact.
D. The agent is guilty of a negligent misrepresentation of material fact.

6. A real estate agent is typically considered to be in what form of agency relationship?

    A. special agency
    B. general agency
    C. universal agency
    D. exclusive agency

7. Allison is an agent with Miller's Creek Realty that has a buyer client who wishes to see a listing obtained by her firm. The broker at Miller's Creek Realty appoints Allison to represent only the interests of the buyer and the listing agent to represent only the interests of the seller. This type of arrangement is an example of:

    A. implied agency
    B. express agency
    C. special agency
    D. designated agency

8. A contract that has no legal standing because it does not meet the minimum standards for a legally enforceable agreement is:

    A. unenforceable
    B. valid
    C. void
    D. voidable

9. A substitution of one contract for another where the original contract is voided is:

    A. exchange
    B. novation
    C. voidable
    D. unilateral

10. A contract in which one party makes a promise of compensation if another party renders a service in return is which of the following?

    A. unilateral
    B. multilateral
    C. trilateral
    D. bilateral

11. Which of the following statements about offers is correct?

    A. They must not be illusory.
    B. They may not be revoked.
    C. They must be accompanied by earnest money.
    D. They must be notarized.

12. A buyer made an offer to purchase a seller's land at a price to be mutually agreed upon in the future. Which of the following best describes this offer?

    A. option
    B. illusory
    C. unilateral
    D. fraudulent

13. A total transfer of contractual rights and obligations to another party is a(n):

    A. novation.
    B. assignment.
    C. accord and satisfaction.
    D. carryover contract.

14. Ralph and Sandra are both agents at Healdsburg Realty. Ralph presents an offer, on behalf of his buyer client to Sandra, the listing agent. Sandra presents the offer to her seller who counteroffers in writing for more money. Ralph presents this counteroffer to his buyer who signs his acceptance in Ralph's presence. After the buyer signs, but before Ralph has notified Sandra, she contacts Ralph to inform him that her seller wishes to withdraw the counteroffer and sell to someone else for more money. Which of the following is true?

    A. There is a valid contract since Ralph's buyer accepted in his presence and both Ralph and Sandra are dual agents.
    B. Sandra's seller can withdraw since neither Sandra nor her seller had yet been informed of the buyer's acceptance.
    C. Sandra's seller can withdraw since the actual paperwork had not yet been returned to Sandra and the earnest money had not yet been deposited.
    D. Ralph had no authority to present the counteroffer on behalf of Sandra's seller.

15. A prospective purchaser has made an offer to the owner's agent who in turn has mailed the offer to his seller. The seller has received this offer, signed it, and now mailed it back to his agent. While the documents are in the mail, another offer for more money is made to the seller's agent. The agent calls the seller to inform him about this new offer, and the seller instructs him to disregard the signed agreement because he wants to accept this new offer. Which of the following is true?

   A. The first offer has been legally accepted because it had been mailed back to the agent.

   B. The second offer has been legally accepted.

   C. The agent cannot present this new offer until there is resolution to the first offer.

   D. The first offer has not been accepted and the seller is free to sell it to the second buyer.

16. An option to purchase differs from a right of first refusal in that:

   A. they are actually two names commonly used to describe the same thing.

   B. in an option the purchaser is required to purchase the property if the seller decides to sell.

   C. in a right of first refusal the seller is not required to sell if the buyer wants to buy.

   D. in an option the seller is not required to sell if the buyer decides to buy.

17. A buyer made an offer to purchase that stated "this offer shall remain open until 12:00 noon on August 20 at which point it shall become null and void." He further stipulates "he will not terminate this offer prior to that time for any reason whatsoever." On Thursday, August 19, before hearing back from the seller, the buyer contacts the seller to inform him that he has changed his mind. The buyer is:

   A. in breach of contract as he agreed not to terminate his offer prior to noon on the 20th.

   B. in breach of agreement and will not be entitled to a refund of his earnest money deposit although he cannot be sued in a court of law.

   C. not in breach of contract even though he terminated prior to noon on the 20th.

   D. not in breach of contract with the seller but is liable for payment of his buyer agent's commission if one was agreed to.

18. On Monday, the buyer, Jeff, signs a full price and conditions offer to purchase Sara's house and mails it to her for review. Sara receives it in the mail late on Tuesday afternoon, at which time she reads the offer and decides that she will accept it. When Sara gets to the office on Wednesday, she signs Jeff's offer and mails it back to him at his proper address. Jeff receives her acceptance on Thursday morning. What Sara does not realize is that Jeff had changed his mind and mailed a letter of revocation of his offer early Tuesday morning. Unfortunately, Sara did not receive the letter of revocation until Thursday afternoon. Is there a binding contract of sale?

    A. No. Jeff has adequately withdrawn his offer when he mailed the letter of revocation to Sara on Tuesday morning.
    B. Yes. Sara created a binding contract when she signed Jeff's offer on Wednesday and mailed it back to him at his proper address.
    C. No. Jeff's revocation does not count until it is actually received on Thursday.
    D. Yes. It was a binding contract when Jeff received the actual acceptance from Sara on Thursday morning.

19. As a result of a provisional broker's negligence in filling in the provisions in a contract of sale, the seller incurred a financial loss. Liability for this loss may be imposed upon:

    A. the agent only.
    B. the employing broker only.
    C. both the agent and the employing broker.
    D. neither the agent nor the employing broker.

20. A listing contract creates an agency relationship in which:

    A. the broker is a general agent.
    B. the seller is principal.
    C. the seller is a special agent.
    D. the broker is a universal agent.

21. A seller tells his broker that he is very anxious to sell and will accept $5,000 less than the listed price. The broker may share this information with:

    A. sales agents in her office.
    B. a cooperating MLS agent acting as a buyer's agent.
    C. the buyer.
    D. anyone interested in the property.

22. Which of the following types of listing agreements allow for the seller to personally sell her own property without having to pay the broker a commission?

    A. net and exclusive agency
    B. exclusive agency and exclusive right to sell
    C. open and exclusive agency
    D. open and exclusive right to sell

23. Amy shows her listing to a buyer who makes an offer that was ultimately accepted by the seller. Before the closing, the buyer has a job transfer that necessitates she move to another town. The seller sympathizes with the purchaser and allows her to withdraw from the contract and releases her from all further obligation. The seller:

    A. owes Amy the selling "side" of the commission.
    B. owes Amy only the expenses incurred by her in selling the property to this particular client.
    C. does not owe Amy a commission since the property was not ultimately closed.
    D. owes Amy the full commission even though the seller has released the buyer from the obligation in this transaction.

24. The clause that is inserted into a listing agreement that protects the broker in the event the seller and buyer try to delay entering into a contract of sale so they can avoid the commission to the agent is known as:

    A. protection agreement clause.
    B. automatic removal clause.
    C. extender clause.
    D. nothing. It is illegal to insert a clause of this type.

25. A pending sales contract agreement can best be described as:

    A. bilateral executed.
    B. unilateral executory.
    C. bilateral executory.
    D. unilateral executed.

26. Champion Realty has received an offer on one of its listings. The seller lives in Maryland and the offer was emailed to him where he signed electronically to accept the offer with no modifications to the original agreement. Once the form was signed electronically it was emailed back to the listing agent at Champion. The agent at Champion then called and told the buyer agent at XYZ Realty the seller had signed the acceptance with no changes. The next day the seller wants to terminate the sale due to having received a better offer. He is claiming there is no contract since he did not "actually" sign the offer but rather used an electronic means to indicate acceptance. Which of the following best describes this situation?

    A. Electronic signatures are legal and it became a contract once the listing agent notified the buyer agent.
    B. It is not a contract since there was no "real" signature on the acceptance.
    C. An electronic acceptance would be legal only if the buyer had signed electronically as well.
    D. Electronic signatures can be legal and this became a contract once the signed offer was emailed back to the listing agent.

27. Amy has verbally accepted a buyer's offer to purchase her house. A week later the buyer calls to inform her that he wishes to terminate his agreement. Which of the following best describes this situation?

    A. This agreement is illegal and has no legal recognition at all.
    B. A verbal acceptance to sell real estate is only valid if the offer was made verbally as well.
    C. This is a voidable contract since it was not in writing.
    D. This is a valid contract and the buyer can be held liable for damages by Amy.

28. The type of listing agreement in which the seller agrees to only have the brokerage firm enter the listing in the local MLS and place a sign in the yard might best be described as a(n):

    A. open listing agreement.
    B. limited services agreement.
    C. exclusive agency listing agreement.
    D. exclusive right to sell agreement.

APPENDIX A Exam Preparation Tips and Strategies and Practice National and State Examinations

Real Property Ownership/Interest

29. All of the following are considered an example of a property owner's "bundle of rights" EXCEPT:
    A. right of possession.
    B. right to build whatever you wish on the property.
    C. right to sell, lease, or convey.
    D. right of quiet enjoyment.

30. The owner(s) of the real property may hold title in all of the following ways EXCEPT:
    A. tenancy in common.
    B. lessees.
    C. severalty.
    D. joint tenancy.

31. Nancy and Kim owned a parcel of property in joint tenancy. Nancy decides to sell her portion to Yvonne, and Kim will continue to own her share. After the transaction closes, how will Kim be considered to hold ownership of her portion?
    A. severalty
    B. joint tenancy
    C. tenancy in common
    D. tenancy by entirety

32. The type of tenancy in which a tenant remains in possession after the lease term has expired but without obtaining the landlord's consent is an example of:
    A. tenancy for years.
    B. periodic tenancy.
    C. tenancy at will.
    D. tenancy at sufferance.

33. A property held in the name of a large corporation will likely be held as:
    A. severalty.
    B. tenancy in common.
    C. joint tenancy.
    D. tenancy by entireties.

34. A trespass on another's land as a result of an intrusion by some structure or other object is an:
    A. encroachment.
    B. easement.
    C. estate.
    D. emblement.

35. Which of the following statements is correct?

   A. Spot zoning is legal in all cases.
   B. Protective covenants are enforced by court injunction.
   C. Protective covenants are government restrictions.
   D. All nonconforming uses are illegal.

36. Easements are created in all of the following ways EXCEPT:

   A. prescription.
   B. lis pendens.
   C. condemnation.
   D. dedication.

37. A property owner in a recently re-zoned area was permitted to continue to use his property in a manner that did not comply with the new zoning requirements. This use is described as which of the following?

   A. exclusive-use zoning
   B. deviation
   C. nonconforming use
   D. private control of land use

38. Wendy has been notified that her property is subject to being acquired by eminent domain. One of the requirements that must be met in order to acquire her property in this manner is that:

   A. it must be for a public purpose.
   B. she does not have to sell if the price being offered is not suitable to her.
   C. she must first be given constructive notice.
   D. a lis pendens must first be filed.

39. Which of the following is an example of an exempt property under the Americans with Disability Act (ADA)?

   A. public school building
   B. model home in a new subdivision
   C. office building
   D. personal residence

40. Which of the following is NOT an example of a public land use control?

   A. protective covenants
   B. zoning regulations
   C. building codes
   D. fire codes

41. Which of the following best illustrates the example of an easement appurtenant?

    A. a right of way across one property to access the adjoining property
    B. a municipal water and sewer line easement
    C. a major oil or gas pipeline project easement
    D. a purely personal right to walk across a neighbor's property to access the beach

Real Estate Finance

42. Regulation Z of the Truth in Lending Act allows which of the following to be placed within an advertisement for a real estate loan without requiring a full disclosure of all credit financing terms?

    A. number of payments
    B. down payment
    C. the full annual percentage rate spelled out in full, that is, not abbreviated as APR
    D. dollar amount of the finance charges

43. A short sale exists when:

    A. the seller owes more than the property will sell for.
    B. the seller owes more than the property is worth and the seller is unwilling, or unable, to pay the difference.
    C. a property is sold quickly typically for all cash and closes in a matter of a few days.
    D. the property is acquired by the lender for nonpayment and re-sold to an investor who buys these type properties in bulk.

44. Who is the oldest and largest of the secondary mortgage markets?

    A. Federal National Mortgage Association (FNMA)
    B. Government National Mortgage Association (GNMA)
    C. Federal Home Loan Mortgage Association (FHLMC)
    D. Washington National Mortgage Association (WNMA)

45. A title theory state is associated with a:

    A. mortgage lien.
    B. deed of trust.
    C. requirement for the acquisition of title insurance.
    D. requirement to record title to the property in a public register of deeds.

46. A loan-to-value (LTV) is traditionally based upon:

    A. the purchase price only.
    B. the relationship of the loan amount in relation to the CMA amount.
    C. the appraised value or the purchase price whichever is more.
    D. the purchase price or appraised value, whichever is less

47. A contract for deed (land contract):

    A. is when the purchaser acquires possession but no title until loan is repaid in full.
    B. stipulates the buyer acquires legal title upon closing the purchase.
    C. stipulates the seller retains equitable title after the closing.
    D. is never recorded until the loan is repaid.

48. Which of the following is true regarding VA mortgage loans?

    A. These loans are not eligible to be assumed.
    B. They can only be assumed by another veteran.
    C. The unmarried surviving spouse of a veteran who died as a result of service-related injuries can use the VA benefits their previous spouse had acquired.
    D. A veteran is allowed to purchase a house as a rental investment using earned VA benefits.

49. Which of the following is NOT considered to be one of the six elements considered to constitute a loan application according to RESPA?

    A. address of the property pledged as collateral
    B. driver's license of the applicant
    C. estimated value of the property
    D. Social Security number of the applicant

50. An alienation clause makes a mortgage:

    A. defeasible.
    B. non-assumable.
    C. unable to be sold in the secondary market.
    D. adjustable.

51. The primary function of the FHA is to:

    A. make mortgage loans.
    B. make loans for low-income housing.
    C. insure loans that protect lenders from financial loss.
    D. purchase mortgages on the secondary market.

52. Which of the following regulates the advertisement of credit terms available for a house offered for sale?

    A. RESPA
    B. Fannie Mae
    C. Equal Credit Opportunity Act
    D. Regulation Z

53. What is the purpose of a deed of trust?

    A. secure the payment of a note
    B. provide protection for the mortgagor
    C. create personal liability of the buyer
    D. prevent assumption

54. Which lien has priority to mortgage foreclosure sale proceeds?

    A. mortgage lien
    B. income tax lien
    C. real property tax lien
    D. mechanic's lien

55. Which of the following requires immediate payment of the principal balance when the borrower is in default on a loan?

    A. equity of redemption
    B. prepayment penalty
    C. right of lender to possession
    D. acceleration

Real Property

56. In which of the following types of legal description must the description close the loop?

    A. government rectangular survey system
    B. recorded plat
    C. metes and bounds
    D. informal reference

57. An acre contains how many square feet?

    A. 640
    B. 4,356
    C. 6,400
    D. 43,560

58. Adherence to which of the following maximizes land value?

    A. principle of contribution
    B. principle of change
    C. principle of anticipation
    D. principle of highest and best use

59. A competitive market analysis is performed when:

    A. assessing property.
    B. pricing property.
    C. appraising property.
    D. condemning property.

60. The principle providing that the highest value of a property has a tendency to be established by the cost of purchasing or constructing a building of equal utility and desirability is the principle of:

    A. highest and best use.
    B. competition.
    C. supply and demand.
    D. substitution.

61. Which appraisal method is most appropriate to a unique property such as a church or post office?

    A. market data approach
    B. cost approach
    C. income approach
    D. capitalization approach

62. Which appraisal method is most appropriate to vacant land?

    A. market data approach
    B. cost approach
    C. income approach
    D. none of the above

63. The direct sales comparison approach takes into consideration all of the following factors EXCEPT:

    A. comparable properties sold within the last six months.
    B. the method of financing of comparable sales.
    C. the price the seller thinks the property is worth.
    D. the age and condition of comparable properties.

64. A gift of real property by will is a:

   A. remise.
   B. demise.
   C. devise.
   D. bequest.

65. A person has died intestate. As a result, the property will be distributed to:

   A. probate.
   B. the state the property is located in.
   C. his or her heirs.
   D. eminent domain.

66. Which of the following is NOT a benefit of recording a deed?

   A. It protects the grantee against future conveyances by the grantor.
   B. It protects the grantee against the grantor's creditors.
   C. It provides constructive notice to all that title is now vested in the grantee.
   D. It is the point when a deed conveys title from the grantor to the grantee.

67. Which of the following would create a defect affecting title?

   A. an un-violated protective covenant
   B. municipal water and sewer easement
   C. a 5-foot-wide maintenance easement for the neighboring property
   D. a concrete driveway that extends slightly over the property line

68. The type of deed the grantee would want to receive in order to gain the maximum benefit of protection from the grantor would be a:

   A. non-warranty deed.
   B. quitclaim deed.
   C. general warranty deed
   D. special warranty deed.

69. Title insurance policies protect the lender against:

   A. losses due to default by the borrower.
   B. losses due to fire and other casualty.
   C. losses due to claims against the property.
   D. risk of injury by a guest of the property owner.

Marketing Regulations (Purchase and Rental)

70. The Residential Lead-Based Paint Hazard Reduction Act requires that a buyer of pre-1978 residential property be provided with all of the following EXCEPT:

    A. a 10-day period in which to have the presence of lead-based paint determined.
    B. a disclosure of any known lead-based paint present in the home.
    C. the EPA pamphlet titled "Protect Your Family from Lead in Your Home."
    D. certification by HUD that the home is "lead free."

71. A real estate agent has been showing his buyer client homes in a subdivision when he sees a For Sale by Owner sign in front of a house that contains the owner's phone number. Unfortunately, a search of the records indicates this owner has registered his home phone number on the Do Not Call Registry. Which of the following is correct?

    A. The agent may call the owner to request more information because the phone number was posted on the sign.
    B. The agent cannot call the owner in order to request more information because the phone number is listed on the Do Not Call registry.
    C. The agent can call the owner because the Do Not Call restrictions do not apply to licensed real estate agents.
    D. The agent cannot legally call; however, the potential buyer may without restriction.

72. The Fair Housing Act of 1968 prohibits discrimination in the rental of all of the following EXCEPT:

    A. offices.
    B. apartments.
    C. houses.
    D. residential lots.

73. Inducing an owner to list property by telling the owner that persons of a particular national origin are moving into the neighborhood is called:

    A. steering.
    B. redlining.
    C. blockbusting.
    D. profiteering.

74. Robert is the manager of an apartment complex that has buildings 1–6 occupied by families with children and buildings 7–10 for those without children. George and Anna, and their two children, are being told by Robert that although they easily qualify for the lease, there aren't any vacancies in a building that allows children. Which of the following best describes this situation?

    A. This is legal because there aren't any units available in a "children allowed" building.
    B. This is an example of redlining.
    C. This is an example of steering.
    D. This is an example of blockbusting.

75. Which of the following does NOT describes radon gas?

    A. It is the second leading cause of lung cancer.
    B. A level above 4.0 pico curries is considered to be a material fact.
    C. High levels of radon can often be mitigated.
    D. It is a gas that is detectable by its sulphur smell.

76. Larry Lender is being asked for a mortgage loan on a house in a predominately minority neighborhood. Because of his concern regarding the long term economic potential for houses in that area he charges a higher interest rate and down payment than he normally would charge that particular buyer given his credit score and income. This can be best described as an example of:

    A. redlining
    B. steering.
    C. blockbusting.
    D. a legal practice given the economic projection.

77. Angela has a listing that is being sold because the prior owner died in the home. Which of the following best describes her responsibility to disclose this fact in her advertising?

    A. She has no responsibility to advertise or disclose this fact due to caveat emptor.
    B. She has no responsibility to advertise this fact.
    C. She must disclose the death as it constitutes a material fact.
    D. This must be disclosed by the seller.

78. Jackson is in the process of acquiring a new residential listing. He states that the listing fee will be 6% of the sales price. When the seller asks why everyone seems to charge the same rate he should:

    A. state that 6% is the "going rate" pretty much all over town.
    B. state that is the MLS rate that has been agreed to by its members.
    C. state that is the rate that the REALTORS® all charge.
    D. state that each firm sets their own rates independent of any other firm's rate.

79. L.B. is a broker that received a call from a prospective buyer a month ago inquiring about a particular property. When L.B. told the buyer this house has just been sold the buyer asks him to keep him in mind should a similar property come on the market. A house very similar has just been listed but when L.B. goes to call this buyer he discovers that he is registered on the Do Not Call registry. What should L.B. do?

    A. He can legally call this buyer because the buyer had asked him 30 days ago to call if a similar property comes on the market.
    B. L.B. cannot call this particular buyer as his phone number is on the registry.
    C. L.B. can call this buyer for up to 180 days from the date of the first call.
    D. L.B. can only call this buyer if he had signed a buyer agency agreement when they first spoke.

Property Management

80. A person living on the managed premises as a salaried employee engaged to rent and lease apartments is called a(n):

    A. property manager.
    B. rental agent.
    C. employee manager.
    D. resident manager.

81. All of the following are required of property managers EXCEPT:

    A. showing and leasing property.
    B. deciding owner's objectives.
    C. collecting rent.
    D. providing for the protection of tenants.

82. The first step in creating an owner-manager relationship is which of the following?
    A. management proposal
    B. management report
    C. management agreement
    D. management fee

83. A property manager's fee is often a combination of a base fee and a percentage of which of the following?
    A. gross potential income
    B. gross operating income
    C. gross effective income
    D. net operating income

84. Periodic financial reports provided to the owner are called:
    A. stabilized budgets.
    B. operating reports.
    C. management statements.
    D. property management reports.

85. A property manager's duties typically include all EXCEPT which of the following?
    A. maintaining the property
    B. collecting rents and security deposits
    C. instituting legal actions on behalf of the owner
    D. giving the owner legal advice regarding eviction procedures

86. In qualifying and selection of tenants the property manager's duties would include all EXCEPT:
    A. obtaining a copy of the prospective tenant's credit report.
    B. obtaining a copy of the prospective tenant's criminal background check.
    C. determining the prospective tenant's "track record" of paying rent and fulfilling rental obligations.
    D. inquiring of the tenant's familial status so the prospective tenant can be placed in units where other families with children are located

87. The principal functions of a property manager include all of the following EXCEPT:

    A. renting space, collecting rents, and paying expenses for the property.
    B. investing the owner's proceeds to acquire more quality rental investment properties.
    C. producing the best possible net operating income from the property.
    D. maintaining and increasing the value of the principal's investment.

Real Estate Calculations

88. A purchaser has contracted to buy a home for $167,900 and the lender has agreed to make him an 85% LTV mortgage at 6.25%. The appraisal has just been completed and the property appraised for only $165,000. What would be the maximum loan amount the lender will make on this purchase?

    A. $139,815
    B. $140,250
    C. $142,715
    D. $143,150

89. A buyer has recently contracted to purchase a duplex that rents for $750 per month per side. If closing is to occur on the 21st of the month, how would the resulting entry for rental income appear on the settlement statement?

    A. $450 debit – seller, credit - buyer
    B. $1,050 debit – seller, credit - buyer
    C. $525 credit – buyer, debit - seller
    D. $225 debit – seller, credit - buyer

90. If a real estate agent listed and sold a property for $90,000 and received 60% of the 7% commission paid to her employing broker, how much did the agent receive?

    A. $2,520
    B. $2,646
    C. $3,780
    D. $5,400

91. A property was recently sold for $170,000, and the monthly payment on the $160,000 fully amortizing mortgage loan at 6% APR for a 20-year term is $1,146. What would be the outstanding loan balance due after the first monthly payment?

    A. $159,654
    B. $158,854
    C. $159,200
    D. $169,654

APPENDIX A Exam Preparation Tips and Strategies and Practice National and State Examinations

92. In making a mortgage loan of $190,000, a lending institution charged sufficient discount points to increase the yield on the loan from 8% to 8 1/8%. The cost of the points was:

   A. $190
   B. $237.50
   C. $1,900
   D. $3,800

93. A triangular tract of land is 8,000 feet deep and has highway frontage of 250 yards. If Ajax Realty Company listed this property at 9% commission and sold it for $15,000 per acre, what was Ajax's commission? (Round sales price and commission to the nearest whole dollar amount.)

   A. $18,596
   B. $3,099
   C. $9,298
   D. $27,893

94. If the closing date is November 10 and the seller has paid the real property taxes of $2,880 for the current tax year, which of the following is the correct closing statement entry for taxes?

   A. seller's debit $2,480; buyer's credit
   B. seller's credit $400; buyer's debit
   C. buyer's credit $400; seller's debit
   D. buyer's debit $2,480; seller's credit

95. Kevin is planning to purchase flooring for his large meeting room. He has been told it will require 88.6 square yards of flooring. The room is 20 feet wide. Without taking into account any walls or other waste how long is this room (rounded)?

   A. 30
   B. 44
   C. 13
   D. 40

96. Cameron has purchased a house and obtained a mortgage loan of $235,000 at 6.5% interest for a term of 30 years. Her monthly P&I payment is $1,485. If she keeps the loan until it is fully amortized what will be the total amount of interest that she will pay over the life of this loan?

   A. $534,600
   B. $458,250
   C. 299,730
   D. $235,000

97. Edward is the property manager of an eight-unit apartment building. The units rent for $600 per month each. Last month one of the units was vacant the entire month and another unit was vacant for 10 days. If Edward is paid a 10% management fee, how much did he earn last month?

   A. $400
   B. $380
   C. $360
   D. $460

98. Ed recently sold his house for $150,000, which is 25% more than he originally paid. How much did he originally pay for the home?

   A. $112,500
   B. $120,000
   C. $150,000
   D. $187,500

99. Dan has contracted to purchase a home for $269,000 with closing set for September 9. He has paid $2,500 in earnest money deposit and $500 as a due diligence fee at the time of his original offer. He has located a lender who agrees to make him a mortgage of $200,000 at an interest rate of 4.5% with one point for loan origination fee and 1% discount point. Dan will be responsible for the payment of interim interest for September. Property taxes for the year are $3,600 have not yet been paid. The taxes are being required to be paid off by the lender at the closing. In addition, the following items will be paid at the closing by the party who would traditionally pay for them: attorney fees $1,200, title insurance $538, survey $450, deed preparation $80, recording fees $35, and revenue stamps using state rate. Dan has paid $450 for the appraisal and $65 for the credit report during the time of loan application. How much money in certified funds will Dan need to bring to the closing? (Round answer to nearest whole dollar amount.)

   A. $75,763
   B. $75,263
   C. $74,713
   D. $73,883

100. Ella has recently contracted to sell her home for $179,000 and has agreed to pay the broker a sales commission of 5%. The outstanding loan balance as of the March 17 date of closing is $103,650. Property taxes are estimated to be $1,080 and are to be prorated. The seller has agreed to pay $80 for deed preparation in addition to revenue stamps. At the time of the offer, the buyer paid a $1,500 earnest money deposit and a $300 due diligence fee. In addition, the seller has also agreed to pay $250 as a carpet cleaning fee. How much will Ella "net" at the closing?

  A. $65,897
  B. $65,643
  C. $65,481
  D. $65,181

SAMPLE STATE SECTION PRACTICE EXAM

This section consists of 40 questions that are specific to North Carolina. For a more detailed listing of the subject areas that comprise this section, refer to the North Carolina Real Estate Commission booklet Real Estate Licensing in North Carolina. *Answers are provided in the Answer Key following the appendix.*

1. Which of the following does NOT require a real estate license in NC?

  A. auctioning of real property
  B. a firm selling its own property through the actions of its own employees
  C. offering to buy property for another as an agent
  D. offering to list property for another as an agent

2. An unlicensed salaried assistant of a real estate broker is soliciting listings for her broker. Is this legal?

  A. This is legal as long as the broker does the actual listing presentation and contracting.
  B. This is legal as long as the assistant is not paid any portion of the commission.
  C. It is not legal for the unlicensed assistant to solicit listings for her broker.
  D. This is not legal unless the assistant and the broker have permission from the broker-in-charge.

3. Betty Broker owns three real estate offices in town. Which of the following is correct?

  A. She can be the broker-in-charge of all three offices.
  B. She can designate a provisional broker to manage one of the offices under her supervision.
  C. She can be broker-in-charge of two or more offices if they are within 5 miles of each other.
  D. Each office must have its own broker-in charge.

4. A broker-in-charge may represent both the buyer and seller in the purchase and sale of a property if:

   A. he acts in a designated agency capacity.
   B. both parties agree in writing.
   C. the broker tells each party that he will be working in this capacity.
   D. This is never allowed under North Carolina Real Estate Commission Rules and Regulations.

5. The North Carolina Real Estate Commission has the authority to:

   A. regulate commissions or fees charged by licensees.
   B. discipline a REALTOR® for breach of the code of ethics.
   C. fine a licensee for violation of license law.
   D. fine a developer whose agent violates the North Carolina Time Share Act.

6. Who may legally work at two different real estate firms for compensation in NC?

   A. a provisional broker if he or she first has written consent of both firms in advance
   B. a non-provisional broker can work at as many firms as he or she so desires assuming the firms are willing to compensate him.
   C. a non-provisional broker may work at two separate firms is he or she has written consent of each firm
   D. a provisional or non-provisional status broker is not allowed to work at more than one firm at a time

7. A licensee must notify the North Carolina Real Estate Commission:

   A. within 10 days of a change of his residence address.
   B. of all criminal convictions by the time of license renewal.
   C. of a change of name within 30 days.
   D. of all disciplinary actions taken by any governmental licensing authority within 60 days of the charges being filed.

8. Which of the following is correct in regards to the practice of designated agency?

   A. No material facts can be learned by either party prior to the agent being named as a designated agent. If either agent has learned any material facts about the other party prior to becoming a designated agent they will be prohibited from becoming designated.
   B. A listing agent can practice designated agency with both his or her seller and buyer clients as long as both have consented in writing.
   C. Any personal information learned before becoming a designated agent can be kept confidential if both parties agree in advance.
   D. A broker-in-charge can practice designated agency with a provisional broker that is associated with another branch office of the firm.

9. Larry Agent has reviewed the *Working with Real Estate Agents* brochure with his buyer. The buyer verbally agrees to have Larry show him some houses as a buyer agent. Larry has located a house listed with his firm that the buyer wants to purchase. At the same time the offer to purchase was prepared, Larry and his buyer also entered into a written buyer agency agreement allowing for both dual and designated agency. Which of the following is true?

   A. All agency documentation must have been in writing at the time of first substantial contact.

   B. Larry must have had his Dual Agency Agreement in writing before showing the house.

   C. Larry should have entered into a verbal Dual Agency Agreement before showing the listing to the buyer.

   D. Larry has complied with all required agency disclosure and documentation requirements.

10. Barney Buyer is visiting an open house held by Sellsmor Homes Realty. He tours the house but decides this is not really the house for him. Which of the following statements is correct regarding this situation?

    A. First substantial contact never occurred and no further agency disclosure was required.

    B. First substantial contact occurred as soon as Barney entered the house and he should have been given the *Working with Real Estate Agents* brochure at the time.

    C. The agent was required to have Barney sign a written Buyer Agency Agreement before allowing him to tour the home.

    D. The agent was required to at least have an oral Buyer Agency Agreement with Barney before allowing him to tour the home.

11. After discussion with the buyer, including the preparation of the *Working with Real Estate Agents* brochure, the broker has agreed to serve in the capacity of a buyer agent. The agent must have the buyer sign a written Buyer Agency Agreement by what specific point in time?

    A. at the point when the buyer agreed to have the broker serve as a buyer agent

    B. at the point of first substantial contact

    C. at the time the broker will present an offer on the buyer's behalf

    D. at the point an offer made by the buyer becomes a contract

12. A buyer makes an offer to the seller that includes a $2,500 earnest money deposit (EMD) and a check for $1,000 due diligence fee. The buyer's agent emails the offer to the listing agent who later calls the buyer agent to tell him the seller has signed the offer. The buyer agent discusses with the listing agent how he will drop the EMD and due diligence fees by the listing firm some time tomorrow. That night, when the buyer agent calls the buyer to share the news that the seller has signed his acceptance, the buyer informs his broker that he has changed his mind and no longer wishes to purchase the house. He demands the return of his EMD check and due diligence fee. The seller agrees to the return of the EMD but refuses to agree to the return of the due diligence fee. What should the buyer agent do with the due diligence fee?

    A. give it to the listing agent to forward to his seller since it legally belongs to the seller
    B. put it in his trust account until both parties sign a release or await court order
    C. return it to the buyer
    D. forward it to the local clerk of court office within 90 days

13. How many days does a provisional broker licensee have to deposit earnest deposits into the trust account?

    A. no later than three banking days from receipt
    B. no later than three banking days from acceptance
    C. the same day received
    D. none

14. Which of the following is NOT true in order to place trust monies in an interest-bearing account?

    A. the broker must have written permission from both the buyer and seller
    B. the written permission must stipulate who is to receive all or a portion of the interest
    C. the trust account must be located in a bank that is physically located in NC
    D. permission must be "highlighted" differently than other parts of a pre-printed contract form.

15. A buyer makes a written offer to purchase a property and includes a $2,500 earnest money deposit. The seller makes a counteroffer for more money. The buyer verbally accepts. The listing agent deposits the money in the trust account at this point in time. When the buyer receives the seller's counteroffer, he refuses to sign even though he had verbally agreed earlier. The seller is angry and tells the buyer that he will not return the earnest deposit since the buyer has reneged on his word. In fact, the seller demands that the listing agent give him the deposit. What must the real estate agent do regarding the earnest money in this situation?

    A. He must give it back to the buyer because the contract was not accepted in writing.
    B. He must retain the deposit in the trust account until he obtains written permission from the buyer and seller or await a court order.
    C. He must give it to the seller since the seller is his principal.
    D. He must return the EMD to the buyer if it is still before 5 p.m. of the due diligence date.

16. A listing broker advised a prospective buyer that the property the buyer was considering was scheduled for annexation into the city limits. This disclosure constituted which of the following?

    A. violation of fiduciary relationship owed to the seller by broker
    B. impermissible disclosure of a material fact
    C. required disclosure of a material fact to the buyer
    D. violation of disclosure of seller's personal information by broker

17. Bob owns a building lot in Holly Springs that he and his wife purchased when they both attended graduate school in Raleigh. Although they paid only $10,000 for the lot many years ago, it has a current tax value of $18,000. Bob and his wife now realize they will not be moving back to NC so they decide to sell. They contact Arnold, who is a real estate broker, to list the property. Arnold tells Bob that he has a builder friend who might be interested in purchasing the lot quickly. Two days later Arnold emails Bob a copy of the listing contract for $20,000 and once it is signed he immediately emails a contract to purchase from the builder friend for full asking price. Bob and his wife sign the contract and the property is closed. Three months later Bob learns from an old college friend, who still lives in the area, that these lots are very much in demand and that they are selling for close to $40,000. After some research by Bob he learns that his friend is correct. As a result of this finding:

    A. Arnold has not likely violated any rules since Bob could list his property for whatever price he wanted and he seemed happy with the list price at the time.

B. Arnold has likely violated his agency duties by not performing an appraisal in order to determine the market value of the lot.

C. Arnold has likely violated his duties to Bob by not performing a CMA in order to determine the probable selling price of the lot.

D. Arnold has not likely violated any rules since Bob has an obligation to do his research before signing an agreement to sell.

18. While a broker was inspecting a property for listing, the property owner told the broker the house contained 2,400 square feet of heated living area. Relying on this information, the broker listed the property and represented it to prospective buyers as containing 2,400 square feet. After purchasing the property, the buyer accurately determined that there were only 1,850 square feet and sued for damages for the difference in value between 2,400 square feet and 1,850 square feet. Which of the following is correct?

    A. The broker is not liable because he relied on the seller's positive statement as to the square footage.
    B. The seller is not liable because the broker, not the seller, represented the property to the buyer as containing 2,400 square feet.
    C. Neither the broker nor the seller is liable since it is the buyer's responsibility to check the square footage.
    D. Both the broker and the seller are liable.

19. A broker deposited a buyer's check for $6,000 earnest money in her escrow account. Prior to the closing and at the seller's written request, the broker paid $1,200 from the escrow account for repairs for damage caused by termites in the house. This expense was necessary so the seller could provide the required repairs the buyer had requested resulting from his home inspection. Which of the following statements about this transaction is correct?

    A. Since the $1,200 disbursement from the broker's escrow account was made at the seller's request and benefited both buyer and seller, the broker acted properly.
    B. The broker's action constituted an act of commingling and was improper.
    C. The broker properly disbursed the funds since he did not need permission from either buyer or seller to disburse funds for this purpose.
    D. The broker acted improperly since both the buyer's and seller's consent is needed to disburse any escrow funds before the transaction is closed.

20. The right to occupy a property for five or more periods of time involving five or more years is considered:

    A. a periodic lease.
    B. an interest in personal property.
    C. a time-share.
    D. adverse possession.

21. Funds paid to a time-share developer:

    A. belong to the seller immediately upon transfer of the money.
    B. belong to the buyer for 10 days from date of contract.
    C. must be immediately placed with an independent escrow agent to hold in a trust account.
    D. must be returned to the buyer if a time-share instrument has not been recorded in 90 days.

22. A provisional broker licensee on active status has just taken continuing education classes for the first time. These classes were taken before the deadline for completion. He took the BICUP course and one elective. What will be his license status as of July 1?

    A. active
    B. inactive
    C. expired
    D. canceled

23. A broker licensee on provisional status has just been hired by a local lender to assist them in the preparation of a CMA/BPO. The lender is asking for this assistance in order to help them understand how much the property might be sold for so they can better set the limits for the equity line of credit the borrower is requesting to be set up. Which of the following best summarizes this situation?

    A. as long as the provisional broker has local real estate knowledge and access to MLS there should be no problem with this assignment
    B. a provisional broker is not allowed to undertake this assignment but a non-provisional broker would be fine with taking this project
    C. a provisional broker is not allowed to complete the CMA that is being requested
    D. the lender can pay the fee for this CMA directly to the provisional broker

24. A broker licensee may be disciplined by the NC Real Estate Commission for which of the following actions?

    A. utilizing an offer to purchase and contract form, provided by the buyer, that does not contain all the items listed in Commission rule .0112
    B. in response to a question asked by the buyer the broker discloses there had been a murder in the home after the seller had clearly marked "no representation" on the Residential Property Owner And Disclosure Statement
    C. the broker refuses to answer a buyer's question regarding if someone previously residing in the home had been tested and found to be HIV positive
    D. drafting a financing contingency addendum at the buyer's request

25. Downtown Realty has recently listed a property on January 15, 2017, that closed on March 1, 2017. Unfortunately a complaint was filed with the NC Real Estate Commission regarding alleged improper activities in this transaction. After an investigation and hearing, the Commission made their ruling on October 30, 2019, by announcing Downtown Realty was not guilty of any impropriety in this case. What would be the minimum date that Downtown Realty must keep all trust account files associated with this case?

    A. March 1, 2017
    B. January 15, 2020
    C. March 1, 2020
    D. October 30, 2022

26. In North Carolina, unpaid property taxes lawfully constitute a lien against the property as of what date?

    A. January 1 of the current tax year
    B. September 1 of the current tax year
    C. July 1, the start of the new fiscal year
    D. January 1 of the following year

27. According to the NCAR/NCBA Offer to Purchase and Contract form, the final date for the buyer to undertake due diligence in the purchase of a home is best represented by which of the following?

    A. the due diligence date, if the buyer wishes to obtain a refund of his due diligence fee and his earnest money deposit
    B. the closing date, but the buyer will not be entitled to a refund of his due diligence fee or his earnest money deposit
    C. loan commitment date, and there will be no refund of the due diligence fee, but there is a refund for the earnest money deposit
    D. due diligence is NOT allowed to be undertaken after the due diligence date

28. Which of the following is NOT an acceptable means of paying the (Additional) Earnest Money Deposit in section 1d of the NCAR/NCBA Offer to Purchase and Contract form?

    A. cash
    B. personal check
    C. official bank check
    D. wire transfer

29. According to the North Carolina Good Funds Settlement Act, monies cannot be disbursed until after:

   A. the closing statements have been signed by the buyer.
   B. the purchaser has first been given a three-day right of rescission.
   C. the deed has been recorded.
   D. the attorney has completed the settlement meeting.

30. Which of the following is true regarding closing statements in North Carolina?

   A. The broker is not responsible for its accuracy as long as it is prepared by an attorney.
   B. The broker must deliver an accurate closing statement to the buyer and seller at the closing.
   C. The Closing Disclosure form is not required to be used as long as the parties use a form that is considered "substantially equivalent" on all federally related mortgages.
   D. The broker does not have to personally prepare the closing statement.

31. The maximum tenant security deposit that can lawfully be collected on a North Carolina residential lease that is for a nine-month fixed term but mandates the rent is to be paid monthly would be:

   A. 1 month.
   B. 1 ½ months.
   C. 2 months.
   D. no limit.

32. According to the Statute of Frauds, which of the following leases must be in writing in order to be enforceable?

   A. all residential leases for less than a one-year term
   B. all residential leases for more than a one-year term
   C. all residential leases in North Carolina
   D. a lease for more than three years

33. The area occupied by the stairway, in a two-story house, is calculated as a part of:

   A. the first floor.
   B. the floor from which it descends.
   C. both the first and second floor.
   D. neither floor.

34. Protective covenants would not typically be allowed to restrict which of the following?

    A. architectural style
    B. building materials used in construction
    C. the number of family members who can occupy the property at one time
    D. minimum size of the building

35. Which of the following statements are NOT true in regards to the North Carolina subdivision streets disclosure law?

    A. The developer must declare whether the streets will be publicly or privately maintained prior to selling the lot.
    B. Agents must disclose to buyers whether new subdivision streets will be publicly or privately maintained prior to selling the lot.
    C. If the street has been dedicated for public use, and construction is approved by the North Carolina Department of Transportation, the street will automatically be publicly maintained.
    D. Buyers of new lots must sign a disclosure form indicating if the street is private and explaining that the street will not be constructed to the minimum standards of a publicly maintained street.

36. The lowest concrete part of a house is the:

    A. slab.
    B. footing.
    C. pier.
    D. sill.

37. The vertical masonry structures placed inside the foundation wall in order to support the subflooring are:

    A. sills.
    B. headers.
    C. piers.
    D. joists.

38. Which of the following are tax-deductible expenses resulting from home ownership?

    A. property taxes and insurance
    B. maintenance and repairs
    C. mortgage interest and property taxes
    D. depreciation and replacement costs

39. Which of the following is true regarding the $500,000 exemption, in the sale of a personal residence, for a married couple filing jointly?

    A. A married couple can use the $500,000 joint exemption ONLY if both meet the ownership and occupancy requirement.
    B. A married couple can use the $500,000 joint exemption if only one meets the ownership requirement, but BOTH meet the occupancy requirement.
    C. A married couple can use the $500,000 joint exemption only once in a lifetime.
    D. A married couple cannot qualify to use the $500,000 joint exemption if EITHER of them has ever used the $250,000 exemption for a single taxpayer.

40. A homeowner in NC had constructed a three-bedroom house with two full baths in a rural area that necessitated the installation of an on-site septic system. It was properly permitted at that time. A few years later the homeowner constructed a fourth bedroom, but no extra bathroom, in the basement area. He did not obtain any permits at that time as he was constructing the addition by himself. He now wants to list the property for sale with a broker. What would be the maximum intended occupancy for this house according to NC guidelines?

    A. In a rural area there are typically no guidelines for maximum occupancy.
    B. 4
    C. 6
    D. 8

PROBLEM TOPICS ON STATE SECTION OF LICENSE EXAMINATION

Problem Topics on State Section of License Examination

The following information is collected from a report published by the North Carolina Real Estate Commission in February 2016, the last such date a report is available. Please note that there have been several modifications to the state section of the examination since that time so only those items appearing from that report that are still a part of the current exam format effective April 1, 2019, are included in this report.

Note: "Comments" refers to the Comments section of Appendix C.

1. **NC Real Estate License Law and Commission Rules** (25 Questions)

   A. **Requirement for Real Estate License**

   Miscellaneous activities requiring a license and exempt activities. Licensees need to know (1) that a real estate license is required to sell time-shares and (2) the statutory exemptions from the license requirement. Particular attention should be given to permitted activities of unlicensed assistants.

   B. **License Categories and Status**

   Active/Inactive Status. Licensees must pay their license renewal fee to retain their license even on inactive status. *See Rule 58A .0504.*

   Firm License. Only entities, other than a sole proprietorship, need a firm license. *See G.S. 93A-1 and Rule 58A .0502(a).*

   C. **North Carolina Real Estate Commission** (No problem topics)

   D. **License Administrative/Maintenance Requirements**

   Postlicensing education requirement. Candidates need to know: What courses have to be taken? When must they be taken? What are the consequences of not taking the courses within the prescribed time frames? Note that there is no restriction on how quickly postlicensing courses may be completed and no prescribed sequence for completing the courses. *See Rule 58A .1902.*

   License expiration and CE requirement. Know the difference between an expired license versus an inactive license. *See Rules 58A .0503 and 58A .1702.*

   E. **Agency Relationships, Contracts, Disclosures and Practices**

   Dual Agency or not? Know when a dual agency situation exists and when it does NOT exist when working with more than one party and/or firm. *See Rule 58A .0104(j-n)*

   Oral Buyer Agency. Know when oral buyer agency must be reduced to writing. *See Rule 58A .0104(a).*

   Broker's responsibility to provide seller client with relevant information. Part of the listing agent's duties is to perform a comparable market analysis and assist the seller client in determining the appropriate listing price and sales price to net the needed seller proceeds.

   Working with Real Estate Agents **brochure.** Confusion exists about its delivery and ability to create agency relationships. *See Rule 58A .0104(c).*

   F. **Selected Regulatory Practices**

   Advertising. Be able to apply the advertising rule about authority to advertise and the use of blind ads to fact situations. *See Comments and Rule 58A .0105.*

   Confidentiality of Offers. Brokers cannot disclose any material terms of an offer without the permission of the offerror. *See Rule 58A.0115.*

Disclosure of Bonus to Licensee. Know the disclosure requirements to his/her principal (the buyer) of any possible incentive for selling agents with regard to a property being shown to the buyer client.

G. **Prohibited Practices**

Provisional Broker Compensation. Know that a provisional broker can only be paid directly from his/her supervising broker. *See G.S. 93A-6(a)(6).*

H. **Time-Shares** (No problem topics)

2. **Other North Carolina Laws and Practices** (15 Questions)

    A. **Property Taxation**

- **Ad Valorem taxes.** Understand how NC ad valorem taxes are computed. *See chapter 3 in text.*

    B. **Sales Contracts and Practices**

- **Preprinted sales contract forms.** Know that a licensee can offer any preprinted sales contract form for consumer use that meets the criteria enumerated in *Rule 58A .0112.*
- **Standard Offer to Purchase and Contract (OPC) Form (2).** Students need to know the standard provisions of this most commonly used form. *See form in Chapter 10 of this text.*

    C. **Closing Procedures** (No problem topics)

    D. **Laws Governing Residential Tenancies**

- **Tenant's Recourse in the Event of a Landlord Breach.** Understand the concept of constructive eviction. Remember that a tenant can never legally withhold rent while in possession of the rental unit.

    E. **Residential Square Footage Guidelines**

- **Agent's Responsibility for Square Footage.** The primary responsibility for verification of square footage falls on the listing agent. Buyer agents should generally be able to rely on the listing agent's information.

    F. **Miscellaneous Laws and Legal Concepts.** (No problem topics)

3. **General Real Estate Topics**

    A. **Basic Home Construction**

- **Terminology.** Be able to differentiate between "footing," "foundation wall," and "pier." *See Chapter 19 in this text.*

    B. **Federal Income Taxation of Home Ownership/Sale**

- **Terminology.** Students need to know the definition of "basis."

APPENDIX B

REAL ESTATE MATH

When solving real estate math problems, it may be helpful to remember and use these hints:

1. *Memorize* the formulas.
2. Write them down before solving the problem.
3. Write out *all* important information as you are solving the problem.
4. Draw a diagram, if applicable.
5. Remember that the size of an acre is 43,560 square feet.
6. Check your answers for logic.

SECTION 1 BASIC REAL ESTATE MATH

FINANCE CALCULATIONS

Principal and Simple Interest

Chapter 11, Real Estate Financing, covers the important calculations of principal and interest and the related financial arithmetic. For review, the following is reproduced from Figure 11.2 in Chapter 11 to summarize the calculations discussed.

Example: Assume a home purchase price of $87,500 with a conventional mortgage of 80% of the sales price at a rate of 8.5% for 30 years.

1. Amount of the loan = $87,500 × 80% = $70,000.
2. Figure 11.1 is given in a factor per $1,000; therefore, divide $70,000 by 1,000 = 70 (the number of units of $1,000).
3. Go to the 8.5% row, read across to the 30-year column, and read the figure of $7.69. This is the payment per month per $1,000 of the loan.
4. Multiply 70 × $7.69 = $538.30. This is the monthly payment of principal and interest to amortize (kill, pay off) a loan of $70,000 at 8.5% for 30 years.

Debt Service and the Reduction in the Balance of a Loan

Calculate how much of a payment goes to interest and what the balance will be on a loan after one payment is made.

Solution: Interest (I) is equal to principal (P) times interest rate (R) times the time period (T = 1 for annual interest; 1/12 for monthly interest)

or I = P × R × T

or loan balance annual interest × 1/12 = monthly interest

$$\frac{\text{loan balance} \times \text{annual interest}}{12} = \text{monthly interest}$$

If a loan balance was $70,000 at 8.5% interest for 30 years, using the chart in Figure 11.1, you retrieve the 8.5%, 30-year factor of $7.69.

Multiplying: 70 × $7.69 = $538.30 P&I

The interest portion is:

$$\frac{\$70,000 \times 8.5\%}{12} = \$495.83$$

Subtracting: $538.30 P&I
−495.83 I
$42.47 P

That is, of the total payment of $538.30, only $42.47 goes to reducing the principal in the first month.

Therefore: $70,000.00 Original principal
− 42.47 Principal reduction
$69,957.53 New balance

To figure the new balance at the end of the second month, apply the same formulas as used above. This time, use $69,957.53 as the loan balance.

The interest portion is:

$$\frac{\$69,957.53 \times 8.5\%}{12} = \$495.83$$

Subtracting: $538.30 P&I
−495.53 I (for second month)
$42.77 P

That is, of the total payment of $538.30, $42.77 is applied to the principal in the second month. Note that this is slightly more than the amount applied to the principal in the first month.

Therefore, subtracting

$69,957.53 Principal at end of first month
−42.77 Principal reduction in second month
$69,914.76 New balance at end of second month

Additionally, consider the following financial calculations.

Example: Calculate the interest paid over the life of a loan.

Solution: Take the monthly payment (P&I) times the number of months in the loan (years times 12). This will equal the total amount of payments (total P&I). Subtract the principal of the loan (P); the remainder is the amount that went to interest (I).

Example: A $70,000 loan at 8.5% for 30 years

From the amortization chart, find the factor $7.69 (per $1,000).
P&I = 70 × $7.69 = $538.30
Number of payments is 30 years × 12 = 360.
Total of payments is $538.30 × 360 = $193,788.
Subtract the principal (P) of $70,000.
Total interest paid over life of loan is $123,788.

Loan Origination and Discount Points

Calculate the service charges to originate a loan.

Solution: Assume there will be two parts to the charges:

1. Origination fee, 1%
2. Discount points, *each of which will also cost 1% of the loan*

Example: The costs to originate a $70,000 loan with 2.5 discount points would be:

1. Origination fee: 1% × $70,000 = $ 700
2. Discount points: 2.5% × $70,000 = $1,750
   Total Costs $2,450

Discount Points, Yields

Calculate (1) the cost of discount points and (2) the effect (yield) of points.

Solution: 1. Each point costs (somebody) 1% of the amount borrowed. Therefore, multiply the number of points times 1% times the loan amount.

Example: Sales price of $87,500 with an 80% loan and 2 1/2 discount points equals
Loan amount = $87,500 × 80% = $70,000
Discount points = $70,000 × 2.5 × .01 = $1,750

Solution: 2. The effect or yield of discount points is calculated by the rule of thumb that each point raises the effective yield to the lender by 1/8%.

Example: An 8% loan with 3 points is a yield of 8% + 3/8% = 8 3/8%. Also, the cost to raise the yield of a $50,000 loan from 8% to 8 1/2% would be:

8% to 8 1/2% is 1/2%, or 4/8%, or 4 points (4%)

Thus, $50,000 times 4% = $2,000.

CLOSING STATEMENT PRORATIONS AND CALCULATIONS

Proration of Real Estate Taxes

The information regarding the preparation of the closing statement, including prorations, is contained within Chapter 12, Closing the Real Estate Transaction. Students should be prepared to complete a closing narrative by using the North Carolina Closing Worksheet as well as basic prorations and basic calculations seeking to determine how much cash that a buyer will need in order to close as well as to determine how much cash the seller will take home from the closing. Although the closing narrative will not typically require proration of interest on an assumed mortgage, there is one practice example included in order to address the possibility of a question on the National portion of the exam. For additional comments, please refer to the appendix section detailing preparation for the State portion of the examination.

MISCELLANEOUS CALCULATIONS

Brokerage Commissions

Problems involving commissions are readily solved by a simple formula illustrated as follows:

$$\frac{I}{R \times V} \quad \frac{\text{Income}}{\text{Rate} \times \text{Value}}$$

In this formula, I represents income, R represents rate, and V represents value. In these problems, one of the three elements is the unknown quantity that will be the answer to the problem. The other two elements are provided. When using the formula, simply cover the letter representing the unknown quantity and perform the calculation indicated. For example, if the unknown quantity or answer sought is income, covering the I in the formula reveals that rate is to be multiplied by value (R × V). The result of this multiplication will be the income. If the known quantities are income and rate and the unknown quantity is value, covering the V results in an indicated calculation of dividing rate into income. The result of this division will be the value.

To clarify the formula and its application in solving for any one of three possible unknowns, the following material is presented to demonstrate its use. The formula can also be written to solve for different unknowns, as follows:

$$\text{Rate} = \frac{\text{Income}}{\text{Value}}$$

$$\text{Value} = \frac{\text{Income}}{\text{Rate}}$$

Or, as discussed, the formula can be written and applied as follows: The horizontal line separating income from R × V indicates that in solving for rate, value is to be divided into income. When value is the unknown, rate is to be divided into income. The multiplication sign between R and V shows that rate is to be multiplied by value to solve for income when income is the unknown quantity. Simply cover the unknown item, and perform the indicated calculations.

Commission Problems

1. A real estate broker sold a property for $80,000. Her rate of commission was 6%. What was the amount of commission in dollars?

    Solution: Commission value = $80,000, rate = 0.06, income is unknown
    $80,000 × 0.06 = $4,800

    Answer: $4,800 commission

2. A real estate broker earned a commission of $3,000 in the sale of a residential property. His rate of commission was 6%. What was the selling price of the property?

    Solution: Income = $3,000, rate = 0.06, value is unknown

    $$\frac{\$3{,}000}{0.06} = \$50{,}000$$

    Answer: $50,000 sales price

3. A real estate broker earned a commission of $1,500 in the sale of a property for $25,000. What was her rate of commission?

    Solution: Value = $25,000, income = $1,500, rate is unknown

    $$\frac{\$1{,}500}{\$25{,}000} = 0.06$$

    Answer: 6% commission rate

4. A real estate agent sells a property for $70,000. The commission on this sale to the real estate firm with whom the agent is associated is 6%. The selling agent receives 60% of the commission paid to the real estate firm. What is the firm's share of the commission in dollars?

Solution: Value = $70,000, rate = 0.06, income is unknown

$70,000 × 0.06 = $4,200

100% − 60% = 40% (firm's percentage of commission)

$4,200 × 0.40 = $1,680

Answer: $1,680 firm's share of the commission

5. A broker's commission was 10% of the first $50,000 of the sales price of a property and 8% on the amount of sales price over $50,000. The broker received a total commission of $7,000. What was the total selling price of the property?

Solution:

Step 1: Rate = 0.10, value = $50,000, income is unknown $50,000 × 0.10 = $5,000 commission on first $50,000 of sales price

Step 2: Total commission minus commission on first $50,000 = commission on amount over $50,000

$7,000 − $5,000 = $2,000 commission on selling price over $50,000

Step 3: $2,000 = income, 0.08 = rate, value is unknown

$$\frac{\text{Income}}{\text{Rate}} = \text{value}$$

$$\frac{\$2,000}{0.08} = \$25,000$$

Step 4: $50,000 + $25,000 = $75,000

Answer: $75,000 total selling price

6. A seller advises a broker that he expects to net $50,000 from the sale of his property after the broker's commission of 6% is deducted from the proceeds of the sale. For what price must the property be sold to provide a $50,000 net return to the seller after paying the broker a 6% commission on the total sales price?

Solution: 100% = Gross sales price

100% − 6% = 94%

94% = Net to owner

$50,000 = 94% × sales price

Solving for the sales price

$$\frac{\$50,000}{94\%} = \text{Minimum sales price} = \$53,191.49$$

Answer: $53,191.49 gross selling price

Interest Problems

Interest problems also use the income, rate, value formula. The amount of interest is the income, the percentage return on the money owed or invested is the rate, and the amount of money invested or borrowed is the value.

1. On October 1, a mortgagor made a $300 payment on her mortgage, which is at the rate of 10%. Of the $300 total payment for principal and interest, the mortgagee allocated $200 to the payment of interest. What is the principal balance due on the mortgage on the date of payment?

    Solution: $200 × 12 months = $2,400 annual interest income

    $$\frac{\text{Income}}{\text{Rate}} = \text{Value}$$

    $$\frac{\$2,400}{10\%} = \$24,000$$

    Answer: $24,000 mortgage balance due

2. If an outstanding mortgage balance is $16,363.64 on the payment due date and the amount of the payment applied to interest is $150, what is the annual rate of interest charged on the loan?

    Solution: $150 × 12 months = $1,800 annual interest

    $$\frac{\text{Income}}{\text{Value}} = \text{Rate}$$

    $$\frac{\$1,800.00}{\$16,363.64} = 0.11 \text{ or } 11\%$$

    Answer: 11% interest rate

3. If $27,000 is invested at 8.25%, what will be the annual income resulting from the investment?

    Solution: Rate is 8.25%, value is $27,000, and income is unknown

    Value × Rate = Income

    $27,000 × 8.25% = $2,227.50

    Answer: $2,227.50 annual income

4. A mortgage loan of $50,000 at 11% interest requires monthly payments of principal and interest in the amount of $516.10 to fully amortize the loan for a term of 20 years. If the loan is paid over the 20-year term, how much interest does the borrower pay?

Solution: 20 years × 12 months per year = 240 payments

240 × $516.10 = $123,864 total amount paid (P & I)

Total amount paid − Principal borrowed = Interest paid

$123,864 − $50,000 = $73,864

Answer: $73,864 interest paid

Net Sales Price

A seller wants to net a certain amount after paying expenses on the sale of his property.

Solution:

Step 1: When the expenses are a fixed amount, such as painting or repairs, the first step is to add these to the desired after-expense amount.

Step 2: When paying a percentage commission, such as 6% of the sales price, perform the following step:

100% − 6% = 94%

That is, the net price desired is 94% of the sales price needed. Therefore, if the seller wants to net $50,000 after paying $800 for repairs and a 7% commission:

$50,000 + $800 = $50,800 the net amount needed

100% − 7% = 93%

Therefore, $50,800 = 93% of the sales price needed.

Solving for the sales price:

$$\frac{\$50,800}{93\%} = \$54,624 \text{ minimum sales price}$$

Equity Problems/Percent Change Problems

Calculate the percent change in an item, such as the percent increase in equity on a home.

Solution: Determine the dollar change or quantity change in the item in question. Then divide the *amount of change* by the *original value* of the item. Multiply your answer by 100 to convert it to a percentage.

1. A home was purchased for $38,000 with a $30,000 loan. Ten years later, the home had a fair market value of $62,000 and the loan balance was amortized to $25,000. Calculate the percent change in equity.

Solution: The dollar change in equity is calculated by subtracting all liens from the current fair market value.

The original purchase price minus the original loan balance gives the original equity ($38,000 − $30,000 = $8,000).

The current fair market value minus the current lien balance gives the current equity ($62,000 − $25,000 = $37,000).

The current equity minus the original equity produces the *dollar change* in equity ($37,000 − $8,000 = $29,000).

To calculate the *percent change in equity,* divide the *dollar change in equity* by the *original equity* and multiply by 100 ($29,000 ÷ $8,000 × 100 = 362.50%).

2. A buyer purchased a home for $50,000 with an 80% loan. A few years later, the home was worth $60,000 and the loan was paid down to $35,000. What was the percent change in equity?

Solution: Step 1: Calculate the original equity.

$50,000 value × 80% loan = $40,000

$50,000 value $40,000 loan = $10,000 equity

Step 2: Calculate the new equity.

$60,000 − $35,000 = $25,000 equity

Step 3: Calculate the change in equity.

$25,000 − $10,000 = $15,000 change in equity

Step 4: Divide the amount of change by the original equity

$$\frac{\$15,000}{\$10,000} = 150$$

Step 5: Multiply 1.5 by 100% to change 1.50 to 150%.

Answer: 150% increase in equity

Area Problems

Problems involving the determination of the size of an area in square feet, cubic feet, number of acres, and so on, are frequent in the real estate brokerage business. When taking a listing, the broker should determine the number of square feet of heated area in the house. In establishing the lot size, the number of square feet should be determined so it can be translated into acreage, if desired. For measures and formulas to use in solving area problems, see Table B.1.

Determining the Surface Area of a Rectangle or Square

The surface area of a rectangle or square is determined by multiplying the width by the length. In a square, the width and length are the same. In terms of a simple formula,

AREA = LENGTH × WIDTH

or

A = L × W (for a rectangle)

or

A = S × S (for a square)

TABLE B.1 Measures and formulas

LINEAR MEASURE

12 inches = 1 ft

39.37 inches = 1 meter (metric system)

3 ft = 1 yd

16½ ft = 1 rod, 1 perch, or 1 pole

66 ft = 1 chain

5,280 ft = 1 mile

SQUARE MEASURE

144 sq inches = 1 sq ft

9 sq ft = 1 sq yd

30= sq yd = 1 sq rod

160 sq rods = 1 acre

2.47 acres = 1 hectare or 10,000 square meters (metric system)

43,560 sq ft = 1 acre

640 acres = 1 sq mile

1 sq mile = 1 section

36 sections = 1 township

CIRCULAR MEASURE

360 degrees = circle

60 minutes = 1 degree

60 seconds = 1 minute

TAX VALUATION

Per $100 of Assessed Value: Divide the AV by 100; then multiply by tax rate.

$$\frac{\text{assessed value}}{100} \times \text{tax rate}$$

Per Mill: Divide the AV by 1,000; then multiply by tax rate.

e

FORMULAS

1 side × 1 side = area of a square

width × length = area of a rectangle

½ base × height = area of a triangle

½ height ×(base$_1$ + base$_2$) = area of a trapezoid

½ × sum of the bases = distance between the other two sides at the midpoint of the height of a trapezoid

length × width × depth = volume (cubic measure) of a cube or a rectangular solid

1. A rectangular lot measures 90 feet by 185 feet. How many square feet does this lot contain?

   Solution: $A = L \times W$
   $= 90 \times 185$
   $= 16{,}650$ square feet (SF or sq. ft.)

   Answer: 16,650 SF

2. An acre of land has a width of 330 feet. If this acre of land were rectangular in shape, what would be its length?

   Solution: Since $A = L \times W$, you can transpose this formula to solve for the length by applying the arithmetic operation of dividing both sides of the equation by WIDTH, or:

   $$\frac{A}{W} = L$$

   A number to learn at this time is that there are *43,560 square feet per acre.* Therefore, since you know the area in square feet and the width, you can solve for length.

   $43{,}560 = 330 \times L$

   or $\dfrac{43{,}560}{330} = 132$

   Answer: The lot is 132 feet deep.

3. If a parcel of land contained 32,670 square feet, what percentage of an acre would it be?

   Solution: $\dfrac{32{,}670}{43{,}560} = 0.75$

   $0.75 = 75\%$

   Answer: 75%

4. A room measures 15 feet by 21 feet. You want to install wall-to-wall carpet and need to calculate the exact amount of carpet required.

   Solution: Since carpet is sold by the square yard, you need to convert square feet to square yards.

   The number of square feet per square yard is $3 \times 3 = 9$ sq. ft. per square yard. Therefore, to convert size in square feet to size in square yards, you need to divide by 9.

   Area = $15 \times 21 = 315$ sq. ft.

   Answer: $\dfrac{315}{9} = 35$ square yards of carpet

APPENDIX B Real Estate Math   677

5. A property owner's lot is 80 feet wide and 120 feet deep (long). The lot is rectangular. The property owner plans to have a fence constructed along both sides and across the rear boundary of the lot. The fence is to be 5 feet high. The property owner has determined that the labor cost in constructing the fence will be $1.25 per linear foot. The material cost will be $3.00 per square yard. What is the total cost of constructing the fence?

   Solution: Step 1: Determine the linear footage to establish the labor cost.

   2×120 feet $+ 80$ feet $= 320$ linear feet

   320 feet $\times \$1.25$ per linear foot $= \$400$ labor cost

   Step 2: Establish the number of square yards in the fence to determine material cost.

   5 feet $\times 320$ feet $= 1{,}600$ square feet

   $1{,}600$ sq. ft. $\div 9$(9 sq. ft. in 1 sq. yd.) $= 177.78$ square yards

   177.78 square yards $\times \$3$/square yard $= \$533.34$ material cost

   $\$533.34 + \$400 = \$933.34$ total cost

   Answer: $933.34 total cost

6. The property owner in the above problem wants a fence post placed every 10 linear feet for the total length of the fence. How many fence posts are required?

   Solution: $\dfrac{320 \text{ linear feet}}{10} = 32$

   $32 + 1 = 33$

   Answer: 33 posts

7. The property owner in the preceding two problems decides to enclose the property with a fence across the front of the property. How many fence posts will be required to enclose the entire property if the fence post interval is maintained at 10 feet?

   Solution: $(2 \times 80 \text{ feet}) + (2 \times 120 \text{ feet}) = 400$ feet

   $\dfrac{400}{10} = 40$

   Answer: Total fence posts required for 400 linear feet is 40.

8. If a rectangular map measures 10 inches × 16 inches and 1 square inch of map surface represents an area of 20 square miles, how many square miles is represented by the map in total?

   Solution: 10 inches × 16 inches = 160 square inches

   160 × 20 sq. mi. = 3,200 sq. mi.

   Answer: 3,200 square miles

9. A triangular lot measures 200 feet along the street and 500 feet in depth (length) on the side that is perpendicular to the front lot line. If the lot sold for 10 cents per square foot, what is the selling price?

   Solution: Try to visualize a triangle as half a rectangle. Instead of measuring a triangle in length and width, label the dimensions as base and height. Therefore, you can visualize the formula for a triangle as half of the product of height times base, or:

   $$A = \frac{h \times b}{2} =$$

   $$\frac{500 \times 200}{2} = 50,000 \text{ square feet}$$

   50,000 square feet × $0.10 = $5,000

   Answer: $5,000 sales price

10. A new 20′ × 25′ garage and a 20′ × 90′ driveway is to be installed. Both the garage floor and the driveway will be paved with concrete at a cost of $0.35 per square foot. What will be the minimum cost to pave the new garage and driveway?

    Solution: Step 1: Area = length × width
    Area of Garage 20 × 25
    = 500
    Area of Driveway 20 × 90
    =1,800
    Total Area: 500 + 1,800
    = 2,300 square feet
    Step 2: Cost = 2,300 × $0.35
    Cost = $805

    Answer: $805 cost

11. What percentage of the lot is occupied by the house shown in the diagram?

    Solution: Step 1: Divide lot into one triangle and one rectangle.
    Area of triangle = 1/2 base × height
    A = 1/2 × 250 feet × 150 feet
    A = 18,750 square feet
    Area of rectangle = length × width
    A = 400 feet × 150 feet
    A = 60,000 square feet
    Total lot area = 18,750 sq. ft. + 60,000 sq. ft.
    Lot area = 78,750 square feet

Step 2: Divide house into two rectangles.

Area of small rectangle = L × W

A = 30 feet × 30 feet

A = 900 square feet

Area of large rectangle = L × W

A = 150 feet × 30 feet

A = 4,500 square feet

Total house area = 900 sq. ft. + 4,500 sq. ft.

A = 5,400 square feet

Step 3: Percentage of lot occupied by house = house footage ÷ lot footage

$$\frac{5,400}{78,750} \times 0.0686$$

0.0686 = 6.86%

Answer: 6.86% of lot occupied by house

12. How many square feet are in the following lot?

    Solution: Divide the figure into common shapes you can work with, such as a rectangle and two triangles. By drawing two parallel lines, you carve the figure into a rectangle that measures 80 × 240 feet and two triangles that have a height of 240 feet. You can figure the base of each by subtracting the 80 feet of the rectangle from the total of 160 feet, which is a total of 80 feet for the two triangles, or 40 feet each.

    Step 1: Area of the rectangle is:

    A = 80 × 240 = 19,200 square feet

    Step 2: Calculate the area of each triangle.

    A = ½ base × height

    $$A = \frac{40 \times 240}{2} = 4,800$$

    Since there are two triangles: 2 × 4,800 = 9,600 square feet.

    Answer: Total area is, therefore,

    19,200 sq. ft. + 9,600 sq. ft. = 28,800 square feet.

    Note: This figure is a trapezoid, and its area can also be determined by using the formula for a trapezoid:

    Area of trapezoid = 1/2 height × (base$_1$ + base$_2$)

    A = 120 (160 + 80)

    A = 28,800

13. A house measures 28 feet wide by 52 feet long and sells for $64,000. What is its price per square foot?

    Solution: Step 1: Calculate the area.

    A = 28 × 52 = 1,456 square feet

    Step 2: Divide the price by the area.

    Answer: $\dfrac{\$64,000}{1,456} = \$43.96 \text{ per square foot}$

    Caution: Since there is always a possibility of getting mixed up and dividing the wrong way, always check your answer before looking at the answer choices.

    For example: $43.96 per square foot × 1,456 = $64,000

    If you were to look at the answer choices before doing this check, you might find your answer even though it is *wrong*; the test often includes all likely wrong answers as distracter items.

14. A rectangular lot that measures 250 feet by 350 feet sells for $10,000. What is the price per square foot?

    Solution: Step 1: A = 250 × 350 = 87,500 square feet

    Step 2: Divide the price by the size

    $\dfrac{\$10,000}{87,500} = \$0.114$

    Caution: As discussed in the problem above, check your answer before looking at the answer sheet. It is easy to come up with an answer of $8.75, which is, of course, wrong, but is guaranteed to be a choice in the answers.

15. The perimeter of a rectangular lot (see below) is 1,800 yards. The length is twice the width plus 6 yards. What is the length in feet?

    Solution: Perimeter of a rectangle = (2 × width) + (2 × length)

    Length = 2W + 6 yards

    Width = W

    Therefore:

    6 × width + 12 yards = perimeter (1,800 yards)

    6 × width = 1,800 − 12

    6W = 1,788 yards

    $W = \dfrac{1,788}{6}$

    W = 298 yards

$2 \times 298 + 6 =$ length
$596 + 6 = 602$ yards
$602 \times 3 = 1{,}806$ (length in feet)

Answer: 1,806 feet

16. A house with the area shown originally cost $15 per square foot to build. If it were built today, it would cost $56,000. How much has the cost per square foot increased (in dollars)?

    Solution: Divide the house into 3 triangles and 1 square.
    Area of a triangle = 1/2 bh
    $A = 1/2 (40 \times 20)$
    $A = 400$ sq. ft.
    $3 \times 400 = 1200$ sq. ft.
    Area of a square = 1 side × 1 side
    $A = 20 \times 20$
    $A = 400$
    Total area = 1,200 + 400
    Total area = 1,600 square feet
    $56{,}000 \div 1{,}600 = \$35$ cost per square foot today
    $\$35 - \$15 = \$20$ per square foot cost increase

    Answer: $20 per square foot

Property Management Fee Calculations

Go over the following examples. Apply the information given in the first problem to all of the problems.

1. John of AAA Realty manages Gail's property for an 8% monthly fee. In August, Unit A and Unit B were occupied. Each unit rents for $570 per month. The rent for both units has been paid in full and on time. How much of the rent does Gail actually receive?

    a. Gross rent collected is the sum of the total rents:

    $$\begin{array}{r}\$570 \\ +570 \\ \hline \$1{,}140\end{array}$$

    b. The property management fee is the gross rent collected times the monthly fee:
    $$\$1{,}140 \times 8\% = \$91.20$$

    c. Gail's check equals the gross rent minus the fee:
    $$\begin{array}{r}\$1{,}140.00 \\ -91.20 \\ \hline \$1{,}048.80\end{array}$$

2. In September, Unit A was rented for the entire month, but Unit B was rented for only 14 days. How much does Gail receive this month?

   a. Prorate the amount collected for Unit B:

   $$\frac{\$570}{30 \text{ (days in month)}} \times 14 \text{ (occupied days)} = \$266$$

   b. Gross rent collected:

   $$\begin{array}{r} \$570 \\ +266 \\ \hline \$836 \end{array}$$

   c. Gross rent times monthly fee:

   $$\$836 \times 8\% = \$66.88$$

   d. Gail's check equals the gross rent minus the fee:

   $$\begin{array}{r} \$836.00 \\ -66.88 \\ \hline \$769.12 \end{array}$$

3. In October, Gail's units were both rented. However, the plumbing in Unit A needed repair at a cost of $86, and Unit B was sprayed for insects at the normal rate of $25. These bills were deducted from the individual proceeds received from each unit. How much did she receive from Unit A? From Unit B? How much did she receive altogether?

   a. Determine the separate management fees for each unit:

Unit A	Unit B
$570 × 8% = $45.60	$570 × 8% = $45.60

   b. Determine the individual proceeds before the bills: $570.00 $570.00

$570.00	$570.00
−45.60	−45.60
$524.40	$524.40

   c. Subtract the individual expenses from each unit: $524.40 $524.40

$524.40	$524.40
−86.00	−25.00
$438.40 from Unit A	$499.40 from Unit B

   d. Add proceeds from Unit A and Unit B to find the total:

   $$\begin{array}{r} \$438.40 \\ +499.40 \\ \hline \$937.80 \end{array}$$

Real Estate Taxation Problems

You need to understand certain terms to solve problems involving real property taxes. *Assessed value* (AV) is the value established by a tax assessor. The tax value or assessed value is usually a percentage of the estimated market value (MV) of the property and can be as much as 100% of market value. The amount of tax is calculated by multiplying the assessed value by the tax rate, which is expressed in dollars per $100 of assessed value in North Carolina.

1. If the market value of a property is $80,000 and the assessed value is 100% of the market value, what is the annual tax if the rate is $1.50 per $100 of tax value?

    Solution: The assessed value is 100% of the market value, or $80,000 MV 100% = $80,000 AV.

    The tax rate is applied per $100 of the assessed value; therefore, divide the AV by 100 and multiply by the tax rate to calculate the annual taxes, or

    Answer: $\dfrac{\$80,00}{100} \times \$1.50 = \$1,200$

2. A property is sold at the market value. The annual real property tax is $588.80 at a tax rate of $1.15 per $100 of tax value. Assessed value is 80% of market value. What is the selling price?

    Solution: Applying the $\dfrac{I}{R \times V}$ formula $V = \dfrac{I}{R}$

    we know the tax income = I = $588.80;

    the rate = R = $1.15 ÷ 100, which is 1.15% or .0115; and V = assessed value.

    Substituting these known items into the formula:

    $V = \dfrac{\$588.80}{.0115} = \$51,200$

    Since the assessed value is 80% of the market value:

    $51,200 = 80\% \times MV$

    Solving for MV:

    $MV = \dfrac{51,200}{80\%} = \$64,000$

    Market value = Selling price = $64,000

    Answer: $64,000 selling price

3. If the assessed value of a property is $68,000, the annual tax paid is $850, and the tax value is 100% of the assessed value, what is the tax rate?

   Solution: $\dfrac{\$68,00}{100} = \$680$

   $\dfrac{\$8,50}{\$680} = \$1.25$

   Answer: Tax rate is $1.25 per $100 of tax value.

4. The real property tax revenue required by a town is $140,800. The assessed valuation of the taxable property is $12,800,000. The tax value is 100% of the assessed value. What must the tax rate be per $100 of assessed valuation to generate the necessary revenue?

   Solution: $\dfrac{\text{Income}}{\text{Value}} = \text{Rate}$

   $\dfrac{\$140,800}{\$12,800,000} = \$0.011 \text{ (rate per \$1.00)}$

   $\$0.011 \times 100 = \$1.10 \text{ per } \$100$

   Answer: Tax rate is $1.10 per $100 of assessed value.

SECTION 2 PRACTICE WORKING IN REAL ESTATE MATH

This section is a "work-along" practice section that summarizes real estate math. The only way to assure yourself that you have mastered this area is to put the pencil to the paper, first verifying the examples presented and then doing the problems on your own. When you complete this section, you can be confident of successfully completing the math problems on the state exam and can look forward to treating these questions as easy bonus points toward your passing score.

Answers to the practice problems are provided in the Answer Key section at the back of the book.

BROKERAGE COMMISSIONS

These problems can be seen as an application of the income, rate, value rule where

$$I = R \times V$$

That is, you solve for the missing element (in this case, the commission income) by multiplying rate times value.

APPENDIX B Real Estate Math

1. On sales

   a. For example, $72,500 sale at 6% commission equals

   $72,500 × 6% = $4,350

You try one:

   b. A $45,900 sale at 3% commission equals

Answer:

2. On rentals

   a. For example, gross rent of $250 per unit with a total of 4 units at 10% commission equals

   4 × $250 × 10% = $100

You try one:

   b. A duplex rents for $295 per unit at 15% property management fee. What will the property management fee be?

Answer:

   c. On gross effective rentals, subtract for vacancy factor. For example, income of $2,500 per month, 7% vacancy, 10% commission =

   $2,500 − 7% ($2,500) × 10% = $232.50 commission

You try one:

   d. $4,300 full rent, 10% vacancy, 7% commission. What will the property management fee be?

Answer:

3. Commission splits

   a. For example, a sale of $72,500 with total commission of 6%, with 25% of the commission going to the listing agent. How much commission will the company receive? How much commission will the listing agent receive?

   $72,500 × 6% = $4,350

   $4,350 × 25% = $1,087.50

You try one:

   b. $54,000 sale with 7% commission to office, 15% of office income to agent. How much commission does the agent receive?

Answer:

NET TO SELLER (NET LISTING)

1. If a seller wants to net $50,000 after paying a 6% commission, what is the minimum sales price she must receive? This is a percentage relationship.

    100% minus 6% = 94%

    Therefore, the $50,000 the seller wants to net is 94% of the sales price.

    $50,000 = 94% Sales price

    Solving for the sales price:

    $$\text{Sales price} = \frac{\$50,000}{94\%} = \$53,191$$

    You try some:

    a. A seller wants to net $65,000 after paying a 7% commission. What must the minimum sales price be?

    Answer:

    b. What would the minimum sales price need to be if the seller wanted to net $75,000 after paying a 5% commission and $800 for repairs?

    Note: Add repairs to net price before dividing by 95%.

    Answer:

PROFIT/LOSS/EQUITY (INCLUDING PERCENT CHANGE)

Rule: Compare the amount of change in a factor to the beginning value of that factor.

1. For example, if you buy a property for $38,000 and sell it for $62,000, your amount of profit would be:

    $62,000
    −38,000
    ─────
    $24,000

    $$\text{The percent profit} = \frac{\text{Amount of profit}}{\text{Original value}} = \frac{\$24,000}{\$38,000} \times 100\% = .6316 \text{ or } 63.16\%$$

    You try one:

2. You buy a property for $72,000 and sell it for $69,000. What is the loss and percentage of loss?

    Answer:

3. Equity and percentage change in equity problems

   Rules:
   - Equity is the difference between value and obligations.
   - Compare the amount of the change (not the total new equity) to the starting amount.

     a. For example, if the value of the property is $50,000 and the outstanding loan is $40,000, the equity is $10,000. Applying the percent change rule, if the value later is $60,000 and the loan is paid down to $30,000, the new equity is $30,000. The percentage change in equity is the amount of the change in equity (that is, $30,000 [new] minus $10,000 [old] = $20,000) compared to the original, or:

     $$\frac{\text{Amount of change}}{\text{Original}} = \frac{\$30,000 - \$10,000}{\$10,000} = \frac{\$20,000}{\$10,000} = 2$$

     Note: Multiply 2 by 100% to change to a percentage: 2 × 100% = 200%

     You try one:

     b. A property with an original value of $38,000 with an 80% loan now has a value of $72,000, and the loan is paid down to $26,000. What is the percentage change in equity?

     Answer:

Area Calculations

1. Convert acres to square feet and vice versa.

   a. For example, a lot measures 250 feet by 350 feet. How many square feet is it, and what portion of an acre is it?

   250 × 350 = 87,500 square feet

   Rule: There are 43,560 square feet per acre. Divide this number into the total square feet to find the number of acres.

   $$\frac{87,500}{43,560} = 2.009 \text{ acres}$$

   You try one:

   b. A lot measures 165 feet by 175 feet. How many acres is this?

   Answer:

2. Formulas for calculating the area of various-shaped lots.

   a. Squares: Multiply the two sides.
   A = S × S

b. Rectangles: Multiply the length by the width.
A = L × W

c. Triangles: Visualize a triangle as half a rectangle.
$$A = \frac{Base \times Height}{2}$$

d. Parallelograms: Ignore the width. You need to multiply the height by the base.
A = Height × Base

e. Trapezoids: Multiply 1/2 the height by the sum of the bases.
A = 1=2 height × (base$_1$ + base$_2$)

Examples

f. A square 20 feet each side
= 20 × 20 = 400 square feet

g. A rectangle 200 feet wide and 300 feet long
= 200 × 300 = 60,000 square feet

h. A triangle with a base of 30 feet and a height of 20 feet
$$\frac{20 \times 30}{2} = 300 \, square \, feet$$

i. A parallelogram with a height of 50, a side of 60, and a base of 75
= 50 × 75 = 3,750 (Ignore the side!)

j. A trapezoid with one base 40, the other 80, and a height of 70
$$\frac{70}{2} \times (40 + 80) = 4,200$$

You try some:

k. A square 75 feet on the side =

l. A rectangle 37 feet by 64 feet =

m. A triangle with a 50-foot base and a 75-foot height =

n. A parallelogram with a 180-foot height, a 200-foot side, and a 350-foot base =

o. A trapezoidal lot with 275 feet on the front, 500 feet on the back, and 360 feet deep =

3. Cost/price per square foot, acre, or front foot
Rules:

- Divide price by size (think $ ÷ sq. ft.).
- Check your work by reversing your calculations; that is, the Check/Step.

a. A home with 1,600 square feet sells for $72,000. What is the price per square foot?

$$\frac{Price}{size} = \frac{\$72,000}{1,600 \text{ square feet}} = \$45$$

You try some:

b. A 1,400-square foot home sells for $38,500. What is the price per square foot?

Answer:

c. A half-acre of land sells for $22,500. What is the cost per square foot?

Answer:

d. A lot with 360 front feet sells for $92,000. What is the cost per front foot?

Answer:

Don't forget the Check/Step in each example!

AD VALOREM TAXES (GIVEN THE RATE AND THE ASSESSED VALUE)

Rule: Divide the assessed value (AV) by 100 and multiply by the tax rate.

1. If the assessed value is $62,500 and the tax rate is $0.75 per $100 of AV, what are the taxes per year?

$$\frac{\$62,500}{100} \times \$0.75 = \$468.75$$

To calculate a monthly payment to tax escrow, simply divide the annual tax bill by 12.

You try one:

2. The AV is $69,000 and the rate is $1.25. What is the monthly payment to escrow?

Answer:

EXCISE TAX

Rule: The rate is $1.00 per $500 or any fraction thereof of total purchase price. The loan amount or any assumed value does not affect excise tax.

1. A home sells for $96,000 cash. How much in excise tax must the seller pay?
$96,000

$$\frac{\$96,000}{500} = \$912$$

You try some:

2. What is the excise tax on a $45,900 sale?
   Answer:

3. What is the excise tax on a sale of $135,600 with the assumption of a $55,000 existing loan?
   Answer:

4. What is the excise tax on a sale of $125,000 with a 90% new first mortgage?
   Answer:

FINANCIAL CALCULATIONS

1. Simple interest
   Rule: I = P × R × T
   Interest = Principal × Rate × Time

   a. What is the interest for the month on a loan balance of $45,000 at 8.25% annual interest?

   $$\frac{\$45,000 \times 8.25\%}{12} = \$309.38 \left(\text{a month is } 1/2 \text{ of a year}\right)$$

   You try one:

   b. What is the monthly interest on a loan of $28,700 at 9% interest?
   Answer:

2. Total interest paid over the life of a loan
   Rule: Calculate the total of the payments ($ per month 12 months per year number of years) minus the amount borrowed.
   Note: This is not the I = P × R × T rule, which will, of course, be one of the wrong answer choices.

   a. If the monthly payment of P&I is $230.97 at 9% interest for 30 years on a loan of $28,700, what is the total interest paid over the life of the loan?
   $230.97 × 12 × 30 = $83,149.20 total paid
   $83,149.20 paid − $28,700 borrowed = $54,449.20

   You try one:

   b. What is the interest paid on a loan of $55,000 with payments of $625 per month for 25 years?
   Answer:

3. Use of an amortization chart
   Rule: Divide the amount of the loan by $1,000, find the appropriate row and column in the chart (on page 249) (per thousands), and multiply the two numbers to find the monthly P&I.

a. A loan of $45,000 at 9% for 15 years

$$=\frac{\$45,000}{\$1,000}=45$$

45 × (factor from chart) =
45 × $10.15 = $456.75

You try one:

b. What is the payment for a $134,900 loan at 8.75% for 30 years?
Answer:

c. What is the total interest paid on the above loan?
Answer:

4. Debt service/mortgage reduction

Rule: Use the I = P × R × T rule to calculate the monthly interest, and subtract this from the P&I. Subtract this principal amount from the previous balance.

a. What is the balance on a loan of $28,700 at 9% after the first payment of $231? I = P × R × T

$$\frac{\$28,700 \times 9\%}{12} = \$215.25$$

$231.00 P & I
−215.25 I
─────────
$15.75 P

$28,700 − $15.75 = $28,684.25

You try one:

b. What is the balance after one payment on a loan of $56,000 at 13.5% with payments of $642?
Answer:

5. Origination fees and discount points

Rule: Each point costs 1% times the loan amount

a. What would be the cost of points on a $96,000 loan with 2.5 points?
= $96,000 × 2.5% = $2,400

You try one:

b. A sale of $117,500 with a 90% loan will cost how much for 4.5 points?
Answer:

6. Yield on a loan

   Rule: Each point is assumed to raise the effective yield to the lender of 1/8 of a percent.

   a. What is the effective yield to the lender of a 10% loan if he charges 6 points?
      6 points × 1/8 each = 6/8 = ¾
      10 + 3/4 = 10.75

   You try one:

   b. What is the yield on a 9.75% loan with 4 points?

   Answer:

   c. What is the cost of points to raise the yield of a given loan to a certain effective rate? To raise a $50,000 loan from 9% to 9 3/8% would be 3 points times the loan amount = $50,000 × 3% = $1,500.

   You try one:

   d. What is the cost of points to raise a $65,000 loan at 10.50% to 11%?

   Answer:

PRORATIONS AT CLOSING

1. Calculate the entry on a closing statement for real estate tax.

   Solution: For example, closing is on March 17 and real estate tax is $1,332 per year, unpaid.

   Step 1: Figure the days used.
   Jan.–Feb. = 2 × 30 = 60
   Plus 17 days of March +17
   77 days used

   Step 2: Figure the daily rate.
   $$\frac{1,332}{360} = \$3.70$$

   Step 3: Figure the dollars used.
   $3.70 day × 77 days × $284.90 used

   Step 4: This entry will show as a $284.90 debit to the sellers since they owe this much for the tax year but have not paid. As a check on this figure, you could figure the buyer's portion of the year independently and ensure that the buyer's and seller's portions add up to the whole tax.

2. Prorate an insurance policy paid for by the seller and assumed by the buyer.

   Solution: For example, closing is on April 27 and insurance of $500 per year was paid by the seller on October 1 of the previous year.

   Step 1: Figure the used portion of the policy.

   Oct.– Mar. = 6 months × 30 days = 180 days

   plus the 27 days of April   +27

   207 days

   Step 2: Figure the daily rate.

   $$\frac{\$500}{360} = \$1.3888 \text{ per day}$$

   Step 3: Figure the dollar amount used.

   207 days × $1.3888 per day = $287.50 used

   Step 4: Now do NOT snatch defeat from the jaws of victory by searching the answer sheet for this number until you take a moment to THINK about what you are doing.

the seller paid	$500.00
but only used	287.50
therefore, is due a refund (credit)	$212.50

PREPARATION OF CLOSING STATEMENTS

Sample "Net Owed by Buyer" Closing Statement*

A buyer made a $5,000 earnest money deposit and contracted to purchase a house for $105,000. The buyer will be obtaining a $70,000 new first mortgage loan and paying the lender a 1-point loan origination fee. The buyer also will be giving the seller a $20,000 second purchase money mortgage. The balance of the purchase price will be paid in cash at closing. Real estate taxes for the current year are estimated to be $1,440 and are unpaid. Additional closing expenses that must be paid by the buyer total $375. What is the net amount owed by the buyer at closing on April 15?

Solution: Step 1: Calculate loan origination fee:

1% (1 point) × $70,000 = $700

Step 2: Prorate real estate taxes:

$$\frac{\$1400}{360} = \$4$$

$4 × 105 days (Jan. 1 – Apr. 15) = $420 (seller's share)

---

*Sample problems provided by the North Carolina Real Estate Commission, Education Department. Reproduced by permission.

Step 3: Make credit/debit adjustments to the purchase price:

Purchase price	$105,000
Deduct earnest money	− 5,000
Deduct first mortgage	− 70,000
Deduct second mortgage	− 20,000
Deduct seller's share of RE taxes	− 420
Add loan origination fee	+ 700
Add additional closing expenses	+ 375
Amount owed (cash needed) by buyer	$ 10,655

Sample "Net to Seller" Closing Statement*

A seller has contracted to sell his house for $95,000 and has agreed to pay a 7% brokerage fee to the listing broker. The buyer is obtaining a $75,000 new first mortgage loan. As of the day of closing, the outstanding principal balance on the seller's existing mortgage loan is $56,925 and accrued interest due for November is $545. Real estate taxes for the current year are $960 and have been paid by the seller. The seller must pay $90 in miscellaneous closing costs as well as the cost of excise tax at the cost of $1.00 per $500 or fraction thereof. How much will the seller net at closing on November 30?

Solution: Step 1: Calculate the brokerage fee:

$$7\% \times \$95,000 = \$6,650$$

Step 2: Prorate the real estate (RE) taxes:

$$\frac{\$960}{12} = \$80 \text{ (buyer's share)}$$

Step 3: Calculate excise tax:

$$\frac{\$95,000}{500} = 190$$

$$190 \times \$1.00 = \$190$$

Step 4: Make credit/debit adjustments to sales price:

Sales price	$ 95,000
Add buyer's share of RE taxes	+ 80
Deduct principal balance of seller's mortgage	− 56,925
Deduct accrued interest on seller's mortgage	− 545
Deduct brokerage fee	− 6,650
Deduct miscellaneous closing costs	− 90
Deduct cost of excise tax	− 190
Net due to seller	$ 30,680

---

*Sample problems provided by the North Carolina Real Estate Commission, Education Department. Reproduced by permission.

You try some:

Practice Problem Number 1.   The closing date is March 3 for the sale of a $45,700 home. There is a $2,000 earnest money deposit, the real estate taxes are $300 per year and are not paid yet, and the personal property tax of $150 is also unpaid. The buyer is paying $225 for a new insurance policy, has miscellaneous expenses of $900, and will be obtaining a new mortgage for 95% of the sales price. The seller will pay excise tax (as discussed earlier in this chapter) as well as a real estate commission of 5%. Calculate the balance owed by the buyer and the balance due to the seller.

Practice Problem Number 2.   The sale of a $60,000 home is closed July 17. The earnest money deposit is $5,000. The real property taxes of $575 and personal property taxes of $400 are unpaid. The seller's existing mortgage is $35,000, and he will pay excise tax and a 6% broker's fee. The buyer is paying $400 for a new insurance policy, is paying $1,400 in miscellaneous expenses, and is obtaining a loan for 90% of the sales price. Calculate the balance owed by the buyer and the balance due to the seller.

SUMMARY

The practice problems in this chapter correspond directly to the calculations required on the state exam. Be sure to practice each problem so you have no surprises in the math section and can use it to boost your overall exam score, rather than burden it.

APPENDIX C

NORTH CAROLINA REAL ESTATE LICENSE LAW, NORTH CAROLINA REAL ESTATE COMMISSION RULES, AND LICENSE LAW AND RULE COMMENTS

Chapter 93A.

Real Estate License Law.

Article 1.

Real Estate Brokers and Salespersons.

§ 93A-1. License required of real estate brokers.

From and after July 1, 1957, it shall be unlawful for any person, partnership, corporation, limited liability company, association, or other business entity in this State to act as a real estate broker, or directly or indirectly to engage or assume to engage in the business of real estate broker or to advertise or hold himself or herself or themselves out as engaging in or conducting such business without first obtaining a license issued by the North Carolina Real Estate Commission (hereinafter referred to as the Commission), under the provisions of this Chapter. A license shall be obtained from the Commission even if the person, partnership, corporation, limited liability company, association, or business entity is licensed in another state and is affiliated or otherwise associated with a licensed real estate broker in this State. (1957, c. 744, s. 1; 1969, c. 191, s. 1; 1983, c. 81, ss. 1, 2; 1995, c. 351, s. 19; 1999-229, s. 1; 2005-395, s. 1.)

§ 93A-2. Definitions and exceptions.

(a) A real estate broker within the meaning of this Chapter is any person, partnership, corporation, limited liability company, association, or other business entity who for a compensation or valuable consideration or promise thereof lists or offers to list, sells or offers to sell, buys or offers to buy, auctions or offers to auction (specifically not including a mere crier of sales), or negotiates the purchase or sale or exchange of real estate, or who leases or offers to lease, or who sells or offers to sell leases of whatever character, or rents or offers to rent any real estate or the improvement thereon, for others.

(a1) The term broker-in-charge within the meaning of this Chapter means a real estate broker who has been designated as the broker having responsibility for the supervision of brokers on provisional status engaged in real estate brokerage at a particular real estate office and for other administrative and supervisory duties as the Commission shall prescribe by rule.

(a2) The term provisional broker within the meaning of this Chapter means a real estate broker who, pending acquisition and documentation to the Commission of the education or experience prescribed by either G.S. 93A-4(a1) or G.S. 93A-4.3, must be supervised by a broker-in-charge when performing any act for which a real estate license is required.

(b) The term real estate salesperson within the meaning of this Chapter shall mean and include any person who was formerly licensed by the Commission as a real estate salesperson before April 1, 2006.

(c) The provisions of G.S. 93A-1 and G.S. 93A-2 do not apply to and do not include:

    (1) Any partnership, corporation, limited liability company, association, or other business entity that, as owner or lessor, shall perform any of the acts aforesaid with reference to property owned or leased by them, where the acts are performed in the regular course of or as incident to the management of that property and the investment therein. The exemption from licensure under this

subsection shall extend to the following persons when those persons are engaged in acts or services for which the corporation, partnership, limited liability company, or other business entity would be exempt hereunder:

    a. The officers and employees whose income is reported on IRS Form W-2 of an exempt corporation.

    b. The general partners and employees whose income is reported on IRS Form W-2 of an exempt partnership.

    c. The managers, member-managers, and employees whose income is reported on IRS Form W-2 of an exempt limited liability company.

    d. The natural person owners of an exempt closely held business entity. For purposes of this subdivision, a closely held business entity is a limited liability company or a corporation, neither having more than two legal owners, at least one of whom is a natural person.

    e. The officers, managers, member-managers, and employees whose income is reported on IRS Form W-2 of a closely held business entity when acting as an agent for an exempt business entity if the closely held business entity is owned by a natural person either (i) owning fifty percent (50%) or more ownership interest in the closely held business entity and the exempt business entity or (ii) owning fifty percent (50%) or more of a closely held business entity that owns a fifty percent (50%) or more ownership interest in the exempt business entity. The closely held business entity acting as an agent under this sub-subdivision must file an annual written notice with the Secretary of State, including its legal name and physical address. The exemption authorized by this sub-subdivision is only effective if, immediately following the completion of the transaction for which the exemption is claimed, the closely held business entity has a net worth that equals or exceeds the value of the transaction.

When a person conducts a real estate transaction pursuant to an exemption under this subdivision, the person shall disclose, in writing, to all parties to the transaction (i) that the person is not licensed as a real estate broker or salesperson under Article 1 of this Chapter, (ii) the specific exemption under this subdivision that applies, and (iii) the legal name and physical address of the owner of the subject property and of the closely held business entity acting under sub-subdivision e. of this subdivision, if applicable. This disclosure may be included on the face of a lease or contract executed in compliance with an exemption under this subdivision.

(2) Any person acting as an attorney-in-fact under a duly executed power of attorney from the owner authorizing the final consummation of performance of any contract for the sale, lease or exchange of real estate.

(3) Acts or services performed by an attorney who is an active member of the North Carolina State Bar if the acts and services constitute the practice of law under Chapter 84 of the General Statutes.

(4) Any person, while acting as a receiver, trustee in bankruptcy, guardian, administrator or executor or any person acting under order of any court.

(5) Any person, while acting as a trustee under a written trust agreement, deed of trust or will, or that person's regular salaried employees. The trust agreement, deed of trust, or will must specifically identify the trustee, the beneficiary, the corpus of trust, and the trustee's authority over the corpus.

(6) Any salaried person employed by a licensed real estate broker, for and on behalf of the owner of any real estate or the improvements thereon, which the licensed broker has contracted to manage for the owner, if the salaried employee's employment is limited to: exhibiting units on the real estate to prospective tenants; providing the prospective tenants with information about the lease of the units; accepting applications for lease of the units; completing and executing preprinted form leases; and accepting security deposits and rental payments for the units only when the deposits and rental payments are made payable to the owner or the broker employed by the owner. The salaried employee shall not negotiate the amount of security deposits or rental payments and shall not negotiate leases or any rental agreements on behalf of the owner or broker. However, in a vacation rental transaction as defined by G.S. 42A-4(6), the employee may offer a prospective tenant a rental price and term from a schedule setting forth prices and terms and the conditions and limitations under which they may be offered. The schedule shall be written and provided by the employee's employing broker with the written authority of the landlord.

(7) Any individual owner who personally leases or sells the owner's own property.

(8) Any housing authority organized in accordance with the provisions of Chapter 157 of the General Statutes and any regular salaried employees of the housing authority when performing acts authorized in this Chapter with regard to the sale or lease of property owned by the housing authority or the subletting of property which the housing authority holds as tenant. This exception shall not apply to any person, partnership, corporation, limited liability company, association, or other business entity that contracts with a housing authority to sell or manage property owned or leased by the housing authority. (1957, c. 744, s. 2; 1967, c. 281, s. 1; 1969, c. 191, s. 2; 1975, c. 108; 1983, c. 81, ss. 4, 5; 1985, c. 535, s. 1; 1995, c. 351, s. 20; 1999-229, ss. 2, 3; 1999-409, s. 1; 2001-487, s. 23(a); 2005-395, ss. 2, 3; 2011-217, s. 1; 2011-235, s. 1; 2015-286, s. 2.1; 2016-98, s. 1.8.)

§ 93A-3. Commission created; compensation; organization.

(a) There is hereby created the North Carolina Real Estate Commission, hereinafter called the Commission. The Commission shall consist of nine members, seven members to be appointed by the Governor, one member to be appointed by the General Assembly upon the recommendation of the President Pro Tempore of the Senate in accordance with G.S. 120-121, and one member to be appointed by the General Assembly upon the recommendation of the Speaker of the House of Representatives in accordance with G.S. 120-121. At least three members of the Commission shall be licensed real estate brokers. At least two members of the Commission shall be persons who are not involved directly or indirectly in the real estate or real estate appraisal business. Members of the Commission shall serve three-year terms, so staggered that the terms of three members expire in one year, the terms of three members expire in the next year, and the terms of three members expire in the third year of each three-year period. The members of the Commission shall elect one of their members to serve as chairman of the Commission for a term of one year. The Governor may remove any member of the Commission for misconduct, incompetency, or willful neglect of duty. The Governor shall have the power to fill all vacancies occurring on the Commission, except vacancies in legislative appointments shall be filled under G.S. 120-122.

(b) The provisions of G.S. 93B-5 notwithstanding, members of the Commission shall receive as compensation for each day spent on work for the Commission a per diem in an amount established by the Commission by rule, and mileage reimbursement for transportation by privately owned automobile at the business standard mileage rate set by the Internal Revenue Service per mile of travel along with actual cost of tolls paid. The total expense of the administration of this Chapter shall not exceed the total income therefrom; and none of the expenses of said Commission or the compensation or expenses of any office thereof or any employee shall ever be paid or payable out of the treasury of the State of North Carolina; and neither the Commission nor any officer or employee thereof shall have any power or authority to make or incur any expense, debt or other financial obligation binding upon the State of North Carolina. After all expenses of operation, the Commission may set aside an expense reserve each year. The Commission may deposit moneys in accounts, certificates of deposit, or time deposits as the Commission may approve, in any federally insured depository institution or any trust institution authorized to do business in this State. Moneys also may be invested in the same classes of securities referenced in G.S. 159-30(c).

(c) The Commission shall have power to make reasonable bylaws, rules and regulations that are not inconsistent with the provisions of this Chapter and the General Statutes; provided, however, the Commission shall not make rules or regulations regulating commissions, salaries, or fees to be charged by licensees under this Chapter.

(c1) The provisions of G.S. 93A-1 and G.S. 93A-2 notwithstanding, the Commission may adopt rules to permit a real estate broker to pay a fee or other valuable consideration to a travel agent for the introduction or procurement of tenants or potential tenants in vacation rentals as defined in G.S. 42A-4. Rules adopted pursuant to this subsection may include a definition of the term "travel agent", may regulate the conduct of permitted transactions, and may limit the amount of the fee or the value of the consideration that may be paid to the travel agent. However, the Commission may not authorize a person or entity not licensed as a broker to negotiate any real estate transaction on behalf of another.

(c2) The Commission shall adopt a seal for its use, which shall bear thereon the words "North Carolina Real Estate Commission." Copies of all records and papers in the office of the Commission duly certified and authenticated by the seal of the Commission shall be received in evidence in all courts and with like effect as the originals.

(d) The Commission may employ an Executive Director and professional and clerical staff as may be necessary to carry out the provisions of this Chapter and to put into effect the rules and regulations that the Commission may promulgate. The Commission shall fix salaries and shall require employees to make good and sufficient surety bond for the faithful performance of their duties. The Commission shall reimburse its employees for travel on official business. Mileage expenses for transportation by privately owned automobile shall be reimbursed at the business standard mileage set by the Internal Revenue Service per mile of travel along with the actual tolls paid. Other travel expenses shall be reimbursed in accordance with G.S. 138-6. The Commission may, when it deems it necessary or convenient, delegate to the Executive Director, legal counsel for the Commission, or other Commission staff, professional or clerical, the Commission's authority and duties under this Chapter, but the Commission may not delegate its authority to make rules or its duty to act as a hearing panel in accordance with the provisions of G.S. 150B-40(b).

(e) The Commission shall be entitled to the services of the Attorney General of North Carolina, in connection with the affairs of the Commission, and may, with the approval of the Attorney General, employ attorneys to represent the Commission or assist it in the enforcement of this Chapter. The Commission may prefer a complaint for violation of this Chapter before any court of competent jurisdiction, and it may take the necessary legal steps through the proper legal offices of the State to enforce the provisions of this Chapter and collect the penalties provided therein.

(f) The Commission is authorized to acquire, hold, convey, rent, encumber, alienate, and otherwise deal with real property in the same manner as a private person or corporation, subject only to the approval of the Governor and Council of State. The rents, proceeds, and other revenues and benefits of the ownership of real property shall inure to the Commission. Collateral pledged by the Commission for any encumbrance of real property shall be limited to the assets, income, and revenues of the Commission. Leases, deeds, and other instruments relating to the Commission's interest in real property shall be valid when executed by the executive director of the Commission. The Commission may create and conduct education and information programs relating to the real estate business for the information, education, guidance and protection of the general public, licensees, and applicants for license. The education and information programs may include preparation, printing and distribution of publications and articles and the conduct of conferences, seminars, and lectures. The Commission may claim the copyright to written materials it creates and may charge fees for publications and programs. (1957, c. 744, s. 3; 1967, c. 281, s. 2; c. 853, s. 1; 1971, c. 86, s. 1; 1979, c. 616, ss. 1, 2; 1983, c. 81, ss. 1, 2, 6-8; 1989, c. 563, s. 1; 1993, c. 419, s. 9; 1999-229, s. 4; 1999-405, s. 2; 1999-431, s. 3.4(a); 2000-140, s. 19(a); 2001-293, ss. 1, 2; 2002-168, s. 3; 2005-374, s. 1; 2005-395, s. 4; 2007-366, s. 1; 2011-217, s. 2; 2017-25, s. 1(j).)

§ 93A-4. Applications for licenses; fees; qualifications; examinations; privilege licenses; renewal or reinstatement of license; power to enforce provisions.

(a) Any person, partnership, corporation, limited liability company, association, or other business entity hereafter desiring to enter into business of and obtain a license as a real estate broker shall make written application for such license to the Commission in the form and manner prescribed by the Commission. Each applicant for a license as a real estate broker shall be at least 18 years of age. Each applicant for a license as a real estate broker shall, within three years preceding the date the application is made, have satisfactorily completed, at a school approved by the Commission, an education program consisting of at least 75 hours of instruction in subjects determined by the Commission, or shall possess real estate education or experience in real estate transactions which the Commission shall find equivalent to the education program. Each applicant for a license as a real estate broker shall be required to pay a fee. The application fee shall be one hundred dollars ($100.00) unless the Commission sets the fee at a higher amount by rule; however, the Commission shall not set a fee that exceeds one hundred twenty dollars ($120.00). The application fee shall not increase by more than five dollars ($5.00) during a 12-month period.

(a1) Each person who is issued a real estate broker license on or after April 1, 2006, shall initially be classified as a provisional broker and shall, within three years following initial licensure, satisfactorily complete, at a school approved by the Commission, a postlicensing education program consisting of 90 hours of instruction in subjects determined by the Commission or shall possess real estate education or experience in real estate transactions which the Commission shall find equivalent to the education program. The Commission may, by rule, establish a schedule for completion of the prescribed postlicensing education that requires provisional brokers to complete portions of the 90-hour postlicensing education program in less than three years, and provisional brokers must comply with this schedule in order to be entitled to actively engage in real estate brokerage. Upon completion of the postlicensing education program, the provisional status of the broker's license shall be terminated. When a provisional broker fails to complete all 90 hours of required postlicensing education within three years following initial licensure, the broker's license shall be placed on inactive status. The broker's license shall not be returned to active status until he or she has satisfied such requirements as the Commission may by rule require. Every license cancelled after April 1, 2009, because the licensee failed to complete postlicensing education shall be reinstated on inactive status until such time as the licensee satisfies the requirements for returning to active status as the Commission may by rule require.

(a2) An approved school shall pay a fee of ten dollars ($10.00) per licensee to the Commission for each licensee completing a postlicensing education course conducted by the school, provided that these fees shall not be charged to a community college, junior college, college, or university located in this State and accredited by the Southern Association of Colleges and Schools.

(b) Except as otherwise provided in this Chapter, any person who submits an application to the Commission in proper manner for a license as real estate broker shall be required to take an examination. The examination may be administered orally, by computer, or by any other method the Commission deems appropriate. The Commission may require the applicant to pay the Commission or a provider contracted by the Commission the actual cost of the examination and its administration. The cost of the examination and its administration shall be in addition to any other fees the applicant is required to pay under subsection (a) of this section. The examination shall determine the applicant's qualifications with due regard to the paramount interests of the public as to the applicant's competency. A person who fails the license examination shall be entitled to know the result and score. A person who passes the exam shall be notified only that the person passed the examination. Whether a person passed or failed the examination shall be a matter of public record; however, the scores for license examinations shall not be considered public records. Nothing in this subsection shall limit the rights granted to any person under G.S. 93B-8.

An applicant for licensure under this Chapter shall satisfy the Commission that he or she possesses the competency, honesty, truthfulness, integrity, good moral character, and general fitness, including mental and emotional fitness, necessary to protect the public interest and promote public confidence in the real estate brokerage business. The Commission may investigate the moral character and fitness, including the mental and emotional fitness, of each applicant for licensure as the applicant's character and fitness may generally relate to the real estate brokerage business, the public interest, and the public's confidence in the real estate brokerage business. The Commission may also require an applicant to provide the Commission with a criminal record report. All applicants shall obtain criminal record reports from one or more reporting services designated by the Commission to provide criminal record reports. Applicants are required to pay the designated reporting service for the cost of these reports. Criminal record reports, credit reports, and reports relating to an applicant's mental and emotional fitness obtained in connection with the application process shall not be considered public records under Chapter 132 of the General Statutes. If the results of any required competency examination and investigation of the applicant's moral character and fitness shall be satisfactory to the Commission, then the Commission shall issue to the applicant a license, authorizing the applicant to act as a real estate broker in the State of North Carolina, upon the payment of any privilege taxes required by law.

Notwithstanding G.S. 150B-38(c), in a contested case commenced upon the request of a party applying for licensure regarding the question of the moral character or fitness of the applicant, if notice has been reasonably attempted, but cannot be given to the applicant personally or by certified mail in accordance with G.S. 150B-38(c), the notice of hearing shall be deemed given to the applicant when a copy of the notice is deposited in an official depository of the United States Postal Service addressed to the applicant at the latest mailing address provided by the applicant to the Commission or by any other means reasonably designed to achieve actual notice to the applicant.

(b1) The Department of Public Safety may provide a criminal record check to the Commission for a person who has applied for a license through the Commission. The Commission shall provide to the Department of Public Safety, along with the request, the fingerprints of the applicant, any additional information required by the Department of Public Safety, and a form signed by the applicant consenting to the check of the criminal record and to the use of the fingerprints and other identifying information required by the State or national repositories. The applicant's fingerprints shall be forwarded to the State Bureau of Investigation for a search of the State's criminal history record file, and the State Bureau of Investigation shall forward a set of the fingerprints to the Federal Bureau of Investigation for a national criminal history check. The Commission shall keep all information pursuant to this subsection privileged, in accordance with applicable State law and federal guidelines, and the information shall be confidential and shall not be a public record under Chapter 132 of the General Statutes.

The Department of Public Safety may charge each applicant a fee for conducting the checks of criminal history records authorized by this subsection.

(b2) Records, papers, and other documentation containing personal information collected or compiled by the Commission in connection with an application for examination, licensure, certification, or renewal or reinstatement, or the subsequent update of information shall not be considered public records within the meaning of Chapter 132 of the General Statutes unless admitted into evidence in a hearing held by the Commission.

(c) All licenses issued by the Commission under the provisions of this Chapter shall expire on the 30th day of June following issuance or on any other date that the Commission may determine and shall become invalid after that date unless reinstated. A license may be renewed 45 days prior to the expiration date by filing an application with and paying to the Executive Director of the Commission the license renewal fee. The license renewal fee shall be forty-five dollars ($45.00) unless the Commission sets the fee at a higher amount by rule; however, the Commission shall not set the license renewal fee at an amount that exceeds sixty dollars ($60.00). The license renewal fee may not increase by more than five dollars ($5.00) during a 12-month period. The Commission may adopt rules establishing a system of license renewal in which the licenses expire annually with varying expiration dates. These rules shall provide for prorating the annual fee to cover the initial renewal period so that no licensee shall be charged an amount greater than the annual fee for any 12-month period. The fee for reinstatement of an expired, revoked, or suspended license shall be an amount equal to two times the license renewal fee at the time the application for reinstatement is submitted. In the event a licensee fails to obtain a reinstatement of such license within six months after the expiration date thereof, the Commission may, in its discretion, consider such person as not having been previously licensed, and thereby subject to the provisions of this Chapter relating to the issuance of an original license, including the examination requirements set forth herein. Duplicate licenses may be issued by the Commission upon payment of a fee of five dollars ($5.00) by the licensee. Commission certification of a licensee's license history shall be made only after the payment of a fee of ten dollars ($10.00).

(d) The Commission is expressly vested with the power and authority to make and enforce any and all reasonable rules and regulations connected with license application, examination, renewal, and reinstatement as shall be deemed necessary to administer and enforce the provisions of this Chapter. The Commission is further authorized to adopt reasonable rules and regulations necessary for the approval of real estate schools, instructors, and textbooks and rules that prescribe specific requirements pertaining to instruction, administration, and content of required education courses and programs.

(e) Nothing contained in this Chapter shall be construed as giving any authority to the Commission nor any licensee of the Commission as authorizing any licensee to engage in the practice of law or to render any legal service as specifically set out in G.S. 84-2.1 or any other legal service not specifically referred to in said section. (1957, c. 744, s. 4; 1967,

c. 281, s. 3; c. 853, s. 2; 1969, c. 191, s. 3; 1973, c. 1390; 1975, c. 112; 1979, c. 614, ss. 2, 3, 6; c. 616, ss. 2-5; 1983, c. 81, ss. 2, 9, 11; c. 384; 1985, c. 535, ss. 2-5; 1995, c. 22, s. 1; 1999-200, s. 1.; 2000-140, s. 19(b); 2002-147, s. 11; 2002-168, s. 4; 2003-361, s. 1; 2005-395, s. 5; 2007-366, s. 2; 2011-217, s. 3; 2013-280, s. 1; 2014-100, s. 17.1(o); 2016-117, s. 4(a).)

§ 93A-4.1. Continuing education.

(a) The Commission shall establish a program of continuing education for real estate brokers. An individual licensed as a real estate broker is required to complete continuing education requirements in an amount not to exceed eight classroom hours of instruction a year during any license renewal period in subjects and at times the Commission deems appropriate. Any licensee who fails to complete continuing education requirements pursuant to this section shall not actively engage in the business of real estate broker.

(a1) The Commission may, as part of the broker continuing education requirements, require real estate brokers-in-charge to complete during each annual license period a special continuing education course consisting of not more than four classroom hours of instruction in subjects prescribed by the Commission.

(b) The Commission shall establish procedures allowing for a deferral of continuing education for brokers while they are not actively engaged in real estate brokerage.

(c) The Commission may adopt rules not inconsistent with this Chapter to give purpose and effect to the continuing education requirement, including rules that govern:

(1) The content and subject matter of continuing education courses.
(2) The curriculum of courses required.
(3) The criteria, standards, and procedures for the approval of courses, course sponsors, and course instructors.
(4) The methods of instruction.
(5) The computation of course credit.
(6) The ability to carry forward course credit from one year to another.
(7) The deferral of continuing education for brokers not engaged in brokerage.
(8) The waiver of or variance from the continuing education requirement for hardship or other reasons.
(9) The procedures for compliance and sanctions for noncompliance.

(d) The Commission may establish a nonrefundable course application fee to be charged to a course sponsor for the review and approval of a proposed continuing education course. The fee shall not exceed one hundred twenty-five dollars ($125.00) per course. The Commission may charge the sponsor of an approved course a nonrefundable fee not to exceed seventy-five dollars ($75.00) for the annual renewal of course approval.

An approved course sponsor shall pay a fee of ten dollars ($10.00) per licensee to the Commission for each licensee completing an approved continuing education course conducted by the sponsor.

The Commission shall not charge a course application fee, a course renewal fee, or any other fee for a continuing education course sponsored by a community college, junior college, college, or university located in this State and accredited by the Southern Association of Colleges and Schools.

(e) The Commission may award continuing education credit for an unapproved course or related educational activity. The Commission may prescribe procedures for a licensee to submit information on an unapproved course or related educational activity for continuing education credit. The Commission may charge a fee to the licensee for each course or activity submitted. The fee shall not exceed fifty dollars ($50.00). (1993, c. 492, s. 1; 1999-229, s. 5; 2003-361, s. 2; 2005-395, s. 6; 2011-217, s. 4.)

§ 93A-4.2. Broker-in-charge qualification.
To be qualified to serve as a broker-in-charge of a real estate office, a real estate broker shall possess at least two years of full-time real estate brokerage experience or equivalent part-time real estate brokerage experience within the previous five years or real estate education or experience in real estate transactions that the Commission finds equivalent to such experience and shall complete, within a time prescribed by the Commission, a course of study prescribed by the Commission for brokers-in-charge not to exceed 12 classroom hours of instruction. A provisional broker may not be designated as a broker-in-charge. (2005-395, s. 7.)

§ 93A-4.3. Elimination of salesperson license; conversion of salesperson licenses to broker licenses.
(a) Effective April 1, 2006, the Commission shall discontinue issuing real estate salesperson licenses. Also effective April 1, 2006, all salesperson licenses shall become broker licenses, and each person holding a broker license that was changed from salesperson to broker on that date shall be classified as a provisional broker as defined in G.S. 93A-2(a2).

(b) A provisional broker as contemplated in subsection (a) of this section who was issued a salesperson license prior to October 1, 2005, shall, not later than April 1, 2008, complete a broker transition course prescribed by the Commission, not to exceed 24 classroom hours of instruction, or shall demonstrate to the Commission that he or she possesses four years' full-time real estate brokerage experience or equivalent part-time real estate brokerage experience within the previous six years. If the provisional broker satisfies this requirement by April 1, 2008, the provisional status of his or her broker license will be terminated, and the broker will not be required to complete the 90-classroom-hour broker postlicensing education program prescribed by G.S. 93A-4(a1). If the provisional broker fails to satisfy this requirement by April 1, 2008, his or her license will be placed on inactive status, if not already on inactive status, and he or she must complete the 90-classroom-hour broker postlicensing education program prescribed by G.S. 93A-4(a1) in order to terminate the provisional status of the broker license and to be eligible to return his or her license to active status.

(c) An approved school or sponsor shall pay a fee of ten dollars ($10.00) per licensee to the Commission for each licensee completing a broker transition course conducted by the school or sponsor, provided that these fees shall not be charged to a community college, junior college, college, or university located in this State and accredited by the Southern Association of Colleges and Schools.

(d) A provisional broker as contemplated in subsection (a) of this section, who was issued a salesperson license between October 1, 2005, and March 31, 2006, shall, not later than April 1, 2009, satisfy the requirements of G.S. 93A-4(a1). Upon satisfaction of the requirements of G.S. 93A-4(a1), the provisional status of the broker's license will be terminated. If the provisional broker fails to satisfy the requirements of G.S. 93A-4(a1) by April 1, 2009, the broker's license shall be cancelled, and the person will be subject to the requirements for licensure reinstatement prescribed by G.S. 93A-4(a1).

(e) A broker who was issued a broker license prior to April 1, 2006, shall not be required to complete either the 90-classroom-hour broker postlicensing education program prescribed by G.S. 93A-4(a1) or the broker transition course prescribed by subsection (b) of this section.

(f) For the purpose of determining a licensee's status, rights, and obligations under this section, the Commission may treat a person who is issued a license on or after the October 1, 2005, or April 1, 2006, dates cited in subsections (a), (b), (d), or (e) of this section as though the person had been issued a license prior to those dates if the only reason the person's license was not issued prior to those dates was that the person's application was pending a determination by the Commission as to whether the applicant possessed the requisite moral character for licensure. If a license application is pending on April 1, 2006, for any reason other than a determination by the Commission as to the applicant's moral character for licensure, and if the applicant has not satisfied all education and examination requirements for licensing in effect on April 1, 2006, the applicant's application shall be cancelled and the application fee refunded.

(g) No applications for a real estate salesperson license shall be accepted by the Commission between September 1, 2005, and September 30, 2005. (2005-395, s. 7.)

§ 93A-4A: Recodified as G.S. 93A-4.1 by Session Laws 2005-395, s. 6.

§ 93A-5. Register of applicants and roster of brokers.

(a) The Executive Director of the Commission shall keep a register of all applicants for license, showing for each the date of application, name, place of residence, and whether the license was granted or refused. Said register shall be prima facie evidence of all matters recorded therein.

(b) The Executive Director of the Commission shall also keep a current roster showing the names and places of business of all licensed real estate brokers, which roster shall be kept on file in the office of the Commission and be open to public inspection.

(c) The Commission shall file reports annually as required by G.S. 93B-2. (1957, c. 744, s. 5; 1969, c. 191, s. 4; 1983, c. 81, ss. 2, 9, 12.; 2000-140, s. 19(b); 2005-395, s. 8; 2011-217, s. 5.)

§ 93A-6. Disciplinary action by Commission.

(a) The Commission has power to take disciplinary action. Upon its own initiative, or on the complaint of any person, the Commission may investigate the actions of any person or entity licensed under this Chapter, or any other person or entity who shall assume to act in such capacity. If the Commission finds probable cause that a licensee has violated any of the provisions of this Chapter, the Commission may hold a hearing on the allegations of misconduct.

The Commission has power to suspend or revoke at any time a license issued under the provisions of this Chapter, or to reprimand or censure any licensee, if, following a hearing, the Commission adjudges the licensee to be guilty of:
    (1) Making any willful or negligent misrepresentation or any willful or negligent omission of material fact.

(2) Making any false promises of a character likely to influence, persuade, or induce.

(3) Pursuing a course of misrepresentation or making of false promises through agents, advertising or otherwise.

(4) Acting for more than one party in a transaction without the knowledge of all parties for whom he or she acts.

(5) Accepting a commission or valuable consideration as a real estate broker on provisional status for the performance of any of the acts specified in this Article or Article 4 of this Chapter, from any person except his or her broker-in-charge or licensed broker by whom he or she is employed.

(6) Representing or attempting to represent a real estate broker other than the broker by whom he or she is engaged or associated, without the express knowledge and consent of the broker with whom he or she is associated.

(7) Failing, within a reasonable time, to account for or to remit any monies coming into his or her possession which belong to others.

(8) Being unworthy or incompetent to act as a real estate broker in a manner as to endanger the interest of the public.

(9) Paying a commission or valuable consideration to any person for acts or services performed in violation of this Chapter.

(10) Any other conduct which constitutes improper, fraudulent or dishonest dealing.

(11) Performing or undertaking to perform any legal service, as set forth in G.S. 84-2.1, or any other acts constituting the practice of law.

(12) Commingling the money or other property of his or her principals with his or her own or failure to maintain and deposit in a trust or escrow account in a bank as provided by subsection (g) of this section all money received by him or her as a real estate licensee acting in that capacity, or an escrow agent, or the custodian or manager of the funds of another person or entity which relate to or concern that person's or entity's interest or investment in real property, provided, these accounts shall not bear interest unless the principals authorize in writing the deposit be made in an interest bearing account and also provide for the disbursement of the interest accrued.

(13) Failing to deliver, within a reasonable time, a completed copy of any purchase agreement or offer to buy and sell real estate to the buyer and to the seller.

(14) Failing, at the time a sales transaction is consummated, to deliver to the broker's client a detailed and accurate closing statement showing the receipt and disbursement of all monies relating to the transaction about which the broker knows or reasonably should know. If a closing statement is prepared by an attorney or lawful settlement agent, a broker may rely on the delivery of that statement, but the broker must review the statement for accuracy and notify all parties to the closing of any errors.

(15) Violating any rule adopted by the Commission.

(b) The Commission may suspend or revoke any license issued under the provisions of this Chapter or reprimand or censure any licensee when:

(1) The licensee has obtained a license by false or fraudulent representation;

(2) The licensee has been convicted or has entered a plea of guilty or no contest upon which final judgment is entered by a court of competent jurisdiction in

this State, or any other state, of any misdemeanor or felony that involves false swearing, misrepresentation, deceit, extortion, theft, bribery, embezzlement, false pretenses, fraud, forgery, larceny, misappropriation of funds or property, perjury, or any other offense showing professional unfitness or involving moral turpitude which would reasonably affect the licensee's performance in the real estate business;

(3) The licensee has violated any of the provisions of G.S. 93A-6(a) when selling, leasing, or buying the licensee's own property;

(4) The broker's unlicensed employee, who is exempt from the provisions of this Chapter under G.S. 93A-2(c)(6), has committed, in the regular course of business, any act which, if committed by the broker, would constitute a violation of G.S. 93A-6(a) for which the broker could be disciplined; or

(5) The licensee, who is also licensed as an appraiser, attorney, home inspector, mortgage broker, general contractor, or member of another licensed profession or occupation, has been disciplined for an offense under any law involving fraud, theft, misrepresentation, breach of trust or fiduciary responsibility, or willful or negligent malpractice.

(c) The Commission may appear in its own name in superior court in actions for injunctive relief to prevent any person from violating the provisions of this Chapter or rules adopted by the Commission. The superior court shall have the power to grant these injunctions even if criminal prosecution has been or may be instituted as a result of the violations, or whether the person is a licensee of the Commission.

(d) Each broker shall maintain complete records showing the deposit, maintenance, and withdrawal of money or other property owned by the broker's principals or held in escrow or in trust for the broker's principals. The Commission may inspect these records periodically, without prior notice and may also inspect these records whenever the Commission determines that they are pertinent to an investigation of any specific complaint against a licensee.

(e) When a person or entity licensed under this Chapter is accused of any act, omission, or misconduct which would subject the licensee to disciplinary action, the licensee, with the consent and approval of the Commission, may surrender the license and all the rights and privileges pertaining to it for a period of time established by the Commission. A person or entity who surrenders a license shall not thereafter be eligible for or submit any application for licensure as a real estate broker during the period of license surrender.

(f) In any contested case in which the Commission takes disciplinary action authorized by any provision of this Chapter, the Commission may also impose reasonable conditions, restrictions, and limitations upon the license, registration, or approval issued to the disciplined person or entity. In any contested case concerning an application for licensure, time share project registration, or school, sponsor, instructor, or course approval, the Commission may impose reasonable conditions, restrictions, and limitations on any license, registration, or approval it may issue as a part of its final decision.

(g) A broker's trust or escrow account shall be a demand deposit account in a federally insured depository institution lawfully doing business in this State which agrees to make its records of the broker's account available for inspection by the Commission's representatives.

(h) The Executive Director shall transmit a certified copy of all final orders of the Commission suspending or revoking licenses issued under this Chapter to the clerk of superior court of the county in which the licensee maintains his or her principal place of business. The clerk shall enter the order upon the judgment docket of the county. (1957, c. 744, s. 6; 1967, c. 281, s. 4; c. 853, s. 3; 1969, c. 191, s. 5; 1971, c. 86, s. 2; 1973, c. 1112; c. 1331, s. 3; 1975, c. 28; 1979, c. 616, ss. 6, 7; 1981, c. 682, s. 15; 1983, c. 81, s. 13; 1987, c. 516, ss. 1, 2; 1989, c. 563, s. 2; 1993, c. 419, s. 10; 1999-229, s. 6; 2000-149, s. 19(b); 2001-487, s. 23(b); 2002-168, s. 5; 2005-374, s. 2; 2005-395, s. 9; 2011-217, s. 6.)

§ 93A-6.1. Commission may subpoena witnesses, records, documents, or other materials.

(a) The Commission, Executive Director, or other representative designated by the Commission may issue a subpoena for the appearance of witnesses deemed necessary to testify concerning any matter to be heard before or investigated by the Commission. The Commission may issue a subpoena ordering any person in possession of records, documents, or other materials, however maintained, that concern any matter to be heard before or investigated by the Commission to produce the records, documents, or other materials for inspection or deliver the same into the custody of the Commission's authorized representatives. Upon written request, the Commission shall revoke a subpoena if it finds that the evidence, the production of which is required, does not relate to a matter in issue, or if the subpoena does not describe with sufficient particularity the evidence, the production of which is required, or if for any other reason in law the subpoena is invalid. If any person shall fail to fully and promptly comply with a subpoena issued under this section, the Commission may apply to any judge of the superior court resident in any county where the person to whom the subpoena is issued maintains a residence or place of business for an order compelling the person to show cause why he or she should not be held in contempt of the Commission and its processes. The court shall have the power to impose punishment for acts that would constitute direct or indirect contempt if the acts occurred in an action pending in superior court.

(b) The Commission shall be exempt from the requirements of Chapter 53B of the General Statutes with regard to subpoenas issued to compel the production of a licensee's trust account records held by any financial institution. Notwithstanding the exemption, whenever the Commission issues a subpoena under this subsection, the Commission shall send a copy to the licensee at his or her address of record by regular mail. (1999-229, s. 7; 2005-395, s. 10; 2011-217, s. 7.)

§ 93A-7. Power of courts to revoke.

Whenever any person, partnership, association or corporation claiming to have been injured or damaged by the gross negligence, incompetency, fraud, dishonesty or misconduct on the part of any licensee following the calling or engaging in the business herein described and shall file suit upon such claim against such licensee in any court of record in this State and shall recover judgment thereon, such court may as part of its judgment or decree in such case, if it deem it a proper case in which so to do, order a written copy of the transcript of record in said case to be forwarded by the clerk of court to the chairman of the said Commission with a recommendation that the licensee's certificate of license be revoked. (1957, c. 744, s. 7; 1983, c. 81, s. 2.)

§ 93A-8. Penalty for violation of Chapter.

Any person violating the provisions of this Chapter shall upon conviction thereof be deemed guilty of a Class 1 misdemeanor. (1957, c. 744, s. 8; 1993, c. 539, s. 657; 1994, Ex. Sess., c. 24, s. 14(c).)

§ 93A-9. Licensing foreign brokers.

(a) The Commission may issue a broker license to an applicant licensed in a foreign jurisdiction who has satisfied the requirements for licensure set out in G.S. 93A-4 or such other requirements as the Commission in its discretion may by rule require.

(b) The Commission may issue a limited broker's license to a person or an entity from another state or territory of the United States without regard to whether that state or territory offers similar licensing privileges to residents in North Carolina if the person or entity satisfies all of the following:

(1) Is of good moral character and licensed as a real estate broker or salesperson in good standing in another state or territory of the United States.

(2) Only engages in business as a real estate broker in North Carolina in transactions involving commercial real estate and while the person or entity is affiliated with a resident North Carolina real estate broker.

(3) Complies with the laws of this State regulating real estate brokers and rules adopted by the Commission.

The Commission may require an applicant for licensure under this subsection to pay a fee not to exceed three hundred dollars ($300.00). All licenses issued under this subsection shall expire on June 30 of each year following issuance or on a date that the Commission deems appropriate unless the license is renewed pursuant to the requirements of G.S. 93A-4. A person or entity licensed under this subsection may be disciplined by the Commission for violations of this Chapter as provided in G.S. 93A-6 and G.S. 93A-54.

Any person or entity licensed under this subsection shall be affiliated with a resident North Carolina real estate broker, and the resident North Carolina real estate broker shall actively and personally supervise the licensee in a manner that reasonably assures that the licensee complies with the requirements of this Chapter and rules adopted by the Commission. A person or entity licensed under this subsection shall not, however, be affiliated with a resident North Carolina real estate provisional broker. The Commission may exempt applicants for licensure under this subsection from examination and the other licensing requirements under G.S. 93A-4. The Commission may adopt rules as it deems necessary to give effect to this subsection, including rules establishing: (i) qualifications for licensure; (ii) licensure and renewal procedures; (iii) requirements for continuing education; (iv) conduct of persons and entities licensed under this subsection and their affiliated resident real estate brokers; (v) a definition of commercial real estate; and (vi) any requirements or limitations on affiliation between resident real estate brokers and persons or entities seeking licensure under this subsection. (1957, c. 744, s. 9; 1967, c. 281, s. 5; 1969, c. 191, s. 6; 1971, c. 86, s. 3; 1983, c. 81, s. 2.; 2000-140, s. 19(b); 2003-361, s. 3; 2005-395, s. 11; 2011-217, s. 8.)

§ 93A-10. Nonresident licensees; filing of consent as to service of process and pleadings.

Every nonresident applicant shall file an irrevocable consent that suits and actions may be commenced against such applicant in any of the courts of record of this State, by the service of any process or pleading authorized by the laws of this State in any county in which the plaintiff may reside, by serving the same on the Executive Director of the Commission, said consent stipulating and agreeing that such service of such process or pleadings on said Executive Director shall be taken and held in all courts to be valid and binding as if due service had been made personally upon the applicant in this State. This consent shall be duly acknowledged, and, if made by a corporation, shall be executed by an officer of the corporation. The signature of the officer on the consent to service instrument shall be sufficient to bind the corporation and no further authentication is necessary. An application from a corporation or other business entity shall be signed by an officer of the corporation or entity or by an individual designated by the Commission. In all cases where process or pleadings shall be served, under the provisions of this Chapter, upon the Executive Director of the Commission, such process or pleadings shall be served in duplicate, one of which shall be filed in the office of the Commission and the other shall be forwarded immediately by the Executive Director of the Commission, by registered mail, to the last known business address of the nonresident licensee against which such process or pleadings are directed. (1957, c. 744, s. 10; 1983, c. 81, ss. 3, 10; 2003-361, s. 4.)

§ 93A-11. Reimbursement by real estate independent contractor of brokers' workers' compensation.

(a) Notwithstanding the provisions of G.S. 97-21 or any other provision of law, a real estate broker may include in the governing contract with a real estate broker on provisional status whose nonemployee status is recognized pursuant to section 3508 of the United States Internal Revenue Code, 26 U.S.C. § 3508, an agreement for the broker on provisional status to reimburse the broker for the cost of covering that broker on provisional status under the broker's workers' compensation coverage of the broker's business.

(b) Nothing in this section shall affect a requirement under any other law to provide workers' compensation coverage or in any manner exclude from coverage any person, firm, or corporation otherwise subject to the provisions of Article 1 of Chapter 97 of the General Statutes. (1995, c. 127, s. 1.; 2000-140, s. 19(b); 2011-217, s. 9.)

§ 93A-12. Disputed monies.

(a) A real estate broker licensed under this Chapter or an attorney licensed to practice law in this State may deposit with the clerk of court in accordance with this section monies, other than a residential security deposit, the ownership of which are in dispute and that the real estate broker or attorney received while acting in a fiduciary capacity.

(b) The disputed monies shall be deposited with the clerk of court in the county in which the property for which the disputed monies are being held is located. At the time of depositing the disputed monies, the real estate broker or attorney shall certify to the clerk of court that the persons who are claiming ownership of the disputed monies have been notified in accordance with subsection (c) of this section that the disputed monies are to be deposited with the clerk of court and that the persons may initiate a special proceeding with the clerk of court to recover the disputed monies.

(c) Notice to the persons who are claiming ownership to the disputed monies required under subsection (b) of this section shall be provided by delivering a copy of the notice to the person or by mailing it to the person by first-class mail, postpaid, properly addressed to the person at the person's last known address.

(d) A real estate broker or attorney shall not deposit disputed monies with the clerk of court until 90 days following notification of the persons claiming ownership of the disputed monies.

(e) Upon the filing of a special proceeding to recover the disputed monies, the clerk shall determine the rightful ownership of the monies and distribute the disputed monies accordingly. If no special proceeding is filed with the clerk of court within one year of the disputed monies being deposited with the clerk of court, the disputed monies shall be deemed unclaimed and shall be delivered by the clerk of court to the State Treasurer in accordance with the provisions of Article 4 of Chapter 116B of the General Statutes. (2005-395, s. 12.; 2011-350, s. 1.)

§ 93A-13. Contracts for broker services.

No action between a broker and the broker's client for recovery under an agreement for broker services is valid unless the contract is reduced to writing and signed by the party to be charged or by some other person lawfully authorized by the party to sign. (2011-165, s. 2.)

§ 93A-14: Reserved for future codification purposes.

§ 93A-15: Reserved for future codification purposes.

Article 2.

Real Estate Education and Recovery Fund.

§ 93A-16. Real Estate Education and Recovery Fund created; payment to fund; management.

(a) There is hereby created a special fund to be known as the "Real Estate Education and Recovery Fund" which shall be set aside and maintained by the North Carolina Real Estate Commission. The fund shall be used in the manner provided under this Article for the payment of unsatisfied judgments where the aggrieved person has suffered a direct monetary loss by reason of certain acts committed by any real estate broker. The Commission may also expend money from the fund to create books and other publications, courses, forms, seminars, and other programs and materials to educate licensees and the public in real estate subjects. However, the Commission shall make no expenditures from the fund for educational purposes if the expenditure will reduce the balance of the fund to an amount less than two hundred thousand dollars ($200,000).

(b) On September 1, 1979, the Commission shall transfer the sum of one hundred thousand dollars ($100,000) from its expense reserve fund to the Real Estate Education and Recovery Fund. Thereafter, the Commission may transfer to the Real Estate Education and Recovery Fund additional sums of money from whatever funds the Commission may have, provided that, if on December 31 of any year the amount remaining in the fund is less than fifty thousand dollars ($50,000), the Commission may determine that each person or entity licensed under this Chapter, when renewing a license, shall pay in addition to the license renewal fee, a fee not to exceed ten dollars ($10.00) per broker as shall be determined by the Commission for the purpose of replenishing the fund.

(c) The Commission shall invest and reinvest the monies in the Real Estate Education and Recovery Fund in the same manner as provided by law for the investment of funds by the clerk of superior court. The proceeds from such investments shall be deposited to the credit of the fund.

(d) The Commission shall have the authority to adopt rules and procedures not inconsistent with the provisions of this Article, to provide for the orderly, fair and efficient administration and payment of monies held in the Real Estate Education and Recovery Fund. (1979, c. 614, s. 1; 1983, c. 81, ss. 1, 2; 1987, c. 516, ss. 3-5.; 2000-140, s. 19(b); 2001-487, s. 23(c); 2005-395, s. 13; 2011-217, s. 10.)

§ 93A-17. Grounds for payment; notice and application to Commission.

(a) An aggrieved person who has suffered a direct monetary loss by reason of the conversion of trust funds by any licensed real estate broker shall be eligible to recover, subject to the limitations of this Article, the amount of trust funds converted and which is otherwise unrecoverable provided that:

(1) The act or acts of conversion which form the basis of the claim for recovery occurred on or after September 1, 1979;

(2) The aggrieved person has sued the real estate broker in a court of competent jurisdiction and has filed with the Commission written notice of such lawsuit within 60 days after its commencement unless the claim against the Real Estate Education and Recovery Fund is for an amount less than three thousand dollars ($3,000), excluding attorneys' fees, in which case the notice may be filed within 60 days after the termination of all judicial proceedings including appeals;

(3) The aggrieved person has obtained final judgment in a court of competent jurisdiction against the real estate broker on grounds of conversion of trust funds arising out of a transaction which occurred when such broker was licensed and acting in a capacity for which a license is required; and

(4) Execution of the judgment has been attempted and has been returned unsatisfied in whole or in part.

Upon the termination of all judicial proceedings including appeals, and for a period of one year thereafter, a person eligible for recovery may file a verified application with the Commission for payment out of the Real Estate Education and Recovery Fund of the amount remaining unpaid upon the judgment which represents the actual and direct loss sustained by reason of conversion of trust funds. A copy of the judgment and return of execution shall be attached to the application and filed with the Commission.

(b) For the purposes of this Article, the term "trust funds" shall include all earnest money deposits, down payments, sales proceeds, tenant security deposits, undisbursed rents and other such monies which belong to another or others and are held by a real estate broker acting in that capacity. Trust funds shall also include all time share purchase monies which are required to be held in trust by G.S. 93A-45(c) during the time they are, in fact, so held. Trust funds shall not include, however, any funds held by an independent escrow agent under G.S. 93A-42 or any funds which the court may find to be subject to an implied, constructive or resulting trust.

(c) For the purposes of this Article, the terms "licensee" and "broker" shall include only individual persons licensed under this Chapter as brokers. The terms "licensee" and "broker" shall not include a time share developer, time share project, independent escrow agent, corporation or other entity licensed under this Chapter. (1979, c. 614, s. 1; 1983, c. 81, ss. 2, 14; 1987, c. 516, s. 6; 1999-229, s. 8.; 2000-140, s. 19(b); 2005-395, s. 14; 2011-217, s. 11.)

§ 93A-18. Hearing; required showing.

Upon application by an aggrieved person, the Commission shall conduct a hearing and the aggrieved person shall be required to show that the aggrieved person:

(1) Is not a spouse of the judgment debtor or a person representing the spouse;

(2) Is making application not more than one year after termination of all judicial proceedings, including appeals, in connection with the judgment;

(3) Has complied with all requirements of this Article;

(4) Has obtained a judgment as described in G.S. 93A-17, stating the amount owing thereon at the date of application;

(5) Has made all reasonable searches and inquiries to ascertain whether the judgment debtor is possessed of real or personal property or other assets liable to be sold or applied in satisfaction of the judgment;

(6) After searching as described in subdivision (5) of this section, has discovered no real or personal property or other assets liable to be sold or applied, or has discovered certain of them, describing them, but the amount so realized was insufficient to satisfy the judgment, stating the amount realized and the balance remaining due on the judgment after application of the amount realized;

(7) Has diligently pursued the aggrieved person's remedies, which include attempting execution on the judgment against all the judgment debtors, which execution has been returned unsatisfied; and

(8) Knows of no assets of the judgment debtor and has attempted collection from all other persons who may be liable for the transaction for which the aggrieved person seeks payment from the Real Estate Education and Recovery Fund if there be any such other persons. (1979, c. 614, s. 1; 1987, c. 516, s. 7; 2001-487, s. 23(d); 2011-217, s. 12.)

§ 93A-19. Response and defense by Commission and judgment debtor; proof of conversion.

(a) Whenever the Commission proceeds upon an application as set forth in this Article, counsel for the Commission may defend such action on behalf of the fund and shall have recourse to all appropriate means of defense, including the examination of witnesses. The judgment debtor may defend such action on his or her own behalf and shall have recourse to all appropriate means of defense, including the examination of witnesses. Counsel for the Commission and the judgment debtor may file responses to the application, setting forth answers and defenses. Responses shall be filed with the Commission and copies shall be served upon every party by the filing party. If at any time it appears there are no triable issues of fact and the application for payment from the fund is without merit, the Commission shall dismiss the application. A motion to dismiss may be supported by affidavit of any person or persons having knowledge of the facts and may be made on the basis that the application or the judgment referred to therein do not form a basis for meritorious recovery within the purview of G.S. 93A-17, that the applicant has not complied with the provisions of this Article, or that the liability of the fund with regard to the particular licensee or transaction has been exhausted; provided, however, notice of the motion shall be given at least 10 days prior to the time fixed for hearing. If the applicant or judgment debtor fails to appear at the hearing after receiving notice of the hearing, the applicant or judgment debtor waives the person's rights unless the absence is excused by the Commission.

(b) Whenever the judgment obtained by an applicant is by default, stipulation, or consent, or whenever the action against the licensee was defended by a trustee in bankruptcy, the applicant, for purposes of this Article, shall have the burden of proving the cause of action for conversion of trust funds. Otherwise, the judgment shall create a rebuttable presumption of the conversion of trust funds. This presumption is a presumption affecting the burden of producing evidence. (1979, c. 614, s. 1; 1983, c. 81, s. 2; 1987, c. 516, s. 8; 1999-229, s. 9; 2001-487, s. 23(e).)

§ 93A-20. Order directing payment out of fund; compromise of claims.

Applications for payment from the Real Estate Education and Recovery Fund shall be heard and decided by a majority of the members of the Commission. If, after a hearing, the Commission finds the claim should be paid from the fund, the Commission shall enter an order requiring payment from the fund of whatever sum the Commission shall find to be payable upon the claim in accordance with the limitations contained in this Article.

Subject to Commission approval, a claim based upon the application of an aggrieved person may be compromised; however, the Commission shall not be bound in any way by any compromise or stipulation of the judgment debtor. If a claim appears to be otherwise meritorious, the Commission may waive procedural defects in the application for payment. (1979, c. 614, s. 1; 1983, c. 81, s. 2; 1987, c. 516, s. 9; 1999-229, s. 10; 2011-217, s. 13.)

§ 93A-21. Limitations; pro rata distribution; attorney fees.

(a) Payments from the Real Estate Education and Recovery Fund shall be subject to the following limitations:
   (1) The right to recovery under this Article shall be forever barred unless application is made within one year after termination of all proceedings including appeals, in connection with the judgment.
   (2) The fund shall not be liable for more than fifty thousand dollars ($50,000) per transaction regardless of the number of persons aggrieved or parcels of real estate involved in such transaction.
   (3) Payment from the fund shall not exceed in the aggregate twenty-five thousand dollars ($25,000) for any one licensee within a single calendar year, and in no event shall it exceed in the aggregate seventy-five thousand dollars ($75,000) for any one licensee.
   (4) The fund shall not be liable for payment of any judgment awards of consequential damages, multiple or punitive damages, civil penalties, incidental damages, special damages, interest, costs of court or action or other similar awards.

(b) If the maximum liability of the fund is insufficient to pay in full the valid claims of all aggrieved persons whose claims relate to the same transaction or to the same licensee, the amount for which the fund is liable shall be distributed among the claimants in a ratio that their respective claims bear to the total of such valid claims or in such manner as the Commission, in its discretion, deems equitable. Upon petition of counsel for the Commission, the Commission may require all claimants and prospective claimants to be joined in one proceeding to the end that the respective rights of all such claimants to the Real Estate Education and Recovery Fund may be equitably resolved. A person who files an application for payment after the maximum liability of the fund for the licensee or transaction has been exhausted shall not be entitled to payment and may not seek judicial review of the Commission's award of payment to any party except upon a showing that the Commission abused its discretion.

(c) In the event an aggrieved person is entitled to payment from the fund in an amount which is equal to or less than the maximum amount of money which may be awarded in small claims court under G.S. 7A-210, the Commission may allow such person to recover from the fund reasonable attorney's fees incurred in effecting such recovery. Reimbursement for attorney's fees shall be limited to those fees incurred in effecting recovery from the fund and shall not include any fee incurred in obtaining judgment against the licensee. (1979, c. 614, s. 1; 1983, c. 81, ss. 2, 15; 1987, c. 516, ss. 10-13; 1999-229, s. 11; 2011-217, s. 14.)

§ 93A-22. Repayment to fund; automatic suspension of license.

Should the Commission pay from the Real Estate Education and Recovery Fund any amount in settlement of a claim or toward satisfaction of a judgment against a licensed real estate broker, any license issued to the broker shall be automatically suspended upon the effective date of the order authorizing payment from the fund. No such broker shall be granted a reinstatement until the fund has been repaid in full, including interest at the legal rate as provided for in G.S. 24-1. (1979, c. 614, s. 1; 1983, c. 81, s. 2; 1987, c. 516, s. 14.; 2000-140, s. 19(b); 2001-487, s. 23(f); 2005-395, s. 15; 2011-217, s. 15.)

§ 93A-23. Subrogation of rights.

When the Commission has paid from the Real Estate Education and Recovery Fund any sum to the judgment creditor, the Commission shall be subrogated to all of the rights of the judgment creditor to the extent of the amount so paid and the judgment creditor shall assign all right, title, and interest in the judgment to the extent of the amount so paid to the Commission and any amount and interest so recovered by the Commission on the judgment shall be deposited in the Real Estate Education and Recovery Fund. (1979, c. 614, s. 1; 1983, c. 81, s. 2; 1987, c. 516, s. 15; 2001-487, s. 23(g); 2011-217, s. 16.)

§ 93A-24. Waiver of rights.

The failure of an aggrieved person to comply with this Article shall constitute a waiver of any rights hereunder. (1979, c. 614, s. 1.)

§ 93A-25. Persons ineligible to recover from fund.

No real estate broker who suffers the loss of any commission from any transaction in which he or she was acting in the capacity of a real estate broker shall be entitled to make application for payment from the Real Estate Education and Recovery Fund for the loss. (1979, c. 614, s. 1.; 2000-140, s. 19(b); 2001-487, s. 23(h); 2011-217, s. 17.)

§ 93A-26. Disciplinary action against licensee.

Nothing contained in this Article shall limit the authority of the Commission to take disciplinary action against any licensee under this Chapter, nor shall the repayment in full of all obligations to the fund by any licensee nullify or modify the effect of any other disciplinary proceeding brought under this Chapter. (1979, c. 614, s. 1; 1983, c. 81, s. 2.)

§§ 93A-27 through 93A-31. Reserved for future codification purposes.

Article 3.

Private Real Estate Schools.

§ 93A-32. Definitions.

As used in this Article:
(1) "Commission" means the North Carolina Real Estate Commission.
(2) "Private real estate school" means any real estate educational entity which is privately owned and operated by an individual, partnership, corporation, limited liability company, or association, and which conducts, for a profit or tuition charge, real estate broker prelicensing or postlicensing courses prescribed by G.S. 93A-4(a) or (a1), provided that a proprietary business or trade school licensed by the State Board of Community Colleges under G.S. 115D-90 to conduct courses other than those real estate courses described herein shall not

be considered to be a private real estate school. (1979, 2nd Sess., c. 1193, s. 1; 1983, c. 81, ss. 1, 2; 1989, c. 563, s. 3; 1993, c. 419, s. 11; c. 553, s. 29.1.; 2000-140, s. 19(b); 2005-395, s. 16.)

§ 93A-33. Commission to administer Article; authority of Commission to conduct investigations, issue licenses, and promulgate regulations.

The Commission shall have authority to administer and enforce this Article and to issue licenses to private real estate schools as defined herein which have complied with the requirements of this Article and regulations promulgated by the Commission. Through licensing applications, periodic reports required of licensed schools, periodic investigations and inspections of schools, and appropriate regulations, the Commission shall exercise general supervisory authority over private real estate schools, the object of such supervision being to protect the public interest and to assure the conduct of quality real estate education programs. To this end the Commission is authorized and directed to promulgate such regulations as it deems necessary which are not inconsistent with the provisions of this Article and which relate to the subject areas set out in G.S. 93A-34(c). (1979, 2nd Sess., c. 1193, s. 1; 1983, c. 81, s. 2.)

§ 93A-34. License required; application for license; fees; requirements for issuance of license.

(a) No person, partnership, corporation or association shall operate or maintain or offer to operate in this State a private real estate school as defined herein unless a license is first obtained from the Commission in accordance with the provisions of this Article and the rules and regulations promulgated by the Commission under this Article. For licensing purposes, each branch location where a school conducts courses shall be considered a separate school requiring a separate license.

(b) Application for a license shall be filed in the manner and upon the forms prescribed by the Commission for that purpose. The Commission may by rule set nonrefundable application fees not to exceed two hundred fifty dollars ($250.00) for each school location and fifty dollars ($50.00) for each real estate broker prelicensing or postlicensing course. The application for a license shall be accompanied by the appropriate fees and shall contain the following:

(1) Name and address of the applicant and the school;
(2) Names, biographical data, and qualifications of director, administrators and instructors;
(3) Description of school facilities and equipment;
(4) Description of course(s) to be offered and instructional materials to be utilized;
(5) Information on financial resources available to equip and operate the school;
(6) Information on school policies and procedures regarding administration, record keeping, entrance requirements, registration, tuition and fees, grades, student progress, attendance, and student conduct;
(7) Copies of bulletins, catalogues and other official publications;
(8) Copy of bond required by G.S. 93A-36;
(9) Such additional information as the Commission may deem necessary to enable it to determine the adequacy of the instructional program and the ability of the applicant to operate a school in such a manner as would best serve the public interest.

(c) After due investigation and consideration by the Commission, a license shall be issued to the applicant when it is shown to the satisfaction of the Commission that the applicant and school are in compliance with the following standards, as well as the requirements of any supplemental regulations of the Commission regarding these standards:

(1) The program of instruction is adequate in terms of quality, content and duration.
(2) The director, administrators and instructors are adequately qualified by reason of education and experience.
(3) There are adequate facilities, equipment, instructional materials and instructor personnel to provide instruction of good quality.
(4) The school has adopted adequate policies and procedures regarding administration, instruction, record keeping, entrance requirements, registration, tuition and fees, grades, student progress, attendance, and student conduct.
(5) The school publishes and provides to all students upon enrollment a bulletin, catalogue or similar official publication which is certified as being true and correct in content and policy by an authorized school official, and which contains the following information:
   a. Identifying data and publication date;
   b. Name(s) of school and its full-time officials and faculty;
   c. School's policies and procedures relating to entrance requirements, registration, grades, student progress, attendance, student conduct and refund of tuition and fees;
   d. Detailed schedule of tuition and fees;
   e. Detailed course outline of all courses offered.
(6) Adequate records as prescribed by the Commission are maintained in regard to grades, attendance, registration and financial operations.
(7) Institutional standards relating to grades, attendance and progress are enforced in a satisfactory manner.
(8) The applicant is financially sound and capable of fulfilling educational commitments made to students.
(9) The school's owner(s), director, administrators and instructors are of good reputation and character.
(10) The school's facilities and equipment comply with all applicable local, State and federal laws and regulations regarding health, safety, and welfare, including the Americans with Disabilities Act and other laws relating to accessibility standards for places of public accommodation.
(11) The school does not utilize advertising of any type which is false or misleading, either by actual statement, omission or intimation.
(12) Such additional standards as may be deemed necessary by the Commission to assure the conduct of adequate instructional programs and the operation of schools in a manner which will best serve the public interest. (1979, 2nd Sess., c. 1193, s. 1; 1983, c. 81, ss. 1, 2; 1989, c. 563, s. 4; 1993, c. 419, s. 12.; 2000-140, s. 19(b); 2005-395, s. 17.)

§ 93A-35. Duration and renewal of licenses; transfer of school ownership.

(a) All licenses issued shall expire on June 30 following the date of issuance.

(b) Licenses shall be renewable annually on July 1, provided that a renewal application accompanied by the appropriate renewal fees has been filed not later than June 1 in the form and manner prescribed by the Commission, and provided further that the applicant and school are found to be in compliance with the standards established for issuance of an original license. The Commission may by rule set nonrefundable renewal fees not to exceed one hundred twenty-five dollars ($125.00) for each school location and twenty-five dollars ($25.00) for each real estate broker prelicensing and postlicensing course.

(c) In the event a school is sold or ownership is otherwise transferred, the license issued to the original owner is not transferable to the new owner. Such new owner must make application for an original license as prescribed by this Article and Commission regulations. (1979, 2nd Sess., c. 1193, s. 1; 1983, c. 81, ss. 1, 2; 1989, c. 563, s. 5; 1993, c. 419, s. 13.; 2000-140, s. 19(b); 2011-217, s. 18.)

§ 93A-36. Execution of bond required; applicability to branch schools; actions upon bond.

(a) Before the Commission shall issue a license the applicant shall execute a bond in the sum of five thousand dollars ($5,000), payable to the State of North Carolina, signed by a solvent guaranty company authorized to do business in the State of North Carolina, and conditioned that the principal in said bond will carry out and comply with each and every contract or agreement, written or verbal, made and entered into by the applicant's school acting by and through its officers and agents with any student who desires to enter such school and to take any courses offered therein and that said principal will refund to such students all amounts collected in tuition and fees in case of failure on the part of the party obtaining a license from the Commission to open and operate a private real estate school or to provide the instruction agreed to or contracted for. Such bond shall be required for each school for which a license is required and shall be first approved by the Commission and then filed with the clerk of superior court of the county in which the school is located, to be recorded by such clerk in a book provided for that purpose. A separate bond shall not be required for each branch of a licensed school.

(b) In any and all cases where the party licensed by the Commission fails to fulfill its obligations under any contract or agreement, written or verbal, made and entered into with any student, then the State of North Carolina, upon the relation of the student(s) entering into said contract or agreement, shall have a cause of action against the principal and surety on the bond herein required for the full amount of payments made to such party, plus court costs and six percent (6%) interest from the date of payment of said amount. Such suits shall be brought in Wake County Superior Court within one year of the alleged default. (1979, 2nd Sess., c. 1193, s. 1; 1983, c. 81, s. 2; 1999-229, s. 12.)

§ 93A-37. Contracts with unlicensed schools and evidences of indebtedness made null and void.

All contracts or agreements entered into on or after October 1, 1980, by private real estate schools, as defined in this Article, with students or prospective students, and all promissory notes or other evidence of indebtedness taken on or after October 1, 1980, in lieu of cash payments by such schools, shall be null and void unless such schools are duly licensed as required by this Article on the date of such contract or agreement or taking of any promissory note or other evidence of indebtedness. (1979, 2nd Sess., c. 1193, s. 1.)

§ 93A-38. Suspension, revocation or denial of license.

The Commission shall have the power to suspend, revoke, deny issuance, or deny renewal of license to operate a private real estate school. In all proceedings to suspend, revoke or deny a license, the provisions of Chapter 150B of the General Statutes shall be applicable. The Commission may suspend, revoke, or deny such license when it finds:

(1) That the applicant for or holder of such license has refused or failed to comply with any of the provisions of this Article or the rules or regulations promulgated thereunder;

(2) That the applicant for or holder of such license has knowingly presented to the Commission false or misleading information relating to matters within the purview of the Commission under this Article;

(3) That the applicant for or holder of such license has presented to its students or prospective students false or misleading information relating to its instructional program, to the instructional programs of other institutions or to employment opportunities;

(4) That the applicant for or holder of such license has failed to comply with the provisions of any contract or agreement entered into with a student;

(5) That the applicant for or holder of such license has at any time refused to permit authorized representatives of the Commission to inspect the school, or failed to make available to them upon request full information relating to matters within the purview of the Commission under the provisions of this Article or the rules or regulations promulgated thereunder; or

(6) That the applicant for or holder of such license or any officer of a corporate licensee or corporation applying for a license, any partner of a partnership licensee or partnership applying for a license, or any member of a limited liability company licensee or limited liability company applying for a license has pleaded guilty, entered a plea of nolo contendere or been found guilty of a crime involving moral turpitude in any state or federal court. (1979, 2nd Sess., c. 1193, s. 1; 1983, c. 81, s. 2; 1987, c. 827, s. 1; 2005-395, s. 18.)

Article 4.

Time Shares.

§ 93A-39. Title.

This Article shall be known and may be cited as the "North Carolina Time Share Act." (1983, c. 814, s. 1.)

§ 93A-40. Registration required of time share projects; real estate license required.

(a) It shall be unlawful for any person in this State to engage or assume to engage in the business of a time share salesperson without first obtaining a real estate broker license issued by the North Carolina Real Estate Commission under the provisions of Article 1 of this Chapter, and it shall be unlawful for a time share developer to sell or offer to sell a time share located in this State without first obtaining a certificate of registration for the time share project to be offered for sale issued by the North Carolina Real Estate Commission under the provisions of this Article.

(b)   A person responsible as general partner, corporate officer, joint venturer or sole proprietor who intentionally acts as a time share developer, allowing the offering of sale or the sale of time shares to a purchaser, without first obtaining registration of the time share project under this Article shall be guilty of a Class I felony. (1983, c. 814, s. 1; 1987, c. 516, s. 16.; 2000-140, s. 19(b); 2005-395, s. 19.)

§ 93A-41. Definitions.

When used in this Article, unless the context otherwise requires, the term:

(1)   "Commission" means the North Carolina Real Estate Commission;

(2)   "Developer" means any person or entity which creates a time share or a time share project or program, purchases a time share for purpose of resale, or is engaged in the business of selling its own time shares and shall include any person or entity who controls, is controlled by, or is in common control with the developer which is engaged in creating or selling time shares for the developer, but a person who purchases a time share for his or her occupancy, use, and enjoyment shall not be deemed a developer;

(3)   "Enrolled" means paid membership in exchange programs or membership in an exchange program evidenced by written acceptance or confirmation of membership;

(4)   "Exchange company" means any person operating an exchange program;

(5)   "Exchange program" means any opportunity or procedure for the assignment or exchange of time shares among purchasers in the same or other time share project;

(5a)   "Independent escrow agent" means a licensed attorney located in this State or a financial institution located in this State;

(6)   "Managing agent" means a person who undertakes the duties, responsibilities, and obligations of the management of a time share program;

(7)   "Person" means one or more natural persons, corporations, partnerships, associations, trusts, other entities, or any combination thereof;

(7a)   "Project broker" means a natural person licensed as a real estate broker and designated by the developer to supervise brokers at the time share project;

(8)   "Purchaser" means any person other than a developer or lender who owns or acquires an interest or proposes to acquire an interest in a time share;

(9)   "Time share" means a right to occupy a unit or any of several units during five or more separated time periods over a period of at least five years, including renewal options, whether or not coupled with a freehold estate or an estate for years in a time share project or a specified portion of a time share project. "Time share" shall also include a vacation license, prepaid hotel reservation, club membership, limited partnership, vacation bond, or a plan or system where the right to use a time share unit or units for periods of time is awarded or apportioned on the basis of points, vouchers, split, divided, or floating use, even if on a competitive basis with other purchasers;

(9a)   "Time share instrument" means an instrument transferring a time share or any interest, legal or beneficial, in a time share to a purchaser, including a contract, installment contract, lease, deed, or other instrument;

(10) "Time share program" means any arrangement for time shares whereby real property has been made subject to a time share;

(11) "Time share project" means any real property that is subject to a time share program;

(11a) "Time share registrar" means a natural person who is designated by the developer to record or cause time share instruments and lien releases to be recorded and to fulfill the other duties imposed by this Article;

(12) "Time share salesperson" means a person who sells or offers to sell on behalf of a developer a time share to a purchaser; and

(13) "Time share unit" or "unit" means the real property or real property improvement in a project which is divided into time shares and designated for separate occupancy and use. (1983, c. 814, s. 1; 1985, c. 578, s. 1; 1999-229, ss. 13, 14.; 2000-140, s. 19(b); 2005-395, s. 20; 2011-217, s. 19.)

§ 93A-42. Time shares deemed real estate.

(a) A time share which in whole or in part burdens or pertains to real property in this State is deemed to be an interest in real estate, and shall be governed by the law of this State relating to real estate.

(b) A purchaser of a time share which burdens or pertains to real property located in the State may in accordance with G.S. 47-18 register the time share instrument by which the purchaser acquired the interest and upon such registration shall be entitled to the protection provided by Chapter 47 of the General Statutes for the recordation of other real property instruments. A time share instrument transferring or encumbering a time share shall not be rejected for recordation because of the nature or duration of that estate, provided all other requirements necessary to make an instrument recordable are complied with. An instrument concerning a time share which burdens or pertains to no real property located in this State shall not be recorded in the office of the register of deeds in any county in this State.

(c) The developer shall record or cause to be recorded a time share instrument:

(1) Not less than six days nor more than 45 days following the execution of the contract of sale by the purchaser; or

(2) Not later than 180 days following the execution of the contract of sale by the purchaser, provided that all payments made by the purchaser shall be placed by the developer with an independent escrow agent upon the expiration of the 10-day escrow period provided by G.S. 93A-45(c).

(d) The independent escrow agent provided by G.S. 93A-42(c)(2) shall deposit and maintain the purchaser's payments in an insured trust or escrow account in a federally insured depository institution or a trust institution authorized to do business in this State. The trust or escrow account may be interest-bearing and the interest earned shall belong to the developer, if agreed upon in writing by the purchaser; provided, however, if the time share instrument is not recorded within the time periods specified in this section, then the interest earned shall belong to the purchaser. The independent escrow agent shall return all payments to the purchaser at the expiration of 180 days following the execution of the contract of sale by the purchaser, unless prior to that time the time share instrument has been recorded. However, if prior to the expiration of 180 days following the execution of the contract of sale, the developer and the purchaser provide their written consent to the independent escrow agent, the developer's obligation to record the time share instrument and the escrow period may be extended for an additional period of 120 days. Upon recordation of the time share instrument, the independent escrow agent shall pay the purchaser's funds to the developer. Upon request by the Commission, the independent escrow agent shall promptly make available to the Commission inspection of records of money held by the independent escrow agent.

(e) In no event shall the developer be required to record a time share instrument if the purchaser is in default of the purchaser's obligations.

(f) Recordation under the provisions of this section of the time share instrument shall constitute delivery of that instrument from the developer to the purchaser. (1983, c. 814, s. 1; 1985, c. 578, ss. 2, 3; 1989, c. 302; 2001-487, s. 23(i); 2011-217, s. 20; 2017-25, s. 1(k).)

§ 93A-42.1. Construction and validity of declarations adopted prior to the Time Share Act.

(a) All provisions contained in time share declarations adopted and recorded at the appropriate register of deeds office prior to July 1, 1984, are severable.

(b) The rule against perpetuities may not be applied to defeat any provision of time share declarations or bylaws adopted and recorded at the appropriate register of deeds office prior to July 1, 1984.

(c) Except as otherwise provided in the time share declaration, the board of directors of a time share project may, by an affirmative vote of two-thirds of the board, amend a provision within the time share declaration, provided that the provision to be changed meets all of the following criteria:
    (1) The provision was adopted as part of the original time share declaration recorded prior to July 1, 1984.
    (2) The provision either converts or provides a mechanism to convert ownership of time share units to tenancy in common.

(d) Title or interest in a time share project or unit is not rendered unmarketable or otherwise affected by reason of an insubstantial failure of the time share declaration to comply with this section. Whether a substantial failure to comply with this section impairs marketability shall be determined by the laws of this State relating to marketability.

(e) This section shall not otherwise impair the ability of the individual time share owner's right under the time share declaration, bylaws, or the laws of this State to vote to terminate the time share project or to amend the declaration to provide for the termination of the time share project and interests. (2014-99, s. 1.)

§ 93A-43. Partition.

When a time share is owned by two or more persons as tenants in common or as joint tenants either may seek a partition by sale of that interest but no purchaser of a time share may maintain an action for partition by sale or in kind of the unit in which such time share is held. (1983, c. 814, s. 1.)

§ 93A-44. Public offering statement.
Each developer shall fully and conspicuously disclose in a public offering statement:
(1) The total financial obligation of the purchaser, which shall include the initial purchase price and any additional charges to which the purchaser may be subject;
(2) Any person who has or may have the right to alter, amend or add to charges to which the purchaser may be subject and the terms and conditions under which such charges may be imposed;
(3) The nature and duration of each agreement between the developer and the person managing the time share program or its facilities;
(4) The date of availability of each amenity and facility of the time share program when they are not completed at the time of sale of a time share;
(5) The specific term of the time share;
(6) The purchaser's right to cancel within five days of execution of the contract and how that right may be exercised under G.S. 93A-45;
(7) A statement that under North Carolina law an instrument conveying a time share must be recorded in the Register of Deeds Office to protect that interest; and
(8) Any other information which the Commission may by rule require.

The public offering statement shall also contain a one page cover containing a summary of the text of the statement. (1983, c. 814, s. 1.)

§ 93A-45. Purchaser's right to cancel; escrow; violation.
(a) A developer shall, before transfer of a time share and no later than the date of any contract of sale, provide a prospective purchaser with a copy of a public offering statement containing the information required by G.S. 93A-44. The contract of sale is voidable by the purchaser for five days after the execution of the contract. The contract shall conspicuously disclose the purchaser's right to cancel under this subsection and how that right may be exercised. The purchaser may not waive this right of cancellation. Any oral or written declaration or instrument that purports to waive this right of cancellation is void.

(b) A purchaser may elect to cancel within the time period set out in subsection (a) by hand delivering or by mailing notice to the developer or the time share salesperson. Cancellation under this section is without penalty and upon receipt of the notice all payments made prior to cancellation must be refunded immediately.

(c) Any payments received by a time share developer or time share salesperson in connection with the sale of the time share shall be immediately deposited by the developer or salesperson in a trust or escrow account in a federally insured depository institution or a trust institution authorized to do business in this State and shall remain in such account for 10 days or cancellation by the purchaser, whichever occurs first. Payments held in such trust or escrow accounts shall be deemed to belong to the purchaser and not the developer. In lieu of such escrow requirements, the Commission shall have the authority to accept, in its discretion, alternative financial assurances adequate to protect the purchaser's interest during the contract cancellation period, including but not limited to a surety bond, corporate bond, cash deposit or irrevocable letter of credit in an amount equal to the escrow requirements.

(d) If a developer fails to provide a purchaser to whom a time share is transferred with the statement as required by subsection (a), the purchaser, in addition to any rights to damages or other relief, is entitled to receive from the developer an amount equal to ten percent (10%) of the sales price of the time share not to exceed three thousand dollars ($3,000). A receipt signed by the purchaser stating that the purchaser has received the statement required by subsection (a) is prima facie evidence of delivery of the statement. (1983, c. 814, s. 1; 1985, c. 578, s. 4.; 2000-140, s. 19(b); 2001-487, s. 23(j); 2017-25, s. 1(*l*).)

§ 93A-46. Prizes.

An advertisement of a time share which includes the offer of a prize or other inducement shall fully comply with the provisions of Chapter 75 of the General Statutes. (1983, c. 814, s. 1.)

§ 93A-47. Time shares proxies.

No proxy, power of attorney or similar device given by the purchaser of a time share regarding the management of the time share program or its facilities shall exceed one year in duration, but the same may be renewed from year to year. (1983, c. 814, s. 1.)

§ 93A-48. Exchange programs.

(a) If a purchaser is offered the opportunity to subscribe to any exchange program, the developer shall, except as provided in subsection (b), deliver to the purchaser, prior to the execution of (i) any contract between the purchaser and the exchange company, and (ii) the sales contract, at least the following information regarding the exchange program:

(1) The name and address of the exchange company;
(2) The names of all officers, directors, and shareholders owning five percent (5%) or more of the outstanding stock of the exchange company;
(3) Whether the exchange company or any of its officers or directors has any legal or beneficial interest in any developer or managing agent for any time share project participating in the exchange program and, if so, the name and location of the time share project and the nature of the interest;
(4) Unless the exchange company is also the developer a statement that the purchaser's contract with the exchange company is a contract separate and distinct from the sales contract;
(5) Whether the purchaser's participation in the exchange program is dependent upon the continued affiliation of the time share project with the exchange program;
(6) Whether the purchaser's membership or participation, or both, in the exchange program is voluntary or mandatory;
(7) A complete and accurate description of the terms and conditions of the purchaser's contractual relationship with the exchange company and the procedure by which changes thereto may be made;

(8) A complete and accurate description of the procedure to qualify for and effectuate exchanges;

(9) A complete and accurate description of all limitations, restrictions, or priorities employed in the operation of the exchange program, including, but not limited to, limitations on exchanges based on seasonality, unit size, or levels of occupancy, expressed in boldfaced type, and, in the event that such limitations, restrictions, or priorities are not uniformly applied by the exchange program, a clear description of the manner in which they are applied;

(10) Whether exchanges are arranged on a space available basis and whether any guarantees of fulfillment of specific requests for exchanges are made by the exchange program;

(11) Whether and under what circumstances an owner, in dealing with the exchange company, may lose the use and occupancy of the owner's time share in any properly applied for exchange without being provided with substitute accommodations by the exchange company;

(12) The expenses, fees or range of fees for participation by owners in the exchange program, a statement whether any such fees may be altered by the exchange company, and the circumstances under which alterations may be made;

(13) The name and address of the site of each time share project or other property which is participating in the exchange program;

(14) The number of units in each project or other property participating in the exchange program which are available for occupancy and which qualify for participation in the exchange program, expressed within the following numerical groupings, 1-5, 6-10, 11-20, 21-50 and 51, and over;

(15) The number of owners with respect to each time share project or other property which are eligible to participate in the exchange program expressed within the following numerical groupings, 1-100, 101-249, 250-499, 500-999, and 1,000 and over, and a statement of the criteria used to determine those owners who are currently eligible to participate in the exchange program;

(16) The disposition made by the exchange company of time shares deposited with the exchange program by owners eligible to participate in the exchange program and not used by the exchange company in effecting exchanges;

(17) The following information which, except as provided in subsection (b) below, shall be independently audited by a certified public accountant in accordance with the standards of the Accounting Standards Board of the American Institute of Certified Public Accountants and reported for each year no later than July 1, of the succeeding year:

    a. The number of owners enrolled in the exchange program and such numbers shall disclose the relationship between the exchange company and owners as being either fee paying or gratuitous in nature;

    b. The number of time share projects or other properties eligible to participate in the exchange program categorized by those having a contractual relationship between the developer or the association and the exchange company and those having solely a contractual relationship between the exchange company and owners directly;

c. The percentage of confirmed exchanges, which shall be the number of exchanges confirmed by the exchange company divided by the number of exchanges properly applied for, together with a complete and accurate statement of the criteria used to determine whether an exchange requested was properly applied for;
d. The number of time shares or other intervals for which the exchange company has an outstanding obligation to provide an exchange to an owner who relinquished a time share or interval during the year in exchange for a time share or interval in any future year; and
e. The number of exchanges confirmed by the exchange company during the year; and

(18) A statement in boldfaced type to the effect that the percentage described in sub-subdivision c. of subdivision (17) of this subsection is a summary of the exchange requests entered with the exchange company in the period reported and that the percentage does not indicate a purchaser's/owner's probabilities of being confirmed to any specific choice or range of choices, since availability at individual locations may vary.

The purchaser shall certify in writing to the receipt of the information required by this subsection and any other information which the Commission may by rule require.

(b) The information required by subdivisions (a)(2), (3), (13), (14), (15), and (17) shall be accurate as of December 31 of the year preceding the year in which the information is delivered, except for information delivered within the first 180 days of any calendar year which shall be accurate as of December 31 of the year two years preceding the year in which the information is delivered to the purchaser. The remaining information required by subsection (a) shall be accurate as of a date which is no more than 30 days prior to the date on which the information is delivered to the purchaser.

(c) In the event an exchange company offers an exchange program directly to the purchaser or owner, the exchange company shall deliver to each purchaser or owner, concurrently with the offering and prior to the execution of any contract between the purchaser or owner and the exchange company the information set forth in subsection (a) above. The requirements of this paragraph shall not apply to any renewal of a contract between an owner and an exchange company.

(d) All promotional brochures, pamphlets, advertisements, or other materials disseminated by the exchange company to purchasers in this State which contain the percentage of confirmed exchanges described in (a)(17)c. must include the statement set forth in (a)(18). (1983, c. 814, s. 1; 2001-487, s. 23(k).)

§ 93A-49. Service of process on exchange company.

Any exchange company offering an exchange program to a purchaser shall be deemed to have made an irrevocable appointment of the Commission to receive service of lawful process in any proceeding against the exchange company arising under this Article. (1983, c. 814, s. 1.)

§ 93A-50. Securities laws apply.

The North Carolina Securities Act, Chapter 78A, shall also apply, in addition to the laws relating to real estate, to time shares deemed to be investment contracts or to other securities offered with or incident to a time share; provided, in the event of such applicability of the North

Carolina Securities Act, any offer or sale of time shares registered under this Article shall not be subject to the provisions of G.S. 78A-24 and any real estate broker registered under Article 1 of this Chapter shall not be subject to the provisions of G.S. 78A-36. (1983, c. 814, s. 1.; 2000-140, s. 19(b); 2005-395, s. 21.)

§ 93A-51. Rule-making authority.

The Commission shall have the authority to adopt rules and regulations that are not inconsistent with the provisions of this Article and the General Statutes of North Carolina. The Commission may prescribe forms and procedures for submitting information to the Commission. (1983, c. 814, s. 1.)

§ 93A-52. Application for registration of time share project; denial of registration; renewal; reinstatement; and termination of developer's interest.

(a) Prior to the offering in this State of any time share located in this State, the developer of the time share project shall make written application to the Commission for the registration of the project. The application shall be accompanied by a fee in an amount fixed by the Commission but not to exceed one thousand five hundred dollars ($1,500), and shall include a description of the project, copies of proposed time share instruments including public offering statements, sale contracts, deeds, and other documents referred to therein, information pertaining to any marketing or managing entity to be employed by the developer for the sale of time shares in a time share project or the management of the project, information regarding any exchange program available to the purchaser, an irrevocable appointment of the Commission to receive service of any lawful process in any proceeding against the developer or the developer's time share salespersons arising under this Article, and such other information as the Commission may by rule require.

Upon receipt of a properly completed application and fee and upon a determination by the Commission that the sale and management of the time shares in the time share project will be directed and conducted by persons of good moral character, the Commission shall issue to the developer a certificate of registration authorizing the developer to offer time shares in the project for sale. The Commission shall within 15 days after receipt of an incomplete application, notify the developer by mail that the Commission has found specified deficiencies, and shall, within 45 days after the receipt of a properly completed application, either issue the certificate of registration or notify the developer by mail of any specific objections to the registration of the project. The certificate shall be prominently displayed in the office of the developer on the site of the project.

The developer shall promptly report to the Commission any and all changes in the information required to be submitted for the purpose of the registration. The developer shall also immediately furnish the Commission complete information regarding any change in its interest in a registered time share project. In the event a developer disposes of, or otherwise terminates its interest in a time share project, the developer shall certify to the Commission in writing that its interest in the time share project is terminated and shall return to the Commission for cancellation the certificate of registration.

(b) In the event the Commission finds that there is substantial reason to deny the application for registration as a time share project, the Commission shall notify the applicant that such application has been denied and shall afford the applicant an opportunity for a hearing before the Commission to show cause why the application should not be denied. In all proceedings to deny a certificate of registration, the provisions of Chapter 150B of the General Statutes shall be applicable.

(c) The acceptance by the Commission of an application for registration shall not constitute the approval of its contents or waive the authority of the Commission to take disciplinary action as provided by this Article.

(d) All certificates of registration granted and issued by the Commission under the provisions of this Article shall expire on the 30th day of June following issuance thereof, and shall become invalid after such date unless reinstated. Renewal of such certificate may be effected at any time during the month of June preceding the date of expiration of such registration upon proper application to the Commission and by the payment of a renewal fee fixed by the Commission but not to exceed one thousand five hundred dollars ($1,500) for each time share project. The developer shall, when making application for renewal, also provide a copy of the report required in G.S. 93A-48. Each certificate reinstated after the expiration date thereof shall be subject to a fee of fifty dollars ($50.00) in addition to the required renewal fee. In the event a time share developer fails to reinstate the registration within 12 months after the expiration date thereof, the Commission may, in its discretion, consider the time share project as not having been previously registered, and thereby subject to the provisions of this Article relating to the issuance of an original certificate. Duplicate certificates may be issued by the Commission upon payment of a fee of one dollar ($1.00) by the registrant developer. Except as prescribed by Commission rules, all fees paid pursuant to this Article shall be nonrefundable. (1983, c. 814, s. 1; 1985, c. 578, s. 5; 1987, c. 827, s. 1; 1999-229, s. 15.; 2000-140, s. 19(b); 2005-395, s. 22.)

§ 93A-53. Register of applicants; roster of registrants; registered projects; financial report to Secretary of State.

(a) The Executive Director of the Commission shall keep a register of all applicants for certificates of registration, showing for each the date of application, name, business address, and whether the certificate was granted or refused.

(b) The Executive Director of the Commission shall also keep a current roster showing the name and address of all time share projects registered with the Commission. The roster shall be kept on file in the office of the Commission and be open to public inspection.

(c) The Commission shall include a copy of the roster of time share projects current on the preceding June 30 and a statement of the income received by the Commission in connection with the registration of time share projects during the fiscal year ending on June 30 with the report required by G.S. 93B-2. (1983, c. 814, s. 1; 2011-217, s. 21.)

§ 93A-54. Disciplinary action by Commission.

(a) The Commission has power to take disciplinary action. Upon its own motion, or on the verified complaint of any person, the Commission may investigate the actions of any time share salesperson, developer, or project broker of a time share project registered under this Article, or any other person or entity who shall assume to act in such capacity. If the Commission finds probable cause that a time share salesperson, developer, or project broker has violated any of the provisions of this Article, the Commission may hold a hearing on the allegations of misconduct.

The Commission has the power to suspend or revoke at any time a real estate license issued to a time share salesperson or project broker, or a certificate of registration of a time share project issued to a developer; or to reprimand or censure such salesperson, developer, or project broker; or to fine such developer in the amount of five hundred dollars ($500.00) for each violation of this Article, if, after a hearing, the Commission adjudges either the salesperson, developer, or project broker to be guilty of:

(1) Making any willful or negligent misrepresentation or any willful or negligent omission of material fact about any time share or time share project;

(2) Making any false promises of a character likely to influence, persuade, or induce;

(3) Pursuing a course of misrepresentation or making of false promises through agents, salespersons, advertising or otherwise;

(4) Failing, within a reasonable time, to account for all money received from others in a time share transaction, and failing to remit such monies as may be required in G.S. 93A-45 of this Article;

(5) Acting as a time share salesperson or time share developer in a manner as to endanger the interest of the public;

(6) Paying a commission, salary, or other valuable consideration to any person for acts or services performed in violation of this Article;

(7) Any other conduct which constitutes improper, fraudulent, or dishonest dealing;

(8) Performing or undertaking to perform any legal service as set forth in G.S. 84-2.1, or any other acts not specifically set forth in that section;

(9) Failing to deposit and maintain in a broker's trust or escrow account as defined by G.S. 93A-6(g) all money received from others in a time share transaction as may be required in G.S. 93A-45 of this Article or failing to place with an independent escrow agent the funds of a time share purchaser when required by G.S. 93A-42(c);

(10) Failing to deliver to a purchaser a public offering statement containing the information required by G.S. 93A-44 and any other disclosures that the Commission may by regulation require;

(11) Failing to comply with the provisions of Chapter 75 of the General Statutes in the advertising or promotion of time shares for sale, or failing to assure such compliance by persons engaged on behalf of a developer;

(12) Failing to comply with the provisions of G.S. 93A-48 in furnishing complete and accurate information to purchasers concerning any exchange program which may be offered to such purchaser;

(13) Making any false or fraudulent representation on an application for registration;

(14) Violating any rule or regulation promulgated by the Commission;

(15) Failing to record or cause to be recorded a time share instrument as required by G.S. 93A-42(c), or failing to provide a purchaser the protection against liens required by G.S. 93A-57(a); or

(16) Failing as a time share project broker to exercise reasonable and adequate supervision of the conduct of sales at a project or location by the brokers and salespersons under the time share project broker's control.

(a1) The clear proceeds of fines collected pursuant to subsection (a) of this section shall be remitted to the Civil Penalty and Forfeiture Fund in accordance with G.S. 115C-457.2.

(b) Following a hearing, the Commission shall also have power to suspend or revoke any certificate of registration issued under the provisions of this Article or to reprimand or censure any developer when the registrant has been convicted or has entered a plea of guilty or no contest upon which final judgment is entered by a court of competent jurisdiction in this State, or any other state, of the criminal offenses of: embezzlement, obtaining money under false pretense, fraud, forgery, conspiracy to defraud, or any other offense involving moral turpitude which would reasonably affect the developer's performance in the time share business.

(c) The Commission may appear in its own name in superior court in actions for injunctive relief to prevent any person or entity from violating the provisions of this Article or rules promulgated by the Commission. The superior court shall have the power to grant these injunctions even if criminal prosecution has been or may be instituted as a result of the violations, or regardless of whether the person or entity has been registered by the Commission.

(d) Each developer shall maintain or cause to be maintained complete records of every time share transaction including records pertaining to the deposit, maintenance, and withdrawal of money required to be held in a trust or escrow account, or as otherwise required by the Commission, under G.S. 93A-45 of this Article. The Commission may inspect these records periodically without prior notice and may also inspect these records whenever the Commission determines that they are pertinent to an investigation of any specific complaint against a registrant.

(e) When a licensee is accused of any act, omission, or misconduct under this Article which would subject the licensee to disciplinary action, the licensee may, with the consent and approval of the Commission, surrender the licensee's license and all the rights and privileges pertaining to it for a period of time to be established by the Commission. A licensee who surrenders a license shall not be eligible for, or submit any application for, licensure as a real estate broker or registration of a time share project during the period of license surrender. For the purposes of this section, the term licensee shall include a time share developer. (1983, c. 814, s. 1; 1985, c. 578, ss. 6-10; 1987, c. 516, ss. 17, 18; 1998-215, s. 138.; 2000-140, s. 19(b); 2001-487, s. 23(l); 2005-395, s. 23; 2011-217, s. 22.)

§ 93A-55. Private enforcement.

The provisions of the Article shall not be construed to limit in any manner the right of a purchaser or other person injured by a violation of this Article to bring a private action. (1983, c. 814, s. 1.)

§ 93A-56. Penalty for violation of Article.

Except as provided in G.S. 93A-40(b) and G.S. 93A-58, any person violating the provisions of this Article shall be guilty of a Class 1 misdemeanor. (1983, c. 814, s. 1; 1985, c. 578, s. 11; 1987, c. 516, s. 19; 1993, c. 539, s. 658; 1994, Ex. Sess., c. 24, s. 14(c).)

§ 93A-57. Release of liens.

(a) Prior to any recordation of the instrument transferring a time share, the developer shall record and furnish notice to the purchaser of a release or subordination of all liens affecting that time share, or shall provide a surety bond or insurance against the lien from a company acceptable to the Commission as provided for liens on real estate in this State, or such underlying lien document shall contain a provision wherein the lienholder subordinates its rights to that of a time share purchaser who fully complies with all of the provisions and terms of the contract of sale.

(b) Unless a time share owner or a time share owner who is his predecessor in title agree otherwise with the lienor, if a lien other than a mortgage or deed of trust becomes effective against more than one time share in a time share project, any time share owner is entitled to a release of his time share from a lien upon payment of the amount of the lien attributable to his time share. The amount of the payment must be proportionate to the ratio that the time share owner's liability bears to the liabilities of all time share owners whose interests are subject to the lien. Upon receipt of payment, the lien holder shall promptly deliver to the time share owner a release of the lien covering that time share. After payment, the managing agent may not assess or have a lien against that time share for any portion of the expenses incurred in connection with that lien. (1983, c. 814, s. 1; 1985, c. 578, s. 12.)

§ 93A-58. Registrar required; criminal penalties; project broker.

(a) Every developer of a registered project shall, by affidavit filed with the Commission, designate a natural person to serve as time share registrar for its registered projects. The registrar shall be responsible for the recordation of time share instruments and the release of liens required by G.S. 93A-42(c) and G.S. 93A-57(a). A developer may, from time to time, change the designated time share registrar by proper filing with the Commission and by otherwise complying with this subsection. No sales or offers to sell shall be made until the registrar is designated for a time share project.

The registrar has the duty to ensure that the provisions of this Article are complied with in a time share project for which the person is registrar. No registrar shall record a time share instrument except as provided by this Article.

(b) A time share registrar is guilty of a Class I felony if he or she knowingly or recklessly fails to record or cause to be recorded a time share instrument as required by this Article.

A person responsible as general partner, corporate officer, joint venturer or sole proprietor of the developer of a time share project is guilty of a Class I felony if the person intentionally allows the offering for sale or the sale of time share to purchasers without first designating a time share registrar.

(c) The developer shall designate for each project and other locations where time shares are sold or offered for sale a project broker. The project broker shall act as supervising broker for all time share salespersons at the project or other location and shall directly, personally, and actively supervise all such persons at the project or other location in a manner to reasonably ensure that the sale of time shares will be conducted in accordance with the provisions of this Chapter. (1985, c. 578, s. 13; 1987, c. 516, s. 20; 1993, c. 539, s. 1289; 1994, Ex. Sess., c. 24, s. 14(c).; 2000-140, s. 19(b); 2001-487, s. 23(m); 2005-395, s. 24.)

§ 93A-59. Preservation of time share purchaser's claims and defenses.

(a) For one year following the execution of an instrument of indebtedness for the purchase of a time share, the purchaser of a time share may assert against the seller, assignee of the seller, or other holder of the instrument of indebtedness, any claims or defenses available against the developer or the original seller, and the purchaser may not waive the right to assert these claims or defenses in connection with a time share purchase. Any recovery by the purchaser on a claim asserted against an assignee of the seller or other holder of the instrument of indebtedness shall not exceed the amount paid by the purchaser under the instrument. A holder shall be the person or entity with the rights of a holder as set forth in G.S. 25-3-301.

(b) Every instrument of indebtedness for the purchase of a time share shall set forth the following provision in a clear and conspicuous manner:

"NOTICE

FOR A PERIOD OF ONE YEAR FOLLOWING THE EXECUTION OF THIS INSTRUMENT OF INDEBTEDNESS, ANY HOLDER OF THIS INSTRUMENT OF INDEBTEDNESS IS SUBJECT TO ALL CLAIMS AND DEFENSES WHICH THE PURCHASER COULD ASSERT AGAINST THE SELLER OF THE TIME SHARE. RECOVERY BY THE PURCHASER SHALL NOT EXCEED AMOUNTS PAID BY THE PURCHASER UNDER THIS INSTRUMENT."

(1985, c. 578, s. 13.)

§§ 93A-60 through 93A-69. Reserved for future codification purposes.

Article 5.

Real Estate Appraisers.

§§ 93A-70 through 93A-81: Repealed by Session Laws 1993, c. 419, s. 7.

Article 6.

Broker Price Opinions and Comparative Market Analyses.

§ 93A-82. Definitions.

As used in this Article, the terms "broker price opinion" and "comparative market analysis" mean an estimate prepared by a licensed real estate broker that details the probable selling price or leasing price of a particular parcel of or interest in property and provides a varying level of detail about the property's condition, market, and neighborhood, and information on comparable properties, but does not include an automated valuation model. (2012-163, s. 2.)

§ 93A-83. Broker price opinions and comparative market analyses for a fee.

(a) Authorized. – A person licensed under this Chapter, other than a provisional broker, may prepare a broker price opinion or comparative market analysis and charge and collect a fee for the opinion if:
    (1) The license of that licensee is active and in good standing; and
    (2) The broker price opinion or comparative market analysis meets the requirements of subsection (c) of this section.

(3) The requirements of this Article shall not apply to any broker price opinion or comparative market analysis performed by a licensee for no fee or consideration.

(b) For Whom Opinion May Be Prepared. – Notwithstanding any provision to the contrary, a person licensed under this Chapter may prepare a broker price opinion or comparative market analysis for any of the following:

(1) An existing or potential seller of a parcel of real property.
(2) An existing or potential buyer of a parcel of real property.
(3) An existing or potential lessor of a parcel of or interest in real property.
(4) An existing or potential lessee of a parcel of or interest in real property.
(5) A third party making decisions or performing due diligence related to the potential listing, offering, sale, option, lease, or acquisition price of a parcel of or interest in real property.
(6) An existing or potential lienholder or other third party for any purpose other than as the basis to determine the value of a parcel of or interest in property, for a mortgage loan origination, including first and second mortgages, refinances, or equity lines of credit.
(7) The provisions of this subsection do not preclude the preparation of a broker price opinion or comparative market analysis to be used in conjunction with or in addition to an appraisal.

(c) Required Contents of a Broker Price Opinion or Comparative Market Analysis. – A broker price opinion or comparative market analysis shall be in writing and conform to the standards provided in this Article that shall include, but are not limited to, the following:

(1) A statement of the intended purpose of the broker price opinion or comparative market analysis.
(2) A brief description of the subject property and property interest to be priced.
(3) The basis of reasoning used to reach the conclusion of the price, including the applicable market data or capitalization computation.
(4) Any assumptions or limiting conditions.
(5) A disclosure of any existing or contemplated interest of the broker issuing the broker price opinion, including the possibility of representing the landlord/tenant or seller/buyer.
(6) The effective date of the broker price opinion.
(7) The name and signature of the broker issuing the broker price opinion and broker license number.
(8) The name of the real estate brokerage firm for which the broker is acting.
(9) The signature date.
(10) A disclaimer stating that "This opinion is not an appraisal of the market value of the property, and may not be used in lieu of an appraisal. If an appraisal is desired, the services of a licensed or certified appraiser shall be obtained. This opinion may not be used by any party as the primary basis to determine the value of a parcel of or interest in real property for a mortgage loan origination, including first and second mortgages, refinances, or equity lines of credit."
(11) A copy of the assignment request for the broker price opinion or comparative market analysis.

(d) Rules. – The North Carolina Real Estate Commission shall have the power to adopt rules that are not inconsistent with the provisions in this Article.

(e) Additional Requirements for Electronic or Form Submission. – In addition to the requirement of subsection (c) of this section, if a broker price opinion is submitted electronically or on a form supplied by the requesting party, the following provisions apply:

 (1) A signature required by subdivision (7) of subsection (c) of this section may be an electronic signature, as defined in G.S. 47-16.2.

 (2) A signature required by subdivision (7) of subsection (c) of this section and the disclaimer required by subdivision (10) of subsection (c) of this section may be transmitted in a separate attachment if the electronic format or form supplied by the requesting party does not allow additional comments to be written by the licensee. The electronic format or form supplied by the requesting party shall do the following:

  a. Reference the existence of a separate attachment.

  b. Include a statement that the broker price opinion or comparative market analysis is not complete without the attachment.

(f) Restrictions. – Notwithstanding any provisions to the contrary, a person licensed pursuant to this Chapter may not knowingly prepare a broker price opinion or comparative market analysis for any purpose in lieu of an appraisal when an appraisal is required by federal or State law. A broker price opinion or comparative market analysis that estimates the value of or worth a parcel of or interest in real estate rather than sales or leasing price shall be deemed to be an appraisal and may not be prepared by a licensed broker under the authority of this Article, but may only be prepared by a duly licensed or certified appraiser, and shall meet the regulations adopted by the North Carolina Appraisal Board. A broker price opinion or comparative market analysis shall not under any circumstances be referred to as a valuation or appraisal.

(g) No Report of Predetermined Result. – A broker price opinion or comparative market analysis shall not include the reporting of a predetermined result. (2012-163, s. 2; 2012-194, s. 61.)

SUBCHAPTER 58A – REAL ESTATE BROKERS

SECTION .0100 - GENERAL BROKERAGE

21 NCAC 58A .0101   PROOF OF LICENSURE
(a) The pocket card issued by the Commission annually to each broker shall be retained by the broker as evidence of licensure. Each broker shall produce a legible form of the card as proof of licensure whenever requested while engaging in real estate brokerage.
(b) Every licensed real estate business entity or firm shall prominently display its license certificate or a copy of its license certificate in each office maintained by the entity or firm. A broker-in-charge shall also display his or her license certificate in the office where he or she is broker-in-charge.
(c) A replacement real estate license or pocket card may be obtained by:
    (1) submitting a written request to the Commission that includes the broker or firm's:
        (A) legal name;
        (B) license number;
        (C) physical and mailing address;
        (D) phone number;
        (E) email address;
        (F) proof of legal name change pursuant to Rule .0103 of this Section, if applicable; and
        (G) signature; and
    (2) paying a five dollar ($5.00) duplicate license fee.

History Note: Authority G.S. 93A-3(c); 93A-4;
        Eff. February 1, 1976;
        Readopted Eff. September 30, 1977;
        Amended Eff. July 1, 2017; July 1, 2005; April 1, 2004; October 1, 2000; September 1, 1998; August 1, 1998; April 1, 1997; February 1, 1989;
        Pursuant to G.S. 150B-21.3A, rule is necessary without substantive public interest Eff. May 1, 2018.

21 NCAC 58A .0102   BRANCH OFFICE

History Note: Authority G.S. 93A-3(c);
        Eff. February 1, 1976;
        Readopted Eff. September 30, 1977;
        Amended Eff. September 1, 1983;
        Repealed Eff. May 1, 1984.

21 NCAC 58A .0103   BROKER NAME AND ADDRESS
(a) Upon initial licensure, every broker shall notify the Commission of the broker's current personal name, firm name, trade name, residence address, firm address, telephone number, and email address. All addresses provided to the Commission shall be sufficiently descriptive to enable the Commission to correspond with and locate the broker.
(b) Every broker shall notify the Commission in writing of each change of personal name, firm name, trade name, residence address, firm address, telephone number, and email address within 10 days of said change. A broker notifying the Commission of a change of legal name or firm name shall also provide evidence of a legal name change for either the individual or firm, such as a court order or name change amendment from the Secretary of State's Office.
(c) In the event that any broker shall advertise or operate in any manner using a name different from the name under which the broker is licensed, the broker shall first file an assumed name certificate in compliance with G.S. 66–71.4 and shall notify the Commission in writing of the use of such a firm name or assumed name. An individual broker shall not advertise or operate in any manner that would mislead a consumer as to the broker's actual identity or as to the identity of the firm with which he or she is affiliated.
(d) A broker shall not include the name of a provisional broker or an unlicensed person in the legal or assumed name of a sole proprietorship, partnership, or business entity other than a corporation or limited liability company. No broker shall use a business name that includes the name of any current or former broker without the permission of that broker or that broker's authorized representative.

History Note: Authority G.S. 55B-5; 66-68; 93A-3(c); 93A-6(a)(1);
Eff. February 1, 1976;
Readopted Eff. September 30, 1977;
Amended Eff. July 1, 2017; July 1, 2016; April 1, 2013; August 1, 1998; February 1, 1989; May 1, 1984;
Pursuant to G.S. 150B-21.3A, rule is necessary without substantive public interest Eff. May 1, 2018.

21 NCAC 58A .0104   AGENCY AGREEMENTS AND DISCLOSURE
(a) Every agreement for brokerage services in a real estate transaction and every agreement for services connected with the management of a property owners association shall be in writing and signed by the parties thereto. Every agreement for brokerage services between a broker and an owner of the property to be the subject of a transaction shall be in writing and signed by the parties at the time of its formation. Every agreement for brokerage services between a broker and a buyer or tenant shall be express and shall be in writing and signed by the parties thereto not later than the time one of the parties makes an offer to purchase, sell, rent, lease, or exchange real estate to another. However, every agreement between a broker and a buyer or tenant that seeks to bind the buyer or tenant for a period of time or to restrict the buyer's or tenant's right to work with other agents or without an agent shall be in writing and signed by the parties thereto from its formation. A broker shall not continue to represent a buyer or tenant without a written, signed agreement when such agreement is required by this Rule. Every written agreement for brokerage services of any kind in a real estate transaction shall be for a definite period of time, shall include the broker's license number, and shall provide for its termination without prior notice at the expiration of that period, except that an agency agreement between a landlord and broker to procure tenants or receive rents for the landlord's property may allow for automatic renewal so long as the landlord may terminate with notice at the end of any contract period and any subsequent renewals. Every written agreement for brokerage services that includes a penalty for early termination shall set forth such a provision in a clear and conspicuous manner that shall distinguish it from other provisions of the agreement. For the purposes of this Rule, an agreement between brokers to cooperate or share compensation shall not be considered an agreement for brokerage services and, except as required by Rule .1807 of this Subchapter, need not be memorialized in writing.
(b) Every listing agreement, written buyer agency agreement, or other written agreement for brokerage services in a real estate transaction shall contain the following provision: "The broker shall conduct all brokerage activities in regard to this agreement without respect to the race, color, religion, sex, national origin, handicap, or familial status of any party or prospective party." The provision shall be set forth in a clear and conspicuous manner that shall distinguish it from other provisions of the agreement. For the purposes of this Rule, the term, "familial status" shall be defined as it is in G.S. 41A-3(1b).
(c) In every real estate sales transaction, a broker shall, at first substantial contact with a prospective buyer or seller, provide the prospective buyer or seller with a copy of the publication "Working with Real Estate Agents," set forth the broker's name and license number thereon, review the publication with the buyer or seller, and determine whether the agent will act as the agent of the buyer or seller in the transaction. If the first substantial contact with a prospective buyer or seller occurs by telephone or other electronic means of communication where it is not practical to provide the "Working with Real Estate Agents" publication, the broker shall at the earliest opportunity thereafter, but in no event later than three days from the date of first substantial contact, mail or otherwise transmit a copy of the publication to the prospective buyer or seller and review it with him or her at the earliest practicable opportunity thereafter. For the purposes of this Rule, "first substantial contact" shall include contacts between a broker and a consumer where the consumer or broker begins to act as though an agency relationship exists and the consumer begins to disclose to the broker personal or confidential information. The "Working with Real Estate Agents" publication may be obtained on the Commission's website at www.ncrec.gov or upon request to the Commission.
(d) A real estate broker representing one party in a transaction shall not undertake to represent another party in the transaction without the written authority of each party. The written authority shall be obtained upon the formation of the relationship except when a buyer or tenant is represented by a broker without a written agreement in conformity with the requirements of Paragraph (a) of this Rule. Under such circumstances, the written authority for dual agency shall be reduced to writing not later than the time that one of the parties represented by the broker makes an offer to purchase, sell, rent, lease, or exchange real estate to another party.
(e) In every real estate sales transaction, a broker working directly with a prospective buyer as a seller's agent or subagent shall disclose in writing to the prospective buyer at the first substantial contact with the prospective buyer that the broker represents the interests of the seller. The written disclosure shall include the broker's license number.

If the first substantial contact occurs by telephone or by means of other electronic communication where it is not practical to provide written disclosure, the broker shall immediately disclose by similar means whom he or she represents and shall immediately mail or otherwise transmit a copy of the written disclosure to the buyer. In no event shall the broker mail or transmit a copy of the written disclosure to the buyer later than three days from the date of first substantial contact with the buyer.

(f) In every real estate sales transaction, a broker representing a buyer shall, at the initial contact with the seller or seller's agent, disclose to the seller or seller's agent that the broker represents the buyer's interests. In addition, in every real estate sales transaction other than auctions, the broker shall, no later than the time of delivery of an offer to the seller or seller's agent, provide the seller or seller's agent with a written confirmation disclosing that he or she represents the interests of the buyer. The written confirmation may be made in the buyer's offer to purchase and shall include the broker's license number.

(g) The provisions of Paragraphs (c), (d) and (e) of this Rule do not apply to real estate brokers representing sellers in auction sales transactions.

(h) A broker representing a buyer in an auction sale transaction shall, no later than the time of execution of a written agreement memorializing the buyer's contract to purchase, provide the seller or seller's agent with a written confirmation disclosing that he or she represents the interests of the buyer. The written confirmation may be made in the written agreement.

(i) A firm that represents more than one party in the same real estate transaction is a dual agent and, through the brokers associated with the firm, shall disclose its dual agency to the parties.

(j) When a firm represents both the buyer and seller in the same real estate transaction, the firm may, with the prior express approval of its buyer and seller clients, designate one or more individual brokers associated with the firm to represent only the interests of the seller and one or more other individual brokers associated with the firm to represent only the interests of the buyer in the transaction. The authority for designated agency shall be reduced to writing not later than the time that the parties are required to reduce their dual agency agreement to writing in accordance with Paragraph (d) of this Rule. An individual broker shall not be so designated and shall not undertake to represent only the interests of one party if the broker has actually received confidential information concerning the other party in connection with the transaction. A broker-in-charge shall not act as a designated broker for a party in a real estate sales transaction when a provisional broker under his or her supervision will act as a designated broker for another party with a competing interest.

(k) When a firm acting as a dual agent designates an individual broker to represent the seller, the broker so designated shall represent only the interest of the seller and shall not, without the seller's permission, disclose to the buyer or a broker designated to represent the buyer:
  (1) that the seller may agree to a price, terms, or any conditions of sale other than those established by the seller;
  (2) the seller's motivation for engaging in the transaction unless disclosure is otherwise required by statute or rule; and
  (3) any information about the seller that the seller has identified as confidential unless disclosure of the information is otherwise required by statute or rule.

(l) When a firm acting as a dual agent designates an individual broker to represent the buyer, the broker so designated shall represent only the interest of the buyer and shall not, without the buyer's permission, disclose to the seller or a broker designated to represent the seller:
  (1) that the buyer may agree to a price, terms, or any conditions of sale other than those established by the seller;
  (2) the buyer's motivation for engaging in the transaction unless disclosure is otherwise required by statute or rule; and
  (3) any information about the buyer that the buyer has identified as confidential unless disclosure of the information is otherwise required by statute or rule.

(m) A broker designated to represent a buyer or seller in accordance with Paragraph (j) of this Rule shall disclose the identity of all of the brokers so designated to both the buyer and the seller. The disclosure shall take place no later than the presentation of the first offer to purchase or sell.

(n) When an individual broker represents both the buyer and seller in the same real estate sales transaction pursuant to a written agreement authorizing dual agency, the parties may provide in the written agreement that the broker shall not disclose the following information about one party to the other without permission from the party about whom the information pertains:
  (1) that a party may agree to a price, terms, or any conditions of sale other than those offered;

(2) the motivation of a party for engaging in the transaction, unless disclosure is otherwise required by statute or rule; and
(3) any information about a party that the party has identified as confidential, unless disclosure is otherwise required by statute or rule.

(o) A broker who is selling property in which the broker has an ownership interest shall not undertake to represent a buyer of that property except that a broker who is selling commercial real estate as defined in Rule .1802 of this Subchapter in which the broker has less than 25 percent ownership interest may represent a buyer of that property if the buyer consents to the representation after full written disclosure of the broker's ownership interest. A firm listing a property owned by a broker affiliated with the firm may represent a buyer of that property so long as any individual broker representing the buyer on behalf of the firm does not have an ownership interest in the property and the buyer consents to the representation after full written disclosure of the broker's ownership interest.

(p) A broker or firm with an existing listing agreement for a property shall not enter into a contract to purchase that property unless, prior to entering into the contract, the listing broker or firm first discloses in writing to their seller-client that the listing broker or firm may have a conflict of interest in the transaction and that the seller-client may want to seek independent counsel of an attorney or another licensed broker. Prior to the listing broker entering into a contract to purchase the listed property, the listing broker and firm shall either terminate the listing agreement or transfer the listing to another broker affiliated with the firm. Prior to the listing firm entering into a contract to purchase the listed property, the listing broker and firm shall disclose to the seller-client in writing that the seller-client has the right to terminate the listing and the listing broker and firm shall terminate the listing upon the request of the seller-client.

History Note: Authority G.S. 41A-3(1b); 41A-4(a); 93A-3(c); 93A-6(a);
Eff. February 1, 1976;
Readopted Eff. September 30, 1977;
Amended Eff. July 1, 2015; July 1, 2014; July 1, 2009; July 1, 2008; April 1, 2006; July 1, 2005; July 1, 2004; April 1, 2004; September 1, 2002; July 1, 2001; October 1, 2000; August 1, 1998; July 1, 1997; August 1, 1996; July 1, 1995;
Pursuant to G.S. 150B-21.3A, rule is necessary without substantive public interest Eff. May 1, 2018.

21 NCAC 58A .0105   ADVERTISING
(a) Authority to Advertise.
(1) A broker shall not advertise any brokerage service or the sale, purchase, exchange, rent, or lease of real estate for another or others without the consent of his or her broker-in-charge and without including in the advertisement the name of the firm or sole proprietorship with which the broker is affiliated.
(2) A broker shall not advertise or display a "for sale" or "for rent" sign on any real estate without the written consent of the owner or the owner's authorized agent.

(b) Blind Ads. A broker shall not advertise the sale, purchase, exchange, rent, or lease of real estate for others in a manner indicating the offer to sell, purchase, exchange, rent, or lease is being made by the broker's principal only. Every such advertisement shall indicate that it is the advertisement of a broker or firm and shall not be confined to publication of only contact information, such as a post office box number, telephone number, street address, internet web address, or e-mail address.

(c) A person licensed as a limited nonresident commercial broker shall comply with the provisions of Rule .1809 of this Subchapter in connection with all advertising concerning or relating to his or her status as a North Carolina broker.

History Note: Authority G.S. 93A-2(a1); 93A-3(c); 93A-9;
Eff. February 1, 1976;
Readopted Eff. September 30, 1977;
Amended Eff. July 1, 2015; April 1, 2013; July 1, 2009; January 1, 2008; April 1, 2006; July 1, 2004; October 1, 2000; August 1, 1998; April 1, 1997; July 1, 1989; February 1, 1989;
Pursuant to G.S. 150B-21.3A, rule is necessary without substantive public interest Eff. May 1, 2018;
Amended Eff. July 1, 2018.

21 NCAC 58A .0106   DELIVERY OF INSTRUMENTS
(a) Except as provided in Paragraph (b) of this Rule, every broker shall deliver a copy of any written agency agreement, contract, offer, lease, rental agreement, option, or other related transaction document to their customer or client within three days of the broker's receipt of the executed document.
(b) A broker may be relieved of the duty to deliver copies of leases or rental agreements to a property owner pursuant to Paragraph (a) of this Rule if the broker:
  (1) obtains the prior written authority of the property owner to enter into and retain copies of leases or rental agreements on behalf of the property owner;
  (2) executes the lease or rental agreement on a pre-printed form, the material terms of which may not be changed by the broker without prior approval by the property owner, except as may be required by law; and
  (3) delivers to the property owner an accounting within 45 days following the date of execution of the lease or rental agreement that identifies:
    (A) the leased property;
    (B) the name, phone number, and home address of each tenant; and
    (C) the rental rates and rents collected.
(c) Paragraph (b) of this Rule notwithstanding, upon the request of a property owner, a broker shall deliver a copy of any lease or rental agreement within five days.

History Note: *Authority G.S. 93A-3(c);*
                  Eff. February 1, 1976;
                  Readopted Eff. September 30, 1977;
                  Amended Eff. July 1, 2017; July 1, 2005; July 1, 2001; October 1, 2000; May 1, 1990; July 1, 1989; February 1, 1989;
                  Pursuant to G.S. 150B-21.3A, rule is necessary without substantive public interest Eff. May 1, 2018;
                  Amended Eff. July 1, 2018.

21 NCAC 58A .0107   HANDLING AND ACCOUNTING OF FUNDS

History Note: *Authority G.S. 93A-3(c); 93A-9;*
                  Eff. February 1, 1976;
                  Readopted Eff. September 30, 1977;
                  Amended Eff. January 1, 2012; April 1, 2006; July 1, 2005; July 1, 2004; July 1, 2003; September 1, 2002; August 1, 2000; August 1, 1998; July 1, 1996; July 1, 1993; May 1, 1990.
                  Repealed Eff. April 1, 2013.

21 NCAC 58A .0108   RETENTION OF RECORDS
(a) Brokers shall retain records of all sales, rental, and other transactions conducted in such capacity, whether the transaction is pending, completed, or terminated. The broker shall retain records for three years after all funds held by the broker in connection with the transaction have been disbursed to the proper party or parties or the conclusion of the transaction, whichever occurs later. If the broker's agency agreement is terminated prior to the conclusion of the transaction, the broker shall retain such records for three years after the termination of the agency agreement or the disbursement of all funds held by or paid to the broker in connection with the transaction, whichever occurs later.
(b) Records shall include copies of the following:
  (1) contracts of sale;
  (2) written leases;
  (3) agency contracts;
  (4) options;
  (5) offers to purchase;
  (6) trust or escrow records;
  (7) earnest money receipts;
  (8) disclosure documents;
  (9) closing statements;
  (10) brokerage cooperation agreements;

(11) declarations of affiliation;
(12) broker price opinions and comparative market analyses prepared pursuant to G.S. 93A, Article 6, including any notes and supporting documentation;
(13) sketches, calculations, photos, and other documentation used or relied upon to determine square footage;
(14) advertising used to market a property; and
(15) any other records pertaining to real estate transactions.

(c) All records shall be made available for inspection and reproduction by the Commission or its authorized representatives without prior notice.

(d) Brokers shall provide a copy of the written agency disclosure and acknowledgement thereof when applicable, written agency agreement, contract, offer, lease, rental agreement, option, or other related transaction document to the firm or sole proprietorship with which they are affiliated within three days of receipt.

History Note: *Authority G.S. 93A-3(c);*
Eff. February 1, 1976;
Readopted Eff. September 30, 1977;
Amended Eff. July 1, 2004; September 1, 2002; August 1, 1998; February 1, 1989; February 1, 1998;
Temporary Amendment Eff. October 1, 2012;
Amended Eff. July 1, 2018; July 1, 2016; April 1, 2013.

21 NCAC 58A .0109   BROKERAGE FEES AND COMPENSATION

(a) A licensee shall not receive, either directly or indirectly, any commission, rebate or other valuable consideration of more than nominal value from a vendor or a supplier of goods and services for an expenditure made on behalf of the licensee's principal in a real estate transaction without the written consent of the licensee's principal.

(b) A licensee shall not receive, either directly or indirectly, any commission, rebate, or other valuable consideration of more than nominal value for services which the licensee recommends, procures, or arranges relating to a real estate transaction for a party, without full and timely disclosure to such party.

(c) In a real estate sales transaction, a broker shall not receive any compensation, incentive, bonus, rebate, or other consideration of more than nominal value:

(1) from his principal unless the compensation, incentive, bonus, rebate, or other consideration is provided for in a written agency contract prepared in conformity with the requirements of 21 NCAC 58A .0104.
(2) from any other party or person unless the broker provides full and timely disclosure of the incentive, bonus, rebate, or other consideration, or the promise or expectation thereof to the broker's principal. The disclosure may be made orally, but must be confirmed in writing before the principal makes or accepts an offer to buy or sell.

(d) Full disclosure shall include a description of the compensation, incentive, bonus, rebate, or other consideration including its value and the identity of the person or party by whom it will or may be paid. A disclosure is timely when it is made in sufficient time to aid a reasonable person's decision-making.

(e) Nothing in this rule shall be construed to require a broker to disclose to a person not his principal the compensation the broker expects to receive from his principal or to disclose to his principal the compensation the broker expects to receive from the broker's employing broker. For the purpose of this Rule, nominal value means of insignificant, token, or merely symbolic worth.

(f) The Commission shall not act as a board of arbitration and shall not compel parties to settle disputes concerning such matters as the rate of commissions, the division of commissions, pay of brokers, and similar matters.

(g) Except as provided in (h) of this rule, a licensee shall not undertake in any manner, any arrangement, contract, plan or other course of conduct, to compensate or share compensation with unlicensed persons or entities for any acts performed in North Carolina for which licensure by the Commission is required.

(h) A broker may pay or promise to pay consideration to a travel agent in return for procuring a tenant for a vacation rental as defined by the Vacation Rental Act if:

(1) the travel agent only introduces the tenant to the broker, but does not otherwise engage in any activity which would require a real estate license;
(2) the introduction by the travel agent is made in the regular course of the travel agent's business; and
(3) the travel agent has not solicited, handled or received any monies in connection with the vacation rental.

For the purpose of this Rule, a travel agent is any person or entity who is primarily engaged in the business of acting as an intermediary between persons who purchase air, land, and ocean travel services and the providers of such services. A travel agent is also any other person or entity who is permitted to handle and sell tickets for air travel by the Airlines Reporting Corporation (ARC). Payments authorized hereunder shall be made only after the conclusion of the vacation rental tenancy. Prior to the creation of a binding vacation rental agreement, the broker shall provide a tenant introduced by a travel agent a written statement advising him or her to rely only upon the agreement and the broker's representations about the transaction. The broker shall keep for a period of three years records of a payment made to a travel agent including records identifying the tenant, the travel agent and their addresses, the property and dates of the tenancy, and the amount paid.

(i) Nothing in this Rule shall be construed to permit a licensee to accept any fee, kickback or other valuable consideration that is prohibited by the Real Estate Settlement Procedures Act (12 USC 2601 et. seq.) or any rules and regulations promulgated by the United States Department of Housing and Urban Development pursuant to said Act or to fail to make any disclosure required by said Act or rules.

History Note: Authority G.S. 93A-3(c) ; 93A-6(a)(1); 93A-6(a)(4);
Eff. February 1, 1976;
Readopted Eff. September 30, 1977;
Amended Eff. October 1, 2008; April 1, 2006; July 1, 2005; September 1, 2002; August 1, 2000; August 1, 1998; April 1, 1997; July 1, 1989; November 1, 1987;
Pursuant to G.S. 150B-21.3A, rule is necessary without substantive public interest Eff. May 1, 2018.

21 NCAC 58A .0110   BROKER-IN-CHARGE

(a) Every real estate firm shall designate one BIC for its principal office and one BIC for each of its branch offices. No office of a firm shall have more than one designated BIC. A BIC shall not serve as BIC for more than one office unless each of those offices share the same physical office space and delivery address.

(b) Every broker who is a sole proprietor shall designate himself or herself as a BIC if the broker:

- (1) engages in any transaction where the broker is required to deposit and maintain monies belonging to others in a trust account;
- (2) engages in advertising or promoting his or her services as a broker in any manner; or
- (3) has one or more other brokers affiliated with him or her in the real estate business.

(c) A licensed real estate firm shall not be required to have a BIC if it:

- (1) is organized for the sole purpose of receiving compensation for brokerage services furnished by its qualifying broker through another firm or broker;
- (2) is treated for tax purposes as a Subchapter S corporation by the United States Internal Revenue Service;
- (3) has no principal or branch office; and
- (4) has no licensed person associated with it other than its qualifying broker.

(d) A broker who maintains a trust or escrow account for the sole purpose of holding residential tenant security deposits received by the broker on properties owned by the broker in compliance with G.S. 42-50 shall not be required to be a BIC.

(e) In order for a broker to designate as a BIC for a sole proprietor, real estate firm, or branch office, a broker shall apply for BIC Eligible status by submitting an application on a form available on the Commission's website. The BIC Eligible status form shall include the broker's:

- (1) name;
- (2) license number;
- (3) telephone number;
- (4) email address;
- (5) criminal history and history of occupational license disciplinary actions;
- (6) certification of compliance with G.S. 93A-4.2, including that:
  - (A) his or her broker license is on active status;
  - (B) the broker possesses at least two years of full-time or four years of part-time real estate brokerage experience within the previous five years or shall be a North Carolina licensed attorney with a practice that consisted primarily of handling real estate closings and related matters in North Carolina for three years immediately preceding application; and

(C) the broker completed the 12-hour Broker-in-Charge Course no earlier than one year prior to application and no later than 120 days after application; and
- (7) signature.

(f) A broker who holds BIC Eligible status shall submit a form to become the designated BIC for a sole proprietor, real estate firm, or branch office. The BIC designation form shall include:
- (1) the broker's:
  - (A) name;
  - (B) license number;
  - (C) telephone number;
  - (D) email address; and
  - (E) criminal history and history of occupational license disciplinary actions; and
- (2) the firm's:
  - (A) name; and
  - (B) license number, if applicable;

(g) A designated BIC shall:
- (1) assure that each broker employed at the office has complied with Rules .0503, .0504, and .0506 of this Subchapter;
- (2) notify the Commission of any change of firm's business address or trade name and the registration of any assumed business name adopted by the firm for its use;
- (3) be responsible for the conduct of advertising by or in the name of the firm at such office;
- (4) maintain the trust or escrow account of the firm and the records pertaining thereto;
- (5) retain and maintain records relating to transactions conducted by or on behalf of the firm, including those required to be retained pursuant to Rule .0108 of this Section;
- (6) supervise provisional brokers associated with or engaged on behalf of the firm at such office in accordance with the requirements of Rule .0506 of this Subchapter;
- (7) supervise all brokers employed at the office with respect to adherence to agency agreement and disclosure requirements; and
- (8) notify the Commission in writing that he or she is no longer serving as BIC of a particular office within 10 days following any such change.

(h) A broker holding BIC Eligible status shall take the Broker-in-Charge Update Course during the license year of designation, unless the broker has satisfied the requirements of Rule .1702 of this Subchapter prior to designation.

(i) A broker's BIC Eligible status shall terminate if the broker:
- (1) made any false statements or presented any false, incomplete, or incorrect information in connection with an application;
- (2) fails to complete the 12-hour Broker-in-Charge Course pursuant to Paragraph (e) of this Rule;
- (3) fails to renew his or her broker license pursuant to Rule .0503 of this Subchapter, or the broker's license has been suspended, revoked, or surrendered; or
- (4) fails to complete the Broker-in-Charge Update Course and a four credit hour elective course pursuant to Rules .1702 and .1711 of this Subchapter, if applicable.

(j) In order to regain BIC Eligible status after a broker's BIC Eligible status terminates, the broker shall complete the 12-hour Broker-in-Charge Course prior to application and then submit a BIC Eligible status form pursuant to Paragraph (e) of this Rule.

(k) A nonresident commercial real estate broker licensed under the provisions of Section .1800 of this Subchapter shall not act as or serve in the capacity of a broker-in-charge of a firm or office in North Carolina.

History Note: *Authority G.S. 93A-2; 93A-3(c); 93A-4; 93A-4.1; 93A-4.2; 93A-9;*
Eff. September 1, 1983;
Amended Eff. July 1, 2014; May 1, 2013; July 1, 2010; July 1, 2009; January 1, 2008; April 1, 2006; July 1, 2005; July 1, 2004; April 1, 2004; September 1, 2002; July 1, 2001; October 1, 2000; August 1, 1998; April 1, 1997; July 1, 1995; July 1, 1994;
Pursuant to G.S. 150B-21.3A, rule is necessary without substantive public interest Eff. May 1, 2018;
Amended Eff. July 1, 2018.

21 NCAC 58A .0111   DRAFTING LEGAL INSTRUMENTS

(a) A broker acting as an agent in a real estate transaction shall not draft offers, sales contracts, options, leases, promissory notes, deeds, deeds of trust or other legal instruments by which the rights of others are secured; however, a broker may complete preprinted offers, option contracts, sales contracts or lease forms in a real estate transaction when authorized or directed to do so by the parties.

(b) A broker may use electronic, computer, or word processing equipment to store preprinted offer and sales contract forms which comply with Rule .0112, as well as preprinted option and lease forms, and may use such equipment to complete and print offer, contract and lease documents. Provided, however, a broker shall not alter the preprinted form before it is presented to the parties. If the parties propose to delete or change any word or provision in the form, the form must be marked to indicate the change or deletion made. The language of the form shall not be modified, rewritten, or changed by the broker or their clerical employees unless directed to do so by the parties.

(c) Nothing contained in this Rule shall be construed to prohibit a broker from making written notes, memoranda or correspondence recording the negotiations of the parties to a real estate transaction when such notes, memoranda or correspondence do not themselves constitute binding agreements or other legal instruments.

History Note: Authority G.S. 93A-3(c);
Eff. July 1, 1988;
Amended Eff. April 1, 2013; April 1, 2006; October 1, 2000; February 1, 1989;
Pursuant to G.S. 150B-21.3A, rule is necessary without substantive public interest Eff. May 1, 2018.

21 NCAC 58A .0112   OFFERS AND SALES CONTRACTS

(a) A broker acting as an agent in a real estate transaction shall not use a preprinted offer or sales contract form unless the form describes or specifically requires the entry of the following information:

(1) the names of the buyer and seller;
(2) a legal description of the real property sufficient to identify and distinguish it from all other property;
(3) an itemization of any personal property to be included in the transaction;
(4) the purchase price and manner of payment;
(5) any portion of the purchase price that will be paid by a promissory note, including the amount, interest rate, payment terms, whether or not the note is to be secured, and any other terms contained in the promissory note deemed material by the parties;
(6) any portion of the purchase price that is to be paid by the assumption of an existing loan, including the amount of such loan, costs to be paid by the buyer or seller, the interest rate and number of discount points and a condition that the buyer must be able to qualify for the assumption of the loan and must make every reasonable effort to qualify for the assumption of the loan;
(7) the amount of earnest money, if any, the method of payment, the name of the broker or firm that will serve as escrow agent, an acknowledgment of earnest money receipt by the escrow agent, and the criteria for determining disposition of the earnest money, including disputed earnest money, consistent with Commission Rule .0116 of this Subchapter;
(8) any loan that must be obtained by the buyer as a condition of the contract, including the amount and type of loan, interest rate and number of discount points, loan term, and who shall pay loan closing costs, and a condition that the buyer shall make every reasonable effort to obtain the loan;
(9) a general statement of the buyer's intended use of the property and a condition that such use must not be prohibited by private restriction or governmental regulation;
(10) the amount and purpose of any special assessment to which the property is subject and the responsibility of the parties for any unpaid charges;
(11) the date for closing and transfer of possession;
(12) the signatures of the buyer and seller;
(13) the date of offer and acceptance;
(14) a provision that title to the property must be delivered at closing by general warranty deed and must be fee simple marketable title, free of all encumbrances except ad valorem taxes for the current year, utility easements, and any other encumbrances specifically approved by the buyer or a provision otherwise describing the estate to be conveyed with encumbrances, and the form of conveyance;
(15) the items to be prorated or adjusted at closing;
(16) who shall pay closing expenses;

(17) the buyer's right to inspect the property prior to closing and who shall pay for repairs and improvements, if any;
(18) a provision that the property shall at closing be in substantially the same condition as on the date of the offer (reasonable wear and tear excepted), or a description of the required property condition at closing;
(19) a provision setting forth the identity of each real estate agent and firm involved in the transaction and disclosing the party each agent and firm represents; and
(20) any other provisions or disclosures required by statute or rule.

(b) A broker acting as an agent in a real estate transaction shall not use a preprinted offer or sales contract form containing:
(1) any provision concerning the payment of a commission or compensation, including the forfeiture of earnest money, to any broker or firm; or
(2) any provision that attempts to disclaim the liability of a broker for his or her representations in connection with the transaction.

A broker or anyone acting for or at the direction of the broker shall not insert or cause such provisions or terms to be inserted into any such preprinted form, even at the direction of the parties or their attorneys.

(c) The provisions of this Rule shall apply only to preprinted offer and sales contract forms which a broker acting as an agent in a real estate transaction proposes for use by the buyer and seller. Nothing contained in this Rule shall be construed to prohibit the buyer and seller in a real estate transaction from altering, amending or deleting any provision in a form offer to purchase or contract nor shall this Rule be construed to limit the rights of the buyer and seller to draft their own offers or contracts or to have the same drafted by an attorney at law.

History Note: *Authority G.S. 93A-3(c);*
Eff. July 1, 1988;
Amended Eff. July 1, 2014; July 1, 2010; July 1, 2009; April 1, 2006; October 1, 2000; July 1, 1995; July 1, 1989; February 1, 1989;
Pursuant to G.S. 150B-21.3A, rule is necessary without substantive public interest Eff. May 1, 2018.

21 NCAC 58A .0113   REPORTING CRIMINAL CONVICTIONS AND DISCIPLINARY ACTIONS

Any broker who is convicted of any felony or misdemeanor, or who is disciplined by or enters into a conciliation agreement or consent order with any governmental agency in connection with any occupational license, or whose notarial commission is restricted, suspended, or revoked, shall file with the Commission a Criminal Conviction Disciplinary Action Reporting Form of such conviction or action within 60 days of the final judgment, order, or disposition in the case. The Criminal Conviction Disciplinary Action Reporting Form is available on the Commission's website at www.ncrec.gov or upon request to the Commission. In the Form, the broker shall set forth the broker's:
(1) full legal name;
(2) physical and mailing address;
(3) real estate license number;
(4) telephone number;
(5) email address;
(6) social security number;
(7) date of birth; and
(8) description of the criminal conviction and disciplinary action, including the jurisdiction and file number.

History Note: *Authority G.S. 93A-3(c); 93A-6(a); 93A-6(a)(10); 93A-6(b)(2);*
Eff. August 1, 1996;
Amended Eff. July 1, 2016; July 1, 2009; January 1, 2008; April 1, 2006; July 1, 2003; July 1, 2000;
Pursuant to G.S. 150B-21.3A, rule is necessary without substantive public interest Eff. May 1, 2018.

21 NCAC 58A .0114   RESIDENTIAL PROPERTY AND OWNERS' ASSOCIATION DISCLOSURE STATEMENT

(a) Every owner of real property subject to a transfer of the type governed by Chapter 47E of the General Statutes shall complete the following Residential Property and Owners' Association Disclosure Statement and furnish a copy of the complete statement to a buyer in accordance with the requirements of G.S. 47E-4. The form shall bear the seal of the North Carolina Real Estate Commission and shall read as follows:

[N.C. REAL ESTATE COMMISSION SEAL]

STATE OF NORTH CAROLINA
RESIDENTIAL PROPERTY AND OWNERS' Association DISCLOSURE STATEMENT

Instructions to Property Owners

1. The Residential Property Disclosure Act (G.S. 47E)("Disclosure Act") requires owners of residential real estate (single-family homes, individual condominiums, townhouses, and the like, and buildings with up to four dwelling units) to furnish buyers a Residential Property and Owners' Association Disclosure Statement ("Disclosure Statement"). This form is the only one approved for this purpose. A disclosure statement must be furnished in connection with the sale, exchange, option, and sale under a lease with option to purchase where the tenant does not occupy or intend to occupy the dwelling. A disclosure statement is not required for some transactions, including the first sale of a dwelling which has never been inhabited and transactions of residential property made pursuant to a lease with option to purchase where the lessee occupies or intends to occupy the dwelling. For a complete list of exemptions, see G.S. 47E-2.

2. You must respond to each of the questions on the following pages of this form by filling in the requested information or by placing a check (√) in the appropriate box. In responding to questions, you are only obligated to disclose information about which you have actual knowledge.

   a. If you check "Yes" for any question, you must explain your answer and either describe any problem or attach a report from an attorney, engineer, contractor, pest control operator or other expert or public agency describing it. If you attach a report, you will not be liable for any inaccurate or incomplete information contained in it so long as you were not grossly negligent in obtaining or transmitting the information.

   b. If you check "No," you are stating that you have no actual knowledge of any problem. If you check "No" and you know there is a problem, you may be liable for making an intentional misstatement.

   c. If you check "No Representation," you are choosing not to disclose the conditions or characteristics of the property, even if you have actual knowledge of them or should have known of them.

   d. If you check "Yes" or "No" and something happens to the property to make your Disclosure Statement incorrect or inaccurate (for example, the roof begins to leak), you must promptly give the buyer a corrected Disclosure Statement or correct the problem.

3. If you are assisted in the sale of your property by a licensed real estate broker, you are still responsible for completing and delivering the Disclosure Statement to the buyers; and the broker must disclose any material facts about your property which he or she knows or reasonably should know, regardless of your responses on the Statement.

4. You must give the completed Disclosure Statement to the buyer no later than the time the buyer makes an offer to purchase your property. If you do not, the buyer can, under certain conditions, cancel any resulting contract (See **"Note to Buyers"** below). You should give the buyer a copy of the Disclosure Statement containing your signature and keep a copy signed by the buyer for your records.

Note to Buyers

> If the owner does not give you a Residential Property and Owners' Association Disclosure Statement by the time you make your offer to purchase the property, you may under certain conditions cancel any resulting contract without penalty to you as the buyer. To cancel the contract, you must personally deliver or mail written notice of your decision to cancel to the owner or the owner's agent within three calendar days following your receipt of the Disclosure Statement, or three calendar days following the date of the contract, whichever occurs first. However, in no event does the Disclosure Act permit you to cancel a contract after settlement of the transaction or (in the case of a sale or exchange) after you have occupied the property, whichever occurs first.

5. In the space below, type or print in ink the address of the property (sufficient to identify it) and your name. Then sign and date.

> Property Address: _____
> Owner's Name(s): _____
> Owner(s) acknowledge(s) having examined this Disclosure Statement before signing and that all information is true and correct as of the date signed.
>
> Owner Signature: _____ Date _____, __
> Owner Signature: _____ Date _____, __
>
> Buyers acknowledge receipt of a copy of this Disclosure Statement; that they have examined it before signing; that they understand that this is not a warranty by owners or owners' agents; that it is not a substitute for any inspections they may wish to obtain; and that the representations are made by the owners and not the owners' agents or subagents. Buyers are strongly encouraged to obtain their own inspections from a licensed home inspector or other professional. As used herein, words in the plural include the singular, as appropriate.
>
> Buyer Signature: _____ Date _____, ___
> Buyer Signature: _____ Date _____, ___

Property Address/Description: _____
_____

The following questions address the characteristics and condition of the property identified above about which the owner has actual knowledge. Where the question refers to "dwelling," it is intended to refer to the dwelling unit, or units if more than one, to be conveyed with the property. The term "dwelling unit" refers to any structure intended for human habitation.

	Yes	No	No Representation
1. In what year was the dwelling constructed? _____ Explain if necessary: _____			☐
2. Is there any problem, malfunction or defect with the dwelling's foundation, slab, fireplaces/chimneys, floors, windows (including storm windows and screens), doors, ceilings, interior and exterior walls, attached garage, patio, deck or other structural components including any modifications to them?	☐	☐	☐
3. The dwelling's exterior walls are made of what type of material? ☐ Brick Veneer ☐ Wood ☐ Stone ☐ Vinyl ☐ Synthetic Stucco ☐ Composition/Hardboard ☐ Concrete ☐ Fiber Cement ☐ Aluminum ☐ Asbestos ☐ Other _____ (Check all that apply)			☐
4. In what year was the dwelling's roof covering installed? _____ (Approximate if no records are available.) Explain if necessary: _____			☐

5. Is there any leakage or other problem with the dwelling's roof? ☐ ☐ ☐

6. Is there any water seepage, leakage, dampness or standing water in the dwelling's basement, crawl space, or slab? ☐ ☐ ☐

7. Is there any problem, malfunction or defect with the dwelling's electrical system (outlets, wiring, panel, switches, fixtures, generator, etc.)? ☐ ☐ ☐

8. Is there any problem, malfunction or defect with the dwelling's plumbing system (pipes, fixtures, water heater, etc.)? ☐ ☐ ☐

9. Is there any problem, malfunction or defect with the dwelling's heating and/or air conditioning? ☐ ☐ ☐

10. What is the dwelling's heat source? ☐ Furnace ☐ Heat Pump ☐ Baseboard ☐ Other_____ (Check all that apply)
Age of system: _____ ☐

11. What is the dwelling's cooling source? ☐ Central Forced Air ☐ Wall/Window Unit(s) ☐ Other_____ (Check all that apply)
Age of system: _____ ☐

12. What is the dwelling's fuel sources? ☐ Electricity ☐ Natural Gas ☐ Propane ☐ Oil ☐ Other_____ (Check all that apply)
If the fuel source is stored in a tank, identify whether the tank is ☐ above ground or ☐ below ground, and whether the tank is ☐ leased by seller or ☐ owned by seller.
(Check all that apply) ☐

13. What is the dwelling's water supply source? ☐ City/County ☐ Community System ☐ Private Well ☐ Shared Well ☐ Other_____
(Check all that apply) ☐

14. The dwelling's water pipes are made of what type of material? ☐ Copper ☐ Galvanized ☐ Plastic ☐ Polybutylene ☐ Other_____
(Check all that apply) ☐

15. Is there any problem, malfunction or defect with the dwelling's water supply (including water quality, quantity or water pressure)? ☐ ☐ ☐

16. What is the dwelling's sewage disposal system? ☐ Septic Tank ☐ Septic Tank with Pump ☐ Community System ☐ Connected to City/County System ☐ City/County System available ☐ Straight pipe (wastewater does not go into a septic or other sewer system [note: use of this type of system violates State law])
☐ Other_____
(Check all that apply) ☐

17. If the dwelling is serviced by a septic system, do you know how many bedrooms are allowed by the septic system permit? If your answer is "Yes," how many bedrooms are allowed? _____ ☐ No records available. ☐ ☐ ☐

18. Is there any problem, malfunction or defect with the dwelling's sewer and/or septic system? ☐ ☐ ☐

19. Is there any problem, malfunction or defect with the dwelling's central vacuum, pool, hot tub, spa, attic fan, exhaust fan, ceiling fans, sump pump, irrigation system, TV cable

wiring or satellite dish, garage door openers, gas logs, or other systems?

20. Is there any problem, malfunction or defect with any appliances that may be included in the conveyance (range/oven, attached microwave, hood/fan, dishwasher, disposal, etc.)?

21. Is there any problem with present infestation of the dwelling, or damage from past infestation of wood destroying insects or organisms which has not been repaired?

22. Is there any problem, malfunction or defect with the drainage, grading or soil stability of the property?

23. Are there any structural additions or other structural or mechanical changes to the dwelling(s) to be conveyed with the property?

24. Is the property to be conveyed in violation of any local zoning ordinances, restrictive covenants, or other land-use restrictions, or building codes (including the failure to obtain proper permits for room additions or other changes/improvements)?

25. Are there any hazardous or toxic substances, materials, or products (such as asbestos, formaldehyde, radon gas, methane gas, lead-based paint) which exceed government safety standards, any debris (whether buried or covered) or underground storage tanks, or any environmentally hazardous conditions (such as contaminated soil or water, or other environmental contamination) which affect the property?

26. Is there any noise, odor, smoke, etc. from commercial, industrial or military sources which affects the property?

27. Is the property subject to any utility or other easements, shared driveways, party walls or encroachments from or on adjacent property?

28. Is the property subject to any lawsuits, foreclosures, bankruptcy, leases or rental agreements, judgments, tax liens, proposed assessments, mechanics' liens, materialmens' liens, or notices from any governmental agency that could affect title to the property?

29. Is the property subject to a flood hazard or is the property located in a federally-designated flood hazard area?

30. Does the property abut or adjoin any private road(s) or street(s)?

31. If there is a private road or street adjoining the property, is there in existence any owners' association or maintenance agreements dealing with the maintenance of the road or street?

If you answered "yes" to any of the questions listed above (1-31) please explain (attach additional sheets if necessary):

_____
_____
_____

In lieu of providing a written explanation, you may attach a written report to this Disclosure Statement by a public agency, or by an attorney, engineer, land surveyor, geologist, pest control operator, contractor, home inspector, or other expert, dealing with matters within the scope of that public agency's functions or the expert's license or expertise.

The following questions pertain to the property identified above, including the lot to be conveyed and any dwelling unit(s), sheds, detached garages, or other buildings located thereon.

	Yes	No	No Repre-sentation

32. Is the property subject to governing documents which impose various mandatory covenants, conditions, and restrictions upon the lot or unit? ☐ ☐ ☐

If you answered "yes" to the question above, please explain (attach additional sheets if necessary):

_____
_____
_____

33. Is the property subject to regulation by one or more owners' association(s) including, but not limited to, obligations to pay regular assessments or dues and special assessments? If your answer is "yes," please provide the information requested below as to each owners' association to which the property is subject [insert N/A into any blank that does not apply]: ☐ ☐ ☐

(specify name) _____ whose regular assessments ("dues") are $ _____ per _____. The name, address and telephone number of the president of the owners' association or the association manager are

_____
_____

(specify name) _____ whose regular assessments ("dues") are $ _____ per _____. The name, address and telephone number of the president of the owners' association or the association manager are

_____
_____

* If you answered "Yes" to question 33 above, you must complete the remainder of this Disclosure Statement. If you answered "No" or "No Representation" to question 33 above, you do not need to answer the remaining questions on this Disclosure Statement. Skip to the bottom of the last page and initial and date the page.

	Yes	No	No Repre-sentation

34. Are any fees charged by the association or by the association's management company in connection with the conveyance or transfer of the lot or property to a new owner? If your answer is "yes," please state the amount of the fees: ☐ ☐ ☐

_____
_____

35. As of the date this Disclosure Statement is signed, are there any dues, fees or special assessment which have been duly approved as required by the applicable declaration or by-laws, and that are payable to an association to which the lot is subject? If your answer is "yes," please state the nature and amount of the dues, fees or special assessments to which the property is subject: ☐ ☐ ☐

_____
_____

36. As of the date this Disclosure Statement is signed, are there any unsatisfied judgments against or pending lawsuits involving the property or lot to be conveyed? If your answer is "yes," please state the nature of each pending lawsuit and the amount of each unsatisfied judgment: ☐ ☐ ☐

_____
_____
_____

37. As of the date this Disclosure Statement is signed, are there any unsatisfied judgments against or pending lawsuits involving the planned community or the association to which the property and lot are subject, with the exception of any action filed by the association for the collection of delinquent assessments on lots other than the property and lot to be conveyed? If your answer is "yes," please state the nature of each pending lawsuit and the amount of each unsatisfied judgment: ☐ ☐ ☐

_____
_____
_____

38. Which of the following services and amenities are paid for by the owners' association(s) identified above out of the association's regular assessments ("dues")? (Check all that apply.)

	Yes	No	No Representation
Management Fees	☐	☐	☐
Exterior Building Maintenance of Property to be Conveyed			
Master Insurance			
Exterior Yard/Landscaping Maintenance of Lot to be Conveyed	☐	☐	☐
Common Areas Maintenance	☐	☐	☐
Trash Removal	☐	☐	☐
Recreational Amenity Maintenance (specify amenities covered) _____	☐	☐	☐
Pest Treatment/Extermination	☐	☐	☐
Street Lights	☐	☐	☐
Water	☐	☐	☐
Sewer	☐	☐	☐
Storm Water Management/Drainage/Ponds	☐	☐	☐
Internet Service	☐	☐	☐
Cable	☐	☐	☐
Private Road Maintenance	☐	☐	☐
Parking Area Maintenance	☐	☐	☐
Gate and/or Security	☐	☐	☐
Other: (specify)	☐	☐	☐

_____
_____

Buyer Initials and Date _____ Owner Initials and Date _____
Buyer Initials and Date _____ Owner Initials and Date _____

(b) The form described in Paragraph (a) of this Rule may be reproduced, but the text of the form shall not be altered or amended in any way.

(c) The form described in Paragraph (a) of this Rule as amended effective July 1, 2018, applies to all properties placed on the market on or after July 1, 2018. The form described in Paragraph (a) of this Rule as amended effective July 1, 2014, applies to all properties placed on the market prior to July 1, 2018. If a corrected disclosure statement required by G.S. 47E-7 is prepared on or after July 1, 2018, for a property placed on the market prior to July 1, 2018, the form described in Paragraph (a) of this Rule as amended effective July 1, 2018, shall be used.

History Note: Authority G.S. 47E-4(b); 47E-4(b1); 93A-3(c); 93A-6;
  Eff. October 1, 1998;

Amended Eff. July 1, 2014; January 1, 2013; January 1, 2012; July 1, 2010; July 1, 2009; January 1, 2008; July 1, 2006; September 1, 2002; July 1, 2000;
Pursuant to G.S. 150B-21.3A, rule is necessary without substantive public interest Eff. May 1, 2018;
Amended Eff. July 1, 2018.

21 NCAC 58A .0115   DISCLOSURE OF OFFERS PROHIBITED
A broker shall not disclose the price or other material terms contained in a party's offer to purchase, sell, lease, rent, or to option real property to a competing party without the express authority of the offering party.

History Note: *Authority G.S. 93A-3(c); 93A-6;*
Eff. July 1, 2008;
Pursuant to G.S. 150B-21.3A, rule is necessary without substantive public interest Eff. May 1, 2018.

21 NCAC 58A .0116   HANDLING OF TRUST MONEY
(a) Except as provided in Paragraph (b) of this Rule, all monies received by a broker acting in his or her fiduciary capacity (hereinafter "trust money") shall be deposited in a trust or escrow account as defined in Rule .0117(b) of this Section no later than three banking days following the broker's receipt of such monies.
(b) Exceptions to the requirements of Paragraph (a):
    (1)   All monies received by a provisional broker shall be delivered upon receipt to the broker with whom he or she is affiliated.
    (2)   All monies received by a non-resident commercial broker shall be delivered as required by Rule .1808 of this Subchapter.
    (3)   Earnest money or tenant security deposits paid by means other than currency and received by a broker in connection with a pending offer to purchase or lease shall be deposited in a trust or escrow account no later than three days following acceptance of the offer to purchase or lease; the date of acceptance of the offer or lease shall be set forth in the purchase or lease agreement.
    (4)   A broker may accept custody of a check or other negotiable instrument made payable to the seller of real property as payment for an option or due diligence fee, or to the designated escrow agent in a sales transaction, but only for the purpose of delivering the instrument to the seller or designated escrow agent. While the instrument is in the custody of the broker, the broker shall, according to the instructions of the buyer, either deliver it to the named payee or return it to the buyer. The broker shall safeguard the instrument and be responsible to the parties on the instrument for its safe delivery as required by this Rule. A broker shall not retain an instrument for more than three business days after the acceptance of the option or other sales contract.
(c) Prior to depositing trust money into a trust or escrow account that bears interest, the broker having custody over the money shall first secure written authorization from all parties having an interest in the money. Such authorization shall specify and set forth in a conspicuous manner how and to whom the interest shall be disbursed.
(d) In the event of a dispute between buyer and seller or landlord and tenant over the return or forfeiture of any deposit other than a residential tenant security deposit held by the broker, the broker shall retain the deposit in a trust or escrow account until the broker has obtained a written release from the parties consenting to its disposition or until disbursement is ordered by a court of competent jurisdiction. Alternatively, the broker may deposit the disputed monies with the appropriate Clerk of Superior Court in accordance with the provisions of G.S. 93A-12. If it appears that one of the parties has abandoned his or her claim to the funds, the broker may disburse the money to the other claimant according to the written agreement. Before doing so, however, the broker must first make a reasonable effort to notify the absent party and provide that party with an opportunity to renew his or her claim to the funds. Tenant security deposits shall be disposed of in accordance with G.S. 42-50 through 56 and G.S. 42A-18.
(e) A broker may transfer an earnest money deposit from his or her trust or escrow account to the closing attorney or other settlement agent no more than 10 days prior to the anticipated settlement date. A broker shall not disburse prior to settlement any earnest money in his or her possession for any other purpose without the written consent of the parties.
(f) A broker shall not disburse trust money to or on behalf of a client in an amount exceeding the balance of trust money belonging to the client and held in the trust account.
(g) Every broker shall safeguard any money or property of others that comes into the broker's possession in a manner consistent with the Real Estate License Law and Commission rules. A broker shall not convert the money or

property of others to his or her own use, apply such money or property to a purpose other than that it was intended for, or permit or assist any other person in the conversion or misapplication of such money or property.

History Note: *Authority G.S. 93A-3(c); 93A-6;*
Eff. April 1, 2013;
Amended Eff. July 1, 2015;
Pursuant to G.S. 150B-21.3A, rule is necessary without substantive public interest Eff. May 1, 2018.

21 NCAC 58A .0117   ACCOUNTING FOR TRUST MONEY
(a) A broker shall create, maintain and retain records sufficient to identify the ownership of all funds belonging to others. Such records shall be sufficient to show proper deposit and disbursement of such funds into and from a trust or escrow account and to verify the accuracy and proper use of the trust or escrow account.
(b) A trust or escrow account shall satisfy the requirements of G.S. 93A-6(g) and shall be designated as a "Trust Account" or "Escrow Account." All bank statements, deposit tickets and checks drawn on said account shall bear the words "Trust Account" or "Escrow Account." A trust account shall provide for the full withdrawal of funds on demand without prior notice and without penalty or deduction to the funds.
(c) A broker shall create, maintain or retain, as required by Rule .0108 of this Section, the following records:
- (1) bank statements;
- (2) canceled checks and other evidence or memoranda of payments from the trust or escrow account, whether by transfer between accounts, wire payments, or payments by electronic means, that shall be referenced to the corresponding journal entry or check stub entries and to the corresponding sales transaction ledgers or for rental transactions, the corresponding property or owner ledgers. Checks and other evidence or memoranda of payments from the account shall identify the payee by name and shall bear a notation identifying the purpose of the disbursement. When a payment is used to disburse funds for more than one sales transaction, owner, or property, the check or other evidence or memoranda of payment shall bear a notation identifying each sales transaction, owner, or property for which disbursement is made, including the amount disbursed for each, and the corresponding sales transaction, property, or owner ledger entries. When necessary, the check notation may refer to the required information recorded on a supplemental disbursement worksheet that shall be cross-referenced to the corresponding check or payment. In lieu of retaining canceled checks, a broker may retain digitally imaged copies of the canceled checks or substitute checks provided that such images are legible reproductions of the front and back of such instruments with no smaller images than 1.1875 x 3.0 inches and provided that the broker's bank retains for a period of at least five years the original checks, "substitute checks" as described in 12 C.F.R. 229.51 or the capacity to provide substitute checks as described in 12 C.F.R. 229.51 and makes the original or substitute checks available to the broker and the Commission upon request. The description of "substitute checks" contained in 12 C.F.R. 229.51 is incorporated by referencing, including subsequent amendments and additions. The regulation may be accessed at www.gpo.gov at no charge.
- (3) deposit tickets or other evidence or memoranda of deposits or payments into the account, whether by transfer between accounts, wire payments, or payments by electronic means:
  - (A) for a sales transaction, the deposit ticket or other evidence or memoranda of deposits or payments into the account shall identify the purpose and remitter of the funds deposited, the property, the parties involved, and a reference to the corresponding sales transaction ledger;
  - (B) for a rental transaction, the deposit ticket or other evidence or memoranda of deposits or payments into the account shall identify the purpose and remitter of the funds deposited, the tenant, and the corresponding property or owner ledger;
  - (C) for deposits of funds belonging to or collected on behalf of a property owner association, the deposit ticket or other evidence or memoranda of deposits or payments into the account shall identify the property or property interest for which the payment is made, the property or interest owner, the remitter, and the purpose of the payment;
  - (D) when a single deposit ticket or payment is used to deposit funds collected for more than one sales transaction, property owner, or property, the required information may either be recorded on the ticket or other evidence or memoranda of deposits or payments into the

account for each sales transaction, owner, or property, or it may refer to the same information recorded on a supplemental deposit worksheet that shall be cross-referenced to the corresponding deposit ticket;

(4) a separate ledger for each sales transaction, for each property or owner of property managed by the broker and for company funds held in the trust account:

    (A) the ledger for a sales transaction shall identify the property, the parties to the transaction, the amount, date, and purpose of the deposits and from whom received, the amount, date, check number, and purpose of disbursements and to whom paid, and the running balance of funds on deposit for each deposit and disbursement entry;

    (B) the ledger for a rental transaction shall identify the particular property or owner of property, the tenant, the amount, date, and purpose of the deposits and from whom received, the amount, date, check number, and purpose of disbursements and to whom paid, and the running balance of funds on deposit for each deposit and disbursement entry. Monies held as tenant security deposits in connection with rental transactions may be accounted for on a separate tenant security deposit ledger for each property or owner of property managed by the broker. For each security deposit, the tenant security deposit ledger shall identify the remitter, the date the deposit was paid, the amount, the tenant, landlord, and subject property as well as the check number, amount, date, payee, purpose and a running balance for each disbursement. When tenant security deposit monies are accounted for on a separate ledger as provided in this Rule, deposit tickets, canceled checks and supplemental worksheets shall reference the corresponding tenant security deposit ledger entries;

    (C) a broker may maintain a maximum of one hundred dollars ($100.00) in company funds in a trust account for the purpose of paying service charges incurred by the account. In the event that the services charges exceed one hundred dollars ($100.00) monthly, the broker may deposit an amount each month sufficient to cover the service charges. A broker shall maintain a separate ledger for company funds held in the trust account identifying the date, amount and running balance for each deposit and disbursement;

(5) a general journal, check register or check stubs identifying in chronological order each bank deposit and disbursement of monies to and from the trust or escrow account, including the amount and date of each deposit and a reference to the corresponding deposit ticket and any supplemental deposit worksheet, and the amount, date, check number, and purpose of disbursements and to whom paid. The journal or check stubs shall also show a running balance for each entry into the account;

(6) a payment record for each property or interest for which funds are collected and deposited into a property owner association trust account as required by Rule .0118 of this Section. Payment record(s) shall identify the amount, date, remitter, and purpose of payments received, the amount and nature of the obligation for which payments are made, and the amount of any balance due or delinquency;

(7) copies of earnest money checks, due diligence fee checks, receipts for cash payments, contracts, and closing statements in sales transactions;

(8) copies of leases, security deposit checks, property management agreements, property management statements, and receipts for cash payments in leasing transactions;

(9) copies of covenants, bylaws, minutes, management agreements and periodic statements relating to the management of property owner associations;

(10) copies of invoices, bills, and contracts paid from the trust account; and

(11) copies of any documents not otherwise described in this Rule that are necessary to verify and explain record entries.

(d) Records of all receipts and disbursements of trust or escrow monies shall be maintained in such a manner as to create an audit trail from deposit tickets and canceled checks to check stubs or journals and to the ledger sheets.

(e) Brokers shall reconcile their trust or escrow accounts monthly. The trust account reconciliation shall be performed in the following manner as of a specific cutoff date selected by the broker:

(1) a trial balance shall be prepared showing a list of the property or owner ledgers, their balances, and the total of all of the property or owner ledger balances as of the cutoff date;

(2) a bank statement shall be reconciled by deducting from the statement's ending balance the amount of any outstanding checks and then adding to the balance the amount of any deposits-in-transit as of the cutoff date; and

(3) the trial balance, reconciled bank statement balance, and the journal balance shall be compared as of the cutoff date. If the amounts on the trial balance, journal balance and reconciled bank balance do not agree, the broker shall investigate the reason for any variation between the balances and make the necessary corrections to bring the balances into agreement.

A broker shall maintain and retain a worksheet for each monthly trust account reconciliation showing the balance of the journal or check stubs, the trial balance and the reconciled bank statement balance to be in agreement as of the cutoff date.

(f) In addition to the records required by Paragraph (c) of this Rule, a broker acting as agent for the landlord of a residential property used for vacation rentals shall create and maintain either a subsidiary ledger sheet for each property or owner of such properties on which all funds collected and disbursed are identified in categories by purpose or an accounts payable ledger for each owner or property and each vendor to whom trust monies are due. If a broker maintains a subsidiary ledger, the broker shall reconcile the subsidiary ledgers to the corresponding property or property owner ledger on a monthly basis. If a broker maintains an accounts payable ledger, the broker shall record on the ledger monies collected on behalf of the owner or property identifying the date of receipt of the trust monies, from whom the monies were received, rental dates, and the corresponding property or owner ledger entry including the amount to be disbursed for each and the purpose of the disbursement. The broker may also maintain an accounts payable ledger in the format described above for vacation rental tenant security deposit monies and vacation rental advance payments.

(g) Upon the written request of a client, a broker shall, no later than ten days after receipt of the request, furnish the client with copies of any records retained as required by Rule .0108 of this Section that pertain to the transaction to which the client was a party.

(h) All trust or escrow account records shall be made available for inspection by the Commission or its authorized representatives in accordance with Rule .0108 of this Section.

History Note: Authority G.S. 93A-3(c); 93A-6;
Eff. April 1, 2013;
Amended Eff. July 1, 2014;
Pursuant to G.S. 150B-21.3A, rule is necessary without substantive public interest Eff. May 1, 2018.

21 NCAC 58A .0118 TRUST MONEY BELONGING TO PROPERTY OWNERS' ASSOCIATIONS

(a) The funds of a property owners' association, when collected, maintained, disbursed or otherwise controlled by a broker, are trust money and shall be treated as such in the manner required by Rules .0116 and .0117 of this Section. Such trust money shall be deposited into and maintained in a trust or escrow account dedicated exclusively for trust money belonging to a single property owners' association and shall not be commingled with funds belonging to other property owners' associations or other persons or parties. A broker who undertakes to act as manager of a property owners' association or as the custodian of trust money belonging to a property owners' association shall provide the association with periodic statements that report the balance of association trust money in the broker's possession or control and account for the trust money the broker has received and disbursed on behalf of the association. Such statements must be made in accordance with the broker's agreement with the association, but not less frequently than every 90 days.

(b) A broker who receives trust money belonging to a property owners' association in his or her capacity as an officer of the association in a residential development in which the broker is a property owner and for which the broker receives no compensation is exempt from the requirements of Rules .0116 and .0117 of this Section. However, the broker shall not convert trust money belonging to the association to his or her own use, apply such money or property to a purpose other than that for which it was intended or permit or assist any other person in the conversion or misapplication of such money or property.

History Note: Authority G.S. 93A-3(c); 93A-6;
Eff. April 1, 2013;
Amended Eff. July 1, 2014;
Pursuant to G.S. 150B-21.3A, rule is necessary without substantive public interest Eff. May 1, 2018.

STATE OF NORTH CAROLINA
MINERAL AND OIL AND GAS RIGHTS MANDATORY DISCLOSURE STATEMENT

Instructions to Property Owners

1. The Residential Property Disclosure Act (G.S. 47E) ("Disclosure Act") requires owners of certain residential real estate such as single-family homes, individual condominiums, townhouses, and the like, and buildings with up to four dwelling units, to furnish purchasers a Mineral and Oil and Gas Rights Disclosure Statement ("Disclosure Statement"). This form is the only one approved for this purpose.
2. A disclosure statement is not required for some transactions. For a complete list of exemptions, see G.S. 47E-2(a). **A DISCLOSURE STATEMENT IS REQUIRED FOR THE TRANSFERS IDENTIFIED IN G.S. 47E-2(b),** including transfers involving the first sale of a dwelling never inhabited, lease with option to purchase contracts where the lessee occupies or intends to occupy the dwelling, and transfers between parties when both parties agree not to provide the Residential Property and Owner's Association Disclosure Statement.
3. You must respond to each of the following by placing a check √ in the appropriate box.

MINERAL AND OIL AND GAS RIGHTS DISCLOSURE

Mineral rights and/or oil and gas rights can be severed from the title to real property by conveyance (deed) of the mineral rights and/or oil and gas rights from the owner or by reservation of the mineral rights and/or oil and gas rights by the owner. If mineral rights and/or oil and gas rights are or will be severed from the property, the owner of those rights may have the perpetual right to drill, mine, explore, and remove any of the subsurface mineral and/or oil or gas resources on or from the property either directly from the surface of the property or from a nearby location. With regard to the severance of mineral rights and/or oil and gas rights, Seller makes the following disclosures:

	Yes	No	No Representation
_____ Buyer Initials 1. Mineral rights were severed from the property by a previous owner.	☐	☐	☐
_____ Buyer Initials 2. Seller has severed the mineral rights from the property.	☐	☐	
_____ Buyer Initials 3. Seller intends to sever the mineral rights from the property prior to transfer of title to the Buyer.	☐	☐	
_____ Buyer Initials 4. Oil and gas rights were severed from the property by a previous owner.	☐	☐	☐
_____ Buyer Initials 5. Seller has severed the oil and gas rights from the property.	☐	☐	
_____ Buyer Initials 6. Seller intends to sever the oil and gas rights from the property prior to transfer of title to Buyer.	☐	☐	

Note to Purchasers

If the owner does not give you a Mineral and Oil and Gas Rights Disclosure Statement by the time you make your offer to purchase the property, or exercise an option to purchase the property pursuant to a lease with an option to purchase, you may under certain conditions cancel any resulting contract without penalty to you as the purchaser. To cancel the contract, you must personally deliver or mail written notice of your decision to cancel to the owner or the owner's agent within three calendar days following your receipt of this Disclosure Statement, or three calendar days following the date of the contract, whichever occurs first. However, in no event does the Disclosure Act permit you to cancel a contract after settlement of the transaction or (in the case of a sale or exchange) after you have occupied the property, whichever occurs first.

Property Address: _____

Owner's Name(s): _____

Owner(s) acknowledge having examined this Disclosure Statement before signing and that all information is true and correct as of the date signed.

Owner Signature: _____ Date _____, ____

Owner Signature: _____ Date _____, ____

Purchaser(s) acknowledge receipt of a copy of this Disclosure Statement; that they have examined it before signing; that they understand that this is not a warranty by owner or owner's agent; and that the representations are made by the owner and not the owner's agent(s) or subagent(s).

Purchaser Signature: _____ Date _____, ____

Purchaser Signature: _____ Date _____, ____

REC 4.25
1/1/15

21 NCAC 58A .0119   MINERAL AND OIL AND GAS RIGHTS MANDATORY DISCLOSURE STATEMENT

(a) Every owner of real property subject to a transfer of the type governed by G.S. 47E-1 and 47E-2(b) shall complete a disclosure statement form prescribed by the Commission and designated "Mineral and Oil and Gas Rights Mandatory Disclosure Statement," and shall furnish a copy of the completed form to a purchaser as required by G.S. 47E-4.1. The form shall bear the seal of the North Carolina Real Estate Commission and shall include the following:

- (1) instructions to property owners regarding transactions when the disclosure statement is required;
- (2) the text and format of the disclosure statement form as required by G.S. 47E-4.1(a);
- (3) a note to purchasers regarding their rights under G.S. 47E-5 in the event they are not provided with a disclosure statement as required by G.S. 47E-4.1;
- (4) the identification of the subject property and the parties to the transaction;
- (5) an acknowledgment by the owner(s) that the disclosure statement is true and correct as of the date signed; and
- (6) an acknowledgment by the buyer(s) of the receipt of a copy of the disclosure statement.

(b) The disclosure statement form described in Paragraph (a) of this Rule shall be available on the Commission's website at www.ncrec.gov or upon request to the Commission.

(c) The disclosure statement form described in Paragraph (a) of this Rule may be reproduced, but the text of the form shall not be altered or amended in any way.

(d) Every broker representing a party in a real estate transaction governed by G.S. 47E-1 and 47E-2(b) shall inform each client of the client's rights and obligations under G.S. Chapter 47E.

(e) The disclosure statement form described in Paragraph (a) of this Rule applies to all contracts executed on or after January 1, 2015.

History Note: *Authority G.S. 47E-4.1; 47E-4.1(b); 47E-5; 47E-8; 93A-3(c); 93A-6;*
Temporary Adoption Eff. January 1, 2015;
Eff. July 1, 2015.

SECTION .0200 - GENERAL PROVISIONS

21 NCAC 58A .0201	**DEFINITIONS**
21 NCAC 58A .0202	**BOARD: DESCRIPTION: OFFICES**
21 NCAC 58A .0203	**MAILING ADDRESS**
21 NCAC 58A .0204	**PURPOSE**

History Note: *Authority G.S. 93A-3(a),(c),(d);*
Eff. February 1, 1976;
Readopted Eff. September 30, 1977;
Amended Eff. April 11, 1980; September 1, 1979;
Repealed Eff. June 1, 1981.

SECTION .0300 – APPLICATION FOR LICENSE

21 NCAC 58A .0301   FORM
An individual or business entity who wishes to file an application for a broker license shall make application on a form prescribed by the Commission and may obtain the required form upon request to the Commission. The application form for an individual calls for the applicant's name and address, the applicant's social security number, proof of the applicant's identity, places of residence, education, prior real estate licenses, and other information necessary to identify the applicant and determine the applicant's qualifications and fitness for licensure. The application form for a business entity is described in Rule .0502 of this Section.

History Note: *Authority G.S. 93A-3(c); 93A-4(a),(b),(d);*
Eff. February 1, 1976;
Readopted Eff. September 30, 1977;

Amended Eff. April 1, 2006; July 1, 2000; February 1, 1991; February 1, 1989; August 1, 1988; December 1, 1985;
Pursuant to G.S. 150B-21.3A, rule is necessary without substantive public interest Eff. May 1, 2018.

21 NCAC 58A .0302   LICENSE APPLICATION AND FEE
(a) The fee for an original application of a broker or firm license shall be one hundred dollars ($100.00).
(b) An applicant shall update information provided in connection with a license application in writing to the Commission or submit a new application form that includes the updated information without request by the Commission to ensure that the information provided in the application is current and accurate. Failure to submit updated information prior to the issuance of a license may result in disciplinary action against a broker or firm in accordance with G.S. 93A-6(b)(1). Upon the request of the Commission, an applicant shall submit updated information or provide additional information necessary to complete the application within 90 days of the request or the license application shall be canceled.
(c) The license application of an individual shall be canceled if the applicant fails to:
　　(1)　pass a scheduled license examination within 180 days of filing a complete application pursuant to Rule .0301 of this Section; or
　　(2)　appear for and take any scheduled examination without having the applicant's examination postponed or absence excused pursuant to Rule .0401 of this Subchapter.

History Note:　*Authority G.S. 93A-4; 93A-6(b)(1); 93A-9;*
　　　　　　　Eff. February 1, 1976;
　　　　　　　Readopted Eff. September 30, 1977;
　　　　　　　Amended Eff. July 1, 2017; April 1, 2006; July 1, 2004; April 1, 2004; July 1, 2003; October 1, 2000; August 1, 1998; July 1, 1998; July 1, 1996; February 1, 1989;
　　　　　　　Pursuant to G.S. 150B-21.3A, rule is necessary without substantive public interest Eff. May 1, 2018.

21 NCAC 58A .0303   PAYMENT OF APPLICATION FEES

History Note:　*Authority G.S. 93A-3(c); 93A-4(a),(d);*
　　　　　　　Eff. February 1, 1976;
　　　　　　　Readopted Eff. September 30, 1977;
　　　　　　　Amended Eff. April 1, 2004; July 1, 2000; December 1, 1985;
　　　　　　　Expired Eff. June 1, 2018 pursuant to G.S. 150B-21.3A.

21 NCAC 58A .0304   WAIVER OF 75-HOUR PRELICENSING EDUCATION REQUIREMENT
The Commission shall grant a waiver of the 75-hour education program pursuant to G.S. 93A-4(a) if an applicant submits:
　　(1)　an application pursuant to Rule .0301 of this Section;
　　(2)　a written request for a waiver of the 75-hour education program; and either
　　(3)　a transcript and copy of a baccalaureate or higher degree in the field of real estate, real estate brokerage, real estate finance, real estate development, or a law degree conferred on the applicant from any college or university accredited by a college accrediting body recognized by the U. S. Department of Education; or
　　(4)　a course completion certificate or transcript evidencing the completion of a prelicensing education program in another state that:
　　　　(a)　consisted of at least 75-hours of instruction;
　　　　(b)　was completed within one year prior to license application while the applicant was a resident of said state; and
　　　　(c)　is parallel to the topics and timings described in the Commission's Prelicensing course syllabus.

History Note:　*Authority G.S. 93A-4;*
　　　　　　　Eff. July 1, 1993;
　　　　　　　Amended Eff. July 1, 2017; April 1, 2006; October 1, 2000;

Pursuant to G.S. 150B-21.3A, rule is necessary without substantive public interest Eff. May 1, 2018.

SECTION .0400 - EXAMINATIONS

21 NCAC 58A .0401   SCHEDULING EXAMINATIONS
(a) An applicant who is required and qualified to take the licensing examination shall be provided a notice of examination eligibility that shall be valid for a period of 180 days and for a single administration of the licensing examination. Upon receipt of the notice of examination eligibility, the applicant shall contact the Commission's authorized testing service to pay for and schedule the examination in accordance with procedures established by the testing service. The testing service will schedule applicants for examination by computer at their choice of one of the testing locations and will notify applicants of the time and place of their examinations.
(b) An applicant may postpone a scheduled examination provided the applicant makes the request for postponement directly to the Commission's authorized testing service in accordance with procedures established by the testing service. An applicant's examination shall not be postponed beyond the 180 day period allowed for taking the examination without first refiling another complete application with the Commission. A request to postpone a scheduled licensing examination without complying with the procedures for re-applying for examination described in Rule .0403 of this Section shall be granted only once unless the applicant satisfies the requirements for obtaining an excused absence stated in Paragraph (c) of this Rule.
(c) An applicant may be granted an excused absence from a scheduled examination if the applicant provides evidence that the absence was the direct result of an emergency situation or condition which was beyond the applicant's control and which could not have been reasonably foreseen by the applicant. A request for an excused absence must be promptly made in writing and must be supported by documentation verifying the reason for the absence. The request must be submitted directly to the testing service in accordance with procedures established by the testing service. A request for an excused absence from an examination shall be denied if the applicant cannot be rescheduled and examined prior to expiration of the 180 day period allowed for taking the examination without first refiling another complete application with the Commission.

History Note: *Authority G.S. 93A-4(b),(d);*
Eff. February 1, 1976;
Readopted Eff. September 30, 1977;
Amended Eff. April 1, 2004; October 1, 2000; July 1, 1996; July 1, 1989; February 1, 1989;
Pursuant to G.S. 150B-21.3A, rule is necessary without substantive public interest Eff. May 1, 2018.

21 NCAC 58A .0402   EXAMINATION SUBJECT MATTER, FORMAT, AND PASSING SCORES
(a) The real estate licensing examination shall test applicants on the following general subject areas:
- (1)   real estate law;
- (2)   real estate brokerage law and practices;
- (3)   the Real Estate License Law, rules of the Commission, and the Commission's trust account guidelines;
- (4)   real estate finance;
- (5)   real estate valuation (appraisal);
- (6)   real estate mathematics; and
- (7)   related subject areas.

(b) The real estate licensing examination shall consist of two sections, a "national" section on general real estate law, principles, and practices and a "state" section on North Carolina real estate law, principles, and practices. Unless the "national" section is waived by the Commission for an applicant based on its authority under G.S. 93A-9, an applicant shall pass both sections of the examination in order to pass the examination.
(c) In order to pass the real estate licensing examination, an applicant shall attain a score for each required section of the examination that is at least equal to the passing score established by the Commission for each section of the examination in compliance with psychometric standards for establishing passing scores for occupational licensing examinations as set forth in the "Standards for Educational and Psychological Testing" jointly promulgated by the American Educational Research Association, the American Psychological Association, and the National Council on Measurement in Education. The "Standards for Educational and Psychological Testing" are incorporated by referencing, including subsequent amendments and editions. A copy of the "Standards for Educational and

Psychological Testing" is available for inspection at the North Carolina Real Estate Commission's office, whose address is posted on its website at www.ncrec.gov. Copies of the "Standards for Educational and Psychological Testing" may be ordered from the American Education Research Association through its website at www.aera.net at a charge of sixty-nine dollars and ninety-five cents ($69.95) per copy plus shipping.

(d) An applicant who passes one or both sections of the examination will receive only a score of "pass" for the section(s) passed; however, an applicant who fails one or both sections of the examination shall be informed of their actual score for the section(s) failed. An applicant who is required to pass both sections of the examination shall do so within his or her 180-day examination eligibility period, and if the applicant passes only one section during his or her 180-day examination eligibility period, then that passing score shall not be recognized if the applicant subsequently re-applies to the Commission for a license.

(e) A passing examination score obtained by a license applicant for both sections of the examination, or for the "state" section if that is the only section an applicant is required to pass, shall be recognized as valid for a period of one year from the date the examination was passed. During this time, the applicant shall satisfy any remaining requirements for licensure that were pending at the time of examination. The running of the one-year period shall be tolled upon mailing the applicant the letter set forth in 21 NCAC 58A .0616(c) informing the applicant that his or her moral character is in question, and shall resume running when the applicant's application is either approved for license issuance, denied, or withdrawn. The application of an applicant with a passing examination score who fails to satisfy all remaining requirements for licensure within one year shall be canceled and the applicant shall be required to reapply and satisfy all requirements for licensure, including retaking and passing the license examination, in order to be eligible for licensure.

History Note: Authority G.S. 93A-3(c); 93A-4(b); 93A-4(d);
Eff. February 1, 1976;
Readopted Eff. September 30, 1977;
Amended Eff. July 1, 2015; January 1, 2012; April 1, 2006; July 1, 2000; July 1, 1996; July 1, 1989; December 1, 1985; May 1, 1982; April 11, 1980;
Pursuant to G.S. 150B-21.3A, rule is necessary without substantive public interest Eff. May 1, 2018.

21 NCAC 58A .0403   RE-APPLYING FOR EXAMINATION
(a) An individual whose license application has been canceled pursuant to Rule .0302(c) of this Subchapter and whose 180 day examination eligibility period has expired who wishes to be rescheduled for the real estate license examination must re-apply to the Commission by filing a complete license application as described in Rule .0301 of this Subchapter and paying the prescribed application fee. Subsequent examinations shall then be scheduled in accordance with Rule .0401 of this Section.
(b) An individual whose license application has been canceled pursuant to Rule .0302(c) of this Subchapter who wishes to be rescheduled for the license examination before the expiration of his or her 180 day examination eligibility period may utilize an abbreviated electronic license application and examination rescheduling procedure by directly contacting the Commission's authorized testing service, paying both the license application fee and the examination fee to the testing service, and following the testing service's established procedures.
(c) An applicant who fails one or both sections of the license examination shall not be allowed to retake the failed section(s) of the examination for at least 10 calendar days.

History Note: Authority G.S. 93A-4(b),(d);
Eff. February 1, 1976;
Readopted Eff. September 30, 1977;
Amended Eff. February 1, 1988; December 1, 1985; April 11, 1980;
Temporary Amendment Eff. April 24, 1995 for a period of 180 days or until the permanent rule becomes effective, whichever is sooner;
Amended Eff. January 1, 2012; April 1, 2004; October 1, 2000; August 1, 1995.
Pursuant to G.S. 150B-21.3A, rule is necessary without substantive public interest Eff. May 1, 2018.

21 NCAC 58A .0404   EXAMINATION RELATED CONDUCT
(a) When taking a license examination, an applicant shall not:

(1) cheat or attempt to cheat on the examination by any means, including giving or receiving assistance or using notes of any type;
(2) communicate with any person other than an examination supervisor for any purpose in any manner;
(3) have in his or her possession or utilize in any manner study materials or notes or any device that may be used to:
  (A) communicate with others;
  (B) access information; or
  (C) record or store photographs, visual images, audio or other information about the examination;
(4) have in his or her possession or utilize a calculator that:
  (A) permits the storage, entry or retrieval of alphabetic characters; or
  (B) is not silent, hand-held and either battery-powered or solar-powered;
(5) have in his or her possession a wallet, pocketbook, bag or similar item that can be used to store materials prohibited by this Rule;
(6) refuse to demonstrate to the examination supervisor that pockets on any item of clothing do not contain materials prohibited by this Rule;
(7) leave or attempt to leave the testing area with any materials provided for the purpose of taking the examination or with any information, notes or other information about the content of the examination; or
(8) refuse to comply with the instructions of the Commission and the Commission's test provider for taking the examination; or
(9) disrupt in any manner the administration of the examination.

(b) Violation of this Rule shall result in dismissal from an examination, invalidation of examination scores, forfeiture of examination and application fees and denial of a real estate license, as well as for disciplinary action if the applicant has been issued a license.

History Note: Authority G.S. 93A-4(d);
Eff. December 1, 1985;
Amended Eff. July 1, 2014; April 1, 2006; July 1, 2000;
Pursuant to G.S. 150B-21.3A, rule is necessary without substantive public interest Eff. May 1, 2018.

21 NCAC 58A .0405 CONFIDENTIALITY OF EXAMINATIONS

Licensing examinations are confidential. No applicant or licensee shall obtain, attempt to obtain, receive, or communicate to other persons examination questions or answers. Violation of this Rule is grounds for denial of a real estate license if the violator is an applicant and disciplinary action if the violator is a licensee or becomes a licensee prior to the discovery of the violation by the Commission.

History Note: Authority G.S. 93A-3(c); 93A-4(d); 93A-6;
Eff. December 1, 1985;
Amended Eff. January 1, 2012; July 1, 2009;
Pursuant to G.S. 150B-21.3A, rule is necessary without substantive public interest Eff. May 1, 2018.

21 NCAC 58A .0406 EXAMINATION REVIEW

History Note: Authority G.S. 93A-4(d);
Eff. December 1, 1985;
Amended Eff. April 1, 2006; October 1, 2000; July 1, 1989; February 1, 1989;
Repealed Eff. January 1, 2012.

SECTION .0500 - LICENSING

21 NCAC 58A .0501 CHARACTER

History Note: Authority G.S. 93A-4(b),(d);
Eff. February 1, 1976;
Readopted Eff. September 30, 1977;
Amended Eff. October 1, 2000; July 1, 1989; February 1, 1989; May 1, 1984; September 1, 1979;
Repealed Eff. July 1, 2003.

21 NCAC 58A .0502   FIRM LICENSING
(a) Every business entity other than a sole proprietorship shall apply for and obtain from the Commission a firm license prior to engaging in business as a real estate broker.
(b) An entity that changes its business form other than by conversion shall submit a new firm license application upon making the change and obtain a new firm license. An entity that converts to a different business entity in conformity with and pursuant to applicable North Carolina General Statutes shall not be required to apply for a new license. However, such converted entity shall provide the information required by this Rule in writing to the Commission within 10 days of the conversion and shall include the duplicate license fee pursuant to Rule .0101(c) of this Subchapter.
(c) Firm license application forms shall be available on the Commission's website or upon request to the Commission and shall require the applicant to set forth:
  (1) the legal name of the entity;
  (2) the name under which the entity will do business;
  (3) the type of business entity;
  (4) the address of its principal office;
  (5) the entity's NC Secretary of State Identification Number if it is required to be registered with the Office of the NC Secretary of State;
  (6) each federally insured depository institution lawfully doing business in this State where the entity's trust account(s) will be held, if applicable;
  (7) the name, real estate license number, and signature of the proposed qualifying broker for the firm;
  (8) the address of and name of the proposed broker-in-charge for each office as defined in Rule .0110(a) of this Subchapter, along with a completed broker-in-charge designation form described in Rule .0110(f) of this Subchapter for each proposed broker-in-charge;
  (9) any past criminal conviction of and any pending criminal charge against any principal in the company or any proposed broker-in-charge;
  (10) any past revocation, suspension, or denial of a business or professional license of any principal in the company or any proposed broker-in-charge;
  (11) if a general partnership, a description of the applicant entity, including a copy of its written partnership agreement or if no written agreement exists, a written description of the rights and duties of the partners, and the name of each partner. If a partner is an entity rather than a natural person, the name of each officer, partner, or manager of that entity, or any entity therein;
  (12) if a limited liability company, a description of the applicant entity, including a copy of its written operating agreement or if no written agreement exists, a written description of the rights and duties of the managers, and the name of each manager. If a manager is an entity rather than a natural person, the name of each officer, partner, or manager of that entity, or any entity therein;
  (13) if a business entity other than a corporation, limited liability company, or partnership, a description of the organization of the applicant entity, including a copy of its organizational documents evidencing its authority to engage in real estate brokerage;
  (14) if a foreign business entity, a Certificate of Authority to transact business in North Carolina issued by the NC Secretary of State and an executed consent to service of process and pleadings; and
  (15) any other information required by this Rule.
(d) When the authority of a business entity to engage in the real estate business is unclear in the application or in law, the Commission shall require the applicant to declare in the firm license application that the applicant's organizational documents authorize the firm to engage in the real estate business and to submit organizational documents, addresses of affiliated persons, and similar information. For purposes of this Rule, the term "principal," when it refers to a person or entity, means any person or entity owning 10 percent or more of the business entity, or who is an officer, director, manager, member, partner, or who holds any other comparable position.
(e) After filing a firm license application with the Commission, the entity shall be licensed provided that it:
  (1) has one principal holding a broker license on active status in good standing who will serve as the qualifying broker; and

(2) employs and is directed by personnel licensed as a broker in accordance with this Chapter.

The qualifying broker of a partnership of any kind shall be a general partner of the partnership; the qualifying broker of a limited liability company shall be a manager of the company; and the qualifying broker of a corporation shall be an officer of the corporation. A licensed business entity may serve as the qualifying broker of another licensed business entity if the qualifying broker-entity has as its qualifying broker a natural person who is licensed as a broker. The natural person who is qualifying broker shall assure to the Commission the performance of the qualifying broker's duties with regard to both entities. A provisional broker may not serve as a qualifying broker.

(f) The licensing of a business entity shall not be construed to extend to the licensing of its partners, managers, members, directors, officers, employees or other persons acting for the entity in their individual capacities regardless of whether they are engaged in furthering the business of the licensed entity.

(g) The qualifying broker of a business entity shall assume responsibility for:
- (1) designating and assuring that there is at all times a broker-in-charge for each office and branch office of the entity as "office" and "branch office" are defined in Rule .0110(a) of this Subchapter;
- (2) renewing the real estate broker license of the entity;
- (3) retaining the firm's current pocket card at the firm and producing it as proof of firm licensure upon request and maintaining a photocopy of the firm license certificate and pocket card at each branch office thereof;
- (4) notifying the Commission of any change of business address or legal or trade name of the entity and the registration of any assumed business name adopted by the entity for its use;
- (5) notifying the Commission in writing of any change of his or her status as qualifying broker within 10 days following the change;
- (6) securing and preserving the transaction and trust account records of the firm whenever there is a change of broker-in-charge at the firm or any office thereof and notifying the Commission if the trust account records are out of balance or have not been reconciled as required by Rule .0117 of this Subchapter;
- (7) retaining and preserving the transaction and trust account records of the firm upon termination of his or her status as qualifying broker until a new qualifying broker has been designated with the Commission or, if no new qualifying broker is designated, for the period of time records are required to be retained by Rule .0108 of this Subchapter;
- (8) notifying the Commission if, upon the termination of his or her status as qualifying broker, the firm's transaction and trust account records cannot be retained or preserved or if the trust account records are out of balance or have not been reconciled as required by Rule .0117 of this Subchapter; and
- (9) notifying the Commission regarding any revenue suspension, revocation of Certificate of Authority, or administrative dissolution of the entity by the NC Secretary of State within 10 days of the suspension, revocation, or dissolution.

(h) Every licensed business entity and every entity applying for licensure shall conform to all the requirements imposed upon it by the North Carolina General Statutes for its continued existence and authority to do business in North Carolina. Failure to conform to such requirements shall be grounds for disciplinary action or denial of the entity's application for licensure.

(i) Upon receipt of notice from an entity or agency of this State that a licensed entity has ceased to exist or that its authority to engage in business in this State has been terminated by operation of law, the Commission shall cancel the license of the entity.

History Note: Authority G.S. 55-11A-04; 93A-3(c); 93A-4;
Eff. February 1, 1976;
Readopted Eff. September 30, 1977;
Amended Eff. July 1, 2017; July 1, 2015; July 1, 2014; July 1, 2009; January 1, 2008; April 1, 2006; July 1, 2005; April 1, 2004; July 1, 2003; October 1, 2000; August 1, 1998; January 1, 1997; July 1, 1994; May 1, 1990;
Pursuant to G.S. 150B-21.3A, rule is necessary without substantive public interest Eff. May 1, 2018.

21 NCAC 58A .0503   LICENSE RENEWAL

(a) All real estate licenses issued by the Commission under G.S. 93A, Article 1 shall expire on June 30 following issuance. Any broker desiring renewal of his or her license shall renew on the Commission's website within 45 days prior to license expiration and shall submit a renewal fee of forty-five dollars ($45.00).

(b) During the renewal process, every individual broker shall provide an email address to be used by the Commission. The email address may be designated by the broker as private in order to be exempt from public records disclosures pursuant to G.S. 93A-4(b2). A broker who does not have an email address is not required to obtain an email address to comply with this Rule.

(c) During the renewal process, every designated broker-in-charge shall disclose:
    (1) each federally insured depository institution lawfully doing business in this State where the trust account(s) for the broker-in-charge or the entity for which the broker-in-charge is designated is held, if applicable; and
    (2) any criminal conviction or occupational license disciplinary action that occurred within the previous year.

History Note: *Authority G.S. 93A-3(c); 93A-4; 93A-4.1; 93A-6;*
Eff. February 1, 1976;
Readopted Eff. September 30, 1977;
Amended Eff. July 1, 1994; February 1, 1991; February 1, 1989;
Temporary Amendment Eff. April 24, 1995 for a period of 180 days or until the permanent rule becomes effective, whichever is sooner;
Amended Eff. July 1, 2017; July 1, 2014; April 1, 2013; April 1, 2006; January 1, 2006; July 1, 2004; December 4, 2002; April 1, 1997; July 1, 1996; August 1, 1995;
Pursuant to G.S. 150B-21.3A, rule is necessary without substantive public interest Eff. May 1, 2018;
Amended Eff. July 1, 2018.

21 NCAC 58A .0504   ACTIVE AND INACTIVE LICENSE STATUS

(a) Except for licenses that have expired or that have been revoked, suspended or surrendered, all licenses issued by the Commission shall be designated as being either on active status or inactive status. Subject to compliance with Rule .0110 of this Subchapter, the holder of a license on active status may engage in any activity requiring a real estate license and may be compensated for the provision of any lawful real estate brokerage service. The holder of a license on inactive status shall not engage in any activity requiring a real estate license, including the referral for compensation of a prospective seller, buyer, landlord or tenant to another real estate broker or any other party. A broker holding a license on inactive status must renew the license and pay the prescribed license renewal fee in order to continue to hold the license. The Commission may take disciplinary action against a broker holding a license on inactive status for any violation of G.S. 93A or any rule adopted by the Commission, including the offense of engaging in an activity for which a license is required.

(b) A license issued to a provisional broker shall, upon initial licensure, be assigned to inactive status. A license issued to a firm or a broker other than a provisional broker shall be assigned to active status. Except for persons licensed under the provisions of Section .1800 of this Subchapter, a broker may change the status of his or her license from active to inactive status by submitting a written request to the Commission. A provisional broker's license shall be assigned by the Commission to inactive status when the provisional broker is not under the active, direct supervision of a broker-in-charge. A firm's license shall be assigned by the Commission to inactive status when the firm does not have a qualifying broker with an active license. Except for persons licensed under the provisions of Section .1800 of this Subchapter, a broker shall also be assigned to inactive status if, upon the second renewal of his or her license following initial licensure, or upon any subsequent renewal, he or she has not satisfied the continuing education requirement described in Rule .1702 of this Subchapter.

(c) A provisional broker with an inactive license who desires to have the license placed on active status must comply with the procedures prescribed in Rule .0506 of this Section.

(d) A broker, other than a provisional broker, with an inactive license who desires to have the license placed on active status shall file with the Commission a request for license activation on a form provided by the Commission containing identifying information about the broker, a statement that the broker has satisfied the continuing education requirements prescribed by Rule .1703 of this Subchapter, the name and address of any broker-in-charge, the date of the request, and the signature of the broker. Upon the mailing or delivery of this form, the broker's status will be considered to be active. If the broker is eligible for license activation, the Commission shall send a written acknowledgement of the license activation to the broker and his or her affiliated broker-in-charge, if any. If neither the broker nor his or her affiliated broker-in-charge receive from the Commission a written acknowledgment of the license activation within 30 days of the date shown on the form, the broker shall immediately terminate his or her real estate brokerage activities pending receipt of the written acknowledgment from the Commission. If either the broker or his or her affiliated broker-in-charge, if any, is notified that he or she is not eligible for license activation due to a continuing education deficiency, the broker shall terminate all real estate brokerage activities until such time as the continuing education deficiency is satisfied and a new request for license activation is submitted to the Commission.

(e) Upon an active, non-provisional broker's affiliation with a firm and broker-in-charge, the broker-in-charge of the office where the broker will be engaged in the real estate business shall notify the Commission of the affiliation on a form provided by the Commission containing identifying information about the affiliating broker and the broker-in-charge, and the signature of the broker-in-charge. If neither the broker nor the broker-in-charge receive from the Commission a written acknowledgment of the license affiliation within 30 days of the date shown on the form, the broker and his or her broker-in-charge shall cease representing the broker as being affiliated with such broker-in-charge pending receipt of the written acknowledgment from the Commission.

(f) A firm with an inactive license which desires to have its license placed on active status shall file with the Commission a request for license activation containing identifying information about the firm and its qualifying broker and satisfy the requirements of Rule .0110 of this Subchapter. If the qualifying broker has an inactive license, he or she must satisfy the requirements of Paragraph (d) of this Rule. Upon the mailing or delivery of the completed form by the qualifying broker, the firm may engage in real estate brokerage activities requiring a license; however, if the firm's qualifying broker does not receive from the Commission a written acknowledgment of the license activation within 30 days of the date shown on the form, the firm shall immediately terminate its real estate brokerage activities pending receipt of the written acknowledgment from the Commission. If the qualifying broker is notified that the firm is not eligible for license activation due to a continuing education deficiency on the part of the qualifying broker, the firm must terminate all real estate brokerage activities until such time as the continuing education deficiency is satisfied and a new request for license activation is submitted to the Commission.

(g) A person licensed as a broker under Section .1800 of this Subchapter shall maintain his or her license on active status at all times as required by Rule .1804 of this Subchapter.

History Note: *Authority G.S. 93A-3(c); 93A-4(d); 93A-4.1; 93A-6; 93A-9;*
Eff. February 1, 1976;
Readopted Eff. September 30, 1977;
Amended Eff. April 1, 2013; February 1, 2012; January 1, 2012; July 1, 2009; April 1, 2006; July 1, 2005; July 1, 2004; October 1, 2000; April 1, 1997; July 1, 1996; July 1, 1995; July 1, 1994; February 1, 1989; December 1, 1985;
Pursuant to G.S. 150B-21.3A, rule is necessary without substantive public interest Eff. May 1, 2018.

21 NCAC 58A .0505   REINSTATEMENT OF A LICENSE
(a) The fee for reinstatement of a license that has been expired, revoked, or surrendered for less than two years shall be an amount equal to two times the current renewal license fee pursuant to Rule .0503 of this Section.
(b) The reinstatement application form is available on the Commission's website and shall include the applicant's:
        (1)   legal name;
        (2)   mailing, physical, and email address;
        (3)   telephone number;
        (4)   previous license number;
        (5)   Secretary of State identification number, if applicable;
        (6)   social security number and date of birth, if applicable;
        (7)   qualifying broker and broker-in-charge's legal name and license number, if applicable;
        (8)   criminal record report prepared within six months of application;
        (9)   certification; and
        (10)   signature.
(c) An individual seeking reinstatement of a license that has been expired for less than six months shall:
        (1)   submit the reinstatement fee pursuant to Paragraph (a) of this Rule;
        (2)   disclose any criminal conviction or disciplinary action pursuant to Rule .0113 of this Section, including any conviction or disciplinary action incurred while the individual's license was expired; and

(3) satisfy the license activation requirements of Rule .1703 of this Subchapter, if applicable.

(d) An individual seeking reinstatement of a license that has been expired for six months but no more than two years or revoked or surrendered for no more than two years shall:
  (1) submit a complete reinstatement application pursuant to Paragraph (b) of this Rule;
  (2) submit the reinstatement fee pursuant to Paragraph (a) of this Rule; and
  (3) pass:
      (A) one Postlicensing course within six months prior to submitting his or her reinstatement application;
      (B) the "National" and "State" sections of the current license examination within 180 days after submitting his or her reinstatement application; or
      (C) the "State" section of the current license examination within 180 days after submitting his or her reinstatement application if the individual possesses an active broker license in another state.

(e) An individual seeking reinstatement of a license that has been expired, revoked, or surrendered for more than two years shall submit an original license application and fee pursuant to G.S. 93A-4 and Rules .0301 and .0302 of this Subchapter.

(f) A license shall be reinstated with the same license number and status, either full or provisional, it held before expiration, revocation, or surrender if reinstated within three years from the expiration, revocation, or surrender and shall be effective as of the date of reinstatement, not the date of original licensure. If a license is reinstated after three years from the expiration, revocation, or surrender, the license shall be on provisional broker status pursuant to G.S. 93A-4(a1).

(g) A business entity seeking reinstatement of a license shall submit:
  (1) the reinstatement fee pursuant to Paragraph (a) of this Rule if the license has been expired for less than six months;
  (2) the reinstatement fee and a complete reinstatement application pursuant to Paragraphs (a) and (b) of this Rule if the license has been expired for six months but no more than two years or revoked or surrendered for no more than two years;
  (3) an original firm license application pursuant to G.S. 93A-4 and Rules .0301, .0302, and .0502 of this Subchapter if the license has been expired, revoked, or surrendered for more than two years.

(h) A broker seeking reinstatement of a license shall satisfy to the Commission that he or she possesses the character requisites pursuant to G.S. 93A-4(b).

History Note: *Authority G.S. 93A-3(c); 93A-4; 93A-4.1;*
Eff. February 1, 1976;
Readopted Eff. September 30, 1977;
Temporary Amendment Eff. April 24, 1995 for a period of 180 days or until the permanent rule becomes effective, whichever is sooner;
Amended Eff. July 1, 2017; January 1, 2012; July 1, 2009; January 1, 2008; April 1, 2004; July 1, 2000; August 1, 1998; July 1, 1996; August 1, 1995; July 1, 1995;
Pursuant to G.S. 150B-21.3A, rule is necessary without substantive public interest Eff. May 1, 2018;
Amended Eff. July 1, 2018.

21 NCAC 58A .0506   PROVISIONAL BROKER TO BE SUPERVISED BY BROKER
(a) This Rule shall apply to all real estate provisional brokers.
(b) A provisional broker may engage in or hold himself or herself out as engaging in activities requiring a real estate license only while his or her license is on active status and he or she is supervised by the broker-in-charge of the real estate firm or office with which the provisional broker is affiliated. A provisional broker may be supervised by only one broker-in-charge at a time.
(c) Upon a provisional broker's affiliation with a real estate broker or brokerage firm, the broker-in-charge of the office where the provisional broker will be engaged in the real estate business shall immediately file with the Commission a provisional broker supervision notification on a form provided by the Commission containing identifying information about the provisional broker and the broker-in-charge, a statement from the broker-in-charge certifying that he or she will supervise the provisional broker in the performance of all acts for which a license is required, the date that the broker-in-charge assumes responsibility for such supervision, and the signature of the broker-in-charge. If the provisional broker is on inactive status at the time of associating with a broker or brokerage

firm, the broker-in-charge shall also file, along with the provisional broker supervision notification, a request for license activation on a form provided by the Commission containing identifying information about the provisional broker, the statement of the broker-in-charge that he or she has verified that the provisional broker has satisfied the continuing education requirements prescribed by Rule .1703 of this Subchapter, and the postlicensing education requirements, if applicable, prescribed by Rule .1902 of this Subchapter, the date of the request, and the signature of the proposed broker-in-charge. Upon the mailing or delivery of the required form(s), the provisional broker may engage in real estate brokerage activities requiring a license under the supervision of the broker-in-charge; however, if the provisional broker and broker-in-charge do not receive from the Commission a written acknowledgment of the provisional broker supervision notification and, if appropriate, the request for license activation, within 30 days of the date shown on the form, the broker-in-charge shall immediately terminate the provisional broker's real estate brokerage activities pending receipt of the written acknowledgment from the Commission. If the provisional broker and broker-in-charge are notified that the provisional broker is not eligible for license activation due to a continuing education or postlicensing education deficiency, the broker-in-charge shall cause the provisional broker to immediately cease all activities requiring a real estate license until such time as the continuing education or postlicensing education deficiency is satisfied and a new provisional broker supervision notification and request for license activation is submitted to the Commission.

(d) A broker-in-charge who certifies to the Commission that he or she will supervise a provisional broker shall actively and directly supervise the provisional broker in a manner that reasonably assures that the provisional broker performs all acts for which a real estate license is required in accordance with the Real Estate License Law and Commission rules. A supervising broker who fails to supervise a provisional broker as prescribed in this Rule may be subject to disciplinary action by the Commission.

(e) Upon the termination of the supervisory relationship between a provisional broker and his or her broker-in-charge, the provisional broker and the broker-in-charge shall provide written notification of the date of termination to the Commission not later than 10 days following said termination.

History Note: *Authority G.S. 93A-2(b); 93A-3; 93A-9;*
Eff. February 1, 1976;
Readopted Eff. September 30, 1977;
Amended Eff. April 1, 2013; April 1, 2006; July 1, 2005; July 1, 2004; October 1, 2000; August 1, 1998; July 1, 1996; July 1, 1995; July 1, 1993.

21 NCAC 58A .0507   PAYMENT OF FEES

Checks, credit cards, and other forms of payment given the Commission for fees due which are returned unpaid shall be considered cause for license denial, suspension, or revocation.

History Note: *Authority G.S. 93A-3(c); 93A-4(c),(d); 150A-11;*
Eff. February 1, 1976;
Readopted Eff. September 30, 1977;
Amended Eff. September 1, 2002; May 1, 1984;
Pursuant to G.S. 150B-21.3A, rule is necessary without substantive public interest Eff. May 1, 2018.

21 NCAC 58A .0508   DUPLICATE LICENSE FEE

History Note: *Authority G.S. 93A-3(c); 93A-4(c),(d); 150A-11;*
Eff. February 1, 1976;
Readopted Eff. September 30, 1977;
Repealed Eff. May 1, 1984.

21 NCAC 58A .0509   DUPLICATE LICENSE FEE

History Note: *Authority G.S. 93A-4(c),(d);*
Eff. December 1, 1985;
Amended Eff. February 1, 1989;
Repealed Eff. July 1, 2017.

21 NCAC 58A .0510   CANCELLATION OF SALESPERSON LICENSE UPON BROKER LICENSURE

History Note: *Authority G.S. 93A-3(c); 93A-4(d);*
Eff. July 1, 1996;
Amended Eff. October 1, 2000;
Repealed Eff. April 1, 2006.

21 NCAC 58A .0511   LICENSING OF PERSONS LICENSED IN ANOTHER JURISDICTION
(a) For purposes of this Rule, "Jurisdiction" shall mean a state, territory, or possession of the United States or Canada.
(b) An individual seeking a real estate license who, at the time of application, holds a current real estate salesperson or broker license in another jurisdiction that has been on active status in good standing within the three years prior to application may satisfy the 75-hour prelicensing education program and examination requirements prescribed in G.S. 93A-4 by electing to either:
- (1) pass the "State" section of that examination. A person qualifying for licensure under this provision shall be issued a North Carolina broker license on a status comparable to the category of license held by the person in the jurisdiction where the qualifying license is held; or
- (2) be issued a North Carolina broker license on provisional status only and then comply with the provisions of G.S. 93A-4(a1).

(c) Brokers who were licensed in North Carolina by reciprocity shall be entitled to retain such license indefinitely, unless suspended, revoked, or surrendered pursuant to G.S. 93A-6, so long as the license is renewed or is reinstated pursuant to Rule .0505 of this Section.
(d) A military-trained or military spouse applicant seeking a temporary practice permit shall submit an application on a form available on the Commission's website. The military-trained or military spouse temporary permit application shall include applicant's:
- (1) legal name;
- (2) mailing, physical, and email address;
- (3) telephone number;
- (4) social security number;
- (5) date of birth;
- (6) criminal background report prepared within six months of application;
- (7) occupational licensing history, including any disciplinary actions;
- (8) pending liens or judgements;
- (9) certification of equivalent training or experience, by submission of either a:
  - (A) military occupational specialty certificate that is substantially equivalent to or exceeds the requirements for licensure;
  - (B) certification that the applicant has engaged in the active practice of brokerage for at least two of the five years preceding the date of the application; or
  - (C) certification, issued within six months of application, of a current real estate salesperson or broker license in another jurisdiction that has been on active status within 3 years of application;
- (10) certification; and
- (11) signature.

(e) An applicant who is issued a temporary practice permit pursuant to Paragraph (d) of this Rule shall remain a provisional broker for the duration of the permit.

History Note: *Authority G.S. 93A-3(c); 93A-4; 93A-4.1; 93A-9(a); 93B-15.1;*
Eff. January 1, 2012;
Amended Eff. April 1, 2013; February 1, 2012;
Pursuant to G.S. 150B-21.3A, rule is necessary without substantive public interest Eff. May 1, 2018;
Amended Eff. July 1, 2018.

21 NCAC 58A .0512   DEATH OR INCAPACITY OF SOLE PROPRIETOR
(a) If a licensed real estate broker engaged in business as a sole proprietor pursuant to G.S. 93A-2(a) dies or becomes incapacitated, the Commission shall issue a temporary license to the executor or administrator of the estate

of the deceased sole proprietor broker or to the court-appointed fiduciary of the incapacitated sole proprietor broker upon receipt of the following:
  (1) a written notification to the Commission of the date of the broker's death or disability; and
  (2) a certified copy of the court order appointing the executor, administer, or fiduciary.
(b) A temporary license shall be valid only for the purpose of distributing trust money held or paying commissions owed by the sole proprietor broker at the time of death or incapacity, but shall not otherwise entitle the holder to undertake any action for which a real estate license is required.
(c) The temporary license shall be valid for one year from issuance.

History Note: Authority G.S. 93A-2;
         Eff. July 1, 2018.

SECTION .0600 – REAL ESTATE COMMISSION HEARINGS

21 NCAC 58A .0601   COMPLAINTS/INQUIRIES/MOTIONS/OTHER PLEADINGS
(a) There shall be no specific form required for complaints. To be sufficient, a complaint shall be in writing, identify the respondent licensee and shall reasonably apprise the Commission of the facts which form the basis of the complaint.
(b) When investigating a complaint, the scope of the Commission's investigation shall not be limited only to matters alleged in the complaint. In addition, a person making a complaint to the Commission may change his or her complaint by submitting the changes to the Commission in writing.
(c) When a complaint has not been submitted in conformity with this Rule, the Commission's legal counsel may initiate an investigation if the available information is sufficient to create a reasonable suspicion that any licensee or other person or entity may have committed a violation of the provisions of the Real Estate License Law or the rules adopted by the Commission.
(d) There shall be no specific forms required for answers, motions, or other pleadings relating to contested cases before the Commission, except they shall be in writing. To be sufficient, the document must reasonably apprise the Commission of the matters it alleges or answers. To be considered by the Commission, every answer, motion, request or other pleading must be submitted to the Commission in writing or made during the hearing as a matter of record.
(e) During the course of an investigation of a licensee, the Commission, through its legal counsel or other staff, may send the licensee a Letter of Inquiry requesting the licensee to respond. The Letter of Inquiry, or attachments thereto, shall set forth the subject matter being investigated. Upon receipt of the Letter of Inquiry, the licensee shall respond within 14 calendar days. Such response shall include a full and fair disclosure of all information requested. Licensees shall include with their written response copies of all documents requested in the Letter of Inquiry.
(f) Hearings in contested cases before the Commission shall be conducted according to the provisions of G.S. 150B, Article 3A.
(g) Persons who make complaints are not parties to contested cases, but may be witnesses.

History Note: Authority G.S. 93A-3(d); 93A-6(a); 150B-38(h);
         Eff. February 1, 1976;
         Readopted Eff. September 30, 1977;
         Amended Eff. July 1, 2000; August 1, 1998; May 1, 1992; February 1, 1989; November 1, 1987;
         Pursuant to G.S. 150B-21.3A, rule is necessary without substantive public interest Eff. May 1, 2018.

21 NCAC 58A .0602   PRIMA FACIE CASE

History Note: Authority G.S. 93A-3(c); 93A-6(a); 150A-11;
         Eff. February 1, 1976;
         Readopted Eff. September 30, 1977;
         Amended Eff. April 22, 1980;
         Repealed Eff. September 1, 1983.

21 NCAC 58A .0603   REQUEST FOR HEARING
21 NCAC 58A .0604   NOTICE OF HEARING

21 NCAC 58A .0605　　WHO SHALL HEAR CONTESTED CASES
21 NCAC 58A .0606　　FAILURE TO APPEAR

History Note:　　Authority G.S. 93A-3(c); 150A-11; 150A-25(a);
　　　　　　　　　　Eff. February 1, 1976;
　　　　　　　　　　Readopted Eff. September 30, 1977;
　　　　　　　　　　Repealed Eff. May 1, 1984.

21 NCAC 58A .0607　　PETITION TO REOPEN PROCEEDING
(a) After a final decision has been reached by the Commission in a contested case, a party may petition the Commission to reconsider a case. Petitions will not be granted except when the petitioner can show that the reasons for reconsidering the case are to introduce newly discovered evidence which was not presented at the initial hearing because of some justifiable, excusable or unavoidable circumstance. Upon the running of the 30 day period for seeking judicial review, such petitions will have no effect.
(b) Decisions on petitions to reopen cases are within the discretion of the Commission.

History Note:　　Authority G.S. 150B-38(h);
　　　　　　　　　　Eff. February 1, 1976;
　　　　　　　　　　Readopted Eff. September 30, 1977;
　　　　　　　　　　Amended Eff. February 1, 1989; May 1, 1984;
　　　　　　　　　　Pursuant to G.S. 150B-21.3A, rule is necessary without substantive public interest Eff. May 1, 2018.

21 NCAC 58A .0608　　ANSWER

History Note:　　Authority G.S. 93A-3(c); 150A-11; 150A-25(b);
　　　　　　　　　　Eff. February 1, 1976;
　　　　　　　　　　Repealed Eff. May 1, 1984.

21 NCAC 58A .0609　　INTERVENTION

History Note:　　Authority G.S. 93A-3(c); 150A-11; 150A-23(d);
　　　　　　　　　　Eff. February 1, 1976;
　　　　　　　　　　Readopted Eff. September 30, 1977;
　　　　　　　　　　Amended Eff. May 1, 1984;
　　　　　　　　　　Repealed Eff. February 1, 1989.

21 NCAC 58A .0610　　SUBPOENAS
(a) Subpoenas issued in preparation for, or in the conduct of, a contested case pending before the Commission shall be issued in the name of the Commission and shall be signed by the Commission's legal counsel, chairman, vice chairman, the officer presiding at the hearing if a member of the Commission other than the chairman or vice chairman has been designated to preside.
(b) After a notice of hearing in a contested case has been issued and served upon a respondent or, in a case concerning an application for licensure, the applicant, the respondent, or the attorney for the respondent or applicant may request subpoenas for the attendance of witnesses and the production of evidence. The subpoenas may be signed by the respondent or applicant, or the respondent's or applicant's attorney.
(c) All subpoenas issued in connection with a contested case pending before the Commission shall be on a form approved by the Commission. Subpoena forms shall be provided by the Commission without charge upon request.
(d) Motions to quash a subpoena issued in preparation for, or in connection with, a contested case pending before the Commission shall be submitted to the Commission in writing and shall clearly state the grounds therefor. The disposition of any motion to quash a subpoena shall be made by the chairman of the Commission in his or her discretion. If the chairman is unavailable, then the vice chairman or other Commission member designated to preside over the hearing may dispose of such a motion in the chairman's place.

History Note:　　Authority G.S. 93A-6(a); 150B-38(h); 150B-39(c); 150B-40;
　　　　　　　　　　Eff. February 1, 1976;

Readopted Eff. September 30, 1977;
Amended Eff. October 1, 2000; August 1, 1996; May 1, 1992; February 1, 1989; May 1, 1984;
Pursuant to G.S. 150B-21.3A, rule is necessary without substantive public interest Eff. May 1, 2018.

21 NCAC 58A .0611   ANSWERS AND OTHER PLEADINGS

History Note: *Authority G.S. 93A-3(c); 150B-11;*
Eff. July 1, 1988;
Repealed Eff. February 1, 1989.

21 NCAC 58A .0612   PRESIDING OFFICER

The Commission may designate any of its members to preside over the hearing in a contested case. When no designation is made, the Chairman of the Commission shall preside, or, in his or her absence, the Vice Chairman shall preside. The presiding officer shall rule on motions or other requests made in a contested case prior to the conduct of the hearing in that case except when the ruling on the motion would be dispositive of the case. When the ruling on a motion or request would be dispositive of the case, the presiding officer shall make no ruling and the motion or request shall be determined by a majority of the Commission.

History Note: *Authority G.S. 93A-3(c); 150B-40(b);*
Eff. May 1, 1992;
Amended Eff. October 1, 2000.

21 NCAC 58A .0613   SCOPE

History Note: *Authority G.S. 93A-3(c);*
Eff. May 1, 1992;
Repealed Eff. August 1, 1998.

21 NCAC 58A .0614   SUMMARY SUSPENSION

(a) If the Commission finds that the public health, safety, or welfare requires emergency action, it may, pursuant to G.S. 150B-3(c), summarily suspend a license without a hearing or opportunity for the licensee to be heard. A motion for summary suspension shall be presented to the Chairman of the Commission by counsel for the State and may be presented ex parte. The motion shall be supported by an affidavit of a person with first-hand knowledge of the facts alleged which require emergency action.

(b) The Commission shall, when it summarily suspends a license, immediately schedule a hearing, to occur at the earliest practicable date, on the merits of the charges set out in a notice of hearing issued contemporaneously with the order of summary suspension. The motion, supporting affidavit, order for summary suspension and notice of hearing shall be served on the licensee as soon as possible and the summary suspension shall be effective no earlier than the date of service of the summary suspension order on the licensee. The order of summary suspension shall remain in effect until the Commission vacates it.

(c) A summarily suspended licensee may petition the Commission to vacate the summary suspension order. If the Chairman of the Commission finds that the summary suspension order was issued in error or on insufficient factual grounds to justify emergency action, the Chairman of the Commission may vacate the summary suspension order.

(d) Neither an order of summary suspension nor a denial of a motion to vacate an order of summary suspension is a final agency decision.

History Note: *Authority G.S. 93A-6(a); 150B-3(c);*
Eff. August 1, 1998;
Pursuant to G.S. 150B-21.3A, rule is necessary without substantive public interest Eff. May 1, 2018.

21 NCAC 58A .0615   SETTLEMENTS

The Commission may consider disposing of any contested matter before it by consent order or upon stipulation of the respondent and the Commission's legal counsel. The Commission may approve or reject any proposal to dispose of a contested matter by consent or stipulation, however, any matter to which a respondent and the Commission's legal counsel have stipulated which is rejected by the Commission shall not thereafter bind the parties or the Commission. Except as may be otherwise allowed by the presiding officer, all proposals to dispose of a contested matter must be in written form and signed by the respondent not later than two days prior to the date set for the hearing of the matter, excluding any days during which the Commission's offices are closed.

History Note: Authority G.S. 93A-3(d); 93A-6(a); 150B-38(h);
Eff. July 1, 2000;
Pursuant to G.S. 150B-21.3A, rule is necessary without substantive public interest Eff. May 1, 2018.

21 NCAC 58A .0616   PROCEDURES FOR REQUESTING HEARINGS WHEN APPLICANT'S CHARACTER IS IN QUESTION
(a) When the moral character of an applicant for licensure or approval is in question, the applicant shall not be licensed or approved until the applicant has affirmatively demonstrated that the applicant possesses the requisite honesty, truthfulness, integrity, good moral character, and general fitness, including mental and emotional fitness, necessary to protect the public interest and promote public confidence in the real estate brokerage business. For the purposes of this Rule, applicant means any person or entity making application for licensure as a real estate broker or for licensure or approval as a prelicensing or continuing education instructor, director, coordinator, school or sponsor.
(b) When the applicant is an entity, it shall be directed and controlled by persons who possess the requisite honesty, truthfulness, integrity, good moral character, and general fitness, including mental and emotional fitness, necessary to protect the public interest and promote public confidence in the real estate brokerage business.
(c) When the character of an applicant is in question, the Commission shall defer action upon the application until the applicant is notified by letter. The letter informing the applicant that his or her moral character is in question shall be sent by certified mail, return receipt requested, to the address shown upon the application. The applicant shall have 60 days from the date of receipt of this letter to request a hearing before the Commission. If the applicant fails to request a hearing within this time or if a properly addressed letter is returned to the Commission undelivered, applicant's right to a hearing shall be considered waived and the application shall be deemed denied. If the applicant makes a timely request for a hearing in accordance with the provisions of this Rule, the Commission shall provide the applicant with a Notice of Hearing and hearing as required by G.S. 150B, Article 3A.
(d) Nothing in this Rule shall be interpreted to prevent an unsuccessful applicant from reapplying for licensure or approval if such application is otherwise permitted by law.

History Note: Authority G.S. 93A-4;
Eff. September 1, 2002;
Amended Eff. April 1, 2013; January 1, 2012; April 1, 2006;
Pursuant to G.S. 150B-21.3A, rule is necessary without substantive public interest Eff. May 1, 2018.

SECTION .0700 - PETITIONS FOR RULES

21 NCAC 58A .0701   PETITION FOR RULE-MAKING HEARINGS
(a) Any person wishing to file a petition requesting the adoption, amendment or repeal of a rule by the Commission shall file a written petition with the executive director.
(b) The petition shall include the following information:
    (1)   name, address and occupation of petitioner;
    (2)   a summary of the proposed action (adoption, amendment, or repeal of a rule or rules);
    (3)   a draft of the proposed rule or other action;
    (4)   a complete statement of the reason for the proposed action; and
    (5)   an identification of the persons or class of persons most likely to be affected by the proposed action.
(c) The Commission shall decide whether to allow or deny a rule-making petition.

History Note: Authority G.S. 150B-16;
Eff. February 1, 1976;
Readopted Eff. September 30, 1977;

Amended Eff. February 1, 1989; May 1, 1984;
Pursuant to G.S. 150B-21.3A, rule is necessary without substantive public interest Eff. May 1, 2018.

21 NCAC 58A .0702 DISPOSITION OF PETITIONS
21 NCAC 58A .0703 ADDITIONAL INFORMATION

History Note: *Authority G.S. 93A-3(c); 150A-12; 150A-16;*
Eff. February 1, 1976;
Readopted Eff. September 30, 1977;
Repealed Eff. May 1, 1984.

SECTION .0800 - RULE MAKING

21 NCAC 58A .0801 REQUEST TO PARTICIPATE

History Note: *Authority G.S. 93A-3(c); 150A-11; 150A-12(e);*
Eff. February 1, 1976;
Readopted Eff. September 30, 1977;
Repealed Eff. May 1, 1984.

21 NCAC 58A .0802 WRITTEN SUBMISSIONS
21 NCAC 58A .0803 PRESIDING OFFICER: POWERS AND DUTIES

History Note: *Authority G.S. 93A-3(c); 150B-12;*
Eff. February 1, 1976;
Readopted Eff. September 30, 1977;
Amended Eff. February 1, 1989; May 1, 1984;
Expired Eff. June 1, 2018 pursuant to G.S. 150B-21.3A.

21 NCAC 58A .0804 STATEMENT OF REASONS FOR DECISION

History Note: *Authority G.S. 93A-3(c); 150A-11; 150A-12(e);*
Eff. February 1, 1976;
Readopted Eff. September 30, 1977;
Repealed Eff. May 1, 1984.

21 NCAC 58A .0805 RECORD OF PROCEEDINGS

History Note: *Authority G.S. 93A-3(c); 150B-12;*
Eff. February 1, 1976;
Readopted Eff. September 30, 1977;
Amended Eff. February 1, 1989; November 1, 1987;
Expired Eff. June 1, 2018 pursuant to G.S. 150B-21.3A.

SECTION .0900 - DECLARATORY RULINGS

21 NCAC 58A .0901 SUBJECTS OF DECLARATORY RULINGS

History Note: *Authority G.S. 93A-3(c); 150A-17;*
Eff. February 1, 1976;
Readopted Eff. September 30, 1977;
Repealed Eff. May 1, 1984.

21 NCAC 58A .0902 **REQUESTS FOR RULINGS: DISPOSITION OF REQUESTS**
(a) All requests for declaratory rulings shall be written and filed with the Commission. The request must contain the following information:
- (1) the name, address and signature of petitioner;
- (2) a concise statement of the manner in which petitioner is aggrieved by the rule or statute in question, or its potential application to him or her;
- (3) a statement of the interpretation given the statute or rule in question by petitioner;
- (4) a statement of the reasons, including any legal authorities, in support of the interpretation given the statute or rule by petitioner.

(b) The Commission shall either deny the request, stating the reasons therefore, or issue a declaratory ruling. The Commission may deny a request for a declaratory ruling when the Commission determines that:
- (1) the petition does not comply with the requirements of Paragraph (a) of this Rule;
- (2) the subject matter is one concerning which the Commission is without authority to make a decision binding the agency or the petitioner;
- (3) the petitioner is not aggrieved by the rule or statute in question or otherwise has insufficient interest in the subject matter of the request;
- (4) there is reason to believe that the petitioner or some other person or entity materially connected to the subject matter of the request is acting in violation of the real estate license law or the rules adopted by the Commission; or
- (5) the subject matter of the request is the subject of litigation, legislation, or rulemaking.

(c) The Commission shall not issue a declaratory ruling when the petitioner or his or her request is the subject of, or materially related to, an investigation by the Real Estate Commission or contested case before the Commission.

History Note: *Authority G.S. 93A-3(c); 150B-4(a);*
Eff. February 1, 1976;
Readopted Eff. September 30, 1977;
Amended Eff. April 1, 2006; October 1, 2000; May 1, 1992; February 1, 1989; May 1, 1984;
Pursuant to G.S. 150B-21.3A, rule is necessary without substantive public interest Eff. May 1, 2018.

21 NCAC 58A .0903 **DISPOSITION OF REQUESTS**
21 NCAC 58A .0904 **APPLICABILITY OF RULING**

History Note: *Authority G.S. 93A-3(c); 150A-17;*
Eff. February 1, 1976;
Readopted Eff. September 30, 1977;
Repealed Eff. May 1, 1984.

21 NCAC 58A .0905 **RECORD OF RULING**

History Note: *Authority G.S. 93A-3(c); 150B-17;*
Eff. February 1, 1976;
Readopted Eff. September 30, 1977;
Amended Eff. November 1, 1987;
Expired Eff. June 1, 2018 pursuant to G.S. 150B-21.3A.

SECTION .1000 - SCHOOLS

This Section .1000 of Title 21 Subchapter 58A of the North Carolina Administrative Code (T21.58A .1000); SCHOOLS; has been transferred and recodified to Section .0100 of Title 21 Subchapter 58C of the North Carolina Administrative Code (T21.58C .0100), effective November 27, 1989.

SECTION .1100 - REAL ESTATE PRE-LICENSING COURSES

21 NCAC 58A .1101 **PURPOSE AND APPLICABILITY**

History Note: *Authority G.S. 93A-4(a),(d);*
Eff. September 1, 1979;
Amended Eff. February 1, 1989; September 1, 1984;
Transferred and Recodified to 21 NCAC 58C .0301 Eff. November 27, 1989.

21 NCAC 58A .1102   PROGRAM STRUCTURING

History Note: *Authority G.S. 93A-4(a),(d);*
Eff. September 1, 1979;
Amended Eff. February 1, 1989; September 1, 1984; September 1, 1983; January 1, 1981;
Transferred and Recodified to 21 NCAC 58C .0302 Eff. November 27, 1989.

21 NCAC 58A .1103   COURSE DURATION

History Note: *Authority G.S. 93A-4(a),(d);*
Eff. September 1, 1979;
Amended Eff. September 1, 1984;
Repealed Eff. February 1, 1989.

21 NCAC 58A .1104   COURSE CONTENT

History Note: *Authority G.S. 93A-4(a),(d);*
Eff. September 1, 1979;
Amended Eff. February 1, 1989; November 1, 1987; May 1, 1987; September 1, 1984;
Transferred and Recodified to 21 NCAC 58C .0303 Eff. November 27, 1989.

21 NCAC 58A .1105   COURSE COMPLETION STANDARDS

History Note: *Authority G.S. 93A-4(a),(d);*
Eff. September 1, 1979;
Amended Eff. April 1, 1987; September 1, 1984;
Recodified Paragraphs (d) and (e) to Rule 58A .1113 (a) and (b) Eff. January 6, 1989;
Amended Eff. February 1, 1989;
Transferred and Recodified to 21 NCAC 58C .0304 Eff. November 27, 1989.

21 NCAC 58A .1106   EXAMINATIONS

History Note: *Authority G.S. 93A-4(a),(d);*
Eff. September 1, 1979;
Amended Eff. September 1, 1983;
Repealed Eff. September 1, 1984.

21 NCAC 58A .1107   COURSE SCHEDULING

History Note: *Authority G.S. 93A-4(a),(d);*
Eff. September 1, 1979;
Amended Eff. February 1, 1989; August 1, 1980;
Transferred and Recodified to 21 NCAC 58C .0305 Eff. November 27, 1989.

21 NCAC 58A .1108   TEXTBOOKS

History Note: *Authority G.S. 93A-4(a),(d);*
Eff. September 1, 1979;
Amended Eff. February 1, 1989; September 1, 1984; September 1, 1983;
Transferred and Recodified to 21 NCAC 58C .0306 Eff. November 27, 1989.

21 NCAC 58A .1109 INSTRUCTORS

History Note: Authority G.S. 93A-4(a),(d);
Eff. September 1, 1979;
Amended Eff. February 1, 1989; September 1, 1984; January 1, 1981;
Transferred and Recodified to 21 NCAC 58C .0307 Eff. November 27, 1989.

21 NCAC 58A .1110 CHANGES IN COURSE DURATION: TEXTBOOKS: PRIMARY INSTRUCTORS

History Note: Authority G.S. 93A-4(a),(d);
Eff. September 1, 1979;
Repealed Eff. January 1, 1981.

21 NCAC 58A .1111 CERTIFICATION OF COURSE COMPLETION

History Note: Authority G.S. 93A-4(a),(d);
Eff. September 1, 1979;
Amended Eff. February 1, 1989; September 1, 1984; January 1, 1981;
Transferred and Recodified to 21 NCAC 58C .0309 Eff. November 27, 1989.

21 NCAC 58A .1112 COURSES PRIOR TO SEPTEMBER 1, 1979

History Note: Authority G.S. 93A-4(a),(d);
Eff. September 1, 1979;
Repealed Eff. January 1, 1981.

21 NCAC 58A .1113 COURSE RECORDS

History Note: Authority G.S. 93A-4(a),(d);
Eff. September 1, 1984;
Recodified from Rule 58A .1105 (d) and (e) Eff. January 6, 1989;
Transferred and Recodified to 21 NCAC 58C .0310 Eff. November 27, 1989.

SECTION .1200 - CERTIFICATION OF REAL ESTATE INSTRUCTORS

21 NCAC 58A .1201 APPLICABILITY: REQUIREMENT FOR CERTIFICATION
21 NCAC 58A .1202 APPLICATION FOR INSTRUCTOR CERTIFICATION
21 NCAC 58A .1203 CRITERIA FOR CERTIFICATION
21 NCAC 58A .1204 DURATION OF CERTIFICATION
21 NCAC 58A .1205 DENIAL: REVOCATION: SUSPENSION OF INSTRUCTOR CERTIFICATION

History Note: Authority G.S. 93A-4(a),(d);
Eff. September 1, 1979;
Amended Eff. November 1, 1987; April 1, 1987; September 1, 1984; January 1, 1981;
Repealed Eff. February 1, 1989.

21 NCAC 58A .1206 CHANGES IN SCHOOL AFFILIATION OR ADDRESS

History Note: Authority G.S. 93A-4(a),(d);
Eff. January 1, 1981;
Amended Eff. November 1, 1987;
Repealed Eff. February 1, 1989.

SECTION .1300 - PRIVATE REAL ESTATE SCHOOLS

21 NCAC 58A .1301　　APPLICABILITY

History Note:　　*Authority G.S. 93A-4(a),(d); 93A-33;*
Eff. October 1, 1980;
Amended Eff. February 1, 1989; December 1, 1987;
Transferred and Recodified to 21 NCAC 58C .0201 Eff. November 27, 1989.

21 NCAC 58A .1302　　APPLICATION FOR ORIGINAL LICENSE

History Note:　　*Authority G.S. 93A-4(a),(d); 93A-33;*
Eff. October 1, 1980;
Repealed Eff. December 1, 1987.

21 NCAC 58A .1303　　SCHOOL NAME

History Note:　　*Authority G.S. 93A-4(a),(d); 93A-33;*
Eff. October 1, 1980;
Amended Eff. September 1, 1984;
Transferred and Recodified to 21 NCAC 58C .0203 Eff. November 27, 1989.

21 NCAC 58A .1304　　COURSES

History Note:　　*Authority G.S. 93A-4(a),(d); 93A-33;*
Eff. October 1, 1980;
Amended Eff. February 1, 1989; September 1, 1984;
Transferred and Recodified to 21 NCAC 58C .0204 Eff. November 27, 1989.

21 NCAC 58A .1305　　ADDITIONAL COURSE OFFERINGS

History Note:　　*Authority G.S. 93A-4(a),(d); 93A-33;*
Eff. October 1, 1980;
Amended Eff. February 1, 1989; November 1, 1987;
Transferred and Recodified to 21 NCAC 58C .0205 Eff. November 27, 1989.

21 NCAC 58A .1306　　ADMINISTRATION

History Note:　　*Authority G.S. 93A-4(a),(d); 93A-33;*
Eff. October 1, 1980;
Amended Eff. April 1, 1987;
Transferred and Recodified to 21 NCAC 58C .0206 Eff. November 27, 1989.

21 NCAC 58A .1307　　FACILITIES AND EQUIPMENT

History Note:　　*Authority G.S. 93A-4(a),(d); 93A-33;*
Eff. October 1, 1980;
Amended Eff. February 1, 1989; November 1, 1987; September 1, 1984;
Transferred and Recodified to 21 NCAC 58C .0207 Eff. November 27, 1989.

21 NCAC 58A .1308　　BULLETINS

History Note:　　*Authority G.S. 93A-4(a),(d); 93A-33;*
Eff. October 1, 1980;
Amended Eff. December 1, 1987;

Transferred and Recodified to 21 NCAC 58C .0208 Eff. November 27, 1989.

21 NCAC 58A .1309   ENROLLMENT CONTRACTS

History Note: Authority G.S. 93A-4(a),(d); 93A-33;
Eff. October 1, 1980;
Transferred and Recodified to 21 NCAC 58C .0209 Eff. November 27, 1989.

21 NCAC 58A .1310   ADMISSIONS POLICY AND PRACTICE

History Note: Authority G.S. 93A-4(a),(d); 93A-33;
Eff. October 1, 1980;
Transferred and Recodified to 21 NCAC 58C .0210 Eff. November 27, 1989.

21 NCAC 58A .1311   RECORDS

History Note: Authority G.S. 93A-4(a),(d); 93A-33;
Eff. October 1, 1980;
Amended Eff. February 1, 1989; September 1, 1984;
Transferred and Recodified to 21 NCAC 58C .0211 Eff. November 27, 1989.

21 NCAC 58A .1312   ENFORCEMENT OF INSTITUTIONAL STANDARDS

History Note: Authority G.S. 93A-4(a),(d); 93A-33;
Eff. October 1, 1980;
Transferred and Recodified to 21 NCAC 58C .0212 Eff. November 27, 1989.

21 NCAC 58A .1313   PERFORMANCE BOND

History Note: Authority G.S. 93A-4(a),(d); 93A-33;
Eff. October 1, 1980;
Amended Eff. December 1, 1987;
Transferred and Recodified to 21 NCAC 58C .0213 Eff. November 27, 1989.

21 NCAC 58A .1314   ADVERTISING AND RECRUITMENT ACTIVITIES

History Note: Authority G.S. 93A-4(a),(d); 93A-33;
Eff. October 1, 1980;
Amended Eff. February 1, 1989; April 1, 1987; September 1, 1984;
Transferred and Recodified to 21 NCAC 58C .0214 Eff. November 27, 1989.

21 NCAC 58A .1315   QUARTERLY REPORTS

History Note: Authority G.S. 93A-4(a),(d); 93A-33;
Eff. October 1, 1980;
Amended Eff. September 1, 1984;
Transferred and Recodified to 21 NCAC 58C .0215 Eff. November 27, 1989.

21 NCAC 58A .1316   CHANGES DURING THE LICENSING PERIOD

History Note: Authority G.S. 93A-4(a),(d); 93A-33;
Eff. October 1, 1980;
Amended Eff. February 1, 1989; September 1, 1984;
Transferred and Recodified to 21 NCAC 58C .0216 Eff. November 27, 1989.

21 NCAC 58A .1317   RENEWAL OF LICENSES

History Note: Authority G.S. 93A-4(a),(d); 93A-33;
Eff. October 1, 1980;
Amended Eff. February 1, 1989; December 1, 1987;
Transferred and Recodified to 21 NCAC 58C .0217 Eff. November 27, 1989.

21 NCAC 58A .1318   LICENSING EXAM CONFIDENTIALITY: SCHOOL PERFORM./LICENSING

History Note: Authority G.S. 93A-4(a),(d); 93A-33;
Eff. October 1, 1980;
Amended Eff. April 1, 1987; September 1, 1984;
Transferred and Recodified to 21 NCAC 58C .0218 Eff. November 27, 1989.

SECTION .1400 – REAL ESTATE EDUCATION AND RECOVERY FUND

21 NCAC 58A .1401   APPLICATION FOR PAYMENT
(a) Any person or entity desiring to obtain payment from the Real Estate Education and Recovery Fund shall file an application with the Commission on a form provided by the Commission. The form shall require the following information concerning the applicant and the claim: the applicant's name and address, the amount of the claim, a description of the acts of the broker which constitute the grounds for the claim and a statement that all court proceedings are concluded. With the form, the applicant shall submit copies of the civil complaint, judgment, and the return of execution marked as unsatisfied. If the application is incomplete or not filed in correct form, or if the Commission is without jurisdiction over the claim or the parties, counsel for the Commission may file a motion to dismiss the application. The Commission shall conduct a hearing on the motion at which the only issues to be determined shall be whether the application is complete or in correct form or whether the Commission has jurisdiction over the claim or the parties.
(b) Forms for application for payment from the Real Estate Education and Recovery Fund shall be available from the Commission on request.

History Note: Authority G.S. 93A-3(c); 93A-17;
Eff. February 1, 1988;
Amended Eff. April 1, 2013; September 1, 2002;
Pursuant to G.S. 150B-21.3A, rule is necessary without substantive public interest Eff. May 1, 2018.

21 NCAC 58A .1402   MULTIPLE CLAIMS
(a) If at any time the Commission has notice of more than one application or potential claim for payment from the Real Estate Education and Recovery Fund arising out of the conduct of a single broker, the Commission may, in its discretion, direct that all applications filed before a date determined by the Commission be consolidated for hearing and payment.
(b) Upon directing that claims be consolidated as provided in Paragraph (a) of this Rule, the Commission shall issue to the broker and the applicants and potential claimants an Order of Consolidation setting forth the deadline for filing all applications to be consolidated. Upon the passing of the deadline, the Commission may, in its discretion, either extend the deadline or issue to the broker and all applicants a notice of the time, date and place set for the hearing on the consolidated applications.
(c) In exercising its discretion as provided in Paragraphs (a) and (b) of this Rule, the Commission shall consider the following factors:
    (1) the number of claim applications or potential claims of which it has notice;
    (2) the amount of each claim;
    (3) the status of the underlying civil action in each claim;
    (4) the length of time each claim has been pending since the Commission first received notice of the claim; and
    (5) whether consolidation of such claims or the extension of the deadline for filing applications to be consolidated will promote the fair and efficient administration and payment of monies from the Real Estate Education and Recovery Fund.

History Note: *Authority G.S. 93A-16(d); 93A-17; 93A-20;*
Eff. February 1, 1988;
Amended Eff. May 1, 2013; July 1, 2000; February 1, 1989;
Pursuant to G.S. 150B-21.3A, rule is necessary without substantive public interest Eff. May 1, 2018.

21 NCAC 58A .1403   **NOTICE OF HEARING: ORDER/PAYT FROM/REAL ESTATE EDUCATION AND RECOVERY FUND**

(a) The Commission shall give notice of the time, place and date of a hearing on a claim for payment from the Real Estate Education and Recovery Fund to any applicant and the broker.

(b) After conducting a hearing, the Commission shall issue an order either authorizing payment or denying the claim, in whole or in part. This order shall be served upon the broker and any applicant.

(c) The existence of subsequent notices of potential claims or subsequent applications shall not be considered by the Commission in the issuance of an Order for Payment in those cases where the award is allowable but must be reduced pursuant to the provisions of G.S. 93A-21.

History Note: *Authority G.S. 93A-16(d); 93A-20;*
Eff. February 1, 1988;
Amended Eff. April 1, 2013; February 1, 1989;
Pursuant to G.S. 150B-21.3A, rule is necessary without substantive public interest Eff. May 1, 2018.

21 NCAC 58A .1404   **EXHAUSTED LIABILITY LIMITS**

Applications for payment from the Real Estate Education and Recovery Fund received or considered by the Commission after the liability of the Real Estate Education and Recovery Fund as described in G.S. 93A-21 has been exhausted shall be dismissed.

History Note: *Authority G.S. 93A-3(c); 93A-21;*
Eff. February 1, 1988;
Amended Eff. April 1, 2013; February 1, 1989;
Pursuant to G.S. 150B-21.3A, rule is necessary without substantive public interest Eff. May 1, 2018.

SECTION .1500 - FORMS

21 NCAC 58A .1501   **LICENSING AND GENERAL BROKERAGE FORMS**

History Note: *Authority G.S. 93A-4(d); 150B-11(1);*
Eff. July 1, 1989;
Repealed Eff. July 1, 1998.

21 NCAC 58A .1502   **FORMS FOR SCHOOL APPROVAL OR LICENSURE**

History Note: *Authority G.S. 93A-4(d); 150B-11(1);*
Eff. July 1, 1989;
Amended Eff. May 1, 1990;
Repealed Eff. July 1, 1998.

SECTION .1600 - DISCRIMINATORY PRACTICES PROHIBITED

21 NCAC 58A .1601   **FAIR HOUSING**

Conduct by a licensee which violates the provisions of the State Fair Housing Act constitutes improper conduct in violation of G.S. 93A-6(a)(10).

History Note: *Authority G.S. 41A-4; 41A-5; 41A-6; 93A-3(c);*

Eff. July 1, 1989;
Amended Eff. April 1, 1997;
Pursuant to G.S. 150B-21.3A, rule is necessary without substantive public interest Eff. May 1, 2018.

SECTION .1700 – MANDATORY CONTINUING EDUCATION

21 NCAC 58A .1701   PURPOSE AND APPLICABILITY
This Section describes the continuing education requirement for real estate brokers authorized by G.S. 93A-4.1, establishes the continuing education requirement to change a license from inactive status to active status, establishes attendance requirements for continuing education courses, establishes the criteria and procedures relating to obtaining an extension of time to complete the continuing education requirement, establishes the criteria for obtaining continuing education credit for an unapproved course or related educational activity, and addresses other similar matters.

History Note: *Authority G.S. 93A-3(c); 93A-4.1;*
Eff. July 1, 1994;
Amended Eff. April 1, 2006; October 1, 2000;
Pursuant to G.S. 150B-21.3A, rule is necessary without substantive public interest Eff. May 1, 2018.

21 NCAC 58A .1702   CONTINUING EDUCATION REQUIREMENT
(a) Except as provided in Rules .1708 and .1711 of this Section, a broker shall complete eight credit hours of real estate continuing education courses approved pursuant to 21 NCAC 58H within one year prior to the expiration of the license as follows:
    (1)   four credit hours of elective courses; and
    (2)   four hours of either:
        (A)   the "General Update Course;" or
        (B)   for a broker with BIC Eligible status, the "Broker-In-Charge Update Course" in lieu of the "General Update Course."
(b) A BIC or broker who takes the General Update Course rather than the Broker-In-Charge Update Course shall receive continuing education credit for taking such course only for the purpose of retaining his or her license on active status and shall not be considered to have satisfied the requirement to take the Broker-In-Charge Update Course in order to retain his or her BIC Eligible status.
(c) Continuing education courses shall be completed upon the second renewal following the initial licensure and upon each subsequent annual renewal.
(d) The broker shall provide the course completion certificate upon request of the Commission.
(e) No continuing education shall be required to renew a broker license on inactive status. In order to change a license from inactive status to active status, the broker shall satisfy the continuing education requirement described in Rule .1703 of this Section.
(f) No continuing education shall be required for a broker who is a member of the U.S. Congress or the North Carolina General Assembly in order to renew his or her license on active status.
(g) For purposes of this Rule, the terms "active status" and "inactive status" shall have the same definition as those in Rule .0504 of this Subchapter.
(h) For continuing education purposes, the term "initial licensure" shall include the first time that a license of a particular type is issued to a person, the reinstatement of a canceled, revoked or surrendered license, and any license expired for more than six months.

History Note: *Authority G.S. 93A-3(c); 93A-4.1;*
Eff. July 1, 1994;
Amended Eff. July 1, 2017; July 1, 2014; April 1, 2006; July 1, 2005; April 1, 2004; October 1, 2000; August 1, 1998; July 1, 1996;
Pursuant to G.S. 150B-21.3A, rule is necessary without substantive public interest Eff. May 1, 2018;
Amended Eff. July 1, 2018.

21 NCAC 58A .1703   CONTINUING EDUCATION FOR LICENSE ACTIVATION
(a) A broker requesting to change an inactive license to active status on or after the broker's second license renewal following his or her initial licensure shall have completed the continuing education as described in Paragraph (b) or (c) of this Rule, whichever is appropriate.
(b) If the inactive broker's license has not been on active status since the preceding July 1 and the broker has a deficiency in his or her continuing education record for the previous license period, the broker shall make up the deficiency and satisfy the continuing education requirement pursuant to Rule .1702 of this Section for the current license period in order to activate the license. Any deficiency may be made up by completing, during the current license period or previous license period, approved continuing education elective courses; however, such courses shall not be credited toward the continuing education requirement for the current license period. When crediting elective courses for purposes of making up a continuing education deficiency, the maximum number of credit hours that will be awarded for any course is four hours.
(c) If a broker's license has been on inactive status for more than two years and the broker has a deficiency in his or her continuing education record, the broker shall:
  (1) cure the continuing education deficiency for the current license year; and
  (2) complete two Postlicensing courses no more than six months prior to activation.

History Note: *Authority G.S. 93A-3(c); 93A-4.1;*
    Eff. July 1, 1994;
    Amended Eff. July 1, 2017; April 1, 2006; July 1, 2000; July 1, 1995;
    Pursuant to G.S. 150B-21.3A, rule is necessary without substantive public interest Eff. May 1, 2018;
    Amended Eff. July 1, 2018.

21 NCAC 58A .1704   NO CREDIT FOR PRELICENSING OR POSTLICENSING COURSES
No credit toward the continuing education requirement shall be awarded for completing a real estate prelicensing or postlicensing course.

History Note: *Authority G.S. 93A-3(c); 93A-4.1;*
    Eff. July 1, 1994;
    Amended Eff. April 1, 2006.
    Pursuant to G.S. 150B-21.3A, rule is necessary without substantive public interest Eff. May 1, 2018.

21 NCAC 58A .1705   ATTENDANCE AND PARTICIPATION REQUIREMENTS
(a) In order to receive credit for completing an approved continuing education course, a broker shall:
  (1) attend at least 90 percent of the scheduled instructional hours for the course;
  (2) provide his or her legal name and license number to the course sponsor;
  (3) present his or her pocket card or photo identification card, if necessary; and
  (4) personally perform all work required to complete the course.
(b) With the instructor or the sponsor's permission, a 10 percent absence allowance shall be permitted at any time during the course, except that it may not be used to skip the last 10 percent of the course unless the absence is:
  (1) approved by the instructor; and
  (2) for circumstances beyond the broker's control that could not have been reasonably foreseen by the broker, such as:
    (A) an illness;
    (B) a family emergency; or
    (C) acts of God.
(c) With regard to the Commission's 12-hour Broker-In-Charge Course that is taught over two days, a broker shall attend at least 90 percent of the scheduled instructional hours on each day of the course and the 10 percent absence allowance referred to in Paragraph (b) of this Rule shall apply to each day of the course.

History Note: *Authority G.S. 93A-3(c); 93A-4.1;*
    Eff. July 1, 1994;
    Amended Eff. July 1, 2017; July 1, 2010;

Pursuant to G.S. 150B-21.3A, rule is necessary without substantive public interest Eff. May 1, 2018.

21 NCAC 58A .1706 REPETITION OF COURSES
A continuing education course may be taken only once for continuing education credit within a single license period.

History Note: Authority G.S. 93A-3(c); 93A-4A;
Eff. July 1, 1994;
Pursuant to G.S. 150B-21.3A, rule is necessary without substantive public interest Eff. May 1, 2018.

21 NCAC 58A .1707 ELECTIVE COURSE CARRY-OVER CREDIT
A maximum of four hours of continuing education credit for an approved elective course taken during the current license period may be carried over to satisfy the continuing education elective requirement for the next following license period if the licensee receives no continuing education elective credit for the course toward the elective requirement for the current license period or the previous license period. However, if a continuing education elective course is used to wholly or partially satisfy the elective requirement for the current or previous license period, then any excess hours completed in such course which are not needed to satisfy the four-hour elective requirement for that license period may not be carried forward and applied toward the elective requirement for the next following license period.

History Note: Authority G.S. 93A-3(c); 93A-4A;
Eff. July 1, 1994;
Amended Eff. July 1, 1995;
Pursuant to G.S. 150B-21.3A, rule is necessary without substantive public interest Eff. May 1, 2018.

21 NCAC 58A .1708 EQUIVALENT CREDIT
(a) The Commission shall award a broker continuing education credit for teaching a Commission Update Course. A broker seeking continuing education credit for teaching a Commission Update Course shall submit a form, available on the Commission's website, that requires the broker to set forth the:
  (1)   broker's name, license number, instructor number, address, telephone number, and email address;
  (2)   Update Course number;
  (3)   sponsor's name and number;
  (4)   sponsor's address; and
  (5)   date the course was taught.
(b) The Commission shall award a broker continuing education elective credit for teaching a Commission approved continuing education elective for the first time any given continuing education elective is taught. A broker seeking continuing education credit under this Paragraph shall submit a form, available on the Commission's website, that requires the broker to set forth the:
  (1)   broker's name, license number, address, telephone number, and email address;
  (2)   course title;
  (3)   course number;
  (4)   sponsor's name and number;
  (5)   sponsor's address; and
  (6)   date the course was taught.
(c) The Commission may award continuing education elective credit for completion of an unapproved course that the Commission finds equivalent to the elective course component of the continuing education requirement set forth in 21 NCAC 58H .0407(a). The broker shall submit a course completion certificate issued by the course sponsor, a copy of the course description or course outline, and a fifty dollar ($50.00) fee for each course for which the broker seeks credit. A broker seeking continuing education credit for a course that is not approved by the Commission shall submit a form, available on the Commission's website, that requires the broker to set forth the:
  (1)   broker's name, license number, address, telephone number, and email address;
  (2)   course title;
  (3)   number of instructional hours;

(4) course instructor's name; and
(5) course sponsor's name, address, telephone number, and email address.

(d) The Commission may award continuing education elective credit for developing a continuing education elective course that is approved by the Commission pursuant to 21 NCAC 58H .0400. However, a broker shall only receive credit for the year in which the continuing education elective is approved. A broker seeking continuing education credit under this Paragraph shall submit a form, available on the Commission's website, that requires the broker to set forth the broker's name, license number, address, telephone number, and email address. Along with the form, the broker shall submit the course title, the course number, the date of the course approval, and a fifty dollar ($50.00) fee for each course for which the broker seeks credit.

(e) The Commission may award continuing education elective credit for authoring a real estate textbook. However, a broker shall receive credit for any single textbook only once. A broker seeking continuing education credit under this Paragraph shall submit a form, available on the Commission's website, that requires the broker to set forth the broker's name, license number, address, telephone number, and email address. Along with the form, the broker shall submit the title page of the textbook, showing the title, publisher, and publication date, the table of contents, and a fifty dollar ($50.00) fee for each textbook for which the licensee seeks credit.

(f) The Commission may award continuing education elective credit for authoring of a scholarly article on a real estate topic published in a professional journal or periodical. A broker shall receive credit for any single article only once. A broker seeking continuing education credit under this Paragraph shall submit a form, available on the Commission's website, that requires the broker to set forth the broker's name, license number, address, telephone number, and email address. Along with the form, the broker shall submit a copy of the article, proof of publication, and a fifty dollar ($50.00) fee for each article for which the broker seeks credit.

(g) In order for any application for equivalent credit to be considered and credits applied to the current licensing period, a complete application, the appropriate fee, and all supporting documents shall be received by the Commission no later than 5:00 p.m. on June 10.

History Note: Authority G.S. 93A-3(c); 93A-4.1;
Eff. July 1, 1994;
Amended Eff. July 1, 2017; April 1, 2006; July 1, 2001; July 1, 2000; March 1, 1996; July 1, 1995;
Pursuant to G.S. 150B-21.3A, rule is necessary without substantive public interest Eff. May 1, 2018.

21 NCAC 58A .1709   EXTENSIONS OF TIME TO COMPLETE CONTINUING EDUCATION

(a) A broker on active status may request an extension of time to satisfy the continuing education requirement for the current license period if the broker was unable to obtain the necessary education due to an incapacitating illness, military deployment, or other circumstance that existed for a portion of the license period and that constituted a severe hardship.

(b) Requests for an extension of time shall be submitted on a form available on the Commission's website that requires the broker to set out the broker's name, mailing address, license number, telephone number, email address, and a description of the incapacitating illness or other circumstance. The requesting broker shall submit, along with the form, supporting documentation, such as a written physician's statement, deployment orders, or other corroborative evidence, demonstrating that compliance with the continuing education requirement would have been impossible or burdensome.

(c) All requests for an extension of time shall be received by the Commission by 5:00 p.m. on June 10 of the licensing period for which the extension is sought.

(d) If an extension of time is granted, the broker shall be permitted to renew his or her license on active status. The broker's license shall automatically change to inactive status if the broker fails to satisfy the continuing education requirement prior to the end of the extension period.

(e) In no event shall an extension of time be granted that extends the continuing education requirement deadline beyond June 10 of the license year following the license year in which the request is made.

History Note: Authority G.S. 93A-3(c); 93A-4.1;
Eff. July 1, 1994;
Amended Eff. July 1, 2017; August 1, 2014; October 1, 2000;
Pursuant to G.S. 150B-21.3A, rule is necessary without substantive public interest Eff. May 1, 2018.

21 NCAC 58A .1710 DENIAL OR WITHDRAWAL OF CONTINUING EDUCATION CREDIT
(a) The Commission shall deny continuing education credit claimed by a broker or reported by a course sponsor for a broker, and shall withdraw continuing education credit previously awarded by the Commission to a broker upon finding that the broker:
- (1) or course sponsor provided incorrect or incomplete information to the Commission concerning continuing education completed by the broker;
- (2) failed to comply with the attendance requirement established by Rule .1705 of this Section; or
- (3) was mistakenly awarded continuing education credit due to an administrative error.

(b) If an administrative error or an incorrect report by a course sponsor results in the denial or withdrawal of continuing education credit for a broker, the Commission shall, upon the written request of the broker, grant the broker an extension of time to satisfy the continuing education requirement.

(c) A broker who obtains or attempts to obtain continuing education credit through misrepresentation of fact, dishonesty, or other improper conduct shall be subject to disciplinary action pursuant to G.S. 93A-6.

History Note: *Authority G.S. 93A-3(c); 93A-4.1;*
Eff. July 1, 1994;
Amended Eff. July 1, 2017; July 1, 1995;
Pursuant to G.S. 150B-21.3A, rule is necessary without substantive public interest Eff. May 1, 2018.

21 NCAC 58A .1711 CONTINUING EDUCATION REQUIRED OF NONRESIDENT BROKERS
(a) To be considered a nonresident for continuing education purposes, a real estate broker licensed in North Carolina shall not have a North Carolina business address, mailing address, or residence address at the time he or she applies for license renewal if he or she seeks to renew his or her license on active status. A nonresident North Carolina broker who wishes to renew his or her license on active status may satisfy the continuing education requirement by any one of the following means:
- (1) A nonresident broker may, at the time of license renewal, hold a real estate license on active status in another state and certify on a form prescribed by the Commission that the broker holds such license. If at any time after renewal there is a change in the status of the out-of-state license, the nonresident broker shall notify the Commission within 10 days and request that his or her North Carolina license be placed on inactive status, or provide evidence to the Commission that he or she has satisfied either Subparagraph (a)(2) or (a)(3) of this Rule or the requirements of Rule .1702 of this Section.
- (2) A nonresident broker may, within one year preceding license expiration, complete the Commission-prescribed Update course plus one Commission-approved continuing education elective course, or complete two Commission-approved continuing education elective courses.
- (3) A nonresident broker may, within one year preceding license expiration, complete eight classroom hours in courses approved for continuing education credit by the real estate licensing agency in the broker's state of residence or in the state where the course was taken. To obtain credit for a continuing education course completed in another state and not approved by the Commission, the broker must submit a written request for continuing education credit accompanied by a fee of fifty dollars ($50.00) per request and evidence that the course was completed and that the course was approved for continuing education credit by the real estate licensing agency in the broker's state of residence or in the state where the course was taken.
- (4) A nonresident broker may obtain eight hours equivalent credit for a course or courses not approved by the Commission or for related educational activities as provided in Rule .1708 of this Section. The maximum amount of continuing education credit the Commission will award a nonresident broker for an unapproved course or educational activity shall be eight hours.

(b) When requesting to change an inactive license to active status, or when applying for reinstatement of a license expired for not more than six months, a nonresident broker may satisfy the continuing education requirements described in Rules .0505 and .1703 of this Subchapter by complying with any of the options described in Paragraph (a) of this Rule, except that the requirements in Subparagraphs (a)(2) and (a)(3) of this Rule restricting the taking of courses to one year preceding license expiration shall not be applicable.

(c) No carry-over credit to a subsequent license period shall be awarded for a course taken in another state that has not been approved by the North Carolina Real Estate Commission as an elective course pursuant to 21 NCAC 58H .0406.

History Note: Authority G.S. 93A-3(c); 93A-4.1;
Eff. July 1, 1994;
Amended Eff. July 1, 2017; July 1, 2015; January 1, 2008; April 1, 2006; October 1, 2000; March 1, 1996; July 1, 1995;
Pursuant to G.S. 150B-21.3A, rule is necessary without substantive public interest Eff. May 1, 2018;
Amended Eff. July 1, 2018.

SECTION .1800 - LIMITED NONRESIDENT COMMERCIAL LICENSING

21 NCAC 58A .1801   GENERAL PROVISIONS
(a) Any person resident in a state or territory of the United States other than North Carolina may perform the acts or services of a real estate broker in North Carolina in transactions involving commercial real estate if said person first applies for and obtains a limited nonresident commercial real estate broker license as provided in this Section.
(b) Corporations, business associations and entities shall be ineligible for licensure under this Section.
(c) Nothing in this Section shall be construed to limit the rights of any person duly licensed as a real estate broker in North Carolina under the provisions of G.S. 93A-4 or 93A-9(a).

History Note: Authority G.S. 93A-4; 93A-9;
Eff. July 1, 2004;
Amended Eff. April 1, 2006;
Pursuant to G.S. 150B-21.3A, rule is necessary without substantive public interest Eff. May 1, 2018.

21 NCAC 58A .1802   DEFINITIONS
For the purposes of this Section:
(1) "Commercial Real Estate" means any real property or interest therein, whether freehold or non-freehold, which at the time the property or interest is made the subject of an agreement for brokerage services:
  (a) is lawfully used primarily for sales, office, research, institutional, warehouse, manufacturing, industrial or mining purposes or for multifamily residential purposes involving five or more dwelling units;
  (b) may lawfully be used for any of the purposes listed in Subitem (1)(a) of this Rule by a zoning ordinance adopted pursuant to the provisions of G.S. 153A, Article 18 or G.S. 160A, Article 19 or which is the subject of an official application or petition to amend the applicable zoning ordinance to permit any of the uses listed in Subitem (1)(a) of this Rule which is under consideration by the government agency with authority to approve the amendment; or
  (c) is in good faith intended to be immediately used for any of the purposes listed in Subitem (1)(a) of this Rule by the parties to any contract, lease, option, or offer to make any contract, lease, or option.
(2) "Qualifying state" means the state or territory of the United States where an applicant for, and the holder of, a limited nonresident commercial license issued under this Section is licensed in good standing as a real estate broker or salesperson. The qualifying state must be the state or territory where the applicant or limited nonresident commercial licensee maintains his or her primary place of business as a real estate broker or salesperson. Under no circumstances may North Carolina be a qualifying state.

History Note: Authority G.S. 93A-4; 93A-9;
Eff. July 1, 2004;

Pursuant to G.S. 150B-21.3A, rule is necessary without substantive public interest Eff. May 1, 2018.

21 NCAC 58A .1803   REQUIREMENTS FOR LICENSURE; APPLICATION AND FEE
(a) A person desiring to obtain a broker license under this Section shall demonstrate to the Real Estate Commission that:
- (1) he or she is a resident of a state or territory of the United States other than North Carolina;
- (2) he or she is licensed as a real estate broker or salesperson in a qualifying state and that said license is on active status and not in abeyance for any reason. If licensed as a salesperson, he or she shall also demonstrate that he or she is acting under the supervision of a broker in accordance with the applicable governing statutes or regulations in the qualifying state; and
- (3) he or she possesses the requisite honesty, truthfulness, integrity, and moral character for licensure as a broker in North Carolina.

A person applying for licensure under this Section shall not be required to show that the state or territory where he or she is currently licensed offers reciprocal licensing privileges to North Carolina brokers.
(b) A person desiring to be licensed under this Section shall submit an application on a form prescribed by the Commission and shall show the Commission that he or she has satisfied the requirements set forth in Paragraph (a) of this Rule. In connection with his or her application a person applying for licensure under this Rule shall provide the Commission with a certification of license history from the qualifying state where he or she is licensed. He or she shall also provide the Commission with a report of his or her criminal history from the service designated by the Commission. An applicant for licensure under this Section shall be required to update his or her application as required by Rule .0302(c) of this Subchapter.
(c) The fee for persons applying for licensure under this Section shall be one hundred dollars ($100.00) and shall be paid in the form of a certified check, bank check, cashier's check, money order, or by credit card. Once paid, the application fee shall be non-refundable.
(d) If the Commission has received a complete application and the required application fee and if the Commission is satisfied that the applicant possesses the moral character necessary for licensure, the Commission shall issue to the applicant a limited nonresident commercial real estate broker license.

History Note: Authority G.S. 93A-4; 93A-9;
Eff. July 1, 2004;
Amended Eff. April 1, 2006;
Pursuant to G.S. 150B-21.3A, rule is necessary without substantive public interest Eff. May 1, 2018.

21 NCAC 58A .1804   ACTIVE STATUS
Broker licenses issued under this Section shall be issued on active status and shall remain valid only so long as the licensee's license in the qualifying state remains valid and on active status. In addition, a license issued to a salesperson under this Section shall remain valid only while the salesperson is acting under the supervision of a real estate broker in accordance with the applicable laws and rules in the qualifying state. Individuals licensed under this Section shall immediately notify the Commission if his or her license in the qualifying state lapses or expires, is suspended or revoked, made inactive, or is placed in abeyance for any reason.

History Note: Authority G.S. 93A-4; 93A-9;
Eff. July 1, 2004;
Amended Eff. April 1, 2006;
Pursuant to G.S. 150B-21.3A, rule is necessary without substantive public interest Eff. May 1, 2018.

21 NCAC 58A .1805   RENEWAL
(a) A license issued under this Section shall expire on June 30 following issuance unless it is renewed in accordance with the provisions of Rule .0503 and .1711 of this Subchapter.
(b) The Commission shall not renew a license issued under this Section unless the licensee has demonstrated that he or she has complied with the requirements of Paragraph (a) of this Rule and that his or her license in the qualifying state is on active status in good standing and is not lapsed, expired, suspended, revoked, or in abeyance for any reason.

History Note: Authority G.S. 93A-4; 93A-9;
Eff. July 1, 2004;
Pursuant to G.S. 150B-21.3A, rule is necessary without substantive public interest Eff. May 1, 2018.

21 NCAC 58A .1806   LIMITATIONS
(a) A person licensed under this Section may act as a real estate broker in this state only if:
- (1) he or she does not reside in North Carolina;
- (2) the real property interest which is the subject of any transaction in connection with which he or she acts as a broker in this state is commercial real estate as that term is defined in Rule .1802 of this Section; and
- (3) he or she is affiliated with a resident North Carolina real estate broker as required in Rule .1807 of this Section.

(b) A nonresident commercial real estate broker licensed under the provisions of Section .1800 of this Subchapter shall not act as or serve in the capacity of a broker-in-charge of a firm or office in North Carolina.

History Note: Authority G.S. 93A-4; 93A-9;
Eff. July 1, 2004;
Amended Eff. April 1, 2006;
Pursuant to G.S. 150B-21.3A, rule is necessary without substantive public interest Eff. May 1, 2018.

21 NCAC 58A .1807   AFFILIATION WITH RESIDENT BROKER
(a) No person licensed under G.S. 93A-9(b) shall enter North Carolina to perform any act or service for which licensure as a real broker is required unless he or she has first entered into a brokerage cooperation agreement and declaration of affiliation with an individual who is a resident in North Carolina licensed as a North Carolina real estate broker.

(b) A brokerage cooperation agreement as contemplated by this Rule shall be in writing and signed by the resident North Carolina broker and the non-resident commercial licensee. It shall contain:
- (1) the material terms of the agreement between the signatory licenses;
- (2) a description of the agency relationships, if any, which are created by the agreement among the nonresident commercial licensee, the resident North Carolina broker, and the parties each represents;
- (3) a description of the property or the identity of the parties and other information sufficient to identify the transaction which is the subject of the affiliation agreement; and
- (4) a definite expiration date.

(c) A declaration of affiliation shall be written and on the form provided by the Commission and shall identify the nonresident commercial licensee and the affiliated resident North Carolina licensee. It shall also contain a description of the duties and obligations of each as required by the North Carolina Real Estate License Law and rules adopted by the Commission. The declaration of affiliation may be a part of the brokerage cooperation agreement or separate from it.

(d) A nonresident commercial licensee may affiliate with more than one resident North Carolina broker at any time. However, a nonresident commercial licensee may be affiliated with only one resident North Carolina broker in a single transaction.

(e) A resident North Carolina broker who enters into a brokerage cooperation agreement and declaration of affiliation with a nonresident commercial licensee shall:
- (1) verify that the nonresident commercial licensee is licensed in North Carolina;
- (2) actively and directly supervise the nonresident commercial licensee in a manner which reasonably insures that the nonresident commercial licensee complies with the North Carolina Real Estate License Law and rules adopted by the Commission;
- (3) promptly notify the Commission if the nonresident commercial licensee violates the Real Estate License Law or rules adopted by the Commission;
- (4) insure that records are retained in accordance with the requirements of the Real Estate License Law and rules adopted by the Commission; and

(5) maintain his or her license on active status continuously for the duration of the brokerage cooperation agreement and the declaration of affiliation.

(f) The nonresident commercial licensee and the affiliated resident North Carolina broker shall each retain in his or her records a copy of brokerage cooperation agreements and declarations of affiliation from the time of their creation and for at least three years following their expiration. Such records shall be made available for inspection and reproduction by the Commission or its authorized representatives without prior notice.

History Note: Authority G.S. 93A-4; 93A-9;
Eff. July 1, 2004;
Amended Eff. April 1, 2006; July 1, 2005;
Pursuant to G.S. 150B-21.3A, rule is necessary without substantive public interest Eff. May 1, 2018.

21 NCAC 58A .1808   TRUST MONIES

A nonresident commercial broker acting as real estate broker in North Carolina shall deliver to the North Carolina resident broker with whom he or she is affiliated all money belonging to others received in connection with the nonresident commercial broker's acts or services as a broker. Upon receipt of the funds, the resident North Carolina broker shall cause the funds to be deposited in a trust account in accordance with the provisions of Rule .0116 of this Subchapter.

History Note: Authority G.S. 93A-4; 93A-6(d); 93A-6(g); 93A-9;
Eff. July 1, 2004;
Amended Eff. July 1, 2014; April 1, 2006;
Pursuant to G.S. 150B-21.3A, rule is necessary without substantive public interest Eff. May 1, 2018.

21 NCAC 58A .1809   ADVERTISING

In all advertising involving a nonresident commercial licensee's conduct as a North Carolina real estate broker and in any representation of such person's licensure in North Carolina, the advertising or representation shall conspicuously identify the nonresident commercial licensee as a "Limited Nonresident Commercial Real Estate Broker".

History Note: Authority G.S. 93A-4; 93A-9;
Eff. July 1, 2004;
Amended Eff. April 1, 2006;
Pursuant to G.S. 150B-21.3A, rule is necessary without substantive public interest Eff. May 1, 2018.

21 NCAC 58A .1810   PAYMENT OF FEES

Commissions, fees, or other compensation earned by a nonresident commercial licensee shall not be paid directly to the licensee if said licensee is employed by or working for a real estate broker or firm. Instead, such fees or compensation shall be paid to the licensee's employing broker or firm.

History Note: Authority G.S. 93A-4; 93A-9;
Eff. July 1, 2004;
Pursuant to G.S. 150B-21.3A, rule is necessary without substantive public interest Eff. May 1, 2018.

SECTION .1900 – POST-LICENSING EDUCATION

21 NCAC 58A .1901   PURPOSE AND APPLICABILITY

This Section prescribes specific procedures relating to the postlicensing education requirement for real estate brokers as prescribed by G.S. 93A-4(a1).

History Note: Authority G.S. 93A-4;
Eff. April 1, 2006;

Pursuant to G.S. 150B-21.3A, rule is necessary without substantive public interest Eff. May 1, 2018.

21 NCAC 58A .1902   POSTLICENSING EDUCATION REQUIREMENT
(a) The 90 classroom hour postlicensing education program shall consist of three 30 classroom hour courses prescribed by the Commission which may be taken in any sequence. A provisional broker as described in G.S. 93A-4(a1) or G.S. 93A-4.3(d) must satisfactorily complete at least one of the 30-hour courses during each of the first three years following the date of his or her initial licensure as a broker in order to retain his or her eligibility to actively engage in real estate brokerage. Upon completion of all three courses by a provisional broker, the provisional status of the broker's license shall be terminated by the Commission. The three courses shall be devoted to:
  (1)   real estate brokerage relationships and responsibilities;
  (2)   real estate contracts and transactions; and
  (3)   specialized topics, including commercial real estate, rental management, real estate finance, real estate appraisal, real estate development, and real estate regulation.
(b) If a provisional broker as describe in G.S. 93A-4(a1) or G.S. 93A-4.3(d) fails to complete the required postlicensing education described in Paragraph (a) of this Rule by the end of either the first or second year following the date of his or her initial licensure as a broker, his or her license shall be placed on inactive status. Between the end of the first year after initial licensure and the end of the third year after initial licensure, a provisional broker who is subject of the postlicensing education requirement and who desires to activate a license that is on inactive status shall make up any postlicensing education deficiency as well as satisfy the continuing education requirements for license activation described in Rule .1703 of this Subchapter, satisfy the requirement for supervision by a broker-in-charge described in Rule .0506 of this Subchapter and file with the Commission a request for license activation as described in Rule .0504 of this Subchapter.
(c) If a provisional broker as described in G.S. 93A-4(a1) or G.S. 93A-4.3(d) fails to complete all three postlicensing courses within three years following the date of his or her initial licensure, his or her license shall be placed on inactive status. In order to activate the license, the provisional broker shall demonstrate completion of all three postlicensing courses within the previous three years, which will terminate the provisional status of the broker's license, and shall satisfy the continuing education requirements for license activation described in Rule .1703 of this Subchapter.

History Note: *Authority G.S. 93A-4; 93A-4(a1);*
Eff. April 1, 2006;
Amended Eff. January 1, 2012;
Pursuant to G.S. 150B-21.3A, rule is necessary without substantive public interest Eff. May 1, 2018.

21 NCAC 58A .1903   EXTENSIONS OF TIME TO COMPLETE POSTLICENSING EDUCATION
A provisional broker as described in G.S. 93A-4(a1) or G.S. 93A-4.3(d) may request and be granted an extension of time to satisfy the postlicensing education requirement for any of the first three years following the date of his or her initial licensure as a broker if the licensee provides evidence satisfactory to the Commission that he or she was unable to obtain the necessary education due to an incapacitating illness or other circumstance which existed for a substantial portion of the year in question and which constituted a severe and verifiable hardship such that to comply with the education requirement would have been impossible or unreasonably burdensome. The Commission shall not grant an extension of time when the reason for the request is a business or personal conflict or when, in the opinion of the Commission, the principal reason for the provisional broker's failure to obtain the required education in a timely manner was unreasonable delay on the part of the provisional broker in obtaining such education. If an extension of time is granted, the provisional broker may retain his or her license on active status until expiration of the extension period, but the license shall be automatically changed to inactive status at the end of the extension period unless the licensee obtains the required postlicensing education prior to that time. If an extension of time is not granted, the provisional broker's license shall be treated as described in Rule .1902(b) or (c) of this Section. A request for an extension of time must be submitted on a form provided by the Commission.

History Note: *Authority G.S. 93A-4;*
Eff. April 1, 2006;
Amended Eff. January 1, 2012;

Pursuant to G.S. 150B-21.3A, rule is necessary without substantive public interest Eff. May 1, 2018.

21 NCAC 58A .1904   DENIAL OR WITHDRAWAL OF POSTLICENSING EDUCATION CREDIT
(a) The Commission may deny Postlicensing education credit claimed by a provisional broker or reported by a school for a provisional broker, and may withdraw Postlicensing education credit previously awarded by the Commission to a provisional broker and make appropriate license status changes for that broker upon finding that:
- (1) the provisional broker or school provided incorrect or incomplete information to the Commission concerning Postlicensing education completed by the provisional broker;
- (2) the provisional broker was mistakenly awarded Postlicensing education credit due to an administrative error; or
- (3) the provisional broker attended a Postlicensing course while concurrently attending a different Postlicensing course at the same school or a different school if such concurrent attendance in the two courses resulted in the provisional broker participating in Postlicensing course sessions for more than 30 instructional hours in any given seven-day period.

(b) When Postlicensing education credit is denied or withdrawn by the Commission under Paragraph (a) of this Rule, the provisional broker shall remain responsible for satisfying the Postlicensing education requirement in G.S. 93A-4(a1).

(c) A broker who obtains or attempts to obtain Postlicensing education credit through misrepresentation of fact, dishonesty or other improper conduct is subject to disciplinary action pursuant to G.S. 93A-6.

History Note: *Authority G.S. 93A-4;*
Eff. April 1, 2006;
Amended Eff. July 1, 2017; July 1, 2009;
Pursuant to G.S. 150B-21.3A, rule is necessary without substantive public interest Eff. May 1, 2018.

21 NCAC 58A .1905   WAIVER OF 90-HOUR POSTLICENSING EDUCATION REQUIREMENT
(a) A provisional North Carolina real estate broker may apply for a waiver of one or more of the three 30-hour Postlicensing courses described in Rule .1902 of this Section in the following circumstances:
- (1) the broker has obtained equivalent education that is parallel to the topics and timings described in the Commission's Postlicensing course syllabi. In this case, the waiver request shall include the course(s):
  - (A) jurisdiction of delivery;
  - (B) title;
  - (C) credit hours earned;
  - (D) beginning and end dates; and
  - (E) detailed subject matter description.
- (2) the broker has obtained full-time experience as a licensed broker or salesperson in another state for at least five of the seven years immediately prior to application for waiver, which shall include the applicant's:
  - (A) employer;
  - (B) title at employer;
  - (C) dates of employment;
  - (D) hours per week devoted to brokerage;
  - (E) approximate number of transactions;
  - (F) areas of practice;
  - (G) approximate percentage of time devoted to each area of practice;
  - (H) detailed description of applicant's role and duties;
  - (I) managing broker's name, telephone number, and email address; and
  - (J) official certification of licensure issued within the six months preceding application from a jurisdiction within a state, territory, or possession of the United States or Canada in which the applicant holds a current real estate license that has been active within the three years prior to application.

(3) the broker has obtained full-time experience as a licensed North Carolina attorney practicing primarily in real estate matters for the two years immediately preceding application, which shall include the applicant's:
    (A) firm or practice name;
    (B) law license number;
    (C) dates of employment;
    (D) hours per week devoted to real estate law practice;
    (E) approximate number of closings conducted;
    (F) detailed description of practice; and
    (G) manager or supervising attorney's name, telephone number, and email address.

(b) The Commission shall not consider education or experience obtained in violation of any law or rule as fulfilling the requirements for waiver of the 90-hour postlicensing education requirement.

History Note: Authority G.S. 93A-4(a1);
                         Eff. July 1, 2017.

SECTION .2000 - ANNUAL REPORTS

21 NCAC 58A .2001   FILING

History Note: Authority G.S. 93B-2(d);
                         Eff. July 1, 2010;
                         Expired Eff. June 1, 2018 pursuant to G.S. 150B-21.3A.

21 NCAC 58A .2002   ESCROW ACCOUNT
(a) The Commission shall establish an escrow account or accounts with a financial institution or institutions lawfully doing business in this state into which the Commission shall deposit and hold fees tendered during any period of time when, pursuant to G.S. 93B-2(d). The Commission's authority to expend funds has been suspended. The Commission shall keep funds deposited into its escrow account or accounts segregated from other assets, monies, and receipts for the duration of the suspension of the Commission's authority to expend funds.
(b) The Commission may deposit into and maintain in its escrow account such monies as may be required to avoid or eliminate costs associated with the account or accounts.

History Note: Authority G.S. 93B-2(d);
                         Eff. July 1, 2010.

SECTION .2100 - BROKERS IN MILITARY SERVICE

21 NCAC 58A .2101   APPLICABILITY
This Section shall apply to every broker whose license is not revoked, suspended, or surrendered, or who is otherwise the subject of a disciplinary order, and who is eligible for an extension of time to file a tax return under the provisions of G.S. 105-249.2 and 26 U.S.C. 7508.

History Note: Authority G.S. 93B-15(b);
                         Eff. July 1, 2010;
                         Pursuant to G.S. 150B-21.3A, rule is necessary without substantive public interest Eff. May 1, 2018;
                         Amended Eff. July 1, 2018.

21 NCAC 58A .2102   POSTPONEMENT OF FEES
(a) A Broker described in 21 NCAC 58A .2101 shall not be required to pay renewal fees accrued during the time to be disregarded described in 26 U.S.C. 7508 until the June 30 immediately following the end of such time. The provisions of 21 NCAC 58A .0504 notwithstanding, during such time and until the June 30 immediately thereafter, the license of a broker other than a provisional broker shall remain on active status. During such time, the license of a provisional broker shall not expire, but shall remain on active status only if the provisional broker remains under the supervision of a broker-in-charge.

(b) All fees postponed by operation of this subsection shall be due and payable on June 30 immediately following the time to be disregarded as described in 26 U.S.C. 7508.

History Note: Authority G.S. 93A-3(c); 93B-15(b);
Eff. July 1, 2010;
Pursuant to G.S. 150B-21.3A, rule is necessary without substantive public interest Eff. May 1, 2018.

21 NCAC 58A .2103 POSTPONEMENT OF CONTINUING EDUCATION
(a) A broker described by 21 NCAC 58A .2101 shall not be required to complete the continuing education required as a condition of license renewal for any June 30 license expiration date if that date falls during the time to be disregarded described in 26 U.S.C. 7508 until the June 10 immediately following the end of such time to be disregarded. If such time ends on or after May 1, the broker shall have until September 1 of the same year to complete the required continuing education.
(b) If a broker entitled to a postponement of continuing education under this Rule accumulates a deficiency in his or her continuing education of 16 or more hours because of the length of the time to be disregarded under 26 U.S.C. 7508, the broker may satisfy the deficiency by satisfying the requirements of 21 NCAC 58A .1703(c) established for an inactive broker returning to active status.
(c) The license of a broker entitled to postponement of continuing education under this Rule shall not be placed on inactive status for failure to complete continuing education until the deadline for completion set out in Paragraph (a) of this Rule has passed.

History Note: Authority G.S. 93A-3(c); 93B-15(b);
Eff. July 1, 2010;
Pursuant to G.S. 150B-21.3A, rule is necessary without substantive public interest Eff. May 1, 2018.

21 NCAC 58A .2104 POSTPONEMENT OF POSTLICENSING EDUCATION
A broker described by Rule .2101 of this Section who is a provisional broker shall not be required to complete any postlicensing education during the period to be disregarded under 26 U.S.C. 7508 until the 180th day following the ending of such period. The broker's license shall not be placed on inactive status or cancelled for his or her failure to complete the required postlicensing education prior to the deadline established in this Rule.

History Note: Authority G.S. 93A-3(c); 93B-15(b);
Eff. July 1, 2010;
Amended Eff. July 1, 2016;
Pursuant to G.S. 150B-21.3A, rule is necessary without substantive public interest Eff. May 1, 2018.

21 NCAC 58A .2105 PROOF OF ELIGIBILITY
It shall be the responsibility of every broker eligible for the postponement of fees and education requirements established by this Section to demonstrate his or her eligibility and the beginning and ending of the time to be disregarded as described in 26 U.S.C. 7508.

History Note: Authority G.S. 93A-3(c); 93B-15(b);
Eff. July 1, 2010;
Amended Eff. July 1, 2016;
Pursuant to G.S. 150B-21.3A, rule is necessary without substantive public interest Eff. May 1, 2018.

SECTION .2200 - BROKER PRICE OPINIONS AND COMPARATIVE MARKET ANALYSES

21 NCAC 58A .2201 APPLICABILITY
This Section applies to broker price opinions and comparative market analyses provided for a fee by a real estate broker whose license is not on provisional status pursuant to Article 6, Chapter 93A of the General Statutes.

History Note: Authority G.S. 93A-83(d);
Temporary Adoption Eff. October 1, 2012;
Eff. April 1, 2013;
Pursuant to G.S. 150B-21.3A, rule is necessary without substantive public interest Eff. May 1, 2018.

21 NCAC 58A .2202 STANDARDS

(a) A broker performing a broker price opinion or comparative market analysis for a fee shall comply with all the requirements in G.S. 93A-83 and in this Rule.

(b) A broker shall only accept an assignment to provide a broker price opinion or comparative market analysis for a property if the broker has knowledge of the real estate market, direct access to real estate market sales or leasing data, and brokerage or appraisal experience in the subject property's geographic location.

(c) A broker shall not provide a broker price opinion or comparative market analysis for a property unless the broker can exercise objective, independent judgment free of any influence from any interested party in the performance of his or her analysis of the facts relevant to determination of a probable selling or leasing price.

(d) A broker shall not provide a broker price opinion or comparative market analysis for a property unless the broker has personally inspected the exterior and interior of that property, provided, however, that an inspection of the exterior or interior is not required if this is waived in writing by the party for whom the opinion or analysis is being performed.

(e) When developing a broker price opinion or comparative market analysis for a property or interest therein, a broker shall utilize methodology such as analysis of sales or income of sold or leased properties comparable to the subject property or capitalization as is appropriate for the assignment and type of subject property.

(f) When analyzing sales or income of properties comparable to the property that is the subject of a broker price opinion or comparative market analysis assignment, a broker shall comply with the following standards:

(1) The broker shall select from reliable information sources a minimum of three sold or leased comparable properties for use in his or her analysis that are similar to the subject property with regard to characteristics such as property type, use, location, age, size, design, physical features, amenities, utility, property condition and conditions of sale. The comparable properties selected shall reflect the prevailing factors or market conditions influencing the sale or lease prices of similar properties in the subject property's local market; and

(2) The broker shall make adjustments to the selling or leasing price of selected comparable properties for differences between the characteristics of the comparable properties and the subject property as necessary to produce a credible estimate of the probable selling or leasing price. Adjustments shall be considered for differences in property characteristics such as location, age, size, design, physical features, amenities, utility, condition, economic or functional obsolescence and conditions of sale. The amounts of adjustments shall reflect the values that the local real estate market places on the differences in the characteristics in question.

(g) A broker price opinion or comparative market analysis provided to the party for whom the opinion or analysis is being performed shall address, in addition to matters required to be addressed by G.S. 93A-83 and other provisions of this Rule, the following items:

(1) a description of the comparable properties used in the analysis (including any unsold properties listed for sale or rent that were used as comparable properties);

(2) the adjustments made to the selling or leasing prices of comparable properties;

(3) local real estate market conditions;

(4) if the date on which the sale or lease of a comparable property became final is more than six months prior to the effective date of the broker price opinion or comparative market analysis, an explanation of why the comparable property was used in the analysis and a description of the market conditions affecting the comparable property at the time the sale or lease became final; and

(5) each method used in deriving the estimate of probable selling or leasing price.

(h) In connection with a broker price opinion or comparative market analysis, an estimated probable leasing price may be reported by a broker as a lease rate and an estimated probable selling or leasing price may be reported by a broker either as a single figure or as a price range. When the estimated probable selling or leasing price is stated as a price range and the higher figure exceeds the lower figure by more than 10 percent, the broker shall include an explanation of why the higher figure exceeds the lower figure by more than 10 percent.

History Note: Authority G.S. 93A-83(d);

Temporary Adoption Eff. October 1, 2012;
Eff. April 1, 2013;
Pursuant to G.S. 150B-21.3A, rule is necessary without substantive public interest Eff. May 1, 2018.

SUBCHAPTER 58B – TIME SHARES

SECTION .0100 – TIME SHARE PROJECT REGISTRATION

21 NCAC 58B .0101   APPLICATION FOR REGISTRATION
(a) Every application for time share project registration shall be filed at the Commission's office upon a form prescribed by the Commission. Every such application shall contain or have appended thereto:
  (1)   information concerning the developer's title or right to use the real property on which the project is located, including a title opinion provided by an independent attorney performed within 30 days preceding the date of application;
  (2)   information concerning owners of time shares at the project other than the developer;
  (3)   a description of the improvements and amenities located at the project, including a description of the number and type of time share units;
  (4)   a description of the time share estate to be sold or conveyed to purchasers;
  (5)   information concerning the developer and his or her financial ability to develop the project (including the developer's most recent audited financial statement, any loan commitments for completion of the proposed time share project, a projected budget for the construction, marketing and operation of the time share project until control by purchasers is asserted, and details of any source of funding for the time share project other than consumer sales proceeds), and information concerning the marketing and managing entities and their relationship to the developer;
  (6)   the developer's name and address, past real estate development experience and such other information necessary to determine the moral character of those selling and managing the project;
  (7)   copies of all documents to be distributed to time share purchasers at the point of sale or immediately thereafter; and
  (8)   such information as may be required by G.S. 93A-52.
The form shall also describe the standards for its proper completion and submission.
(b) In accordance with G.S. 93A-52, an application for time share registration shall be considered to be properly completed when it is wholly and accurately filled out and when all required documents are appended to it and appear to be in compliance with the provisions of the Time Share Act, and, where the project is a condominium, the Condominium Act or Unit Ownership Act.
(c) An entity which owns time shares at a time share project where there are one or more existing registered developers may also apply to the Commission for registration of its time shares, provided that the entity does not control a registered developer, is not controlled by a registered developer, and is not in common control of the project with a registered developer.

History Note: Authority G.S. 47A; 47C; 93A-51; 93A-52(a);
Eff. March 1, 1984;
Amended Eff. July 1, 2000; August 2, 1993; February 1, 1989; April 1, 1987;
Pursuant to G.S. 150B-21.3A, rule is necessary without substantive public interest Eff. May 1, 2018.

21 NCAC 58B .0102   REGISTRATION FEE
(a) For the initial registration or subsequent registration of a time share project by a developer proposing to sell or develop 16 or more time shares, the fee shall be one thousand dollars ($1,000). For an initial or subsequent registration of a time share project in which the developer proposes to sell 15 or fewer time shares, the fee shall be seven hundred dollars ($700.00). For any time share registration by a homeowner association for the purpose of re-selling time shares in its own project which it has acquired in satisfaction of unpaid assessments by prior owners, the fee shall be four hundred fifty dollars ($450.00).

(b) Payment of application fees for time share registration shall be made to the Commission by certified check, money order, debit card, or credit card. Applications for registration not accompanied by the appropriate fee shall not be considered by the Commission.

(c) In the event a properly completed application filed with the Commission is denied for any reason, or if an incomplete application is denied by the Commission or abandoned by the developer prior to a final decision by the Commission, the amount of two hundred fifty dollars ($250.00) shall be retained by the Commission from the application fee and the balance refunded to the applicant developer.

History Note: *Authority G.S. 93A-51; 93A-52;*
Eff. March 1, 1984;
Amended Eff. July 1, 2016; April 1, 2013; July 1, 2000;
Pursuant to G.S. 150B-21.3A, rule is necessary without substantive public interest Eff. May 1, 2018.

21 NCAC 58B .0103   RENEWAL OF TIME SHARE PROJECT REGISTRATION

(a) A developer seeking a renewal of a time share project registration shall submit a complete renewal application form during the month of June. A renewal application form is available on the Commission's website at www.ncrec.gov. In the renewal application form, the developer shall set forth:

    (1)   the time share's project name, registration number, and mailing address;
    (2)   the developer's name, telephone number, and email address;
    (3)   the full legal name of brokers that are associated with the time share project and their real estate license numbers;
    (4)   the name of all exchange programs associated with the time share project along with a current copy of the Exchange Disclosure Report pursuant to G.S. 93A-48;
    (5)   the name, address, email address, telephone number, real estate broker license number if applicable, and the assignment date for each of the following:
        (A)   the managing entity;
        (B)   the marketing entity;
        (C)   the registrar, pursuant to G.S. 93A-58(a);
        (D)   the independent escrow agent, pursuant to G.S. 93A-42(a); and
        (E)   the project broker, pursuant to 93A-58(c);
    (6)   a certification that the information contained in the registration filed with the Commission is accurate and current on the date of the renewal application; and
    (7)   the developer's attorney or project broker's signature.

(b) The developer shall submit a nonrefundable fee of eight hundred dollars ($800.00) payable to the North Carolina Real Estate Commission by certified check, money order, debit card, or credit card.

(c) A complete renewal application shall be accompanied by the prescribed fee and shall be received at the Commission's office prior to the expiration of the certificate of registration as described in G.S. 93A-52(d).

(d) Making a false certification on a time share project registration renewal application shall be grounds for disciplinary action by the Commission.

History Note: *Authority G.S. 93A-51; 93A-52(d);*
Eff. March 1, 1984;
Temporary Amendment Eff. May 23, 1985;
Amended Eff. July 1, 2016; April 1, 2013; February 1, 1989; September 1, 1985;
Pursuant to G.S. 150B-21.3A, rule is necessary without substantive public interest Eff. May 1, 2018;
Amended Eff. July 1, 2018.

21 NCAC 58B .0104   AMENDMENTS TO TIME SHARE PROJECT REGISTRATION

(a) A developer shall notify the Commission immediately, but in no event later than 15 days, after any material change in the information contained in the time share project registration.

(b) A material change shall be any change which reflects a difference in:
    (1)   the nature, quality or availability of the purchaser's ownership or right to use the time share;
    (2)   the nature, quality or availability of any amenity at the project;
    (3)   the developer's title, control or right to use the real property on which the project is located;

(4) the information concerning the developer, the managing or marketing entities, or persons connected therewith, previously filed with the Commission;
(5) the purchaser's right to exchange his or her unit; however, a change in the information required to be disclosed to a purchaser by G.S. 93A-48 shall not be a material change; or
(6) the project or time share as originally registered which would be significant to a reasonable purchaser.

(c) Amendments to time share project registrations shall be submitted in the form of substitute pages for material previously filed with the Commission. New or changed information shall be conspicuously indicated by underlining in red ink. Every amendment submitted shall be accompanied by a cover letter signed by the developer or the developer's attorney containing a summary of the amendment and a statement of reasons for which the amendment has been made. The cover letter shall state:
(1) the name and address of the project and its registration number;
(2) the name and address of the developer;
(3) the document or documents to which the amendment applies;
(4) whether or not the changes represented by the amendment required the assent of the time share owners and, if so, how the assent of the time share owners was obtained; and
(5) the recording reference in the office of the register of deeds for the changes, if applicable.

Developers of multiple projects must submit separate amendments and cover letters for each project for which amendments are submitted.

(d) The Commission may, in its discretion, require the developer to file a new time share project registration application in the place of an amendment form. Such refiling shall be without fee.

History Note: *Authority G.S. 93A-51;*
Eff. March 1, 1984;
Amended Eff. October 1, 2000; February 1, 1989; April 1, 1987;
Pursuant to G.S. 150B-21.3A, rule is necessary without substantive public interest Eff. May 1, 2018.

21 NCAC 58B .0105   NOTICE OF TERMINATION
(a) A developer of a registered time share project which, for any reason, terminates its interest, rights, ownership or control of the project or any significant part thereof shall immediately notify the Commission in writing on a form prescribed by the Commission for that purpose. Notice of termination to the Commission shall include the date of termination, the reasons therefor, the identity of the developer's successor, if any, and a report on the status of time share sales to purchasers on the date of termination.
(b) Upon receipt of a properly executed notice of termination of the developer's interest in a time share project, the Commission shall enter a notation of cancellation of registration in the file of the project, and shall notify the developer of cancellation. A developer's failure to give notice of termination as provided herein shall not prevent cancellation of the project's registration under G.S. 93A-52.

History Note: *Authority G.S. 93A-51; 93A-52(a);*
Eff. April 1, 1987;
Pursuant to G.S. 150B-21.3A, rule is necessary without substantive public interest Eff. May 1, 2018.

SECTION .0200 - PUBLIC OFFERING STATEMENT

21 NCAC 58B .0201   GENERAL PROVISIONS
(a) Information contained in a public offering statement shall be accurate on the day it is supplied to a purchaser. Before any public offering statement is supplied to a purchaser, the developer shall file a copy of the statement with the Commission.
(b) In addition to the information required to be contained in a public offering statement by G.S. 93A-44, every public offering statement shall disclose to the purchaser of a time share complete and accurate information concerning:
(1) the real property type of the time share program, whether tenancy-in-common, condominium or other, and a description of the estate the purchaser will own, the term of that estate and the remainder interest, if any, once the term has expired;

(2) the document creating the time share program, a statement that it is the document which governs the program and a reference to the location where the purchaser may obtain or examine a copy of the document;
(3) whether or not the property is being converted to a time share from some other use and, if so, a statement to that effect and disclosure of the prior use of the property;
(4) the maximum number of time shares in the project, each recreational and other commonly used facility offered, and who or what will own each facility, if the project is to be completed in one development or construction phase;
(5) if the project is planned in phased construction or development, the complete plan of phased offerings, including the maximum number of time shares which may be in the project, each recreational and other commonly used facility, who or what will own each facility, and the developer's representations regarding his or her commitment to build out the project;
(6) the association of owners or other entity which will ultimately be responsible for managing the time share program, the first date or event when the entity will convene or commence to conduct business, each owner's voting right, if any, and whether and for how long the developer, as time share owner, will control the entity;
(7) the location where owners may inspect the articles and bylaws of the owners association, or other organizational documents of the entity and the books and records it produces;
(8) whether the entity has lien rights against time share owners for failure to pay assessments;
(9) whether or not the developer has entered into a management contract on behalf of the managing entity, the extent to which the managing entity's powers are delegated to the manager and the location where a copy of the management contract may be examined;
(10) whether or not the developer will pay assessments for time shares which it owns and a statement that the amount of assessments due the managing entity from owners will change over time, as circumstances may change;
(11) whether or not the developer sponsors or will sponsor a rental or resale program and, if so, a summary of the program or programs; and
(12) the developer's role at the project, if the developer is a separate entity from any other registered developer of the time share project.

(c) The inclusion of false or misleading statements in a public offering statement shall be grounds for disciplinary action by the Commission.

History Note: Authority G.S. 93A-44(8); 93A-51;
Eff. March 1, 1984;
Amended Eff. October 1, 2000; August 2, 1993; February 1, 1989; April 1, 1987;
Pursuant to G.S. 150B-21.3A, rule is necessary without substantive public interest Eff. May 1, 2018.

21 NCAC 58B .0202   PUBLIC OFFERING STATEMENT SUMMARY
Every public offering statement shall contain a one page cover prescribed by the Commission and completed by the developer entitled Public Offering Statement Summary. The Public Offering Statement Summary shall read as follows:

PUBLIC OFFERING STATEMENT

SUMMARY

NAME OF PROJECT:

NAME AND REAL ESTATE LICENSE NUMBER OF BROKER:

This Public Offering Statement contains information which deserves your careful study, as you decide whether or not to purchase a time share.
The Public Offering Statement includes general information about the real estate type, the term, and the size of this time share project. It also includes a general description of the recreational and other facilities existing now, or to be provided in the future. The Public Offering Statement will tell you how maintenance and management of the project

will be provided and how the costs of these services will be charged to purchasers. From the Public Offering Statement, you will also learn how the project will be governed and whether purchasers will have a voice in that government. You will also learn that a time share instrument will be recorded to protect your real estate interest in your time share.

The Public Offering Statement contains important information, but is not a substitute for the detailed information contained in the contract of purchase and the legal documents which create and affect the time share program at this project.

Please study this Public Offering Statement carefully. Satisfy yourself that any questions you may have are answered before you decide to purchase. If a salesperson or other representative of the developer has made a representation which concerns you, and you cannot find that representation in writing, ask that it be pointed out to you.

NOTICE

UNDER NORTH CAROLINA LAW, YOU MAY CANCEL YOUR TIME SHARE PURCHASE WITHOUT PENALTY WITHIN FIVE DAYS AFTER SIGNING YOUR CONTRACT. TO CANCEL YOUR TIME SHARE PURCHASE, YOU MUST MAIL OR HAND DELIVER WRITTEN NOTICE OF YOUR DESIRE TO CANCEL YOUR PURCHASE TO (name and address of project). IF YOU CHOOSE TO MAIL YOUR CANCELLATION NOTICE, THE NORTH CAROLINA REAL ESTATE COMMISSION RECOMMENDS THAT YOU USE REGISTERED OR CERTIFIED MAIL AND THAT YOU RETAIN YOUR POSTAL RECEIPT AS PROOF OF THE DATE YOUR NOTICE WAS MAILED. UPON CANCELLATION, ALL PAYMENTS WILL BE REFUNDED TO YOU.

History Note: *Authority G.S. 93A-44; 93A-51;*
Eff. March 1, 1984;
Amended Eff. April 1, 2006; October 1, 2000; February 1, 1989; April 1, 1987;
Pursuant to G.S. 150B-21.3A, rule is necessary without substantive public interest Eff. May 1, 2018.

21 NCAC 58B .0203   RECEIPT FOR PUBLIC OFFERING STATEMENT
(a) Prior to the execution of any contract to purchase a time share, a time share developer or a time share salesperson shall obtain from the purchaser a written receipt for the public offering statement, which shall display, directly over the buyer signature line in type in all capital letters, no smaller than the largest type on the page on which it appears, the following statement: DO NOT SIGN THIS RECEIPT UNLESS YOU HAVE RECEIVED A COMPLETE COPY OF THE PUBLIC OFFERING STATEMENT TO TAKE WITH YOU.
(b) Receipts for public offering statements shall be maintained as part of the records of the sales transaction.

History Note: *Authority G.S. 93A-45(a); 93A-51;*
Eff. February 1, 1988;
Amended Eff. October 1, 2000;
Pursuant to G.S. 150B-21.3A, rule is necessary without substantive public interest Eff. May 1, 2018.

SECTION .0300 - CANCELLATION

21 NCAC 58B .0301   PROOF OF CANCELLATION
(a) The postmark date affixed to any written notice of a purchaser's intent to cancel his or her time share purchase shall be presumed by the Commission to be the date the notice was mailed to the developer. Evidence tending to rebut this presumption shall be admissible at a hearing before the Commission.
(b) Upon receipt of a purchaser's written notice of his or her intent to cancel his or her time share purchase, the developer, or his or her agent or representative, shall retain the notice and any enclosure, envelope or other cover in the developer's files at the project, and shall produce the file upon the Commission's request.
(c) When there is more than one registered developer at a time share project and a purchaser gives written notice of his or her intent to cancel his or her time share purchase that is received by a developer or sales staff other than the one from whom his or her time share was purchased, the developer or sales staff receiving such notice shall promptly deliver it to the proper developer who shall then honor the notice if it was timely sent by the purchaser.

History Note: Authority G.S. 93A-51; 93A-54(d);
                      Eff. September 1, 1984;
                      Amended Eff. October 1, 2000; August 2, 1993; February 1, 1989;
                      Pursuant to G.S. 150B-21.3A, rule is necessary without substantive public interest Eff. May 1, 2018.

SECTION .0400 - TIME SHARE SALES OPERATION

21 NCAC 58B .0401   RETENTION OF TIME SHARE RECORDS
A time share developer and a time share salesperson shall retain or cause to be retained for a period of three years complete records of every time share sale, rental, or exchange transaction made by or on behalf of the developer. Records required to be retained shall include but not be limited to offers, applications and contracts to purchase, rent or exchange time shares; records of the deposit, maintenance and disbursement of funds required to be held in trust; receipts; notices of cancellation and their covers if mailed; records regarding compensation of salespersons; public offering statements; and any other records pertaining to time share transactions. Such records shall be made available to the Commission and its representatives upon request.

History Note: Authority G.S. 93A-51; 93A-54(d);
                      Eff. September 1, 1984;
                      Amended Eff. October 1, 2000;
                      Pursuant to G.S. 150B-21.3A, rule is necessary without substantive public interest Eff. May 1, 2018.

21 NCAC 58B .0402   TIME SHARE AGENCY AGREEMENTS AND DISCLOSURE
Time share sales transactions conducted by licensees on behalf of a time share developer are subject to 21 NCAC 58A .0104.

History Note: Authority G.S. 93A-3(c); 93A-51;
                      Eff. August 1, 1998;
                      Pursuant to G.S. 150B-21.3A, rule is necessary without substantive public interest Eff. May 1, 2018.

SECTION .0500 – HANDLING AND ACCOUNTING OF FUNDS

21 NCAC 58B .0501   TIME SHARE TRUST FUNDS
(a) Except as otherwise permitted by G.S. 93A-45(c), all monies received by a time share developer or a time share salesperson in connection with a time share sales transaction shall be deposited into a trust or escrow account not later than three banking days following receipt and shall remain in such account for ten days from the date of sale or until cancellation by the purchaser, whichever first occurs.
(b) All monies received by a person licensed as a broker in connection with a time share transaction shall be delivered immediately to his or her project broker.
(c) When a time share purchaser timely cancels his or her time share purchase, the developer shall refund to the purchaser all monies paid by the purchaser in connection with the purchase. The refund shall be made no later than 30 days following the date of execution of the contract. Amounts paid by the purchaser with a bankcard or a credit card shall be refunded by a cash payment or by issuing a credit voucher to the purchaser within the 30-day period.
(d) Every project broker shall obtain and keep a written representation from the developer as to whether or not lien-free or lien-subordinated time share instruments can be recorded within 45 days of the purchaser's execution of the time share purchase agreement. When a lien-free or lien-subordinated instrument cannot be recorded within said time period, on the business day following the expiration of the ten day time share payment escrow period, a project broker shall transfer from his or her trust account all purchase deposit funds or other payments received from a purchaser who has not cancelled his or her purchase agreement, to the independent escrow agent in a check made payable to the independent escrow agent. Alternatively, the check may be made payable to the developer with a restrictive endorsement placed on the back of the check providing "For deposit to the account of the independent escrow agent for the (name of time share project) only."

History Note: Authority G.S. 93A-42(c); 93A-51;
Eff. September 1, 1984;
Amended Eff. April 1, 2006; October 1, 2000; February 1, 1989; July 1, 1988; February 1, 1988;
Pursuant to G.S. 150B-21.3A, rule is necessary without substantive public interest Eff. May 1, 2018.

SECTION .0600 - PROJECT BROKER

21 NCAC 58B .0601   DESIGNATION OF PROJECT BROKER
The developer of a registered timeshare project shall designate for each project subject to the developer's control a project broker by filing with the Commission an affidavit on the form prescribed. The developer may from time to time change the designated project broker by filing a new designation form with the Commission within 10 days following the change. A broker licensed under the provisions of Section .1800 of Subchapter 58A shall not be designated as a project broker. Provisional brokers shall not be designated as a project broker.

History Note: Authority G.S. 93A-41(7a); 93A-51; 93A-58(c); 93A-9;
Eff. February 1, 1998;
Amended Eff. April 1, 2006; July 1, 2004;
Pursuant to G.S. 150B-21.3A, rule is necessary without substantive public interest Eff. May 1, 2018.

21 NCAC 58B .0602   DUTIES OF THE PROJECT BROKER
(a) The broker designated by the developer of a time share project to be project broker shall assume responsibility for:
(1) The display of the time share project certificate registration and the license certificates of the real estate brokers associated with or engaged on behalf of the developer at the project;
(2) The determination of whether each licensee employed has complied with Rules .0503 and .0506 of Subchapter 58A;
(3) The notification to the commission of any change in the identity or address of the project or in the identity or address of the developer or marketing or managing entities at the project;
(4) The deposit and maintenance of time share purchase or rental monies in a trust or escrow account until proper disbursement is made; and
(5) The proper maintenance of accurate records at the project including all records relating to the handling of trust monies at the project, records relating to time share sales and rental transactions and the project registration and renewal.

(b) The project broker shall review all contracts, public offering statements and other documents distributed to the purchasers of time shares at the project to ensure that the documents comport with the requirements of the Time Share Act and the rules adopted by the commission, and to ensure that true and accurate documents have been given to the purchasers.
(c) The project broker shall not permit time share sales to be conducted by any person not licensed as a broker and shall not delegate or assign his or her supervisory responsibilities to any other person, nor accept control of his or her supervisory responsibilities by any other person.
(d) The project broker shall notify the commission in writing of any change in his or her status as project broker within ten days following the change.

History Note: Authority G.S. 93A-51; 93A-58(c);
Eff. February 1, 1988;
Amended Eff. April 1, 2006; October 1, 2000; February 1, 1989;
Pursuant to G.S. 150B-21.3A, rule is necessary without substantive public interest Eff. May 1, 2018.

SECTION .0700 - TIME SHARE FORMS

21 NCAC 58B .0701   FORMS FOR TIME SHARE PROJECTS

History Note: Authority G.S. 93A-51; 150B-11(1);

Eff. July 1, 1989;
Expired Eff. June 1, 2018 pursuant to G.S. 150B-21.3A.

SUBCHAPTER 58C - REAL ESTATE PRELICENSING EDUCATION

This Section .0100 of Title 21 Subchapter 58C of the North Carolina Administrative Code (T21.58C .0101 - .0107); SCHOOLS; has been transferred and recodified from Section .1000 of Title 21 Subchapter 58A of the North Carolina Administrative Code (T21.58A .1001 - .1007), effective November 27, 1989.

SECTION .0100 – SCHOOLS

21 NCAC 58C .0101   APPLICABILITY: REQUIREMENT FOR APPROVAL
21 NCAC 58C .0102   APPLICATION FOR APPROVAL
21 NCAC 58C .0103   CRITERIA FOR APPROVAL
21 NCAC 58C .0104   SCOPE, DURATION AND RENEWAL OF APPROVAL

History Note: *Authority G.S. 93A-4;*
Eff. February 1, 1976;
Readopted Eff. September 30, 1977;
Amended Eff. July 1, 2010; April 1, 2006; July 1, 1996; July 1, 1994; May 1, 1990; February 1, 1989; November 1, 1987; September 1, 1984;
Repealed Eff. July 1, 2017.

21 NCAC 58C .0105   WITHDRAWAL OR DENIAL OF APPROVAL

History Note: *Authority G.S. 93A-4; 93A-6;*
Eff. September 1, 1979;
Amended Eff. July 1, 2009; April 1, 2006; July 1, 2000; July 1, 1994; May 1, 1990; February 1, 1989; November 1, 1987;
Repealed Eff. July 1, 2017.

21 NCAC 58C .0106   PROGRAM CHANGES

History Note: *Authority G.S. 93A-4(a),(d);*
Eff. January 1, 1981;
Amended Eff. July 1, 2000; February 1, 1989; November 1, 1987;
Repealed Eff. September 1, 2002.

21 NCAC 58C .0107   USE OF EXAMINATION PERFORMANCE DATA

History Note: *Authority G.S. 93A-4(a),(d);*
Eff. September 1, 1984;
Amended Eff. July 1, 2000; July 1, 1994; May 1, 1990;
Repealed Eff. July 1, 2017.

21 NCAC 58C .0108   STUDENT EVALUATIONS OF INSTRUCTOR PERFORMANCE

History Note: *Authority G.S. 93A-4(a),(d);*
Amended Eff. July 1, 2000;
Repealed Eff. July 1, 2017.

SECTION .0200 - PRIVATE REAL ESTATE SCHOOLS

21 NCAC 58C .0201   APPLICABILITY

History Note: Authority G.S. 93A-4(a),(d); 93A-33;
Eff. October 1, 1980;
Amended Eff. February 1, 1989; December 1, 1987;
Transferred and Recodified from 21 NCAC 58A .1301 Eff. November 27, 1989;
Repealed Eff. July 1, 2017.

21 NCAC 58C .0202   ORIGINAL APPLICATION FEE

History Note: Authority G.S. 93A-33; 93A-34(b);
Eff. July 1, 1990;
Amended Eff. April 1, 2006; July 1, 1994;
Repealed Eff. July 1, 2017.

21 NCAC 58C .0203   SCHOOL NAME
21 NCAC 58C .0204   COURSES
21 NCAC 58C .0205   ADDITIONAL COURSE OFFERINGS
21 NCAC 58C .0206   ADMINISTRATION
21 NCAC 58C .0207   FACILITIES AND EQUIPMENT
21 NCAC 58C .0208   BULLETINS
21 NCAC 58C .0209   ENROLLMENT PROCEDURES AND CONTRACTS
21 NCAC 58C .0210   ADMISSIONS POLICY AND PRACTICE
21 NCAC 58C .0211   RECORDS
21 NCAC 58C .0212   ENFORCEMENT OF INSTITUTIONAL STANDARDS
21 NCAC 58C .0213   PERFORMANCE BOND
21 NCAC 58C .0214   ADVERTISING AND RECRUITMENT ACTIVITIES

History Note: Authority G.S. 93A-4; 93A-4(a),(d); 93A-33; 93A-34;
Eff. October 1, 1980;
Amended Eff. February 1, 1989; December 1, 1987; November 1, 1987; April 1, 1987; September 1, 1984;
Transferred and Recodified from 21 NCAC 58A .1303 Eff. November 27, 1989;
Transferred and Recodified from 21 NCAC 58A .1304 Eff. November 27, 1989;
Transferred and Recodified from 21 NCAC 58A .1305 Eff. November 27, 1989;
Transferred and Recodified from 21 NCAC 58A .1306 Eff. November 27, 1989;
Transferred and Recodified from 21 NCAC 58A .1307 Eff. November 27, 1989;
Transferred and Recodified from 21 NCAC 58A .1308 Eff. November 27, 1989;
Transferred and Recodified from 21 NCAC 58A .1309 Eff. November 27, 1989;
Transferred and Recodified from 21 NCAC 58A .1310 Eff. November 27, 1989;
Transferred and Recodified from 21 NCAC 58A .1311 Eff. November 27, 1989;
Transferred and Recodified from 21 NCAC 58A .1312 Eff. November 27, 1989;
Transferred and Recodified from 21 NCAC 58A .1313 Eff. November 27, 1989;
Transferred and Recodified from 21 NCAC 58A .1314 Eff. November 27, 1989;
Amended Eff. July 1, 2014; January 1, 2012; July 1, 2010; July 1, 2009; January 1, 2008; April 1, 2006; July 1, 2005; July 1, 2001; July 1, 2000; July 1, 1994; July 1, 1993; July 1, 1990;
Repealed Eff. July 1, 2017.

21 NCAC 58C .0215   QUARTERLY REPORTS

History Note: Authority G.S. 93A-4(a),(d); 93A-33;
Eff. October 1, 1980;
Amended Eff. September 1, 1984;
Transferred and Recodified from 21 NCAC 58A .1315 Eff. November 27, 1989;
Repealed Eff. September 1, 2002.

21 NCAC 58C .0216   CHANGES DURING THE LICENSING PERIOD

21 NCAC 58C .0217   **LICENSE RENEWAL AND FEES**
21 NCAC 58C .0218   **LICENSING EXAM CONFIDENTIALITY: SCHOOL PERFORM./LICENSING**

History Note: *Authority G.S. 93A-4; 93A-4(a),(d); 93A-33; 93A-34(b); 93A-35(b);*
Eff. October 1, 1980;
Amended Eff. February 1, 1989; April 1, 1987; December 1, 1987; September 1, 1984;
Transferred and Recodified from 21 NCAC 58A .1316 Eff. November 27, 1989;
Transferred and Recodified from 21 NCAC 58A .1317 Eff. November 27, 1989;
Transferred and Recodified from 21 NCAC 58A .1318 Eff. November 27, 1989;
Amended Eff. July 1, 2009; April 1, 2006, September 1, 2002; July 1, 2000; July 1, 1994; July 1, 1990;
Repealed Eff. July 1, 2017.

21 NCAC 58C .0219   **VIOLATIONS OF THE AMERICANS WITH DISABLITIES ACT**

History Note: *Authority G.S. 93A-3(c); 93A-33;*
Eff. July 1, 1993;
Repealed Eff. July 1, 2017.

21 NCAC 58C .0220   **STUDENT EVALUATIONS OF INSTRUCTOR PERFORMANCE**

History Note: *Authority G.S. 93A-4(a),(d); 93A-33;*
Eff. July 1, 2000;
Repealed Eff. July 1, 2017.

21 NCAC 58C .0221   **TRANSFER OF SCHOOL OWNERSHIP**

History Note: *Authority G.S. 93A-33; 93A-34; 93A-35;*
Eff. July 1, 2014;
Repealed Eff. July 1, 2017.

SECTION .0300 - PRELICENSING AND POSTLICENSING COURSES

21 NCAC 58C .0301   **PURPOSE AND APPLICABILITY**
21 NCAC 58C .0302   **PROGRAM STRUCTURING AND ADMISSION REQUIREMENTS**
21 NCAC 58C .0303   **COURSE CONTENT**
21 NCAC 58C .0304   **COURSE COMPLETION STANDARDS**
21 NCAC 58C .0305   **COURSE SCHEDULING**
21 NCAC 58C .0306   **TEXTBOOKS**
21 NCAC 58C .0307   **INSTRUCTORS**

History Note: *Authority G.S. 93A-4; 93A-4(a1); 93A-4(a),(d); 93A-33; 93A-34; 93A-75(a);*
Eff. September 1, 1979;
Amended Eff. November 1, 1987; May 1, 1987; April 1, 1987; September 1, 1984; September 1, 1983; January 1, 1981; August 1, 1980;
Recodified Paragraphs (d) and (e) to Rule 58A .1113 (a) and (b) Eff. January 6, 1989;
Amended Eff. February 1, 1989;
Transferred and Recodified from 21 NCAC 58A .1101 Eff. November 27, 1989;
Transferred and Recodified from 21 NCAC 58A .1102 Eff. November 27, 1989;
Transferred and Recodified from 21 NCAC 58A .1104 Eff. November 27, 1989;
Transferred and Recodified from 21 NCAC 58A .1105 Eff. November 27, 1989;
Transferred and Recodified from 21 NCAC 58A .1107 Eff. November 27, 1989;
Transferred and Recodified from 21 NCAC 58A .1108 Eff. November 27, 1989;
Transferred and Recodified from 21 NCAC 58A .1109 Eff. November 27, 1989;
Amended Eff. May 1, 1990;
Temporary Amendment Eff. July 5, 1990, For a Period of 180 Days to Expire on January 1, 1991;

Amended Eff. January 1, 1991; February 1, 1991;
Temporary Amendment Eff. April 5, 1991, For a Period of 180 Days to Expire on October 2, 1991;
Temporary Amendment Eff. May 9, 1991, For a Period of 146 Days to Expire on October 2, 1991;
Amended Eff. July 1, 2010; July 1, 2009; January 1, 2008; April 1, 2006; September 1, 2002; October 1, 2000; July 1, 2000; July 1, 1996; July 1, 1994; July 1, 1993; October 1, 1991;
Repealed Eff. July 1, 2017.

21 NCAC 58C .0308   APPRAISAL INSTRUCTORS

History Note: *Filed as a Temporary Amendment Eff. July 5, 1990, For a Period of 180 Days to Expire on January 1, 1991;*
Authority G.S. 93A-33; 93A-75(a);
Eff. May 1, 1990;
Amended Eff. February 1, 1991; January 1, 1991;
Repealed Eff. July 1, 1994.

21 NCAC 58C .0309   COURSE COMPLETION REPORTING

History Note: *Authority G.S. 93A-4(a); 93A-4(a2); 93A-4(d); 93A-33;*
Eff. September 1, 1979;
Amended Eff. February 1, 1989; September 1, 1984; January 1, 1981;
Transferred and Recodified from 21 NCAC 58A .1111 Eff. November 27, 1989;
Amended Eff. July 1, 2014; July 1, 2009; January 1, 2008; April 1, 2006; July 1, 1994; May 1, 1990;
Repealed Eff. July 1, 2017.

21 NCAC 58C .0310   COURSE RECORDS

History Note: *Authority G.S. 93A-4(a),(d); 93A-33;*
Eff. September 1, 1984;
Recodified from Rule 58A .1105 (d) and (e) Eff. January 6, 1989;
Transferred and Recodified from 21 NCAC 58A .1113 Eff. November 27, 1989;
Amended Eff. July 1, 2014; October 1, 2000; May 1, 1990;
Repealed Eff. July 1, 2017.

21 NCAC 58C .0311   INSTRUCTIONAL DELIVERY METHODS
21 NCAC 58C .0312   EXCEPTION FOR PERSONS WITH DISABILITIES

History Note: *Authority G.S. 93A-3(c); 93A-4(a); 93A-34;*
Eff. July 1, 1996;
Amended Eff. April 1, 2006; April 1, 2004; July 1, 2000;
Repealed Eff. July 1, 2017.

21 NCAC 58C .0311   INSTRUCTIONAL DELIVERY METHODS
The principal instructional delivery method utilized in real estate prelicensing and postlicensing courses must provide for the instructor to interact with students either in person in a traditional classroom setting or through an interactive television system or comparable system which permits continuous mutual audio and visual communication between the instructor and all students and which provides for monitoring and technical support at each site where the instructor or students are located. The use of media-based instructional delivery systems such as videotape or digital video disc (DVD), remote non-interactive television, computer-based instructional programs or similar systems not involving continuous mutual audio and visual communication between instructor and students may be employed only to enhance or supplement personal teaching by the instructor. Such delivery systems may not be used to substitute for personal teaching by the instructor. No portion of a course may consist of correspondence instruction.

History Note: Authority G.S. 93A-3(c); 93A-4(a); 93A-34;
Eff. July 1, 1996;
Amended Eff. April 1, 2006; April 1, 2004.

21 NCAC 58C .0312   EXCEPTION FOR PERSONS WITH DISABILITIES
Schools may deviate from Commission rules concerning student attendance, course scheduling, instructional methods, instructional materials, facilities or similar matters as may be necessary in order for a school to comply with the Americans With Disabilities Act or other laws requiring such schools to accommodate persons with disabilities; provided that no deviations from Commission rules are permitted by this Rule with regard to program structuring, course content, academic course completion standards, or instructors. When considering a request for special accommodation under the Americans With Disabilities Act or other similar laws, a school shall make a reasonable inquiry to determine that the person making the request is a qualified individual with a disability and that the requested accommodation is appropriate for the particular disability. A school providing a special accommodation for a student with a disability that requires the school to deviate from Commission rules shall notify the Commission in writing of the accommodation within ten days of the start of the course in which the student is enrolled or, if the accommodation is requested after the start of the course, within ten days of the date the accommodation is first provided.

History Note: Authority G.S. 93A-3(c); 93A-34;
Eff. July 1, 1996;
Amended Eff. July 1, 2000.

21 NCAC 58C .0313   NOTICE OF SCHEDULED COURSES

History Note: Authority G.S. 93A-4(a1),(d); 93A-33;
Eff. January 1, 2008;
Amended Eff. July 1, 2009;
Repealed Eff. July 1, 2017.

SECTION .0400 - APPRAISAL TRADE ORGANIZATION COURSES

21 NCAC 58C .0401	PURPOSE AND APPLICABILITY
21 NCAC 58C .0402	APPLICATION AND FEE
21 NCAC 58C .0403	CRITERIA FOR COURSE RECOGNITION
21 NCAC 58C .0404	CHANGES DURING THE RECOGNITION PERIOD
21 NCAC 58C .0405	ADVERTISING OF RECOGNITION AND EXAMINATION PERFORMANCE
21 NCAC 58C .0406	RENEWAL OF COMMISSION RECOGNITION: FEE
21 NCAC 58C .0407	WITHDRAWAL OR DENIAL OF COMMISSION RECOGNITION

History Note: Authority G.S. 93A-75(a) and (b);
Eff. May 1, 1990;
Amended Eff. July 1, 1993;
Repealed Eff. July 1, 1994.

SECTION .0500 - APPRAISAL CONTINUING EDUCATION COURSES

21 NCAC 58C .0501	PURPOSE AND APPLICABILITY
21 NCAC 58C .0502	APPLICATION AND FEE
21 NCAC 58C .0503	CRITERIA FOR COURSE APPROVAL
21 NCAC 58C .0504	PRE-LICENSING AND PRE-CERTIFICATION COURSES
21 NCAC 58C .0505	CONTINUING EDUCATION CREDIT HOURS
21 NCAC 58C .0506	COURSE OPERATIONAL REQUIREMENTS
21 NCAC 58C .0507	CERTIFICATION OF COURSE COMPLETION
21 NCAC 58C .0508	SUBMISSION OF COURSE ROSTER

21 NCAC 58C .0509	CHANGES DURING THE APPROVAL PERIOD
21 NCAC 58C .0510	COURSE RECORDS
21 NCAC 58C .0511	RENEWAL OF APPROVAL AND FEES
21 NCAC 58C .0512	WITHDRAWAL OR DENIAL OF APPROVAL

History Note: Authority G.S. 93A-75(c), (d); 93A-77;
Eff. July 1, 1991;
Amended Eff. May 1, 1992;
Repealed Eff. July 1, 1994.

SECTION .0600 – PRELICENSING AND POSTLICENSING INSTRUCTORS

21 NCAC 58C .0601	PURPOSE AND APPLICABILITY
21 NCAC 58C .0602	NATURE AND SCOPE OF INSTRUCTOR APPROVAL
21 NCAC 58C .0603	APPLICATION AND CRITERIA FOR ORIGINAL APPROVAL
21 NCAC 58C .0604	INSTRUCTOR PERFORMANCE
21 NCAC 58C .0605	REQUEST FOR EXAMINATIONS AND VIDEO RECORDINGS
21 NCAC 58C .0606	POSTLICENSING COURSE REPORTS
21 NCAC 58C .0607	EXPIRATION, RENEWAL, AND REINSTATEMENT OF APPROVAL
21 NCAC 58C .0608	DENIAL OR WITHDRAWAL OF APPROVAL

History Note: Authority G.S. 93A-4; 93A-4(a),(d); 93A-33; 93A-34;
Eff. October 1, 2000;
Amended Eff. July 1, 2015; January 1, 2012; July 1, 2009; January 1, 2008; April 1, 2006; July 1, 2005; April 1, 2004; September 1, 2002;
Repealed Eff. July 1, 2017.

SUBCHAPTER 58D - REAL ESTATE APPRAISERS

SECTION .0100 - APPLICATION FOR APPRAISER LICENSE OR CERTIFICATE

21 NCAC 58D .0101	FORM
21 NCAC 58D .0102	FILING AND FEES

History Note: Filed as a Temporary Amendment Eff. July 5, 1990, for a Period of 180 Days to Expire on January 1, 1991;
Statutory Authority G.S. 93A-73(a),(b); 93A-77;
Eff. May 1, 1990;
Amended Eff. January 1, 1992; January 1, 1991;
Repealed Eff. July 1, 1994.

SECTION .0200 - APPRAISER LICENSING AND CERTIFICATION

21 NCAC 58D .0201	QUALIFICATIONS FOR APPRAISER LICENSURE AND CERTIFICATION
21 NCAC 58D .0202	CHARACTER
21 NCAC 58D .0203	LICENSE AND CERTIFICATE RENEWAL
21 NCAC 58D .0204	CONTINUING EDUCATION
21 NCAC 58D .0205	INACTIVE STATUS
21 NCAC 58D .0206	EXPIRED LICENSE OR CERTIFICATE
21 NCAC 58D .0207	PAYMENT OF LICENSE AND CERTIFICATE FEES
21 NCAC 58D .0208	REPLACEMENT LICENSE OR CERTIFICATE FEE

21 NCAC 58D .0209   **FEDERAL APPRAISER REGISTRY**

History Note: *Filed as a Temporary Amendment Eff. May 9, 1991, For a Period of 146 Days to Expire on October 2, 1991;*
Filed as a Temporary Amendment Eff. April 5, 1991, For a Period of 180 Days to Expire on October 2, 1991;
Filed as a Temporary Amendment Eff. July 5, 1990, For a Period of 180 Days to Expire on January 1, 1991;
Authority G.S. 93A-73(c); 93A-74(a),(b),(c),(d); 93A-75(d); 93A-77; 93A-79(e); 12 U.S.C. 3332, 3345, and 3347; 12 C.F.R. 34.42;
Eff. May 1, 1990;
Amended Eff. April 1, 1994; July 1, 1993; May 1, 1992; January 1, 1992;
Repealed Eff. July 1, 1994.

21 NCAC 58D .0210   **TEMPORARY PRACTICE**

History Note: *Authority G.S. 93A-77; Title XI, Section 1122 (a); 12 U.S.C. 3351(a);*
Eff. January 1, 1992;
Amended Eff. July 1, 1993;
Repealed Eff. July 1, 1994.

SECTION .0300 - APPRAISER EXAMINATIONS

21 NCAC 58D .0301   **TIME AND PLACE**
21 NCAC 58D .0302   **SUBJECT MATTER AND PASSING SCORES**
21 NCAC 58D .0303   **RE-EXAMINATION**
21 NCAC 58D .0304   **CHEATING AND RELATED MISCONDUCT**
21 NCAC 58D .0305   **CONFIDENTIALITY OF EXAMINATIONS**
21 NCAC 58D .0306   **EXAMINATION REVIEW**

History Note: *Filed as a Temporary Amendment Eff. July 5, 1990, For a Period of 180 Days to Expire on January 1, 1991;*
Authority G.S. 93A-73(c); 93A-77;
Eff. May 1, 1990;
Amended Eff. February 1, 1991; January 1, 1991;
Repealed Eff. July 1, 1994.

SECTION .0400 - GENERAL APPRAISAL PRACTICE

21 NCAC 58D .0401   **USE OF TITLES**
21 NCAC 58D .0402   **DISPLAY OF LICENSES AND CERTIFICATES**
21 NCAC 58D .0403   **ADVERTISING**
21 NCAC 58D .0404   **CHANGE OF NAME OR ADDRESS**
21 NCAC 58D .0405   **CERTIFIED APPRAISALS**
21 NCAC 58D .0406   **APPRAISAL REPORTS**
21 NCAC 58D .0407   **MANAGING APPRAISER**
21 NCAC 58D .0408   **SUPERVISION OF UNLICENSED AND UNCERTIFIED ASSISTANTS**
21 NCAC 58D .0409   **SUPERVISION OF LICENSED AND CERTIFIED RESIDENTIAL APPRAISERS**

History Note: *Filed as a Temporary Amendment Eff. July 5, 1990, For a Period of 180 Days to Expire on January 1, 1991;*
Authority G.S. 93A-71(d),(f),(g); 93A-77;
Eff. May 1, 1990;
Amended Eff. February 1, 1991; January 1, 1991;
Repealed Eff. July 1, 1994.

SECTION .0500 - STANDARDS OF APPRAISAL PRACTICE

21 NCAC 58D .0501   **APPRAISAL STANDARDS**

History Note: Authority G.S. 93A-77;
Eff. May 1, 1990;
Amended Eff. July 1, 1991;
Repealed Eff. July 1, 1994.

SECTION .0600 - APPRAISAL BOARD HEARINGS

21 NCAC 58D .0601	**SCOPE**
21 NCAC 58D .0602	**FORM OF COMPLAINTS AND OTHER PLEADINGS**
21 NCAC 58D .0603	**PRESIDING OFFICER**
21 NCAC 58D .0604	**SUBPOENAS**
21 NCAC 58D .0605	**FINAL DECISIONS**
21 NCAC 58D .0606	**PETITION TO REOPEN PROCEEDING**

History Note: Authority G.S. 93A-77; 150B-38(h);
Eff. May 1, 1992;
Repealed Eff. July 1, 1994.

SECTION .0700 - DECLARATORY RULINGS

21 NCAC 58D .0701   **REQUESTS FOR RULINGS: DISPOSITION OF REQUESTS**

History Note: Authority G.S. 93A-77; 150B-4;
Eff. May 1, 1992;
Repealed Eff. July 1, 1994.

SUBCHAPTER 58E - REAL ESTATE CONTINUING EDUCATION

SECTION .0100 - UPDATE COURSE

21 NCAC 58E .0101	**PURPOSE AND APPLICABILITY**
21 NCAC 58E .0102	**UPDATE COURSE COMPONENT**
21 NCAC 58E .0103	**APPLICATION FOR ORIGINAL APPROVAL**
21 NCAC 58E .0104	**CRITERIA FOR APPROVAL OF UPDATE COURSE SPONSOR**
21 NCAC 58E .0105	**STUDENT FEE FOR UPDATE COURSES**

History Note: Authority G.S. 93A-3(c); 93A-4.1; 93A-4A;
Eff. July 1, 1994;
Amended Eff. July 1, 2014; April 1, 2006; July 1, 2000; July 1, 1995;
Repealed Eff. July 1, 2017.

SECTION .0200 - UPDATE COURSE INSTRUCTORS

21 NCAC 58E .0201	**PURPOSE AND APPLICABILITY**
21 NCAC 58E .0202	**NATURE AND SCOPE OF APPROVAL**
21 NCAC 58E .0203	**APPLICATION AND CRITERIA FOR ORIGINAL APPROVAL**
21 NCAC 58E .0204	**ACTIVE AND INACTIVE STATUS; RENEWAL OF APPROVAL**

21 NCAC 58E .0205	**DENIAL OR WITHDRAWAL OF APPROVAL**
21 NCAC 58E .0206	**REQUEST FOR A VIDEO RECORDING**

History Note: Authority G.S. 93A-3(c); 93A-4.1; 93A-4A;
Eff. July 1, 1994;
Amended Eff. July 1, 2015; July 1, 2014; January 1, 2012; January 1, 2008; April 1, 2004; July 1, 2003; September 1, 2002; July 1, 2000; July 1, 1996; July 1, 1995;
Repealed Eff. July 1, 2017.

SECTION .0300 - ELECTIVE COURSES

21 NCAC 58E .0301	**PURPOSE AND APPLICABILITY**
21 NCAC 58E .0302	**ELECTIVE COURSE COMPONENT**
21 NCAC 58E .0303	**APPLICATION FOR ORIGINAL APPROVAL**
21 NCAC 58E .0304	**CRITERIA FOR ELECTIVE COURSE APPROVAL**
21 NCAC 58E .0305	**ELECTIVE COURSE SUBJECT MATTER**
21 NCAC 58E .0306	**ELECTIVE COURSE INSTRUCTORS**
21 NCAC 58E .0307	**ELECTIVE COURSE CREDIT HOURS**
21 NCAC 58E .0308	**REQUEST FOR A VIDEO RECORDING**
21 NCAC 58E .0309	**STUDENT FEES FOR ELECTIVE COURSES**

History Note: Authority G.S. 93A-3(c); 93A-4.1; 93A-4A;
Eff. July 1, 1994;
Amended Eff. July 1, 2015; July 1, 2014; July 1, 2010; April 1, 2006; July 1, 2005; April 1, 2004; September 1, 2002; October 1, 2000; July 1, 2000; July 1, 1996; September 1, 1996; March 1, 1996; July 1, 1995;
Repealed Eff. July 1, 2017.

21 NCAC 58E .0310   **DISTANCE EDUCATION COURSES**

History Note: Authority G.S. 93A-3(c); 93A-4.1;
Eff. July 1, 1996;
Amended Eff. July 1, 2009; July 1, 2005; July 1, 2000;
Repealed Eff. July 1, 2017.

SECTION .0400 - GENERAL SPONSOR REQUIREMENTS

21 NCAC 58E .0401	**PURPOSE AND APPLICABILITY**
21 NCAC 58E .0402	**SPONSOR ELIGIBILITY**
21 NCAC 58E .0403	**SPONSOR NAME**
21 NCAC 58E .0404	**ADVANCE APPROVAL REQUIRED**
21 NCAC 58E .0405	**CONTINUING EDUCATION COORDINATOR**
21 NCAC 58E .0406	**COURSE COMPLETION REPORTING**

History Note: Authority G.S. 93A-3(c); 93A-4.1; 93A-4A;
Eff. July 1, 1994;
Amended Eff. April 1, 2006; July 1, 2005; September 1, 2002; October 1, 2000; July 1, 1996; July 1, 1995;
Repealed Eff. July 1, 2017.

SECTION .0400 - GENERAL SPONSOR REQUIREMENTS

21 NCAC 58E .0401   **PURPOSE AND APPLICABILITY**
This Section contains miscellaneous general provisions relating to the approval of sponsors to conduct either the update course or elective courses and to the responsibilities of approved sponsors. Matters addressed include:

Sponsor names and eligibility; designation of a continuing education coordinator; renewal of course and sponsor approval; records and reports; grounds for denial or withdrawal of approval, and other related matters.

History Note: *Authority G.S. 93A-3(c); 93A-4A;*
Eff. July 1, 1994.

21 NCAC 58E .0402 SPONSOR ELIGIBILITY
Any legal entity is eligible to seek approval as a sponsor of continuing education courses, provided that the entity seeking approval of a course as a continuing education elective course is either the owner of the proprietary rights to the course or has lawfully acquired from the course owner the right to seek course approval from the Commission and to conduct such course.

History Note: *Authority G.S. 93A-3(c); 93A-4A;*
Eff. July 1, 1994.

21 NCAC 58E .0403 SPONSOR NAME
(a) The official name to be used by any course sponsor in connection with the offering of an approved continuing education course must clearly distinguish the sponsor from any other previously approved continuing education course sponsor. Unless the sponsor is a licensed private real estate school proposing to operate continuing education courses in its own name, the official name also must clearly distinguish the sponsor from any licensed private real estate school. Sponsor applicants proposing to use a sponsor name which does not comply with this standard may be required to adopt a different name as a condition of approval.
(b) Any advertisement or promotional material utilized by an approved course sponsor must include the course sponsor's official name and shall not include any other name for the sponsor.

History Note: *Authority G.S. 93A-3(c); 93A-4A;*
Eff. July 1, 1994.

21 NCAC 58E .0404 ADVANCE APPROVAL REQUIRED
Prospective sponsors of an update course or elective course must obtain written approval from the Commission to conduct such course prior to conducting the course and prior to advertising or otherwise representing that the course is or may be approved for continuing education credit in North Carolina. No retroactive approval to conduct an update course will be granted for any reason. Retroactive approval of an elective course may be granted by the Commission if the course sponsor can provide evidence satisfactory to the Commission that the course was not offered for purposes of satisfying the real estate continuing education requirement and that the sponsor could not reasonably have been expected to anticipate in advance that students would want to receive continuing education elective credit for the course.

History Note: *Authority G.S. 93A-3(c); 93A-4A;*
Eff. July 1, 1994.

21 NCAC 58E .0405 CONTINUING EDUCATION COORDINATOR
A sponsor of an update course or elective course must designate one person to serve as the continuing education coordinator for all Commission-approved continuing education courses offered by the sponsor. The designated coordinator shall serve as the official contact person for the sponsor and shall be responsible for the following:
  (1) Supervising the conduct of all the sponsor's Commission-approved continuing education courses;
  (2) Signing the course completion certificates provided by the sponsor to licensees completing courses; and
  (3) Submitting to the Commission all required fees, rosters, reports and other information.

History Note: *Authority G.S. 93A-3(c); 93A-4A;*
Eff. July 1, 1994;
Amended Eff. July 1, 1995.

21 NCAC 58E .0406 COURSE COMPLETION REPORTING

(a) Course sponsors must prepare and submit to the Commission, along with the per student fee required by G.S. 93A-4.1(d), reports verifying completion of a continuing education course for each licensee who satisfactorily completes the course according to the criteria in 21 NCAC 58A .1705 and who desires continuing education credit for the course. Such reports shall include students' names, students' license numbers, course date, sponsor and course codes and course information presented in the format prescribed by the Commission, and sponsors shall be held accountable for the completeness and accuracy of all information in such reports. Such reports shall be transmitted electronically via the Internet. Sponsors must submit these reports to the Commission in a manner that will assure receipt by the Commission within seven calendar days following the course, but in no case later than June 15 of any approval period for courses conducted during that approval period.

(b) At the request of the Commission, course sponsors must provide licensees enrolled in each continuing education course an opportunity to complete an evaluation of each approved continuing education course on a form provided by the Commission. Sponsors must submit the completed evaluation forms to the Commission with the reports verifying completion of a continuing education course.

(c) Course sponsors shall provide each licensee who satisfactorily completes an approved continuing education course according to the criteria in 21 NCAC 58A .1705 a course completion certificate on a form provided by the Commission. Sponsors must provide the certificates to licensees within fifteen calendar days following the course, but in no case later than June 15 for any course completed prior to that date. The certificate shall be retained by the licensee as his or her proof of having completed the course.

(d) When a licensee in attendance at a continuing education course does not comply with the student participation standards, the course sponsor shall advise the Commission of this matter in writing at the time reports verifying completion of continuing education for the course are submitted. A sponsor who determines that a licensee failed to comply with either the Commission's attendance or student participation standards shall not provide the licensee with a course completion certificate nor shall the sponsor include the licensee's name on the reports verifying completion of continuing education.

(e) Notwithstanding the provisions of Paragraphs (a) and (c) of this Rule, approved course sponsors who are national professional trade organizations and who conduct Commission-approved continuing education elective courses out of state shall not be obligated to submit reports verifying completion of continuing education courses by electronic means, provided that such sponsors submit to the Commission a roster which includes the names and license numbers of North Carolina licensees who completed the course in compliance with the criteria in 21 NCAC 58A .1705 and who desire continuing education credit for the course. A separate roster must be submitted for each class session and must be accompanied by a per student fee required by G.S. 93A-4.1(d), payable to the North Carolina Real Estate Commission. Rosters must be submitted in a manner which assures receipt by the Commission within 15 calendar days following the course, but not later than the last course reporting dates for an approval period specified in Paragraph (a) of this Rule. Such sponsors may also provide each licensee who completes an approved course in compliance with the criteria in 21 NCAC 58A .1705 a sponsor-developed course completion certificate in place of a certificate on a form provided by the Commission. Sponsors must provide the certificates to licensees within fifteen calendar days following the course.

History Note: *Authority G.S. 93A-3(c); 93A-4.1;*
Eff. July 1, 1994;
Amended Eff. April 1, 2006; July 1, 2005; September 1, 2002; October 1, 2000; July 1, 1996; July 1, 1995.

21 NCAC 58E .0407   PER STUDENT FEE

History Note: *Authority G.S. 93A-3(c); 93A-4A;*
Eff. July 1, 1994;
Amended Eff. July 1, 2005; August 1, 1998; July 1, 1996; July 1, 1995;
Repealed Eff. April 1, 2006.

21 NCAC 58E .0408   CHANGE IN SPONSOR OWNERSHIP
21 NCAC 58E .0409   CHANGES DURING APPROVAL PERIOD
21 NCAC 58E .0410   COURSE RECORDS
21 NCAC 58E .0411   RENEWAL OF COURSE AND SPONSOR APPROVAL
21 NCAC 58E .0412   DENIAL OR WITHDRAWAL OF APPROVAL

History Note: Authority G.S. 93A-3(c); 93A-4.1; 93A-4A; 93A-6(a)(15);
Eff. July 1, 1994;
Amended Eff. July 1, 2015; July 1, 2014; July 1, 2010; April 1, 2004; July 1, 2000; July 1, 1996;
Repealed Eff. July 1, 2017.

SECTION .0500 - COURSE OPERATIONAL REQUIREMENTS

21 NCAC 58E .0501	PURPOSE AND APPLICABILITY
21 NCAC 58E .0502	SCHEDULING
21 NCAC 58E .0503	MINIMUM CLASS SIZE
21 NCAC 58E .0504	NOTICE OF SCHEDULED COURSES
21 NCAC 58E .0505	ADVERTISING; PROVIDING COURSE INFORMATION
21 NCAC 58E .0506	CLASSES OPEN TO ALL LICENSEES
21 NCAC 58E .0507	CLASSROOM FACILITIES
21 NCAC 58E .0508	STUDENT CHECK-IN
21 NCAC 58E .0509	INSTRUCTOR CONDUCT AND PERFORMANCE
21 NCAC 58E .0510	MONITORING ATTENDANCE
21 NCAC 58E .0511	STUDENT PARTICIPATION STANDARDS
21 NCAC 58E .0512	SOLICITATION OF STUDENTS
21 NCAC 58E .0513	CANCELLATION AND REFUND POLICIES
21 NCAC 58E .0514	COURSE INSPECTIONS BY COMMISSION REPRESENTATIVE

History Note: Authority G.S. 93A-3(c); 93A-4.1; 93A-4A;
Eff. July 1, 1994;
Amended Eff. July 1, 2015; January 1, 2012; July 1, 2010; July 1, 2009; April 1, 2004; July 1, 2001; October 1, 2000; July 1, 1996; July 1, 1995;
Repealed Eff. July 1, 2017.

21 NCAC 58E .0515 ACCOMMODATIONS FOR PERSONS WITH DISABILITIES

History Note: Authority G.S. 93A-3(c); 93A-4A;
Eff. July 1, 1995;
Amended Eff. July 1, 2000;
Repealed Eff. July 1, 2017.

SECTION .0600 – BROKER-IN-CHARGE ANNUAL REVIEW

21 NCAC 58E .0601	PURPOSE AND APPLICABILITY
21 NCAC 58E .0602	COURSE DESCRIPTION
21 NCAC 58E .0603	AUTHORITY TO CONDUCT COURSE
21 NCAC 58E .0604	COURSE OPERATIONAL REQUIREMENTS

History Note: Authority G.S. 93A-2; 93A-3; 93A-3(c); 93A-4.1; 93A-4.2;
Eff. July 1, 2010;
Repealed Eff. July 1, 2014.

SUBCHAPTER 58F - BROKER TRANSITION COURSE

SECTION .0100 – REQUIREMENTS

21 NCAC 58F .0101	BASIC REQUIREMENT
21 NCAC 58F .0102	COURSE CONTENT
21 NCAC 58F .0103	COURSE SPONSORS AND INSTRUCTORS
21 NCAC 58F .0104	COURSE OPERATIONAL REQUIREMENTS

21 NCAC 58F .0105 COURSE COMPLETION REPORTING AND PER STUDENT FEE
21 NCAC 58F .0106 WITHDRAWAL OF SPONSOR AND INSTRUCTOR APPROVAL

History Note: Authority G.S. 93A-4; 93A-4.3;
Eff. April 1, 2006;
Repealed Eff. July 1, 2009.

SUBCHAPTER 58G – NORTH CAROLINA REAL ESTATE COMMISSION

SECTION .0100 – GENERAL

21 NCAC 58G .0101 PER DIEM
A member of the Real Estate Commission shall receive a per diem payment of two hundred dollars ($200.00) for each day during which the member is engaged in business for or on behalf of the Real Estate Commission.

History Note: Authority G.S. 93A-3(b) and (c);
Eff. April 1, 2006;
Pursuant to G.S. 150B-21.3A, rule is necessary without substantive public interest Eff. May 1, 2018.

21 NCAC 58G .0102 LOCATION
(a) The office of the North Carolina Real Estate Commission is located at 1313 Navaho Drive, Raleigh, North Carolina. The mailing address is Post Office Box 17100, Raleigh, North Carolina 27619-7100.
(b) Forms and information about the office may be obtained from the Commission's website at www.ncrec.gov.

History Note: Authority G.S. 93A–3(c);
Eff. July 1, 2017.

21 NCAC 58G .0103 DEFINITIONS
The following definitions apply throughout this Chapter and to all forms prescribed pursuant to this Chapter:
(1) "Branch Office" means any office in addition to the principal office of a broker that is operated in connection with the broker's real estate business.
(2) "BIC" means a broker-in-charge pursuant to G.S. 93A-2(a1).
(3) "BIC Eligible" means a broker's license status who has satisfied the broker-in-charge qualification requirements and filed application pursuant to G.S. 93A-4.2 and 21 NCAC 58A .0110.
(4) "Commission" means the North Carolina Real Estate Commission.
(5) "Commission's website" means www.ncrec.gov.
(6) "Day" means calendar day unless the rule expressly states otherwise. The first day counted is the day following the act, event, or transaction that triggered the tolling of the designated time period.
(7) "Fee" means a payment made to the Commission by a bank check, certified check, money order, debit card, credit card, or other electronic means and is nonrefundable once the payment has been processed.
(8) "Firm" means a partnership, corporation, limited liability company, association, or other business entity, except for a sole proprietorship.
(9) "Form" means an original form template provided by the Commission and completed by the submitting party.
(10) "Office" means any place of business where acts are performed for which a real estate license is required or where monies received by a broker acting in a fiduciary capacity are handled or records for such trust monies are maintained.
(11) "Principal Office" means the office so designated in the Commission's records by the qualifying broker of a licensed firm or the broker-in-charge of a sole proprietorship.

History Note: Authority G.S. 93A–3(c);
Eff. July 1, 2017;
Amended Eff. July 1, 2018.

SUBCHAPTER 58H - REAL ESTATE EDUCATION

SECTION .0100 – GENERAL

21 NCAC 58H .0101 DEFINITIONS
The following definitions apply throughout this Subchapter and to all forms prescribed pursuant to this Chapter:
- (1) "Instructional hour" means 50 minutes of instruction and 10 minutes of break time.
- (2) "Distance education" means a method of instruction accomplished through the use of media whereby teacher and student are separated by distance or time.
- (3) "End-of-course evaluation" means a student evaluation of the course and the instructor's performance that shall be administered during the class period before administration of the end-of-course examination.
- (4) "End-of-course examination" means an examination administered at the conclusion of a course that tests students' knowledge and mastery of all course subjects mandated by the Commission prescribed course syllabus.
- (5) "Mid-course evaluation" means a student evaluation of the course and the instructor's performance given at the midpoint of the course.
- (6) "Instructor development program" means courses of instruction designed to assist real estate instructors in the performance of Prelicensing, Postlicensing, or Continuing Education instructor duties or in the development of teaching skills.
- (7) "License Examination Performance Record" means the percentage of an instructor's or school's students who, within 30 days of completing a Prelicensing course pursuant to 21 NCAC 58H .0210(a), take and pass the license examination, as defined in 21 NCAC 58A .0402, on their first attempt.
- (8) "Postlicensing course" means any one of the courses comprising the 90 hour Postlicensing education program pursuant to G.S. 93A-4(a1) and 21 NCAC 58A .1902.
- (9) "Prelicensing course" means a single course consisting of at least 75 hours of instruction on subjects prescribed by the Commission pursuant to G.S. 93A-4(a).
- (10) "Private real estate school" means any real estate educational entity that is privately owned and operated by an individual, partnership, corporation, limited liability company, or association, and that conducts, for a profit or tuition charge, Prelicensing or Postlicensing courses.
- (11) "Public real estate school" means any proprietary business or trade school licensed by the State Board of Community Colleges under G.S. 115D-90 or approved by the Board of Governors of the University of North Carolina that conducts Prelicensing or Postlicensing courses.
- (12) "Schools" mean licensed private and approved public real estate schools.
- (13) "Update Courses" mean the General Update Course and the Broker-in-Charge Update Course.

History Note: *Authority G.S. 93A-4; 93A-4.1; 93A-32; 93A-33;*
Eff. July 1, 2017.

SECTION .0200 - REAL ESTATE SCHOOLS

21 NCAC 58H .0201 APPLICABILITY
This Section applies to all real estate schools offering approved Prelicensing and Postlicensing courses. Public real estate schools offering approved Prelicensing and Postlicensing courses shall be exempt from rules in this Section unless a Rule specifically requires compliance.

History Note: *Authority G.S. 93A-4; 93A-33;*
Eff. July 1, 2017.

21 NCAC 58H .0202 APPLICATION FOR ORIGINAL APPROVAL OF A PUBLIC REAL ESTATE SCHOOL

(a) Any entity seeking original approval as a public real estate school to conduct Prelicensing or Postlicensing courses shall apply to the Commission on a form available on the Commission's website and shall set forth the:
- (1) school name;
- (2) school director name and contact information;
- (3) school address;
- (4) school telephone number;
- (5) school website address;
- (6) type of public institution;
- (7) Prelicensing or Postlicensing courses to be offered by the school;
- (8) Update courses to be offered by the school; and
- (9) a signed certification by the school director that courses shall be conducted in compliance with the rules of this Subchapter.

(b) Public real estate schools offering Prelicensing or Postlicensing courses pursuant to Paragraph (a) of this Rule shall be eligible to offer Update courses and continuing education courses.

(c) Approval shall extend only to the courses included in the application for school approval.

History Note: Authority G.S. 93A-4;
Eff. July 1, 2017.

21 NCAC 58H .0203 APPLICATION FOR ORIGINAL LICENSURE OF A PRIVATE REAL ESTATE SCHOOL

(a) Any entity seeking original licensure as a private real estate school to conduct Prelicensing or Postlicensing courses shall apply to the Commission on a form available on the Commission's website and shall set forth the following criteria in addition to the requirements in G.S. 93A-34(b):
- (1) the physical, website, and email addresses and telephone number of the principal office of the school;
- (2) the proposed school director's legal name, real estate license number, if any, email and mailing address, and telephone number;
- (3) the type of school ownership entity and the name, title, real estate license number, if any, mailing address, and ownership percentage of each individual or entity holding at least 10% ownership in the entity;
- (4) the North Carolina Secretary of State Identification Number;
- (5) the criminal history and history of occupational license disciplinary actions of individual school owner(s);
- (6) the physical address of each proposed school location;
- (7) the source of real estate examinations to be used for each course offered;
- (8) a copy of a current fire inspection report;
- (9) a copy of a criminal background check for the previous seven years on the proposed school director;
- (10) a signed Consent to Service of Process and Pleadings form available on the Commission's website, if a foreign entity;
- (11) the Prelicensing or Postlicensing courses to be offered by the school;
- (12) the Update courses to be offered by the school;
- (13) the signature and certification of the school owner(s).

(b) Private real estate school names shall contain the words "Real Estate" and other words identifying the entity as a school, such as "school," "academy," or "institute" that are distinguishable from other licensed private real estate schools and from continuing education course sponsors approved by the Commission.

(c) The school name shall be used in all school publications and advertising.

(d) Each school shall certify that its facilities and equipment are in compliance with all applicable local, state and federal laws and regulations regarding health, safety, and welfare, including the Americans with Disabilities Act.

(e) The original license application fee shall be two hundred dollars ($200.00) for each proposed school location.

(f) The initial fee for a school to offer a Prelicensing or Postlicensing course at any of its locations during the licensing period shall be forty dollars ($40.00) per Prelicensing or Postlicensing course.

(g) Private real estate schools offering Prelicensing or Postlicensing courses pursuant to Paragraph (a) of this Rule shall be eligible to offer Update courses and continuing education courses.

(h) If a school relocates any location during any licensing period, the school owner shall submit an original application for licensure of that location pursuant to this Rule.

History Note: Authority G.S. 93A-4; 93A-33; 93A-34;
                     Eff. July 1, 2017.

21 NCAC 58H .0204   SCHOOL DIRECTOR

(a) All schools shall designate a school director, who shall
- (1) supervise all school operations related to the conduct of Prelicensing and Postlicensing courses;
- (2) ensure compliance with all statutory and rule requirements governing the licensing and operation of the school; and
- (3) act as the school's liaison to the Commission.

(b) Public real estate schools shall designate one permanent employee to serve as the school director.

(c) The school director for a private real estate school shall satisfy one of the following qualification standards:
- (1) hold a baccalaureate or higher degree;
- (2) have at least two years full-time experience within the past 10 years as an instructor or school administrator; or
- (3) possess qualifications that the Commission finds to be equivalent to those described in Subparagraph (1) or (2) of this Rule, such as:
  - (A) a transcript demonstrating completion of 120 semester hours of education at an institution accredited by any college accrediting body recognized by the U. S. Department of Education;
  - (B) currently holding or having held within the past 15 years a military pay grade of an E-8 level, O-1 level, or higher; or
  - (C) a current Distinguished Real Estate Instructor (DREI) designation granted by the Real Estate Educators' Association.

(d) The school director shall approve a guest lecturer prior to the guest lecturer teaching a course session. School directors shall ensure that all guest lecturers possess experience related to the particular subject area the guest lecturer is teaching. Guest lecturers may be utilized to teach collectively up to one-fourth of any Prelicensing or Postlicensing course.

(e) The school director shall ensure that each instructor meets the requirements of Rule .0302 of this Subchapter.

(f) The school director shall ensure each course utilizes a textbook currently approved by the Commission pursuant to Rule .0206 of this Section.

(g) Schools shall notify the Commission within 10 days of any change in school director during the licensing period.

History Note: Authority G.S. 93A-4; 93A-33; 93A-34;
                     Eff. July 1, 2017.

21 NCAC 58H .0205   PRIVATE REAL ESTATE SCHOOL BULLETIN

(a) A private real estate school shall publish a single bulletin addressing Prelicensing and Postlicensing courses offered. The same bulletin shall be used by all locations of a private real estate school.

(b) In addition to the information required by G.S. 93A-34(c)(5), a school's bulletin shall:
- (1) describe the purpose of Prelicensing and Postlicensing courses;
- (2) describe the school's policies and procedures;
- (3) include the name and address of the Commission, along with a statement that any complaints concerning the school or its instructors should be directed to the Commission;
- (4) include a statement that the school shall not discriminate in its admissions policy or practice against any person on the basis of age, sex, race, color, national origin, familial status, handicap status, or religion;
- (5) contain the following prescribed text: "NOTICE: Pursuant to North Carolina Real Estate Commission Rule 21 NCAC 58A .1904, the Commission may deny or withdraw credit for a Postlicensing course that a provisional broker begins taking while already enrolled in another Postlicensing course at the same school or a different school if participating in the two courses concurrently results in the provisional broker attending Postlicensing course sessions that total more than 30 instructional hours in any given seven-day period;" and

(6) include a signed certification that a student received a copy of the bulletin prior to payment of any portion of tuition or registration fee without the right to a full refund.

(c) A private real estate school may provide in its bulletin information about courses that are not approved by the Commission and shall state that such courses are not approved or sanctioned by the Commission.

(d) A private real estate school may not include in its bulletin any promotional information for a particular real estate broker, firm, franchise, or association, even if the entity being promoted owns the school.

(e) A private real estate school shall retain the signed certification required by Paragraph (b)(6) of this Rule pursuant to Rule .0212 of this Section. The certification shall include:

(1) the student's name;
(2) the date;
(3) the title of the course(s) for which the student is enrolling;
(4) the course schedule, including the beginning and end date, and meeting days and times;
(5) the amount of tuition and other required fees being paid by the particular student;
(6) a provision whereby the school certifies that the school's bulletin has been provided to the student and that the student acknowledges receipt of the bulletin;
(7) any provisions needed to address special accommodations or arrangements applicable to a particular student; and
(8) the signatures of both the student and a school official.

History Note: Authority G.S. 93A-4(a); 93A-4(d); 93A-33; 93A-34;
Eff. July 1, 2017.

21 NCAC 58H .0206   APPROVAL OF TEXTBOOKS

(a) A request for approval of a proposed textbook shall be submitted in writing to the Commission along with two copies of the proposed textbook. The criteria for approval shall be:

(1) the textbook shall cover current North Carolina real estate related laws, rules, and practices;
(2) the text shall be grammatically correct; and
(3) the nature and depth of subject matter coverage shall be consistent with the competency and instructional levels prescribed by the Commission for the course for which approval is sought.

(b) Approval of a textbook shall only apply to the edition reviewed by the Commission. A request for approval of a new or updated edition of a previously approved textbook shall be submitted in writing to the Commission, along with two copies of the proposed textbook, and shall include a list with specific page references of all significant changes from the previously approved edition.

(c) Approval of a textbook shall terminate four years after the initial approval or upon the approval of a new edition of a previously approved textbook.

History Note: Authority G.S. 93A-4; 93A-33;
Eff. July 1, 2017.

21 NCAC 58H .0207   SCHOOL ADVERTISING AND RECRUITMENT ACTIVITIES

(a) Any school utilizing its license examination performance record for advertising or promotional purposes shall only use data that:

(1) are limited to the annual examination performance data for the particular school and for all examination candidates in the State;
(2) include the time period covered, the number of first-time candidates examined, and either the number or percentage of first-time candidates passing the examination; and
(3) are presented in a manner that is not misleading or false.

(b) Schools shall not make or publish, by way of advertising or otherwise, any false or misleading statement regarding employment opportunities that may be available as a result of completion of a course offered by that school or acquisition of a real estate license.

(c) Schools shall not use endorsements or recommendations of any person or organization of advertising or otherwise unless such person or organization has consented in writing to the use of the endorsement or recommendation. In no case shall any person or organization be compensated for an endorsement or recommendation.

(d) Schools may offer and advertise courses in addition to those approved by the Commission pursuant to this Subchapter provided that references to such courses are not made or published in a manner that implies approval by the Commission.

(e) Instructional time and materials may be utilized for instructional purposes only.

(f) Schools shall not offer Postlicensing courses only for brokers affiliated with a particular real estate broker, firm, franchise, or association, even if the entity whose affiliated brokers would benefit from the closed course is the school owner.

History Note: Authority G.S. 93A-4(d); 93A-33; 93A-34;
Eff. July 1, 2017.

21 NCAC 58H .0208   PRELICENSING AND POSTLICENSING COURSE SCHEDULING AND NOTIFICATION

(a) All Prelicensing and Postlicensing courses shall have fixed beginning and ending dates. Schools shall not utilize a scheduling system that allows students to enroll late for a course and then complete their course work in a subsequently scheduled course. Late enrollment shall be permitted only if the enrolling student can satisfy the minimum attendance requirement set forth in Rule .0210 of this Section.

(b) Schools shall notify the Commission of all scheduled Prelicensing and Postlicensing course offerings not later than 10 days prior to a scheduled course beginning date.

(c) The notice required by Paragraph (b) of this Rule shall include:
- (1) the school name;
- (2) the school code number; and
- (3) for each scheduled course:
  - (A) the name and course code number;
  - (B) the scheduled beginning and ending dates;
  - (C) the course meeting days and times, including any scheduled lunch breaks; and
  - (D) the name of the instructor and instructor number.

(d) If there is a change or cancellation within five days of the scheduled course date, then the school director shall provide notice to the Commission within 24 hours of the change or cancellation.

(e) Class meetings shall not exceed seven and a half instructional hours per day and shall not exceed 30 instructional hours over any seven day period.

History Note: Authority G.S. 93A-4;
Eff. July 1, 2017.

21 NCAC 58H .0209   PRELICENSING AND POSTLICENSING COURSE ENROLLMENT

(a) A school shall not enroll an individual in a Postlicensing course if the first day of the Postlicensing course occurs while the individual is enrolled in a Prelicensing course or if that individual has not passed the license examination.

(b) A school shall not enroll an individual in a Postlicensing course if the first day of the Postlicensing course occurs while the individual is taking another Postlicensing course at the same school or a different school if such enrollment results in the individual being in class for more than 30 instructional hours in any given seven day period.

History Note: Authority G.S. 93A-4(a1); 93A-33;
Eff. July 1, 2017.

21 NCAC 58H .0210   PRELICENSING AND POSTLICENSING COURSE COMPLETION STANDARDS

(a) To complete a Prelicensing course, a student shall, at a minimum:
- (1) attend at least eighty percent of all scheduled credit hours for the course; and
- (2) obtain a grade of at least seventy-five percent on the end-of-course examination.

(b) To complete a Postlicensing course, a student shall, at a minimum:
- (1) attend at least ninety percent of all scheduled credit hours for the course; and
- (2) obtain a grade of at least seventy-five percent on the end-of-course examination.

(c) The end-of-course examination shall be completed in the classroom and proctored by the instructor or another school staff member. Students shall not use textbooks or notes on the end-of-course examination.

(d) Prelicensing end-of-course examinations may be provided by the Commission for use by a licensed or approved school. If the Commission does not provide such end-of-course examination, or if a school elects not to use a Commission-provided examination, the school shall use an examination that tests students' knowledge and mastery of the course subject matter. Upon the request of the Commission during an application or investigation, the school shall provide a copy of its end-of-course examination.

(e) Postlicensing end-of-course examinations shall be provided by the Commission for use by a licensed or approved school.

(f) A school may, within 30 days of the course ending date, allow a Prelicensing or Postlicensing course student opportunities to make-up a missed end-of-course examination or to retake a failed end-of-course examination without repeating the course. Postlicensing students shall be allowed at least one retake examination opportunity. Any make-up or repeat end-of-course examination shall consist of a different form of the examination than any previously administered in the student's course. If the examination used is not provided by the Commission, at least seventy-five percent of the questions shall be different from those previously included on any end-of-course examination used earlier in the student's course.

(g) Schools, school directors, and instructors shall take steps to protect the security and integrity of course examinations at all times. These steps shall include:

- (1) maintaining examinations and answer keys in a secure place, such as a locked area, accessible only to the instructor or school officials;
- (2) prohibiting students from retaining copies of examinations, answer sheets, and scratch paper containing notes or calculations, or any material that may jeopardize examination security;
- (3) monitoring students at all times when examinations are being administered; and
- (4) prohibiting students from reviewing examinations, answer sheets, scratch paper, or any material used during the examination after students have completed the examination.

(h) Any student who is found to have cheated in any manner on any course examination shall be dismissed from the course and shall not be awarded a passing grade for the course or any credit for partial completion of the course. The school shall report the cheating incident in writing to the Commission within 10 days.

History Note: Authority G.S. 93A-4; 93A-33;
Eff. July 1, 2017.

21 NCAC 58H .0211   PRELICENSING AND POSTLICENSING ROSTER REPORTING

(a) A school shall provide a course completion certificate to each student who completes a Prelicensing or Postlicensing course under Rule .0210 of this Section. Each course completion certificate shall identify the course, date of completion, student, and instructor. The certificate shall be signed by the school director.

(b) For each Prelicensing or Postlicensing course taught, a school shall submit a Roster Report electronically within seven days following the course as follows:

- (1) The Prelicensing Roster Report shall include:
  - (A) each student's legal name;
  - (B) each student's email address and telephone number;
  - (C) each student's unique identification number;
  - (D) the course completion date pursuant to Rule .0210 of this Section;
  - (E) the school's name and number;
  - (F) the course's number; and
  - (G) the instructor's name and number.
- (2) The Postlicensing Roster Report shall include:
  - (A) each student's legal name;
  - (B) each broker's license number;
  - (C) the course completion date pursuant to Rule .0210 of this Section;
  - (D) the school's name and number;
  - (E) the course's name and number; and
  - (F) the instructor's name and number.

(c) Schools shall electronically submit with the Postlicensing Roster Reports the per student fee prescribed by G.S 93A-4(a2).

History Note: Authority G.S. 93A-4; 93A-33;
Eff. July 1, 2017;
Amended Eff. July 1, 2018.

21 NCAC 58H .0212 SCHOOL RECORDS
All school records shall be retained for three years by the school and be made available to the Commission during an investigation or application process. School records shall include:
- (1) enrollment and attendance records;
- (2) each student's end-of-course examination with grade and graded answer sheet;
- (3) a master copy of each end-of-course course examination with its answer key, course title, course dates, and name of the instructor;
- (4) all student evaluations pursuant to Rule .0213(a) of this Section;
- (5) all instructor evaluations pursuant to Rule .0213(c) of this Section;
- (6) class schedules;
- (7) advertisements;
- (8) bulletins, catalogues, and other official publications; and
- (9) statements of consent required by Rule .0207(c) of this Section.

History Note: Authority G.S. 93A-4; 93A-33;
Eff. July 1, 2017.

21 NCAC 58H .0213 EVALUATIONS OF INSTRUCTOR PERFORMANCE
(a) A school shall provide each student an opportunity to complete a mid-course evaluation and an end-of-course evaluation of the instructor in each Prelicensing course and to complete an end-of-course evaluation of the instructor in each Postlicensing course. Each student's evaluation shall be on a form provided by the Commission, include a section for the student's comments, and shall evaluate the instructor's:
- (1) knowledge of the subject matter;
- (2) teaching skills; and
- (3) classroom management.

(b) The school director shall submit a Summary Report electronically within 30 days after course completion pursuant to Rule .0210 of this Section. The Summary Report form shall require the school director to set forth:
- (1) the full name of the instructor being evaluated;
- (2) title of course;
- (3) the number of students who initially enrolled in the course;
- (4) the number of students who met all course requirements pursuant to Rule .0210 of this Section;
- (5) the number of students who met all course requirements except Rule .0210(a)(2) and (b)(2) of this Section;

(c) In addition to the student evaluations in Paragraph (a) of this Rule, school directors shall also ensure all school-affiliated instructors are observed at least once annually for a minimum of one hour of live uninterrupted instruction by either the school director or a Commission-approved Prelicensing or Postlicensing instructor present in the classroom. School directors who are also instructors may, upon written request to the Commission, be evaluated by a Commission monitor. The evaluation shall be based on the instructor's teaching abilities pursuant to Rule .0304 of this Subchapter. The instructor shall receive the written evaluation of his or her instructional performance within 30 days of observation.

History Note: Authority G.S. 93A-4; 93A-33;
Eff. July 1, 2017.

21 NCAC 58H .0214 EXPIRATION AND RENEWAL OF A SCHOOL APPROVAL OR LICENSE
(a) All Commission approvals and licenses issued to real estate schools shall expire annually on June 30 following issuance of approval or licensure.
(b) A school shall file an electronic application for renewal of its approval or license within 45 days immediately preceding expiration of approval or licensure on a form available on the Commission's website. The school renewal application form shall include:
- (1) the school name;
- (2) the school number;

(3) the school director's name;
(4) the school's mailing address, telephone number, and web address, if applicable;
(5) all Commission approved courses offered by the school;
(6) any change in the school's business entity;
(7) court records of any conviction, guilty plea, or plea of no contest to, a misdemeanor or felony violation of state or federal law by a court of competent jurisdiction against the school owner(s) and school director since the last renewal;
(8) records pertaining to any disciplinary action taken against the school owner(s) and school director by an occupational licensing board since the last renewal;
(9) a copy of the current bulletin;
(10) proof of bond as required in G.S. 93A-36;
(11) proof of a current fire inspection; and
(12) the school director's signature.

(c) The private school license renewal fee shall be one hundred dollars ($100.00) for each school location.

(d) The renewal fee for a private real estate school to offer a Prelicensing or Postlicensing course at any of its locations during the licensed period shall be twenty-five dollars ($25.00) per Prelicensing or Postlicensing course.

(e) If a school approval or license has expired, the school shall submit an application for original approval or licensure.

History Note: Authority G.S. 93A-4; 93A-33; 93A-34(b); 93A-35(b); 93A-36;
Eff. July 1, 2017.

21 NCAC 58H .0215   DENIAL, WITHDRAWAL, OR TERMINATION OF SCHOOL APPROVAL OR LICENSE

(a) The Commission may deny or withdraw approval of any public real estate school or suspend, revoke, or deny renewal of the license of any private real estate school upon finding that:

(1) any school official employed by the school has been convicted of, pleaded guilty to, or pleaded no contest to, a misdemeanor or felony violation of state or federal law by a court of competent jurisdiction;
(2) any school official found by a court or government agency of competent jurisdiction to have violated any state or federal regulation prohibiting discrimination;
(3) a school made any false statements or presented any false, incomplete, or incorrect information in connection with an application;
(4) a school provided false, incomplete, or incorrect information in connection with any report the school is required to submit to the Commission;
(5) a school presented to its students or prospective students false or misleading information relating to its instructional program, to the instructional programs of other institutions, or related to employment opportunities;
(6) a school refused at any time to permit authorized representatives of the Commission to inspect the school or audit its courses;
(7) a school director violated the rules of this Subchapter or was disciplined by the Commission under G.S. 93A-6;
(8) a school obtained or used, or attempted to obtain or use, in any manner or form, North Carolina real estate license examination questions;
(9) a school compiled a license examination performance record for first-time examination candidates that is below sixty percent passing for two or more of the previous five annual reporting periods;
(10) a school failed to provide to the Commission a written plan describing the changes the school made or intends to make in its instructional program including instructors, course materials, methods of student evaluation, and completion standards to improve the performance of the school's students on the license examination within 30 days of the Commission's request during an investigation, application process, or following a school's attainment of a licensing examination record for first-time examination candidates that is below 60 percent passing for the previous annual reporting period;
(11) a school provided the Commission a fee that was dishonored by a bank or returned for insufficient funds; or
(12) a school refused or failed to comply with the provisions of this Subchapter.

(b) When ownership of a licensed private real estate school is transferred and the school ceases to operate as the licensed entity, the school license is not transferable and shall terminate on the effective date of the transfer. All courses shall be completed by the effective date of the transfer. The transferring owner shall report course completion(s) to the Commission. The new entity shall obtain an original private real estate school license for each location where the school will conduct courses as required by G.S. 93A-34 and Rule .0203 of this Section prior to advertising courses, registering students, accepting tuition, conducting courses, or otherwise engaging in any school operations.

(c) If a licensed private real estate school transfers an aggregate of 50 percent or more of the ownership interest, the school shall notify the Commission in writing within 10 days of the transfer.

History Note: *Authority G.S. 93A-4(d); 93A-34(c); 93A-35(c); 93A-38;*
Eff. July 1, 2017.

SUBCHAPTER 58H - REAL ESTATE EDUCATION

SECTION .0300 – APPROVED INSTRUCTORS

21 NCAC 58H .0301   PRELICENSING, POSTLICENSING, AND UPDATE COURSE INSTRUCTOR APPROVAL

(a) Approval of an instructor to teach Prelicensing and Postlicensing courses shall authorize the instructor to teach courses only in conjunction with and at schools approved or licensed by the Commission pursuant to Rule .0202 or .0203 of this Subchapter to conduct such courses.

(b) An instructor approved to teach Prelicensing and Postlicensing courses may elect to also teach Update courses upon initial approval, renewal, or any time while holding such approval.

(c) Approved instructors may teach Update courses for any approved Update course sponsor pursuant to Rule .0402 of this Subchapter. An approved instructor may not independently conduct an Update course unless the instructor has also obtained approval as an Update course sponsor.

History Note: *Authority G.S. 93A-4(d); 93A-33; 93A-34;*
Eff. July 1, 2017.

21 NCAC 58H .0302   APPLICATION AND CRITERIA FOR ORIGINAL PRELICENSING, POSTLICENSING, OR UPDATE COURSE INSTRUCTOR APPROVAL

(a) An individual seeking original instructor approval shall submit an application on a form available on the Commission's website that shall require the instructor applicant to indicate the course(s) for which he or she is seeking approval and set forth the instructor applicant's:
- (1) legal name, address, email address, and telephone number;
- (2) real estate license number and instructor number, if any, assigned by Commission;
- (3) criminal and occupational licensing history, including any disciplinary actions;
- (4) education background, including specific real estate education;
- (5) experience in the real estate business;
- (6) real estate teaching experience, if any;
- (7) a signed Consent to Service of Process and Pleadings for nonresident applicants; and
- (8) signature.

(b) An instructor applicant shall demonstrate that he or she possesses good reputation and character pursuant to G.S. 93A-34(c)(9) and has:
- (1) a North Carolina real estate broker license that is not on provisional status;
- (2) completed continuing education sufficient to activate a license under 21 NCAC 58A .1702;
- (3) completed 60 semester hours of college-level education at an institution accredited by any college accrediting body recognized by the U.S. Department of Education; and
- (4) within the previous seven years has either:
  - (A) two years full-time experience in real estate brokerage with at least one year in North Carolina;
  - (B) three years of instructor experience at a secondary or post-secondary level;
  - (C) real estate Prelicensing or Postlicensing instructor approval in another jurisdiction; or

(D) qualifications found to be equivalent by the Commission, including a current North Carolina law license and three years' full time experience in commercial or residential real estate transactions or representation of real estate brokers or firms.

(c) Along with their application, an instructor applicant shall submit a digital video recording of themselves teaching a 50 minute block of a single topic in a Prelicensing, Postlicensing, or Update course that demonstrates the ability to teach the subject in a manner consistent with the course materials. The digital video recording shall comply with Rule .0305(c) of this Section.

(d) The digital video recording requirement described in Paragraph (c) of this Rule shall be waived by the Commission if the instructor applicant has a current:
  (1) approval as either a General Update Course, Prelicensing, or Postlicensing instructor; or
  (2) Distinguished Real Estate Instructor (DREI) designation that has been awarded to the instructor by the Real Estate Educators Association or an equivalent instructor certification.

(e) Prior to teaching any Prelicensing or Postlicensing course, an approved instructor shall take the Commission's New Pre/Postlicensing Instructor Seminar.

(f) Prior to teaching any Update course, an approved instructor shall take the Commission's annual Update Instructor Seminar for the current license period. The Update Instructor Seminar shall not be used to meet the requirement in Rule .0306(b)(4) of this Section.

History Note: Authority G.S. 93A-3(f); 93A-4; 93A-10; 93A-33; 93A-34;
Eff. July 1, 2017.

21 NCAC 58H .0303   DENIAL OR WITHDRAWAL OF INSTRUCTOR APPROVAL

The Commission may deny or withdraw approval of any instructor applicant or approved instructor upon finding that the instructor or instructor applicant:

(1) has failed to meet the criteria for approval described in Rule .0302 of this Section or the criteria for renewal of approval described in Rule .0306 of this Section at the time of application or at any time during an approval period;

(2) made any false statements or presented any false, incomplete, or incorrect information in connection with an application for approval or renewal of approval or any report that is required to be submitted to the Commission;

(3) has failed to submit to the Commission any report, course examination, or video recording required by these Rules;

(4) has failed to demonstrate the ability to teach a Prelicensing, Postlicensing, or Update couse in a manner consistent with the course materials;

(5) taught a Prelicensing course and compiled a license examination performance record for first-time examination candidates that is below 60 percent passing for two or more of the previous five annual reporting periods;

(6) taught a Prelicensing course and failed to provide to the Commission a written plan describing the changes the instructor has made or intends to make in his or her instructional program to improve the performance of the instructor's students on the license examination within 30 days of the Commission's request during an investigation, application process, or following an instructor's attainment of a licensing examination record for first-time examination candidates that is below sixty percent passing for the previous annual reporting period;

(7) has been convicted of, pleaded guilty to, or pleaded no contest to, a misdemeanor or felony violation of state or federal law by a court of competent jurisdiction;

(8) has been found by a court or government agency of competent jurisdiction to have violated any state or federal regulation prohibiting discrimination;

(9) has obtained, used, or attempted to obtain or use, in any manner or form, North Carolina real estate license examination questions;

(10) has failed to take appropriate steps to protect the security of end-of-course examinations pursuant to Rule .0210(g) of this Subchapter;

(11) failed to take any corrective action set out in the plan described in Item (5) of this Rule or as otherwise requested by the Commission;

(12) engaged in any other improper, fraudulent, or dishonest conduct; or

(13) failed to comply with any other provisions of this Subchapter.

History Note: Authority G.S. 93A-4; 93A-33; 93A-34;
Eff. July 1, 2017.

21 NCAC 58H .0304   INSTRUCTOR CONDUCT AND PERFORMANCE
(a) All instructors shall ensure that class sessions are conducted at the scheduled time and for the full amount of time that is scheduled or required. Instructors shall conduct courses in accordance with the Commission's rules, and any applicable course syllabi, instructor guide, or course plan. Instructors shall conduct classes demonstrating the ability to:
- (1) state student learning objectives at the beginning of the course and present accurate and relevant information;
- (2) communicate correct grammar and vocabulary;
- (3) utilize a variety of instructional techniques that require students to analyze and apply course content, including teacher-centered approaches, such as lecture and demonstration, and student-centered approaches, such as lecture discussion, reading, group problem solving, case studies, and scenarios;
- (4) utilize instructional aids, such as:
  - (A) whiteboards;
  - (B) sample forms and contracts;
  - (C) pictures;
  - (D) charts; and
  - (E) videos.
- (5) utilize assessment tools, such as:
  - (A) in-class or homework assignments, and
  - (B) quizzes and midterm examinations for Prelicensing and Postlicensing courses.
- (6) avoid criticism of any other person, agency, or organization;
- (7) identify key concepts and correct student misconceptions; and
- (8) maintain control of the class.

(b) Instructors teaching Prelicensing, Postlicensing, or Update courses shall interact with students either in person in a classroom setting or through an interactive telecommunication system, or comparable system, that permits continuous mutual audio and visual communication between the instructor and students. The school shall provide monitoring and technical support for the instructors or students.

(c) Instructors teaching Prelicensing or Postlicensing courses shall:
- (1) safeguard and protect the security of course examinations;
- (2) not allow students to review or retain copies of end-of-course examinations and any materials used during the examination; and
- (3) only use guest lecturers that have been approved by the school director pursuant to Rule .0204(d) of this Section.

(d) Instructors shall not obtain, use, or attempt to obtain or use, in any manner or form, North Carolina real estate license examination questions.

History Note: Authority G.S. 93A-4; 93A-33; 93A-34;
Eff. July 1, 2017.

21 NCAC 58H .0305   DIGITAL VIDEO RECORDINGS
(a) Upon request of the Commission during an investigation, an approved instructor shall submit a digital video recording of the instructor teaching specified topics of a course, as identified by the Commission which the instructor is approved to teach.

(b) Upon the request of the Commission during an investigation, a continuing education sponsor shall submit a digital video recording depicting a particular Update Course instructor, as designated by the Commission, teaching the Update course.

(c) Any digital video recording submitted to the Commission shall:
- (1) have been made within 12 months of the date of submission;
- (2) be recorded either on a digital video disc (DVD), USB drive, or similar medium;
- (3) be unedited;
- (4) display a visible date and time stamp during the entire video recording;

(5) include a label identifying the instructor, the course title, subject being taught, student materials used, and dates of the video instruction;
(6) have visual and sound quality to allow reviewers to see and hear the instructor; and
(7) show at least a portion of the students present in a live audience.

(d) The deadline for any digital video recording requested during an investigation shall be 30 days after the date of the next scheduled course, but no later than 120 days after the Commission's request.

History Note: Authority G.S. 93A-4; 93A-33; 93A-34;
Eff. July 1, 2017.

21 NCAC 58H .0306   RENEWAL AND EXPIRATION OF INSTRUCTOR APPROVAL
(a) Commission approval of instructors shall expire annually on June 30 following issuance of approval.
(b) Any approved instructor shall file an electronic application for renewal of approval within the 45 days immediately preceding expiration of approval. The instructor renewal application shall set forth the instructor's:
(1) legal name, address, email address, and telephone number;
(2) real estate license number and instructor number assigned by Commission;
(3) any criminal convictions and occupational license disciplinary actions within the past year;
(4) proof of attendance since approval or last renewal of a real estate instructor educational program of at least six hours, such as the:
(A) Commission's Spring Educators Conference or New Instructor Seminar;
(B) NC Real Estate Educators Association's conference or instructor development workshop; or
(C) Real Estate Educators Association's conference or instructor development workshop.
(5) courses for which he or she is seeking approval as an instructor; and
(6) signature.

(c) In order to reinstate an instructor approval that has been expired for less than six months, the former instructor shall meet the requirements set forth in Paragraph (b) of this Rule.
(d) If an instructor approval has been expired for more than six months, the former instructor shall file an application for original approval pursuant to Rule .0302 of this Section.

History Note: Authority G.S. 93A-4; 93A-33; 93A-34;
Eff. July 1, 2017.

SECTION .0400 - CONTINUING EDUCATION

21 NCAC 58H .0401   APPLICABILITY
This Section shall apply to the application, renewal, and conduct of continuing education sponsors, continuing education elective courses, and Update Courses.

History Note: Authority G.S. 93A-4; 93A-33; 93A-34;
Eff. July 1, 2017.

21 NCAC 58H .0402   APPLICATION FOR ORIGINAL APPROVAL OF CONTINUING EDUCATION SPONSOR
(a) Only continuing education sponsors approved by the Commission shall be eligible to offer continuing education courses, including elective courses and Update Courses.
(b) Any entity seeking original approval to be a continuing education sponsor shall make application on a form available on the Commission's website that requires the applicant to set forth:
(1) the legal name of applicant and any assumed business name;
(2) the applicant's mailing address, telephone number, and email address;
(3) the legal name of the individual who will serve as the applicant's continuing education coordinator as defined in Rule .0403 of this Section;
(4) the applicant's form of business entity;
(5) the SOSID issued by the NC Secretary of State, if applicable;
(6) the legal name(s) of the sponsor's owner(s);

(7) a record of any criminal convictions for all individuals listed as owner(s), manager(s), or partner(s);
(8) a record of any discipline related to a professional license for all individuals listed as owner(s), manager(s), or partner(s); and
(9) the signature of the applicant.

(c) Any foreign or out-of-state entity or person applying for original approval shall submit a signed Consent to Service of Process and Pleadings form as required by G.S. 93A-10.

(d) The name of any course sponsor shall not be identical to the name of any other approved continuing education course sponsor or licensed private real estate school.

(e) Continuing education sponsors shall notify the Commission in writing within 10 days of any change in business name, ownership interest, continuing education coordinator, address, business telephone number, or email address.

History Note: Authority G.S. 93A-3(c); 93A-4.1; 93A-10; 93A-34;
Eff. July 1, 2017.

21 NCAC 58H .0403   CONTINUING EDUCATION COORDINATOR

(a) Continuing education sponsors shall designate in writing to the Commission one person to serve as the continuing education coordinator. The continuing education coordinator shall serve as the official contact person for the sponsor and shall be responsible for:
(1) supervising the sponsor's continuing education courses;
(2) ensuring continuing education elective courses are taught by instructors complying with Rule .0407 of this Section;
(3) ensuring elective courses are taught according to the course materials approved by the Commission;
(4) ensuring only approved instructors who have taken the Update Course Seminar for the current license period teach Update Courses;
(5) ensuring students are furnished with the approved course materials pursuant to Rule .0406 of this Section;
(6) signing course completion certificates;
(7) submitting to the Commission all required fees, rosters, reports, and other information; and
(8) submitting to the Commission the name and the instructor number of each elective course instructor within 10 days of employment.

(b) Each continuing education coordinator shall view the Commission's Continuing Education Coordinator video electronically within 30 days of initial designation and annually within 45 days immediately preceding expiration of sponsor approval.

History Note: Authority G.S. 93A-3; 93A-4.1;
Eff. July 1, 2017.

21 NCAC 58H .0404   RENEWAL OF SPONSOR APPROVAL

(a) Commission approval of all continuing education sponsors shall expire annually on June 30 following issuance of approval.

(b) In order to ensure continuous sponsor approval, an approved sponsor shall file an electronic application for renewal of approval within the 45 days immediately preceding expiration of approval. The sponsor approval renewal application shall require the sponsor to set forth:
(1) the legal name of sponsor and any assumed business name;
(2) the sponsor number assigned by the Commission;
(3) the sponsor's mailing address, telephone number, and email address;
(4) the continuing education coordinator's legal name;
(5) any criminal convictions or occupational licensure disciplinary action taken against any individual listed as owner(s) of the sponsor since last approval;
(6) the name and course number of each continuing education elective course approved pursuant to Rule .0406 of this Section the applicant wishes to renew;
(7) a certification that the continuing education coordinator has completed the Commission's video training pursuant to Rule .0403(b) of this Section;

(8) a certification that its facilities and equipment are in compliance with all applicable local, state, and federal laws and regulations regarding health, safety, and welfare, including the Americans with Disabilities Act; and
(9) the signature of the sponsor.

(c) A continuing education sponsor also licensed or approved as a school may renew its continuing education sponsor approval on its school renewal form pursuant to Rule .0214 of this Subchapter.

(d) Continuing education sponsors shall submit a fifty dollar ($50.00) fee for each continuing education elective course the sponsor wishes to renew. No fee is required if the entity making application is a public school or is an agency of federal, state or local government.

(e) Continuing education sponsors shall submit a one hundred dollar ($100.00) materials fee if the sponsor wishes to renew approval to offer Update courses. No fee is required if the entity making application is a public real estate school or is an agency of federal, state, or local government.

History Note: Authority G.S. 93A-3; 93A-4.1;
Eff. July 1, 2017;
Amended Eff. July 1, 2018.

21 NCAC 58H .0405   DENIAL OR WITHDRAWAL OF SPONSOR APPROVAL

(a) The Commission may deny or withdraw approval of any continuing education sponsor upon finding that the sponsor or the continuing education coordinator in the employ of the sponsor:
(1) made any false statements or presented any false, incomplete, or incorrect information in connection with an application for course or sponsor approval or renewal;
(2) provided false, incomplete, or incorrect information in connection with any reports the continuing education sponsor is required to submit to the Commission;
(3) provided the Commission a check for required fees that was dishonored by a bank or returned for insufficient funds;
(4) has been convicted of, pleaded guilty to, or pleaded no contest to, a misdemeanor or felony violation of state or federal law by a court of competent jurisdiction;
(5) has been found by a court or government agency of competent jurisdiction to have violated any state or federal regulation prohibiting discrimination;
(6) has been disciplined by the Commission or any other occupational licensing agency in North Carolina or another jurisdiction;
(7) collected money from brokers for a continuing education course but refused or failed to provide the promised instruction;
(8) intentionally provided false, incomplete, or misleading information relating to real estate licensing, education matters, or the broker's education needs or license status;
(9) failed to submit the CE Roster Reports as required by Rule .0412 of this Section;
(10) failed to submit the per student fee as required by G.S. 93A-4.1(d); or
(11) failed to comply with any other provision of this Subchapter.

(b) A broker shall be subject to discipline pursuant to G.S. 93A-6 if the broker engages in dishonest, fraudulent, or improper conduct in connection with the operations of a continuing education course sponsor if that broker:
(1) has an ownership interest in the course sponsor;
(2) is the designated continuing education coordinator for the course sponsor; or
(3) is an instructor for the course sponsor.

(c) When ownership of an approved continuing education sponsor is transferred to a separate legal entity, the sponsor's approval is not transferable and shall terminate on the effective date of the transfer. All courses shall be completed by the effective date of the transfer. The transferring owner shall report course completion(s) to the Commission. The new entity shall obtain an original continuing education sponsor approval as required by Rule .0402 of this Subchapter prior to advertising courses, registering students, accepting tuition, conducting courses, or otherwise engaging in any sponsor operations.

(d) If an approved continuing education sponsor transfers an aggregate of 50 percent or more of the ownership interest, the sponsor shall notify the Commission in writing within 10 days of the transfer.

History Note: Authority G.S. 93A-3(c); 93A-4.1; 93A-6(a)(15);
Eff. July 1, 2017.

21 NCAC 58H .0406   APPROVAL AND RENEWAL OF ELECTIVE COURSE
(a) Prior to obtaining the Commission's written approval of a continuing education elective course, sponsors shall not offer, advertise, or otherwise represent that any continuing education elective course is, or may be, approved for continuing education credit in North Carolina.
(b) A sponsor seeking original approval of a proposed elective course shall complete an application on a form available on the Commission's website that requires the applicant to set forth the:
- (1) title of the proposed elective course;
- (2) continuing education sponsor's legal name, address, and telephone number;
- (3) continuing education coordinator's legal name;
- (4) continuing education sponsor's sponsor code, if previously approved;
- (5) credit hours awarded for completing the course;
- (6) subject matter of the course;
- (7) identity of the course owner;
- (8) written permission of the course owner, if other than the applicant;
- (9) identity of prospective instructors; and
- (10) continuing education sponsor's signature.

(c) The application for original approval shall be accompanied by a copy of the course guide, which shall include course objectives, learning objectives for each topic, a timed outline, instructional methods and aids to be employed, and all materials that will be provided to students.
(d) If the elective course will be taught by any method other than live, in-person, in-class instruction, the applicant shall submit, along with the application for original approval:
- (1) a full copy of the course on the medium to be utilized for instruction;
- (2) a description of the method by which the sponsor will verify and record student attendance;
- (3) a list of hardware and software or other equipment necessary to both offer and complete the course;
- (4) the contact information for the technical support service for the course; and
- (5) a copy of the student orientation and course tutorial information.

(e) If the course will be taught by any method other than live, in-person, in-class instruction, the applicant shall, if requested, make available, at a date and time satisfactory to the Commission and at the applicant's expense, all hardware and software necessary for the Commission to review the submitted course. In the case of an Internet-based course, the Commission shall be provided access to the course at a date and time set by the Commission and shall not be charged any fee for such access.
(f) A sponsor seeking approval to offer an already approved elective course shall complete an application on a form available on the Commission's website that requires the applicant to set forth the:
- (1) title of the elective course;
- (2) applicant's legal name, address, and telephone number;
- (3) applicant's continuing education coordinator's legal name;
- (4) applicant's continuing education sponsor code, if previously approved;
- (5) identity of the course owner;
- (6) written permission of the course owner, if other than the applicant;
- (7) identity of prospective instructors; and
- (8) continuing education sponsor's signature.

(g) All applicants shall submit a fee of one hundred dollars ($100.00) per elective course. No fee shall be required if the applicant is a public real estate school or is an agency of federal, state, or local government.
(h) Applications submitted pursuant to Paragraph (f) of this Rule shall be deemed approved ten business days after the Commission has received both a complete application and the required one hundred dollar ($100.00) per course fee, unless the Commission notifies the applicant otherwise.
(i) Commission approval of all continuing education elective courses shall expire on June 30.
(j) In order to ensure continuous approval, a course sponsor shall include the name and course number of each previously approved continuing education elective it wishes to renew, along with the required fifty dollar ($50.00) fee, in the sponsor approval renewal application pursuant to Rule .0404 of this Section.
(k) In order to obtain approval for an expired continuing education elective, a course sponsor shall submit an application for original approval.

History Note: Authority G.S. 93A-3(c); 93A-4.1
                  Eff. July 1, 2017.

21 NCAC 58H .0407   CONTINUING EDUCATION ELECTIVE COURSE REQUIREMENTS
(a) Continuing education elective courses shall:
- (1) cover subject matter related to real estate brokerage practice and offer knowledge or skills that will enable brokers to better serve real estate consumers and the public interest;
- (2) consist of at least four hours of instruction;
- (3) offer four continuing education credit hours;
- (4) include handout materials for students that provide the information to be presented in the course; and
- (5) be taught only by an instructor who possesses at least one of the following:
    - (A) a baccalaureate or higher degree in a field directly related to the subject matter of the course;
    - (B) three years' full-time work experience within the previous 10 years that is directly related to the subject matter of the course;
    - (C) three years' full-time experience within the previous 10 years teaching the subject matter of the course; or
    - (D) education or experience or both found by the Commission to be equivalent to one of the above standards.

(b) Sponsors shall obtain approval from the Commission before making any changes in the content of an elective course. Requests for approval of changes shall be in writing. However, changes in course content that are technical in nature do not require approval during the approval period, but shall be reported at the time the sponsor requests renewal of course approval.

History Note: Authority G.S. 93A-3(c); 93A-4.1;
Eff. July 1, 2017.

21 NCAC 58H .0408   COMMISSION CREATED UPDATE COURSES
(a) The Commission shall annually develop Update courses and shall produce instructor and student materials for use by sponsors.
(b) Only approved continuing education sponsors shall offer Update courses. Only approved instructors pursuant to Rule .0302 of this Subchapter shall instruct Update courses.
(c) Continuing education sponsors shall obtain written approval from the Commission prior to offering, advertising, or otherwise representing that any Update course is being offered for continuing education credit in North Carolina.
(d) A continuing education sponsor seeking approval to offer Update courses shall submit an application form available on the Commission's website that shall require the applicant to set forth the:
- (1) continuing education sponsor's legal name, address, and telephone number;
- (2) continuing education coordinator's legal name;
- (3) continuing education sponsor's number assigned by the Commission;
- (4) name and instructor number of prospective instructors; and
- (5) continuing education sponsor's signature.

(e) A continuing education sponsor seeking approval to offer a modified Update course pursuant to Paragraph (k) of this Rule shall also submit the written permission of each of the course owners, if other than the applicant.
(f) A licensed or approved school may obtain approval from the Commission to offer an Update Course by requesting it on the application or renewal of the school license or approval.
(g) The applicant shall submit a one hundred dollar ($100.00) materials fee. No fee shall be required if the applicant is a public school or is an agency of federal, state, or local government.
(h) Sponsors shall use the Commission-developed course materials to conduct Update courses. Sponsors shall provide a copy of the course materials to each broker taking an Update course.
(i) Commission approval to offer Update courses shall expire annually on June 30 following issuance of approval. Sponsors shall apply for renewal of approval to offer Update courses each year along with the renewal of sponsor approval required in Rule .0404 of this Section.
(j) All Update course materials developed by the Commission are the sole property of the Commission and are subject to the protection of federal copyright laws. Violation of the Commission's copyright with regard to these materials shall be grounds for disciplinary action or other action as permissible by law.
(k) With advance approval from the Commission, course sponsors and approved instructors may make modifications to the Update course when the Update course is being promoted to and conducted for a group of

brokers that specialize in a particular area of real estate brokerage. Such modifications shall relate to the same general subject matter addressed in the prescribed Update course and the Update course as modified shall achieve the same educational objectives as the unmodified Update course. Where certain subject matter addressed in the prescribed Update course is not directly applicable to the group of brokers who specialize in the particular area of real estate brokerage being targeted, different subject matter and education objectives may be substituted with the prior written consent of the Commission. All modified Update course materials shall be the joint property of the Commission and the course sponsor or approved instructor approved to make such modifications, or as otherwise determined by written agreement. Violation of the Commission's copyright with regard to these materials shall be grounds for disciplinary action or other action as permitted by law.

History Note: *Authority G.S. 93A-3; 93A-4.1;*
                         Eff. July 1, 2017.

21 NCAC 58H .0409   RECORDS AND COMMISSION REVIEW
(a) All continuing education sponsors shall retain on file for three years records of student registration and attendance for each session of a continuing education course that is conducted and shall make such records available to the Commission upon request during an investigation.
(b) Continuing education sponsors shall admit any Commission authorized representative to monitor any continuing education class without prior notice. Such representatives shall not be required to register or pay any fee and shall not be reported as having completed the course.

History Note: *Authority G.S. 93A-3(c); 93A-4.1;*
                         Eff. July 1, 2017.

21 NCAC 58H .0410   CONTINUING EDUCATION COURSE SCHEDULING AND NOTIFICATION
(a) All continuing education courses shall be scheduled and conducted in a manner that limits class sessions to a maximum of eight instructional hours in any given day. The maximum permissible class session without a break shall be 90 minutes. Courses scheduled for more than four instructional hours in any given day shall include a meal break of at least one hour.
(b) Continuing education sponsors shall not offer, conduct, or allow a student to complete any course and offer continuing education credit between June 11 and June 30, inclusive.
(c) Sponsors shall provide the Commission written notice of all scheduled course offerings at least 10 days prior to the scheduled course date. The notice shall include:
        (1)   the sponsor name;
        (2)   the sponsor number assigned by the Commission;
        (3)   the legal name and instructor number of the course instructor;
        (4)   the course number;
        (5)   the scheduled course date and start time; and
        (6)   the course location.
(d) Continuing education sponsors shall notify the Commission of any schedule changes or course cancellations at least five days prior to the original scheduled course date. If a change or cancellation occurs within five days of the scheduled course date, then the continuing education sponsor shall provide notice to the Commission within 24 hours of the change or cancellation.
(e) The sponsor of any distance education course shall require students to complete the course within 30 days of the date of registration or the date the student is provided the course materials and permitted to begin work, whichever is the later date. The sponsor shall not offer, conduct, or allow a student to complete any course for continuing education credit between June 11 and June 30, inclusive. The sponsor shall advise all students registering for a distance education course, prior to accepting payment for any course, of the deadlines for course completion.
(f) Each sponsor shall certify that its facilities and equipment are in compliance with all applicable local, state, and federal laws and regulations regarding health, safety, and welfare, including the Americans with Disabilities Act.

History Note: *Authority G.S. 93A-3(c); 93A-4.1;*
                         Eff. July 1, 2017.

21 NCAC 58H .0411   CONTINUING EDUCATION COURSE ATTENDANCE

(a) Continuing education sponsors shall require each student who is a licensed broker to provide his or her name and license number at the initial check in for a class session.
(b) A student shall not be issued a Course Completion Certificate, and shall not be reported to the Commission as having completed a course unless the student satisfies the attendance requirement in 21 NCAC 58A .1705.
(c) Sponsors and instructors shall not make any exceptions to this Rule.

History Note: Authority G.S. 93A-3(c); 93A-4.1;
                    Eff. July 1, 2017.

21 NCAC 58H .0412   CONTINUING EDUCATION ROSTER REPORTS AND CERTIFICATES
(a) At the conclusion of any continuing education course, elective or Update, the sponsor shall submit to the Commission a CE Roster Report verifying each broker's completion of the course pursuant to Rule .0411 of this Section. The CE Roster Report shall contain the:
  (1)   sponsor's name;
  (2)   sponsor's number assigned by the Commission;
  (3)   course instructor's name and number;
  (4)   course's name and number;
  (5)   course completion date; and
  (6)   name and license number of each student who completed the course.
(b) Sponsors shall submit the CE Roster Report electronically within seven calendar days following the end of any course, but in no case later than June 15.
(c) Sponsors shall submit the ten dollar ($10.00) per student fee required by G.S. 93A-4.1(d), along with the CE Roster Report.
(d) Sponsors shall provide a course completion certificate to each student who completes an approved continuing education course pursuant to Rule .0411 of this Section. Sponsors shall provide a printed or electronic certificate within 15 days following the course, but in no case later than June 15, for any course completed prior to that date.

History Note: Authority G.S. 93A-3(c); 93A-4.1;
                    Eff. July 1, 2017.

21 NCAC 58H .0413   CONTINUING EDUCATION COURSE COST, CANCELLATION, AND REFUNDS
(a) Sponsors shall establish an all-inclusive cost to be charged to students taking any continuing education course. No separate or additional costs shall be charged to students.
(b) Sponsors shall establish written course cancellation and refund policies. In the event a sponsor cancels a scheduled course, registered students shall be notified within 24 hours. Sponsors shall refund all prepaid payments received from registered students within 30 days of the date of cancellation, or with the student's written permission apply the refund toward another course.

History Note: Authority G.S. 93A-3(c); 93A-4.1;
                    Eff. July 1, 2017.

21 NCAC 58H .0414   ADVERTISING
(a) Sponsors shall not utilize advertising that is false or misleading.
(b) All course advertisement and promotional materials shall specify the number of continuing education credit hours to be awarded by the Commission for the course.
(c) All continuing education course promotional materials shall describe the course costs, the cancellation policy, and refund policies.
(d) Sponsors shall not use endorsements or recommendations of any person or organization, in advertising or otherwise, unless the person or organization:
  (1)   has consented in writing to the use of the endorsement or recommendation; and
  (2)   is not compensated for such use.

History Note: Authority G.S. 93A-3(c); 93A-4.1;
                    Eff. July 1, 2017.

LICENSE LAW AND RULES COMMENTS

Comments on Selected Provisions of the North Carolina Real Estate License Law and Real Estate Commission Rules

INTRODUCTION

These comments on selected North Carolina Real Estate License Law and Real Estate Commission Rules provisions are intended to assist real estate licensees, prelicensing course students and others in understanding the License Law and Commission rules. The comments are organized in a topic format that often differs from the sequence in which the topics are addressed in the License Law and Commission rules. The topics selected for comment here are not only of particular importance in real estate brokerage practice but also are likely to be tested on the real estate license examination. The appropriate references to the License Law and Commission rules are provided beside each listed topic.

REQUIREMENT FOR A LICENSE

General [G.S. 93A-1 and 93A-2]

Any person or business entity who directly or indirectly engages in the business of a real estate broker for compensation or the promise thereof while physically in the state of North Carolina must have a North Carolina real estate broker license. In North Carolina, a real estate licensee may only engage in brokerage as an "agent" for a party to a transaction. Thus, a real estate licensee is commonly and appropriately referred to as a real estate "agent" even though the latter term does not actually appear in the License Law. Note that a real estate "licensee" is NOT automatically a "REALTOR®." A licensed real estate agent is a REALTOR® **only** if he/she belongs to the National Association of REALTORS®, a private trade association. Thus, the term REALTOR® should not be used to generally refer to all real estate licensees.

License Categories [G.S. 93A-2]

There is only one "type" of license, a **broker** license; however, there are several license status categories as described below:

Provisional Broker – This is the "entry level" license status category. A person who has met all the license qualification requirements (including a *75-hour prelicensing course and passing the Commission's license examination*) is initially issued **a broker license on "provisional" status** and is referred to as a **"provisional broker."** A provisional broker generally may perform the same acts as a broker whose license is NOT on provisional status so long as he or she is supervised by a broker who is a designated **broker-in-charge**. A provisional broker may not operate independently in any way. G.S. 93A-2(a2) defines a **"provisional broker"** as "...*a real estate broker who, pending acquisition and documentation to the Commission of the education or experience prescribed by G.S. 93A-4(a1), must be supervised by a broker-in-charge when performing any act for which a real estate license is required.*"

This license status category is comparable to a "salesperson" license in most other states except that it is a **temporary license status category**. Provisional brokers may not retain this status indefinitely – they must complete required **postlicensing education** (one 30-hour course each year for the three years following initial licensure – total of 90 hours) to remove the "provisional" status of their licenses and to remain eligible for "active" license status.

Broker – A "provisional broker" who satisfies all postlicensing education requirements to terminate the "provisional" status of such license becomes a **"broker"** without having to take another license examination. A broker is NOT required to be supervised by a broker-in-charge in order to hold an "active" license. An applicant who is a licensed broker in another US jurisdiction may be licensed directly as a North Carolina **broker NOT on provisional status** by passing the "State" section of the North Carolina license examination. All others must first be licensed in North Carolina as a **provisional broker** and then satisfy the postlicensing education requirement to become a non-provisional broker.

Most frequently, brokers elect to work for another broker or brokerage firm. Brokers may also elect to operate independently as a sole proprietor; however, with limited exceptions, such broker will have to qualify for and designate himself or herself as a **broker-in-charge** in order to operate independently and perform most brokerage activities (discussed further below under "broker-in-charge" and also in a subsequent section on brokers-in-charge that appears near the end of this appendix).

Broker-In-Charge – G.S. 93A-2(a1) defines a **"broker-in-charge"** as "...*a real estate broker who has been designated as the broker having responsibility for the supervision of real estate provisional brokers engaged in real estate brokerage at a particular real estate office and for other administrative and supervisory duties as the Commission shall prescribe by rule.*" Commission Rule A.0110 requires that each real estate office must have a broker who meets the qualification requirements to serve as "broker-in-charge" of the office and who has designated himself or herself as the broker-in-charge of that office. As is the case with "provisional broker," "*broker-in-charge*" *is not a separate license, but only a* **separate license status category**. A broker who is to serve as the broker-in-charge (BIC) of an office (including working independently) must be designated as a BIC with the Commission.

To qualify for designation as a broker-in-charge, a broker's license must be on "active" status but NOT on "provisional" status, the broker must have **two years full-time or four years part-time brokerage experience within the previous five years** (or education/experience the Commission finds equivalent to such experience), and the broker must complete a 12-hour **Broker-In-Charge Course** no earlier than one year prior or 120 days after designation. Broker-in-charge requirements are addressed in detail in a separate subsequent section titled "Broker-In-Charge."

Limited Nonresident Commercial Broker – A broker or salesperson residing in a state other than North Carolina who holds an active broker or salesperson license in the state where his or her primary place of real estate business is located may apply for and obtain a North Carolina **"limited nonresident commercial broker license"** that entitles such licensee to engage in transactions for compensation involving "commercial real estate" in North Carolina. While the non-resident limited broker will remain affiliated with his/her out of state real estate company and will not have a North Carolina broker-in-charge, the non-resident licensee must enter into a "notification of broker affiliation" and a "brokerage cooperation agreement" with a resident North Carolina broker not on provisional status and the licensee must be supervised by the North Carolina broker while performing commercial real estate brokerage in North Carolina. Like a "firm" license, a limited nonresident commercial broker license is a separate license.

Licensing of Business Entities [G.S. 93A-1 and 2; Rule A.0502]

In addition to individuals (persons), "business entities" also must be licensed in order to engage in real estate brokerage. Any corporation, partnership, limited liability company, association or other business entity (other than a sole proprietorship) must obtain a separate real estate **firm** broker license.

Activities Requiring a License [G.S. 93A-2]

Persons and business entities who for consideration or the promise thereof perform the activities listed below as an agent for others are considered to be performing brokerage activities and must have a real estate license unless specifically exempted by the statute (see subsequent section on "Exemptions"). There is no exemption for engaging in a limited number of transactions. A person or entity who performs a brokerage service in even one transaction must be licensed. Similarly, no fee or other consideration is so small as to exempt one from the application of the licensing statute when acting for another in a real estate transaction. *Brokerage activities include*:

1. **Listing (or offering to list) real estate for sale or rent**, including any act performed by a real estate licensee in connection with obtaining and servicing a listing agreement. Examples of such acts include, but are not limited to, soliciting listings, providing information to the property owner, and preparing listing agreements or property management agreements.

2. **Selling or buying (or offering to sell or buy) real estate**, including any act performed by a real estate licensee in connection with assisting others in selling or buying real estate. Examples of such acts include, but are not limited to, advertising listed property for sale, "showing" listed property to prospective buyers, providing information about listed property to prospective buyers (other than basic property facts that might commonly appear in an advertisement in a newspaper, real estate publication or internet website), negotiating a sale or purchase of real estate, and assisting with the completion of contract offers and counteroffers using preprinted forms and communication of offers and acceptances.

3. **Leasing or renting (or offering to lease or rent) real estate**, including any act performed by real estate licensees in connection with assisting others in leasing or renting real estate. Examples of such acts include, but are not limited to, advertising listed property for rent, "showing" listed rental property to prospective tenants, providing information about listed rental property to prospective tenants (other than basic property facts that might commonly appear in an advertisement in a newspaper, real estate publication or internet website), negotiating lease terms, and assisting with the completion of lease offers and counteroffers using preprinted forms and communication of offers and acceptances.

4. **Conducting (or offering to conduct) a real estate auction**. (Mere criers of sale are excluded.) NOTE: An auctioneer's license is also required to auction real estate.

5. **Selling, buying, leasing, assigning or exchanging any interest in real estate, including a leasehold interest, in connection with the sale or purchase of a business**.

6. **Referring a party to a real estate licensee, if done for compensation**. Any arrangement or agreement between a licensee and an unlicensed person that calls for the licensee to compensate the unlicensed person in any way for finding, introducing or referring a party to the licensee has been determined by North Carolina's courts to be prohibited under the License Law. Therefore, *no licensee may pay a finder's fee, referral fee, "bird dog" fee or similar compensation to an unlicensed person.*

Unlicensed Employees — Permitted Activities

The use of unlicensed assistants and other unlicensed office personnel in the real estate industry is very widespread and the Commission is frequently asked by licensees what acts unlicensed persons may lawfully perform. As guidance to licensees, the Commission has prepared the following list of acts that an unlicensed assistant or employee may lawfully perform so long as the assistant or employee is salaried or hourly paid and is not paid on a per-transaction basis.

An unlicensed, salaried employee MAY:
1. Receive and forward phone calls and electronic messages to licensees.
2. Submit listings and changes to a multiple listing service, but only if the listing data or changes are compiled and provided by a licensee.
3. Secure copies of public records from public repositories (i.e., register of deeds office, county tax office, etc.).
4. Place "for sale" or "for rent" signs and lock boxes on property at the direction of a licensee.
5. Order and supervise routine and minor repairs to listed property at the direction of a licensee.
6. Act as a courier to deliver or pick up documents.
7. Provide to prospects basic factual information on listed property that might commonly appear in advertisements in a newspaper, real estate publication or internet website.
8. Schedule appointments for showing property listed for sale or rent.
9. Communicate with licensees, property owners, prospects, inspectors, etc. to coordinate or confirm appointments.
10. Show rental properties managed by the employee's employing broker to prospective tenants and complete and execute preprinted form leases for the rental of such properties.
11. Type offers, contracts and leases from drafts of preprinted forms completed by a licensee.
12. Record and deposit earnest money deposits, tenant security deposits and other trust monies, and otherwise maintain records of trust account receipts and disbursements, under the close supervision of the office broker-in-charge, who is legally responsible for handling trust funds and maintaining trust accounts.
13. Assist a licensee in assembling documents for closing.
14. Compute commission checks for licensees affiliated with a broker or firm and act as bookkeeper for the firm's bank operating accounts.

Exemptions [G.S. 93A-2(c)]

The following persons and organizations are specifically exempted from the requirement for real estate licensure:
1. A **business entity** selling or leasing real estate owned by the business entity when the acts performed are in the regular course of or are incident to the management of that real estate and the investment therein. This exemption extends to officers and employees of an exempt corporation, the general partners of an exempt partnership, and the managers of an exempt limited liability company when engaging in acts or services for which the corporation, partnership or limited liability company would be exempt.
2. A person acting as an **attorney-in-fact** under a power of attorney from the owner authorizing the final consummation of performance of any contract for the sale, lease or exchange of real estate. (Note: This limited exemption applies only to the final completion of a transaction already commenced. The licensing requirement may not be circumvented by obtaining a power of attorney.)
3. An **attorney-at-law** who is an active member of the North Carolina State Bar only when performing an act or service that constitutes the practice of law under Chapter 84 of the General Statutes. Thus, the attorney exemption is strictly limited and attorneys generally may NOT engage in real estate brokerage practice without a real estate license.
4. A person acting as a receiver, trustee in bankruptcy, guardian, administrator or executor or any person acting under a court order.
5. A **trustee** acting under a written trust agreement, deed of trust or will or the trustee's regular salaried employees.
6. **Certain salaried employees of broker-property managers.** (See G.S. 93A-2(c)(6) for details.)
7. An individual owner selling or leasing the owner's own property.
8. A **housing authority** organized under Chapter 157 of the General Statutes and any regular salaried employee with regard to the sale or lease of property owned by the housing authority or to the subletting of property which the housing authority holds as tenant.

THE REAL ESTATE COMMISSION
Composition [G.S. 93A-3(a)]

The Real Estate Commission consists of nine (9) members who serve three-year terms. Seven members are appointed by the Governor and two are appointed by the General Assembly upon the recommendations of the Speaker of the House of Representatives and the President Pro Tempore of the Senate. At least three (3) members must be licensed brokers. At least two (2) members must be "public members" who are NOT involved directly or indirectly in the real estate brokerage or appraisal businesses.

Purpose and Powers [G.S. 93A-3(a), (c) and (f); G.S. 93A-6(a) and (b);G.S. 93A-4(d) and 93A-4.1 & 4.2]

The principal purpose of the Real Estate Commission is to protect the interests of members of the general public in their dealings with real estate brokers. This is accomplished through the exercise of the following statutory powers granted to the Commission:
1. Licensing real estate brokers and brokerage firms, and registering time share projects.
2. Establishing and administering prelicensing education programs for prospective licensees and postlicensing and continuing education programs for licensees.
3. Providing education and information relating to the

real estate brokerage business for licensees and the general public.
4. Regulating the business activities of brokers and brokerage firms, including disciplining licensees who violate the License Law or Commission rules.

It should be noted that the Commission is specifically prohibited, however, from regulating commissions, salaries or fees charged by real estate licensees and from arbitrating disputes between parties regarding matters of contract such as the rate and/or division of commissions or similar matters. [See G.S. 93A-3(c) and Rule A.0109.]

Disciplinary Authority [G.S. 93A-6(a)-(c)]

The Real Estate Commission is authorized to take a variety of disciplinary actions against licensees who the Commission finds guilty of violating the License Law or Commission rules while acting as real estate licensees. These are: **reprimand, censure, license suspension** and **license revocation**. The License Law also permits a licensee under certain circumstances to surrender his/her license with the consent of the Commission. Disciplinary actions taken against licensees are regularly reported in the Commission's periodic newsletter which is distributed to all licensees and also may be reported in local and regional newspapers.

It should be noted that licensees may be subject to the same disciplinary action for committing acts prohibited by the License Law when selling, leasing, or buying real estate for themselves, as well as for committing such acts in transactions handled as agents for others. [G.S. 93A-6(b)(3)]

The Commission also has the power to seek in its own name **injunctive relief** in superior court to prevent any person (licensees and others) from violating the License Law or Commission rules. A typical example of when the Commission might pursue injunctive relief in the courts is where a person engages in real estate activity without a license or during a period when the person's license is suspended, revoked or expired. [G.S. 93A-6(c)]

Any violation of the License Law or Commission rules is a criminal offense (misdemeanor) and may be prosecuted in a court of law. However, a finding by the Commission that a licensee has violated the License Law or Commission rules does not constitute a criminal conviction. [G.S. 93A-8]

PROHIBITED ACTS BY LICENSEES

G.S. 93A-6 provides a list of prohibited acts which may result in disciplinary action against licensees. Discussed below are various prohibited acts, except for those related to handling and accounting for trust funds, broker's responsibility for closing statements, and the failure to deliver certain instruments to parties in a transaction, which are discussed in the subsequent sections on "General Brokerage Provisions" and "Handling Trust Funds."

Important Note

The provisions of the License Law relating to misrepresentation or omission of a material fact, conflict of interest, licensee competence, handling of trust funds, and improper, fraudulent or dishonest dealing generally apply independently of other statutory law or case law such as the law of agency. Nevertheless, other laws may affect the application of a License Law provision. For example, the N.C. Tenant Security Deposit Act requires an accounting to a tenant for a residential security deposit within 30-60 days after termination of a tenancy. License Law provisions (and Commission rules) require licensees to account for such funds within a reasonable time. Thus, in this instance, a violation of the Tenant Security Deposit Act's provisions would also be considered a violation of the License Law.

Similarly, the law of agency and the law of contracts as derived from the common law may impact the application of License Law. Thus, a licensee's agency status and role in a transaction might affect the licensee's duties under the license law. Examples of how an agent's duties under the License Law may be affected by the application of other laws are included at various points in this section on "Prohibited Acts by Licensees."

Misrepresentation or Omission [G.S. 93A-6(a)(1)]

Misrepresentation or omission of a material fact by a licensee is prohibited, and this prohibition includes both "willful" and "negligent" acts. A "willful" act is one that is done intentionally and deliberately, while a "negligent" act is one that is done unintentionally. A **"misrepresentation"** is communicating false information, while an **"omission"** is failing to provide or disclose information where there is a duty to provide or disclose such information.

Material Facts

For purposes of applying G.S. 93A-6(a)(1), whether a fact is "material" depends on the facts and circumstances of a particular transaction and the application of statutory and/or case law. The Commission has historically interpreted **"material facts"** under the Real Estate License Law to include at least:

Facts about the property itself (such as a structural defect or defective mechanical systems);

Facts relating directly to the property (such as a pending zoning change or planned highway construction in the immediate vicinity); and

Facts relating directly to the ability of the agent's principal to complete the transaction (such as a pending foreclosure sale).

Regardless of which party in a transaction a real estate agent represents, the facts described above must be disclosed to both the agent's principal and to third parties the agent deals with on the principal's behalf. In addition, an agent has a duty to disclose to his or her principal any information that may affect the principal's rights and interests or influence the principal's decision in the transaction.

Death or Serious Illness of Previous Property Occupant — Note, however, that G.S. 39-50 and 42-14.2 specifically provide that the fact that a property was occupied by a person who died or had a serious illness while occupying the property is NOT a material fact. Thus, agents do not need to voluntarily disclose such a fact. If a prospective buyer or tenant specifically asks about such a matter, the agent may either decline to answer or respond honestly. If, however, a prospective buyer or tenant inquires as to whether a previous owner or occupant had AIDS, the agent is prohibited by fair housing laws from answering such an inquiry because persons with AIDS are considered to be "handicapped" under such laws and disclosure of the information may have the effect of discriminating against the property owner based on the handicapping condition.

Convicted Sex Offender Occupying, Having Occupied or Residing Near a Property — Note also that the same North Carolina statutes (G.S. §39-50 and §42-14.2) that state the death or serious illness of a previous occupant of a property is not a material fact in a real estate transaction contain a similar provision relating to **convicted sex offenders**. The statutes provide that when offering a property for sale, rent or lease, "…it shall not be a material fact…that a person convicted of any crime for which registration is required by Article 27A of Chapter 14 of the General Statutes [statutes establishing registration programs for sex offenders and sexually violent predators] occupies, occupied or resides near the property; provided, however, that no seller [or landlord or lessor] may knowingly make a false statement regarding such fact." Therefore, an agent involved in a transaction is **not** required to volunteer to a prospective buyer or tenant any information about registered sex offenders as described above. If a buyer or tenant specifically asks about sex offenders in a neighborhood, an agent need only answer truthfully to the best of his/her knowledge. In the absence of a specific inquiry about this matter from the buyer, an agent representing the buyer who knows, for example, that a registered sex offender lives in the immediate area, will probably want to disclose the information in the interest of serving his/her buyer-client even though not required by law to do so. On the other hand, in the absence of a specific inquiry by the buyer, if the agent who knows such information represents the seller, the agent will probably want to check with his/her seller-client before disclosing that information since voluntary disclosure is likely not in the seller's best interest. Any agent also has the option of advising a prospective buyer or tenant about how to check the statewide sex offender registry online at www.sexoffender.ncdoj.gov/search.aspx.

This introductory information should assist in understanding G.S. 93A-6(a)(1), which establishes four separate (although closely related) categories of conduct which are prohibited. These are discussed below, and a few examples of prohibited conduct are provided for each category.

Willful Misrepresentation — *This occurs when a licensee who has "actual knowledge" of a material fact deliberately misinforms a buyer, seller, tenant or landlord concerning such fact.* A misrepresentation is also considered to be "willful" when a licensee who does NOT have actual knowledge of a matter material to the transaction provides incorrect information concerning such matter to a buyer, seller, tenant or landlord *without regard for the actual truth of the matter* (i.e., when a licensee intentionally provides information without knowing whether it is true and the information provided is in fact not true).

Note: The following examples of willful misrepresentation apply regardless of the licensee's status (seller's agent or buyer's agent) or role (listing agent or selling agent).

Example: An agent knows that a listed house has a severe problem with water intrusion in the crawl space during heavy rains. In response to a question from a prospective buyer who is being shown the house during dry weather, the agent states that there is no water drainage problem.

Example: An agent knows that the heat pump at a listed house does not function properly, but tells a prospective buyer that all mechanical systems and appliances are in good condition.

Example: An agent knows that the approximate market value of a house is $225,000, but tells the property owner that the house is worth $250,000 in order to obtain a listing.

Example: An agent is completely unfamiliar with the features or condition of a listed property; however, the agent informs a prospective buyer that the plumbing is in good working order without first checking with the owner. (The agent in such instance is acting without regard for the truth of the matter being represented. If the plumbing in fact needs significant repair, then the agent may be guilty of willful misrepresentation.)

Example: Without checking with the owner, an agent tells a prospective buyer of a listed house that heating and cooling costs are "very reasonable." (Because the agent acted without regard for the truth of the matter, he may be guilty of willful misrepresentation if heating and cooling costs are in fact extraordinarily high.)

Negligent Misrepresentation — *This occurs when a licensee unintentionally misinforms a buyer, seller, tenant or landlord concerning a material fact either because the licensee does not have actual knowledge of the fact, because the licensee has incorrect information, or because of a mistake by the licensee.* If a reasonably prudent licensee *"should reasonably have known"* the truth of the matter that was misrepresented, then the licensee may be guilty of "negligent misrepresentation" even though the licensee was acting in good faith.

Negligent misrepresentation by real estate licensees occurs frequently in real estate transactions. A very common situation is the recording of incorrect information about a property in an MLS listing due to the negligence of the listing agent. When a prospective buyer is subsequently provided the incorrect information from the MLS by the agent working with the buyer, a negligent misrepresentation by the listing agent occurs.

A listing agent is generally held to a higher standard with regard to negligent misrepresentation of material facts about a listed property to a buyer than is a selling agent who is acting as a seller's subagent. This is because (1) The listing agent is in the best position to ascertain facts about the property, (2) the listing agent is expected to take reasonable steps to assure that property data included with the listing is correct and (3) it is generally considered reasonable for a selling agent to rely on the accuracy of the listing data except in those situations where it should be obvious to a reasonably prudent agent that the listing information is incorrect. However, *a buyer's agent may in some cases be held to a higher standard than a seller's subagent because of the buyer's agent's duties to the buyer under the law of agency and the buyer's agent's special knowledge of the buyer's particular situation and needs.*

Example: An agent has previously sold several lots in a subdivision under development and all those lots passed a soil suitability test for an on-site septic system. The agent then sells Lot 35 without checking as to whether this lot satisfies the soil test; however, the agent informs the buyer that Lot 35 will support an on-site septic system when in fact the contrary is true. (While the agent's conduct may not rise to the level of willful disregard for the truth of the matter, the agent was at least negligent in not checking the soil test result on Lot 35 and is therefore guilty of negligent misrepresentation. This result is not affected by the agent's agency status or role in the transaction.)

Example: An owner tells a listing agent with ABC Realty that his house has 1850 heated square feet. Without verifying the square footage, the agent records 1850 square feet on the listing form and in the listing information published in the local MLS. The house is subsequently sold by a sales agent with XYZ Realty who tells the buyer that according to the MLS data, the house has 1850 square feet. The buyer later discovers that the house actually has only 1750 square feet. (In this situation, the listing agent did not make a direct misrepresentation to the buyer; however, he/she initiated the chain of communication which led to the buyer being misinformed, and thus indirectly misrepresented a material fact. Further, the listing agent's failure to verify the square footage constituted negligence. Therefore, the listing agent is guilty of a negligent misrepresentation. Although the selling agent directly communicated the incorrect information to the buyer, he/she probably acted reasonably in relying on the data in MLS. In this case, if the selling agent had no reason to doubt the MLS data, the selling agent is not guilty of a negligent misrepresentation. Note, however, that if the square footage discrepancy had been sufficiently large that a reasonably prudent selling agent should have known the listed data was incorrect, then the selling agent would also have been guilty of negligent misrepresentation. The result in this particular example is not affected by the selling agent's agency status (seller's subagent or buyer's agent), although this might be a factor in other situations.

Willful Omission — *This occurs when a licensee has "actual knowledge" of a material fact and a duty to disclose such fact to a buyer, seller, tenant, or landlord, but deliberately fails to disclose such fact.*

Example: An agent knows that a zoning change is pending that would adversely affect the value of a listed property, but fails to disclose such information to a prospective buyer. The agent has committed a willful omission regardless of the agent's agency status or role in the transaction.

[**Note:** Information about a zoning change, planned major highway or similar matter that would significantly enhance the value of a seller's property must also be disclosed to the seller, even if the licensee is a buyer's agent.]

Example: An agent knows that the city has just decided to extend water and sewer lines to a subdivision that has been plagued for years by serious water quality and sewage disposal problems. This will result in a substantial increase in the value of homes in the subdivision. The agent, who is working with a buyer to purchase a house in the subdivision, does not inform the seller of the city's recent decision. The agent has committed a willful omission and this result is not affected by the agent's agency status or role in the transaction.

Example: An agent knows that a listed house has a major defect (e.g., crumbling foundation, no insulation, malfunctioning septic tank, leaking roof, termite infestation, or some other problem) but fails to disclose such information to a prospective buyer. The agent has committed a willful omission and this result is not affected by the agent's agency status or role in the transaction.

Example: A selling agent working with a buyer as a subagent of the seller learns that the buyer is willing to pay more than the price in the buyer's offer, but fails to disclose this information to the seller (or listing agent) when presenting the offer. The selling agent has committed a willful omission. If, however, the selling agent were acting as a buyer's agent, then the result would be different because the agent does not represent the seller and has a duty not to disclose to the seller confidential buyer information that would be harmful to the buyer's interest.

Example: A buyer's agent becomes aware that the seller with whom his buyer is negotiating is under pressure to sell quickly and may accept much less than the listing price. Believing such information should always be kept confidential, the buyer's agent does not provide the buyer with this information. The buyer's agent is guilty of a willful omission. An agent must disclose to his/her principal any information that might affect the principal's decision in the transaction.

Example: Suppose in the immediately preceding example that the seller's property is listed with the firm of the buyer's agent and the firm's policy is to practice traditional dual agency in in-house sales situations where it represents both the seller and the buyer. In this situation, the buyer's agent would not be considered to have committed a willful omission under the License Law by not disclosing the information about the seller's personal situation to the buyer. NOTE: This assumes, however, that the buyer's agent properly disclosed his/her status as a buyer's agent to the seller or seller's agent upon "initial contact," that dual agency was properly authorized by both the seller and buyer prior to showing the seller's property to the buyer, the authorization was timely reduced to writing in the agency agreements that also limit the disclosure of information in dual agency situations (as is the case with the agency agreement forms provided by the North Carolina Association of REALTORS® for use by its members).

Negligent Omission — *This occurs when a licensee does NOT have actual knowledge of a material fact and consequently does not disclose the fact, but a reasonably prudent licensee "should reasonably have known" of such fact.* In this case, the licensee may be guilty of "negligent omission" if he/she fails to disclose this fact to a buyer, seller, tenant or landlord, even though the licensee acted in good faith in the transaction.

The prohibition against negligent omission creates a *"duty to discover and disclose" material facts* which a reasonably prudent licensee would typically have discovered in the course of the transaction. *A listing agent is typically in a much better position than a selling agent to discover material facts relating to a listed property and thus, will be held to a higher standard than will a selling agent acting as a seller's subagent. On the other hand, a buyer's agent in some circumstances may be held to a higher standard than a seller's subagent because of the buyer's agent's duties to the buyer under the law of agency, particularly if the buyer's agent is aware of a buyer's special needs with regard to a property.* Again we see how the agency relationships between agents and principals to a transaction and the licensee's role in the transaction can affect a licensee's duties and responsibilities under the License Law.

Instances of negligent omission occur much less frequently than instances of negligent misrepresentation. This is because most facts about a listed property are recorded on a detailed property data sheet from which information is taken for inclusion in MLS listings. If incorrect information taken from an MLS listing is passed on to a prospective purchaser, then a "misrepresentation," rather than an "omission," has occurred. Nevertheless, there are examples of negligent omission which can be cited.

Example: A listing agent lists for sale a house located adjacent to a street that is about to be widened into a major thoroughfare. The thoroughfare project has been very controversial and highly publicized. The city recently finalized its decision to proceed with the project and the plans for the street widening are recorded in the city planner's office. A buyer, working with a selling agent, makes an offer to buy the house. The listing agent does not disclose the street widening plans to the buyer or selling agent and claims later that he/she was not aware of the plans. In this situation, both the listing and selling agents are probably guilty of negligent omission because each "should reasonably have known" of the street widening plans, clearly a material fact, and should have disclosed this fact to the buyer. This result is not affected by whether the selling agent is a buyer agent or seller's subagent.

Example: A seller has a 30,000 square foot commercial property for sale which cannot be expanded under local zoning laws. The buyer is looking for property in the 25,000 - 30,000 square foot range, but has told his buyer's agent that he needs a property where he can expand to 50,000 square feet or more in the future. The seller does not think to advise the buyer's agent that the property cannot be expanded, and the buyer's agent makes no inquiry about it although he is aware of the buyer's special needs. If the buyer purchases the property without knowing about the restriction on expansion, the buyer's agent is guilty of a negligent omission for failing to discover and disclose a special circumstance that the agent knew was especially important to his/her client.

Example: When listing a house, a listing agent is told by the seller that one area of the roof leaks badly when it rains, but the moisture so far is being contained in the attic. The listing agent forgets to note this on the MLS data sheet and forgets to disclose the leaking roof problem to prospective buyers and selling agents. The listing agent is guilty of a negligent omission. Because the agent's failure to disclose the leaking roof problem was unintentional, the listing agent is not guilty of a willful omission; however, his/her forgetfulness resulting in his/her failure to disclose the defect constitutes a negligent omission.

Making False Promises [G.S. 93A-6(a)(2)]

Real estate brokers are prohibited from "making any false promises of a character likely to influence, persuade or induce." The promise may relate to any matter which might influence, persuade or induce a person to perform some act he/she might not otherwise perform.

Example: An agent promises a prospective apartment tenant that the apartment will be repainted before the tenant moves in. The agent then fails to have the work done after the lease is signed.

Example: An agent promises a property owner that

if he/she lists his/her house for sale with the agent's firm, then the firm will steam-clean all the carpets and wash all the windows. The firm then fails to have the work done after the listing contract is signed.

Other Misrepresentations [G.S. 93A-6(a)(3)]

Real estate brokers are prohibited from pursuing a course of misrepresentation (or making of false promises) through other agents or salespersons or through advertising or other means.

> **Example:** In marketing subdivision lots for a developer, a broker regularly advertises that the lots for sale are suitable for residential use when in fact the lots will not pass a soil suitability test for on-site sewage systems.
>
> **Example:** A broker is marketing a new condominium complex which is under construction. Acting with the full knowledge and consent of the broker, the broker's agents regularly inform prospective buyers that units will be available for occupancy on June 1, when in fact the units won't be available until at least September 1.

Conflict of Interest [G.S. 93A-6(a)(4) and (6); Rule A.0104(d)] and (i)

Undisclosed Dual Agency. G.S. 93A-6(a)(4) prohibits a real estate agent from *"acting for more than one party in a transaction without the knowledge of all parties for whom he or she acts."* Commission Rule A.0104(d) and (i) takes this a step further by providing that a broker or brokerage firm representing one party in a transaction shall not undertake to represent another party in the transaction without the express written authority (i.e., authorization of dual agency) of each party (subject to one exception, explained as part of the dual agency discussion in the "General Brokerage Provisions" section). A typical violation of this provision occurs when the agent has only one principal in a transaction but acts in a manner which benefits another party without the principal's knowledge. In such a situation, the agent violates the duty of loyalty and consent owed to his principal.

> **Example:** A house is listed with Firm X. When showing the house to a prospective buyer not represented by Firm X, an agent of Firm X advises the buyer to offer substantially less than the listing price because the seller must move soon and is very anxious to sell the property fast. The agent and Firm X are contractually obligated to represent only the seller. By advising the prospective buyer as indicated in this example, the agent is acting to benefit the buyer without the seller's knowledge and consent. This act violates both the License Law and the Law of Agency.
>
> **Example:** An agent with Firm Y assists her sister in purchasing a house listed with Firm X without advising Firm X or the seller of her relationship with the buyer. The agent is "officially" acting as a subagent of the seller in the transaction. In this situation, there is an inherent conflict of interest on the part of the agent. If the agent does not disclose her relationships to both parties, then the agent violates both the License Law and Law of Agency. In fact, since her allegiance lies with her sister, the agent should instead act as a buyer's agent from the outset. The same would be true if the buyer were a close friend or business associate of the agent, or in any way enjoyed a special relationship to the agent which would clearly influence the agent to act in behalf of the buyer rather than the seller.

Self-dealing. G.S. 93A-6(a)(4) also prohibits any **"self-dealing"** on the part of an agent. For example, if an agent attempts to make a secret profit in a transaction where he is supposed to be representing a principal, then the agent violates this "conflict of interest" provision.

> **Example:** An agent lists a parcel of undeveloped property which is zoned for single-family residential use. The agent knows that this property is about to be rezoned for multi-family residential use, which will greatly increase the property's value. Rather than informing the seller of this fact, the agent offers to buy the property at the listed price, telling the seller that he wants to acquire the property as a long-term investment. The deal closes. Several months later, after the rezoning has been accomplished, the agent sells the property at a substantial profit.

Representing Another Broker without Consent. G.S. 93A-6(a)(6) prohibits a licensee from "representing or attempting to represent a real estate broker other than the broker by whom he or she is engaged or associated, without the express knowledge and consent of the broker with whom he or she is associated." While brokers may work for or be associated with more than one real estate company at the same time, *so long as* they have the express consent of all brokers-in-charge, provisional brokers may never engage in brokerage activities for more than one company at a time.

Improper Brokerage Commission [G.S. 93A-6(a)(5) and (9)]

A broker may NOT pay a commission or valuable consideration to any person for acts or services performed in violation of the License Law. [G.S. 93A-6(a)(9)] *This provision flatly prohibits a broker from paying an unlicensed person for acts which require a real estate license.* Following are examples of prohibited payments:

> **Example:** The payment by brokers of commissions to previously licensed sales associates who failed to properly renew their licenses for any acts performed after their licenses had expired. [Note that payment could properly be made for commissions earned while the license was on active status, even if the license is inactive or expired at time of payment. The determining factor is whether the license was on active status at the time all services were rendered which generated the commission?]
>
> **Example:** The payment of a commission, salary or fee by brokers to unlicensed employees or independent

contractors (e.g., secretaries, "trainees" who haven't passed the license examination, etc.) for performing acts or services requiring a real estate license.

Example: The payment by licensees of a "finder's fee," "referral fee," "bird dog fee," or any other valuable consideration to unlicensed persons who find, introduce, or bring together parties to a real estate transaction. This is true even if the ultimate consummation of the transaction is accomplished by a licensee and even if the act is performed without expectation of compensation. Thus, a licensee may NOT compensate a friend, relative, former client or any other unlicensed person for "referring" a prospective buyer, seller, landlord or tenant to such licensee. This prohibition extends to "owner referral" programs at condominium or time share complexes and "tenant referral" programs at apartment complexes.

In addition, a *provisional* broker may NOT accept any compensation for brokerage services from anyone other than his employing broker or brokerage firm. Consequently, *a broker may not pay a commission or fee directly to a provisional broker of another broker or firm. Any such payment must be made through the provisional broker's employing broker or firm.* [G.S. 93A-6(a)(5)]

Note: *See also the discussion of Rule A.0109 on "Brokerage Fees and Compensation" under the subsequent section titled "General Brokerage Provisions."*

Unworthiness and Incompetence [G.S. 93A-6(a)(8)]

This broad provision authorizes the Real Estate Commission to discipline any licensee who, based on his or her conduct and consideration of the public interest, is found to be unworthy or incompetent to work in the real estate business. A wide range of conduct may serve as the basis for a finding of unworthiness or incompetence, including conduct which violates other specific provisions of the License Law or Commission rules. Here are a few examples of improper conduct which do not specifically violate another License Law provision but which might support a finding of unworthiness or incompetence.

1. Failure to properly complete (fill in) real estate contracts or to use contract forms which are legally adequate.
2. Failure to diligently perform the services required under listing contracts or property management contracts.
3. Failure to provide accurate closing statements to sellers and buyers or accurate income/expense reports to property owners.

Improper Dealing [G.S. 93A-6(a)(10)]

This broad provision prohibits a real estate licensee from engaging in "any other conduct [not specifically prohibited elsewhere in the License Law] which constitutes **improper, fraudulent or dishonest dealing**." The determination as to whether particular conduct constitutes "improper, fraudulent or dishonest dealing" is made by the Real Estate Commission on a case-by-case basis. Therefore, a broad range of conduct might be found objectionable under this provision, depending on the facts in a case.

One category of conduct which violates this provision is any breach of the duty to exercise skill, care, and diligence in behalf of a client under the Law of Agency. (Note that other breaches of Agency Law duties constituting either a "misrepresentation or omission," a "conflict of interest" or a "failure to properly account for trust funds" are covered by other specific statutory provisions.)

Another category of conduct which violates this provision is any violation of the State Fair Housing Act. This is mentioned separately under the "Discriminatory Practices" heading.

Example: An agent assists a prospective buyer in perpetrating a fraud in connection with a mortgage loan application by preparing two contracts — one with false information for submission to the lending institution, and another which represents the actual agreement between seller and buyer. (This practice is commonly referred to as "dual contracting" or "contract kiting.")

Example: A broker lists a property for sale and agrees in the listing contract to place the listing in the local MLS, to advertise the property for sale, and to use his best efforts in good faith to find a buyer. The broker places a "For Sale" sign on the property, but fails to place the property in the MLS for more than 30 days and fails to otherwise advertise the property during the listing period. (The broker has failed to exercise reasonable skill, care and diligence in behalf of his client as required by the listing contract and the Law of Agency.)

Example: An agent is aware that the owners of a house listed with his company are out of town for the weekend, yet the agent gives a prospective buyer the house keys and allows such prospect to look at the listed house without accompanying the prospect. (The agent has failed to exercise reasonable skill, care and diligence in behalf of his client.)

Discriminatory Practices [G.S. 93A-6(a)(10); Rule A.1601]

Any conduct by a licensee that violates the provisions of the State Fair Housing Act is considered by the Commission to constitute "improper conduct" and to be a violation of the License Law.

Practice of Law [G.S. 93A-4(e); G.S. 93A-6(a)(11); Rule A.0111]

Real estate licensees may not perform for others any legal service described in G.S. 84-2.1 or any other legal service. Following are several examples of real estate-related legal services which licensees may NOT provide.

1. Drafting legal documents such as deeds, deeds of trust, leases and real estate sales contracts for others. Although licensees may "fill in" or "complete" pre-

printed real estate contract forms which have been drafted by an attorney, they may NOT under any circumstances complete or fill in deed or deed of trust forms.
2. Abstracting or rendering an opinion on legal title to real property.
3. Providing "legal advice" of any nature to clients and customers, including advice concerning the nature of any interest in real estate or the means of holding title to real estate. (Note: Although providing advice concerning the legal ramifications of a real estate sales contract is prohibited, merely "explaining" the provisions of such a contract is not only acceptable, but highly recommended.)

Violating any Commission Rule [G.S. 93A-6-(a)(15)]

The law also has a "catch-all" provision that subjects a licensee to disciplinary action for violating any rule adopted by the Commission.

Note: The provisions of G.S. 93A-6(a)(12)-(14) are addressed elsewhere in these "Comments" under the "General Brokerage Provisions" section.

Other Prohibited Acts [G.S. 93A-6(b)]

In addition to those prohibited acts previously discussed, G.S. 93A-6(b) prescribes several other specific grounds for disciplinary action by the Commission, including:
1. Where a licensee has obtained a license by false or fraudulent representation (e.g., falsifying documentation of prelicensing education, failing to disclose prior criminal convictions, etc.).
2. Where a licensee has been convicted of, or pled guilty or no contest to, a number of listed misdemeanors or felonies plus any other offense that shows professional unfitness or involves moral turpitude that would reasonably affect the licensee's performance in the real estate business.
3. Where a broker's unlicensed employee, who is exempt from licensing under G.S. 93A-2(c)(6) (property management exception), has committed an act which, if committed by the broker, would have constituted a violation of G.S. 93A-6(a) for which the broker could be disciplined.
4. Where a licensee who is also licensed as an appraiser, attorney, home inspector, mortgage broker, general contractor, or another licensed profession or occupation has been disciplined for an offense under any law involving fraud, theft, misrepresentation, breach of trust or fiduciary responsibility, or willful or negligent malpractice..

Lastly, be aware that under (b)(3), licensees may be disciplined for violating any of the 15 provisions under subsection (a) when selling, buying, or leasing their own property.

GENERAL BROKERAGE PROVISIONS

Discussed below are selected Commission rules related to general brokerage.

Agency Agreements and Disclosure [G.S. 93A-13 and Rule A.0104]

Provided below is a brief summary of the various provisions of the Commission's rule regarding agency agreements and disclosure. For a much more in-depth discussion of this rule and its application, the reader is referred to the Commission's *North Carolina Real Estate Manual*.

Agency Agreements. G.S. 93A-13 and Rule A.0104(a) requires all agency agreements for brokerage services (in both sales and lease transactions) to be in writing and signed by the parties thereto. Rule A .0104(a):

- Requires agency agreements with **property owners** (both sellers and lessors) of any type of property to be in writing prior to the broker providing any services;
- Allows an express **oral buyer/tenant agency agreement** from the outset of the relationship, *but the agreement must be reduced to writing no later than the time any party to the transaction makes an offer*. As a practical matter, this oral agreement needs to address all key aspects of the relationship, including agent compensation, authorization for dual agency, etc.

(Note: A buyer/tenant agency agreement must be in writing from the outset if it seeks to limit the buyer/tenant's right to work with other agents or binds the client to the agent for any definite time period. In other words, *an oral buyer/tenant agency agreement must be "non-exclusive" and must be for an indefinite period and terminable by the client at any time.***)**

Further, every **written** agency agreement of any kind must also:
- *Provide for its existence for a definite period of time* and terminate without prior notice at the expiration of that period. [Exception: an agency agreement between a broker and a landlord to procure tenants for the landlord's property may allow for automatic renewal so long as the landlord may terminate with notice at the end of any contract or renewal period.]
- *Contain the Rule A.0104(b) non-discrimination (fair housing) provision*, namely: "The broker shall conduct all brokerage activities in regard to this agreement without respect to the race, color, religion, sex, national origin, handicap or familial status of any party or prospective party." (This provision must be set forth in a clear and conspicuous manner which shall distinguish it from other provisions of the agency agreement.)
- *Include the license number of the individual licensee* who signs the agreement.

Allowing an agent to work with a buyer under an express *oral* buyer agency agreement is intended to address the problem of buyers being reluctant to sign a written buyer agency agreement at the outset of their relationship with a buyer agent. The idea underlying this approach is to allow an agent to work temporarily with a prospective buyer as a buyer's agent under an oral agreement while the agent establishes a rapport with the buyer that makes the buyer feel more comfortable with signing a written buyer agency agreement.

Although the rule allows oral buyer/tenant agency agreements until the point in time when any party is ready to make an offer, it nevertheless is highly advisable that agents have such agreements reduced to writing and signed by the buyer/tenant at the earliest possible time in order to avoid misunderstanding and conflict between the buyer/tenant and agent. Recall also that the agent must obtain a written buyer/tenant agency agreement from the client not later than the time either party to the transaction extends an offer to the other.

If the buyer will not sign a written buyer agency agreement prior to making or receiving an offer, then the agent may not continue to work with the buyer as a buyer's agent. Moreover, the agent may not begin at this point to work with the buyer as a seller's subagent unless the agent (1) fully advises the buyer of the consequences of the agent switching from buyer's agent to seller's agent (including the fact that the agent would have to disclose to the seller any information, including "confidential" information about the buyer, that might influence the seller's decision in the transaction), (2) obtains the buyer's consent, and (3) obtains the consent of the seller and listing firm, which is the seller's agent. The foregoing applies equally to brokers working with tenants as a tenant agent.

Agency Disclosure Requirement. While Rule A.0104(a) requires all agency agreements, whether for lease or sales transactions, to be in writing, the *Rule A.0104(c) agency disclosure requirement applies only to* **sales** *transactions. It requires licensees to provide prospective buyers and sellers, at* **"first substantial contact,"** *with a copy of the* **Working with Real Estate Agents** *brochure, to review the brochure with them and then reach an agreement regarding their agency relationship.* The licensee providing the brochure should also include his/her name and license number on the brochure. Note that the obligation under this rule is not satisfied merely by handing the prospective seller or buyer the brochure to read. The agent is required to review the contents of the brochure with the prospective buyer or seller and then reach agreement with the prospective buyer or seller as to whether the agent will work with the buyer or seller as his/her agent or as the agent of the other party.

In the case of a prospective **seller**, the agent may either (1) act as the seller's agent, which is the typical situation and requires a written agreement from the outset of their relationship, or (2) work with the seller as a buyer's agent if the agent already represents a prospective buyer.

In the case of a prospective **buyer**, the agent may either (1) act as the buyer's agent under either an oral or written agreement as addressed in Rule A.0104(a), or (2) work with the buyer as a seller's agent, disclosure of which must be in writing from the outset.

Disclosure of Agency Status by Sellers' Agents and Subagents to Prospective Buyers: Paragraph (e) of Rule A.0104, like paragraph (c), requires a seller's agent or subagent in sales transactions to disclose his/her agency status in writing to a prospective buyer at the "first substantial contact" with the buyer. It is recommended that sellers' agents make this required written disclosure using the form provided for this purpose in the *Working with Real Estate Agents* brochure that must be provided to buyers (as well as to sellers) at first substantial contact. This form has a place for the buyer to acknowledge receipt of the brochure and disclosure of agency status, thereby providing the agent with written evidence of having provided the brochure and disclosure. The disclosure may, however, be made using a different form — *the most important point is that the disclosure be made in writing in a timely manner.* The reason for this requirement is that buyers tend to assume that an agent they contact to work with them in locating a property for purchase is "their" agent and working primarily in their interest. This may or may not be the case in reality. *The purpose of the disclosure requirement is to place prospective buyers on notice that the agent they are dealing with is NOT "their" agent before the prospective buyer discloses to the agent information which the buyer would not want a seller to know because it might compromise the buyer's bargaining position.*

Most frequently, **"first substantial contact"** will occur at the first "face-to-face" meeting with a prospective buyer. However, the point in time that "first substantial contact" with a prospective buyer occurs will vary depending on the particular situation and may or may not be at the time of the first or initial contact with the prospective buyer. Many first contacts are by telephone and do not involve discussions which reach the level that would require disclosure, although some initial phone contacts, especially those with out-of-town buyers, could reach this level.

"First substantial contact" occurs at the point in time when a discussion with a prospective buyer begins to focus on the buyer's specific property needs and desires or on the buyer's financial situation. Typically, that point in time is reached when the agent is ready to solicit information from the prospective buyer that is needed to identify prospective properties to show the buyer. Therefore, *an agent planning to work with a prospective buyer as a seller's agent or subagent should assure that disclosure of his/her agency status is made in writing to the prospective buyer prior to obtaining from the prospective buyer any personal or confidential information that the buyer would not want a seller to know.*

A few **examples of such personal or confidential information include:** *The maximum price a buyer is willing to pay for a property; the buyer's ability to pay more than the price offered by the buyer; or the fact that a buyer has a special interest in purchasing the seller's property rather than some other similar property.* In any event, the disclosure must be made prior to discussing with the prospective buyer his/her specific needs or desires regarding the purchase of a property. As a practical matter, this means the *disclosure will always need to be made prior to showing a property to a prospective buyer.* The best policy is to simply make the disclosure at the earliest possible time.

If first substantial contact occurs by telephone or by means of other electronic communication where it is not practical to provide written disclosure, the agent shall immediately disclose by similar means whom he/she represents and shall immediately, but in no event later than three days from the date of first substantial contact, mail or otherwise transmit a copy of the written disclosure to the buyer.

Disclosure of Agency Status by Buyers' Agents to Sellers or Sellers' Agents. Paragraph (f) of Rule A.0104 *requires a buyer's agent to disclose his/her agency status to a seller or seller's agent at the* **"initial contact"** *with the seller or seller's agent.* "Initial contact" will typically occur when a buyer's agent telephones or otherwise contacts the listing firm to schedule a showing. The initial disclosure may be oral, but a written confirmation of the previous oral disclosure must be made (except in auction sale transactions) no later than the time of delivery of an offer to purchase. The written confirmation may be (and usually is) included in the offer to purchase. In fact, Commission Rule A.0112(a)(19) requires that any preprinted offer to purchase and contract form used by an agent include a provision providing for confirmation of agency status by each real estate agent (and firm) involved in the transaction.

Consent to Dual Agency. Paragraph (d) of Rule A.0104 requires generally that an agent must obtain the written authority of all parties prior to undertaking to represent those parties as a dual agent. It is important to note that this requirement applies to all real estate transactions (sales and lease/rentals), not just sales transactions. [In sales transactions, this written authority to act as a dual agent is usually included in the listing and buyer agency contracts. If those contracts do not grant such authority, then the agent must have both the seller and buyer consent to the dual agency prior to beginning to act as a dual agent for both parties.]

Paragraph (d) of Rule A.0104 currently *requires written authority for dual agency from the formation of the relationship except situations where a buyer/tenant is represented by an agent working under an oral agency agreement as permitted by A.0104(a), in which case written authority for dual agency must be obtained no later than the time one of the parties represented by the agent working as a dual agent makes an offer to purchase, sell, rent, lease, or exchange real estate to the other party.* Thus, it is permissible for the agent to operate for a limited period of time under an oral dual agency agreement. It is very important to remember that G.S. 93A-6(a)(4) still requires agents to obtain the consent of all parties prior to beginning to act as a dual agent for those parties. Therefore, it is essential that agents electing to operate as a dual agent for a limited period of time without obtaining this authority in writing still explain fully the consequences of their acting as a dual agent and obtain the parties' oral consent.

As a practical matter in sales transactions, agents will frequently have already obtained written authority to act as a dual agent for in-house sales transactions at the time the initial written listing or buyer agency agreement is executed. However, under Paragraph (a) of Rule A.0104, many buyer's agents may elect to work with their buyer clients for a period of time under an oral buyer agency agreement. Paragraph (d) permits such buyer's agents to also operate for a limited period of time as a dual agent under an oral agreement in order to deal with situations where a buyer client is interested in a property listed with the agent's firm. Note that, *although an oral dual agency agreement for a limited period of time is permitted by Commission rules, it is strongly recommended that agents have any dual agency agreement in writing from the outset of the dual agency arrangement.* This will provide the agent with some evidence that the matter of dual agency was discussed with the parties and that they consented to it. Such evidence could prove quite useful if a party later asserts that the agent did not obtain their consent for dual agency in a timely manner.

Auction Sales Exemption. Paragraph (g) of Rule A.0104 provides that the provisions of Paragraphs (c), (d) and (e) of the Rule shall not apply to real estate licensees representing sellers in auction sales transactions. Note that in auction sales, the real estate agents involved almost invariably work only as seller's agents and this fact is considered to be self-evident. Thus, there is no need for agents to distribute and review the *Working with Real Estate Agents* brochure, no need for disclosure of agency status by the seller's agents, and no dual agency. For the unusual situation where a buyer may be represented by an agent in an auction sale transaction, Paragraph (h) of Rule A.0104 provides that such a buyer's agent shall, no later than the time of execution of a written agreement memorializing the buyer's contract to purchase, provide the seller or seller's agent with a written confirmation that he/she represents the buyer.

Dual Agency Status of Firm. Paragraph (i) of Rule A.0104 codifies in the Commission's rules the common law rule that *a firm which represents more than one party in the same real estate sales transaction is a dual agent, and further states that the firm, through the brokers affiliated with the firm, shall disclose its dual agency to the parties.* In other words, dual agency is not limited to those situations where an individual agent is working with both a buyer client and seller client (or lessor and commercial tenant) in the same transaction. If one agent of a firm is working with a buyer client of the firm and another agent of the same firm is working with a seller client of the firm in a transaction involving the sale of the seller client's property to the buyer client, then the firm is a dual agent (as it holds both agency agreements). However, a firm functions through its employees, namely, its associated agents; thus, under the common law, whenever the firm is a dual agent of certain parties in a transaction, all licensees affiliated with that firm are also dual agents of those parties in that transaction.

Designated Agency. Paragraphs (j) - (m) of Rule A.0104 authorize real estate firms to engage in a form of dual agency practice referred to in the rule as **"designated agency"** in certain **sales transactions involving in-house dual agency**. *"Designated agency involves appointing or "designating" an individual agent(s) in a firm to represent only the interests of the seller and another individual agent(s) to represent only the interests of the buyer when a firm has an in-house dual agency situation.*

The principal advantage of the designated agency approach over the "standard" dual agency approach is that each of a firm's clients (seller and buyer) receive fuller representation by their designated agent. In the typical dual agency situation, client advocacy is essentially lost because the dual agent may not seek an advantage for (i.e., "advocate" for) one client to the detriment of the other client. The dual agent must remain completely neutral and impartial at all times. Designated agency returns "advocacy" to the services provided by the respective designated agents and allows them to more fully represent their respective clients.

Authority to practice designated agency must be in writing no later than the time a written dual agency agreement is required under A.0104(d). Additional required procedures for practicing designated agency are clearly spelled out in Paragraphs (j) - (m) and are not discussed further here. For more detailed coverage of dual and designated agency, the reader is once again referred to the Commission's *North Carolina Real Estate Manual*.

Dual Agency by Individual Agent. Paragraph (n) of Rule A.0104 authorizes individual agents representing both the buyer and seller in the same real estate sales transaction pursuant to a written dual agency agreement to include in the agreement a provision authorizing the agent not to disclose certain "confidential" information about one party to the other party without permission from the party about whom the information pertains. This provision is intended to allow individual dual agents to treat confidential information about their clients in a manner similar to that allowed for firms practicing designated agency.

Brokers As Parties to Transactions. There is an inherent conflict of interest presented by a broker representing the very party against whom the broker, as an interested party, is negotiating. Paragraph (o) of Rule A.0104 prohibits a broker who is selling property in which the broker has an ownership interest from representing a buyer of the property. Except that a broker who is selling commercial real estate, as defined in Rule .1802 of this Subchapter, in which the broker has less than 25% ownership interest may represent a buyer of that property if the buyer consents to the representation after full written disclosure of the broker's ownership interest. However, a firm listing a property owned by a broker affiliated with the firm may represent a buyer of that property so long as the individual broker representing the buyer does not have an ownership interest in the property and the buyer consents to the representation after full disclosure. Paragraph (p) of Rule A.0104 prohibits a listing broker or firm from purchasing a property listed by that broker or firm unless they first disclose to the seller in writing that a potential conflict of interest exists and that the seller may want to seek independent counsel. Prior to the listing broker entering into a purchase contract, the individual listing broker and firm must either terminate the listing agreement or transfer the listing to another broker in the firm. Prior to the firm entering into a purchase contract, the listing broker and firm must disclose to the seller in writing that the seller has the right to terminate the listing. The broker or firm must terminate the listing upon the request of the seller.

Broker Name and Address [Rule A.0103]

A broker must notify the Commission in writing (may include online) within 10 days of each change in personal name, firm name, trade name, residence address and firm address, telephone number, and email address.

If a broker intends to advertise in any manner using a firm name or assumed name which does not set forth the surname of the broker, the broker must first register the firm name or assumed name with the county *register of deeds office in each county in which the broker intends to engage in brokerage activity* and must also notify the Commission of the use of such firm name or assumed name. For individuals and partnerships, a name is "assumed" when it does not include the surname of the licensee(s). For a firm required to be registered with the Secretary of State, a name is "assumed" when it is different from the firm's legal name as registered with the Secretary of State. Note: most franchisees operate under assumed names. An Assumed Name certificate can be filed in the Register of Deeds office for uploading to the statewide database maintained by the Secretary of State.

A licensee operating as a sole proprietorship, partnership or business entity other than a corporation or limited liability company may NOT include in its legal or assumed name the name of an unlicensed person or a provisional broker.

A broker who proposes to use a business name that includes the name of another active, inactive or cancelled broker must have the permission of that broker or his or her authorized representative. This rule provision is intended to prohibit a broker or firm from using without proper authorization the name of some other broker or former broker who is not currently associated with the broker or firm, such as a former associate or a deceased broker.

Advertising [Rule A.0105]

A licensee must have the proper authority to advertise. A broker may not advertise or display a "for sale" or "for rent" sign on a property without the written consent of the owner or the owner's authorized agent. A broker may not advertise any brokerage service for another without the consent of his or her broker-in-charge and without including in any advertisement the name of the firm or sole proprietorship with which the broker is associated.

The rule also prohibits any advertisement by a licensee that indicates an offer to sell, buy, exchange, rent or lease real property is being made by the licensee's principal without the involvement of a broker – i.e., a **"blind ad."** *All advertising by a licensee must indicate that it is the advertisement of a broker or brokerage firm.*

Delivery of Instruments [G.S. 93A-6(a); Rule A.0106]

Among other things, this rule, which implements G.S. 93A-6(a)(13), *requires agents to deliver to their customer or client copies of any required written agency agreement, contract, offer, lease, rental agreement, option or other related transaction document within three days of the broker's receipt* of the executed document. Regarding offers, this does NOT mean that agents may in every case wait up to three days to present an offer to a seller. Rather, it means that an agent must, as soon as possible, present to the seller any offer received by the agent. If the agent is the "selling agent," then the offer should be immediately presented to the "listing agent" who should, in turn, immediately present the offer to the seller. The "three-day" provision is included only to allow for situations where the seller is not immediately available (e.g., seller is out of town), and represents an outside time limit within which offers must always be presented. In all cases where the seller is available, the offer should be presented as soon as possible.

The same rule also means that a prospective buyer who signs an offer must immediately be provided a copy of such offer. (A photocopy is acceptable for this purpose.) Do NOT wait until after the offer is accepted (or rejected) by the seller.

In addition, this rule means that an offer must be immediately presented to a seller even if there is a contract pending on the property. Of course, in this instance, it is essential that the agent also advise the seller that serious legal problems could result from the seller's acceptance of such offer and that the seller should contact an attorney if he is interested in treating the offer as a "back-up" offer or in attempting to be released from the previously signed contract.

Copies of any signed sales contract or lease must also be promptly delivered to the parties within the three-day period. Clients should be provided a copy of the agency agreement upon signing, since both parties presumably are present, but certainly within three days of receipt by the broker.

Finally, G.S. 93A-6(a)(14) requires a broker to provide his/her client a detailed and accurate closing statement showing the receipt and disbursement of all monies relating to the transaction about which the broker knows or reasonably should know. A broker may rely on a closing statement prepared by an attorney but must review the statement for accuracy.

Retention of Records [Rule A.0108]

Brokers are required to retain records pertaining to their brokerage transactions for three years from the successful or unsuccessful conclusion of the transaction or the disbursement of all trust monies pertaining to that transaction, whichever occurs later. However, if the broker's agency agreement is terminated prior to the conclusion of the transaction, the broker shall retain transaction records for three years after the agency agreement is terminated or the disbursement of all funds held by or paid to the broker in connection with the transaction, whichever occurs later. Documents that must be retained include sale contracts, leases, offers (even those not accepted), agency contracts, earnest money receipts, trust account records, disclosure documents, closing statements, broker cooperation agreements, broker price opinions and comparative market analyses (including notes and supporting documentation), advertising, sketches, and any other records relating to a transaction.

Rule A .0108(d) also requires an individual broker to provide a copy of such records including written agency disclosures, agency agreements, and contracts to the firm or sole proprietorship with which they are affiliated within three days of the broker's receipt of such documents.

Brokerage Fees and Compensation [Rule A.0109]

This rule addresses various issues associated with the disclosure of and sharing of compensation received by a real estate licensee.

Disclosure to principal of compensation from a vendor or supplier of goods or services. Paragraph (a) prohibits a licensee from receiving any form of valuable consideration from a vendor or supplier of goods or services in connection with an expenditure made on behalf of the licensee's principal in a real estate transaction without first obtaining the written consent of the principal.

> **Example:** A broker manages several rental units for various owners and routinely employs Ajax Cleaning Service to clean the units after the tenants leave. The broker pays Ajax a $50 per unit fee for its services out of rental proceeds received and deposited in his trust account. Ajax then "refunds" to the broker $10 for each $50 fee it receives, but the property owners are not aware that the broker receives this payment from Ajax in addition to his regular brokerage fee. The broker in this situation is making a secret profit without the property owners' knowledge and is violating the rule.

Disclosure to a party of compensation for recommending, procuring or arranging services for the party. Paragraph (b) prohibits a licensee from receiving any form of valuable consideration for recommending, procuring, or arranging services for a party to a real estate transaction without full and timely disclosure to such party. The party for whom the services are recommended, procured, or arranged does not have to be the agent's principal.

> **Example:** An agent sells a listed lot to a buyer who wants to build a house on the lot. Without the buyer's knowledge, the agent arranges with ABC Homebuilders for ABC to pay the agent a 3% referral fee if the agent recommends ABC to the buyer and the buyer employs ABC to build his house. The agent then recommends ABC to the buyer, ABC builds the buyer's house for $100,000 and ABC secretly pays

the agent $3,000 for his referral of the buyer. The agent has violated this rule. (Note that the buyer in this situation likely paid $3,000 more for his house than was necessary because it is very likely the builder added the agent's referral fee to the price he charged the buyer for building the house. The main point here is that the buyer had the right to know that the agent was not providing disinterested advice when recommending the builder.)

Example: A selling agent in a real estate transaction, while acting as a subagent of the seller, recommends to a buyer who has submitted an offer that the buyer apply to Ready Cash Mortgage Company for his mortgage loan. The agent knows that Ready Cash will pay him a "referral fee" of $100 for sending him the buyer's business if the loan is made to the buyer, but the agent does not disclose this fact to the buyer. If the agent subsequently accepts the referral fee from the lender, he will have violated this rule. (The buyer has the right to know that the agent's recommendation is not a disinterested one.)

Disclosure to principal of compensation for brokerage services in sales transactions. Paragraph (c) deals with disclosure to a licensee's principal of the licensee's compensation in a **sales** transaction from various sources other than in situations addressed in paragraphs (a) and (b). A broker may not receive any compensation, incentive, bonus, rebate or other consideration of more than nominal value (1) from his or her principal unless the compensation, etc. is provided for in a written agency contract or (2) from any other party or person unless the broker provides to his or her principal a full and timely disclosure of the compensation.

Example: ABC Homebuilders offers to pay any broker who procures a buyer for one of ABC's inventory homes a **bonus** of $1,000 that is in addition to any brokerage commission the broker earns under any agency contract and/or commission split agreements. Any broker working with a buyer-client who is considering the purchase of one of ABC's homes must comply with the disclosure requirement and disclose the bonus to the buyer in a timely manner. **Note:** If ABC Homebuilders also offers a bonus of $2,000 on a second sale of one of its homes and $3,000 on a third sale, and if a buyer's broker has already sold one of ABC's homes, then the broker must disclose to his or her buyer principal the entire bonus program and that his or her bonus will be at least $2,000 if the buyer purchases an ABC home.

Nominal compensation. Compensation is considered to be "nominal" if it is of insignificant, token or merely symbolic worth. The Commission has cited gifts of a $25 bottle of wine or a $50 dinner gift certificate as being examples of "nominal" compensation paid to a broker that do not require the consent of the broker's principal.

Full and timely disclosure. Paragraph (d) of Rule A.0109 explains what is meant by "full and timely disclosure" in paragraphs (a), (b) and (c). "Full" disclosure includes a description of the compensation, incentive, etc. including its value and the identity of the person or party by whom it will or may be paid. The disclosure is "timely" when it is made in sufficient time to aid a reasonable person's decision-making. In a sales transaction, the disclosure may be made orally, but must be confirmed in writing before the principal makes or accepts an offer to buy or sell.

Restrictions on compensation disclosure requirement. Paragraph (e) clarifies that a broker does NOT have to disclose to a person who is not his or her principal the compensation the broker expects to receive from his or her principal, and further clarifies that a broker does NOT have to disclose to his principal the compensation the broker expects to receive from the broker's employing broker/firm (i.e., the individual broker's share of the compensation paid to the broker's employing broker/firm).

Commission will not arbitrate commission disputes. G.S 93A-3(c) provides that the Commission shall not make rules or regulations regulating commission, salaries, or fees to be charged by licensees. Paragraph (f) of Rule A.0109 augments that statutory provision by providing that the Commission will not act as a board of arbitration regarding such matters as the rate of commissions, the division of commissions, pay of brokers and similar matters.

Compensation of unlicensed persons by brokers prohibited. G.S. 93A-6(a)(9) authorizes the Commission to take disciplinary action against a licensee for paying any person for acts performed in violation of the License Law. Paragraph (g) of Rule A.0109 simply augments this statutory provision by providing an affirmative statement that a licensee shall not in any manner compensate or share compensation with unlicensed persons or entities for acts performed in North Carolina for which a license is required. [Note that NC brokers may split commissions or pay referral fees to licensees of another state so long as the out-of-state licensee does not provide any brokerage services while physically in North Carolina.] One narrow, limited exception to this restriction is provided in Paragraph (h) – licensees may pay referral fees to travel agents who contact them to book vacation rentals only, so long as well-defined procedures are followed.

RESPA prohibitions control. Finally, Paragraph (i) of Rule A.0109 provides that nothing in this rule permits a licensee to accept any fee, kickback, etc. that is prohibited by the federal Real Estate Settlement Procedures Act (RESPA) or implementing rules, or to fail to make any disclosure required by that act or rules.

Broker-In-Charge [Rule A.0110].

Requirement to Have a Broker-In-Charge. Paragraph (a) of Rule A.0110 states the general rule that each real estate firm is required to have a broker designated by the Commission who meets the qualification requirements to serve as **"broker-in-charge"** of the firm's principal office and a different broker to serve in the same capacity at each branch office. It is important to note, as discussed previously under "License Requirement," that **"broker-in-charge"** *is not a separate license*, but only a separate license status category. No broker may be broker-in-charge of more than one office location at a time, and no office of a firm shall have more than one designated broker-in-charge. Rule A.0110(a) describes the lone exception in the rare circumstance when two or more firms share the same office space. Note that G .0103 defines the terms "office," "principal office" and "branch office" – these definitions are not repeated here.

Exception to BIC Requirement for Certain Firms. Paragraph (c) of Rule A.0110 provides: A licensed real estate firm is not required to have a BIC if it: (1) has been organized for the sole purpose of receiving compensation for brokerage services furnished by its qualifying broker through another firm or broker; (2) is treated for tax purposes as a Subchapter S corporation by the U.S. Internal Revenue service; (3) has no principal or branch office; and (4) has no licensed or unlicensed person associated with it other than its qualifying broker.

Sole Proprietors. In addition to each firm having to have a broker-in-charge for each office, *most broker-sole proprietors (including sole practitioners) also must be a broker-in-charge.*

Rule A.0110 (b) provides that a broker who is a **sole proprietor** shall designate himself or herself as a broker-in-charge if the broker: (1) engages in any transaction where the broker is required to deposit and maintain monies belonging to others in a trust account; (2) engages in advertising or promoting his or her services as a broker in any manner; OR (3) has one or more other brokers affiliated with him or her in the real estate business. Note, however, that maintenance of a trust account by a broker solely for holding residential tenant security deposits received by the broker on properties owned by the broker in compliance with G.S. 42-50 shall not, standing alone, subject the broker to the requirement to be designated as a broker-in-charge.

The most misunderstood of the three broker-in-charge triggering requirements for sole proprietors cited above is # (2): *"... engages in advertising or promoting his or her services as a broker in any manner."* Acts of a sole proprietor that trigger the BIC requirement under # (2) include, but are not limited to: Placing an advertisement for his or her services as a broker in any form or any medium; distributing business cards indicating he or she is a real estate broker; orally soliciting the real estate business of others; or listing a property for sale (which inherently involves holding oneself out as a broker and advertising).

Therefore, *a broker-sole proprietor may lawfully provide only limited brokerage services without designating himself or herself as a BIC.* A couple of examples of *permissible* brokerage activities by a broker-sole proprietor who is NOT a designated BIC include receiving a referral fee from another broker or brokerage firm for referring business to the broker or firm or representing a relative or friend as a buyer's broker in a sales transaction provided the broker has not solicited the business, has not advertised or promoted his or her services, and does not hold earnest money beyond the time it is required to be deposited in a trust account.

The practical effect of these requirements is that a broker who will be operating independently in most cases must also designate himself or herself as a BIC. The real significance of these requirements for a sole proprietor will be better understood when the qualification requirements to serve as a BIC are subsequently discussed.

Requirements for BIC-Eligible Status. Paragraph (e) of Rule A .0110 states that, in order for a broker to be designated as a BIC for a sole proprietorship, real estate firm, or branch office, the broker must FIRST have BIC Eligible status. A broker must request BIC Eligible status on a form provided by the Commission.

The qualifying requirements for BIC Eligible Status, pursuant to paragraph (e) of Rule A .0110, are:

- Broker license must be on "active" status but NOT on "provisional" status. A provisional broker is ineligible to serve as broker-in-charge, as is a broker whose license is inactive or expired.

- Broker must have at least 2 years of full-time or 4 years of part-time real estate brokerage experience within the previous 5 years or be a North Carolina licensed attorney with a practice that consisted primarily of handling real estate closings and related matters in North Carolina for 3 years immediately preceding application. The requirement is for actual brokerage experience, not just having a license on "active" status. Note that by submission of the request form to the Commission, a broker certifies that he or she possesses the required experience. The Commission may at its discretion require the broker to provide evidence of possessing the required experience.

- After obtaining BIC Eligible status, a broker must complete the Commission's 12-hour Broker-In-Charge Course within 120 days of designation (unless the 12-hour course has been taken within the previous year). Failure to complete this course within 120 days will result in the broker losing BIC Eligible status. The broker must then take the course before he or she may again be granted BIC Eligible status.

Requesting Designation as Broker-in-Charge (BIC). A broker who has BIC Eligible status may request BIC Designation on a form provided by the Commission at any time so long as the broker continuously maintains his/her BIC Eligible status. The broker may also request BIC Eligible status and BIC Designation simultaneously.

Broker-In-Charge (BIC) Duties. The designated broker-in-charge is the primary person the Commission will hold responsible for the supervision and management of an office. See paragraph (g) of Rule A.0110 for a list of the specific responsibilities of a broker-in-charge.

Maintaining BIC Eligible Status. To maintain BIC Eligible status, paragraph (g) of Rule A.0110 requires that a broker must:

• Renew his or her broker license in a timely manner each license year and keep the license on active status at all times.

• Complete each license year the four-hour mandatory Broker-in-Charge Update Course (BICUP) as well as any approved four-hour CE elective.

The broker must begin taking the BICUP course during the same license year of designation, unless the broker completed the General Update (GENUP) course prior to designation.

The BICUP Course satisfies the broker's four-hour mandatory continuing education Update course requirement. If a broker with BIC Eligible status fails to take both the BICUP and one elective CE course by June 10 in any given year when required, then the broker will lost BIC Eligible status, and BIC designation if applicable, the following July 1.

Termination of BIC Eligible Status and Broker-In-Charge Designation. Paragraph (i) of Rule A.0110 provides that a broker's BIC Eligible status, and, if currently designated as a BIC, his or her BIC designation, shall be terminated if the broker: made any false statements or presented any false, incomplete, or incorrect information in connection with an application; fails to complete the 12-hour Broker-in-Charge Course pursuant to Paragraph (e) of the Rule; fails to timely renew his or her broker license, or the broker's license has been suspended, revoked, or surrendered; or fails to timely complete the Broker-in-Charge Update Course (BICUP) and a four credit hour elective course in any license year.

Regaining Lost BIC Eligible Status and BIC Designation. Pursuant to Rule A .0110(m), once a broker's BIC Eligible status has been terminated, the broker must complete the following steps in the order prescribed to regain the status:

1. The broker must first have a license on active status. If the license has expired, it must first be reinstated. If the license is inactive due to a CE deficiency, then the licensee must first complete whatever CE is necessary to reactivate the license and in either case, must then submit a reactivation form to the Commission requesting that the license be placed back on active status. A broker who has lost his or her BIC Eligible status should not take either the 12-hour BIC Course or the BICUP course prior to officially reactivating his/her license with the Commission.

2. Once back on active status, the broker must possess the experience required for initial designation and must first complete the 12-hour BIC Course prior to requesting BIC Eligible status and re-designation as a BIC regardless of when the broker may have previously taken the 12-hour course. There are no exceptions to this requirement to retake the 12-hour course prior to re-designation.

Notice to Commission When BIC Status Ends. A BIC must notify the Commission in writing within 10 days upon ceasing to serve as BIC of a particular office. [See Paragraph (g).]

Exception for certain Subchapter S corporations. See Paragraph (c).

Nonresidents. Nonresident individuals and firms holding a NC broker and/or firm license and engaging in brokerage activity in NC are subject to the same requirements as NC resident brokers/firms with regard to when they must have a designated broker-in-charge. Thus, a nonresident company engaging in brokerage in NC must have a broker-in-charge of the company who holds an active NC broker license for purposes of its NC business, although the office need not be physically located in North Carolina. Similarly, a nonresident NC broker sole practitioner engaging in activity that triggers the broker-in-charge requirement for a resident NC broker sole practitioner (see previous discussion on this subject) also must be designated as a broker-in-charge for NC brokerage purposes as without a BIC, a company has no office anywhere.

Education Exception for Certain Nonresident NC Brokers-In-Charge: A nonresident NC broker who has attained BIC Eligible status and been designated as the broker-in-charge of an office NOT located in NC and who has no office, primary residence or mailing address in North Carolina is NOT required to complete four-hour mandatory Broker-in-Charge Update (BICUP) Course to maintain BIC Eligible status. [See Rule 58A .1711.] However, a nonresident broker who has attained BIC-Eligible status IS REQUIRED to complete the 12-hour BIC Course pursuant to paragraph (e) of Rule A .0110.

Drafting Legal Instruments [Rule A.0111]

This rule prohibits licensees from drafting legal instruments, e.g., contracts, deeds, deeds of trust, etc., but does allow them to fill in the blanks on preprinted sales or lease contract forms, which is not construed to be the unauthorized practice of law.

Offers and Sales Contracts [Rule A.0112]

This rule specifies what minimum terms must be contained in any preprinted offer or sales contract form a licensee, acting as an agent, proposes for use by a party in a real estate transaction.

Reporting Criminal Convictions [Rule A.0113]

Licensees are required to report to the Commission any criminal convictions for a felony or misdemeanor, any disciplinary action taken against them by any other occupational licensing board, or any restriction, suspension or revocation of a notarial commission within sixty (60) days of the final judgment or order in the case. This reporting requirement is ongoing in nature. *Note that Driving While Impaired (DWI) is a misdemeanor and must be reported!*

Residential Property and Owners' Association Disclosure Statement [Rule A.0114]

State law (Chapter 47E of the General Statutes) requires that most residential property owners complete a disclosure form to give to prospective purchasers. The form seeks to elicit information about the condition of the property by asking various questions, to which owners may answer "yes," "no," or "no representation." Failure to provide a buyer with this form may allow the buyer to cancel the contract by notifying the seller in writing within three calendar days of contract acceptance.

Note: Licensees in residential real estate transactions have a duty under G.S. 47E-8 to inform their clients of the client's rights and obligations under the statute. The Real Estate Commission also views the Real Estate License Law as imposing on licensees working with sellers and buyers certain additional responsibilities to ensure statutory compliance and serve their clients' interests. Licensees are expected to "assist" sellers with completion of the form but should not complete the form for a seller or advise a seller as to what representation (or No Representation) to make. That being said, licensees should be certain to advise sellers that the licensee is obligated by law to disclose all material facts about or relating to the seller's property to prospective buyers regardless of what representation the seller makes on the disclosure form. See the Commission's *North Carolina Real Estate Manual* for a full discussion of the disclosure law and an agent's duties.

Sellers must also provide a Mineral and Oil and Gas Mandatory Disclosure Statement (MOGS) to buyers prior to making an offer to purchase and contract. The form has been developed by the Real Estate Commission and is available for download from the Commission's website, www.ncrec.gov. It is a separate form and is in addition to the Residential Property and Owner's Association Statement. A disclosure statement is not required for some transaction. For a complete list of exemptions, see G.S. 47E-2.

Broker's Responsibility for Closing Statements [G.S. 93A-6(a)(14)]

The cited statute requires a broker, "…at the time a sales transaction is consummated, to deliver to the broker's client a detailed and accurate closing statement showing the receipt and disbursement of all monies relating to the transaction about which the broker knows or reasonably should know." The statute goes on to provide that if a closing statement is prepared by an attorney or lawful settlement agent, a broker may rely on the delivery of that statement, but *the broker must review the statement for accuracy and notify all parties to the closing of any errors.* Since virtually every residential transaction in North Carolina is closed by an attorney (or lawful settlement agent), it is standard practice for brokers to adopt the attorney's settlement statement to satisfy this License Law requirement.

Commission Guidelines. A settlement statement is a detailed report of all monies received and disbursed by the settlement agent in connection with a real estate sales transaction. It is essential that the settlement statement be accurate and that a copy be provided to each party. The settlement statement is prepared by the settlement agent – the individual conducting the closing, which in North Carolina is almost always the closing attorney or a nonlawyer assistant working under the supervision of the closing attorney.

The TRID (Tila-RESPA Integrated Disclosures) rule became effective October 3, 2015, and applied to loan applications received on or after October 3, 2015. The TRID rule replaced the HUD-1 settlement statement (RESPA) and final Truth-in-Lending statement (TILA) with two Closing Disclosure (CD) documents, one for the borrower and a separate one for the seller. Closing disclosures are disclosures only and are not equivalent to a settlement statement. While the HUD-1 is no longer used in TRID-governed transactions, other types of settlement statements may be used, such as settlement/closing statements created and published by the American Land Title Association (ALTA). Also, the HUD-1 may be used as the settlement statement in non-TRID-governed transactions, such as cash transactions, construction loans, or purchases of investment property.

The Commission has published in its North Carolina Real Estate Manual the following guidelines regarding brokers' responsibilities for settlement statements:

- A broker must confirm the accuracy of all entries about which s/he has direct knowledge. Such items include, but may not be limited to: the sale price; amount of the due diligence fee and earnest money deposit; amount of the brokerage commission and split; any amounts due either party under the offer to purchase and contract, e.g., closing costs paid by seller, as well as any sums paid by or due to third parties related to the transaction, if the broker knows or should know about the expense.
- As to amounts paid by or due to third parties, brokers generally may assume that the amounts for charges and fees as stated on the settlement statement are correct unless there is something that would lead a reasonable broker to suspect that an amount is incorrect. As to all debits and credits related to the transaction, whether paid before or at closing, the broker must:
  1) review and confirm that all charges and credits have been properly debited or credited to the seller or buyer and are entered in the correct column; and
  2) review and confirm the accuracy of the calculations for all prorated items, escrow reserves, interim interest, excise tax and the "bottom line figures," i.e., total settlement charges to each party, cash from borrower-buyer, and cash to seller.
- If a broker is aware of any expense related to the transaction paid to or by either party or any third party that is not included on the settlement statement, the broker must notify both the settlement agent and the lender of the omission, as the settlement statement should reflect all expenses and payments related to the transaction, not just monies the settlement agent

disburses.
- A broker should notify the settlement agent if the broker believes there are any errors or omissions on the statement.

HANDLING TRUST FUNDS

This section addresses those aspects of handling trust funds that are taught in the Real Estate Broker Prelicensing Course and tested on the real estate license examination for entry-level brokers. All brokers are encouraged to take the Basic Trust Account course for a fuller treatment of this subject. The Basic Trust Account course schedule is available on the Commission's website at www.ncrec.gov.

Definition of Trust Money

In the context of real estate transactions, "**trust money**" is most easily defined as *money belonging to others received by a real estate broker who is acting* **as an agent** *in a real estate transaction.* It is *also any money held by a licensee who acts as the temporary custodian of funds belonging to others.* Such money must be held in trust even if the circumstances are only collateral to the licensee's role as an agent in a real estate related matter, e.g., a listing agent receives monies from his out of town seller for yard maintenance while the property is being marketed. The most common examples of trust money are:
- Earnest money deposits
- Down payments
- Tenant security deposits
- Rents
- Homeowner association dues and assessments, and
- Money received from final settlements

In the case of resort and other short-term rentals, trust money also includes:
- Advance reservation deposits
- State (and local, if applicable) sales taxes on the gross receipts from such rentals

Trust or Escrow Account [G.S. 93A-6(a)(12) & (g); 93A-45(c); Rule A.0116, .0117]

One of the most basic tenets of broker accountability when handling trust money is that it must be deposited into a trust or escrow account as described below. A "trust account" or "escrow account" (the terms are synonymous for Commission purposes) is simply a bank account into which trust money (and *only* trust money) is deposited. The three primary features of a trust or escrow account are that it is:
1) **separate**, containing only monies belonging to others,
2) **custodial**, meaning *only the broker or the broker's designated employee has disbursement control over the account,* but no one who has funds in the account has that ability, **and**
3) **available on demand**, that is, the funds may be withdrawn at any time without prior notice.

Type and Location of Trust Account. A broker's trust account or escrow account must be:

1) a demand deposit account
2) in a federally insured depository institution
3) lawfully doing business in North Carolina
4) that agrees to make the account records available for inspection by Commission representatives. [G.S. 93A-6(g)]

Thus, for the purpose of holding most trust money, the bank can be located outside North Carolina if the foregoing conditions are met.

Designation of Trust Account and FDIC Insurance. A broker-in-charge who must maintain a trust account must ensure that the bank properly designates the account and that the words "trust account" or "escrow account" appear on all signature cards, bank statements, deposit tickets and checks. Even though the escrow account typically is in the name of the company or broker, so long as the broker properly designates the account as a "trust" or "escrow" account and keeps accurate records that identify each owner of the funds and/or depositor (buyer, seller, lessor, lessee, etc.), the depositors are protected from the funds being "frozen" or attached if the broker/trustee becomes insolvent, incapacitated, dies, has tax liens, becomes involved in a lawsuit, etc. Failure to properly designate an account titled in the name of the company/broker as a trust or escrow account may result in attachment of the account by others to collect a judgment or denial of FDIC insurance coverage as to each individual's interest in the account.

So long as the account is properly designated as a trust/escrow account, *all deposits are insured by the Federal Deposit Insurance Corporation (FDIC) up to $250,000* **per each individual** *for whom funds are held.* Thus, a broker's trust account may contain $500,000 total, but *all funds are fully insured so long as no one individual's interest in the account exceeds $250,000.* (**Note**, however, that an individual still may be underinsured if the individual maintains accounts in his/her individual name at the same financial institution as the broker's trust/escrow account.)

When a Trust Account Is Required. A broker must open and maintain a trust account when the broker or any affiliated licensee takes possession of trust money. A broker who is inactive or otherwise not using his/her real estate license is not required to open or maintain a trust account because s/he should not be engaged in brokerage nor receiving monies belonging to others. Similarly, if an *active* practicing broker does not collect or otherwise handle the funds of others, no trust account is required. Note: A broker who leases residential property he or she owns to tenants may be required to maintain a trust account under 42-50 NC Residential Landlord Tenant law.

Number of Trust Accounts. Except for brokers who are managing homeowner or property owner association funds, a broker holding trust money is only required to have one trust account. All earnest money deposits, tenant security deposits, rents, and other trust monies may be deposited into this one common trust account. However, brokers who are active in both sales and property management often find it helpful to use more than one trust account. For example, they may wish to keep a "general sales trust account" for earnest money deposits, settlement proceeds, etc., and a "rental trust account" for tenant security deposits, rents, and related receipts. Although it is not required, many brokers involved in property management and leasing elect to maintain an additional "security deposit trust account" to keep tenant security deposits separate from rents and other related receipts. However, **Rule A.0118(a)** requires brokers who handle homeowner or property owner association funds to maintain a *separate trust account for each property owner association or homeowner association they manage*. The funds of one homeowner association are not to be commingled with funds from any other association nor with any general trust monies. The broker also must provide the association with periodic written statements not less than once each quarter reporting all monies received, disbursed, and due, but not paid (i.e., delinquent), as well as the balance of funds in the account.

"Commingling" Prohibited. [G.S. 93A-6(a)(12)] The basic statutory provision relating to a licensee's handling of the money or property of others states that a broker may not "commingle" his or her own money or property with the money or property of others. This means that a broker may not maintain funds belonging to others in the same bank account that contains his or her personal or business funds. Funds belonging to others must be held in a trust account and, except as described below regarding "bank service charges on trust accounts," a broker may not deposit his or her own funds in that trust account. The prohibition against commingling also means, for example, that a broker who has an ownership interest in property is precluded from depositing monies (e.g., earnest money, rent, security deposits, etc.) related to that property in his brokerage trust account.

Bank Service Charges on Trust Accounts. Trust accounts usually are subject to the same service charges as regular checking accounts. Whenever possible, brokers should arrange for the depository/bank either to bill the broker for these expenses or charge these expenses to the broker's personal or general operating account. However, if such arrangements cannot be made, the Commission will permit a broker to deposit and maintain in his trust account a maximum of $100.00 of his personal funds (or such other amount as may be required) to cover (not avoid) such charges. So, if a broker's monthly service charges and other fees typically are $100, then the broker may deposit up to $200 of his/her own money to *cover* these charges. A broker who deposits any of his/her own money in the trust account to cover bank charges must be careful to properly enter and identify these personal funds in his/her trust account records by use of a personal funds ledger. While this technically constitutes "commingling," it is permissible commingling to avoid the greater evil of using other people's money to pay these bank charges.

Interest-Bearing Trust Account. Both G. S. 93A-6(a)(12) and Rule A.0116(c) permit a broker to deposit trust money into an interest-bearing trust account so long as the broker first obtains written authorization for deposit in an interest-bearing account from all parties having an interest in the monies being held. Such authorization must specify how and to whom the interest will be paid. If the authorization is contained in an offer, contract, lease or other transaction instrument, it must be set forth in a conspicuous manner that distinguishes it from other provisions of the instrument. Remember, however, that all trust accounts must be a *demand account*, so investment of trust monies in any type of security, such as a government bond or a fixed term certificate of deposit, is prohibited.

Broker-In-Charge Responsible for Trust Accounts. [Rule A.0117; Rule A.0110(g)(4)] Rule A.0117(a) requires a broker to maintain complete records showing the deposit, maintenance and withdrawal of money belonging to the broker's principals or *held in escrow or in trust for the broker's principals*. Paragraph (h) of that rule also provides that the Commission may inspect trust account records periodically without prior notice and whenever the records are pertinent to investigation of a complaint against a licensee. Rule A.0110(g)(4) refines this requirement by specifying that a **broker-in-charge (BIC)** *is responsible for the proper maintenance of real estate trust accounts and records pertaining thereto*.

Custodian of Trust Account Records Other Than the Broker-In-Charge. While a broker-in-charge may transfer possession of trust money to a bookkeeper, secretary, or some other clerical employee to record and deposit the funds in a trust account and to maintain trust account records, the broker-in-charge nonetheless remains responsible for the care and custody of such funds. Brokers-in-charge should closely and diligently supervise the acts of all persons having access to the trust account, since final accountability for the accuracy and integrity of the account rests with the broker-in-charge. *Access to trust money should be limited and carefully controlled.*

Disbursement of Earnest Money [Rule A0116(e)] This rule permits a broker-in-charge to transfer an earnest money deposit from his/her trust account to the closing attorney or other settlement agent not more than ten (10) days prior to the anticipated settlement date. Earnest money may **not** be disbursed prior to settlement for any other purpose without the written consent of the parties. Thus, earnest money may not be used by the broker to pay for inspection reports or other services on behalf of the buyer prior to settlement without the written consent of the seller, and vice-versa.

Disputed Trust Funds. Rule A.0116(d) addresses disputed trust funds as follows: "In the event of a dispute between buyer and seller or landlord and tenant over the return or forfeiture of any deposit other than a residential tenant security deposit held by a broker, the broker shall retain said deposit in a trust or escrow account until the broker has obtained a written release from the parties consenting to its disposition or until disbursement is ordered by a court of competent jurisdiction." The rule also references the G.S. 93A-12 procedures for depositing disputed funds with the Clerk of Court as well as when one party abandons his or her claim to the disputed funds. However, these procedures are beyond the scope of these materials and are more important for brokers-in-charge to know.

Handling of Trust Money [Rule A.0116(a), (b) & (g)]

The **general rule** is that all trust monies received by a licensee must be deposited in a trust account **within three banking days of receipt**. **Exception: Earnest money** received with offers to purchase and **tenant security deposits** in connection with leases must be deposited in a trust account *not later than three banking days following* **acceptance** *of the offer to purchase or lease agreement* **unless** *the deposit is tendered in* **cash** *in which event it must be deposited within* **three banking days following receipt, even if the contract or lease has not been accepted.** In part, this is because cash is immediately available and may be refunded within a day of deposit, unlike checks which may require a few days to clear.

Understand that a broker *may* choose to immediately deposit a check received for an earnest money deposit or tenant security deposit and is *not required* to wait until contract acceptance unless so instructed by the buyer/tenant. Of course, early deposit may cause problems if the offer to purchase or lease is not accepted and the prospective buyer or tenant understandably wants their deposit to be immediately returned. The date of acceptance should be shown in the purchase or lease agreement to determine when the three banking days begins.

Receipt of Trust Money by Provisional Broker. [Rule A.0116(b)(1)&(2), Rule A.1808.] *All trust money received by a* **provisional broker** *must be delivered immediately to the provisional broker's broker-in-charge.* In other words, provisional brokers may not retain or hold trust money any longer than absolutely necessary to deliver the trust money to his/her broker-in-charge. Similarly, trust monies received by a **nonresident limited commercial broker** are to be delivered immediately to and held by the resident North Carolina broker with whom the nonresident is affiliated. Brokers-in-charge should have written policies that clearly state the procedures to be followed when *any agent* affiliated with the company, whether a provisional or non-provisional broker, receives trust monies.

Handling Option Money and Due Diligence Fee. Rule A.0116(b)(4) states in part: "A broker may accept custody of a **check or other negotiable instrument** *made payable to the seller* of real property as payment for an **option or due diligence fee**, but only for the purpose of delivering the instrument to the seller. While the instrument is in the custody of the broker, the broker shall, according to the instructions of the buyer, either deliver it to the seller or return it to the buyer. The broker shall safeguard the instrument and shall be responsible to the parties on the instrument for its safe delivery as required by this Rule. A broker shall not retain such an instrument for more than three business days after the acceptance of the option or other sales contract."

The rule is basically self-explanatory. In the rule, "custody" means possession. Recall that option money or a due diligence fee is paid directly to the seller, to whom the check is written as payee, and so it is not appropriate for a broker to deposit these checks into his/her trust account because the check is not payable to the broker or real estate company as is the case with earnest money checks. Either the listing agent or buyer's agent may hold the check or negotiable instrument until negotiations are completed and a contract is formed, at which point the check should be delivered to the seller as soon as possible.

If, however, a buyer for some reason gives a broker *cash for the option money or due diligence fee*, then the broker must *immediately deposit the cash in his/her trust account* pending contract formation as *cash must* **always** *be deposited into a trust account within* **three banking days of receipt — no exceptions**. If the parties enter into a contract, then the broker would write a check from the trust account payable to the seller, noting in the memo section and trust account records that it is for the option fee or due diligence fee from the buyer.

Safeguarding Trust Money; Improper Use of Trust Money. [Rule A.0116(g)] This rule places on *every licensee* the responsibility to safeguard the money or property of others coming into his or her possession according to the requirements of the License Law and Commission rules. In addition, it states that: "A broker shall not convert the money or property of others to his or her own use, apply such money or property to a purpose other than that for which it was intended or permit or assist any other person in the conversion or misapplication of such money or property."

BROKER PRICE OPINION AND COMPARATIVE MARKET ANALYSIS
[G.S. 93A, Article 6; Commission Rules Chapter 58A, Section .2200]

Definitions. General Statute §93A-82 of the North Carolina Real Estate License Law and General Statute §93E-1-4(7c) of the North Carolina Appraisers Act both define a **"broker price opinion" ("BPO")** and a **"comparative market analysis" ("CMA")** as "…an estimate prepared by a licensed real estate broker that details the probable selling price or leasing price of a particular parcel of or interest in property and provides a varying level of detail about the property's condition, market, and neighborhood, and information on comparable properties, but does not include an automated valuation model." Thus, *the terms "BPO" and "CMA" have exactly the same legal meaning* even though an estimate provided for a seller or buyer client or prospective client is most commonly referred to as a CMA and an estimate performed for a third party for a purpose other than mortgage loan origination (for example, a foreclosure or short sale decision) is typically referred to as a BPO.

- A "non-provisional" broker with a current license on "active" status may prepare a broker price opinion

(BPO) or comparative market analysis (CMA) for a fee for a variety of persons and entities for a variety of reasons, not just for actual or prospective brokerage clients. Note, however, that a provisional broker may NOT perform a BPO or CMA for a fee for anyone. [G.S. §93A-83(a) and (b)]

- A broker may **NOT** prepare a BPO (or CMA) for an existing or potential lienholder or other third party where the BPO is to serve as the basis to determine the **value** of a property *for the purpose of originating a mortgage loan*, including first and second mortgages, refinances or equity lines of credit. [G.S. §93A-83(b)(6)]
- A BPO or CMA may only estimate the *"probable selling price"* or *"probable leasing price"* of a property, not the "value" of a property. Moreover, if a BPO or CMA does propose to estimate the "value" or "worth" of a property, it shall be legally considered a "real estate appraisal" that may only be prepared by a licensed or certified real estate appraiser, not by a real estate broker. [G.S. §93A-83(f)]
- A BPO or CMA provided *for a fee* must be performed in accordance with the requirements of Article 6 of the Real Estate License Law and standards set forth in rules adopted by the North Carolina Real Estate Commission. [Rules, Ch. 58, Section A.2200]
- A BPO or CMA must be *in writing* and must address those matters specifically required by the statute or Commission rule. [G.S. §93A-83(c)]

Standards for BPOs and CMAs Performed for Compensation. Article 6 of the Real Estate License Law provides a number of standards that must be followed when a broker is performing a BPO/CMA for a fee. Additionally, the Commission has adopted rules (Section A.2200) setting forth specific standards for brokers when performing such standards. A broker performing a BPO/CMA utilizes the same valuation concepts and methodology as an appraiser performing an appraisal; however, the analysis associated with a BPO/CMA is less comprehensive and detailed than with an appraisal, and the regulatory standards for brokers performing BPOs/CMAs are less stringent than those required for real estate appraisers performing appraisals. [See G.S. 93A-83 and especially Commission Rule 58A.2202.]

Reporting Probable Selling/Leasing Price as a "Range." In recognition of the fact that brokers performing BPOs/CMAs are not expected to be as precise in their analysis and adjustments to comparable properties as an appraiser when performing an appraisal, the Commision's rules permit reporting in a BPO/CMA of probable selling price or leasing price (lease rate) as either a single figure or as a **price range.** The applicable rules also states: "When the estimate states a price range and the higher figure exceeds the lower figure by more than ten (10%), the broker shall include an explanation as to why the variance is more than 10 percent. [Rule A.2202(h)]

Use of Income Analysis Methodology Now Required Where Appropriate. The revised statutes eliminated the old Appraisers Act restriction that a broker's CMA for actual or prospective clients *and for compensation* was permitted only if the sales comparison approach was the only method used to derive an indication of the probable sales price. A broker performing a BPO or CMA to determine an estimated *"probable selling price or leasing price"* is now *required* to utilize methods involving the analysis of income where appropriate (i.e., income capitalization or gross rent multiplier methodology for income-producing properties) as well as the sales comparison method. [G.S. §93A-83(c)(3) and Commission Rule A.2202(e)]

Competence to Perform BPO/CMA. Although Article 6 of the License Law and Section A.2200 of the Commission's rules do not specifically require a broker to perform a BPO/CMA in **competent** manner, the reader should remember that the License Law has always made incompetence a basis for disciplinary action and those provisions also apply to the performance of BPOs and CMAs. If a broker is not qualified by way of education and experience to properly utilize the appropriate methodology required for a particular property (for example, income capitalization for a commercial property), then the broker is expected to decline the assignment.

CMAs/BPOs Performed for NO FEE. Any broker *(non-provisional or provisional)* has always been permitted to perform a BPO/CMA for any party when NO FEE is charged, and this continues to be the case under the revised law and rules. Note that *the Commission does not consider compensation of a broker for general brokerage services under a brokerage agreement to constitute a "fee" under Article 6 of N.C.G.S. §93A.* "General brokerage services" means services provided under a brokerage agreement to property owners in connection with listing/selling/leasing property and to prospective buyers or tenants in connection with purchasing or leasing a property. Such services include the provision by a licensee of a CMA or BPO. Similarly, the possibility of entering into a brokerage agreement (and earning a brokerage fee) does not constitute a "fee" when a licensee performs a CMA/BPO for a *prospective* client without charging a fee for the CMA/BPO. *It is important for licensees to remember, however, that the Commission expects every CMA/BPO performed by a licensee to be performed in a competent manner and without any undisclosed conflict of interest, even if no fee is received for the CMA/BPO. Thus, as a practical matter, a licensee performing a CMA/BPO for no fee should still look to the standards described in Commission Rule 58A .2202 for guidance regarding the proper performance of a CMA/BPO.*

For a full explanation of the law and rules governing BPOs and CMAs, and a Sales Comparison Analysis Illustration, the reader is referred to the Commission's *North Carolina Real Estate Manual,* **which may be ordered through the Commission's website at <u>www.ncrec.gov</u>.**

RESIDENTIAL SQUARE FOOTAGE GUIDELINES

APPENDIX D

INTRODUCTION

It is often said that the three most important factors in making a homebuying decision are "location," "location," and "location." Other than "location," the single most-important factor is probably the size or "square footage" of the home. Not only is it an indicator of whether a particular home will meet a homebuyer's space needs, but it also affords a convenient (though not always accurate) method for the buyer to estimate the value of the home and compare it with other properties.

Although real estate agents are not required by the Real Estate License Law or Real Estate Commission rules to report the square footage of properties offered for sale (or rent), when they do report square footage, it is essential that the information they give prospective purchasers be accurate. At a minimum, information concerning square footage should include the amount of *living area* in the dwelling. The following guidelines and accompanying illustrations are designed to assist real estate brokers in measuring, calculating, and reporting (both orally and in writing) the *living area* contained in detached and attached single-family residential buildings. When reporting square footage, real estate agents should carefully follow these *Guidelines* or any other standards that are comparable to them, including those approved by the American National Standards Institute, Inc. (ANSI), which are recognized by the North Carolina Real Estate Commission as comparable standards.* Agents should be prepared to identify, when requested, the standard used.

Real estate appraisers and lenders generally adhere to more detailed criteria in arriving at the *living area* or "gross living area" of residential dwellings. This normally includes distinguishing "above-grade" from "below-grade" area, which is also required by many multiple listing services. "Above-Grade" is defined as space on any level of a dwelling which has *living area* and no earth adjacent to any exterior wall on that level. "Below-Grade" is space on any level which has *living area*, is accessible by interior stairs, and has earth adjacent to any exterior wall on that level. If earth is adjacent to any portion of a wall, the entire level is considered "below-grade." Space that is "at" or "on grade" is considered "above-grade."

While real estate agents are encouraged to provide the most complete information available about properties offered for sale, the *Guidelines* recognize that the separate reporting of "above-grade" and "below-grade" area can be impractical in the advertising and marketing of homes. For this reason, *real estate agents*

---

*The following materials were consulted in the development of these *Guidelines*: The *American National Standard for Single-Family Residential Buildings; Square Footage-Method for Calculating* approved by the American National Standards Institute, Inc.; *House Measuring & Square Footage* published by the Carolina Multiple Listing Services, Inc.; and materials compiled by Bart T. Bryson, MAI, SRA, and Mary L. D'Angelo. Copyright ©1999 by North Carolina Real Estate Commission. All rights reserved. 0,000 copies of this public document were printed at a cost of $.000 per copy. REC 3.40 5/1/05 *are permitted under these Guidelines to report square footage of the dwelling as the total "living area"* without a separate distinction between "above-grade" and "below-grade" areas. However, to help avoid confusion and concern, agents should alert purchasers and sellers that the appraisal report may reflect differences in the way *living area* is defined and described by the lender, appraiser, and the *North Carolina Building Code* which could affect the amount of *living area* reported.

LIVING AREA CRITERIA

Living area (sometimes referred to as "heated living area" or "heated square footage") is space that is intended for human occupancy and is:

1. ***heated*** by a conventional heating system or systems (forced air, radiant, solar, etc.) that are permanently installed in the dwelling—not a portable heater—which generates heat sufficient to make the space suitable for year-round occupancy;

2. ***finished***, with walls, floors and ceilings of materials generally accepted for interior construction (e.g., painted drywall/ sheet rock or panelled walls, carpeted or hardwood flooring, etc.) and with a ceiling height of at least 7 feet, except under beams, ducts, etc. where the height must be at least 6 feet 4 inches *[Note: In rooms with sloped ceilings (e.g., finished attics, bonus rooms, etc.) you may also include as living area the portion of the room with a ceiling height of at least 5 feet if at least half of the finished area of the room has a ceiling height of at least 7 feet.]*; and

3. ***directly accessible from other living area*** (through a door or by a heated hallway or stairway).

Determining whether an area is considered *living area* can sometimes be confusing. Finished rooms used for general living (living room, dining room, kitchen, den, bedrooms, etc.) are normally included in *living area*. For other areas in the dwelling, the determination may not be so easy. *For example, the following areas are considered* **living area** *if they meet the criteria (i.e., heated, finished, directly accessible from living area):*

- ***Attic***, but note in the listing data that the space is located in an attic (Fig. 2). *[Note: if the ceiling is sloped, remember to apply the "ceiling height" criteria.]*

- ***Basement (or "Below-Grade")***, but note in the listing data that the space is located in a basement or "below-grade" (Fig. 1). *[Note: For reporting purposes, a "basement" is defined as an area below the entry level of the dwelling which is accessible by a **full** fight of stairs and has earth adjacent to some portion of at least one wall above the floor level.]*

- ***Bay Window***, if it has a floor, a ceiling height of at least 7 feet, and otherwise meets the criteria for *living area* (Fig. 2).

- ***Bonus Room (e.g., Finished Room over Garage)*** (Fig. 3). *[Note: If the ceiling is sloped, remember to apply the "ceiling height" criteria.]*

- *Breezeway* (enclosed).
- *Chimney*, if the chimney base is inside *living area*. If the chimney base is outside the *living area* but the hearth is in the *living area*, include the hearth in the *living area* but not the chimney base (Fig. 1).
- *Closets*, if they are a functional part of the *living area*.
- *Dormers* (Fig. 6).
- *Furnace (Mechanical) Room*. Also, in order to avoid excessive detail, if the furnace, water heater, etc. is located in a small closet in the *living area*, include it in *living area* even if it does not meet other *living area* criteria (Fig. 4).
- *Hallways*, if they are a functional part of the *living area*.
- *Laundry Room/Area* (Fig. 6).
- *Office* (Fig. 1).
- *Stairs*, if they meet the criteria and connect to *living area* (Fig. 1, 2, 3, 4, 5, 6). Include the stairway with the area from which it descends, **not to exceed the area of the opening in the floor**. If the opening for the stairway exceeds the length and width of the stairway, deduct the excess open space from the upper level area. Include as part of the lower level area the space beneath the stairway, regardless of its ceiling height.
- *Storage Room* (Fig. 6).

OTHER AREA

Note in the listing data and advise purchasers of any space that does not meet the criteria for *living area* but that contributes to the value of the dwelling; for example, unfinished basements, unfinished attics (with permanent stairs), unfinished bonus rooms, shops, decks, balconies, porches, garages, and carports.

HELPFUL HINTS

Concealed in the walls of nearly all residential construction are pipes, ducts, chases, returns, etc. necessary to support the structure's mechanical systems. Although they may occupy *living area*, to avoid excessive detail, do **not** deduct the space from the *living area*.

When measuring and reporting the *living area* of homes, be alert to any remodeling, room additions (e.g., an enclosed porch) or other structural modifications to assure that the space meets all the criteria for *living area*. **Pay particular attention to the heating criteria, because the heating system for the original structure may not be adequate for the increased square footage**. Although agents are not required to determine the adequacy of heating systems, they should at least note whether there are heat vents, radiators or other heat outlets in the room before deciding whether to include space as *living area*.

When an area that is not part of the *living area* (e.g., a garage) shares a common wall with the *living area*, treat the common wall as the exterior wall for the *living area*; therefore, the measurements for the living area will include the thickness of the common wall, and the measurements for the other area will not.

Interior space that is open from the floor of one level to the ceiling of the next higher level is included in the square footage for the lower level only. However, any area occupied by interior balconies, lofts, etc. on the upper level or stairs that extend to the upper level is included in the square footage for the upper level.

MEASURING

The amount of *living area* and "other area" in dwellings is based upon **exterior measurements**. A 100-foot-long tape measure is recommended for use in measuring the exterior of dwellings, and a 30-foot retractable tape for measuring interior and hard-to-reach spaces. A tape measure that indicates linear footage in "tenths of a foot" will greatly simplify your calculations. For best results, take a partner to assist you in measuring. But if you do not have someone to assist you, a screwdriver or other sharp tool can be used to secure the tape measure to the ground.

Begin at one corner of the dwelling and proceed with measuring each exterior wall. **Round off your measurements to the nearest inch** (or 10th-of-a-foot if your tape indicates footage in that manner). Make a sketch of the structure. Write down each measurement as you go, and record it on your sketch. A clipboard and graph paper are helpful in sketching the dwelling and recording the measurements. Measure *living area* and "other area," but identify them separately on your sketch. Look for offsets (portions of walls that "jut out"), and adjust for any "overlap" of exterior walls (Fig. 3) or "overhang" in upper levels (Fig. 5).

When you cannot measure an exterior surface (such as in the case of attics and below-grade areas), measure the perimeter walls of the area from the inside of the dwelling. Remember to add **6 inches** for each exterior wall and interior wall that you encounter in order to arrive at the exterior dimensions (Fig. 2, 3, 4, 6).

Measure all sides of the dwelling, making sure that the overall lengths of the front and rear sides are equal, as well as the ends. Then inspect the interior of the dwelling to identify spaces which cannot be included in *living area*. You may also find it helpful to take several photographs of the dwelling for later use when you return to your office.

CALCULATING SQUARE FOOTAGE

From your sketch of the dwelling, identify and separate *living area* from "other area." If your measurements are in inches (rather than 10ths-of-a-foot), convert your figures to a decimal as follows:

1" = .10 ft	7" = .60 ft.
2" = .20 ft	8" = .70 ft.
3" = .25 ft	9" = .75 ft.
4" = .30 ft	10" = .80 ft.
5" = .40 ft	11" = .90 ft.
6" = .50 ft	12" = 1.00 ft.

Calculate the *living area* (and other area) by multiplying the length times the width of each rectangular space. Then add your subtotals and round off your figure for total square footage to the nearest **square foot**. Double-check your calculations. When in doubt, re-check them and, if necessary, re-measure the house.

ATTACHED DWELLINGS

When measuring an "attached" single-family home (e.g., townhouse, duplex, condominium, etc.), use the same techniques just described. If there is a common wall, measure to the inside surface of the wall and add **6 inches**. *[Note: In the case of condominiums, do not include the thickness of exterior or common walls.]* Do not include any "common areas" (exterior hallways, stairways, etc.) in your calculations.

PROPOSED CONSTRUCTION

For proposed construction, your square footage calculations will be based upon dimensions described in blueprints and building plans. When reporting the projected square footage, be careful to disclose that you have calculated the square footage based upon plan dimensions. Therefore, the square footage may differ in the completed structure. Do not rely on any calculations printed on the plans.

AGENTS' RESPONSIBILITY

Real estate agents are expected to be able to accurately calculate the square footage of most dwellings. When reporting square footage, whether to a party to a real estate transaction, another real estate agent, or others, a real estate agent is expected to provide accurate square footage information that was compiled using these *Guidelines* or comparable standards. While an agent is expected to use reasonable skill, care, and diligence when calculating square footage, it should be noted that the Commission does not expect absolute perfection. Because all properties are unique and no guidelines can anticipate every possibility, minor discrepancies in deriving square footage are not considered by the Commission to constitute negligence on the part of the agent. Minor variations in tape readings and small differences in rounding off or conversion from inches to decimals, when multiplied over distances, will cause reasonable discrepancies between two competent measurements of the same dwelling. In addition to differences due to minor variations in measurement and calculation, discrepancies between measurements may also be attributable to reasonable differences in interpretation. For instance, two agents might reasonably differ about whether an addition to a dwelling is sufficiently finished under these *Guidelines* to be included within the measured living area. Differences which are based upon an agent's thoughtful judgment reasonably founded on these or other similar guidelines will not be considered by the Commission to constitute error on the agent's part. Deviations in calculated square footage of less than 5% will seldom be cause for concern.

As a general rule, the most reliable way for an agent to obtain accurate square footage data is by personally measuring the dwelling unit and calculating the square footage. It is especially recommended that *listing agents* use this approach for dwellings that are not particularly unusual or complex in their design.

As an alternative to personally measuring a dwelling and calculating its square footage, an agent may rely on the square footage reported by other persons when it is reasonable under the circumstances to do so. Generally speaking, an agent working with a buyer (either as a buyer's agent or as a seller's agent) may rely on the listing agent's square footage representations except in those unusual instances when there is an error in the reported square footage that should be obvious to a reasonably prudent agent. For example, a buyer's agent would not be expected to notice that a house advertised as containing 2,200 square feet of living area in fact contained only 2,000 square feet. On the other hand, that same agent, under most circumstances, would be expected to realize that a house described as containing 3,200 square feet really contained only 2,300 square feet of living area. If there is such a "red flag" regarding the reported square footage, the agent working with the buyer should promptly point out the suspected error to the buyer and the listing agent. The listing agent should then verify the square footage and correct any error in the information reported.

It is also appropriate for an agent to rely upon measurements and calculations performed by other professionals with greater expertise in determining square footage. A new agent who may be unsure of his or her own calculations should seek guidance from a more experienced agent. As the new agent gains experience and confidence, he or she will become less reliant on the assistance of others. In order to ensure accuracy of the square footage they report, even experienced agents may wish to rely upon a competent state-licensed or state-certified appraiser or another agent with greater expertise in determining square footage. For example, an agent might be confronted with an unusual measurement problem or a dwelling of complex design. The house described in Figure 8 in these *Guidelines* is such a property. When an agent relies upon measurements and calculations personally performed by a competent appraiser or a more expert agent, the appraiser or agent must use these *Guidelines* or other comparable standards and the square footage reported must be specifically determined in connection with the current transaction. An agent who relies on another's measurement would still be expected to recognize an obvious error in the reported square footage and to alert any interested parties.

Some sources of square footage information are by their very nature unreliable. For example, an agent should **not** rely on square footage information determined by the property owner or included in property tax records. An agent should also **not** rely on square footage information included in a listing, appraisal report, or survey prepared in connection with an earlier transaction.

In areas where the prevailing practice is to report square footage in the advertising and marketing of homes, agents whose policy is **not** to calculate and report square footage must disclose this fact to prospective buyer and seller clients before entering into agency agreements with them.

ILLUSTRATIONS

For assistance in calculating and reporting the area of homes, refer to the following illustrations showing the *living area* shaded. To test your knowledge, an illustration and blank "Worksheet" for a home with a more challenging floor plan has also been included. (A completed "Worksheet" for the Practice Floor Plan can be found on page 830.) In reviewing the illustrations, assume that for those homes with basements, attics, etc., the exterior measurements shown have been derived from interior measurements taking into account walls and partitions. Where there is a common wall between *living area* and other area, the measurements shown in the illustrations include the thickness of the common wall in *living area* except in the condominium example where wall thickness is not included.

APPENDIX D Residential Square Footage Guidelines

ONE STORY WITH BASEMENT AND CARPORT

(Figure 1)

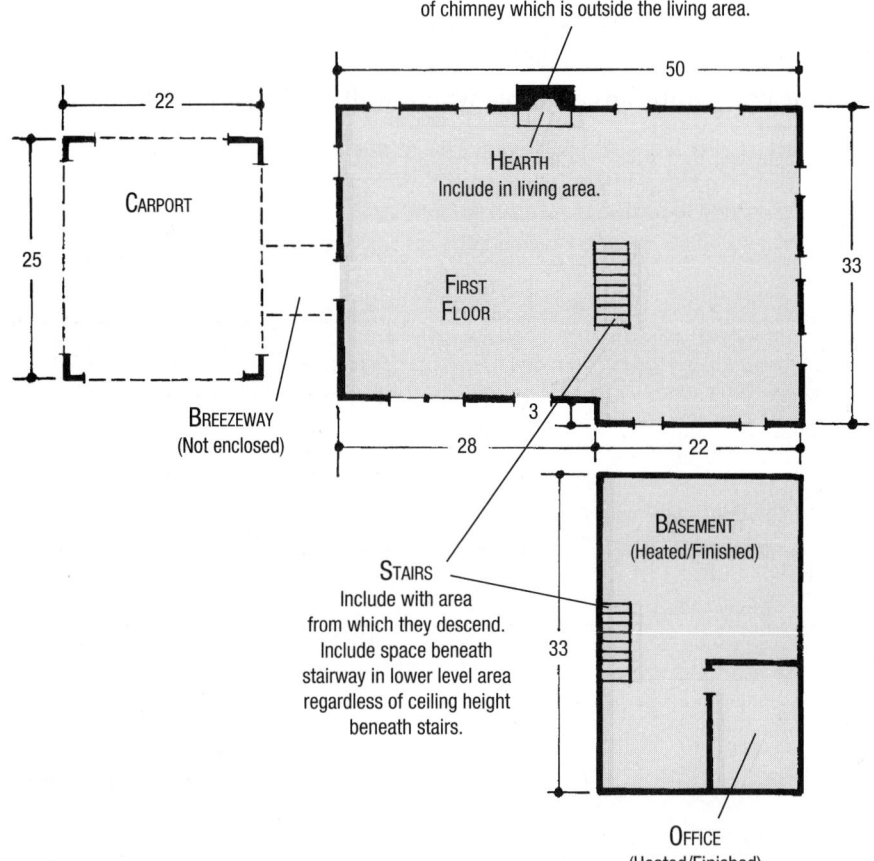

Chimney
Do not include in living area the portion of chimney which is outside the living area.

Hearth
Include in living area.

Carport

Breezeway
(Not enclosed)

First Floor

Stairs
Include with area from which they descend. Include space beneath stairway in lower level area regardless of ceiling height beneath stairs.

Basement
(Heated/Finished)

Office
(Heated/Finished)

APPENDIX D Residential Square Footage Guidelines

ONE STORY WITH BASEMENT AND CARPORT WORKSHEET

\multicolumn{4}{c}{LIVING AREA}			
AREA	DIMENSIONS	SUBTOTAL	TOTAL
1st Floor	50 x 30	1,500	
	3 x 22	+ 66	1,566
Basement	22 x 33		<u>726</u>
Total			2,292
\multicolumn{4}{c}{OTHER AREA}			
AREA	DIMENSIONS	SUBTOTAL	TOTAL
Carport	22 x 25		550

REPORT: ONE-STORY DETACHED HOUSE WITH 2,292 SQUARE FEET OF LIVING AREA OF WHICH 726 SQUARE FEET ARE IN A FINISHED BASEMENT, PLUS A 550-SQUARE-FOOT CARPORT.

APPENDIX D Residential Square Footage Guidelines

Two Story With Open Foyer And Finished Attic

(Figure 2)

Attic
Add 1 ft. (6" for each exterior side wall) to inside measurements. Thus, 19' inside measurement equals 20' exterior measurement. In this example, do NOT add for front and rear walls since the allowable square foot age (5' ceiling height) does not extend to the kneewalls.

Stairway with Open Area
1. Calculate area of open space (10' x 12' = 120 sf).
2. Subtract from second floor area (1,200 − 120 = 1,080 sf).
3. Add stairway (6' x 4' = 24 + 1,080 = 1,104 sf).

Bay Window (Floored)
Include in living area if it is floored and has ceiling height of at least 7 ft.
1. Calculate area of triangles (3' x 4' ÷ 2 = 6 sf x 2 = 12 sf).
2. Add area of triangles (12 sf) to remaining area of bay window (6' x 4' = 24 sf) = 36 sf.

3 Ft. Knee-wall
In rooms with sloped ceilings, do not include any area with a ceiling height of less than 5ft.

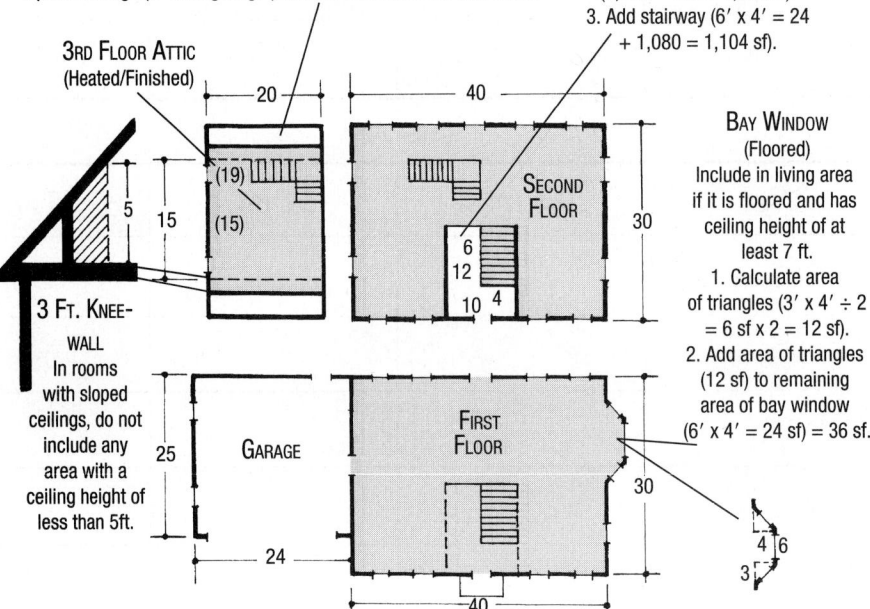

Two Story With Open Foyer And Finished Attic Worksheet

_____	LIVING AREA		
AREA	DIMENSIONS	SUBTOTAL	TOTAL
1st Floor	40 x 30	1,200	
Bay Window		36	1,236
2nd Floor	40 x 30	1,200	
	10 x 12	− 120	
	4 x 6	+ 24	1,104
Fin. Attic	20 x 15		<u>300</u>
Total			2,640
OTHER AREA			
AREA	DIMENSIONS	SUBTOTAL	TOTAL
Garage	25 x 24		600

REPORT: TWO-STORY DETACHED HOUSE WITH 2,640 SQUARE FEET OF LIVING AREA OF WHICH 300 SQUARE FEET ARE IN A FINISHED ATTIC, PLUS A 600-SQUARE-FOOT GARAGE.

Two Story With "Bonus Room" Over Garage

(Figure 3)

BONUS ROOM
If the "Bonus Room" is accessible from living area through a door,
hallway or stairway, include in living area; otherwise, report as other area.

Add 6" to inside measurements for each exterior wall.
Thus, 14' x 23.5' inside measurement equals 15' x 24' exterior measurements.
In rooms with sloped ceilings, do not include any space with a ceiling height of less than 5 ft. in height.

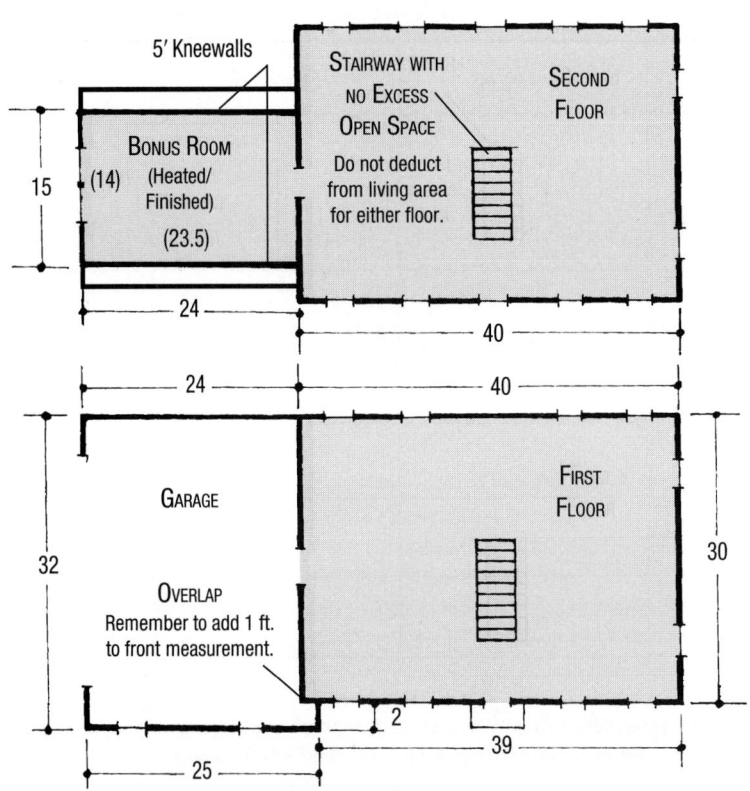

APPENDIX D Residential Square Footage Guidelines

Two Story With "Bonus Room" Over Garage Worksheet

\multicolumn{4}{c}{Living Area}			
Area	Dimensions	Subtotal	Total
1st Floor	40 x 30		1,200
2nd Floor	40 x 30		1,200
Bonus Room	15 x 24		<u>360</u>
Total			2,760
\multicolumn{4}{c}{Other Area}			
Area	Dimensions	Subtotal	Total
Garage	24 x 32	768	
	1 x 2	+ 2	770

Report: Two-story detached house with 2,760 square feet of living area of which 360 square feet are in a "bonus room" over the garage, plus a 770-square-foot garage.

SPLIT FOYER

(Figure 4)

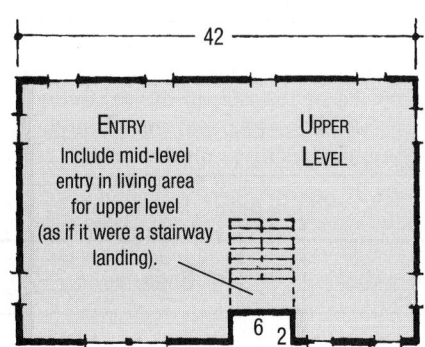

ENTRY
Include mid-level entry in living area for upper level (as if it were a stairway landing).

UPPER LEVEL

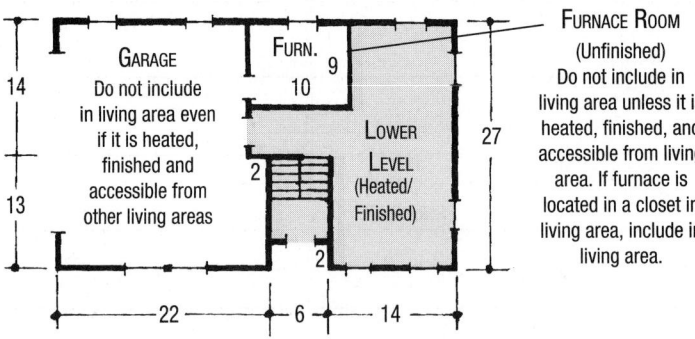

GARAGE
Do not include in living area even if it is heated, finished and accessible from other living areas

FURN.

LOWER LEVEL
(Heated/Finished)

FURNACE ROOM
(Unfinished)
Do not include in living area unless it is heated, finished, and accessible from living area. If furnace is located in a closet in living area, include in living area.

APPENDIX D Residential Square Footage Guidelines

SPLIT FOYER WORKSHEET

\multicolumn{4}{c}{LIVING AREA}			
AREA	DIMENSIONS	SUBTOTAL	TOTAL
Upper Level	27 x 42	1,134	
	6 x 2	− 12	1,122
Lower Level	22 x 27	594	
	6 x 2	− 12	
	13 x 2	− 26	
	9 x 10	− 90	<u>466</u>
Total			1,588
\multicolumn{4}{c}{OTHER AREA}			
AREA	DIMENSIONS	SUBTOTAL	TOTAL
Garage	27 x 20	540	
	2 x 13	+ 26	566
Furnace Room	9 x 10		90

REPORT: SPLIT-FOYER DETACHED HOUSE WITH 1,588 SQUARE FEET OF LIVING AREA, PLUS A 566-SQAURE-FOOT GARAGE AND 90-SQUARE-FOOT FURNACE ROOM.

Split (Tri-) Level With Overhang

(Figure 5)

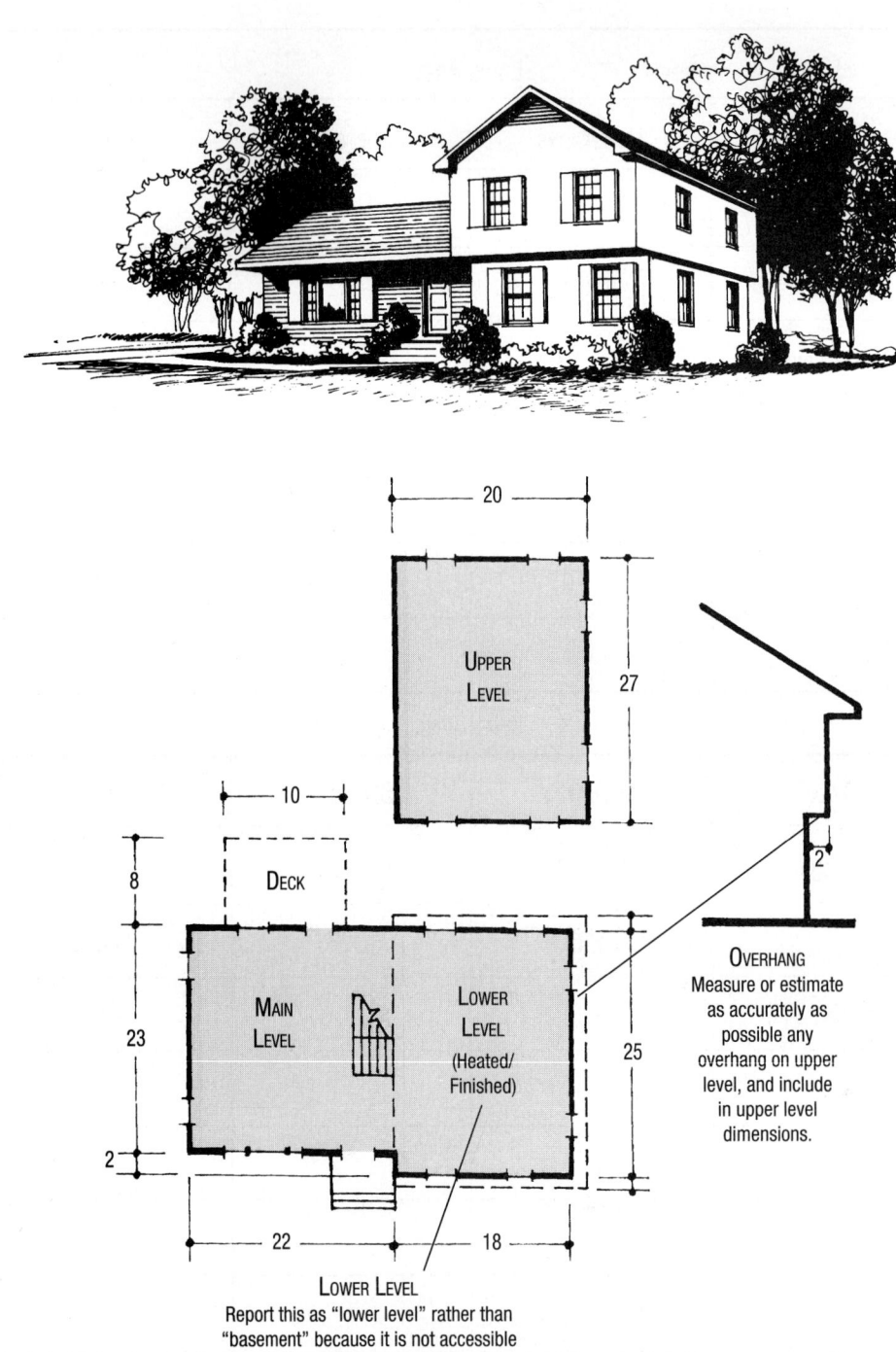

Overhang Measure or estimate as accurately as possible any overhang on upper level, and include in upper level dimensions.

Lower Level Report this as "lower level" rather than "basement" because it is not accessible by a full flight of stairs.

APPENDIX D Residential Square Footage Guidelines

SPLIT (TRI-) LEVEL WITH OVERHANG WORKSHEET

LIVING AREA			
AREA	DIMENSIONS	SUBTOTAL	TOTAL
Main Level	22 x 23		506
Lower Level	18 x 25		450
Upper Level	27 x 20		<u>540</u>
Total			1,496
OTHER AREA			
AREA	DIMENSIONS	SUBTOTAL	TOTAL
Deck	8 x 10		80

REPORT: SPLIT-LEVEL DETACHED HOUSE WITH 1,496 SQUARE FEET OF LIVING AREA, PLUS AN 80-SQUARE-FOOT DECK.

ONE AND ONE-HALF STORY

(Figure 6)

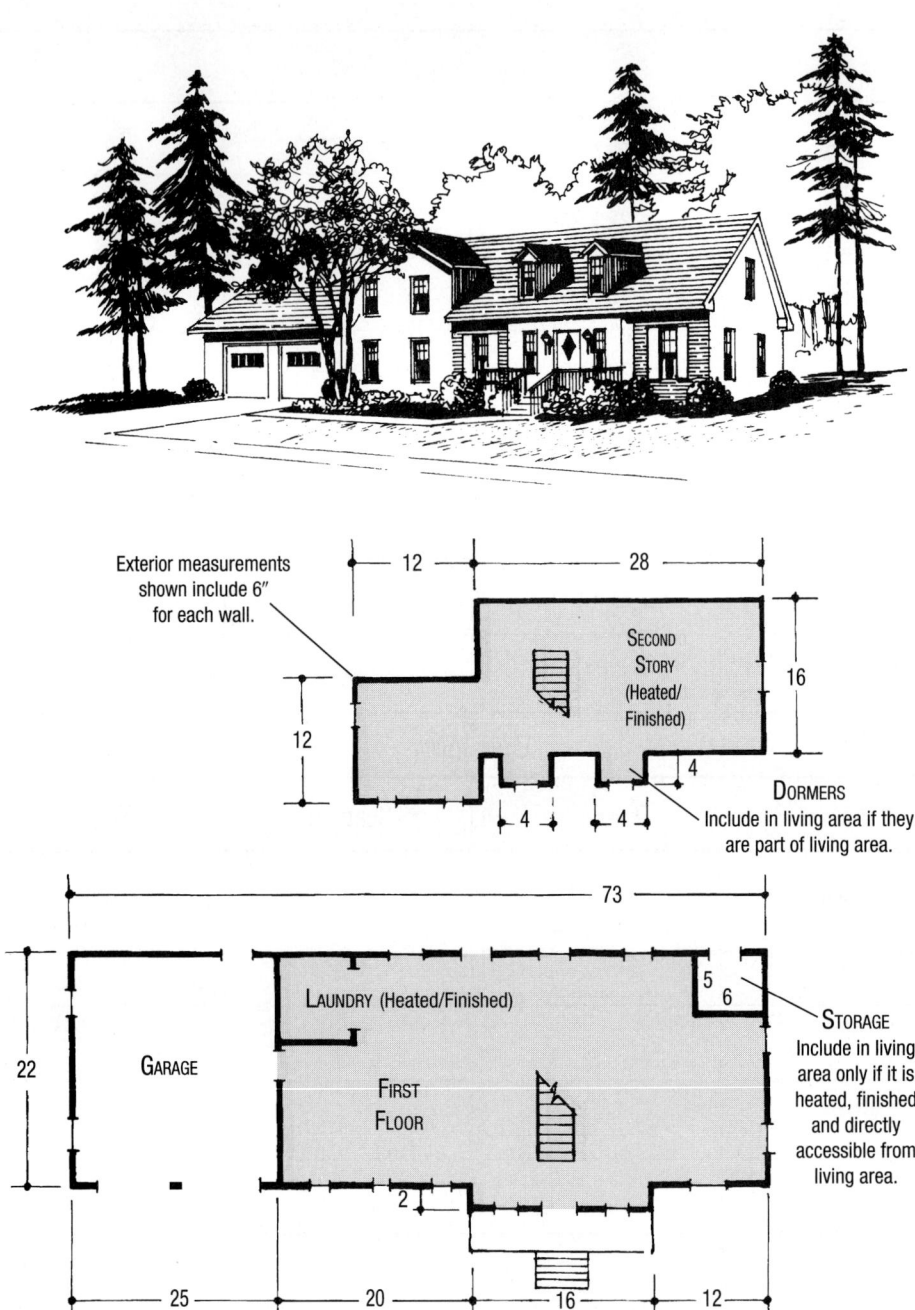

ONE AND ONE-HALF STORY WORKSHEET

\	LIVING AREA		
AREA	DIMENSIONS	SUBTOTAL	TOTAL
1st Floor	48 x 22	1,056	
	16 x 2	+ 32	
	5 x 6	– 30	1,058
2nd Floor	16 x 28	448	
	4 x 4	+ 16	
	4 x 4	+ 16	
	12 x 12	+ 144	624
Total			1,682
	OTHER AREA		
AREA	DIMENSIONS	SUBTOTAL	TOTAL
Garage	22 x 25		550
Storage	5 x 6		30

REPORT: ONE AND ONE-HALF STORY DETACHED HOUSE WITH 1,682 SQUARE FEET OF LIVING AREA, PLUS A 550-SQUARE-FOOT GARAGE.

APPENDIX D Residential Square Footage Guidelines

CONDOMINIUM

(Figure 7)

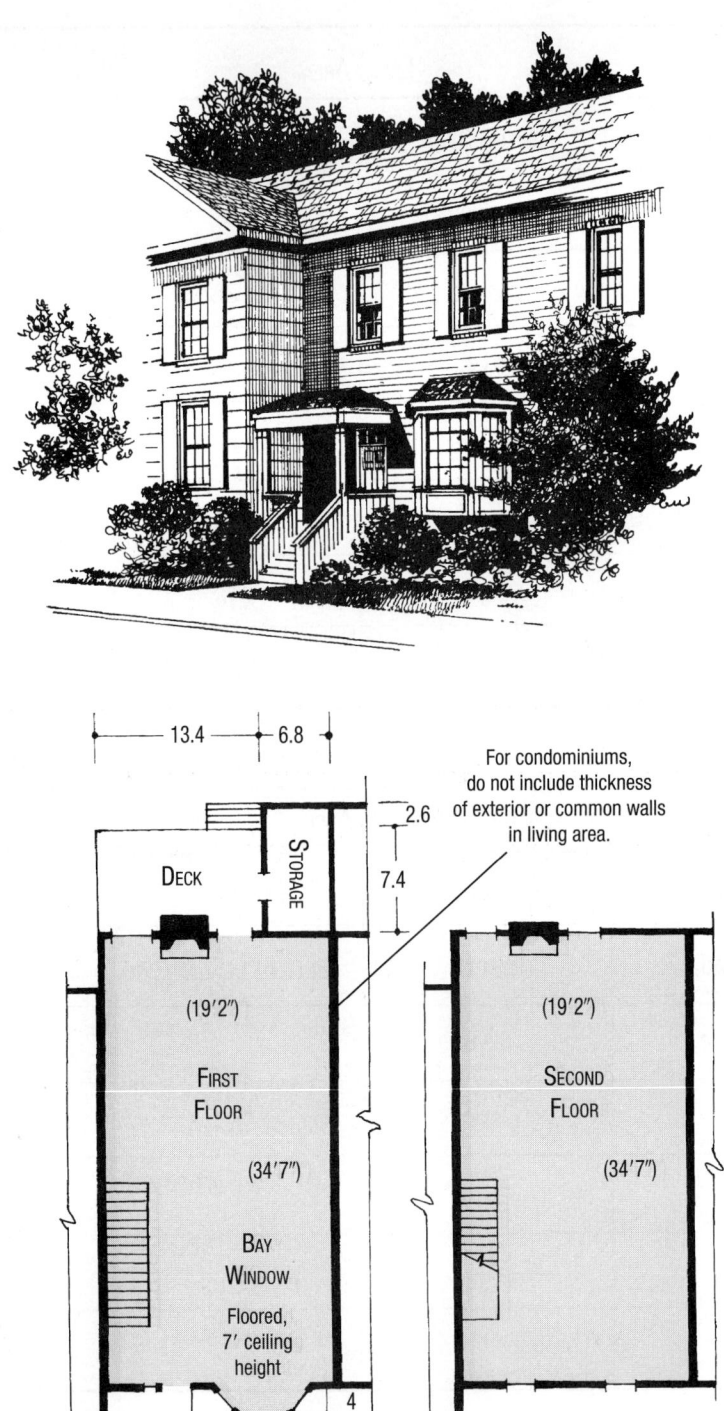

APPENDIX D Residential Square Footage Guidelines

Condominium Worksheet

\	Living Area		
Area	Dimensions	Subtotal	Total
1st Floor	34.6 x 19.2	664.3	
Bay Window		48.0	712
2nd Floor	34.6 x 19.2	664.3	664
Total			1,376
	Other Area		
Area	Dimensions	Subtotal	Total
Deck	13.4 x 7.4	99.2	99
Storage	10 x 6.8		68

Report: Two-story condominium with 1,364 square feet of living area, plus a 99-square-foot deck.

APPENDIX D Residential Square Footage Guidelines

PRACTICE FLOOR PLAN
(Figure 8)

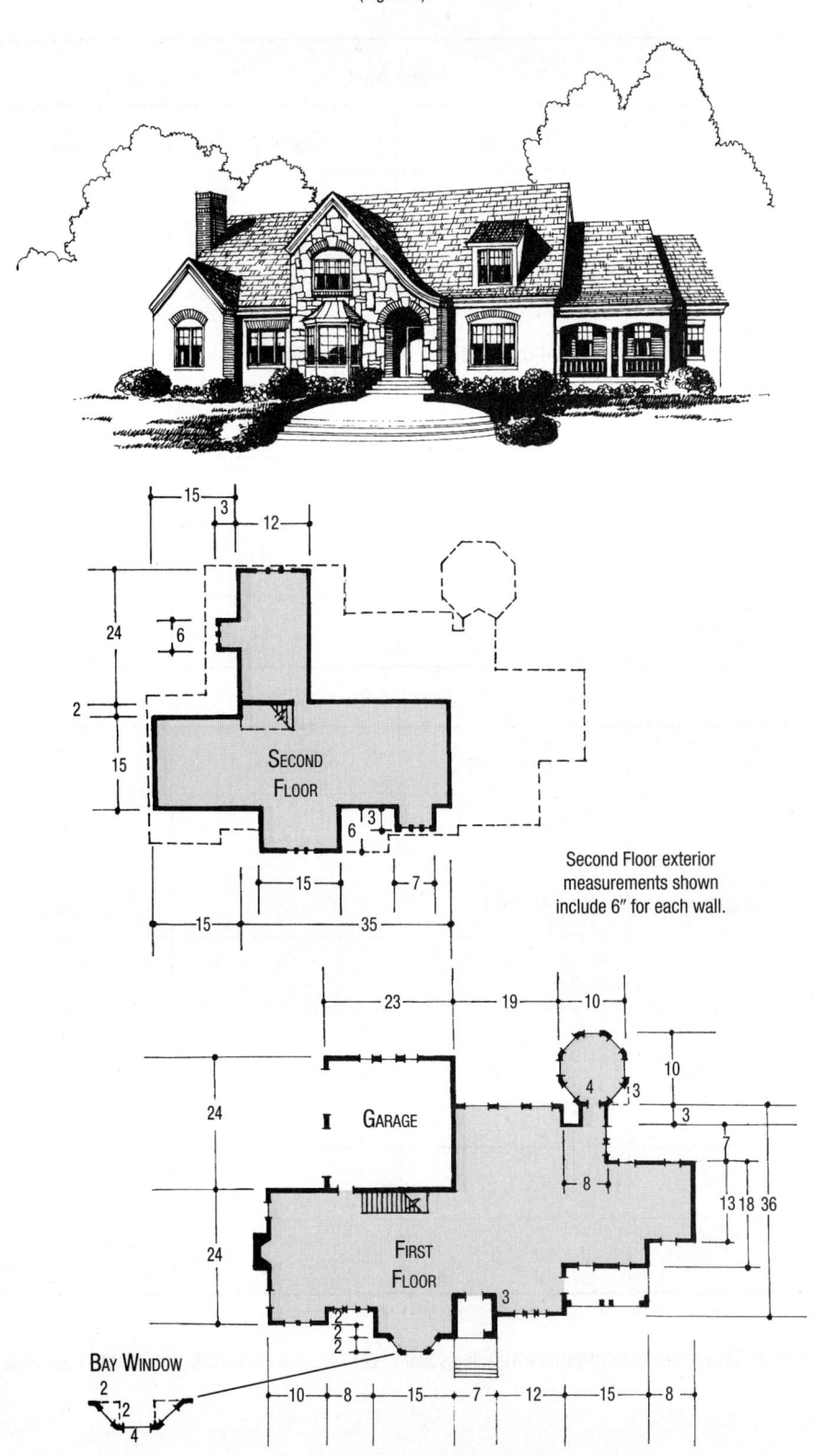

APPENDIX D Residential Square Footage Guidelines

PRACTICE FLOOR PLAN WORKSHEET

Living Area			
Area	Dimensions	Subtotal	Total

Other Area			
Area	Dimensions	Subtotal	Total

REPORT:

APPENDIX D Residential Square Footage Guidelines

PRACTICE FLOOR PLAN
(Zoned to facilitate calculations)

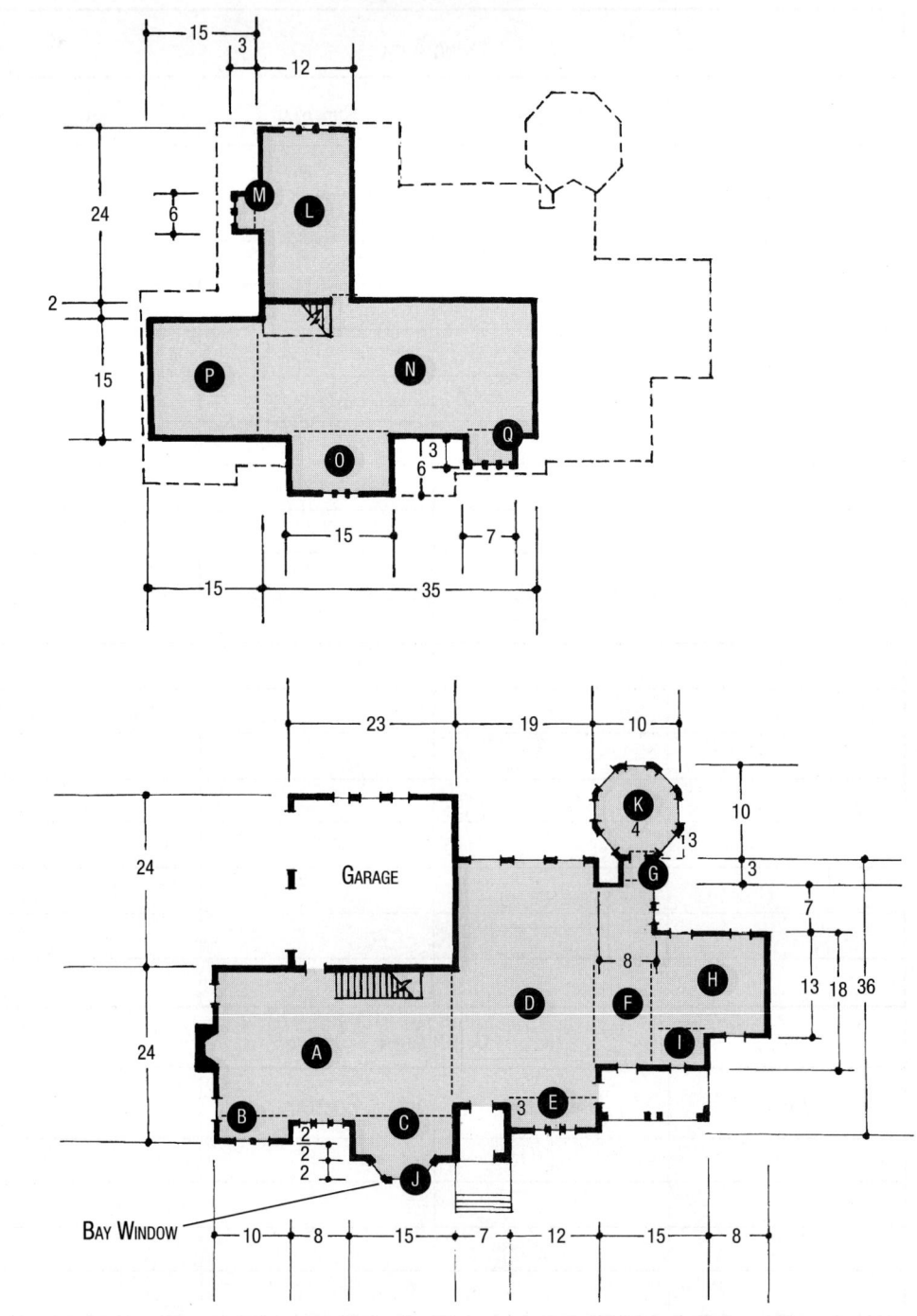

APPENDIX D Residential Square Footage Guidelines

PRACTICE FLOOR PLAN WORKSHEET

Living Area			
Area	Dimensions	Subtotal	Total
1st Floor A	22 x 33	726	
1st Floor B	2 x 10	20	
1st Floor C	4 x 15	60	
1st Floor D	19 x 33	627	
1st Floor E	3 x 12	36	
1st Floor F	8 x 25	200	
1st Floor G	4 x 3	12	
1st Floor H	15 x 13	195	
1st Floor I	7 x 5	35	
Bay Window J		12	
Oct. Window K		82	2,005
2nd Floor L	24 x 12	288	
2nd Floor M	3 x 6	18	
2nd Floor N	17 x 35	595	
2nd Floor O	15 x 6	90	
2nd Floor P	15 x 15	225	
2nd Floor Q	3 x 7	21	1,237
Total			3,242

Other Area			
Area	Dimensions	Subtotal	Total
Garage	24 x 23		552

REPORT: ONE AND ONE-HALF STORY DETACHED HOUSE WITH 3,242 SQUARE FEET OF LIVING AREA, PLUS A 552-SQUARE-FOOT GARAGE.

APPENDIX D Residential Square Footage Guidelines

Floor Plan Worksheet

Living Area			
Area	Dimensions	Subtotal	Total
Other Area			
Area	Dimensions	Subtotal	Total

Report:

APPENDIX D Residential Square Footage Guidelines

Floor Plan Worksheet

Living Area			
Area	Dimensions	Subtotal	Total
Other Area			
Area	Dimensions	Subtotal	Total

Report:

APPENDIX D Residential Square Footage Guidelines

Notes

SAFETY ISSUES FOR REAL ESTATE BROKERS

APPENDIX E

This text has focused on what you need to know to protect the interest of your clients and to help you avoid lawsuits and disciplinary action by the Real Estate Commission by providing you the knowledge to practice real estate in a professional and legally correct manner. An important aspect of the real estate business that still remains to discuss is the issue of personal safety while conducting business. Before you encounter your first potential client or customer, you should know how to protect yourself from those who seek to lure you into a dangerous situation on the pretext of buying or listing real estate.

Every year, too many real estate agents are assaulted, robbed, raped, or even murdered during or as a result of real estate activity. Most of these attacks can be prevented by using common sense and following proven safety practices. Agents frequently must talk to strangers and often are alone with people they barely know. The nature of the real estate business requires that agents exercise safety precautions by being aware of their surroundings, anticipating and avoiding danger, and being prepared to escape a dangerous situation.

This discussion is not meant to be all-encompassing and you may choose not to follow all of these suggestions. Adopt those pertinent to your situation, and continue to develop knowledge of safety procedures through your company's training program, seminars, and reading. Every company should have policies and procedures to ensure the safety of its employees and agents. Learn and follow these policies and build on that knowledge by accessing the wealth of additional information on safety including the "North Carolina Real Estate Agent Safety Guide," a joint publication of the NC Real Estate Commission and NCAR, continuing education courses, and materials produced by the National Association of REALTORS®.

Safety is important at the office, in advertising, between the office or property and your car, in your car, and on property being shown to an individual or at an open house. The following suggestions may help create a safer office environment.

1. An office location that is not isolated after normal business hours.
2. Well-lit parking lot and lights around perimeter of building, especially areas that would give a criminal an easy place to hide.
3. A security system to prevent unauthorized entry.
4. A personal security system that can be worn as a watch or pendant by agents when working alone at the office on evenings or weekends.
5. Security cameras, preferably with the images transmitted and stored off premises.
6. A single, monitored point of entry. *Note:* All doors must be able to be easily exited in case of fire.
7. An information center containing the following pertinent information about agents, clients, and customers, which could help locate an agent in case of disappearance.
   - Information about clients and customers containing a picture ID, make and model of car, and license tag number, as well as other information needed to verify identity.
   - An itinerary sheet showing routes, addresses, and call-in and return times.

You should carefully establish and consistently apply criteria for this in order to avoid even the appearance of profiling members of a specific race, sex, national origin, or any other protected category.

Advertising often is overlooked as a hazard. Modify your advertising to protect your safety, beginning with these suggestions.

1. Consider not putting your picture on your cards or ads, especially if you are a woman. If you use a picture, avoid "glamour shots."
2. Use cell phone numbers, not home phone number on cards and ads.
3. Never advertise a house as vacant.
4. Do not include personal information in advertising.

An agent's vehicle is an essential tool for the practice of real estate. The following actions may help as you move to and from your vehicle, whether entering or leaving the office or a property alone or with customers or clients.

1. Observe activity around property before getting out of your car.
2. Check your car including the backseat before entering.
3. Lock doors while driving and when leaving car unattended.
4. Fill up your car with gas when it is half-full. Do not risk running out of gas.
5. Keep vehicle in good mechanical condition with routine maintenance and high-quality, puncture-resistant tires. Do not risk being stranded in a remote area.
6. Park your car on the street, if possible, when showing houses or sitting an open house. Position car for a fast getaway should it become necessary.
7. Keyless entry and automatic ignitions are great safety tools that you may want to consider on your next car if you do not presently have them. On-Star, a system using GPS tracking and telecommunications technology, is also a great safety tool available on selected new cars. It tracks the location of the car and sends help when necessary. It also offers services such as unlocking car doors, alerting drivers to routine maintenance, and tracking and stopping the car if stolen.
8. An inexpensive portable GPS and a well-charged cell phone may provide a measure of safety. If you do not have a GPS, On-Star, or equivalent system, have a good map and a cell phone with you and know your route before leaving the office.
9. Some guidelines suggest keeping an extra key in a hidden magnetized box on the outside of a car; however, a criminal may be able to easily locate it. It may be better to always have an extra key hidden in your clothes, but easily accessible.

Agents should always use common sense when showing property, including but not limited to the following practices.

1. Never meet a potential client, especially one you do not know, at a property, a hotel, or anywhere away from the office.

2. Always carry a well-charged cell phone. Keep the phone easily accessible, not in the bottom of a purse. Have your cell phone programmed to speed dial 911, the office, and home.
3. Always make sure someone else—a coworker, friend, or family member—has seen your client or customer and that your client or customer knows he has been seen and can be identified. Even better, leave a client profile sheet and an itinerary sheet with the office staff or your family.
4. Avoid wearing expensive jewelry or carrying a large sum of money.
5. Check in with home or office periodically. Office and family should have an action plan for when they have not heard from you as scheduled and cannot reach you.
6. Have a code for when you are uncomfortable, but not so much so that you want to call 911. Some suggest calling the office and saying something similar to "Will you please locate the red file for 123 Happy Lane and tell me the dimensions of the lot?" That may be a little too obvious. Many people are accustomed to hearing Code Blue, Code Red, or Doctor White coming over hospital loudspeakers and may associate a color, especially red, with a distress call. No matter what the code is, it should be understood by everyone in your office or home.
7. Keep your keys readily available.
8. Wear comfortable shoes suitable for running. If you find yourself in danger while you are wearing shoes that would hamper running, kick them off and run barefoot.
9. Have your car parked for an easy getaway.
10. Always allow your client or customer to enter the home or room before you. Remain between the client and the exit.

An open house is potentially dangerous for the agent. Although agents and their seller-clients may never be willing to forego having an open house, agents may reduce the danger with the following precautions.

1. Never sit an open house alone in a remote area. Regardless of location, it is preferable to not sit any open house alone. Have your car parked for an easy escape.
2. Open only one entrance. Assure that open house guests do not leave another door unlocked through which they could later return and enter. You should be able to exit through any door, but only allow access through one entrance.
3. Take the same precautions as with showing houses.
4. Ask owners to secure valuables out of sight or off premises. Do the same for your own valuables.
5. Have specific times to check in with your family or the office.
6. Have someone call you periodically if you do not call them as scheduled.

7. Meet the neighbors when you are setting up for an open house. They may be able to provide assistance if needed.
8. Keep control. Do not allow groups to split up as you are showing the home, especially if it is occupied.

An open house is safest for the agent and the homeowner's possessions if there are two people to control traffic flow. A large group or two groups working together could out-maneuver the saviest agent working alone. It is sad to think you may need a bodyguard at an open house, but there are deceased agents who might still be alive if a trusted second person had been with them.

Perhaps the greatest danger an agent faces is being alone with clients and customers about whom he or she knows little or nothing. All is not always as it appears. Be alert and heed warning signs. If a customer's or client's strange behavior concerns you, pay attention to your instincts. Diplomatically end the relationship as soon as possible if you see signs of current drug or alcohol abuse; violent or irrational behavior toward his or her family, you, or others; or inappropriate remarks of a violent or sexual nature. If you sense immediate danger, forget the diplomacy and get out immediately. No commission is worth risking your life.

If someone wants to harm you, embarrassment is irrelevant. You do not care what they think. Those who do not want to harm you will likely understand. Do not let the desire for a commission or the fear of embarrassment prevent you from leaving a dangerous situation.

The most important key to your safety is to plan ahead. Knowing what you will do in the event of an emergency can help you retain your wits and survive. A self-defense course may give you more confidence and enable you to remain calm and think clearly. Even if you are strong and proficient in self-defense, it is wiser to avoid or escape danger when possible. Fight only if you must. If you can neither run away nor fight, try talking with your assailant. You may be able to negotiate your release. Practicing safe habits every day and having the tools and skills at your disposal can help you practice real estate safely.

REAL ESTATE FORMS AND ADDENDA

APPENDIX F

Additional Provisions Addendum (2A11-T)	p. 890
Back-Up Contract Addendum (2A1-T)	p. 892
Buyer Possession before Closing Agreement (2A7-T)	p. 895
Confirmation of Compensation (770)	p. 897
Contingent Sale Addendum (2A2-T)	p. 898
Due Diligence Request and Agreement (310-T)	p. 900
Exclusive Right to Sell Listing Agreement (Vacant Lot/Land) (103)	p. 901
FHA/VA Financing Addendum (2A4-T)	p. 908
Internet Advertising Addendum (105)	p. 910
Lead-Based Paint or Lead-Based Hazard Addendum (2A9-T)	p. 912
Notice to Seller That Buyer is Exercising Their Right to Terminate the Offer to Purchase and Contract (Form 2-T) (350-T)	p. 914
Notice to Seller That Buyer Is Exercising Their Right to Terminate the Offer to Purchase and Contract—Vacant Lot/Land (Form 12-T) (351-T)	p. 916
Professional Services Disclosure and Election (Form 760 G) (760)	p. 918
Residential Property and Owners' Association Disclosure Statement	p. 922
Response to Buyer's Offer (340-T)	p. 926
Seller Possession after Closing Agreement (2A8-T)	p. 927
Short Sale Addendum (2A14-T)	p. 929
Short Sale Addendum to Exclusive Right to Sell Listing Agreement (104)	p. 933
Unrepresented Seller Disclosure and Fee Agreement (105)	p. 935

ADDITIONAL PROVISIONS ADDENDUM

Property: _____

Seller: _____

Buyer: _____

This Addendum is attached to and made a part of the Offer to Purchase and Contract ("Contract") between Seller and Buyer for the Property.

> **NOTE:** All of the following provisions which are marked with an "X" shall apply to the attached Offer to Purchase and Contract or Offer to Purchase and Contract – Vacant Lot/Land ("Contract"). Those provisions marked "N/A" shall not apply.

1. _____ **EXPIRATION OF OFFER:** This offer shall expire unless unconditional acceptance is delivered to Buyer on or before _____ ❏ AM ❏ PM, on _____, **TIME BEING OF THE ESSENCE**, or until withdrawn by Buyer, whichever occurs first.

2. _____ (To be used with Offer to Purchase and Contract Form 2-T only) **SEPTIC SYSTEM INSTALLATION/ MODIFICATION:** As a part of the Buyer's Due Diligence, Buyer intends to obtain an Improvement Permit or written evaluation from the County Health Department ("County") for a (check only ONE) ❏ conventional or ❏ other_____ _____ _____ ground absorption sewage system for a _____ bedroom home. Except for the costs for clearing the Property, all costs and expenses of obtaining such Permit or written evaluation shall be borne by Buyer unless otherwise agreed. Seller shall be responsible for clearing that portion of the Property required by the County to perform its tests and/or inspections by no later than _____.

   > **NOTE**: Insert a date that will allow testing to be completed prior to the end of the Due Diligence Period.

3. _____ **RENTAL/INCOME/INVESTMENT PROPERTY:** The Property shall be conveyed subject to existing leases and/or rights of tenants. Seller shall deliver to Buyer on or before_____, true and complete copies of all existing leases, rental agreements, outstanding tenant notices, written statements of all oral tenant agreements, statement of all tenant's deposits, uncured defaults by Seller or tenants, and claims made by or to tenants, if any.

   > **NOTE**: Insert a date that will allow review to be completed prior to the end of the Due Diligence Period).

   Any security deposit held in connection with any lease(s) shall be transferred to Buyer at Settlement and otherwise in accordance with North Carolina Tenant Security Deposit Act (N.C.G.S. § 42-54) Seller ❏ will ❏ will not transfer to Buyer any pet fee/deposit at Settlement.

   > **NOTE**: DO NOT USE THIS PROVISION FOR PROPERTY SUBJECT TO THE NORTH CAROLINA VACATION RENTAL ACT. A VACATION RENTAL ADDENDUM SHOULD BE USED IN SUCH CASES.

4. _____ **AGREED-UPON REPAIRS AND/OR IMPROVEMENTS:** Seller agrees, prior to Settlement Date and at Seller's expense, to complete the following items:_____
   _____
   _____
   _____
   _____
   _____
   _____
   _____
   _____.

   Buyer shall have the right to verify, prior to Settlement, that the above items have been completed in a good and workmanlike manner.

Page 1 of 2

This form jointly approved by:
North Carolina Bar Association
North Carolina Association of REALTORS®, Inc.

Buyer initials _____ _____   Seller initials _____ _____

STANDARD FORM 2A11–T
Revised 7/2015
© 7/2018

APPENDIX F Real Estate Forms and Addenda 891

5. _____ **MANUFACTURED (MOBILE) HOME:** The Property shall include the following manufactured (mobile) home(s) located on the Property: VIN(s): _____ or ❏ VIN(s) unknown Other description (*year, model, etc.*): _____

IN THE EVENT OF A CONFLICT BETWEEN THIS ADDENDUM AND THE CONTRACT, THIS ADDENDUM SHALL CONTROL, EXCEPT THAT IN THE CASE OF SUCH A CONFLICT AS TO THE DESCRIPTION OF THE PROPERTY OR THE IDENTITY OF THE BUYER OR SELLER, THE CONTRACT SHALL CONTROL.

THE NORTH CAROLINA ASSOCIATION OF REALTORS®, INC. AND THE NORTH CAROLINA BAR ASSOCIATION MAKE NO REPRESENTATION AS TO THE LEGAL VALIDITY OR ADEQUACY OF ANY PROVISION OF THIS FORM IN ANY SPECIFIC TRANSACTION. IF YOU DO NOT UNDERSTAND THIS FORM OR FEEL THAT IT DOES NOT PROVIDE FOR YOUR LEGAL NEEDS, YOU SHOULD CONSULT A NORTH CAROLINA REAL ESTATE ATTORNEY BEFORE YOU SIGN IT.

Date: _____

Buyer: _____

Date: _____

Buyer: _____

Entity Buyer: _____
(Name of LLC/Corporation/Partnership/Trust/etc.)

By: _____

Name: _____

Title: _____

Date: _____

Date: _____

Seller: _____

Date: _____

Seller: _____

Entity Seller: _____
(Name of LLC/Corporation/Partnership/Trust/etc.)

By: _____

Name: _____

Title: _____

Date: _____

STANDARD FORM 2A11–T
Revised 7/2015
© **7/2018**

BACK-UP CONTRACT ADDENDUM

NOTE: This Addendum should NOT be used in a short sale transaction. Use ONLY the Short Sale Addendum (form 2A14-T)

Property: _____

Seller: _____

Buyer: _____

This Addendum is attached to and made a part of the Offer to Purchase and Contract ("Back-Up Contract") between Seller and Buyer for the Property.

Buyer and Seller acknowledge that Seller has previously entered into an Offer to Purchase and Contract or an Offer To Purchase and Contract - Vacant Lot/Land (the "Primary Contract") with _____ [insert last name only] (the "Primary Buyer" under the Primary Contract), that the Primary Contract is currently pending, and that this Back-up Contract is accepted in a secondary or back-up position to the Primary Contract under the following terms and conditions:

1. **Condition.** It is a condition of this Back-up Contract that the Primary Contract is terminated as described below before Buyer and Seller shall be obligated to perform under this Back-up Contract.

2. **Termination of Primary Contract.** Termination of the Primary Contract shall be evidenced by:
   (a) written release signed by all parties thereto; or
   (b) written notice of termination from Seller to Primary Buyer that Seller is exercising a right to terminate the Primary Contract; or
   (c) written notice of termination from Primary Buyer to Seller that Primary Buyer is exercising a right to terminate the Primary Contract; or
   (d) final judgment of a court of competent jurisdiction that the Primary Contract is invalid, illegal, unenforceable, or is otherwise terminated.

NOTE: For example, NCAR Forms 350-T, 351-T, 352-T, 353-T, 390-T or 391-T may be used to evidence the release or notices called for in this paragraph.

3. **Indemnification/Hold Harmless.** Seller shall indemnify Buyer and hold Buyer harmless from any and all claims, damages and costs, including reasonable attorneys' fees, incurred by Buyer as a result of Buyer's reliance upon any wrongful or ineffective termination of the Primary Contract by Seller.

4. **Modification of Primary Contract.** Modification of the terms or conditions of the Primary Contract, including extensions of time, shall not constitute a termination of the Primary Contract and shall not cause this Back-up Contract to move into a primary position.

5. **Access to Primary Contract.** Buyer and Seller agree that Buyer may not examine or otherwise have access to the Primary Contract without written permission from Seller and Primary Buyer. Seller represents that the Primary Contract calls for a settlement date of _____ (date).

6. **Initial Earnest Money Deposit.** Buyer and Seller agree that any Initial Earnest Money Deposit shall be deposited within three (3) banking days following the Effective Date of this Back-up Contract even while this Back-up Contract is in secondary position.

7. **Closing on Primary Contract.** In the event the Primary Contract closes, then this Back-up Contract shall become null and void, and any Earnest Money Deposit shall be refunded to Buyer.

8. **Notification of Termination of Primary Contract.** In the event the Primary Contract is terminated, Seller shall promptly provide Buyer:
   (a) written notice stating that this Back-up Contract has become primary ("Notice of Primary Status"); and
   (b) written evidence that the Primary Contract has been terminated as provided in paragraph 2 above.

Page 1 of 3

This form jointly approved by:
North Carolina Bar Association
North Carolina Association of REALTORS®, Inc.

STANDARD FORM 2A1-T
Revised 7/2018
© 7/2018

Buyer initials _____ _____   Seller initials _____ _____

9. **Due Diligence/Settlement Dates.**
    (a) Due Diligence Fee. Any Due Diligence Fee provided for in this Contract shall be due and payable within five (5) days after delivery to Buyer of Notice of Primary Status.
    (b) Due Diligence Period. The Due Diligence Period of this Contract shall extend through 5:00 p.m. on the last day of a _____ _____ day period following Seller's delivery to Buyer of Notice of Primary Status.
    (c) Settlement Date. The Settlement Date of this Contract shall be on a date that is _____ days following Seller's delivery to Buyer of Notice of Primary Status.

> **NOTE**: Instead of inserting dates in the "Due Diligence Period" and "Settlement Date" blanks in the Contract, insert "See attached Back-Up Contract Addendum"

10. **Buyer's Right to Terminate**. Buyer may terminate this Back-up Contract without liability by giving written notice of termination to Seller at any time prior to receipt by Buyer of Notice of Primary Status and any Earnest Money Deposit shall be refunded to Buyer.

11. **Automatic Termination**. In any event, Buyer must receive Notice of Primary Status from Seller no later than 5 p.m. on _____, ***TIME BEING OF THE ESSENCE***, or this Back-up Contract shall become null and void and any Earnest Money Deposit shall be refunded to Buyer.

IN THE EVENT OF A CONFLICT BETWEEN THIS ADDENDUM AND THE BACK-UP CONTRACT THIS ADDENDUM SHALL CONTROL, EXCEPT THAT IN THE CASE OF SUCH A CONFLICT AS TO THE DESCRIPTION OF THE PROPERTY OR THE IDENTITY OF THE BUYER OR SELLER, THE BACK-UP CONTRACT SHALL CONTROL.

THE NORTH CAROLINA ASSOCIATION OF REALTORS®, INC. AND THE NORTH CAROLINA BAR ASSOCIATION MAKE NO REPRESENTATION AS TO THE LEGAL VALIDITY OR ADEQUACY OF ANY PROVISION OF THIS FORM IN ANY SPECIFIC TRANSACTION. IF YOU DO NOT UNDERSTAND THIS FORM OR FEEL THAT IT DOES NOT PROVIDE FOR YOUR LEGAL NEEDS, YOU SHOULD CONSULT A NORTH CAROLINA REAL ESTATE ATTORNEY BEFORE YOU SIGN IT.

Date: _____   Date: _____

Buyer: _____   Seller: _____

Date: _____   Date: _____

Buyer: _____   Seller: _____

Entity Buyer: _____   Entity Seller: _____
(Name of LLC/Corporation/Partnership/Trust/etc.)   (Name of LLC/Corporation/Partnership/Trust/etc.)

By: _____   By: _____

Name: _____   Name: _____

Title: _____   Title: _____

Date: _____   Date: _____

> **NOTE**: The following is a suggested notice that may be copied for the purpose of complying with the notice provision contained in paragraph 8 of the Back-Up Contract Addendum. DO NOT DETACH THE ORIGINAL OF THIS FORM FROM THE BACK-UP CONTRACT.

NOTICE TO BUYER THAT BACK-UP CONTRACT IS NOW IN EFFECT

NOTICE is hereby given to _____ (insert name of Buyer) from Seller under the Back-up Contract between them dated _____ that Seller has terminated the Primary Contract with _____ (Primary Buyer), as evidenced by the **ATTACHED** (initial any one of the following):

- (a) _____ _____ written release signed by all parties thereto; or
- (b) _____ _____ written notice of termination from Seller to Primary Buyer that Seller is exercising a right to terminate the Primary Contract; or
- (c) _____ _____ written notice of termination from Primary Buyer to Seller that Primary Buyer is exercising a right to terminate the Primary Contract; or
- (d) _____ _____ final judgment of a court of competent jurisdiction that the Primary Contract is invalid, illegal, unenforceable, or is otherwise terminated.

and that the Back-up Contract entered into between Seller and Buyer has become primary and its terms and conditions are now in effect.

Seller: _____ Date: _____

Seller: _____ Date: _____

Seller: _____ Date: _____

STANDARD FORM 2A1-T
Revised 7/2018
© 7/2018

BUYER POSSESSION BEFORE CLOSING AGREEMENT
THIS AGREEMENT IS AN ADDENDUM TO THE OFFER TO PURCHASE AND CONTRACT

> **_WARNINGS_ TO _BUYERS AND SELLERS_:**
> - THIS FORM MAY NOT BE USED FOR LONG-TERM OCCUPANCY, LEASE PURCHASE OR LEASE OPTION TRANSACTIONS.
> - THIS FORM DOES NOT ADDRESS IMPORTANT ISSUES TYPICALLY ADDRESSED IN A RESIDENTIAL LEASE, AND SHOULD ONLY BE USED FOR SHORT-TERM OCCUPANCY.
> - YOU ARE ADVISED TO CONFIRM WITH AN INSURANCE PROFESSIONAL THE TERMS OF COVERAGE UNDER YOUR PROPERTY AND CASUALTY INSURANCE POLICY BEFORE USING THIS ADDENDUM.

Property: _____

Seller: _____

Buyer: _____

This Agreement is attached to and made a part of the Offer to Purchase and Contract ("Contract") between Seller and Buyer for the Property. For valuable consideration, the receipt and legal sufficiency of which are acknowledged, Buyer and Seller agree:

1. **Term of Possession.** Buyer may take possession of the Property at 8:00 a.m. on _____ ("Commencement Date"). This Agreement shall terminate at the earlier of Closing or the termination of the Contract (the entire period is referred to as the "Term"). *TIME IS OF THE ESSENCE* with regard to the beginning and ending of the Term.

2. **Buyer's Waiver and Acceptance of Property Condition.** By taking possession of the Property on or after the Commencement Date, Buyer waives any further Due Diligence rights under Paragraph 4 of the Contract, and Buyer waives the contingency under Paragraph 11 of the Contract relating to the condition of the Property at Closing, and accepts the Property in its condition at the Commencement Date. Buyer's waiver and acceptance is subject to any other agreements between the parties that are a part of the Contract, including, but not limited to, any agreements with respect to repairs or improvements to the Property and any Seller warranties or agreements that may survive Closing.

3. **Buyer's Obligation to Maintain Property.** Prior to Closing, Buyer shall not alter, modify, or damage the Property, or fail to maintain the Property in its same condition as of the Commencement Date, and shall make no changes in the Property, decorating or otherwise, without the written consent of Seller. Seller shall not be obligated to maintain the Property after the Commencement Date, subject to any obligation that may be imposed on Seller by law. In the event Closing does not occur, Buyer shall pay all costs necessary to correct any alteration, modification or damage to the Property to restore the Property to the condition it was in at the Commencement Date. This paragraph shall not be deemed to modify the rights and obligations of the parties under Paragraph 12 of the Contract relating to the risk of loss or damage to the Property by fire or other casualty.

4. **Rent.** Prior to the Commencement Date, Buyer shall pay Seller a lump sum of $_____ ("Rent") for the Term. In the event that Buyer is the Delaying Party under Paragraph 13 of the Contract, Buyer shall pay additional rent in the sum of $_____ per day from the Settlement Date until Closing.

5. **Termination of Possession.** Buyer shall immediately vacate the Property if the Contract is terminated. If Buyer does not then immediately vacate the Property, Buyer shall continue to be bound by all the terms and conditions of this Agreement and Buyer shall in addition pay Seller a hold-over fee of $_____ per day for each day Buyer remains in possession of the Property from the date of termination of the Contract until Buyer vacates the Property or is evicted.

6. **Utilities.** Buyer shall have all utilities registered in Buyer's name as of the Commencement Date and shall pay the costs of all utilities (sewer, water, gas, electricity, etc.) during the Term.

7. **Lawn Maintenance; Trash.** Buyer shall be responsible for lawn maintenance and trash removal after the Commencement Date.

8. **Insurance on Buyer's Property.** Buyer shall keep any personal property owned by Buyer on or in the Property insured for the benefit of Buyer in such amount and to such extent as Buyer determines desirable.

9. **Insurance on Seller's Property.** Seller shall procure and/or maintain in effect a policy or policies of fire and hazard insurance adequately covering the Property and Seller's personal property, if any, located on the Property. Risk of loss or damage to the Property

This form jointly approved by:
North Carolina Bar Association
North Carolina Association of REALTORS®, Inc.

STANDARD FORM 2A7-T
Revised 7/2018
© 7/2018

Buyer initials _____ _____   Seller initials _____ _____

by fire or other casualty remains with Seller until Closing under Paragraph 12 of the Contract.

10. **Buyer's Indemnification.** Buyer shall indemnify and hold Seller harmless from and against any and all liability, fines, suits, claims, demands, actions, costs and expenses of any kind or nature whatsoever caused by, or arising out of, or in any manner connected with any damage to the Property or any injury or death to a person or persons arising out of Buyer's use and/or occupancy of the Property after the Commencement Date, including intentional or negligent acts by Buyer, Buyer's family, invitees, and/or agents and employees of Buyer.

11. **Subletting; Assignment.** Buyer shall not sublet the Property or assign this Agreement.

12. **Association Dues and Charges.** Seller shall pay the owner's association dues and other like charges, if any, during the Term.

13. **Pets.** Check one: ❏ pets are allowed on the Property ❏ no pets are allowed on the Property.

14. **Eviction.** In the event of Buyer's breach of this Agreement or the Contract, Buyer may be evicted from the Property pursuant to a summary ejectment proceeding brought before the magistrate in the county where the Property is located, as provided in Chapter 42 of the North Carolina General Statutes.

15. **Costs of Legal Proceedings.** The losing party in any legal proceeding brought by Buyer or Seller against the other party for breach of any provision of this Agreement (including an action for summary ejectment) shall be liable for the costs and expenses of the prevailing party, including reasonable attorneys' fees (at all tribunal levels).

EXCEPT AS SPECIFICALLY MODIFIED HEREIN, ALL OF THE TERMS AND CONDITIONS OF THE CONTRACT SHALL REMAIN IN FULL FORCE AND EFFECT.

IN THE EVENT OF A CONFLICT BETWEEN THIS AGREEMENT AND THE CONTRACT, THIS AGREEMENT SHALL CONTROL, EXCEPT THAT IN THE CASE OF SUCH A CONFLICT AS TO THE DESCRIPTION OF THE PROPERTY OR THE IDENTITY OF THE BUYER OR SELLER, THE CONTRACT SHALL CONTROL.

THE NORTH CAROLINA ASSOCIATION OF REALTORS®, INC. AND THE NORTH CAROLINA BAR ASSOCIATION MAKE NO REPRESENTATION AS TO THE LEGAL VALIDITY OR ADEQUACY OF ANY PROVISION OF THIS FORM IN ANY SPECIFIC TRANSACTION. IF YOU DO NOT UNDERSTAND THIS FORM OR FEEL THAT IT DOES NOT PROVIDE FOR YOUR LEGAL NEEDS, YOU SHOULD CONSULT A NORTH CAROLINA REAL ESTATE ATTORNEY BEFORE YOU SIGN IT.

Date: _____
Buyer: _____
Date: _____
Buyer: _____
Entity Buyer: _____
(Name of LLC/Corporation/Partnership/Trust/etc.)
By: _____
Name: _____
Title: _____
Date: _____

Date: _____
Seller: _____
Date: _____
Seller: _____
Entity Seller: _____
(Name of LLC/Corporation/Partnership/Trust/etc.)
By: _____
Name: _____
Title: _____
Date: _____

STANDARD FORM 2A7-T
Revised 7/2018
© 7/2018

CONFIRMATION OF COMPENSATION
See Guidelines (Standard Form 770G) on proper use of this form.

Property Address:_____("Property")

Buyer or Seller:_____("Client")

Real Estate Firm:_____("Firm")

1. **Disclosure.** A real estate firm is required by law to timely disclose to their client the receipt of (or promise or expectation of receiving) any compensation, incentive, bonus, rebate and/or other valuable consideration of more than nominal value ("Compensation") from any other party or person in a real estate sales transaction and confirm such disclosure in writing before making or accepting any offer.

2. **Confirmation.** Firm hereby confirms that in connection with the sale or purchase of the Property, Firm expects to receive the following Compensation **(check all applicable boxes)**:

☐ Monetary: $_____ or _____ percent of sales price of Property received/to be received from _____
_____

☐ Non-monetary: (describe) _____ received/to be received from _____ estimated value: $_____

☐ Other: _____
_____
_____

THE NORTH CAROLINA ASSOCIATION OF REALTORS, INC. MAKES NO REPRESENTATION AS TO THE LEGAL VALIDITY OR ADEQUACY OF ANY PROVISION OF THIS FORM IN ANY SPECIFIC TRANSACTION.

Firm _____
    Real Estate Firm Name

By: _____ Date: _____
    Individual agent signature

ACKNOWLEDGEMENT BY CLIENT

Client hereby acknowledges receipt of a completed copy of this form.

Client: _____ Date: _____

Client: _____ Date: _____

Client: _____ Date: _____

Entity Client: _____
    (Name of LLC/Corporation/Partnership/Trust/etc.)

By _____ Date: _____

Name: _____ Title: _____

North Carolina Association of REALTORS®, Inc.

STANDARD FORM 770
REV 7/2014
© 7/2018

CONTINGENT SALE ADDENDUM

Seller's Property: _____

Seller: _____

Buyer: _____

This Addendum is attached to and made a part of the Offer to Purchase and Contract ("Contract") between Seller and Buyer for the Seller's Property.

1. **Closing Contingency for Buyer's Real Property located at:** _____
_____ ("Buyer's Property"):

    (a) **Contract For Buyer's Property**: If Buyer's Property is under contract as of the Effective Date of this Contract with Seller OR goes under contract after the Effective Date of this Contract, then Buyer shall deliver a copy of the contract for Buyer's property ("Contract for Buyer's Property") to Seller and it shall be a condition of this Contract that closing on the sale of Buyer's Property occurs on or before the Settlement Date of this Contract, subject to the terms of this Addendum. If Buyer fails to deliver to Seller a copy of a Contract for Buyer's Property by the expiration of the Due Diligence Period this Contract shall be null and void and the Earnest Money Deposit shall be refunded to Buyer. In any instance when Buyer is providing to Seller a copy of a Contract for Buyer's Property, Buyer may mark out any confidential information, such as the purchase price and the buyer's identity, prior to providing the copy to Seller.

    (b) **Closing on Contract For Buyer's Property**: If there is a Contract For Buyer's Property, but the closing on the sale of Buyer's Property has not occurred by the Settlement Date of this Contract, then Buyer may terminate this Contract within three days following the Settlement Date of this Contract by written notice to Seller, ***TIME BEING OF THE ESSENCE***, and the Earnest Money Deposit shall be refunded to Buyer.

    (**WARNING: If Buyer does not terminate this Contract as set out in (b) above, and Buyer fails to timely complete Settlement and Closing as provided in this Contract, Buyer risks the loss of the Earnest Money Deposit**).

2. **Termination of Contract for Buyer's Property**. If any Contract for Buyer's Property previously delivered to Seller terminates for any reason, Buyer shall within 3 days provide Seller written notice and reasonable documentation of such termination. In the event of any such termination, then Buyer may terminate this Contract by written notice to Seller any time prior to Buyer's delivery of another Contract for Buyer's Property or the expiration of Buyer's 3-day right of termination set forth in subparagraph 1(b) above, and Seller may terminate this Contract by written notice to Buyer any time prior to Buyer's delivery of another Contract for Buyer's Property. In either event, the Earnest Money Deposit shall be refunded to Buyer. If Seller elects to terminate the Contract under this paragraph during the Due Diligence Period, Seller also must refund any Due Diligence Fee as a condition of such termination.

3. **Listing of Buyer's Property for Sale.** If Buyer has not entered into a Contract For Buyer's Property as of the Effective Date of this Contract, Buyer's Property (*check only ONE of the following options*):
    ❑ is listed with and actively marketed by _____
    ❑ will be listed with and actively marketed by _____ on or before _____
    ❑ Buyer is attempting to sell the Buyer's Property without the assistance of a real estate broker.

IN THE EVENT OF A CONFLICT BETWEEN THIS ADDENDUM AND THE CONTRACT, THIS ADDENDUM SHALL CONTROL, EXCEPT THAT IN THE CASE OF SUCH A CONFLICT AS TO THE DESCRIPTION OF THE SELLER'S PROPERTY OR THE IDENTITY OF THE BUYER OR SELLER, THE CONTRACT SHALL CONTROL.

This form jointly approved by:
North Carolina Bar Association
North Carolina Association of REALTORS®, Inc.

STANDARD FORM 2A2–T
Revised 7/2016
© 7/2018

Buyer initials _____ _____ Seller initials _____ _____

THE NORTH CAROLINA ASSOCIATION OF REALTORS®, INC. AND THE NORTH CAROLINA BAR ASSOCIATION MAKE NO REPRESENTATION AS TO THE LEGAL VALIDITY OR ADEQUACY OF ANY PROVISION OF THIS FORM IN ANY SPECIFIC TRANSACTION. IF YOU DO NOT UNDERSTAND THIS FORM OR FEEL THAT IT DOES NOT PROVIDE FOR YOUR LEGAL NEEDS, YOU SHOULD CONSULT A NORTH CAROLINA REAL ESTATE ATTORNEY BEFORE YOU SIGN IT.

Date: _____

Buyer: _____

Date: _____

Buyer: _____

Date: _____

Buyer: _____

Entity Buyer: _____
(Name of LLC/Corporation/Partnership/Trust/etc.)

By: _____

Name: _____

Title: _____

Date: _____

Date: _____

Seller: _____

Date: _____

Seller: _____

Date: _____

Seller : _____

Entity Seller: _____
(Name of LLC/Corporation/Partnership/Trust/etc.)

By: _____

Name: _____

Title: _____

Date: _____

[THIS SPACE INTENTIONALLY LEFT BLANK]

APPENDIX F Real Estate Forms and Addenda

DUE DILIGENCE REQUEST AND AGREEMENT
[See Guidelines for completing this form (Standard form # 310G)]

_____, as Buyer,

and _____, as Seller,

have entered into an Offer to Purchase and Contract ("Contract") regarding the purchase and sale of the following property (insert property address): _____

_____ ("Property").

1. Based upon Buyer's Due Diligence, the Buyer requests and the Seller agrees to the following: _____

_____
_____
_____
_____
_____
_____
_____
_____

In the event the parties have agreed to any adjustment in the condition of the Property, then such adjustment shall be completed prior to Settlement in a good and workmanlike manner. Seller shall notify Buyer upon completion of the above and provide Buyer with documentation thereof. Buyer shall have the right to verify that the items above have been completed in a good and workmanlike manner. Unless otherwise indicated in the Contract or this Agreement, such verification shall be at Buyer's expense.

> **NOTE:** If the parties agree herein to a change in the Purchase Price or the amount Seller agrees to pay toward Buyer's expenses associated with the purchase of the Property, the Agreement to Amend Contract (Form 4-T) should be completed and signed by the parties to reflect the change. However, the parties' failure to complete and sign Form 4-T will not affect the validity of any agreement reached hereunder. Buyer is advised to confirm with Buyer's lender that this amount will not exceed the amount lender will allow Seller to contribute.

> **NOTE**: Unless otherwise agreed, Buyer retains the right to conduct Due Diligence during the period agreed to in Paragraph 1(j), Due Diligence Period, of the Offer to Purchase and Contract. Buyer is advised to consult with Buyer's lender regarding this Agreement and/or any Agreement to Amend Contract prior to the expiration of the Due Diligence Period.

2. **Release of Inspection Reports**: Buyer ☐ does ☐ does not agree to release any inspection reports to Seller.

3. **Agreement:** This agreement shall become effective on the date it has been signed by both parties. All changes, additions or deletions hereto must be in writing and signed by all parties.

THE NORTH CAROLINA ASSOCIATION OF REALTORS®, INC. MAKES NO REPRESENTATION AS TO THE LEGAL VALIDITY OR ADEQUACY OF ANY PROVISION OF THIS FORM IN ANY SPECIFIC TRANSACTION.

Buyer: _____ Date _____   Seller: _____ Date _____

Buyer: _____ Date _____   Seller: _____ Date _____

Entity Buyer: _____   Entity Seller: _____
(Name of LLC/Corporation/Partnership/Trust/etc.)   (Name of LLC/Corporation/Partnership/Trust/etc.)

By: _____   By: _____
Name: _____   Name: _____
Title: _____   Title: _____
Date: _____   Date: _____

Page 1 of 1

North Carolina Association of REALTORS®, Inc.

STANDARD FORM 310-T
Revised 7/2018
© 7/2018

APPENDIX F Real Estate Forms and Addenda   901

EXCLUSIVE RIGHT TO SELL LISTING AGREEMENT (VACANT LOT/LAND)

This EXCLUSIVE RIGHT TO SELL LISTING AGREEMENT ("Agreement") is entered into between _____ as Seller(s) ("Seller") of the property described below (the "Property"), and _____ as Listing Firm ("Firm"). The individual agent who signs this Agreement on behalf of the Firm shall, on behalf of the Firm, be primarily responsible for ensuring that the Firm's duties hereunder are fulfilled; however, it is understood and agreed that other agents of the Firm may be assigned to fulfill such duties if deemed appropriate by the Firm. For purposes of this Agreement, the term "Firm," as the context may require, shall be deemed to include the individual agent who signs this Agreement and any other agents of the Firm.

Seller represents that as of the Effective Date the Seller is not (or will not be, if the Property is currently listed) a party to a listing agreement with any other real estate firm regarding the Property. Seller also represents that Seller has received a copy of the "WORKING WITH REAL ESTATE AGENTS" brochure and has reviewed it with Firm.

1. TERM OF AGREEMENT.
 (a) **Term:** The term of this Agreement ("Term") shall begin on its Effective Date and shall end at midnight on its Expiration Date.
 (b) **Effective Date**. This Agreement shall become effective and the Seller and Firm's respective rights and obligations under this Agreement shall commence ("Effective Date") as follows (*check appropriate box*):
  ❑ The Effective Date shall be the date that this Agreement has been signed by both Seller and Firm
  ❑ The Property is currently listed for sale exclusively with another real estate firm. Seller represents that the current listing agreement expires on _____. The Effective Date of this Agreement shall commence immediately upon the expiration of the current listing agreement. (**NOTE**: According to Article 16 of the REALTORS® Code of Ethics: *"REALTORS® shall not engage in any practice or take any action inconsistent with exclusive representation or exclusive brokerage relationship agreements that other REALTORS® have with clients."*)
  (c) **Expiration Date**. This Agreement shall terminate at midnight on _____ ("Expiration Date").

2. PROPERTY. The Property that is the subject of this Agreement shall include all that real estate described below together with all appurtenances thereto.
 Street Address: _____
 City: _____ Zip _____
 County: _____, North Carolina

 NOTE: Governmental authority over taxes, zoning, school districts, utilities and mail delivery may differ from address shown.
 Legal Description: (Complete *ALL* applicable)
 - Plat Reference: Lot/Unit_____, Block/Section_____, Subdivision/Condominium _____ _____, as shown on Plat Book/Slide _____ at Page(s) _____
 - The PIN/PID or other identification number of the Property is: _____
 - Other description: _____
 Some or all of the Property may be described in Deed Book _____ at Page _____

3. LISTING PRICE. Seller lists the Property at a price of $_____ on the following terms:
❑ Cash ❑ FHA ❑ VA ❑ USDA ❑ Conventional ❑ Loan Assumption ❑ Seller Financing ❑ Other _____.
Seller agrees to sell the Property for the Listing Price or for any other price or on any other terms acceptable to Seller.

4. FIRM'S COMPENSATION.
 (a) **Fee**. Seller agrees to pay Firm a total fee of _____ % of the gross sales price of the Property, OR _____ ("Fee"), which shall include the amount of any compensation paid by Firm as set forth in paragraph 5 below to any other real estate firm, including individual agents and sole proprietors ("Cooperating Real Estate Firm").
 (b) **Fee Earned**. The Fee shall be deemed earned under any of the following circumstances:
  (i) If a ready, willing and able buyer is procured by Firm, a Cooperating Real Estate Firm, the Seller, or anyone else during the Term of this Agreement at the price and on the terms set forth herein, or at any price and upon any terms acceptable to the Seller;
  (ii) If the Property is sold, optioned, exchanged, conveyed or transferred, or the Seller agrees, during the Term of this Agreement or any renewal hereof, to sell, option, exchange, convey or transfer the Property at any price and upon any terms whatsoever; or
  (iii) If the circumstances set out in (i) or (ii) above have not occurred, and if , within _____ days after the Expiration Date (the "Protection Period"), Seller either directly or indirectly sells, options, exchanges, conveys or transfers, or agrees to sell, option, exchange, convey or transfer the Property upon any terms whatsoever, to any person with whom Seller, Firm, or any

Page 1 of 8
North Carolina Association of REALTORS®, Inc.
STANDARD FORM 103
Revised 7/2018
© 7/2018

Individual agent initials _____ Seller initials _____ _____

Cooperating Real Estate Firm communicated regarding the Property during the Term of this Agreement or any renewal hereof, provided the names of such persons are delivered or postmarked to the Seller within 15 days after the Expiration Date. HOWEVER, Seller shall NOT be obligated to pay the Fee if a valid listing agreement is entered into between Seller and another real estate broker and the Property is subsequently sold, optioned, exchanged, conveyed or transferred during the Protection Period.

(c) **Fee Due and Payable.** Once earned as set forth above, the Fee will be due and payable at the earlier of: (i) closing on the Property;

(ii) The Seller's failure to sell the Property (including but not limited to the Seller's refusal to sign an offer to purchase the Property at the price and terms stated herein or on other terms acceptable to the Seller, the Seller's default on an executed sales contract for the Property, or the Seller's agreement with a buyer to unreasonably modify or cancel an executed sales contract for the Property); or

(iii) Seller's breach of this Agreement.

(d) **Transfer of Interest in Business Entity.** If Seller is a partnership, corporation or other business entity, and an interest in the partnership, corporation or other business entity is transferred, whether by merger, outright purchase or otherwise, in lieu of a sale of the Property, and applicable law does not prohibit the payment of a fee or commission in connection with such sale or transfer, the Fee shall be calculated on the fair market value of the Property, rather than the gross sales price, multiplied by the percentage of interest so transferred, and shall be paid by Seller at the time of the transfer.

(e) **Additional Compensation.** If additional compensation, incentive, bonus, rebate and/or other valuable consideration ("Additional Compensation") is offered to the Firm from any other party or person in connection with a sale of the Property, Seller will permit Firm to receive it in addition to the Fee. Firm shall timely disclose the promise or expectation of receiving any such Additional Compensation and confirm the disclosure in writing before Seller makes or accepts an offer to sell. (**NOTE**: NCAR Form #770 may be used to confirm the disclosure of any such Additional Compensation)

(f) **Attorney Fees and Costs.** If Firm is the prevailing party in any legal proceeding brought by Firm against Seller to recover any or all of the Fee, Firm shall be entitled to recover from Seller reasonable attorney fees and court costs incurred by Firm in connection with the proceeding.

5. **COOPERATION WITH/COMPENSATION TO OTHER FIRMS.** Firm has advised Seller of Firm's company policies regarding cooperation and the amount(s) of any compensation that will be offered to other brokers, including but not limited to, seller subagents, buyer agents or both, brokers who do or do not participate in a listing service and brokers who are or are not REALTORS®. Seller authorizes Firm to (*Check ALL applicable authorizations*):

- ❏ Cooperate with subagents representing the Seller and offer them the following compensation:_____% of the gross sales price or $_____; and/or,
- ❏ Cooperate with buyer agents representing the buyer and offer them the following compensation:_____% of the gross sales price or $_____; and/or,
- ❏ Cooperate with and compensate other Cooperating Real Estate Firms according to the Firm's attached policy.

Firm will promptly notify Seller if compensation offered to a Cooperating Real Estate Firm is different from that set forth above. Agents with Cooperating Real Estate Firms must orally disclose the nature of their relationship with a buyer (subagent or buyer agent) to Firm at the time of initial contact with Firm, and confirm that relationship in writing no later than the time an offer to purchase is submitted for the Seller's consideration. Seller should be careful about disclosing confidential information because agents representing buyers must disclose all relevant information to their clients.

6. **FIRM'S DUTIES.** Firm agrees to provide Seller the benefit of Firm's knowledge, experience and advice in the marketing and sale of the Property. Seller understands that Firm makes no representation or guarantee as to the sale of the Property, but Firm agrees to use its best efforts in good faith to find a buyer who is ready, willing and able to purchase the property. In accordance with the REALTORS® Code of Ethics, Firm shall, with Seller's approval, in response to inquiries from buyers or Cooperating Real Estate Firms, disclose the existence of offers on the Property. Where Seller authorizes disclosure, Firm shall also disclose whether offers were obtained by the individual agent who signs this Agreement, another agent of the Firm, or by a Cooperating Real Estate Firm. Seller acknowledges that real estate brokers are prohibited by N.C. Real Estate Commission rule from disclosing the price or other material terms contained in a party's offer to purchase, sell, lease, rent or option real property to a competing party without the express authority of the party making the offer.

Seller acknowledges that Firm is required by law to disclose to potential purchasers of the Property all material facts pertaining to the Property about which the Firm knows or reasonably should know, and that REALTORS® have an ethical responsibility to treat all parties to the transaction honestly. Seller further acknowledges that Firm is being retained solely as a real estate professional, and understands that other professional service providers are available to render advice or services to Seller, including but not limited to an attorney, insurance agent, tax advisor, surveyor, structural engineer, home inspector, environmental consultant, architect, or contractor. Although Firm may provide Seller the names of providers who claim to perform such services, Seller understands that Firm cannot guarantee the quality of service or level of expertise of any such provider. Seller agrees to pay the full amount due for all services directly to the service provider whether or not the transaction closes. Seller also agrees to indemnify and hold Firm harmless from and against any and all liability, claim, loss, damage, suit, or expense that Firm may incur either as a result of Seller's selection and use of any such provider or Seller's election not to have one or more of such services performed.

THE AGENT (FIRM) SHALL CONDUCT ALL BROKERAGE ACTIVITIES IN REGARD TO THIS AGREEMENT WITHOUT RESPECT TO THE RACE, COLOR, RELIGION, SEX, NATIONAL ORIGIN, HANDICAP OR FAMILIAL STATUS OF ANY PARTY OR PROSPECTIVE PARTY TO THE AGREEMENT. FURTHER, REALTORS® HAVE AN ETHICAL DUTY TO CONDUCT SUCH ACTIVITIES WITHOUT RESPECT TO THE SEXUAL ORIENTATION OR GENDER IDENTITY OF ANY PARTY OR PROSPECTIVE PARTY TO THIS AGREEMENT.

7. **MARKETING.**

(a) **Commencement of Marketing**. The Firm is authorized to commence marketing the Property as described in subparagraph (b) below on the Effective Date OR, if selected ❑ on (insert date only if applicable) _____("Delayed Marketing Date").

> **NOTE**: If a Delayed Marketing Date is selected, Seller understands and acknowledges the following:
> - THE PROPERTY MAY NOT BE SHOWN BY ANY REAL ESTATE AGENT, INCLUDING FIRM'S AGENTS, PRIOR TO THE DELAYED MARKETING DATE.
> - FIRM IS OBLIGATED TO PRESENT TO SELLER ANY OFFERS ON THE PROPERTY THAT MAY BE SUBMITTED TO FIRM PRIOR TO THE DELAYED MARKETING DATE.
> - IT IS IN THE BEST INTEREST OF MOST SELLERS TO GET THE HIGHEST POSSIBLE PRICE ON THE BEST TERMS FOR THEIR PROPERTY, AND MAXIMIZING EXPOSURE OF THEIR PROPERTY ADVANCES THAT INTEREST. ACCEPTING AN OFFER ON THE PROPERTY BEFORE IT IS FULLY EXPOSED TO THE WIDEST GROUP OF POTENTIAL BUYERS MAY DENY SELLER THE BEST OPPORTUNITY TO ATTRACT OFFERS AT THE HIGHEST PRICE AND BEST TERMS.

(b) **Marketing Authorization**.

❑ **Signs**. To place "For Sale," "Under Contract," "Sale Pending," or other similar signs on the Property (where permitted by law and relevant covenants) and to remove other such signs.

❑ **On-Site Marketing**. To conduct on-site marketing of the Property at such times as Seller and Firm may subsequently agree.

❑ **Listing Service**. To submit pertinent information concerning the Property to any listing service of which Firm is a member or in which any of Firm's agents participate and to furnish to such listing service notice of all changes of information concerning the Property authorized in writing by Seller. Seller authorizes Firm, upon execution of a sales contract for the Property, to notify the listing service of the pending sale and the expiration date of any due diligence period, and upon closing of the sale, to disseminate sales information, including sales price, to the listing service, appraisers and real estate brokers.

❑ **Lock/Key Boxes**. The Seller ❑ does ❑ does not authorize Firm to place lock/key boxes on the Property.

❑ **Advertising Other Than On The Internet**. To advertise the Property in non-Internet media, and to permit other firms to advertise the Property in non-Internet media to the extent and in such manner as Firm may decide.

❑ **Internet Advertising**. To display information about the Property on the Internet either directly or through a program of any listing service of which the Firm is a member or in which any of Firm's agents participate. Seller further authorizes other firms who belong to any listing service of which the Firm is a member or in which any of Firm's agents participate to display information about the Property on the Internet in accordance with the listing service rules and regulations, and also authorizes any listing service of which the Firm is a member or in which any of Firm's agents participate to use, license or sell to others information about the Property entered into the listing service. Seller specifically authorizes the display of the address of the Property, automated estimates of the market value of the Property and third-party comments about the Property. If seller desires to limit or prohibit Internet advertising as set forth above, seller must complete an opt-out form in accordance with listing service rules.

> **NOTE:** NCAR Form #105 may be used to limit or prohibit Internet advertising and explains how such limitations may or may not be effective.

(c) **"Coming Soon" Advertising**. ❑ (Check only if applicable). If applicable, Firm is authorized to market the Property as "Coming Soon," commencing on the Effective Date, in any media Firm may in its discretion select, provided that any "Coming Soon" advertising shall be conducted in accordance with any restrictions and requirements of any listing service in which the Property will be included, a copy of which ❑ are ❑ are not attached to this Agreement.

(d) **Seller Acknowledgement**. Seller acknowledges and understands that while the marketing services selected above will facilitate the showing and sale of the Property, there are risks associated with allowing access to and disseminating information about the Property that are not within the reasonable control of the Firm, including but not limited to:

(i) unauthorized use of a lock/key box,

(ii) control of visitors during or after a showing or an open house, including the taking and use of photographs and videos of the Property

(iii) inappropriate use of information about the Property placed on the Internet or furnished to any listing service in which the Firm participates, and

(iv) information about the Property placed on the Internet by or through any listing service in which the Firm participates which is inaccurate or dated.

Seller therefore agrees to release and discharge Firm and Firm's agents from any and all claims, demands, rights and causes of action of whatsoever kind and nature not caused by Firm's negligence arising directly or indirectly out of any such marketing services.

> **WARNING:** IT MAY BE A CRIME UNDER FEDERAL AND STATE LAWS TO LISTEN TO OR RECORD AN ORAL COMMUNICATION THROUGH THE USE OF ANY ELECTRONIC, MECHANICAL, OR OTHER DEVICE WITHOUT THE CONSENT OF A PARTY TO THAT COMMUNICATION. If there is a video/audio/surveillance device(s) on the Property, Seller is advised: (i) that no audio surveillance device may be turned on during any showings, open houses, investigations, examinations or inspections of the Property; and (ii) that the placement of any video surveillance device should not violate a visitor's reasonable expectation of privacy.

8. **EARNEST MONEY.** Unless otherwise provided in the sales contract, any initial and additional earnest money deposits and any other earnest monies paid in connection with any transaction shall be held by the Firm, in escrow, until the consummation or termination of the transaction. Any earnest money forfeited by reason of the buyer's default under a sales contract shall be divided equally between the Firm and Seller. In no event shall the sum paid to the Firm because of a buyer's default be in excess of the fee that would have been due if the sale had closed as contemplated in the sales contract. In accordance with NC General Statutes Section 93A-12, if a dispute regarding the return or forfeiture of any earnest money deposit arises between Seller and the buyer, the escrow agent holding the deposit may deposit the disputed monies with the appropriate Clerk of Court following written notice to the parties. In the event of any such dispute, Seller directs Firm to disclose Seller's last known mailing address to the escrow agent upon request to enable the escrow agent to comply with the notice requirement of such law.

9. **SELLER REPRESENTATIONS.**
   (a) **Flood Hazard Disclosure/Insurance.** To the best of Seller's knowledge, the Property ❑ is ❑ is not located partly or entirely within a designated Special Flood Hazard Area.
   (b) **Owners' Association.** To the best of Seller's knowledge there ❑ is ❑ is not an owners' association which imposes various mandatory covenants, conditions and restrictions upon the Property. If there is an owners' association, Seller agrees to promptly complete an Owners' Association Disclosure and Addendum For Properties Exempt from Residential Property Disclosure Statement (Standard Form 2A12-T) at Seller's expense and to attach it as an addendum to any contract for the sale of the Property. Seller authorizes and directs any owners' association or any management company of the owners' association to release to Firm true and accurate copies of the following items affecting the Property, including any amendments:
   - Seller's statement of account
   - master insurance policy showing the coverage provided and the deductible amount
   - Declaration and Restrictive Covenants
   - Rules and Regulations
   - Articles of Incorporation
   - Bylaws of the owners' association
   - current financial statement and budget of the owners' association
   - parking restrictions and information
   - architectural guidelines

   (c) **Ownership.** Seller represents that Seller:
   ❑ has owned the Property for at least one year;
   ❑ has owned the Property for less than one year
   ❑ does not yet own the Property

If Seller does not yet own the Property, Seller agrees to promptly provide Firm information pertaining to Seller's acquisition of the Property, such as a copy of a sales contract or option for the Property, and to keep Firm timely informed of all developments pertaining to Seller's acquisition of the Property.

   (d) **Receipt of Sample Forms.**
   ❑ Seller acknowledges receipt of a sample copy of an Offer to Purchase and Contract—New Construction (form #800-T) or Offer to Purchase and Contract—Vacant Lot/Land (form 12-T) as may be appropriate for review purposes.
   ❑ Seller acknowledges receipt of a sample copy of a Professional Services Disclosure and Election form (form #760) for review purposes.

   (e) **Access.** Seller represents that the Property has legal access to a public right of way. If access is by private road/easement/other, Seller further represents that there ❑ is ❑ is not an agreement regarding the maintenance of such private road/easement/other means of access. If applicable, Seller agrees to promptly provide Firm information pertaining to any such agreement.

(f) **Current Liens**. Seller represents to the best of Seller's knowledge:
   (1) The Property ❏ is ❏ is not encumbered by a deed of trust or mortgage. *Complete any of the following where applicable:*
      (i) There is a first deed of trust or mortgage on the Property securing a loan held by:
         Lender Name: _____
         Approximate balance: $_____ Lender Phone#: _____
         Lender Address: _____
      (ii) There is a second deed of trust or mortgage on the Property securing a loan held by:
         Lender Name: _____
         Approximate balance: $_____ Lender Phone#: _____
         Lender Address: _____
      (iii) There is a deed of trust or mortgage on the Property securing an equity line of credit held by:
         Lender Name: _____
         Approximate balance: $_____ Lender Phone#: _____
         Lender Address: _____
   (2) Seller is current on all payments for the loans identified in numbered items (i), (ii) and (iii) above except as specified in (7) below.
   (3) Seller is not in default on any loan identified in numbered items (i), (ii) and (iii) above and has not received any notice(s) from the holder of any loan identified in numbered items (i), (ii) and (iii) above or from any other lien holder of any kind, regarding a default under the loan, threatened foreclosure, notice of foreclosure, or the filing of foreclosure except as specified in (7) below.
   (4) There are not any liens secured against the Property for Federal, State or local income taxes, unpaid real property taxes, unpaid condominium or homeowners' association fees, mechanics', laborers' or material men's liens, or other liens affecting the Property, and Seller has no knowledge of any matter that might result in a lien affecting the Property except as specified in (7) below.
   (5) There are not any judgments against Seller affecting the Property, and Seller has no knowledge of any matter that might result in a judgment that may potentially affect the Property except as specified in (7) below.
   (6) There are not any Uniform Commercial Code (UCC) fixture filings affecting the Property, and Seller has no knowledge of any matter that might result in a UCC fixture filing affecting the Property except as specified in (7) below.
   (7) Specify any information, including approximate balances, required by Seller representations (2) through (6) above **NOTE**: Outstanding liens may affect Seller's net proceeds: _____
   _____
   _____
   _____

(g) **Bankruptcy**. Seller currently:
   (1) ❏ is ❏ is not under bankruptcy protection under United States law.
   (2) ❏ is ❏ is not contemplating seeking bankruptcy protection during the term of this Agreement.
(h) **Lease(s)**. To the best of Seller's knowledge, the Property ❏ is ❏ is not subject to any lease(s). If applicable, Seller agrees to promptly provide Firm a copy of any such lease(s) or a written statement of the terms of any oral lease(s).
(i) **Special Assessments**. To the best of Seller's knowledge, there are no Proposed or Confirmed Special Assessments (as defined in the sample contract form provided to Seller) regarding the Property except as follows (Insert "none" or the identification of such assessments, if any): _____
_____

(j) **Manufactured (Mobile) Home**. Complete ONLY if there is a manufactured (mobile) home(s) on the Property that Seller intends to include as a part of the sale of the Property: VIN(s): _____
or ❏ VIN(s) unknown. Other description (*year, model, etc.*): _____
_____

If, during the term of this Agreement, Seller becomes aware that any of the representations set forth in this paragraph 9 are incorrect or no longer accurate, Seller shall promptly notify Firm and cooperate with Firm in taking appropriate corrective action.

10. **SELLER'S DUTIES**. Seller agrees to cooperate with Firm in the marketing and sale of the Property, including but not limited to:
   (a) providing to Firm, in a timely manner, accurate information about the Property of which Seller may be aware, including but not limited to presence of or access to any water supply, sewer and/or septic system; problems with drainage, grading or soil stability; environmental hazards; commercial or industrial nuisances (noise, odor, smoke, etc.); utility or other easements, shared driveways, or encroachments from or on adjacent property; lawsuits, foreclosures, bankruptcy, tenancies, judgments, tax liens, proposed assessments, mechanics' liens, materialmens' liens, or notice from any governmental agency; flood hazard; cemetery/grave sites; or abandoned well;

(b) making the Property available for showing (including working, existing utilities) at reasonable times and upon reasonable notice;

(c) providing Firm as soon as reasonably possible after the execution of this Agreement copies of the following documents (where relevant) in the possession of Seller:

(1) restrictive covenants affecting the Property;

(2) bylaws, articles of incorporation, rules and regulations, and other governing documents of the owners' association and/or the subdivision;

(3) title insurance policies, attorney's opinions on title, surveys, covenants, deeds, notes and deeds of trust and easements relating to the Property.

Seller authorizes (1) any attorney presently or previously representing Seller to release and disclose any title insurance policy in such attorney's file to Firm, (2) the Property's title insurer or its agent to release and disclose all materials in the Property's title insurer's (or title insurer's agent's) file to Firm, and (3) the owners' association manager (or other authorized representative) to release and disclose copies of all documents referenced in subparagraphs (c)(1) and (c)(2) above. Seller acknowledges and understands that Firm is under no obligation to acquire any of the information referenced in this subparagraph (c) or to verify the accuracy of any such information that may be provided to Firm.

(d) immediately referring to Firm all inquiries or offers it may receive regarding the Property; showing the Property only by appointment made by or through Firm; and conducting all negotiations through Firm.

(e) executing and delivering at Settlement a GENERAL WARRANTY DEED conveying fee simple marketable title to the Property, including legal access to a public right of way, free of all encumbrances except ad valorem taxes for the current year, utility easements, rights-of-way, and unviolated restrictive covenants, if any, and those encumbrances that the buyer agrees to assume in the sales contract.

Seller represents that the Seller has the right to convey the Property, and that there are currently no circumstances that would prohibit the Seller from conveying fee simple marketable title as set forth in the preceding sentence, except as follows *(insert N/A if not applicable)*: _____

_____

> **NOTE**: If any sale of the Property may be a "short sale," consideration should be given to attaching NCAR form 104 as an addendum to this Agreement.

(f) providing Firm, in a timely manner, any information necessary (including any information omitted under Paragraph 9) to enable Firm to prepare an estimate of Seller's net proceeds at settlement. Seller acknowledges and understands that any such estimate is an approximation only and that Seller should verify the accuracy of the calculations.

(g) if required by N.C.G.S. §44A-11.1, timely designating a Lien Agent, and providing Firm as soon as reasonably possible a copy of the appointment of Lien Agent.

11. PHOTOGRAPHS AND OTHER MATERIALS: PHOTOGRAPHS AND OTHER MATERIALS: Firm is specifically authorized to use, for any purposes whatsoever, any and all photographs, drawings, video, advertising copy or other information obtained by or provided to Firm pursuant to this Agreement (including but not limited to any information concerning the price and terms of the sale of the Property, the description of the Property and the length of time the Property is on the market) ("Materials"), both before and after the sale or, in the event there is not a sale, after this Agreement has expired. Seller shall not have or acquire any rights to use any of the Materials created by, on behalf of, or at the direction of Firm or an agent of Firm either during or after the Term of this Agreement without Firm's written consent. If Seller provides any Materials to Firm ("Seller Materials"), Seller represents that Seller owns the Seller Materials or otherwise has the legal right to provide the Seller Materials to Firm, and Seller grants to Firm and any listing service in which Firm or its agents participate a non-exclusive, perpetual license to use the Seller Materials, including the rights to display, reproduce, distribute or make derivative works from the Seller Materials. Seller agrees to indemnify and hold Firm and its agents harmless for any and all claims resulting from use of the Seller Materials under the terms of this license.

12. ADDITIONAL TERMS AND CONDITIONS. The following additional terms and conditions shall also be a part of this Agreement: _____

_____

_____

13. DUAL AGENCY. Seller understands that the potential for dual agency will arise if a buyer who has an agency relationship with Firm becomes interested in viewing the Property. Firm may represent more than one party in the same transaction only with the knowledge and informed consent of all parties for whom Firm acts.

(a) **Disclosure of Information**. In the event Firm serves as a dual agent, Seller agrees that without permission from the party about whom the information pertains, Firm shall not disclose to the other party the following information:

(1) that a party may agree to a price, terms, or any conditions of sale other than those offered;

(2) the motivation of a party for engaging in the transaction, unless disclosure is otherwise required by statute or rule; and

(3) any information about a party which that party has identified as confidential unless disclosure is otherwise required by statute or rule.

Individual agent initials _____ Sellers initials _____ _____

(b) **Firm's Role as Dual Agent**. If Firm serves as agent for both Seller and a buyer in a transaction involving the Property, Firm shall make every reasonable effort to represent Seller and buyer in a balanced and fair manner. Firm shall also make every reasonable effort to encourage and effect communication and negotiation between Seller and buyer. Seller understands and acknowledges that:
    (1) Prior to the time dual agency occurs, Firm will act as Seller's exclusive agent;
    (2) In its separate representation of Seller and buyer, Firm may obtain information which, if disclosed, could harm the bargaining position of the party providing such information to Firm;
    (3) Firm is required by law to disclose to Seller and buyer any known or reasonably ascertainable material facts. Seller agrees Firm shall not be liable to Seller for (i) disclosing material facts required by law to be disclosed, and (ii) refusing or failing to disclose other information the law does not require to be disclosed which could harm or compromise one party's bargaining position but could benefit the other party.
(c) **Seller's Role**. Should Firm become a dual agent, Seller understands and acknowledges that:
    (1) Seller has the responsibility of making Seller's own decisions as to what terms are to be included in any purchase and sale agreement with a buyer client of Firm;
    (2) Seller is fully aware of and understands the implications and consequences of Firm's dual agency role as expressed herein to provide balanced and fair representation of Seller and buyer and to encourage and effect communication between them rather than as an advocate or exclusive agent or representative; Seller has determined that the benefits of dual agency outweigh any disadvantages or adverse consequences;
    (3) Seller may seek independent legal counsel to assist Seller with the negotiation and preparation of a purchase and sale agreement or with any matter relating to the transaction which is the subject matter of a purchase and sale agreement.

Should Firm become a dual agent, Seller waives all claims, damages, losses, expenses or liabilities, other than for violations of the North Carolina Real Estate License Law and intentional wrongful acts, arising from Firm's role as a dual agent. Seller shall have a duty to protect Seller's own interests and should read any purchase and sale agreement carefully to ensure that it accurately sets forth the terms which Seller wants included in said agreement.

(d) **Authorization** *(initial only ONE)*.
    _____ _____Seller authorizes the Firm to act as a dual agent, representing both the Seller and the buyer, subject to the terms and conditions set forth in Paragraph 13.
    _____ _____Seller desires exclusive representation at all times during this agreement and does NOT authorize Firm to act in the capacity of dual agent. *If Seller does not authorize Firm to act as a dual agent, the remainder of this paragraph shall not apply.*

(e) **Designated Agent Option** (*Initial only if applicable*).
    _____ _____ Seller hereby authorizes the Firm to designate an individual agent(s) to represent the Seller. The individual designated agent(s) shall represent only the interests of the Seller to the extent permitted by law.

> **NOTE**: When dual agency arises, an individual agent shall not practice designated agency and shall remain a dual agent if the individual agent has actually received confidential information concerning a buyer client of the Firm in connection with the transaction or if designated agency is otherwise prohibited by law.

14. **MEDIATION.** If a dispute arises out of or related to this Agreement or the breach thereof, and if the dispute cannot be settled through negotiation, the parties agree first to try in good faith to settle the dispute by mediation before resorting to arbitration, litigation, or some other dispute resolution procedure. If the need for mediation arises, the parties will choose a mutually acceptable mediator and will share the cost of mediation equally.

15. **WIRE FRAUD WARNING.**

> **IF SELLER'S PROCEEDS WILL BE WIRED, IT IS RECOMMENDED THAT SELLER PROVIDE WIRING INSTRUCTIONS AT CLOSING IN WRITING IN THE PRESENCE OF THE ATTORNEY. IF SELLER IS UNABLE TO ATTEND CLOSING, SELLER MAY BE REQUIRED TO SEND AN ORIGINAL NOTARIZED DIRECTIVE TO THE CLOSING ATTORNEY'S OFFICE CONTAINING THE WIRING INSTRUCTIONS. THIS MAY BE SENT WITH THE DEED, LIEN WAIVER AND TAX FORMS IF THOSE DOCUMENTS ARE BEING PREPARED FOR SELLER BY THE CLOSING ATTORNEY. AT A MINIMUM, SELLER SHOULD CALL THE CLOSING ATTORNEY'S OFFICE TO PROVIDE THE WIRE INSTRUCTIONS. THE WIRE INSTRUCTIONS SHOULD BE VERIFIED OVER THE TELEPHONE VIA A CALL TO SELLER INITIATED BY THE CLOSING ATTORNEY'S OFFICE TO ENSURE THAT THEY ARE NOT FROM A FRAUDULENT SOURCE.**
>
> **SELLER SHOULD CALL THE CLOSING ATTORNEY'S OFFICE AT A NUMBER THAT IS INDEPENDENTLY OBTAINED. TO ENSURE THAT SELLER'S CONTACT IS LEGITIMATE, SELLER SHOULD NOT RELY ON A PHONE NUMBER IN AN EMAIL FROM THE CLOSING ATTORNEY'S OFFICE, SELLER'S REAL ESTATE AGENT OR ANYONE ELSE.**

> Seller acknowledges and understands that there are risks associated with wire transfers that are not within the reasonable control of Firm, and Seller hereby agrees to release and discharge Firm and Firm's agents from any and all claims, demands, rights and causes of action of whatsoever kind and nature not caused by gross negligence of Firm or Firm's agents arising directly or indirectly out of any wire transfer Seller sends or receives/was to receive in connection with any real estate transaction in which Firm represents Seller.

16. **ENTIRE AGREEMENT/CHANGES/TERMINATION.** This Agreement constitutes the entire agreement between Seller and Firm and there are no representations, inducements, or other provisions other than those expressed herein. This Agreement may be signed in multiple originals or counterparts, all of which together constitute one and the same instrument. All changes, additions, or deletions to this Agreement must be in writing and signed by both Seller and Firm. Seller acknowledges and understands that this Agreement constitutes a binding contract between Seller and Firm. Although Seller may at any time withdraw from the fiduciary relationship existing between Seller and Firm, the contract created by this Agreement may not be terminated by Seller or Firm prior to its Expiration Date without legally sufficient cause. Any such termination shall be by mutually-acceptable written agreement signed by both Seller and Firm.

Seller and Firm each acknowledge receipt of a signed copy of this Agreement.

THE NORTH CAROLINA ASSOCIATION OF REALTORS®, INC. MAKES NO REPRESENTATION AS TO THE LEGAL VALIDITY OR ADEQUACY OF ANY PROVISION OF THIS FORM IN ANY SPECIFIC TRANSACTION.

Seller: _____ _____ _____
                 Print Name   Signature   Date

Contact Information: _____ _____ _____ _____
                      Home   Work   Cell   Email

Mailing Address: _____

Seller: _____ _____ _____
                 Print Name   Signature   Date

Contact Information: _____ _____ _____ _____
                      Home   Work   Cell   Email

Mailing Address: _____

Entity Seller: _____
            (Name of LLC/Corporation/Partnership/Trust/etc.)

By: _____ Date: _____

Name: _____ Title: _____

Contact Information: _____ _____ _____ _____
                    Home   Work   Cell   Email

Mailing Address: _____

Firm: _____ Phone: _____
       Print Real Estate Firm Name

By: _____ _____ _____
     Individual Agent Signature   Individual License Number   Date

Office: _____

Address: _____

Office Phone: _____ Fax: _____ Email _____

FHA/VA FINANCING ADDENDUM

Property: _____

Seller: _____

Buyer: _____

This Addendum is attached to and made a part of the Offer to Purchase and Contract ("Contract") between Seller and Buyer for the Property.

> **FHA FINANCING:** ☐ **U.S. DEPARTMENT OF HOUSING AND URBAN DEVELOPMENT**
> **FEDERAL HOUSING ADMINISTRATION**
>
> **AMENDATORY CLAUSE** – It is expressly agreed that, notwithstanding any other provisions of this contract, the purchaser shall not be obligated to complete the purchase of the property described herein or to incur any penalty for forfeiture of earnest money deposits or otherwise unless the purchaser has been given in accordance with HUD/FHA or DVA requirements a written statement issued by the Federal Housing Commissioner, the Department of Veterans Affairs or a Direct Endorsement lender, setting forth the appraised value of the property of not less than $_____. The purchaser shall, however, have the privilege and option of proceeding with the consummation of the contract without regard to the amount of the appraised valuation. <u>The appraised valuation is arrived at to determine the maximum mortgage the Department of Housing and Urban Development will insure. HUD does not warrant the value nor the condition of the property. The purchaser should satisfy himself/herself that the price and condition of the property are acceptable.</u>

> **VA FINANCING:** ☐
>
> **VA NOTICE TO BUYER** – It is expressly agreed that, notwithstanding any other provisions of this contract, the Buyer shall not incur any penalty by forfeiture of earnest money deposits or otherwise be obligated to complete the purchase of the Property described herein, if the contract purchase price or cost exceeds the reasonable value of the Property established by the Department of Veterans Affairs. The Buyer shall, however, have the privilege and option of proceeding with the consummation of this contract without regard to the amount of the reasonable value established by DVA. If Buyer elects to complete the purchase at an amount in excess of the reasonable value established by DVA, Buyer shall pay such excess amount in cash from a source which Buyer agrees to disclose to the DVA and which Buyer represents will not be from borrowed funds except as approved by DVA. If DVA reasonable value of the Property is less than the sales price, Seller shall have the option of reducing the sales price to an amount equal to the DVA reasonable value and the parties to the sale may close at such lower sales price with appropriate adjustments to the sales contract.
>
> If Buyer obtains a VA loan, the DVA may or may not require well/water, septic/sewer, and/or wood destroying insect inspections to be performed. If required to be performed, such inspections may or may not be required to be at Seller's expense. If such inspections are required to be performed and are required to be at Seller's expense, Seller agrees to pay the cost of such inspections, subject to the limit set forth in Paragraph 8(i) of the Contract.

IN THE EVENT OF A CONFLICT BETWEEN THIS ADDENDUM AND THE CONTRACT, THIS ADDENDUM SHALL CONTROL, EXCEPT THAT IN THE CASE OF SUCH A CONFLICT AS TO THE DESCRIPTION OF THE PROPERTY OR THE IDENTITY OF THE BUYER OR SELLER, THE CONTRACT SHALL CONTROL.

THE NORTH CAROLINA ASSOCIATION OF REALTORS®, INC. AND THE NORTH CAROLINA BAR ASSOCIATION MAKE NO REPRESENTATION AS TO THE LEGAL VALIDITY OR ADEQUACY OF ANY PROVISION OF THIS FORM IN ANY SPECIFIC TRANSACTION. IF YOU DO NOT UNDERSTAND THIS FORM OR FEEL THAT IT DOES NOT PROVIDE FOR YOUR LEGAL NEEDS, YOU SHOULD CONSULT A NORTH CAROLINA REAL ESTATE ATTORNEY BEFORE YOU SIGN IT.

Page 1 of 2

This form jointly approved by:
North Carolina Bar Association
North Carolina Association of REALTORS®, Inc.

STANDARD FORM 2A4-T
Revised 7/2014
© 7/2018

Buyer initials _____ _____   Seller initials _____ _____

APPENDIX F Real Estate Forms and Addenda

REAL ESTATE CERTIFICATION – The seller, the purchaser, and the broker hereby certify that the terms of the sales contract are true to the best of their knowledge and belief and it is agreed that any other agreement entered into by any of the parties is fully disclosed and attached to the sales contract. The seller, the purchaser, and the broker fully understand that it is a federal crime punishable by fine or imprisonment or both to knowingly make any false statement concerning any of the above facts as applicable under the provisions of Title 18, United States Code, Sections 1012 and 1014.

I CERTIFY I HAVE READ & UNDERSTAND THE ABOVE STATEMENTS:

BUYER/BORROWER _____ DATE _____

BUYER/CO-BORROWER _____ DATE _____

Entity Buyer/Borrower: _____
(Name of LLC/Corporation/Partnership/Trust/etc.)

By: _____ Date: _____

Name: _____ Title: _____

SELLING FIRM _____ By: _____
(Firm Name)   (Signature)

SELLER _____ DATE _____

SELLER _____ DATE _____

Entity Seller: _____
(Name of LLC/Corporation/Partnership/Trust/etc.)

By: _____ Date: _____

Name: _____ Title: _____

LISTING FIRM _____ By: _____
(Firm Name)   (Signature)

THE MORTGAGE LENDER MUST RECEIVE AN ORIGINAL SIGNATURE COPY

STANDARD FORM 2A4-T
Revised 7/2014
© 7/2018

INTERNET ADVERTISING ADDENDUM
(**Note**: This form should be used only if a seller has elected to limit or prohibit Internet advertising of their property)

This INTERNET ADVERTISING ADDENDUM hereby modifies the attached: *(Check the appropriate box)*

❑ NCAR Form 101 (Exclusive Right to Sell Listing Agreement)   dated _____
❑ NCAR Form 103 (Exclusive Right to Sell Listing Agreement (Vacant Lot/Land))   dated _____
❑ NCAR Form 401 (Exclusive Property Management Agreement (Long-Term Rental))   dated _____
❑ NCAR Form 601 (Exclusive Right to Sell Listing Agreement – Auction Sales)   dated _____
❑ Other: _____   dated _____

Seller: _____ ("Seller")

Real Estate Firm/Agent/Broker: _____ ("Firm")

Property Address: _____ ("Property")

1. **DEFINITIONS:**
   (a) "**Automated Valuation Model**" or "**AVM**" means a service or computer function that uses statistical calculations to estimate the value of a property based upon data from public records, multiple listing service ("MLS"), and other sources and incorporating certain assumptions. The accuracy of AVMs has sometimes been criticized because they do not take into consideration all relevant factors in valuing a property.
   (b) "**IDX site**" means a web site operated by a broker participating in the MLS on which the broker can advertise the listings of other brokers in MLS, subject to certain MLS rules. The consumer visiting an IDX site is not required to register on the site or to have a brokerage relationship with the broker displaying listings on the site.
   (c) "**Third-party commentary**" means comments and reviews regarding the Property left on a web site by someone other than the operator of the web site.
   (d) "**Virtual office web site**" (**VOW**) means a web site operated by a broker participating in the MLS that delivers brokerage services to consumers over the world wide web. Visitors to a VOW are required to register on the site (with their name and a real email address) and enter a brokerage relationship with the broker operating the VOW. The broker operating the VOW can then show the visiting customer/client nearly all the information available to the broker in MLS. The seller(s) of a listing have the right to opt out of certain kinds of data display under the MLS's VOW policy. The MLS imposes various other rules and restrictions on VOWs.

2. **DISPLAY OF PROPERTY ON THE INTERNET:** (*Seller must choose (a), (b), or (c)*)
   (a) ❑ Seller permits display of information about the Property on the Internet subject to the limitations set forth in paragraphs 3, 4 and/or 5 below.
   (b) ❑ Seller authorizes Firm to display information about the Property on the Internet but does NOT authorize participants of any listing service (MLS) of which the Firm is a member or in which any of Firm's agents participate to display information about the Property on the Internet. **Seller acknowledges and understands that if Seller selects this option, the Property will not be eligible for inclusion in any listing service (MLS).**
   (c) ❑ Seller does NOT authorize the display of information about the Property on the Internet. **Seller acknowledges and understands that consumers who conduct searches for listings on the Internet will not see information about the Property in response to their search.**

   If (a) or (b) above is selected, complete paragraphs 3, 4 and 5 below. If (c) above is selected, do not complete paragraphs 3, 4 and 5 below.

3. **DISPLAY OF THE PROPERTY ADDRESS ON INTERNET:** Seller ❑ permits ❑ does not permit display of the Property address (house and unit numbers and street name) in marketing of the Property on the Internet. Seller's election in this section affects all Internet display, including on Firm's web site, IDX and VOW sites, and third-party sites such as Zillow, Trulia and Realtor.com. If Seller does not permit address display on the Internet, brokers participating in MLS can still disclose the address to clients/customers via other means, including email, fax, mail, hand delivery, and orally.

Page 1 of 2

North Carolina Association of REALTORS®, Inc.

Individual agent initials _____ Seller initials _____ _____

STANDARD FORM 105
Revised 7/2014
© 7/2018

4. **DISPLAY OF AUTOMATED VALUATIONS ON VOWS/IDX SITES:** Seller ❑ permits ❑ does not permit an automated valuation of the Property or a link to an automated valuation of it to be displayed adjacent to the Property on the IDX sites and VOWs of other brokers. Seller's election here affects only the web sites of other real estate brokers, and does not affect display of automated valuations of the Property on third-party web sites such as Zillow, Trulia and Realtor.com.

5. **DISPLAY OF THIRD-PARTY COMMENTARY ON VOWS/IDX SITES:** Seller ❑ permits ❑ does not permit third-party commentary regarding the Property or a link to third-party commentary regarding it to be displayed adjacent to the property on the IDX sites and VOWs of other brokers. Seller's election here affects only the web sites of other real estate brokers, and does not affect display of third-party commentary regarding the Property on third-party web sites such as Zillow, Trulia and Realtor.com.

THE NORTH CAROLINA ASSOCIATION OF REALTORS®, INC. MAKES NO REPRESENTATION AS TO THE LEGAL VALIDITY OR ADEQUACY OF ANY PROVISION OF THIS FORM IN ANY SPECIFIC TRANSACTION.

Date: _____

Seller Signature: _____

Date: _____

Seller Signature: _____

Entity Seller: _____
(Name of LLC/Corporation/Partnership/Trust/etc.)

By: _____

Name: _____

Title: _____

Date: _____

Date: _____

Firm: _____

By: _____
            Individual Agent Signature

Page 2 of 2

STANDARD FORM 105
Revised 7/2014
© 7/2018

LEAD-BASED PAINT OR LEAD-BASED PAINT HAZARD ADDENDUM

Property: _____

Seller: _____

Buyer: _____

This Addendum is attached to and made a part of the Offer to Purchase and Contract ("Contract") between Seller and Buyer for the Property.

During the Due Diligence Period, Buyer shall have the right to obtain a risk assessment or inspection of the Property for the presence of lead-based paint and/or lead-based paint hazards* at Buyer's expense. Buyer may waive the right to obtain a risk assessment or inspection of the Property for the presence of lead-based paint and/or lead-based paint hazards at any time without cause.

*Intact lead-based paint that is in good condition is not necessarily a hazard. See EPA pamphlet "Protect Your Family From Lead in Your Home" for more information.

Disclosure of Information on Lead-Based Paint and Lead-Based Paint Hazards

Lead Warning Statement
Every Buyer of any interest in residential real property on which a residential dwelling was built prior to 1978 is notified that such property may present exposure to lead from lead-based paint that may place young children at risk of developing lead poisoning. Lead poisoning in young children may produce permanent neurological damage, including learning disabilities, reduced intelligence quotient, behavioral problems, and impaired memory. Lead poisoning also poses a particular risk to pregnant women. The Seller of any interest in residential real property is required to provide the Buyer with any information on lead-based paint hazards from risk assessments or inspections in the Seller's possession and notify the Buyer of any known lead-based paint hazards. A risk assessment or inspection for possible lead-based hazards is recommended prior to purchase.

Seller's Disclosure (initial)

_____ (a) Presence of lead-based paint and/or lead-based paint hazards (check one below):
❑ Known lead-based paint and/or lead-based paint hazards are present in the housing (explain).
_____
_____

❑ Seller has no knowledge of lead-based paint and/or lead-based paint hazards in the housing.

_____ (b) Records and reports available to the Seller (check one)
❑ Seller has provided the Buyer with all available records and reports pertaining to lead-based paint and/or lead-based paint hazards in the housing (list documents below).
_____
_____

❑ Seller has no reports or records pertaining to lead-based paint and/or lead-based paint hazards in the housing.

Buyer's Acknowledgement (initial)

_____ (c) Buyer has received copies of all information listed above.
_____ (d) Buyer has received the pamphlet *Protect Your Family from Lead in Your Home*.
_____ (e) Buyer has (check one below):
❑ Received the opportunity during the Due Diligence Period to conduct a risk assessment or inspection for the presence of lead-based paint and/or lead-based paint hazards; or
❑ Waived the opportunity to conduct a risk assessment or inspection for the presence of lead-based paint and/or lead-based paint hazards.

Page 1 of 2

This form jointly approved by:
North Carolina Bar Association
North Carolina Association of REALTORS®, Inc.

STANDARD FORM 2A9–T
Revised 7/2015
© 7/2018

Buyer Initials _____ _____   Seller Initials _____ _____

Agent's Acknowledgment (initial)

_____ (f) Agent has informed the Seller of the Seller's obligations under 42 U.S.C. 4852d and is aware of his/her responsibility to ensure compliance.

Certification of Accuracy

The following parties have reviewed the information above and certify, to the best of their knowledge, that the information provided by the signatory is true and accurate.

IN THE EVENT OF A CONFLICT BETWEEN THIS ADDENDUM AND THE CONTRACT, THIS ADDENDUM SHALL CONTROL, EXCEPT THAT IN THE CASE OF SUCH A CONFLICT AS TO THE DESCRIPTION OF THE PROPERTY OR THE IDENTITY OF THE BUYER OR SELLER, THE CONTRACT SHALL CONTROL.

THE NORTH CAROLINA ASSOCIATION OF REALTORS®, INC. AND THE NORTH CAROLINA BAR ASSOCIATION MAKE NO REPRESENTATION AS TO THE LEGAL VALIDITY OR ADEQUACY OF ANY PROVISION OF THIS FORM IN ANY SPECIFIC TRANSACTION. IF YOU DO NOT UNDERSTAND THIS FORM OR FEEL THAT IT DOES NOT PROVIDE FOR YOUR LEGAL NEEDS, YOU SHOULD CONSULT A NORTH CAROLINA REAL ESTATE ATTORNEY BEFORE YOU SIGN IT.

Buyer:_____ Date:_____

Buyer:_____ Date:_____

Entity Buyer:_____
(Name of LLC/Corporation/Partnership/Trust/etc.)

By: _____ Date:_____

Name:_____ Title:_____

Agent:_____ Date:_____

Seller:_____ Date:_____

Seller:_____ Date:_____

Entity Seller: _____
(Name of LLC/Corporation/Partnership/Trust/etc.)

By: _____ Date_____

Name:_____ Title:_____

Agent:_____ Date:_____

STANDARD FORM 2A9-T
Revised 7/2015
© 7/2018

APPENDIX F Real Estate Forms and Addenda

NOTICE TO SELLER THAT BUYER IS EXERCISING THEIR UNILATERAL RIGHT TO TERMINATE THE OFFER TO PURCHASE AND CONTRACT (FORM 2-T)

Buyer: _____ ("Buyer")

Seller: _____ ("Seller")

Property Address: _____ ("Property")

1. **Contract.** Buyer and Seller entered into a contract for the purchase and sale of the Property on the Offer to Purchase and Contract (form 2-T) ("Contract"). The Effective Date of the Contract is _____.

2. **Termination by Buyer.** Buyer hereby terminates the Contract for the following reason(s) (check all applicable boxes):

   ❑ Non-receipt of a signed copy of the N.C. Residential Property Disclosure Statement prior to the signing of the Contract (see Paragraph 5(d) of Contract)

   ❑ Exercise by Buyer of right to terminate during the Due Diligence Period (see paragraph 4(f) of the Contract)

   ❑ Improvements on the Property have been destroyed or materially damaged by fire or other casualty (See Paragraph 12 of the Contract)

   ❑ Seller's delay in Settlement and Closing beyond the time permitted under the terms of the Contract (see Paragraph 13) and any amendment thereof (see Agreement to Amend Contract, form 4-T).

   ❑ Exercise by Buyer of right to terminate under Paragraph 10 of Back-Up Contract Addendum (form 2A1-T) prior to receipt by Buyer of written notice from Seller that Back-Up Contract has become primary

   ❑ Exercise by Buyer of right to terminate under Paragraph 1 of Contingent Sale Addendum (form 2A2-T) because Buyer has not closed on the sale of Buyer's Property by the Settlement Date

   ❑ Exercise by Buyer of right to terminate under Paragraph 2 of Contingent Sale Addendum (form 2A2-T) because the Contract For Buyer's Property has terminated (**NOTE**: Notice must be accompanied by reasonable documentation of termination of Contract For Buyer's Property)

   ❑ Exercise by Buyer of right to terminate under Paragraph 4 of Short Sale Addendum (form 2A14-T) at any time prior to receipt of Notice of Approval of Short Sale

   ❑ Exercise by Buyer of right to terminate as provided in the FHA/VA Financing Addendum (Form 2A4-T)

THE NORTH CAROLINA ASSOCIATION OF REALTORS®, INC. MAKES NO REPRESENTATION AS TO THE LEGAL VALIDITY OR ADEQUACY OF ANY PROVISION OF THIS FORM IN ANY SPECIFIC TRANSACTION.

_____ _____ _____
Buyer   Date   Time

_____ _____ _____
Buyer   Date   Time

Mailing Address: _____

Entity Buyer: _____
(Name of LLC/Corporation/Partnership/Trust/etc.)

By: _____ Date: _____ Time: _____

Name: _____ Title: _____

North Carolina Association of REALTORS®, Inc.

STANDARD FORM 350-T
Revised 7/2016
© 7/2018

RELEASE OF EARNEST MONEY DEPOSIT BY SELLER*

Property Address: _____

Seller acknowledges that Buyer is entitled to a refund of the Earnest Money Deposit received in connection with the Contract as a result of Buyer's termination of the Contract for the reason(s) set forth above, and hereby agrees that Escrow Agent may disburse the Earnest Money Deposit to Buyer.

_____   _____
Seller   Date

_____   _____
Seller   Date

Mailing Address: _____

*As set forth in Paragraph 1(f) of the Contract, in the event of a dispute between Seller and Buyer over the return or forfeiture of the Earnest Money Deposit held in escrow by a broker, the broker is required by state law (and Escrow Agent, if not a broker, has agreed) to retain said Earnest Money Deposit in the Escrow Agent's trust or escrow account until a written release from the parties consenting to its disposition has been obtained or until disbursement is ordered by a court of competent jurisdiction. Alternatively, if the broker or an attorney licensed to practice law in North Carolina ("Attorney") is holding the Earnest Money Deposit, the broker or Attorney may deposit the disputed monies with the appropriate clerk of court in accordance with the provisions of N.C.G.S. §93A-12.

STANDARD FORM 350-T
Revised 7/2016
© 7/2018

APPENDIX F Real Estate Forms and Addenda

NOTICE TO SELLER THAT BUYER IS EXERCISING THEIR UNILATERAL RIGHT TO TERMINATE THE OFFER TO PURCHASE AND CONTRACT—VACANT LOT/LAND (FORM 12-T)

Buyer: _____ ("Buyer")

Seller: _____ ("Seller")

Property Address: _____ ("Property")

1. **Contract.** Buyer and Seller entered into a contract for the purchase and sale of the Property on the Offer to Purchase and Contract—Vacant Lot/Land (form 12-T) ("Contract"). The Effective Date of the Contract is _____.

2. **Termination by Buyer.** Buyer hereby terminates the Contract for the following reason(s) (check all applicable boxes):
   - ❏ Exercise by Buyer of right to terminate during the Due Diligence Period (see Paragraph 2 of the Contract)
   - ❏ Seller's delay in Settlement and Closing beyond the time permitted under the terms of the Contract (see Paragraph 10) and any amendment thereof (see Agreement to Amend Contract, form 4-T).
   - ❏ Exercise by Buyer of right to terminate under Paragraph 8 of Back-Up Contract Addendum (form 2A1-T) prior to receipt by Buyer of written notice from Seller that Back-Up Contract has become primary
   - ❏ Exercise by Buyer of right to terminate under Paragraph 1 of Contingent Sale Addendum (form 2A2-T) because Buyer has not closed on the sale of Buyer's Property by the Settlement Date
   - ❏ Exercise by Buyer of right to terminate under Paragraph 2 of Contingent Sale Addendum (form 2A2-T) because the Contract For Buyer's Property has terminated (**NOTE**: Notice must be accompanied by reasonable documentation of termination of Contract For Buyer's Property)
   - ❏ Exercise by Buyer of right to terminate under Paragraph 4 of Short Sale Addendum (form 2A14-T) at any time prior to receipt of Notice of Approval of Short Sale

THE NORTH CAROLINA ASSOCIATION OF REALTORS®, INC. MAKES NO REPRESENTATION AS TO THE LEGAL VALIDITY OR ADEQUACY OF ANY PROVISION OF THIS FORM IN ANY SPECIFIC TRANSACTION.

_____   _____   _____
Buyer   Date   Time

_____   _____   _____
Buyer   Date   Time

Mailing Address: _____

Entity Buyer: _____
(Name of LLC/Corporation/Partnership/Trust/etc.)

By: _____ Date: _____ Time: _____

Name: _____ Title: _____

Page 1 of 2

North Carolina Association of REALTORS®, Inc.

STANDARD FORM 351-T
Revised 7/2016
© 7/2018

RELEASE OF EARNEST MONEY DEPOSIT BY SELLER*

Seller acknowledges that Buyer is entitled to a refund of the Earnest Money Deposit received in connection with the Contract as a result of Buyer's termination of the Contract for the reason(s) set forth above, and hereby agrees that Escrow Agent may disburse the Earnest Money Deposit to Buyer.

_____   _____
Seller   Date

_____   _____
Seller   Date

Mailing Address: _____

*As set forth in Paragraph 1(f) of the Contract, in the event of a dispute between Seller and Buyer over the return or forfeiture of the Earnest Money Deposit held in escrow by a broker, the broker is required by state law (and Escrow Agent, if not a broker, has agreed) to retain said Earnest Money Deposit in the Escrow Agent's trust or escrow account until a written release from the parties consenting to its disposition has been obtained or until disbursement is ordered by a court of competent jurisdiction. Alternatively, if the broker or an attorney licensed to practice law in North Carolina ("Attorney") is holding the Earnest Money Deposit, the broker or Attorney may deposit the disputed monies with the appropriate clerk of court in accordance with the provisions of N.C.G.S. §93A-12.

APPENDIX F Real Estate Forms and Addenda   919

PROFESSIONAL SERVICES DISCLOSURE AND ELECTION
[See Guidelines (Form 760G) for instructions on completing this form]

Property Address:_____("Property")
Buyer or Seller:_____
Real Estate Firm: _____("Firm")

1. There are professional services that typically are performed in connection with the purchase and sale of real estate. Buyer or Seller understands that Firm cannot give advice in certain matters that may relate to the purchase or sale of the Property, including but not limited to matters of law, taxation, financing, surveying, wood-destroying insect infestation, structural soundness of engineering.

REGARDING EACH PROFESSIONAL SERVICE LISTED BELOW, BUYER OR SELLER SHOULD EITHER SELECT THE SERVICE PROVIDER LISTED OR ELECT NOT TO HAVE THE SERVICE PERFORMED:

Service	Selected (initial)	Waived (initial)	Name(s) of Service Providers(s)	Who Orders
Accountant/CPA /Tax Advisor				
Appraisal				
Attorney (e.g. Title Exam/Title Insurance/Seller Document-Deed prep/Closing)				
NFIP Elevation Certificate				
Home Inspections				
Home Warranty				
HVAC Inspection				
Mortgage Loan				
Property Insurance				
Radon Inspection				
Septic Inspection				
Survey* (see note below)				
Well/Water Inspection				
Wood Infestation				

Page 1 of 2
North Carolina Association of REALTORS®, Inc.

STANDARD FORM 760
Revised 7/2018
©7/2018

Individual Agent initials _____   Buyer or Seller initials _____ _____

2. Buyer or Seller acknowledges Firm has recommended that Buyer or Seller consult with a professional for an opinion regarding each service listed above to be performed pursuant to Buyer or Seller's purchase or sale of the property. Buyer or Seller hereby agrees to indemnify and hold Firm harmless from and against any and all liability, claim, loss, damage, suit, or expense that Firm may incur either as a result of Buyer or Seller's selection and use of any of the listed service providers or Buyer or Seller's election not to have one or more of the listed services performed.

---

*NOTE REGARDING SURVEYS: Situations arise all too often that could have been avoided if the buyer had obtained a new survey from a NC registered surveyor. A survey will normally reveal such things as encroachments on the Property from adjacent properties (fences, driveways, etc.); encroachments from the Property onto adjacent properties; road or utility easements crossing the Property; violations of set-back lines; lack of legal access to a public right-of-way; and indefinite or erroneous legal descriptions in previous deeds to the Property. Although title insurance companies may provide lender coverage without a new survey, the owner's policy contains an exception for easements, set-backs and other matters which would have been shown on a survey. Many such matters are not public record and would not be included in an attorney's title examination. In addition, if the buyer does not obtain their own survey, they would have no claim against a surveyor for inaccuracies in a prior survey.

OTHER IMPORTANT NOTES:
- ALTHOUGH FIRM MAY PROVIDE BUYER OR SELLER THE NAMES OF PROVIDERS WHO CLAIM TO PERFORM SERVICES IN ONE OR MORE OF THE LISTED AREAS, BUYER OR SELLER UNDERSTANDS THAT FIRM CANNOT GUARANTEE THE QUALITY OF SERVICE OR LEVEL OF EXPERTISE OF ANY SUCH PROVIDER.
- BUYER OR SELLER AGREES TO PAY THE FULL AMOUNT DUE FOR ALL SERVICES DIRECTLY TO THE SERVICE PROVIDER WHETHER OR NOT THE TRANSACTION CLOSES.

THE NORTH CAROLINA ASSOCIATION OF REALTORS®, INC. MAKES NO REPRESENTATION AS TO THE LEGAL VALIDITY OR ADEQUACY OF ANY PROVISION OF THIS FORM IN ANY SPECIFIC TRANSACTION.

_____
Buyer or Seller

Date: _____

_____
Buyer or Seller

Date: _____

Entity Buyer or Seller:
_____
(Name of LLC/Corporation/Partnership/Trust/etc.)

By: _____

Name: _____

Title: _____

Date: _____

_____
Signature of individual agent

_____
Real Estate Firm (print name)

Date: _____

STANDARD FORM 760
Revised 7/2018
©7/2018

STATE OF NORTH CAROLINA
RESIDENTIAL PROPERTY AND OWNERS' ASSOCIATION DISCLOSURE STATEMENT

Instructions to Property Owners

1. The Residential Property Disclosure Act (G.S. 47E) ("Disclosure Act") requires owners of residential real estate (single-family homes, individual condominiums, townhouses, and the like, and buildings with up to four dwelling units) to furnish buyers a Residential Property and Owners' Association Disclosure Statement ("Disclosure Statement"). This form is the only one approved for this purpose. A disclosure statement must be furnished in connection with the sale, exchange, option, and sale under a lease with option to purchase where the tenant does not occupy or intend to occupy the dwelling. A disclosure statement is not required for some transactions, including the first sale of a dwelling which has never been inhabited and transactions of residential property made pursuant to a lease with option to purchase where the lessee occupies or intends to occupy the dwelling. For a complete list of exemptions, see G.S. 47E-2.

2. You must respond to each of the questions on the following pages of this form by filling in the requested information or by placing a check (√) in the appropriate box. In responding to the questions, you are only obligated to disclose information about which you have actual knowledge.

    a. If you check "Yes" for any question, you must explain your answer and either describe any problem or attach a report from an attorney, engineer, contractor, pest control operator or other expert or public agency describing it. If you attach a report, you will not be liable for any inaccurate or incomplete information contained in it so long as you were not grossly negligent in obtaining or transmitting the information.

    b. If you check "No," you are stating that you have no actual knowledge of any problem. If you check "No" and you know there is a problem, you may be liable for making an intentional misstatement.

    c. If you check "No Representation," you are choosing not to disclose the conditions or characteristics of the property, even if you have actual knowledge of them or should have known of them.

    d. If you check "Yes" or "No" and something happens to the property to make your Disclosure Statement incorrect or inaccurate (for example, the roof begins to leak), you must promptly give the buyer a corrected Disclosure Statement or correct the problem.

3. If you are assisted in the sale of your property by a licensed real estate broker, you are still responsible for completing and delivering the Disclosure Statement to the buyers; and the broker must disclose any material facts about your property which he or she knows or reasonably should know, regardless of your responses on the Disclosure Statement.

4. You must give the completed Disclosure Statement to the buyer no later than the time the buyer makes an offer to purchase your property. If you do not, the buyer can, under certain conditions, cancel any resulting contract (See **"Note to Buyers"** below). You should give the buyer a copy of the Disclosure Statement containing your signature and keep a copy signed by the buyer for your records.

Note to Buyers: If the owner does not give you a Residential Property and Owners' Association Disclosure Statement by the time you make your offer to purchase the property, you may under certain conditions cancel any resulting contract without penalty to you as the buyer. To cancel the contract, you must personally deliver or mail written notice of your decision to cancel to the owner or the owner's agent within three calendar days following your receipt of the Disclosure Statement, or three calendar days following the date of the contract, whichever occurs first. However, in no event does the Disclosure Act permit you to cancel a contract after settlement of the transaction or (in the case of a sale or exchange) after you have occupied the property, whichever occurs first.

---

5. In the space below, type or print in ink the address of the property (sufficient to identify it) and your name. Then sign and date.

Property Address: _____

Owner's Name(s): _____

Owner(s) acknowledge(s) having examined this Disclosure Statement before signing and that all information is true and correct as of the date signed.

Owner Signature: _____ Date _____, ____

Owner Signature: _____ Date _____, ____

Buyers acknowledge receipt of a copy of this Disclosure Statement; that they have examined it before signing; that they understand that this is not a warranty by owners or owners' agents; that it is not a substitute for any inspections they may wish to obtain; and that the representations are made by the owners and not the owners' agents or subagents. Buyers are strongly encouraged to obtain their own inspections from a licensed home inspector or other professional. As used herein, words in the plural include the singular, as appropriate.

Buyer Signature: _____ Date _____, ____

Buyer Signature: _____ Date _____, ____

REC 4.22
REV 7/18

APPENDIX F Real Estate Forms and Addenda

Property Address/Description: _____

The following questions address the characteristics and condition of the property identified above about which the owner has *actual knowledge*. Where the question refers to "dwelling," it is intended to refer to the dwelling unit, or units if more than one, to be conveyed with the property. The term "dwelling unit" refers to any structure intended for human habitation.

<u>Yes</u> <u>No</u> <u>No Representation</u>

1. In what year was the dwelling constructed? _____.
   Explain if necessary: _____

2. Is there any problem, malfunction or defect with the dwelling's foundation, slab, fireplaces/chimneys, floors, windows (including storm windows and screens), doors, ceilings, interior and exterior walls, attached garage, patio, deck or other structural components including any modifications to them?..

3. The dwelling's exterior walls are made of what type of material? ☐ Brick Veneer ☐ Wood ☐ Stone ☐ Vinyl ☐ Synthetic Stucco ☐ Composition/Hardboard ☐ Concrete ☐ Fiber Cement ☐ Aluminum ☐ Asbestos ☐ Other _____ (Check all that apply)

4. In what year was the dwelling's roof covering installed? _____ (Approximate if no records are available) Explain if necessary: _____

5. Is there any leakage or other problem with the dwelling's roof?..

6. Is there any water seepage, leakage, dampness or standing water in the dwelling's basement, crawl space, or slab?

7. Is there any problem, malfunction or defect with the dwelling's electrical system (outlets, wiring, panel, switches, fixtures, generator, etc.)?..

8. Is there any problem, malfunction or defect with the dwelling's plumbing system (pipes, fixtures, water heater, etc.)?

9. Is there any problem, malfunction or defect with the dwelling's heating and/or air conditioning?..................

10. What is the dwelling's heat source? ☐ Furnace ☐ Heat Pump ☐ Baseboard ☐ Other _____
    _____ (Check all that apply)...
    Age of system: _____

11. What is the dwelling's cooling source? ☐ Central Forced Air ☐ Wall/Window Unit(s) ☐ Other _____
    _____ (Check all that apply) ....
    Age of system: _____

12. What are the dwelling's fuel sources? ☐ Electricity ☐ Natural Gas ☐ Propane ☐ Oil ☐ Other _____
    _____ (Check all that apply) If the fuel source is stored in a tank, identify whether the tank is ☐ above ground or ☐ below ground, and whether the tank is ☐ leased by seller or ☐ owned by seller. (Check all that apply)..

13. What is the dwelling's water supply source? ☐ City/County ☐ Community System ☐ Private Well ☐ Shared Well ☐ Other _____ (Check all that apply)..

14. The dwelling's water pipes are made of what type of material? ☐ Copper ☐ Galvanized ☐ Plastic ☐ Polybutylene ☐ Other _____ (Check all that apply)..

15. Is there any problem, malfunction or defect with the dwelling's water supply (including water quality, quantity, or water pressure)?..

16. What is the dwelling's sewage disposal system? ☐ Septic Tank ☐ Septic Tank with Pump ☐ Community System ☐ Connected to City/County System ☐ City/County System available ☐ Straight pipe (wastewater does not go into a septic or other sewer system [note: use of this type of system violates State law]) ☐ Other _____ (Check all that apply)

17. If the dwelling is serviced by a septic system, do you know how many bedrooms are allowed by the septic system permit?
    If your answer is "yes," how many bedrooms are allowed? _____
    ☐ No records available

18. Is there any problem, malfunction or defect with the dwelling's sewer and/or septic system?........................

19. Is there any problem, malfunction or defect with the dwelling's central vacuum, pool, hot tub, spa, attic fan, exhaust fan, ceiling fans, sump pump, irrigation system, TV cable wiring or satellite dish, garage door openers, gas logs, or other systems?..

20. Is there any problem, malfunction or defect with any appliances that may be included in the conveyance (range/oven, attached microwave, hood/fan, dishwasher, disposal, etc.)?..

Buyer Initials and Date_____ Owner Initials and Date_____

Buyer Initials and Date_____ Owner Initials and Date_____

	Yes	No	No Representation

21. Is there any problem with present infestation of the dwelling, or damage from past infestation of wood destroying insects or organisms which has not been repaired?..

22. Is there any problem, malfunction or defect with the drainage, grading or soil stability of the property?...........

23. Are there any structural additions or other structural or mechanical changes to the dwelling(s) to be conveyed with the property?..

24. Is the property to be conveyed in violation of any local zoning ordinances, restrictive covenants, or other land-use restrictions, or building codes (including the failure to obtain proper permits for room additions or other changes/improvements)?...

25. Are there any hazardous or toxic substances, materials, or products (such as asbestos, formaldehyde, radon gas, methane gas, lead-based paint) which exceed government safety standards, any debris (whether buried or covered) or underground storage tanks, or any environmentally hazardous conditions (such as contaminated soil or water, or other environmental contamination) which affect the property?...

26. Is there any noise, odor, smoke, etc. from commercial, industrial, or military sources which affects the property?

27. Is the property subject to any utility or other easements, shared driveways, party walls or encroachments from or on adjacent property?..

28. Is the property the subject of any lawsuits, foreclosures, bankruptcy, leases or rental agreements, judgments, tax liens, proposed assessments, mechanics' liens, materialmens' liens, or notices from any governmental agency that could affect title to the property?..

29. Is the property subject to a flood hazard or is the property located in a federally-designated flood hazard area?

30. Does the property abut or adjoin any private road(s) or street(s)?...

31. If there is a private road or street adjoining the property, is there in existence any owners' association or maintenance agreements dealing with the maintenance of the road or street?...

If you answered "yes" to any of the questions listed above (1-31) please explain (attach additional sheets if necessary):
_____
_____

In lieu of providing a written explanation, you may attach a written report to this Disclosure Statement by a public agency, or by an attorney, engineer, land surveyor, geologist, pest control operator, contractor, home inspector, or other expert, dealing with matters within the scope of that public agency's functions or the expert's license or expertise.

The following questions pertain to the property identified above, including the lot to be conveyed and any dwelling unit(s), sheds, detached garages, or other buildings located thereon.

	Yes	No	No Representation

32. Is the property subject to governing documents which impose various mandatory covenants, conditions, and restrictions upon the lot or unit?

If you answered "yes" to the question above, please explain (attach additional sheets if necessary):
_____
_____

33. Is the property subject to regulation by one or more owners' association(s) including, but not limited to, obligations to pay regular assessments or dues and special assessments? If your answer is "yes," please provide the information requested below as to each owners' association to which the property is subject [insert N/A into any blank that does not apply]:

•(specify name)_____ whose regular assessments ("dues") are $_____ per _____. The name, address, and telephone number of the president of the owners' association or the association manager are_____
_____
_____

•(specify name)_____ whose regular assessments ("dues") are $_____ per _____. The name, address, and telephone number of the president of the owners' association or the association manager are_____
_____
_____

* **If you answered "Yes" to question 33 above, you must complete the remainder of this Disclosure Statement. If you answered "No" or "No Representation" to question 33 above, you do not need to answer the remaining questions on this Disclosure Statement. Skip to the bottom of the last page and initial and date the page.**

Buyer Initials and Date_____   Owner Initials and Date_____

Buyer Initials and Date_____   Owner Initials and Date_____

No
Yes No Representation

34. Are any fees charged by the association or by the association's management company in connection with the conveyance or transfer of the lot or property to a new owner? If your answer is "yes," please state the amount of the fees:_____

35. As of the date this Disclosure Statement is signed, are there any dues, fees, or special assessments which have been duly approved as required by the applicable declaration or bylaws, and that are payable to an association to which the lot is subject? If your answer is "yes," please state the nature and amount of the dues, fees, or special assessments to which the property is subject: _____

36. As of the date this Disclosure Statement is signed, are there any unsatisfied judgments against, or pending lawsuits *involving the property or lot to be conveyed*? If your answer is "yes," please state the nature of each pending lawsuit, and the amount of each unsatisfied judgment:_____

37. As of the date this Disclosure Statement is signed, are there any unsatisfied judgments against, or pending lawsuits *involving the planned community or the association to which the property and lot are subject*, with the exception of any action filed by the association for the collection of delinquent assessments on lots other than the property and lot to be conveyed? If your answer is "yes," please state the nature of each pending lawsuit, and the amount of each unsatisfied judgment:_____

38. Which of the following services and amenities are paid for by the owners' association(s) identified above out of the association's regular assessments ("dues")? (Check all that apply).

No
Yes No Representation

Management Fees..

Exterior Building Maintenance of Property to be Conveyed..

Master Insurance..

Exterior Yard/Landscaping Maintenance of Lot to be Conveyed......................................

Common Areas Maintenance...

Trash Removal..

Recreational Amenity Maintenance (specify amenities covered)_____

Pest Treatment/Extermination..

Street Lights...

Water..

Sewer..

Storm water Management/Drainage/Ponds..

Internet Service..

Cable..

Private Road Maintenance...

Parking Area Maintenance...

Gate and/or Security..

Other: (specify) _____

Buyer Initials and Date_____   Owner Initials and Date_____

Buyer Initials and Date_____   Owner Initials and Date_____

APPENDIX F   Real Estate Forms and Addenda

RESPONSE TO BUYER'S OFFER

TO:_____

RE: OFFER TO PURCHASE _____
                                    Property Address

_____

Dated:_____

[*check only ONE box*]

❏ Thank you for your offer to purchase the above property (the "Property"). I/we cannot accept the offer as written and hereby reject it. However, while this is not a counter offer, I/we would favorably consider the following changes:

_____
_____
_____
_____
_____
_____
_____

If the above changes are acceptable to you, please submit another offer with the noted changes.

It is further understood that until an offer has been accepted, I/we are free to consider and may accept any other offers to purchase presented that contain terms and conditions satisfactory to me/us in my/our sole discretion.

❏ Thank you for your offer to purchase the above property (the "Property"). I/we cannot accept the offer as written and hereby reject it.

THE NORTH CAROLINA ASSOCIATION OF REALTORS®, INC. MAKES NO REPRESENTATION AS TO THE LEGAL VALIDITY OR ADEQUACY OF ANY PROVISION OF THIS FORM IN ANY SPECIFIC TRANSACTION.

_____   _____   _____
Seller   Date   Time

_____   _____   _____
Seller   Date   Time

Entity Seller: _____
              (Name of LLC/Corporation/Partnership/Trust/etc.)

By: _____ Date: _____ Time: _____

Name: _____ Title: _____

Page 1 of 1

North Carolina Association of REALTORS®, Inc.

STANDARD FORM 340-T
Revised 7/2017
© 7/2018

SELLER POSSESSION AFTER CLOSING AGREEMENT
THIS AGREEMENT IS AN ADDENDUM TO THE OFFER TO PURCHASE AND CONTRACT

> ***WARNINGS* TO *BUYERS AND SELLERS*:**
> - **THIS FORM MAY ONLY BE USED FOR SHORT-TERM OCCUPANCY.**
> - **THIS FORM DOES NOT ADDRESS IMPORTANT ISSUES TYPICALLY ADDRESSED IN A RESIDENTIAL LEASE DRAFTED FOR A LONG-TERM OCCUPANCY.**
> - **YOU ARE ADVISED TO CONFIRM WITH AN INSURANCE PROFESSIONAL THE TERMS OF COVERAGE UNDER YOUR PROPERTY AND CASUALTY INSURANCE POLICY BEFORE USING THIS ADDENDUM.**

Property: _____

Seller: _____

Buyer: _____

This Agreement is attached to and made a part of the Offer to Purchase and Contract ("Contract") between Seller and Buyer for the Property. For valuable consideration, the receipt and legal sufficiency of which are acknowledged, Seller and Buyer agree:

1. **Term of Possession.** Seller may remain in possession of the Property for a period of _____ days after the Closing (insert a number of days) until 5 p.m. on the last day (the entire period including any extension agreed to by Buyer and Seller in writing is referred to as the "Term"). **TIME IS OF THE ESSENCE** with regard to the end of the Term.

2. **Seller Acknowledgment of Property Condition and Obligation to Maintain Property.** Seller acknowledges that all appliances, systems and equipment are in good working order except for the following (describe any appliances, systems and equipment that are not in working order at the time of this Agreement): _____
_____.

Seller shall be responsible for the maintenance and repair of all appliances, systems and equipment on the Property other than any appliances, systems and equipment described above. Buyer shall not be obligated to maintain the Property after Closing while Seller remains in possession of the Property, subject to any obligation that may be imposed on Buyer by law.

Seller shall maintain the Property in its same condition as at Closing and shall make no changes in the Property, decorating or otherwise, without the written consent of Buyer. In the event that the Property is altered, modified, damaged or not maintained by Seller in its condition at Closing, Seller shall pay all costs necessary to correct any alterations, modifications or damage to the Property to restore the Property back to its condition at Closing; provided, the risk of loss or damage to the Property by fire or other casualty shall pass to Buyer at Closing without limiting Seller's obligation to indemnify and hold Buyer harmless as set forth below.

3. **Rent.** Seller shall credit Buyer at Closing a non-refundable lump sum of $_____ for the Term ("Rent").

4. **Termination of Possession.** Without a written extension signed by the Parties, Seller shall vacate the Property no later than the end of the Term. If Seller has not vacated the Property by that time, Seller shall continue to be bound by all of the terms and conditions of this Agreement, and Seller shall in addition pay Buyer a hold-over fee of $_____ per day for each day Seller remains in possession of the Property from the end of the Term until Seller vacates the Property or is evicted.

5. **Utilities.** Seller shall keep all utilities registered in Seller's name and shall pay the costs of all utilities (sewer, water, gas, electricity, etc.) during the Term.

6. **Lawn Maintenance; Trash.** Seller shall be responsible for lawn maintenance and trash removal during the Term.

7. **Insurance on Seller's Property.** Seller shall procure and/or maintain in effect a policy or policies of insurance adequately covering Seller's personal property and insuring against any public liability which may arise out of, or by virtue of, the use and occupancy of the Property by Seller, Seller's family and/or agents and employees of Seller.

Page 1 of 2

This form jointly approved by:
North Carolina Bar Association
North Carolina Association of REALTORS®, Inc.

STANDARD FORM 2A8-T
Revised 7/2018
© 7/2018

Buyer Initials _____ _____   Seller Initials _____ _____

8. **Insurance on Buyer's Property.** As of Closing, Buyer shall keep the Property, together with any improvements and any personal property owned by Buyer on or in the Property, insured for the benefit of Buyer in such amount and to such extent as Buyer determines desirable.

9. **Seller's Indemnification.** Seller shall indemnify and hold Buyer harmless from and against any and all liability, fines, suits, claims, demands, actions, costs and expenses of any kind or nature whatsoever caused by, or arising out of, or in any manner connected with any damage to the Property or any injury or death to a person or persons arising out of Seller's use and/or occupancy of the Property during the Term, including intentional or negligent acts by Seller, Seller's family, invitees, and/or agents and employees of Seller.

10. **Subletting; Assignment.** Seller shall not sublet the Property or assign this Agreement.

11. **Association Dues and Charges.** Buyer shall pay the owner's association dues and other like charges, if any, during the Term.

12. **Pets.** Check one: ❑ pets are allowed on the Property ❑ no pets are allowed on the Property.

13. **Eviction.** In the event of Seller's breach of this Agreement, Seller may be evicted from the Property pursuant to a summary ejectment proceeding brought before the magistrate in the county where the Property is located, as provided in Chapter 42 of the North Carolina General Statutes.

14. **Costs of Legal Proceedings.** The losing party in any legal proceeding brought by Buyer or Seller against the other party for breach of any provision of this Agreement (including an action for summary ejectment) shall be liable for the costs and expenses of the prevailing party, including reasonable attorneys' fees (at all tribunal levels).

EXCEPT AS SPECIFICALLY MODIFIED HEREIN, ALL OF THE TERMS AND CONDITIONS OF THE CONTRACT SHALL REMAIN IN FULL FORCE AND EFFECT.

IN THE EVENT OF A CONFLICT BETWEEN THIS AGREEMENT AND THE CONTRACT, THIS AGREEMENT SHALL CONTROL, EXCEPT THAT IN THE CASE OF SUCH A CONFLICT AS TO THE DESCRIPTION OF THE PROPERTY OR THE IDENTITY OF THE BUYER OR SELLER, THE CONTRACT SHALL CONTROL.

THE NORTH CAROLINA ASSOCIATION OF REALTORS®, INC. AND THE NORTH CAROLINA BAR ASSOCIATION MAKE NO REPRESENTATION AS TO THE LEGAL VALIDITY OR ADEQUACY OF ANY PROVISION OF THIS FORM IN ANY SPECIFIC TRANSACTION. IF YOU DO NOT UNDERSTAND THIS FORM OR FEEL THAT IT DOES NOT PROVIDE FOR YOUR LEGAL NEEDS, YOU SHOULD CONSULT A NORTH CAROLINA REAL ESTATE ATTORNEY BEFORE YOU SIGN IT.

Date:_____ Date:_____

Buyer:_____ Seller:_____

Date:_____ Date:_____

Buyer:_____ Seller:_____

Entity Buyer:_____ Entity Seller:_____
(Name of LLC/Corporation/Partnership/Trust/etc.) (Name of LLC/Corporation/Partnership/Trust/etc.)

By: _____ By: _____

Name: _____ Name: _____

Title : _____ Title: _____

Date:_____ Date: _____

STANDARD FORM 2A8-T
Revised 7/2018
© 7/2018

SHORT SALE ADDENDUM

> **NOTE**: The Back-Up Contract Addendum (form 2A1-T) should NOT be used in conjunction with this form when more than one contract of sale is being signed by Seller, as this form manages multiple contracts when necessary

Property: _____

Seller: _____

Buyer: _____

This Addendum is attached to and made a part of the Offer to Purchase and Contract ("Contract") between Seller and Buyer for the Property.

1. **Short Sale Defined**: For purposes of this Contract, a "Short Sale" is a sale where:
   (a) the Purchase Price is or may be insufficient to enable Seller to pay the costs of sale, which include but are not limited to the Seller's closing costs and payment in full of all loans or debts secured by deeds of trust on the Property due and owing to one or more lender(s) and/or other lienholders ("Lienholders");
   (b) Seller does not or may not have sufficient liquid assets to pay the costs of sale; and,
   (c) the Lienholders agree to release or discharge their liens upon payment of an amount less than the amount secured by their liens with or without the Seller being released from any further liability.

2. **Short Sale Approval Risks: Buyer and Seller understand and agree that**:
   - No Lienholder is required or obligated to approve a Short Sale
   - Lienholders may require some terms of the Contract be amended in exchange for approval of a Short Sale, including acceleration of the Due Diligence Period and Settlement Date
   - Buyer and Seller are not obligated to agree to any of Lienholders' proposed terms
   - Seller may not be financially able to make any repairs to the Property that Buyer may request. The Seller's inability to make repairs shall not affect any rights that Buyer may have to terminate the Contract.
   - The costs of Due Diligence and any Due Diligence Fee usually are not refundable to Buyer in the event the Short Sale is not approved.
   - Lienholders' approval may take several weeks or months to obtain, and neither the Seller nor any real estate agent representing Seller or Buyer can guarantee the timeliness of Lienholders' review, approval or rejection.
   - NEITHER THE BUYER, THE SELLER, THE CLOSING ATTORNEY NOR THE BROKERS IN THIS TRANSACTION HAVE ANY CONTROL OVER LIENHOLDERS' APPROVAL, OR ANY ACT, OMISSION OR DECISION BY ANY LIENHOLDERS IN THE SHORT SALE PROCESS.

3. **Contingency:** This Contract is contingent upon Seller obtaining written approval for a Short Sale from all Lienholders whose approval is necessary to enable Seller to close and convey title in accordance with the Contract, which approval shall be effective through Closing upon terms which are acceptable to Seller ("Short Sale Approval").

4. **Notice of Seller's Acceptance of Lienholders' Approval and Parties' Right to Terminate:** Upon obtaining written Short Sale Approval from all necessary Lienholders, Seller agrees to promptly provide Buyer with written notice of Seller's acceptance of Lienholders' approval ("Notice of Approval of Short Sale"). Until Notice of Approval of Short Sale, either party may terminate the Contract by written notice to the other party and the Earnest Money Deposit shall be refunded to Buyer.

5. **Due Diligence/Settlement Date:**
   (a) Buyer and Seller agree that the Due Diligence Period of this Contract shall extend through 5:00 p.m. on the fifteenth (15th) day (or the _____ day, if this blank is completed) following Seller's delivery to Buyer of Notice of Approval of Short Sale, *TIME BEING OF THE ESSENCE*.
   (b) Buyer acknowledges that it could be of substantial benefit to Buyer to conduct any and all Due Diligence soon after the Effective Date. Doing so enables Buyer to inform Seller of defects or other matters that may affect Lienholder approval,

Page 1 of 4

This form jointly approved by:
North Carolina Bar Association
North Carolina Association of REALTORS®, Inc.

STANDARD FORM 2A14-T
Revised 7/2015
© 7/2018

Buyer initials _____ _____ Seller initials _____ _____

allows Buyer to determine that the Property is suitable and that Buyer can obtain financing, and allows the parties to avoid unnecessary delays.

(c) Buyer and Seller agree that the Settlement Date of this Contract shall be on the thirtieth (30th) day (or the _____ day, if this blank is completed) following Seller's delivery to Buyer of Notice of Approval of Short Sale.

> **NOTE**: Instead of inserting dates in the "Due Diligence Period" and "Settlement Date" blanks in the Contract, insert "See attached Short Sale Addendum".

6. **Other Offers/Additional Contracts:**
   (a) Rules of the NC Real Estate Commission require offers from other buyers received by the Seller's Agent to be presented to the Seller. The NC Real Estate Commission also requires the Seller's Agent to inform Lienholders of all offers and contracts of sale on the Property received after a request for a Short Sale has been submitted by such Agent to any Lienholder.
   (b) Seller hereby represents to Buyer that there ☐ is ☐ is not an existing contract of sale on the Property ("Existing Sales Contract")
   (c) Offers from other buyers may be accepted by the Seller and become sales contracts ("Additional Sales Contract") Seller or Lienholders may, prior to the Notice of Approval of Short Sale, elect to substitute any Existing or Additional Sales Contract for approval by Lienholders and withdraw this Contract or any Existing or Additional Sales Contract from consideration by Lienholders.
   (d) Unless this Contract has been terminated, Seller shall promptly notify Buyer in writing of the occurrence of any of the following events:
      (i) Seller's acceptance of any Additional Sales Contract; or
      (ii) Seller's or Lienholders' substitution of any Existing or Additional Sales Contract for this Contract for Lienholder approval; or
      (iii) Short Sale Approval of any Additional Sales Contract; or
      (iv) Seller's closing on any Existing or Additional Sales Contract.
   (e) If not sooner terminated by Buyer or Seller hereunder, this Contract shall become null and void upon the completion of closing of any Existing or Additional Sales Contract whether or not Seller notifies Buyer of any such closing, and any Earnest Money Deposit shall be refunded to Buyer.

7. **Foreclosure:** Seller represents that to the best of Seller's knowledge, a foreclosure proceeding ☐ has not ☐ has been filed with respect to the Property. Further, if during the Short Sale process a foreclosure proceeding is filed, the Seller shall disclose such foreclosure filing to the Buyer. Buyer and Seller understand that if Closing does not occur before the completion of a foreclosure of the Property, Seller will lose all rights and interest in the Property. In such event, the Contract shall be void, and the Earnest Money Deposit shall be refunded to Buyer.

8. **Bankruptcy:** Seller represents that Seller ☐ is ☐ is not under bankruptcy protection under United States law. If Seller files a bankruptcy proceeding, Seller shall promptly disclose such filing in writing to Buyer.

9. **Tax Consequences and Advice:** Seller is advised to seek advice from an attorney, a certified public accountant or other professional regarding the credit, legal and tax consequences of a Short Sale.

IN THE EVENT OF A CONFLICT BETWEEN THIS ADDENDUM AND THE CONTRACT, THIS ADDENDUM SHALL CONTROL, EXCEPT THAT IN THE CASE OF SUCH A CONFLICT AS TO THE DESCRIPTION OF THE PROPERTY OR THE IDENTITY OF THE BUYER OR SELLER, THE CONTRACT SHALL CONTROL.

THE NORTH CAROLINA ASSOCIATION OF REALTORS®, INC. AND THE NORTH CAROLINA BAR ASSOCIATION MAKE NO REPRESENTATION AS TO THE LEGAL VALIDITY OR ADEQUACY OF ANY PROVISION OF THIS FORM IN ANY SPECIFIC TRANSACTION. IF YOU DO NOT UNDERSTAND THIS FORM OR FEEL THAT IT DOES NOT PROVIDE FOR YOUR LEGAL NEEDS, YOU SHOULD CONSULT A NORTH CAROLINA REAL ESTATE ATTORNEY BEFORE YOU SIGN IT.

Date:_____

Buyer _____

Date:_____

Buyer _____

Entity Buyer:
_____
(Name of LLC/Corporation/Partnership/Trust/etc.)

By: _____

Name: _____

Title: _____

Date:_____

Date: _____

Seller _____

Date: _____

Seller _____

Entity Seller:
_____
(Name of LLC/Corporation/Partnership/Trust/etc.)

By: _____

Name: _____

Title: _____

Date _____

[THIS SPACE INTENTIONALLY LEFT BLANK]

STANDARD FORM 2A14-T
Revised 7/2015
© 7/2018

APPENDIX F Real Estate Forms and Addenda

> **NOTE**: The following is a suggested notice that may be copied for the purpose of complying with the notice provision contained in paragraph 4 of the Short Sale Addendum. DO NOT DETACH THE ORIGINAL OF THIS FORM FROM THE CONTRACT.

NOTICE OF APPROVAL OF SHORT SALE

NOTICE is hereby given to _____(insert name of Buyer) from Seller under the Contract between them dated _____ that Seller has obtained written approval for a Short Sale upon terms which are acceptable to Seller from all Lienholders whose approval is necessary to enable Seller to close and convey title in accordance with the Contract.

Seller: _____
                                                                                                              Date

Seller: _____
                                                                                                              Date

[THIS SPACE INTENTIONALLY LEFT BLANK]

STANDARD FORM 2A14-T
Revised 7/2015
© 7/2018

SHORT SALE ADDENDUM TO
EXCLUSIVE RIGHT TO SELL LISTING AGREEMENT
(to be used with NCAR standard form 101 or 103)

Property Address: _____

The additional provisions set forth below are hereby made a part of the Exclusive Right to Sell Listing Agreement for the Property between Seller: _____
and Firm: _____

1. **Short Sale Defined:** For purposes of the Agreement between Seller and Firm, a "Short Sale" is a sale where:
   - The purchase price is or may be insufficient to enable Seller to pay the costs of sale, which include but are not limited to the Seller's closing costs and payment in full of all loans or debts secured by deeds of trust on the Property due and owing to one or more lender(s) and/or other lienholders ("Lienholders")
   - Seller does not or may not have sufficient liquid assets to pay any deficiencies and
   - The Lienholders agree to release or discharge their liens upon payment of an amount less than the amount owed, with or without the Seller being released from any further liability.

2. **Acknowledgement of Short Sale:** Seller acknowledges that any sale of the above Property may or would be a Short Sale. Seller further acknowledges that other options may be available to Seller, including but not limited to negotiating a modification of existing loans or liens, refinancing, bankruptcy, foreclosure, or deed in lieu of foreclosure. Nevertheless, Seller desires to make special arrangements with Firm and any potential Buyer of the Property for a Short Sale. Seller acknowledges that the ability of Firm to successfully market the Property could be limited by any need for a Short Sale

3. **Potential Credit and Tax Consequences:** Seller understands that:
   - A Short Sale may have a negative impact on the credit rating or credit score of Seller
   - A Short Sale may result in taxable income to Seller, even though Seller does not receive any cash proceeds from the sale.
   Seller is advised to seek advice from an attorney, a certified public accountant or other professional regarding the credit, legal and tax consequences of a Short Sale.

4. **Lienholders' Conditions:** Seller understands that the Lienholders:
   - Are not obligated to approve a Short Sale
   - Are not obligated to release Seller from further liability even if Lienholders approve a Short Sale
   - May impose conditions prior to consideration or approval of a Short Sale, such as obtaining a current appraisal, requiring Seller to demonstrate financial hardship or provide income tax returns, pay stubs, evidence of financial assets or other financial information
   Seller acknowledges that Firm has no control over Lienholders' approval, or any act, omission or decision by any Lienholders in the Short Sale process, and that Firm has not made any promise that a Short Sale of the Property will be successful.

5. **Duties of Seller to Close a Short Sale:** Seller understands that a Short Sale may require Seller to:
   - Deposit with the settlement agent additional funds belonging to Seller to pay obligations of the Seller at closing, and/or
   - Obtain approval of any contract of sale for the Property from the Lienholders, and/or
   - Pay from Seller's other assets at closing or after the sale is completed some or all of the difference between the sales price and the costs of sale

6. **Authorization of Firm:** Seller hereby authorizes Firm to take the following additional actions with regard to the listing and sale of the Property:
   - Market the Property as a Short Sale or "pre-foreclosure" property in the multiple listing services and other advertising or promotional materials
   - Continue to market the Property for sale according to the rules of the multiple listing service until the Short Sale is fully approved and agreed upon by all necessary parties;
   - Disclose or provide any requested information or documentation to the Lienholders (and to the buyer and/or buyer's agent) in order to obtain approval of a Short Sale
   - Contact and communicate directly with the loss mitigation or other similar departments or divisions of Lienholders to obtain loan or lien status, account and payoff-related information and to facilitate a Short Sale
   - Provide comparable sale information or broker price opinions or other data or information documenting the current fair market value of the Property to the Lienholders
   - Provide any and all mortgage and/or other lien account payoff information to settlement agent, prospective buyers and/or buyer's agents
   - Coordinate and allow inspection of the Property by authorized representatives of Lienholders;

Page 1 of 2

North Carolina Association of REALTORS®, Inc.

Individual agent initials _____ Seller initials _____ _____

STANDARD FORM 104
Revised 7/2014
© 7/2018

- Include as a part of any contract of sale that would be a Short Sale a "Short Sale Addendum" (standard form 2A14-T), a copy of which Seller acknowledges has been provided to Seller by Firm

7. **Provision of Information by Seller:** Seller shall be obligated to:
   - Promptly furnish Firm and/or Lienholders with such information or documentation as Lienholders may deem necessary to substantiate and justify the need for a Short Sale, including but not limited to:
     o Providing copies of financial information such as pay stubs, income tax returns, bank statements, proof of Seller's assets and liabilities, homeowner or condominium association lien status letters (when applicable),
     o Composing and providing a hardship letter detailing Seller's financial difficulties.

8. **Lienholder List:** Seller hereby represents to Firm that to the best of Seller's knowledge, the Listing Agreement contains an accurate list of all Lienholders having any lien or encumbrance upon the Property, including the amount now owed by Seller with respect to each such lien or encumbrance.

9. **Potential Foreclosure or Judicial Sale:** Seller understands that:
   - During a Short Sale process a foreclosure or other judicial sale of the Property could occur if Seller is in default of Seller's financial obligations
   - Seller shall remain at all times responsible to be aware of the status of any such sale and to promptly inform Firm of all information possessed by Seller about any sale
   - If a foreclosure or other judicial proceeding is filed with respect to the Property, Firm is required by law to timely disclose it to any prospective buyer
   - Once a foreclosure or other judicial proceeding is filed with the Clerk of Superior Court, Firm may continue to solicit and negotiate offers to purchase between Buyer and Seller. Firm may also contact, communicate with, obtain information from and supply information to Lienholders and to the parties to the foreclosure proceeding.

10. **Limitation of Firm:** While Seller and Seller's attorney may negotiate with Lienholders regarding any foreclosure or the terms of Lienholders' approval of a Short Sale, Firm should avoid negotiating with Lienholders as such conduct may constitute the practice of law.

11. **Disclosure of Offers/Contracts:** Seller understands that in a Short Sale, any offers that may be received by Firm must be presented to Seller according to the Rules of the NC Real Estate Commission, and that the NC Real Estate Commission also requires Firm to inform Lienholders of all offers and contracts of sale on the Property received after a request for a Short Sale has been submitted to any Lienholder.

12. **Firm's Compensation**: Seller understands and acknowledges that Firm's entitlement to the fee set forth in the Listing Agreement shall not be affected by a Short Sale or any other sale of the Property.

IN THE EVENT OF A CONFLICT BETWEEN THIS ADDENDUM AND THE EXCLUSIVE RIGHT TO SELL LISTING AGREEMENT OR THE EXCLUSIVE RIGHT TO SELL LISTING AGREEMENT (VACANT LAND), THIS ADDENDUM SHALL CONTROL.

THE NORTH CAROLINA ASSOCIATION OF REALTORS®, INC. MAKES NO REPRESENTATION AS TO THE LEGAL VALIDITY OR ADEQUACY OF ANY PROVISION OF THIS FORM IN ANY SPECIFIC TRANSACTION.

Date: _____   Date: _____

Seller Signature: _____   Firm: _____

Date: _____   By: _____
                                                Individual Agent Signature

Seller Signature: _____

Entity Seller: Entity Firm:
_____   _____
(Name of LLC/Corporation/Partnership/Trust/etc.) (Name of LLC/Corporation/Partnership/Trust/etc.)

By: _____   By: _____

Name: _____   Name: _____

Title: _____   Title: _____

Date: _____   Date: _____

STANDARD FORM 104
Revised 7/2014
© 7/2018

UNREPRESENTED SELLER DISCLOSURE AND FEE AGREEMENT
(Selling Agent Represents the Buyer)

This Agreement is entered into on (Date) _____, by and between
_____ as "Seller",
and _____ ("Firm").

RECITALS:

A. Seller is the owner of property commonly known as _____
_____ (the "Property").

B. Seller is endeavoring to sell the Property without the assistance of a licensed real estate agent; however, Firm has a client, _____ ("Client") who would like to see the Property.

C. If Seller sells the Property to Firm's Client, Seller agrees to pay Firm a fee of _____
_____ ("Fee").

D. THE AGENT (FIRM) SHALL CONDUCT ALL BROKERAGE ACTIVITIES IN REGARD TO THIS AGREEMENT WITHOUT RESPECT TO THE RACE, COLOR, RELIGION, SEX, NATIONAL ORIGIN, HANDICAP OR FAMILIAL STATUS OF ANY PARTY OR PROSPECTIVE PARTY TO THE AGREEMENT. FURTHER, REALTORS® HAVE AN ETHICAL DUTY TO CONDUCT SUCH ACTIVITIES WITHOUT RESPECT TO THE SEXUAL ORIENTATION OR GENDER IDENTITY OF ANY PARTY OR PROSPECTIVE PARTY TO THIS AGREEMENT.

Accordingly, the parties agree as follows:

1. **FEE:** The Fee will be deemed earned if Seller enters into a contract to sell the Property to Firm's Client at any time within _____ days from the date Seller signs this Agreement. Once earned, the Fee will be due and payable at the earlier of closing or Seller's failure to sell the Property as a result of Seller's default on the contract. HOWEVER, if, prior to the expiration of this Agreement and the execution of a contract to sell the Property, Seller enters into a valid listing agreement with any real estate firm, Seller shall NOT be obligated to pay the Fee if the listing firm offers compensation to Firm through a multiple listing service or otherwise.

2. **BUYER AGENCY:** Seller acknowledges that Firm is the agent representing Client with respect to the Property. As the agent of Client, the Firm has the duty to act on behalf of the Client, and will not be acting on behalf of Seller. This duty requires that all information regarding this transaction given to the Firm by Seller be disclosed to Client. For example, if Seller discloses to Firm that Seller is compelled by outside circumstances to sell by a certain date, or that Seller is prepared to lower the price, the Firm would be required to disclose this information to Client. Seller is advised to keep this in mind when communicating with Firm. By signing this Agreement, Seller acknowledges that this Client agency relationship has been previously orally disclosed to Seller when Firm first discussed an appointment to show Property to Client.

[THIS SPACE INTENTIONALLY LEFT BLANK]

North Carolina Association of REALTORS®, Inc.

STANDARD FORM 150
Revised 7/2014
© 7/2018

DO NOT SIGN THIS FORM UNTIL YOU HAVE RECEIVED AND READ THE "WORKING WITH REAL ESTATE AGENTS" BROCHURE

Seller and Firm each acknowledge receipt of a signed copy of this document.

THE NORTH CAROLINA ASSOCIATION OF REALTORS®, INC. MAKES NO REPRESENTATION AS TO THE LEGAL VALIDITY OR ADEQUACY OF ANY PROVISION OF THIS FORM IN ANY SPECIFIC TRANSACTION.

SELLER: **FIRM:**

Date: _____ _____

Seller: _____ By: _____

Date: _____ Date: _____

Seller: _____

Entity Seller:

_____
(Name of LLC/Corporation/Partnership/Trust/etc.)

By: _____

Name: _____

Title: _____

Date: _____

Page 2 of 2

STANDARD FORM 150
Revised 7/2014
© 7/2018

ANSWER KEY

END-OF-CHAPTER REVIEW QUESTIONS

Chapter 1: Basic Real Estate Concepts

1. C
2. B
3. D
4. D
5. D
6. D
7. B
8. C
9. C
10. B
11. C
12. A
13. B
14. B
15. B
16. A
17. B
18. D
19. D
20. B

Chapter 2: Property Ownership and Interests

1. C
2. B
3. A
4. D
5. D
6. A
7. B
8. B
9. B
10. D
11. D
12. A
13. C
14. B
15. B
16. A
17. D
18. A
19. B
20. D
21. A
22. A
23. D
24. C
25. B
26. C
27. C
28. A
29. C
30. D
31. A

Chapter 3: Property Taxation and Assessments

1. B
2. B
3. D
4. C

$100,000/$100 = 1,000 # of $100 increments

$1.45 × 1,000 = $1,450 Taxes for the year

$1,450/12 = $121 Taxes per month (rounded)

5. D
6. D
7. C

$240,000 × 75% = $180,000 Assessed value

$0.95 + $0.36 = $1.31 Combined tax rate per $100

$180,000/$100 = 1,800 # of $100 increments

$1.30 × 1,800 = $2,340 Taxes per year

8. B

$130,000/$100 = 1,300 # of $100 increments

$1,495/1,300 = $1.15 Tax rate per $100

9. A

$18,057,000 / $100 = 180,570 # of $100 units

$162,513 / 180,570 = $0.90 Tax Rate per $100

10. C

$215,000 / $100 = 2,150 # of $100 increments

$1.40 × 2,150 = $3,010 annual taxes for year

11. C

$175,000 × 70% = $122,500 Assessed value

.1 × .0125 = .0250 25 mills

$122,500 × .0250 = $3,062.50 Taxes per year

12. D

$8.50 × 95 = $807.50 Cost of Assessment

Chapter 4: Transfer of Title to Real Property

1. A	11. C	21. C
2. C	12. A	22. D
3. A	13. A	23. B
4. C	14. A	24. D
5. D	15. B	25. C
6. D	16. C	26. D
7. B	17. C	27. B
8. A	18. B	28. B
9. D	19. A	
10. D	20. D	

$103,250 is rounded up to $103,500

$103,500 / $500 = 207 # of $500 increments

$1 × 207 = $207 Cost of excise (revenue) stamps

29. A

43,560 × 3.45 = 150.282 Sq. Ft. in "A"

150.282 / 900 = 167 Width of "A"

167 × 780 = 130,260 Sq. Ft. in "B"

130,260 / 43,560 = 2.99 Acres in lot "B"

30. D

$138,600 / 165 = $840 Price per front foot

31. A

43,560 × 6.48 = 282,268.8 Sq. Ft. in 6.48 acres

$79,035 / 282,268.8 = $0.28 Cost per sq. ft.

50 × 225 = 11,250 Sq. Ft. sold

$0.28 × 11,250 = $3,150 Sales Price

32. C

.5 × 750 × 825 = Sq. Ft. in each portion

309,375 / 43,560 = 7.10 Acres in each portion

33. A

$329,560 is rounded up to the nearest $500 increment of $330,000

$330,000 / $500 = 660 # of $500 increments in sales price

$1 X 660 = $660 cost of stamps

34. D

43,560 ×.3817 = 16,627 Sq. Ft. in lot

Chapter 5: Land Use Controls

1. D	10. A	19. A
2. D	11. B	20. D
3. B	12. C	21. C
4. C	13. C	22. D
5. B	14. D	23. D
6. B	15. B	24. D
7. D	16. B	25. D
8. C	17. D	26. B
9. C	18. B	

Chapter 6: Environmental Issues in Real Estate

1. A	5. C	9. B
2. D	6. A	10. C
3. B	7. D	
4. C	8. A	

Chapter 7: Real Estate Brokerage and the Law of Agency

1. A	10. D	19. D
2. D	11. D	20. C
3. D	12. D	21. B
4. C	13. D	22. D
5. D	14. B	23. D
6. C	15. A	24. C
7. C	16. B	25. D
8. A	17. B	26. C
9. A	18. A	

Chapter 8: Agency Contracts (Sales) and Related Practices

1. B
2. C
3. D
4. B
5. A
6. C
7. C
8. D
9. B
10. A
11. D
12. A
13. A

100% − 5% = 95% Percent that $180,500 is of the sales price

$180,500/95% = $190,000 Sales price

14. D

$25,000 + $121,900 + $3,500 = $150,400 94% of sales price

$150,400/94% = $160,000 Sales price

15. C

$225,000 × 6% = $13,500 Total commission

$13,500 × 6% = $810 Franchise fee

$13,500 − $810 = $12,690 Commission minus franchise fee

$12,690 × 55% = $6,979.50 Agent commission

16. B

$240,000 × 5% = $12,000 Total commission

$12,000 × 50% = $6,000 Selling firm's share of commission

$6,000 × 95% = $5,700 Commission after franchise fee

$5,700 × 65% = $3,705 Christy's share

17. C

$150,000 × 7% = $10,500 Commission at 7%

$150,000 × 6% = $9,000 Commission at 6%

$150,000 + $150,000 = $300,000 Sales price at 7% + 6%

$380,000 − $300,000 = $80,000 Sales price at 5%

$80,000 × 5% = $4,000 Commission at 5%

$10,500 + $9,000 + $4,000 = $23,500 Total commission

18. A

$210,000 - $150,000 = $60,000 Amount of profit

$60,000/$150,000 = 40% Percentage of profit

40%/4 = 10% Average percent of profit per year

19. B

$160,000 - $150,000 = $10,000 Increase in equity

$10,000/$25,000 = 40% Percent of increase in equity

20. C

$30,000 = Original equity

$120,000 × 10% = $12,000 Increase in equity

$12,000/$30,000 = 40% Percent of increase in equity

Chapter 9: Real Estate Contracts

1. C
2. C
3. D
4. C
5. A
6. D
7. B
8. D
9. A
10. D
11. C
12. D
13. C
14. A
15. C

Chapter 10: Sales Contracts and Practices

1. C
2. A
3. D
4. B
5. B
6. C
7. C
8. B
9. C
10. C
11. D
12. D
13. D
14. D
15. B

Chapter 11: Real Estate Finance

1. D
2. A
3. D
4. B
5. C
6. A
7. D
8. A
9. C
10. C
11. B

$73,000 \times 12\% = \$8,760$ Annualized interest

$\$8,760/12 = \$730$ Interest for the month

12. B	16. C	20. D
13. A	17. B	21. D
14. A	18. A	22. D
15. A	19. D	

$\$172,000 \times 80\% = \$137,600$ Loan amount

6 3/8 (51/8) − 5 ¾ (46/8) = 5/8 or 5 points

$\$137,600 \times 5\% = \$6,880$ Cost of points

23. C	26. D	29. D
24. B	27. A	30. B
25. B	28. B	31. C

$\$118,000 \times 85\% = \$100,300$ Loan amount

$\$100,300/\$1,000 = 100.3$ # of $1,000 borrowed

$\$6.16 \times 100.3 = \$617.85$ Principal & interest per month (debt service)

32. B

$\$184,300.00 \times 5.75\% = \$10,597.25$ Annualized interest

$\$10,597.25/12 = \$883.10$ Interest 1st month

$\$1,075.52 − \$883.10 = \$192.42$ Principal 1st month

$\$184,300.00 − \$192.42 = \$184,107.58$ Loan balance after 1st payment

33. B

$\$195,000.00 \times 80\% = \$156,000$ Loan amount (principal)

$\$885.75 \times 360$ months $= \$318,870.00$ Total principal & interest paid over life of the loan

$\$318,870.00 − \$156,000 = \$162,870.00$ Total interest paid over the life of the loan

34. C

$\$155,000/\$182,350 = 85\%$ Loan to value ratio

Chapter 12: The Closing Real Estate Transaction

1. A
2. A
3. B
4. D
5. A
6. C

   $160,000 × 1% = $1,600 Cost of one discount point

7. C

   $600/30 = $20 Rent per day

   $20 × 10 days = $200 (Rent income for 21–30)

8. C
9. D

   $151,050/$500 = 302.1 (round up to 303*)

   $1 × 303 = $303 Cost of revenue (excise) stamps

   *NC collects $1 per $500 of sales price or ANY portion thereof.

10. D
11. B
12. D
13. C
14. C
15. C
16. A
17. B

    June 26 – 30 = 5 Days inclusive (buyer pays day of closing for interim interest

    $243,250 × 5.25% = $12,770.63 Annualized interest

    $12,770.63 / 360 = $35.47 Interest per day

    $35.47 × 5 = $177.37 Debit - buyer

18. C

    September 22 – 30 8 days

    $600 × 2 = $1,200 Total rents for month

    $1,200 / 30 = $40 Rents per day

    $40 × 8 – $320 Debit – Seller, Credit – Buyer

19. C

    January 1 – March 19 = 79 days

    $864 / 360 = $2.40 Taxes per day

    $2.40 × 79 = $189.60 Debit – Seller, Credit – Buyer

20. D

October 21 – December 30 = 69 days

$360 / 360 = $1 Assessment per day

$1 × 69 = $69 Debit – Buyer, Credit - Seller

21. C

January 1 – November 27 = 327 Days – Seller

November 27 – December 30 = 33 Days – Buyer

$594 / 360 = $1.65 Taxes per day

$1.65 × 327 = $539.55 Debit – Seller

$1.65 × 33 = $54.45 Debit – Buyer

22. C

27 – 30 = 4 days inclusive

$178,000 × 5.5% = $9,790 Annualized interest

$9,790 / 360 = $27.19 Interest per day

$27.19 × 4 = $108.76 Debit – Buyer

23. D

December 11 – 30 19 days

$810 / 360 = $2.25 Taxes per day

$2.25 × 19 = $42.75 Debit – Buyer, Credit – Seller

24. B

ITEM	BUYER DEBIT	BUYER CREDIT
Sales Price	$250,000	
New Mortgage		$200,000
Loan Origination Fee	$2000	
Discount Points	$3000	
Interim Interest	$305.60	
Attorney Fees	$950	
Survey	$450	
Title Insurance	$500	
Termite Report	$75	
Earnest Money Deposit		$2,500

Due Diligence Fee		$200
Subtotals	$257,280.60	$202,700.00
Due from Buyer		$54,580.60
Totals	$257,280.60	$257,280.60

(Interim interest)

October 21 – 30 = 10 days inclusive

$200,000 × 5.5% = $11,000 Annualized interest

$11,000 / 360 = $30.56 Interest per day

$30.56 × 10 = $305.60 Debit – Buyer

(Taxes)

$2,750 / 360 = $7.64 Taxes per day

January 1 – October 21 = 291 Days – Seller

October 21 – December 30 = 69 Days – Buyer

$7.64 × 291 = $2,223.24 Debit – Seller

$7.64 × 69 = $527.16 Debit - Buyer

25. A

ITEM	SELLER DEBIT	SELLER CREDIT
Sales Price		$319,000
Due Diligence Fee	$1,000	
Loan Payoff	$191,415	
Property Taxes	$1,265.60	
HOA Fees		$11.20
Deed Preparation	$80	
Revenue Stamps	$638	
Commission	$15,950	
Subtotals	$210,349.60	$319,011.20
Balance Due/Seller	$108,661.60	
Totals	$319,011.20	$319,011.20

(Taxes)

January 1 – April 23 = 113 Days - Seller

$4,032 / 360 = $11.20 Taxes per day

$11.20 × 113 = $1,265.60 Debit – Seller, Credit – Buyer

(HO Assoc. Fees)

April 23 – 30 = 7 Days - Buyer

$48 / 30 = $1.60 Assessment per day

$1.60 × 7 = $11.20 Debit – Buyer, Credit - Seller

Chapter 13: Property Valuation

1. D	6. C	11. B
2. B	7. A	12. B
3. A	8. A	13. B
4. C	9. C	14. D
5. A	10. A	15. C

$480,000/11% = $4,363,636 Estimate of property value

16. D	22. A	28. B
17. B	23. D	29. B
18. B	24. C	30. B
19. D	25. D	31. B
20. D	26. B	
21. C	27. C	

Subject	Comp #1	$159,000	Comp #2	$160,000	Comp #3	$175,000
Appreciation	2%	+ 3,180	2%	+3,200	2%	$3,500
1,650 sf	1,550 sf	+ 5,000	1,600 sf	+2,500	1,725 sf	– 3,750
2 baths	1 ½ baths	+ 1,000	2 baths fireplace	(0)	2 ½ baths fireplace	– 1,500
Fireplace	No fireplace	+ 3,000		(0)		(0)
1 car gar. Total	1 car gar.	$0 $171,180	no gar.	+ 7,000	1 car gar.	(0)
				$172,700		$173,250

32. B

Subject	Comp #1	$180,000
Appreciation	4 months	+ 3,600
1,750 sf	1,675 sf	+ 5,250
2 ½ baths	3 baths	– 1,100
2 car gar. Probable value	1 car gar.	+ 6,000
		$193,750

33. A

Chapter 14: Property Insurance Basics

1. C
2. B
3. D
4. C
5. C
6. A
7. D
8. A

Chapter 15: Relationship of Landlord and Tenant

1. D
2. B
3. B
4. C
5. B
6. B
7. B
8. C
9. D
10. C
11. B
12. D
13. C
14. A
15. B
16. B
17. D
18. B
19. A
20. B
21. C
22. D
23. B

Chapter 16: Real Estate Management

1. C
2. C
3. A
4. C
5. C
6. A
7. B
8. D
9. C

$850 × 6 = $5,100 Rents due for 6 units

$850/30 = $28.333 Rent per day – 1 unit

$28.333 × 18 = $510 Rents for 18 days (rounded)

$5,100 + $510 = $5,610 Total rents collected

$5,610 × 9% = $504.90 Management fee earned (rounded to whole dollar)

10. B

$950 × 5 = $4,750 total rents collected for the month

$4,750 × 8% = $380 management fee earned

Chapter 17: Fair Housing

1. B
2. C
3. D
4. D
5. B
6. C

7. C	10. A	13. C
8. B	11. C	14. B
9. B	12. B	15. B

Chapter 18: Federal Taxation of Home Ownership

1. C
2. D
3. C
4. D

$80,000 + $5,000 + $20,000 = $105,000 Adjusted basis

5. A

$150,000 − $10,000 = $140,000 Amount realized

$140,000 − $105,000 = $35,000 Capital gain

6. D	8. B	10. C
7. A	9. D	

Chapter 19: Basic House Construction

1. A	10. B	19. A
2. B	11. B	20. D
3. B	12. A	21. C
4. D	13. D	22. D
5. B	14. D	23. B
6. B	15. D	24. A
7. D	16. C	25. D
8. A	17. B	
9. D	18. D	

Chapter 20: Basic Real Estate Investment

1. A	3. A	5. C
2. C	4. D	

Appendix A: Practice Exam Preparation Tips and Strategies and Practice National and State Examinations

Sample National Examination

Agency Relationships and Contracts

1. C	11. A	21. A
2. C	12. B	22. C
3. A	13. B	23. D
4. B	14. A	24. C
5. D	15. D	25. C
6. A	16. C	26. A
7. D	17. C	27. C
8. C	18. B	28. B
9. B	19. C	
10. A	20. B	

Real Property Ownership/Interest

29. B	34. A	39. D
30. B	35. B	40. A
31. C	36. B	41. A
32. D	37. C	
33. A	38. A	

Real Estate Finance

42. C	47. A	52. D
43. B	48. C	53. A
44. A	49. B	54. C
45. B	50. B	55. D
46. D	51. C	

Real Property

56. C	61. B	66. D
57. D	62. A	67. D
58. D	63. C	68. C
59. B	64. C	69. C
60. D	65. C	

Marketing Regulations (Purchase and Rental)

70. D
71. A
72. A
73. C
74. C
75. D
76. A
77. A
78. D
79. A

Property Management

80. D
81. B
82. A
83. C
84. D
85. D
86. D
87. B

Real Estate Calculations

88. B

$165,000 × 85% = $140,250 Maximum loan amount

89. A

$750 × 2 = $1,500 Total monthly rent

$1,500 / 30 = $50 Rent per day

$50 × 9 = $450 Debit – seller, Credit - buyer

90. C

$90,000 × 7% = $6,300 Total commission

$6,300 × 60% = $3,780 Agent's share

91. A

$160,000 × 6% = $9,600   Annualized interest

$9,600 / 12 = $800   Interest for 1st month

$1,146 – $800 = $346   Principal paid 1st month

$160,000 – $346 = $159,654   Loan balance due after 1 payment

92. C

8% – 8 1/8% = 1/8 of 1% or one point

$190,000 × 1% = $1,900   Cost of 1 point

93. C

250 X 3 = 750   Feet

800 X 750 X .5 = 300,000   Total square feet

Answers to Chapter Review Questions   951

300,000 / 43,560 = 6.887   Total acres in tract

$15,000 × 6.887 = 103,305   Sales price

$103,305 × 9% = $9,298   Total sales commission

94. B

$2,880/360 = $8.00 Taxes per day

20 days (Nov) + 30 days (Dec) = 50 Days buyer owes seller

$8.00 × 50 = $400 Debit-buyer; credit-seller

95. D

3 × 3 = 9   Sq. feet per yard

88.6 × 9 = 797.4   Total square feet

797.4 / 20 = 39.87 (rounded to 40)   Length of room

96. C

$1,485 × 360 = $534,600   Total P&I paid over life of loan

$534,600 − $235,000 = $299,600   Total interest paid over life of loan

97. A

$600 / 30 = $20   Rent per day per unit

20 × 20 = $400   Rent for partially vacant unit

$600 × 6 = $3,600   Rent for 6 units

$3,600 + $400 = $4,000   Total rent paid for month

$4,000 × 10% = $400   Property management fee

98. B

$150,000/125% = $120,000 Original purchase price

99. B

Pre-paid Interim Interest

$200,000 × 4.5% = $9,000   Annualized Interest

$9,000 / 360 = $25   Interest per day

$25 × 22 = $550   Debit to Buyer

Property Taxes

$3,600 / 360 = $10 Property Taxes per day

$10 × 249 = $2,490 Debit to Buyer

100. D

ITEM	SELLER DEBIT	SELLER CREDIT
Sales Price		$179,000
Commission	$8,950	
Loan Payoff	$103,650	
Property Taxes	$231.00	
Deed Prepreparation	$80.00	
Revenue Stamps	$358.00	
Due Diligence Fee	$300.00	
Carpet Cleaning Fee	$250.00	
Subtotals	$113,819	$179,000
Balance Due/Seller	$65,181	
Totals	$179,000	$179,000

Property Taxes

$1,080 / 360 = $3   Property Taxes per day

$3 X 77 = $231   Debit to Seller

Sample State Examination Section

1. B
2. C
3. D
4. B
5. D
6. C
7. A
8. D
9. C
10. A
11. C
12. C
13. D
14. C
15. B
16. C
17. C
18. D
19. D
20. C
21. B
22. B
23. C
24. D
25. D
26. A
27. B
28. B
29. C
30. D
31. C
32. D
33. C
34. C
35. C
36. B
37. C
38. C
39. B
40. C

Appendix B: Real Estate Math

Brokerage Commissions

1. **b. $1,377**

   $45,900 × 3% = $1,377 Sales commission

2. **b. $88.50**

   $295 × 2 = $590 Rent per month for both sides

   $590 × 15% = $88.50 Property management commission

2. **d. $270.90**

   $4,300 × 90% = $3,870 Gross rent collected for month

   $3,870 × 7% = $270.90 Property management commission

3. **b. $567.00**

   $54,000 × 7% = $3,780 Commission to office

   $3,780 × 15% = $567 Agent commission

Net to Seller

1. **a. $69,892.47**

   $65,000/93% = $69,892.47 Minimum sales price

   b. $79,789.47

   $75,000 + $800 = $75,800 95% of sales price

   $75,800/95% = $79,789.47 Minimum sales price

Profit/Loss/Equity

2. **$3,000, 4.167%**

   $72,000 − $69,000 = $3,000 Amount of loss

   $3,000/$72,000 = 4.167% % of loss

3. **b. 605.26%**

   $38,000 × 20% = $7,600 Original equity

   $72,000 − $26,000 = $46,000 Current equity

   $46,000/$7,600 = 6.0526 (605.26%) % change in equity

Area

1. **b. 0.66 acres**

   165 × 175 = 28,875 sq. ft.

   28,875/43,560 = 0.66 acres

2. **k. 5,625 sq. ft.**

   75′ × 75′ = 5,625 sq. ft.

   l. 2,368 sq. ft.

   37′ × 64′ = 2,368 sq. ft.

   m. 1,875 sq. ft.

   .5 × 75′ × 50′ = 1,875 sq. ft.

   n. 63,000 sq. ft.

   350′ × 180′ = 63,000 sq. ft.

   o. 139,500 sq. ft.

   (500′ + 275′)/2 = 387.50 Avg. of the parallel sides

   360′ × 387.50 = 139,500 sq. ft.

3. **b. $27.50/sq. ft.**

   $38,500/1,400 = $27.50 Cost per sq. ft.

   c. $1.03/sq. ft.

   43,560/2 = 21,780 sq. ft. in ½ acre

   $22,500/21,780 = $1.03 Cost per sq. ft.

   d. $255.56/front ft.

   $92,000/360 = $255.56 Cost per front ft.

Property Taxes

2. **$71.88**

   $69,000/$100 = 690 # of $100 increments

   $1.25 × 690 = $862.50 Property taxes per year

   $862.50/12 = $71.88 Property taxes per month

Revenue Stamps (Excise Tax)

2. **$92**

   $45,900/$500 = 91.8 (Round up to 92) # of $500

   $1 × 92 = $92 Cost of revenue (excise) stamps

3. **$272**

   $135,600/$500 = 271.20 (Round up to 272) # of $500

   $1 × 272 = $272 Cost of revenue (excise) stamps

Answers to Chapter Review Questions   955

4. **$250**

   $125,000/$500 = 250 # of $500

   $1 × 250 = $250 Cost of revenue (excise) stamps

Finance

1. **b. $215.25**

   $28,700 × 9% = $2,583 Annualized interest

   $2,583/12 = $215.25 Monthly interest

2. **b. $132,500**

   25 × 12 = 300 Months in 25 years

   $625 × 300 = $187,500 Total P&I paid in 25 years

   $187,500 − $55,000 = $132,500 Total interest paid in 25 years

3. **b. $1,061.66**

   $134,900/$1,000 = 134.9 # of $1,000 Borrowed

   $7.87 × 134.9 = $1,061.66 Monthly P&I payment

3. **c. $247,298.68**

   $1,061.66 × 360 = $382,197.60 Total P&I paid

   $382,198.68 − $134,900 = $247,298.68 Total interest paid

4. **b. $55,988**

   $56,000 × 13.5% = $7,560 Annualized interest

   $7,560/12 = $630 Interest due for the month

   $642 − $630 = $12 Principal paid for the month

   $56,000 − $12 = $55,988 Balance after payment

5. **b. $4,758.75**

   $117,500 × 90% = $105,750 Loan amount

   $105,750 × 4.5% = $4,758.75 Cost of points

6. **b. 10.25**

   4 points × 1/8 each = 4/8 = 1/2 (.50) Inc. due to points

   9.75 + .50 = 10.25 Yield

6. **d. $2,600**

   11% 10.50% = .50 (or ½ or 4/8) Increase needed

   4/8 = 4 points

   $65,000 × 4% = $2,600 Cost of points

Closing Statements

Problem No. 1

Balance Owed by Buyer		Balance Due to Seller	
Sales Price	$45,700	Sales Price	$45,700
Insurance	225	RE Tax	52.50
Misc	900	Pers Tax	150
E/M	2,000	Excise Tax	92
RE Tax	52.50	Broker's Fee	2,285
Mortgage	43,415	Balance Due	$43,120.50
Balance Owed	$1,357.50		

Problem 2

Balance Owed by Buyer		Balance Due to Seller	
Sales Price	$60,000	Sales Price	$60,000
Insurance	400	RE Tax	314.65
Misc	1,400	Pers Tax	400
E/M	5,000	Mortgage	35,000
RE Tax	314.65	Excise Tax	120
Mortgage	54,000	Broker's Fee	3,600
Balance Owed	$2,485.35	Balance Due	$20,565.35

GLOSSARY

This glossary presents definitions of real estate terms that appear in the text. Many of these terms have other meanings in other contexts; all definitions here refer to real estate. Numbers in parentheses indicate the chapters in which the terms are discussed. We also include definitions of terms that are not specifically discussed in this text but may be included in the license examinations.

abandonment The surrender or release of a right, a claim, or an interest in real property. (2)

acceleration clause A provision in a mortgage or deed of trust that permits the lender to declare the entire principal balance of the debt immediately due and payable if the borrower is in default. (11)

access A way of approach or entrance onto a property. (2)

accord and satisfaction A new agreement by contracting parties that is satisfied by full performance, thereby terminating a prior contract. (9)

acknowledgment A formal statement before an authorized official (e.g., notary public) by a person who executed a deed, contract, or other document that it was (is) his or her free act. (4)

acquisition cost The basis used by the FHA in calculating the loan amount. (11) The purchase plus the closing costs incurred in purchasing the property. (17)

acquisition debt The debt incurred in the purchase of a personal residence. Can be used similar to acquisition cost. (17)

acre A land area of 43,560 square feet.

actual age Chronological age. (13)

actual eviction The removal of a tenant by the landlord because the tenant breached a condition of a lease or other rental contract. (14)

actual notice The knowledge that a person has of a fact. (4, 7)

adjoining lands Lands that share a boundary line. (2)

adjustable rate mortgage (ARM) One in which the interest rate changes according to changes in a predetermined index. (11)

adjusted basis The value of property used to determine the amount of gain or loss realized by the owner upon sale of the property; equals acquisition cost plus capital improvements minus depreciation taken. (17)

adjusted sales price Sales price minus allowable selling expenses. Also called amount realized. (17)

adjustments In the sales comparison approach to value, additions or subtractions to sales prices of comparable properties to make comparables like the subject property. (13)

administrator A man appointed by a court to administer the estate of one who has died intestate. (4)

administrator's deed One executed by an administrator to convey title to estate property. (4)

administratrix A woman appointed by a court to administer the estate of one who has died intestate. (4)

ad valorem Latin meaning "according to value"; the basis for taxes on real property. (2)

adverse possession A method of acquiring title to real property by conforming to statutory requirement. A form of involuntary alienation of title. (4)

agency The fiduciary relationship between a principal and an agent. (7)

agency agreement An employment contract between principal and agent that sets forth all the terms and conditions of employment including specifying the authority given to the agent and the compensation of the agent. (8)

agent A person authorized by another to act on his or her behalf. (7)

agreement A contract. Mutual assent between two or more parties. (9)

air rights Rights in the air space above the surface of land. (2)

alienation Transfer of title to real property. (2)

alienation clause A clause in a mortgage or deed of trust that entitles the lender to declare the entire principal balance of the debt due and payable immediately if the borrower sells the property during the mortgage term. This clause prohibits the ability of a borrower to assume the loan. Also known as a due-on-sale clause. (11)

amendment A change or modification of a zoning ordinance by the local legislative authority. (5)

amenities Benefits resulting from the ownership of a particular property. (13)

Americans with Disabilities Act A federal law protecting the rights of individuals with physical or mental impairments. (16)

amortization The gradual reduction of a mortgage loan through periodic payments of principal and interest over a specific term to satisfy a mortgage loan. (11)

amortization schedule A printed list of periodic payments of principal and interest over a specific term to satisfy a mortgage loan. Usually shows total payment, amount going to principal and interest and the loan balance after each payment, as well as total principal and interest paid to date. (11)

amount realized The sales price minus any allowable expenses of sale. The "net" sales price. (17)

annual Yearly.

annual percentage rate (APR) The actual effective rate of interest charged on a loan expressed on an annual basis; not the same as the simple interest rate. It takes into account certain closing costs and discount points charged by the lender; therefore, it may be higher than simple interest. (11)

anticipation In valuing property, value based on the present value of anticipated future benefits of ownership. (13)

apparent authority A fact situation that creates the appearance of an agent's authority. (7)

appraisal An estimate of property value based on factual data. (13)

appraisal by capitalization Also called income approach; an approach to the appraisal of income-producing real estate that estimates the property's value based on the amount of net income the property will produce over its life. (13)

appraisal process An organized and systematic program for estimating real property value. (13)

appraisal report A report containing an estimate of property value and the data on which the estimate is based. (13)

appreciation An increase in property value. (13)

approaches to value Methods of estimating real property value such as market data, cost, and income approaches. (13)

appurtenance All rights or privileges that result from ownership of a particular property and that move with the title. (2)

arm's length transaction Any transaction where there is no relationship, such as family, business, etc., between the purchaser and the seller such as family.

appurtenant easement A right of use in the adjoining land of another that moves with the title to the property benefiting from the easement. (2)

arrears Delinquent in meeting an obligation. The payment of interest for a prior period as scheduled. (11)

asbestos Tiny fibers that can become airborne when contact is made (friable) and then trapped within the soft lung tissue and cause a variety of lung related diseases including cancer. There is no safe level of asbestos exposure. (6)

asking price The price specified in a listing contract. (8)

assessed value The value to which a local tax rate is applied to calculate the amount of real property tax. (3)

assessment A levy against property. (3)

assessor An local government official who has the responsibility for establishing the value of property for tax purposes. (3)

assignee One to whom contractual rights are transferred. (9)

assignment A complete transfer of all legal rights and obligations by one party to another. (9)

assignment of a lease The transfer by a lessee of the remaining term of a lease without reversion of interest to the lessee. (14)

assignor One transferring contractual rights to another. (9)

assumable mortgage One that does not contain an alienation clause. (11)

attorney-in-fact A person appointed to perform legal acts for another under a power-of-attorney. (9)

auction A form of property sale in which people bid against one another. (10)

availability (also called scarcity) An economic characteristic of land describing that land as a commodity having a fixed supply base. (1)

balloon payment One in which the scheduled payment will not fully amortize the loan over the term. Therefore, it requires a final payment called a balloon payment, larger than the uniform payments, to satisfy the debt fully. (11)

base lines East-west lines in the Government Rectangular Survey System method of property description (not used in North Carolina). (4)

base rent The fixed or minimum rent portion in a percentage lease. (14)

basis The value of property for income tax purposes. Adjusted basis is original acquisition cost (purchase price plus allowable closing costs) plus capital improvements less accrued depreciation. (17)

before tax cash flow Cash flow that exists after the payment of debt sevice (P&I). Is also referred to a cash flow after debt service and cash throwoff. (19)

beneficiary The recipient of a gift of personal property by will. (4). The lender in a deed of trust. (11)

bequest A gift of personal property by will. (4)

bilateral contract An agreement based on mutual promises of specified consideration. (9)

bill of sale An instrument transferring ownership of personal property. (1)

blanket mortgage One in which two or more parcels of real property are pledged to secure the payment of the note. (11)

blockbusting For profit, to induce or attempt to induce any person to sell or rent any dwelling by representations regarding the entry or prospective entry into the neighborhood of a person or persons of a particular race, color, religion, sex, familial status, handicap, or national origin. (16)

bona fide Latin meaning "in good faith."

boot The difference between the purchase price and the value of what is being exchanged that is paid in cash or other property. (17)

breach of condition Failure of landlord or tenant to perform his or her respective duties under the terms of the lease, thereby giving the other party grounds for terminating the lease agreement. (14)

breach of contract Failure without legal excuse to perform a promise that forms the whole or part of a contract. (9)

breach of duty The failure to fulfill an agent's duty to his or her principal. This includes disloyalty; disobedience; lack of skill, care, and diligence; and failure to either properly disclose information or to accurately account for funds. (7)

broker A person or an organization acting as agent for others in negotiating the purchase and sale of real property or other commodities for a fee. (1, 7)

brokerage The business of bringing buyers and sellers together and assisting in negotiations for the terms of sale of real estate. (7, 16)

broker price opinion See competitive market analysis. (7)

building codes Public controls regulating construction that establish minimum construction standards. (5)

bundle of rights The rights of an owner of a freehold estate to possession, enjoyment, control, and disposition of real property. (2)

buydown loan A loan with a reduced interest rate that a seller, developer, or buyer has obtained by paying money up front. (11)

buyer agency agreement A contract in which a buyer engages an agent to act on the buyer's behalf in purchasing a property. (8)

buyer's agent A real estate agent who acts solely on behalf of the buyer and owes all fiduciary duties of agency to the buyer. (7, 8)

capacity of parties The ability of parties to perceive and understand what they are contracting to do. All parties to a contract must be mentally competent and must have reached the age of majority. (9)

capital gain Profit made on the sale of real property. (17)

capital improvement An item that adds value to the property, adapts the property to new uses, or prolongs the life of property. Maintenance is not a capital improvement. (13, 17)

capitalization The process of converting future income into an indication of the present value of a property by applying a capitalization rate to net annual income. (13)

capitalization formula Investment or value of real estate times the capitalization rate equals the annual net income of the real estate. (13)

capitalization rate The rate of interest appropriate to the investment risk as a return on and return of the investment. (13)

capital loss Loss incurred on the sale of real property. (17)

cash flow Regular income produced by a rental property after deducting operating expenses and debt service. (13, 19)

cash on cash The relationship of the cash flow generated relative to the amount of cash invested in order to acquire the investment. Also known as equity dividend rate. (19)

caveat emptor Literally "let the buyer beware." Does not relieve agent's obligation of disclosing material facts. (7)

certificate of eligibility A statement provided to veterans of military service setting forth the amount of loan guarantee to which they are entitled at that time. (11)

Certificate of Occupancy (CO) A document issued by a local government agency after a satisfactory inspection of a structure, authorizing the occupancy of the structure. (5)

certificate of reasonable value (CRV) A document establishing the value of a property as the basis for the loan guarantee by the Department of Veterans Affairs to the lender. (11)

chain of title The successive conveyances of title to a particular parcel of land. (4)

change The principle stating that change is continually affecting land use and therefore continually altering value. (13)

chattel Personal property. (1)

chronological age Actual age of a structure. (13)

civil penalty Payment or redress for a private civil wrong imposed by a civil, not a criminal, proceeding. (7)

Civil Rights Act of 1866 A federal law that prohibits all discrimination on the basis of race. (16)

Civil Rights Act of 1968 Title VIII, commonly known as the Fair Housing Act, as amended in 1974 and 1988, prohibits discrimination in housing on the basis of race, color, national origin, religion, sex, handicap, or familial status (children). (16)

civil suit An action in a court of equity that seeks financial compensation for loss caused by another. (16)

client The principal, to whom the agent owes fiduciary duties. (7)

closing The consummation of a real estate contract. Also called settlement. (1, 12)

closing costs Expenses incurred in the purchase and sale of real property paid at the time of settlement or closing. (12)

closing statement An accounting of the funds received and disbursed in a real estate transaction. (12)

cloud on a title A claim against a title to real property. (4)

cluster zoning A form of zoning providing for several types of land use within a zoned area. (5)

Code of Ethics A standard of conduct required by license laws and by the National Association of REALTORS®. (1, 12)

collateral Property pledged as security for the payment of a debt. (11)

color of title A defective claim to a title. (4)

commercial property Property producing rental income or used in business. (15)

commingle To mix the money or property of others by an agent with the agent's personal or business funds or other property. (7)

commission A fee paid for the performance of services, such as a broker's commission. (1)

commissioner's deed A form of judicial deed executed by a commissioner. (4)

commitment A promise, such as a promise by a lending institution to make a certain mortgage loan. (11)

common areas Property to which title is held by co-owners as a result of ownership of a condominium unit. (2)

common law By judicial precedent or tradition as opposed to a written statute. (2)

community-based planning A form of land use control originating in the grassroots of a community. (5)

community planning A plan for the orderly growth of a city or a county to result in the greatest social and economic benefits to the people. (5)

community property A form of co-ownership limited to husband and wife. Does not include the right of survivorship. North Carolina is not a community property state. (2)

comparable A property that is similar to a property being appraised by the direct sales comparison approach. (13)

comparative market analysis (CMA) Presentation and analysis of the competition in the marketplace for a particular property for the purpose of arriving at a market price or listing price. Also referred to as a Broker Price Opinion (BPO). (13)

competent parties Persons and organizations legally qualified to manage their own affairs, including entering into contracts. (9)

competition The principle stating that when the net profit generated by a property is excessive, the result will be to create very strong competition. (13)

complete performance Execution of a contract by virtue of all parties having fully performed all terms. (9)

Comprehensive Environmental Response, Compensation, and Liability Act (CERCLA) Federal law that established the "superfund" to address clean-up of contaminated waste sites. Requires the offending party to clean up the contaminated area at their expense. If the offending party cannot be found the current owner may have liability. (6)

condemnation The exercise of the power of eminent domain. The taking of private property for public use by paying just compensation. (2)

condominium A form of ownership of real property recognized in all states that consists of individual ownership of some aspects and co-ownership of other aspects of the property. (2)

conforming loans Those processed on uniform loan forms and according to FNMA/FHLMC guidelines. (11)

conformity The homogeneous uses of land within a given area, which results in maximizing land value. (13)

Conner Act Requires certain documents (e.g., deeds, purchase contracts, and leases over three years) to be recorded to be enforceable against third parties. (4)

consideration Anything of value as recognized by law offered as an inducement to contract such as money, action, or forbearance, or a promise to act or a promise to forbear. (9)

construction loan A short-term loan, secured by a mortgage, to obtain the funds to construct an improvement on land. Usually considered to be the riskiest of all mortgage loans. Most prevalent example of a term loan. (11)

constructive eviction The right of a tenant to move out and stop paying rent resulting from some action or inaction by the landlord that renders the premises unsuitable for the use agreed to in a lease or another rental contract. (14)

constructive notice Notice of a fact on the public record that is considered to be known to everyone, even though he or she has not actually been notified of such fact. Everyone is bound by this knowledge. (4)

Consumer Price Index (CPI) An index of the change in prices of various commodities and services that provides a measure of the rate of inflation. (14)

contingency A condition in a contract relieving a party of liability if a certain event occurs. (9)

contract An agreement between competent parties upon legal consideration to do or abstain from doing some legal act. (9)

contract for deed A contract of sale and a financing instrument wherein the seller agrees to convey title when the buyer completes the purchase price installment payments. Also called installment land contract, land contract, and conditional sales contract. (10)

contractual capacity Having the ability to understand the terms of a contract and the consequences of nonperformance. (9)

contribution The principle that for any given part of a property, its value is the result of the contribution that part makes to the total value by being present or the amount that it subtracts from total value as a result of its absence. (13)

conventional life estates Those created by intentional act of the parties. (2)

conventional loan One in which the federal government does not insure or guarantee the payment to the lender. (11)

conveyance Transfer of title to real property. (2)

cooperating broker One who participates in the sale of a property through the listing broker. (7)

cooperative A form of ownership in which stockholders in a corporation occupy property owned by the corporation under a lease. (2)

co-owners See co-ownership.

co-ownership Title to real property held by two or more persons (co-owners) at the same time. There are many forms of co-ownership, including tenancy in common, tenancy by the entirety, and joint tenancy. Also called concurrent ownership. (2)

corporation A form of organization existing as a legal entity. An artificial person. (2)

corporeal Tangible things. (2)

cost A measure of expenditure of labor and material made sometime in the past. (13)

cost approach An appraisal method whereby the cost of constructing a substitute structure is calculated, depreciation is deducted, and land value is added. (13)

costs of acquisition The allowable costs of acquiring real property that can be added to the purchase price to determine the basis. (17)

counteroffer A promise or a request by an offeree that terminates the original offer from an offeror by rejecting it and substituting a new offer in its place. (9)

covenant A promise in writing. (5)

covenant against encumbrances A promise in a deed that there are no encumbrances against the title except those set forth in the deed. (4)

covenant of quiet enjoyment A promise in a deed (or lease) that the grantee (or lessee) will not be disturbed in his or her use of the property because of a defect in the grantor's (or lessor's) title. (4)

covenant of right to convey A promise in a deed that the grantor has the legal capacity to convey the title. (34)

covenant of seisin A promise in a deed assuring the grantee that the grantor has the title being conveyed. (4)

covenant of warranty A promise in a deed that the grantor will guarantee and defend the title against lawful claimants. (4)

credit In a closing statement, money to be received or credit given for money or a stated obligation. (12)

creditor One to whom a debt is owed. (2)

cul-de-sac A dead-end street with a circular turnaround at the dead end. (4)

cumulative-use zoning A type of zoning permitting a higher priority use even though different from the type of use designated for the area. (5)

curable A condition of property that exists when correction is physically possible and the cost of correction is less than the value increase. (13)

curtesy A husband's interest in the real property of his wife. (2)

customer The "third party" in a transaction; the agent works with the customer but not for him. (7)

damages The amount of financial loss as a result of the action of another. (9)

debit In a closing statement, an expense, money, or charge against the seller or buyer. (12)

debt service Principal and interest payments on a debt. (11)

declaration of restrictions The instrument used to record restrictive covenants on the public record. (2)

decree An order of a court. (2)

dedication An appropriation of land or an easement therein by the owner to the public. (2)

deed A written instrument that transfers an interest in real property when signed by grantor and delivered to the grantee. (4)

deed in lieu of foreclosure A conveyance of title to the lender by a borrower in default to avoid a record of foreclosure. Also called friendly foreclosure. (11)

deed of correction A deed executed to correct an error in a prior deed. Also called a deed of confirmation. (4)

deed of gift A warranty or quitclaim deed conveying title as a gift to the grantee. (4)

deed of release A deed executed by a mortgage lender to release a title from the lien of a mortgage when the debt has been satisfied. Also used to release a dower right. (4)

deed of surrender A deed executed by a life tenant to convey his or her estate to the remainder or reversionary interest. (4)

deed of trust A form of security instrument pledging real property as security for the loan by conveying legal title to a third party, who is called a trustee until the loan is paid in full. (11)

deed restrictions Limitations on land use appearing in deeds. Also known as restrictive, or protective, covenants. (5)

default Failure to perform an mortgage obligation. (11)

defeasance clause to defeat the mortgage. The clause in a mortgage or a deed of trust giving the borrower the right to redeem the title and have the mortgage lien released at any time prior to default by paying the debt in full. (11)

defeasible Subject to being defeated by the occurrence of a certain event. (2)

defeasible fee A title that is subject to being lost if certain conditions occur. (2)

deficiency judgment A judgment obtained by a lender for the difference between the amount of foreclosure sale proceeds and the amount needed to satisfy the mortgage debt. (11)

demise To convey an estate for years. Synonymous with lease or let. (14)

density The number of persons or structures per acre. (5)

Department of Housing and Urban Development (HUD) A federal agency involved with housing. (11, 16)

depreciated value The original basis of a property less the amount of depreciation taken at any point in time. (13)

depreciation Loss in value from any cause. (13)

descent The distribution of property of one who has died intestate to legally qualified heirs. (4)

description by reference A valid legal description that refers to a recorded plat or other publicly recorded document. (4)

devise A gift of real property by will. (4)

devisee The recipient of a gift of real property by will. (4)

direct sales comparison approach The primary approach in estimating the value of vacant land and single-family owner-occupied dwellings. Also called market data approach. (13)

disability A physical or mental impairment that substantially limits one or more of a person's major life activities. (16)

disclosure of information The prompt and total communication to the principal by the agent of any information that is material to the transaction for which the agency was created. (7)

discount points A percentage of the loan amount required by the lender for making a mortgage loan at a more attractive interest rate. There will be one point charged for every 1/8 of 1% between the interest rate and the desired yield. Each point will cost 1% of the loan amount. (11)

discriminatory advertising Any advertising that states or indicates a preference, limitation, or discrimination on the basis of race, color, religion, sex, familial status, handicap, or national origin in offering housing for sale or rent. (16)

disintermediation The loss of funds available to lending institutions for making mortgage loans caused by the withdrawal of funds by depositors for making investments that provide greater yields. (11)

dominant tenement Land benefiting from an appurtenant easement. (2)

do not call registry A federal program that allows homeowner's to register their residential phone numbers in order to eliminate, with some exceptions, unsolicited phone calls from telemarketers. (8)

double entry An amount of money showing on the closing statement for both buyer and seller. It is an amount collected from one party and given to the other party, therefore, a debit to the first party and a credit to the other party. (12)

dower A wife's interest in the real property of her husband. (2)

dual agency Representing two parties at the same time or in the same transaction. This practice is illegal unless all parties are properly informed and consent to the agency. (7)

due diligence The ability of the buyer to conduct research to determine issues relative to things of interest to the buyer such as property condition, zoning, protective covenants, appraised value, insureability, etc. (10)

due diligence date The date stated in the contract in which the buyer has the right to conduct due diligence without risk of losing the earnest money. (10)

due diligence fee A non-refundable amount of money paid by the buyer, to the seller, to compensate the seller for the buyer's rights of due diligence. There is no fee required by law but may be imposed by seller or offered by the buyer. (10)

due-on-sale clause See alienation clause. (11)

duress The inability of a party to exercise his or her free will because of fear of another party. (9)

earnest money A deposit of money made by a buyer at the time of making an offer to demonstrate the earnest intent to purchase. Also called binder, good faith deposit, or escrow deposit. (10)

easement A nonpossessory right of use in the land of another. (2)

easement by necessity Created by operation of law to allow access to land locked property. (2)

easement by dedication A portion of property set aside for use by the public (e.g. roadways, parks). (2)

easement in gross A personal right of use in the land of another without the requirement that the holder of the right own adjoining land. (2)

economic (external) obsolescence A loss in value caused by such things as changes in surrounding land use patterns and failure to adhere to the principle of highest and best use. Always associated with things located outside the boundaries of the property. (13)

economic life The period of time during which a property is economically beneficial to the owner. (13)

effective age The age of a property as it appears to be based on its appearances. (13)

effective date The date the contract has been both signed and proper notice has been delivered to the offeror that the offeree has accepted in writing. (10)

effective demand A desire for property accompanied by the financial ability to satisfy the desire by purchasing the property. (13)

effective gross income Scheduled gross income minus allowances for vacancy and other non-payment of rent by the tenant. (13)

effective interest rate The actual rate of interest being paid. (11)

ejectment A legal action to evict a tenant from property. (14)

emblements Personal property growing in the soil that requires planting and cultivation. Annual crops. Also, the right of former owners to reenter property to cultivate and harvest annual crops that were planted by them. (2)

eminent domain The power of government to take private property for public use. (2)

employment authority A document or contract giving a real estate agent the right to act for a principal with certain specific guidelines in a real estate contract (i.e., a listing contract or a buyer's agency contract). (7)

enabling acts Laws passed by state legislatures authorizing cities and counties to regulate land use within their jurisdictions. (5)

encapsulate To enclose in order to prevent the release of fibers such as is the case involving friable asbestos. (6)

encroachment A trespass on the land of another as a result of an intrusion by some structure or other object. (2)

encumbrance A claim, lien, charge, or liability attached to and binding upon real property. (2)

enforceable A contract in which the parties may be required legally to perform. (9)

environmental impact statement A statement required by the national Environmental Policy Act that must be submitted before initiating or changing a land use that may adversely affect the environment. (5)

Environmental Policy Act A federal law that requires filing an environmental impact statement with the EPA prior to changing or initiating a land use or development. (5)

Environmental Protection Agency (EPA) A federal agency that oversees land, air and water through development and enforcement of regulations use. (5)

Equal Credit Opportunity Act (ECOA) A federal law prohibiting discrimination in consumer loans. (11)

equitable title As opposed to legal title. Equitable title is title that will be conveyed once certain contract obligations are performed. An interest in real estate such that a court will take notice and protect the owner's rights. (10)

equity dividend rate See cash on cash. **equity of redemption** The right of the borrower to pay off what is owed and redeem the title to the property prior to final foreclosure sale. Also known as right of redemption. (11)

escalated lease One in which the rental amount changes in proportion to the lessor's costs of ownership and operation of the property. (14)

escheat The power of government to take title to property left by a person who has died without leaving a will or qualified heirs. (2)

escrow account (a) An account maintained by a real estate broker in an insured bank for the deposit of other people's money; also called trust account. (2, 10) (b) An account maintained by the borrower with the lender in certain mortgage loans, also known as an impound account or reserve account, to accumulate the funds to pay an annual insurance premium, a real property tax, and/or a homeowner's association assessment. (11)

estate An interest in real property sufficient to give the owner of the estate the right to possession of real property. (2)

estate at sufferance Describes the situation of someone continuing to occupy property after lawful authorization has expired. A form of leasehold estate. (14)

estate at will A leasehold estate that may be terminated at the will of either party. (114)

estate for years A leasehold estate of definite duration. (14)

estate from period to period A leasehold estate that automatically renews itself for consecutive periods until terminated by notice given by either party. Also called estate from year to year and periodic tenancy. (114)

estate in real property An interest sufficient to provide the right to use, possession, and control of land and establishes the degree and duration of ownership. (2)

estoppel The prevention of a person from making a statement contrary to a previous statement. (7)

estovers The right of a life tenant or lessee to cut timber on the property for fuel or to use in making repairs. (2)

et al. Latin for "and others."

et ux. Latin for "and wife."

eviction A landlord's action that interferes with the tenant's use or possession of the property. Eviction may be actual or constructive. (114)

excise tax A state tax that a grantor must affix to a deed. It provides a rough indication of purchase price and is a valuable data source for the broker's records. Also known as revenue stamps. (4)

exclusive agency A listing given to one broker only (exclusive), who is entitled to the commission if the broker or any agent of the listing broker effects a sale, but it imposes no commission obligation on the owner who sells the property to a person who was not interested in the property by efforts of the listing broker or an agent of the listing broker. (8)

exclusive buyer agency A relationship in which the agent represents only the interests of the buyer and not the seller. (7)

exclusive right to sell A listing given to one broker only who is entitled to the commission if anyone sells the property during the term of the listing contract. (8)

exclusive-use zoning A type of zoning in which only the specified use may be made of property within the zoned district. (5)

executed contract An agreement that has been fully performed. (9)

execution The signing of a contract or another legal document. (4, 9)

executor A man appointed in a will to see that the terms of the will are carried out. (4)

executory contract An agreement that has not been fully performed. (9)

executrix A woman appointed in a will to see that the terms of the will are carried out. (4)

express agency Any oral or written agreement establishing a trust relationship between a principal and agent. (7)

express authority That authority specifically granted in a contract. (7)

express contract One created verbally or in writing by the parties. (9)

extender clause A clause in a listing contract protecting the broker's commission entitlement for a specified time after expiration of the contract. (8)

Fair Housing Act of 1968 (as amended) A federal prohibition of discrimination in the sale, rental, or financing of housing on the basis of race, color, religion, sex, national origin, handicap, or familial status. (16)

fair market value A price for property agreed upon between buyer and seller in a competitive market with neither party being under undue pressure. (13)

Fannie Mae (FNMA) The shortened name for the Federal National Mortgage Association. (7)

Federal Home Loan Mortgage Corporation (Freddie Mac) A secondary mortgage market institution (corporation) that only purchases conventional loans. (11)

Federal Housing Administration (FHA) The federal agency that insures mortgage loans to protect lending institutions. (11)

Federal National Mortgage Association (Fannie Mae) A privately owned corporation that purchases FHA, VA, and conventional mortgages. (11)

Federal Reserve Bank Regulates monetary policy by controlling the money supply and the discount rate. (11)

fee simple absolute An inheritable freehold estate in land that is the greatest form of real property ownership. (2)

fee simple determinable A defeasible fee (title) that terminates automatically if conditions of the title are violated. (2)

fee simple subject to a condition subsequent A defeasible fee (title) by which the grantor or his heirs may reenter the property and bring legal action to terminate the grantee's estate and regain title and possession if conditions of title are violated. (2)

FHA-insured loan A mortgage loan in which the payments are insured by the Federal Housing Administration. (11)

fiduciary A person, such as an agent, who is placed in a position of trust in relation to the person for whose benefit the relationship is created. Essentially the same as a trustee. (7)

first mortgage One that is superior to later recorded mortgages. Also known as a senior mortgage. (11)

first substantial contact A flexible standard that typically occurs when an agent and a prospective buyer discuss in any detail the buyer's interest in purchasing property. (7)

fit premises Residential property that is in fit condition for human habitation. In North Carolina a landlord is required to do whatever is necessary to put and maintain fit premises. (114)

fixed-rate loan One in which the interest does not change. (11)

fixture Personal property that has become real property by having been permanently attached to real property. (2)

flat fee listing Commission arrangement in which the broker takes a listing based on a specified payment of money by the seller to the broker at time of listing. (8)

foreclosure The legal procedure in which the lender sells the collateral in order to pay off the existing loan in the event of default by the borrower. The process used to terminate the borrower's equity, or right, of redemption. (11)

foreclosure under power of sale See nonjudicial foreclosure. (11)

foreshore The land between high and low watermarks. (2)

fraud An intentional false statement of a material fact. (7)

Freddie Mac (FHLMC) The shortened name for the Federal Home Loan Mortgage Corporation, an agency that purchases mortgages, especially conventional mortgages, in the secondary mortgage market. (11)

freehold An interest in land of at least a lifetime and is therefore generally identified with the concept of title or ownership. (2)

free market An economic condition in which buyer and seller are able to negotiate a purchase and sale without undue pressure, urgency, or outside influences other than the law of supply and demand. (1)

friable A term used to reference asbestos fibers that can become airborne when contact is made. (6)

friendly foreclosure An absolute conveyance of title to the lender by the mortgagor in default to avoid a record of foreclosure. Also called a deed in lieu of foreclosure. (11)

front foot A linear foot of property frontage on a street or highway.

fruits of industry (fructus industriales) Growing things on real estate that require planting each season and cultivation (e.g., annuals, crops). These are typically considered personal property and not real property. (2)

fruits of the soil (fructus naturales) Growing things that do not require planting or cultivation but grow naturally and are perennial (e.g., forest trees and native shrubs). They are designated in law as real property as long as they are attached to the soil. (2)

full performance The usual manner of terminating contracts. (9)

full-service leases A lease requiring each tenant to pay a portion of the overall operating expenses for the building and common areas in addition to a base rent; common in large office buildings and shopping centers. (14)

functional obsolescence A loss in value resulting from such things as faulty design, inadequacies, overadequacies, and out-of-date equipment. (13)

future interest (also called future estate) The right in real property of a person holding a remainder or reversionary interest who will vest at some time in the future in a property during the tenancy of a life tenant. (2)

gain realized The excess of the amount realized over the adjusted basis. (17)

general agency Full authority over one particular field of business or aspect of personal affairs of the principal (e.g., a property manager managing an apartment complex for the owner). (7)

general agent One who is authorized to conduct a broad scope of business for his or her principal but whose authority is limited in some way (e.g., one who is authorized to manage another's business). (7)

general lien One that attaches to all property of the debtor within the jurisdiction of the court. (2)

general warranty deed A deed in which there is an unlimited warranty of title. (4)

Ginnie Mae (GNMA) A nickname for Government National Mortgage Association, a U.S. government agency that purchases FHA and VA mortgages. (7)

Government National Mortgage Association (Ginnie Mae) A government agency that purchases FHA and VA mortgages. (11)

government rectangular survey system A type of land description by townships and sections. (4)

graduated lease One in which the rental amount changes in specified amounts over the lease term. (14)

graduated payment mortgage (GPM) One in which the payments are lower in the early years but increase on a scheduled basis until they reach an amortizing level. (11)

grantee One who receives title to real property by deed. (4)

grantor One who conveys title to real property by deed. (4)

gross effective income Gross potential income less deductions for vacancy and credit losses plus other income. (13)

gross income Income received without the subtraction of expenses. (11)

gross lease One in which the lessor pays all costs of operating and maintaining the property and real property taxes. (14)

gross rent multiplier A number used to estimate the value of income property. Also called gross income multiplier. (13)

ground lease A lease of unimproved land. Also called a land lease. (10)

habitable Suitable for the type of occupancy intended. (14)

handicap A mental or physical impairment that limits at least one major human activity that qualifies the person with the impairment to protection under the Fair Housing Act. (16)

heir A person legally eligible to receive property of a decedent. (4)

hereditaments All the corporeal and incorporeal attributes of real estate that can be inherited. (2)

highest and best use The use of land that will preserve its utility and yield a net income in the form of rent that forms, when capitalized at the proper rate of interest, the highest present value of the land. (1, 13)

hold over The act of a tenant remaining in possession of property after the termination of a lease. (14)

homogeneous Similar and compatible land uses. (5)

Housing and Urban Development (HUD) An agency of the federal government concerned with housing programs and laws. (11, 16)

Human Relations Commission See North Carolina Human Relations Commission.

hypothecation Pledging property as security for the payment of a debt without giving up possession. (11)

illusory offer One that does not obligate the offeror. (9)

immobility A physical characteristic of land describing the impossibility of relocating land from one place to another. (1)

implied contract One created by deduction from the conduct of the parties rather than from the direct words of the parties. Opposite of an express contract. (9)

implied warranty One presumed by law to exist in a deed though not expressly stated. (4)

improved land Land on which structures or roads exist. (2)

improvements Structures, walls, roads, and so on. (1)

income approach The primary method of estimating the value of properties that produce rental income. Also called appraisal by capitalization. (13)

income property One that produces rental income. (13)

incompetent A person who is not capable of managing his or her own affairs. (9)

incurable That which is not physically correctable or not economically practical to correct. (13)

indestructibility A physical characteristic of land meaning that land is a permanent commodity and cannot be destroyed. (1)

index lease One in which the rental amount is changed in proportion to changes in a measure such as the Consumer Price Index. (14)

ingress and egress The right to enter (ingress) and to exit (egress) from a parcel of land. (2)

injunction An instruction of a court to discontinue a specified activity. (5)

installment land contract See contract for deed.

installment sale A transaction in which the seller receives the purchase price in more than one payment. (11)

instrument A written legal document such as a contract, note, and mortgage. (9)

insured conventional loan One in which the loan payment is insured by private mortgage insurance to protect the lender. (11)

interest Money paid for the use of money. (11) Also an ownership or right. (2)

interim financing Short-term or temporary financing, such as a construction loan. (11)

interim interest Interest paid on the loan amount from the date of closing through the end of the closing month inclusive. Typically is prepaid at the time of closing. (12)

Interstate Land Sales Full Disclosure Act A federal law regulating the interstate sale of land under certain conditions. (5)

intestate A person who has died without leaving a valid will. (4)

intestate succession Distribution of property by descent as provided by statute. (2)

invalid Not legally enforceable. (9)

irrevocable That which cannot be changed or canceled.

joint tenancy A form of co-ownership that includes the right of survivorship. (2)

judgment A court determination that one party is indebted to another. When properly filed, it creates a lien on the debtor's property. (2)

judgment lien A general lien resulting from a court decree. (2)

judicial deed One executed by an official with court authorization. (4)

judicial foreclosure A court proceeding to require that property be sold to satisfy a mortgage lien. (11)

jumbo loans When a loan amount is higher than the conforming limit.

junior mortgage One that is subordinate to a prior mortgage. Any loan in which there is another loan of higher priority. (11)

jurisdiction The extent of the authority of a court. (2)

land The surface of the earth, the area above and below the surface, and everything attached naturally (trees, crops) thereto. (2)

land contract See contract for deed. (10)

landlocked With regard to property, without access to a public road. (2)

landlord One who owns real property and leases it to another. Also referred to as lessor. (14)

lateral support The right of land to be supported in its natural state by adjacent land. (2)

lawful Legal, not prohibited by law. (9)

Lead-Based Paint Hazard Reduction Act Federal law that requires disclosure of known lead-based paint on residential properties constructed prior to 1978. There is a mandated addendum that must be used as well as delivery of a EPA pamphlet outlining the risks of lead-based paint exposure. Buyers are given a 10-day period in which to assess the presence of lead-based paint although this right may be waived. (6)

lead poisoning Health risks of high exposure to lead-based products such as paint, glazes, and solders. Typical risk is to the central nervous system. (6)

lease A contract wherein a landlord gives a tenant the right of use and possession of property for a limited time in return for rent. (14)

leasehold estate Nonfreehold estate. A leasehold estate is of limited duration and provides the right to possession and control, but not title. (2, 14)

legal capacity The ability to contract. (9)

legal description A description of land recognized by law. (4)

legal entity A person or organization with legal standing or capacity. (9)

legal title Belongs to the party who actually holds the deed. (10)

less-than-freehold estate Nonfreehold estates. (2, 14)

lessee A tenant under a lease. (14)

lessor A landlord under a lease. (14)

leverage The use of borrowed funds, which allows an owner to control an investment greater than the owner's equity in the investment. The larger the percentage of borrowed money, the greater the leverage. (1)

levy Imposition of a tax executing a lien. (3)

lien A claim that one person has against the property of another for some debt or charge which entitles the lien holder to have the claim satisfied from the property of the debtor. (2)

lien foreclosure sale A sale of real property at public auction to satisfy a specific or general lien against the property. These sales do not have the consent of the owner/debtor, and title is typically conveyed by trustee's deed. (4)

lien theory The legal theory that a mortgage creates a lien against the real property pledged in the mortgage to secure the payment of a debt. (11)

life estate A freehold estate created for the duration of the life or lives of certain named person or persons. A noninheritable estate. (2)

life estate in remainder A form of life estate in which certain persons called remaindermen are designated to receive the title upon termination of the life tenancy. (2)

life estate in reversion A form of life estate that reverts to the creator of the estate in fee simple upon termination. (2)

life estate pur autre vie An estate in which the duration is measured by the life of someone other than the life tenant. (2)

life tenant One holding a life estate. (2)

liquidated damages A predetermined amount of money to be paid and received as compensation for a breach of contract. (8, 9)

liquidity The ability to convert an asset into cash. (11)

lis pendens Literally "a lawsuit pending." Notice of pending litigation whose outcome potentially will affect title to all or part of a new owner's property. (2)

listing contract An agreement whereby a property owner employs a real estate broker to look for a buyer for the property described in the contract and promises to compensate the agent. (1, 8)

litigation A lawsuit.

littoral rights The rights of owners bordering large bodies of water such as oceans to access of that water body. (2)

loan assumption The transfer of loan obligations to a purchaser of the mortgaged property. (11)

loan commitment The obligation of a lending institution to make a certain mortgage loan. (11)

loan-to-value ratio The relationship between the amount of a mortgage loan or the sales price, whichever is lower and the lender's opinion of the value of the property pledged to secure the payment of the loan. (11)

location (situs) An economic characteristic of land having the greatest effect on value of any other characteristic. (1)

long term capital gain Profit made on the sale of real property where the asset was held for at least one year. (17)

loyalty An absolute duty of an agent to a principal to serve the best interest of the principal. (7)

Maggie Mae (MGIC) A secondary mortgage market corporation of the Mortgage Guaranty Insurance Corporation. (11)

management plan A long-range program prepared by a property manager for the management of a property. (15)

management proposal A program for operating a property submitted to the owner by a property manager. (15)

marital life estates Those created by the exercise of the right of dower, curtesy, or a statutory substitute. (2)

marketable title One that is free from reasonable doubt and that a court would require a purchaser to accept. (4)

Marketable Title Act North Carolina legislation designed to extinguish old defects in the title by providing that when a chain of title can be established for 30 years without conflicts, claims outside this chain are extinguished. This Act has exceptions. (4)

market value The value in terms of money agreed upon by a willing buyer and seller, neither being under undue pressure and each being knowledgeable of market conditions at the time. (13)

master plan Created for the purpose of providing for the orderly growth of a community that will result in the greatest social and economic benefits to the people in the community. (5)

material fact An important fact that may affect a person's judgment. (7)

mechanics' liens Statutory liens available to persons supplying labor (mechanic) or material (materialmen) to the construction of an improvement on land if they are not paid. (2)

metes and bounds A system of land description by distances and directions. This description must "close" by ending up precisely where it began. (4)

mill rate (mills) A tax rate based upon the theory of .1 of 1 cent, or .001 of the tax value. A mill rate of 15 would represent 15 × .001 or .015 times the tax value. This method is not used in NC but may appear on the national portion of the state examination. (3)

mineral lease A nonfreehold (leasehold) estate in the area below the surface of land. (2)

mineral rights The right to take minerals from the earth; the landowner holds these rights or can sell or lease them to others. (2)

minor A person who has not attained the statutory age of majority (18). (9)

misdemeanor A criminal violation punishable by a fine and/or imprisonment. It is not considered as severe an offense as a felony. (7)

mitigate To lessen the risk such as in the case of radon gas in the home. Mitigation often consists of filling in holes and cracks where the gas can enter the home as well as ventilation to release trapped gasses. (6)

modification by improvement An economic characteristic of land providing that the economic supply of land is increased by improvements made to land and on land. (1)

mortgage A written instrument used to pledge a title to real property to secure the payment of a promissory note. (11)

mortgage banker A form of organization that makes and services mortgage loans from its own monies. (11)

mortgage broker One who arranges a mortgage loan between a lender and borrower for a fee. (11)

mortgagee The lender in a mortgage loan receiving a mortgage from the borrower/mortgagor. (11)

mortgagee's policy A policy that insures a mortgagee against defects in a title pledged by a mortgagor to secure payment of a mortgage loan. (4)

mortgage insurance premium (MIP) A fee charged by the Federal Housing Administration (FHA) to insure FHA loans. There is both an upfront fee, which can be added to the loan amount or paid in cash at closing, and an annual fee, which can be paid with the monthly payments. (11)

mortgage satisfaction Full payment of a mortgage loan. (11)

mortgaging clause The clause in a mortgage or deed of trust that demonstrates the intention of the mortgagor to mortgage the property to the mortgagee. (11)

mortgagor The borrower in a mortgage loan who executes and delivers a mortgage to the lender. (11)

multiple listing A type of listing by an organized method of sharing or pooling listings by member brokers. (7)

multiple listing service (MLS) An organized method of sharing or pooling listings by member brokers. (7)

mutual assent The voluntary agreement of all parties to a contract as evidenced by an offer and acceptance. (9)

National Association of REALTORS® The largest and most prominent trade organization of real estate licensees. (1)

negative amortization When the loan payment amount is not sufficient to cover interest due, the shortfall is added back into principal, causing principal to grow larger after payment is made. (11)

negative covenants or easements Promises on the part of the purchasers of property in the subdivision to limit their use of their property to comply with the requirements of the restrictive/protective covenants. (5)

negligent misrepresentation An unintended misrepresentation of a material fact that the party did not make knowingly but should have known the truth by exercising due skill, care, and diligence. (7)

negligent omission An unintended failure to communicate a known material fact. An unintended failure to communicate unknown material fact by a person responsible for disclosing it because this person did not exercise the due skill, care, and diligence that would have revealed the fact. (7)

net income Gross income less operating expenses. Also called net operating income. (13)

net lease One in which the lessee pays a fixed amount of rent plus the costs of operation of the property. (14)

net listing Not a type of listing but a method of establishing the listing broker's commission as all money above a specified net amount to the seller. (7)

net operating income Gross operating income minus operating expenses. (13)

nonconforming use A use of land that does not conform to the use permitted by a zoning ordinance for the area but is allowed to continue because it preceded the zoning ordinance. (5)

non-exclusive buyer agency A type of buyer agency in which the buyer is free to utilize other buyer agents and is not obligated to just one agent. This is the type of buyer agency that would exist if the agency agreement is not reduced to writing. (8)

nonfreehold estate An estate (interest in land) of less than freehold (lifetime, ownership), i.e., rental property. (2, 14)

non-friable A term used to describe asbestos that will not typically result in airborne particles when physical contact is made. (6)

nonhomogeneity A physical characteristic of land describing that land as a unique commodity. (1)

nonjudicial foreclosure A form of foreclosure that does not require court action to conduct a foreclosure sale. Also called foreclosure under power of sale. (11)

nonrecourse note A note in which the borrower has no personal liability for payment. (11)

North Carolina Condominium Act Legislation passed in 1986 that set requirements for the sale or resale of condominiums. Requirements include disclosure, right to rescind contract for seven days, special escrow rules, and timely provision of required documents. (2)

North Carolina Fair Housing Act of 1983 State fair housing law that is almost identical to the federal fair housing laws; however, it provides no exemptions for owners selling their own property, and it broadens rental exemption slightly. (16)

North Carolina Human Relations Commission A state agency that, as a substantially equivalent agency to HUD, is currently enforcing the 1968 Fair Housing Act and its 1988 amendments. (16)

North Carolina Residential Rental Agreements Act A North Carolina statute that affects residential rentals in North Carolina by setting forth the mutually dependent obligations and duties of landlords and tenants, as well as the remedies available for breach of contract by the landlord. (14)

North Carolina Tenant Security Deposit Act A North Carolina statute that requires a landlord or his or her agent to ensure that residential rental deposits are placed in a trust account or guaranteed with a bond and specifies the amount and permitted use of such deposits. The tenant must be notified of the disposition of such deposits. (14)

notary public A person authorized by a state to take oaths and acknowledgments. (4)

notice of lis pendens A notice on the public record warning all persons that a title to real property is the subject of a lawsuit and any lien resulting from the suit will attach to the title held by a purchaser from the defendant. (2)

novation The substitution of a new contract for a prior contract. (9)

null and void Invalid, without legal force or effect. (9)

obsolescence A loss in property value caused by external or functional factors. (13)

occupancy Physical possession of property. (2)

offer A promise made to another conditional upon acceptance by a promise or an act made in return. (7)

offer and acceptance Necessary elements for the creation of a contract. (7)

offeree One to whom an offer is made. (10)

offeror One making an offer. (10)

offer to purchase and contract A bilateral enforceable contract for the sale of real property. (1, 9, 10)

omission The failure to disclose information. (7)

open-end mortgage One that may be refinanced without rewriting the mortgage. (11)

open listing A listing given to one or more brokers wherein the broker procuring a sale is entitled to the commission but imposes no commission obligation on the owner in the event the owner sells the property to a person who was not interested in the property by one of the listing brokers. (8)

operating budget A yearly budget of income and expense for a particular property prepared by a property manager. (15)

operating expenses The costs of operating a property held as an investment. (13)

operating statement A report of receipts and disbursements in evidence of net income of rental property. (13, 15)

operation of law The manner in which the rights and/or liabilities of parties may be changed by the application of law without the act or cooperation of the parties. (2)

opinion of title An attorney's report based on a title examination, setting forth the examiner's opinion of the quality of a title to real property. (4)

option A contract giving one (optionee) the exclusive right to buy a specified property from the owner (optionor) at a specified price for a specified period of time. (10)

optionee One who receives an option. (10)

optionor One who gives an option. (10)

option to purchase A contract whereby a property owner (optionor) sells a right to purchase his or her property to a prospective buyer (optionee). (10)

ordinance A law enacted by a local government. (5)

origination fee A service charge made by a lending institution for making a mortgage loan. (11)

overlay district A zoning device that superimposes a particular zoning over one or more zoning areas. Examples are flood zones and historic preservation districts. (5)

override clause Also called extender, or carry-over, clause. It provides for seller to pay the full commission to broker for any sale to registered prospects within the specified period after the termination of the contract. (8)

ownership The right to use, control, possess, and dispose of property. (2)

ownership in severalty Title to real property held in the name of one person only. (2)

owners association The organization of owners having the responsibility of providing for the operation and maintenance of the common areas of a condominium or residential subdivision. Also called property owners association. (2)

package mortgage One in which personal property as well as real property is pledged to secure payment of the note. (11)

paid outside closing (POC) Items paid by the buyer or seller before closing, which appear on the closing statement, but are not included in totals. (12)

Parol Evidence Rule Rule of evidence and law that states the written words contain all of the agreement and that oral statements not agreeing with the written word are to be disregarded. (9)

partition A legal proceeding dividing property of co-owners so that each holds title in severalty to a specific portion of the property. (2)

party wall A common wall used by two adjoining structures. (2)

peaceable self-help The illegal activity of landlords to bar tenants from a premise, e.g., locking out. (14)

percentage lease One in which the rental amount is a combination of a fixed amount plus a percentage of the lessee's gross sales. (14)

periodic tenancy A lease that automatically renews for successive periods unless terminated by either party. Also called an estate from year to year. (14)

permanence A physical characteristic of land referring to its indestructibility.

personal property All property that is not land and is not permanently attached to land. Everything that is movable. (1, 2)

personalty Personal property or chattels. (1)

physical deterioration A loss in value caused by unrepaired damage or inadequate maintenance. (13)

PITI Letters following the amount of a mortgage payment designating that the payment includes principal, interest, taxes, and insurance. (11)

planned unit development (PUD) A type of zoning ordinance which permits a special use; thereby enabling a designated area or subdivision to have a combination of property types, such as, residential housing, recreation facilities, and business establishments. (5)

planning A program for the development of a city or a county designed to provide for orderly growth. (5)

plat A property map. (4)

plat books Books wherein plats are recorded on the public record. (4)

pledge To provide property as security for the payment of a debt or for the performance of a promise. (11)

point of beginning A reasonably easy-to-locate point tied to a well-established reference point from which a surveyor begins the metes and bounds description. After sighting all distances and directions of the perimeter of the property, the description must close, that is, return to the point of beginning. (4)

points See discount points.

police power The power of government to regulate the use of real property for the benefit of the public interest. (2)

population density The relationship of the number of people to a given land area. (5)

power of attorney An instrument appointing an attorney-in-fact. (7)

power of sale clause Gives the trustee the right to sell the property if the buyer defaults. (11)

prepaid items Funds paid at closing to start an escrow account required in certain mortgage loans. Also called prepaids. (11, 12)

prepayment penalty clause States that a financial penalty is imposed on a borrower for paying a mortgage loan prior to the expiration of the full mortgage term or before a time specified in the loan. (11)

prescription A method of acquiring an easement by continuous and uninterrupted use without permission. (2)

prescriptive easement One obtained by open, continued, and uninterrupted use without the owner's permission. (2)

price The amount of money paid for a property. (13)

prima facie Latin meaning "on the fact of it." A fact presumed to be true unless disproved by contrary evidence.

primary mortgage market The activity of lenders making mortgage loans to individual borrowers. (11)

prime rate The interest rate a lender charges the most creditworthy customers. (11)

principal (a) In the law of agency, one who appoints an agent to represent him or her. (7) (b) The amount of money on which interest is either owed or received. (11)

principal residence The home the owner or renter occupies most of the time. (11, 17)

private land use controls The regulations of land use by individuals or nongovernment organizations in the form of deed restrictions and restrictive covenants. (5)

private mortgage insurance (PMI) A form of insurance required in high loan-to-value ratio conventional loans to protect the lender in case of borrower default in loan payment.

private property That which is not owned by government. (2)

privity of contract One of two sets of rights and duties between parties in a lease; arises from contractual promises expressed in the lease. (14)

privity of estate One of two sets of rights and duties between parties in a lease; arises from traditional property law. (14)

probable selling price Estimating price of property being listed. (13)

probate The procedure for proving a will's validity. (4)

profit, or profit à prendre The right to participate in the profits of the land of another. (2)

promissory note A written promise to pay a debt as set forth in the writing. (11)

promulgate To put in effect by public announcement.

procuring cause of sale The theory based upon the commission being earned by the party who is the primary factor in introducing the property as well as the predominant factor in concluding the transaction while not being violation of the laws of agency. (7)

property management Comprehensive, orderly, continuing program analyzing all investment aspects of a property and coordinating the leasing and maintenance of the property to ensure a financially successful project. (15)

property management agreement An employment contract setting up the agency relationship between the property owner and the real estate agent that gives the agent the responsibility of managing the property, including such responsibilities as negotiating, leasing, repairing and maintaining the property, collecting rents, and accounting for funds. (8, 15)

property management report A periodic financial report prepared by a property manager for the owner. (15)

property manager One who manages properties for an owner(s) as the owner's agent. (15)

property report Disclosure required under Interstate Land Sales Disclosure Act. (5)

proprietary lease A lease for an apartment unit in a development owned by a corporation in which the lessee owns stock entitling him to lease a unit. (2)

prorating Dividing certain settlement costs between buyer and seller. (12)

protective agreement Any agreement that serves to protect the agent's rights to be paid a commission. (10)

provisional broker In real estate in North Carolina, a person licensed as a broker with a provisional status attached to the license, who can perform the same real estate functions as a broker who does not have a provisional status, but under the supervision of a broker-in-charge (BIC).

public land use controls The regulation of land use by government organizations in the form of zoning laws, building codes, subdivision ordinances, and environmental protection laws. (5)

public offering statement A statement disclosing all material facts about a property. State and federal laws require a developer to provide prospective purchasers such a statement in certain circumstances. (2)

public record A record providing constructive notice of real property conveyances and other matters. (2, 4)

pur autre vie French meaning "for the life of another." A life estate measured by the life of someone other than the life tenant. (2)

purchase money mortgage A mortgage given by a buyer to a seller to secure the payment of all or part of the purchase price. (11)

quantity survey method A method for estimating replacement or reproduction cost. (13)

quiet enjoyment The use or possession of property that is undisturbed by an enforceable claim of superior title. (4)

quitclaim To relinquish or release a claim to real property. (4)

quitclaim deed A deed that contains no warranty of title. It is used to remove a cloud on a title. It conveys whatever interest, if any, the grantor has. (4)

radon A colorless, odorless gas that occurs naturally in the earth from decaying uranium deposits. Radon gas is considered to be the second leading cause of lung cancer. The E.P.A. has established 4.0 picocuries as the maximum "safe" level of radon in the home. (6)

rate of return The percentage of the net income produced by a property or another investment. (13)

ready, willing, and able Describes a buyer who is ready to buy, willing to buy, and financially able to pay the asking price. (7)

real estate Land and everything that is permanently attached to land. Interchangeable with the terms real property and realty. (1)

real estate broker A person or organization who negotiates real estate sales, exchanges, or rentals for others for compensation or a promise of compensation. (1)

Real Estate Commission The state agency responsible for the administration and enforcement of real estate license laws. (1)

real estate investment trust (REIT) A form of business trust owned by shareholders who make mortgage loans. (11)

real estate market A local activity in which real property is sold, exchanged, leased, or rented at prices set by competing forces. (1)

Real Estate Settlement Procedures Act (RESPA) Law requiring advance disclosure of settlement costs and other specified information mandating specific closing statement forms and prohibiting kickbacks. (12)

realized gain Actual profit resulting in a sale. (17)

real property Land and everything permanently attached to land, including all rights and interests in the land. (1)

REALTOR® A registered trademark of the National Association of REALTORS®. Its use is limited to members only. (1)

realty Land and everything permanently attached to land. (1)

reconciliation The process of weighted evaluation of the estimate derived from the three approaches to determine a single reliable estimate of value. (13)

recording The registration of a document on the public record. (4)

rectangular survey See government survey system.

redemption See equity of redemption.

redlining The refusal of lending institutions to make loans for the purchase, construction, or repair of a dwelling because the area in which the dwelling is located is integrated or populated by minorities. (16)

referral fee A percentage of a broker's commission paid to another broker for referring a buyer or a seller. (7)

refinancing Obtaining a new mortgage loan to pay and replace an existing mortgage. (11)

registration certificate Document from Real Estate Commission showing a time-share is properly registered. It must be obtained before marketing the property. (2)

Regulation Z Requirements issued by the Federal Reserve Board in implementing the Truth-in-Lending Law, which is a part of the Federal Consumer Credit Protection Act. (11)

reject To refuse to accept an offer; to kill the offer. (9)

release clause A provision in a mortgage to release certain properties from the mortgage lien when the principal is reduced by a specified amount. (11)

release of liability The procedure by which a mortgage holder agrees not to hold a borrower responsible for a mortgage on a property when that property has been bought by someone else who has assumed the seller's loan and the responsibility for it. (11)

remainder A future interest in a life estate. (2)

remainderman One having a future interest in a life estate. (2)

replacement cost The amount of money required to replace a structure with another structure of comparable utility. (13)

replacement reserve A fund to replace assets when they wear out. (13)

reproduction cost The amount of money required to build an exact duplicate of a structure. (13)

rescission Cancellation of a contract when another party is in default. (9)

residential eviction remedies Judicial eviction, also known as summary ejectment, is the only legal residential eviction remedy in North Carolina. (14)

Residential Property Disclosure Act The North Carolina act that requires the seller to deliver to the buyer, prior to the first offer being presented, a mandatory disclosure form that stipulates disclosures regarding residential property unless exempt. (7)

resident manager A person employed to manage a building who lives on the premises. (15)

residual income The income allocated to the land under the principle of highest and best use. (13)

residual method A method used by the U.S. Department of Veteran Affairs to determine the veteran's ability to meet the financial obligations of his or her house payment. It is the residual income remaining after taxes, debts, and housing expenses are subtracted from gross income. (11)

RESPA See Real Estate Settlement Procedures Act.

restrictive/protective covenants Limitations on land use binding on all property owners. A form of private land use control. (5)

retainer fee A small monetary compensation paid by the buyer up front for an agent's services. (7)

retaliatory eviction statute The doctrine protecting a tenant from eviction for having asserted his or her rights. Provides an automatic defense for up to one year after such an event. (14)

return on investment The amount of money that is obtained relative to the amount that was initially invested. (19)

reverse mortgage Mortgage allowing elderly homeowners to borrow against the equity in their homes to help meet living expenses while continuing to occupy their home. (11)

reversionary interest A return of title to the holder of a future interest, such as the grantor in a life estate not in remainder. (2)

revocation The withdrawal of an offer. (9)

right of first opportunity The right that a buyer has to purchase a property at a stipulated price should the seller decide to sell. If the seller decides to sell and the buyer does not purchase the property the seller may offer it to another party for a specified period of time. If the purchase does not occur the original buyer will still have the right to purchase and the process is repeated in the future. (10)

right of first refusal A written agreement that provides for a potential buyer to have the first opportunity to purchase a property before it is offered to anyone else or to purchase the property on the same terms as an offer received from another offeror. This agreement may appear in a lease or in articles of association. It does not have to be in another document. It can stand on its own. The seller is not obligated to sell, but if he does, he must give the holder of this right, the first opportunity to purchase the property before it is offered to anyone else. (10)

right of survivorship The right of an owner to receive the title to a co-owner's share upon death of the co-owner, as in the case of joint tenancy and tenancy by the entirety. (2)

riparian rights The rights of an owner of property adjoining a watercourse such as a river, including access to and use of the water. (2)

run with the land Rights that move from grantor to grantee along with a title. (5)

sale and leaseback A transaction whereby an owner sells his or her property to an investor who immediately leases the property to the seller as agreed in the sales contract. (14)

sales contract An agreement between buyer and seller on the price and other terms and conditions of the sale of property. (10)

savings and loan associations (S&Ls) A major source of funds for financing residential real estate. (11)

scheduled gross income Income that would be obtained if all units were fully rented for 100% of the time. (13)

scarcity A short supply in comparison with demand. (1, 13)

secondary mortgage market The market in which mortgages are sold by lenders. (11)

second mortgage One next in priority after a first mortgage. Often referred to as a junior mortgage. (11)

section An area of land described by the rectangular survey system consisting of 640 acres and being 1 mile square. (4)

seisin Possession of a freehold estate in land. (4)

seizin An alternative spelling of seisin. (4)

servient tenement Land encumbered by an easement. (2)

setback The distance from a front or interior property line to the point where a structure can be located. (5)

settlement The consummation of a real estate contract. Also called closing. (12)

Settlement Cost: A HUD Guide A booklet explaining aspects of loan settlement required by RESPA. (12)

settlement costs Expenses paid by buyers and sellers at the time of consummation of a real estate sales contract. Also called closing costs. (12)

severalty A type of ownership or estate in which only one person holds title to a piece of real property. (2)

sexual harassment An unsolicited overt request or demand for sexual acts when submission to such conduct is a condition of the execution or continuation of a lease or the according of tenant's rights under a lease. (16)

Sherman Antitrust Act A federal law that prohibits price fixing; in the case of real estate, it prohibits brokers to agree to charge certain rates of commission to listing sellers. (7)

short term capital gain Profit made from the sale of real property where title was held for less than one year. (17)

single entry An item that appears as a debit or credit on either the buyer's or seller's closing statement, but not on both. (12)

situs Location of land. (1)

soil evaluation test An analysis of the absorbency of the soil to bear the output of a septic tank. (12)

special agency Limited authority to act on behalf of the principal, such as created by a listing. (7)

special agent One who is limited to a very narrow duty on behalf of his or her principal, e.g., as a real estate agent to find a buyer. (7)

special assessment A levy by a local government against real property for part of the cost of making an improvement to the property, such as paving streets, installing water lines, and making sidewalks. (3)

special use An exception, or special use, built into a zoning ordinance that must be granted if the criteria for the exception are met. (5)

special warranty deed A deed containing a limited warranty of title limited to the time the seller owned the property. (4)

specific lien One that attaches to one particular property only. (2)

specific performance An instruction of a court requiring a defaulting party to a contract to buy and sell real property to carry out his or her obligations under the contract. (1, 9)

spot zoning The rezoning of a particular property in a zoned area to permit a use different from that authorized for the rest of the area. It is illegal unless there is a clearly established, reasonable basis for it. (5)

square foot method A technique to estimate the total cost of construction in which the total number of square feet to be constructed is multiplied by a cost per square foot to derive total cost. (13)

statement of record A document disclosing specific information that the developer must file with HUD before offering unimproved lots in interstate commerce by telephone or through the mail. (5)

Statute of Frauds A law in effect in all states requiring certain contracts to be in writing to be valid. (4, 9)

statute of limitations State laws establishing the time period within which certain lawsuits may be brought. (2)

statutory redemption period A statutory time period after a foreclosure sale during which the borrower may still redeem the title. (11)

steering The practice of directing prospective purchasers or tenants toward or away from specific neighborhoods because they belong to a protected class under the Fair Housing Act. (16)

straight-line depreciation A depreciation method whereby the property is depreciated in equal annual installments over the years of useful life. (13)

strict foreclosure A proceeding in which a court gives a borrower in default a specified time period to satisfy the debt to prevent transfer of the title to the mortgaged property to the lender. Illegal in North Carolina. (11)

subagent A person appointed by an agent to assist in performing some or all of the tasks of the agency. (7)

subdivision regulation (ordinance) Public control of the development of residential subdivisions. (5)

subjacent support The right to have one's land supported from below. (2)

subject to a loan A method of taking title to a property with a mortgage on it without becoming liable for the note payments. (11)

sublet The transfer of only part of a lease term with reversion to the lessee. Also referred to as a sublease or sandwich lease. (14)

subordinate Lower in priority. (9)

substitution The principle providing that the highest value of a property has a tendency to be established by the cost of purchasing or constructing another property of equal utility and desirability, provided the substitution could be made without unusual delay. (13)

substitution of entitlement The process by which one veteran pledges entitlement for a VA loan he or she is assuming in order to free up the entitlement of the original veteran/borrower. (11)

success fee Buyer's agent's compensation that may be received from the seller if the seller or seller's agent has offered compensation to the buyer's agent. (7)

suit to quiet title A suit brought before the court to eliminate a cloud on a title or to establish title (i.e., in an adverse possession claim). (4)

supply and demand The principle stating that the greater the supply of any commodity in comparison to demand, the lower the value. Conversely, the smaller the supply and the greater the demand, the higher the value. (13)

survivorship The right of the surviving co-owner(s) to receive automatically a deceased co-owner's title of property immediately without probate. (2)

taking title subject to a mortgage Accepting a title pledged to secure a mortgage and with no personal liability for the payment of the note. (11)

taxable gain The amount of profit or gain subject to tax (recognized gain minus applicable exclusion amount if any). (17)

taxation One of the four powers of government. The power of government to tax, among other things, real property. (3)

tax basis The value of property for income tax purposes; consists of original cost plus allowable costs of acquisition. (14)

tax-free exchange (tax deferred exchange) Trading of like-kind properties held as an investment or for use in business. (14, 19)

tax shelter A method of tax avoidance such as protecting income from taxation by allowable depreciation. (15)

tenancy by the entirety A form of co-ownership limited to husband and wife with the right of survivorship. (2)

tenancy in common A form of co-ownership that does not include the right of survivorship. (2)

tenant Lessee. A person possessing real property with the owner's permission. (14)

tenement Land and all corporeal and incorporeal rights in land. (2)

term loan One that requires the borrower to pay interest only during the mortgage term with the principal due at the end of the term. (11)

testate To have died leaving a valid will. (4)

testator A man who has died and left a valid will. (4)

testatrix A woman who has died and left a valid will. (4)

third party The person or party in a transaction other than the principal and his or her agent. In a subagency relationship, the buyer is a third party; in a buyer's agency relationship, the seller is the third party. (7)

time share As defined by Article IV of the North Carolina Real Estate Law, a time share is the right to occupy one unit or one of several units, for at least five non-consecutive periods, over a span of at least 5 years, whether it is deemed a freehold or leasehold estate. No matter what terminology is used to describe the arrangement, if it meets this definition, it is a time share. (2)

title Total body of facts or evidence on which ownership is based or approved. (2)

title examination A search of the public record to determine the quality of a title to real property. (4)

title insurance An insurance policy protecting the insured from a financial loss caused by a defect in a title to real property. (4)

title theory The legal theory followed in some states that a mortgage conveys a title to real property to secure the payment of a debt. (11)

title transfer tax A tax imposed on the conveyance of title to real property by deed. (4)

Torrens System A system of title recordation. (4)

tort A civil wrong by an agent for which the principal can be held accountable, i.e., negligence, misrepresentation, or fraud. (7)

town house A dwelling unit in a housing complex in which the owner or owners of an individual unit own the unit and land under the unit, and the homeowners association owns and maintains the common areas. (2)

township A unit pertaining to the Government Rectangular Survey System that measures six miles square and is divided into 36 equal parcels that are 1 mile square called sections. (4)

toxic mold Mold that is considered to be of a greater health risk. Not all mold is considered "toxic" and professional analysis is recommended in order to determine the extent, and effect, of the mold. (6)

tract An area of land.

trade fixtures Items installed by a commercial tenant that are removable upon termination of the tenancy. (2)

transferability The ability to transfer property ownership from seller to buyer. (13)

trapezoid An area with two parallel sides and two nonparallel sides.

trespass Unlawful entry on the land of another. (2)

trust account An account maintained by a real estate broker in an insured bank for the deposit of other people's money. Also called escrow account. (7)

trust deed See deed of trust. (11)

trustee One who holds title to property for the benefit of another called a beneficiary. (11)

trustor One who conveys title to a trustee. (11)

Truth-in-Lending Law See Regulation Z. (11)

Truth-in-Lending Simplification and Reform Act (TILSRA) Part of the Federal Consumer Credit Protection Act. It requires four chief disclosures: annual percentage rate, finance charge, amount financed, and total of payments. (11)

undivided interest Ownership of fractional parts not physically divided. (2)

undue influence Improper or wrongful influence by one party over another whereby the will of a person is overpowered so that he or she is induced to act or prevented from acting on free will. (7)

Uniform Commercial Code (UCC) A standardized and comprehensive set of commercial laws regulating security interests in personal property. (2)

unilateral contract An agreement wherein one party makes a promise of compensation to the other party and the second party returns an action in response to the promise, although he is not legally obligated to do so. (9)

uninsured conventional loan One in which the loan payment is not insured to protect the lender. Typically less that 80% LTV. (11)

unintentional misrepresentation An innocent false statement of a material fact. (7)

unit in place method The technique used in appraising real estate under the cost approach, in which the cost of replacement or reproduction is grouped by stages of construction. (13)

universal agency Complete authority over all activity of the principal. May be created by an unlimited power of attorney. (7)

up-front mortgage insurance premium (UFMIP) An insurance premium charged at the time an FHA loan is closed to insure the mortgage lender against default by the borrowers on an FHA loan. (11)

urea-formaldehyde A type of foam insulation that was used back in the mid to late 70s that released harmful gasses that are considerd a respiratory risks. The installation of this product was later banned by the Consumer Product Safety Council although existing insulation was allowed to remain. (6)

useful life The period of time that a property is expected to be economically useful. (13)

usury Charging a rate of interest higher than the rate allowed by law. (11)

utility Capable of serving a useful purpose. (13)

vacancy rate A projected rate of the percentage of rental unit vacancies that will occur in a given year. (15)

VA-guaranteed loan A mortgage loan in which the loan payment is guaranteed to the lender by the Departmentof Veterans Affairs. (11)

valid contract An agreement that is legally binding and enforceable. (9)

value The amount of money (or goods) considered of equal worth to the subject property. There are many types of value, e.g., market value, book value, assessed value, and so on. (13)

value in exchange The amount of money a property may command for its exchange. This is the market value and is a negotiated value. (13)

value in use A subjective value that is not market value, derived from the usefulness of the property. (13)

variance A permitted deviation from specific requirements of a zoning ordinance because of the special hardship to a particular property owner. (5)

vendee Purchaser.

vendor Seller.

void contract An agreement that is absolutely unenforceable and has no legal force or effect. (9)

voidable contract One which appears valid, but may be avoided by one of the parties without legal consequences because it contains a defect. If the party who may avoid the contract based on the defect, does not identify the defect and takes action to avoid the contract, the contract is valid and enforceable. (9)

voluntary alienation The transfer of title freely by the owner. (4)

waste A violation of the right of estovers. (2)

weighted average In the direct sales comparison method of appraisal, reconciliation by giving more weight to comparables most similar to subject property. (13)

will The legal instrument to dispose of a decedent's property according to his or her instructions. See devise, bequest. (4)

willful misrepresentation A deliberate false statement concerning a material fact by one who knows the true fact and is responsible for disclosing it. (7)

willful omission A deliberate failure to inform a party of a known material fact when one has an obligation to that party to relay all material facts. (7)

words of conveyance Wording in a deed demonstrating the definite intention to convey a particular title to real property to a named grantee. (4)

yield The return on an investment. (11)

zoning A public law regulating land use. (5)

zoning ordinance A statement setting forth the type of use permitted under each zoning classification and specific requirements for compliance. (5)

INDEX

acceleration clause, 344
acceptance, 255–256
   communication, 315–317
   of deed, 76
   effective date and, 329
   electronically submitted, 320–321
   oral, 314–315
   sales contract procedures, 313–317
   written, 329
accord and satisfaction, 263
accounting, 158–159
acknowledgment, 75–76, 352
acquired immune deficiency syndrome (AIDS), 166, 579
   stigmatized properties, 168
acquisition, costs of, 588
acquisition debt, 586
acreage, calculating, 88
ADA (Americans with Disabilities Act), 564–565, 578–579
Additional Provisions Addendum, 313
adjustable rate mortgage (ARM), 368–369
adjusted basis, 588, 590
ad valorem, 58
   calculating, 63
adverse possession, 73–74
advertising, 222
   discriminatory, 572
   Federal Fair Housing Act of 1968, 571–572
   Regulation Z, 389–390
aesthetic zoning, 102–103
age
   appraisal, 472
   chronological, 478
   effective, 478

age/life (straight-line) method, 477–478
agency. *See also* dual agency
   agent compensation and, 139
   breach of duty, 147
   buyer, 142, 144, 181, 186
   communication requirements for contracts, 145
   definition of, 134
   designated, 182–184
   exclusive seller, 140–141
   express, 138
   general, 136
   general concepts and definitions, 134–136
   implied, 137–138
   math concepts, 241–243
   multi-agent firm, 140–141
   practices, 139
   single, 140
   special or limited, 136–137
   status, 145
   termination of, 146–147
   universal, 136
agency agreement
   dual, 137, 181–182
   language of, 198
   NCAR standard, 181–182
   nondiscrimination and, 198
   period of time, 197–198
   renewal and/or amendment, 215
   for rental properties, 566
   types of, 197
   written, 151
agency contracts (sales) and related practices, 192–250
   antitrust law, 218–219

buyer agency contracts, 226–237
buyer's agent procedures and, 240–243
general requirement for, 197–198
listing contracts and practices, 198–218
listing procedures, 221–226
math, 193
MLS arrangements, 218
solicitation of clients or customers, laws affecting, 219–220
working with buyers, 238–239
agency disclosure
   of material facts, 146
   nonexclusive buyer agency contracts and, 226–231
   of status, 151
agency relationships, 139–154
   disclosure of, 147–148
   first substantial contract, 148–153
   in rental properties, 548–560
agent, 13, 134
   accounting, 158–159
   apparent authority, 139
   authority, scope of, 138–139
   buyer's, 149–150, 238, 240–243
   buyers and, 238–239
   communication requirement, 140
   compensation, agency and, 139
   confidentiality, 156
   disclosure, 136
   disclosure of information, 158
   dual, 150–151
   fiduciary duty, 139

implied authority, 138–139
land use control and
    responsibility of, 114
liability, 114
listing, 141, 148, 217–218, 244
loyalty, 155
obedience, 155–156
principal duties to, 184–185
property management
    agreement and, 551
seller's, 141–142, 149, 151
skill, care, and diligence,
    156–157
working with, 149–153
agent duties and liabilities, 114,
    154–160, 167, 170
breach of duties, liability of,
    178–179
civil liability, 178
criminal liability, 178
disclosure, 162–163, 166, 180
honesty and fairness, 160
to principal, 154, 185–186
under real estate license law and
    commission rules, 159
seller duties versus, 223
to third parties, 160, 163
agreement of parties, 263–264
AIDS. *See* acquired immune
    deficiency syndrome
air rights, 19–20
alienation, 67
involuntary, 73–74, 89–90
right of, 31
voluntary, 72, 89–90
alienation clause, 344
ambiguity, in contracts, 267
amendment
agency agreement, 215
Federal Fair Housing
    Amendments Act of 1988,
    569
zoning, 101, 116
Americans with Disabilities Act
    (ADA), 564–565, 578–579
amortization, 336
chart, 337
negative, 369
amount realized, 588

annual percentage rate (APR), 426
anticipation, 460, 490
antitrust law, 218–219, 246
apparent authority, 139
appraisal, 60–61
age, 472
basic concepts, 455–462
BPO, 455–457
CMA, 455–457
comparables, 461, 464, 473–475
construction type and quality, 472
cost, 456
date of sale, 473
definition of, 455
due diligence, 404
fees, 433
financing method, 473
home inspection versus, 385
location, 472
lot/land value, 472
market value, 456–457
methods, 463, 490
North Carolina Appraisal
    Board, 455
physical characteristics and
    amenities, 472–473
price, 456
report, 486–487, 490
sales comparison approach,
    463–475
seller and, 473
size, 472
uniform residential appraisal
    report, 466–471
URAR, 457, 466–471
VA, 363
valuation versus evaluation,
    457–458
appraised value, 341, 456
concepts of, 458–459
in exchange, 457
in use, 457
appraiser
licensure and certification, 455
North Carolina Appraisers Act,
    455–456, 488–489
appraiser regulation, 455
appreciation, 624
definition of, 7

appreciation rate, 474
appurtenance, 53
air rights, 19–20
definition of, 2–3, 19
lateral and subjacent support, 21
riparian rights, 20–21
subsurface rights, 19
appurtenant easement, 47–48
APR (annual percentage rate), 426
architectural types and styles,
    599–601, 616
Cape Cod, 600–601
ranch style, 601
Tudor style, 601
Victorian, 600–601
area-related math, 87–89
ARM (adjustable rate mortgage),
    368–369
arrears, 335
asbestos
friable, 125–126, 130
health risks of, 130
nonfriable, 126, 130
"as is" sale, 163, 171–177
assessed value, 58, 63
assessment, 305–306
by city and town, 62
by country, 62
improvements and, 64
property, 58–65
special, 62
assignment, 265–266, 354,
    541–542
lease provisions, 524
property insurance, 503, 506
sublease versus, 525
attorney, closing
commission, 411
fees, 433
selecting and providing
    information to, 402–409
auction sales, 152
contract law and, 261
"Without Reserve," 261
"With Reserve," 261
authority
apparent, 139
employment, 186
implied, 138–139

back taxes, 336
Back-Up Contract Addendum, 310–311
balloon framing, 606
balloon payment, 370–371
bankruptcy, 265
   lease and, 532
banks
   commercial, 377
   the Fed, 374–375
   savings, 377
bargain and sale deed, 80
basis, 586, 591
   adjusted, 588, 590
beneficiary, 72, 350
bequest, 72
BIC. *See* broker-in-charge
bilateral contract, 253
bill of sale
   personal property, 21
   title conveyed by, 2
binding contract, 314–315
blanket mortgage, 372
blockbusting, 571, 580
boot, 595
borrower
   analysis, 384
   mortgage, 352–353
   rights of, 352–353, 394
bounds, 67–68, 89
   sample, 69
boycotting, 246
BPO. *See* broker price opinion
breach by landlord, 511
breach of condition, 538
breach of contract, 265
breach of duty, 185
   agency, 147
   by tenant, 531–532
breakdown method, 478–480
bridge loan, 372–373
broker, 11
   buyer's, 196
   commission, entitlement to, 193–198, 244–245
   cooperating with other, 141
   definition of, 8–10
   expired or inactive, legal payment to, 196–197
   firms and, relationship between, 137
   independent, listing with, 140–141
   individual, dual agency, 184
   license status, 196
   out-of-state, 195–196
   ownership interest, 143
   REALTOR® compared with, 8
   settlement statement and, 446–447
   solicitation of, 219
   transactional, 135
brokerage, 573–574
brokerage commission, math, 241–243
brokerage fee, 214
brokerage relationships, 133–191
   agency and subagency relationships, 139–154
   agent duties to principal, 185–186
   classification of, 136–137
   creation of, 137–139
   disclosure, laws governing, 167–179
   dual agency, 179–184
   duties and liabilities of agents, 154–160
   general agency concepts and definitions, 134–136
   material facts, 160–167
   principal duties to agent, 184–185
   subagency relationships, 139–154
brokerage service agreements, 240
broker-in-charge (BIC), 11
   PB and, 184
broker price opinion (BPO), 454–457, 487–489, 491
   standards, 489
buffer zones, 103
building codes, 106–107, 115
   North Carolina Uniform Residential Building Code, 614–615
   "stick-built" state building codes, 54
building permit, 615

bundle of rights, 51
   definition of, 17
   diminished, 42
   of personal property, 21
buydown loan, 370
buyer
   CD for, 416–420
   due diligence, 304, 403–407
   first substantial contact, 238–239
   installment land contracts advantages and disadvantages, 326
   land use controls and, 96
   liability, 395
   loan, 404
   obligations, 305
   offers to, copies of, 323
   as principal, 142–144
   ready, willing, and able, 194, 245, 253
   seller's agent and, 151
   seller subagents and, 239
   working with, 238–239
buyer agency, 144, 181
   agreement, 142, 186
buyer agency contracts
   exclusive, 226–231
   nonexclusive, 226–231
   oral, 244, 246
   provisions of, 231, 247
Buyer Possession before Closing Agreement Addendum, 312
buyer representations, 304
   OTPC, 296–297
buyer responsibilities, 169–170
buyer's agent, 149–150, 238
   procedures for, 240–243
buyer's broker, commission and, 196

CAN-SPAM Act, 221, 246
Cape Cod, 600–601
capital gain, 587–588
   computing, 591
   depreciation and, 594
   formula, 589
   occupancy rule, 593
   reporting features, 594
   taxation of, rules for, 592–594

capital improvement, 588
capitalization, 481
    formula, 484–485
capitalization approach, 481–485
capital loss, 587–588
carbon monoxide alarms, 510
cash flow, 484, 622–623
    positive, 7
cash sale, 357
caveat emptor, 169–170, 185
CD. *See* Closing Disclosure
CERCLA (Comprehensive Environmental Response, Compensation, and Liability Act), 129–131
Certificate of Occupancy (CO), 106, 615
certificate of reasonable value (CRV), 363
CFPB (Consumer Financial Protection Bureau), 386–387, 448
chain of title, 82
change, economic principle of, 462, 490
chattel, 2, 21
children, lead-based paint hazards and, 121, 125
chronological age, 478
civil penalty, 178
Civil Rights Act of 1866, 568–569, 577
    discrimination prohibited in, 580
Civil Rights Act of 1968, 568–569, 580
civil suit, 575
client, 134
    educating, 221
    solicitation of, 219–220
closing, 303, 386
    attorney, 402–409, 411, 433
    delay in, OTPC, 298, 308
    escrow method, 410
    methods, 410
    practice problem, sample, 427–429
    preclosing, 402, 408–409
    procedures, 409–412
    as recordation of deed, 410

RESPA, 412–421
risk of loss before, 505
sales transaction, 401–454
settlement meeting method, 410–411, 446
worksheet problems, 444
closing costs, 589
    net proceeds estimate, 225
    taxation, 597
Closing Disclosure (CD), 413, 425–426, 448
    for buyer, 416–420
    for sellers, 414–415
closing statement
    double entry, 430
    prepaids, 435–446
    property tax on, 438
    prorations, 435–446
    settlement statement entries and calculation, 426–435
    single entry, 430
cloud on title, 80
CLUE (Comprehensive Loss Underwriting Exchange), 504
cluster zoning, 103
CMA. *See* comparative market analysis
CO (Certificate of Occupancy), 106, 615
co-brokerage, seller subagency and, 239
co-brokered sales
    commission, 195
    out-of-state broker, 195–196
Code of Ethics (1913), 8
co-insurance, 505–506
    clause, 500–501
color of title, 73–74
commercial banks, 377
Commercial Real Estate Broker Lien Act, 44–45
commission, 590
    agent duties under, 159
    brokerage, math, 241–243
    broker entitlement to, 193–198, 244–245
    buyer's broker and, 196
    closing attorney, 411
    co-brokered sales, 195

computation, 430
exclusive right to sell, 200
flat fee listing, 214–216
in-house sales, 194–195
minimum, 214
net listing, 216
as percentage of final sales price, 214
property management, 565
rule requirements, 245–246
sales, 434–435
in sales contracts, 277
splits, 195
to travel agents, 519
commitment, loan, 386
communication
    of acceptance, 315–317
    agency and, requirements for contracts, 145
    agent requirement, 140
comparable, 461, 464, 473–475
    plus adjustment, 475
comparative market analysis (CMA), 222, 224, 454–457, 464, 487–489, 491
    standards, 489
compensatory damages, 267
competition, 461, 490
Comprehensive Environmental Response, Compensation, and Liability Act (CERCLA), 129–131
Comprehensive Loss Underwriting Exchange (CLUE), 504
concrete slab, 602
condemnation, 50, 74, 538
condition, 111, 500, 505
    breach of, 538
    fee simple subject to condition subsequent, 28–29
    lease, 523
    OTPC, 298
condominium, 52–53
    creation of, 36–37
    financing, 37–38
    homeowner's policy, 498
    offering for sale or resale, 38
    rights, 36–37
    sale or resale, 38–39

confidential information, 149, 151, 182
confidentiality, 156
conflicts of interest, dual agency, 180
conforming loans, 359, 382
conformity, 460–461, 490
Connor Act, 85–86, 90, 373–374, 540
consent, requirements for reality of, 259–262
consideration, 252
   adequate, 257–258
   earnest money and, 258
   lease, 523
   sufficient, 257
construction
   architectural types and styles, 599–601, 616
   basic, 599–620
   ceiling framing and roof, 606–607
   contractor licensing, 615
   doors, 610
   electrical systems, 614
   exterior walls, 607–608, 617
   FHA/VA minimum standards, 615
   flooring, 603–605, 616
   footing, 602
   foundations, 602–603, 616
   foundation walls, 602–603
   framing, 603–607, 616
   government regulation, 614–615, 618
   heating/air conditioning, 612–613, 617
   insulation, 611, 617
   loan, 371–372, 395
   location on site, 601
   moisture control, 611, 616
   plumbing systems, 614
   roofing, 610
   type and quality, 472
   walls, 605–606, 616–617
   windows, 608–610, 617
   wood-destroying insects, 616
   wood-frame, 616
constructive eviction, 510–511, 538, 541
constructive notice, 77
Consumer Financial Protection Bureau (CFPB), 386–387, 448
Consumer Protection Act, 386
Contingent Sale Addendum, 311–312
contract for deed, 323
contract law, 251–271
   agreement of parties, 263–264
   auction sales and, 261–262
   capacity of parties, 258
   consent requirements, 259–262
   consideration, 257–258
   counteroffer, 256
   full performance, 264
   impossibility of performance, 264–265
   lawful objective, 258
   money damages, 267–268
   mutual assent, 255
   operation of law, 265–267
   performance dates and times, 262
   rescission, 268
   specific performance, 268
   Statute of Frauds, 262–263
   termination of offer, 257
   terms and classifications, 251–254
   UETA, 263
   valid contract, 255–258
contract modification, handling, 318–320
contract requirements
   communication, 145
   FHA-insured loan, 362–363
   VA-guaranteed loan, 364
contracts. *See also* listing contract; sales contracts and related procedures
   acceptance, 313–317
   accord and satisfaction of, 263
   bilateral, 253
   breach of, 265
   discharge of, 263
   estate and, 509–510
   express, 252
   fixtures and, 23
   full performance, 264
   implied, 252
   land, 263, 323–326, 330
   mutual assent, 255
   offer, 277–313
   operation of law and, 265–267
   oral, 244, 246, 262
   property management, 549–559
   undue influence and, 261
   unilateral, 253
   valid, 253–258
   written, 262–263
contractual agreements, dual agency, 146
contractual capacity, 258
contribution, 461, 490
conventional loan, 359–360, 395
cooperative, 39–40, 53
co-ownership, 33
   property insurance, 502
cost approach, 476–481, 490
   calculations, 481
   depreciation, estimating, 477
   valuation calculation, 454
costs, 489
   of acquisition, 588
   appraisal, 456
   closing, 225, 589, 597
   replacement and reproduction, 476–477
   square footage, 88–89
counteroffer, 256
   acceptance of, 319–320
   communication requirements, 145
   handling, 318–320
county transfer tax, 82
covenants
   definition of, 110
   against encumbrances, 75, 78
   negative, 111
   of quiet enjoyment, 17, 78, 537
   restrictive or protective, 47, 111–115, 223
   of right to convey, 78
   run with the land, 2, 19, 111
   of seisin, 78
   of title in deeds, 82
   of warranty, 78–80
credit, 427, 430

credit report, 433
credit reporting, 390–391
credit unions, 378
CRV (certificate of reasonable value), 363
cumulative-use zoning, 99
curable, 479
curtesy, 31
customer, 135
    solicitation of, 219–220

damages
    compensatory, 267
    lease, 530
    liquidated, 264, 267, 302, 322, 329
    money, 267–268
    to rental properties, 535
    security deposits and, 514
death, stigmatized properties, 168
debit, 427, 430
debt service, 335–336, 484
declaration of restrictions, 47
dedication, 105
deed
    acknowledgment, 75–76
    bargain and sale, 80
    consideration, 76
    covenant, 110
    covenants of title in, 82
    date, 77
    definition of, 2
    delivery and acceptance, 76
    general warranty, 77–80, 90
    of gift, 81
    grantor, 75
    judicial, 73
    in lieu of foreclosure, 355
    marriage and, 350–351
    named parties, 75
    nonessential elements of, 76–82
    preparation, 434
    property description, 75
    quitclaim, 80, 90
    recordation of, 77, 90, 410
    seal, 76–77
    sheriff's, 81
    special purpose, 81
    special warranty, 80

    title transfer by, 72, 74–76
    trustee, 81
    types, 77
    valid, essential elements of, 74–76
    validity, 90
    witnessing, 77
    words of conveyance, 75
    writing, 76
deed of trust, 345–352
    borrower, rights of, 352–353
    clauses and covenants, 351–352
    essential elements, 351
    purpose of, 394
    sample, 346–349
    transaction, relationships in, 350
    valid, 394
deed restrictions, 115
    definition of, 110
    individual, 110–111
defaults, 345
defeasance clause, 350
defeasible fee, 28
deficiency judgment, 355
demand, 458
Department of Housing and Urban Development (HUD), 575
    Interstate Land Sales Full Disclosure Act, 108
    manufactured housing standards, 25
    Residential Lead-Based Paint Hazard Reduction Act, 121, 124
Department of Veterans Affairs (VA). *See also* VA-guaranteed loan
    appraisal, 363
    construction standards, 615
    FHA/VA Financing Addendum, 312
depreciation, 490
    age/life (straight-line) method to estimating, 477–478
    breakdown method to estimating, 478–480
    capital gain and, 594
    causes, 479

    cost approach to estimating, 477
    estimating, 477–480
    market abstraction method to estimating, 478
descent, 72
designated agency, 182–184
    facts and limitations, 183–184
destruction of property, 265
devise, 72
devisee, 72
disability, 578
discharge of contracts, 263
disclosure. *See also* Closing Disclosure
    of agency material facts, 146
    of agency relationships, 147–148
    of agency status, 151
    agent, 136
    agent duty of, 162–163, 180
    "as is" sale, 171–177
    consumer legislation, 169
    of dual agency, 180–182, 186
    duty to, 166
    flood hazard, 206
    of information, 149, 158, 180, 238
    laws governing, 167–179
    lead-based paint, 122–123, 177, 222
    of loan servicing, 413
    of material facts, 146, 161, 166
    of material facts, agency and, 146
    Mineral and Oil and Gas Rights Mandatory Disclosure Statement, 176
    North Carolina Residential Property Disclosure Act, 170–171
    of personal information, 149, 180, 238
    Regulation Z, 388–389
    Residential Property and Owners' Association Disclosure Statement, 222
    Residential Property Disclosure Act, 171–175
    of seller subagency, 147–148, 151, 239

stigmatized and psychologically affected properties, 167–169
street maintenance, requirements, 105–106
synthetic stucco, 177, 206, 222
TILSRA/Real Estate Settlement Procedures Act integrated, 382–386
discount points, 339–340, 587, 589–590
   calculating, 392–394, 430
discount rate, 375
discrimination, 579. *See also* fair housing
   agency agreement language and, 198
   Civil Rights Act of 1866 and prohibition of, 580
   nondiscrimination language, 147
   North Carolina Fair Housing Act of 1983 and unfair, 576
   restrictive or protective covenants, 111
   tenants and, 515
discriminatory advertising, 572
disintermediation, 379
doctrine of prior appropriation, 21
Dodd-Frank Act, 386
Do Not Call Registry, 219–220, 244
double entry, 430–431, 447
dower, 31
down payment
   FHA-insured loan, 366
   VA-guaranteed loan, 366
dual agency, 144
   agreement, 137, 181–182
   basics, 179–180
   conflicts of interest, 180
   contractual agreements, 146
   designated agency, 182–184
   disclosure of, 180–182, 186
   exclusive right to sell listing, 209–210
   individual broker, 184
   intentional, disclosed, 181–182
   recognizing, 179
   unintentional, undisclosed, 180–181

dual agent, 150–151
due diligence, 273
   appraisal, 404
   buyer's, 304, 403–407
   date, selection of, 409
   homeowner's association, 407
   inspections and, 405–406
   OTPC, 295–296
   period, 303
   process, of buyer, 403–407
   property insurance and, 405
   property survey and, 405
   repair-related issues, 407
   restrictive covenants and, 407
   septic/sewer system and, 406–407
due diligence fee, 303, 329, 432
   handling, 321–323
due-on-sale clause, 344
duress, 261
dwelling, 569

earnest money, 206, 258, 263, 268, 301–302
   deposit, 431–432
   forfeiture of, 322, 329
   handling, 321–323
easement
   appurtenant, 47–48
   creation of, 49
   express, 49–50
   general classification of, 47
   in gross, 48–49
   implied, 50
   negative, 111
   by operation of law, 50–51
   termination of, 51
ECOA (Equal Credit Opportunity Act), 391
economic feasibility, 458
economic obsolescence, 5, 478–479
effective age, 478
effective date, 303, 329
effective demand, 458
elderly housing, 569
electronically submitted acceptance, 320–321

electronically submitted offer, 320–321
email, CAN-SPAM Act, 221
emblements, 19
eminent domain, 50, 52, 74, 533
employment authority, 186
enabling acts, 97
encroachment, 51
encumbrance, 53
   covenants against, 75, 78
   to real property, 42–51
endorsement, 499–500, 505
environmental issues, 120–132
   asbestos, 125–126
   CERCLA, 129–130
   formaldehyde, 127–128
   health risks, 121
   lead poisoning, 121–125
   leaking underground storage tanks, 129
   lease provisions, 524
   radon, 126–127
   toxic mold, 128–129
Environmental Protection Agency (EPA)
   "Protect Your Family from Lead in Your Home" pamphlet, 124, 130, 177
   radon recommendations, 126
   "Renovate Right" pamphlet, 125
   Residential Lead-Based Paint Hazard Reduction Act, 121, 124
environmental protection laws, 115
EPA. *See* Environmental Protection Agency
Equal Credit Opportunity Act (ECOA), 391
equal opportunity housing, 578
equitable title, 324
equity, 336–337, 623–624
   calculating, 624
   growing equity mortgage, 370
   percentage of increase in, 242–243
   of redemption, 352–353
equity build-up, 624
equity debt, 586

escheat, 52, 74
escrow account, 366–367
　reserves, 413
escrow agent, 302–303
escrow items, computation of, 430
escrow method, of closing, 410
estate
　contract and, 509–510
　definition of, 26
　freehold, 27–31, 52–53
　of inheritance, 27–29
　in land, types of, 26–32
　nonfreehold, 32, 54
　not of inheritance, 29–32
　from period to period, 520
　pur autre vie, 29
　in real property, 26–32
　at sufferance, 32, 520–521
　at will, 32, 520
　for years, 32, 519
　from year to year, 32
estoppel, 138
　theory of, 139
estovers, right to, 31–32
evaluation, valuation versus, 457–458
eviction
　constructive, 510–511, 538, 541
　expedited, 518
　judicial, 538
　residential eviction remedies, 515, 540
　retaliatory eviction statute, 512
　Vacation Rental Act, 516
excise tax, 81–82, 434
exclusion, 500
exclusive agency, 199, 244
　exclusive listing versus, 200
　listing, 194, 245
exclusive buyer agency, 142
exclusive buyer agency contract, 226–231
　form, 232–237
exclusive listing
　agreement, 197
　exclusive agency versus, 200

exclusive right to sell, 193–194, 244, 245
　commission, 200
　exclusive agency versus, 200
exclusive right to sell listing
　dual agency, 209–210
　earnest money, 206
　extender clause, 212
　fees, 203–204
　firm's duties, 204–205
　fixtures and exclusions, 202–203
　home inspection, 209
　home warranty, 203
　listing price, 203
　marketing, 205–206
　mediation, 210
　personal property, 203
　photographs and other materials, 209
　property, 202
　seller representation, 206–208
　seller's duties, 208–209
　wire fraud warning, 210
Exclusive Right to Sell Listing Agreement, 202–211, 224
　sample, 212–214
　term of agreement, 202
exclusive-use zoning, 99
executed contract, 253
executor, 72
executory contracts, 253
executrix, 72
express agency, 138
express contract, 252
extender clause, 212

facilitator, 135
factory-built (manufactured) housing, 25–26, 54
Fair Credit Reporting Act (FCRA), 390–391
fair housing, 568–584
　ADA, 578–579
　Civil Rights Act of 1866, 577
　Federal Fair Housing Act of 1968, 569–574
　laws, 564–565
　in North Carolina, 577–578

　North Carolina Fair Housing Act of 1983, 574–576
　sexual harassment, 579
familial status, 569
Fannie Mae. *See* Federal National Mortgage Association (FNMA, Fannie Mae)
Farm Service Agency (FSA), 367
fascia, 607
faxed offer, 321
FCRA (Fair Credit Reporting Act), 390–391
FDIC (Federal Deposit Insurance Corporation), 376
Fed (Federal Reserve Bank), 374–375
Federal Deposit Insurance Corporation (FDIC), 376
Federal Emergency Management Agency (FEMA), 107, 503
Federal Fair Housing Act of 1968
　advertising, 571–572
　definitions, 569–574
　enforcement, 575
　exemptions, 574–575, 579–580
　prohibited acts, 572–573, 581
Federal Fair Housing Amendments Act of 1988, 569
Federal Home Loan Mortgage Corporation (FHLMC, Freddie Mac)
　conventional loan guidelines, 359–360
　mortgages purchased by, 382, 396
Federal Housing Administration (FHA). *See also* FHA-insured loan
　construction standards, 615
　FHA/VA Financing Addendum, 312
Federal National Mortgage Association (FNMA, Fannie Mae)
　conventional loan guidelines, 359–360
　mortgages purchased by, 381, 396
Federal Reserve Bank (the Fed), 374–375

federal tax liens, 46
fees
　appraisal, 433
　attorney, 433
　brokerage, 214
　exclusive right to sell listing, 203–204
　flat fee listing, 214–216
　homeowners association, 407
　loan, 340–342, 432
　property management, 547–548
　property management agreement, 550
　recording, 434
　referral, 216
　retainer, 196
　travel agent referral, 519, 548
fee simple absolute, 27–28, 52–53
fee simple absolute title, 75
fee simple subject to condition subsequent, 28–29
FEMA (Federal Emergency Management Agency), 107, 503
FHA. *See* Federal Housing Administration
FHA 203(b) regular loan program, 361–363
　changes to, 362
FHA-insured loan, 360–361, 395–396
　condominium, 37–38
　contract requirements, 362–363
　down payment, 366
　escrow account, 366
　loan assumption policies, 362, 366–367
　maximum loan amount, 361
　MIP, 361
　qualification, 361–362
FHLMC. *See* Federal Home Loan Mortgage Corporation
fiduciary, 135
fiduciary duty, agent, 139
Financial Institutions Reform, Recovery, and Enforcement Act (FIRREA), 376, 455
financing, 333
　condominium, 37–38
　the Fed and, 374–375

FHA-insured loan, 360–361, 366–367
FSA mortgage loans, 367
illegal, 573
legislation, 386–391, 396
loan types, 367–373
math concepts, 392–394
methods, 395
mortgage basics, 342–356
mortgage priorities, 373–374
primary sources of, 376–391
principal, interest, taxes, and insurance, 335–342
RD mortgage loans, 367
residential, sources of, 395
residential first mortgage loans, 358–363
sale of mortgaged properties, 356–358
VA-guaranteed loan, 363–367
fire insurance policy, 506
FIRREA (Financial Institutions Reform, Recovery, and Enforcement Act), 376, 455
first contact, dual agency disclosure, 182
first (or senior) mortgage, 373
first substantial contact, 148–153, 238–239
　examples, 152–153
　first contact versus, 154
fit premises, 510
　of vacation rental, 517
fixed rate loans, 368
fixed rental lease, 521
fixture, 52
　exclusive right to sell listing, 202–203
　lease provisions, 524
　OTPC, 295, 304
　total circumstance test, 22–23, 201
　trade, 24
flashing, 603
flat fee listing, 214–216
flipping, 622
flood hazard area, 107, 114
　disclosure, 206
flood insurance, 503–504, 506

flood zone maps, FEMA, 114
flooring, 603–605
　subfloor, 605
FNMA. *See* Federal National Mortgage Association
footing, 602
foreclosure, 73, 394–395
　deed in lieu of, 355
　judicial, 353–354
　nonjudicial, 354
　under power of sale, 354
　strict, 354
foreshore, 20
formaldehyde, 127–128
　causes, 131
　remediation, 128
formula
　capital gain, 589
　capitalization, 484–485
For Sale by Owner (FSBO), 201
foundations, 602–603, 616
foundation vents, 603
framing, 603–607
　balloon, 606
　ceiling, 606–607
　platform, 605
　post-and-beam, 606
fraud, 259–260. *See also* Statute of Frauds
Freddie Mac. *See* Federal Home Loan Mortgage Corporation
freehold estate, 27–31, 52–53, 539
free market, 10
friable, 125–126, 130
frieze board, 607
front foot, 64
fruits of industry (*fructus industriales*), 19, 52
fruits of the soil (*fructus naturales*), 19
FSA (Farm Service Agency)
　mortgage loans, 367
FSBO (For Sale by Owner), 201
full performance, 264
full-service leases, 522
full-service listing agreements, 199–214
　exclusive agency listing, 199
　exclusive right to sell, 200

limited service listing contracts, 200
listing contract provisions, 201, 212–214
open listing, 199
protection agreement and, 200–201
functional obsolescence, 478–480

gable roof, 606–607
gambrel roof, 607
general agency, 136
general warranty deed, 77–80, 90
gift
  deed of, 81
  right to dispose of property by, 17
Ginnie Mae. *See* Government National Mortgage Association
girder, 603–604
GNMA. *See* Government National Mortgage Association
government agencies, mortgage funds and, 378–379
Government National Mortgage Association (GNMA, Ginnie Mae), mortgages purchased by, 381–382, 396
government ownership, 110
government rectangular survey system, 68–71, 89
GPM (graduated payment mortgage), 369
grace period, 266
graduated lease, 522
graduated payment mortgage (GPM), 369
Gramm-Leach-Bliley Act, 425
grantee, 75
  rights to recovery, 80
grantor, 75, 350
GRM. *See* gross rental multiplier
gross effective income, 483
gross lease, 521, 540
gross rental income, 486
gross rental multiplier (GRM), 485–486, 490
  application, 486
  calculating, 486

ground (land) lease, 523
growing equity mortgage, 370

handicap, 571
haunted, stigmatized properties, 168–169
hazard insurance, 497, 506
hazardous waste
  CERCLA, 129–130
  cleanup, 130
headers, 605
heating, ventilation, and air conditioning (HVAC), 612
heating/air conditioning systems, 612–614, 617
  solar heat, 613, 618
HELOC (home equity line of credit), 360
hereditaments, 18–19
  definition of, 3
highest and best use, 13, 462, 490
  definition of, 6
highway access controls, 107–108, 115
hip roof, 606–607
historic preservation zoning, 102
holdover tenant, 521
home equity line of credit (HELOC), 360
home equity mortgages, 360, 372
home inspection, 209, 363
  appraisal versus, 385
home office, 594, 596
homeowner, tax deductions for, 586
homeowner insurance, 434
  common, 498–500
  computation, 430
  declaration page, 499
  HO-2 Policy, 499
  HO-3 Policy, 498–499
  policy, 497–499
  property description and, 499
  standardized, 497–498
  standardized policy provisions, 499–500
homeowner's association, 407

home warranty, 308
  exclusive right to sell listing, 203
  OTPC, 298
honesty and fairness, 160
HUD. *See* Department of Housing and Urban Development
HVAC (heating, ventilation, and air conditioning), 612
hypothecation, 345

illegal financing, 573
illegal use, 116
illusory offer, 255
immobility
  definition of, 4–5
  real estate market and, 10
implied agency, 137–138
implied authority, 138–139
implied contract, 252
improvements
  as appurtenance, 25
  assessments and, 64
  capital, 588
  definition of, 2
  land use controls and, 114
  modification by, 3–4
  to personal property, 24–25
  private, 24–25
  public, 25
  uplifting, 524
income
  gross effective, 483
  gross rental, 486
  net, 484
  NOI, 481–482, 484–485
  potential gross, 482
  rental, 440–441, 486
income approach, 481–485
  operating statement analysis, 482–485
  valuation calculation, 454, 490
income property, value of, 486
incurable, 479
independent broker, listing with, 140–141
indestructibility, 5
index lease, 522

individual broker dual agency, 184
individual investors, mortgage funds and, 378
informal reference, 70–71
information
    confidential, 149, 151, 182
    disclosure of, 149, 158, 180, 238
    listing, accuracy of, 165
    personal, 149, 180, 182, 238
in-house sales, 144
    commissions, 194–195
injunction, 97
innocent misrepresentation, 260
inspections, 209, 363
    appraisal versus, 385
    due diligence and, 405–406
    of premises, lease, 533
installment land contracts, 323–326, 330
    advantages and disadvantages, 326
    buyer, 326
    provisions, 324–325
installment sale, 594–595
insulation, 611, 617
insurable interest, 500–501
insured, 497–498
    conventional loan, 359
insurer, 497–498
intangible property, 17
interest, 335
    calculations, 392–393
    insurable, 500–501
    interim, 430, 435, 441–443
    leasehold, 519
    mortgage, 586–587, 596
    mortgagee insurable, 502–503
    ownership, 179
    payments, 338
    reversionary, 30
    total, 339
interest rate
    APR, 426
    ARM, 368–369
    fixed rate loan, 368
    indices, 368
    LIBOR, 368
    T-bill, 368–369
    VA-guaranteed loan, 365–366

interim interest, 441–442
    calculating, 442–443
    prepaid, 430, 435
Internal Revenue Service (IRS), 590
interpretation of contracts, 266–267
Interstate Land Sales Full Disclosure Act, 115
    exemptions, 108
    government ownership, 110
    onsite septic systems, 109–110
intestate, 72
intestate succession, 30, 72
investment, 13, 621–626
    advantages to, 622
    basic concepts, 623–625
    land as, 5
    land use and, 6–7
    objectives, 7
    return on, 625
    risks, 7
    speculation versus, 622–623
    tax-related benefits, 625
involuntary alienation, 73–74, 89–90
IRS (Internal Revenue Service), 590

Joint Forms Committee, 275
joint tenancy, 34, 52
joist, 603–604
judgment lien, 45
judicial deed, 73
judicial eviction, 538
judicial foreclosure, 353–354
junior mortgage, 373, 395
"junk fax" laws and rules, 220

kickbacks for referrals, 413, 448
Know Before You Owe, 383, 412, 448

lake, 54
land
    definition of, 2, 18
    economic characteristics, 3–4

    estate in, types of, 26–32
    immobility of, 4–5
    indestructibility, 5
    lease, 523
    modification by improvement, 3–4
    nonhomogeneity of, 5
    permanence of investment, 4
    physical characteristics, 4–5
    run with, 2, 19, 111
    scarcity of, 3
    situs, 4
    types, special, 107–110
    value of, 480–481
    value of, appraisal, 472
land contracts, 263
    installment, 323–326, 330
landlord
    covenant of quiet enjoyment and, 537
    default, 532
    definition of, 509
    duties, 539, 564
    late payment fees, 515
    Law of Negligence, 511–512
    lease provisions and, 523–524
    obligations, 510, 529, 535
    property manager and, 564
    right to enter premises, 526, 530
    rules and regulations, 530
    statutory duties, 510–511
    tenant and, 508–545
    tenant remedies for breach by, 511
    Vacation Rental Act and, 516–519
land trusts, 42
land use and investment
    general concepts of, 6–7
    highest and best use, 6
    public and private land use restrictions, 6–7
land use controls, 13, 95–119
    buyers and, 96
    definition of, 6–7
    historical development of, 96
    improvements and, 114
    private, 110–115
    public, 96, 97–107, 114–115

purpose of, 114
real estate agents and, 114
real estate practitioners and, 96
regulation of special land types, 107–110
lateral support, 21
Law of Negligence, 511–512
laws
anti-spam, 221, 246
antitrust, 218–219, 246
basic contract, 251–271
disclosure, 167–179
do not call, 219–220, 246–247
fair housing, 564–565
"junk fax," 220, 246–247
license, 159
North Carolina Homestead Exemption Law, 32
North Carolina Real Estate License Law, 147, 167, 170
operation of, 265
solicitation of clients or customers, 219–220
LE. *See* Loan Estimate
lead-based paint, 305
ban, 121
children and, 121, 125
disclosure, 177, 222
disclosure form, 122–123
Lead-Based Paint or Lead-Based Paint Hazard Addendum, 312
North Carolina Lead-Based Paint or Lead-Based Paint Hazard Addendum, 122–124
pre-1978 residential dwellings, 121, 124, 130
property management agreement and, 554, 558
Lead-Based Paint or Lead-Based Paint Hazard Addendum, 312
lead poisoning, 121–125
groups at high risk for, 130
LHMP, 124–125
Residential Lead-Based Paint Hazard Reduction Act, 121, 124

lease
alterations to property, 530, 536
bankruptcy and, 532
breach of condition, 538
consideration, 523
damages, 530
default, 524
definition of, 509
eminent domain and casualties, 533
environmental matters, 524
expiration of, 537
fixed rental, 521
fixtures, 524
full-service, 522
graduated, 522
gross, 521, 540
ground, 523
index, 522
inspection of premises, 533
joint and several liability, 533
landlord default, 532
legal description, 523
legal purpose, 523
liability, 533
mineral, 19, 523
mutual agreement, 523
NCAR Residential Rental Contract, 527–534
net, 521–522, 540
occupants, 531
percentage, 522
pet deposit, 513, 530
provisions, common, 523–539
recordation of, 538–539
renewal, 525, 527
rental application, 531
repairs (nonresidential property), 524
Statute of Frauds and, 538, 540, 542
tenant breach, 531–532
tenant insurance, 532
tenant's use, 524
termination, 527, 536–538, 540
terminology, 540–541
terms and conditions, 523
types, 521–523, 540–541
uplifting improvements, 524

utility bills/service contracts, 529–530, 535
leaseback, 523
lease contracts, 263
leasehold estates, 32, 53, 541. *See also* nonfreehold estates
leasehold interest, ownership and, 519
lease with option to purchase, 328
legal description, 75, 523
legally void, 254
legal title, 324
lender
borrower analysis, 384
escrows required by, 435
property analysis, 385
reserves required by, 435
rights of, 353–356, 394
lessee, 509. *See also* tenant
lessor, 509. *See also* landlord
leverage, 622, 624
levy, 43
LHMP. *See* North Carolina Lead-Based Paint Hazard Management Program
liability. *See also* agent duties and liabilities
buyer, 395
insurance, 497
lease, 533
misrepresentation, 165
principal, 184–185
release of, 365
seller, 395
LIBOR (London Interbank Offered Rate), 368
license agreement, personal easement compared with, 49
licensee
ownership interest, 179
preprinted sales contract and, 274, 329
license law, agent duties under, 159
licensing, 9
lien, 42–46
federal tax, 46
general, 43, 45–46
judgment, 45
mechanic's, 44

mortgage, 43
personal property tax, 4
priority of, 46
property tax, 45, 61
sale, foreclosure, 73
special assessment, 43, 62
specific, 43–44, 350
tax, 45–46, 61–62, 336
lien foreclosure sale, 73
lien theory, 345, 394
life estate, 29–30, 52
life insurance companies, 378
life tenant, 29–30, 52
    rights and responsibilities of, 31–32
like-kind exchange, 595
limited service agreements, 214–216
liquidated damages, 264, 267, 302, 322, 329
liquidity, 353, 623
lis pendens, 47
listing agent, 148, 244
    firing, 217–218
    subagents and, 141
listing contract, 198–218, 243, 245
    definition and purpose of, 198–199
    exclusive right to sell, 202–214
    full-service listing agreements, 199–214
    limited service listing contracts, 200
    termination of, 217–218
    terms, 194, 244
    types, 199
listing duration, 216–217
listing information, accuracy of, 165
listing price, 224
    exclusive right to sell listing, 203
listing procedures
    final, 222–226
    preliminary, 221–222
littoral rights, 20
living (revocable) trusts, 42
loan application, 389, 412, 448
    procedures, 382–383

loan assumption, 357–358, 443
    FHA, 362, 366–367
    VA, 362, 366–367
loan cap, 369
Loan Estimate (LE), 413, 421–424, 448
    tolerance limits, 425
loan fees, 340–342, 432
loan origination fee (LOF), 587, 590
    calculating, 392–394, 430
loan payoff, 432
loans
    amount, calculating, 385
    analysis, 386
    ARM, 368–369
    balance, calculating, 338
    balloon payment, 370–371
    blanket mortgage, 372
    bridge loan, 372–373
    buydown loan, 370–371
    construction loan, 371–372
    first (or senior) mortgage, 373
    fixed rate-level-payment plan, 368
    graduated payment plan, 369
    growing equity mortgage, 370
    junior mortgage, 373
    by mortgage priorities, 373
    nonconforming, 359
    open-end mortgage, 372
    package mortgage, 372–373
    purchase money mortgage, 371
    by purpose or special feature, 371–373
    by repayment terms, 367–371
    term loan, 369
loan servicing, disclosure of, 413
loan-to-value (LTV) ratio, 335, 340–342
    application of, 393–394
    of FHA-insured loans, 360
loan underwriting, 384
loan values, 340–342
location, 4
    appraisal, 472
    on site, 601
LOF. *See* loan origination fee

London Interbank Offered Rate (LIBOR), 368
losses
    capital, 587–588
    real property potential, 506
    risk of, 298, 308, 505
    on sale, math, 242–243
loyalty, 155
LTV ratio. *See* loan-to-value ratio

Machinery Act, 60, 63
mailbox rule, 329
management plan, 560–561
management proposal, 560
mandatory evacuation, 518
mansard roof, 607
manufactured housing. *See* factory-built housing
marital life estates, 29–30
Marketable Title Act, 87, 90
market abstraction method, 478
marketing, 222
    rental property, 552, 561
market value, 58, 61, 63, 456–457, 489
marriage
    capital gains and, 593–594
    deeds and, 350–351
    tenancy by entirety and, 35–36
master plan, 98
material facts, 160–167
    disclosure of, 161, 166
    misrepresentation, 164–166
    omission, 166–167
    quick review of, 163–164
math
    agency and, 241–243
    agency contract (sales), 193
    area-related, 87–88
    brokerage commission, 241–243
    estimating net to seller, 242–243
    finance, 392–394
    profit/loss on sale, 242–243
measurements, 223
mechanic's lien, 44
mental capacities, 258
meridian, 68
metes, 67–68, 89
    sample, 69

mill rate, 59–60, 64
    calculating, 63
mills, 59
Mineral and Oil and Gas Rights Mandatory Disclosure Statement, 176
mineral lease, 523
    definition of, 19
MIP. *See* mortgage insurance premium
misdemeanor, 178
misrepresentation, 164–166
    innocent, 260
    liability, 165
    negligent, 165, 260
    willful, 164–165, 259–260
mistake, mutual, 259
MLS. *See* multiple listing service
modification by improvement, 3–4
modular housing, 26, 54
monetary damages, 267–268
monetary policy, 374–375
mortgage. *See also* residential first mortgage loans, categories of; secondary mortgage market
    ARM, 368–369
    basics, 342–356
    blanket, 372
    clauses and covenants, 351–352
    essential elements, 351
    first (or senior), 373
    GPM, 369
    growing equity, 370
    home equity, 360, 372
    interest, 586–587, 596
    junior, 373, 395
    lien, 43
    new first mortgage loan, 432
    open-end, 372
    package, 372–373
    paperwork, 410
    pooling, 380
    primary mortgage market, 396
    priorities, 373–374
    purchased, 381–382, 396
    purchase money, 371
    purpose of, 394
    RD mortgage loan, 341, 367
    recordation, effect of, 373–374
    releases, 374
    reverse, 360
    senior, 373
    subordination of, 374
    theory, 345
    types, 395
    valid, 394
mortgage banker, 377–378
mortgage borrower, rights of, 352–353
mortgage broker, 377–378
mortgaged properties
    cash sale of, 357
    loan assumption, 357–358
    sale of, 356–358
    taking title subject to a loan, 358
mortgagee, 345
    insurable interest, 502–503
mortgage funds
    commercial banks, 377
    credit unions, 378
    employers, 379
    government agencies, 378–379
    individual investors, 378
    life insurance companies, 378
    mortgage bankers and, 377–378
    mortgage brokers and, 377–378
    primary sources of, 376–379
    REITs, 378
    savings banks, 377
    S&Ls, 376–377
mortgage insurance premium (MIP), 360
    FHA, 361
mortgage interest, 586–587, 596
mortgage lien, 43
mortgage loan yields, using rule of thumb values, 393–394
mortgage note, 342–344
mortgagor, 345
moving expenses, 590–591
multi-agent firm, listing with, 140–141
multiple listing service (MLS), 244
    arrangements, 218
    co-brokered sales, 195
mutual agreement, 523
mutual assent, 255
mutual mistake, 259

NAR. *See* National Association of REALTORS®
National Association of Real Estate Boards, 8
National Association of REALTORS® (NAR), 8, 186
    A Buyers' and Sellers' Guide to Multiple Offer Negotiations, 318
    co-brokered sales, 195
National Flood Insurance Program (NFIP), 503
navigable waterway, 54
NCAR. *See* North Carolina Association of REALTORS®
NCBA/NCAR. *See* North Carolina Bar Association/North Carolina Association of REALTORS®
NCDOT (North Carolina Department of Transportation), 106
N.C.G.S. *See* North Carolina General Statute
NCHRC (North Carolina Human Relations Commission), 575
negative amortization, 369
negative covenants or easements, 111
Negligence, Law of, 511–512
negligent misrepresentation, 163, 165, 260
negligent omission, 163, 166–167
negotiable note, 344
net income, 484
net lease, 521–522, 540
net listing, 216, 244–245
net operating income (NOI), 481–482, 484–485
net proceeds estimate, 224–225
    math, 242–243
new first mortgage loan, 432
New York standard policy form, 497
NFIP (National Flood Insurance Program), 503

NOI (net operating income), 481–482, 484–485
nonconforming loans, 359
nonconforming use, 99–101, 116
nonexclusive buyer agency agreement, 226–231
nonfreehold estates, 32, 54, 539
    estate at sufferance, 520–521
    estate at will, 520
    estate for years, 519
    estate from period to period, 520
nonfriable, 126, 130
nonhomogeneity, 5
nonjudicial foreclosure, 354
nonnavigable waterway, 54
nonnegotiable note, 344
nonrecourse note, 355–356
North Carolina Appraisal Board, 455
North Carolina Appraisers Act, 455–456
    revision, 488–489
North Carolina Association of REALTORS® (NCAR), 146
    agency agreements, 182–183
    forms, 274
        North Carolina Real Estate Commission versus, 275
        offers and sales contracts form, 275–276
        Residential Rental Contract, 527–534
        Response to Buyer's Offer, 320
North Carolina Bar Association/North Carolina Association of REALTORS® (NCBA/NCAR) addenda forms, 310–313
    Additional Provisions Addendum, 313
    Back-Up Contract Addendum, 310–311
    Buyer Possession before Closing Agreement Addendum, 312
    Contingent Sale Addendum, 311–312
    FHA/VA Financing Addendum, 312
    Form for Sale/Purchase of Vacant Lot/Land, 313
    forms, 274–275, 403
    Lead-Based Paint or Lead-Based Paint Hazard Addendum, 312
    OTPC, 23, 112, 277–292, 301–313
    Seller Possession after Closing Agreement Addendum, 312
    Short Sale Addendum, 313
    Vacation Rental Addendum, 313
North Carolina Condominium Act (1986), 38, 53
North Carolina Department of Transportation (NCDOT), 106
North Carolina Fair Housing Act of 1983, 568–569, 580
    enforcement and penalties, 576–577
    exemptions, 576, 581
    prohibitions, 581
North Carolina General Statute (N.C.G.S.), 186
    93A-13, 197
    136-102.6, 106
    153A-335, 103
    agent duties to third party and, 163
North Carolina Good Funds Settlement Act, 411
North Carolina Homestead Exemption Law, 32
North Carolina Human Relations Commission (NCHRC), 575
North Carolina Lead-Based Paint Hazard Management Program (LHMP), 124–125
    exemptions, 125
    RRP and, 130
    violations, 125
North Carolina Leaking Petroleum Underground Storage Tank Cleanup Act, 129
North Carolina Lending Acts, 391
North Carolina Licensing Law, 455–456
North Carolina Real Estate Commission, 8
    disciplinary action, 157
    material facts and, 161–162
    NCAR versus, 275
    Rule 58A, 138
    Rule 58A.0104, 181–182
    Rule A.0104(a), 197
    Rule A.0104(c), 240
    Rule A.0104(d), 180
    Rule A.0104(e), 151
    sales contract forms, 274
    Working with Real Estate Agents brochure, 148, 152–154, 186, 239
North Carolina Real Estate License Law, 147, 167, 170
North Carolina Real Estate Licensing Examine, 2
North Carolina Residential Property Disclosure Act, 170–171
North Carolina Residential Rental Agreements Act, 510–512, 539, 541
North Carolina's Uniform Electronic Transaction Act, 321
North Carolina Tax Rate, 63
North Carolina Tenant Security Deposit Act, 512–515, 539–541, 562
North Carolina Unfair and Deceptive Trade Practices Act, 169
North Carolina Uniform Residential Building Code, 614–615
novation, 264, 352

obsolescence
    economic, 5, 478–479
    functional, 478–480
occupancy
    capital gains and, 593
    CO, 106, 615
    lease, 531
ocean, 54
offer, 255–256
    binding, 314
    copies to buyer and seller, 323
    electronically submitted, 320–321

faxed, 321
illusory, 255
multiple, 317–318
NCAR, 275–276
OTPC, 23, 277–292, 301–313
to purchase and contract, 277–313
Response to Buyer's Offer, 320
sales contract procedures, 313–317
submitting, 317–318
termination of, 257
offeree, 255, 314
offeror, 255, 314
Offer to Purchase and Contract (OPC), 403
   North Carolina Residential Property Disclosure Act and, 170
   OTPC, 23
   right to cancel, 171
Offer to Purchase and Contract Standard Form 2-T (OTPC), 23, 112, 277–292
   assignments, 309
   buyer obligations, 305
   buyer representations, 296–297, 304
   closing delay and, 298, 308
   completing, guidelines for, 293–300
   condition of property at closing, 308
   due diligence, 295–296, 304
   entire agreement, 299, 309
   execution, 299, 309
   fixtures, 295, 304
   home warranty, 298, 308
   notice, 309
   parties, 309
   personal property, 295, 304
   possession, 298, 308
   prorations and adjustments, 307–308
   provisions and conditions, 298
   risk of loss, 298, 308
   sections, 291–292, 301–313
   seller obligations, 297–298, 306–307
   seller representations, 297, 305–306
   survival, 309
   tax-deferred exchange, 299, 309
   taxes on real property, 298
   terms and definitions, 293–295, 301–303
oil and gas rights, 306
omission
   negligent, 163, 166–167
   willful, 163, 166
on center, 604
onsite septic system, 109–110
OPC. See Offer to Purchase and Contract
open-end mortgage, 372
open listing, 199, 244–245
operating budget, 561
   sample, 562
operating expenses, 483–484
operating statement, analysis of, 482–485
operation of law
   assignment of contracts, 265–266
   interpretation of contracts, 266–267
   time is of essence, 266
option, 327–330
   lease with option to purchase, 328
optionee, 327, 330
optioner, 327, 330
option to purchase, 328, 525
oral contracts
   buyer agency, 244, 246
   Statute of Frauds and, 262
ordinances. See subdivision regulations
OTPC. See Offer to Purchase and Contract Standard Form 2-T
out-of-state broker, 195–196
overlay district, 102
override clause protection period, 216–217
owners associations, 306, 530
ownership, 2, 52–53
   broker, 143
   combination (hybrid) forms of, 36–42
   concurrent (joint), 33–36
   government, 110
   interest, 179
   leasehold interest and, 519
   licensee, 179
   of personal property, 21
   powers of government and, 52
   of real property, 33–42, 51
   of real property, taxes and, 596
   in severalty, 33, 52
   townhouse, 39

package mortgage, 372–373
package policy, 497
Parol Evidence Rule, 266
partition, 33
party wall, 49–50
payoff, loan, 432
PB (provisional broker), 184
percentage lease, 522
percolation, 406
peril, 497, 506
periodic cap, 369
periodic tenancy, 519
permanence, 4, 5
permissible variations, 389
personal information, 182
   disclosure of, 149, 180, 238
personal property, 2, 12, 304
   bundle of rights of, 21
   exclusive right to sell listing, 203
   factory-built (manufactured) housing, 25–26
   fixture, 22–24
   improvements, 24–25
   OTPC, 295
   ownership of, 21
   tax lien, 45, 61
personal residence basis, sale of, 587–592
personalty, 2, 21
pet deposit, 513, 530, 536
pets, property management agreement, 553
physical deterioration, 478–480
piers, 602, 618
P&I payment, 335
   calculating, 392–393

PITI (principal, interest, taxes, and insurance), 335, 340–341
planned unit developments (PUDs), 99
planning, 97–103
plat, 70
   sample, 71
plumbing systems, 614
PMI. *See* private mortgage insurance
point of beginning (POB), 68
police powers, 52, 96
positive cash flow, 7
possession
   adverse, 73–74
   Buyer Possession before Closing Agreement Addendum, 312
   early, 504
   late, 504
   OTPC, 298, 308
   right of, 509
   right to possession of property, 17
   Seller Possession after Closing Agreement Addendum, 312
potential gross income, 482
power of sale clause, 350
preclosing, 402, 408–409
preemptive rights, agreements for, 328–329
prepaid items, 366
   computation of, 430
   interim interest, 430, 435
prepaids
   closing statement, 435–446
   mortgage interest, 441–442
   real property tax, 437–440
prepayment penalty, 591
   clause, 344, 367
prescription, 50
present value, 491
price, 194, 456, 489
   probable sales, 455
   sales, 431
price fixing, 219, 246
primary mortgage market, 396
principal, 134, 335
   agent and duties of, 184–185
   agent duties to, 154, 185–186

breach of duties, liabilities and consequences of, 185
duties and liabilities of, 184–185
reduction, 338
third party and duties of, 185
principal, interest, taxes, and insurance (PITI), 335, 340–341
private land
   use controls, 110–115
   use restrictions, 6–7
private mortgage insurance (PMI), 342, 359
   computation, 430
probable sales price, 455, 491
probate, 72
procuring cause of sale, 193
profit or profit à prendre, 18
promissory note, 342–344, 394
   sample, 343
property
   analysis, 385, 561
   appurtenance, 19–21
   assessment, 58–65
   concept of, 17–26
   destruction of, 265
   exclusive right to sell listing, 202
   facts about, 160–161
   insurance, 405
   intangible, 17
   mortgaged, sale of, 356–358
   personal, 21–26
   real, 18–19
   tangible, 17
   types requiring management, 547
property data sheet, 217, 224
property description, 75, 89
   adequacy of, 67
   government rectangular survey system, 68–71
   insurance and, 499
   methods, 67–68
   by reference, 69–70
   survey, 71–72
property insurance, 496–507
   assignment, 503, 506
   basic concepts and terminology, 497

co-insurance, 500–501, 505–506
co-ownership, 502
definitions, 500
early or late possession by parties, 504
eligibility, 506
fire insurance policy, 506
flood, 503–504, 506
homeowner's policy, 497–498
insurability issues, 504
insurable interest, 500–501
insurance company liability, 501
legal issues, 500–505
policy interpretation, 501–502
residential sales transaction concerns, 504–505
risk of loss before recordation/closing, 505
tenant, 532
unoccupied building exclusion, 501–504
property management, 536, 546–567
   commission, 565
   contracts, 549–559
   fee, 547–548
   purposes of, 546–547
   types of property requiring, 547
property management agreement, 549, 565
   agent and, 551
   default and, 558
   fees, 550
   lead-based paint/hazard disclosure, 554, 558
   marketing, 552
   owner responsibilities and, 552, 558
   pets, 553
   sample, 550–557
   security deposit, 553, 558
   sewage, 553
   termination, 555
property management report, 564, 566
property manager
   collecting rents and security deposits, 563
   duties of, 559–560, 565

fee, calculating, 547–548
landlord duties performed by, 564
legal actions instituted by, 563
management plan preparation, 560–561
marketing and renting property, 561
owner relationship with, 546–547
principal functions of, 560–565
property maintenance, 563–564
qualifying and selecting tenants, 561–563
property map, 70
property report, 108
property survey, 71–72
due diligence and, 405
property taxes, 58–65. *See also* real property tax
calculating, 63
on closing statement, 438
property tax lien, 45, 61
property values, 58. *See also* assessed value; market value
prorated items, 447
computation of, 430
prorating, 435, 447
prorations, 307–308
calculating, 436–437
closing statement, 435–446
real property taxes, 437–440
rental income, 440–441
30-day month/360-day year method, 436
365-day year/actual days in month method, 436–437
protection agreements, 199–201, 244
provisional broker (PB), 184
psychologically affected properties, 167–169
public housing, 515
public land
use controls, 97–107
use restrictions, 6–7
public land use controls, 96–107, 114–115
enforcement of, 113

examples of, 115
subdivision regulations, 103–107
urban and regional planning, 103
zoning, 97–103
publicly recorded documents, 70
PUDs (planned unit developments), 99
puffing, 166
pur autre vie, 29
purchase
effect of, 589–592
lease with option to, 328
offer to, 277–313
option to, 277–313, 327–329, 525
right of first opportunity to, 328–329
purchase money mortgage, 371
purchase price, 301
pure race system, 46, 374

qualified fee, 28
quantity survey method, 477
quiet enjoyment, covenant of, 17, 78, 537
quitclaim deed, 80, 90

radon, 126–127, 131
remediation, 127
testing, 127
rafter, 603
ranch style, 601
RD (Rural Development) mortgage loan, 341, 367
ready, willing, and able buyer, 194, 245
bilateral contract and, 253
real estate
basic concepts, 2–5
careers, 12
terminology and definitions, 2–3
real estate business
scope of, 8–12
specialties, 13
real estate investment trusts (REITs), 378

real estate market
characteristics, 10
historical trends, 10–11
immobility and, 10
recessions and, 11, 13
supply and demand, 10
real estate practitioners, 11–12
land use controls and, 96
Real Estate Settlement Procedures Act (RESPA), 448. *See also* TILA/RESPA Integrated Disclosure
requirements, 412–421
violations, penalties for, 421
real property, 2, 12–13
encumbrances to, 42–51
estates in, 26–32
hereditaments, 18–19
ownership of, 33–42, 51
potential losses, 506
risk factors, 506
tenements, 18
title transfer to, 66–94
real property tax, 586
computation, 430
OTPC, 298
ownership and, 596
prepaid, 437–440
prorating, 437–440
real property (ad valorem) tax, 43
real property valuation, 453–495
appraisal, basic concepts of, 455–462
appraiser regulation, 455
BPO, 487–489
CMA, 487–489
cost approach, 476–481
process, 462–463
sales comparison approach, 454, 490–491
REALTOR®
broker compared with, 8
Code of Ethics, 219
definition of, 8–10
REALTOR ASSOCIATE®, 8
realty, 2
recessions, real estate market and, 11, 13
reconciliation, 475, 486–487, 490

recordation
    closing as, 410
    of deed, 77, 90, 410
    effect of, 373–374
    of leases, 538–539
    risk of loss before, 505
    statement of record, 108
    title, 85–86
recording, 77, 90
    contracts, 86
    fees, 434
    procedures, 86
redlining, 573, 581
referral
    fee, 216, 548
    kickbacks, 413, 448
Regulation Z
    advertising, 389–390
    disclosure, 388–389
    penalties, 390
REITs. *See* real estate investment trusts
release of liability, 365
relocation, 9
remainderman, 30
renovation, repair, and painting (RRP)
    issues, 407
    led-based paint hazards and, 125
    LHMP and, 130
    "Renovate Right" pamphlet, 125
rental income
    gross, 486
    prorations, 440–441
rental properties
    agency agreements for, 566
    agency relationships in, 144–145, 548–560
    covenant of quiet enjoyment and, 537
    damage to, 535
    maintenance, 563–564
    management, 536
    marketing, 552, 561
    normal wear and tear, 513–514
    renting, 561
replacement cost, 476–477

replacement reserve, 484
reproduction cost, 476–477
rescission, 268
residential eviction remedies, 515, 540
residential financing, sources of, 395
residential first mortgage loans, categories of, 358–359
    conventional loans, 359–360
    FHA 203(b) regular loan program, 361–363
    FHA-insured loans, 360–361
Residential Lead-Based Paint Hazard Reduction Act, 121, 124
Residential Property and Owners' Association Disclosure Statement, 222
Residential Property Disclosure Act, 170–175
    "no representation" answer, 178–179
resident manager, 559
RESPA (Real Estate Settlement Procedures Act), 448
restrictive or protective covenants, 47
    discriminatory, 111
    due diligence and, 407
    enforcement of, 113–115
    examples of, 112
    termination of, 113
retainer fee, 196
retaliatory eviction statute, 512
return on investment, 625
reverse mortgage, 360
reversionary interest, 30
R-factor, 607, 611
ridge board, 606
right of assignment, 353
right of first opportunity to purchase, 328–329
right of first refusal, 328, 330, 526
right of possession, 509
right of quiet enjoyment of property, 17, 78
    rental property, 537

right of redemption, 352–353
rights
    air, 19–20
    of alienation, 31
    of borrower, 352–353, 394
    bundle of, 17, 21, 42, 51
    condominium, 36–37
    of deed of trust borrower, 352–353
    to estovers, 31–32
    landlord, 526, 530
    of lender, 353–356, 394
    littoral, 20
    of mortgage borrower, 352–353
    to recovery, grantee's, 80
    riparian, 20–21, 54
    run with the land, 2, 19
    subsurface, 19
    of tenants in public housing, 515
    water, 20
right to control use of property and profits within limits of law, 17
right to dispose of property by gift, sale, or will, 17
right to enter premises, landlord, 526, 530
right to exclude others, 17
right to possession of property, 17
riparian boundaries, 54
    processes affecting, 20–21
riparian rights, 20–21, 54
risk of loss
    before closing, 505
    OTPC, 298, 308
roof, 617
    gable, 606–607
    gambrel, 607
    hip, 606–607
    mansard, 607
    soffit, 607
RRP. *See* renovation, repair, and painting
run with the land, covenants, 2, 19, 111
Rural Development (RD), 341, 367

sale. *See also* agency contracts and related practices
  "as is," 163, 171–177
  auction, 152, 261
  bargain and sale deed, 80
  bill of, 2, 21
  cash, 357
  co-brokered, 195–196
  due-on-sale clause, 344
  effect of, 589–592
  foreclosure under power of, 354
  FSBO, 201
  in-house, 144, 194–195
  installment, 594–595
  lien foreclosure, 73
  to organizations, 380–382
  of personal residence basis, 587–592
  power of sale clause, 350
  profit/loss of, math for, 242–243
  right to dispose of property by, 17
  short, 356
  Short Sale Addendum, 313
  taxation, 585–598
  "Without Reserve" auction sales, 261
  "With Reserve" auction sales, 261
sale and leaseback, 523
sale price, 431, 589
sale proceeds, distribution of, 355
sales commission, 434–435
sales comparison approach,
  valuation calculation, 454, 463–475, 490–491
  key points about, 464–475
sales contracts and related procedures, 272
  dates and times, 329
  drafting, 273–274
  form, appropriate, 274–277
  NCAR, 275–276
  offer and acceptance, 313–317
  offer to purchase and contract, 277–313
  option to purchase real estate, 327–329
  OTPC, 277–292, 301–313
  preprinted form, 274–277

savings and loan associations (S&Ls), 376–377
savings banks, 377
scarcity, 458, 489
  definition of, 3
secondary mortgage market, 354, 379–382, 396
  activities among lending institutions, 380
  sale to organizations, 380–382
section, 68
security deposits, 528
  collecting, 563
  maximum amounts, 513–514
  normal wear and tear, 513–514
  North Carolina Tenant Security Deposit Act, 512–515, 526, 539–541
  other damage, 514
  permitted uses, 512–513, 535
  property management agreement, 553, 558
self-dealing, 181
seller
  appraisal and, 473
  CD for, 414–415
  copies of offers to, 323
  duties of, 223
  installment land contracts advantages and disadvantages, 326
  liability, 395
  submitting offers to, 317–318
seller obligations, OTPC, 297–298, 306–307
Seller Possession after Closing Agreement Addendum, 312
seller representation
  exclusive right to sell listing, 206
  OTPC, 297, 305–306
seller responsibilities, 169–170
seller's agent, 149
  buyer and, 151
  cooperating firm acting as, 141–142
seller subagency
  buyers and, 239
  disclosure of, 151, 239

senior mortgage, 373
septic systems
  due diligence and, 406–407
  private, 109–110
setback, 97
settlement, 303, 402
  North Carolina Good Funds Settlement Act, 411
  RESPA, 412–421, 448
settlement meeting method, of closing, 410, 446
  procedures after meeting, 411
settlement statement
  accuracy, 448
  appraisal fees, 433
  attorney fees, 433
  broker and, 446–447
  credit report, 433
  deed preparation, 434
  due diligence fee, 432
  earnest money deposit, 431–432
  entries and calculations, 426–435
  entries and calculations, practice, 443–446
  excise tax, 434
  homeowner's insurance policy, 434
  loan fees, 432
  loan payoff, 432
  new first mortgage loan, 432
  preliminaries, 447
  prepaid interim interest, 435
  proration, 435
  recording fees, 434
  reserves and escrows required by lender, 435
  sales commission, 434–435
  sales price, 431
  survey, 433–434
  title insurance, 433
several liability, 533
severalty, ownership in, 33, 52
sewage
  due diligence and, 406–407
  property management agreement, 553
sex offenders, stigmatized properties, 168

sexual harassment, 515, 579
sheathing, 604
sheriff's deed, 81
short sale, 356
Short Sale Addendum, 313
sill, 609, 617
single agency, 140
single entry, 430–431, 448–449
situs (location), 4
smoke detectors, 510, 535
soffit, 607
solicitation
    of active clients or other firms or brokers, 219
    CAN-SPAM Act, 221
    of clients or customers, laws affecting, 219–220
    do not call laws and rules, 219–220
    "junk fax" laws and rules, 220
special assessment, 62, 303
special land types
    highway access controls, 107–108
    Interstate Land Sales Full Disclosure Act, 108
    regulation of, 107–110
special or limited agency, 136–137
special purpose deed, 81
special use, 101–102
special use permit, 116
special warranty deed, 80
specific lien, 43–44, 350
specific performance, 268
    definition of, 5
speculation, 622–623
spot zoning, 103, 116
square footage
    calculating, 88–89, 244, 245
    cost/price, 88–89
    heated, 245
square-foot method, 477
square yards, calculating, 88–89
statement of record, 108
state tax liens, 46
Statute of Frauds, 76, 86, 198, 262
    lease and, 538, 540, 542
    option agreement under, 327

statutory cartway proceeding, 51
statutory redemption period, 353
steering, 571, 581
"stick-built" state building codes, 54
stigmatized properties, 167–169
straight-line method, 477–478
straight-piping, 110
street maintenance disclosure requirements, 105–106
strict foreclosure, 354
studs, 603
subagency
    definition of, 141
    disclosure of seller, 147–148
    relationships, 139–154, 186
    seller, 151
subagent, 134, 150
    listing agent and, 141
subdivision, restrictive or protective covenants, 111–112, 115
subdivision regulations (ordinances), 103–107, 115
    required statutory provisions, 104–105
    requirements, 104
    street maintenance disclosure requirements, 105–106
subjacent support, 21
subject to a loan, 358
sublease, 524–525
    assignment versus, 525
sublet, 525
substitution, 460, 490
substitution of entitlement, 365
subsurface rights, 19
success fee, 196
suit to quiet title, 74
supply and demand, 10, 458–460, 490
survey, 433–434
    government rectangular survey system, 68–71, 89
    property, 71–72, 405
    quantity survey method, 477
survivorship, 34
synthetic stucco, disclosure, 177, 206, 222

tangible property, 17
taxable gain, computing, 591–592
tax advantages, 7
tax assessor, 58
taxation, 52
    assessed rate, 61
    calculation, 63
    of capital gains, rules for, 592–594
    closing costs, 597
    excise tax, 81–82, 434
    home office, 594, 596
    of home ownership/sale, 585–598
    listing property to, 60
    ownership of real property and, 596
    real estate investment, 625
    tax collection, 61–62
    tax rate and, calculation, 59–63
    timetable for listing, 61–62
    transfer tax, 589
    vacation rental, 595–596
tax basis, 591
tax-deductible expense, 586
tax-deferred exchange, OTPC, 299, 309
taxes
    back, 336
    capital gain, 592
    excise tax, 81–82
    federal tax lien, 46
    payment, 64, 90
    property, 58–65
    on real property, OTPC, 298
tax lien, 336
    federal, 46
    personal property, 45, 61
    property, 61
    special priority of, 62
tax rates
    assessed, 61
    calculation, 59–63
    North Carolina Tax Rate, 63
T-bill rate, 368–369
telemarketers, 220
tenancy
    in common, 33–34
    by entirety, 35–36, 52
    joint, 34, 52
    periodic, 519

tenant
    breach, 531–532
    breach by landlord against, 511
    definition of, 509
    discrimination against, 515
    duties, 531, 539
    holdover, 521
    homeowner's policy, 498
    insurance, 532
    landlord and, 508–545
    late payment fees, 515
    Law of Negligence, 511–512
    lease provisions and, 523–524
    obligations, 510, 528–529, 535
    property sale and protection of, 517–518
    in public housing, rights of, 515
    qualifying and selecting, 561–563
    retaliatory eviction statute and, 512
    sexual harassment of, 515
    statutory duties, 511
    at sufferance, 521
    Vacation Rental Act and, 516–519
tenements, 18
    definition of, 3
term loan, 369
testamentary trusts, 42
testate, 72
testator, 72
testatrix, 72
third party, 134–135
    agent duties and liabilities to, 160, 163
    principal duties to, 185
TILA (Truth in Lending Act), 408
TILA/RESPA Integrated Disclosure (TRID), 382–383, 408, 412–413
TILSRA. *See* Truth in Lending Simplification and Reform Act
time is of essence clauses, 266
time sharing, 54
    key facts, 40–41
title, 2
    action to quiet, 74, 87
    attorney's opinion of, 83
    chain of, 82
    cloud on, 80
    color of, 73–74
    covenants of title in deeds, 82
    equitable, 324
    fee simple absolute, 75
    liquidation of, 353
title, transfer of, 66–94
    by descent (intestate succession), 72
    methods, 72–82
    by will, 72
title assurance, 82–87
title conveyance, 89
    bill of sale, 2
title examination, 90
    procedures, 82–83
title insurance, 84–86, 90, 433
    calculating, 84
    leasehold policy, 85
    mortgagee's policy, 85
    owner's policy, 85
title recordation, 85–86
title search, 83, 403
title theory, 345, 350–351, 394
tolerance limits, 389
Torrens System, 87
total circumstance test, fixture, 22–23, 201
townhouse, 39
township, 68, 89
toxic mold, 128–129, 131
    remediation, 129
transactional broker, 135
transaction parties, relationships between, 137
transferability, 459, 489
transferable warranties, 223
transfer tax, 589
travel agent, vacation rental referral fees, 519, 548
Treasury bill (T-bill) rate, 368–369
TRID (TILA/RESPA Integrated Disclosure), 382–383, 408, 412–413
truss, 604–605, 617
trust, 41–42
    deed of, 345–352
    land, 42
    living (revocable), 42
    REITs, 378
    testamentary, 42
trustee, 350
    deed, 81
trustor, 350
Truth in Lending Act (TILA), 408. *See also* TILA/RESPA Integrated Disclosure
Truth in Lending Simplification and Reform Act (TILSRA), 387–388
    Regulation Z, 388
Tudor style, 601

UCC (Uniform Commercial Code), 24, 408
UETA (Uniform Electronic Transaction Act), 263, 329
UFMIP. *See* upfront mortgage insurance premium
underground storage tanks, leaking, 129
undue influence, 261
Unfair and Deceptive Trade Practices Act, 260
Uniform Commercial Code (UCC), 24, 408
Uniform Electronic Transaction Act (UETA), 263, 329
Uniform Residential Appraisal Report (URAR), 457, 466–471
unilateral contract, 253
uninsured, conventional loan, 359
uniqueness. *See* nonhomogeneity
unit-in-place method, 477
universal agency, 136
unoccupied building, property insurance exclusion, 501–504
upfront mortgage insurance premium (UFMIP), 360
    FHA, 361
uranium, 126
URAR (Uniform Residential Appraisal Report), 457, 466–471
urban and regional planning, 103, 115
usury, 339–340

utilities bills, in lease, 529–530, 535
utility, 458, 489

VA. *See* Department of Veterans Affairs
vacant lot, 313
vacation rental
    fit premises of, 517
    taxation, 595–596
    travel agent referral fees, 519, 548
Vacation Rental Act, 516–519, 540
    agreements in writing, 516–517
    purpose of, 516
    rents and deposits procedures, 517
Vacation Rental Addendum, 313
VA-guaranteed loan, 395–396
    condominium, 37–38
    contract requirements, 364
    down payment, 366
    eligibility, 363–364
    escrow account, 366
    funding fee, 364
    history of loan guarantees, 365
    interest rate negotiability, 365–366
    loan assumption policies, 366–367
    qualifying for, 364
    restoration of entitlement, 365
valid contract, 253–254
    elements of, 255–258
valuation
    calculation, 454
    evaluation versus, 457–458
    process, 462–463
    real property, 453–495
value
    approaches to, 463–486
    concepts, 458–459
    cost approach, 476–481

CRV, 363
    economic principles of, 459–462
    estimate of, 481
    in exchange, 457, 489
    forces and factors influencing, 459
    income approach, 481–485
    of income property, 486
    land, estimating, 480–481
    lot/land, 472
    market, 456–457
    present, 491
    sales comparison approach, valuation calculation, 463–475
    in use, 457
vapor barrier, 603
variance, zoning, 101
veterans, "certificate of eligibility," 365
Victorian, 600–601
voidable contract, 254
void contract, 254
voluntary alienation, 72, 89–90

warranty
    covenants of, 78–80
    general warranty deed, 77–80, 90
    home, 203, 298, 308
    special warranty deed, 80
    transferable, 223
watercourse, 54. *See also* riparian rights
water rights, 20–21
weather stripping, 610
weepholes, 608
wetlands, 107
will
    right to dispose of property by, 17
    title transfer by, 72

willful misrepresentation, 163–165, 259–260
willful omission, 163, 166
windows, 617
    fixed, 610
    sliding, 608–609
    swinging, 609
"Without Reserve" auction sales, 261
"With Reserve" auction sales, 261
words of conveyance, 75
writ of attachment, 46
written contracts, 262–263

year to year estate, 32
yield, 339–340
yield spread premium, 413

zones, 115
    buffer, 103
zoning, 97–103
    aesthetic, 102–103
    air rights and, 19–20
    amendments, 101, 116
    cluster, 103
    codes, changes in, 101
    concepts and terms, 99–103
    cumulative-use, 99
    exclusive-use, 99
    historic preservation, 102
    illegal use, 101
    nonconforming use, 99–101
    overlay district, 102
    restrictions, 223
    special use permit, 101–102
    spot, 103, 116
    types, 99
    variance, 101
zoning map, 98
zoning ordinance, 98–99, 115